The Cambridge Handbook of Literacy

Edited by

DAVID R. OLSON

University of Toronto

NANCY TORRANCE

University of Toronto

CAMBRIDGE UNIVERSITY PRESS
Cambridge, New York, Melbourne, Madrid, Cape Town, Singapore, São Paulo, Delhi

Cambridge University Press
32 Avenue of the Americas, New York, NY 10013-2473, USA

www.cambridge.org
Information on this title: www.cambridge.org/9780521680523

First published 2009

Printed in the United States of America

A catalog record for this publication is available from the British Library.

Library of Congress Cataloging in Publication data

The Cambridge handbook of literacy / edited by David R. Olson, Nancy Torrance.
p. cm.
Includes bibliographical references and index.
ISBN 978-0-521-86220-2 (hardback) – ISBN 978-0-521-68052-3 (pbk.)
1. Literacy. I. Olson, David R., 1935– II. Torrance, Nancy. III. Title.
LC149.C28 2008
302.2′244 – dc22 2008045809

ISBN 978-0-521-86220-2 hardback
ISBN 978-0-521-68052-3 paperback

The Cambridge Handbook of Literacy

This *Handbook* marks the transformation of the topic of literacy from the narrower concerns with learning to read and write to an interdisciplinary inquiry into the various forms of writing and reading in the full range of social and psychological functions in both modern and developing societies. It does so by exploring the nature and development of writing systems, the relationships between speech and writing, the history of the social uses of writing, the evolution of conventions of reading, the social and developmental dimensions of acquiring literate competencies, and, more generally, the conceptual and cognitive dimensions of literacy as a set of social practices. Contributors to the volume are leading scholars drawn from such disciplines as linguistics, literature, history, anthropology, psychology, the neurosciences, cultural psychology, and education.

David R. Olson is University Professor Emeritus of the Ontario Institute for Studies in Education of the University of Toronto. He has written extensively on language, literacy, and cognition, including the widely anthologized article, "From Utterance to Text: The Bias of Language in Speech and Writing" (1977). His book *The World on Paper* (Cambridge University Press, 1994) has been translated into several languages. He is co-editor with Nancy Torrance of *The Handbook of Education and Human Development* (1996), co-editor with Michael Cole of *Technology, Literacy and the Evolution of Society: Implications of the Work of Jack Goody* (2006), co-editor with Janet Astington and Paul Harris of *Developing Theories of Mind* (Cambridge University Press, 1988), co-editor with Nancy Torrance of *Literacy and Orality* (Cambridge University Press, 1991), and co-editor with Nancy Torrance and Angela Hildyard of *Literacy, Language and Learning* (Cambridge University Press, 1985). His most recent authored books are *Psychological Theory and Educational Reform: How School Remakes Mind and Society* (Cambridge University Press, 2003) and *Jerome Bruner: The Cognitive Revolution in Educational Theory* (2007).

Nancy Torrance has worked as a senior research officer/research associate in the Centre for Applied Cognitive Science and the International Centre for Educational Change at the Ontario Institute for Studies in Education of the University of Toronto. She has worked extensively with David Olson on a theory of the social development of literacy and the acquisition of literacy in young children and with Lorna Earl on the evaluation of school reform efforts in Manitoba, Ontario, and England. She is co-editor with David Olson of several volumes, including *On the Making of Literate Societies: Literacy and Social Development* (2001), *The Handbook of Education and Human Development: New Models of Learning, Teaching and Schooling* (1996), *Literacy and Orality* (Cambridge University Press, 1991), and, with David Olson and Angela Hildyard, *Literacy, Language and Learning* (Cambridge University Press, 1985).

Contents

List of Contributors

RUTH A. BERMAN,
Linguistics Department, Tel-Aviv University

DOUGLAS BIBER,
Applied Linguistics, Northern Arizona University

JENS BROCKMEIER,
Department of Psychology and Education, Free University of Berlin; Department of Psychology, University of Manitoba

A.-M. CHARTIER,
Service d'histoire de l'éducation, Institut national de recherche pédagogique (INRP/ENS Paris)

KARINE CHEMLA,
REHSEIS, CNRS, and University Paris Diderot – Paris 7

STEPHEN CHRISOMALIS,
Department of Anthropology, Wayne State University

PETER T. DANIELS,
Scholar on writing systems of the world, Jersey City, New Jersey

TERESA M. DOBSON,
Department of Language and Literacy Education, University of British Columbia

NICHOLAS EVERETT,
Department of History, University of Toronto

JOSEPH P. FARRELL,
Ontario Institute for Studies in Education of the University of Toronto

ALISON F. GARTON,
School of Psychology, Edith Cowan University

JAMES PAUL GEE,
Department of Educational Psychology, University of Wisconsin–Madison

USHA GOSWAMI,
Centre for Neuroscience in Education, University of Cambridge and St. John's College

NILOOFAR HAERI,
Department of Anthropology, Johns Hopkins University

ROY HARRIS,
Faculty of Medieval and Modern Languages and St. Edmund's Hall, Oxford University

BRUCE D. HOMER,
Educational Psychology Program, City University of New York Graduate Center

MARTIN INGVAR,
Stockholm Brain Institute, Karolinska Institutet

LISBETH LARSSON,
Litteraturvetenskapliga institutionen, Göteborgs universitet

ELIZABETH LONG,
Department of Sociology, Rice University

HEATHER MURRAY,
Department of English, University of Toronto

STEPHEN P. NORRIS,
Centre for Research in Youth, Science Teaching and Learning, University of Alberta

DAVID R. OLSON,
Human Development and Applied Psychology, Ontario Institute for Studies in Education of the University of Toronto

KARL MAGNUS PETERSSON,
Max Planck Institute for Psycholinguistics and Donders Institute for Brain, Cognition, and Behaviour

LINDA M. PHILLIPS,
Canadian Centre for Research on Literacy, University of Alberta

CHRIS PRATT,
School of Psychological Science, La Trobe University

DORIT RAVID,
Constantiner School of Education and Department of Communications Disorders, Tel-Aviv University

ALEXANDRA REIS,
Cognitive Neuroscience Research Group, Department of Psychology, University of Algarve

CATHERINE E. SNOW,
Harvard Graduate School of Education, Harvard University

CAROLYN STEEDMAN,
Department of History, Warwick University

THOMAS G. STICHT,
International Consultant, Adult Education and Applied Behavioral and Cognitive Sciences, El Cajon, California

BRIAN STREET,
Language in Education, King's College, London

ROSALIND THOMAS,
Faculty of Classics, Balliol College, Oxford University

LILIANA TOLCHINSKY,
Department of Linguistics, University of Barcelona

NANCY TORRANCE,
Ontario Institute for Studies in Education of the University of Toronto

YACHING TSAI,
Chinese University of Hong Kong

PAOLA UCCELLI,
Harvard Graduate School of Education, Harvard University

FRITS VAN HOLTHOON,
University of Groningen

DANIEL A. WAGNER,
International Literacy Institute, Graduate School of Education, University of Pennsylvania

FENG WANG,
Peking University

WILLIAM S.-Y. WANG,
Chinese University of Hong Kong; Academia Sinica; International Institute of Advanced Studies, Kyoto

JOHN WILLINSKY,
Department of Language and Literacy Education, University of British Columbia

Preface

Literacy is both an urgent practical concern and a metaphor for modernism itself. Further, the uses of literacy are so pervasive and diverse, affecting every aspect of personal and social life for an increasingly large proportion of humankind, that the prospect of addressing it as a single topic almost certainly invites skepticism. Entire fields of study are devoted to special aspects or uses of literacy – for example, theories of literature, science, and law – not to mention those that specifically address the topics of learning to read and write. Indeed, the specialized uses of writing for such purposes as tomb inscriptions, shopping lists, field notes, billboards, traffic signs, cattle brands, laws, constitutions, equations, treatises, epics, love notes, advertisements, and other forms of dissembling are so diverse as to warrant describing them as different 'literacies,' each with its own set of conventions and pattern of implications. What unites them – visual signs that represent linguistic forms – is such a small part of a social practice that they scarcely bear mention. Yet, attention to specific uses of literacy may lead us to overlook the more general questions of just how literacy is used to regulate and inform social practices, sometimes so dramatically as to warrant the description of an entire society as literate. Certainly, this was the concern of economist Harold Innis (1951) when he proposed that different forms of social organization were the result of "the bias of communication." So, while it is appropriate for some purposes to focus on the diverse uses of written signs, it is appropriate for other purposes to look at the relationships among those uses. Neither focus has a monopoly on significance and the chapters that constitute this *Handbook* attempt to provide some balance between the examination of basic principles of reading, writing, and literacy and the extraordinary diversity to which those principles have been exploited for various social and personal purposes, both historically and in the present.

The very concept of literacy implies that writing and reading are social practices involving both writers and readers in what Brian Stock (1983) has called a "textual community" and Karel van der Toorn (2007) has called a "scribal culture." Even Robinson Crusoe and Samuel Pepys, who wrote for themselves alone, employed established conventional forms of expression and canons of interpretation that constitute literary traditions. Much of a society's significant work is conducted within those traditions, whether in science and politics or in diaries and personal letters. Not only do such traditions have a history, they also compete for dominance – for example, between science and religion. In other cases, patterns of use and interpretation are so divergent that readers – unwilling to make the effort – judge them as unintelligible. Just because they are social practices does not mean that they are not, at the same time, uniquely personal. A reader meditating and reading a prayer book is engaged in a social practice and yet may be doing it in a personal – indeed, idiosyncratic – way. The history of literacy is replete with examples of reading the same texts in widely divergent ways, ways that in some cases come to define a tradition and in other cases to be suppressed as heresy. "It is written" may serve as either a citation of authority or an invitation to dissent.

Yet, the fact that writing and reading have assumed both a prominent place and such diverse forms invites again the question of just what writing is: its relation to other forms of communication, the conventions of interpretation involved, and the competencies recruited and developed in becoming a reader and a writer. The general public, including those of us embedded in literate culture as well as those excluded from it, continues to place the highest value on literacy. Whether expressed through international agencies such as the United Nations, or through the mandates set out by national governments, or, indeed, through teachers and parents themselves, the demand for general and high levels of literacy for the world's children and adults is unequivocal. These mandates assume that there is such a thing as 'general literacy' and that it can be achieved most effectively through universal education. Indeed, education is not inappropriately thought of as the induction of the young into the dominant literate practices of the larger society.

Advocacy for literacy and literacy standards, like the concept of literacy itself, is ambiguous. The primary definition of literacy is "the ability to read and write," but it also carries a second definition: "an acquaintance with literature" – that is, what we may think of as having a liberal education. Much of the debate in government policy over literacy plays on this ambiguity, offering literacy skills for the masses while reserving a liberal education for an advantaged elite. In examining the rise of mass public education in Britain, historian Michael Clanchy (1979, p. 263) noted that:

> Opponents of government policy were worried that schools might succeed in educating people to a point where there would be a surplus of scholars and critics who might undermine the social hierarchy. Such fears were allayed by reformers emphasizing elementary practical literacy and numeracy (the three Rs of reading, writing and arithmetic) rather than a liberal education in the classical tradition, which remained as much the preserve of an elite of *litterati* [sic] in 1900 as it had been in 1200.

This ambiguity continues in the ongoing debates about basic and higher levels of literacy. Basic literacy – the ability to understand and produce written texts to some minimally acceptable standard, the preoccupation of the primary (and even secondary[1]) school years – is in tension with the 'literary' literacy that is at the core of more elite – that is, specialized – literary and scientific discourse. Some progress has been made in closing this gap by showing that learning to read and write is not only the attainment of cognitive skills but also an introduction to important social or communicative practices, such as managing information for various intellectual purposes or entertaining and expressing oneself. At the same time, schools continue to be faced with the complex task of balancing the needs of the individual learners with the needs of the society that mandates and supports the school.

The current focus on literacy derives in large part from the now almost universal concern over standards of literacy: nations vying with each other for top billing, international organizations promoting universal literacy, and developing countries enlarging their still meager investments in early education. Just what this goal implicates remains subject to debate. As this volume indicates, there is growing agreement that literate competence includes not only the basic skills of writing and reading but also competence with the more specialized intellectual or academic language that provides "ready and informed access to an encyclopedic range of linguistic varieties" (Langacker, 1991; Berman and Ravid, Chapter 6, this volume). Such varieties are produced in social contexts for special purposes and involve special conventions for their use – conventions that are mastered only through extended participation and practice. The challenge is to identify the kinds of competence that are sufficiently general to allow access to this range of activities. To this end, the study of literacy has found its way into a number of human and social sciences as well as the cognitive and brain sciences. This enlarged scope necessarily draws a number of disciplines, including history, anthropology, linguistics, literature, sociology, and the neurosciences, into a field previously dominated by psychology, education, and international development. The task is to explore the relationships among these lines of inquiry.

Structure of the *Handbook*

Five major transformations in our understanding of literacy have both helped if not to define, then at least to structure the field of literacy studies and provide a basis for the organization of this *Handbook*.

Literacy as a Scientific Subject

The first transformation is the increasing recognition that literacy is not simply one empirical fact among others but rather, for better or worse, a fact that has permeated a host of social and intellectual practices from meditation to regulation. This reflects Derrida's famous – if overstated – claim that the "factum of phonetic writing is massive: it commands our entire culture and our entire science, and it is certainly not just one fact among others" (1976, pp. 30–31). As the chapter by Brockmeier and Olson attempts to show, literacy is less a topic than a perspective, an "episteme" that organizes much of the current work in the human and social sciences.

Literacy and Language

The second transformation is the deeper understanding that reading and writing are not simply skills to be acquired but rather components of a distinctive mode of communication with a complex relation to the primary mode of communication – namely, listening and speaking – as well as to other modes of expression and communication (Olson, 1994). Exploring the ways that these two primary modes, the oral and the literate, are related – as discrete symbolic forms with distinctive communicative potentials, as instruments that serve distinctive social and intellectual functions, as forms of competence that recruit somewhat specialized brain processes – is the focus of Part II of the *Handbook*.

In Part II, Peter T. Daniels examines the evolution of the major writing systems of the world and shows how modern forms of writing may be traced back to three language systems in which a single sign could represent a monosyllabic word. Roy Harris shows that the usual assumption that speech is available to consciousness and, hence, readily available for transcription is false; the search for unambiguously interpreted visual signs is what led to the discovery of the implicit properties of speech. Stephen Chrisomalis provides historical evidence for the coevolution of written signs for language and signs for numbers, with written signs offering one solution to the problems faced by complex societies. Douglas Biber examines an extensive corpus of oral and written texts to locate the dimensions of similarity as well as the unique properties and advantages of each mode. Ruth Berman and Dorit Ravid show how the distinctive academic potentials of language result from the unique interaction between genre and the written mode; this potential is mastered only by relatively sophisticated writers. Catherine Snow and Paola Uccelli argue for the importance of instructional approaches that will help students develop the "academic language" that is needed for achievement in domains such as maths and science, as well as domains more traditionally associated with language such as literature and language arts. Usha Goswami presents recent neuroscientific research showing that the brain processes critical to reading primarily center on phonological processing even when nonalphabetic scripts are involved. Karl Magnus Petersson, Martin Ingvar, and Alexandra Reis introduce the new lines of cognitive neuroscience research that attempt to isolate the brain functions involved in language and literacy by showing that language is represented in the brain in somewhat different ways in literate as opposed to nonliterate adults.

Literacy and Literatures

The third transformation is the shift from the study of reading and writing as cognitive processes of special interest to psychologists and educators to the broader study of literacy as a set of social practices, or 'literacies.' The former research tradition was well established in the nineteenth century as a branch of psychology by such luminaries as Cattell (1900) and Huey (1908). Reading was seen as a mechanical, cognitive process sufficiently uniform that it was assumed to be the same across all history, culture, and development. The transformation was to recognize that different readers in different historical periods or in different cultural contexts might create and engage with written documents in dramatically distinctive ways. Reading privately, reading in groups, reading and writing in school, reading and writing in science, searching for information, making lists, writing curses, writing recipes and programs, signing contracts, and so forth involve special conventions for use and make different demands on readers. Such activities are 'social practices' often embedded in larger social and institutional contexts. Learning to read and write in these contexts is, in part, to learn the conventions, norms, and standards for compliance if one is to read a prayer book, a law text, or a scientific article. Consequently, literacy has come to be seen as not only familiarity with a script but also as familiarity with more specific literate practices ranging from those of the dominant institutions such as literature, law, and science to local literacy practices such as exchanging personal letters and organizing reading circles.

In Part III, Elizabeth Long provides an autobiographical account of the social dimensions of quite different ways of reading, thereby undercutting the "ideology of the solitary reader." Heather Murray examines the two senses of "conventions" of reading: the assumptions that readers make about how to "take" a text and the coming together of readers as in a collective. She sets out the history of these conventions in nineteenth-century Upper Canada as readers came together in various groups or reading circles for mutual enjoyment and enlightenment. Carolyn Steedman examines eighteenth-century diaries for indications of how the idea of a life came to be seen as bound up with having a life story, centering on a private self shaped not only by experience but also by one's reading and learning to read and otherwise complying with the demands of literate institutions. Lisbeth Larsson traces the relationships between women's reading habits and perceptions of women's literacy to women's more generalized self-perceptions. Karine Chemla examines ancient mathematical texts and shows that reading them requires not only mathematical knowledge but also the conventions for writing and reading about that knowledge. Stephen Norris and Linda Phillips examine a number of conceptions of "scientific literacy" and show that they all collapse an important distinction. Norris and

Phillips defend a *fundamental* sense of scientific literacy as the knowledge of the special conventions involved in writing and reading about science and they reject a *derived* or metaphorical extension of the term that includes knowledge of the substantive content of science possessed by the experts in the field. Two chapters examine how information technology is altering not only our conception of literacy but also our literate practices. The first, by Teresa Dobson and John Willinsky, examines what happens to knowledge and to notions of competence when confronted by the new demands of digital literacy. The second, by James Gee, examines how literacy is implicated in computer games and popular culture and argues that even learning to read should be seen as involving not only mapping from signs to sounds but also as introducing specialized situational contexts of meaning.

Literacy and Society

The fourth transformation is a revised conception of the relation between literacy and social change. Just as reading and writing were once seen as involving a more or less mechanical and universal set of cognitive processes, the social implications of literacy were seen as similarly universal – the same across all history, culture, and development. In a word, literacy was seen as the route to social and democratic development. Indeed, to this day, social commentators link illiteracy not only with crime and poverty but also with authoritarian and dictatorial regimes and the absence of the rule of law. As literacy has come to be seen as a constituent of rather diverse and distinctive social practices, with different properties, uses, and consequences in different kinds of society, it has come to be recognized that literacy is as likely to be an instrument of social control as it is an instrument of liberation; much depends on context and use. Whereas eighteenth-century philosophers such as Vico, Condorcet, and Rousseau had advanced theories linking the evolution of the alphabet to the advance of Western civilization, only in the late twentieth century did historians such as Cipolla (1969), Harris (1989), Thomas (1989), Kaestle et al. (1991), and Lockridge (1974) show that the presumed link between writing and civil society was far less clear than advertised. At the same time, anthropologists such as Street (1984); Heath (1991); Finnegan (1988); Besnier (1991); Barton, Hamilton, and Ivanic (2000); Boyarin (1993); Waquet (2003); and others showed that literacy may be taken up in radically different ways in different societies at different times and with different consequences. The diverse relationships between literacy and society are explored in Part IV of the *Handbook*.

Brian Street provides a detailed criticism of the notion that literacy is a single uniform process with uniform social implications. He provides ethnographic evidence that shows how different societies exploit writing and reading in radically different ways, yet in ways appropriate to those societies. Rosalind Thomas examines the sometimes contradictory ways in which educated elites in classical Roman and Greek societies used, and misused, writing for intellectual and social purposes. Nicholas Everett guides us through the late Middle Ages to show how literate elites defined and managed intellectual and social life while maintaining a radical discontinuity from the laity, a gap that remained until the invention of print and mass literacy. The much-misrepresented and little-understood topic of Chinese literacy in both historical and modern terms is addressed by linguists Feng Wang, Yaching Tsai, and William S.-Y. Wang. The reciprocal relationships between literacy and culture are central to their analysis. Niloofar Haeri examines the contradictory relationships between classical Arabic – a sacred and elite form of language and literacy – and the requirements of mass education and mass literacy. She argues the need for urgent reform if the Arab world is to overcome the low literacy rates associated with uneven social development. Frits van Holthoon examines the relation among literacy, modernization, and the evolution of "civil society" in the early modern period.

Literacy and Education

A fifth transformation involves a new understanding of the processes involved in the acquisition of literacy by both children and adults. Whereas a tradition going back to antiquity acknowledged that literacy, unlike speech, had to be taught and that learning required little more than attention and practice, modern research has indicated the wide range of relevant knowledge that must be brought by the learner to the learning task if high levels of literacy are to be achieved. These competencies include both cultural predispositions and rich implicit knowledge of language that must be recovered and reconfigured in the process of learning and in the design of successful educational programs. The study of an adult's learning to be literate brings these assumptions and predispositions to the fore in that, unlike children, adults take up literacy only when they see it as relevant and instrumental to the achievement of their own purposes and goals.

Nowhere is the transformation of an understanding of literacy and literacy acquisition more conspicuous than in the pedagogies devised. A.-M. Chartier traces the evolution of these pedagogies in Western Europe from the sixteenth to the twentieth centuries as attention shifted from a focus on signs to a focus on understanding and, at the same time, from a focus on literal memory of texts to a focus on semantic understanding. Liliana Tolchinsky shows how aspects of the visual forms of writing come to be learned by children both before and as they work out the complex relationships between speech and writing. Bruce Homer examines the ways that one's knowledge of an oral language must be "meta"-represented in order for visual signs to become signs for spoken language; the result is an increasingly high level of metarepresentational competence, specifically for the management of text. Alison Garton and Chris Pratt examine literacy from a sociocultural perspective to show how, especially for middle-class families, literacy development is embedded in oral social practices in the home. Becoming literate is a matter of increased competence in participating in various roles in these social processes.

Although much of literacy research is confined to modern Western classrooms, important advances in understanding literacy and literacy development come from attempts to advance literacy competence around the world in both children and adults in societies with low or negligible levels of literacy. Joseph Farrell examines the extensive current attempts to enhance literacy levels around the world under the aegis of the United Nations' declaration of literacy as a human right by distinguishing between programs that are effective from those that are not. Without exception, those programs that are successful give extraordinary attention to the agency of the learners, providing them with materials that they either alone or in small groups *can work through themselves*. Thomas Sticht examines the implications of the ironic fact that whereas even in developed countries, a substantial segment of the society – perhaps as many as one in ten – lacks functional literacy skills, the persons so described neither experience their literacy limitations as a problem nor are they willing to invest the effort to become more literate. He considers possible routes for addressing this anomaly. Daniel Wagner examines the role that new technologies have begun to play in literacy programs in the attempt to meet the increasing concerns about international development. David Olson considers some of the implications of these more recent advances in the study of literacy for the formulation of realistic educational goals and policies. These include broadening rather than narrowing what we mean by being literate, recognizing the conceptual challenge in achieving a high level of literate competence, and acknowledging the difficulties of imposing literacy on reluctant learners.

These themes, then, spell out the structure of the *Handbook*. Although the book attempts to sample appropriately from a burgeoning field, it also builds on and relies to a large extent on work not well represented in the volume. Literacy has long been the eminent domain of the educational sciences. The standard compendium of work on the topic is the three-volume *Handbook of Reading Research*. The first volume (Pearson, Barr, Kamil & Mosenthal, Eds.) appeared in 1984 and summarized various lines of research on reading, such as word identification and comprehension, family and social variables associated with literacy, and pedagogies seen as facilitating reading acquisition. In the eight-hundred–page second volume (Barr, Kamil, Mosenthal, & Pearson, Eds.) published in 1991, two of the three sections were devoted to literacy. By the third volume (Kamil, Mosenthal, Pearson, & Barr, Eds.), published in 2000, all five sections of the book were allocated to or at least described in terms of literacy. The *Handbook of Children's Literacy* (Nunes & Bryant, Eds., 2004) takes the topic out of the school and into the society more generally. The recent *Handbook of Research on Writing* (Bazerman, Ed., 2008) sets out complementary research on writing and learning to write. Two useful anthologies should also be mentioned. The one authored by Cushman, Kintgen, Kroll, and Rose (2001) is a collection of thirty-eight previously published works on themes including technology, cognition, history, development, culture, and social change. Beck and Olah (2001) offer an anthology of major works on literacy published by the *Harvard Educational Review*. Extensive reviews of the diversity and effectiveness of local, national, and international literacy programs for both children and adults is well represented in the UNESCO-sponsored volume *Literacy: An International Handbook* (Wagner, Venezky, & Street, Eds., 1999). *The Making of Literate Societies* (Olson & Torrance, Eds., 2001) presents a series of reports on indigenous local literacy programs sponsored by non-governmental organizations (NGOs) in Africa, Asia, and the Americas. A major section of the *International Handbook of Educational Policy* (Bascia, Cumming, Datnow, Leithwood, & Livingstone, Eds., 2005) is devoted to the topic of "literacies" with an emphasis on how research and theory, as well as technology, bear on literacy policy and practices around the world, noting that programs are often planned without acknowledging that the targeted learners often do not feel a need for literacy.

Unlike the pedagogical thrust of those handbooks and anthologies, this volume highlights the shift from a prescriptive to a descriptive orientation to literacy. Most studies of literacy, particularly studies of reading and writing, are almost exclusively devoted to exploring ways of extending either the range (to other societies) or the depth (in individuals) of literate competence, primarily through the school. Studies of reading failure, understandably, are motivated by the desire to advance the literacy skills of poor readers. From that perspective, literacy tends to be seen as an intrinsic 'good'; the problem for research was to devise ways of making its resources available to everyone (Scribner, 1984). Hence, the focus was primarily prescriptive and pedagogical, exploring ways of teaching reading or exploring factors that limited the acquisition and spread of literacy. This, of course, remains the primary concern of policy makers and educators and remains a central concern, whether addressed through either international comparisons or literacy programs.

The descriptive as opposed to the prescriptive approach to literacy arose as disciplines other than psychology and education began to address issues of literacy. There is now a rich literature reflecting the shift from literacy as a cognitive skill to literacy as a social practice, a shift first evident in the debates about the cognitive consequences of literacy. This perspective came into focus through both the psychological writings of Vygotsky (1962, 1978) and the historical and anthropological research of Goody and Watt (1968), Havelock (1982, 1991), Ong (1976), and, of course, McLuhan (1962). More recent psychological and anthropological studies of literacy were increasingly critical of any simple or single link between literacy and social change. This is an area of considerable dispute as scholars try to work out precise relationships between the cognitive processes specifically recruited in learning to deal with a writing system (Morais & Kolinsky, 2004; Olson, 1994; Vernon & Ferreiro, 1999) and those recruited by the social uses of writing and reading in diverse social contexts (Basso, 1974; Besnier, 1991; Boyarin, 1993; Heath, 1983; Howsam, 1991; Murray, 2002; Scribner & Cole, 1981; Street, 1995; Willinsky, 1990).

It is overly optimistic to say that these overlapping spheres of research have begun to define a coherent field with its own expertise, its own distinctive literature, and its own research methods. Contacts among workers in these areas are seriously limited and sometimes marked by disciplinary rivalry. Some attempts at cooperation appear in the numerous emerging graduate programs in many universities bearing such names as Language and Literacy, Literacy Studies, Written Culture, and The History of the Book. Although research on the various aspects of literacy now appears in the books and journals of a number of disciplines, there is still no standard text or document that helps to define literacy as a field, or to alert researchers of their potential colleagues, or, most usefully, to suggest promising areas of interdisciplinary research and theory. Contributors to *The Cambridge Handbook of Literacy* aim to satisfy that need.

The *Handbook* is addressed to senior undergraduates; to graduate students in the fields of education, psychology, linguistics, history, anthropology, sociology, and literary theory; and to academics and informed laypersons interested in the scholarly analysis of the role of literacy in mind and society.

David R. Olson and Nancy Torrance,
Editors
Toronto, November 30, 2008

Note

1 The province of Ontario requires all students to meet a literacy standard if they are to graduate from secondary school. This standard is defined independently of specialized disciplinary knowledge.

References

Barr, R., Kamil, M. L., Mosenthal, P. B., & Pearson, P. D. (Eds.) (1991). *Handbook of reading research: Vol. II*. New York: Longman.

Barton, D., Hamilton, M., & Ivanic, R. (2000). *Situated literacies*. London: Routledge.

Bascia, N., Cumming, A., Datnow, A., Leithwood, K., & Livingstone, D. (Eds.) (2005). *International handbook of educational policy: Vols. 1 and 2*. Dordrecht, The Netherlands: Springer.

Basso, K. (1974). The ethnography of writing. In R. Bauman & J. Sherzer. (Eds.), *Explorations in the ethnography of speaking* (pp. 425–432). Cambridge: Cambridge University Press.

Bazerman, C. (Ed.) (2008). *Handbook of research on writing: History, society, school, individual, text*. New York: L. Erlbaum Associates.

Beck, S., & Olah, L. (Eds.) (2001). *Perspectives of language and literacy*. Reprint Series #35, *Harvard Educational Review*.

Berman, R. A., & Ravid, D. (this volume). *Becoming a literate language user: Oral and written text construction across adolescence*.

Besnier, N. (1991). Literacy and the notion of person on Nukulaelae Atoll. *American Anthropologist*, 93, 570–587.

Boyarin, J. (Ed.) (1993). *The ethnography of reading*. Berkeley: University of California Press.

Cattell, J. M. (1900). On relations of time and space in vision. *Psychological Review*, 7, 325–343.

Cipolla, C. M. (1969). *Literacy and development in the West*. Baltimore, MD: Penguin.

Clanchy, M. (1979). *From memory to written record: England* 1066–1307. Cambridge, MA: Harvard University Press.

Cushman, E., Kintgen, E., Kroll, B., & Rose, M. (2001). *Literacy: A critical sourcebook*. Boston: Bedford/St. Martin's.

Derrida, J. (1976). *Of grammatology* (G. C. Spivak, Trans.). Baltimore, MD: Johns Hopkins University Press.

Finnegan, R. (1988). *Literacy and orality: Studies in the technology of communication*. Oxford: Blackwell Press.

Goody, J., & Watt, I. (1968). The consequences of literacy. In J. Goody (Ed.), *Literacy in traditional societies*. Cambridge: Cambridge University Press.

Harris, W. (1989). *Ancient literacy*. Cambridge, MA: Harvard University Press.

Havelock, E. (1982). *The literate revolution in Greece and its cultural consequences*. Princeton, NJ: Princeton University Press.

Havelock, E. (1991). The oral-literate equation: A formula for the modern mind. In D. R. Olson & N. Torrance (Eds.), *Literacy and orality* (pp. 11–27). Cambridge/New York: Cambridge University Press.

Heath, S. B. (1983). *Ways with words: Language, life and work in communities and classrooms.* Cambridge/New York: Cambridge University Press.

Heath, S. B. (1991). The sense of being literate. In R. Barr, M. L. Kamil, P. Mosenthal, & P. D. Pearson (Eds.), *Handbook of reading research: Vol. II* (pp.3–26). New York: Longman.

Howsam, L. (1991). *Cheap bibles.* Cambridge: Cambridge University Press.

Huey, E. B. (1908). *The psychology and pedagogy of reading. With a review of the history of reading and writing and of methods, texts, and hygiene in reading.* New York: Macmillan.

Innis, H. (1951). *The bias of communication.* Toronto: University of Toronto Press.

Kaestle, C. F., Damon-Moore, H., Stedman, L. C., Tinsley, K., & Trollinger, W. V. (1991). *Literacy in the United States: Readers and reading since 1800.* New Haven, CT: Yale University Press.

Kamil, M. L., Mosenthal, P. B., Pearson, P. D., & Barr, R. (Eds.) (2000). *Handbook of reading research: Vol. III.* Mahwah, NJ: Erlbaum.

Langacker, R. (1991). *Concept, image and symbol: The cognitive basis of grammar.* Berlin: Mouton de Gruyter.

Lockridge, K. (1974). *Literacy in colonial New England.* New York: Norton.

McLuhan, M. (1962). *The Gutenberg galaxy.* Toronto: University of Toronto Press.

Messick, B. (1993). *The calligraphic state: Textual domination and history in a Muslim society.* Berkeley: University of California Press.

Morais, J., & Kolinsky, R. (2004). The linguistic consequences of literacy. In T. Nunes and P. Bryant (Eds.), *Handbook of children's literacy.* Dordrecht, The Netherlands: Kluwer.

Murray, H. (2002). *Come, bright improvement: The literary societies of nineteenth-century Ontario.* Toronto: University of Toronto Press.

Nunes, T., & Bryant, P. (2004). *Handbook of children's literacy.* Dordrecht, The Netherlands: Kluwer.

Olson, D. R. (1994). *The world on paper: The conceptual and cognitive implications of writing and reading.* Cambridge/New York: Cambridge University Press.

Olson, D. R., & Torrance, N. (Eds.) (2001). *The making of literate societies.* New York: Blackwell.

Ong, W. (1976). *The presence of the word.* New Haven, CT: Yale University Press.

Pearson, P. D., Barr, R., Kamil, M. L., & Mosenthal, P. B. (Eds.) (1984). *Handbook of reading research: Vol. I.* White Plains, NY: Longman.

Scribner, S. (1984). Literacy in three metaphors. *American Journal of Education,* 93, 6–21.

Scribner, S., & Cole, M. (1981). *The psychology of literacy.* Cambridge, MA: Harvard University Press.

Stock, B. (1983). *The implications of literacy.* Princeton, NJ: Princeton University Press.

Street, B. V. (1984). *Literacy in theory and practice.* Cambridge: Cambridge University Press.

Street, B. V. (1995). *Social literacies: Critical approaches to literacy in development, ethnography and education.* London: Longman.

Thomas, R. (1989). *Oral tradition and written record in classical Athens.* Cambridge: Cambridge University Press.

van der Toorn, K. (2007). *Scribal culture and the making of the Hebrew bible.* Cambridge, MA: Harvard University Press.

Vernon, S., & Ferreiro, E. (1999). Writing development: A neglected variable in the consideration of phonological awareness. *Harvard Educational Review,* 69(4), 395–415.

Vygotsky, L. S. (1962). *Thought and language.* Cambridge, MA: MIT Press.

Vygotsky, L. S. (1978). *Mind in society: The development of higher psychological processes.* M. Cole, V. John-Steiner, S. Scribner, & E. Souberman (Eds.). Cambridge, MA: Harvard University Press.

Wagner, D. A., Venezky, R. L., & Street, B. V. (Eds.) (1999). *Literacy: An international handbook.* Boulder, CO: Westview Press.

Waquet, F. (2003). *Parler comme un livre: L'oralite´ et le savoir, XVIe-XXe siècle. L'évolution de l'humanite.* Paris: Albin Michel.

Willinsky, J. (1990). *The new literacy: Redefining reading and writing in the schools.* New York: Routledge.

Part I

LITERACY AS A SCIENTIFIC SUBJECT

CHAPTER 1

The Literacy Episteme

From Innis to Derrida

Jens Brockmeier and David R. Olson

The significance of a basic medium to its civilization is difficult to appraise since the means of appraisal are influenced by the media, and indeed the fact of appraisal appears to be peculiar to certain types of media. A change in the type of medium implies a change in the type of appraisal and hence makes it difficult for one civilization to understand another.

Harold Innis (1950/1986, p. 6)

Samuel Johnson loved writing. From early on, he was a gifted and prolific writer. While working on his *Dictionary of the English Language*, he also regularly contributed to *The Gentleman's Magazine* and wrote a series of semiweekly essays in publications that ran under such titles as *The Idler* and *The Rambler*. For Dr. Johnson and his mid-eighteenth-century readers, it was common to view writing and reading as one of a gentleman's noblest pastimes. Besides, it was the art of writing and reading that distinguished man from uncivilized savages, as Thomas Astle, the Keeper of Records at the Tower of London, summarized the widespread opinion of the day in his *The Origin and Progress of Writing* (1784/1876).

Although clerical uses of writing had long been established practices in London's branch offices, commercial chambers, boards, courts, and navy colleges, for a true gentleman, reading and writing were seen as a form of amusement. It was what Bourdieu would have called a "clubby habitus," shared by that small fragment of the population that happened to have enough education to participate and enough time and money to indulge. Why would one spend one's leisure time dealing with *lettres*? In addition to pleasure, it provided distinction. In a time of long working days and hardship for most, what could be more representative of a privileged gentleman's status than sitting comfortably in an armchair and reading *The Idler*?

If we compare the world of letters and armchairs inhabited by Dr. Johnson and the readers of his *Gentleman's Magazine* to the state of the world today, it is obvious why it has become next to impossible to give a clear and bounded definition of literacy: the array of phenomena referred to as literacy has become unclear and unbounded itself. Perhaps Dr. Johnson still could have included in his famous *Dictionary of the English Language* an entry on literacy such as "The quality or state of being literate; esp. ability to read and write; knowledge of letters; condition in respect to education." (He did not. The entry is from the current edition of the *Oxford English Dictionary*, which dates the first appearance of the term *literacy* to the 1880s.) In today's cultural semiosphere, however, not only the concept of literacy has exploded – or imploded, for that matter – but also all related concepts and ideas that might have been valid in Dr. Johnson's linguistic and social universe. The spectrum ranges from the idea that literacy is linked to a specific class, gender, educational status, and mental attitude to the very concepts of "dictionary" and "the English language" – as if there were one dictionary or one English language in a world where countless dialects in countless ethnic and cultural contexts serve a myriad of continuously evolving uses, enriching the language by hundreds of new entries every day.

Whereas the readers of *The Gentlemen's Magazine* could still choose whether they wanted to dedicate some of their time to the letters rather than to, say, hunting, dancing, or military services, today no member of any class or social field in a modern society has a choice at all: the ability to actively participate in the life of a modern society, including the common life, depends to a large extent on the ability to read and write. At the same time, these ways of participating have become infinitely more diverse and call for a variety of literate competences and practices (see Street, Chapter 18, this volume). They also include the new repertoire of literacy competences and practices that has emerged with the digital revolution: in the 1980s, with the public uptake of the computer; in the 1990s, with the rise of the Internet and the use of hypermedia; and, more recently, with the emergence of a networked information economy (see Dobson & Willinsky, Chapter 16, this volume). To be sure, in a developed culture of literacy, there is not much left of the "clubby" feel to reading and writing.

Literacy has not only become essential for all fundamental social, societal, economic, and political conditions under which we live, it also has become inextricably tied to our private, psychological lives, our diaries, our confessions, and our last wills and testaments. So pervasive is our involvement in literacy that such concepts as writing, reading, and text have become traveling concepts, theoretical metaphors, and methodological shorthands that have effortlessly crossed borders between disciplines and discourses. We read pictures, cities, landscapes, and decipher texts of cultures, lives, and minds. Recent decades have seen an unprecedented general interest in issues of writing – a general cultural concern with literacy and literacies that goes far beyond the waves of intellectual fashion. "The study of literacy," Wagner (1999, p. 1) concluded, "combines all the social science disciplines, from psychology and linguistics to history, anthropology, sociology, and demographics, but the field itself broadens beyond research to both policy and practice, from childhood though adulthood." In fact, issues of literacy have been discussed far beyond the academic realm. Literacy is high on the agendas of organizations such as the United Nations, World Bank, World Health Organization, and many other nongovernmental organizations. Literacy has become part of the human rights agenda; as an educational right, literacy has sponsored global strategies for improved education, human development, and well-being.

If we consider these different institutional orders in which literacy plays a role – whether in research and scholarship, communication and entertainment, public and political administration, politics and international development, as well as the more private and local uses of writing and reading – it becomes clear that, unlike in the days of Dr. Johnson, there is no such thing as a clear and bound definition or empirically based concept of literacy simply because the range of activities encompassed by the concept of literacy has expanded and continues to expand enormously. Even in taking a more theoretical stance, it is somewhat misleading to speak of literacy as the focus of a paradigm of academic study and research, with a paradigm understood, following Kuhn (1962), as a perspectival framework of assumptions and beliefs that organizes concepts, models, theories, and research methodologies for scientific knowledge in a particular domain. The far-reaching cross-disciplinary interest in literacy is not merely tied to the rise of a new paradigm in the human sciences; indeed, it cannot be reduced to an academic phenomenon at all.

Thus, it seems that we are faced with a dilemma. On the one hand, to understand the specific empirical properties and implications of literacy, it is necessary to abandon the notion of a single competence that we may think of as literacy and to embrace the broad range of particular competencies and practices that, in turn, may be analyzed in linguistic, cognitive, semiotic, technological, and cultural terms. On the other hand, we cannot overlook the underlying relationships and common themes within this diversity – themes that can be adequately understood only if located within an overarching cultural discourse. This discourse we call the *literacy episteme*.

In this chapter, we define what is meant by the literacy episteme, proposing that it is only within such a larger cultural-historical trajectory that we can capture the astonishing rise of a set of activities and issues subsumed under the notion of literacy (or writing) to an area of academic and applied inquiry that, by now, is well established – as, not least of all, this *Handbook* demonstrates. Only within such an overarching order, we suggest, do these practices and problems take on an epistemic form and become subjects of thought and theoretical curiosity as well as public attention. Only within the literacy episteme can the social, intellectual, and cultural implications of writing become epistemic objects: "things" that appear as intelligible objects of theory and investigation and whose investigation is considered to be fulfilling societal demands and cultural interests.

The notion of the literacy episteme brings into play a long-standing epistemological tradition, in both philosophy and the human sciences. In the twentieth century, this tradition increasingly was concerned with the significance of language for thought and culture, including an appreciation of writing as a special form and practice of language. Philosophical discourse on the nature of man shifted from Descartes' "one who thinks" to Wittgenstein's "one who speaks" and, even more recently, as we try to show, to "one who writes." But, this turn to language and writing may be seen as the more recent phase of a much longer tradition; it began with philosophers' search for the general conditions that make human knowledge possible. Since Kant, such conditions have been described as the a priori of our empirical knowledge. What we show in this chapter is that the literacy episteme can be understood as an historical priori, a sort of epistemological background for our understanding of writing and its implications and uses in shaping a cultural discourse of literacy.

Because the historical fabric of the literacy episteme comprises both material and conceptual factors, we give particular prominence to the work of two scholars: the Canadian economist and theorist of communication, Harold Innis, and the French philosopher, Jacques Derrida, who, albeit in different ways, have drawn attention to the materiality of the conceptual and thus to the physicality of language and communication as materialized in writing. Further, we suggest that, regardless of these theoretical debates, the rise of the literacy episteme is not simply the result of accumulative scholarship, scientific discovery, or century-long debates on the very nature of language. Rather, it is the result, if not the side effect, of more profound sociocultural changes in the twentieth century, among which the revolutions in modes of communication – perhaps most significantly the digital revolution – have played a crucial role.

The Literacy Episteme and its Scope

The notion of an episteme is meant to enable us to understand what organizes the theoretical order of a culture, assuming that the organizing forces are themselves not just theoretical. We also could say that an episteme is the cultural order of ideas and concepts that define, at a given moment in history, what knowledge is and how we gain and transmit it.

To illustrate this, let us consider a few examples. On a smaller scale, such an epistemic definition is operative in the material and symbolic practices carried out in an experimental laboratory. A molecular-biology laboratory for synthesizing proteins, for example, may be viewed as constituting a specific epistemic system. Within this system, some things are assumed, some are made visible, and yet others ruled out of court. Typically, in their talking and thinking, the laboratory researchers do not differentiate between a computer-generated inscription – endless columns of numeric entries or graphs registering the course of measurements during an experiment – and what they conclude about certain protein connections. Within the universe of "laboratory life" (Latour & Woolgar, 1979), the inscription or writing becomes indistinguishable from "what it represents." The inscriptions are the "real things" the researchers deal with, model, and operate on and whose experimental reality is, in this way, continuously fixed and practically acknowledged (Rheinberger, 1997). In a similar case, a number of high-tech physics laboratories recently examined a state they call "supercool," or the "ultracold." The ultracold is artificially created – it is the amazing domain of almost absolute zero that exists only in that ultracold laboratory. But, within the epistemic system of the laboratory, it has been turned from something unattainable into something with which we can interact (Hacking, 2006). Philosophers of science have called these states and creations *epistemic objects*. Although they exist only within a specific epistemic matrix, their "reality" is taken for granted in the fullest of all senses. Is it possible to view the diverse forms and practices of literacy as members of one such family, one episteme?

Chamberlin (2002) pointed out that even the hunting practices of hunter-gatherers can be understood as reading practices. In this way, Chamberlin moves the notion of reading to encompass a broad spectrum of practices of deciphering all kinds of signs and "traces." Such practices, at the same time, interpret and constitute a specific epistemic reality. "Hunters read visible signs," Chamberlin (2002, p. 82) writes, "but they know them to be signs of the visible, almost exactly as other readers of signs such as nuclear physicists do. A track, even when it's very clear, tells you where an animal (or a neutron) was, not where it is. To figure that out, a hunter uses a combination of experience and imagination." Chamberlin concludes, "The hunter's imagination shapes reality through re-presentation."

Another much-discussed example of an epistemic object is the social, psychological, and cultural dimensions of the "self." Geertz (1983) and other social scientists and historians argued that the idea of an individual, bound, self-referential, and independent self is a very specific – Geertz calls it "peculiar" – Western creation. Even within the Western tradition, the self has become a "substantial" epistemic thing only in modern times, with our principles of individual human rights and responsibilities. Is this to say that the historical Julius Caesar did not have a "self"? Well, he certainly had an *anima*, as he would have replied, but he did not have anything that resembled what we today mean by a "self" because, as a speaker of Roman Latin, he simply did not have the words to talk about his "self" apart from his being a general, politician, writer, husband, citizen, and believer in the Roman gods.

The historian of concepts, Reinhard Koselleck (1985), made the case that whenever people want to express more complex ideas, these ideas are inextricably mingled with the linguistic concepts they have at hand. The meanings of these concepts, however, do not depend only on people's "ideas" and "intentions" but also on the historical network of meanings into which these concepts are inserted. For Koselleck, there is an "historical semantic" that underlies the cultural-historical context of use that gives concepts and other linguistic expressions their specific meanings. Outside of this historical context, concepts such as the Roman *anima* are meaningless – that is, without use. In turn, in referring to the epistemic reality of one's "self," we bind ourselves into an epistemic community that via further linguistic and communicative practices (e.g., greeting formulas, pronouns, autobiographical narratives, and written identity documents) continuously confirms one's sense of self or identity (Kroskrity, 2001; Wang & Brockmeier, 2002). The meaning of such expressions is best understood in terms of use, as Wittgenstein (1953) insisted – meaning as use within a given cultural grammar or, as we may say, epistemic system.

Taylor (1989) made a similar point, emphasizing that things and discourses that are part of an episteme also have a moral dimension. He maintained that the "moral ontology" of a culture changes from one historical episteme to another. A moral ontology is constituted by the set of concepts and assumptions that lay out what we believe to be good and bad, right and wrong, ethically appropriate and inappropriate. For example, the particular moral value that Western cultures allot to the "self" is a crucial element of its ontology. To advance our line of argument, we associate with Taylor's moral ontology an "epistemic ontology": the system of beliefs and rules that sets out what is considered knowledge worth knowing and that motivates us to consider some "things" as real. This epistemic ontology expands on the traditional idea of a relationship between the knowing subject and the (potential) object of knowledge – a relationship that defines the horizon of our intellectual imagination.

This notion of an episteme as a framework within which objects of knowledge, ways of knowing, and ways of being in the world are organized in a particular epoch is borrowed from Michel Foucault (1970) who described it as an "historical a priori." Foucault's paradigm case is the "episteme of Man," the amalgamation of ideas, forms of knowledge, social and cultural practices, and institutions emerging in the eighteenth century that created, among others, the bourgeois "individual" as well as the cluster of concepts and discourses that since then have been revolving around it. According to Foucault, the episteme of Man is the cultural system of representation that shaped the modern idea of human being and thinking, giving epistemic reality to concepts such as the self and the individual mind, conscience, consciousness and the unconscious, and normalcy and deviance. Foucault (1970, p. 127) wrote that historically a priori conditions organize the "emergence of statements, the law of their coexistence with others, the specific form of their mode of being, the principles according to which they survive, become transformed, and disappear."

The notion of an historical a priori contrasts sharply with the original Kantian notion. For Kant, the term *a priori* denotes what is considered the transcendental dimension of human knowledge, those categories that cannot be derived from experience because they are necessary preconditions of experience itself. Categories of space and time are such transcendental concepts in that they are prior to and make possible all forms of experience, including historical experience. For Foucault, however, those categories (and the discourses, as he put it, to which they belong) are historical, tied to a time and a concrete world as well as to ways of acting and understanding. Instead of claiming to be universal and merely categorical (i.e., intellectual) conditions, they draw the attention to the cultural context in which ideas, institutions, and practices emerge. On this account, such categories can be viewed as historical forms of life rather than transcendental (or logical, linguistic, or cognitive) universals. It is in this sense that we have used the concept of episteme to describe the cultural discourse of literacy. The literacy episteme can be understood as an historical a priori. It defines the terms under which we conceptualize what we have called a fully developed "culture of literacy" (Brockmeier & Olson, 2002).

To see literacy as an episteme rather than as simply a skill, a competence, a social practice, or a universal good – that is, as a frame rather than a content – has brought to the fore two ideas that had been absent from academic and public discourse on language. One is that writing is a peculiar form of language and not simply a secondary representation of speech. This seems to be, by now, a widely accepted view, even if the question of just what exactly makes writing a particular form of language has led to new debates. The other idea is that the prototypical form of written language – extended, monological prose, traditionally conceived of as a dominant feature of our civilization and hallmark of high culture – is an historical form. It came to have its pride of place – in science, in philosophy, in government, in the courts, in church, in school, and in public discourse – with Dr. Johnson as one of its articulate promoters. But, like all historical phenomena, language forms wax and wane. Perhaps what we are witnessing with the rise of the literacy episteme is the final dissolution of Dr. Johnson's privileged claim of cultural superiority for writing and bookishness, a process in which writing is forfeiting its dominant role in both the management of knowledge and information and in the organization of bureaucratic societies. "Minerva's owl begins its flight only in the gathering dusk," Innis (1951, p. 3) quotes Hegel at the beginning of his book on the interplay among communication, culture, and history.

The Rise of the Literacy Episteme

Describing the rise of the literacy episteme as a phenomenon of the twentieth century is not to say that matters of writing and reading were not dealt with in earlier times. Beginning with Plato's critique of writing as failing to live up to the rhetorical, mnemonic, and moral standards of oral discourse, the phenomenon of writing has been discussed in philosophical, religious, social, and political contexts. We might think of authors such as Luther, Erasmus, and the early Protestants; philosophers of the Enlightenment including Rousseau, Vico, and Turgot; and archival practitioners such as the Keeper of the Records at the Tower of London, Thomas Astle.

However, the 'discovery' of writing and literacy – that is, its constitution as an epistemic subject in the second half of the last century – has a different epistemic quality. On the theoretical side of this process, we witness nothing less than a breakthrough: within a couple of years in the 1960s, there was an unparalleled concentration of publications on issues of literacy, followed by the institutionalization of a new academic field of research. At the same time, the United Nations became a leading advocate of the Basic Rights of the Child, which included access to basic education and, more specifically, literacy and numeracy (see Farrell, Chapter 28, this volume). This new interest in writing and the new focus on literacy are even more stunning because modern linguistic theory, following de Saussure, was concerned almost exclusively with the spoken form. In fact, the significance of writing had been ignored and dismissed for centuries – an attitude that can be traced back to Aristotle's infamous definition and Plato's even more fundamental repudiation of the written word. Derrida (1976) argued that there is a tradition of adopting a dismissive attitude toward writing that is deeply rooted in Western metaphysics, even if it found its most systematic expression in modern linguistic thought.

An episteme, we have maintained, is not just about books and thoughts; however, books can be indicators and symptoms of more than just bookishness. This is particularly true for the series of books published in the 1960s by a number of authors from different disciplines and different countries. Today, from a distance of four decades, we see those publications as precise and reliable indicators of a new perspective; they set the stage for a new epistemic ontology of language. Havelock (1991, p. 12) provided a first-person account of the origins of this perspective, pointing out that the almost concurrent appearance of these books marked a turning point in the Western attitude toward writing, a "watershed . . . that had been reached, or perhaps more accurately they point to a dam starting to burst," releasing a flood of cultural interest and intellectual activity devoted to showing the importance of literacy as well as attempting to understand it.

Although most of these remarkable books – we look into their contents presently – focused primarily on the implications of writing and printing in the contexts of specific academic debates, they were eagerly received by readers with their own problems and concerns, especially those attempting to understand the impact of newer media such as television and the computer, and by those concerned with issues of human and social development, issues of education and training in modern societies, and issues of international development centered around the newly formed United Nations. In the 1950s and 1960s, there was a strong sense that education and literacy were pivotal for social and cultural progress and that they could be used as powerful means to reach this goal. As Cole and Cole (2006) observed, this was a time when many countries were still emerging from the aftermath of World War II and centuries of colonialism: "There appeared to be a general consensus that the former colonized societies should be brought into more equitable interaction with their former colonizers in the industrialized world. Many people conceived of this process of change as a process of development in all spheres of life – the political, the economic, and the psychological." Referring to the role of UNESCO in the 1950s, Cole and Cole say, "in all spheres, people believed that literacy (ordinarily equated with formal education) was an essential engine of change" (pp. 308–309).

What Havelock described as a bursting dam is the sudden 'discovery' of literacy as an epistemic subject, its constitution as a prestigious subject, worthy of intellectual attention and academic investigation, and bringing with it the possibility of important social change. Havelock, the renowned Harvard and Yale classicist, is a case in point. His *Preface to Plato* (1963) was soon to become a milestone in the history of the literacy episteme. It set out to present Havelock's view of a "literate revolution" when the alphabet was introduced into the oral culture of ancient Greece, affecting all spheres of society and the individual mind. In a lecture presented at the University of Toronto three months before he died, Havelock described what he called "the breakthrough: 1962–63." He saw this breakthrough constituted by the appearance of four publications "that, in retrospect, can be said to have made a joint announcement": *The Gutenberg Galaxy* by McLuhan, *La Pensee Sauvage* by Levi-Strauss, and *The Consequences of Literacy* by Goody and Watt, as well as Havelock's own *Preface to Plato*. The statement they made was that orality and, thus, literacy "had to be put on the map. As a subject of intellectual interest, it's time was arriving" (Havelock, 1991, p. 12). We take a closer look at these breakthrough publications and, while adding some more to them, consider how all of them have changed the map of the emerging literacy episteme.

It is interesting that Havelock himself saw the breakthrough as the recognition of the oral as a mode of information storage and retrieval. He credits Milman Parry and his student, Alfred Lord, with the idea – well summarized in Lord's *The Singer of Tales* (1960) – that the recurring formulaic phrases in the Homeric epics (e.g., "rosy fingered dawn," "the wine dark sea," "Hector, tamer of horses") are a product of *oral* composition, the epithets being essential aids to memory. By comparing the Homeric tradition with an oral epic tradition that Parry and Lord found still existing in Serbia and Bosnia, they concluded that Homer was an oral poet. Havelock's contribution to the story was to show that by the time of Plato, oral methods of composition of extended texts had been rejected in favor of models based on written prose – even if Plato, as mentioned, was also the first critic of writing. Writing – in particular, alphabetic writing – he claimed, made the transcription of the oral epics possible; by looking at the written marks, one could mentally reconstruct the very voice of the speaker/poet. More important, Havelock claimed that because the alphabet bypassed the memory problem, it was possible to compose in a way that resembled ordinary speech and yet be preserved through time. This, Havelock argued, was the beginning of the distinction between the knower and the known and the birth of prose (for the current state of research on orality and literacy in ancient Greece, see Thomas, Chapter 19, this volume).

The idea of such differences among forms of language, modes of thought, the uses of memory, and, ultimately, the organization of societies based on the alternative "technologies" of orality and literacy caught the imagination of an entire generation of intellectuals and researchers. There may be no book more emblematic of this new fascination with matters of speech and writing than Lévi-Strauss's *La Pensée Sauvage*, published in 1962. Lévi-Strauss, who had made structuralism an intellectual mass movement, played a central role in associating the new look at writing with a new valuation of traditional, nonliterate or oral cultures: a move shifting the moral ontology. The resulting picture showed a fundamentally binary structure, to be sure, not unfamiliar to structuralists: a clear-cut distinction between speech and writing – the former viewed as a medium of natural human communication and authenticity, the latter as an unnatural and violent alienation of the voice and, in effect, a distortion of human nature. Lévi-Strauss's title, *La Pensée Sauvage*, was emphatic. It proclaimed a new view of a type of thought that most anthropologists and philosophers had until then considered the "primitive" (Malinowski, 1954), "pre-logical" (Lévy-Bruhl, 1923), and "mythic" (Cassirer, 1957) thought of native people in "traditional societies." For Lévi-Strauss, "savage thinking" became a positive quality – in fact, a value associated with "natural" orality that was to be seen as in sharp contrast with the "artificial" structures of Western literacy. Havelock (1991, p. 21) insisted that what Lévi-Strauss was investigating was not la *pensée sauvage* but rather la *pensée oraliste*. Oral thinking, in this view, was a thinking uncorrupted by writing (with "writing" exclusively understood in terms of the Western alphabet). How the dichotomy of orality and literacy – each linked to a specific "technology of the intellect" – powerfully affected the imagination of many is well laid out in Ong's (1967) *The Presence of the Word*, a book that radicalized and extended what critics called the theory of the "great divide."

Only a few months after publication of Lévi-Strauss's *La Pensée Sauvage*, Goody and Watt (1963) presented the first version of their cross-cultural studies, *The Consequences of Literacy*. The enormous influence of Goody's work on a broad spectrum of sociological-anthropological research on the relationships among literacy, thought, and society recently became the subject of an extensive reevaluation (Olson & Cole, 2006a). Goody's fundamental interest was in the development of Eurasian and African societies and the emergence of the "culture of cities" with the growth of bureaucratic institutions that overrode traditional forms of social organization, including families and tribes. In this development, the technologies of communication, especially writing, were crucial for the emergence of a variety of new social and cultural forms as well as corresponding psychological processes. In Goody's view, the beginning of writing in the Middle East was linked to the task of managing economic surplus and later to various forms of literature. Like Havelock, he saw ancient Greece and the invention of the alphabet as a paradigm case: given the historically unique combination of social, cultural, and material factors in Greek society, an efficient writing system, once introduced, could have a momentous impact on the development of science, philosophy, history, and democracy – creating, in effect, a new psychological mentality.

Goody, a Cambridge anthropologist, is best known for his detailed fieldwork among the LoDagaa peoples of Ghana. In addition to describing their social system, funeral rites, and rules of inheritance, as any good anthropologist would do, Goody was particularly attentive to their extended oral poetic tradition, embodied in *The Myth of the Bagra*. This interest was kindled by his experience as a prisoner of war who escaped and lived in a remote Italian village in the more or less complete absence of books – an even more peculiar experience for a Cambridge don. Yet, he became aware that this, in some ways, was a literate society, with its church, school, train schedules, postal system, taxes, and bureaucracy. The attraction of the LoDagaa was the striking contrast: here was a people whose social life was unaffected by writing, and Goody attributed many features of that society to the fact that its knowledge and traditions were preserved through songs and other oral rituals. Although Goody staunchly disavowed that an oral society is a primitive one, he is often taken to be the primary spokesperson for a "great divide" between the oral and the literate, the traditional and the civilized, *Gemeinschaft* and *Gesellschaft* societies, between us and them.

The influence that Goody's views exerted on various disciplines might have been that it offered a number of readily identifiable factors that could be applied to either any historical and contemporary social system or to systematic changes over time (Olson & Cole, 2006b, p. x). At the same time, this approach did, perhaps, sponsor a reductionist – unidirectional or monocausal – focus just on writing systems despite Goody's acknowledgment that "only to a limited extent can the means of communication, to use Marx's terminology from a different context, be separated from the relations of communication, which together form the mode of communication" (1977, p. 46).

Also in 1963, the book of another classicist, Hermann Koller, titled *Dichtung und Musik im frühen Griechenland* (*Poetry and Music in Early Greece*), independent of Havelock's and Goody's work, supported the hypothesis of a changing relationship between ancient orality and literacy but now in the domain of music and poetry. Koller drew on Snell's classic work, *The Discovery of the Mind* (1960), which advanced arguments that were comparable to those made with a wider scope in the volume, *L'écriture et la psychologie des peuples* (*Writing and Folk Psychology*), edited by Cohen et al. (1963). With a still wider scope, and certainly with an incomparably more spectacular thrill, there was the publication of Marshall McLuhan's *The Gutenberg Galaxy* in 1962. It put the entire study of the media and technologies of communication into an explicitly global and historical perspective and added to it what we today would call the global media hype. Media revolutions, McLuhan proclaimed on all channels, are revolutions of consciousness. New media are not merely new forms of communication of existing concepts, but rather they transform the very contents. McLuhan's slogan, "the medium is the message," albeit primarily based on the experience of first-generation television broadcasting, reverberated in all quarters of the 1960s culture and counterculture in the West. Indeed, it has never stopped.

Let us add a few more books to this list. Even scientists contributed to the emerging new epistemic ontology of the literacy episteme. In 1963, biologist Ernst Mayr published his *Species and Evolution*, a classic synthesis of evolutionary biology. Mayr claimed that language played a pivotal role in the evolution of the human species because it allowed for cultural development to be superimposed on biological structures. A similar view was articulated by the prehistorian and paleontolgist, André Leroi-Gourhan. In his *La Geste e la Parole* (*Gesture and Speech*) (Volume 1, *Technique et Langage;* Volume 2, *La Mémorire e les Rythmes*), published in 1964–65 (in English in 1993), he drew an evolutionary and cultural-historical line of development from the first traces of prehistoric writing practices to the manifold inscriptions that accompanied and, in fact, made possible the biological-cultural emergence of modern humans on their way to the computer age. For Leroi-Gourhan, this was the line of a continuous "externalization of memory," a line of thought productively developed by Donald (1991).

The significance of another influential scientist, Lev S. Vygotsky, investigating the interrelationships among language, writing, culture, and the mind, is widely acknowledged. In 1962, Vygotsky's *Thought and Language* was published for the first time in English, with an introduction by Jerome Bruner, a leading proponent of the "cognitive revolution" of the 1960s, who subsequently oriented his research more toward the psychological fabric of language, mind, and culture. Why did the work of Vygotsky and his student and colleague, Alexander Luria, become such an influential source for many researchers who then would contribute to the rise of the literacy episteme? As Cole and Cole (2006, p. 310) noted, the basic assumption of the "Vygotskian perspectives" (Wertsch, 1985) unfolding in those years was that "the human mind is formed through the active appropriation of the cultural store of the past, embodied in material artifacts, rituals, belief systems, writing systems, and the modes of social interaction they entail."

Although Vygotsky developed his ideas in the 1920s and 1930s in the Soviet Union, it was no accident that they came to fruition in the West in the cultural climate of the 1960s. Many of Vygotsky's claims about the role of literacy and schooling echo the views of Goody and Havelock (and several of the social and human scientists and scholars previously mentioned). They have become part of the semiotic and sociocultural tradition of psychological research on both oral and written language that has developed, not least, in the wake of Vygotsky and Luria (Brockmeier, 1998; Cole, 1996; Olson, 1994).

Widening the Frame: Innis and Derrida

So far, we have left out of the picture the work of two scholars who we first introduced. Innis and Derrida both contributed importantly to the rise of the literacy episteme through two different if partly overlapping developments. In one, literacy appears as a momentous factor within a practical, economic, social, and political trajectory; this is the focus of Innis, the economist and historian of communication. The other, at the theoretical end of the literacy episteme, places writing and language at the heart of the history of philosophy in the twentieth century. Whereas traditional Western philosophizing had assumed that conceptual thought derived from experience itself, thereby excluding language and writing, Derrida attempted to show that language and writing provide the basis of all conceptual thought.

Following Heidegger and Wittgenstein, the most influential philosophers in the first half of the last century, Derrida insisted that there had been what was called the *Sprachvergessenheit* – forgetfulness of language – in traditional philosophical thinking. Like them, Derrida argued that neither the world nor our selves are given to us "as such" and "in itself" – that is, in sheer spiritual or mental immediacy. Rather, our experience of the world – our being in the world – is inescapably mediated by sign and symbol systems, the imprint of human culture, among which language towers most prominently. We view Derrida's work on writing as part of this theoretical shift. In the twentieth century's effort to overcome forgetfulness of language, he took a further step, drawing attention not only to language "as such" and "in itself" but also to written language as central to the human experience, including that of language and thought. His readings of Western philosophy of language and metaphysics made clear that in place of a notion of writing, there is a void – a void that results from a consistent *Schriftvergessenheit* – forgetfulness of writing – in the Western tradition.

By including both Innis and Derrida in our range of vision, our time focus on the early 1960s widens: Innis's two books, *Empire and Communications* and *The Bias of Communication*, were published in 1950 and 1951; Derrida's two main books dealing with writing, *De la Grammatologie* (*Of Grammatology*) and *L'écriture et la Différence* (*Writing and Difference*), were published in 1967 (in English in 1976 and 1978).

Harold Innis was a Canadian economist best known for his extensive studies on the nature and structure of systems of transportation and communication. His work on the fur trade and on the pulp and paper industry was concerned not only with economic aspects but also with how those activities affected their social and intellectual lives. The implications of this work for the social development and economy of Canada were sufficiently clear to make him an important consultant to government. Late in his career, he published two books, *Empire and Communication* and *The Bias of Communication*. In the former, he compared ancient empires of Egypt, Greece, and Rome with those of the modern period, tracing their structure in part to forms of communication: the Egyptians writing on stone, thereby preserving empire through time; the Romans writing on paper, which enabled them to not only dominate but also to organize and control a far-flung empire. One focus of Innis's explorations of the relationships among communication, media, and culture was the significance of time and space for these relationships:

> *The concepts of time and space reflect the significance of media to civilization. Media that emphasize time are those that are durable in character, such as parchment, clay, and stone. The heavy materials are suited to the development of architecture and sculpture. Media that emphasizes space are apt to be less durable and light in character, such as papyrus and paper. The latter are suited to wide areas in administration and trade. . . . Materials that emphasize time favour decentralization and hierarchical types of institutions, while those that emphasize space favour centralization and systems of government less hierarchical in character. Large-scale political organizations such as empires must be considered from the standpoint of two dimensions, those of space and time (Innis, 1950/1986, p. 5).*

Innis's *The Bias of Communication* is not only a discussion of how communication media influence our lives but also is a lament for the loss of the direct, personal, and more traditional forms of oral communication.

Derrida's contribution to the literacy episteme might be situated, we suggested, at the end of the theoretical spectrum opposite to Innis's. At first sight, it might be difficult to see a match between the interests of the Canadian scholar, studying the history of the fur trade around the Hudson Bay, and the interests of the French intellectual, deconstructing metaphysical constructs such as "phallogocentrism." However, there are surprising commonalities. One is a keen sensibility for issues of power and violence. For Innis, writing and communication are factors of power and the struggle for hegemony in an economic and political field. His point of reference is "the Empire"; an empire is "an indication of the efficiency of communication" (Innis, 1950/1986, p. 5). For Derrida, writing is a factor of power and the struggle for hegemony in the field of Western philosophy and in the politics of ideas. Both scholars aim to fuse two orders that traditional academic discourse has always tried to keep apart: the order of material (i.e., political, economic, and social) interests and the order of thoughts and concepts.

These visions and their underlying assumptions show great proximity to the work of Foucault who, in his discourse theory of power and knowledge (Foucault, 1970, 1972), offered a systematically and historically elaborated theory of such "fusion." Then there also is their interest in – in fact, the insistence on – taking the interface of language, communication, thought, and history as the point of departure for such an inquiry. Both Innis and Derrida would not have had any difficulty in making sense, each in his work, of the Wittgensteinian conviction that "to imagine a language means to imagine a form of life" (Wittgenstein, 1953, §19).

The task Derrida sets for himself in his *De la Grammatologie* and *L'écriture et la Différence* is to examine and challenge a tradition of metaphysics in which the status of writing has been constantly subordinated to that of speech. This tradition is revealed as an ongoing attempt to repress the fact that the written sign has its own specificity, materiality, and significance. As both a consequence and presupposition of this repression, Derrida argues, philosophy and linguistics have advanced the idea that words can communicate thoughts or meanings without any direct link to the material sign, their inscription. The sign, on this account, appears as a nonessential auxiliary to spoken language. Not only is the sign external to the essence of speech, it also is taken as entirely transparent. In other words, thoughts or meanings are given in an unmediated and immediate fashion. They are conveyed like the sound of the voice (*phone*) that pervades the air without resistance. Derrida calls this the vision of *phonocentrism* or *phonologism*, and he views it as the dominant Western model of writing: "this factus of phonetic writing is massive: it commands our entire culture and our entire science, and it is certainly not just one fact among others" (Derrida, 1976, pp. 30–31).

The phonocentric model is not restricted to the philosophy of language. Derrida devotes one of his exemplary critiques of the phonocentric subordination of writing to de Saussure's linguistics and another to Lévi-Strauss's anthropology, which was modeled on de Saussureian structuralism. In metaphysics, linguistics, and structural anthropology, Derrida (1976) states, "phonologism" is undoubtedly the exclusion or abasement of writing. But it is also the granting of authority to a science which is held to be the model for all the so-called sciences of man. In both these senses Lévi-Strauss's structuralism is a phonologism" (p. 102). We also could add here the name of another highly influential linguist: Noam Chomsky. As has often been pointed out, de Saussure and Chomsky conceived of language as a closed and internally (i.e., "structurally") regulated system, without paying heed to the social and pragmatic functions of language and the role language plays in a culture and as a form of life. As a consequence, scientific linguistics in the wake of de Saussure and Chomsky dismissed and, in effect, rejected all concrete forms of use in which language exists, including the material use of signs and, thus, writing. Instead, it has been based on the conviction that the nature of language is determined by "fixed codes," which, according to Harris (1981), is the "language myth" of linguistic thought.

Historically, the exclusion of writing from the notion of language can be traced back to Aristotle's (1963) view, previously discussed, that spoken words are the symbols of mental experience and written words are the symbols of spoken words. Simply stated, writing is speech "put down." Some writers have noted a contradiction in Aristotle: the material of reference for his distinctions of forms on which he built his momentous formal logic is forms of written and not spoken language (Simon, 1989; Stetter, 1999). Still, the Aristotelian paradigm went on to dominate not only medieval thinking about language and the significance of writing (Stock, 1983), but also modern and even twentieth-century philosophy, linguistics, and psychology of language (e.g., Derrida, 1976; Harris, 1986; Olson, 1994). Significantly, the three most influential linguistic theories about the origin and development of writing, those of Gelb (1963), Cohen (1958), and Diringer (1968), described the history of writing systems as teleologically evolving toward the phonocentric ideal of the Western alphabet, which postulates the precise representations, or "perfect transcription," of sound patterns by visible signs.

Such is the theoretical situation in which Derrida outlined his new theory of *écriture*, drawing attention to the specificity and materiality of writing. Moreover, the concept of writing is extended and dissociated from any underlying alphabetic teleology, which he dismissed as ethnocentric. Writing is given priority for the understanding of speech and language in general. At the same time, Derrida aimed to explain why Western thought about language consistently avoided recognizing, much less investigating the materiality of the linguistic sign. Phonocentrism, he argued, is not just a mistake, failure, or shortcoming of philosophers of language and linguists who were unable to capture the semiotic particularities of writing, but rather it is part of a bigger intellectual and moral project. Examining the works of philosophers of the Enlightenment (Rousseau), German idealists (Hegel), phenomenologists (Husserl), and structuralists (de Saussure and Lévi-Strauss), Derrida argued that privileging of the voice is but a consequence of viewing writing as a mere secondary representation – as an appendage that only has function and meaning in as far as it is a transparent symbol of the immaterial word. This patently reflects a deeply rooted conviction of the superiority of mental or spiritual immediacy. This "metaphysics of immediacy" is not simply a linguistic fixation but rather the symptom of a more fundamental tendency that relates phonocentrism to logocentrism. *Logocentrism* is the assumption that both spoken and written signs are only hints and external expressions of deeper meanings and truths, truths that lie in either thoughts of men or, ultimately, the minds of gods. It is not surprising, then, that the first and last concerns in the Western tradition are spiritual and ethereal entities, such as *logos* and the Divine Word, soul and spirit, Hegel's *Geist* (i.e., mind/spirit), and Kant's transcendental subject, all of which Derrida scoffingly rejects.

It is clear that on this account, the priority of the immaterial voice over writing (and the traditional oppositions of presence and absence, substance and form, essence and appearance) proves to be interwoven with a complex fabric of philosophical and religious motives. We have to be aware of these motives if we want to understand why phonocentrism and logocentrism are bound into a moral ontology that privileges the mind over the body and the spiritual and intelligible over the sensible and material.

Why Did the Dam Burst?

Somewhere between Innis and Derrida, the dam, which kept the issue of writing and literacy out of reach, started to burst, to use Havelock's expression once again. A cultural pressure must have built up that finally released a flood of interest and intellectual curiosity, of social and economic commitment devoted to both the evocation of the importance of literacy and to the attempt of understanding it. Today, there can be no doubt that the emergence of this novel orientation – the literacy episteme – cannot be explained only within theoretical and academic confines but rather needs to be situated within the trajectories of far-reaching social, cultural, and technological transformations. In fact, our focus on the intellectual construction of concepts and theories is only half the story, for scientific and cultural communities are not only constituted by a shared epistemic and moral ontology but also by institutional realities. As Innis already underlined, structures of communication are always also material realities, shaped by manifest social, economic, political, and military interests.

Much recent research within and on the literacy episteme has dealt with these interests and the different institutional orders of literacy (Olson & Torrance, 2001), which include, for example, the supervisory activities of authorities and powerful organizations. A case in point of how these realities make themselves felt is the mega-institution of schooling. There are many different theories and ideas about how to teach children proper spoken and written language. That these theories and ideas are not just theoretical becomes clear when teachers, academics, politicians, and institutions come onto the scene with the power to enforce norms of linguistic practice. When teachers have the power to enforce – through testing and grading – children's spelling and thereby implement certain literacy standards, we encounter the significance of institutional knowledge and power. The institutional norms and disciplinary standards of "academic literacies" (Lea & Street, 1999) similarly aim to shape scientific discourse, including discourse on spoken and written language (as in this *Handbook*). Various authors have pointed out that academic discourse is not the neutral linguistic expression of new findings and insights that it often claims to be but rather that body of genre conventions – rules of composition and style that the institutions of science have legitimized as in conformity with established epistemic codes (e.g., Bazerman, 1988; Berkenkotter & Huckin, 1995; Geissler, 1994; Proctor, 2002). Indeed, it may be argued that such science is possible only within this institutional order.

New technologies of communication have provided another powerful incentive toward recognizing the reality of literacy. Many scholars today have suggested viewing twentieth-century transformations in literacy and cultural modes of communication as inextricably intermingled with the profound changes in the material technologies of communication. Not many, however, realized the significance of twentieth-century electronic media revolutions for the shift in our knowledge about orality and literacy as early as Innis's colleague, McLuhan. But McLuhan set the tone. Through his well-orchestrated demonstrations of a mutual connection between technological development and cultural change in Western means of communication, reflection, and imagination, he was perhaps the most timely and media-eloquent prophet of the new episteme. Still, as we have seen, McLuhan was essentially alone in beginning to reflect on the fact that television and its predecessors, radio and telephone, were transforming the reach of the spoken word, of orality, while also establishing a spectrum of new and specific literacies. All of these new phenomena raised new questions and cast new light on old questions. What actually is meant by *orality* and *literacy* (terms that now became ubiquitous), and what is the difference between their 'old' and 'new' (i.e., electronically mediated) forms? And how does oral discourse relate to non-oral, literate discourse, and how do both affect the mind?

These questions were publicly addressed and discussed in various cultural milieus in North America and Western Europe – only rarely, however, in established academic contexts. Havelock (1991) noted many years later that it would be misleading to view the appearance of this new sensitivity as the conscious and coordinated emergence of a new awareness of a problem or even of a new vision; rather, it might be more helpful to view it as a reaction to something else. "Was this grouping as it occurred," Havelock (1991, p. 12) asked, "a pure accident or did it reflect a common and widespread response, even if an unconscious one, in France, England, the United States, and Canada, to a shared experience of a technological revolution in the means of human communication?"

If the shared experience of the transformation of the dominant modes of communication in the West, which McLuhan (1962, 1964) believed to have culminated in the "global village" of 1960s television culture, can be seen as the cultural backdrop of the rise of the literacy episteme, as we have proposed, then this experience fully unfolded and radicalized with the electronic revolutions of the 1970s, 1980s, and 1990s – that is, with the emergence of the personal computer, e-mail, Internet, and the many other digital means of communication, archivation, and information handling that came with them. But let us be clear about this: it was not new technology alone that led to the momentous changes of the "digital age," changes that included the emergence of a new sensitivity for the cultural significance of literacy. Another development overlapped and intermingled with the technological one, to the point that it became difficult to distinguish between the two. This was the development of increased concern with traditional literacy.

The literacy levels of school children were increasingly seen as inadequate; campaigns like *A Nation at Risk* and the perceived "illiteracy" of even educated adults drew increased attention, public pressure, and, in some cases, increased public funding during this period (see Sticht, Chapter 29, this volume). In part, this concern was fueled by the exponential increase of all kinds of printed documents, a flood of writing unimaginable to previous generations – which, to a degree, has also been a consequence of the "digital revolution." Since those legendary years at the beginning of the 1960s, probably more books, newspapers, journals, and other written documents have been printed and published than in all the centuries since Gutenberg. The entire unfathomable universe of Gutenberg print is right now in the process of being once again multiplied in countless virtual libraries and public and private libraries (if these terms still make any sense in the digital world).

It seems that only now two features of an advanced culture of literacy have unmistakably come to the fore: that it is based in a radical sense on a documentary tradition, in terms of both society and mind (Olson, 2006), and that it is not just about 'writing' and the alphabet but also about the fusion of many sign systems, media, modes of communication, and corresponding practices in one symbolic space – a space of signs and symbols that, again, embraces both society and the mind (Brockmeier, 2000).

In the 1950s and 1960s, authors such as Innis, McLuhan, and Goody and Watt were not the only ones who defined the vision that revolutions of media and modes of communication redraw the maps for culture and the mind. However, they were among the first who noticed and anticipated interdependencies that would develop in the decades to come in countless variations and be applied to every facet of the "digital culture" (for a survey, see Castells, 2001; Levinson, 1999). Entire new disciplines (e.g., Information Studies, Communication, Cultural Studies, and Media Studies) were built on this thesis, and transdisciplinary discussions on the meaning and implication of the "media hypothesis" have not ceased since then.

The argument presented in this chapter is that the new focus on sign mediation (or semiotic mediation) of culture and thought – with literacy being just one but crucial mode of such mediation – appears to be an advanced version of the effort to overcome traditional *Sprachvergessenheit* (i.e., forgetfulness of language) in philosophy and the human sciences. This effort has now also included overcoming *Schriftvergessenheit* (i.e., forgetfulness of writing).

Arguably, the technological, social, and cultural changes of modern communication have had a greater and further-reaching impact on our thoughts about language than all mainstream linguistic thinking. It says much about the closed and self-referential discourse of Western academia that the question of the particular nature of writing could be posed clearly for the first time only after the traditional phonocentric and logocentric dogmas about the relationship between speech and writing had been questioned from the outside, subjected "to the brash counterpropaganda of a McLuhan and to the inquisitorial skepticism of a Derrida," as Harris (1986, p. 158) stated it. Harris went on to maintain that it says even more "that the question could not be posed clearly until writing itself had dwindled to microchip dimensions."

In the last few decades, there has been a significant increase in the number of linguists "willing to consider writing as a form of language in its own right" (Harris, 1995, p. 3). However, these changes within the discipline of linguistics began to take place only after the dam had already burst under the pressure of technological and cultural innovation and the flood of a novel discourse had given shape to the new literacy episteme. It is worth noting that the first systematic linguistic theory of writing proposed in light of the new episteme was *Signs of Writing* by Harris (1995), an outspoken outsider and critic of traditional phonocentric linguistics.

Literacy, we may conclude, can never again be ignored. It has become a part of the discourse in all of the human sciences. It is not surprising that as the concept has been assimilated by various disciplines and social movements, the entire notion of literacy itself has changed. We can no longer simply compare the literate with the illiterate, the spoken with the written, the word with the text, the primitive with the civilized as some of the pioneers of the literacy episteme did. Literacy today is understood in many different cultural configurations. It has a place in countless social practices and activities, in institutional settings, and on political agendas, as well as in many theoretical perspectives and empirical research paradigms. As a consequence, there are several different concepts and definitions of literacy to be found (also in this *Handbook*). Most writers today agree that it is necessary to distinguish diverse forms and practices of writing and literacy, to distinguish the potential of writing for specific purposes from the concrete uses made of writing by particular individuals or in particular societies, and, on occasion, to distinguish the different uses and implications of writing even within a society or cultural milieu. In other words, there is no scholar of literacy today who considers writing as a simple cause of change as many did at the onset of the literacy episteme. Simplifying and reductionist claims have given way to differentiated views according to which, as formulated, for example, by Besnier (1991, p. 570), "the value of literacy in a society is defined by the ideology that surrounds it, the social practices with which it is associated, and the power structure in which reading and writing activities are enacted." This is in line with statements of literacy policy as presented, for example, by UNESCO: "literacy must be seen as an activity embedded in social and cultural practice" rather than as "a deficit or lack in the learner [to] be remedied by ready-made packages of knowledge and skill" (Olson & Torrance, 2001, p. xii). Further, as mentioned previously, there is growing consensus that there is not just literacy but also a spectrum of different literacies, a spectrum that keeps expanding with the digital revolution – as does the ontology of the literacy episteme.

As a consequence, many different theoretical and empirical approaches have been developed to investigate this growing spectrum of literacies. At the same time, however, research has also aimed at looking for the common basis of these diverse activities to determine both what is distinctive about writing as opposed to alternative means of expression, communication, and reflection, and the psychological competencies that may be general to many of them. The goal of this research is a more precise understanding of what we may mean by something as vague yet as important as literate competence as the ability to use written language as a form of life. This includes not only examining literacy as one social practice among others but also how social practices of communication, recordkeeping, and sharing are themselves altered by the availability of a notational system. It is widely assumed, perhaps optimistically, by educators that literacy skills are generalizable and that the skills involved in creating and using texts are sufficiently important that they justify an enormous investment in education. Although some have seen here the danger of imposing a too sharp distinction between general literacy skills and the specialized knowledge accessible through literacy, there does seem to be a consensus that at least some forms of competence are sufficiently general that they can be taught and learned in such a way that they may be applied to any domain, whether in science or literature, economics or politics. There is no doubt that it is the belief in that generalized competence – a specialized way with words – that has driven much of public schooling and literacy policy.

Let us point out a last consequence of the literacy episteme. We have argued in this chapter that the rise of the literacy episteme, which seemed to have been possible only in the wake of a fundamental shift in the technological and cultural settings of mass communication, at the same time has witnessed how the once universal cultural hegemony of writing itself has been coming to an end. The gentleman in the parlor reading *The Idler*, a literacy practice in Dr. Johnson's days considered the peak of educated and cultured living, has become but an ironic vignette to be used in a handbook to illustrate how much has changed since the rise of the literacy episteme. That is not to say that the practice of writing is coming to an end – indeed, literate practices flourish as never before. Rather, the intellectual and cultural attitude – an attitude originated in class, privilege, and the modernist outlook upon the world that has regarded the traditional form of writing and its institutions as the epitome and guaranty of civilization – not only of Western civilization but also of human civilization as such, has come to an end. In its place is a renewed interest in and recognition of the diverse forms and uses of this most recognizable of all human technologies: the written word.

References

Aristotle (1963). *Categories and de interpretatione* (transl. by J. L. Ackrill). Oxford: Clarendon Press.

Astle, T. (1784/1876). *The origin and progress of writing, as well hieroglyphic as elementary, illustrated by engravings taken from marbles, manuscripts and charters, ancient and modern: also, some account of the origin and progress of printing* (1st ed. 1784 by the Author). London: Chatto & Windus.

Bazerman, C. (1988). *Shaping written knowledge: The genre and activity of the experimental article in science*. Madison, WI: University of Wisconsin Press.

Berkenkotter, C., & Huckin, T. (1995). *Genre knowledge in disciplinary communication: Cognition/culture/power*. Mahwah, NJ: Erlbaum.

Besnier, N. (1991). Literacy and the notion of person on Nukulaelae Atoll. *American Anthropologist*, 93 (3), 570–587.

Brockmeier, J. (1998). *Literales Bewußtsein. Schriftlichkeit und das Verhältnis von Sprache und Kultur [The literate mind: Literacy and the relationship between language and culture]*. Munich: Fink.

Brockmeier, J. (2000). Literacy as symbolic space. In J. W. Astington (Ed.), *Minds in the making* (pp. 43–61). Oxford: Blackwell.

Brockmeier, J., & Olson, D. R. (2002). Introduction: What is a culture of literacy? In J. Brockmeier, M. Wang, & D. R. Olson (Eds.), *Literacy, narrative and culture* (pp. 1–15). Richmond: Curzon/Routledge.

Cassirer, E. (1957). *The Philosophy of symbolic forms (Volume 3)*. (R. Manheim, Trans.). New Haven, Conn: Yale University Press.

Castells, M. (2001). *The internet galaxy*. Oxford and New York: Oxford University Press.

Chamberlin, E. (2002). Hunting, tracking and reading. In J. Brockmeier, M. Wang, & D. R. Olson (Eds.), *Literacy, narrative and culture* (pp. 67–85). Richmond: Curzon/Routledge.

Cohen, M. (1958). *La grande invention de l'écriture et son évolution*. Paris: Klincksieck.

Cohen, M., et al. (1963). *L'écriture et la psychologie des peuples*. Centre International de synthèse. Paris: Colin.

Cole, M. (1996). *Cultural psychology: A once and future discipline*. Cambridge, MA: Harvard University Press.

Cole, M., & Cole, J. (2006). Rethinking the Goody myth. In D. R. Olson & M. Cole (Eds.), *Technology, literacy, and the evolution of society: Implications of the work of Jack Goody* (pp. 305–324). Mahwah, NJ: Erlbaum.

Derrida, J. (1967). *De la grammatologie*. Paris: Editions de Minuit.

Derrida, J. (1976). *Of grammatology*. Baltimore, MD: Johns Hopkins University Press (French 1967).

Derrida, J. (1978). *Writing and difference*. London: Routledge & Kegan Paul (French 1967).

Derrida, J. (1993). *Speech and phenomena, and other essays on Husserl's theory of signs*. Evaston, IL: Northwestern University Press (French 1972).

Diringer, D. (1968). *The alphabet: A key to the history of mankind* (1st ed. 1948). London: Hutchinson.

Donald, M. (1991). *Origins of the modern mind: Three stages in the evolution of culture and cognition*. Cambridge, MA: Harvard University Press.

Foucault, M. (1970). *The order of things: An archeology of the human sciences*. London: Tavistock Publications (French 1966).

Foucault, M. (1972). *The archeology of knowledge*. New York: Harper and Row (French 1969).

Geertz, C. (1983). *Local knowledge: Further essays in interpretive anthropology*. New York: Basic Books.

Geisler, C. (1994). *Academic literacy and the nature of expertise: Reading, writing, and knowing in academic philosophy*. Hillsdale, NJ: Lawrence Erlbaum.

Gelb, I. J. (1963). *A study of writing* (1st ed. 1952). Chicago: University of Chicago Press.

Goody, J. (1977). *The domestication of the savage mind*. Cambridge: Cambridge University Press.

Goody, J. (1987). *The interface between the written and the oral*. Cambridge: Cambridge University Press.

Goody, J., & Watt, I. (1963). The consequences of literacy. *Comparative Studies in Society and History*, 5, 304–345.

Hacking, I. (2002). *Historical ontology*. Cambridge, MA: Harvard University Press.

Hacking, I. (2006). *Another new world is being constructed right now: The ultracold*. Max-Planck-Institute Preprints 316. Berlin: Max-Planck-Institute for Historical Epistemology.

Harris, R. (1981). *The language myth*. London: Duckworth.

Harris, R. (1986). *The origin of writing*. London: Duckworth.

Harris, R. (1995). *Signs of writing*. London and New York: Routledge.

Havelock, E. A. (1963). *Preface to Plato*. Cambridge, MA, and London: Belknap Press of Harvard University Press.

Havelock, E. A. (1986). *The muse learns to write: Reflections on orality and literacy from antiquity to the present*. New Haven, CT: Yale University Press.

Havelock, E. A. (1991). The oral-literature equation: A formula for the modern mind. In D. R. Olson & N. Torrance (Eds.), *Literacy and orality* (pp. 11–27). Cambridge: Cambridge University Press.

Innis, H. (1986). *Empire and communications*. Victoria, BC: Press Porcépic (1st ed. 1950).

Innis, H. (1951). *The bias of communication*. Toronto: University of Toronto Press.

Koller, H. (1963). *Dichtung und Musik im frühen Griechenland*. Bern and Munich: Francke.

Koselleck, R. (1985). *Futures past: On the semantics of historical time*. Cambridge, MA, and London: MIT Press.

Kroskrity, P. V. (2001). Identity. In A. Duranti (Ed.), *Key terms in language and culture* (pp. 106–109). Oxford: Blackwell.

Kuhn, T. S. (1962). *The structure of scientific revolutions*. Chicago: The University of Chicago Press.

Latour, B., & Woolgar, B. (1979). *Laboratory life: The social construction of scientific facts*. Beverly Hills, CA: Sage Publications.

Lea, M., & Street, B. (1999). Writing as academic literacies: Understanding textual practices in higher education. In C. Candlin & K. Hyland (Eds.), *Writing: texts, processes and practices* (pp. 62–81). London: Longman.

Leroi-Gourhan, A. (1964, 1965). *La geste e la parole* (Gesture and Speech) (*Vol. 1, Techique et langage; Vol. 2, La mémorire e les rythmes*). Paris: A. Michel.

Leroi-Gourhan, A. (1993). *Gesture and speech*. Cambridge, MA: MIT Press.

Levinson, P. (1999). *Digital McLuhan: A guide to the information millennium*. London and New York: Routledge.

Lévi-Strauss, C. (1962). *La pensée sauvage*. Paris: Plon.

Levy-Bruhl, L. (1923). *Primitive mentality*. London: George Allen & Unwin.

Lord, A. B. (1960). *The singer of tales*. Cambridge, MA: Harvard University Press.

Malinowski, B. (1954). *Magic, science and religion, and other essays*. Garden City, NY: Doubleday.

Mayr, E. (1963). *Animal species and evolution*. Cambridge, MA: Belknap Press of Harvard University Press.

McLuhan, M. (1962). *The Gutenberg galaxy. The making of typographic man*. Toronto: University of Toronto Press.

McLuhan, M. (1964). *Understanding media: The extensions of man*. New York: McGraw-Hill.

Olson, D. R. (1994). *The world on paper: The cognitive and conceptual implication of writing and reading*. Cambridge: Cambridge University Press.

Olson, D. R. (2006). The documentary tradition in mind and society. In D. R. Olson & M. Cole (Eds.), *Technology, literacy, and the evolution of society: Implications of the work of Jack Goody* (pp. 289–304). Mahwah, NJ: Erlbaum.

Olson, D. R., & Cole, M. (Eds.) (2006a). *Technology, literacy, and the evolution of society: Implications of the work of Jack Goody*. Mahwah, NJ: Erlbaum.

Olson, D. R., & Cole, M. (Eds.) (2006b). In the Preface to *Technology, literacy, and the evolution of society: Implications of the work of Jack Goody* (pp. ix–xvii). Mahwah, NJ: Erlbaum.

Olson, D. R., & Torrance, N. (Eds.) (2001). In the Preface to *On the making of literate societies: Literacy and social development* (pp. x–xiii). Oxford: Blackwell.

Ong, W. J. (1967). *The presence of the word*. New Haven, CT: Yale University Press.

Ong, W. J. (1982). *Orality and literacy: The technologizing of the word*. London: Methuen.

Procter, M. (2002). The essay as a literary and academic form: Closed gate or open door? In J. Brockmeier, M. Wang, & D. R. Olson (Eds.), *Literacy, narrative and culture* (pp. 170–83). Richmond: Curzon/Routledge.

Rheinberger, H.-J. (1997). *Toward a history of epistemic things: Synthesizing proteins in the test tube*. Stanford, CA: Stanford University Press.

Simon, J. (1989). *Philosophie des Zeichens [Philosophy of the sign]*. Berlin: de Gruyter.

Snell, B. (1960). *The discovery of the mind: The Greek origins of European thought*. New York: Harper & Row (German 1953).

Stetter, C. (1999). *Schrift und Sprache [Writing and language]*. Frankfurt/Main: Suhrkamp.

Stock, B. (1983). *The implications of literacy: Written language and models of interpretation in the eleventh and twelfth centuries*. Princeton, NJ: Princeton University Press.

Taylor, C. (1989). *Sources of the self: The making of the modern identity*. Cambridge: Cambridge University Press.

Vygotsky, L. S. (1962). *Thought and language*. Cambridge, MA: MIT Press.

Wagner, D. A. (1999). Rationales, debates, and new directions: An introduction. In D. A. Wagner, R. L. Venetzky, & B. V. Street (Eds.), *Literacy: An international handbook* (pp. 1–8). Boulder, CO: Westview.

Wang, Qi, & Brockmeier, J. (2002). Autobiographical remembering as cultural practice: Understanding the interplay between memory, self, and culture. *Culture & Psychology, 8* (1), 45–64.

Wertsch, J. V. (Ed.) (1985). *Culture, communication and cognition: Vygotskian perspectives*. Cambridge: Cambridge University Press.

Wittgenstein, L. (1953). *Philosophical investigations*. Oxford: Blackwell.

Part II

LITERACY AND LANGUAGE

CHAPTER 2

Grammatology

Peter T. Daniels

The aim of this book is to lay a foundation for a full science of writing. . . . To the new science we could give the name "grammatology," following partially the term "grammatography" which was used [in 1861] in a title of a book on writing published in England.

(Gelb, 1952, p. 23)[1]

Without writing, there is no literacy. But writing does not guarantee literacy.

In Mesopotamia it is clear, and in the other loci of the invention of writing it is surmised, that writing began not for recording connected discourse – that is, language – but for recording commercial transactions.[2] This chapter, then, describes the varieties of writing systems that have arisen over the past five millennia, outlining their development and showing how they relate to the languages they record. As an experiment in clarity, we proceed not in historical order but rather from most familiar to less familiar, along several dimensions.

The English alphabet is known to all readers of this book, so it is our starting point. It can be considered but a slight development from the Roman alphabet (devised for the Latin language), combining a form that was SET IN STONE more than two thousand years ago; a form standardized in the court of Charlemagne twelve hundred years ago; and an *Italian Renaissance hand* based on it seven hundred years ago. The *forms* of written characters are of little consequence for literacy studies, and it suffices to direct the reader to the two reliable, detailed accounts in English (Diringer, 1968 and Jensen, 1969; they are not superseded by Daniels & Bright, 1996, which, although it includes historical information, primarily treats the synchronic use of scripts).[3]

In *function*, though, the English alphabet has diverged considerably from the Latin, and English orthography is often claimed to be a stumbling block in the way of literacy acquisition. An overview of the way this came about introduces many of the concepts needed for a functional interpretation of the history of writing (Daniels, 2007).

For a century or so, many movements have been afoot to "simplify" English spelling. Perhaps the most visible have been those of the Simplified Spelling Board in the United States (advocated by Melville Dewey [or Melvil Dui] and used in every edition of the Dewey Decimal Classification until his death in 1931 [Dewey, 1932] and, in part, beyond) and the Simplified Spelling Society in the United Kingdom (Upward, 1996), each of which proposes a small number of rules (eighteen for the former, just three for the latter!) to be applied to "traditional orthography" (t.o.) resulting in more rational symbol–sound correspondences. Such enterprises have not succeeded – and are unlikely to – in part because of the immense pool of literate English-readers who would resist the re-education needed to access new materials, and in part because the four-hundred-plus years of written English that can now be read with little difficulty would become inaccessible to generations trained only in an orthography that omitted "redundant letters" (to take a term from Upward's title). A phenomenon that has produced extremely compressed English orthography is text-messaging, or texting (Cook, 2004, pp. 201–203; Crystal, 2006, pp. 262–264), but this may prove transitory as message capacity increases and input methods simplify.[4]

The last time a spelling "reform" succeeded for English was toward the close of the eighteenth century, when "American" spelling came into use in the new nation. This is usually attributed to Noah Webster (1758–1843), educator and lexicographer, but it is an exaggeration: far from all the orthographic changes he advocated found acceptance; most or all of them can be found in proposals current in England before and during his career (Mickelthwait, 2000); and they don't amount to much anyway – ultimately *-er* for *-re* and *-or* for *-our*, and the still controversial *-ize* for *-ise*. Spelling reforms can only succeed via the intervention of a government or of a national language academy with the authority to enforce decrees (Neijt, 2006); such has never existed in the English-speaking world, where norms are set by publishers, lexicographic enterprises (notably Oxford University Press in the British sphere and Merriam-Webster in the American), and a few exceptional individuals (Webster; Samuel Johnson [1709–1784]).

The contrast between the methodology of Dr. Johnson and that of James A. H. Murray's (1837–1915) *Oxford* [originally *New*] *English Dictionary* (*OED*) (which prevailed everywhere until the advent of electronic databases), described by Reddick (1996) and Murray (1977), respectively, reveals the importance of often overlooked technological advances. Johnson's amanuenses copied his illustrative quotations onto sheets of paper, which were then cut up and either pasted or recopied into the manuscript; the *OED*'s readers used slips of paper of uniform size, which could be sorted and filed. Mass production of uniformly sized paper of uniform thickness developed only in the 1830s; index cards came even later, and with them the flexible library catalog only in the 1850s.[5] Eisenstein's (1979) principal observation is that religious reformation and the modern conception of science were made possible by the invention of printing with movable type (through both widespread distribution and reliable reproduction of written materials); she also notes that alphabetizing, essential for both dictionaries and the indexing of books, could not be practically accomplished without both printing and paper (p. 89f.). Entertainment in the form of prose fiction, too (as opposed to storytelling and the composition and recitation of more easily memorized and re-created poetic diction), also became possible with printing.

Paper – handmade paper – was a Chinese invention of the second century BCE; by the early first century CE, it was used for writing. In the early eighth century at the latest, the thing and its manufacture had come to the nascent Islamic civilization, which in turn brought it to Europe by the eleventh century. Printing would not have been feasible without paper: parchment was far too costly to be used in quantity, and papyrus had become scarce (Bloom, 2001; Lewis, 1974).

In Europe, printing dates from the middle of the fifteenth century, and its development – it was not a single invention, but rather the combination of the existing technologies of the wine (or oil) press, the chemistry of ink, the metallurgy of casting, and the goldsmith's ability to manipulate tiny sculptural forms – was the achievement of Johannes Gutenberg (ca. 1390–1468) and associates in Mainz. The Gothic forms of letters used in their first products – most famously, of course, the 42-line Bible of 1455 – were those in use in northern Europe. They did not travel well (though German was still, decreasingly, printed with their descendant the Fraktur style until the mid twentieth century), and when printing reached Venice shortly thereafter, it was natural for Nicholas Jenson (ca. 1420–1480) to cut Roman types imitating the standardized manuscript hand developed at Charlemagne's behest by Alcuin of York (ca. 732–804) more than 650 years earlier. At the turn of the sixteenth century, Aldus Manutius (1449–1515) looked back only two centuries to Petrarch (1304–1374) for a more compact form, now known as *italic*. The gross uniformity of roman-alphabet forms over the ensuing centuries can be ascribed to the uniformitization imposed by print; another realm with an area of a size similar to Europe's, the Indian Subcontinent, did not know printing in some areas until the nineteenth century. With the advent of the press, regional variation – earlier no greater than that found in European areas of traditions of similar age – crystallized into more than half a dozen distinctive but clearly related local standard scripts.

So much for the formal contribution of printing to the history of literacy: functionally, printing, insofar as a consistent orthography is used, fixes the spellings of words. Before the standardization imposed by printing (and the subsequent systematization by dictionaries like Johnson's), people wrote essentially as they spoke. People from different dialect areas spelled words differently. People learned different conventions in different scribal schools. (These early variations are useful in untangling the history of a language, but they can be problematic for those literate in the standard language.) The introduction of printing to England by William Caxton (1422?–1491) in 1475 came at a particularly inopportune time, for it fixed the spelling of English vowels just before a wholesale change took place over several generations: the Great English Vowel Shift. Before it – in Chaucer's day – English vowels were pronounced as indicated by the Latin values of the letters used for them; after it, they were pronounced largely as they are today, at odds with their spelling as understood by all other users of Roman alphabets. The sound(s) represented by ⟨gh⟩ changed differently in different areas or circumstances, leading to the variety heard in *bough, cough, dough, rough, through*. Other languages that have undergone extensive changes in pronunciation since their orthography became fixed include French and Thai.

Why Latin? Because Latin was the language of the Church of Rome – the church that sent missionaries throughout Europe to convert the heathen. (The Roman Empire had had no interest in bringing literacy to its subject peoples.) Centers of learning – abbeys – were scattered about Europe. Manuscripts were kept and copied there, and for some languages, the earliest vernacular writing was interlinear glosses in Latin texts. The most celebrated were (in the seventh century) in Ireland and (in the ninth century) in Charlemagne's court at Aix, led by the aforementioned Alcuin of York. Parchment was the preferred medium, and the codex was the almost exclusive format. Codices were initially associated with early Christian texts, apparently in deliberate contrast to the scrolls used for Classical (pagan) books. The Romans were also very fond of inscribing texts on marble walls, and it is the forms perfected for such inscriptions in the first century CE, adapted to the pen, that comprise the alphabet in use to this day.

This perfected Roman alphabet was the outcome of about seven centuries of graphic development, after the first attempts to write Latin. The Latin alphabet was borrowed from the Etruscan alphabet, and the

Etruscan alphabet came from a form of the first alphabet, the Greek alphabet (Carrasquer Vidal, 2006b).[6] Etruscan was just one among a score or more languages of Italy whose alphabets, numbering about a dozen distinctive ones, developed from the Greek – some directly, most in a sort of shared cultural achievement during the second half of the first millennium BCE (Baldi, 2002, pp. 118–167). One can only speculate about why the Celtic languages of continental Europe found comparatively far less use for writing (Eska 2004, pp. 858–860) and the Germanic none at all until runes were devised after the turn of the era, adapting a Northern Italic alphabet to carving in wood (Lowe, 2006). (In Ireland, the Latin alphabet became a code, *ogham*, that found limited employment on funerary stones; Simpson, 2006.)

One variety of Germanic, exceptionally, was extensively recorded – to the extent of a Bible translation, at any rate, and related literature – namely, the Gothic language. The Greek and Roman churches had begun to go their somewhat separate ways early in the fourth century. Both traditions proselytized: the Roman church, as we have seen, used Latin language and writing; but the Greek (Orthodox) church welcomed translations into vernaculars and, with them, the provision of distinctive national alphabets (Gamkrelidze, 1994).[7] The earliest of these was the Coptic (for the Egyptian language), which simply supplements the Greek alphabet with seven letters taken from demotic Egyptian. The alphabet for Gothic, spoken around present-day Moldova, also closely resembles the Greek model. Two national alphabets dating to the early fifth century – both traditionally attributed to Mesrop Mashtots – the Armenian and Georgian, reflect the structure and order of the Greek alphabet, but their letterforms are distinct innovations. A recently discovered palimpsest manuscript in the "Caucasian Albanian" alphabet, of unknown date, has been identified as the Northeast Caucasian language Udi. The latest Eastern Orthodox alphabet has become the most widespread: in the later ninth century, the missionaries Constantine (later Cyril) and Methodius devised the Glagolitic alphabet (modeled on contemporary cursive Greek)[8] for a form of Slavic; not long after, the Cyrillic alphabet (modeled on formal Greek plus some Glagolitic letters) was created for Old Bulgarian. As Cyrillic became the alphabet for Russian, it subsequently served as the basis for the alphabets of most of the languages of the Russian Empire and the Soviet Union. Thus all the alphabets ever used in the world – the Roman-based, the Cyrillic-based, and the handful of national scripts just mentioned – derive from the Greek alphabet, a creation of ca. 800 BCE or a little earlier. (There had been considerable variation in the local ["epichoric"] forms of Greek alphabets, but a standard one was adopted in Athens in 402 BCE.)

An *alphabet* is usually said to be the type of writing system in which one sound corresponds to one symbol – but this description would hold for any type of writing system, with distinctions among them made according to what counts as "one sound." In alphabets, "one sound" is a *phoneme* or (less fraught with theory) a *segment*, a single consonant or vowel. Usually, when an alphabet is created for or adapted to a previously unwritten language, that is the goal, whether those doing the work are modern missionaries with training in phonology (Pike, 1947) or ancient experimenters thousands of years before the invention of linguistics (O'Connor, 1992). Examples of the kinds of language change that cause the spoken language to deviate from standardized spelling are: the merging of phonemes (*here/hear*), the split of phonemes (*thigh/thy*), and the loss of phonemes (*bough/cough*, etc.). Change of phonemes affects not the transparency of spelling but its relation to the spelling of other languages using a similar writing system (compare *table* in English and French). Ways that alphabets provide for sounds not found in the model or earliest inventory of letters include inventing letters, combining letters, altering letters, borrowing letters, adding to letters, adding diacritics,[9] and simplifying letters (Daniels, 2006a).

There was, however, writing before there was an alphabet. Greek legend itself

(Herodotus 5.58) knows that Greek writing was received from the Phoenicians.[10] But Phoenician writing was not an alphabet (according to the above definition), for no provision whatsoever is made for noting vowels. This typological distinction is very important, and the label *abjad* has proven useful for a script comprising symbols for consonants only (Daniels, 1990, 2005).[11] The relationship between Phoenician and Greek writing is very clear. Letters for the same or similar sounds are similar or identical; the conventional order of the letters ('alphabetical order') is the same; and the names of the Greek letters – *alpha, beta,* and so forth – have no meaning in Greek but correspond exactly to the Phoenician names (as reconstructed on the basis of the Hebrew names, which are attested from the third century BCE) – **alp, *bayt,* and so forth – which do have meanings in Semitic languages.

The great difference between the Phoenician abjad and the Greek alphabet is that the latter includes letters for vowels, and this difference needs to be explained. Two hoary explanations are still found in the literature, both popular and even technical. The more pernicious one attributes the invention of vowel letters to "Greek genius" or even "Aryan genius" – the implication, sometimes even explicit, being that the "Semitic mind" was too dull to accomplish such an achievement.[12] The other explanation, born more of ignorance than prejudice, claims that Indo-European languages (such as Greek) "need" to write vowels, whereas Semitic languages (such as Phoenician, Hebrew, and Arabic) do not "need" to write vowels. The reason is supposedly that in Indo-European, word roots contain vowels, but in Semitic, word roots comprise only consonants (three of them) and the vowels provide only "grammatical detail."[13] The refutation is simple: such major Indo-European languages as Persian and Urdu have been written for centuries with Arabic script, making no special provision for notating vowels.[14]

In fact, the explanation of the origin of the Greek vowel letters seems to be a simple case of misunderstanding. We can imagine a Greek-speaking merchant in a marketplace observing a Phoenician-speaking counterpart keeping records of inventory, sales, and so on, running a business more efficiently than might have been thought possible, using perhaps ink or perhaps a stylus to make marks or scratches on a potsherd or a wax tablet. The would-be Greek scribe asks how it's done, and the Phoenician obligingly writes the characters and recites the letter names, since each letter name begins with the sound the letter stands for. Six of the seven Greek vowel letters (*omega* was a later addition) correspond in shape, sequential order, and name to Phoenician letters for consonants that do not occur in Greek. These consonants – glottal stop, [h w y], and voiced and voiceless pharyngeal fricatives – are not phonemic in Greek, and the Greek-speaker will not even register their presence in the speech stream. Thus, when for the first letter the Phoenician says ['alp], meaning /'alp/, the Greek hears it as /alp/ and understands the letter to stand for the sound /a/, even though the Phoenician is not aware of /a/ as a sound that could be notated. So if the Greek had learned Phoenician well, there would be no vowel letters!

It is sometimes suggested that the basis for the Greek alphabet was not the Phoenician abjad but the closely related Aramaic abjad (e.g., Segert, 1963), on two grounds. First, a number of the Greek letter names end with *-a,* which corresponds to nothing in the Phoenician language but resembles the Aramaic definite article; if the Aramaic letter names were *alpā, bētā,* and so on, then they could have been borrowed into Greek without alteration. However, the Aramaic explanation for the Greek *-a* is unnecessary; the Greek language is not hospitable to final consonant clusters or even to most final single consonants, and the vowel is added to resolve the difficulty. The second pro-Aramaic argument involves a feature of Aramaic orthography (it was adopted into Hebrew orthography early on, as well), the use of *matres lectionis* ('mothers of reading') – that is, certain consonant letters used to note certain vowels. This practice seems to have originated in a sound change: /bayt/ was spelled ⟨byt⟩; the diphthong /ay/ contracted to /ê/; but the spelling with ⟨y⟩ was retained (and similarly for /ô/ < /aw/); and analogically, other long vowels, particularly at the end of a word, came to be written with some consonant letters as well. However, if the Greek merchant had learned the letters from an Aramaic-speaking source, there would have been no confusion over how to notate long vowels and diphthongs and no impetus to write every vowel – even the short vowels that would not be accounted for in Aramaic orthography until centuries later.

But this consideration need not remain hypothetical. Persian and Urdu have already been mentioned, but we need not look only to modern times. During the first millennium BCE, Aramaic became the principal language of administration of the parade of empires that ruled Mesopotamia and its environs. By the middle of the second century BCE, the successors of Alexander in the East had given way to two Iranian dynasties, the Arsacid (or Parthian) and, from 224 CE, the Sassanian. The sparse records of these empires reveal that gradually, over several centuries, Aramaic gave way to Iranian languages, while the Aramaic abjad remained in use for these languages – in reduced forms, no less, whose orthography is remarkably uniform across several centuries and many varieties – culminating in Pahlavi (Henning, 1958).[15]

Aramaic was the vector of religion even more than of politics, and Christian and Manichaean missionaries brought their forms of writing eastward (Thompson, 2006a): first to write the Iranian language Sogdian (fourth century CE). *Matres lectionis* stand for vowels other than short *ă*. The Sogdian script was adapted to write the Turkic language Uyghur (eighth century).[16] *Matres lectionis* stand for vowels without distinguishing the front and back vowels that are so characteristic of Turkic languages. The Uyghur script was adapted to write the Mongolic language Mongolian (1310).[17] *Matres lectionis* again do not distinguish such vowel pairs, but some letters now represent vowels exclusively. Finally, in separate developments, the script for the Tungusic language Manchu (1599, reformed 1632)[18] (Li, 2000), and the 'Clear script' for Mongolian (1648) were provided with distinct letters for the vowels, thereby becoming alphabets.

The situation just described demands a pause for reflection. The persistence of this single approach to writing – the abjad with increasingly refined use of *matres lectionis* – bespeaks a continuous scribal tradition, passed down from master to pupil, from scriptorium to scriptorium, from chancery to chancery, across countless polities and five language families, over nearly three thousand years. Beside this record, do not even the celebrated cases pale, of Mesopotamian cuneiform, Egyptian hieroglyphs, and Chinese characters, each of which enjoyed or continues to enjoy a similar life span, but each associated with but a single culture?

Yet while that progression of script adoptions was making its way across Inner Asia, another sequence of script adaptations was taking place across South and East Asia that is equally or even more remarkable (Daniels, 2000a). Aramaic writing reached the northwest regions of India, perhaps as early as the early fifth century BCE with the Achaemenid (Persian) Empire. Attested in the mid third century but perhaps originating in the fourth or even fifth century is the first of two scripts of India, known as Kharoṣṭhi (used especially for Gāndhārī Prakrit), from present-day northwest Pakistan and areas northeast and northwest of there; its use declined during the third century CE (Salomon, 1998, pp. 42–56). The Kharoṣṭhi letters clearly derive from Aramaic letters (though when and where the model was found remains unclear) – but Kharoṣṭhi is an entirely new type of script. Vowels other than /a/ are notated not with letters of their own, or with consonant letters reused as *matres lectionis*, but with appendages in the form of four distinctive strokes for /e i o u/ attached to the preceding consonant letter. In the event of a consonant cluster (an infrequent occurrence in Prakrit), the first consonant is written attached to the second (forming a *conjunct*), with the vowel appendage on the whole. (A word-initial vowel is denoted with a letter that alone represents /a/ and, with the appendages, the other vowels.) My term for this type is *abugida*.[19]

The other Indic script, historically far more important, is called Brāhmī. It too is first attested in the mid third century but probably was not devised any earlier. Formally, its connection with some form of Aramaic is less clear, and it is written from left to right; but functionally, it is clearly a development from Kharoṣṭhi. The bare letter form still represents a consonant with /a/, but the vowel appendages now distinguish short and long vowels (including /ā/), and there is a separate letter for each word-initial vowel. When in the first centuries CE it became usual to write Sanskrit, the conjunct device became more elaborate, and clusters of as many as five consonants are attested (*-rtsny-*). Over the centuries and across the Subcontinent, Brāhmī diversified greatly (periods of centralized political power were rare) and, as noted previously, only with the arrival of British printing presses – mostly in the nineteenth century – did ten script standards crystallize: six for Indic languages and four for Dravidian languages (Salomon, 2003; Shackle, 2006;[20] Daniels, 2008). A very wide variety of manuscript samples can be seen in Grierson (1903–1927).

The significance of the two Indic scripts in this context is that before there was writing in India, there was a sophisticated grammatical tradition, associated with the name of Pāṇini, who lived perhaps in the fifth century BCE.[21] Consonants and vowels had been identified as different kinds of speech entities (Deshpande, 1994), and it must have only made sense to notate them, and in different ways, after the sheer practicality of writing was appreciated. As for why /a/ is not notated, it is not impossible that the absence of *matres lectionis* for /a/ in Aramaic led the first Gāndhārī-writer to believe that the /a/ was intended to be inherent in the consonant letters.

From the grammarian-mediated transmission of writing from Aramaic to Indic, we turn to another presumably grammarian-mediated transmission of writing that yielded a script better suited to its new language: Tibetan (Thompson, 2006b). The languages involved in the script transmissions discussed so far have been "inflecting" (Semitic, Indo-European) or "agglutinative" (Turkic, Mongolic, Tungusic); but Tibetan is "isolating."[22] And wisely, whoever adapted some form of Brāhmī-derived script for Tibetan – traditionally, Thon mi Saṃbhoṭa before 650 CE – did away with the system of conjuncts that can cross syllable boundaries, instead grouping separate consonant letters, horizontally and vertically within each syllable, and adding an obligatory dot after the last consonant of each syllable. (Vowels other than /a/ are still marked on each syllable, so Tibetan writing is still an abugida.) And, there was a Tibetan grammatical tradition.

A short-lived but interesting development of Tibetan was a script ordered by Kubla Khan for writing all the languages of his empire – Tibetan, Uyghur, Mongolian, and Chinese. The Tibetan monk 'Phags pa delivered the script that bears his name in 1269 (it was used for only about a century, and mostly only for Mongolian). It comprises squared-up versions of Tibetan letters, and added to it are symbols for additional consonants and a plethora of vowels needed for the other languages, both word-initial vowel letters and syllable-following vowel appendages. 'Phags pa is written in columns from left to right (Thompson, 2006b, pp. 710–712).

The third occurrence of a script adaptation based in grammatical learning is also the first creation of a script for which we have documentation and explanation (Ledyard, 1966).[23] Korea's King Sejong (r. 1418–1450) undertook far-reaching reforms; among them was his linked desire to bring both Buddhism and its scriptures, and literacy, to the Korean people. (Until then, and long after, records even in the Korean language were kept only in Chinese characters and therefore were all but inaccessible. They were difficult even for those who had devoted years to a classical Chinese education because the plethora of grammatical endings [Korean is agglutinative] were not recorded in the script that served [isolating] Chinese well.) King Sejong, or his advisory committee, was deeply familiar with the Chinese grammatical tradition and with 'Phags pa script as well. It is highly plausible that the accidental resemblance of several 'Phags pa letters to configurations of the vocal tract suggested that these resemblances be made deliberate and systematic, and so they are. The Korean "alphabet" goes beyond the representation of segments to the iconic representation of phonetic features. Moreover, probably in imitation of the Chinese writing system, the letters comprising each syllable are grouped into a compact square resembling a simple Chinese character (Kim, 2006).[24]

The two progressions of script transmissions – the northern route by consistent scribal training, the more southerly route by grammatically informed scholarship – have brought us to East Asia, and we may resume our reverse chronological treatment of the world's writing systems with another basic type: the *logosyllabary*. In this type, which survives to the present only in the Chinese script (Boltz, 2003) and its Japanese derivative, each discrete character in the writing system represents a single morpheme of the associated language.[25] The earliest attested Chinese inscriptions, dating from the later Shang dynasty, ca. 1250 BCE, already reveal a writing system of considerable sophistication, which would place its creation at least several centuries earlier. These are the Oracle Bone Inscriptions, on animal scapulae or turtle plastrons, in which a question was addressed to the spirit world, the bone was fired, the resulting cracks were interpreted, and the emergent response was also recorded. A significant percentage, but by no means all, of the characters attested in the thousands of surviving examples have been identified and their descendants traced to their equivalents in use today (Branner, 2006). Familiarity with three thousand or so different characters suffices for practical modern literacy.[26]

Hardly any Chinese characters originated as pictures of the things they name (a very small percentage did). Almost every character is combined from two parts, known as the *semantic* or *radical* and the *phonetic*. The former gives a hint of the meaning of the character; the latter gives an indication of the sound of the character. Phonetic indications can be more or less transparent in Modern Chinese; they were close to exact when the system was codified, some two thousand years ago, but significant change and diversification has taken place in the Chinese language(s) during that time. It must be stressed that Chinese characters do not represent "ideas"; rather, they represent specific morphemes in the Chinese language.[27]

As with Korean, early Japanese writing (beginning before the late seventh century CE) was initially done with Chinese characters, and again the results were unsatisfactory: characters were used for Japanese words (but not for grammatical affixes), but because there is no historical/genetic relationship at all between the two languages, the phonetic portions of characters played no part in reading native Japanese words. Instead of the Korean resolution – of at first doing nothing and later inventing an entirely new writing system – already in seventh- and eighth-century Japan some characters came to be used for their sound values alone, usually taking on a simplified shape, to represent the syllables comprising grammatical affixes (Seeley, 1991/2000).[28]

This is our first exposure to the last of the script types we mention: the *syllabary*. In a syllabary, each character represents a syllable, and (unlike in an abugida) there is no graphic resemblance among the characters that denote syllables beginning with the same consonant or among the characters that denote syllables containing the same vowel.[29] Over the centuries, two syllabaries emerged for Japanese: one, more cursive, called *hiragana*, is used for grammatical affixes on the words written with Chinese characters (*kanji*); the other, called *katakana*, has functions similar to those of italics in English writing – for foreign words, emphasis, and so on – and is also used for loan words in Japanese. The characters in the two syllabaries (which together are referred to as the *kana*), which were not standardized until the twentieth century, are simplified from a limited selection of Chinese characters. Some hiragana and katakana for the same sound have the same parent character, but most such pairs derive from different ancestors (Unger, 2006, p. 96).

After this exploration of the writing systems of Asia, we can return to our reverse chronological survey by filling in the background to the Phoenician abjad. Phoenician and Aramaic are the two representatives of the North Semitic branch of West Semitic writing. Phoenician, attested from ca. 1000 BCE, was less cursive (and its modern-day representative, the Samaritan abjad, retains that characteristic);[30] Aramaic, attested from ca. 950 CE, was more rounded even in its early exemplars, and over the centuries this tendency (visible even in rock-cut inscriptions) led in many varieties to the connection of letters within words. The most familiar variety today is the Arabic abjad; the northern Asian progression is also a scion of the large family of Aramaic scripts.[31]

The Aramaic practice of *matres lectionis* developed in two ways in later scripts. During the first millennium BCE, those used for Aramaic languages added more and more of them: first for long vowels, then even for some or most short vowels. Mandaic is sometimes said to have grown into a pure alphabet, but that is an exaggeration – /o/ is written the same as /u/, and the letter for /e/ has several additional functions (Daniels, 1997b, p. 36). Arabic, on the other hand, writes every long vowel with a letter (the writing of /ā/ has even usurped the function of the letter for glottal stop;[32] /ī/ with ⟨y⟩ and /ū/ with ⟨u⟩). Biblical Hebrew orthography involves the more limited use of *matres* seen in, and presumably borrowed from, earlier Aramaic; modern Israeli Hebrew uses almost as many as were found in the Rabbinic Aramaics of the Talmuds, Targums, and so on.

The Bible and the Qur'ān were sacred even in their very texts, and as the languages in which they were written grew and changed, there was a perceived need to record the precise vowel sounds used in their accurate recitation. Their sacral character meant that the sequence of consonants could not be interrupted (for instance, to insert vowel letters in imitation of the Greek alphabet). Scholars of both languages solved this dilemma (from the seventh century CE) by placing "points" (dots, dashes, curls) above, below, and within the consonant letters.[33] Throughout the centuries, this pointing has remained optional (except in manuscripts of the Qur'ān; conversely, a Torah scroll used in Jewish liturgy will never exhibit pointing), being used outside children's books primarily to clarify proper names and poetry.

But the Syriac, Hebrew, and Arabic abjads were not the first ones to be supplemented with a device for notating all the vowels. That honor goes to the Ethiopic script, the sole survivor of the South Semitic family of West Semitic abjads (Gragg, 2006a). This comprised the Old North Arabian (Macdonald, 2004) and Old South Arabian branches; Ethiopic derived from the latter (Uhlig, 1990).[34] In the middle of the fourth century, King Ezana of Aksum converted to Christianity, and his inscriptions invoking pagan gods are unvocalized; his inscriptions invoking Jesus are vocalized – and the vocalization is in the Indian abugida format! There is little or no resemblance between the vowel appendages for Brāhmī and for Ethiopic, and a vowelless consonant is notated with the symbol for a short high central vowel, but similarities between the Ethiopian and the Indian (Martomite) liturgies suggest that the vocalization system was introduced by missionaries from Christian India (Friedrich, 1966: p. 93), who might not have had a perfect recollection of how the script worked (Daniels, 1992a).

Underlying both the northern and southern branches of the Semitic family of abjads is a script, attested sparsely beginning in Egypt's late Middle Kingdom period (ca. 1850–1700 BCE), whose earliest examples are labeled Proto-Sinaitic (they were excavated at the site of a mine in the Sinai peninsula) and later examples, scattered about the Levant, are called (Proto-)Canaanite (Dobbs-Allsopp, 2006). They[35] can be tentatively interpreted as recording a West Semitic language, though most of them contain little more than the names of owners of objects, or of deities to whom objects are dedicated. It is clear that the shapes (but not the sounds) of the letters of this script are taken from Egyptian hieroglyphs (Hamilton, 2006), but why and how this happened demands explanation. This can be taken as a second example of script transfer by misunderstanding: a would-be Semitic scribe would have had no opportunity to attend an Egyptian scribal school and master Egyptian writing so as to use it for another language; at best, the notion that what was written was consonants could have filtered down in some casual manner. A selection of symbols was chosen from the array of hieroglyphs, assigned sounds on the basis of the names of the things they depicted and according to a phonological analysis of the language performed by the inventor. The outcome was the twenty-nine letters of the earliest Semitic abjad.

The oldest sizable corpus of abjad-written texts comes from the city-state of Ugarit, on the Syrian coast of the Mediterranean, dating to the fourteenth century BCE. Most of these texts are in a language very similar to the ancestor of Hebrew, and among them are literary compositions showing strong resemblances to Biblical texts. Ugaritic writing is unique in two respects: (1) it takes the form of combinations of wedges impressed with a stylus on clay (like Mesopotamian cuneiform), though the ensuing letters resemble the Canaanite letters and not the Mesopotamian syllabic signs; and (2) to the letters for the 27 consonants, it adds two additional glottal-stop letters – and each of the three glottal-stop letters represents a glottal stop when it is followed by one of the three vowels /a i u/. One can only speculate on what might have developed; the script was abandoned when the city was destroyed at the beginning of the twelfth century BCE.

Mesopotamian cuneiform (Gragg, 2006b), which was used for well over three thousand years (ca. 3200 BCE – second/third century CE; Geller, 1997), was devised for Sumerian,[36] a language with no known relatives, ancient or modern. Initially logographic – reminiscent of Chinese writing as applied to Korean or Japanese – in symbiosis with its use for the Semitic language Akkadian (Cooper, 1999), it became logosyllabic (i.e., a character could represent a word's meaning and sound, or just its sound; the sounds could be V, CV, VC, or CVC syllables) and could record Sumerian speech in, presumably, full detail. It was adapted to Akkadian and a number of other languages of the ancient Near East with more or less perspicacity: a major complication was that characters could be used in these other languages not only for their syllabic value but also for their meaning alone. These instances, known as *logograms*, could be facilitated by the addition of a *phonetic complement* (a character or two indicating the pronunciation of the start or end of the word) and/or, more usually, a *semantic determinative* – one of a small set of characters that indicate the class to which the item represented by the word belongs (e.g., personal name, bird, wooden object).[37]

Egyptian writing, too, whose period of use was almost exactly coextensive with that of cuneiform, made use of logograms, phonograms (either alone or as phonetic complements), and semantic determinatives.[38] The greatest functional difference from Sumerian cuneiform is that the sounds denoted are not syllables but from one to three consonants. Influence from Sumerian writing on the invention of Egyptian writing has long been supposed, but because the two systems differ in both appearance and structure, only recently has a plausible mechanism been proposed for such influence (Daniels, 2006b). This could represent the third (chronologically, the first) example of script transfer by misunderstanding.[39] The Egyptian protoscribe learned that each Sumerian character represented an occurrence of the same word. In Sumerian, the sound of the base word rarely changed even when inflections were added. But in Egyptian, inflections took the form not only of prefixes and suffixes, but also (as in its distant relative Semitic; cf. n. 13) of vowel alternations within the base word. Thus when the same word was written with the same character, as in Sumerian, it was not the same sounds that were always written, but only the same consonants. Thus the phonetic material denoted by Egyptian writing was the consonants only.[40]

Every script mentioned so far had its origin in the Old World, and only in the last half-century did it become possible to say anything at all about the nature of indigenous New World scripts. Only in the last quarter-century has reading any of them become possible (Marcus, 2006), and the greatest strides have been made with Maya writing. Of special interest is the structure of the script: it is logosyllabic and employs phonetic complements and (to a very limited extent) semantic determinatives.

As an appendix to this survey of scripts whose legacy dates back thousands of years, we may mention a phenomenon that seems to have originated in the early nineteenth century, with the Cherokee Indian Sequoyah. Living with his tribe in or near Echota, Georgia, in the 1820s, he was aware that the Americans around him communicated with each other via marks on paper, but he spoke no English and knew nothing of English writing. He felt his people should have such a boon, so he set about devising a script; after some false starts, he hit on a CV syllabary for writing Cherokee. Not long after, Momolu Duwalu Bukele did the same for his language, Vai, spoken in Liberia; there is reason to believe that he was aware of Sequoyah's accomplishment (Tuchscherer & Hair, 2002). Like the Cherokee, the Vai script found great acceptance among the language's speakers, and Vai mercenary soldiers seem to have brought the idea of writing one's native language to a number of peoples of West Africa. Similar achievements occurred in Alaska, South America, and Oceania, and always the outcome was a CV syllabary.[41]

The foregoing superficial survey of the world's writing systems and a few interesting facts about them has laid the groundwork for some theoretical observations having to do with the typology and history of writing. For more than a century, exactly three types of writing system have conventionally been recognized: logography, syllabography, and alphabet;[42] these categories are often found in popular treatments of writing and in elementary linguistics textbooks. The apotheosis of this scheme is found in Gelb's (1952: 252) *Principle of Unidirectional Development* "from word to syllabic to alphabetic writing," which also continues to be reiterated in such works. The difficulties with this principle are twofold: first, "the alphabet" developed only once, in the leap from Phoenician to Greek, which casts doubt on any general or necessary principle; and second, no syllabary has ever given rise to any other type of script. To get around these objections, Gelb must define the vowelless West Semitic script family as encoding "monosyllables ending in a vowel, with differences in vowels not indicated" (p. 196)[43] and the Indic and Ethiopic scripts that represent syllables as alphabets with "vowels indicated by diacritic marks attached to the signs or by internal modification" (p. 198).

These troublingly counterintuitive redefinitions of script type are resolved by recognizing the two additional types: abjad and abugida. We can then observe that logosyllabaries do give rise to syllabaries (Sumerian/Akkadian, Chinese > Japanese, Mayan), but also to a logoconsonantary (Sumerian > Egyptian); that a logoconsonantary gave rise to an abjad (Egyptian > West Semitic); and that an abjad gave rise to an alphabet and an abugida (Phoenician > Greek, Aramaic > Kharoṣṭhi).[44] This observation has the additional advantage of removing the alphabet from the privileged position as the "optimal" or "perfect" or "ultimate" type of writing system it had been awarded by perhaps unthinking "alphabetolaters" (Schmidt, 1991).

Identifying the difference between syllabaries proper and abugidas was one of two breakthroughs that shed bright light on the origins of writing. The other was my perhaps belated[45] discovery that a good start had been made on deciphering Maya writing – and that it was structurally identical to Sumerian writing, with a logographic core and phonetically written satellites. What this meant was that there were three known independent ancient origins of writing[46] – the Sumerian, the Chinese,[47] and the Mayan – all of which served societies that had developed some degree of urbanism, and that the three languages involved were similar in basic structure: most of their morphemes are just a single syllable. It is noteworthy that no writing system was independently invented in urbanized societies relying on languages with different sorts of basic morpheme structure: Indo-European, Semitic, or the Quechua of the Inca Empire in Peru.[48] Urbanization is important because a need for keeping records arises as communities grow and their occupants specialize; some sort of recordkeeping seems well-nigh universal in such societies. The complex arrays of knotted strings in Inca *quipus* are a celebrated example.

Setting down thoughts in the form of pictograms seems to be a universal human preoccupation, dating back at least to the Aurignacian period (28,000–22,000 BCE), whatever the language of the people involved. Perhaps in many cultures, the pictograms represented specific words rather than general thoughts. But only when the languages involved were essentially monosyllabic did the pictograms become writing – at this point, a definition of *writing* is germane: *A system of more or less permanent marks used to represent an utterance in such a way that it can be recovered more or less exactly without the intervention of the utterer*. And an utterance cannot be recovered more or less exactly unless the writing system can reproduce the sounds of speech with systematic fidelity (DeFrancis, 1989). Since writing represents language, it must represent the sounds of speech.

But what is special about monosyllabicity? Considerable psycholinguistic and even philological evidence for the primacy of the syllable over the segment in the processing of language and speech among those who have not learned an alphabet has been summarized (Daniels, 1992b, pp. 90–93), but this has perhaps proved too abstruse for the semiotician, the philologist, or the anthropologists to assimilate. Some critics resort to ridicule, respectively: "For Daniels, an 'abjad,' unlike a full consonant-and-vowel alphabet, is more primitive than a syllabary" (Watt, 1998, p. 121);[49] "has a particular affection for the syllable" (Mair, 2005, p. 103); and several contributors to Houston (2004), none of whom admits to having consulted Daniels (1992b).

The example of modern inventions of writing (Sequoyah et seq.) alerts us to the salience of the syllable in the stream of speech. The examples of ancient inventions of writing (Sumerian, Chinese, Maya) show that when the word (or morpheme) represented by a pictogram is a single syllable, the salience of the word in the stream of language coincides with the salience of the syllable in the stream of speech. It hardly seems a great leap of intellect to reuse a word-character for its sound but not its meaning: Sumerian *ti* 'arrow' for *ti* 'life' (Gelb, 1952, p. 110f.); Mandarin *k'iu* 'fur coat' for *k'iu* 'to seek' (Karlgren, 1926, p. 34); Maya **baah* 'pocket gopher' for the sound *ba* (Robertson, 2004, p. 30); and, where applicable, similarly for the sounds of grammatical affixes and particles and for the sounds of proper names, especially those taken from another language such that they have no semantic content in the language being written.

This survey of the world's writing systems from a functional point of view permits an integrated approach to a number of questions that have hitherto not even been asked, and it suggests the excessive pessimism of Coulmas's remark (2003, p. 208): "The history of writing, therefore, cannot rely much on universal tendencies, but has to investigate the spread and transmutation of every script in its own right." A new collection (Baines, Bennet, & Houston, 2008) brings the intriguing suggestion that not only the origin and dispersal of scripts can be investigated globally and typologically, but also the disuse of writing systems under different circumstances. Does a society ever abandon literacy entirely?

Notes

1 I have previously used *grammatology* as the name of the subfield of linguistics that studies writing systems, but I now prefer *graphonomy*, which was proposed by C. F. Hockett in 1951 (pub. 2003) and used in his *Course* (1958, 539), because (a) it is shorter, (b) Gelb's term was hijacked (with acknowledgment) by Derrida (1967) for something completely different, and (c) some have interpreted *grammatology* as the label for an approach to the study of writing rather than for that study itself (Watt, 1998, pp. 120ff.).

2 In Mycenae, although Linear B was fully capable of recording language, it seems not to have been used for that purpose.

3 References regarding specific scripts are largely restricted to ones not found in these resources. A compact source of information not covered here is Daniels (2001).

4 Two once-well-known schemes for replacing or supplementing English orthography are now of only historical interest. George Bernard Shaw asserted that if English were spelled phonetically according to the usage of Received Pronunciation (RP), the lower classes would necessarily give up their inferior dialects and improve their station in life (1941; excerpted so as to obscure the class prejudice by Tauber, 1963, pp. 111–136). Finding no acceptable proposal therefore during his lifetime, he made provision in his will to finance a "Proposed British alphabet," the eventual outcome being a competition for such a scheme. The winner, known as the Shaw Alphabet, was finally drafted by Kingsley Read and used for the publication of a single work, Shaw's *Androcles and the Lion* (ibid., pp. 163–200). It is impractical in the extreme, as the shapes represent the phonetic features of the phonemes of the recorded speech of King George V (r. 1910–1936) with minimal differentiation and no redundancy whatsoever. (Shaw apparently did not invent, or even cite, the specious example ⟨ghoti⟩ frequently attached to his name [*gh* as in *rough*, *o* as in *women*, *ti* as in *nation*; thus, "fish"]; none of those three writings can occur in the position in which they are found in that example.)

The "initial teaching alphabet" or ita (one of its principles is the non-use of differently shaped capital letters) was intended to introduce reading via near one-to-one correspondences between symbol and phoneme. To the ordinary minuscules excluding q and x, it adds ligatures and variants that cleverly mimic traditional orthography: e.g., ⟨a⟩ represents (RP) /a/, ⟨æ⟩ represents /eː/ (i.e., "long a"), and ⟨o œ⟩ are paired similarly; ⟨z⟩ represents /z/ spelled (t.o.) ⟨z⟩, and the same letter reversed represents /z/ spelled ⟨s⟩ as in *horses*. It was devised by James Pitman in 1959, published in 1960, and introduced in 1961 in a limited number of British schools, with wider acceptance over the next few years. Pitman and St. John (1969) summarize considerable research showing that children taught with ita learned to read (both ita and t.o.) more quickly than children taught with t.o.; but about learning to write t.o., they are silent: research was either not done or suppressed, and anecdotal evidence from adults raised on ita indicates that they did not master t.o. spelling. Pitman contributed an essay to Tauber (1963, pp. 190–198) recounting his discussions with Shaw and comparing the purposes and achievements of the two schemes.

5 Hastings (1929). The ninth edition of *Encyclopædia Britannica* 14 (1882), p. 539, notes that "card-catalogues are used comparatively little in England, but are found to act satisfactorily in many American libraries," but in the eleventh edition, it was deemed necessary to provide a description of a card catalog for the British reader (16 [1911], p. 560).

6 The attentive reader will observe a bewildering lack of consistency in the titles of articles in the *Encyclopedia of Language and Linguistics*, 2nd ed. This, as well as the absence of a trio of survey articles totaling twenty thousand words, was the result of unconscionable bureaucratic interference and bungling on the part of the publisher and cannot be said to reflect on the editor.

7 The illustrations in its condensation, Gamkrelidze (2006), are very poorly reproduced.

8 A *cursive* ("running") script is one written with few or no lifts of the pen, often characteristic of manuscript as opposed to inscribed forms of scripts.

9 A *diacritic* is a mark on a letter, usually recurring in an alphabet, that notes a systematic (to at least some extent) differentiation of the sound of the letter. The invention of the diacritic is usually attributed to the Bohemian reformer Jan Hus (1372–1415), for whose work see Schröpfer (1968). Adaptations of the Roman alphabet worldwide have tended to favor the use of diacritics, while adaptations of the Cyrillic alphabet have tended to favor the various ways of increasing the inventory of letters.

10 Robert Graves (1960, §52) spins a bizarre, mystical tale out of late baseless traditions that somehow drags in "the ancient Irish alphabet."

11 *Abjad* is an Arabic word. Arabic alphabetical order is not that inherited from its Semitic forebears, still found in Greek *a b g d* etc. and easily recognizable in the English alphabet. Instead, Arabic groups together letters of similar shape, thus *a b t th* etc. In some circumstances, however, primarily when the letters are used as numerals, the ancient values prevail, so that "4" is written not with *th* but with *d*. The term for this ancient order is *abjad* (*j* < **g*), and as a label for a script type, it offers a nice parallel for *alphabet*, which comprises the first two letters of the Greek alphabet.

12 Note the assumption (often not even left implicit) that the alphabet is the best type of writing system – although a statement as apodictic as "It is generally accepted that on all grounds an alphabetical system of writing is best" (Berry, 1958, p. 753) is rarely found. Note that criteria for evaluating "goodness" of writing system type are never made explicit. Likely they come down to nothing more than "the way *we* do it." Eric Havelock, an avowed adherent of Marshall McLuhan's "Toronto school," goes so far as to claim regarding "the so-called literatures of the ancient Near East . . . the basic complexity of human experience is not there. . . . One need only compare what is narrated in the so-called Epic of Gilgamesh with what is narrated in Homer . . . to realize the difference" (1976, 33f.) – and all because Homer used an alphabet! For Sumerian, Akkadian, and Biblical poetry as fully expressive and fully responsive to modern critical approaches, see Black (1998), Reiner (1985), and Robinson (1947), respectively.

13 The very concept of the Semitic lexical root and grammatical vowel pattern is an artifact of the Arabic writing system used by the eighth-century grammarians who first formulated the notion, and it is under psycholinguistic (Shimron, 2003) as well as philological (Gray, 1934) challenge.

14 Arabic script has been adopted throughout the Islamic world for languages of the most diverse typology belonging to many families (Daniels, 1997a).

15 This despite the availability, since probably the fourth century CE, of the alphabetic script devised under Greek influence for recording the Zoroastrian scripture, the Avesta, composed much earlier in ancient Iranian and transmitted orally until that time (the earliest extant manuscripts date only to the thirteenth century, but some letterforms derive from Pahlavi shapes current in the fourth century). Avestan is a rare example of a subphonemic alphabet – it records phonetic distinctions of no functional significance in the language – making the interpretation of some characters difficult or impossible on the basis of comparative Iranistics (Hoffmann & Narten, 1989).

16 Sogdian, like its Aramaic forebears, is read horizontally from right to left. Uyghur is written vertically, with columns proceeding left to right. This change of orientation can be attributed both to the prevailing Chinese esthetic, with its columns rather than rows of characters, and to the practice of Syriac scribes of writing their manuscripts from top to bottom (to avoid smearing ink), in columns left to right, and rotating them to read right to left, in rows from top to bottom. Cf. n. 33.

17 An attempted revival of Classical Mongolian script after Mongolia was freed by the fall of the Soviet Union from the obligation to use an adaptation of the Cyrillic alphabet seems not to have succeeded.

18 Perhaps with Korean influence (King, 1987).

19 *Abugida* is an Ethiopic word for the historic order of the Ethiopic characters (cf. nn. 11, 34.

20 This article is incorrectly attributed to Shackle and Skjærvø. The latter's contribution is the two columns devoted to Central Asian Brahmi (546b–547a), a supplement to Skjærvø, 2006.

21 The conventional order of the characters of the Indic scripts by phonetic features is a further indication of their grammarian

background. It supplanted a random-looking order used for Kharoṣṭhi that began with ⟨a ra pa ca . . . ⟩; Salomon (2005) has identified the early Kharoṣṭhi order of the vowel markers as ⟨(a) e i o u⟩, conforming not only to the order in the Greek alphabet but also to the position of the marker from top to bottom of the consonant letter.

22 These terms come from a nineteenth-century morphological typology useful only for communicating a gross "feel" for a language; it has no historic or evolutionary implications whatsoever. In an "inflecting" language, grammatical relations are signaled by affixes that might combine several functions, such as Latin *-us* 'masculine singular nominative.' In an "agglutinative" language, each grammatical relation is marked by a single affix. In an "isolating" language, grammatical relations are not marked by affixes but by word order; typically, each (lexical) morpheme is a syllable unto itself.

23 Ledyard's dissertation underwent a partial revision in anticipation of publication in Seoul. The revision was interrupted due to external circumstances but was nonetheless published without the author's supervision. The author subsequently renounced the basis for the revision and considers the dissertation definitive (pers. comm., 4 Feb. 2006); it is supplemented by Ledyard (1997).

24 Korean script, now known as *hangul* 'people's writing,' did not find widespread use in place of Chinese characters until 1910, and only after World War II were Chinese characters expunged from Korean texts, even more thoroughly in North Korea than in South Korea.

25 A *morpheme* is a minimal meaningful unit of a language. The term *word* is best avoided in discussions of Chinese, because in dictionaries of modern Chinese, entries are usually two-character units, and there is no agreement on whether these or single-character entities should be called words.

26 Compare the number of English words whose pronunciations deviate from what the spelling might suggest: *to too two, bomb comb tomb*. These might amount to as many as three thousand items that need to be remembered individually, while each one, like Chinese, includes a greater or lesser indication of the pronunciation.

27 Thus the term *ideogram* is utterly inappropriate in this context, even though its use persists in Francophone circles. Nor does it relate to *pictogram*, which simply refers to a standardized, usually stylized image of some object and can represent an idea, a word, a morpheme, or a sound.

28 It was also possible to write entire texts syllabically, with no words at all written with Chinese logograms; this came to be seen as writing by and for women, who did not have the opportunity of acquiring a Classical education.

29 Typically, but not necessarily, syllabaries are found for languages with the simplest possible canonical form of syllable, Consonant + Vowel (CV). Japanese also has syllables comprising a vowel only, and can follow CV with either vowel length or /n/. A syllabary would be thoroughly impractical for English because English allows a very large variety of syllables, some of them as long as *splints*. Whorf (1940/1956, p. 223) drew up a "structural formula of the monosyllabic word in English" that is frighteningly complex – unfortunately, the graphic devices employed in his chart are not explained.

30 Samaritan represents the Old Hebrew variety of Phoenician writing. Old Hebrew is first found in the Moabite Stone of the ninth century BCE and then in a variety of monumental inscriptions and ostraca (i.e., writings in ink on potsherds) down to the Babylonian Exile of the seventh century. It was supplanted, except by the isolated Samaritans, for writing Hebrew by a form of Aramaic script (see n. 31) but was revived for certain religious and then nationalistic purposes in the centuries flanking the turn of the era.

31 Klugkist (1982, p. 278), who investigated the Middle Aramaic scripts (5th c. BCE – 6th c. CE), identifies no fewer than forty-eight archeologically recovered varieties (though he counted separately successive stages of several of them). Among them are lapidary Imperial Aramaic, cursive Imperial Aramaic, Nabataean, Palmyran, Old Syriac, Hatran, Assyrian, Elymaic, and Manichaean; still in use are Nabataean's direct descendant Arabic, Mandaic, the convergence of Jewish Babylonian and Jewish Palestinian as Hebrew, and Syriac.

32 Glottal stop is obligatorily written with a mark not part of the sequence of consonant letters; a handful of /ā/'s are not notated with letters. These and other morphophonemic peculiarities originate in the fact that the Qur'ān was originally written down in a

variety of Arabic that had lost the glottal stop and most case endings, while the vowel pointing was added somewhat later to reflect a variety that had not (Versteegh, 1997, p. 56).

33 The pointing of both Hebrew and Arabic was imitated from the pointing of Syriac, the principal literary Aramaic language of many of the Eastern churches. In Eastern Syriac, dots used originally to differentiate homographic words developed in time into an inventory sufficient to notate all vowels. In Western Syriac, these were replaced by vowel symbols that were miniature Greek letters. The Greek letters appear rotated with respect to their usual orientation, evidencing the rotation between writing and reading (n. 16).

34 A further distinction of the South Semitic group of scripts is a completely different alphabetical order from that of the North Semitic group, beginning ⟨ h l ḥ m . . . ⟩ rather than ⟨ ' b g d . . . ⟩. Neither order can be explained, and there is no discernable connection between them.

35 Except for a pair of inscriptions recently found at Wadi el-Hol, in Egypt's Western Desert, which appear to use the same script but resist interpretation as either Semitic or Egyptian.

36 As demonstrated by Steinkeller (1995), who observes Sumerian phonetic elements within some of the characters of the very earliest stage of cuneiform.

37 Another writing system on the fringe of cuneiform was the Old Persian cuneiform, which gives the appearance of a melding of Akkadian and Aramaic writing. The characters, built of wedges (though seemingly never impressed on clay – the only known example has recently been identified [Stolper, 2007]), denote syllables or consonants; the script was used only for inscribing royal inscriptions of the Achaemenid Empire alongside translations into Elamite and Akkadian, and Gershevitch (1979) makes the intriguing, if not entirely plausible, suggestion that only one or a handful of scribes could read it at any one time.

38 There were three varieties: hieroglyphs ('sacred writing'), the stylized but recognizable pictures used in monumental inscriptions and the most formal manuscripts; hieratic ('priestly'), a range of cursive forms of hieroglyphs, used in most manuscripts on papyrus; and demotic ('popular'), which emerged much later (7th c. BCE – 5th c. CE), is not in one-to-one correspondence with hieroglyphs, and records a late form of the Egyptian language.

39 The recently discovered written materials in Egypt that may (or may not) antedate the earliest Sumerian writing must not be facilely interpreted as proving an independent invention of writing in Egypt: they are very difficult to interpret and do not appear to be readily connected with the undisputed writing that came later (Baines, 2004). Cf. n. 48.

40 Additional scripts from the area of the Aegean Sea that supported minimal to no literate culture may relate to Egyptian (Carrasquer Vidal, 2006a): Luvian hieroglyphs for a language closely related to Hittite (ca. 1800–700 BCE), and Linear B (ca. 1550–1200) and the Cypriote syllabary (8th–5th c.) for two stages of Greek.

41 This contrasts with scripts devised by people who knew how to write in some language, or who were even familiar with phonetics; these tend to be abugidas or alphabets. This distinction was long obscured by the customary pairing of the Cherokee and Cree writing systems in surveys: the latter was devised by a missionary who was familiar with the phonetically based shorthand of Isaac Pitman. Cree Syllabics employs a geometric shape in four rotations or reflections for each consonant followed by each of the four vowels.

42 The earliest widely known expression of this scheme is in Taylor (1883), but it is not presented there either as innovative or as "common wisdom" (Daniels, 2002, pp. 93–97). It was first enunciated by Peter Stephen Du Ponceau (1838, p. xxxi).

43 Cf. Gelb (1958), Daniels (2000b).

44 The sixth script type, the featural, appears when those familiar with phonetics turn to script creation: Korean hangul, various shorthand systems, and iconic phonetic notations.

45 In April 1984 (cf. Daniels, 2002, p. 99); the crucial step was announced in Lounsbury (1973).

46 Some undeciphered ancient scripts (Robinson, 2002) could also represent independent inventions: "Proto-Elamite" (which need have no connection at all with the Elamite language known from cuneiform documents of later periods), Indus Valley.

47 The formerly popular suggestion that Chinese writing was inspired by Sumerian (or Akkadian?) cuneiform writing, by "stimulus diffusion," is untenable because by the time Chinese writing must have been coming into

existence (ca. 1500 BCE, or perhaps even earlier), the pictographic origins of Sumerian writing had been forgotten – the idea of recording syllables with pictograms of the things those syllabic words stood for could not have been communicated (Daniels, 1992c).

48 It is this line of reasoning that leads me to insist that Egyptian writing is not autochthonous and to propose the "misunderstanding of Sumerian" route for its origin.

49 It is Watt, not I, who invokes a notion of "primitivity." It is Watt who claims that the development of a syllabary from an alphabet would be a "retrogression" – this is his own imagined corollary to Gelb's Principle of Unidirectional Development.

References

Baines, John. (2004). The earliest Egyptian writing: Development, context, purpose. In Stephen D. Houston (Ed.), *The first writing: Script invention as history and process* (pp. 150–189). Cambridge: Cambridge University Press.

Baines, John, John Bennet, & Stephen Houston (Eds.) (2008). *The disappearance of writing systems: Perspectives on literacy and communication*. London: Equinox.

Baldi, Philip. (2002). *The foundations of Latin*. Berlin: Mouton de Gruyter.

Berry, Jack. (1958). The making of alphabets. In Eva Siverstein (Ed.), *Proceedings of the VIII International Congress of Linguists* (pp. 752–764). Oslo: University Press.

Black, Jeremy. (1998). *Reading Sumerian poetry*. Ithaca, NY: Cornell University Press.

Bloom, Jonathan M. (2001). *Paper before print: The history and impact of paper in the Islamic world*. New Haven, CT: Yale University Press.

Boltz, William. (2003). *Origin and early development of the Chinese writing system* (Rev. ed.). American Oriental Series 78. New Haven, CT: American Oriental Society.

Branner, David Prager. (2006). China: Writing system. *Encyclopedia of language and linguistics*, 2nd ed. Keith Brown (Ed.), *2*, 331–341. Oxford: Elsevier.

Carrasquer Vidal, Miguel. (2006a). Aegean scripts. *Encyclopedia of language and linguistics*, 2nd ed. Keith Brown (Ed.), *1*, 69–82. Oxford: Elsevier.

Carrasquer Vidal, Miguel. (2006b). Europe alphabets, ancient classical. *Encyclopedia of language and linguistics*, 2nd ed. Keith Brown (Ed.), *4*, 267–278. Oxford: Elsevier.

Cook, Vivian. (2004). *The English writing system*. The English Language Series. London: Arnold.

Cooper, Jerrold S. (1999). Sumerian and Semitic writing in most ancient Mesopotamia. In K. Van Lerberghe and G. Voet (Eds.), *Languages and cultures in contact: At the crossroads of civilizations in the Syro-Mesopotamian realm* (pp. 61–77). Orientalia Lovaniensia Analecta 96. Leuven: Peeters.

Coulmas, Florian. (2003). *Writing systems*. Cambridge Textbooks in Linguistics. Cambridge: Cambridge University Press.

Crystal, David. (2006). *Language and the Internet*. 2nd ed. Cambridge: Cambridge University Press.

Daniels, Peter T. (1990). Fundamentals of grammatology. *Journal of the American Oriental Society*, *110*, 727–731.

Daniels, Peter T. (1992a). Contacts between Semitic and Indic scripts. In Amir Harrack (Ed.), *West Asia and North Africa*. Contacts between cultures: Selected papers from the 33rd International Congress of Asian and North African Studies, Toronto, August 15–25, 1990 1 (pp. 146–52). Lewiston, NY: Edwin Mellen.

Daniels, Peter T. (1992b). The syllabic origin of writing and the segmental origin of the alphabet." In Pamela Downing, Susan D. Lima, & Michael Noonan (Eds.), *The linguistics of literacy* (pp. 83–110). Typological Studies in Language 21. Amsterdam and Philadelphia: John Benjamins.

Daniels, Peter T. (1992c). What do the "paleographic" tablets tell us of Mesopotamian scribes' knowledge of the history of their script? *Mār Šipri: Newsletter of the Committee on Mesopotamian Civilization, American Schools of Oriental Research*, *5/1*, 1–4.

Daniels, Peter T. (1997a). The protean Arabic abjad. In Asma Afsaruddin & A. H. Mathias Zahniser (Eds.), *Humanism, culture, and language in the Near East: Studies in honor of George Krotkoff* (pp. 369–384). Winona Lake, IN: Eisenbrauns.

Daniels, Peter T. (1997b). Scripts of Semitic languages. In Robert Hetzron (Ed.), *The Semitic languages* (pp. 16–45). London: Routledge.

Daniels, Peter T. (2000a). On writing syllables: Three episodes of script transfer.

Studies in the Linguistic Sciences (Urbana), 30, 73–86.

Daniels, Peter T. (2000b). Syllables, consonants, and vowels in West Semitic writing. *Lingua Posnaniensis*, 42, 43–55.

Daniels, Peter T. (2001). Writing systems. In Mark Aronoff & Janie Rees-Miller, *Handbook of linguistics* (pp. 43–80). Malden, MA: Blackwell.

Daniels, Peter T. (2002). The study of writing in the twentieth century: Semitic studies interacting with non-Semitic. *Israel Oriental Studies*, 20, 85–117.

Daniels, Peter T. (2005). Reply to Victor H. Mair. *Word*, 56 (3).

Daniels, Peter T. (2006a). On beyond alphabets. *Written Language and Literacy*, 9, 7–24.

Daniels, Peter T. (2006b). Three models of script transfer. *Word*, 57 (3).

Daniels, Peter T. (2007). *Littera ex occidente*: Toward a functional history of writing. In Cynthia L. Miller (Ed.), *Studies in Semitic and Afroasiatic linguistics presented to Gene B. Gragg* (pp. 53–70). Studies in Ancient Oriental Civilization 60. Chicago: Oriental Institute.

Daniels, Peter T. (2008). Writing systems of major and minor languages. In Braj Kachru, Yamuna Kachru, & S. N. Sridhar (Eds.), *Language in South Asia* (pp. 283–305). Cambridge: Cambridge University Press.

Daniels, Peter T., & William Bright (Eds.) (1996). *The world's writing systems*. New York: Oxford University Press.

DeFrancis, John. (1989). *Visible speech: The diverse oneness of writing systems*. Honolulu: University of Hawaii Press.

Derrida, Jacques. (1967). *De la grammatologie*. Paris: Minuit.

Deshpande, M. M. (1994). Phonetics, ancient Indian. *Encyclopedia of language and linguistics*, R. E. Asher & J. M. Y. Simpson (Eds.) (pp. 3053–3058). Oxford: Pergamon.

Dewey, Melvil. (1932). *Decimal clasification and relativ index: For libraries and personal use in arranjing for immediate reference books, pamflets, clippings, pictures, manuscript notes and other material.* 13th ed. Revised and enlarged by Dorkas Fellows and Myron Warren Getchell. Lake Placid, NY: Forest Press.

Diringer, David. (1968). *The alphabet: A key to the history of mankind*. 3rd ed., 2 vols. New York: Funk & Wagnalls.

Dobbs-Allsopp, F. W. (2006). Asia, ancient southwest: Scripts, earliest. *Encyclopedia of language and linguistics*, 2nd ed. Keith Brown (Ed.), 1, 495–500. Oxford: Elsevier.

Du Ponceau, Peter Stephen. (1838). A dissertation on the nature and character of the Chinese system of writing. *Transactions of the Historical and Literary Committee of the American Philosophical Society*, 2, vii–xxxii, 1–123.

Eisenstein, Elizabeth L. (1979). *The printing press as an agent of change: Communications and cultural transformations in early-modern Europe*. Cambridge: Cambridge University Press.

Eska, Joseph F. (2004). Continental Celtic. In Roger D. Woodard (Ed.), *The Cambridge encyclopedia of the world's ancient languages* (pp. 857–880). Cambridge: Cambridge University Press.

Friedrich, Johannes. (1966). *Geschichte der Schrift*. Heidelberg: Winter.

Gamkrelidze, Thomas V. (1994). *Alphabetic writing and the Old Georgian script: A typology and provenience of alphabetic writing systems*. Delmar, NY: Caravan.

Gamkrelidze, Thomas V. (2006). Europe, Christian: Alphabets. *Encyclopedia of language and linguistics*, 2nd ed. Keith Brown (Ed.), 4, 295–305. Oxford: Elsevier.

Gelb, I. J. (1952). *A study of writing*. Chicago: University of Chicago Press. (2nd ed., 1963.)

Gelb, I. J. (1958). New evidence in favor of the syllabic character of West Semitic writing. *Bibliotheca Orientalis*, 15, 2–7.

Geller, M. J. (1997). The last wedge. *Zeitschrift für Assyriologie*, 87, 43–95.

Gershevitch, Ilya. (1979). The alloglottography of Old Persian. *Transactions of the Philological Society*, 114–190.

Gragg, Gene B. (2006a). Asia, ancient southwest: Scripts, South Semitic. *Encyclopedia of language and linguistics*, 2nd ed. Keith Brown (Ed.), 1, 512–518. Oxford: Elsevier.

Gragg, Gene B. (2006b). Mesopotamian cuneiform script. *Encyclopedia of language and linguistics*, 2nd edition. Keith Brown (Ed.), 8, 27–31. Oxford: Elsevier.

Graves, Robert. (1960). *The Greek myths*, Revised edition, 2 volumes. Harmondsworth, England: Penguin.

Gray, Louis H. (1934). *Introduction to Semitic comparative linguistics*. New York: Columbia University Press.

Grierson, George A. (1903–1927). *Linguistic survey of India*. 11 volumes in 19 parts. Calcutta: Office of the Superintendent of Government Printing.

Hamilton, Gordon J. (2006). *The origins of the West Semitic alphabet in Egyptian scripts.*

Catholic Biblical Quarterly Monograph Series 40. Washington, DC: Catholic Biblical Association of America.

Hastings, Charles Harris. (1929/1967). Reminiscences and observations on the card distribution work of the Library of Congress. In William Warner Bishop & Andrew Keogh, *Essays offered to Herbert Putnam by his colleagues and friends on his thirtieth anniversary as Librarian of Congress* (pp. 195–206) (Reprint 1967). Freeport, NY: Books for Libraries.

Havelock, Eric. (1976). *Origins of Western literacy*. Toronto: Ontario Institute for Studies in Education.

Henning, Walter B. (1958). Mitteliranisch. In Bertold Spuler (Ed.), *Iranistik, part 1: Linguistik* (pp. 20–130). Handbuch der Orientalistik 1/4/1. Leiden: Brill.

Hockett, Charles F. (1958). *A course in modern linguistics*. New York, NY: Macmillan.

Hockett, Charles F. (2003). Two lectures on writing. Prepared for publication by Peter T. Daniels. *Written Language and Literacy*, *6*, 131–175.

Hoffmann, Karl, & Johanna Narten. (1989). *Der Sasanidische Archetypus: Untersuchungen zu Schreibung und Lautgestalt des Avestischen*. Wiesbaden: Reichert.

Houston, Stephen D. (Ed.) (2004). *The first writing: Script invention as history and process*. Cambridge: Cambridge University Press.

Jensen, Hans. (1969). *Sign, symbol and script*. 3rd ed. Translated by George Unwin. New York: Putnam.

Karlgren, Bernhard. (1926/1980). *Philology and ancient China*. Oslo: Aschehoug; Cambridge: Harvard University Press. (Reprint, 1980) Philadelphia: Porcupine.

Kim, Chin-Wu. (2006). Korean script: History and description. *Encyclopedia of language and linguistics*, 2nd ed. Keith Brown (Ed.), *6*, 239–243. Oxford: Elsevier.

King, Ross. (1987). The Korean elements in the Manchu script reform of 1632. *Central Asiatic Journal*, *31*, 197–217.

Klugkist, A. C. (1982). Midden-Aramese Schriften in Syrië, Mesopotamië, Perzië en aangrenzende gebieden. Ph.D. dissertation, University of Groningen.

Ledyard, Gari K. (1966). The Korean language reform of 1446: The origin, background, and early history of the Korean alphabet. Ph.D. dissertation, University of California, Berkeley.

Ledyard, Gari K. (1997). The international linguistic background of the correct sounds for the instruction of the people. In Young-Key Kim-Renaud (Ed.), *The Korean alphabet: Its history and structure* (pp. 31–87). Honolulu: University of Hawai'i Press.

Lewis, Naphtali. (1974). *Papyrus in classical antiquity*. Oxford: Clarendon. *Supplement*. (1989). Papyrologica Bruxellensia 23. Brussels: Fondation Égyptologique Reine Élisabeth.

Li, Gertraude Roth. (2000). *Manchu: A textbook for reading documents*. Honolulu: University of Hawai'i Press.

Lounsbury, Floyd. (1973). On the derivation and reading of the 'Ben-Ich' prefix. In Elisabeth P. Benson (Ed.), *Mesoamerican writing systems* (pp. 99–143). Washington, DC: Dumbarton Oaks Research Library and Collections.

Lowe, K. A. (2006). Runes. *Encyclopedia of language and linguistics*, 2nd ed. Keith Brown (Ed.), *10*, 688–691. Oxford: Elsevier.

Macdonald, M. C. A. (2004). Ancient North Arabian. In Roger D. Woodard (Ed.), *The Cambridge encyclopedia of the world's ancient languages* (pp. 488–533). Cambridge: Cambridge University Press.

Mair, Victor H. (2005). [Review of *Writing systems: A linguistic approach*, by Henry Rogers]. *Word*, *56*, 101–107.

Marcus, Joyce. (2006). Mesoamerica: Scripts. *Encyclopedia of language and linguistics*, 2nd ed. Keith Brown (Ed.), 8, 16–27. Oxford: Elsevier.

Mickelthwait, David. (2000.) *Noah Webster and the American dictionary*. Jefferson, NC: McFarland.

Murray, K. M. Elisabeth. (1977). *Caught in the web of words: James Murray and the Oxford English Dictionary*. New Haven, CT: Yale University Press. (Reprint, 1979) Oxford: Oxford University Press.

Neijt, Anneke. (2006). Spelling reform. *Encyclopedia of language and linguistics*, 2nd ed. Keith Brown (Ed.), *12*, 68–71. Oxford: Elsevier.

O'Connor, M. (1992). Writing systems and native-speaker analyses. In Walter R. Bodine (Ed.), *Linguistics and Biblical Hebrew* (pp. 231–254). Winona Lake, IN: Eisenbrauns.

Pike, Kenneth L. (1947). *Phonemics: A technique for reducing languages to writing*. Ann Arbor: University of Michigan Press.

Pitman, James, & John St. John. (1969). *Alphabets and reading: The initial teaching alphabet*. New York: Pitman.

Reddick, Allen. (1996). *The making of Johnson's dictionary 1746–1773*. (Rev. ed.) Cambridge: Cambridge University Press.

Reiner, Erica. (1985). *Your thwarts in pieces your mooring rope cut: Poetry from Babylonia and Assyria*. Michigan Studies in the Humanities 5. Ann Arbor: Horace H. Rackham School of Graduate Studies at the University of Michigan.

Robertson, John S. (2004). The possibility and actuality of writing. In Stephen D. Houston (Ed.), *The First Writing* (pp. 16–38). Cambridge: Cambridge University Press.

Robinson, Andrew. (2002). *Lost languages: The enigma of the world's undeciphered scripts*. New York: McGraw-Hill.

Robinson, T. H. (1960). *The poetry of the Old Testament*. London: Duckworth.

Salomon, Richard. (1998). *Indian epigraphy: A guide to the study of inscriptions in Sanskrit, Prakrit, and the other Indo-Aryan languages*. New York: Oxford University Press.

Salomon, Richard. (2003). Writing systems of the Indo-Aryan languages. In George Cardona & Dhanesh Jain (Eds.), *The Indo-Aryan Languages* (pp. 67–103). London: Routledge.

Salomon, Richard. (2005). On alphabetical order in India, and elsewhere. Paper presented at the Plenary Session on Writing, American Oriental Society annual meeting, Philadelphia, March 20.

Schmidt, David L. (1991). Some implications of alphabetolatry for writing system analysis. In David L. Schmidt & Janet S. Smith (Eds.), *Literacies: Writing systems and literate practices* (pp. 1–9). University of California, Davis Working Papers in Linguistics 4.

Schröpfer, Johannes. (1968). *Hussens Traktat "Orthographia Bohemica": Die Herkunft des diakritischen Systems in der Schreibung slavischer Sprachen und die älteste zusammenhängende Beschreibung slavischer Laute*. Slavistische Studienbücher 4. Wiesbaden: Harrassowitz.

Seeley, Christopher. (1991/2000). *A history of writing in Japan*. Leiden: Brill. (Reprint, 2000.) Honolulu: University of Hawai'i Press.

Segert, Stanislav. (1963). Altaramäische Schrift und Anfänge des griechischen Alphabets. *Klio*, *41*, 38–57.

Shackle, Christopher. (2006). South and Southeast Asia: Scripts. *Encyclopedia of language and linguistics*, 2nd ed. Keith Brown (Ed.), *11*, 544–557. Oxford: Elsevier.

Shaw, [George] Bernard. (1941). Preface to *The miraculous birth of language*, by Richard Albert Wilson (pp. ix–xxxvii). London: Dent.

Shimron, Joseph. (Ed.) (2003). *Language processing and acquisition in languages of Semitic, root-based, morphology*. Language Acquisition & Language Disorders 28. Amsterdam and Philadelphia: John Benjamins.

Simpson, J. M. Y. (2006). Ogam. *Encyclopedia of language and linguistics*, 2nd ed. Keith Brown (Ed.), 9, 15–18. Oxford: Elsevier.

Skjærvø, P. Oktor. (2006). Iran: Scripts, Old Persian, Aramaic, Avestan. *Encyclopedia of language and linguistics*, 2nd ed. Keith Brown (Ed.), 6, 12–16. Oxford: Elsevier.

Steinkeller, Piotr. (1995). [Review of *Zeichenliste der archaischen Texte aus Uruk*, by M. W. Green and Hans J. Nissen (1987)]. *Bibliotheca Orientalis*, 52, 689–713.

Stolper, Matthew W. (2007). An Old Persian administrative tablet from the Persepolis fortification archive. Paper presented at the American Oriental Society annual meeting, San Antonio, March 19.

Tauber, Abraham. (Ed.) (1963). *George Bernard Shaw on language*. New York: Philosophical Library.

Taylor, Isaac. (1883). *The alphabet: An account of the origin and development of letters*. 2 vols. London: Kegan Paul, Trench. 2nd ed., London: Edward Arnold, 1899.

Thompson, Mikael A. (2006a). Asia, Inner: Scripts. *Encyclopedia of language and linguistics*, 2nd ed., Keith Brown (Ed.), *1*, 519–534. Oxford: Elsevier.

Thompson, Mikael A. (2006b). Tibet: Scripts. *Encyclopedia of language and linguistics*, 2nd ed. Keith Brown (Ed.), 12, 707–712. Oxford: Elsevier.

Tuchscherer, Konrad, & P. E. H. Hair. (2002). Cherokee and West Africa: Examining the origins of the Vai script. *History in Africa*, *29*, 427–486.

Uhlig, Siegbert. (1990). *Introduction to Ethiopian palaeography*. Äthiopistische Forschungen 28. Stuttgart: Steiner.

Unger, J. Marshall. (2006). Japan: Writing system. *Encyclopedia of language and linguistics*, 2nd ed. Keith Brown (Ed.), 6, 95–102. Oxford: Elsevier.

Upward, Christopher. (1996.) *Cut spelling: A handbook to the simplification of written English by omission of redundant letters*. 2nd ed. Birmingham: The Simplified Spelling Society.

Versteegh, Kees. (1997). *The Arabic language*. New York: Columbia University Press.

Watt, W. C. (1998). The old-fashioned way. [Review of *The world's writing systems* (Peter T. Daniels & William Bright, Eds.)]. *Semiotica, 122*, 99–138.

Whorf, Benjamin Lee. (1940/1956). Linguistics as an exact science. *Technology Review, 43*, 61–63, 80–83. Cited from John B. Carroll (Ed.), *Language, thought, and reality: Selected writings of Benjamin Lee Whorf* (pp. 220–232). Cambridge, MA: MIT Press.

CHAPTER 3

Speech and Writing

Roy Harris

Introduction

Differences in vocabulary and syntax between written documents and everyday speech have long been recognized. So has the fact that the vocal sounds produced in the oral delivery of written texts differ from those of colloquial conversation. But attention to these differences seems often to have obscured a more general and more fundamental question. How does writing relate to speech?

One might have supposed that the first logical requirement for tackling this question would be to define 'writing' on the one hand and 'speech' on the other, before proceeding to examine the connexions between the two. But even a slight historical acquaintance with the topic shows that what has often happened is that this logic has been swept aside in favour of allowing a priori assumptions about the relationship itself to dictate definitions of both.

The most naive of these assumptions, that writing is 'visible speech', goes back to Graeco-Roman antiquity. It has been perpetuated for centuries, particularly in countries where the usual form of writing is alphabetic. It still informs the work of many educationists, linguists, psychologists, philosophers and historians of writing systems. The complementary assumption that reading aloud makes 'writing audible' is no less simplistic. The facts of the matter are more complex and more difficult to grasp, because they have been overlaid by so many cultural prejudices, the latter often passing for 'common sense'. Speech and writing are both completely independent, having quite different semiological foundations. But certain forms of speech and certain forms of writing can, in certain circumstances, be made to function as the basis for mutually complementary activities.

Another misconception associated with the relationship is the idea that writing something down is a communicational 'substitute' for uttering it aloud. This popular view was already common enough in the Athens of their day for Socrates and Plato to think it worth while pointing out to their contemporaries what a gross mistake it was. But in spite of this early warning, the 'visible speech' thesis and the 'substitution' thesis have gone hand in hand now for so long that they have become what might well be called 'the writing myth' of the Western tradition. The perpetuation of this myth is largely due to the establishment of pedagogic programmes in which children are taught to write by explicitly correlating individual letters (*A*, *B*, *C*, and so forth) with sounds. It is far less solidly entrenched in non-Western societies that never adopted alphabetic writing.

A third component of this Occidental myth has already been alluded to above: this is the tacit reductivism by which the terms *speech* and *writing* (or their counterparts in other languages) are themselves restricted in application so as to fit prior assumptions about the relationship. In this way, the opposition between two diverse modes of communication is reduced to a distinction between the vocalization of words and their inscription. Thus it becomes possible – and even customary – to exclude from what purport to be studies of writing (e.g., Gelb, 1963; Sampson, 1985) such important developments as mathematical and musical notation, or to regard these as marginal matters of no great consequence. Any serious analysis of the relationship between speech and writing cannot afford to adopt this blinkered perspective. Speech is not just the audible product of a talking head, any more than writing is just a collection of visible marks left on a surface by the hand of a writer. Unfortunately, phoneticians often encourage the former fallacy, while grammatologists and graphologists promote the latter. The whole concept of 'literacy' is thereby distorted. The depths of the contrast between speech and writing are flattened out, and its full social and psychological dimensions hidden.

It is impossible in the scope of one paper to explore the many facets of the relationship between speech and writing across the whole gamut of the literate societies of the world. Here the discussion will focus mainly on the landmark contributions to it in European thinking. The term *scriptism* is sometimes used to designate a tendency to treat speech as if it were writing. There seems to be no parallel term to designate a tendency to treat writing as if it were speech. But this is no less common, as can been seen from the use of expressions like 'it says here . . . ' in reference to written texts.

Socrates and Plato on Speech and Writing

In *Phaedrus*, Plato puts into the mouth of Socrates a remarkable tirade against writing, which begins with the tale of the Egyptian god, Ammon, rebuking Theuth, the legendary inventor of writing, who claimed that his invention would enhance both wisdom and memory. On the contrary, maintained Ammon, reliance on writing weakens the memory and substitutes information for wisdom. Those who practice it thereby disguise their own ignorance and become conceited, laying claim to knowledge they do not themselves possess. According to Socrates, truth does not lend itself to expression in writing, because a text, once written down, is divorced from its author and the relevant circumstances of composition. A written text raises questions but cannot answer them, and is consequently open to interpretation by ignorant people who are in no position to judge what the writer meant. (The same point, that texts are deaf to questions, is also made in passing in *Protagoras*.) Thus we are misled if we are simple-minded enough to believe that what is written down can function as an alternative to – much less a definitive version of – what was said on some particular occasion.

This may be read as Plato's explanation of why Socrates, the foremost philosopher of his day, refused to commit any of his teachings to writing. (He was by no means the only philosopher of antiquity to do so.) But Ammon's argument is also a classic example of treating writing as if it ought to be answerable to the same requirements as speech, that is, putting an assumption about the relationship before any serious comparison of the practices.

What was Plato's own view? An attack on writing similar to that presented in *Phaedrus* appears in what has come down to us as *Letter VII*, although its authenticity has been doubted. Even if it is not from the hand of Plato, its author was certainly someone well acquainted with Plato's position. *Letter VII* rejects the pretentions of those who have written treatises on philosophy, particularly when purporting to be based upon Plato's own philosophical teachings. Any pretence of trying to write about philosophy is dismissed out of hand: 'no treatise by me concerning it exists or ever will exist'. The reader is told that no serious student of any subject ever tried to commit his mature understanding of that subject to writing. The usual excuse that writing provides useful assistance to the memory will not do, since 'there is no danger of a man forgetting the truth, once his soul has grasped it'.

This does not quite tally with what Socrates says in *Phaedrus*, for there Socrates seems at least to allow the possibility of a philosopher using writing for his own amusement or as a private aid to recollecting truths already recognized. What is condemned is the use of writing to make a definitive or final statement concerning some philosophical topic.

How is it, then, that speech can succeed where writing fails? And is there something suspect about the fact that these unpopular truths about writing are themselves expressed in written form (viz. in the edited text of *Phaedrus*, and in a letter ostensibly addressed by Plato to the friends of Dion, although doubtless intended for wider circulation)? Plato, like the author of *Letter VII* (if that is a forgery), was far too astute a debater to fall into such an obvious trap. The remarks about writing in both places are presented as a salutary warning to the naive, not as the conclusion to any detailed examination of the two modes of communication: they have roughly the same standing as might nowadays be accorded to a caution to the effect that one cannot always believe what is shown on television. Such a caution would be pointless if there were not many people foolish enough to be deceived in this way.

What is reflected by the attitude to writing expressed in *Phaedrus* and *Letter VII* might superficially seem to reflect a situation characteristic of the transition from a primary oral to a literate society, in which the newer form of communication is still regarded with suspicion by traditionalists. But Socrates and Plato are not just being 'old-fashioned'. (Had that been the case, Plato would hardly have recommended in his *Laws* compulsory instruction in reading and writing for all children of both sexes – a notably 'progressive' educational policy.) When they compare writing unfavourably to speech, they are thinking of speech not just as the use of the voice, but as the face-to-face engagement of one individual with another and one human personality with another. They would probably have agreed with Marshall McLuhan (1964, p. 77) that 'the spoken word involves all of the senses dramatically' (not just hearing) and is thus immeasurably richer in texture than any legible marks that appear on the page.

The crucial point, as far as Socrates and Plato are concerned, is that truth is something that can be found – and even then, not easily – only by this process of total engagement between speakers, and through their patient commitment to inquiry by a series of questions and answers (the famous 'Socratic method'). Even if such a search could be attempted by exchanging letters, that exchange would inevitably lack the immediacy and impact of *viva voce* contact and reaction. The function of speech, declares Socrates, 'is to influence the soul'. And the recognition of truth is one that emerges not from solitary contemplation or inspired insight but from the direct and reciprocal action of one seeker's rational mind on another's.

It is not part of their case to argue that writing is totally useless for mundane purposes (such as keeping records or drafting speeches). Socrates and Phaedrus are themselves poring over the manuscript of a speech by Lysias, and Socrates goes out of his way to make the point that Lysias is not to be condemned just because he is a professional logographer: 'there is nothing inherently disgraceful in speech-writing'. Rather, the objection is that, by divorcing the expression of an opinion both from the person who holds it and from the context of inquiry in which it was arrived at, writing can distort the very facts that it claims to present. This is not for any failing on the part of the writer, but is intrinsic to that particular means of communication.

It is ironic that Plato himself may have contributed unwittingly to the 'visible speech' fallacy by the comparison he draws in *Phaedrus* between writing and painted portraits. In *Phaedrus*, texts and pictures are both mute, and equally inadequate as representations, because they can capture no more than superficial appearances. What a person looks like as depicted by the painter tells us very little about the real person. Both painting and writing are lifeless attempts to represent living things.

Did Plato later modify these sceptical views? It can be argued that he must have done, since otherwise, like his master Socrates, he would have left nothing in writing to posterity. His later work even abandons the dialogue form as a preferred mode of exposition. It has been suggested that Plato suffered from presbyopia and that being forced to rely on dictation to secretaries motivated his distaste for writing. But in *Timaeus*, the wise Egyptian priest attributes the ignorance of the Greeks to their failure to preserve written records, and in the *Laws*, the Guardian of Plato's model state is recommended to preserve in writing all materials suitable for the education of children. The state laws themselves are envisaged as being codified in writing. Clinias argues that their written form is essential, since written laws 'remain fixed and permanent, ready to stand up to scrutiny for ever'.

But it hardly takes a great philosopher to point out that no one can ensure that the written form is proof against later misinterpretation. Subsequent legal history, from Plato down to the present day, amply demonstrates the error of supposing that writing permanently 'fixes' the legislator's meaning. If it did, endless unnecessary court battles would be pre-empted. Meaning aside, even the identification of the verbal forms originally used in the formulation of a law requires a text to be interpreted by a reader. As Socrates insists in *Phaedrus*, writing cannot somehow speak for itself. It is never writing that imposes its own interpretation on the reader, but the reader who invariably imposes an interpretation on the text.

A more likely explanation of Plato's antipathy to writing has nothing to do with his eyesight, but is based on his known aversion to poetry as a traditional source of wisdom. Plato may well have felt – although he nowhere makes this explicit – that the (relatively recent) new lease on life accorded to Homer by the availability of manuscripts of the Homeric poems was a retrograde step in Greek culture, and he felt that it diverted attention from philosophy. He might have been depressed at the prospect that, in an increasingly literate Greece, the lies and fancies of the poets were to be preserved in perpetuity, ready to corrupt the minds of each fresh generation. He had already perceived, with misgivings, what has been described as 'the way in which writing itself tends to canonize knowledge'.

Moreover, the false appearance of permanence that writing carries with it may well have seemed to Plato a cheap substitute for the reliability and invariance promised by acquaintance with the sempiternal Forms – the ultimate basis of human knowledge in Plato's epistemology.

It is nowhere suggested, either in *Phaedrus* or in *Letter VII*, that the trouble with writing is the substitution of a visual for an auditory sign. The transposition of sensory modalities is an irrelevance. If Socrates had lived to see the invention of the gramophone record or the tape recorder, he would doubtless have condemned those too. It is not a question of how 'accurately' or 'inaccurately' writing captures vocal sounds. It is a question of divorcing the simulacrum from the original, and in ways which are beyond any possibility of recovery.

Aristotle on Symbols

Plato's pupil, Aristotle, presents a quite different perspective on speech and writing. If ancient Greece ever had a 'literate revolution' (Havelock, 1982), Aristotle was the first major thinker to come to terms with it. Writing suits Aristotle's purposes perfectly. As teacher and polymath, he sees his function as being to establish and document the current state of research and theory in the intellectual world of his day.

Education, according to Aristotle (*Politics VIII*), has four basic branches: reading, writing, gymnastic exercises and music, with drawing sometimes added as a fifth. Reading and writing are useful in four spheres of activity: in making money, in household management, for purposes of instruction, and in taking part in civic affairs. But apart from these practical matters, Aristotle is also interested in putting forward a theory of writing: he compares writing with speech on a strictly semiological basis (*De Interpretatione* 16A) – which has nothing at all to do with its practical utility – and is the first philosopher in the Western tradition to do so.

The basis of Aristotle's theory of writing is his concept of the symbol (*symbolon*), widely misunderstood both in antiquity and ever since. For Aristotle, a symbol is not a 'representation' of anything; even less is it a copy or imitation or embodiment of anything, or a symbolic act in the modern sense. It is a token or tally, directly corresponding to another such item, with which it correlates. It thus constitutes one half of a complementary pair, the 'symbolic' connexion between the two being established by agreement and shown by some physical connexion between them. The source of Aristotle's symbol is the ancient commercial practice of sealing a bargain by breaking any small object in two, one half being retained by each party to the contract, to be shown subsequently, if need be, as proof of identity. An approximate modern analogy would be the present-day cloakroom ticket, which enables the holder to reclaim an item deposited earlier.

By transferring such a model to language, Aristotle – it scarcely needs pointing out – was venturing into the realm of metaphor, and various points about the way he uses this metaphor are worthy of note. But why appeal to metaphor at all? Because the current metalinguistic terminology of his day simply had no established words for describing or discussing the kind of relationship that Aristotle is keen to put in place. And here we see again how an assumption about the relationship takes priority over analysis of the things allegedly related.

Aristotle's semiology is basically reocentric: meaning has to be derived from *realia* in the external world. He recognizes two types of sign – oral and written – and four basic elements involved. One of these is psychological – an 'affection of the soul', or, as it would be expressed in modern terminology, a mental impression or concept. Aristotle's semantic schema relates this internal 'affection of the soul' to three external elements: sounds, letters, and things (the latter comprising the whole panoply of *realia*, including people and everything else in the universe, whether animate or inanimate, whether of natural or human origin). Thus a city (say, Athens) counts as an object, the name of that object would be the sounds we utter in order to refer to that particular city, and thirdly there would be the written form of the name – a sequence of letters. The latter two elements vary from language to language, but the thing itself (the city in question) remains the same, as does the corresponding 'affection of the soul'. It is an important premise of Aristotelian semiology that the universe is the same for all observers: there is no question of Athens being one city in the mind of Aristotle, but a rather different city in the mind of Plato (even though they may live in different parts of it). Similarly, a horseman does not have a different concept of a horse from someone who never rides.

This is where the *symbolon* metaphor begins to do its theoretical work. It would not be a *symbolon* if, in the minds of the parties to the contract, what each had agreed on was different. For, in that case, the contract would be null and void. Language, for Aristotle, has to provide the possibility of common understanding: otherwise, it would be a source of endless confusion.

The other key aspect of the *symbolon* is that, although it takes the shape of a physical object, what makes it a *symbolon* is, precisely, what has been agreed by the parties involved. This is central to Aristotle's notion of language as resting on a set of conventions.

What is interesting, and perhaps unexpected, about Aristotle's schema is that the written form is a *symbolon* of the spoken. In other words, Aristotle tacitly assumes a standardized orthography. (There is no room in the metaphor for a *symbolon* which sometimes takes one form, sometimes another.) The background to this is almost certainly the fact that at the time when Aristotle first arrived in Athens as a young man, Athens had just officially adopted the Ionic alphabet. Even so, Aristotle must have been fully aware of the fact that it is possible for a spoken word to have more than one spelling. So his account of the relationship between spoken and written forms of a given name is, in effect, an idealization rather than an empirical description. But there is a reason for this (see below).

The third important function of the *symbolon* metaphor is that it distinguishes the relationship between two of Aristotle's four elements from the relationship which obtains between things and affections of the soul. The latter relationship is *not* 'symbolic'. Affections of the soul are not symbols but images or likenesses of external things. Exactly what kind of image or likeness is involved Aristotle never explains. But the crucial point is that the *symbolon* is not a *representation* of the thing, whereas that is just what an affection of the soul is. The latter is in some sense a natural reflection of the original object (the city, the horse, etc.), whereas *symbola* are not natural products at all, but artificial devices invented by human beings for their own convenience.

But is this the only reason why Aristotle posits a symbolic relationship between spoken and written forms? It also helps explain to some extent the more enigmatic connexion between sounds and affections of the soul. (More enigmatic because, whereas we can utter and hear sounds as public phenomena, what is going on in the soul is not directly available for public perception.) However, we readily grasp the fact that in order to write down what a person says, one must first hear the sounds uttered. These belong to a quite different modality of perception from the symbols employed by the scribe, but the phenomenon of writing seems in itself to be evidence of the possibility of establishing some kind of one-to-one correspondence between the two quite disparate modes. By analogy, that may help us to grasp how, in turn, the sounds uttered stand in relation to the quite different mental units of which our inner thoughts are composed; or at least to grasp that there must *be* such units in the mind, even if we are not at all clear about what mental form they take.

From an integrationist perspective, the importance of the invention of glottic writing is this. The fact that speech and writing have different biomechanical bases automatically opens up a gap between statement and utterance. Into that theoretical and psychological gap is inserted 'the sentence' – an abstraction that, allegedly, can be 'expressed' perfectly well in either form. With the arrival of 'the sentence', a new forum is created for the discussion of human thinking, and along with that comes the concomitant demand or expectation that all thinking (reasoning) worth bothering about has to be presented in sentential form. (This expectation is already realized by the time of Aristotle, because the sentence is the basis of the Aristotelian syllogism.)

This new forum, however, is also an intellectual cage or enclosure imposing its own limitations. It cannot accommodate non-sentential modes of thought. Here we can identify the basis of the long-held anthropological prejudice that people in pre-literate cultures are somehow mentally inferior. (The idea is that their failure to progress to literacy somehow cripples their minds. So just as a Western child who could speak but could not learn to write would be regarded as subnormal or handicapped, whole societies are implicitly condemned.)

In other words, in a literate society, writing provides a model for construing the relationship between speech and thought, a model which is not available in a pre-literate society. Whether Aristotle himself consciously saw the matter in those terms is not evident from the surviving texts, but the above hypothesis fits the account he gives, and would explain why he treats the written form as a fully fledged metasymbol in its own right (and not, like Plato, as a specious and superficial *substitute* for speech).

Grammar

Grammar (*techne grammatike, ars grammatica*) had its origin it the pedagogic practices associated with teaching children their letters (*grammata*). The methods had changed little by the time Quintilian describes them in the first century. They are based on one-to-one correspondences between letter-shapes and sounds, with a common name for both. Thus, for example, '*alpha*' designates both the first letter of the Greek alphabet and also its sound. This conflation must have further reinforced the tendency to assimilate the spoken system to the writing system, while subtly enhancing the importance of the latter, since the durability of the written shape contrasts favourably with the ephemerality of its audible counterpart.

Corroboration of this comes from the fact that grammarians and philosophers use the same terms for the units of both systems. Plato refers to the *grammata* of a word even in contexts where the units under discussion are clearly sounds, not letters. In *Cratylus*, an attempt is made to correlate articulations with meanings. And when Socrates suggests that originally *alpha* signified greatness and *eta* length because of 'the size of the letters', confusion seems complete. In Latin, the indiscriminate use of the terms *littera* and *elementum* matches that in Greek of *gramma* and *stoicheion*. However, as Françoise Desbordes (1990) points out, it would be a mistake to infer from such curious statements as 'the human voice consists of letters' that the ancients actually believed that, in speech, armies of invisible little marks issued forth from the speaker's mouth (p. 113). Plotinus, nevertheless, comes quite close to this absurdity when he describes sounds as letters written in the air. What all this shows is the extent to which in the ancient world speech was conceptualized on the model of writing. This brand of scriptism is the intellectual hallmark of a literate society.

It also explains why, as historians of linguistics have noted, Greek and Roman grammarians made virtually no progress with the study of phonetics. It made them oblivious, as Robins (1997) observes, to dialectal differences other than those corresponding to spelling variations. 'More seriously, an improper analogy was accepted between the relation of discrete letters to a text and that of allegedly discrete sounds to a spoken utterance' (p. 30). In this connexion, Robins cites Priscian's famous comparison between sounds and atoms: 'Just as atoms come together and produce every corporeal thing, so likewise do speech sounds (*elementa vocis*) compose articulate speech as it were some bodily entity'. The atomic comparison might conceivably be justified for written texts, but hardly for speech.

The earliest Greek grammatical treatise that has survived (traditionally attributed to Dionysius Thrax) explains the *grammata* as being so called because they are produced by scratching a surface, even though Dionysius proceeds to subclassify them by phonetic criteria. The alternative term *stoicheia* is explained by reference to the fact that they are arranged in rows, another feature that would hardly have occurred to anyone in a pre-literate society. The definition of grammar itself (by reference to the usage of poets and prose writers) confirms the extent to which thinking about language is dominated by the scriptist perspective.

Although it was eventually recognized in antiquity that the units provided by the alphabet did not entirely match the inventory of segmental speech sounds, and that in any case they were inadequate to render features of stress and intonation, this did not lead to any rethinking of the basic assumption that words were combinations of 'letters'. The solution was the introduction of new letters and diacritics, that is, reform of the writing system, not redefinition of the word.

Quintilian, who describes *grammar* as 'a necessity for boys and the delight of old age', does question the adequacy of the traditional alphabet for the writing of Latin. Commenting on the spelling of the words *servus* and *vulgus*, he complains that Latin lacks the Aeolic digamma. He also notes that Latin has a vowel 'intermediate' between *u* and *i*, and that in the word written *here*, the vowel is neither exactly *e* nor *i*. He gives it as his personal view that, with due deference to customary usage (*consuetudo*), a word should be spelt as it is pronounced (*quomodo sonat*). The statement is highly significant, although the significance is not quite what it might initially appear to be. Once it is felt that spelling and pronunciation are mismatched, or even *can* be mismatched, this is treated as a defect in communication that must be dealt with. There seem to be only two options available. One is to change the spelling to conform with pronunciation and the other is to change the pronunciation to conform with spelling. Either policy will, in principle, restore the internal consistency that the mismatch disrupts. Quintilian opts for changing the spelling, presumably because he is a teacher of rhetoric and not a *grammaticus*. That is exactly what one would expect a rhetorician to say, given that the pinnacle of his art is oral performance in public. Speech is supreme and writing ancillary. At the same time, however, the notion of spelling words *as they are pronounced* presupposes that the letters do have fixed phonetic correlates as their 'values'. So mispronunciation becomes a failure to assign the correct values to the letters. It follows that those who cannot read or write cannot possibly know how to speak correctly. The prestige of the alphabet is restored after all.

The Stoic theorists of grammar went even further. As Desbordes (1990, pp. 101–103) points out, in effect, they made writing criterial for the definition of human speech. That is to say, they treated the vocal apparatus as a physiological mechanism for sound production and distinguished its products into two categories: speech and mere noise. The former was 'articulated' and the latter lacked articulation. The distinction hinged on whether the sound produced could be written down.

The Stoic insistence that the *grammata* are simultaneously the ultimate elements of both speech and writing is a manifestation of what W.T. Stace (1949) once called 'the Parmenidean dogma'. In other words, in order to preserve the metaphysical principle that 'everything comes from something', writing has to be accounted for as a transference of 'the same' substance into a different 'form'. Hence the importance for the Stoics of the idea (stressed by Diogenes Laertius) that sound, although it gives no tangible product, is actually corporeal, a material body. In support of this view, Diogenes Laertius cites Archedemus, Diogenes of Babylon, Antipater and Chrysippus – an impressive array of authorities. Thus speech provides the material substrate for the visible sign that is writing. By this point, clearly, the relationship between speech and writing has been taken out of the school classroom altogether and been given a philosophical interpretation with far-reaching implications.

Thus the notion that all ancient writers were careless about distinguishing between spoken and written units does not stand up to serious scrutiny. In any case, as Saussure (1922) pointed out many centuries later, any accusation of scriptist bias would be more apposite if levelled at the founders of nineteenth-century comparative philology. Saussure berates Bopp for failing to distinguish between sounds and letters: 'Reading Bopp, we might think that a language is inseparable from its alphabet' (p. 46). He pokes fun at Grimm for supposing that the fricative digraph *th* must represent two consonants because it has two letters. He might also have been equally scathing (had it occurred to him) about some of his own contemporaries, such as Max Müller, who still spoke of 'letters' as the basic phonetic units. Müller even entitled one of his lectures on speech sounds 'The physiological alphabet' (Müller, 1864) and declared that 'Letters are formed in different places by active and passive organs, the normal places being those marked by the contact between the root of the tongue and the palate, the tip of the tongue and the teeth [. . .]' and so on.

This is all the more remarkable in that by the latter half of the nineteenth century most students of phonetics had realized that the first step in the analytic study of speech sounds had to be, as Henry Sweet put it in 1890, its 'emancipation from spelling'. The snag was that, once the emancipation was achieved, writing had to be immediately reintroduced in order to make phonetic transcription possible, and the transcription systems proposed were all alphabetically based. So there is a certain air of the conjuror's performance about the emancipatory programme. Spelling is dismissed in full view of the audience, only to be produced magically on stage out of the empty hat.

Called upon to explain the 'new' relationship between letters and sounds, phoneticians tended to shift uncomfortably from one foot to the other. For in practice they were by no means in agreement about what phonetic distinctions needed to be recognized or explicitly represented, and even less in agreement about the vexed question of 'spelling reform', at that time attracting the attention of the general public. In the absence of any sound theoretical basis for establishing a universal inventory of discrete speech sounds, they tended to fall back on authoritarian pronouncements drawn from the scriptist tradition of pre-emancipation days. Sweet's introduction to *The History of Language* (1900) might almost have been taken from a misunderstood treatise by one of the Stoic philosophers. There readers are told that 'every sentence or word by which we express our ideas has a certain definite form of its own by virtue of the sounds of which it is made up', that not all vocal sounds are speech sounds, that this difference depends on 'articulation', and, finally, that this articulation is 'logical articulation'. Thus, according to Sweet, the call of the cuckoo and the bleat of a sheep are 'fairly articulate' from a 'formal point of view', but lacking in logical articulation. This is even more of a muddle than any of which the Stoics were guilty. In *The Practical Study of Languages* (1899), it becomes clear that Sweet subscribed to the old idea that writing has a regulatory or corrective function *vis-à-vis* speech: specifically, he held that a scientific form of writing (i.e., phonetic notation) is essential in order to enable the learner to 'correct' the unreliable impressions of the ear and guard against 'mishearings' and 'mispronunciations'. But this remedial function is incomprehensible unless it is first assumed that letters are indeed able in some magical way to capture the authentic sounds that a native speaker 'should' produce. So it did not take long for writing, resuscitated by the phonetician, to resume its old role as the authoritative representation of human language, in the form of what Alexander Melville Bell in 1867 had christened 'visible speech'. *Plus ça changeait, plus c'était la même chose.*

The 'Primacy of Speech'

Modern linguistics reacted to what was seen as the tyrannical hold of writing over Western perceptions of language by elaborating the doctrine of the 'primacy of speech'. This had the effect of marginalizing the study of writing and writing systems, now seen as 'artificial' constructs devised and maintained by elites for their own advantage, as opposed to communication based on the 'natural' processes of speech.

It was claimed that there are at least four respects in which speech takes priority over writing: (1) as far as is known, all human communities had a spoken language before they had, if they ever had, a corresponding written language; (2) all normal children learn their native language in its spoken form before learning the corresponding written form; (3) speech serves a wider range of communicational purposes than writing; and (4) writing originated as a representation of speech. These four 'priorities' have been termed, respectively, 'phylogenetic priority', 'ontogenetic priority', 'functional priority' and 'structural priority' (Lyons, 1972). But while it is clear that those who claim that language is essentially 'rooted in speech', and that 'nothing is a language in the fullest and clearest sense' unless it includes the production, reception and interpretation of sounds originating in the vocal tract (Black, 1972, p. 79), it is often less clear which of the various 'priorities' they consider decisive, or what difference it would make if only some – or none – of them held. For it does not follow from any of the four that the use of vocal sound as a medium of expression must be treated as criterial, to the exclusion of writing, in defining either language or languages, except in the case of those languages which happen to have no written form. But no one has ever argued that it would be impossible to devise a system of writing for any known spoken language, should the need arise. On the other hand, there are certainly forms of writing, including some in everyday use, that cannot be 'read aloud' in any language. The implications of this will be considered further below.

Since the latter part of the nineteenth century, the primacy of speech has been affirmed dogmatically by a number of eminent linguists. A typical example is Leonard Bloomfield, who simply asserts – without argument: 'Writing is not language, but merely a way of recording language by means of visible marks' (Bloomfield, 1935, p. 21). Bloomfield's pronouncement is still repeated uncritically today (e.g., Rogers, 2005, p. 2), even though it enlists the topos of 'visible speech' in support of a manifestly preposterous position. For if the claim is taken seriously, it would follow that Bloomfield's book itself cannot be a linguistic product, but merely a record of things Bloomfield had at one time said. Whereas the plain fact is that it makes no difference to anyone who can read English whether Bloomfield ever uttered the contents of his book aloud or not. It can even be read and understood by people who would be quite incapable of grasping what Bloomfield was saying if he *had* ever spoken it aloud.

An interesting case is that of Saussure, who also affirmed the primacy of speech, even though it is doubtful whether that doctrine is compatible with his own theoretical approach to linguistics. In Saussure's *Cours de linguistique générale*, we are told that *la langue* is a 'system of signs expressing ideas, and hence comparable to writing' (Saussure, 1922, p. 33). This seems to imply that written signs are signs in their own right, and do not owe this semiological status to their connexion with speech. However, only a few pages later, it is stated that *langue* and *écriture* are 'two separate systems of signs', but that the sole reason for the existence of the latter is to represent the former (Saussure, 1922, p. 45). In other words, the written sign is a metasign.

Saussure nevertheless insists that the object of study in linguistics is not a combination of the written word and the spoken word, but the spoken word alone. So the study of writing, while legitimately included in semiology, is at the same time banished from linguistics.

This compromise is patently an awkward one, since, if the written sign is a metasign, then in Saussurean terms that means that the *signifié* of any given written sign must actually be a linguistic sign, or some element thereof. But it is difficult to see how this can be the case, since a system of signs, in Saussurean semiology, is structured solely by its own internal relations and oppositions. A system which borrows all (or indeed any) of its *signifiés* from outside is an impossibility, just as it would be impossible for English words to have French meanings. Such a hybridization makes no theoretical sense at all.

The reason why Saussure finds himself in this impasse is not difficult to detect. If he denied any connexion between writing systems and *la langue*, he would have to sacrifice diachronic linguistics, since he admits that the bulk of a linguist's knowledge about dead languages has to come from written documents. On the other hand, if he admitted the written sign as a linguistic sign in its own right, he would have to admit a fundamental bifurcation of linguistics, depending on whether the linguistic community studied was literate or pre-literate. And this would play havoc with his basic linguistic axioms, as well as with his conception of the sign as a simple bi-partite entity.

The Independence of Speech and Writing

Some writers have taken up again Sweet's scriptist notion of the overriding regulatory function of writing. In a chapter which he pointedly called 'The primacy of writing', F.W. Householder argued that in (American) English, cases in which pronunciation adapts to spelling are more numerous than the other way round and, furthermore, the 'rules' which relate written forms to their pronunciation are much simpler than the 'rules' which relate the pronunciation of words to their spellings (Householder, 1971). One possible explanation would be that although American children learn to speak before they learn to write, the written forms, once learnt, serve to explain and regularize the spoken forms the child is already familiar with. On this view, written English would provide a first elementary metalanguage – the letters of the alphabet – which made it possible for learners to describe, compare and analyse the oral forms they heard, and thus the continuous process of learning new spoken words would come to be guided by fitting them into the framework supplied by spelling.

This thesis was later developed and generalized by David Olson (1993, 1994). According to him, we are dealing with a universal process underlying the history of all literate societies: it would thus be illusory to suppose that writing systems owe their origins to the need to 'represent' oral structures already recognized. On the contrary, it is the development of a writing system which facilitates conceptualization of a corresponding oral structure. In Olson's view, the word itself as a discrete linguistic unit is a graphic conception.

These suggestions seem to be pointing the way to a neo-Stoic view of language, in which speech and writing are seen in literate societies as complementary realizations of the linguistic sign. But without the support of any explicit semiological analysis, such suggestions remain in a kind of theoretical limbo, and their exact implications about the relationships between spoken and written signs are far from clear.

At the other end of the spectrum, the most radical claim for the semiological independence of speech and writing is one advanced on the basis of integrational linguistics (Harris, 1995). Integration, as the integrationist understands it, involves the non-random linking of sequences of activities, mental or physical or both. Some of these are integrated by means of signs, as when the flow of different streams of traffic at a crossroads is regulated by means of traffic lights, or when the starter's gun galvanizes the competitors at the start of a race into simultaneous action, or when the movements of a passenger alighting at a train station are oriented by seeing the sign 'EXIT'. Signs, for the integrationist, do not exist except in the context of some such pattern of integration. (The trafffic lights do not function as signs when the roads are deserted, or the starter's gun if no one hears it, or the 'EXIT' sign when it is obscured by scaffolding.)

The integrational sign is not a simple bi-partite unit with a 'form' and a 'meaning'. It has no such determinate structure 'given' in advance. It is treated as a complex of which any number of different facets may be identified, depending on the case. It is not an abstract invariant, as in structuralist semiology, nor a particular instantiation of any such invariant. It is the unique product of a particular communication situation.

A sign has an integrational function in that it typically involves the contextualized application of biomechanical skills within a certain macrosocial framework, thereby contributing to the integration of activities which would otherwise remain unintegrated. Speech and writing can therefore be related semiologically only through the integration of certain patterns of activity, which, in themselves, are biomechanically quite disparate. The biomechanical proficiency requisite for using a manual instrument, such as a pen, has nothing to do with the biomechanical proficiency involved in identifying an auditory signal, such as the utterance of a word. Being able to do the former does not mean being able to do the latter, or vice versa. But a person who can use a pen to write down what is said has somehow learnt to integrate these activities.

From an integrationist perspective, the underlying formal substratum of writing is not visual but spatial. Spatial relations hold the key to the way a written text is presented and processed. Vision simply gives access to the spatial organization.

But if speech requires an auditory continuum and writing requires a spatial continuum, on what basis can these two modes of communication be integrated? The answer is that signs from both modes can be integrated on the basis of time, since the temporal dimension is one they both share. Time, being common to all sensory modalities, is the primary axis along which, for human beings, the various senses are themselves integrated. There is no order of human experience that is a-temporal.

What has to happen, therefore, if speech and writing are to be integrated is that a temporal correlation must be established which allows an auditory sequence of items to match a spatial pattern of items. Such a matching is possible because oral delivery of an utterance takes time, just as it takes time to execute an inscription (or to arrange a set of objects); and this requirement explains both the characteristic limitations and the characteristic forms of what integrationists call 'glottic' writing, which is one major subdivision of writing as a whole. Non-glottic writing involves the integration of activities other than speech, and includes various forms of mathematical, musical and dance notation. For integrationists, non-glottic writing is of particular interest because, as mentioned above, its texts cannot be 'read aloud'. They deploy forms of spatial display (such as grids and tabulations) which are rendered meaningless by any attempt to 'translate' rows and columns into a single sequence of signs.

The traditional forms of glottic writing actually utilize only a few of the theoretically available possibilities for setting up the temporal correlations required for the semiological integration of spoken and written signs. The whole question has been confused by widespread acceptance of Saussure's misguided axiom concerning the so-called 'linearity' of the linguistic sign. The term *linearity* is a misnomer. The properties of a line are not those of the speech signal produced by the human voice. (In order to approximate linearity, the vocal apparatus would have to be biomechanically much simpler than, in fact, it is.) The term *linear*, paradoxically, highlights precisely those characteristics of the written form which it derives from the use of spatial relations, thus actually setting it apart from speech and other forms of auditory communication.

There is no counterpart in speech to the use of a surface, which is the commonest way in writing of articulating spatial relations. Nor is there any counterpart in speech to varying the disposition of marks on a surface in accordance with the changing spatial relations between surface and reader. In brief, writing is revealed by integrational analysis as a far more powerful and flexible form of communication than speech ever was – or could be – before the advent of modern technologies. These technologies, beginning with the development of sound recording and now extended by all kinds of computer-based devices, have reduced the gap between the two by a previously unimaginable margin. They have actually made possible genuine – as opposed to metaphorical – forms of 'visible speech', a landmark that was passed with the invention of the sound spectrogram.

Conclusion

There has been no room here to discuss the important changes in the perception of the relationship between speech and writing brought about by technical changes in the writing process and their dissemination. The impact of printing – and the consequent mass-production and depersonalization of the written text – stands out historically as one of the most fundamental. For the development of handwriting, it is now possible to consult Sirat (2006), a definitive survey of the topic. Further changes still may confidently be expected in the not-too-distant future. Is it going too far to anticipate that the computer keyboard opens up the prospect of an era in which 'writing', in the collective sense of semiological forms based on spatial relations, will become the major mode of human communication, while speech is increasingly reduced to mere supplementation of what writing has created? If so, that progression will be following a path already traced out in mathematics and the exact sciences.

References

Black, M. (1972). *The labyrinth of language*. Harmondsworth, England: Penguin.

Bloomfield, L. (1935). *Language*. London: Allen & Unwin.

Desbordes, F. (1990). *Idées romaines sur l'écriture*. Lille: Presses Universitaires de Lille.

Gelb, I. J. (1963). *A study of writing*, 2nd ed. Chicago: Chicago University Press.

Harris, R. (1995). *Signs of writing*. London: Routledge.

Havelock, E. A. (1982). *The literate revolution in Greece and its cultural consequences*. Princeton, NJ: Princeton University Press.

Householder, F. W. (1971). *Linguistic speculations*. Cambridge: Cambridge University Press.

Lyons, J. (1972). Human language. In R. A. Hinde (Ed.), *Non-Verbal Communication*. Cambridge: Cambridge University Press.

McLuhan (1964). *Understanding Media*. New York: McGraw-Hill Book Company.

Müller, F. M. (1864). *Lectures on the science of language*. Second Series. London: Longman, Green, Longman, Roberts & Green.

Olson, D. R. (1993). How writing represents speech. *Language & Communication*, 13 (1), 1–17.

Olson, D. R. (1994). *The world on paper*. Cambridge: Cambridge University Press.

Robins, R. H. (1997). *A short history of linguistics*, 4th ed. London: Longman.

Rogers, H. (2005). *Writing systems: A linguistic approach*. Oxford: Blackwell.

Sampson, G. (1985). *Writing systems*. London: Hutchinson.

Saussure, F. de (1922). *Cours de linguistique générale*, 2me éd. Paris: Payot.

Sirat, C. (2006). *Writing as handwork: A history of handwriting in Mediterranean and Western culture*. Turnhout, Belgium: Brepols Publishers.

Stace, W. T. (1949). The Parmenidean dogma. *Philosophy*, 34 (90), 195–204.

Sweet, H. (1899). *The practical study of languages*. London: Dent.

Sweet, H. (1900). *The history of language*. London: Dent.

CHAPTER 4

The Origins and Co-Evolution of Literacy and Numeracy

Stephen Chrisomalis

The origins and early histories of literate and numerate traditions and practices are interwoven in complex ways. During the past thirty years, a body of research in Near Eastern archaeology has linked the development of literacy to the earlier development of numerical notation and computational devices (Damerow, 1996; Nissen, Damerow, & Englund, 1993; Schmandt-Besserat, 1978, 1984, 1992). Several of these scholars go further and propose that cognitive changes result from human interaction with representational systems. This research tradition follows in the footsteps of the important theoretical work of Goody (1968, 1977, 1986), whose scholarship on the cognitive effects of literacy regards numerate practices such as multiplication tables and account-books as vitally important developments. Moreover, archaeologists studying the Upper Paleolithic period have linked the development of numerical notation to the general origins of graphic representation and art (d'Errico, 1989, 2001; Marshack, 1964, 1972). These bodies of work have been used by psychologists and linguists studying literacy and numeracy to add a historical dimension to these subjects (Olson, 1994; Tolchinsky, 2003; Wiese, 2003).

Both the Paleolithic and Mesopotamian research traditions have come under heavy criticism, however, and their conclusions require careful scrutiny. Because archaeology is a historical science (like paleontology or geology), its conclusions are necessarily constrained by the often spotty material database of the archaeological record and, because it (unlike psychology or cultural anthropology) accesses mental processes only very indirectly, one must exercise caution to prevent over-interpretation based on modern conceptions and theoretical prejudices. Finally, because archaeology is not generally an experimental science, conclusions drawn from one site or region must be analyzed in light of data from other sites and regions before drawing more general cognitive or historical conclusions.

Despite these methodological and epistemological challenges, it is highly fruitful to study the origins of writing and numeration when studying ancient literacy and numeracy. We can analyze notations as material culture ('writing' and 'numerals') and then extend our analysis to the way in which ancient humans used them ('literacy' and 'numeracy'). Comparative cross-cultural research can shed light on the similarities and differences among social contexts and the constellation of literate and numerate practices used in each. General theoretical works on writing (Coulmas, 1989; Daniels & Bright, 1996; Gelb, 1963; Sampson, 1985) and numerical notation (Guitel, 1975; Ifrah, 1998; Menninger, 1969; Chrisomalis, forthcoming) allow a detailed and rigorous comparison of both the structures of representational systems and their social aspects. The connections between ancient literacy and numeracy are particularly evident through a study of their interdependent origins.

Tallies, Numerals, and Scripts

The prehistory of graphic numeration is substantially longer than the recorded history of written language. Some artifacts from the Upper Paleolithic period (approximately thirty thousand to ten thousand years before the present) appear to have been numerical markings, lunar calendars, or similar tallies or mnemonic devices (Absolon, 1957; d'Errico, 1989; d'Errico & Cacho, 1994; Marshack, 1964, 1972).[1] The amateur archaeologist, Alexander Marshack, analyzed hundreds of artifacts – primarily engraved bones from European sites – that were marked with notches or grooves resulting from intentional human activity, and he concluded that many were lunar calendrical notations. He further linked the origins of numerals to the origin of graphic representation in general, specifically Paleolithic art. Marshack's research has come under criticism from scholars who contend that what he interpreted as calendars or tallies need not have served such functions and/or that the numerical patterns he identified could have been purely decorative (d'Errico, 1989; d'Errico & Cacho, 1994). The structures of the notational systems must have varied regionally and are thus open to wide latitude in interpretation.

Despite these difficulties, however, Upper Paleolithic humans were certainly *capable* of using notations to mark seasonal, lunar, or physiological cycles; to count successes in hunting; or to count objects. As members of our subspecies *Homo sapiens sapiens*, they were anatomically indistinguishable from modern humans. Notations of the type hypothesized by Marshack for the Upper Paleolithic are nearly ubiquitous in the ethnographic record (Goldschmidt, 1940; Lagercrantz, 1968, 1970, 1973; Marshack, 1985). Perishable materials such as wood and string, which are common materials for notational artifacts, do not survive tens of millennia in the archaeological record. The corpus of surviving Upper Paleolithic notational artifacts thus reflects only a small proportion of what once may have existed. Given the complexity and representational power of the vast body of Upper Paleolithic art (some of which occurs on the same artifacts as tallying notations), it is not credible to deny outright that Upper Paleolithic humans made tallying notations. Yet, absent any reliable way of distinguishing numerical signs from decorative marks, and lacking information on social and functional context, we cannot learn much about the representational capabilities of early humans.

All of the Upper Paleolithic artifacts to which a numerical function has been attributed contain relatively unstructured notations in which one mark represents one object. This relatively simple method of quantifying employs the principle of one-to-one correspondence in which the cardinality of some set of objects is determined by mentally matching them with an equal number of marks (Wiese, 2003, pp. 18–20). Yet, far from being archaic, this technique is widespread even in Western societies where Hindu-Arabic numerals predominate – for instance, the practice of marking lines to make a tally (sometimes crossed off in groups of five). Tallying is widespread because its function is quite different from writing numerical totals. Tallies are marked sequentially, producing an open-ended count, and tally-marks (whether knots, notches, stones, or something else) are *iconic* – that is, they represent one object each. Wiese (2003, pp. 131–150) claims that, in fact, such tallying could be done by individuals who lacked language.

In contrast, numerical notation systems are *structured symbolic systems* of permanent, trans-linguistic graphic marks for recording numbers. They include the Hindu-Arabic numerals, the Roman numerals, and more than 100 other systems used during the past five thousand years, few of which are still used (Chrisomalis, forthcoming). They assign different numerical values to a set of signs and combine them using a structure in which some number (i.e., the base of the system) and its powers are specially notated. The Hindu-Arabic system has a base of 10 and uses the sign-set {0,1,2,3,4,5,6,7,8,9}. Quantifying using numerical notation is *symbolic*. One cannot simply count signs or marks, but rather one must know the values of different signs and understand the rules that dictate how signs combine. Although a Roman numeral such as CCXXXVIII seems tally-like, one cannot simply add additional signs to it if an adjustment to the numeral is desired. The use of V = 5, X = 10, L = 50, C = 100, instead of IIIII, IIIIIIIIII, and so on, is significant from the perspective of the writer, because numerical notation is written nonsequentially to record a single total for later consultation whereas tallies are marked sequentially as part of the act of counting. The difference is also cognitively significant for the reader, because base-structured numeral-phrases are simpler to read than long strings of repeated symbols.

In turn, numerical notation differs from lexical numeration, which conveys numerical meanings in a specific language using a set of spoken or written numeral words. Numerical notation is essentially language-independent and, as such, constitutes an "open" rather than a "closed" recording system (Houston, 2004a, p. 275). The number 47 is read as *forty-seven* by English speakers, *quarante-sept* by French speakers, and *siebenundvierzig* by German speakers. Nearly every language has a lexical numeral system, whereas numerical notation may or may not be present in a society (Chrisomalis, 2004; Divale, 1999; Gordon, 2004; Hurford, 1987). Although both lexical numerals and numerical notation systems are *symbolic* systems and tend to be structured using one or more numerical bases, numerical notation is not simply a shorthand for lexical numeration because the two systems follow different rules. No natural language expresses 3642 as something like "three six four two," and no language expresses 30 as "ten ten ten" even though many numerical notation systems, such as the Roman numerals, use representations like XXX = 30. This distinction probably results from as-yet undertheorized differences between visual and auditory media of numerical expression.

Although Gelb's (1963, p. 253) classic definition of writing as "a system of intercommunication by means of conventional visible marks" seems to include numerical notation, Gelb never intended this implication and preferred a narrow definition of writing that treated pictographic and semasiographic notations (including all precolonial American scripts) as evolutionary precursors to "true" writing. Although Boone (1994, 2000) rightly assaults Gelb's ethnocentric denial of the legitimacy of New World writing, her own similar definition of writing as "the communication of relatively specific ideas in a conventional manner by means of permanent visible marks" (1994, p. 15) equally includes numerical notation. Scripts and numerical notation need to be treated in parallel, however, rather than as two aspects of a single phenomenon. Whereas writing systems generally represent ideas linguistically, numerical notation systems do so nonlinguistically. Not all scripts are associated with numerical notation systems; for instance, the earliest Canaanite script and the Irish Ogham script always express numbers using number words. Similarly, some numerical notation systems, like the Inca *quipu* discussed below, are not associated with phonetic scripts. Moreover, when both written numerals and numerical notation occur in a text, each often serves a different function. For instance, the text of the Bible is written using lexical numerals, but chapters and verses are numbered using numerical notation. The patterns of invention and borrowing of numerals and scripts differ. The Western (Hindu-Arabic) numerals developed initially in India and passed into Europe via the Arab world, whereas the Roman alphabet is of Greek, Phoenician, and, ultimately, Egyptian ancestry.

Perhaps the most significant distinction is that although it is impossible to have *literacy* without a writing system, it is perfectly possible to have numeracy without numerical notation. Numerical notation complements verbal numeration systems and tallying systems without replacing them. Lack of written notation is no bar to the proficient use of numbers (Barnes, 1982; Rosin, 1984). Yet, there are differences between the ways that nonliterates and literates use numbers. Numerate technologies such as ordinal lists, multiplication tables, and bookkeeping systems drastically alter the way in which literate people use and manipulate numbers (Goody, 1977, 1986). The emergence of specialized practitioners of technology, magic, and science correlates well with the emergence of highly complex stratified states. In turn, these states are often (but not always) literate.

Yet, despite these differences, writing and numerals share much in common. Both are structured sets of relatively permanent visual marks used to communicate information. They occur in many of the same contexts and are often interchangeable within a word or phrase (e.g., *4th* versus *fourth*). The majority of writing systems have adjoining numerical notations, and few structured numerical notations (i.e., those with a base) occur outside written contexts. Most important for the present discussion, their origins are significantly intertwined.

The Origins of Writing and Numerical Notation

Prior to the twentieth century, the predominance of Biblical scholars among philologists, archaeologists, and epigraphers meant that enormous importance was attached to Mesopotamian representation systems, following the monogenetic principle based on a strict interpretation of the Bible (see Daniels, 1996, for a useful summary of the history of scholarship on writing systems). Gelb (1963) was the most vigorous modern proponent of the theory that true writing originated only once, in Mesopotamia, and diffused from there throughout the Old World. Whereas fewer scholars have given close attention to the history of numerical notation, thinkers such as Seidenberg (1960, 1962, 1986) similarly asserted that all numeration (both lexical and graphic!) developed in Mesopotamia and then spread throughout the world (including the Americas).

Most scholars now reject the principle of monogenesis, although the number of episodes of independent invention is still debated. Numerical notation systems were invented at least five times independently of any preexisting numerical notation system (i.e., in Mesopotamia, Egypt, China, lowland Mesoamerica, and Peru) and possibly up to five additional times (i.e., highland Mesoamerica, the Indus Valley, Italy, India, and Crete). This contrasts with only three to five likely instances of 'pristine' or independent script development (certainly Mesopotamia, China, and lowland Mesoamerica and probably Egypt and the Indus Valley). In two cases (i.e., Peru and highland Mesoamerica), numerical notation existed without phonetic writing, whereas all of the other script traditions had both writing and written numeration.

It is likely, although generally indemonstrable, that in each society, the inventors of numerical notation systems used base-structured lexical numerals and simple tallying or recording devices; similarly, writing systems may have developed from iconographic traditions, pot-marks, or numerical notation systems. Writing systems and numerical notation systems do not simply *emerge*; rather, they are *invented* by human beings in specific sociohistorical circumstances and for specific purposes. If there were a universal human tendency to record visually language or numbers, numerical notation and writing would be ubiquitous in the archaeological and historical records. Although the *potential* for representing language and numbers exists in all humans, it is realized only when there is sufficient need and interest to do so.

I now briefly consider seven instances in which scripts and/or numerical systems were developed. In four cases (i.e., Mesopotamia, Egypt, lowland Mesoamerica, and Shang China), both scripts and numerical notation systems were probably invented independently. I also discuss two cases – the Inca Empire of Peru and the highland Mesoamerican tributary state centered around the Aztecs – in which distinct numerical notations developed in the absence of phonetic script traditions. The similarities and differences observed pave the way for a broader understanding of the co-evolution of writing and numeration.

Mesopotamia

As early as 8000 BCE, some Near Eastern agriculturalists began to use small clay tokens in basic geometric shapes: cones, spheres, cylinders, cubes, and so forth. The archaeologist, Denise Schmandt-Besserat, proposed that these tokens formed part of a notational system for recording information related to agricultural practices (Schmandt-Besserat, 1992). She further suggested that they represented a precursor to a more complex token-based economic system that emerged around 4000–3500 BCE in Mesopotamia (i.e., the area delimited roughly by the Tigris and Euphrates Rivers) and some regions to the east, in modern Iran. Amiet (1966) first identified hollow clay spheres (called *bullae*, or *envelopes*) at the site of Susa (in modern Iran), some of which contained small clay objects of different shapes and some of which were impressed on the outer surface with tokens prior to inserting them into the envelope. The envelopes may well have been 'double documents' through which transfers of goods such as livestock could be conducted while minimizing the risk of fraud or error. A literate official could see the quantity of goods from the impressed token-marks on the outside, but if there were any doubt, the *bulla* could be broken open and the tokens inside counted and matched with the actual quantity received. In turn, Schmandt-Besserat contends, around 3200 BCE, the users of this system realized that they no longer needed to use the tokens but rather could simply record the necessary information using clay tablets, leading to the earliest ancestor of the well-known cuneiform writing – a system called *proto-cuneiform*. Schmandt-Besserat's archaeological conclusions have been heavily criticized by scholars of writing systems and Near Eastern archaeologists (see especially Lieberman, 1980; Zimansky, 1993). Nevertheless, it has been widely disseminated and is currently the best-known general theory of the origin of writing.

The proto-cuneiform texts are attested primarily from the site of Uruk, in southern Iraq, where almost five thousand clay tablets were found. Smaller numbers of these documents were found to the north, at Jemdet Nasr, Khafaji, and Tell Uqair, and a related system was used to the east, at the site of Susa, where the script used is known as "Proto-Elamite" (Englund, 2004; Potts, 1999). Approximately 85 percent of the proto-cuneiform texts record economic data by juxtaposing numerical signs with ideograms depicting the objects being counted – mainly livestock, agricultural produce, and people – with the remainder being "lexical lists" (Nissen, Damerow, & Englund, 1993). Statistically analyzing the corpus of proto-cuneiform texts, Nissen, Damerow, and Englund established conclusively that at least fifteen distinct numerical notation systems (of which five were particularly common) were used at Uruk, each enumerating a distinct category of discrete objects or unit of measurement using a dizzying array of numerical bases and ratios between sign-values.

Damerow (1996), a developmental psychologist, went further, asserting that the multiplicity of numerical systems shows that there was no abstract number concept among the Uruk accountant-scribes; there was, therefore, an incomplete conceptual connection between "three bushels of wheat", "three months", and "three women". In effect, he argued, the archaic character of this early writing and numerical notation represents both a sociohistorical stage in the evolution of society and a cognitive stage of individual development. Schmandt-Besserat used the data from the token system to arrive at similar conclusions – she argued that they represent concrete rather than abstract numbers and, following Conant (1896), that the development of written numeration and writing represented an important conceptual leap. Both theories are *unilinear* in character – they see the development of numeration and writing as proceeding in a series of stages that are more or less invariant cross-culturally. Yet, their data are strictly Mesopotamian, casting doubt on the enterprise.

The essentially simultaneous development of the proto-cuneiform numerals and writing corresponds well with the growing complexity of the city-state of Uruk and the administrative demands of managing a system of trade and tribute that spread throughout Mesopotamia. The documents, largely economic in function, originated to help solve these problems. How the clay *bullae* relate to proto-cuneiform writing, however, is quite unclear. It is entirely possible that they are two distinct and largely unrelated technologies, the one developed for verifying economic transactions, the other for recording those transactions. Nevertheless, the theory that writing and numerical notation developed at Uruk around 3300–3200 BCE relative to bureaucratic and administrative needs is secure.

Egypt

The earliest Egyptian writing and numeration emerged during the Late Predynastic period (ca. 3300–3100 BCE) in contexts related to royal iconography and linked to Egyptian artistic conventions. The Narmer mace-head, a royal ceremonial object found at Hierakonpolis that may describe Egypt's unification around 3100 BCE, is a very early example of early Egyptian hieroglyphic writing and numeration. Its hieroglyphs phonetically represent the name of Narmer and describe an exaggerated tally of booty of 400,000 bulls, 1,422,000 goats, and 120,000 prisoners (Arnett, 1982). Such objects were probably not used for generalized royal propaganda, given the limited extent of Predynastic literacy, but they may have aided the king in emphasizing his power among other elites. Although the classification of the early Egyptian writing is still debatable, it probably included both logograms and phonetic signs for consonants. The numerals are much more easily interpreted; they are a base-10 additive system in which signs for the powers of 10 were repeated as necessary and linked in numerical phrases structured from the highest to lowest value.

Recent finds at the royal Tomb U-j at Abydos, dating to approximately 3250 BCE, have added to our knowledge of the contexts of the earliest Egyptian writing (Dreyer, 1998). Numerous bone and ivory tags have been recovered, alongside a number of labeled pots, some of which are inscribed with numerals and others with what appear to be precursors of later Egyptian hieroglyphs. Later, in the Early Dynastic Period (2920–2575 BCE), tags were attached to containers of grave goods in royal tombs, and the Tomb U-j tags may well have been precursors of this practice. This raises the intriguing possibility that the tomb tags were part of an administrative system, perhaps notating the provenance, nature, and/or amount of goods sent to Abydos.

Baines (2004) argued, however, that no direct administrative function was served by tagging goods in this fashion. Instead, he asserted, they simply emphasized the prestige and mystery of the Egyptian elite, which was growing enormously in power at the time. No other Late Predynastic Egyptian sites have revealed tags or labelled pots. Therefore, the notations may have been used only at Abydos and been of interest only to a small coterie of officials, without serving a particular purpose within broader trade or tribute systems. Although the Tomb U-j tags and pot-labels may have served some as-yet undiscovered administrative function, the best evidence currently available suggests that like the palettes, mace-heads, and other Predynastic notated artifacts, the earliest Egyptian writing and numeration served iconographic and display functions related to elite interests. This limited-function writing was perfectly useful but need not have been capable of expressing thoughts in a fully phonetic manner and need not have served economic functions.

It was once held that Egyptian writing developed suddenly as a fully mature script and that this suggested it had been borrowed from Mesopotamia rather than developed indigenously. The discovery of the Tomb U-j tags tends to refute this hypothesis because it establishes a very early origin of Egyptian writing in a rarefied, elite, probably noneconomic context and provides evidence of an Egyptian 'proto-writing' period centuries in advance of full phonetic writing. Moreover, whereas the Mesopotamian numerical systems were purely ideographic, in Egypt, unlike most early numerical notation systems, the hieroglyphic numeral-signs also had phonetic values. This distinction further supports the idea of independent development. There is no attested Egyptian bookkeeping system from this period that remotely resembles the proto-cuneiform system. Even by the end of the Old Kingdom around 2150 BCE, Egyptians were not using writing as a general-purpose information-recording system; it was potentially function-independent but not actually so (Baines, 1983, p. 577).

Lowland Mesoamerica

Of the civilizations of lowland Mesoamerica, by far the best known is that of the Maya, whose classical period extended from approximately AD 200 to AD 900 and who dominated the Yucatan peninsula and much of the lowland rainforest until the Spanish conquest. Several million people still speak Maya languages, the descendants of Classic Maya. Yet, the earliest Mesoamerican writing was not Maya but rather originated several centuries earlier among the civilizations of the Olmec and Zapotec during the Middle Formative period (900–400 BCE). The so-called bar and dot numerical notation systems and allied calendrical systems were the first lowland Mesoamerican representational systems to be deciphered (Bowditch 1910; Morley, 1915). The use of a dot for 1 and a bar for 5, combined in additive sets to represent any number from 1 to 19, coupled with a sign for zero, was ubiquitous in lowland Mesoamerican scripts from their inception. The system is tremendously simple in comparison to the often-obscure, homonymy-laden, and still incompletely understood scripts of lowland Mesoamerica, and it is a shared conventional representation that contrasts with the diversity of Mesoamerican scripts (Marcus, 1992).

Recent finds near the Olmec site of La Venta (along Mexico's Gulf Coast) uncovered a cylinder seal and greenstone plaque containing glyphic writing and numeration dating to 650 BCE (Pohl, Pope, & von Nagy, 2002). Its discoverers identified the calendrical date "3 Ajaw" on the cylinder seal, written using dot notation. This may refer only to a date but, alternately, by analogy with the later Mesoamerican practice of using day-names as personal names, it may refer to an individual, "King 3 Ajaw"; the seal was interpreted as a tool for printing a royal stamp on perishable materials (Pohl et al., 2002, pp. 1985–1986). Although the evidence from La Venta is still highly fragmentary, if it is confirmed, then the earliest evidence of Mesoamerican writing is related to royal inscriptions and iconography, and the earliest numbers on those inscriptions were used for calendrical purposes, including day-name onomastics.

This assertion is confirmed by the slightly more abundant and slightly later evidence for writing among the Zapotecs, who lived in the Valley of Oaxaca in south-central Mexico. Monument 3 from San José Mogote contains the day-name "1 Earthquake" written with a stylized dot for 1, whereas the nearly contemporaneous Stela 12 from the nearby site of Monte Albán contains the first combined bar and dot numeral – a bar plus three dots for 8 – apparently indicating a day of the Zapotec month (Marcus, 1976, pp. 45–46). There is considerable debate as to whether Monument 3 dates to 600–500 BCE or several centuries later, closer to 300–200 BCE (Justeson & Mathews, 1990). Regardless, the fact that this inscription – distant both geographically and temporally from La Venta – is also a combination of a numeral-sign and a calendrical glyph suggests that we are not far off in postulating an original calendrical function for all Mesoamerican writing.

Much of the theoretical analysis of the function of lowland Mesoamerican writing has focused on how elites used scripts and iconography to distort history and promote their own interests (Marcus, 1992). Nevertheless, Houston (2004b, p. 235) rightly cautions against using terms such as 'royal propaganda' when describing the function of early Mesoamerican writing or, by extension, any early writing system. Although writing was restricted to elites, its purpose may have been much more closely connected to royal rituals and communication with supernatural entities than to narrowly self-interested ideological elite goals. Calendrical calculations may have been important to maintaining Olmec and Zapotec elites' power (e.g., by promoting the idea that kings could predict and even control astronomical events), but there is no direct evidence for this. In Mesoamerica, at least, the use of day-names as personal names suggests that writing and numeration may have emerged as part of a complex set of ritual practices relating to naming practices (Stuart, 2001). This function has closer parallels to astrology or Hebrew *gematria* than it does to an elite class disseminating propaganda. Early Mesoamerican writing, being the province of a tiny elite and being connected to complex calendrical practices, would certainly have reinforced the distinction between elites and commoners. Nevertheless, barring the discovery of further evidence, one cannot infer much about the immediate utility of Mesoamerican writing for sustaining elite power.

The use of numbers in personal names and day-names, two of the earliest recorded functions of the Mesoamerican scripts, suggests that they developed in tandem. Conversely, there is no evidence to suggest that narrowly construed administrative or record-keeping functions were central to the development of either Zapotec or Olmec writing. Rather, a set of as-yet poorly understood royal practices related to calendrics and onomastics motivated the development of both writing and bar-and-dot numeration in the Middle Formative period.

Shang China

The earliest graphic notations identified in East Asia are marks on pots and tortoise shells dating from 6600–6200 BCE found at Jiahu in Henan Province (Li et al., 2003). Yet, although there are parallels between the graphic form of some of these Neolithic pot-marks and later Chinese graphemes and numerals, the marks do not occur in long series. Even if they did have conventional meanings, there is no way to verify them. Not until the latter part of the Shang Dynasty (approximately 1200 BCE) do systematic notations appear on East Asian artifacts, in the form of *jiaguwen*, or "oracle-bone inscriptions." Found primarily at Anyang in Henan Province, the oracle-bone inscriptions are primarily records of royal divinations written on bones and tortoise carapaces. They record quantities of sacrifices made, tribute received, and animals hunted, thus telling us much about the daily life of elites at Anyang, but they were primarily divinatory artifacts.

The oracle-bone inscriptions include both logosyllabic signs and numerals that are, in heavily modified form, the ancestors of the modern Chinese script and numerals. In many respects, the linguistic representation of Old Chinese on the oracle bones is incomplete, and the graphemes tend to be more pictorial and less abstract than their mature forms (Boltz, 1996). Eventually, pictorial signs came to be used as *rebuses*, referring to homonyms of the depicted object, and as *determinatives*, or general semantic indicators of the sign's meaning. Although most early numerical systems are additive – that is, they repeat identical signs in order to indicate multiples of some power of the base, like the Roman numerals – the Shang numerals were not. Whereas the signs for 1 through 4, and 10 through 40, were additive combinations of one to four signs for 1 or 10, respectively, the other numerals were multiplicative combinations of a multiplier-sign and a power-sign (Djamouri, 1994; Needham & Ling, 1959, Tables 22, 23). For instance, the number 567 would be written as (5 100 6 10 7). Over time, even the additive combinations became more abstract; in the Shang and Zhou periods, the sign for 4 was ☰, four horizontal strokes; however, from the Han Dynasty onward (206 BCE – AD 220), the sign used was 四, the standard ideogram used in modern Chinese.

It is striking that far from being a general-purpose notation system, the oracle-bone inscriptions are virtually all limited to recording the results of divination rituals, although a few seem to record deliveries of materials or other preparations for those rituals (Bagley, 2004, p. 214). Not until much later, during the Eastern Zhou Dynasty (770–256 BCE), is a wider variety of historical and ritual texts attested, including writing with ink on bamboo or cloth and numbers stamped on coins (Boltz, 1996). The restricted function of the oracle bones suggests that divination was the original function for which Chinese writing and numerical notation developed and that only later did the range of functions expand, turning a special-purpose notation into a more general one. There is no reason, other than analogy from Mesopotamia, to think that economic functions were among the early uses of Chinese writing or to postulate a long and unattested prehistory for the oracle-bone notations. Bagley's (2004, p. 236) suggestion that we should look for a numerical precursor to the oracle bones (analogous to Mesopotamian tokens) wrongly assumes that all civilizations develop writing in a similar path as Mesopotamia. Similarly, Keightley's (1987, p. 112) suggestion that following the parallel of the Minoan-Mycenean civilization, Shang writing emerged in the context of complex tasks relating to measurement, such as pot-making and jade-working, is intriguing but currently unprovable. The most parsimonious interpretation of the origin of Chinese writing is one based on its attested function – namely, that it developed indigenously in contexts relating to divinatory and ritual practices in the nascent Shang royal court at Anyang.

Peru

The *quipus* (in modern Quechua, *khipus*) were bundles of cotton or wool cords on which series of knots were placed to convey information. *Quipus* were used as an administrative and record-keeping mechanism throughout much of the Andean region prior to the sixteenth century, most notably by the Inca Empire, which ruled an enormous territory along 3,000 km of the Pacific coast of South America, encompassing dozens of ethnolinguistic groups. Approximately six hundred *quipus* survive today, of which approximately three-quarters can be partly deciphered as a decimal, place-value numerical notation system.

Quipus are frequently classified with unstructured tallying systems in which one mark equals one object (see, e.g., Birket-Smith, 1966; Ifrah, 1998, p. 70). This is a gross miscategorization. The *quipus* encoded a complex system for notating numbers and linking those numbers to various types of countable objects, and they may have recorded even more complex syntactical information. Although the precise way in which *quipus* encoded non-numerical meanings is unknown, the numerals written on *quipus* are recorded in a potentially infinite, decimal, place-value system. *Quipus* enabled Inca administrators to record census and tribute data in a complex and unambiguous fashion and to transmit information to local administrative centers, and for local accountants to return information to the Inca capital of Cusco (Urton & Brezine, 2005).

The early history of the *quipus* is poorly known. The recent and still-unpublished find at the urban site of Caral (ca. 2700 BCE) of a *quipu*-like bundle of knotted cotton strings wrapped around thin sticks may or may not have been a number-recording system. Relatively simple knotted tallies that lack a numerical base and the place-value concept are widespread throughout the circum-Pacific region (Birket-Smith, 1966). Some ceramic vessels from the Moche civilization (ca. AD 200–700) bear designs suggestive of *quipus* (Bennett, 1963, p. 616). Most surviving *quipus*, however, probably date from the period of Inca rule (AD 1438–1532). Unfortunately, of the six hundred or so surviving Inca-period *quipus*, only two have adequate provenances (Urton, 2001, p. 131).

There can be little doubt that the *quipus* were readable in a context-independent manner and encoded information at least as semantically complex as found in the Mesopotamian proto-cuneiform texts. It is difficult to believe that *quipus* encoded enormously complex numerical data without providing the reader any indication as to what was being enumerated. Attempts to decipher non-numerical information show some promise, such as the identification of a set of three figure-eight knots as a toponym for the city of Puruchuco (Urton & Brezine, 2005). Furthermore, approximately one-quarter of extant *quipus* apparently do not encode numerical information, raising the possibility that the knots on these *quipus* recorded some other type of information. Given the administrative needs of managing an enormously complex and diverse multicultural empire, a relatively 'open' but semantically simple notation system would be far more useful than one closely linked to the phonetic values of a particular language (e.g., Quechua, the language used by the Inca).

Nevertheless, the *quipus* were probably not used for recording narrative directly. We must be cautious in inferring ethnocentrically that any notational system must have served all the functions of modern writing. Whatever else the *quipu* notation may have been, it was primarily an accounting system used for imperial administration. Urton's (1997, p. 179) speculation that there were two precolonial *quipu* systems, one for recording quantity and another for recording narrative, is interesting but as yet unconfirmed. Moreover, viewing *quipus* as 'proto-writing' is inappropriate; although they seem to have been as flexible as proto-cuneiform for recording information, it is unwarranted to assume that the notation would have developed over time in the direction of phonetic writing (Cooper, 2004, p. 93).

Highland Mesoamerica

The Valley of Mexico, located in the central Mexican highlands around modern Mexico City, was the center of a complex tributary state of dozens of ethnic and political entities that paid tribute to the Aztec capital of Tenochtitlan from the late fourteenth through the early sixteenth centuries (i.e., the time of the Spanish conquest of Mexico). Although sharing a common calendar, certain ritual practices, and certain other cultural features with the Maya, highland Mesoamerica was largely distinct from the lowlands, including its visual notation systems.[2]

From the tenth until the sixteenth centuries AD, peoples of central Mexico (i.e., first the Oto-Manguean-speaking Mixtecs and later the Aztecs and related peoples of the Valley of Mexico) used complex pictorial codices written on deerskin parchment or bark-paper to record and communicate information. The codices depicted deities, historical figures, toponyms, and numbers in specific, conventionalized, and unambiguous ways. As well, the Aztecs used some phoneticism in the form of the rebus principle to suggest the names of people and places; for instance, *tochtli* ("rabbit") for the town of Tochpan (Nicholson, 1973). Yet, there is limited evidence for the representation of submorphemic linguistic units through graphemes. Whereas the lowland iconographic tradition of the Maya and the Zapotec clearly demarcated "art" from "writing" within individual texts, in the Aztec–Mixtec tradition, art and writing were one and the same (Boone, 1994, p. 20). The Classical Nahuatl word *tlacuiloliztli* meant both "writing" and "painting" (Boone, 2004, p. 315). The Aztec and Mixtec script tradition is thus "open" and language-independent, relying on notational convention but not phonetic representation for its communicative force (Houston, 2004b).

Some early Mixtec writings (i.e., tenth–thirteenth centuries AD), as well as a few inscriptions from the early highland city of Teotihuacan (i.e., sixth–eighth centuries AD), used Maya-like bar-and-dot numerals (Caso, 1965, p. 955; Langley, 1986, p. 143; Smith, 2003, p. 242). Thereafter, however, the peoples of central Mexico ceased to use bar-and-dot numerals, instead using groups of dots (without bars) to represent 1 through 19; numbers higher than 20 were never expressed. In the fifteenth century, the Aztecs modified this highland dot-only system into a new and distinct numerical notation. In addition to the dot for 1, signs for powers of 20 were developed using depictions of objects: for 20, a flag (*pantli*); for 400, a feather (*tzontli*, literally "hairs"); and for 8,000, a bag used to hold copal incense (*xiquipilli*) (Harvey, 1982, p. 190). These combined additively, so that 1,074 would be written with two 400-signs, thirteen 20-signs, and fourteen 1-signs. Although groups of six or more signs were grouped in rows of five, there was no special sign for 5, as in the bar-and-dot system.

The most important function of the Aztec numerals was to record the results of economic transactions, such as amounts of cacao beans, grain, clothing, and other goods received from different regions of their tributary system (Payne & Closs, 1986, pp. 226–230). Numerals were also used in Aztec annals and historical documents, such as the record of the massacre of twenty thousand prisoners in the Codex Telleriano-Remensis (Boone, 2000, p. 43). In contrast, for writing day-names and dates, the Aztecs continued to use dot-only numerals until the Spanish conquest (Boone, 2000, pp. 43–44). For managing the economic needs of a large tributary state and for recording large (and sometimes surely inflated) numbers in historical annals, it was vitally important to be able to write large numbers. For more conservative ritual and calendric functions, however, numbers higher than 19 were simply not especially useful.[3]

Whereas Classic Maya writing was phonetic, language-dependent, distinct from art, and (probably) largely monumental, Aztec writing was nonphonetic, language-independent, conceptually interlinked with art, and written in codices. Maya writing seems to have been primarily historical, genealogical, and calendrical, whereas Aztec writing also was used to record information about trade, land measurements, and similar administrative subjects. Maya numerals used a sub-base of 5, whereas Aztec numerals were strictly base-20. Thus, despite the known cultural connection between the highland and lowland Mesoamerican civilizations (as demonstrated most clearly through their common calendar), the Aztec writing and numerical systems are fundamentally independent from their earlier lowland counterparts. It is pointless to regard them as either a precursor to some later stage (cut off by the Spanish conquest) or a degraded version of the lowland traditions.

Early Writing and Numerals: Summary

In all four cases of independent script development (i.e., Mesopotamia, Egypt, lowland Mesoamerica, and China), numerical notation was present in the earliest attested texts. Similarly, the partially independently developed script tradition of highland Mesoamerica also used numerals from its inception. Finally, at a minimum, the Andean *quipus* represented numerals as well as some indication of the referents being quantified. There is minimal evidence, except in Mesopotamia, for Houston's (2004c, p. 351) suggestion that numerical notation is a substantially older and distinct trajectory from writing. In all other cases, base-structured numerical notation emerged contemporaneously with the earliest writing. This mutual co-emergence can hardly be coincidental.

Postgate, Wang, and Wilkinson (1995) noted, however, that because many writing materials used for everyday administration are perishable, absence of evidence does not refute the utilitarian origin of writing. It is possible, they asserted, that utilitarian documents have decayed, leaving only monumental texts, oracle bones, and other well-preserved materials. They proposed, accordingly, that early, unattested, and possibly unrecoverable administrative writings – analogous to the Mesopotamian tokens and proto-cuneiform script – preceded and led to the development of the later script traditions of Mesoamerica, China, and Egypt.

Yet, the comparative evidence does not support the hypothesis of an administrative origin of writing. Although numerals were used alongside each early script, the functions of numeration were as diverse as the functions of writing: divinatory records in Shang China, display and elite iconography in Egypt, calendrics and onomastics in Mesoamerica, administrative record-keeping in Mesopotamia, and so on. Numerals are not simply arithmetical aids, but rather special-purpose representational systems for numbers, regardless of their specific functions. If there are as-yet unattested numerical precursors of writing, they are likely to relate to the later attested functions of writing in each local context. Even historically related script traditions can be employed for radically different purposes; the almost obsessive use of numerals for calendrical notation in lowland Mesoamerica contrasts strongly with the Aztec tribute records and censuses. To assume without direct evidence that scripts emerged out of administrative needs, therefore, is tendentious.

The evolutionary sequence described for Mesopotamia is roughly correct, at least for the Uruk IV period onward: cuneiform emerged out of the earlier proto-cuneiform bookkeeping system that used only number-signs and ideograms. This development probably related to the expansion of functions for which writing was perceived to be useful, which required that ways be found to represent ideas other than objects. Yet, we should not expect writing to emerge out of bookkeeping or economic systems wherever it is independently invented. Instead, in each society, writing and numeration essentially developed simultaneously for highly context-dependent functions related to elite interests, ranging from display (Egypt) to divination (China) to calendrics (Maya) to bookkeeping (Uruk). Although the Andean *quipus* and the Mesopotamian proto-cuneiform texts are similar in structure and function, this does not imply that the *quipus* would have inevitably developed into phonetic writing. Similarly, Aztec writing – despite the occasional use of the rebus principle for phonetic representation of names – was perfectly adequate for the needs of the Aztec tributary state. There is limited evidence from these early periods for the spread of writing beyond the elite and their immediate retainers and officials. Each system was limited in function and although some scripts eventually became increasingly generalized, no early writing system was used as generally as modern systems.

Yet, if there is no functional explanation for the co-evolution of writing and numeration, why would they develop together at all? The answer, I suspect, is that the linkage is conceptual but not functional. Tallies, pictorial art, and related notation systems are iconic, not symbolic; they describe properties of objects but do not symbolize them abstractly. Numerical notation (beyond the level of tallying) and writing (whether logographic, syllabic, or alphabetic) are both symbolic systems. It may be that the development of the concept of symbolizing ideas visually leads to two parallel systems: one for visually representing numbers and another for visually representing language or ideas.

One would then wish to establish why, of all the types of societies that have existed – from tiny hunter-gatherer bands to immense industrial states – numerical notations and writing systems tend to develop in ancient civilizations. No sociopolitically simple society ever independently developed phonetic writing. The four instances of independent script development discussed herein (i.e., Mesopotamia, Egypt, lowland Mesoamerica, and Shang China) all occurred in societies at roughly the same degree of political stratification and surplus appropriation (Trigger, 2003, pp. 584–603). Yet, writing is not an *inevitable* consequence of state formation because many states (e.g., the precolonial West African states or the Vedic civilization of India) developed neither phonetic writing nor numerical notation, and some (e.g., the Inca) developed numerical notation without phonetic writing. Writing is thus one solution to a set of problems faced by complex societies, but not the only solution. The stimulus for the development of writing and numerical notation cannot be simply economic growth or else we would expect to see a much narrower range of functions for early writing. Instead, writing and written numeration record information in a relatively permanent way that allows information to be transmitted between strangers. They also facilitate ritual, political, and technical practices that arise in states with agricultural surpluses and serve elite interests. This more general utility, rather than specific needs such as accounting, might explain why writing developed in similarly complex societies yet in completely different spheres of activity.

A remaining issue is why numerical notation would develop at all. It is perfectly possible for users of a script to write all numbers out phonetically and, indeed, this is true of a small minority of scripts. Yet, the fact that this situation is cross-culturally rare suggests that there is something about numbers that leads people to symbolize numbers differently from language. One might wish to contend that numbers comprise, for some reason, the first domain that humans symbolize visually, and only later do they develop visual symbols for other ideas, for words, and for sounds. The Paleolithic and ethnographic evidence for widely prevalent tallying notations suggests that this might be so. Numerals might still be generally ancestral to writing systems (although there is little direct evidence for this). Yet, even if this were so, the functional side of the argument – in which administrative necessity gives rise to numerical notation and then writing – could not be sustained.

Comparative archaeological evidence demonstrates conclusively that although numerals tend to appear alongside the first writing in several ancient societies, the reasons why and functions for which writing and numerals co-evolve are complex and cross-culturally variable. The well-understood Mesopotamian case, therefore, should not be treated as the basis for a universal theory; thus, the functional correlates and prerequisites of writing are more complex than previously thought. This, in turn, casts doubt on all unilinear theories of the origins of writing and the cognitive consequences of literacy and numeracy. It is to be hoped that future theories of the origins of writing will weigh seriously this comparative archaeological evidence.

Notes

1 The evidence for written numeration or tallying in the Middle Paleolithic period (300,000–30,000 BCE), such as the engraved red ochres from Blombos Cave, South Africa (ca. 70,000 BCE), is even more speculative (Cain, 2006; d'Errico et al., 2001).

2 An apt Old World parallel might be Mesopotamia and Egypt, which – despite sharing some cultural features and engaging in trade – were in other ways highly divergent.

3 Whereas Western calendrics uses phrases such as "3250 years," the Aztec system represents time through a series of time units, each having no more than 19 subunits, as if we were to write in English, "3 millennia, 2 centuries, 5 decades."

References

Absolon, K. (1957). Dokumente und Beweise der Fähigkeiten des fossilen Menschen zu zählen im mährischen Paläolithikum. *Artibus Asiae*, 20 (2–3), 123–150.

Amiet, P. (1966). Il y a 5000 ans les Elamites inventaient l'écriture. *Archeologia*, 12, 20–22.

Arnett, W. S. (1982). *The Predynastic origin of Egyptian hieroglyphs*. Washington, DC: University Press of America.

Bagley, R. W. (2004). Anyang writing and the origin of Chinese writing. In Stephen D. Houston (Ed.), *The first writing: Script invention as history and process* (pp. 190–249). Cambridge: Cambridge University Press.

Baines, J. (1983). Literacy and ancient Egyptian society. *Man*, 18 (3), 572–599.

Baines, J. (2004). The earliest Egyptian writing: development, context, purpose. In Stephen D. Houston (Ed.), *The first writing: Script invention as history and process* (pp. 150–189). Cambridge: Cambridge University Press.

Barnes, R. H. (1982). Number and number use in Kedang, Indonesia. *Man* (N.S.), 17, 1–22.

Bennett, W. C. (1963). Lore and learning: Numbers, measures, weights and calendars. In Julian Steward (Ed.), *Handbook of South American Indians*, vol. 5. (pp. 601–619). New York: Cooper Square.

Birket-Smith, K. (1966). The Circumpacific distribution of knot records. *Folk*, 8/9, 15–24.

Boltz, W. O. (1996). Early Chinese writing. In Peter T. Daniels & William Bright (Eds.), *The world's writing systems* (pp. 191–199). New York: Oxford University Press.

Boone, E. H. (1994). Introduction: Writing and recording knowledge. In Elizabeth Hill Boone & Walter Mignolo (Eds.), *Writing without words* (pp. 3–26). Durham, NC: Duke University Press.

Boone, E. H. (2000). *Stories in red and black: Pictorial histories of the Aztecs and Mixtecs*. Austin: University of Texas.

Boone, E. H. (2004). Beyond writing. In Stephen D. Houston (Ed.), *The first writing: Script invention as history and process* (pp. 313–348). Cambridge: Cambridge University Press.

Bowditch, C. P. (1910). *The numeration, calendar systems and astronomical knowledge of the Mayas*. Cambridge: Cambridge University Press.

Cain, C. R. (2006). Implications of the marked artifacts of the Middle Stone Age of Africa. *Current Anthropology*, 47 (4), 675–681.

Caso, A. (1965). Mixtec writing and calendar. In Robert Wauchope & Gordon R. Willey (Eds.), *Handbook of Middle American Indians*, vol. 3, part 2, pp. 948–961. Austin: University of Texas.

Chrisomalis, S. (2004). A cognitive typology for numerical notation. *Cambridge Archaeological Journal*, 14 (1), 37–52.

Chrisomalis, S. (forthcoming). *A comparative history of numerical notation*. New York: Cambridge University Press.

Conant, L. L. (1896). *The number concept*. New York: Macmillan.

Cooper, J. S. (2004). Babylonian beginnings: the origin of the cuneiform writing system in comparative perspective. In Stephen D. Houston (Ed.), *The first writing: Script invention as history and process* (pp. 71–99). Cambridge: Cambridge University Press.

Coulmas, F. (1989). *The writing systems of the world*. Oxford: Blackwell.

Damerow, P. (1996). *Abstraction and representation: Essays on the cultural evolution of thinking*. Dordrecht: Kluwer.

Daniels, P. T. (1996). The study of writing systems. In Peter T. Daniels & William Bright (Eds.), *The world's writing systems* (pp. 3–18). New York: Oxford University Press.

Daniels, P. T., & Bright, W. (Eds.) (1996). *The world's writing systems*. New York: Oxford University Press.

d'Errico, F. (1989). Paleolithic lunar calendars: A case of wishful thinking? *Current Anthropology*, 30 (1), 117–118.

d'Errico, F. (2001). Memories out of mind: The archaeology of the oldest memory systems. In A. Nowell (Ed.), *In the mind's eye: Multidisciplinary approaches to the evolution of human cognition* (pp. 33–49). Ann Arbor, MI: International Monographs in Prehistory.

d'Errico, F., & Cacho, C. (1994). Notation versus decoration in the Upper Paleolithic: A case-study from Tossal de la Roca, Alicante, Spain. *Journal of Archaeological Science*, 21, 185–200.

d'Errico, F., Henshilwood, C. S., & Nilssen, P. (2001). An engraved bone fragment from c. 70,000-year-old Middle Stone Age levels at Blombos Cave, South Africa: Implications for the origin of symbolism and language. *Antiquity*, 75 (288), 309–318.

Divale, W. (1999). Climatic instability, food storage, and the development of numerical counting: A cross-cultural study. *Cross-Cultural Research*, 33 (4), 341–368.

Djamouri, R. (1994). L'emploi des signes numériques dans les inscriptions Shang. In Alexei Volkov (Ed.), *Sous les nombres, le monde* (pp. 13–42). Extrême-Orient, Extrême-Occident 16. Paris: Université de Paris.

Dreyer, G. (1998). *Umm el-Qaab I*. Mainz: Verlag Philipp von Zabern.

Englund, R. K. (2004). The state of decipherment of proto-Elamite. In Stephen D. Houston (Ed.), *The first writing: Script invention as history and process* (pp. 100–149). Cambridge: Cambridge University Press.

Gelb, I. J. (1963). *A study of writing* (2nd ed.). Chicago: University of Chicago Press.

Goldschmidt, W. R. (1940). A Hupa "calendar." *American Anthropologist*, 42 (1), 176–177.

Goody, J. (Ed.) (1968). *Literacy in traditional societies*. Cambridge: Cambridge University Press.

Goody, J. (1977). *The domestication of the savage mind*. Cambridge: Cambridge University Press.

Goody, J. (1986). *The logic of writing and the organization of society*. Cambridge: Cambridge University Press.

Gordon, P. (2004). Numerical cognition without words: Evidence from Amazonia. *Science*, 306 (5695), 496–499.

Guitel, G. (1975). *Histoire comparée des numérations écrites*. Paris: Flammarion.

Harvey, H. R. (1982). Reading the numbers: Variation in Nahua numerical glyphs. In M.E.R.G.N. Jansen & Th. J.J. Leyenaar (Eds.), The *Indians of Mexico in Pre-Columbian and modern times* (pp. 190–205). Leiden: Rutgers.

Houston, S. D. (2004a). Writing in early Mesoamerica. In Stephen D. Houston (Ed.), *The first writing: Script invention as history and process* (pp. 274–312). Cambridge: Cambridge University Press.

Houston, S. D. (2004b). The archaeology of communication technologies. *Annual Review of Anthropology*, 33, 223–250.

Houston, S. D. (2004c). Final thoughts on first writing. In Stephen D. Houston (Ed.), *The first writing: Script invention as history and process* (pp. 349–353). Cambridge: Cambridge University Press.

Hurford, J. R. (1987). *Language and number*. Oxford: Basil Blackwell.

Ifrah, G. (1998). *The universal history of numbers*. Translated by David Bellos, E. F. Harding, Sophie Wood, & Ian Monk. New York: John Wiley and Sons.

Justeson, J. S., & Mathews, P. (1990). Developmental trends in Mesoamerican hieroglyphic writing. *Visible Language*, 24, 86–132.

Keightley, D. N. (1987). Archaeology and mentality: The making of China. *Representations*, 18, 91–128.

Lagercrantz, S. (1968). African tally-strings. *Anthropos*, 63, 115–128.

Lagercrantz, S. (1970). Tallying by means of lines, stones, and sticks. *Paideuma*, 16, 52–62.

Lagercrantz, S. (1973). Counting by means of tally sticks or cuts on the body in Africa. *Anthropos*, 68, 569–588.

Langley, J. C. (1986). *Symbolic notation of Teotihuacan*. Oxford: BAR.

Li, X., Harbottle, G., Zhang, J., & Wang, C. (2003). The earliest writing? Sign use in the seventh millennium BC at Jiahu, Henan Province, China. *Antiquity*, 77 (295), 31–44.

Lieberman, S. J. (1980). Of clay pebbles, hollow clay balls, and writing: A Sumerian view. *American Journal of Archaeology*, 84, 339–358.

Marcus, J. (1976). The origins of Mesoamerican writing. *Annual Review of Anthropology*, 5, 35–67.

Marcus, J. (1992). *Mesoamerican writing systems*. Princeton, NJ: Princeton University Press.

Marshack, A. (1964). Lunar notation on Upper Paleolithic remains. *Science*, 146 (3645), 743–745.

Marshack, A. (1972). *The roots of civilization*. New York: McGraw-Hill.

Marshack, A. (1985). A lunar-solar year calendar stick from North America. *American Antiquity*, 50 (1), 27–51.

Menninger, K. (1969). *Number words and number symbols*. Translation by Paul Broneer of *Zahlwort und Ziffer* (Gottingen: Vandenhoeck). Cambridge: MIT Press.

Morley, S. G. (1915). *An introduction to the study of the Maya hieroglyphs*. Bureau of American Ethnology, Bulletin #57. Washington, DC: Smithsonian Institution.

Needham, J., & Ling, W. (1959). *Science and civilization in China. Vol. 3: Mathematics and the sciences of the heavens and the earth*. Cambridge: Cambridge University Press.

Nicholson, H. B. (1973). Phoneticism in the late pre-Hispanic Central Mexican writing system. In Elizabeth P. Benson (Ed.), *Mesoamerican writing systems* (pp. 1–46). Washington, DC: Dumbarton Oaks.

Nissen, H. J., Damerow, P., & Englund, R. K. (1993). *Archaic bookkeeping*. Translation of *Frühe Schrift und Techniken der Wirtschaftsverwaltung im alten Vorderen Orient*, Paul Larsen, trans. Chicago: University of Chicago.

Olson, D. R. (1994). *The world on paper: The conceptual and cognitive implications of writing and reading*. Cambridge: Cambridge University Press.

Payne, S. E., & Closs, M. P. (1986). A survey of Aztec numbers and their uses. In M.P. Closs (Ed.), *Native American Mathematics* (pp. 213–236). Austin, TX: University of Texas Press.

Pohl, M. E. D., Pope, K. O., & von Nagy, C. (2002). Olmec origins of Mesoamerican writing. *Science*, 298 (6 December 2002), 1984–1987.

Postgate, N., Wang, T., & Wilkinson, T. (1995). The evidence for early writing: Utilitarian or ceremonial? *Antiquity*, 69, 459–480.

Potts, D. T. (1999). *The archaeology of Elam: Formation and transformation of an ancient Iranian state*. Cambridge: Cambridge University Press.

Rosin, R. T. (1984). Gold medallions: The arithmetic calculations of an illiterate. *Anthropology and Education Quarterly*, 15 (1), 38–50.

Sampson, G. (1985). *Writing systems: A linguistic introduction*. Stanford, CA: Stanford University Press.

Schmandt-Besserat, D. (1978). The earliest precursor of writing. *Scientific American*, 238 (6), 38–47.

Schmandt-Besserat, D. (1984). Before numerals. *Visible Language*, 18 (1), 48–60.

Schmandt-Besserat, D. (1992). *Before writing*. Austin: University of Texas Press.

Seidenberg, A. (1960). The diffusion of counting practices. *University of California Publications in Mathematics*, 3 (4), 215–299.

Seidenberg, A. (1962). The ritual origin of counting. *Archive for the History of Exact Sciences*, 2, 1–40.

Seidenberg, A. (1986). The zero in the Mayan numerical notation. In Michael P. Closs (Ed.), *Native American Mathematics* (pp. 371–386). Austin: University of Texas Press.

Smith, M. (2003). *The Aztecs* (2nd ed.). Oxford: Blackwell.

Stuart, D. S. (2001). *Proper names and the origins of literacy*. Working paper, Peabody Museum, Harvard University.

Tolchinsky, L. (2003). *The cradle of culture and what children know about writing and numbers before being taught*. Mahwah, NJ: Lawrence Erlbaum.

Trigger, B. G. (2003). *Understanding early civilizations*. Cambridge: Cambridge University Press.

Urton, G. (1997). *The social life of numbers*. Austin: University of Texas Press.

Urton, G. (2001). A calendrical and demographic tomb text from northern Peru. *Latin American Antiquity*, 12 (2), 127–147.

Urton, G., & Brezine, C. (2005). Khipu accounting in ancient Peru. *Science*, 309 (12 August 2005), 1065–1067.

Wiese, H. (2003). *Numbers, language, and the human mind*. Cambridge: Cambridge University Press.

Zimansky, P. (1993). Review of Denise Schmandt-Besserat, *Before writing*. *Journal of Field Archaeology*, 20, 513–517.

CHAPTER 5

Are There Linguistic Consequences of Literacy? Comparing the Potentials of Language Use in Speech and Writing

Douglas Biber

Introduction

A major issue for discourse studies during the last three decades concerns the ways in which literacy influences language use: are there systematic linguistic differences between spoken and written language that can be associated with literacy as a technology (i.e., writing considered as a physical mode of communication distinct from speech)? Answers to this question have run the gamut, from claiming that written language is fundamentally different from spoken language to recent claims that there are essentially no linguistic differences associated with literacy in itself.

Earlier research on this question sometimes took an extreme position, arguing that there are fundamental linguistic differences between speech and writing. For example, researchers such as O'Donnell (1974), Olson (1977), and Chafe (1982) argued that written language generally differs from speech in being more structurally complex, elaborated, and/or explicit. This view was moderated in the 1980s, when researchers such as Tannen (1982), Beaman (1984), and Chafe and Danielewicz (1986) argued that it is misleading to generalize about overall differences between spoken and written language because communicative task is also an important predictor of linguistic variation; therefore, equivalent communicative tasks should be compared to isolate the existence of mode differences.

Multi-dimensional (MD) studies of register variation in English (e.g., Biber, 1986, 1988) went a step further by analyzing linguistic variation among the range of registers within both speech and writing. These studies found "dimensions" of variation that distinguished between stereotypical "oral" versus "literate" registers, but they also found that there are few (if any) absolute linguistic differences between speech and writing. Rather, particular spoken and written registers are more or less similar/different with respect to several underlying "dimensions" of variation.

At the opposite extreme from the earlier research on this question, some scholars in the 1990s began to claim that there are essentially no linguistic correlates of literacy as a technology. Many of these researchers take an ethnographic perspective, studying literacy practices in communities where writing is used for specific, local functions. Having noticed that those functions do not necessarily include the stereotypical purposes of informational exposition, these researchers made general claims minimizing the importance of literacy as a technology; for example:

> *Literacy can be used (or not used) in so many different ways that the technology it offers, taken on its own, probably has no implications at all.* (Bloch, 1993, p. 87)

> *It seems quite evident that speech may have all the characteristics Olson ascribes to text and written prose may have none of them. . . . Thus, the characteristics of linguistic performance at issue here have no intrinsic relation to whether performance is spoken or written.* (Halverson, 1991, p.625)

> *In sum, orality and literacy share many common features and the features that have been identified with one or the other have more to do with the context in which language is used than with oral versus literate use.* (Hornberger, 1994, p. 114)

This chapter argues that none of these extreme views is correct. Rather, the spoken and written modes differ in their potential for linguistic variation: speech is highly constrained in its typical linguistic characteristics, whereas writing permits a wide range of linguistic expression, including linguistic styles not attested in speech. Thus, written texts can be highly similar to spoken texts or they can be dramatically different. This difference is attributed to the differing production circumstances of the two modes: real-time production in speech versus the opportunity for careful revision and editing in writing. As a result, the written mode provides the *potential* for styles of linguistic expression not found in the spoken mode.

I present evidence for these systematic linguistic differences between the modes from a survey of corpus-based research studies carried out in the past twenty years. First, I present a survey of how particular grammatical features are used in spoken and written registers. In addition, I survey the results from MD studies of register variation in English, Spanish, Somali, and Korean, which have adopted both synchronic and diachronic perspectives. Both bodies of research consistently uncover the same patterns of linguistic variation: (1) few, if any, absolute differences between speech and writing generally; (2) significant differences in the typical linguistic characteristics of the two modes; and (3) a significant difference in the range of linguistic variation within each mode, with writing allowing much more diversity in linguistic expression than speech. The following three sections document these linguistic patterns from synchronic, diachronic, and cross-linguistic perspectives.

Linguistic Variation within and across the Two Modes

One analytical approach that has proven to be especially productive for studying spoken/written linguistic variation is corpus-based analysis: a research approach that focuses on the analysis of a large body of texts that have been systematically collected to represent particular registers, usually employing computational tools. The corpus-based approach enables identification of the linguistic features that are typically used in each register, as well as analysis of the extent to which a feature is especially common or rare (see Biber, Conrad, & Reppen, 1998; and McEnery, Xiao, & Tono, 2006, for introductions to this analytical approach).

Two recent books provide detailed corpus-based descriptions of the use of lexico-grammatical features in spoken and written registers. The first study – the *Longman Grammar of Spoken and Written English* (LGSWE) (Biber et al., 1999) – applies corpus-based analyses to show how any grammatical feature can be described for both its structural characteristics and its patterns of use across spoken and written registers. The analyses in the LGSWE are based on texts from four registers: conversation, fiction, newspaper language, and academic prose (approximately twenty million words of text overall, with approximately four million to five million words from each of the four registers). The second study (Biber, 2006) describes the typical linguistic characteristics of university spoken and written registers (both academic and nonacademic).

I focus here on seven of the registers described in the earlier studies: conversation, classroom teaching, and office hours within speech; and university textbooks, course syllabi, institutional texts (e.g., university catalogs or handbooks), and fiction within writing. In addition to the physical-mode difference, these seven registers differ from one another with respect to interactiveness, production circumstances, communicative purpose, target audience, and so forth. For example, among the spoken registers described herein, conversation has the stereotypical characteristics of speech: it is highly interactive, speaker and hearer are present together in the same situation, speakers discuss personal topics, and there is usually no preplanning of the language. Classroom teaching differs from conversation in several respects: the speaker and hearer interact much less, the primary speaker (i.e., the instructor) has a primary purpose of conveying information, and he or she has usually preplanned the discourse. However, conversation and classroom teaching are similar in that the language in both situations is produced in real-time: the speaker is constructing utterances while he or she is actually speaking. Furthermore, once an utterance is produced, it exists in the ongoing discourse – a new 'repaired' utterance can be added, but the original utterance cannot be taken back, revised, or edited.

Written registers have dramatically different production circumstances: writers can take as much time as they want to plan exactly what they want to write, and if they write something unintended, they can delete/add/revise/edit the language of the text. Thus, the final written text that an external reader sees might bear little resemblance to the initial words that the author produced, and readers usually have no overt indication of the extent to which the author has revised the original draft. Nearly all written registers offer the opportunity for extensive planning and revising during production, even if the author does not avail himself or herself of this opportunity.

Beyond that, the four written registers included here differ from one another in several key respects. Textbooks have a focused informational purpose, with few overt references to the author. Textbooks might make generic reference to the student reader, but they are written for a general audience rather than a specific set of addressees. Institutional university writing is similar to textbooks in this regard. It differs in purpose, however, in that it is much more directive than textbooks. Course syllabi, conversely, are more personal: the course instructor often expresses his or her own personal attitudes and expectations, the communicative purposes are both informational and directive, and the text is addressed to the specific set of students who are taking a course. Finally, fiction is included here because it represents a completely different type of register in the written mode. The production circumstances for a fictional story or novel are similar to those for a textbook. However, the communicative purposes of fiction are completely different: creating a fictional world and narrating a story rather than conveying technical information. In addition, fiction usually includes dialogue: conversations constructed in writing by the author. These fictional conversations can be revised and edited, unlike spoken face-to-face conversation that occurs in real-time.

Table 5.1 summarizes many of the most important linguistic characteristics of these seven registers, based on a survey of the patterns of use documented in the LGSWE (Biber et al., 1999) and Biber (2006). Part A lists features that are especially common in the written registers. Many of these features are nouns or features that can be used for noun-phrase modification, such as adjectives, prepositional phrases, or relative clauses. Despite the differences in communicative purpose, these features tend to be common in all three written university registers. Text Sample 1, from a textbook, illustrates many of the typical linguistic characteristics of informational written prose. Notice especially the dense use of nouns and the use of complex noun phrases, with nouns and adjectives as premodifiers and prepositional phrases and relative clauses as postmodifiers.

Text Sample 1: Textbook, Graduate Social Science

Nouns are **bold underlined**; adjectives are underlined; prepositional phrases as nominal modifiers are in *italics*; relative clauses are marked by [. . .].

As we shall see below, the structural **components** *of the* ***lifeworld*** become **subsystems** *of a general* ***system*** *of* ***action***, [to which the physical **substratum** *of the* ***lifeworld*** is reckoned

Table 5.1. Distinctive Linguistic Characteristics of Written University Registers, Compared to Spoken University Registers and Fiction [Based on Biber et al. 1999 and Biber 2006]

	Spoken University Registers		*Other Speech*	*Written University Registers*			*Other Writing*
Linguistic Feature	*Classroom Teaching*	*Office Hours*	*Conversation*	*Textbooks*	*Course Syllabi*	*Institutional Writing*	*Fiction*
Part A: Features generally more common in written university registers (and fiction)							
diversified vocabulary (e.g., *sanctimonious*)				*			
nouns/nominalizations (e.g., *term, assumption*)				***	***	***	*
rare nouns (e.g., *abscission, ambivalence*)				*			
common abstract / process nouns (e.g., *system, factor, problem*)					*	*	*
style adverbs (e.g., *generally, typically*)				*			
adjectives (e.g., *important, likely*)				*	*	*	*
linking adverbials (e.g., *however, for example*)				***	*	*	
passive voice (e.g., *was determined*)				*	*	*	
relative clauses (e.g., *the sequence which determines . . .*)				*	*	*	*
prepositional phrases (e.g., *patterning of behavior by households*)				***	***	***	*
noun + *that*-clause (e.g., *the fact/assumption that . . .*)				*			
mental verb + *to*-clause (e.g., *remember to . . .*)				*	***	*	
adjective + *to*-clause (e.g., *unlikely/difficult to . . .*)				*	*		
noun + *to*-clause (e.g., *the opportunity to learn*)						*	

	Spoken University Registers		*Other Speech*	*Written University Registers*			*Other Writing*
Linguistic Feature	*Classroom Teaching*	*Office Hours*	*Conversation*	*Textbooks*	*Course Syllabi*	*Institutional Writing*	*Fiction*
Part B: Features generally more common in spoken registers (and fiction)							
verbs (e.g., *get, go, see*)	***	***	***				***
progressive aspect (e.g., *bringing, making*)	*	*	*				*
adverbs (e.g., *here, now, again*)	*	*	*				*
stance adverbs:							
certainty adverbs (e.g., *really, actually*)	***	***	***				
likelihood adverbs (e.g., *probably, maybe*)	*	***	*				
pronouns (e.g., *I, you, it*)	*	***	***				*
discourse markers (e.g., *ok, well*)	*	***	***				
adverbial clauses:							
conditional clauses (e.g., *if you read . . .*)	*	***	*		*	*	
causative clauses (e.g., *because . . .*)	*	***	*				
temporal clauses (e.g., *when/while . . .*)			*				*
that-clauses							
certainty verb + *that*-clause (e.g., *I know [that] . . .*)	***	***	*				*
likelihood verb + *that*-clause (e.g., *I think/guess [that] . . .*)	*	***	***				*
communication V + *that*-cls (e.g., *he said [that] . . .*)	*	*	*				*
WH-clauses (e.g., *you know how to . . .*)	*	***	***				*

*** = extremely common; much more frequent than in other registers
* = very common; more frequent than in other registers

along with the **behavior system**]. The **proposal** [I am advancing here], by **contrast**, attempts to take into **account** the methodological **differences** *between the internalist and the externalist* ***viewpoints*** [connected with the two conceptual **strategies**]. From the **participant perspective** *of* ***members*** *of a* ***lifeworld*** it looks as if **sociology** *with a* ***systems****, theoretical* ***orientation*** considers only one *of the three* ***components*** *of the* ***lifeworld****,* namely, the institutional **system**, [for which **culture** and **personality** merely constitute complementary **environments**]. From the **observer perspective** *of* ***systems theory***, on the other **hand**, it looks as if **lifeworld analysis** confines itself to one societal **subsystem** [specialized in maintaining structural **patterns** (**pattern maintenance**)]; in this **view**, the **components** *of the* ***lifeworld*** are merely internal **differentiations** *of this* ***subsystem*** [which specifies the **parameters** *of societal* ***self-maintenance***].

Part B of Table 5.1, in contrast, lists linguistic features that are especially common in the spoken registers. These are mostly features relating to pronouns (rather than nouns), the verb phrase (verbs and adverbs), and finite clauses. It is surprising that there are several types of dependent clauses included here: finite adverbial clauses (e.g., *if I'm lucky*), *that* complement clauses controlled by verbs (e.g., *I don't think [that] he does*), and WH clauses (e.g., *I don't know what's happening*). Text Sample 2 illustrates the use of these features in an advising session from office hours:

Text Sample 2: Office Hours; School of Business

> Pronouns are **bold underlined**; verbs are *underlined italics*; finite adverbial clauses and finite complement clauses are marked by [. . .].
>
> **Instructor:** Now here*'s* [what **you** *should do*] [if **you** *want* **me** to *go* over your graduation papers] **you** *gotta do* **it** this semester [because [if **you** wait until the summer or the fall] –
> **Student:** uh huh
> **Instructor:** then **you***'ll have to go* through somebody else and **it***'ll* just *take* longer]
> **Student:** yeah so **I** *can do* **that** then and what *do* **I** – *do* **you** just *file?*

Classroom teaching also illustrates the dense use of many of these same features, even when it is not directly interactive. For example:

Text Sample 3: Classroom Teaching; English

> Pronouns are **bold underlined**; verbs are *underlined italics*; finite adverbial clauses and finite complement clauses are marked by [. . .].
>
> **Instructor:** [What **I** *want* **you** to *do* in your free writes] *is* kind of *reflect* on [what *do* **you** *think* [he *means* here]]. Maybe – and [what **you** *could answer*] *is would* **you** *want* to *live* in that kind of place. *Would* **you** *want* to *live* there? And [if **you** *do*], Why? and *do* not, Why? And how *does* Rymmer *give* **you** clues? **I** *think* [Rymmer, especially in a poem like **this**, **he** *talks* about this hollowness at his core, sort of the absence of the bona fide, legitimate purpose to the whole thing]. **I** *think* [clues like **this** *are embedded* throughout that *suggest* [that Rymmer*'s* pretty negative, or skeptical about this whole project]], right? And [what **I** *wanna know*] *is*, [if **you** *do want* to *live* there], why *is* **that**, and [if **you** *don't*], what *is* **it** about Rymmer's writing, or Rymmer's ideas that *lead* **you** to *believe* [that **you** *wouldn't want* to *live* there].

It is more interesting for our purposes here that classroom teaching is different from written informational prose in that it does *not* make dense use of nouns and complex noun-phrase structures, even though both registers have informational communicative purposes. Text Sample 3 is dramatically different from Text Sample 1 in this regard. Text Sample 3 is typical of most classroom teaching in that the instructor uses comparatively few nouns overall and few complex noun phrases (e.g., with embedded prepositional phrases or relative clauses). Rather, the linguistic complexity of this passage is expressed primarily through the dense use of finite dependent clauses: adverbial clauses with *if* or *because* and complement clauses (i.e., *WH* or *that*).

Thus, communicative purpose has a surprisingly small effect on the typical linguistic characteristics of spoken discourse. That is, whether a speech event is interactive and interpersonal (as in normal conversation) or primarily monologic and informational (as in classroom teaching), it is characterized by the same set of typical linguistic features: verbs, pronouns, finite adverbial and complement clauses, and so forth. All of these speech events are characterized by the relative absence of nouns and complex noun-phrase structures.

Considering the overall patterns of linguistic variation, Table 5.1 shows three general distributional patterns: (1) linguistic features that are common in informational writing tend to be rare in the spoken registers, and vice versa; (2) spoken registers are surprisingly similar to one another in their typical linguistic characteristics, regardless of differences in communicative purpose, interactiveness, and preplanning; and (3) in contrast, written registers have a much wider range of linguistic diversity.

I attribute the linguistic uniformity among spoken registers to their shared production circumstances. Spoken texts are normally produced in real-time. As a result, spoken registers share a heavy reliance on finite clausal syntax. Conversely, it seems that the dense use of complex noun-phrase structures – typical of some types of written prose – is simply not normally feasible given the production constraints of the spoken mode.

In contrast, we find large linguistic differences among written registers, corresponding to differences in purpose, interactiveness, author involvement, and so forth. Thus, fiction is very different from the language of textbooks and other university registers in Table 5.1. Other written registers such as letters, memoranda, or e-mail messages reflect such differences to an even greater extent. The following text sample from an e-mail message can be contrasted with Text Sample 1, illustrating the wide range of linguistic variation possible in writing. Notice especially the use of conversational linguistic features, such as contractions, first- and second-person pronouns, verbs, and adverbs, as follows:

Text Sample 4: Personal E-mail Message

> Hey there,
> How's it going? It won't be long now before you're down here (or at least close to where I am now). I need your arrival time, flight number, etc. We are getting to CC earlier than I planned, so I will pick up the car on the 8th and may do something with these folks before you arrive. Let me know if you have any other questions too before you head for Japan.
>
> Cheers, LC

Thus, the production circumstances in writing give the author maximum flexibility, permitting styles of linguistic expression similar to those typical of speech, as well as styles of expression that are apparently not feasible in speech.

Multi-Dimensional Studies of Spoken and Written Registers in English

The MD analytical approach was originally developed to investigate the linguistic patterns of variation among spoken and written registers (see, e.g., Biber, 1988, 1995; Conrad & Biber, 2001). Studies in this research tradition have used large corpora of naturally occurring texts to represent the range of spoken and written registers in a language. These registers are compared with respect to 'dimensions' of variation (identified through a statistical factor analysis), comprising constellations of linguistic features that typically co-occur in texts (discussed in the next section). Each dimension is distinctive in three respects, as follows:

1. It is defined by a distinctive set of co-occurring linguistic features.
2. It is associated with distinctive communicative functions.
3. There are distinctive patterns of register variation associated with each dimension.

MD analysis is based on the assumption that all registers have distinctive linguistic patterns of use (associated with their defining situational characteristics). Thus, MD studies of speech and writing set out to describe the linguistic similarities and differences among a range of spoken registers and, similarly, among a range of written registers – and to then compare speech and writing within the context of a comprehensive analysis of register variation.

MD analysis uses statistical factor analysis to reduce a large number of linguistic variables to a few basic parameters of linguistic variation. In MD analyses, the distribution of individual linguistic features is analyzed in a corpus of texts. Factor analysis is then used to identify the systematic co-occurrence patterns among those linguistic features – the 'dimensions' – and then texts and registers are compared along each dimension. Each dimension comprises a group of linguistic features that usually co-occur in texts (e.g., nouns, attributive adjectives, prepositional phrases); these co-occurrence patterns are identified statistically using factor analysis. The co-occurrence patterns are then interpreted to assess their underlying situational, social, and cognitive functions.

Several general patterns and conclusions about spoken and written language have emerged from MD studies:

1. Some dimensions are strongly associated with spoken and written differences; other dimensions have little or no relation to speech and writing.
2. There are few, if any, absolute linguistic differences between spoken and written registers.
3. However, there are strong and systematic linguistic differences between stereotypical speech and stereotypical writing – that is, between conversation and written informational prose.
4. The spoken and written modes differ in their linguistic potential: they are not equally adept at accommodating a wide range of linguistic variation. In particular, there is an extremely wide range of linguistic variation among written registers because writers can choose to employ linguistic features associated with stereotypical speech. In contrast, there is a more restricted range of linguistic variation among spoken registers. As in the previous discussion, I attribute this last pattern to the real-time production circumstances of the spoken mode, making it difficult to employ many of the linguistic features associated with stereotypical informational writing.

The MD study of discourse complexity reported in Biber (1992) clearly illustrates these patterns. That study used confirmatory factor analysis to compare the statistical adequacy of competing MD models. A five-dimensional model best accounted for the patterns of "linguistic complexity" among a wide range of spoken and written registers. Those dimensions were interpreted as "Reduced Structure," "Integrated Structure," "Elaboration of Reference," "Passive Constructions," and "Framing Elaboration."

None of these dimensions is associated with an absolute distinction between spoken and written texts; rather, the mode interacts with other situational characteristics (e.g., an informational purpose) to determine the relationships among registers with respect to the dimensions. However, when all five dimensions are considered together, they identify a fundamental distinction between written and spoken registers: spoken registers are limited in the types of complexity they can exploit, whereas written registers show much greater differences with respect to both their types and extent of discourse complexity.

Figures 5.1 and 5.2 show this distinction between the linguistic complexity profiles of written and spoken registers: written registers differ widely in both the extent and types of linguistic complexity, whereas spoken registers follow a single pattern with respect to their types of complexity, differing only with respect to extent. Thus, Figure 5.1 shows that written registers use much of the available complexity space defined by the five dimensions. In contrast, spoken registers follow a single complexity profile in Figure 5.2: noncomplex in permitting the use of reduced structures, moderately complex in the use of referential elaboration, noncomplex in the use of integrated structures, highly complex with respect to the use of framing elaboration, and noncomplex with respect to the use of passive

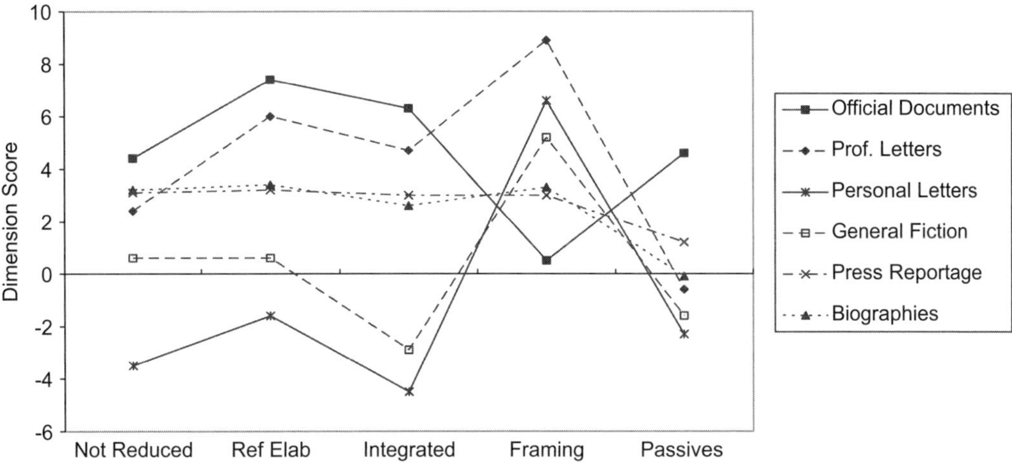

Figure 5.1. Complexity dimension scores for six written registers.

constructions. (The only departure from this profile is shown by the broadcasting register, which is unmarked in all dimensions.)

These two figures further support the claim that there is a fundamental difference in linguistic expression associated with the production differences between speech and writing. Written production gives the addressor maximum freedom to manipulate the linguistic characteristics of a text in accordance with a number of situational parameters, including communicative purpose, interactiveness, and degrees of personal involvement. As a result, we find a wide range of linguistic styles within writing. In contrast, the real-time production circumstances of spoken registers restrict the types of linguistic complexity that are possible. Thus, Figure 5.2 shows some linguistic differences in the *extent* to which spoken registers employ the linguistic features of a dimension (e.g., associated with situational differences in purpose and involvement), but all spoken registers follow only a single basic profile in their reliance on particular *types* of complexity. In summary, the exploitation of complexity features is restricted by mode, so that written registers differ greatly in both the types and extent of discourse complexity, whereas spoken

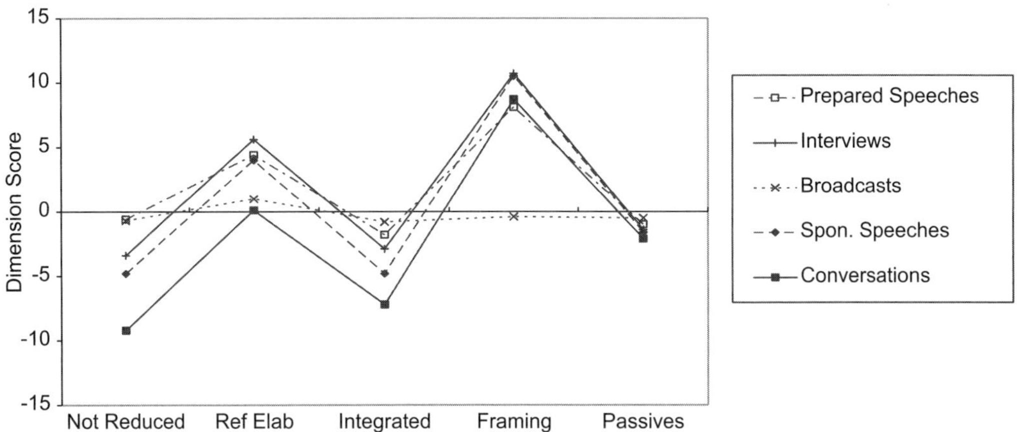

Figure 5.2. Complexity dimension scores for five spoken registers.

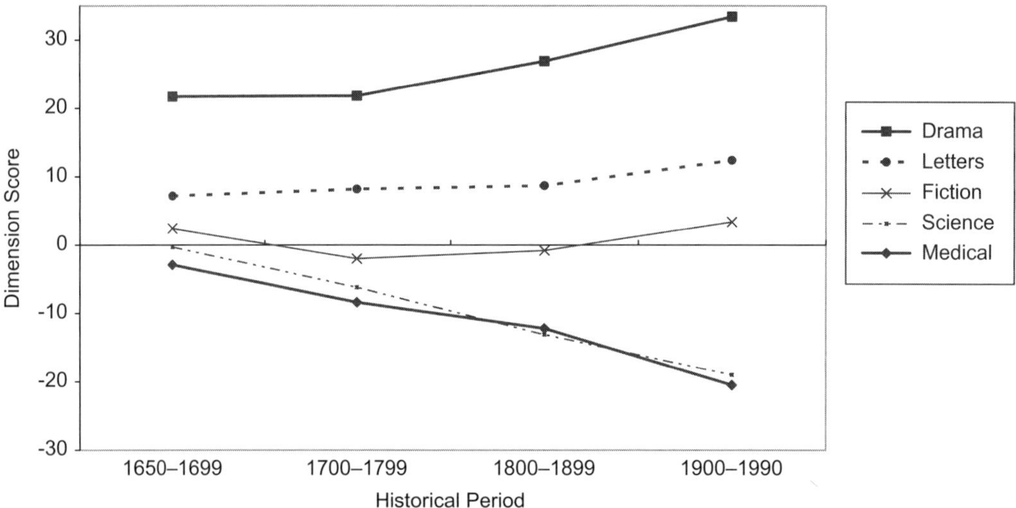

Figure 5.3. Historical change along Dimension 1: Involved versus Informational.

registers are mostly restricted to differences of extent.

Historical Evidence

Historical corpus-based studies help us to better understand the nature of the differences between the spoken and written modes. For example, Biber and Finegan (1997) documented the historical patterns of change for nine registers from the ARCHER Corpus, including speech-based registers (e.g., drama), personal/popular written registers (e.g., letters and fiction), and specialized expository written registers (e.g., medical and scientific prose). The study used MD analysis, based on the Biber (1988) study of synchronic spoken/written registers.

Figure 5.3 plots the historical patterns of change with respect to Dimension 1: Involved versus Informational Production. This dimension is composed of two sets of features: the co-occurring 'positive' features include verbs, pronouns, stance devices, and finite dependent clauses; this pole of the dimension is interpreted as 'involved, interactive discourse.' In contrast, the co-occurring 'negative' features in Dimension 1 include nouns, attributive adjectives, long words, and prepositional phrases; this constellation of features is interpreted as 'informational production.'

Figure 5.3 shows that all registers in the seventeenth century were relatively similar to one another along this dimension. Drama was already relatively 'involved' as were letters, to a lesser extent. These two registers commonly used the positive Dimension 1 features (e.g., verbs, pronouns), whereas negative Dimension 1 features were relatively rare in those texts. In contrast, fiction and medical/science prose were unmarked in Dimension 1 in the seventeenth century, with a dense use of neither positive nor negative features.

Figure 5.3 further shows that this pattern of register variation changed dramatically in the following three centuries. On the one hand, drama shifted to be characterized by much larger positive Dimension 1 scores. (There are two possible interpretations of this shift: (1) speakers in conversation changed over time to adopt more involved styles of expression; or (2) authors changed over time to better capture the actual patterns of natural conversation.) The two personal/popular written registers – letters and fiction – remained relatively stable during those centuries: fiction actually became somewhat less involved in the eighteenth century (see Biber & Finegan,

1989), whereas both registers have gradually shifted toward more involved styles during the two most recent centuries.

On the other hand, the most dramatic shift in linguistic style has been for the two specialist expository registers (i.e., science prose and medical prose), which both evolved to an extreme 'informational' style in Dimension 1, characterized by the dense use of nouns, attributive adjectives, prepositional phrases, and so forth. The previous section showed that the dense use of these features in present-day English is associated exclusively with informational purposes in the written mode; thus, classroom teaching – a spoken register with informational purposes – does not make dense use of these features. Figure 5.3 further shows that these linguistic styles of expression are apparently not 'natural' in any register. Thus, no register in the seventeenth or eighteenth century was characterized by the extremely dense use of complex noun-phrase constructions. Rather, this linguistic style of expression evolved gradually in the following centuries, with the most notable shift in the twentieth century.

This historical change can be attributed to two influences: (1) an increasing need for written prose with dense informational content, associated with the 'informational explosion' of recent centuries; and (2) an increasing awareness among writers of the production possibilities of the written mode, permitting extreme manipulation of the text. Specifically, it seems that the extremely dense use of complex noun-phrase constructions (described in the previous section) is not normally feasible in speech, regardless of the communicative purpose. As a result, we did not have models for this style of linguistic expression in earlier centuries. It was only as research specialists developed a communicative need for such styles that authors became aware that the written mode provided the production possibilities that allowed linguistic styles of expression not attested in the spoken mode. Here again, it is important to note that the written mode does not necessitate these distinctive linguistic styles; letters and fiction in Figure 5.1 are both relatively 'involved' in their linguistic styles. Rather, it seems that the written mode provides possibilities for styles of linguistic expression not normally possible in speech and that authors have only gradually come to exploit those possibilities in the past four centuries.

Biber and Clark (2002) undertook a more detailed investigation of these linguistic changes, focusing specifically on noun-phrase structures in drama, fiction, and medical prose (from the ARCHER Corpus). This study showed how the use of nonclausal 'compressed' types of noun modification – attributive adjectives, nouns as premodifiers, and prepositional phrases as postmodifiers – has increased dramatically in the past three centuries. (Clausal modifiers, like relative clauses, have remained relatively constant in frequency across those periods.) For example:

Attributive adjectives:
gradually expanding cumulative effect
Nouns as premodifiers:
baggage inspection procedures
Prepositional phrases as postmodifiers:
a high incidence ***of*** *heavy alcohol consumption* ***amongst*** *patients . . .*

However, as Figures 5.4 through 5.6 show, the increase in nonclausal modifiers has occurred only in informational written prose (medical prose in this study; see also Biber, 2003).

In contrast, drama and fiction have shown only slight increases, if at all. Furthermore, as Figure 5.7 illustrates, this increase has accelerated dramatically in the last fifty years, resulting in the extremely wide range of linguistic variation among written registers that characterizes present-day use.

These developments can be interpreted as resulting from the same factors as discussed previously: communicative forces on the one hand – the 'informational explosion' and the concomitant need to present information as economically as possible; and, on the other hand, the potential for careful

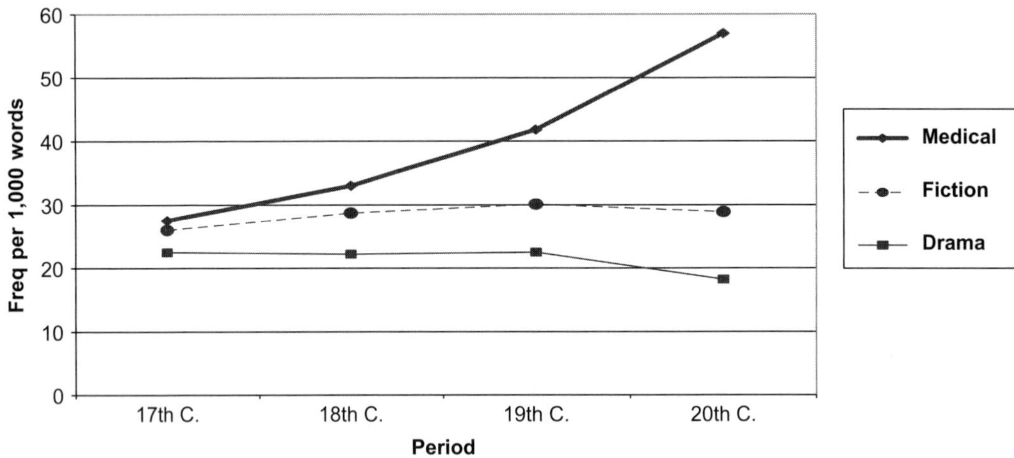

Figure 5.4. Attributive adjectives across periods.

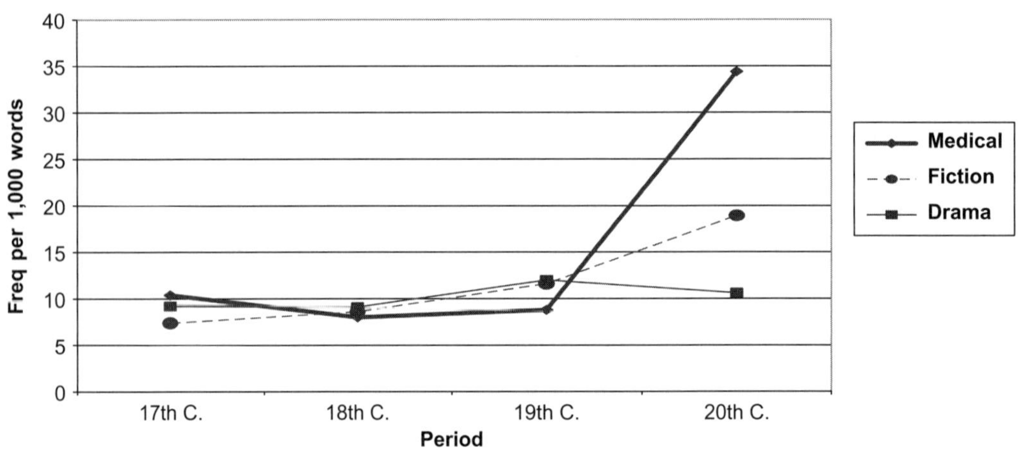

Figure 5.5. Noun–noun sequences across periods.

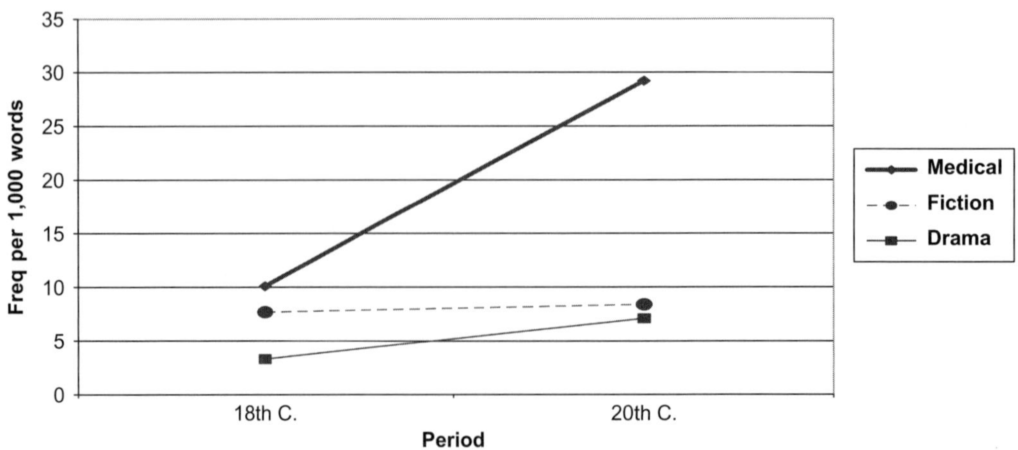

Figure 5.6. Prepositional phrases as postnominal modifiers, across periods.

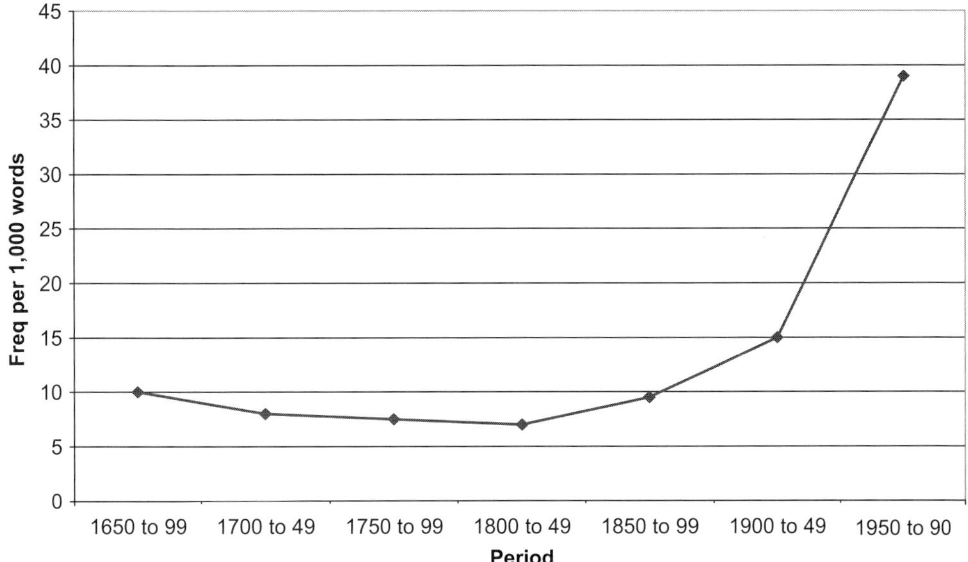

Figure 5.7. Noun–noun sequences in medical prose, across fifty-year periods.

production in the written mode, enabling the dense use of extremely complex, compressed noun-phrase structures.

Cross-Linguistic Evidence

Finally, several MD studies of spoken/written register variation in languages other than English have been carried out, using the same methods as those outlined previously. These include major studies of Spanish (Biber et al., 2006), Korean (Kim & Biber, 1994), and Somali (Biber, 1995; Biber & Hared, 1992). These languages all show important differences in the linguistic potentials of the spoken and written modes, and the overall patterns of variation are quite similar: in all three languages, those written registers that have expository, informational purposes are systematically different in their linguistic characteristics from spoken as well as other written registers. These linguistic differences include a dense integration of structure, greater lexical specificity, and a greater use of nominal elaboration in the written expository registers.

The specific patterns of spoken/written register variation in these languages differ from one another to some extent. For example, the study of Korean includes several scripted spoken registers, such as scripted public speeches or scripted TV documentaries. These registers are produced in writing but performed in speech; as a result, it is not surprising that they pattern more similarly to written registers than spoken registers (see, e.g., Biber, 1995, Figure 6.10).

The findings from the studies of Spanish, Korean, and Somali are all different from English in that they include a fundamental dimension that defines a near dichotomy between spoken and written registers:

Dimension 1 in Korean: 'Fragmented versus Elaborated Structure' (see Biber, 1995, Figure 6.10)
Dimension 2 in Somali: 'Lexical Elaboration' (see Biber, 1995, Figure 6.17)
Dimension 1 in Spanish: 'Oral versus Literate Discourse' (see Biber et al., 2006, Figure 1)

These dimensions are similar to Dimension 1 in English in that they are composed of noun-phrase features (e.g., nouns, attributive adjectives, prepositions, or postpositions) and features indicating vocabulary diversity (e.g., high type-token ratio, use of rare words). However, they differ from the English Dimension 1 in that nearly *all* written registers (i.e., personal, popular, and expository) are characterized by the dense use of these linguistic features, in opposition to all spoken registers.

The MD analysis of Somali provides one of the most dramatic illustrations of the new linguistic styles of expression that are made possible through the written mode. Before 1972, all public written communication in Somalia was carried out in Arabic, Italian, or English. The history of Somali literacy began abruptly on October 21, 1972, when Siyaad Barre, the president of Somalia, announced the development of a new standardized orthography for Somali and declared that Somali would be the sole official language of government and education. This proclamation was implemented in short order. For example, mass literacy campaigns were conducted from October 1972 to January 1973 and from July 1974 to February 1975. Within a very short period following 1972, there was a national newspaper in Somali (i.e., *Xiddigta Oktoobar*) and two periodical news magazines (i.e., *Waaga Cusub* and *Codka Macalinka*). Folk stories, a number of nonfiction pamphlets, and government memoranda also appeared quickly in Somali; textbooks and longer fictional or historical works began appearing after two or three years. Thus, Somali provides an ideal case study to investigate what happens to the range of register variation in a language following the introduction of written registers.

Figure 5.8 plots the distribution of spoken and written registers along Dimension 2 from the MD analysis of Somali. This dimension is composed of vocabulary features: once-occurring words, a high type-token ratio, nominalizations, and compound verbs have the largest negative weights on the dimension (see Biber, 1995, Table 6.19). In this case, registers with positive dimension scores are marked by the relative absence of the features; registers with negative dimension scores are marked by the dense use of the features. Figure 5.8 shows a remarkable expansion in the range of register variation following the introduction of native Somali written registers in 1972. Nearly all written registers show a greater reliance on diverse and elaborated vocabulary than any spoken register, whereas written registers such as newspaper editorials and commentary articles are extreme in their use of these features.

Of course, these written registers in Somali were influenced by foreign models (i.e., Italian and English registers) that had been used previously in Somalia for these communicative purposes. Such foreign models were also available in speech, but it is only the written Somali registers that show the extremely dense use of the lexical elaboration features. That is, the production potential of the written mode enabled these new linguistic styles in Somali, which were further motivated by foreign models and the desire for the dense presentation of informational content.

Conclusion

Somali also illustrates an apparent counterexample to the general patterns of spoken/written register variation documented in this chapter: oral poetry. According to Andrzejewski and Lewis (1964, p. 45), a Somali poet can spend days working on a single poem. Somali oral poetry is governed by strict rules of alliteration so that every hemistich must include at least one content word beginning with the chosen sound (i.e., a consonant or vowel). Furthermore, there is a strong preference to avoid repetitions of words. To meet these demands, Somali poets use numerous archaic terms and create new words (Andrzejewski & Lewis, 1964, p. 43). As a result, the best Somali poems can have greater lexical diversity than informational written registers.

For example, in two of the famous classical poems composed by Maxamed Cabdille Xasan, the type-token ratio is between 67 and 69 percent, and the frequency of once-occurring words is 59 to 60 per 100 words of text in the first 500 words. Thus, in a poem of 500 words, there would be approximately 350 different words used, and 295 of those

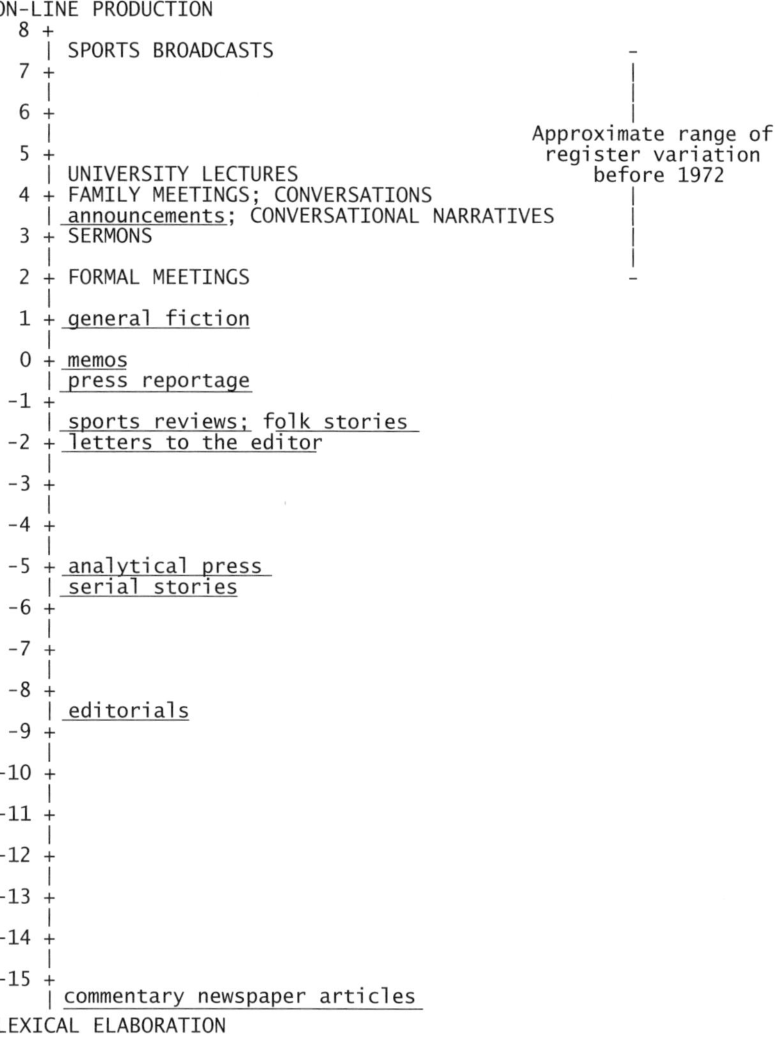

Figure 5.8. Expansion in the range of register variation in Somali, following the addition of written registers in 1972. Somali Dimension 2: 'Lexical Elaboration'.

words would occur only once. In contrast, institutional editorials have an average type-token ratio of 59 percent and an average of 46 once-occurring words per 100 words of text (in the first 500 words). Thus, oral poetry represents a specialized spoken register that exhibits greater lexical elaboration than the most complex written registers.

The case of oral poetry in Somali shows that the production difference between the spoken and written modes documented in this chapter is not an absolute one. That is, a few speakers are specially gifted and able to mentally compose dense, lexically elaborated texts, relying on memory without the aid of writing. Such texts go through multiple rounds of planning, revision, and editing, similar to the process of careful production described previously for written registers. In this case, the process of careful production and revision relies heavily on an exceptional memory – the entire text is planned, revised, and edited in a period of weeks, relying on the powers of memory. The case of Somali oral poets shows that such feats are humanly possible.

However, these are truly exceptional spoken registers. The majority of speech, in any language, is not memorized and has not been mentally revised and edited. Rather, speech is normally produced spontaneously in real-time (even if it has been preplanned, as in the case of university lectures). The study of such spontaneous spoken registers, carried out from several perspectives, has shown repeatedly that spoken registers differ from written registers in that they do not provide the possibility of extreme lexical diversity or the dense use of complex noun-phrase constructions. Rather, such linguistic styles require extensive planning, revision, and editing – processes that are normally possible only in writing.

This does not represent an absolute or necessary difference between speech and writing. Rather, authors can exploit the written mode to produce texts that are similar to the typical linguistic styles of speech. However, the converse is not true – that is, speakers are not normally able to revise and edit their texts because they are constrained by real-time production circumstances. As a result, some written registers have evolved to exploit styles of linguistic expression – with extreme lexical diversity and a dense use of complex noun-phrase structures – that are not normally feasible in the spoken mode. Thus, there are genuine linguistic consequences of literacy; however, the consequences have to do with the linguistic potential of the two modes rather than the necessary linguistic characteristics of them. In particular, this chapter has shown that language production in the written mode enables styles of linguistic expression not normally attested in speech, even though writers often choose not to exploit that linguistic potential.

References

Andrzejewski, B. W., & Lewis, I. M. (1964). *Somali poetry: An introduction.* Oxford: Oxford University Press.

Beaman, K. (1984). Coordination and subordination revisited: Syntactic complexity in spoken and written narrative discourse. In D. Tannen (Ed.), *Spoken and written language: Exploring orality and literacy* (pp. 45–80). Norwood, NJ: Ablex Publishing.

Biber, D. (1986). Spoken and written textual dimensions in English: Resolving the contradictory findings. *Language, 62*, 384–414.

Biber, D. (1988). *Variation across speech and writing.* Cambridge: Cambridge University Press.

Biber, D. (1992). On the complexity of discourse complexity: A multidimensional analysis. *Discourse Processes, 15*, 133–163. Reprinted in S. Conrad & D. Biber (Eds.) (2001, pp. 215–240).

Biber, D. (1995). *Dimensions of register variation: A cross-linguistic comparison.* Cambridge: Cambridge University Press.

Biber, D. (2003). Compressed noun phrase structures in newspaper discourse: The competing demands of popularization vs. economy. In J. Aitchison & D. Lewis (Eds.), *New media discourse.* Routledge.

Biber, D. (2006). *University language: A corpus-based study of spoken and written registers.* Amsterdam: John Benjamins Publishing.

Biber, D., & Clark, V. (2002). Historical shifts in modification patterns with complex noun phrase structures: How long can you go without a verb? In T. Fanego, M. J. López-Couso, & J. Pérez-Guerra (Eds.), *English historical syntax and morphology* (pp. 43–66). Amsterdam: John Benjamins Publishing.

Biber, D., Conrad, S., & Reppen, R. (1998). *Corpus linguistics: Exploring language structure and use.* Cambridge: Cambridge University Press.

Biber, D., Davies, M., Jones, J. K., & Tracy-Ventura, N. (2006). Spoken and written register variation in Spanish: A multi-dimensional analysis. *Corpora*, 1.7–38.

Biber, D., & Finegan, E. (1989). Drift and the evolution of English style: A history of three genres. *Language, 65*, 487–517.

Biber, D., & Finegan, E. (Eds.). (1994). *Sociolinguistic perspectives on register.* Oxford: Oxford University Press.

Biber, D., & Finegan, E. (1997). Diachronic relations among speech-based and written registers in English. In T. Nevalainen & L. Kahlas-Tarkka (Eds.), *To explain the present: Studies in changing English in honor of Matti Rissanen* (pp. 253–276). Helsinki: Societe Neophilologique. Reprinted in S. Conrad & D. Biber (Eds.) (2001, pp. 66–83).

Biber, D., & Hared, M. (1992). Dimensions of register variation in Somali. *Language Variation and Change, 4*, 41–75.

Biber, D., Johansson, S., Leech, G., Conrad, S., & Finnegan, E. (1999). *Longman grammar of spoken and written English*. London: Longman.

Bloch, M. (1993). The uses of schooling and literacy in a Zafimaniry village. In B. V. Street (Ed.), *Cross-cultural approaches to literacy* (pp. 87–109). Cambridge: Cambridge University Press.

Chafe, W. (1982). Integration and involvement in speaking, writing, and oral literature. In D. Tannen (Ed.), *Spoken and written language: Exploring orality and literacy* (pp. 35–54). Norwood, NJ: Ablex Publishing Co.

Chafe, W. L., & Danielewicz, J. (1986). Properties of spoken and written language. In R. Horowitz & S. J. Samuels (Eds.), *Comprehending oral and written language* (pp. 82–113). New York: Academic Press.

Conrad, S., & Biber, D. (Eds.). (2001). *Variation in English: Multi-dimensional studies*. London: Longman.

Halverson, J. (1991). Olson on literacy. *Language in Society*, 20, 619–640.

Hornberger, N. H. (1994). Continua of biliteracy. In B. M. Ferdman, R.-M. Weber, & A. G. Ramirez (Eds.), *Literacy across languages and cultures* (pp. 103–139). Albany: State University of New York Press.

Kim, Y., & Biber, D. (1994). A corpus-based analysis of register variation in Korean. In D. Biber & E. Finegan (Eds.), *Sociolinguistic perspectives on register* (pp. 157–181). Oxford: Oxford University Press.

McEnery, T., Xiao, R., & Tono, Y. (2006). *Corpus-based language studies*. London: Routledge.

O'Donnell, R. C. (1974). Syntactic differences between speech and writing. *American Speech*, 49, 102–110.

Olson, D. (1977). From utterance to text: The bias of language in speech and writing. *Harvard Educational Review*, 47 (3), 257–281.

Tannen, D. (1982). The oral/literate continuum in discourse. In D. Tannen (Ed.), *Spoken and written language: Exploring orality and literacy* (pp. 1–16). Norwood, NJ: Ablex Publishing.

CHAPTER 6

Becoming a Literate Language User

Oral and Written Text Construction across Adolescence[1]

Ruth A. Berman and Dorit Ravid

Introduction

This chapter considers how the language of literacy is acquired in the school years, taking into account lexical items, syntactic constructions, and entire texts. Its focus is on "linguistic literacy" (Ravid & Tolchinsky, 2002), in the sense of ready and informed access to an encyclopedic range of linguistic varieties (Langacker, 1991), ranging across different modalities (e.g., speech and writing), discourse genres (e.g., narrative and non-narrative, research and journalism), registers of use from literary or formal to everyday colloquial, and communicative functions (e.g., referential, interactive, entertaining).

Within this broad spectrum, we view written language as the core of literate language use, taking as a point of departure Olson's view of literacy as "a set of social practices that exploit the affordances of writing for particular ends" (2006b, p. 177). True, command of both spoken as well as written language and the ability to move skillfully and flexibly between the two are hallmarks of linguistic literacy. Yet the written mode of expression occupies a privileged cognitive position for maturely literate individuals. As Chafe (1994) points out, writing represents a "special mode of consciousness," one that is realized through Slobin's (2003) "thinking for writing." This involves the ability to control and shape the flow of information in discourse through linguistic means, while viewing the text as a whole (Strömqvist, Nordqvist, & Wengelin, 2004). Consequently, in constructing a piece of written language, what Chafe terms the "roving eye of consciousness" imposes cognitive demands on memory, executive functions, and top-down processing that are not readily met before adolescence (Steinberg, 2005). Current psycholinguistic studies of language development beyond early childhood reflect important changes in morphosyntax, lexicon, and discourse (Berman, 2004a, 2007; Berman & Nir-Sagiv, 2007; Ravid, 2006a). We suggest that these could not have been achieved without the platform of written language.

Olson's (1994) insight into the different strengths of speech and writing is particularly relevant in this connection. He pointed out that spoken language has expressive powers and illocutionary force that excel in conveying the sender's communicative intent to the addressee, whereas writing (and reading) fosters explicit thought about language. A key motivation of this chapter is to provide developmental evidence for the prediction deriving from Olson's model: that reflection on language is enabled by gaining command of written language and that, once learned, written language, in fact, takes over as a model for thinking about language in general. To this end, we move beyond writing as a notational system (i.e., Olson's "script-as-model") to the domain of text construction, examining written language as a special style of discourse in later language development (Berman, 2008).

Our narrative revolves around three orthogonal motifs. First, it deals with text *production* – hence, with speaking and writing rather than listening and reading. Concern is with authentic texts constructed by nonexpert, ordinary language users rather than with edited texts produced by specialist writers, journalists, translators, and so forth. In developmental perspective, the texts that school-goers construct provide optimal hunting grounds for unveiling their linguistic abilities, in a period when command of written language is opening up new avenues to linguistic knowledge (Jisa, 2004a; Ong, 2002; Ravid & Zilberbuch, 2003a).

Second, we examine the "language of literacy" as reflected in different types of texts constructed by speaker-writers from middle childhood across adolescence. That is, our concern is with *later, school-age language*, as manifesting three major developments: an extended repertoire of linguistic items, categories, and constructions; new pathways for integrating formerly unrelated elements and systems into complex linguistic schemata and syntactic architectures; and more efficient and explicit modes for representing and thinking about language. Current research shows that in this period, language use diverges markedly from what has been observed for young children (Berman, 2004b, 2007; Nippold, 1998), although not yet reaching the level of educated adult usage (Jisa, 2004a,b; Ravid & Zilberbuch, 2003b). For example, derivational morphology plays an increasingly important role at the interface between vocabulary and syntax (Carlisle, 2000; Ravid, 2004a); vocabulary is extended to allow for greater lexical diversity and semantically more specific encoding of concepts (Nippold, 2002; Seroussi, 2004; Strömqvist et al., 2002); and syntax relies increasingly on more marked, less frequent constructions such as passive voice, center-embedded clauses, and nonfinite subordination (Berman & Nir-Sagiv, 2007, 2008; Friedman & Novogrotsky, 2004; Ravid & Saban, 2008; Scott, 2004). These developments in school-age language knowledge go hand in hand with increased command of metalinguistic abilities and access to higher-order, nonliteral language (Ashkenazi & Ravid, 1998; Karmiloff-Smith, 1986; Nippold & Taylor, 2002; Tolchinsky, 2004).

A third motif is the inherent *interface of modality and genre*, in the present context – of speech versus writing and narratives versus expository discussions. Here, we aim to show that broadly speaking, modality affects the *how* and genre the *what* of text construction: modality will be more marked as a special style of communication in terms of *process* and genre as a special discourse style in terms of *product*. We hope to demonstrate how the modality/genre interface shapes the language of text construction by focusing on local linguistic expression in lexicon and grammar, including both clause-internal and clause-linking syntax.[2]

The basic methodology presented here for a range of studies in different languages elicited four text types (i.e., written and spoken, narrative and expository) from the same participants across different age groups: schoolchildren aged nine and ten and twelve and thirteen; sixteen- and seventeen-year-old high school students; and graduate-level university students. In an initial study (henceforth, Project I), participants were asked to tell and write a story and also to give a talk and write a composition about violence in schools (Berman, 2003; Berman & Ravid, 1999, for Hebrew;

Gayraud, 2000, for French). In a subsequent cross-linguistic project (Project II), other participants in the same age groups were shown a short video clip depicting scenes of (unresolved) interpersonal conflict in a school setting and were then asked to tell a story and write a story and to give a talk or write a composition discussing the topic of interpersonal conflict or of "problems between people" (Berman, 2005a; Berman & Verhoeven, 2002a).[3] This design allowed us to examine the modality/genre interface across carefully controlled conditions, and it has been extended with minor modifications to a range of populations in Hebrew.[4] Because our motivations were research-oriented rather than primarily teaching goals (Macbeth, 2006), participants were not given explicit instructions on how to structure their texts or what kind of language to use.

We present major findings on developing text construction from middle childhood across adolescence that have emerged from studies of the two authors with their students and associates in the past decade – with details from English and Hebrew supplemented by data from other languages. The issue is considered from two interlocking perspectives: (1) the language used in oral and written texts produced in personal-experience narratives and expository discussions; and (2) the special nature of written language use in these two genres.

The Language of Oral and Written Text Construction

As a point of departure, we take a key finding of our study of information density in spoken and written narratives produced by four age groups of school and university students in English and Hebrew (Ravid & Berman, 2006). Across the population, irrespective of age and language, the written texts contained 90 percent of novel, referentially informative material. In contrast, the spoken texts consisted in equal parts (i.e., 50 percent each) of novel information and ancillary, procedural or noninformative material – the latter in the form of reiterations, repetitions, repairs, and other disfluencies as well as pragmatic discourse markers. We concluded that what makes written language more informatively dense can be attributed, in part, at least, to the complex linguistic usage that it affords. The section that follows charts the units – lexical, syntactic, and discursive – that we analyzed in assessing discourse-embedded linguistic complexity.

Consider, first, the factor of *unit size* in monologic text construction. Linguists have largely neglected this apparently superficial facet of discourse performance as irrelevant to more abstract knowledge or linguistic competence. However, from a psycholinguistic, usage-based perspective (Bybee, 2006), surface phenomena are often indicative of underlying systematicity. For example, language acquisition research considers mean length of utterance (MLU) as a measure of early grammatical development in different languages (Brown, 1973; Dromi & Berman, 1982). In education, Loban's (1976) study of oral and written language of English-speaking children from kindergarten through high school showed that MLUs and mean length of sentences "increased slowly but steadily throughout the school years" (Scott, 2004, p. 111). For current purposes, we consider units ranging from the entire text via syntactic constructions between and within clauses to words and morphemes.

Text length is measured in our studies by two units: number of words and number of clauses. The *word* – our basic lexical unit – is a fundamental and intuitively obvious building block of language, yet it defies simple definition and demarcation – particularly across different developmental phases and typologically different languages (Anderson, 1985; Strömqvist et al., 2002). For example, what constitutes a "word" is not necessarily the same in writing and in speech (Hebrew even has a special word *teva* 'box' for a written word). Consider the problem of English contracted forms like *I've* and *won't*; or compounds that are written as single words in Dutch and German but not necessarily in English (cf. *ashtray*, *high-school*, *apple juice*); or the fact that in Hebrew, several grammatical items that correspond to words in European languages – like those meaning *the, that, in* – are written as part of the next word (Ravid, 2005). Accordingly, we specified 'a word' as any element separated by spaces in our transcription of both spoken and written materials in different languages.

Our basic unit of syntax is the *clause*, defined as "any unit that contains a unified predicate expressing a single situation" (Berman & Slobin, 1994, p. 660). The clause is similar to the simple sentence of traditional grammar, it is semantically and syntactically readily identifiable, and it has served as a robust unit of analysis for both oral and written narrative and expository texts across a wide range of languages (Berman & Verhoeven, 2002b). Text size in words and clauses is illustrated in (1) and (2) from the following oral narratives of junior-high students in English and Hebrew, respectively, numbered by clauses.

(1) Oral Narrative of Seventh-Grade Girl [eJo3fns]: 20 clauses, 143 words[5]

1. *Um this one time I can remember*
2. *I think*
3. *it was like maybe two or three weeks ago*
4. *we were me and my sister were moving our room around*
5. *and um we have these thing these things*
6. *that are like these crate things*
7. *and we have our stuff in it*
8. *and she was helping me move mine*
9. *and I told her*
10. *not to break it*
11. *and we started to put it down*
12. *and she broke it*
13. *and it fell apart*
14. *and then I got mad at her*
15. *and I told her*
16. *she had to fix it*
17. *but she couldn't fix it good*
18. *so I was still mad at her*
19. *and then and then I finally put it back on*
20. *so it was ended*

(2) Oral Narrative of Seventh-Grade Hebrew-Speaking Boy [hJo4mns]: 13 clauses, 88 words[6]

1. *tov, eh kodem~kol eh stam eh hayiti be^ [/] be^ eyze kita daled, gimel mashu*
2. *hayiti imm xaver sheli*
3. *az keilu ravnu imm eyze exad*
4. *ve^ ravnu ito*
5. *az asinu keilu alav eh xerem*
6. *ve^ az asinu*
7. *ve^ kol ha^ kita hayta alav xerem ve^ ze*
8. *ve^ hayom keilu axshav loh hayom keilu, lifney kama zman lifney <kama sha> [//] shana ulay kaxa hitxalnu lahakir oto*
9. *liyot xaverim shelo ve^ ze*
10. *amarnu*
11. *ma shave*
12. *ma'asher she^ niye be^ [/] be^ brogez ve^ ze*
13. *ma asinu be^ ze*

Two main trends emerged for overall text length in mean number of words and of clauses per text. Developmentally, there is a consistent age-related rise, in line with the increase in text length documented for the oral narratives produced by preschoolers, schoolchildren, and adults in five different languages (Berman & Slobin, 1994, p. 31). This emerged clearly in different studies, including the language-specific findings of Project I (Gayraud, 2000; Ravid, 2004b; Ravid & Levie, in press) and also across all seven languages and in all four text types – narrative and expository, spoken and written – in Project II (Berman & Verhoeven, 2002b, p. 23). Moreover, a major difference in mean text size was found between the junior-high and high-school students. These findings were replicated in numerous other studies in Hebrew and Arabic (see endnote 2). Second, cross-modally, in both Projects I and II, in both English and Hebrew, and in all four age groups, the oral texts were typically longer than their written counterparts and the narratives than the expository texts.

However, raw measures of text length are insufficient as criteria of text quality

(Berman & Nir-Sagiv, in press). Processing constraints may account for greater repetitiveness and more disfluencies – hence, greater length – in spoken texts (Ravid & Berman, 2006; Strömqvist et al., 2004), whereas factors of thematic content and global discourse structure may explain why narratives tend to be longer than expository texts (Berman & Katzenberger, 2004; Berman & Nir-Sagiv, 2007; Tolchinsky, Johanssen, & Zamora, 2002). Rather, what critically contributes to the quality of the language in monologic discourse is *linguistic richness*, which we define as lexical density and diversity combined with syntactic depth and complexity (Berman & Nir-Sagiv, 2007; Ravid, 2004b). To evaluate these facets of developing text construction, we typically analyze lexical and syntactic quality through two derived measures – number of elements per clause and proportion of items out of total words – with syntactic connectivity specified by how clauses are packaged together in larger units.

Our point of departure for measuring syntactic complexity is number of words per clause – that is, mean clause length – also an apparently superficial criterion. However, words are not simply strung together linearly across a clause but rather are packaged into the syntactic units termed *phrases*. For example, the written narrative of a Californian high-school boy starts with the clause: *The conflict between [sic] an ex-friend of mine started in my senior year of high school.* The fifteen words in this clause group into the subject-noun phrase *the conflict between an ex-friend of mine*, the verb phrase *started*, and the adverbial phrase *in my senior year of high school*, with the subject consisting of a noun phrase and a prepositional phrase and the adverbial phrase consisting of two prepositional phrases – each with a preposition followed by a noun phrase (*between* + *an ex-friend of mine*; *in* + *my senior year*; *of* + *high school*). This shows how clause length in words and, hence, syntactic density are a function of both number of phrases and number of words per phrase. It also demonstrates that syntactic complexity is inseparable from information or content density: this one clause provides information about two protagonists and the place, time, and circumstances of the events that are about to unfold.

Developmentally, our findings for mean clause length are consistent with those for text size: in different languages and text types, number of words per clause rises as a function of age and schooling, most markedly in the two older age groups. This trend, too, is mediated by the factors of genre and modality but in the opposite direction: clauses in written texts – most markedly in written expository texts – are typically longer than in narratives, and they are shortest in oral narratives. This is in line with our general finding that written language and expository discourse combine to create a favored habitat for rich and complex use of language. Moreover, in both English and Hebrew, this pattern is significant mainly from high-school age, indicative of a general spurt in text-embedded linguistic complexity from adolescence up (Berman & Nir-Sagiv, 2007; Ravid & Levie, in press; Ravid & Zilberbuch, 2003b). Again, these trends are robust across different languages, populations, and methods of elicitation.

To illustrate, Figure 6.1 depicts mean clause length for different age groups and levels of schooling in four different types of texts, for Hebrew Project I data.

Figure 6.1 indicates that the distinction between written and spoken language is more marked in expository texts than in narratives. It also illustrates a typical range for mean clause length for different age groups and levels of schooling. Taken together, our findings clearly indicate that mean clause length constitutes a reliable developmental yardstick for one facet of linguistic complexity in text construction across the school years.

We move now to lexical measures, again starting with a seemingly surface criterion, *word length*. The factor of word length, measured by number of syllables, is widely used in distributionally oriented, corpus linguistics research (Riedemann, 1996; Wimmer & Altmann, 1996), and it has proved

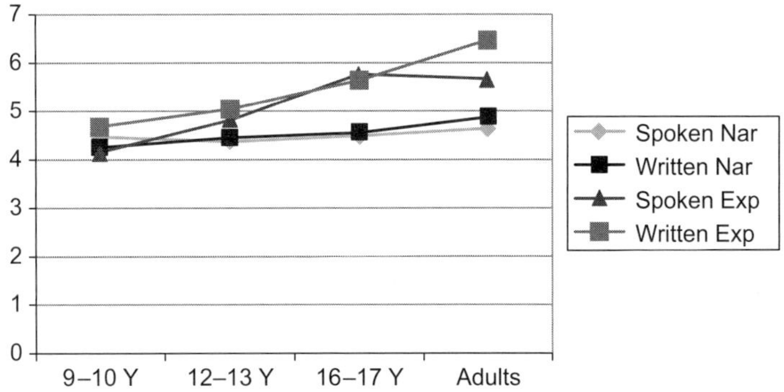

Figure 6.1. Mean number of words per clause by age and text type.

to be developmentally diagnostic of literacy levels when measured by number of letters per word in written language (Malvern, Richards, Chipere, & Durán, 2004). For present purposes, we defined word length in syllables to accommodate both written and spoken usage, as well as languages with different orthographies. Word length seems a particularly appropriate measure for a language with linearly analytical morphology like English, where longer words are not only rarer and more sophisticated but also structurally more complex in terms of their derivational morphology (e.g., Germanic *childishness*, *unforgiving*; Latinate *misinterpretation*, *comprehensible*). It is interesting that this appears to be the case for Hebrew, too, although it is a language with a richly synthetic morphology (Nir-Sagiv, 2005; Ravid, 2006b).

As another illustration, Figure 6.2 shows the development of word length measured by number of words of four or more syllables out of total words in the English sample of Project II.

Figure 6.2 shows clear developmental patterns across the variables of age, modality, and genre. Polysyllabic words are rare in the two younger groups across text types; they occur mainly from high school up and significantly more in the texts of adults. These patterns highlight a key motif of our entire enterprise: *the interface of modality and genre across development*. They reveal spoken narratives and written expository texts as two extremes, with written narratives and spoken expository texts clustering together between them. Thus, long words are rare in spoken narratives even of adults, and they are most common in written

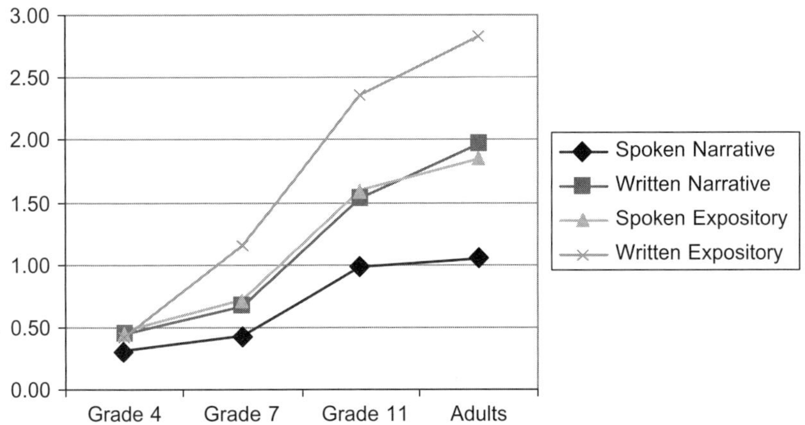

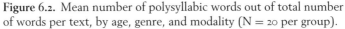

Figure 6.2. Mean number of polysyllabic words out of total number of words per text, by age, genre, and modality (N = 20 per group).

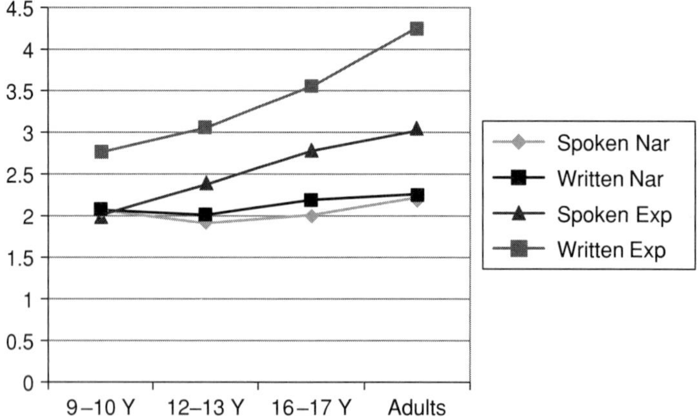

Figure 6.3. Mean number of content words per clause.

expository texts, especially from high school up.

The notion of *lexical density* focuses on open-class lexical items or so-called content words (i.e., nouns, verbs, adjectives). These carry the burden of the referential information of any piece of discourse, and they are indispensable sites for constructing the phrases that comprise syntactic complexity (Ravid, 2004b). As such, the proportion of content words provides a more fine-tuned criterion of text-embedded linguistic complexity than surface length. In fact, two derived measures of lexical density, both as proportion of content words out of total words per text and number of content words per clause, yield consistent patterns across our database.

Figure 6.3 presents typical figures for age- and text-type patterns of lexical density, based on Hebrew Project I.

Across projects, and in both English and Hebrew, texts produced by older participants typically contain a higher proportion of content words than those of the younger age groups. In text type, expository texts have higher lexical density than the narratives produced by the same subjects across age groups, and written texts have higher density on average than their spoken counterparts (Bar-Ilan & Berman, 2007; Nir- Sagiv, Bar-Ilan, & Berman, 2008 ; Ravid, 2004b, 2006a). These trends confirm earlier findings for the higher lexical density of written compared with spoken language, both in a comparable Swedish sample (Strömqvist et al., 2002) and in other unrelated studies (Halliday, 1985; Ure, 1971). Overall, lexical density thus reveals similar trends across age groups, modality, and genre to what was shown by the more coarse-grained measures of mean clause and word length. Furthermore, in lexical density, the expository genre shows an age-related rise, whereas narratives manifest the same level of lexical density across speech and writing. This suggests that once students reach high school, expository discourse constitutes a more suitable means than narratives for evaluating lexical and syntactic abilities.

Another accepted measure of lexical development is that of *lexical diversity*. Thus, when measured by ratio of different word forms to total number of word tokens in a text, the entire database of Project II indicated a significant age-related increase in lexical diversity in different languages, most markedly between junior high and high school and in the expository genre (Berman & Verhoeven, 2002b, pp. 28–31). Here, we do not pursue the topic of lexical diversity in the accepted sense of "type-token ratio" because even the highly sophisticated VOC-D procedure for calculating Voc(abulary) D(ensity) (Malvern et al., 2004) relates to word types as different word *forms* rather than different lexemes or lemmas (e.g., the English *walk*, *walks*, *walked*, and *walking* are four word forms, whereas *walk(s)* as a verb and *walk(s)* yield two different lexemes). The latter criterion appears more relevant for cross-linguistic comparisons of both spoken and written usage, particularly in languages with a rich morphology like Hebrew and when evaluating text-embedded vocabulary use across adolescence and into adulthood.

We found it more rewarding to analyze each class of content words in a *context-sensitive*, functional perspective that captures changes in the lexicon across later language development and that ensures ecological validity within each word class in a given language. One such analysis involves a "*noun scale*" of semantic-pragmatic abstractness and categoriality. Originally devised as a ten-point scale for Hebrew (Ravid, 2006b), this was applied to English by a condensed, similarly motivated four-point scale (Nir-Sagiv, Bar-Ilan, & Berman, 2008; Berman & Nir-Sagiv, 2007). At the lower end are (1) concrete objects and specific people (e.g., *John, a ball, flowers*); and (2) categorical nouns, roles and locations, and generic nouns (e.g., *a / every teacher, the city, people*); whereas the two higher levels include (3) nonabstract, high-register, or rare nouns (e.g., *rival, cult*); abstract but common terms like *fight* and *war*; and metaphorical extensions of concrete terms like *path to success, river of time*; and (4) nouns that are nonimageable, abstract, and low frequency (e.g., *relationship, lack, existence*).

Differences between level of noun abstractness as a function of age and level of literacy are illustrated by the following oral expository texts of three girls in grade school, junior high, and high school in (3), (4), and (5), respectively. All nouns are boldfaced and those ranked as more abstract, at Level 3 or 4, are underlined.

(3) Oral Expository Text of Grade-School Girl [eG16fewd]
I do not think ***<u>fighting</u>*** *is good. You do not make* ***friends*** *that* ***way****. If you do not fight, you can have many many* ***friends****, but when you fight, you can hurt the* ***person's*** ***<u>feelings</u>*** *you are fighting with. You should always be nice and respectful to other* ***people****. And if you are not nice, you will end up not having any* ***friends****. That is why you should not fight.*

This quite typical expository text of a fourth-grade girl contains relatively few open-class items (i.e., twenty out of a total of seventy words) and only eight nouns in all, two of higher level semantics.

(4) Oral Expository Text of Junior High School Girl [eJ18fewd]
Some of the ***<u>conflicts</u>*** *are related. Just because* ***people*** *have known each other for a long* ***<u>time</u>****, and about my* ***<u>age</u>*** *like they start like they're getting new* ***friends*** *and someone may not like those* ***friends*** *and so some of those* ***fights*** *like.* ***<u>Fighting</u>*** *can be a lot about that and like new* ***<u>interests</u>*** *that they haven't realized that they had and you know you aren't interested in them. That's one of the big* ***<u>differences</u>*** *and just a lot of* ***stuff*** *like that.*

The seventh-grade text in (4) contains relatively few open-class items (i.e., twenty-one out of eighty-two), but six of its ten nouns are semantically more abstract. The noun lexicon of the excerpt from an eleventh-grade text, in contrast, consists almost entirely of morphologically derived and semantically abstract, largely Latinate terms (Bar-Ilan & Berman, 2007).

(5) First Part of Oral Expository Text of High School Girl [eH05few]
I just think that ***<u>conflict</u>*** *is just kind of a natural* ***<u>part</u>*** *of social* ***<u>interaction</u>*** *and that it often arises from* ***<u>misunderstandings</u>*** *or a* ***<u>lack</u>*** *of* ***<u>acceptance</u>*** *for* ***<u>differences</u>*** *between* ***people****. And how I personally have very low* ***<u>tolerance</u>*** *for other* ***people*** *you know creating a* ***<u>conflict</u>*** *with me because of a* ***<u>misunderstanding</u>*** *of me or because of some* ***<u>difference</u>*** *that I have. So I mean it's very often isn't a genuine* ***<u>conflict</u>****. Because it's just kind of like, I mean in my* ***<u>view</u>*** *I can only really relate to me personally. There are some other general* ***things*** *obviously in the* ***<u>world</u>*** *that go on. But I don't have enough* ***<u>experience</u>*** *with any of that* ***stuff****. But it's kind of like, if there looks*

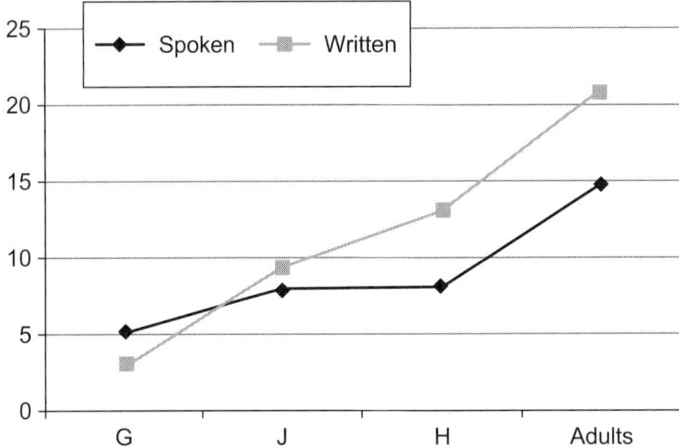

Figure 6.4. Percentage of derived abstract nouns by age and modality.

*like there's going to be a **conflict**, then I just end it before there's a **conflict**. And there doesn't need to be any sort of **relationship** really there.*

The texts in (3) to (5) differ markedly in nominalness in general and in the semantic level of the nouns they contain in particular. As can be expected, nominal abstractness increases as a function of age and level of literacy. Figure 6.4 illustrates the impact of modality on these patterns, by the relative number of abstract-derived nominals across later language development in the Hebrew database of Project II (Ravid, 2006a).

Noun abstractness, as a facet of text-embedded lexical sophistication, rises only gradually with age and schooling in spoken texts and shows a far steeper curve in writing. Again, markedly similar patterns are revealed for the two typologically distinct languages of English and Hebrew.

Number of *adjectives* per clause reveals similar trends as other facets of text-embedded lexical usage. There is an increase with age and schooling, more so in written than in spoken texts, more in expository than narrative texts, and specifically in the written expositories of eleventh-graders and adults. Because adjectives function primarily for noun modification, such an increase reflects richer and more informative text content. For example, an eleventh-grade girl writes in a narrative about a former friend, with adjectives underlined: *There was a scene of exaggerated jealousy which resulted in a verbal argument, a scathing argument, filled with reciprocal accusations and yelling.* Moreover, rich adjectival texture is typically grounded in complex nominal and syntactic structure because adjectives play a role in the construction of noun phrases, as discussed later. Another related facet of lexical density is revealed by the fact that the *category* (in this case, of adjectives) expands and diversifies along with an increase in usage of token members of the category. To date, relevant data on use of adjectives are available only for Hebrew. However, from what is known of vocabulary development across school age in general, similar patterns can be expected in English and other languages: an age-related increase, with more adjectives in written expository texts than elsewhere, in the shape of, for example, sophisticated – *iy* suffixed, denominal adjectives in Hebrew and Latinate-based denominatives, such as *industrial* and *cooperative*, in English.

The features of text-embedded lexical usage reviewed so far apply similarly across different languages. Other aspects of lexical structure and content are more language-specific. One such property is the Germanic-Latinate divide of English vocabulary, which emerged as a critical factor in characterizing the role of linguistic register in developing literacy (Bar-Ilan & Berman, 2007). A Hebrew-specific facet of semantic and structural lexical diversity is use of the seven morphological verb patterns in Hebrew, the *binyan* "conjugation" system of Semitic grammars expressing semantic and syntactic alternations such as voice (i.e., active, middle, passive), causativeness, and transitivity in general (Berman, 1993). With age, Hebrew speaker-writers use a greater variety of different verb patterns for a larger range of semantic and syntactic functions. This is reflected, *inter alia*, by a shift to a more patient-oriented use of intransitive-, middle-, and passive-voice constructions (Alfi-Shabtay, 1999; Berman, 2002b), although for language-specific reasons, Hebrew speaker-writers, like their Spanish counterparts, rely on passive-voice constructions far less than in subject-requiring languages such as Dutch, English, and French (Jisa et al., 2002; Tolchinsky & Rosado, 2005). Again, in all these cases, the relevant forms emerge most prominently in written expository texts, from adolescence up.

To round out this comparison of oral and written texts across different ages and level of schooling, we note two syntactic criteria devised in the framework of Project II: noun-phrase complexity and clause-linking connectivity. The internal structure and content of *noun phrases* provide a qualitative means of evaluating syntactic density. For example, the following relatively 'heavy' (i.e., long and structurally complex) noun phrases occur in the expository text written by a high-school boy, ranging from four to seven words in length, with head nouns underlined: *a result of insecurity, another source of conflict, many people in this world, close contact with someone unknown, their dominant status amongst a group, the other person's point of view, students who are unfamiliar with another student, the relationships in which they are involved*. These noun phrases are heavy in the sense that they contain several layers of embedding (e.g., nouns inside of prepositional phrases or relative clauses) as well as different types of modifying expressions: adjectives, postnominal prepositional phrases, and relative clauses. Multidimensional analyses – including abstractness of head nouns; length in words; and number, type, and depth of modifiers – reveal that in different languages, the proportion of complex noun phrases increases primarily in the written language and in expository texts as a function of age, most markedly from high school up (Ravid & Berman, in press; Ravid et al., 2002). These findings for syntactic complexity closely parallel the trends observed for text-embedded lexical development, indicating that the content lexicon provides an important underpinning for construction of syntax.

Regarding how clauses are packaged together in monologic discourse, we found clear qualitative differences between the two modalities. In written narratives, the majority of clauses inside a "clause package" (as defined in Berman & Nir-Sagiv, 2008; Nir-Sagiv, 2008), across age groups, and increasingly from high school up, are linked by conjunctions as semantically and syntactically conventional markers of different types of coordination and subordination. We take this to reflect development of the notion of 'sentence' as a viable unit of written language. In contrast, spoken texts make far greater use of segment-tagging "discourse markers" such as *and so, well, okay*, and *that's it* that are utterance-initial rather than syntactically motivated (Berman, 1996; Ravid & Berman, 2006). By and large, the texts produced in speech reveal looser connectivity and rely more on thematic and discursive rather than strict syntactic linking of clauses. For example, compared with their written counterparts, they contain higher proportions of direct speech (i.e., syntactically nonmarked complement clauses), juxtaposed main clauses without overt marking between them, and parenthetical asides commenting on what has just been said or is about to be reported. Such constructions are illustrated in the excerpt from a graduate student's oral narrative in (6), with clause boundaries marked by double square brackets.

> (6) *I threw . . . okay let me think of the story* [Parenthetical] . . .]] *I asked her*]] *to put the thumbtacks in her drawer*]] *although I must have a said it in a not so desirable tone*]] *and she shot back with*]] *"Don't tell me*]] *what to do"* [Direct Speech]. *So #*

we um # hmmm, God what was it?]] *We had a little bit of an argument about that*]] *and we . . . # something horrible, what did I say?* [Parenthetical]]] *Okay, so we had a little bit of an argument about that*]], *I didn't like the way* [Juxtaposed]]] *she said that to me*]].

A quantitative outcome of this looser clustering of clauses in spoken narratives is that more clauses tend to be combined together in a single package compared with their written counterparts (Berman & Nir-Sagiv, 2006). Such contrasts between spoken versus written language highlight the importance of supplementing quantitative measures with functionally motivated qualitative criteria.

Across a range of measures, the factor of modality thus has the effect of promoting tighter, more cohesive organization in written texts. Both as a cause and a result of processing constraints, spoken texts are more 'interactive' and more communicatively oriented than their written counterparts, even when they are monologic, and therefore lacking in turn-taking as the hallmark of conversational interaction. Moreover, in linguistic expression, the constraints of online versus offline processing mean that compared with speech, writing allows for greater lexical and syntactic complexity and diversity. As Olson notes, among such "affordances," "Writers draw on an enlarged vocabulary, a more formalized grammar, a more logically organized rhetorical structure" (2006a, p. 140).

However, these differences are always mediated by the factor of *genre* (in this case, narrative or expository discourse). Recall that we found the gap between spoken and written narratives to be less marked than between spoken and written expository discourse across development. We suggest that this is because in relating modality to genre, each genre imposes different demands on the speaker-writer. Constructing narratives is governed by an entrenched narrative schema that is internalized by early school age (Berman & Slobin, 1994; Hickmann, 2003). The major cognitive challenge in producing narratives lies in the domain of psychological interpretation, and this is age-dependent rather than modality-dependent (Ravid & Berman, 2006). In contrast, expository discourse demands that novel ideas be logically organized and elaborated into coherent segments. This is particularly difficult in speech, when texts are produced online, without the offline benefits of reflection and reconsideration provided by writing. Consequently, both the achievements and the challenges of becoming "a literate language user" are most markedly evident in the interface between the expository genre of discourse and the written mode of expression.

Written Language Use in Narrative and Expository Texts

In comparing oral and written language usage, our focus was largely on nominal elements of discourse. In considering the written style that students deploy in acquiring the language of literacy, we shift attention to the predicative components of discourse – mainly in the domains of tense, mood, and voice – where linguistic distinctiveness is more relevant to cross-genre than cross-modal considerations.

Studies in different languages demonstrate key differences in the temporal texture and organization of narrative compared with expository prose – differences to which even the youngest children in our sample were attentive (Berman & Katzenberger, 2004; Berman & Nir-Sagiv, 2004; Ragnarsdóttir et al., 2002; Reilly, Zamora, & McGivern, 2005). Narratives, by their very nature, are anchored in specific past events and these are typically expressed by past tense, which – in languages that mark grammatical aspect – may alternate across imperfective, progressive, and pluperfect aspect (Berman & Slobin, 1994). Expository discourse is typically atemporal, anchored in generalized propositions in the timeless present or in projections on future contingencies in irrealis mood (Kupersmitt, 2006).

In consequence, narratives employ primarily dynamic verbs, with more stative propositions and generalizations dedicated to the interpretive or evaluative elements of the story. By contrast, expository texts make wide use of existential and copular constructions, relying heavily on middle and passive voice to express a patient-oriented rather than agent-oriented perspective (Berman & Nir-Sagiv, 2004; Jisa & Viguié, 2005; Tolchinsky & Rosado, 2005). At the same time, increasingly from high school up, writers use more nominalized constructions in formulating their narrative predications (Berman & Katzenberger, 2004; Ravid & Cahana-Amitay, 2005). The temporal texture of texts also becomes increasingly diversified with age because writers rely on more marked and more mixed types of aspectual categories, including past-progressive and past-perfect in languages like English and Spanish (Kupersmitt, 2006).

We noted previously that from as early as grade-school age, written texts are typically informatively denser and syntactically more tightly packaged than their oral counterparts. To this we now add the fact that they typically deploy *high-register* and quite formal means of linguistic expression, deploying what Blank (2002) terms "book language," including, *inter alia*, reliance on "the literate lexicon" (Ravid, 2004a). The texts written by literate high school students are linguistically "marked" in the sense that they deploy less frequent, more sophisticated language in preference to more common everyday forms of expression. Examples include wider use of passive and not only active voice; heavily complex noun phrases; and morphologically derived, low-frequency, high-register lexical items (in English – often Latinate).

Another major development, part of a more general, cognitively anchored shift around adolescence (Paus, 2005; Steinberg, 2005) that we characterize as a move "from dichotomy to divergence," is the ability to move beyond rigidly genre-typical forms of expression in constructing monologic texts. For example, from high school up but not before, writers introduce timeless, "story-external" generalizations into their narratives and they may make reference to specific, past-tense events in their expository texts (Berman & Nir-Sagiv, 2004, 2007; Ravid & Berman, 2006).

High school students are also able to use language to express more cognitively distanced, knowledge-based attitudes to hypothetical contingencies, analogous to Bruner's "subjunctivizing transformations . . . lexical and grammatical usages that highlight subjective states, attenuating circumstances, alternative possibilities" (1990, p. 53). This is reflected in the use of *modal expressions* (e.g., English *can, be able to*) in evaluating whether a given proposition or state of affairs is necessary, possible, or likely. This particular linguistic system provides an interesting meeting ground between cognition, semantics, lexicon, and syntax in developing written text construction. A series of studies in different languages (Kupersmitt, 2006; Reilly, Jisa, & Berman, 2002; Reilly et al., 2005) reveals that in this connection, too, the impact of genre is critical. Across languages, such expressions were far more common in expository texts as a genre that is anchored in timeless generalizations about current states of affairs that are fleshed out and elaborated by commentary about desirable or possible future contingencies. This is illustrated in the opening paragraph of the essay of a Californian woman graduate student asked to discuss the topic of interpersonal conflict. Elements in (7) that express modal modifications of a proposition are underlined and the semantics of the modality are indicated in small caps.

> (7) *Conflict is a matter that* <u>*I believe*</u> {BELIEF} <u>*needs to be handled*</u> {NECESSITY / OBLIGATORINESS} *in a case by case manner. The manner in which people* <u>*decide to*</u> {INTENTION} *handle conflict* <u>*needs to be*</u> {NECESSITY/OBLIG} *thoughtfully* <u>*considered*</u>*, as the person or people with whom the conflict is with [sic] and the reasons for the conflict* <u>*will warrant*</u> {DESIRABILITY} *a different approach for different instances. Sometimes conflict* <u>*will need to be*</u> {NECESSITY/OBLIG} <u>*addressed*</u> *directly since it* <u>*can harm*</u> {POSSIBILITY} *an individual's well-being. It* <u>*may cause*</u> {POSSIBILITY} *damage emotionally and/or*

physically. In this case I believe {BELIEF} *that the problem must be* {NECESSITY} *addressed. In other cases I believe* {BELIEF} *that it may be worked out* {POSSIBILITY} *within oneself. In this case I only advise it* {DESIRABILITY}. *If addressing* {CONDITION} *the conflict will cause* {LIKELIHOOD/PREDICTION} *additional problems and* {PREDICTION+GAP} *worsen the situation. Along these lines, addressing some conflicts may put* {POSSIBILITY} *an individual in danger and should simply be handled* {ADVISABILITY} *by shrugging it off and/or walking away.*

Nearly every clause in this excerpt modifies the neutral referential content it contains by expressing some kind of propositional attitude, relating to possible states of affairs, the circumstances attendant on them, the consequences that they might incur, and the author's thoughts and feelings about the decisions or actions that should be taken with respect to these contingencies. In structure, these expressions demonstrate the interaction between lexicon and syntax: in English, modal auxiliaries quite typically occur with passive-voice constructions – for example, *needs to be considered, must be addressed, may be worked out,* and *should be handled.* This excerpt also reflects what was found across languages and age groups for the lexicon–syntax interface and for inter-genre distinctiveness: in expository texts, such expressions typically co-occur with impersonal expletive pronouns (e.g., *it*) in a language like English or in subjectless impersonal constructions in Hebrew and Spanish; in narratives, they tend to be "agent-oriented," relating to the protagonist's ability, needs, or desires rather than to the proposition as a whole.

This domain also revealed a clear *developmental shift* across different languages, again most marked from high school up. Nine- to twelve-year-olds – irrespective of whether they were writing in English, French, or Hebrew – typically relied largely on *deontic* types of modal expressions, which refer to prohibitions or prescriptions. In contrast, from adolescence up, writers shifted largely to *epistemic* modalities, relating to possible or probable future contingencies. These differences are clearly shown in the essays of two nine-year-olds – a girl in (8a) and a boy in (8b) – compared with those of eleventh-graders in (9).

(8a) *I think people should discuss their problems or maybe even ask a grownup or someone older than yourself. And people really should get along I think people should treat everyone the same.*

(8b) *I think people should stop using their hand and feet and start using their words and I think people should think before they act, and people should help people if in need instead of ignoring them.*

These fourth-graders, a girl (8a) and a boy (8b), both use the deontic modal *should* (in the sense of advising what is desirable, what people "ought to" do) across their texts. They express prescriptively normative, socially dictated attitudes to the topic of "problems between people." Other deontic devices used by fourth-grade children in different languages in the sample express the prohibitive sense of "shouldn't" or give voice to generalized judgmental evaluations – for example, that "problems are bad" or "fighting is not good" (as in example [3]).

In marked contrast, as illustrated in the adult excerpt in (7), older writers rely mainly on cognitively motivated *epistemic* modals to relate to possible or probable contingencies arising out of interpersonal conflict. This is shown in the underlined elements in the excerpts from eleventh-grade essays in (9): the first (9a) from a boy who starts by explaining why "high school is a focal point of conflict," and the second (9b) from a girl who illustrates her discussion by two specific episodes from her personal experience (three dots represent passages not presented here).

(9a) *Coming from a sheltered environment with the close supervision and intervention of parents and teachers, students are thrust into realization of the so called "real world," where you must now make choices and resolve problems on your own. While you are never really on your own, this new freedom can give the overwhelming feeling of distancing yourself from your parents' control. Students are exposed to many new people and begin to form social cliques or groups. These groups not only follow racial and ethnic lines but also the class bracket that they are placed in such as advanced or remedial. This can have an impact on people because of the exposure or lack of it or jealousy and envy.*

(9b) *Conflict is opposing ideas or stances between two or more people.*

In many ways it is a necessary part of life. On the other hand it can cause disruption and chaos in the relationships of those involved. When people have a difference of opinion, a conflict is usually the result.

This is a good way for those differences to be put aside. For example, I recently started swimming under a new coach . . .

In that way conflict can be a good thing. The results were better than the situation that were achieved beforehand. In other cases, conflict can ruin a friendship. My friend was very close friends . . . This is a situation in which conflict was a bad thing. If the conflict cannot be resolved, then the relationship will suffer . . . In my case I avoid conflict at all costs, sometimes to the point where I void my own opinion in order to prevent a conflict. On the one hand, I very seldom argue with people, on the other hand, my ideas may go unheard . . .

There is a happy medium somewhere, though. Hopefully someday I will realize when a conflict is necessary and use it intelligently, not as a fight but as a discussion to solve a common problem.

Here, sixteen- and seventeen-year-old adolescents express their ideas from abstractly mentalistic, largely individual perspectives, couching their thoughts in epistemic terms that refer to eventualities that can, may, or will arise under given circumstances. They may use many of the same surface forms of language as younger children: in English, by means of the special grammaticized category of modal auxiliaries (e.g., *can, could, may, might, should, will*); in Hebrew or Spanish, by rather different types of constructions. However, even 'basic' modals expand semantically to acquire a range of different senses, so that *can* refers not only to ability but also to possibility and *must* not only to obligation but also to inference.

The essays of older, more literate writers thus reflect semantically more complex use of modal expressions. They also reveal different *attitudes* to the topic under discussion, giving voice to a more individual and personalized set of values than the socially normative prescriptions of children. This is in line with other studies from our project (e.g., Berman, 2005b; Ravid, 2006a; Ravid & Cahana-Amitay, 2005; Tolchinsky et al., 2002) that reflect age-related changes not only in the linguistic structure but also in the thematic content and pragmatic perspectives of the language used by maturely literate although nonexpert writers in expressing their ideas.

Conclusion

The three guiding motifs of this chapter – text production, later language development, and the modality/genre interface – converge to shed light on what is involved in becoming "a literate language user." It entails the ability to use the linguistic repertoire of one's native language in ways that meet the needs of varied communicative contexts in different types of text. Each of the four text types we elicited from the same participants represents a specific communicative setting, from more intimate and conversation-like personal narratives produced in speech to more distanced and formal discussion of an abstract topic produced in writing. Indeed, results of the manifold studies in the projects delineated herein yield a remarkably consistent hierarchy – as depicted in Figure 6.5 – in the language used across the four text types we examined: in lexical density and diversity; in abstractness and richness of the content vocabulary; in level of formality and linguistic register; and in syntactic complexity within and across clauses.

The hierarchy depicted in Figure 6.5 reflects a consistent trend in the linguistic patterning of texts produced by nonexpert

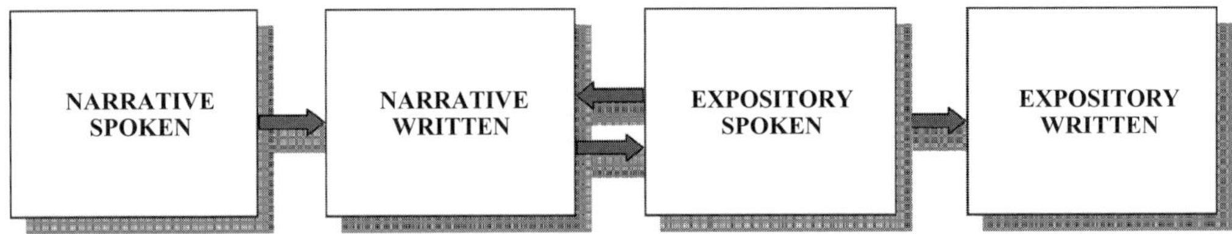

Figure 6.5. Linguistic expression at the interface of modality and genre.

speaker-writers of different languages from age nine across adolescence and into adulthood in meeting the different pragmatic functions involved in telling or writing a story about a personal experience as compared to giving a talk or writing an essay on an abstract topic.

Throughout the projects, the most distinct differences emerged between oral narratives and written expository texts as two extremes in use of complex language along a continuum that, in principle, could be extended in both directions: oral narratives to interactive conversation and written essays to literary composition or research articles. In the two extremes on this hierarchy, the factors of modality and genre operate in tandem to produce internally consistent linguistic usage. In contrast, the two "intermediate" text types – written narratives and spoken expository texts – are more mixed, revealing both the combined impact and the distinct contributions of the two variables of modality and genre. Thus, in writing a narrative text, speaker-writers need to meet the conflicting "communicative charges" (Slobin, 1977) of the written modality, on the one hand, and the personal narrative genre on the other. The first requires a more monitored and reflective style of discourse, whereas the second elicits more personalized, subjective, and less detached forms of expression. Similarly, construction of a spoken expository reflects the dual demands of "thinking for discussing" on an abstract topic (Slobin, 1996, 2001) while also contending with the processing constraints of on-line speech production.

The interface between modality and genre emerges as a facet of what we label "discourse stance": how speaker-writers use language to position themselves with respect to a piece of discourse in a given set of circumstances (Berman, 2005b; Berman, Ragnarsdóttir, & Strömqvist, 2002). From this perspective, discourse stance is a textual property that serves as a pragmatic frame for the organization of different types of discourse – from interactive conversation, via oral narratives, to formal written essays.

Across the studies in our projects, the essay type of text – a written exposition discussing a socially relevant issue – constitutes a preferred site for expression of a detached, more distant discourse stance. This type of writing requires reference to general, knowledge-based concepts and abstract issues and, hence, involves high-level language use, particularly in the school-like settings of our research. In this, it contrasts markedly with the subjectively immediate style of oral personal-experience narratives, whereas the written narrative and oral expository text lie somewhere in between. Taken together, these findings illuminate literate language use as playing a defining role in differentiating between types of discourse along the dimensions of both modality and genre – distinctions that are developmentally most marked from adolescence on.

Notes

1 The authors are indebted to Ronit Levie and Bracha Nir-Sagiv for their help in all phases of data collection and analysis.

2 We deliberately exclude other facets of text construction that have been examined by the authors and their associates, such as top-down, global-level discourse structure and organization, rhetorical devices, and categories of referential content (e.g., Berman, 1997; Berman & Nir-Sagiv, 2007, in

press; Ravid & Berman, 2006; Tolchinsky et al., 2002).

3 Project I was funded by an Israel Science Foundation grant to Ruth Berman and Dorit Ravid for the study of "The Oral/Literate Continuum" (1996–1998) and Project II by a major research grant from the Spencer Foundation, Chicago, to Ruth Berman, PI, for the study of "Developing Literacy in Different Contexts and Different Languages" in seven countries (1997–2000), with Dorit Ravid responsible for the Hebrew-based project in Israel and Judy S. Reilly of San Diego State University for the English-language project in California.

4 In Israel, such studies have included ultra-orthodox Jews, first and second language users, bilinguals, and children of low and high SES background (Abu-Salem, 2004; Ehrlich, 2001; Farah, 2004; Levin, 2003; Rabukhin, 2003; Schleifer, 2003; Segal, 2008; Shalmon, 2002; Tannenbaum, Abugov, & Ravid, 2007).

5 Text ID was identified by language – e, for English; grade level – J for junior high; participant number – 03 = the third student out of twenty in this group; sex – f, for female; and text type – ns = narrative spoken. Texts were transcribed in regular orthography (here, standardized for spelling and punctuation) in English and in broad phonemic transcription in Hebrew.

6 The caret signs (^) indicate morphemes that are separate words in the European languages in our sample but written as part of the next word in Hebrew. This meant we could count them both as part of the next word and as separate lexical items for purposes of comparison with (1) written Hebrew, and (2) other languages.

References

Abu-Salem, R. (2004). The development of narratives in Palestinian Arabic. Unpublished master's thesis, Tel Aviv University [in Hebrew].

Alfi-Shabtay, I. (1999). Passives and alternatives in different text types in Hebrew. In *Developing literacy across genres, modalities, and languages* (pp. 58–67). Tel Aviv University International Literacy Project: Working Papers, Vol. I.

Anderson, S. R. (1985). Inflectional morphology. In T. Shopen (Ed.), *Language typology and syntactic description, Volume III: Grammatical categories and the lexicon* (pp. 150–201). Cambridge: Cambridge University Press.

Ashkenazi, O., & Ravid, D. (1998). Children's understanding of linguistic humor: An aspect of metalinguistic awareness. *Current Psychology of Cognition*, 17, 367–387.

Bar-Ilan, L., & Berman, R. A. (2007). Developing register differentiation: The Latinate-Germanic divide in English. *Linguistics*, 45, 1–36.

Berman, R. A. (1993). Developmental perspectives on transitivity: A confluence of cues. In Y. Levy (Ed.), *Other children, other languages: Issues in the theory of acquisition* (pp. 189–241). Hillsdale, NJ: Erlbaum.

Berman, R. A. (1996). Form and function in developing narrative abilities: The case of "and." In D. Slobin, J. Gerhardt, A. Kyratzis, & J. Guo (Eds.), *Social interaction, context, and language: Essays in honor of Susan Ervin-Tripp* (pp. 243–268). Mahwah, NJ: Lawrence Erlbaum.

Berman, R. A. (1997). Narrative theory and narrative development: The Labovian impact. *Journal of Narrative and Life History*, 7, 235–244.

Berman, R. A. (2002a). Cross-linguistic comparisons in later language development. In S. Strömqvist (Ed.), *The diversity of languages and language learning* (pp. 25–44). Lund, Sweden: Center for Languages and Literature.

Berman, R. A. (2002b). The lexicon–syntax interface: Development of verb usage in written Hebrew. Paper presented at the triennial conference of the International Association for the Study of Child Language (IASCL), Madison, Wisconsin (July).

Berman, R. A. (2003). Genre and modality in developing discourse abilities. In C. L. Moder & A. Martinovic-Zic (Eds.), *Discourse across languages and cultures* (pp. 223–365). Amsterdam: John Benjamins.

Berman, R. A. (Ed.) (2004a). *Language development across childhood and adolescence: Psycholinguistic and cross-linguistic perspectives.* (Trends in Language Acquisition Research Series, Volume 3.) Amsterdam: John Benjamins.

Berman, R. A. (2004b). Between emergence and mastery: The long developmental route of language acquisition. In R. A. Berman (Ed.), *Language development across childhood and adolescence* (pp. 9–34). Amsterdam: John Benjamins.

Berman, R. A. (Ed.) (2005a). Developing discourse stance across adolescence. *Journal of Pragmatics*, 37, 2 (special issue).

Berman, R. A. (2005b). Introduction: Developing discourse stance in different text types and languages. *Journal of Pragmatics*, 37, 105–124.

Berman, R. A. (2007). Developing language knowledge and language use across adolescence. In E. Off & M. Shatz (Eds.), *Handbook of language development* (pp. 346–367). London: Blackwell.

Berman, R. A. (2008). The psycholinguistics of developing text construction. *Journal of Child Language*, 35, 735–771.

Berman, R. A., & Katzenberger, I. (2004). Form and function in introducing narrative and expository texts: A developmental perspective. *Discourse Processes*, 38, 57–94.

Berman, R. A., & Nir-Sagiv, B. (2004). Linguistic indicators of inter-genre differentiation in later language development. *Journal of Child Language*, 31, 339–380.

Berman, R. A., & Nir-Sagiv, B. (2006). Modality-driven versus modality-neutral features of text production. Paper presented to Second Biennial Conference on Cognitive Science, St. Petersburg, Russia (June).

Berman, R. A., & Nir-Sagiv, B. (2007). Comparing narrative and expository text construction across adolescence: A developmental paradox. *Discourse Processes*, 43, 79–120.

Berman, R. A., & Nir-Sagiv, B. (2008). Clause-packaging in narratives: A cross-linguistic developmental study. In J. Guo, E. Lieven, S. Ervin-Tripp, N. Budwig, S. Özçalişkan, & K. Nakamura (Eds.), *Cross-linguistic approaches to the psychology of language: Research in the tradition of Dan I. Slobin* (pp. 149–162). Mahwah, NJ: Lawrence Erlbaum.

Berman, R. A., & Nir-Sagiv, B. (In press). Cognitive and linguistic factors in evaluating expository text quality: Global versus local? In V. Evans & S. Pourcel (Eds.), *New directions in cognitive linguistics*. Amsterdam: John Benjamins.

Berman, R. A., Ragnarsdóttir, H., & Strömqvist, S. (2002). Discourse stance. *Written Languages and Literacy*, 5, 255–289.

Berman, R. A., & Ravid, D. (1999). The oral/literate continuum: Developmental perspectives. Final report submitted to the Israel Science Foundation. Tel Aviv University (September).

Berman, R. A., & Slobin, D. (1994). *Relating events in narrative: A cross-linguistic developmental study*. Hillsdale, NJ: Erlbaum.

Berman, R. A., & Verhoeven, L. (Eds.) (2002a). Cross-linguistic perspectives on the development of text production abilities in speech and writing. *Written Languages and Literacy*, 5, Parts 1 and 2 (special issue).

Berman, R. A., & Verhoeven, L. (2002b). Developing text production abilities in speech and writing: Aims and methodology. *Written Languages and Literacy*, 5, 1–44.

Blank, M. (2002). Classroom discourse: A key to literacy. In K. D. Butler & E. R. Silliman (eds.), *Speaking, reading, and writing in children with language learning disabilities* (pp. 151–174). Mahwah, NJ: Lawrence Erlbaum.

Brown, R. (1973). *A first language: The early stages*. London: Allen & Unwin.

Bruner, J. (1990). *Acts of meaning*. Cambridge, MA: Harvard University Press.

Bybee, J. (2006). From usage to grammar: The mind's response to repetition. *Language*, 82, 529–551.

Carlisle, J. F. (2000). Awareness of the structure and meaning of morphologically complex words: Impact on reading. *Reading and Writing*, 12, 169–190.

Chafe, W. L. (1994). *Discourse, consciousness, and time: The flow of language in speech and writing*. Chicago: Chicago University Press.

Dromi, E., & Berman, R. (1982). A morphemic measure of early language development: Data from Hebrew. *Journal of Child Language*, 9, 403–424.

Ehrlich, S. (2001). Developing writing abilities in junior high-schoolers. Unpublished master's thesis, Tel Aviv University [in Hebrew].

Farah, A. (2004). The development of expositories in Palestinian Arabic. Unpublished master's thesis, Tel Aviv University [in Hebrew].

Friedman, N., & Novogrotsky, R. (2004). The acquisition of relative clause comprehension in Hebrew: A study of SLI and normal development. *Journal of Child Language*, 31, 661–681.

Gayraud, F. (2000). *Le développement de la differentiation oral/écrit vu à travers le lexique*. Thèse de doctorat, Université Lumière, Lyon 2.

Halliday, M. A. K. (1985). *Spoken and written language*. Victoria, Australia: Deakin University.

Hickmann, M. (2003). *Children's discourse: Person, space and time across languages*. Cambridge: Cambridge University Press.

Jisa, H. (2004a). Growing into academic French. In R. A. Berman (Ed.), *Language development across childhood and adolescence* (pp. 135–162). Amsterdam: John Benjamins.

Jisa, H. (2004b). Developing alternatives for indicating discourse stance. In D. Ravid &

H. Bat-Zeev Shyldkrot (Eds.), *Perspectives on language and language development: Essays in honor of Ruth A. Berman* (pp. 357–374). Dordrecht: Kluwer.

Jisa, H., Reilly, J., Verhoeven, L., Baruch, E., & Rosado, E. (2002). Passive voice constructions in written texts. *Written Language and Literacy*, 5, 163–182.

Jisa, H., & Viguié, A. (2005). A developmental perspective on the role of "on" in written and spoken expository texts in French. *Journal of Pragmatics*, 37, 125–144.

Karmiloff-Smith, A. (1986). Some fundamental aspects of language acquisition after five. In P. Fletcher & M. Garman (Eds.), *Studies in language acquisition* (2nd revised ed.) (pp. 455–474). Cambridge: Cambridge University Press.

Kupersmitt, J. (2006). Temporality in texts: A cross-linguistic developmental study of form-function relations in narrative and expository discourse. Unpublished doctoral dissertation, Bar-Ilan University, Israel.

Langacker, R. (1991). *Concept, image, and symbol: The cognitive basis of grammar*. Berlin: Mouton de Gruyter.

Levin, M. (2003). Narrative and linguistic development in English L2 compared to Hebrew L1 across adolescence. Unpublished master's thesis, Tel Aviv University.

Loban, W. (1976). *Language development: Kindergarten through grade twelve*. Champaign, IL: National Council of Teachers of English, Research Report No. 18.

Macbeth, K. P. (2006). Diverse, unforeseen and quaint difficulties: The sensible responses of novices learning to follow instructions in academic writing. *Research in the Teaching of English*, 41, 180–207.

Malvern, D., Richards, B., Chipere, N., & Durán, P. (2004). *Lexical diversity and language development: Quantification and assessment*. Basingstoke: Palgrave Macmillan.

Nippold, M. A. (1998). *Later language development*. Austin, TX: PRO-ED.

Nippold, M. A. (2002). Lexical learning in school-age children, adolescents, and adults: A process where language and literacy converge. *Journal of Child Language*, 29, 474–478.

Nippold, M. A., & Taylor, C. L. (2002). Judgments of idiom familiarity and transparency: A comparison of children and adolescents. *Journal of Speech, Language, and Hearing Research*, 45, 384–391.

Nir-Sagiv, B. (2005). Word length as a criterion of text complexity: A cross-linguistic developmental study. Paper presented at triennial conference of the International Association for the Study of Child Language [IASCL], Berlin (July).

Nir-Sagiv, B. (2008). Clause-packages as constructions in developing narrative discourse. Unpublished doctoral dissertation, Tel Aviv University.

Nir-Sagiv, B., Bar-Ilan, L., & Berman, R. A. (2008). Vocabulary development across adolescence: Text-based analyses. In I. Kupferberg & A. Stavans (Eds.), *Studies in language and language education: Essays in honor of Elite Olshtain* (pp. 47–74). Jerusalem: Magnes Press.

Olson, D. (1994). *The world on paper*. Cambridge: Cambridge University Press.

Olson, D. (2006a). Oral discourse in a world of literacy. *Research in Teaching of English*, 41, 136–142.

Olson, D. (2006b). Continuing the discourse on literacy. *Research in Teaching of English*, 41, 175–179.

Ong, W. J. (1992). Writing is a technology that restructures thought. In P. Downing, S. D. Lima, & M. Noonan (Eds.), *The linguistics of literacy* (pp. 293–319). Amsterdam: John Benjamins.

Ong, W. J. (2002). *Orality and literacy*. London: Routledge.

Paus, T. (2005). Mapping brain maturation and cognitive development during adolescence. *Trends in Cognitive Sciences*, 9, 60–68.

Rabukhin, L. (2003). Text production abilities in bilingual Hebrew-Russian children: A developmental study. Unpublished master's thesis, Tel Aviv University [in Hebrew].

Ragnarsdóttir, H., Cahana-Amitay, D., van Hell, J., Rosado, E., & Viguié, A. (2002). Verbal structure and content in written discourse: Narrative and expository texts. *Written Language and Literacy*, 5, 95–126.

Ravid, D. (2004a). Later lexical development in Hebrew: Derivational morphology revisited. In R.A. Berman (Ed.), *Language development across childhood and adolescence* (pp. 53–82). Amsterdam: John Benjamins.

Ravid, D. (2004b). Emergence of linguistic complexity in written expository texts: Evidence from later language acquisition. In D. Ravid & H. Bat-Zeev Shyldkrot (Eds.), *Perspectives on language and language development: Essays in honor of Ruth A. Berman* (pp. 337–355). Dordrecht: Kluwer.

Ravid, D. (2005). Hebrew orthography and literacy. In R. M. Joshi & P. G. Aaron (Eds.), *Handbook of orthography and literacy* (pp. 339–363). Mahwah, NJ: Erlbaum.

Ravid, D. (2006a). Semantic development in textual contexts during the school years: Noun Scale analyses. *Journal of Child Language, 33*, 791–821.

Ravid, D. (2006b). Word-level morphology: A psycholinguistic perspective on linear formation in Hebrew nominals. *Morphology, 16*, 127–148.

Ravid, D., & Berman, R. A. (2006). Information density in the development of spoken and written narratives in English and Hebrew. *Discourse Processes, 41*, 117–149.

Ravid, D., & Berman, R. A. (in press). Developing noun phrase complexity across adolescence: A text-embedded cross-linguistic analysis. *First Language*.

Ravid, D., & Cahana-Amitay, D. (2005). Verbal and nominal expression in narrating conflict situations in Hebrew. *Journal of Pragmatics, 37*, 157–183.

Ravid, D., & Levie, R. (In press). Adjectives in the development of text production: Lexical, morphological and syntactic analyses. *First Language*.

Ravid, D., & Saban, R. (2008). Syntactic and meta-syntactic skills in the school years: A developmental study in Hebrew. In I. Kupferberg & A. Stavans (Eds.), *Language education in Israel: Papers in honor of Elite Olshtain* (pp. 75–110). Jerusalem: Magnes Press.

Ravid, D., & Tolchinsky, L. (2002). Developing linguistic literacy: A comprehensive model. *Journal of Child Language, 29*, 419–448.

Ravid, D., van Hell, J., Rosado, E., & Zamora, A. (2002). Subject NP patterning in the development of text production: Speech and writing. *Written Language and Literacy, 5*, 69–94.

Ravid, D., & Zilberbuch, S. (2003a). Morpho-syntactic constructs in the development of spoken and written Hebrew text production. *Journal of Child Language, 30*, 395–418.

Ravid, D., & Zilberbuch, S. (2003b). The development of complex nominals in expert and non-expert writing: A comparative study. *Pragmatics and Cognition, 11*, 267–297.

Reilly, J. S., Jisa, H., & Berman, R. A. (2002). Propositional attitudes: Development of modal expression. *Written Language and Literacy, 5*, 183–218.

Reilly, J., Zamora, A., & McGivern, R. F. (2005). Acquiring perspective in English: The development of stance. *Journal of Pragmatics, 37*, 185–207.

Riedemann, H. (1996). Word length distribution in English press texts. *Journal of Quantitative Linguistics, 3*, 265–271.

Schleifer, M. (2003). Development of written text production of native Israeli and Ethiopian immigrant schoolchildren and adolescents: Linguistic and sociocultural perspectives. Unpublished doctoral dissertation, Tel Aviv University.

Scott, C. M. (2004). Syntactic ability in children and adolescents with language and learning disabilities. In R. A. Berman (Ed.), *Language development across childhood and adolescence* (pp. 111–134). Amsterdam: John Benjamins.

Segal, M. (2008). *What's the story? On the development of narrative competence*. Tel Aviv: Mofet Institute [in Hebrew].

Seroussi, B. (2004). Hebrew derived nouns in context: A developmental perspective. *Folia Phoniatrica et Logopaedica, 56*, 273–290.

Shalmon, S. (2002). Text production abilities in children from low-SES: A developmental study. Unpublished master's thesis, Tel Aviv University [in Hebrew].

Shalom, T. (2002). The language of Hebrew teaching textbooks. Unpublished doctoral dissertation, Bar-Ilan University, Israel [in Hebrew].

Slobin, D. I. (1977). Language change in childhood and in history. In J. Macnamara (Ed.), *Language learning and thought* (pp. 185–214). New York: Academic Press.

Slobin, D. I. (1996). From "thought and language" to "thinking for speaking." In J. J. Gumperz & S. C. Levinson (Eds.), *Rethinking linguistic relativity* (pp. 70–96). Cambridge: Cambridge University Press.

Slobin, D. I. (2001). Form-function relations: How do children find out what they are? In M. Bowerman & S. C. Levinson (Eds.), *Language acquisition and conceptual development* (pp. 406–449). Cambridge: Cambridge University Press.

Slobin, D. I. (2003). Language and thought online: Cognitive consequences of linguistic relativity. In D. Gentner & S. Goldin-Meadow (Eds.), *Language in mind: Advances in the investigation of language and thought* (pp. 157–191). Cambridge, MA: MIT Press.

Steinberg, L. (2005). Cognitive and affective development in adolescence. *Trends in Cognitive Sciences*, 9, 69–74.

Strömqvist, S., Johansson, V., Kriz, S., Ragnarsdóttir, R., & Ravid, D. (2002). Towards a cross-linguistic comparison of lexical quanta in speech and writing. *Written Language & Literacy*, 5, 45–68.

Strömqvist, S., Nordqvist, Å., & Wengelin, Å. (2004). Writing the frog story: Developmental and cross-modal perspectives. In S. Strömqvist & L. Verhoeven (Eds.), *Relating events in narrative: Typological and contextual* perspectives (pp. 359–394). Mahwah, NJ: Lawrence Erlbaum.

Tannenbaum, M., Abugov, N., & Ravid, D. (2007). Linguistic patterns in narratives of ultra-orthodox girls. *Pragmatics and Cognition*, 15, 347–378.

Tolchinsky, L. (2004). The nature and scope of later language development. In R. A. Berman (Ed.), *Language development across childhood and adolescence* (pp. 233–248). Amsterdam: John Benjamins.

Tolchinsky, L., Johansson, V., & Zamora, A. (2002). Text openings and closings: Textual autonomy and differentiation. *Language and Literacy*, 5, 219–254.

Tolchinsky, L., & Rosado, E. (2005). The effect of literacy, text type, and modality on the use of grammatical means for agency alternation in Spanish. *Journal of Pragmatics*, 37, 209–237.

Ure, J. (1971). Lexical density and register differentiation. In G. E. Perren & I. L. M. Trim (Eds.), *Applications of linguistics* (pp. 443–452). Cambridge: Cambridge University Press.

Wimmer, G., & Altmann, G. (1996). The theory of word length distribution: Some results and generalizations. In P. Schmidt (Ed.), *Glottometrika* 15 (pp. 112–133). Trier, Germany: WVT.

CHAPTER 7

The Challenge of Academic Language

Catherine E. Snow and Paola Uccelli[1]

Increasingly in recent years, educators have related worries about students' literacy accomplishments to their lack of "academic language skills" (August & Shanahan, 2006; Halliday & Martin, 1993; Pilgreen, 2006; Schleppegrell & Colombi, 2002). Indeed, it seems clear that control over academic language is a requirement for success with challenging literacy tasks, such as reading textbooks or writing research papers and literature reviews. As early as the middle-elementary grades, students are expected to learn new information from content-area texts, so failure to understand the academic language of those texts can be a serious obstacle in their accessing information. Accountability assessments requiring written essays in persuasive or analytic genres are often graded using criteria that refer implicitly to academic-language forms. Even in the primary grades, students are expected in some classrooms to abide by rules for "accountable talk" (Michaels & O'Connor, 2002) which specify features encompassed in the term *academic language*.

Despite the frequent invocations of "academic language" and the widespread concern about its inadequate development, there is no simple definition of what academic language is. What we consider "academic language" in this chapter is referred to in the literature using a variety of terms: *the language of education* (Halliday, 1994a); *the language of school, the language of schooling, the language that reflects schooling* (Schleppegrell, 2001); *advanced literacy* (Colombi & Schleppegrell, 2002); *scientific language* (Halliday & Martin, 1993); or, more specifically, *academic English* (Bailey, 2007; Scarcella, 2003). As suggested by these terms, one approach to characterizing academic language is to resort to the contexts for its use – the language used in school, in writing, in public, in formal settings (see Table 7.1 for a more complete list). Thus, for example, Scarcella (2003) defines academic English as "a variety or register of English used in professional books and characterized by the linguistic features associated with academic disciplines" (p. 9). Similarly, Chamot and O'Malley (1994) identify it with school, defining it as "the language that is used by teachers and students for the purpose of acquiring new knowledge

Table 7.1. Contextual Factors

		Audience		
(Home, friends)		(School)		(College/professional)
Real familiar cooperative interlocutor (assess interlocutor's shared knowledge)	vs.	Pretended distant uncooperative interlocutors (suspend assumptions of situational knowledge)	vs.	Alternative communities with various levels of disciplinary knowledge (become familiar with expectations of audience)
Dialogic/interactive	vs.	Monologic	vs.	Delayed dialogue
		Activity/Modality		
Spontaneous/improvised	vs.	Highly planned		
Process (dynamic)	vs.	Product (synoptic)		
Spoken	vs.	Written	vs.	Other additional media
Situation				
Private	vs.	Public		
Informal	vs.	Formal		
		Sociocultural match of Primary and Secondary discourses		
Closer match (e.g., home and school) • same language • similar discourse patterns	vs.	Partial mismatch	vs.	Full mismatch (e.g., home and school) • different language • different discourse patterns

and skills . . . imparting new information, describing abstract ideas, and developing students' conceptual understanding" (p. 40).

Whereas identifying contexts of use and purposes is important, a comprehensive definition of academic language requires further specification. Scarcella (2003) identifies three dimensions required for academic-language proficiency: linguistic, cognitive, and sociocultural/psychological. Bailey defines being academically proficient as "knowing and being able to use general and content-specific vocabulary, specialized or complex grammatical structures, and multifarious language functions and discourse structures – all for the purpose of acquiring new knowledge and skills, interacting about a topic, or imparting information to others" (Bailey, 2007, pp. 10–11; in press).

Despite these advances in delineating academic language, a conceptualization of academic language within a consensual analytical framework that could guide educationally relevant research is still lacking. Indeed, this topic, which seems as if it should be located in the exact center of educators' concerns, is notably absent from the table of contents in the most up-to-date handbook of educational linguistics (Spolsky & Hult, 2008). Ironically, although academic language skills are widely cited as the obstacle to achievement for struggling readers in general, much of the empirical research on academic language has been done by those studying English Language Learners (ELLs). In other words, learning 'academic English' is recognized as a challenging task for second-language speakers of English, but the challenges faced by native speakers in learning the rules, the structures, and the content of academic English have received much less attention.

One line of thinking about academic language started with Cummins' proposed distinction between Cognitive Academic Language Proficiency (CALP) and Basic Interpersonal Communicative Skill (BICS) – a distinction he presented as relevant to second-language learners. In Cummins' original formulation of this distinction (Cummins, 1980, 1981), BICS was presented as easy and relatively automatically acquired, whereas acquiring CALP was seen as a lengthier process. Cummins was the first to point out cogently that many assessments of second-language proficiency focus exclusively on BICS yet are used to place students in classroom contexts where CALP is required for success (see Kieffer, Lesaux, & Snow, 2008, for an updated version of this argument as it relates to the testing requirements of the U.S. No Child Left Behind Act). Although Cummins' work was crucial in raising awareness of the gulf between conversational and academic language, he did not specify in much detail which particular language skills were encompassed by CALP, in either his original discussions of it or later, somewhat more elaborated formulations (Cummins, 1984, 2001).

A more theory-based approach that has contributed centrally to our understanding of language, in general, and of academic language, in particular, is Systemic Functional Linguistics (SFL) (Halliday, 1994b). SFL studies language in its social context, understanding language as both shaping and resulting from social circumstances. Within this framework, linguists search for systematic relationships between the social context and linguistic features, including lexicogrammatical and discourse elements, in their analysis of the registers of particular genres.[2] In studying academic language, Halliday (1993) emphasized its multidimensional and dynamic nature. On the one hand, he warned us that there is no single academic language, just as there is no single British English, but rather a number of varieties that share certain core features. On the other hand, Halliday highlighted that academic language is continually evolving as the sciences, disciplines, and subdisciplines themselves evolve. In fact, he argued that the evolution of science goes hand in hand with the evolution of scientific language, so that academic or scientific languages are not arbitrary sets of conventions but rather grammatical resources that make scientific thought possible.

Although SFL has proven to be highly relevant in studying the language of school (Schleppegrell, 2001), it is a linguistically sophisticated model originally designed more as a theory of language than as a framework for educational research. An educationally relevant framework would direct less attention to the description of linguistic features per se and more to the skills required in the process of mastering academic language and, thus, potentially to the nature of instruction that would promote those skills. In other words, we argue for the value of practice-embedded approaches to thinking about academic language that would generate more directly useable information. For example, Bailey (2007) derived valuable data about academic-language demands on ELLs from an analysis of content standards, classroom discourse, and the tests they are expected to pass. Scarcella (2003) and Schleppegrell (2001) also adumbrated the nature of academic language by describing the typical failures of ELLs who have advanced conversational skills but who struggle with high school or university writing tasks and by proposing instructional approaches to improving the academic-language skills of ELL students in tertiary-education settings.

Although the problem of academic language may be particularly visible or acute for second-language speakers, in fact, we argue that academic language is intrinsically more difficult than other language registers and that thinking about the educational experiences that promote its development is a crucial task for educators of all students. Furthermore, formulating instructional approaches to academic language is necessary not just for achievement in the domains traditionally associated with language (e.g., literature study, English language arts) but also for achievement in math, science, and other areas where all-purpose academic language forms the core of content-area–specific language. Designing instruction for academic and discipline-specific language, however, requires having a convergent view of what academic language involves, how it should be conceptualized, where its boundaries are, and how it might be assessed.

Certainly, members of the academy can identify violations of academic language in our students' writing and may have learned something about the features of academic language by working hard to stamp them out in writings meant to communicate with practitioners or the general public. Despite these practice-based sources of knowledge about academic language, the central concept remains somewhat inchoate and underspecified. In the absence of a conceptual framework, it is difficult to design instruction to promote academic language, to properly assess academic-language skills, or to understand what normal, expectable progress toward achievement of academic-language skills might look like.

The goal of this chapter is to survey the work on academic language in order to provide an overview of its features as a basis for proposing a pragmatics-based framework that accommodates those many discrete features in a coherent model of communication. Based on this pragmatic framework, we then propose a research agenda focusing on issues that would take our understanding of this important topic a step farther. Given the absence of an agreed-upon set of criteria for academic language, we start by presenting an example of middle-school student writing to illustrate the rules of academic language. We then turn to a more formal inventory, based on theorizing about the differences between oral and written language, between informal and formal language, and between narrative and expository language, because these three distinctions overlap with and contribute to a sharpening of the definition of academic language. It is notable that *academic language*, unlike the categories of written, formal, and expository language, has no clear opposite. We start, then, from the assumption that language can be *more or less* academic – that is, furnished with fewer or more of the traits that are typical of academic language; we have no basis for postulating a separate category of language that has passed some threshold qualifying it as academic.

Academic Language in Use: Some Examples

The example we analyze herein was an end-of-week paragraph produced by a middle-school student participating in the pilot implementation of a program intended to promote knowledge of all-purpose 'academic' vocabulary in particular and use of academic language more generally. The program was designed for use in an urban district in which assessment had suggested that students' reading comprehension challenges might be related to vocabulary limitations. Classroom observations in this district also showed that the vocabulary instruction that occurred was primarily focused on disciplinary terms (e.g., *sonnet, legislation, digestion,* and *rhomboid* in English language arts, social studies, science, and math, respectively), whereas pretesting showed that a significant proportion of the students was struggling with the more all-purpose vocabulary found in their texts, including words like *dramatic, interpret, sufficient,* and *decade*.

The program consisted of week-long units in each of which five 'academic vocabulary' words were targeted. The five target words (and other words of similarly low frequency) were introduced in the context of a paragraph about a topic selected to be engaging to young adolescents and to be somewhat open-ended (i.e., supporting a number of different plausible points of view). The introductory paragraphs were written in a style that might be characterized as 'seriously journalistic' and each briefly presented two or more positions on the topic of the week, with limited elaboration of each position. The instructional program presented focused teaching about the target words (i.e., their varying meanings in different contexts, morphological analyses, and variants of them) as well as contexts for the students to use the words. Thus, some form of debate about the issue in the paragraph was recommended for social studies class and "taking a stand," a short argumentative essay in which each student was asked to develop and justify his or her opinion about the topic of the week, was the standard Friday activity.

It is important to note that these "taking a stand" paragraphs were written in 10 to 15 minutes, were not preceded by explicit instruction in how to construct them, and were not graded. Thus, we can assume that they reflect something of the students' natural and unedited writing style, with the exception that students were encouraged to use the words of the week if possible; complying with this request sometimes led to awkward constructions or even outright errors.

EXAMPLE 1: Female Seventh-Grader, responding to the prompt: *What do you think the function of school is?*

What's the purpose of school **you tell me!** *Well first of all,* school is to get your education. [S]o we can learn what the teachers learn[,] so we can be ready for the 8th grade. Because if we don't get [an] education[,] you can't be what you want to be when [you] grow up. Secondly to get us ready so we can make it to the 8th grade ready and prepared[.] [T]hey don't want to send [us] to the 8th grade because they like us or the[y] just feel sorry for us. No!
[T]hat's not the reason[.] [T]hey want to prepare [us,] make sure we understand the work. When we grow up we also want to get a good job because we are the future leaders of the world. That's [why] we need to work with the function of the school[,] so you [can] show us [how] the world should be.

- **involved style**
- *colloquial expressions*
- redundancy
- simple connectives
- inconsistent perspective-taking(you/we)

As a piece of writing from a seventh-grader, this falls short of excellence on many grounds. First, it is inconsistent in attention to conventions like capitalization, punctuation, and spelling (corrections introduced for readability are indicated in square brackets). Second, the major position expressed (i.e., we go to school to get a good job, to be what we want to be when we grow up) is somewhat obscured by other claims (i.e., attending school is necessary for promotion to higher grades, teachers will not promote students out of pity, teachers want students to learn) whose relationship to the central claim is left unclear. These issues of form and content are rightly important in judging this as a piece of writing, but our focus in this chapter is how we respond to it as a piece of *academic language*. The key question is: What is the most effective pedagogical response to writings like this? Will academic language follow naturally if students are helped to formulate their ideas more fully and precisely, or should one teach the academic forms using the content the students themselves have generated? If we agree that revision and rewriting help to improve the quality of writing (Klein & Olson, 2001), then what would be the best strategies to scaffold effective revision and rewriting geared toward improving academic-language skills more broadly?

Consider Example 1a, a rewritten version of the previous example paragraph that attempts to express the same ideas in a more academic form.

EXAMPLE 1A.

What is the purpose of school?

First, school functions to provide an education, so students can learn what the teachers know and be prepared to continue their education at higher levels. Teachers will not promote students who have not learned the material, so understanding the work is very important. Without an education, attaining one's career goals is very difficult.

Second, getting a good job is dependent on going to school. Today's students are the future leaders of the world. School could help them understand how the world should be.

Analyzing the differences between Examples 1 and 1a reveals some of the key features of academic language. Example 1a eliminates markers of involvement (e.g., you tell me! No!); removes redundancy (the point about getting ready for eighth grade is made twice in Example 1, only once in Example 1a); moves from specific and personal to generic formulations of claims (*eighth grade* becomes *education at higher levels*; *they don't want to send us . . .* becomes *teachers will not promote . . .*); substitutes metadiscourse markers (*first, second*) for more colloquial expressions (*well first of all*); compresses Example 1 clauses into adverbial phrases (*without an education*) and nominalizations (*getting a good job*); and imposes a consistent, distant, third-person perspective, whereas Example 1 shifts between first- and second-person perspectives. Although more academic in style, Example 1a is still not a particularly good response to the topic assigned because it is restricted to the same ideas presented in more or less the same order as Example 1.

The paragraphs written by the middle-grade students participating in this program were not devoid of academic-language features. Some students provided overarching initial or concluding statements, used metadiscourse markers, and incorporated the academic vocabulary they were taught. Nonetheless, the paragraphs, particularly in contrast to the more academic translations one could provide for them, displayed language features inappropriate for academic language (e.g., colloquial expressions, involvement markers, redundancy) and revealed characteristics of academic language that the students did not employ (e.g., grammatical compression, generic statements, impersonal stance, a variety of connectives).

Finally, comparing the student "taking-a-stand" paragraph to the original paragraph designed to stimulate thinking about this topic reveals still more academic-language features.

EXAMPLE 1B. Paragraph prompt.
What is the purpose of school?
Why do we go to school? One **prime** goal of education is to **transmit** knowledge. Another is to **enhance** students' **capacities** to earn a good living. Some would argue that schools should **orient** students toward a set of shared values, in order to **facilitate** the maintenance of a democratic state. Others contend that schools should help students develop an understanding of the **perspectives** of others, to promote social harmony. Still others think schools should teach students to **challenge** authority, **reject** received opinion, and think for themselves. Of course, if we accept this last **version** of what schools should do, then we will have to expect that the curriculum will be massively **adjusted** and classroom activities radically **altered**. **Whereas** thinking for themselves is something educators value, students don't always have the **license** to do so in the classroom.

This adult-written paragraph reveals a number of features not present in the student paragraphs, as follows:

- lexical density
- modal verbs
- endophoric reference
- abstract entity as agent (school)
- wide variety of connectives
- stepwise logical argumentation
- evidence of planning
- detached stance
- authoritative stance
- lots of abstract/low-frequency vocabulary
- elaborate noun phrases (nominalization)
- markers of course of rationale
- deductive/inductive inference

Some of these features, such as the high density of relatively low-frequency words, were deliberately introduced into the paragraph to serve the purposes of the program. Others were required by the argumentative genre; these included the logical progression of the argument and the explicit marking of different points of view. Other features, such as the use of nominalization, were a product of efforts to keep the paragraph brief. Others, such as the authoritative and detached stance, are simply the default academic writing style.

Academic Language: An Inventory of Features

Having explored examples of academic language and its absence in actual practice, we now must confront the issue of how to conceptualize 'academic language.' A first advantage of a coherent characterization of academic language might be the value of sharing it with struggling students. Schleppegrell (2001) argues that only rarely are the linguistic expectations of school-based tasks made explicit to students, despite the fact that students' academic performance is judged considering these expectations. Without explicit discussion of linguistic expectations, academic language constitutes an arcane challenge for many, and some explicit teaching about it might be useful.

Linguists and educational researchers have revealed features about which students might be taught through contrastive analysis of language corpora (e.g., Biber & Reppen, 2002; Chafe & Danielewicz, 1987), evolutionary analysis of scientific language (Halliday & Martin, 1993), explorations of performances at different levels of expertise (Schleppegrell, 2001), in different academic disciplines (Achugar & Schleppegrell, 2005; Schleppegrell, 2007), and in specific genres (Halliday & Martin, 1993; Swales, 1990). Table 7.2 represents an effort to summarize this literature, by organizing the many linguistic features identified under the domains of knowledge involved in academic language in a way that makes them somewhat more tractable.[3] The features listed to the left are more characteristic of colloquial language, whereas the features toward the right are more typical of academic language. Linguistic features are divided into those referring to interpersonal stance, information load, organization of information, lexical choices, and representational congruence (i.e., how grammar is used to depict reality). Of course, the realization of all these features requires knowledge of specific vocabulary and grammatical structures. In addition to these linguistic skills, three core domains of cognitive accomplishment involved in academic-language performance are genre mastery, command of reasoning/argumentative strategies, and disciplinary knowledge.

The typical *interpersonal stance* expected in academic language is *detached* and *authoritative*. As we saw in Example 1, **you tell me!** and **No!** are markers of an involved style that in Schleppegrell's words form part of a "hortatory style that instantiates a context of interaction" (2001, p. 446). In contrast, academic language requires a nondialogical and distant construction of opinion, as well as "an assertive author [or speaker] who presents him/herself as a knowledgeable expert providing objective information" (Schleppegrell, 2001, pp. 444–445) (for an illustration of detached versus involved writing styles, see Schleppegrell, 2001, p. 445).

The *information load* in academic discourse is characterized by *conciseness* and *density*. Academic writing or speech is expected to be short and to the point, conveying information without unjustified repetitions. In Example 1, the repetition of *being ready for 8th grade* stands out as a violation to the flow of information expected in such a piece of writing. In contrast to the typical redundancy of spontaneous speech (Ong, 1982/1995), conciseness is highly valued, with only the minor exceptions of artful pseudo-redundant moves such as those included in abstracts or summaries and conclusions. Besides, academic language packs a lot of information into a few words. This informational density is evident in the high proportion of content words, usually achieved through nominalizations and expanded noun phrases (Chafe & Danielewicz , 1987; Halliday & Martin, 1993; Schleppegrell, 2001).

At the syntactic level of *organization of information*, Halliday (1994b) subdivided the

Table 7.2. Linguistic Features and Core Domains of Cognitive Accomplishments Involved in Academic Language Performance

More Colloquial		*More Academic*		
1. Interpersonal stance				
Expressive/Involved	→	Detached/Distanced (Schleppegrell, 2001)		
Situationally driven personal stances	→	Authoritative stance (Schleppegrell, 2001)		
2. Information load				
Redundancy (Ong, 1995)/ Wordiness	→	Conciseness		
Sparsity	→	Density (*proportion of content words per total words*) (Schleppegrell, 2001)		
3. Organization of information				
Dependency (Halliday, 1993)/Addition (Ong, 1995) (*one element is bound or linked to another but is not part of it*)	→	Constituency (Halliday, 1994b)/Subordination (Ong, 1995) (*embedding, one element is a structural part of another*)		
Minimal awareness of unfolding text as discourse (*marginal role of metadiscourse markers*)	→	Explicit awareness of organized discourse (*central role of textual metadiscourse markers*) (Hyland & Tse, 2004)		
Situational support (*exophoric reference*)	→	Autonomous text (*endophoric reference*)		
Loosely connected/dialogic structure	→	Stepwise logical argumentation/unfolding, tightly constructed		
4. Lexical choices				
Low lexical diversity	→	High lexical diversity (Chafe & Danielewicz, 1987)		
Colloquial expressions	→	Formal/prestigious expressions (e.g., *say/like* vs. *for instance*)		
Fuzziness (e.g., *sort of, something, like*)	→	Precision (*lexical choices and connectives*)		
Concrete/common-sense concepts	→	Abstract/technical concepts		
5. Representational congruence				
Simple/congruent grammar (simple sentences, e.g., *You heat water and it evaporates faster.*)	→	Complex/congruent grammar (complex sentences, e.g., *If the water gets hotter, it evaporates faster.*)	→	Compact/Incongruent grammar (*clause embedding and nominalization*, e.g., *The increasing evaporation of water due to rising temperatures*) (Halliday, 1993)
Animated entities as agents (e.g., *Gutenberg invented printing with movable type.*)	→	Abstract concepts as agents (e.g., *Printing technology revolutionized European book-making.*) (Halliday, 1993)		

(continued)

Table 7.2 (*continued*)

More Colloquial				*More Academic*
➢Genre mastery				
Generic Values (Bhatia, 2002) (narration, description, explanation…)	→	School-based genres (e.g., lab reports, persuasive essay)	→	Discipline-specific specialized genres
➢Reasoning strategies				
Basic ways of argumentation and persuasion	→	Specific reasoning moves valued at school (Reznitskaya et al., 2001)	→	Discipline-specific reasoning moves
➢Disciplinary knowledge				
• **Taxonomies**				
Commonsense understanding	→	Abstract groupings and relations	→	Disciplinary taxonomies and salient relations
• **Epistemological assumptions**				
Knowledge as fact	→	Knowledge as constructed		

traditional category of subordinated clauses into "hypotactic" and "embedded" clauses. Hypotactic clauses are subordinated clauses that are dependent on but not constitutive of other clauses, such as adverbial clauses or those introduced by verbs of saying or thinking (Colombi, 2002). In the following example, clause *a* and clause *b* are hypotactic clauses: *I concluded [that the party was a total failure]$_a$ [because it ended before midnight]$_b$.* In contrast, embedded clauses form part of another clause, such as clause *a* and clause *b* in the following sentence: *The party [which ended before midnight]$_a$ was a total failure [that we hope will not be repeated]$_b$*. Whereas some posit that addition and coordination are characteristic features of colloquial language that contrast with subordination and complex syntax (Ong, 1982/1995), Halliday (1994b) persuasively argued that the crucial distinction is *dependency* (which includes hypotactic subordinated clauses) versus *constituency* (embeddedness). He argued that embedding is a distinctive feature of scientific or academic discourse. If we contrast the subordinated clauses in Examples 1 and 1b, it becomes evident that embedded clauses are used only in the latter text.

Organization of information also involves *explicit marking of text structures*. Explicit awareness of text structure is indexed via discourse and metadiscourse markers that have been widely explored in the literature. In Hyland and Tse's (2004) words: "metadiscourse represents the writer's awareness of the unfolding text as *discourse*: how writers situate their language use to include a text, a writer, and a reader" (p. 167). These authors developed a taxonomy of metadiscourse markers and their functions by studying different types of texts. Additionally, information in academic language needs to be organized according to a *stepwise logical argument structure* that makes sophisticated use of *autonomous endophoric reference* strategies instead of relying on situational context or underspecified references.

At the *lexical level*, a *diverse*, *precise*, and *formal* repertoire that includes appropriate cross-discipline and discipline-specific terms is desirable.

The final level concerns *representational congruence*, or the correspondence between language and the reality it represents. The concept of *grammatical metaphor* plays a central role in Halliday's model. According to Halliday (1994a), in children's commonsense language, nouns refer to things, verbs refer to processes, adjectives denote attributes, and connectives establish relationships. However, when these grammatical categories are extended beyond their prototypes (e.g., when nouns refer to processes like *evaporation* or verbs refer to relationships like *precede*), a grammatical metaphor, which Halliday calls a *compact and incongruent form*, is created. He argued that experience is reconstructed when nominalized forms such as *evaporation* are used; this term has the semantic features both of processes (water evaporates) and of things (because a noun prototypically refers to things). In Halliday's terms, these processes have been transformed metaphorically into virtual objects, "[t]he effect of this is to provide a less dynamic, more synoptic vision of the world, in which reality is as it were held still, rendered fixed, bounded and determinate, so that it can be observed, measured and, if possible, explained" (Halliday, 1994a, p. 14). Halliday emphasized that there would be no noticeable effect of sporadic uses like that but that academic language is profusely populated by these grammatical metaphors (in particular, nominalizations of processes).

Nominalization also creates lexical density. The recursive linguistic principle permits nominalizations to function as embedded clauses of other propositions, allowing long, information-packed sentences. Furthermore, in examples like *The increasing evaporation of water due to rising temperatures is alarming,* not only is the nominalization phrase the subject of a longer sentence, but it also constructs the claim of relationship between rising temperature and evaporation as assumed truth rather than a falsifiable claim, contributing to the authoritative stance previously discussed.

However, grammatical metaphor is not the only case of *representational incongruence*. Another incongruent move of academic language involves using *abstract concepts as agents*. Whereas in colloquial interactions, animate entities are typically the grammatical agents of sentences, academic language often displays abstract concepts as agentive subjects of sentences. For example, in *Gutenberg invented printing with movable type*, a noun that refers to a person is the subject and agent of the sentence. However, the sentence, *Printing technology revolutionized European book-making,* presents a noun that refers to an abstract concept as agent, a less intuitive construction that departs from our commonsense knowledge of the world (Halliday & Martin, 1993).

Finally, all these linguistic features must be coordinated with at least three additional cognitive accomplishments: genre mastery (Bhatia, 2002; Swales, 1990); command of reasoning/argumentative strategies (Reznitskaya, Anderson, Nurlen, Nguyen-Jahiel, Archodidou, & Kim, 2001); and disciplinary knowledge (Achugar & Schleppegrell, 2005; Wignell, Martin, & Eggins, 1993). As students advance in their mastery of these three domains of knowledge, they learn to put features of academic language at the service of genre conventions, persuasive and clear argumentations, and disciplinary-specific relationships and concepts. These are three vast areas of research, which have been the focus of work in fields such as English for Specific Purposes, the "Sydney school" of genre theory, and the Collaborative Reasoning approach, among others. Reviewing these three areas with the detail they deserve would go beyond the scope of this chapter.

As we have seen herein, the claims that have been made in the literature about the characteristics of academic language result in a lengthy list of features. The mere length of the list in Table 7.2 displays the problem with our current conception of academic language: dozens of traits have been identified that contrast with primary or colloquial language and that might function as markers of academic language, but it is unclear that any of them actually defines the phenomenon. Any of these traits might be present in casual spoken language: Is it their co-occurrence that defines some language as academic? Is it their frequency? How, if at all, do these various traits relate to one another? Are some particularly crucial and others merely epiphenomena? Are some causes and others consequences? How does the list in Table 7.2 help us with the tasks of assessment or instruction?

A Pragmatics-Based Approach to Academic Language

The problem with the inventorizing approach reflected in Table 7.2 is the omission

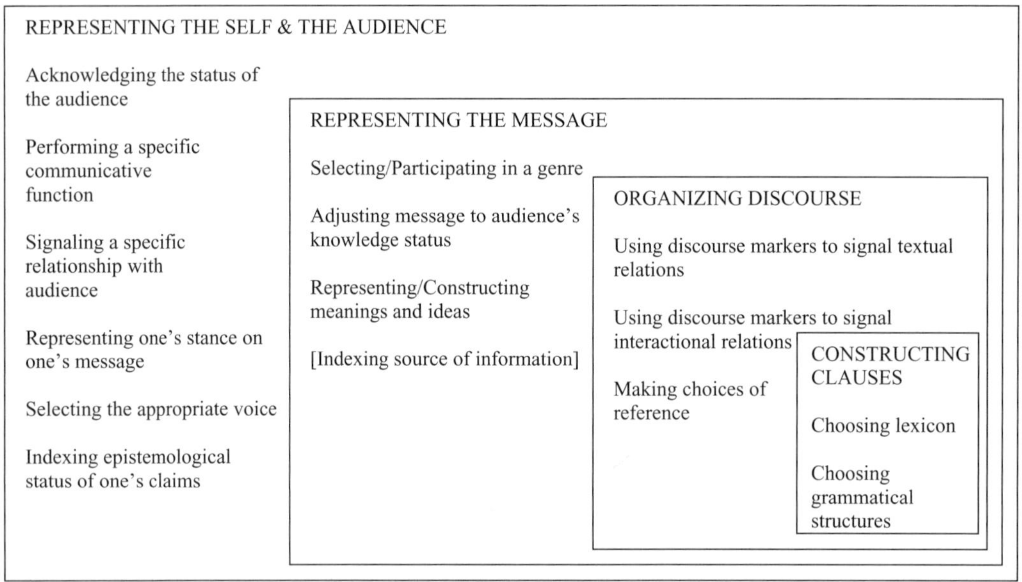

Figure 7.1. Nested challenges within any communicative event.

of attention to the overall rationale for these features of academic language. In other words, we start from the assumption that language forms represent conventionalized solutions to communicative challenges and that decisions about specific forms constitute solutions to those challenges. What are the communicative challenges to which the features of academic language are meant to respond?

In Figures 7.1 and 7.2, we present a first attempt to answer this question (and, in the process, questions about how the traits listed in Table 7.2 relate to one another). Figure 7.1 represents a view of language in which communicative goals are seen as driving decisions about specifics of expression. In this view, all communicative forms are a simultaneous solution to two tasks: representing the self and representing the message. Representing the self involves selecting (or perhaps simply having) a voice and a relationship to the audience; representing the message requires conceptualizing some thought and figuring out what the audience already knows and needs to know about it.

Given a representation of self and message, then discourse and utterance features consistent with those prior frames are realized.

In many communicative exchanges, self-representation is fairly straightforward (e.g., self as purchaser of a kilo of onions, self as student in a first-grade classroom) and the message is relatively uncomplicated (e.g., How much do the Vidalia onions cost? 3 plus 2 equals 5). The rules governing discourse structure, lexical selection, and grammatical formulation for such exchanges are accordingly relatively easy to learn and to implement. Furthermore, formulating some frequently occurring but potentially challenging messages has been greatly simplified by the availability of conventional forms designed to express them (e.g., greetings, requests, apologies, condolences).

We argue, however, that characteristics of academic language represent an accommodation to the two ubiquitous features of communicative tasks – representation of self and of one's message – under particularly challenging conditions (see Figure 7.2).

The first condition is the need to formulate messages that are relatively challenging on any number of grounds – for example, because the content is inherently complicated, because some of the concepts being talked about are abstract or theoretical, because some of the claims being made have an uncertain epistemological status, and so

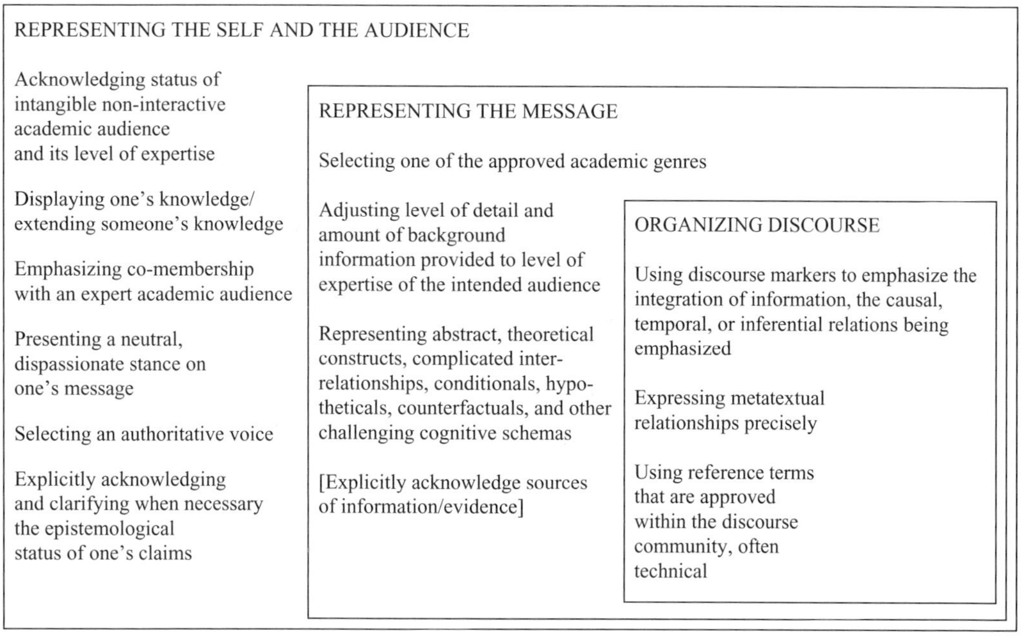

REPRESENTING THE SELF AND THE AUDIENCE

Acknowledging status of intangible non-interactive academic audience and its level of expertise

Displaying one's knowledge/ extending someone's knowledge

Emphasizing co-membership with an expert academic audience

Presenting a neutral, dispassionate stance on one's message

Selecting an authoritative voice

Explicitly acknowledging and clarifying when necessary the epistemological status of one's claims

REPRESENTING THE MESSAGE

Selecting one of the approved academic genres

Adjusting level of detail and amount of background information provided to level of expertise of the intended audience

Representing abstract, theoretical constructs, complicated inter-relationships, conditionals, hypo-theticals, counterfactuals, and other challenging cognitive schemas

[Explicitly acknowledge sources of information/evidence]

ORGANIZING DISCOURSE

Using discourse markers to emphasize the integration of information, the causal, temporal, or inferential relations being emphasized

Expressing metatextual relationships precisely

Using reference terms that are approved within the discourse community, often technical

Figure 7.2. Nested challenges within a communicative event calling for academic language.

on. It is simply more difficult to explain the process by which cells replicate, or the theory of evolution, or the various factors contributing to global warming than it is to negotiate the purchase of onions or respond to an addition problem; therefore, the language required must be more complicated.[4]

The second challenge is to identify the audience and the appropriate relationship between self and audience. An early developmental task is to assess the listener's knowledge so as to provide sufficient information and to gradually free language from situational support. The additional communicative challenges of academic language require learning the traditions that govern discourse among participants in an intangible academic community. The questions of who the audience is and what they know are crucial in appropriately framing the discourse in academic tasks, yet they are not always easy to unravel for students. In face-to-face interactions, speakers learn language by identifying co-occurrences between language forms and situational context via repeated participation in similar speech events with clearly identifiable participants. In those situations, children initially rely on contextual support (e.g., pointing, enactment, gestures, deictics), but they gradually learn to use language as its own context. Of course, autonomous discourse skills develop throughout the school years and are needed in many nonacademic situations as well (e.g., talking on the telephone, telling a story, writing a letter to a friend). From a communicative perspective, what seems to make academic language particularly challenging, in addition to the complexity of the message, is that the components of the communicative situation are less obvious and less accessible. In the academic-discourse world, identifying patterns of co-occurrences between specific situations and linguistic forms is a much harder task. Approaches to this task taken by inexperienced users of academic language range from borrowing oral-language forms[5] to imitating experts' discourse so slavishly as to verge on plagiarism.

Moreover, the producers of academic language need to establish their own level of authoritativeness and negotiate their relationship with a distant and potentially critical or incredulous audience, through the language forms chosen. Impersonal, generic, and distancing forms are required because even if a personal relationship between the producer of academic language and the audience does exist, that relationship is irrelevant to the self being represented under conditions that call for academic language. Thus, the intrusion of spoken-language involvement markers in Example 1 represents a violation of academic-language norms because involvement with the audience is inappropriate under those circumstances. Control over modals and explicit markers of epistemological status (e.g., *probably, likely, undoubtedly, evidently, obviously*) represents acknowledgment of the need to be explicit about the credibility of one's claims. That need derives partly from the obligation to represent the message accurately and partly from the protection of personal authority that comes from making reasoned and modulated claims.

Thus, the challenge lies not only in the audience's physical absence but also more profoundly in the somewhat indeterminate nature of this audience. Figure 7.2 describes the audience as an "intangible noninteractive academic audience." At school, even though teachers are the ones who request assignments, students need to suspend their personal relationship with their teacher and ignore what they know their teacher knows in responding. Instead, they need to imagine a nonfamiliar audience with high levels of language but without specific knowledge of the target topic.

In line with the pragmatics-based model proposed herein, we think that two essential starting points for students are to (1) gain an awareness of the desired relationship among participants in academic communications; and (2) understand that meaning resides not only in *what* they say but also in *how* they communicate it. We are arguing, then, that the long list of academic-language markers reviewed in Table 7.2 can be sorted out usefully by fitting the various items into this pragmatics-based understanding of academic language. Forms that have to do with the largest task – self-representation – are those that express authoritativeness, that perform the function of displaying knowledge to or for someone, that acknowledge co-membership with the audience, that express the speaker's unique voice within the 'academic community,' and that make explicit the epistemological assumptions under which the speaker is operating. Those markers, then, must be integrated with language forms imposed by an adequate representation of the message to be conveyed, which in turn leads to decisions about genre (in the broadest sense), about the audience's level of background knowledge to be presupposed and the level of detail to be included, about the mechanisms for making reference to key concepts and interrelationships, and about the need to acknowledge sources of information. Having established what self and what information will be represented, then text-specific decisions at the level of discourse organization (e.g., How will the organizational structure of the discourse be signaled? How will relationships of temporality, causality, dependency, conditionality, and so forth be talked about? How much anaphoric and exophoric reference is permissible?) and clause constructions can be made.

Figures 7.1 and 7.2 present a relatively simplistic view of the nested relationships among these different levels; clearly, much more work would need to be done to specify implications of a specific decision at any of the levels for decisions at lower or higher levels. Nonetheless, we hope that this representation makes clear that the clause- or discourse-level characteristics typical of academic language may occur under other circumstances, but that the most likely conditions for them are in satisfying the demands that are particular to self-representing as a member of the 'academic-language–using community' and that are imposed by the need to express complex content in efficient and effective ways.

Academic Language: A Research Agenda

The view presented herein makes no clear predictions about the order of development of the various academic-language markers or about an optimal approach to teaching academic language. Indeed, these are issues we would prioritize in a research agenda focused on academic language. Clearly, children start acquiring clause-level skills as soon as they learn to talk; the challenge for teachers is to figure out precisely how the construction of clauses needs to be adapted to contexts in which academic language must be produced and/or comprehended and what new lexical and grammatical knowledge is needed to succeed in those contexts. Similarly, children produce extended discourses from early in their language-acquisition trajectories, and they use in conversational narratives some features that may also be relevant to academic-language texts. So, the specific task of becoming skilled in academic language requires expanding the repertoires available at those two levels for use in nonacademic contexts.

As can be inferred from the model presented herein, the skills required for successful academic-language performance go beyond the traditionally cited lexicogrammatical skills to include a level of metacommunication. For instance, research with Hebrew-speaking children and adults has shown that whereas knowledge of formal sophisticated morphology and syntax increases from age five to age seven, only college-educated adults and some older adolescents are capable of appropriately displaying this knowledge in the construction of texts (Ravid & Tolchinsky, 2002). As stated by Berman (2004) and by Ravid and Tolchinsky (2002), a crucial aspect of later language development, in addition to vocabulary expansion, is learning a variety of sophisticated morpho-syntactic structures and how to use them flexibly for diverse communicative purposes.

We propose, then, two large categories of urgent research questions. One set has to do with the developmental course of academic language and includes attention to issues such as the following: What does normative development look like? How does it relate to literacy development? Which early-developing language skills constitute precursors to later academic language? How do the various components of academic language relate to one another? The second set has to do with instruction – for example: What are effective methods for promoting academic language? Which aspects of the system need explicit instruction and which do not? How can we best embed (or not) academic-language instruction into attention to literacy instruction and content-area learning?

We expand briefly on the research base for these two sets of questions in the following sections.

The Developmental Course and Composition of Academic-Language Skills

What Are the Early Precursors?

Even though the field of academic language is concerned mostly with the study of later language development, it is of crucial importance to recognize that academic-language skills fall on a continuum with earlier language skills. Within this view, exploring earlier language skills that might predict academic-language skills later in life is of particular educational relevance. Specifically, we need research to explore which skills are predictive of later mastery of academic language and, in turn, which contexts are most conducive to efficient learning of academic-language skills.

Reviewing relevant literature, Blum-Kulka (2008) documents preschool children's early development in the areas of conversation and extended discourse, including what she calls *literate discourse*. Blum-Kulka defines *literate discourse* as "include[ing] all those uses of language that involve elements of planning, precision, distancing, internal coherence, and explicitness. It may appear in discursive events that mainly require the skills for constructing a continuous text, such as public lecture or written articles, as well as when the main requirement is conversational skills . . . especially on topics that are remote from the here-and-now" (p. 9).

Within conversational skills, Blum-Kulka includes *thematic coherence, frequency of topical initiatives, capacity for regulation, correction and metapragmatic comments* (e.g., *say it in baby talk*), and *sociolinguistic skills* (i.e., the ability to choose a linguistic style appropriate to the social circumstances of the speech event). Extended discourse skills comprise *structural development* (genre features); *enrichment of linguistic means* (textual fabric, used to structure the text); *conversational autonomy* (free from conversational scaffold from interlocutors); *textual autonomy* (ability to correctly assess the state of knowledge of the interlocutor so that information in text does not assume shared knowledge); and *expansion of range of interest*, among others.

From a theoretical standpoint, we could envision many of these early skills as foundational abilities or rudimentary precursors for later, more sophisticated academic-language skills.

Research on metadiscourse (Hyland & Tse, 2004) also provides an interesting taxonomy of markers that might prove relevant for the study of younger students' oral and written academic language. Whether these metadiscourse elements will be sensitive to developmental changes, in addition to being sensitive to different functions of texts, is an open question that deserves further investigation. Research on the applicability of this taxonomy for pedagogical purposes is another potentially fruitful enterprise. Further research looking at these potential associations would be illuminating, both to construct a comprehensive theoretical model and to inform the design of coherent educational programs.

What Is the Role of Metapragmatic Awareness?

In line with the conceptualization of academic language presented in Figure 7.2, we urge research attention to the question of whether sociolinguistic and stylistic awareness plays a pivotal role in the development of academic language. We might hypothesize that sociolinguistic awareness is a prerequisite to mastering academic language. Systematic linguistic variation can be dialectal, sociolectal, ethnic, or gender-based, as well as determined by genre, register, and modality (Ravid & Tolchinsky, 2002). The ability to switch appropriately across language varieties and registers depends on the opportunities to participate in various communicative situations (Hymes, 1974). Whereas most speakers can at least partially adapt their language forms to specific contexts, expanding these adaptation skills so that students learn how to map language forms onto a variety of situations in a conscious and reflective way may be a crucial step in fostering academic-language proficiency. Moreover, stylistic awareness – that is, being aware of a set of linguistic options that have the potential to realize a variety of alternative meanings – may also be necessary. Schleppegrell's research connects particular language forms with specific expectations in illuminating ways. For instance, she documents how the authoritative stance typical of academic discourse is constructed through impersonal subjects, declarative mood structure, and lexical realization of meanings; and she relates lexical density and nominalization to the function of incorporating more (ideational) content into each clause (Schleppegrell, 2001).

What Is the Effect of Mode?

Academic language is understood as a construct that goes beyond modes of expression and disciplinary boundaries. Bailey (2007) argues for a core set of academic-language skills that cuts across different disciplines and is complemented with additional discipline-specific skills. Within this conceptualization, it is relevant to study how different modes of expression (written versus oral) and skills in specific discipline-based genres (a social studies report versus a science-lab report) influence each other. To what extent skills learned in one mode of expression or in one genre transfer to other domains is an important question, with relevant pedagogical implications.

Whereas nobody would deny a bidirectional influence of spoken and written language, some researchers emphasize one side as the source of more sophisticated skills. Ravid and Tolchinsky's (2002) intriguing model of linguistic literacy proposes a bidirectional influence; however, their model states that basic features (e.g., basic syntax and phonology) are transferred from speaking to writing, whereas sophisticated features originate in writing and, therefore, exposure to and production of written language is the main factor in enriching linguistic literacy. However, some complex features might also transfer from spoken to written language, as Collaborative Reasoning studies demonstrate (Reznitskaya et al., 2001). Reznitskaya and colleagues show that higher levels of argumentation or reasoning can be achieved through the scaffolding of explicit discourse stratagems. To construct a theoretical model that establishes associations or predictive relationships across modes of expression, research needs to assess later language development so that we can begin to understand which skills get transferred under which conditions.

Is Academic Language Truly More Grammatically Complex?

Findings on syntactic complexity of academic language are not uncontroversial. Whereas many authors have pointed to a higher degree of subordination in academic writing versus colloquial speech, others (Poole & Field, 1976) have reported more embedding in spoken language. Tolchinsky and Aparici (2000) found a higher degree of embedding in written than spoken narratives in Spanish but more frequent center-embedded relative clauses in subject position in spoken than written expository texts. As pointed out by Ravid and Tolchinsky (2002) and previously emphasized by Biber (1995), language features should be studied taking into account the influence of register, degree of formality, and planning. In the study of academic-language skills, then, the three domains of knowledge identified in Table 7.2 and all contextual factors mentioned in Table 7.1 should be considered to develop a precise picture of which skills are displayed under which circumstances.

What Is the Normative Developmental Course and the Ultimate Goal?

Teachers' expectations and students' skills vary not only by grade but also by discipline and specific genres within disciplines. In addition, academic-language skills can progress to reach highly sophisticated levels such as those used in sharing professional knowledge among a community of experts. Within this range of possibilities, what should be considered the ideal developmental endpoint for academic-language development and, just as important, the minimal educational standards for different grades and content areas?

Teaching Academic-Language Skills

Which Academic-Language Skills Should Be Instructed?

Teaching about mechanisms for representing complex information – both as an approach to reading comprehension and as an input to academic writing – could be helpful in supporting students' development of academic-language skills. Here again, however, the task may be primarily one of expanding the learner's repertoire of useful stratagems for formulating messages because children from their first months of talking understand the challenge of trying to express complex thoughts with limited language skills. Consider the child lexical forms formerly seen as overgeneralizations, such as calling the postman *daddy* or calling horses *cows*; most child-language researchers would now argue that these are simply immature attempts to comment on similarities or to refer despite lexical gaps (Gelman, Croft, Fu, Clausner, & Gottfried, 1998). Their occurrence suggests that even young children can solve the problem of expressing complex ideas, although in ways that may be unconventional and thus often unsuccessful.

Exposure to talking styles that display features of academic discourse and participation in academic genres is probably essential for mastering academic language. Children who come from families that value the accumulation and display of knowledge for its own sake, who require warrants for claims, and who model and scaffold the organization of extended discourse and sophisticated utterances will probably have a much easier transition into academic language. However, documentation of how some families support their children's academic-language skills is sorely needed.

For school instruction, attention to linguistic form may be a powerful mechanism for improving students' academic-language skills. A traditional grammar approach might be effective, but the value of a discussion about self, audience, purpose, and the appropriate lexical and grammatical means to represent information in specific school tasks should be ascertained. Assuming that teaching grammatical and lexical devices is essential, we agree with a little-cited claim made by Bakhtin (1942) decades ago:

> *Without constantly considering the stylistic significance of grammatical choices, the instruction of grammar inevitably turns into scholasticism. In practice, however, the instructor very rarely provides any sort of stylistic interpretation of the grammatical forms covered in class. Every grammatical form is at the same time a means of representing reality. Particularly in instances where the speaker or writer may choose between two or more equally grammatically correct syntactic forms, the choice is determined not by grammatical but by representative and expressive effectiveness of these forms. Teaching syntax without providing stylistic elucidation and without attempting to enrich the students' own speech does not help them improve the creativity of their own speech productions (quoted in Bazerman, 2005).*

What Are Effective Pedagogical Approaches?

Research-based pedagogical approaches to teaching academic-language skills within specific disciplines or genres are starting to emerge (Lemke, 1990; Schleppegrell, Achugar, & Oteiza, 2004). For instance, content-based instruction (CBI) is a pedagogy for English as a Second Language that integrates language and content-area knowledge with the purpose of improving both dimensions within specific disciplines (Schleppegrell & de Oliveira, forthcoming). These emerging approaches are promising, yet their design and effectiveness are still in need of further study. How to make the linguistic expectations explicit to students, at what level of precision, and how to further develop sociolinguistic and stylistic awareness skills to improve academic-language performance in the classroom are still open research questions.

A related challenge is how to provide instruction without prescription. Many genre-based classroom pedagogies have been critiqued because of their prescriptive and hierarchical nature and the low transferability of skills produced (Fosen, 2000; Kamler, 1994). Developing students' sociolinguistic competence, stylistic awareness, familiarity with linguistic expectations, and command of lexical and grammatical features of specific genres while emphasizing the individual creativity required for an expert mastery of the interplay between form and meaning is a major challenge.

How Do Planning, Revision, and Rewriting Improve the Advancement of Academic-Language Skills?

In a conceptualization of academic language as a construct that cuts across modes of expression, exploring the effect of editing as a way of fostering acquisition and awareness of academic skills seems promising. Whereas encouraging students to edit their own texts seems to be a successful approach to improving writing skills, little research has explored the effect of rereading and revising on students' learning (Klein & Olson, 2001). Research suggests that frequent opportunities for authentic writing improve the quality of students' written products (see Klein & Olson, 2001, for a brief review). Thus, would frequent opportunities for editing texts have a positive effect on academic-language performance? If so, would the skills learned transfer from writing to speaking? How much guidance do students need so that editing can effectively improve academic-language skills?

How Can Schools Provide Intervention in Academic-Language Skills to Students Who Start Far Behind?

Children enter school with different linguistic, sociolinguistic, and pragmatic experiences, and not all of them have been exposed to the forms of communication valued at school. Strategies to make children feel comfortable in expressing who they are and what they bring to school should be at the core of any instructional program. At the same time, schools have the moral obligation to provide all children with equal opportunities to participate in the discourse of academics that is a requisite for later academic success. Children's education can be based in their own culture while also providing explicit teaching of the skills required for success in the academic context of schools (Delpit, 1995). Snow, Cancini, Gonzalez, and Shriberg (1989) found that meeting the expectations of a formal academic register, such as definitional discourse, correlated with academic success. Therefore, children who are less skillful in academic language are less likely to succeed at school. How to provide all children – ELLs and also struggling native English speakers – with equal opportunities of mastering academic language in a way that incorporates and values their primary discourses is yet another challenge.

How Can the Role of Language in Self-Presentation Be Taught?

It is not obvious that all children automatically see language as a form of self-representation. Evidence from children growing up bilingual suggests that they choose the language that is effective for communication (i.e., for formulating a message that is likely to be successful) from a very early age (e.g., Genesee, 2005, 2006; Genesee & Nicoladis, in press; Taeschner, 1983) but that they become aware of the 'otherness' imposed by speaking a minority language in public only somewhat later. Furthermore, understanding the relationship of a language to an identity is rather different from understanding how features within a language express identity. Certainly, students do identity work through language in adolescence (Eckert, 1989), but it is not clear how much metalinguistic awareness they have about those linguistic decisions. Thus, it is worth exploring whether students might benefit from teaching designed to make the problem of self-representation explicit because that is a source of important academic-language features – but, at the same time, a pragmatic force to which they may be blind. One approach to this task might be sociolinguistic exploration of questions like "How does the language of people in power differ from the language of those in subordinate positions?" Another approach might involve text analysis to determine, for example, which markers readers use to infer the writer's level of certainty or to decide whether they consider the writer trustworthy.

Do Students Need Instruction in Metasociolinguistic Awareness?

Another somewhat different approach would be taken if we assumed that students knew the importance of linguistically managing self-representation but lacked a full understanding of the cues signaling the appropriate representation for academic settings. In that case, a metasociolinguistic curriculum might be appropriate, one that specified the factors leading to the need for greater care in representing oneself as knowledgeable or trustworthy (see Table 7.1 for a preliminary list of the situations that do/do not call for academic language). How should talking to one's friends in class differ from talking to them on the playground? How does pursuing an intellectual dispute differ from arguing with one's boyfriend?[6] Charting students' knowledge about these issues might be a research undertaking worth pursuing and might shed light on how to gradually bring them to deeper understandings of the interactions between form and meaning.

A related research area involves exploring the best strategy to help students understand the importance of continuing to expand their language knowledge. For example, would it be fruitful to teach teachers and/or students explicitly about the concept of 'academic language'? Should we also teach students about the multidimensionality of language – discussing, for example, how having a conversation with friends requires a different set of skills than a formal presentation? Would this knowledge be helpful and, if so, at what level of specification? Which purposeful activities would best help promote this learning?

In What Informational Context Should Teachers Teach Academic-Language Expression?

Studying the development of definitional skill, Snow (1990) reported no age differences in the amount of information children provided but significant age differences in "the way they organize that information into the formal structure required" (p. 708). These findings lead us to reflect about whether is it too much to ask of students that they simultaneously learn content and linguistic organization. Should academic language perhaps be taught initially in the context of highly familiar topics or topics for which students have abundant background knowledge?

Which Genres Are the Most Important?

Which discourse varieties should be included under the label "academic language" for the purposes of improving school-relevant linguistic skills? What are the crucial discourse varieties students need to master in school? Should we study mainly the language of the most traditional academic subjects, or should we also include other professional discourses, such as journalistic, legal, medical, or business language? Ravid and Tolchinsky (2002, p. 421) note that discourse varieties "can be thought of as multidimensional spaces within which speakers and writers move, and which can be defined at different depths of focus: for example, . . . the genre of a high school physics textbook versus the less specific genre of natural sciences." What should be the depth of focus in defining academic registers? In other words, should we focus on highly specific genres, such as a laboratory report, a project proposal, and a biography, or should we direct our efforts to clusters of genres that share register features, such as scientific versus persuasive discourse?

Conclusion

We have suggested several possible lines of research focused on understanding the origins of academic-language skill, probing the differential success of different groups of students with it and evaluating different approaches to helping all students master it. The basic question underlying all of these suggestions is one about the source of the challenge: academic language, like all linguistic communication, involves challenges at the level of self-representation, representing a message, constructing discourse, and composing utterances. Where in this nested process do students encounter particular difficulties, and are those difficulties primarily ones of understanding or of performing the task? If we had the answer to these questions, then we would be well on our way to devising effective instruction for students and professional development for teachers to ensure universal improvement in this crucial aspect of academic functioning.

Notes

1 The authors' names are in alphabetical order. The authors would like to thank The Spencer Foundation, which has supported the first author's work on this topic, and the Institute of Education Sciences, which has supported the second author through the grants

"Diagnostic Assessment of Reading Comprehension: Development and Validation" and "Improving Reading Comprehension for Struggling Readers."

2 *Register* is a central notion in SFL. *Register* is defined as "the constellation of lexical and grammatical features that characterizes particular uses of language" (Halliday & Hasan, 1989). As elaborated by Schleppegrell (2001, pp. 431–432): "A register reflects the context of a text's production and at the same time enables the text to realize that context. In other words, the grammatical choices are made on the basis of the speaker's perception of the social context, and those choices then also serve to instantiate that social context. . . . Registers manifest themselves both in choice of words or phrases and also in the way that clauses are constructed and linked." Each genre has its own register features and different genres can share many common register features. *Genres* are purposeful, staged uses of language that are accomplished in particular cultural contexts (Christie, 1985, as quoted in Schleppegrell, 2001). As stated by Schleppegrell, certain lexical and grammatical features are common to many school genres because they are functional for "doing schooling" (Schleppegrell, 2001, p. 432).

3 This table is organized in categories imposed by the authors of this chapter.

4 Note that we are not arguing here that academic language is more complex overall than other forms of language. Language forms constitute adequate responses to a variety of communicative challenges; thus, complexity can be manifested at different levels in various language exchanges. We are simply highlighting one specific dimension of complexity. More colloquial forms can be more complex in other dimensions – for example, in how linkages among clauses are indicated from one part of a discourse to another (Schleppegrell, 2001; Hemphill, 1989).

5 For example, a paper submitted to a special issue of *Hormones and Behavior* that reviewed how the functioning of pheromones as social cues is mediated by brain structures included the sentence, "We thus conclude there is something funky going on in the amygdala."

6 It is worth noting that in one fifth-grade classroom that implemented the Word Generation curriculum, the teacher often closed down the heated student debates on the topic of the week by saying "but we are still going to be friends, right?," thus explicitly marking the distinction between the academic arguments and the normal classroom relationships.

References

Achugar, M., & Schleppegrell, M. J. (2005). Beyond connectors: The construction of cause in history textbooks. *Linguistics and Education, 16* (3), 298–318.

August, D., & Shanahan, T. (2006). Developing literacy in second-language learners: Report of the national literacy panel on language minority children and youth. Mahwah, NJ: Lawrence Erlbaum; Washington, DC: Center for Applied Linguistics.

Bailey, A. (2007). *The language demands of school: Putting academic English to the test.* New Haven, CT: Yale University Press.

Bailey, A. (in press). From Lambie to Lambaste: The conceptualization, operationalization, and use of academic language in the assessment of ELL students. In K. Rolstad (Ed.), *Rethinking school language.* Mahwah, NJ: Lawrence Erlbaum Associates.

Bazerman, C. (2005). An essay on pedagogy by Mikhail M. Bakhtin. *Written Communication,* 22 (3), 333–338.

Berman, R. A. (2004). The role of context in developing narrative abilities. In S. Strömqvist & L. Verhoeven, (Eds.), *Relating events in narrative: Typological and contextual perspectives* (pp. 261–280). Mahwah, NJ: Lawrence Erlbaum.

Bhatia, V. J. (2002). Applied genre analysis: Analytical advances and pedagogical procedures. In A. M. Johns (Ed.), *Genre in the classroom: Multiple perspectives* (pp. 279–284). Mahwah, NJ: Lawrence Erlbaum Associates.

Biber, D. (1995). *Dimensions of register variation: A cross-linguistic comparison.* Cambridge: Cambridge University Press.

Biber, D., & Reppen, R. (2002). What does frequency have to do with grammar teaching? *Studies in Second Language Acquisition,* 24 (2), 199–208.

Blum-Kulka, S. (2008). Language, communication and literacy: Steps in the development of literate discourse. In P. Klein & K. Yablon (Eds.), *Modes of early education and their effect on improving education in school* (pp. 117–155). The Initiative for Applied Research in Education, Israeli Academy of Science. [Report published in Hebrew; chapter available in English]

Chafe, W., & Danielewicz, J. M. (1987). Properties of spoken and written language. In R. Horowitz & S. J. Samuels (Eds.), *Comprehending oral and written language* (pp. 83–113). San Diego, CA: Academic Press.

Chamot, A. U., & O'Malley, J. M. (1994). The CALLA handbook: Implementing the cognitive academic language learning approach. Reading, MA: Addison-Wesley.

Colombi, M. C. (2002). Academic language development in Latino students' writing in Spanish. In M. J. Schleppegrell & M. C. Colombi (Eds.), *Developing advanced literacy in first and second languages: Meaning with power* (pp. 67–86). Mahwah, NJ: Lawrence Erlbaum Associates.

Colombi, M. C., & Schleppegrell, M. J. (2002). Theory and practice in the development of advanced literacy. In M. J. Schleppegrell & M. C. Colombi (Eds.), *Developing advanced literacy in first and second languages: Meaning with power* (pp. 1–20). Mahwah, NJ: Lawrence Erlbaum Associates.

Cummins, J. (1980). The cross-lingual dimensions of language proficiency: Implications for bilingual education and the optimal age issue. *TESOL Quarterly*, 14, 175–187.

Cummins, J. (1981). Age on arrival and immigrant second-language learning in Canada: A reassessment. *Applied Linguistics*, 2, 132–149.

Cummins, J. (1984). Language proficiency and academic achievement revisited: A response. In C. Rivera (Ed.), *Language proficiency and academic achievement* (pp. 71–76). Clevedon, UK: Multilingual Matters.

Cummins, J. (2001). *Negotiating identities: Education for empowerment in a diverse society*. 2nd Edition. Los Angeles: California Association for Bilingual Education.

Delpit, L. (1995). *Other people's children: Cultural conflict in the classroom*. New York: The New Press.

Eckert, P. (1989). *Jocks and burnouts: Social categories and identity in the high school*. New York: Teachers College Press.

Fosen, C. (2000). Genres made real: Genre theory as pedagogy, method, and content. Paper presented at the Annual Meeting of the Conference on Composition and Communication, Minneapolis, MN.

Gelman, S., Croft, W., Fu, P., Clausner, T., & Gottfried, G. (1998). Why is a pomegranate an apple? The role of shape, taxonomic relatedness, and prior lexical knowledge in children's overextensions of *apple* and *dog*. *Journal of Child Language*, 25, 267–291.

Genesee, F. (2005). The capacity of the language faculty: Contributions from studies of simultaneous bilingual acquisition. In J. Cohen, K. T. McAlister, K. Rolstad, & J. MacSwan (Eds.), *Proceedings of the 4th International Symposium on Bilingualism* (pp. 890–901). Somerville, MA: Cascadilla Press.

Genesee, F. (2006). Bilingual first language acquisition in perspective. In E. Hoff & P. McCardle (Eds.), *Childhood bilingualism* (pp. 45–67). Clevedon, UK: Multilingual Matters.

Genesee, F., & Nicoladis, E. (in press). Bilingual acquisition. In E. Hoff & M. Shatz (Eds.), *Handbook of language development*, Oxford: Blackwell.

Halliday, M. A. K. (1993). Some grammatical problems in scientific English. In M. A. K. Halliday & Martin, J. R., *Writing science: Literacy and discursive power* (pp. 69–85). London: Falmer (Critical Perspectives on Literacy and Education); Pittsburgh: University of Pittsburgh Press. (Pittsburgh Series in Composition, Literacy, and Culture).

Halliday, M. A. K. (1994a). A language development approach to education. In N. Bird, et al. (Eds.), *Language and learning*. Papers presented at the Annual International language in Education Conference, Hong Kong, 1993.

Halliday, M. A. K. (1994b). *An introduction to functional grammar*. London: Edward Arnold.

Halliday, M. A. K., & Hasan, R. (1989). *Language context, and text: Aspects of language in a social-semiotic perspective*. Oxford: Oxford university Press.

Halliday, M. A. K., & Martin, J. R. (1993). *Writing science: Literacy and discursive power*. London: Falmer (Critical Perspectives on Literacy and Education); Pittsburgh: University of Pittsburgh Press. (Pittsburgh Series in Composition, Literacy, and Culture).

Hemphill, L. (1989). Topic development, syntax, and social class. *Discourse Processes*, 12 (3), 267–286.

Hyland, K., & Tse, P. (2004). Metadiscourse in academic writing: A reappraisal. *Applied Linguistics*, 25 (2), 156–177.

Hymes, D. (1974). *Foundations in sociolinguistics: An ethnographic approach*. Philadelphia: University of Pennsylvania Press.

Kamler, B. (1994). Gender and genre in early writing. *Linguistics and Education*, 6 (2), 153–182.

Kieffer, M., Lesaux, N., & Snow, C. E. (2008). Promises and pitfalls: Implications of No Child Left Behind for defining, assessing, and serving English language learners. In G. Sunderman (Ed.), *Holding NCLB accountable: Achieving accountability, equity, and school reform* (pp. 57–74). Thousand Oaks, CA: Corwin Press.

Klein, P. D., & Olson, D. R. (2001). Texts, technology, and thinking: Lessons from the Great Divide. *Language Arts*, 78 (3), 227–236.

Lemke, J. L. (1990). *Talking science: Language, learning, and values*. Norwood, NJ: Ablex Publishing.

Michaels, S., & O'Connor, M. C. (2002). *Accountable talk: Classroom conversation that works* [CD-ROM]. Pittsburgh, PA: University of Pittsburgh.

Ong, W. J. (1982/1995). *Orality and literacy: The technologizing of the world*. London/New York: Routledge Press.

Pilgreen, J. (2006). Supporting English learners: Developing academic language in the content area classroom. In A. Terrel & N. L. Hadaway (Eds.), *Supporting the literacy development of English learners* (pp. 41–60). Newark, DE: International Reading Association.

Poole, M. E., & Field, T. W. (1976). A comparison of oral and written code elaboration. *Language and Speech*, 19, 305–311.

Ravid, D., & Tolchinsky, L. (2002). Developing linguistic literacy: A comprehensive model. *Journal of Child Language*, 29 (2), 417–447.

Reznitskaya, A., Anderson, R., Nurlen, B., Nguyen-Jahiel, K., Archodidou, A., & Kim, S. (2001). Influence of oral discussion on written argument. *Discourse Processes*, 32, 155–175.

Scarcella, R. (2003). Academic English: A conceptual framework. The University of California Linguistic Minority Research Institute. Technical Report 2003–1.

Schleppegrell, M. J. (2001). Linguistic features of the language of schooling. *Linguistics and Education*, 14 (4), 431–459.

Schleppegrell, M. J. (2007). The linguistic challenges of mathematics teaching and learning: A research review. *Reading & Writing Quarterly: Overcoming Learning Difficulties*, 23 (2), 139–159.

Schleppegrell, M. J., Achugar, M., & Oteiza, T. (2004). The grammar of history: Enhancing content-based instruction through a functional focus on language. In *TESOL Quarterly: A Journal for Teachers of English to Speakers of Other Languages and of Standard English as a Second Dialect*, 38, 67–93.

Schleppegrell, M. J., & Colombi, M. C. (2002). *Developing advanced literacy in first and second languages: Meaning with power* (pp. 1–20). Mahwah, NJ: Lawrence Erlbaum Associates.

Schleppegrell, M. J., & de Oliveira, L. C. (forthcoming). An integrated language and content approach for history teachers. *Journal of English for Academic Purposes*.

Snow, C. E. (1990). The development of definitional skill. *Journal of Child Language*, 17, 697–710.

Snow, C. E., Cancini, H., Gonzalez, P., & Shriberg, E. (1989). Giving formal definitions: An oral language correlate of school literacy. In D. Bloome (Ed.), *Classrooms and literacy* (pp. 233–249). Norwood, NJ: Ablex.

Spolsky, B., & Hult, F. M. (2008). *Handbook of educational linguistics*. Oxford: Blackwell Publishing.

Swales, J. (1990). *Genre analysis: English in academic and research settings*. Cambridge: Cambridge University Press.

Taeschner, T. (1983). *The sun is feminine: A study on language acquisition in bilingual children*. Berlin: Springer-Verlag.

Tolchinsky, L. & Aparici, M. (2000). Is written language more complex than spoken language? International literacy project working papers in developing literacy across genres, modalities, and languages, Vol. III. Barcelona: Institute of Educational Sciences.

Wignell, P., Martin, J. R., & Eggins, S. (1993). The discourse of geography: Ordering and explaining the experiential world. In M. A. K. Halliday & J. R. Martin (Eds.), *Writing science: Literacy and discursive power* (pp. 136–165). London: Falmer (Critical Perspectives on Literacy and Education); Pittsburgh: University of Pittsburgh Press (Pittsburgh Series in Composition, Literacy, and Culture).

CHAPTER 8

The Basic Processes in Reading

Insights from Neuroscience

Usha Goswami

The development of reading in children who speak different languages may appear to make rather different demands on their brains. Children who are learning to read languages like Chinese and Japanese would seem to require excellent visuospatial skills in order to distinguish between the visually complex characters that represent spoken words in their languages. Children who are learning to read languages like Italian or Spanish would seem to require code-breaking skills because each letter in those alphabetic languages corresponds to a single sound. Hence, once the brain has learned the (approximately) twenty-six–symbol code, reading should be largely a process of phonological assembly. However, the development of reading in deaf children who communicate via sign language seems to make different demands. The deaf brain has to learn to read a language that is not the language of manual communication. Despite these apparently different demands on the brain, however, research in neuroscience suggests mainly biological unity concerning reading development and developmental dyslexia.

As I demonstrate in this chapter, brain-imaging studies suggest that reading across languages begins primarily as a phonological process. The neural structures that are important for spoken language are particularly active in the early phases of learning to read. As expertise develops, an area in the visual cortex, dubbed the *visual word form area* (VWFA), becomes increasingly active during the task of reading (Cohen & Dehaene, 2004). This area is very close to the visual areas that are active during picture naming, but the VWFA does not seem to be a logographic system. This is because the VWFA is also active during nonsense-word reading. Because nonsense words have no word forms in the mental lexicon, the VWFA probably stores orthography–phonology connections at different grain sizes (Goswami & Ziegler, 2006). Finally, in children with developmental dyslexia, there is selective under-activation of the phonological areas of the brain. Targeted remediation – for example, via explicit phonological training – can improve levels of activation in these areas, 'normalising' the neural activity during reading for affected children.

In this chapter, I first discuss briefly the development of reading in typically developing children who are learning to read different languages. Using this cross-language focus, I attempt to pinpoint the critical developmental factors in reading acquisition, the factors for which we can use neuroimaging to give us further insights. I develop a cognitive framework that can also account for developmental dyslexia and then discuss associated neuroimaging studies. To date, there is little neuroimaging data concerning the development of reading in typically developing children. There is significant neuroimaging data from adults who can already read and some neuroimaging data from studies of children with developmental dyslexia. In general, my focus is on studies of children. However, studies of reading in deaf adults are also considered.

The Development of Reading across Languages

Reading and writing require acquisition of the ability to comprehend and communicate using language expressed in visual form. The visual form may comprise an alphabet –, a code in which individual speech sounds are represented by individual symbols – as discussed for Italian and Spanish. The visual form may comprise characters, which may represent whole words or individual syllables in the spoken form, as discussed for Chinese and Japanese. The child may have to learn to comprehend a visual language that is different from the language of communication, as in the case of deaf children or those who must learn to read in their non-native language (e.g., children of immigrants). In all cases, the act of reading is a linguistic act. The visual symbols that must be learned represent a spoken language. To become a fluent reader, therefore, the cognitive skills involved in processing spoken language may be expected to be important.

This is indeed the case. Developmental studies of reading acquisition across languages show that individual differences in reading development are (for the most part) governed by individual differences in phonological skills. Some of the evidence for this claim is discussed herein. Individual differences in reading are not governed by individual differences in visual skills, although in the earliest phases of learning to read character-based languages like Chinese, visual memory skills are important (Siok & Fletcher, 2001). Even children with developmental dyslexia, who struggle to acquire reading, seem to have good visual memory skills (Vellutino, 1979). Although originally conceived as a visual disorder, in which letters reversed themselves on the page (Hinshelwood, 1917), the consensus from more recent research is that developmental dyslexia across languages and scripts is, in general, a *phonological* disorder (see Ziegler & Goswami, 2005, for a recent review). A child who has developmental dyslexia is one who has a serious and specific difficulty with the neural representation of the sounds that comprise words.

The Core Role of Phonology

In fact, children's awareness of the phonological structure of their language, measured before schooling, is the strongest predictor that we have of how well a particular child will learn to read and to spell. This awareness is usually called 'phonological awareness' and is usually defined by performance in tasks requiring children to detect and manipulate component sounds in words, which can be defined at a number of different linguistic levels. First, a single word can comprise a number of syllables (e.g., *helicopter* has four syllables; *toffee* has two syllables). Second, words can share subparts, like the subpart that makes two words rhyme. A word like *fountain* rhymes with *mountain* because the words share their phonology after the first sound (linguists call this first sound the *onset*). A word like *string* rhymes with *sing* even though *string* has an onset consisting of three sounds and *sing* has an onset consisting of one sound. The rhyming part of the syllable, the sound 'ing', is called the *rime* by linguists. So onset-rime is a second linguistic level at which children can develop phonological awareness; phonemes are the third linguistic level. The onset in *string* comprises three phonemes, and the onset in *sing* is a single phoneme. Phonemes are the smallest units of sound in words that change meaning. For example, *string* differs in meaning from *spring* because the phoneme /t/ is replaced by the phoneme /p/.

Most studies measuring phonological awareness in children have focused on the phoneme level of awareness. This is because phonemes usually correspond to alphabetic letters: the alphabet is a code that works (in general) at the phoneme level of phonology. However, syllables are the primary phonological processing units across most of the world's languages. Furthermore, in most of the world's languages, syllable structure is simple. Syllables consist of a consonant (C) and a vowel (V). The CV syllable structure characterises spoken languages as diverse as Chinese, Spanish, Italian and Japanese. Clearly, not all languages with a CV syllable structure use the alphabet as their visual code, although many do. Thus, most syllables in most languages in the world contain two sounds: an onset comprising a single phoneme and a rime comprising a single phoneme. This means that for languages with a CV syllable structure, there is no distinction among phonemes, onsets and rimes. Theoretically, this should make it easier for children who speak those languages to become phonologically aware. Indeed, cross-language research suggests that this is the case (Ziegler & Goswami, 2005).

Spoken English does not have many CV syllables. An analysis of all English monosyllables showed that only 5 percent followed the CV pattern (De Cara & Goswami, 2002). Examples include words like *me* and *do*. Most of the monosyllables in English, 43 percent, followed a CVC structure ('cat', 'rope', 'mill'). Note that the phonological structure can be CVC even if the chosen spelling is CVCV (as in 'vowel e' spellings in English: *rope, cake, mile*). The next most frequent phonological structure was CVCC. This accounted for an additional 21 percent of English monosyllables ('fist', 'belt', 'camp'). A further 15 percent of monosyllables followed a CCVC phonological structure ('drip', 'clog', 'steam'). As might be expected, dividing complex syllables like these into their constituent sounds is more challenging for young children across English-speaking countries (Ziegler & Goswami, 2005).

The Development of Phonological Awareness across Languages

It is usually assumed that phonological awareness develops from the phonological representations that children must develop when acquiring spoken language. During the first four or five years of language development, children know about phonology at an implicit level by being competent users of their language. Whereas the average one-year-old might have a productive vocabulary of approximately 100 words, by the age of six it is estimated that the average child's vocabulary will contain approximately 14,000 words (Dollaghan, 1994). If a child is a competent language user, as most children indeed are when they enter school, all of these words will be represented as phonologically distinct from each other. This very achievement seems to lead to the development of phonological awareness at the syllable and onset-rime levels. Research studies across languages suggest a universal sequence in the development of phonological awareness even though the phonological structure of the syllables comprising some of the languages differs. Children in languages studied so far (primarily the European languages and Chinese) first become aware of relatively 'large' sounds in words, such as syllables. They then become aware of the onset-rime division of the syllable ('cl-og', 'str-ing', 'j-ump'). Finally, they become aware of phonemes. Whereas the awareness of syllables, onsets and rimes develops in most children at the age of three to five years, the development of phoneme awareness depends on, to some extent, when literacy instruction begins (or when direct training in phonemes is given). It also depends on phonological complexity. Children learning to speak languages with CV syllables (e.g., Italian) usually develop phoneme awareness more quickly than children learning to speak languages with complex syllable structures, such as English and German. Nevertheless, illiterate adults do not spontaneously develop awareness of phonemes. Learning to read plays an important developmental role in phoneme awareness.

Word	WIGWAM	
Syllable	WIG	WAM
Onset-Rime	W IG	W AM
Phoneme	W I G	W A M

Figure 8.1. Schematic depiction of hierarchical phonological structure for the English bisyllabic word *wigwam*.

The Sequence of Phonological Development

The development of phonological awareness in young children across languages has been measured by a wide variety of tasks. For example, children may be asked to monitor and correct speech errors (e.g., 'sie' to 'pie'), they may be asked to select the 'odd word out' in terms of sound (e.g., Which word does not rhyme: 'fit', 'pat', 'cat'?), or they may be asked to make a judgment about sound similarity (e.g., Do these two words share a syllable: 'hammer – hammock'?) (Bradley & Bryant, 1983; Chaney, 1992; Treiman & Zukowski, 1991). Older children might be asked to count sounds in words by tapping with a stick (e.g., the component sounds in 'soap' = three taps) or to blend sounds into words (e.g., 'd-ish', or 'd-i-sh' to make 'dish') (Liberman, Shankweiler, Fischer, & Carter, 1974; Metsala, 1999). Clearly, these different tasks also make differing cognitive demands on young children. The best way to investigate the *sequence* of phonological development, therefore, is to equate the cognitive demands of the chosen task across linguistic level. Surprisingly, it is rare to find research studies that have used the same cognitive task to study the emergence of phonological awareness at the different linguistic levels of syllable, onset-rime and phoneme in any language.

The most comprehensive studies in English are those conducted by Anthony and his colleagues (Anthony & Lonigan, 2004; Anthony, Lonigan, Burgess, Driscoll, Phillips, & Cantor, 2002; Anthony, Lonigan, Driscoll, Phillips, & Burgess, 2003). For example, Anthony et al. (2003) used blending and deletion tasks at the word, syllable, onset-rime and phoneme levels. They studied a large group of more than a thousand children, and they included a much wider age range than many studies (i.e., two to six years). Anthony et al. (2003) found that the development of children's phonological awareness followed the hierarchical model outlined previously and shown in schematic form in Figure 8.1. English-speaking children generally mastered word-level skills before they mastered syllable-level skills, syllable-level skills before onset/rime skills, and onset/rime-level skills before phoneme skills.

When making developmental comparisons across languages, counting and oddity tasks have been particularly useful. These tasks, pioneered by Liberman et al. (1974) and by Bradley and Bryant (1983), have been used in numerous languages, with the counting/tapping task being used to measure syllable-versus-phoneme awareness and the oddity task being used to measure onset-rime awareness. Regarding syllable-versus-phoneme awareness, syllable awareness has been found to emerge prior to phoneme awareness in children learning all languages so far studied. For example, Cossu and colleagues (1988) studied the development of syllable-versus-phoneme awareness in Italian preschoolers and school-aged children using a counting task (comparing groups of four-, five- and seven- to eight-year-olds). Syllable awareness was shown by 67 percent of the four-year-olds, 80 percent of the five-year-olds, and 100 percent of the school-age sample (Cossu, Shankweiler, Liberman, Katz, & Tola, 1988). Phoneme awareness was shown by 13 percent of the four-year-olds, 27 percent of the five-year-olds and 97 percent of the school-age sample. A similar study was carried out by Liberman, Shankweiler, Fischer, & Carter (1974) with American children. Syllable awareness was shown by 46 percent of the four-year-olds, 48 percent of the five-year-olds and 90 percent of the six-year-olds. The four- and five-year-olds were pre-readers, and the six-year-olds had been learning to read for about a year. Phonemic awareness was shown by 0 percent of the four-year-olds, 17 percent of the five-year-olds and 70 percent of the six-year-olds. Liberman et al. concluded that whereas syllabic awareness was present in pre-readers, phonemic awareness was dependent on learning to read. Regarding onset-rime awareness, studies using the oddity task have shown that onset-rime awareness emerges long before schooling in studies with Chinese, German, English, and Norwegian children (Bradley & Bryant, 1983; Ho & Bryant, 1997; Hoien, Lundberg, Stanovich, & Bjaalid, 1995; Wimmer, Landerl, & Schneider, 1994, see Ziegler & Goswami, 2005, for a full survey).

In all languages so far studied, therefore, phonological awareness progresses from an awareness of large units of sound, such as syllables, onsets and rimes, to an awareness of 'small' units of sound – phonemes. In all languages so far studied, including character-based scripts, individual differences in phonological awareness are predictive of individual differences in literacy acquisition (Ho & Bryant, 1997; Hoien et al., 1995; Schneider, Roth, & Ennemoser, 2000; see Ziegler & Goswami, 2005, for a summary). Finally, in all languages so far studied, providing children with training in phonological awareness and letter-sound correspondences has a measurable positive impact on progress in literacy (Bradley & Bryant, 1983; Lundberg, Frost, & Petersen, 1988; Schneider, Kuespert, Roth, Vise, & Marx, 1997). Awareness of the phonological structure of one's spoken language is clearly fundamental to the acquisition of literacy.

The Acquisition of Reading and Spelling Skills across Languages

For most children learning to read most languages, acquisition of phoneme awareness is very rapid once they begin learning to read. These children then apply grapheme–phoneme correspondence knowledge to the new words that they encounter in texts and acquire efficient decoding rather rapidly. For English-speaking children learning to read in English, the acquisition of phoneme awareness is somewhat slower as is the acquisition of fluent decoding skills. The causal factors appear to be twofold: the first concerns the phonological structure of the syllable; the second concerns the consistency of the spelling system or orthography. It is relatively easy to learn about phonemes when the language has a CV syllable structure and a transparent orthography. In such languages, a child can learn a set of consistent grapheme–phoneme relationships and apply them to decoding new words. It is relatively difficult to learn about phonemes when the language has a complex syllable structure and an ambiguous orthography. It is also difficult to learn a set of grapheme–phoneme relationships as a basis for decoding new words because the relationships that must be learned are rather variable. English is particularly ambiguous with respect to both spelling-to-sound and sound-to-spelling relationships (Ziegler, Stone, & Jacobs, 1997) because in English, a single letter or letter cluster can have multiple pronunciations (e.g., the letter A in 'car', 'cat', 'cake', 'call'; the cluster 'ough' in 'cough', 'bough', 'through'). A phoneme can also have multiple spellings: consider the vowel sound in 'hurt' 'dirt', and 'Bert'; or the sound /f/ in 'photo' versus 'off' versus 'cough'.

Studies of children learning to read across languages show that the factors of phonological complexity and orthographic consistency have systematic and predictable effects on the acquisition of reading. A large and well-designed cross-language study of early reading acquisition was conducted by Seymour, Aro, & Erskine (2003). They

Table 8.1. Data (% Correct) From the COST A8 Study of Grapheme-Phoneme Recoding Skills for 14 European Languages (adapted from Seymour, Aro, & Erskine, 2003)

Language	*Familiar Real Words*	*Monosyllabic Nonwords*
Greek	98	97
Finnish	98	98
German	98	98
Austrian German	97	97
Italian	95	92
Spanish	95	93
Swedish	95	91
Dutch	95	90
Icelandic	94	91
Norwegian	92	93
French	79	88
Portuguese	73	76
Danish	71	63
Scottish English	34	41

compared early reading in children learning fourteen languages by collating the results of word and nonsense-word reading tests carried out by scientists participating in the European Concerted Action on Learning Disorders as a Barrier to Human Development.[1] These scientists developed a matched set of simple real words and nonwords across languages that were given to children to read during their first year of schooling in different European Union member states (fourteen at that time). All participating schools used a 'phonics-based' instructional approach to reading. Table 8.1 is a summary of the results.

The data show that decoding accuracy came close to ceiling in many European languages during the first year of schooling (i.e., Greece, Spain, Italy and Finland). All of those languages have a transparent spelling system. For four other languages – Portuguese, French, Danish and English – performance was not approaching ceiling; those languages have a less transparent spelling system. English in particular has a very inconsistent orthography, as described previously. The English-speaking children (i.e., a Scottish sample – Scotland traditionally has strong phonics teaching for early reading) performed particularly poorly. It is interesting to compare the performances of the English and German children because English and German have the same phonological structure. In fact, many of the words in English and German are the same words (e.g., wine/Wein; mouse/Maus, garden/garten); nevertheless, German has a consistent orthography. The German children attained 98 percent accuracy for word reading and 94 percent accuracy for nonsense-word reading. The English children attained 34 percent accuracy for real-word reading and 41 percent accuracy for reading simple nonsense words (e.g., 'eb' and 'fip'). These striking differences in reading acquisition by English versus German children have also been demonstrated in smaller studies with careful cognitive matching of the participants (Frith, Wimmer, & Landerl, 1998; Wimmer & Goswami, 1994).

Clearly, the normal neuropsychological development of reading differs depending on the language that a child is learning to read, which is important for the design of neuroimaging studies. Conversely, the same cognitive factor underpins successful reading acquisition in all languages so far studied – namely, phonological awareness. This means that neuroimaging studies that focus on phonology should find biological unity across languages. However, the developmental data show that phonological awareness and orthographic transparency become reciprocal during development. Children who are learning to read languages with a simple phonological structure and a transparent orthography focus on the phoneme level and use largely grapheme–phoneme recoding strategies during reading (e.g., German and Spanish). Children who are learning to read languages with a complex phonological structure and an inconsistent orthography take longer to acquire efficient grapheme–phoneme recoding strategies and develop other reading strategies as well, such as whole-word recognition and rhyme analogy (Ziegler &

Goswami, 2006). Literacy is a more difficult 'learning problem' in a language like English, which could affect the brain. These cross-language factors need to be borne in mind when designing and interpreting neuroimaging studies of reading across languages. Before turning to the neuroimaging literature, however, I first consider what we know about children who have specific difficulties with reading – those with developmental dyslexia – because most neuroimaging studies of children have focused on those with this disability. Should these neuroimaging studies also focus on phonology and word-recoding strategies, or must other factors also be considered when exploring the neural networks supporting reading?

The Development of Reading in Atypical Groups of Children

Children with Developmental Dyslexia

Studies of cognitive factors in reading demonstrate that children with developmental dyslexia in all languages so far studied have difficulties with phonological-awareness tasks. They find it difficult to carry out tasks requiring them to count syllables, recognise rhymes, distinguish the shared phonemes in words, and substitute one phoneme for another (Kim & Davis, 2004, Korean; Wimmer, 1996, German; Porpodas, 1999, Greek; Share & Levin, 1999, Hebrew; see Ziegler & Goswami, 2005, for a comprehensive review). Again, there are interactions between phonological development and the transparency of the spelling system that is being learned. Numerous studies in English in particular have shown that children with developmental dyslexia remain poor at tasks like deciding whether words rhyme (Bradley & Bryant, 1978); in counting or same–different judgment tasks at the different linguistic levels of syllable, onset-rime and phoneme (Swan & Goswami, 1997); and at making oddity judgments about phonemes (Bowey, Cain, & Ryan, 1992). These difficulties persist into the teenage years (Bruck, 1992). Children with developmental dyslexia learning to read other languages can become very accurate in such tasks, although they perform them slowly and with effort (Wimmer, 1993). For consistent orthographies such as German, Italian and Greek, learning a one-to-one mapping system for letters and sounds appears to improve the specificity of dyslexic children's phonological representations. Children with developmental dyslexia in those languages can still perform poorly in phonological-awareness tasks that are less easy to perform using print, such as Spoonerism tasks (Landerl, Wimmer, & Frith, 1997), in which the child has to swap onsets in words (like Reverend Spooner, who told students, 'You have hissed all my mystery lectures'). Nevertheless, German dyslexic children can show age-appropriate phonological skills in such tasks by the age of ten (Wimmer, 1993). However, when German dyslexic children are compared to matched English dyslexic children, the former perform much better, despite both groups of children being dyslexic (Landerl et al., 1997). Again, such data reflect the reciprocal relationship between reading and phonological awareness, highlighting that there are developmental differences across languages.

Concerning reading skills in developmental dyslexia, a similar cross-language picture is found. Dyslexic children learning to read languages with consistent orthographies attain good levels of accuracy in word reading via the application of effortful and slow grapheme–phoneme recoding strategies. In fact, for children with developmental dyslexia, group differences in the accuracy of decoding print are only found in the earliest phases of learning to read. For example, studies of young German and Greek children who later turned out to have specific reading difficulties found that word and nonsense-word reading was significantly poorer than that of age-matched controls in the first year of reading instruction (Porpodas, 1999; Wimmer, 1996). This significant difference soon disappeared, however, for both languages. Although difficulties with phonology remain for children learning to read transparent orthographies, they do not impede reading accuracy; rather, they impede reading *speed* and *spelling* accuracy. Developmental dyslexia in most languages other than English is usually diagnosed on the basis of extremely slow and effortful reading and strikingly poor spelling. The 'phonological deficit' is thus the hallmark of developmental dyslexia across languages rather than levels of reading accuracy attained. Nevertheless, because the dyslexic brain experiences more reading success in some languages than in others, these cross-language differences could affect the neural networks that develop to support reading in individuals with dyslexia in different languages.

Deaf Children

Studies of cognitive factors in reading carried out with children who are deaf also demonstrate that a major problem for reading acquisition is poor phonological awareness. Deaf children do not appear to learn to read 'visually' in some kind of logographic manner. They also develop phonological codes – for example, via lip and cheek cues (i.e., 'speech reading') and vibrational cues. Deaf individuals develop phonological codes even if they use signing as their native language. This has led to the suggestion that the representation of phonology in the brain may be 'amodal', depending on the development of a core phonological system rather than on a system specific to speech (MacSweeney, Waters, Brammer, Woll, & Goswami, 2008).

Phonology is essentially a term used to describe the smallest contrastive units of a language that create new meanings. In signed languages, phonology depends on visual/manual elements, with hand shapes, movements and locations combined to form signs (Sandler & Lillo-Martin, 2006). Of the phonological parameters of signs, *location* is thought to be particularly salient. Location is one of the core factors to determine whether or not signers judge signs to be similar (Hildebrandt & Corina, 2002). Hence, signing deaf children can develop phonological awareness in their manual language by developing awareness of phonological parameters such as location.

When it comes to reading, however, most studies of deaf children have measured the developmental role of awareness of the phonology of spoken language rather than of signs. For studies in English, deaf children who have good phonological awareness in English appear to do better in terms of learning to read. A drawback of these studies, however, is that almost all studies of phonological awareness in deaf children have been conducted after the onset of literacy instruction (Campbell & Wright, 1988; James et al., 2005; Sterne & Goswami, 2000). Nevertheless, deaf children appear to become aware of the same phonological units in spoken language as hearing children (i.e., syllable, onset-rime and phoneme), at least for English (Harris & Beech, 1998; James et al., 2005). Deaf children who develop better phonological-awareness skills also develop better reading skills (Johnson & Goswami, 2005). Again, therefore, the core cognitive skill for reading appears to be phonology.

Neuroimaging of Typical and Atypical Readers

A developmental analysis of the core cognitive factors in reading acquisition clearly gives the primary role to phonology across languages and participant groups. Reading development depends on phonological awareness, whether a child is learning to read an alphabetic language (e.g., in Europe), a character-based script (e.g., in Asian countries), or a second language (e.g., deaf children). The neuroscience of reading in these different types of readers is largely informed by studies of adults; therefore, in the following sections I summarize the data from some of these studies, making links where possible with development. In areas where studies of children were conducted, I then focus most on those studies.

Neuroimaging of Word Recognition and Phonology in Adult Readers

Numerous neuroimaging studies of adult readers are now available in the literature (see Price & McCrory, 2005, for a recent synthesis). The most popular methods for studying brain activation during the act of reading use imaging techniques like fMRI (functional magnetic resonance imaging) and positron emission tomography (PET). Both of these methods measure changes in brain activity over time. In fMRI, changes in blood flow are measured, changes which take approximately 6 to 8 seconds to reach a maximum value after stimulation. In PET, radioactive tracers are injected into the bloodstream and provide an index of brain metabolism. Neurons, of course, communicate on the millisecond scale, with the earliest stages of cognitive information-processing beginning between 100 and 200 milliseconds after stimulus presentation. Electrophysiology (EEG) can record electrical signals reflecting the direct electrical activity of neurons at the time of stimulation. However, EEG methods have been less widely used in the neuroscience of reading because the localisation of function is rather difficult to pinpoint.

Studies of reading based on PET and fMRI have focused on a relatively small range of reading and reading-related tasks. Popular measures include asking participants to read single words while in the scanner and then comparing activation to a resting condition with the eyes closed; asking participants to pick out target visual features such as 'ascenders' while reading print or 'false font' (i.e., false font consists of meaningless symbols matched to letters for visual features like the ascenders in b, d, k); making decisions about phonology while reading words or nonsense words (e.g., Do these items rhyme: leat, jete?), and making lexical decisions (e.g., press one button when a word is presented and a different button when a nonsense word is presented). In EEG studies, participants are typically asked to perform tasks such as lexical decision. Data from EEG studies suggest that the brain has decided whether it is reading a real word or a nonsense word within 180 milliseconds of presentation (Csepe & Szucs, 2003).

In terms of the neural networks that underpin skilled reading, the data from fMRI and PET studies are largely convergent (Price et al., 2003; Rumsey et al., 1997; see Price & McCrory, 2005, for comments on divergence). Data from adult studies in English converge in showing that word recognition in skilled readers depends on a left-lateralised network of frontal, temporo-parietal and occipito-temporal regions (these comprise the language, cross-modal and visual areas of the brain, with [at a simplistic level] semantic-processing thought to occur in temporal and frontal areas, auditory processing in temporal areas, visual processing in occipital areas, and cross-modal processing in parietal areas). Studies of adults reading other orthographies report a largely similar neural network, with some additional recruitment of areas (e.g., left-middle frontal gyrus for Chinese) (see the meta-analysis by Tan, Laird, Li, & Fox, 2005). This core neural network fits with neuropsychological studies of adults with aphasia, which also reveal the importance of Broca's area (i.e., inferior frontal gyrus) and Wernicke's area (i.e., posterior superior temporal gyrus) for the motor production and receptive aspects of speech, respectively. As might be expected, given their importance in comprehending and producing spoken language, these areas along with visual and frontal areas are recruited when we read. Studies comparing typical adult readers to adults with dyslexia suggest that there is reduced activation in left-posterior temporal regions in dyslexia, presumably reflecting problems with phonology (Brunswick, McCrory, Price, Frith, & Frith, 1999). Again, these studies typically use tasks such as word and nonsense-word reading (e.g., 'valley', 'carrot', 'vassey', 'cassot') and often use the false-font task that requires the identification of visual features in words, nonsense words and random symbols. One important caveat in studies of adults with developmental dyslexia is that it is critical to equate participant groups for skill levels in the tasks used in the scanner. For example, nonsense words that can be read as well by the dyslexic adults as by the control group must be used if any group differences found are to be attributed to having dyslexia. Otherwise, differences in neural activation could simply reflect behavioural differences in reading performance.

An interesting study by Paulesu and colleagues (2001) suggested that there is essentially biological unity in terms of neural activity in adults with developmental dyslexia. Paulesu et al. compared the neural networks activated during reading by adults with developmental dyslexia who had learned to read a consistent orthography (Italian), an inconsistent orthography (English), and an intermediate orthography (French) (Paulesu et al., 2001). They reported that a common neural network for reading appeared to be activated across languages. This network depended, in particular, on posterior-inferior temporal areas and middle-occipital gyrus, again suggestive of a core role for phonology. Complementary studies of adults with developmental dyslexia suggest that phonological mechanisms are localised in the temporo-parietal junction (see Eden & Zeffiro, 1998, for a review). When performing tasks such as rhyme judgment, rhyme detection, and word and nonsense-word reading, dyslexic adults usually show reduced activation in temporal and parietal regions, particularly within the left hemisphere.

It is surprising that no neuroimaging studies of deaf individuals performing reading tasks have so far been carried out. However, studies of brain activation related to language-processing by deaf participants suggest activation of a similar network of left-lateralised neural areas to that found in hearing participants listening to language, whether the deaf participants are processing sign language or oral language (Neville et al., 1998). Focussing specifically on phonology yields even fewer studies. Because signing is usually the native language for deaf people and because signing has its own phonology, a potentially fascinating comparison with regard to the neural structures supporting phonological processing in deaf people concerns native versus non-native signers. Recently, MacSweeney et al. (2008) compared the performance of deaf native and deaf non-native signers in two phonology tasks, one based on signing ('Same location?') and one based on speech ('Do they rhyme?'). In the study by MacSweeney and colleagues, both phonology tasks were based on pictures, which ensured that participants had to access their *own* stored phonological representations of sign language or spoken English, respectively. Both phonological similarity tasks were carried out while the adult deaf participants were in the fMRI scanner. The groups being scanned had been matched so that behavioural performance in the two phonological tasks was equivalent.

MacSweeney et al. (2008) reported that the rhyme and location tasks activated a remarkably similar neural network in both deaf native and non-native signers. The network consisted of the posterior portion of the left-frontal cortex, the left-superior parietal lobule and the medial portion of the superior frontal gyrus bordering the anterior cingulate. Hearing control participants given the rhyme task engaged the same phonological processing network recruited by the deaf participants. MacSweeney et al. (2008) argued that the same neural network supported phonological similarity judgments made in both spoken English and sign language despite the very different modalities in which these languages are conveyed. These data suggest that there is an amodal system for phonological representation in the brain. The challenge now is to determine whether this amodal system supports reading development in deaf native versus non-native signers.

Neuroimaging of Word Recognition and Phonology in Children

In comparison to the abundant neuroimaging literature with adults, there are relatively few neuroimaging studies of reading by children, and most available studies are in

English. Nevertheless, there is a high degree of consistency in the neural networks that are recruited by novice and expert readers. For example, work by Turkeltaub and colleagues (2003) compared neural activation in a cross-sectional study of English-speaking children and college students aged seven to twenty-two. The participants were given the feature-detection task based on real words and false font during fMRI scanning. Turkeltaub et al. argued that subtraction of activity in the false-font condition from the real-word condition could be interpreted as neural activity specific to 'implicit reading' (Turkeltaub, Gareau, Flowers, Zeffiro, & Eden, 2003) (see Figure 8.2). The false-font task was chosen because seven-year-olds could perform it as well as adults. The implicit reading-related activity in adults was found to depend on the usual left-hemisphere sites, including the left-posterior temporal and left-inferior frontal cortex and also the right-inferior parietal cortex. When the analyses were restricted to children under the age of nine, the main area engaged was the left-posterior superior temporal cortex. As reading developed, activity in left-temporal and frontal areas increased, whereas activity in right-posterior areas declined.

In further analyses focusing just on the younger children, the researchers investigated the relationships among three core phonological skills and word processing: phonological awareness, phonological memory and rapid automatised naming (RAN), the rapid output of familiar phonological information such as the names of letters. Phonological awareness was measured via performance on the Lindamood Auditory Conceptualisation Test, phonological short-term memory was measured via digit span, and RAN was measured for letters. Partial correlations between activated brain regions and each of the three measures were calculated while controlling for the effects of the other two measures (this was necessary because all of the phonological measures were significantly interrelated). Turkeltaub et al. (2003) reported that the three different measures correlated

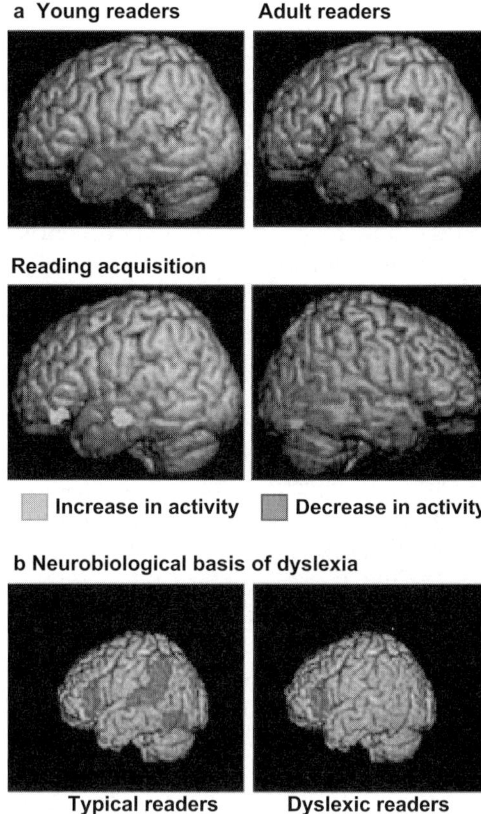

Figure 8.2. Brain areas involved in typical reading development and dyslexia measured with functional MRI. The images in the top panel are from Turkeltaub et al. (2003) and show the early reliance on the left posterior superior temporal cortex in beginning readers and the expansive involvement of left parietal, temporal, and frontal cortices in adult readers. The middle panel shows correlations between brain activity during reading and reading ability (measured on standardized tests) demonstrating increased temporal and frontal involvement as reading develops. Right-hemisphere activation declines as reading is acquired. The bottom panel summarizes the brain regions engaged during reading and reading-related tasks in typically developing readers (left inferior frontal gyrus, left temporo-parietal cortex, left infero-temporal cortex) and dyslexic readers. Figure adapted from Goswami (2006).

with three distinct patterns of brain activity. Phonological awareness appeared to depend on a network of areas in the left-posterior superior temporal cortex and inferior frontal gyrus. Activity in this region was modulated by the level of children's phonological skills. As previously discussed, the left- posterior temporal sulcus was also the primary area recruited by young children at the beginning of reading development. This supports behavioural data in suggesting that phonological recoding to sound is a key early reading strategy. Activity in the inferior frontal gyrus increased with reading ability. Phonological short-term memory (i.e., digit span) appeared to depend on the left-intraparietal sulcus, the dominant site of working memory in adults, with activation also found in the middle-frontal gyri (bilaterally) and right-superior temporal sulcus. RAN appeared to depend on a different bilateral network including right-posterior superior temporal gyrus, right-middle temporal gyrus and left-ventral inferior frontal gyrus. In Turkeltaub et al.'s (2003) study, the VWFA did not become more engaged as reading ability increased. However, recall that the experimental task was the false-font task rather than a direct measure of word-reading. Other studies have found increasing engagement of the VWFA as reading ability increases, suggesting that the VWFA is a type of 'skill zone', with greater activation reflecting increasing expertise with orthography–phonology connections (see Pugh, 2006, for an overview).

A number of neuroimaging studies of reading and reading-related tasks have been carried out on children with developmental dyslexia. For example, a series of studies by Shaywitz and colleagues has shown that children with developmental dyslexia display reduced activation in the normal left-hemisphere posterior sites for reading, along with atypical engagement of right-temporo-parietal cortex (Shaywitz et al., 2002, 2003, 2004). In a landmark study, Shaywitz et al. (2002) studied seventy children with developmental dyslexia aged, on average, thirteen years and seventy-four nonimpaired control children aged, on average, eleven years (however, this was not a reading-level matched control group). The children were asked to perform a variety of tasks in the scanner that were intended to tap different component processes in reading. The tasks were letter identification (e.g., Are T and V the same letter?); single-letter rhyme (e.g., Do V and C rhyme?); nonsense-word rhyming (e.g., Do *leat* and *jete* rhyme?); and reading for meaning (e.g., Are *corn* and *rice* in the same semantic category?). Neural activity in each condition was contrasted with neural activity in a baseline condition based on line-orientation judgments (e.g., Do [\\V] and [\\V] match?). Shaywitz et al. (2002) found that the children with developmental dyslexia showed underactivation in the core brain areas for reading – namely, the left frontal, temporal, parietal and occipital sites familiar from studies with adults. In addition, the children with dyslexia activated right-hemisphere sites in the temporo-parietal cortex. Although interpretation of the data was complicated by behavioural differences in performance in some of the component tasks (e.g., the control group [79 percent] was significantly better at nonsense-word rhyming than the dyslexic group [59 percent]), individual differences in performance on a standardised test of nonsense-word reading were found to be significantly correlated with the degree of activation in left-posterior inferior temporal regions. Therefore, the data showed a satisfactory brain–behaviour correlation.

It is important to find out whether there is neural plasticity for these children – that is, whether the inefficient neural systems that characterize children with developmental dyslexia are malleable and can be altered by the appropriate environmental input. Thus, neuroimaging studies that explore the effects of different educational training programmes for dyslexia are of particular interest. As might be expected from the foregoing analysis, if targeted remediation is provided – usually via intensive tuition in phonological skills and in letter-sound conversion – then neural activity appears to normalise (Shaywitz et al., 2004; Simos et al., 2002; Temple et al., 2003). For example, Shaywitz and colleagues (2004) recruited three groups of children from second and third grade to a remediation study: a group of children with reading disability who received a daily targeted intervention based on phonology and orthography–phonology connections, a group of children with reading disability who were receiving typical community-based interventions offered in their school, and a group of nonimpaired readers who served as the control group. The children receiving the targeted remediation improved their reading accuracy and fluency as well as their reading comprehension. Comparing brain activation following remediation to fMRI scans taken before the intervention began, Shaywitz et al. (2004) found that these children showed increased activation in the left-posterior temporal and inferior-frontal regions associated with efficient reading in typically developing children. The reading-disabled children who were receiving community-based interventions did not show comparable gains, behaviourally or neurally. Shaywitz and Shaywitz (2005) argued that the nature of the remedial educational intervention is crucial for developmental dyslexia and that it should be based on phonology.

These studies, of course, have all been carried out with dyslexic children learning to read in English. Comparable neuroimaging studies of children with developmental dyslexia who are becoming literate in other languages, in general, have yet to be done, as have neuroimaging studies of children who are deaf. However, Siok, Perfetti, Jin, and Tan (2004) reported an fMRI study of eight Chinese children with developmental dyslexia, enabling a cross-language comparison of neural activation. The dyslexic children and age-matched typically developing control children were given homophone-judgment and character-decision tasks during scanning. In the homophone-judgment task, children were shown two Chinese characters and had to decide whether they sounded the same (many words in Chinese are homophones). In the character-decision task, the children were shown a single stimulus and had to decide whether it was a real Chinese character. The character-decision task was intended to measure connections between orthography and semantics, whereas phonological recoding to sound was clearly required by the homophone-judgment task. The control task for the homophone-judgment task required the children to make a decision about similarities in font between two Chinese characters.

Siok et al. (2004) reported that brain activation in the homophone-judgment task for Chinese children with developmental dyslexia did not demonstrate the reduced activation in left temporo-parietal regions typically found in studies of developmental dyslexia in English. Instead, there was reduced activity in the left-middle frontal gyrus, an area involved in visuospatial analysis. Siok et al. (2004) argued for an important neurological difference with respect to impaired Chinese reading and impaired English reading. They argued that whereas the biological marker for reading disability in English was reduced left temporo-parietal activation, for Chinese it was reduced activation of left-middle frontal gyrus. In the character-decision task, however, the normally reading Chinese control children showed greater activity in the VWFA than those with developmental dyslexia. This finding is similar to findings reported in English (Pugh, 2006). Nevertheless, Siok et al. (2004) argued that their findings from the eight children were a major challenge to the biological-unity theory of dyslexia proposed by Paulesu and his colleagues (2001) (based on adult data).

This claim has aroused considerable controversy (Ziegler, 2006). Clearly, accurate visuospatial analysis is mandatory in acquiring a character-based writing system. Nevertheless, as discussed previously, individual differences in visuospatial memory do not predict individual differences in typical reading development in Chinese; therefore, it is unclear why a deficit in visuospatial analysis should be the cause of difficulty in reading acquisition in Chinese. In fact, a problem with Siok et al.'s (2004) study is that the neural difference observed between the Chinese dyslexic children and their controls could have been a product of the impaired reading development of the children being studied. This is because the control children were not matched for reading level and were, in fact, superior in the homophone-judgment task to the dyslexic participants. The children with dyslexia also took significantly longer to make homophone decisions, complicating interpretation of differences in neural activity. The atypical imaging profile reported (i.e., reduced activation in left-middle frontal gyrus, an area associated with the representation and working memory of visuospatial and verbal information) may have been the profile to be expected for the character-reading level achieved by the children.

In response to the controversy, Perfetti, Tan, and Siok (2006) clarified that they did not intend to undermine the view that a phonological deficit is the cross-language signature of developmental dyslexia. Rather, they suggested that biological adaptations to the demands of different scripts may indeed lead researchers to expect some cross-language differences in the neural substrates for reading. This position is, of course, in line with the developmental cognitive framework being argued for in this chapter, which has highlighted the systematic effects of orthographic consistency and phonological complexity on reading development. Clearly, further neuroimaging studies, ideally longitudinal studies with the appropriate (reading level) control groups, are required to continue exploring this interesting possibility.

Finally, Shaywitz and Shaywitz (2005) were able to report on different developmental trajectories and associated neural differences for children at risk of reading difficulties. This was done by examining retrospectively a sample of young adults who had been followed since they were five years old. Shaywitz and Shaywitz (2005) were able to distinguish three groups within this sample: a group of persistently poor readers (PPR), who had met criteria for poor reading in both second/third and ninth/tenth grade; a group of accuracy-improved poor readers (AIR), who had met criteria for poor reading in second/third but not in ninth/tenth grade; and a control group of nonimpaired readers (C), who had never met criteria for poor reading. Both the PPR and AIR groups showed neural under-activation when required to manipulate phonology. For example, in a nonsense-word rhyming task, both groups of young adults still showed relative under-activation in left-superior temporal and occipito-temporal regions. However, when reading real words, brain activation in the two groups diverged. The AIR group again demonstrated under-activation in the normal left-posterior areas for reading, whereas the PPR group activated the left-posterior regions to the same extent as the control group (a much unexpected finding).

Further analyses based on connectivity (i.e., examining the neural areas that were functionally connected to each other during reading) suggested that this achievement depended on memory for the PPR group and not on typical functioning of the left-posterior regions. Whereas the connectivity analyses showed that the control group demonstrated functional connectivity between left-hemisphere posterior and anterior reading systems, the PPR group demonstrated functional connectivity between left-hemisphere posterior regions and right-prefrontal areas associated with working memory and memory retrieval. Shaywitz and Shaywitz (2005) therefore speculated that the PPR group was reading primarily by memory. Because the words used in the scanner were high-frequency simple words, this is quite possible. Recall that comparisons of individuals with dyslexia need to use simpler words in order to equate reading performance in the scanner. However, this complicates the interpretation of neural differences in terms of the possible role of memory. It may also be important that the PPR group had, in general, lower I.Q. scores than the AIR group. Further longitudinal studies of this nature, ideally prospective studies comparing patterns of activation as high-frequency words become over-learned, would clearly be valuable.

Conclusion

The neuroimaging studies available at the time of this writing, although incomplete, nevertheless provide an interesting complement to the cognitive behavioural research on reading acquisition and developmental dyslexia across languages discussed in this chapter (see also Ziegler & Goswami, 2005, 2006). It seems that brains are mostly similar across languages in terms of the neural networks that they develop to support reading. Although orthographies are variable across languages, leading to systematic (and predictable) differences in the psycholinguistic strategies that develop for reading (and also to systematic and predictable differences in the manifestation of developmental dyslexia), in all languages so far studied, phonological awareness is the foundation of reading acquisition. All brains appear to process phonology in the same language-based areas, with dyslexic brains simply processing phonological information less efficiently in these same areas rather than in completely different ways. Although the ease of learning to read a particular language depends on the phonological complexity of the spoken language and the orthographic consistency of the written language (as well as morphology; see Goswami & Ziegler, 2006), it is not clear that the grain size of lexical representations across orthographies fundamentally affects what takes place in the brain. Rather, the VWFA develops to encode orthographic–phonological representations across languages, whether the written form of the languages is alphabetic or character-based. There is some dispute about whether the same left-lateralised network of visual, phonological and semantic (i.e., temporal) areas underpins reading in languages as different as English and Chinese (Perfetti et al., 2006; Siok et al., 2004). Future research focussing on acquiring reading in non-native languages or in second languages that differ markedly in phonological and orthographic characteristics should shed further light on the extent to which there are universal neural networks for literacy.

Note

1 National representatives of this action were H. Wimmer, T. Reinelt (Austria); J. Alegria, J. Morais, J. Leybaert (Belgium); C. Elbro, E. Arnbak (Denmark); H. Lyytinen, P. Niemi (Finland); J-E. Gombert, M-T. Le Normand, L. Sprenger-Charolles, S. Valdois (France); A. Warnke, W. Schneider (Germany); C. Porpodas (Greece); V. Csepe (Hungary); H. Ragnarsdottir (Iceland); C. Cornoldi, P. Giovanardi Rossi, C. Vio, P. Tressoldi, A. Parmeggiani (Italy); C. Firman (Malta); R. Licht, A. M. B. De Groot (Netherlands); F-E. Tonnessen (Norway); L. Castro, L. Cary (Portugal); S. Defior, F. Martos, J. Sainz, X. Angerri (Spain); S. Stromqvist, A. Olofsson (Sweden); and P. Seymour, P. Bryant, U. Goswami (United Kingdom).

References

Anthony, J. L., & Lonigan, C. J. (2004). The nature of phonological awareness: Converging evidence from four studies of preschool and early grade-school children. *Journal of Educational Psychology*, 96, 43–55.

Anthony, J. L., Lonigan, C. J., Burgess, S. R., Driscoll, K., Phillips, B. M., & Cantor, B. G. (2002). Structure of preschool phonological sensitivity: Overlapping sensitivity to rhyme, words, syllables, and phonemes. *Journal of Experimental Child Psychology*, 82, 65–92.

Anthony, J. L., Lonigan, C. J., Driscoll, K., Phillips, B. M., & Burgess, S. R. (2003). Phonological sensitivity: A quasi-parallel progression of word structure units and cognitive operations. *Reading Research Quarterly*, 38 (4), 470–487.

Bowey, J. A., Cain, M. T., & Ryan, S. M. (1992). A reading-level design study of phonological skills underlying fourth-grade children's word reading difficulties. *Child Development*, 63, 999–1011.

Bradley, L., & Bryant, P. E. (1978). Difficulties in auditory organization as a possible cause of reading backwardness. *Nature*, 271, 746–747.

Bradley, L., & Bryant, P. E. (1983). Categorising sounds and learning to read: A causal connection. *Nature*, 310, 419–421.

Bruck, M. (1992). Persistence of dyslexics' phonological awareness deficits. *Developmental Psychology*, 28, 874–886.

Brunswick, N., McCrory, E., Price, C. J., Frith, C. D., & Frith, U. (1999). Explicit and implicit processing of words and pseudowords by adult developmental dyslexics: A search for Wernicke's Wortschatz. *Brain*, 122, 1901–1917.

Campbell, R., & Wright, H. (1988). Deafness, spelling and rhyme: How spelling supports written word and picture rhyming skills in deaf subjects. *Quarterly Journal of Experimental Psychology*, 40 (A), 771–788.

Chaney, C. (1992). Language development, metalinguistic skills and print awareness in 3-year-old children. *Applied Psycholinguistics*, 13, 485–514.

Cohen, L., & Dehaene, S. (2004). Specialization within the ventral stream: The case for the visual word form area. *NeuroImage*, 22, 466–476.

Cossu, G., Shankweiler, D., Liberman, I. Y., Katz, L., & Tola, G. (1988). Awareness of phonological segments and reading ability in Italian children. *Applied Psycholinguistics*, 9, 1–16.

Csepe, V., & Szucs, D. (2003). Number word reading as a challenging task in dyslexia? An ERP study. *International Journal of Psychophysiology*, 51, 69–83.

De Cara, B., & Goswami, U. (2002). Statistical analysis of similarity relations among spoken words: Evidence for the special status of rimes in English. *Behavioural Research Methods and Instrumentation*, 34 (3), 416–423.

Dollaghan, C. A. (1994). Children's phonological neighbourhoods: Half empty or half full? *Journal of Child Language*, 21, 257–271.

Eden, G. F., & Zeffiro, T. A. (1998). Neural systems affected in developmental dyslexia revealed by functional neuroimaging. *Neuron*, 21, 279–282.

Fisher, S. E., & Francks, C. (2006). Genes, cognition and dyslexia: Learning to read the genome. *Trends in Cognitive Sciences*, 10, 250–257.

Frith, U., Wimmer, H., & Landerl, K. (1998). Differences in phonological recoding in German- and English-speaking children. *Scientific Studies of Reading*, 2, 31–54.

Goswami, U. (2006). Neuroscience and education: From research to practice. *Nature Reviews Neuroscience*, 7, 406–413.

Goswami, U., & Ziegler, J. C. (2006). Fluency, phonology and morphology: A response to the commentaries on becoming literate in different languages. *Developmental Science*, 9 (5), 451–453.

Harris, M., & Beech, J. R. (1998). Implicit phonological awareness and early reading development in prelingually deaf children. *Journal of Deaf Studies and Deaf Education*, 3 (3), 205–216.

Hildebrandt, U., & Corina, D. (2002). Phonological similarity in American sign language. *Language and Cognitive Processes*, 17, 593–612.

Hinshelwood, J. (1917). *Congenital Word-blindness*. London: H. K. Lewis.

Ho, C. S.-H., & Bryant, P. (1997). Phonological skills are important in learning to read Chinese. *Developmental Psychology*, 33, 946–951.

Hoien, T., Lundberg, L., Stanovich, K. E., & Bjaalid, I. K. (1995). Components of phonological awareness. *Reading & Writing*, 7, 171–188.

James, D. M., Rajput, K., Brown, T., Sirimanna, T., Brinton, J., & Goswami, U. (2005). Phonological awareness in deaf children who use cochlear implants. *Journal of Speech Language and Hearing Research*, 48, 1511–1528.

Johnson, C., & Goswami, U. (2005). *Phonological skills, vocabulary development and reading development in deaf children with cochlear implants: Current results.* Poster presention at the Society for the Scientific Study of Reading Annual Meeting, Toronto, Canada, June 27–30.

Kim, J., & Davis, C. (2004). Characteristics of poor readers of Korean Hangul: Auditory, visual and phonological processing, *Reading and Writing*, 17 (1–2), 153–185.

Landerl, K., Wimmer, H., & Frith, U. (1997). The impact of orthographic consistency on dyslexia: A German-English comparison. *Cognition*, 63, 315–334.

Liberman, I. Y., Shankweiler, D., Fischer, F. W., & Carter, B. (1974). Explicit syllable and phoneme segmentation in the young child. *Journal of Experimental Child Psychology*, 18, 201–212.

Lundberg, I., Frost, J., & Petersen, O. (1988). Effects of an extensive programme for stimulating phonological awareness in pre-school children. *Reading Research Quarterly*, 23, 163–284.

Metsala, J. L. (1999). Young children's phonological awareness and nonword repetition as a function of vocabulary development. *Journal of Educational Psychology*, 91, 3–19.

Neville, H. J., Bavelier, D., Corina, D., Rauschecker, J., Karni, A., Lalwani, A., et al. (1998). Cerebral organization for language in deaf and hearing subjects: Biological constraints and effects of experience. *Proceedings of the National Academy of Sciences, USA*, 95, 922–929.

Paulesu, E., Démonet, J.-F., Fazio, F., McCrory, E., Chanoine, V., Brunswick, N., et al. (2001). Dyslexia: Cultural diversity and biological unity. *Science, 291* (5511), 2165–2167.

Perfetti, C. A., Tan, L. H., & Siok, W. T. (2006). Brain-behaviour relations in reading and dyslexia: Implications of Chinese results. *Brain and Language*, 98, 344–346.

Porpodas, C. D. (1999). Patterns of phonological and memory processing in beginning readers and spellers of Greek. *Journal of Learning Disabilities*, 32, 406–416.

Price, C. J., Gorno-Tempini M-L. D., Graham, K. S., Biggio, N., Mechelli, A., Patterson, K., et al. (2003). Normal and pathological reading: Converging data from lesion and imaging studies. *NeuroImage*, 20 (Suppl. 1), S30–S41.

Price, C. J., & McCrory, E. (2005). Functional brain imaging studies of skilled reading and developmental dyslexia. In M. J. Snowling & C. Hulme (Eds.), *The science of reading: A handbook*. Oxford: Blackwell Publishing, 473–496.

Pugh, K. (2006). A neurocognitive overview of reading acquisition and dyslexia across languages. *Developmental Science*, 9, 448–450.

Rumsey, J. M., Horwitz, B., Donohue, B. C., Nace, K., Maisog, J. M., & Andreason, P. (1997). Phonological and orthographic components of word recognition: A PET rCBF study. Brain, *120*, 739–759.

Sandler, W., & Lillo-Martin, D. (2006). *Sign language and linguistic universals*. Cambridge: Cambridge University Press.

Schneider, W., Kuespert, P., Roth, E., Vise, M., & Marx, H. (1997). Short- and long-term effects of training phonological awareness in kindergarten: Evidence from two German studies. *Journal of Experimental Child Psychology*, 66, 311–340.

Schneider, W., Roth, E., & Ennemoser, M. (2000). Training phonological skills and letter knowledge in children at-risk for dyslexia: A comparison of three kindergarten intervention programs. *Journal of Educational Psychology*, 92, 284–295.

Seymour, P. H. K., Aro, M., & Erskine, J. M. (2003). Foundation literacy acquisition in European orthographies. *British Journal of Psychology*, 94, 143–174.

Share, D., & Levin, I. (1999). Learning to read and write in Hebrew. In M. Harris & G. Hatano (Eds.), *Learning to read and write: A cross-linguistic perspective*. Cambridge studies in cognitive and perceptual development (pp. 89–111). New York: Cambridge University Press.

Shaywitz, S. E., & Shaywitz, B. A. (2005). Dyslexia (specific reading disability). *Biological Psychiatry*, 57, 1301–1309.

Shaywitz, B. A., Shaywitz, S. E., Blachman, B. A., Pugh, K. R., Fullbright, R. K., Skudlarski, P., et al. (2004). Development of left occipito-temporal systems for skilled reading in children after a phonologically based intervention. *Biological Psychiatry*, 55, (9), 926–933.

Shaywitz, S. E., Shaywitz, B. A., Fulbright, R. K., Skudlarski, P., Mencl, W. E., Constable, R. T., et al. (2003). Neural systems for compensation and persistence: Young adult outcome of childhood reading disability. *Biological Psychiatry*, 54 (1), 25–33.

Shaywitz, B. A., Shaywitz, S. E., Pugh, K. R., Mencl, W. E., Fullbright, R. K., Skudlarski, P., et al. (2002). Disruption of posterior brain systems for reading in children with developmental dyslexia. *Biological Psychiatry*, 52 (2), 101–110.

Simos, P. G., Fletcher, J. M., Bergman, E., et al. (2002). Dyslexia-specific brain activation profile becomes normal following successful remedial training. *Neurology*, 58, 1203–1213.

Siok, W. T., & Fletcher, P. (2001). The role of phonological awareness and visual-orthographic skills in Chinese reading acquisition. *Developmental Psychology*, 37, 886–899.

Siok, W. T., Perfetti, C. A., Jin, Z., & Tan, L. H. (2004). Biological abnormality of impaired reading is constrained by culture. *Nature*, 431, 71–76.

Stanovich, K. E. (1992). Speculations on the causes and consequences of individual differences in early reading acquisition. In P. B. Gough, L. C. Ehri, & R. Treiman (Eds.), *Reading Acquisition* (pp. 307–342). Hillsdale, NJ: Lawrence Erlbaum Associates.

Sterne, A., & Goswami, U. (2000). Phonological awareness of syllables, rhymes and phonemes in deaf children. *Journal of Child Psychology and Psychiatry*, 41 (5), 609–625.

Swan, D., & Goswami, U. (1997). Phonological awareness deficits in developmental dyslexia and the phonological representations hypothesis. *Journal of Experimental Child Psychology*, 66, 18–41.

Tan, L. H., Laird, A. R., Li, K., & Fox, P. T. (2005). Neuroanatomical correlates of phonological processing of Chinese characters and alphabetic words: A meta-analysis. *Human Brain Mapping*, 25 (1), 83–91.

Temple, E., Deutsch, G. K., Poldrack, R. A., Miller, S. L., Tallal, P., Merzenich, M. M., et al. (2003). Neural deficits in children with dyslexia ameliorated by behavioral remediation: Evidence from functional MRI. *Proceedings of the National Academy of Sciences*, 100, 2860–2865.

Treiman, R. (1988). The internal structure of the syllable. In G. Carlson & M. Tanenhaus (Eds.), *Linguistic structure in language processing* (pp. 27–52). Dordrecht, The Netherlands: Kluwer.

Treiman, R., & Zukowski, A. (1991). Levels of phonological awareness. In S. Brady & D. Shankweiler (Eds.), *Phonological processes in literacy*. Hillsdale, NJ: Erlbaum.

Turkeltaub, P. E., Gareau, L., Flowers, D. L., Zeffiro, T. A., & Eden, G. F. (2003). Development of neural mechanisms for reading. *Nature Neuroscience*, 6 (6), 767–773.

Vellutino, F. R. (1979). *Dyslexia*. Cambridge, MA: MIT Press.

Wimmer, H. (1993). Characteristics of developmental dyslexia in a regular writing system. *Applied Psycholinguistics*, 14, 1–33.

Wimmer, H. (1996). The nonword reading deficit in developmental dyslexia: Evidence from children learning to read German. *Journal of Experimental Child Psychology*, 61, 80–90.

Wimmer, H., & Goswami, U. (1994). The influence of orthographic consistency on reading development – word recognition in English and German children. *Cognition*, 51 (1), 91–103.

Wimmer, H., Landerl, K., & Schneider, W. (1994). The role of rhyme awareness in learning to read a regular orthography. *British Journal of Developmental Psychology*, 12, 469–484.

Ziegler, J. C. (2006). Do differences in brain activation challenge universal theories of dyslexia? *Brain & Language*, 98 (3), 341–343.

Ziegler, J. C., & Goswami, U. (2005). Reading acquisition, developmental dyslexia and skilled reading across languages: A psycholinguistic grain size theory. *Psychological Bulletin*, 131 (1), 3–29.

Ziegler, J. C., & Goswami, U. (2006). Becoming literate in different languages: Similar problems, different solutions. *Developmental Science*, 9, 429–453.

Ziegler, J. C., Stone, G. O., & Jacobs, A. M. (1997). What's the pronunciation for -OUGH and the spelling for /u/? A database for computing feedforward and feedback inconsistency in English. *Behavior Research Methods, Instruments, & Computers*, 29, 600–618.

CHAPTER 9

Language and Literacy from a Cognitive Neuroscience Perspective[1]

Karl Magnus Petersson, Martin Ingvar, and Alexandra Reis

Introduction

This chapter consists of two parts. The first presents a general perspective on cognitive neuroscience in which we use natural language as an example to illustrate various issues involved in understanding the human brain from a cognitive point of view. We start with a brief review of some relevant structural and functional facts about neural systems and an outline of the cognitive science perspective on psychological explanation. A framework for describing cognitive systems is Marr's three levels of analysis: the computational, algorithmic, and implementation levels (Marr, 1982). As a first approximation, natural language can be viewed as analyzed at levels 1–3 in theoretical linguistics (Sag, Wasow, & Bender, 2003), psycholinguistics (Gernsbacher, 1994), and neurolinguistics (Brown & Hagoort, 1999), respectively. The second part of the chapter provides a glimpse of the challenges that the human brain poses to our understanding of the same. Here, we review some empirical findings related to illiteracy in the context of literacy, we outline a perspective on the acquisition of reading and writing skills as well as other cognitive skills during (formal) education, and we take the view that the educational system is a structured process for cultural transmission; on this view, the educational system represents an institutionalized structure that subserves important aspects of socialization and cultural transmission.

Cognitive neuroscience typically works with a modified perspective on cognition, learning, and development compared to classical cognitive science, although the underlying ideas are essentially the same. Within this modified framework (Petersson, 2005a), the three descriptive levels can be generalized to (1) the *cognitive level*: a formal theory for structured cognitive states and a corresponding cognitive transition system, which specifies the transitions between cognitive states and the results of information-processing; (2) the *dynamical system level*: given a formal cognitive theory, a state-space is specified and processing is formulated in terms of a dynamical system that embeds the system specification at the cognitive level; and (3) the *implementation level*: given a

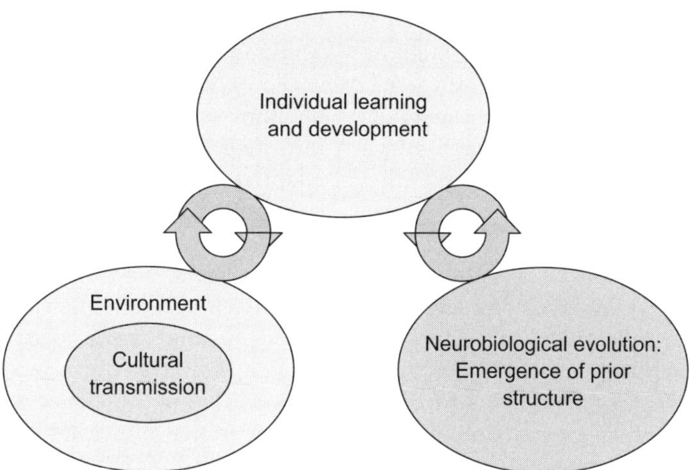

Figure 9.1. An adaptive cognitive system situated in the context of its evolutionary history and its current environment (Petersson, 2005).

dynamical system, this level specifies the physical hardware implementation of the dynamical system – for example, a neural network (Haykin, 1998; Koch & Segev, 1998). In the following discussion, we integrate this perspective with some contemporary ideas on the functional architecture of the human brain; learning and adaptation at different time-scales; and, more broadly, the interaction, via individual learning, among factors determined by neurobiological evolution and the environment of the human cognitive system (including social and cultural transmission) (Figure 9.1). Neurobiological systems are naturally evolved information-processing (i.e., cognitive) systems and, to understand the significance of their different features, it is necessary to consider both their individual developmental (i.e., ontogenesis) and evolutionary histories (i.e., phylogenesis). Neural systems have evolved under tight energy, space, and real-time processing constraints. With respect to perception, for example, the characteristic time-scale of processing must match that of the external world; similarly, for output control, the characteristic time-scale of motor output must match the time it takes to organize a coordinated response that is behaviorally relevant. Moreover, when the outputs from different processing components need to be integrated, then the time-scales of the various processors involved must also match and necessary memory constraints must be met. There are also more general constraints in terms of available energy turnover, the physical and biochemical infrastructure, and spatial constraints. It seems safe to assume that these types of general constraints have had an important influence on the brain from an implementation point of view. However, there are good reasons to believe that the nervous system is not fully specified at a phylogenetic (i.e., genetic) level. The existence of learning and adaptation speaks clearly on this issue. For example, it would also seem too restrictive, ineffective, or costly to prespecify every detail of the functional organization of the human brain, and ontogenetic development and learning represent vital complements for the cognitive system to reach its full potential.

Structural and Functional Complexity of the Brain

The human brain weighs approximately 1.3 kg and is divided into grey and white matter. The grey matter is formed into a convoluted surface of gyri and sulci and is densely packed with neurons, the processing unit of the brain, with their local and more long-range neuronal connectivity (including short-distance interneurons and the dendritic trees and cell bodies, or *somata*, of long-distance inter-regional neurons). The white matter contains predominantly myelinated axons of the inter-regional neurons that constitute the regional and long-range cortico-cortical (e.g., inter-hemispheric tracts) as well as cortico-subcortical interconnectivity (e.g., sensory input and motor output tracts) (Nieuwenhuys, Voogd, & van Huijzen, 1988). In addition to the neocortex, grey matter is also found in the medial temporal lobe (including the hippocampus), the basal ganglia, the cerebellar cortex and nuclei, and various other subcortical nuclei in the midbrain and the brainstem (Nieuwenhuys et al., 1988). Microscopically, the brain is composed of about $\sim 10^{10}$–10^{12} processing units (i.e., neurons), each supporting $\sim 10^{3}$–10^{4} axonal output connections and receiving, on average, the same number of dendritic and somatic input connections. The connectivity comprises, in total, hundreds of trillions of interconnections and many thousand kilometers of cabling (Koch & Laurent, 1999; Shepherd, 1997).

The structural organization of brain connectivity resembles that of a tangled hierarchically structured and recurrently connected network (a "tangled hierarchy"; Hofstadter, 1999) composed of different functionally specialized brain regions, which consist of several types of neurons and synaptic connections (Felleman & Van Essen, 1991; Shepherd, 1997). The functional complexity of the nervous system arises from the nonlinear, nonstationary (i.e., adaptive) characteristics of the processing units (i.e., neurons with synaptic parameters that can change across multiple time-scales of behavioral relevance), and the spatially nonhomogeneous, parallel, and interactive patterns of connectivity (Figure 9.2). This hardware architecture, in principle, can support a wide range of system dynamics and allows for a rich class of nonstationary, nonlinear dynamical models to be instantiated (Maass, Natschläger, & Markram, 2004).

The characteristics of the synaptic connections can change as a consequence of information-processing and support various adaptive and learning mechanisms, thereby supporting the seemingly self-organizing properties of cognition. From this perspective, learning and memory can be seen as a dynamic consequence of information-processing and system plasticity (Petersson, Elfgren, & Ingvar, 1997, 1999). Recent work in cognitive neuroscience suggests that the organizational principles for cognitive functions depend on the patterns of distributed connectivity between functionally specialized brain regions, as well as the functional segregation of interacting processing pathways – the dominant pattern of interconnectivity being recurrent (Arbib, 2003; Frackowiak et al., 2004; Ingvar & Petersson, 2000).

It has been suggested that an information-processing system (Koch, 1999), physical or biophysical, that operates efficiently in the real world needs to obey several constraints: (1) it must operate at sufficiently high speeds; (2) it must have a sufficiently rich repertoire of computational primitives, with the ability to implement linear and nonlinear, high-gain operations; and (3) it must interface efficiently with the physical world via sensory input and motor output interfaces, matching various relevant time-scales. The neuronal membrane potential is the physical variable that can fulfill these requirements: an action potential, the basis for neuronal signaling, changes the potential by $\sim$100 mV within $\sim$1 ms and propagate $\sim$1 cm or more within that time. Moreover, the membrane potential controls a large number of nonlinear gates, ion channels, in each neuron (Koch, 1999). In the following discussion, we assume that important aspects of a neuronal state are well characterized by its membrane potential and a small number of other neuronal state variables (cf. the Hodgkin-Huxley model, which is four-dimensional; Izhikevich, 2007). However, various adaptive phenomena imply that the membrane

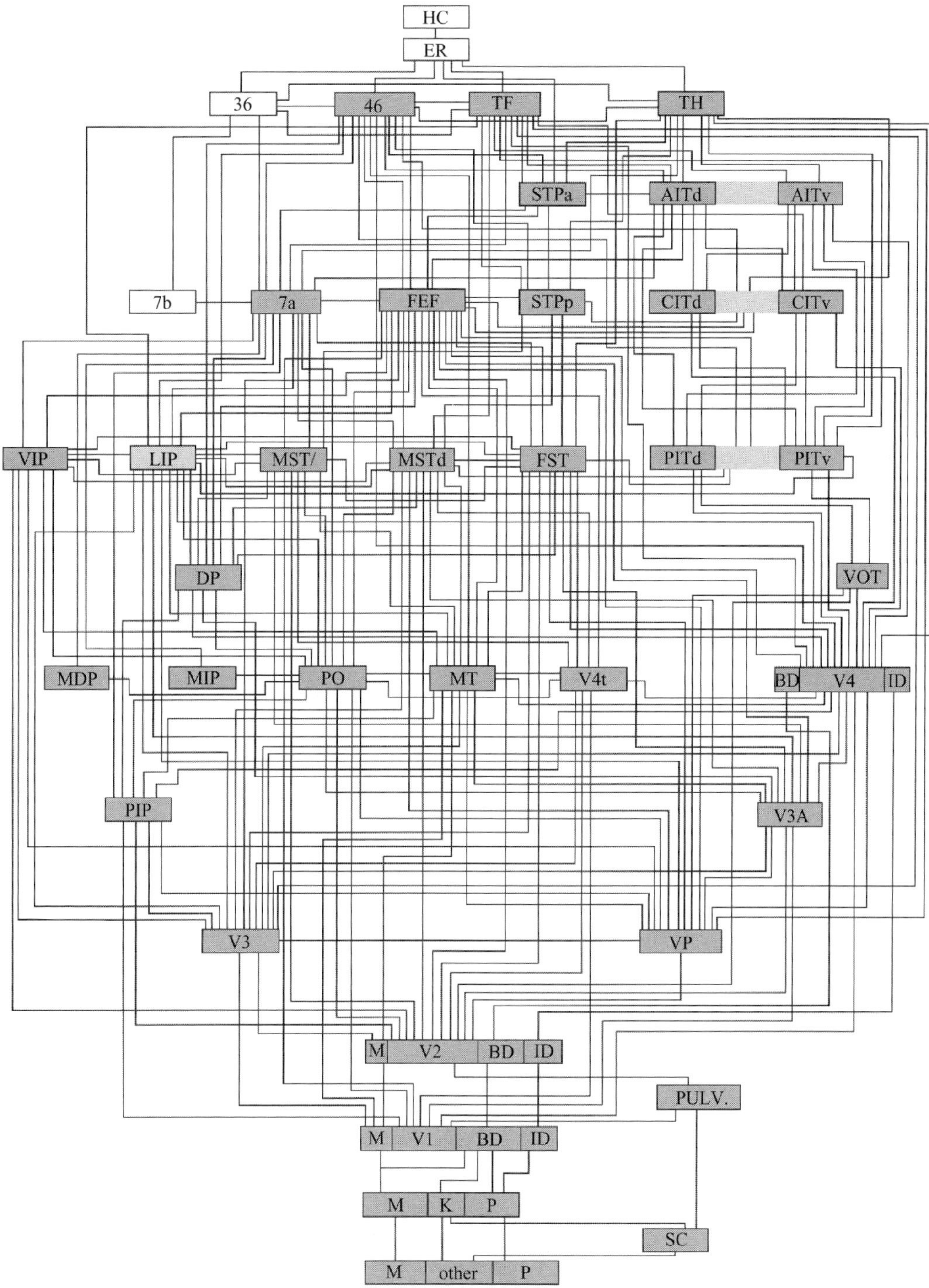

Figure 9.2. The structural organization of the human brain (adapted from Felleman & Van Essen, 1991; courtesy of Frauke Hellwig).

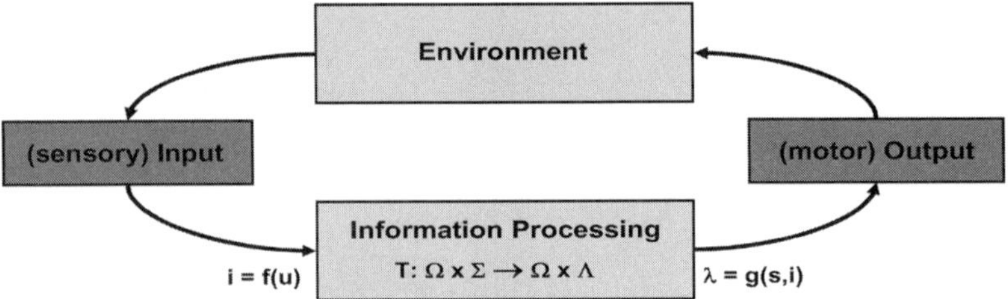

Figure 9.3. Information-processing system. Cognition is equated with internal information-processing in interaction with the environment, the so-called perception-action cycle. Here, the cognitive system is portrayed as interfacing with the external environment through sensory and motor interfaces. However, the processing (sub)system can equally well be viewed as interfacing with other subsystems (Petersson, 2005).

potential is not a complete description of the state of a given neuron at any given point in time (cf. adaptive parameters herein). In any case, a complete state description of the neurons in a neural system provides a description of the state of the neural system as a function of time. We return to this concept in an abstract form in the next section. Ever since the network-circuit hypothesis of McCulloch and Pitts (1943; see also Minsky, 1967) and the neuronal assembly theory of Hebb (1949), several approaches to information-processing in neural systems have suggested that information is represented as distributed neuronal activity and that information-processing emerges from the interactions between different functionally specialized regions and neuronal groups (Arbib, 2003). In short, these approaches suggest that cognitive functions emerge from the global dynamics of interacting subnetworks (Petersson, 2005a).

Information-Processing Models

Cognitive neuroscience approaches the human brain as a cognitive system: a system that functionally can be conceptualized in terms of information-processing (Petersson, 2005a; Petersson, 2008). Here and in the following subsections, we outline some aspects of the information-processing concept; what is important is how these concepts are interrelated and, to a lesser extent, their formal details. In general, we consider a physical (or biophysical) system as an information-processing device when a subclass of its physical states can be viewed as cognitive/representational and when transitions (i.e., dynamical principles $T: \Omega \times \Sigma \rightarrow \Omega \times \Lambda$ in Figure 9.3, which govern the processing of information; here Ω is the space of internal states, Σ is the transduced input space, and Λ is the space of outputs) between these can be conceptualized as a process operating on these states by implementing well-defined operations on the representational structures. Information-processing (i.e., the state transitions) thus can be conceptualized as trajectories in a suitable state-space (i.e., Ω in Figure 9.3). At processing time-step t, the system receives input i(t) in state s(t); then the system changes state to $s(t + \Delta t)$ and optionally outputs $\lambda(t + \Delta t)$ according to:

$$[s(t + \Delta t), \lambda(t + \Delta t)] = T[s(t), i(t)] \quad [9.1]$$

Equation [9.1] describes an input-driven (i.e., forced) discrete-time dynamical system. Note that the memory organization of the system has not been explicitly described here (see Figures 9.4 and 9.5). The characteristics of the memory organization, both short and long term, are crucial because they determine in important respects the expressive power of the processing architecture (for a brief review, see Petersson, 2005b; or, alternatively, Savage, 1998; or Wells, 2005).

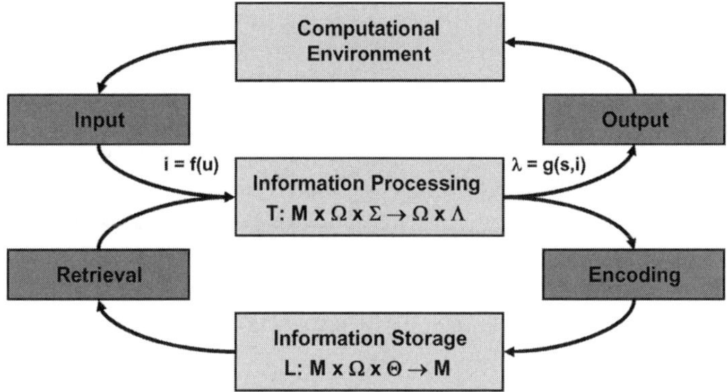

Figure 9.4. Adaptive information-processing system (Petersson, 2005).

As a point of clarification, we use the terms *representational* and *cognitive* interchangeably. It is important to note from the outset that when we are using *representational*, it is not meant to implicitly entail a conceptualization of meaning in terms of a naïve "referential semantics". Rather, *representational* or *cognitive* is here referring to the functional role of a physical state with respect to the relevant processing machinery and thus does not have an independent status separate from the information processing device as such (Eck, 2000; Tanenbaum, 1990). Thus, the "internal semantics" of the system is only in complex and indirect ways related to the exterior of the system (e.g., via the sensorimotor interfaces) (Jackendoff, 2002) and there may be important aspects of processing that only have an internal significance (e.g., because of implementation constraints).

The framework of classical cognitive science and artificial intelligence assumes that information is coded by structured representations (i.e., "data structures") and that cognitive processing is accomplished by the execution of algorithmic operations ("rules"; ~T in Figure 9.3) on the basic representations ("primitive symbols") comprising compositionally structured representations (Newell & Simon, 1976). This processing paradigm suggests that cognitive phenomena can be modeled within the framework of Church-Turing computability and effectively takes the view that isomorphic models of cognition can be found within this framework (Cutland, 1980; Davis, Sigal, & Weyuker, 1994; Lewis & Papadimitriou, 1981). Language modeling in theoretical linguistics and psycholinguistics represents one example in which the classical framework has served reasonably well and all common

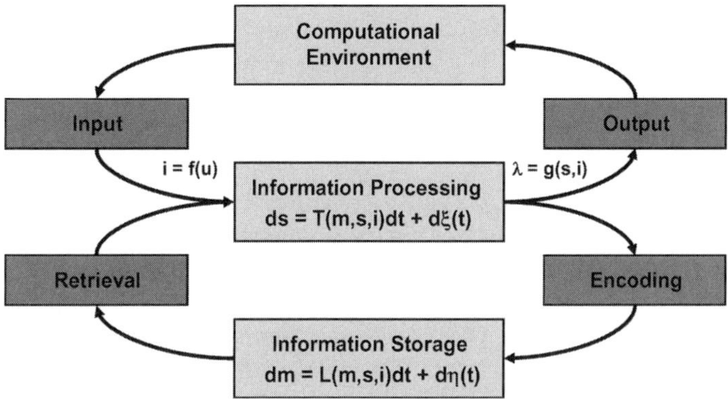

Figure 9.5. Adaptive dynamical system (Petersson, 2005).

formal language models can be described within the classical framework (Partee, ter Meulen, & Wall, 1990).

A Developmental Perspective on Cognition

To incorporate development and learning in this picture, the processing dynamics, T, outlined in the previous section and in Figure 9.3, have to be extended with an adaptive or developmental dynamics ($L{:}M \times \Omega \times \Theta \rightarrow M$ in Figure 9.4). For simplicity, let us focus on some particular cognitive module C, which is fundamental in the sense that all normal individuals develop cognitive capacities related to C; for example, let C be natural language. We can conceptualize the development of the module C as a trajectory in its model space $M = [m \mid m$ can be instantiated by $C]$ driven by the interaction with the environment in conjunction with innately specified developmental processes (Figure 9.1). In other words, at any point in time, t, one can imagine C being in a given state $m_C(t)$. (Note that "state" here refers to the model being instantiated by C rather than a cognitive state in the state-space of the processing system.) If we suppose that C incorporates an innately specified prior structure, we can capture this notion by a structured initial state of C, $m_C(t_0)$. Thus, as C develops, it traces out a trajectory in M determined by its adaptive dynamics L (Figure 9.4). If C and L are such that it (approximately) converges on a final model $m_C[F]$, this will characterize the end-state of the developmental process reached after time Δt_F – that is, $m_C(t_0 + \Delta t_F) \approx m_C[F]$. We thus conceptualize development (as well as learning) in a cognitive system in terms of a forced system of interacting (i.e., coupled) dynamical systems (Figure 9.4). Thus, as C develops, it traces out a trajectory in M determined by its adaptive dynamics L according to:

$$m_C(t + \Delta t) = L(m_C(t), s(t), t) \qquad [9.2]$$

where the explicit dependence on time in L captures the idea of an innately specified developmental process (i.e., maturation) as well as a possible dependence on the previous developmental history of C. Within this adaptive framework, m_C determines the transition function T in the following sense: T can be viewed as parameterized by m_C (i.e., T is a function also of m_C) according to $T = T[m_C]$, and equation [9.1] needs to be modified according to:

$$[s(n+1), \lambda(n+1)] = T[m_C][s(n), i(n)] \qquad [9.1']$$

In other words, $T{:}\ \Omega \times \Sigma \rightarrow \Omega \times \Lambda$ is replaced by $T{:}\ M \times \Omega \times \Sigma \rightarrow \Omega \times \Lambda$ (Petersson, 2005a; Petersson, 2008). This outline is in its essentials similar to Chomsky's well-known hypothesis concerning language acquisition (Chomsky, 1980, 1986) in which the module C is taken to be the faculty of language, L the language acquisition device, and the model space M the set of natural languages, which is determined by an innate universal grammar (see also Jackendoff, 2002). Different aspects of the universal grammar, including constraints and principles (Chomsky, 2000), are captured by M, L, and the initial state $m_C(t_0)$. Chomsky and others have argued extensively that the inherent properties of M, L, and $m_C(t_0)$ are determined by innately specified (genetic) factors, the genetically determined morphogenetic processes, in interaction with the physiochemical processes of cells. From this point of view, natural language acquisition is the result of an interaction between two sources of information: (1) *innate prior structure*, which is likely to be language specific in nature as well as of more general nonlanguage type; and (2) the *environment*, both the linguistic and the extra-linguistic, which can be viewed as an interactive boundary condition for the developing system (Petersson, 2005a). The learning that characterizes language acquisition is largely implicit in nature (Forkstam, Hagoort, Fernandez, Ingvar, & Petersson, 2006; Forkstam & Petersson, 2005a, 2005b; Petersson, Forkstam, & Ingvar, 2004).

In summary, the nervous system is naturally viewed as a (bio-)physical dynamic system and the temporal evolution of a given brain system, determined by its underlying neuronal dynamics, corresponds to transitions between physical states, which we here conceptualize as transitions between cognitive states or information-processing. The brain's recurrent network architecture is a prerequisite for functional integration of functionally specialized brain regions (i.e., *functional modularity*). This serves as a basis for the dynamical systems perspective on cognitive function and suggests a form of functional modularity, which might be called *dynamic functional modularity*, which naturally lends itself to a description in terms of Marr's (1982) three (generalized) levels of analysis: the cognitive level, the dynamical system level, and the implementation level. We thus arrive at a dynamic conceptualization of a cognitive learning system C in terms of (1) a *functional architecture* specifying its structural organization (e.g., network architecture); (2) a *representational dynamics* specifying its information-processing dynamics (e.g., the evolution of membrane potentials and the generation of action potentials); and (3) a *learning dynamics* specifying its adaptive parameters (for information storage in a general sense; e.g., synaptic parameters) and the dynamical principles governing the time evolution of the adaptive parameters (e.g., co-occurrence- or covariance-based Hebbian learning) (Arbib, 2003; Gerstner & Kistler, 2002; Koch, 1999).

In short, a developmental learning system can be conceptualized as coupled dynamical systems, one for processing of information in interaction with (an)other dynamical subsystem(s) for learning, memory, and development (Figure 9.5). That is, an adaptive dynamical system C = <*functional architecture, representational dynamics, learning dynamics*> or, more explicitly: (1) the *functional architecture* is a specification of the structural organization of the system; (2) the *representational dynamics* includes a specification of a state-space, Ω, of state variables s (e.g., membrane potentials) carrying information, and dynamical principles, T, governing the active processing of information; and (3) the *learning dynamics* includes a specification of learning (adaptive) variables/parameters m (e.g., synaptic parameters) for information storage (i.e., memory formation) and dynamical principles L (e.g., Hebbian learning) governing the temporal evolution of the learning variables in the model space M. A more general dynamical formulation, compared to equations [9.1′] and [9.2], is perhaps more natural from a neuroscience perspective; for example, in terms of multidimensional stochastic differential/difference equation (Øksendal, 2000) with additive noise processes $\xi(t)$ and $\eta(t)$:

$$ds = T(s, m, i)dt + d\xi(t) \qquad [9.3]$$

$$dm = L(s, m, i)dt + d\eta(t) \qquad [9.4]$$

Here, the representational dynamics corresponds to equation [9.3] and the learning dynamics corresponds to equation [9.4]. These equations represent a system of coupled stochastic differential/difference equations, which allows information-processing to interact with the learning dynamics and can be directly related to – for example – the interaction between the perception-cognition-action and encoding-storage-retrieval cycles, respectively. Note also that equations [9.3] and [9.4] correspond directly to the classical picture given by equations [9.1′] and [9.2] in Figure 9.4. However, general dynamical system theory (Lasota & Mackey, 1994; Ott, 1993) is in a sense obviously too rich as a framework for formulating explicit models of cognitive brain functions (Petersson, 2005a); what is crucially needed is a specification of cognitively relevant constraints and processing principles as well as constraints and processing principles relevant for the neurobiological networks subserving information-processing in the brain. Thus, in a very important sense, most of the empirical and theoretical work necessary for a deeper understanding of cognitive functions remains to be pursued in order to specify detailed and integrated models of cognition, development, and learning. The point of the discussion so far has been to specify explicitly the form such models can take and how the concepts behind them are interrelated, serving as a foundation for a more profound understanding of developing cognitive systems, most prominently represented by the human brain and its capacity to acquire a natural language. What is important here is to understand how these concepts are interrelated and how they serve as a context and a background to the second part of this chapter. In the second part, we first briefly discuss how cognitive states – viewed as physical states – and operations on these states (i.e., information-processing) can be empirically as well as behaviorally characterized with functional neuroimaging techniques. In the final part, we provide an overview of some recent empirical results related to literacy/illiteracy.

Language and Literacy

Since Broca (1861, Broca's region ~ Brodmann's areas (BA) 6/44/45/47) and Wernicke (1874, Wernicke's region ~ posterior BA 22 and inferior BA 39/40) identified separate brain regions specialized for different aspects of language processing, it is well accepted that the human brain instantiates a distributed network supporting natural language processing. From a cognitive neuroscience perspective, natural language is a brain system of knowledge, a generative system for communicative use (Baggio, Van Lambalgen, & Hagoort, 2007, in press; Chomsky, 1986). During language comprehension, incoming sounds or orthographic patterns trigger memory-retrieval processes that make available phonologic, syntactic, and semantic features of words. These structures are integrated (i.e., unified) at the sentence and discourse levels, typically resulting in a coherent interpretation of the input. Similar processes are at work in language production, resulting in compositionally structured serialized (i.e., linearized) sounds or orthographic patterns in the service of communication. Memory retrieval and structure integration (i.e., unification) play an important role in both comprehension and production (Forkstam & Petersson, 2005a; Hagoort, 2005; Jackendoff, 2002; Shieber, 1986; Vosse & Kempen, 2000).

The neural structures involved in retrieval of stored language knowledge are likely to have evolved from and show an overlap with structures involved in retrieving general knowledge and working memory (Baddeley, 1996, 2000; Baddeley, Gathercole, & Papagno, 1998; Jackendoff, 2002), including prefrontal, temporal, and inferior parietal regions. In addition to the medial temporal lobe memory system, which plays a central role in declarative memory operations (Bastiaansen & Hagoort, 2006; Miller, Li, & Desimone, 1991; Petersson, Gisselgård, Gretzer, & Ingvar, 2006), numerous brain regions have been linked to the retrieval of information from long-term memory and its utilization in working memory, including prefrontal, temporal, parietal, anterior cingulate, and cerebellar regions. Among the cortical regions that have been specifically associated with retrieval of lexical information in the context of language comprehension are the central and posterior parts of the left-middle and superior-temporal gyri, and the posterior-inferior frontal gyrus (Indefrey & Cutler, 2005). Unification operations related to the domains of phonology, syntax, and semantics are thought to be carried out in a set of brain regions including the left-inferior frontal gyrus (i.e., Broca's region and surrounding tissue: BA 6/44/45/47) and possibly the left-posterior superior temporal/inferior parietal region (BA 22/39/40). There appears to be a degree of regional specificity for phonology, syntax, and semantics in the left-inferior frontal gyrus (Bookheimer, 2002; Hagoort, Hald, Baastiansen, & Petersson, 2004; Petersson et al., 2004). The language network, characterized with PET and fMRI, is thus becoming increasingly well understood. However, the resulting picture is static, emphasizing mainly the structural aspects of the language network, and does not capture the dynamic properties of the language-processing device

(Bastiaansen & Hagoort, 2006). Thus, the information obtained with PET and fMRI needs to be complemented with information derived from EEG and MEG, which record neuronal activity on a millisecond time scale (Bastiaansen & Hagoort, 2006). Bastiaansen and Hagoort (2006) provide a review of the rapid, oscillatory changes during language processing and give reasons for why these oscillatory changes provide a window on the neuronal dynamics of the language system. They argue that it has become increasingly clear on the basis of functional neuroimaging studies that the view that there is a one-to-one mapping between a brain area and a specific component of a cognitive function is far too simplistic; they suggest that individual cortical areas can be recruited dynamically in more than one functional network (Mesulam, 1998). Bastiaansen and Hagoort (2006) suggest that the dynamic recruitment of participating cortical and subcortical regions is reflected in the patterns of synchronization and desynchronization of neuronal activity. The idea is that synchronous, repetitive neuronal firing of action potentials facilitates the activation of functional networks because it increases the probability that neurons entrain one another in synchronous firing and that synchronization/desynchronization plays a crucial role in the dynamic linking of regions that are part of a given functional network (Fries, 2005). However, this domain of functional neuroimaging is in its infancy and many issues remain unknown or unexplored. Here it is important to note, relative to the first part of this chapter – which provided a somewhat abstract conceptualization of cognitive systems as coupled dynamical systems on appropriate state-spaces (see Figure 9.5) – that the various functional neuroimaging methods (i.e., PET/fMRI/EEG/MEG) provide techniques for direct or indirect quantitative measurements of aspects of the physical states of the brain, which are the concrete instantiations of the cognitive states referred to previously. Although most of the empirical and theoretical work necessary for a deeper understanding of cognitive functions remains to be developed, the current functional neuroimaging techniques provide powerful and useful tools in this quest for a more detailed and integrated model of cognition.

Aspects of language can also be an object of metalinguistic awareness: explicit processing and the intentional control over aspects of phonology, syntax, semantics, and discourse, as well as pragmatics. Children gradually create explicit representations and acquire processing mechanisms that allow for reflecting and analyzing different aspects of language function and language use (Karmiloff-Smith, Grant, Sims, Jones, & Cuckle, 1996). Children do not learn language passively but rather actively construct representations on the basis of linguistically relevant constraints and abstractions of the linguistic input (Karmiloff-Smith et al., 1996). When children subsequently learn to read, this has repercussions on the phonological representations of spoken language (Morais, 1993; Petersson, Reis, Askelöf, Castro-Caldas, & Ingvar, 2000; Ziegler & Goswami, 2005). During the acquisition of reading and writing skills, a child creates the ability to represent aspects of the phonological component of language by an orthographic representation and relates this to a visuographic input-output code. This is commonly achieved by means of a supervised learning process (i.e., teaching), in contrast to natural language acquisition, which is largely a spontaneous, nonsupervised, and self-organized process.

Reading and writing are cognitive abilities that depend on human cultural evolution (Vygotsky, 1962). Writing is a relatively late invention in human history (i.e., five thousand to six thousand years ago) and it seems unlikely that specific brain structures have developed for the purpose of mediating reading and writing per se. Instead, it is likely that reading and writing skills are supported by pre-adapted brain structures. Dehaene (2005) suggests that cultural acquisitions are only possible to the extent that they can be accommodated within the range of neural plasticity, by adapting (i.e., "customizing"/"configuring") pre-existing neural predispositions. Literacy – reading and writing – as well as printed media represent extensive cultural complexes and, like all cultural expressions, they originate in human cognition and social interaction. Goody's work on literacy emphasizes the role that written communication has played in the emergence, development, and organization of social and cultural institutions in contemporary societies (Goody, 2000). The emergence of writing transformed human culture, including the ability to preserve speech and knowledge in printed media. The invention of new communication media has significant impact on the way information is created, stored, retrieved, transmitted, and used, as well as on the cultural evolution as a whole. Furthermore, reading and writing makes possible an increasingly articulate feedback as well as independent self-reflection and promotes the development of metacognitive skills. Although auditory-verbal language use is oriented toward content, aspects of this knowledge can become explicitly available to the language user in terms of cognitive control and analytic awareness. Thus, it has been suggested that the acquisition of reading and writing skills, as well as formal education more generally, facilitates this through a process of representational construction and reorganization (Karmiloff-Smith, 1992).

In what ways do cognitive and neural processes interact during development, and what are the consequences of this interaction for theories of learning? Quartz and Sejnowski (1997) attempted to sketch a neural framework addressing these issues – so-called neural constructivism – suggesting that there is an active constructive interaction between the developing system and the environment in which it is embedded. Human natural language, a major vehicle for cultural transmission, serves as a good illustration of the issues involved (Hauser, Chomsky, & Fitch, 2002; Nowak, Komarova, & Niyogi, 2002). To effectively solve real-world learning problems, it is typically necessary to incorporate relevant prior structure (i.e., prior knowledge in the form of a structured initial state and prior properties of adaptive acquisition devices) in the functional architecture. Prior innate structure can significantly reduce the complexity of the acquisition problem by constraining the available model space M (for a given cognitive component), thus alleviating the extent of the search problem that a child is confronted with in order to converge on an appropriate final model $m_C[F]$. Chomsky's hypothesis of the existence of a universal competence grammar, determined by the language acquisition device and the initial state of the individual's language faculty, is an example of this (Chomsky, 1965, 1986). It has been suggested that natural language arises from three distinct but interacting adaptive systems: individual learning, cultural transmission, and biological evolution (Christiansen & Kirby, 2003). The adaptive character of evolution as well as individual learning (i.e., "adaptation of the individual's knowledge") is undisputed, but this is less clear for cultural development. Christiansen and Kirby (2003) argued that the knowledge of particular languages persists over time by being repeatedly used to generate language output, and this output represents input to the language-acquisition device of the individual learner of the next generation. It is likely that aspects of natural languages have adapted to the constraints set by the language-acquisition device of individual learners. Constraints on language transmission are thus set by prior structures related to the language-acquisition device determined by the outcome of biological evolution. However, Christiansen and Kirby (2003) suggested that if there are features of language that must be acquired by all learners, and there are constraints or selection pressures on the reliable and rapid acquisition of those features, then an individual who is born with such acquisition properties will have an advantage, exemplifying the so-called Baldwin effect of genetic assimilation, whereby acquired features can become innate. These suggestions are consistent with Chomsky's perspective that the universal competence grammar is determined by the language-acquisition device and the initial state of the individual.

We leave the general discussion at this point and move on to experimental results related to literacy and education as seen from the point of view of cognitive neuroscience. That is, we focus on empirical studies investigating the left-side interaction of Figure 9.1, that which is between the individual and his or her environment with its sources for cultural transmission. In particular, we review some recent cognitive, neuroanatomic, and functional neuroimaging data that, taken together, suggest that formal education influences important aspects of the human brain and provides strong support for the hypothesis that the functional architecture of the brain is modulated by literacy. In particular, we focus on results from a series of experiments with an illiterate population and their matched literate controls living in the south of Portugal.

Literacy from a Cognitive Neuroscience Point of View

Acquiring reading and writing skills as well as other cognitive skills during formal education can be viewed as a structured process of cultural transmission. These institutionalized structures subserve important aspects of socialization and cultural transmission. The study of illiterate subjects and their matched literate controls provides an opportunity to investigate the interaction between neurobiological and cultural factors on the outcome of cognitive development and learning (see Figure 9.1). The careful study of illiteracy can contribute to an understanding of the organization of human cognition without the confounding factor of education and, from a practical point of view, investigations of illiteracy can contribute to disentangling the influence of educational background on cognitive test performance in clinical neuropsychological practice. It is well known that educational variables significantly influence performance on many neuropsychological tests (Lezak, Howieson, & Loring, 2004; Petersson & Reis, 2006; Reis & Petersson, 2003; Silva, Petersson, Faísca, Ingvar, & Reis, 2004) and it is important to distinguish, for example, the effects of brain damage from the influence of individual educational history. This is particularly important because reading and writing skills are still far from universal at the beginning of the twenty-first century. At present, it is estimated that there are close to one billion illiterate humans in the world (about two thirds are women; UNESCO, 2003), whereas the mean educational level is only about three or four years of schooling (Abadzi, 2003).

The Study Population of Southern Portugal

The fishing village of Olhão in southern Portugal, where all of our studies on illiteracy were conducted, is socioculturally homogeneous and most of the population has lived their life within the community. Mobility within the region has been limited and the main source of income is related to agriculture or fishing. Illiteracy occurs in Portugal because of the fact that forty or fifty years ago, it was common for the older daughters of a family to be engaged in daily household activities at home and, therefore, did not attend school. Later in life, they may have started to work outside the family. In larger families, the younger children were generally sent to school when they reached the age of six, whereas the older siblings typically helped out with the younger siblings at home. Thus, the illiterate subjects we investigated are illiterate for reasonably well-defined sociocultural reasons and not because of individual causes (e.g., learning difficulties or early central nervous system pathologies). Literate and illiterate subjects live intermixed and participate actively in this community on similar terms. Illiteracy is not perceived as a functional handicap and the same sociocultural environment influences both literate and illiterate subjects to a similar degree. In addition, most of the literate subjects participating in our studies are not highly educated; typically, they have had only approximately four years of schooling. In the present context, it is important to ensure that the subjects investigated are not cognitively impaired and also that the illiterate subjects are matched to the literate subjects in as many relevant respects as possible – except, of course, for the consequences of not having had the opportunity to receive a formal education. In our studies, we attempted to match the different literacy groups in terms of several relevant variables including, for example, age, gender, sociocultural background, and level of everyday functionality. (For a more detailed characterization of our study population and our selection procedures, see Reis, Guerreiro, & Petersson, 2003.) These protocols and procedures ensure with reasonable confidence that the illiterate subjects are cognitively normal and that their lack of formal education results from specific sociocultural reasons and because of low intelligence, learning disability, or other pathology potentially affecting the brain. The illiterate subjects and their literate controls included in our studies are comparable along socioeconomic dimensions as well.

Functional and Neuroanatomical Differences between Literacy Groups

In an early PET study of literate and illiterate subjects, we compared the two literacy groups on an immediate verbal-repetition task. The subjects were instructed to repeat words or pseudowords, one item presented at a time recorded by a native speaker (Petersson et al., 2000). We chose to investigate the word/pseudoword repetition task because it is known to be a test of phonological processing and awareness and it correlates with reading acquisition (discussed herein). In our view, this task is more ecologically relevant than many other tasks that also tax phonological processing and phonological awareness (e.g., initial phoneme deletion, phoneme counting, phoneme similarity classification, and so forth; discussed herein). Within-group comparisons showed a more prominent left-sided inferior parietal (BA 40) activation in word-versus-pseudoword repetition in the literate group. In the reverse comparison (i.e., pseudowords versus words), the literate group displayed significant activations in the anterior insular cortex (BA 14/15) bilaterally and in the right-inferior frontal/frontal opercular cortices (BA 44/45/47), left perigenual anterior cingulate cortex (BA 24/32), left basal ganglia, and the midline cerebellum. In the illiterate group, a single significant activation was observed in the right-middle frontal/frontopolar region (BA 10). Direct group comparisons largely confirmed these differences. In particular, the significantly greater activation of the left-inferior parietal region (BA 40) in the literate group compared to the illiterate group was related to a greater activation of this region in the word-versus-pseudoword comparison.

A central cognitive capacity related to spoken language is verbal working memory, which supports several higher cognitive functions, including language and reasoning (Baddeley, 1986, 2003). According to the Baddeley–Hitch model, working memory is composed of a central executive with two support systems: the phonological loop for storing verbal information and the visual sketch pad for storing visuospatial information. The phonological loop consists of the phonological store and an articulatory rehearsal process. The functional-anatomical correlate of the phonological store is putatively the left-inferior parietal region (BA 39/40) together with parts of the superior temporal cortex (BA 22; Becker, MacAndrew, & Fiez, 1999), while the articulatory rehearsal process is related to a left-frontal circuit including Broca's region (BA 44) and parts of the left premotor cortex (BA 6; Smith & Jonides, 1998, 1999). Taken together with the behavioral findings outlined herein, the PET results suggest that the functional architecture of auditory-spoken language is influenced by literacy and that the acquisition of reading and writing skills modifies aspects of phonological processing especially, as we will see, of pseudowords.

A complementary approach to the analysis of functional neuroimaging data outlined in the previous paragraph, which investigates differences between conditions and experimental groups in terms of functionally specialized regions, takes a network perspective on cognitive brain function in order to explore functional integration in terms of functional connectivity (Friston, 1994; Ingvar & Petersson, 2000; Petersson et al., 2006). As outlined in the first part of this chapter, information is thought to be represented as distributed activity patterns, whereas information-processing subserving cognitive functions is thought to emerge from the interactions within and between different functionally specialized regions. Structural-equation modeling provides one approach to characterize network interactions and to test network hypotheses explicitly by investigating the covariance structure observed between a set of brain regions. Petersson et al. (2000) employed a network analysis of the PET data described previously to characterize the pattern of interactions between brain regions during immediate verbal repetition in literate and illiterate subjects (for limitations, see Petersson, Nichols, Poline, & Holmes, 1999a, 1999b). The network analysis aimed to characterize the functional organization in terms of effective connections between regions in a functional-anatomical model. Our objective was to construct a simple network model that could explain a sufficient part of the observed covariance structure in both groups during both word and pseudoword repetition. At the same time, we required that the network model should be both theoretically and empirically plausible based on the available literature on the functional organization of language (for details, see Petersson et al., 2000). In terms of network interactions, the results showed no significant difference in the literate group when they repeated words or pseudowords, which suggests that the interactions observed in the functional network support both word or pseudoword repetition in a similar way. There was no significant difference between the literate and illiterate group in the word-repetition condition. In contrast, there were significant differences between word and pseudoword repetition in the illiterate group and between the illiterate and literate groups in the pseudoword condition. The differences between groups were mainly related to the phonological loop – in particular, the interaction between Broca's region and the inferior parietal region.

The absence of a significant difference between word and pseudoword repetition in the literate group relates to the fact that the network interactions were similar in both conditions, which suggests that the literate subjects automatically recruit the same processing network during immediate verbal repetition irrespective of whether they repeat words or pseudowords. In contrast, this was not the case for the illiterate group. Although the functional network investigated was the same as that in the literate group, the interaction patterns between brain regions were different from those observed in the literate group, consistent with the suggestion that phonological processing is differently organized in illiterate individuals when confronting novel but phonotactically legitimate phonological patterns. We suggest that the observed differences are due to the different developmental background of the two groups related to the acquisition of reading and writing skills. The observed differences in interaction patterns related to the phonological loop between literate and illiterate subjects are in line with the suggestion that the parallel interactive processing characteristics of the language system – in particular, with respect to phonology – differ between literate and illiterate subjects (Petersson et al., 2000). Given what is known about preliterate phonological development (Goswami & Bryant, 1990; Jusczyk, 1997; Ziegler & Goswami, 2005) and for theoretical reasons as well (Olson, 1996), and in line with our previous interpretation of our behavioral results, the difference in phonological processing between literate and illiterate subjects is likely related to aspects of subsyllabic phonological structure.

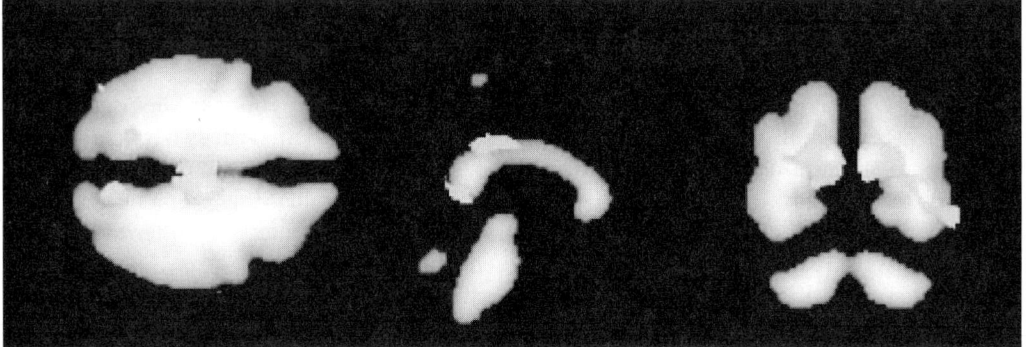

Figure 9.6. Structural MR data suggest that the local thickness of the corpus callosum is thinner in illiterate subjects compared to the literate subjects in the posterior mid-portion (Petersson et al., 2007).

Hemispheric Differences

Early accounts, based on patient descriptions, suggested that illiterates were less prone to develop persistent aphasia following localized cerebral lesions. Later, more systematic studies negated this (Castro-Caldas, Reis, & Guerreiro, 1997). Still, one may wonder whether there are also neuroanatomic correlates corresponding to literacy status; that is, whether a specific form of cultural transmission makes a systematic influence on an ontogenetic level detectable in terms of differences in the functional organization as well as brain morphology. It is well known that the corpus callosum – the large fiber bundle that interconnects the left and the right brain hemisphere – develops during childhood and young adulthood. In particular, there is an active myelination process of the neuronal axons running through this structure to establish efficient communication between the two hemispheres (Giedd, Rumsey, Castellanos, Rajapakse, Kaysen, Vaituzis, et al., 1996). Recent evidence suggests that the posterior mid-body part of the corpus callosum undergoes extensive myelination during the years of reading acquisition – that is, from six to ten years of age (Thompson et al., 2000). The fibers that cross over in this region of the corpus callosum interconnect the left and right parieto-temporal regions (for a general review, see Zaidel & Iacoboni, 2003). The parieto-temporal regions – in particular, in the left hemisphere – is related to language processing, verbal working memory, and reading, and it has been suggested that the corpus callosum plays an important role in the inter-hemispheric exchange of orthographic and phonological information during reading. A previous study of the morphology of the corpus callosum in literate and illiterate subjects suggested that the posterior mid-body region is thinner in the illiterate subjects compared to the literate subjects (Castro-Caldas et al., 1999), a finding that we recently replicated (Petersson, Silva, Castro-Caldas, Ingvar, & Reis, 2007; see Figure 9.6). Petersson et al. (1998) suggested that this may be related to a difference in the inter-hemispheric interactions between the left and right parieto-temporal cortices in the two literacy groups. Behavioral and lesion data have suggested, although not unambiguously, that certain aspects of language processing in illiterate individuals recruit bilateral brain regions to a greater extent than literate subjects (for a review, see Coppens, Parente, & Lecours, 1998).

In a recent study (Petersson et al., 2007), we characterized the hemispheric left-right differences with respect to the inferior parietal regions in two independent datasets from two different samples of illiterate subjects and their matched literate controls. In the first dataset, in which the subjects repeated words and pseudowords, we explored the possibility of a left-right

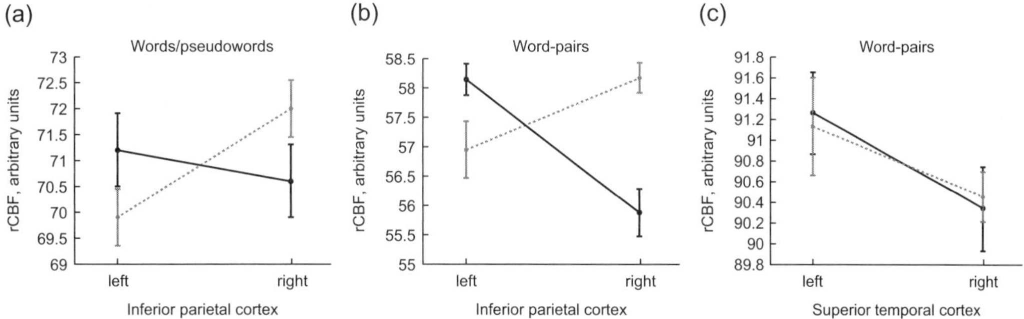

Figure 9.7. Left-right differences. *Left panel*: Participants listened to and repeated words and pseudowords. The diagrams show the level of left- and right-activation levels (levels averaged over conditions) as a function of literacy group (illiterate: red/dashed) in the inferior parietal region. *Middle panel*: Participants listened to and encoded word pairs. *Right panel*: The superior temporal left-right differences in the second experiment.

difference, predicting a greater left-right difference in the literate compared to the illiterate subjects in the inferior parietal region. The left-right comparison in the first sample showed a significant group difference (i.e., group × hemisphere interaction: P = 0.009; Figure 9.7, left panel), which showed a positive left-right difference in the literate group whereas the illiterate subjects showed a negative left-right difference. The group × hemisphere interaction was independent of whether the subjects repeated words (P = 0.017) or pseudowords (P = 0.006). To replicate this finding, we investigated the same inferior parietal region (BA 39/40) in the second sample. Again, the group x hemisphere interaction was independent of whether the subjects listened to semantically related word-pairs (BA 39/40, cluster P = 0.015; FWE-corrected; Figure 9.7, middle panel) or phonologically related word-pairs (BA 39/40, cluster P = 0.005; P = 0.005, FWE-corrected). In the whole brain analysis (Figure 9.8), we observed the same left-right differences in the inferior parietal cortex independent of condition (BA 39/40, cluster P = 0.001, FWE-corrected). The inferior parietal region was part of a larger cluster that extended into the temporo-parietal and occipito-temporal region. In addition, we observed a significant posterior inferior/middle temporal cluster (BA 20/37).

To test the specificity of our results with respect to the left-right differences in the

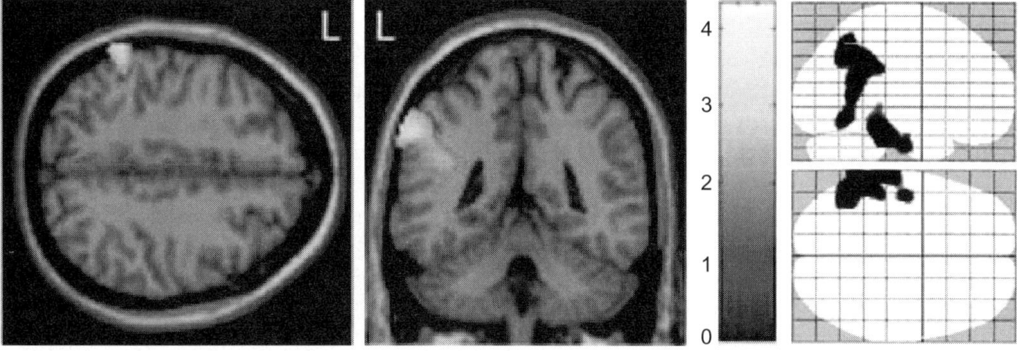

Figure 9.8. Whole-brain analysis of the left-right differences between literacy groups with age as a covariate of no interest. The inferior parietal region that showed greater left-right difference in the literate group compared to the illiterate group (BA 39/40). In addition, there was a significant posterior inferior temporal cluster (BA 20/37).

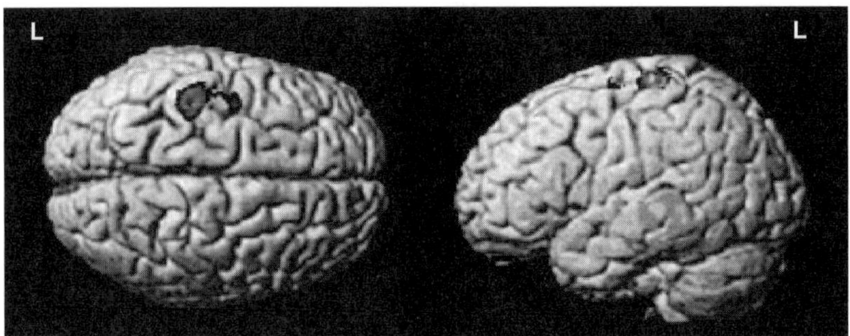

Figure 9.9. Grey-matter intensity differences between literacy groups (literate > illiterate) located in the left-primary motor representation for the right hand.

inferior parietal cortex, we followed up on a suggestion that infants are left-lateralized in the superior temporal gyrus when listening to speech or speech-like sounds (Dehaene-Lambertz, Dehaene, & Hertz-Pannier, 2002), and we also investigated the superior temporal region (BA 22/41/42). The results showed that both literacy groups were similarly left-lateralized in this region (see Figure 9.7, right panel), suggesting that the functional lateralization of early speech-related brain regions are not modulated by literacy in the way that the inferior parietal region is. Consistent with these findings, Ostrosky-Solis and colleagues (2004), recording cortical evoked potentials (ERPs) during a verbal memory task in literate and illiterate subjects, observed hemispheric differences between groups in the parieto-temporal regions. It is well accepted that both hemispheres play a role in language processing. However, the results outlined herein lend support to the suggestion that literacy influences the functional hemispheric balance in inferior parietal language-related regions. One may speculate that acquiring reading and writing skills at the appropriate age shapes not only the local morphology of the corpus callosum but also the degree of functional specialization, as well as the pattern of interaction between the interconnected parieto-temporal regions. Thus, there might be a causal connection among reading and writing acquisition, the development of the corpus callosum, and the hemispheric differences reported herein (Petersson & Reis, 2006).

In recent work with voxel-based morphometry, we investigated a group of twenty-two illiterate subjects and twenty-six matched literate controls to characterize the impact of reading and writing skills on brain morphometry (Reis, Silva, et al., 2007). Preliminary findings suggest relatively subtle grey-matter density differences between literacy groups, including a robust difference located in the left-primary motor representation for the right-hand (literate > illiterate; $P = 0.03$, FWE-corrected), suggesting that this grey-matter intensity difference is related to differences in writing skills or writing habits (Figure 9.9). In contrast, the white-matter intensity differences were more prominent. We first tested for the predicted greater white-matter difference in the posterior mid-body region of the corpus callosum. We placed a spherical region of interest (radius = 10 mm) centered at [0, −20, 24] in the posterior third of the mid-body region of the corpus callosum. We observed significantly greater white-matter intensity in the literate group compared to the illiterate group (cluster $P = 0.02$, with local maximum at [6, −19, 24], $P = 0.04$, SVC FWE-corrected). This cluster was part of a larger significant white-matter cluster ($P < 0.001$, FWE-corrected), which extended toward the white-matter underlying the inferior parietal/parieto-temporal regions, bilaterally, and the right-inferior temporal cortex (Figure 9.7). Further significant white-matter differences were observed in the vicinity of the left-inferior frontal region (literate > illiterate; BA 6/44; cluster $P = 0.05$, FWE-corrected), the posterior part of the left-anterior insula and the anterior part of the corpus callosum (cluster $P < 0.001$, FWE-corrected), the right occipito-temporal cortex (lingual/fusiform gyrus, BA 18/19, cluster $P = 0.001$; FWE-corrected), and mid-cerebellar white-matter (cluster $P = 0.003$; FWE-corrected). There were no significant differences between the two literacy groups in the reverse comparison (Reis, Silva et al., 2007).

In summary, our results suggest that learning to read and write modifies the density of white matter adjacent to brain regions involved in the processing of written language. The fact that the differences between literacy groups were more prominent with respect to white-matter intensity relative to grey-matter intensity might suggest that the acquisition and maintenance of reading and writing skills neuronal connectivity (e.g., degree of myelination) is relatively more affected by literacy and education compared to neuronal density as such, promoting the communication in a functionally dedicated neocortical network.

Cognitive Differences between Literacy Groups

Behavioral studies have demonstrated that literacy and illiteracy, as well as the extent of formal education, influence the performance of several behavioral tasks commonly used in neuropsychological assessment (for recent reviews, see Petersson & Reis, 2006; Petersson, Reis, & Ingvar, 2001). For example, it appears that the acquisition of written language skills modulates aspects of spoken language processing (Mendonça et al., 2002; Silva et al., 2002). Additional results suggest that formal education influences visuospatial skills (Reis, Petersson, Castro-Caldas, & Ingvar, 2001). However, a detailed understanding of which parts of the cognitive system and which processing levels are affected is still lacking. The basic idea is that literacy influences some aspects of spoken language processing related to phonological processing – in particular, the processing of subsyllabic structure, verbal short-term working memory, and visuomotor skills related to or influenced by reading and writing.

Color Makes a Difference: Object Naming

Several studies have indicated that the level of formal education and/or literacy influences performance when subjects name two-dimensional (2D) pictorial representations of objects (Reis, Guerreiro, & Castro-Caldas, 1994). Naming objects or their 2D pictorial representations are common everyday tasks and the performance on simple object-naming tasks is dependent on the systems for visual recognition, lexical retrieval, and organization of speech output, as well as the interaction between these systems (Levelt, 1989). In our study population, practice in interpreting schematic 2D representations commonly took place simultaneously with the acquisition of written Portuguese and other symbolic representations during school attendance. Moreover, reading and writing depend on advanced visual and visuomotor skills in coding, decoding, and generating 2D representations. It is thus likely that the interpretation and production of 2D representations of real objects, as well as the coding and decoding of 2D material in terms of figurative/symbolic semantic content, is more practiced in literate compared to illiterate individuals, who generally have received little systematic practice in interpreting conventional visuosymbolic representations. We thus speculated that there may be differences in 3D and 2D object-naming skills between literate and illiterate individuals. In a simple object-naming experiment in which the participants named common everyday objects, Reis, Petersson et al. (2001) reported differences between literate and illiterate subjects related to 2D object-naming but found no difference when subjects named real 3D objects, with respect to both naming performance and response times. In addition, the two groups dissociated in terms of their error patterns, with the illiterate group more prone to make visually related errors (e.g., pen instead of needle), whereas the literate group tended to make semantically related errors (e.g., necklace instead of bracelet). Although the results with 2D line drawings and real objects were clear in the study of Reis, Petersson et al. (2001), the results with colored photographs did not clearly dissociate between the literacy groups in terms of 2D versus 3D naming skills. Therefore, we speculated that the semantic significance of object color might play a role, particularly for the illiterate subjects because they are prone to be driven by content/substance rather than formal aspects of stimuli or information. In a recent follow-up study (Reis, Faísca, Ingvar, & Petersson, 2006), we presented common everyday objects as black and white (i.e., grey-scaled) as well as colored drawings and photographs in an immediate 2D object-naming task. Consistent with the results already outlined, the literate group performed significantly better than the illiterate group on black and white items, both for line drawings and photographs. In contrast, there was no significant difference between literacy groups on the colored items. It is interesting that the illiterate participants performed significantly better on colored line drawings compared to black and white photographs. Further investigation suggested that the color effect is related to the semantic value of the color in the sense that the effect seems more pronounced for objects with no or little consistency in the color-object relationship compared to objects with a consistent relationship to its color (e.g., lemons are yellow).

The Impact of Literacy on Visuomotor Integration

The impact of literacy and formal education on nonverbal cognitive domains has not been fully explored. In an earlier study, Ostrosky-Solis, Efron, and Yund (1991) made an interesting observation about the visual scanning behavior in nonliterate subjects. The nature of these differences suggests that the acquisition of reading skills might cause literate subjects to adopt more consistent scanning paths. In more recent work, Matute and colleagues (2000) demonstrated that literacy also plays a significant role on visuoconstructional tasks. These results lend support to the idea that the reading level might be related to the mechanisms responsible for variation in performance on visuoperceptual tests (Byrd, Jacobs, Hilton, Stern, & Manly, 2005). These results are consistent with previous findings (Le Carret et al., 2003) that showed that individuals with a lower educational level have less effective visual search strategies and produce fewer successful responses to target items appearing in the lower half of 2 × 2 response matrices. Although the results of these studies suggest poorer strategic search skills in illiterate, low-level literate subjects, and poor readers, it is possible that the low performance is related to poor shape-recognition skills (cf. the previous object-naming subsection). Another line of evidence concerning the effect of reading on visual scanning mechanisms comes from studies performed in literate populations that have acquired orthographies with different reading directions (i.e., left-to-right and right-to-left), suggesting that the reading system biases the visual scanning behavior in certain circumstances. One of the first studies reported an influence of reading habits on visual recognition of English words (read from left to right) and Yiddish words (read from right to left) presented in the left and right visual fields to subjects who could read both languages (Mishking & Forgays, 1952). More recently, Chokron and Imbert (1993) used a line-bisection task to investigate the impact of reading and writing habits on visuomotor integration skills. The authors analyzed the performance of French and Israeli subjects and the bisection performance was found to depend on the reading habits of the subjects. In a recent study, Bramão and colleagues (2007) demonstrated that the acquisition of literacy also modulates visuomotor integration with nonlinguistic stimuli. The results showed that the literate subjects were significantly faster in detecting and touching targets on the left compared with the right side of the screen. In contrast, the presentation side did not affect the performance of the illiterate group. It is clear that the act of reading and writing in an alphabetic language engages cognitive processes related to both the systematic scanning of space as well as motor integration. Consistent with this idea, our results suggest that visual scanning, detection, and pointing at nonlinguistic targets are modulated by literacy and represent new evidence that a preferred left-to-right reading direction influences visual scanning behavior. Reading and writing skills depend on both right-hemisphere (e.g., visuospatial strategies) and left-hemisphere functions (e.g., language and writing), which is likely to promote an increased asymmetry in information transfer between the hemispheres.

Ecological Relevance

Formal education is not only associated with literacy but also with the acquisition of a broader knowledge base of general world knowledge, as well as strategies to process this information in a more elaborate, systematic, and abstract manner. Thus, education catalyzes the development of several cognitive skills in addition to reading and writing. Task selection is thus of importance when investigating populations with different cultural backgrounds – in particular, when the objective is to interpret differences in performance in cognitive terms and it is important in this context that the task is of comparable ecological relevance to the populations investigated (Petersson et al., 2001). This goes beyond matching populations for background variables related to, for example, socioeconomic status (Coppens et al., 1998; Reis & Petersson, 2003). This is illustrated by the results from a study of semantic fluency by Silva et al. (2004).

Verbal fluency tasks (i.e., production tasks in which subjects generate as many words as possible according to some given criterion during a limited amount of time) are commonly used in neuropsychological assessment because they are easy to administer, sensitive to brain damage and cognitive deterioration, and have been applied to groups with different cultural backgrounds. Clear and consistent differences between literacy groups have been reported when a phonological fluency criterion is used. In contrast, several studies using semantic criteria have yielded inconsistent results (Silva et al., 2004). Reis et al. (2003) suggested that the nonconvergence of results could be related to the ecological or cultural relevance of the chosen semantic criterion. To investigate this issue in greater detail, Reis et al. (2001, 2003) decided to use a semantic criterion of equal relevance to female literate and illiterate subjects of southern Portugal and asked the participants to name things one can buy at the supermarket. The relevance of this criterion springs from the fact that almost all of the individuals we investigate do the major part of their regular shopping at supermarkets and at comparable levels over time. Reis, Guerreiro et al. (2001, 2003) found no significant difference between illiterate subjects, subjects with four years of education, and subjects with more than four years of education. Silva et al. (2004) compared the performance of the same illiterate and literate subjects on two time-constrained semantic-fluency tasks, the first using the semantic category of food items (i.e., supermarket-fluency task), and the second, animal names (i.e., animal-fluency task). The literate and illiterate groups performed equally on the supermarket-fluency task, whereas the literate subjects were significantly better on the animal-fluency task. The equal supermarket-fluency performance excludes a simple explanation for the performance differences on the animal-fluency task in terms of general factors, such as cognitive speed. Instead, the interaction between literacy and semantic criteria can be explained in terms of similarities and differences in shared cultural background. Thus, significant educational effects may or may not be observed depending on the choice of semantic criterion; more generally, this emphasizes the importance of developing instruments that are free of educational and cultural biases when investigating cognition in groups of different educational or cultural background.

Short-Term Working Memory and Phonological Processing

Repetition of pseudowords and digit-span tasks are considered good measures of verbal working-memory capacity. These measures have been shown to correlate with reading achievements in children (Baddeley et al., 1998; Gathercole & Baddeley, 1995). Additional research also points toward a role of verbal working memory and the efficiency of phonological processing relative to reading skills (Brady, 1991; Goswami & Bryant, 1990; Ziegler & Goswami, 2005). Verbal short-term working memory is a system subserving the representation and on-line processing of verbal information. In the Baddeley–Hitch model, one role of the phonological loop – a subsystem for short-term storage of phonologically represented information – is to store unfamiliar sound patterns. This suggests that the phonological loop might serve as an integral part of a learning device for spoken and written language acquisition (Baddeley et al., 1998). Several researchers have investigated the relationship between reading and metalinguistic awareness, including phonological awareness (e.g., Morais, 1993). With respect to phonological awareness, this research indicated that illiterate subjects have some difficulty in dealing with tasks requiring explicit phonological processing. For example, the results of Morais et al. (1979) showed that illiterate subjects found it more difficult to add or remove phonemes at the beginning of words as well as pseudowords. One may ask to what extent these tasks are equally natural to literate and illiterate individuals (i.e., of similar ecological relevance), thus complicating the interpretation of these findings. Generally speaking, it is still unclear what type of relationship exists among phonological processing, verbal working memory, and the acquisition of orthographic knowledge. Moreover, it appears that the phonological processing difficulties in illiterate subjects are not limited to phonological awareness per se but rather involve aspects of subsyllabic phonological processing as well as skills related to verbal working memory (e.g., phonological recoding in working memory). In the following subsections, we review results on short-term memory span, pseudoword processing, and word awareness in sentence context.

Digit and Spatial Span

Several studies have suggested that there is a difference in digit span between literacy groups (Ardila, Rosselli, & Rosas, 1989; Reis, Guerreiro, Garcia, & Castro-Caldas, 1995). However, Reis et al. (2003) showed that the difference in digit span is not a simple effect of literacy as such. Instead, digit span seems to be dependent on the extent of formal education: illiterate participants had a mean digit span of 4.1 ($\pm$ 0.9), significantly below literate digit span; however, literate subjects with four years of education (5.2 $\pm$ 1.4) also performed significantly below the literate subjects with nine years of education (7.0 $\pm$ 1.8). Thus, it appears that education more generally contributes to the observed difference (overall effect, $P < .001$). In a recent follow-up study, we compared literate and illiterate participants directly on the digit span and spatial span subtasks of the Wechsler Memory Scale (WMS-III; Wechsler, 1997). Consistent with the results just described, there was a significant difference between literacy groups on the digit span ($P = .004$) but there was no significant difference on the spatial span task ($p = .3$). These results suggest that illiterate subjects have a lower verbal span compared to literate subjects, whereas this is not the case for spatial span. For example, it is possible that the phonological working memory representations are in some sense more effective in literate compared to illiterate individuals (Petersson & Reis, 2006).

Word and Pseudoword Processing

Reis and Castro-Caldas (1997) concluded that illiterate individuals performed similarly to literate individuals on word repetition, whereas there was a significant difference on pseudoword repetition (literate > illiterate). We have suggested that this is related to an inability to handle certain aspects of subsyllabic phonological structure and indicates that the phonological representations or the processing of these representations are differently developed in the two literacy groups (Petersson et al., 2000; Petersson et al., 2001). Alternatively, the system for orthographic representations may support phonological processing as an auxiliary interactive processing network (Petersson et al., 2001) (see also Olson, 1996, for a theoretical perspective). This latter possibility suggests that there might a bidirectional reciprocal influence between orthography and phonology; that is, orthography ↔ phonology rather than orthography → phonology or phonology → orthography. Not only do literate subjects have access to additional representational means (i.e., orthography), but also aspects of the phonological representation itself might be modified by reading acquisition, along similar lines as the phonological grain-size theory of Ziegler and Goswami (2005).

Because several aspects of auditory-verbal language may differ between literate and illiterate individuals, it is of interest to isolate the different sources contributing to these differences in phonological processing. In particular, it is important to study the differences in phonological processing relatively independent of lexicality effects (e.g., vocabulary size and frequency effects) and articulatory mechanisms. To do so, we used an immediate auditory-verbal serial recognition paradigm (Gathercole, Pickering, Hall, & Peacker, 2001) in a recent follow-up study (Petersson et al., 2004). Immediate serial recognition is independent of articulatory speech output. In addition, serial recognition of pseudowords is (relatively) independent of lexicality effects. In this experiment, we compared illiterate and literate subjects on immediate recognition of lists of 3 CVCV-syllable items (C = consonant, V = vowel). The lists varied in lexicality (i.e., words/pseudowords) and phonological similarity (i.e., dissimilar/similar). The participants were asked to judge whether two lists (presented one after the other) contained items presented in the same or different order. Group comparisons showed significant differences: the literate group performing better than the illiterate group, in all conditions (i.e., pseudoword/dissimilar, $P < .001$; pseudoword/similar, $P = .03$; word/similar $P = .003$), except for phonologically different words ($P = .2$). Of the four conditions, the phonologically different word condition is, of course, the easiest to handle from a phonological point of view. Words are more familiar than pseudowords and the phonological contrast is greater in the different compared to the similar condition. These results are thus consistent with the differences in pseudoword repetition and digit-span performance and further support the idea that there are differences in verbal working-memory capacity and phonological processing between the two literacy groups. In addition, the results on immediate serial recognition suggest that these differences are (relatively) independent of lexicality effects, articulatory organization (e.g., output phonology), and other speech-output mechanisms.

Words in Sentence Context

Little is known about how adult illiterate subjects perceive words in a sentence context. Awareness of words as independent lexical units has been investigated in children, both before and after reading acquisition (e.g., Barton, 1985; Hamilton & Barton, 1983; Karmiloff-Smith et al., 1996), and also in illiterate adults (Cary & Verhaeghe, 1991). The results show that explicit knowledge of words as independent lexical units is dependent on literacy. Cary and Verhaeghe (1991) suggested that the difficulty for illiterate subjects is to efficiently identify closed-class words because of their relative lack of semantic content. However, given the prominent syntactic role of closed-class words in sentence processing, including sentence comprehension, and the fact that illiterate and literate individuals acquire spoken language on similar terms, we were interested in whether the effects related to closed-class words could be given a phonological explanation. In two recent studies, we revisited these issues (Mendonça et al., 2003; Mendonça et al., 2002). In both studies, we investigated the awareness of words in sentence context with the aim of clarifying the role of literacy in the recognition of words as independent lexical units and the possible relationship to the known phonological-processing characteristics of illiterate subjects. We presented short sentences that varied in their constituent structure in random order to the participants. All determiners, prepositions, pronouns, and adverbs were included in the closed-class category. We divided this class into phonologically stressed and nonstressed words, in which the latter are characterized by the absence of a stressed vowel. Subjects were instructed to attentively listen to the sentences, to immediately repeat them, and to identify its constituent words. The results of both studies showed that there was no significant difference in sentence repetition and, consistent with previous findings, the literate segmentation performance was significantly better than the illiterate (see Petersson & Reis, 2006, for further details). In particular, the illiterate group showed a specific pattern of merging of words, or "clitization" (or "blending of words"). There are few mergers between the major syntactic constituents, meaning that illiterates are sensitive to the major syntactic structure of the sentence, whereas increasing rates of mergers were observed within phrase-internal constituents. Comparing the stressed and the nonstressed closed-class words (Mendonça et al., 2003) showed that mergers related to closed-class words were observed significantly more often with nonstressed compared to stressed closed-class words in the illiterate group ($P < .001$).

Overall, then, the present results corroborate previous suggestions that recognition of words as independent phonological units in sentence context depends on literacy. However, our results show that the segmentation failures did not distribute evenly over closed-class words (not even within subtypes) but rather occurred more often with phonologically nonstressed than phonologically stressed closed-class words. The illiterate subjects are thus more sensitive to phonologically stressed closed-class words, which they are able to efficiently segment. We suggest that illiterate segmentation performance is closely related to sentence internal prosody and phonological stress. Thus, the difficulty seems to be a phonological phenomenon rather than related to lexical semantics. In addition, the clitization phenomenon seems not to be related to phrase structure per se because the illiterate group respected phrasal boundaries; blending mainly occurred within phrases and rarely across phrasal boundaries or boundaries between major sentence constituents. A contributing factor to segmentation difficulties may be verbal working-memory capacity because the performance of the illiterate group increased from the start to the end of sentences. In other words, the linear sentence position also plays a role. Thus, illiterate sentence segmentation appears to depend on factors related to phonology, syntactic structure, and linear position, and not on factors related to lexical semantics.

Semantic Intrusions and the Awareness of Phonological Form

Kolinsky, Cary, and Morais (1987) investigated the notion of phonological word length in literate and illiterate subjects. Even when explicitly asked to attend to the abstract phonological properties of words, the illiterate group still found it difficult to ignore their semantic content and thus failed to inhibit the intrusion of semantic information when attempting to solve the task based on a form criterion. Similar findings related to the processing of meaning have been reported in various experimental settings (Reis & Castro-Caldas, 1997; Silva et al., 2004). For example, Reis and Castro-Caldas (1997) showed that illiterate individuals exhibit greater difficulty on tasks that focus on formal rather than substantive aspects of the stimulus material (e.g., phonological versus semantic aspects of words), results that have been replicated in a Greek population (Kosmidis, Tsapkini, & Folia, 2007; Kosmidis, Tsapkini, Folia, Vlahou, & Kiosseoglou, 2004). Kolinsky and colleagues (1987) suggested that learning to read plays an important role in the development of the ability to focus on the phonological form of words.

In a recent experiment (Reis, Faísca, Mendonça, Ingvar, & Petersson, 2007), literate and illiterate participants listened to words and pseudowords during a phonological ("sound") length decision task, in which the participants were asked to decide which item in a pair was the longest in phonological ("sound") terms. In the word condition, we manipulated the relationship between word length and size of the denoted object, yielding three subconditions: (1) *congruent*, the longer word denoted the larger object; (2) *incongruent*, the longer word denoted the smaller object; and (3) *neutral*, only phonological length of the words varied, denoting objects of similar size. Pseudoword pairs were constructed based on the real-word pairs by changing the consonants and maintaining the vowels as well as length. Two effects were of interest in the results: (1) the literate subjects showed no effect of semantic interference, whereas this was clearly the case in the illiterate group; and (2) whereas the literates performed at similar levels on words and pseudowords, the illiterate group performed significantly better on pseudowords compared to words. In fact, the mean performance in the pseudoword condition was slightly better than in the neutral-word condition. These results suggest that the illiterate subjects show a greater difficulty in inhibiting the influence of semantic interference, the intrusion of lexical semantics in the decision process.

Conclusion

In the first part of this chapter, we outlined a framework for investigating developmental learning systems as coupled dynamical systems, and we indicated the extreme complexity involved in attempting to understand the human brain from a cognitive neuroscience point of view. We concluded that in an important sense, most of the empirical and theoretical work necessary for a deeper understanding of human cognition remains to be pursued in order to specify integrated models of cognition, development, and learning. In the second part, we briefly discussed how cognitive states – viewed as physical states – and operations on these states (i.e., information-processing) can be empirically characterized with functional neuroimaging techniques as well as behaviorally. In the final part, we took the perspective that the educational system can be viewed as an institutionalized process for structured cultural transmission. With this perspective, the study of illiterate subjects and their literate controls becomes an approach to investigate the interactions between neurobiological and cultural factors on the outcome of learning and cognitive development. The results reviewed herein suggest that literacy influences important aspects of cognition – most prominently, the processing of phonological structure, verbal working memory, and object-recognition/naming. Literacy and education also influence corresponding structural and functional properties of the brain. Taken together, the evidence provides strong support for the hypothesis that certain structural and functional properties of the brain are modulated by literacy and formal education. Literacy and formal education influence the development of the human brain and its capacity to interact with the environment. This includes the culture of the individual who, through acquired cognitive skills, actively can participate in, interact with, and contribute to the process of cultural transmission.

Note

1 This work was supported in part by Fundação para a Ciência e Tecnologia (POCTI/46955/PSI/2002), EU grant QLK6-CT-99-02140, the Swedish Medical Research Council (8276, 127169), the Knut and Alice Wallenberg Foundation, and the Swedish Dyslexia Foundation. The author also wants to thank Dr. Francisco Reis, Catarina Silva, Luís Faísca, Susana Mendonça, and Alexandra Mendonça for their contribution to this work; and Giosué Baggio, Christian Forkstam, and Julia Uddén for helpful comments on the manuscript.

References

Abadzi, H. (2003). *Improving adult literacy outcomes: Lessons from cognitive research for developing countries*. Washington, DC: The World Bank, Operation Evaluation Department.

Arbib, M. A. (Ed.) (2003). *The handbook of brain theory and neural networks* (2nd ed.). Cambridge, MA: MIT Press.

Ardila, A., Rosselli, M., & Rosas, P. (1989). Neuropsychological assessment in illiterates: Visuospatial and memory abilities. *Brain and Cognition, 11*, 147–166.

Baddeley, A. (1986). *Working memory*. Oxford: Oxford University Press.

Baddeley, A. (1996). Working memory: The interface between memory and cognition. In S. E. Gathercole (Ed.), *Models of short-term memory*. Hove, UK: Psychology Press.

Baddeley, A. (2000). The episodic buffer: A new component of working memory? *Trends in Cognitive Sciences*, 4 (11), 417–423.

Baddeley, A. (2003). Working memory: Looking back and looking forward. *Nat. Rev. Neurosci.*, 4, 829–839.

Baddeley, A., Gathercole, S., & Papagno, C. (1998). The phonological loop as a language learning device. *Psychological Review*, 105, 158–173.

Baggio, G., Van Lambalgen, M., & Hagoort, P. (2007, in press). Language, linguistics, and cognition. In M. Stokhof & J. Groenendijk (Eds.), *Handbook of philosophy of linguistics*. Amsterdam: Elsevier.

Barton, D. (1985). Awareness of language units in adults and children. In A. W. Ellis (Ed.), *Progress in the psychology of language* I. Hillsdale, NJ: Lawrence Erlbaum Associates.

Bastiaansen, M., & Hagoort, P. (2006). Oscillatory neuronal dynamics during language comprehension. In C. Neuper & W. Klimesch (Eds.), *Event-related dynamics of brain oscillations* (pp. 179–196). Amsterdam: Elsevier.

Becker, J. T., MacAndrew, D. K., & Fiez, J. A. (1999). A comment on the functional localization of the phonological storage subsystem of working memory. *Brain and Cognition, 41*, 27–38.

Bookheimer, S. (2002). Functional MRI of language: New approaches to understanding the cortical organization of semantic processing. *Annual Review of Neuroscience*, 25, 151–188.

Brady, S. A. (1991). The role of working memory in reading disability. In S. A. Brady & D. P. Shankweiler (Eds.), *Phonological processes in literacy* (pp. 129–151). Hillsdale, NJ: Lawrence Erlbaum Associates.

Bramão, I., Mendonça, A., Faísca, L., Ingvar, M., Petersson, K. M., & Reis, A. (2007). The impact of reading and writing skills on a visuomotor integration task: A comparison between illiterate and literate subjects. *Journal of the International Neuropsychological Society*, 13, 359–364.

Broca, P. (1861). Remarques sur le siege de la faculte de langage articulation suivies d'une observation d'aphemie (perte de la parole). *Bulletine Societe d'Anatomie*, 36, 330–357.

Brown, C. M., & Hagoort, P. (Eds.). (1999). *The neurocognition of language*. Oxford, UK: Oxford University Press.

Byrd, D. A., Jacobs, D. M., Hilton, H. J., Stern, Y., & Manly, J. J. (2005). Source of errors on visuoperceptual tasks: Role of education, literacy, and search strategy. *Brain and Cognition*, 58, 251–257.

Cary, L., & Verhaeghe, A. (1991). Efeito da prática da linguagem ou da alfabetização no conhecimento das fronteiras formais das unidades lexicais: Comparação de dois tipos de tarefas. *Actas das Jornadas de Estudos dos Processos Cognitivos* (pp. 33–49): Sociedade Portuguesa de Psicologia: Secção de Psicologia Cognitiva.

Castro-Caldas, A., Miranda Cavaleiro, P., Carmo, I., Reis, A., Leote, F., Ribeiro, C., et al. (1999). Influence of learning to read and write on the morphology of the corpus callosum. *European Journal of Neurology*, 6, 23–28.

Castro-Caldas, A., Reis, A., & Guerreiro, M. (1997). Neuropsychological aspects of illiteracy. *Neuropsychological Rehabilitation*, 7, 327–338.

Chokron, S., & Imbert, M. (1993). Influence of reading habits on line bisection. *Cognitive Brain Research*, 1, 219–222.

Chomsky, N. (1965). *Aspects of the theory of syntax*. Cambridge, MA: MIT Press.

Chomsky, N. (1980). On the biological basis of language capacities. In N. Chomsky, *Rules and representations* (pp. 185–216). Oxford, UK: Blackwell.

Chomsky, N. (1986). *Knowledge of language*. New York: Praeger.

Chomsky, N. (2000). *New horizons in the study of language and mind*. Cambridge, UK: Cambridge University Press.

Christiansen, M. H., & Kirby, S. (2003). Language evolution: Consensus and controversies. *Trends in Cognitive Sciences*, 7, 300–307.

Coppens, P., Parente, M. A. M. P., & Lecours, A. R. (1998). Aphasia in illiterate individuals. In P. Coppens, Y. Lebrun, & A. Basso (Eds.), *Aphasia in atypical populations* (pp. 175–202). London: Lawrence Erlbaum.

Cutland, N. J. (1980). *Computability: An introduction to recursive function theory*. Cambridge, UK: Cambridge University Press.

Davis, M. D., Sigal, R., & Weyuker, E. J. (1994). *Computability, complexity, and languages: Fundamentals of theoretical computer science* (2nd ed.). San Diego, CA: Academic Press.

Dehaene, S. (2005). Evolution of human cortical circuits for reading and arithmetic: The neuronal recycling hypothesis. In S. Dehaene, J.-R. Duhamel, M. D. Hauser, & G. Rizzolatti (eds.), *From monkey brain to human brain. A Fyssen Foundation Symposium* (pp. 133–157). Cambridge, MA: MIT Press.

Dehaene-Lambertz, G., Dehaene, S., & Hertz-Pannier, L. (2002) Functional neuroimaging of speech perception in infants. *Science*, 298, 2013–2015.

Eck, D. J. (2000). *The most complex machine: A survey of computers and computing*. Natick, MA: A K Peters.

Felleman, D. J., & Van Essen, D. C. (1991). Distributed hierarchical processing in the primate cerebral cortex. *Cerebral Cortex*, 1, 1–47.

Forkstam, C., Hagoort, P., Fernandez, G., Ingvar, M., & Petersson, K. M. (2006). Neural correlates of artificial syntactic structure classification. *NeuroImage*, 32, 956–967.

Forkstam, C., & Petersson, K. M. (2005a). Syntactic classification of acquired structural regularities. *Proceedings of the Cognitive Science Society*, 696–701.

Forkstam, C., & Petersson, K. M. (2005b). Towards an explicit account of implicit learning. *Current Opinion in Neurology*, 18, 435–441.

Frackowiak, R. S. J., Friston, K. J., Frith, C., Dolan, R., Price, C., Zeki, S., et al. (Eds.). (2004). *Human brain function* (2nd ed.). San Diego, CA: Academic Press.

Fries, P. (2005). A mechanism for cognitive dynamics: Neuronal communication through neuronal coherence. *Trends in Cognitive Sciences*, 9, 474–480.

Friston, K. (1994). Functional and effective connectivity. *Human Brain Mapping*, 2, 56–78.

Gathercole, S. E., & Baddeley, A. D. (1995). *Working memory and language*. Hillsdale, NJ: Lawrence Erlbaum Associates.

Gathercole, S. E., Pickering, S. J., Hall, M., & Peacker, S. M. (2001). Dissociable lexical and phonological influences on serial recognition and serial recall. *The Quarterly Journal of Experimental Psychology*, *54A* (1), 1–30.

Gernsbacher, M. A. (Ed.) (1994). *Handbook of psycholinguistics*. San Diego, CA: Academic Press.

Gerstner, W., & Kistler, W. (2002). *Spiking neuron models: Single neurons, populations, plasticity*. Cambridge, UK: Cambridge University Press.

Giedd, J. N., Rumsey, J. M., Castellanos, F. X., Rajapakse, J. C., Kaysen, D., Vaituzis, A. C., et al. (1996). A quantitative MRI study of the corpus callosum in children and adolescents. *Developmental Brain Research*, 91, 274–280.

Goody, J. (2000). *The power of the written tradition*. Washington: Smithsonian Institution Press.

Goswami, U., & Bryant, P. E. (1990). *Phonological skills and learning to read*. Hillsdale, NJ: Earlbaum.

Hagoort, P. (2005). On Broca, brain, and binding: A new framework. *Trends in Cognitive Sciences*, 9, 416–423.

Hagoort, P., Hald, L., Baastiansen, M., & Petersson, K. M. (2004). Integration of word meaning and world knowledge in language comprehension. *Science, 304*, 438–441.

Hamilton, M. E., & Barton, D. (1983). Adult's definition of "word": The effects of literacy and development. *Journal of Pragmatics, 7*, 581–594.

Hauser, M. D., Chomsky, N., & Fitch, W. T. (2002). The faculty of language: What is it, who has it, and how did it evolve? *Science, 298* (5598), 1569–1579.

Haykin, S. (1998). *Neural networks: A comprehensive foundation* (2nd ed.). Upper Saddle River, NJ: Prentice Hall.

Hebb, D. O. (1949). *Organization of behavior*. New York: Wiley.

Hofstadter, D. R. (1999). *Godel, Escher, Bach: An eternal golden braid* (20th anniversary edition). New York: Basic Books.

Indefrey, P., & Cutler, A. (2005). Prelexical and lexical processing in listening. In M. Gazzaniga (Ed.), *The cognitive neurosciences III*. Cambridge, MA: MIT Press.

Ingvar, M., & Petersson, K. M. (2000). Functional maps – cortical networks. In A. W. Toga & J. C. Mazziotta (Eds.), *Brain mapping: The systems* (pp. 111–140). San Diego, CA: Academic Press.

Izhikevich, E. M. (2007). *Dynamical systems in neuroscience: The geometry of excitability and bursting*. Cambridge, MA: MIT Press.

Jackendoff, R. (2002). *Foundations of language: Brain, meaning, grammar, evolution*. Oxford, UK: Oxford University Press.

Jusczyk, P. W. (1997). *The discovery of spoken language*. Cambridge, MA: MIT Press.

Karmiloff-Smith, A. (1992). *Beyond modularity: A developmental perspective on cognitive science*. Cambridge, MA: MIT Press.

Karmiloff-Smith, A., Grant, J., Sims, K., Jones, M. C., & Cuckle, P. (1996). Rethinking metalinguistic awareness: Representing and accessing knowledge about what counts as a word. *Cognition, 58*, 197–219.

Koch, C. (1999). *Biophysics of computation: Information processing in single neurons*. New York: Oxford University Press.

Koch, C., & Laurent, G. (1999). Complexity and the nervous system. *Science, 284*, 96–98.

Koch, C., & Segev, I. (1998). *Methods in neuronal modeling: From ions to networks* (2nd ed.). New York: Oxford University Press.

Kolinsky, R., Cary, L., & Morais, J. (1987). Awareness of words as phonological entities: The role of literacy. *Applied Psycholinguistics, 8*, 223–237.

Kosmidis, M. K., Tsapkini, K., & Folia, V. (2007). Lexical processing in illiteracy: Effect of literacy or education? *Cortex, 42*, 1021–1027.

Kosmidis, M. K., Tsapkini, K., Folia, V., Vlahou, C., & Kiosseoglou, G. (2004). Semantic and phonological processing in illiteracy. *Journal of the International Neuropsychological Society, 10*, 818–827.

Lasota, A., & Mackey, M. C. (1994). *Chaos, fractals, and noise: Stochastic aspects of dynamics*. New York: Springer-Verlag.

Le Carret, N., Rainville, C., Lechevallier, N., Lafont, S., Letenneur, L., & Fabrigoule, C. (2003). Influence of education on the Benton Visual Retention test performance as mediated by a strategic search component. *Brain and Cognition, 53*, 408–411.

Levelt, W. J. M. (1989). *Speaking: From intention to articulation*. Cambridge, MA: MIT Press.

Lewis, H. R., & Papadimitriou, C. H. (1981). *Elements of the theory of computation*. Englewood Cliffs, NJ: Prentice-Hall.

Lezak, M. D., Howieson, D. B., & Loring, D. W. (2004). *Neuropsychological assessment* (4th ed.). New York: Oxford University Press.

Maass, W., Natschläger, T., & Markram, H. (2004). Computational models for generic cortical microcircuits. In J. Feng (Ed.), *Computational neuroscience: A comprehensive approach* (pp. 575–605). Boca Raton, FL: Chapman & Hall/CRC.

Marr, D. (1982). *Vision: A computational investigation into the human representation and processing of visual information*. New York: W. H. Freeman and Company.

Matute, E., Leal, F., Zarabozo, D., Robles, A., & Cedillo, C. (2000). Does literacy have an effect on stick construction tasks? *Journal of the International Neuropsychological Society, 6*, 668–672.

McCulloch, W. S., & Pitts, E. (1943). A logical calculus of the ideas immanent in nervous activity. *Bulletin of Mathematical Biophysics, 5*, 115–133.

Mendonça, A., Mendonça, S., Reis, A., Faisca, L., Ingvar, M., & Petersson, K. M. (2003, November 10–12). *Reconhecimento de unidades lexicais em contexto frásico: O efeito da literacia*. Paper presented at the Congresso em Neurociências Cognitivas, Évora, Portugal.

Mendonça, S., Faisca, L., Silva, C., Ingvar, M., Reis, A., & Petersson, K. M. (2002). The role of literacy in the awareness of words as independent lexical units. *Journal of the International Neuropsychological Society, 8*, 483.

Mesulam, M. M. (1998). From sensation to cognition. *Brain, 121*, 1013–1052.

Miller, E. K., Li, L., & Desimone, R. (1991). A neural mechanism for working and recognition memory in inferior temporal cortex. *Science, 254*, 1377–1379.

Minsky, M. L. (1967). *Computation: Finite and infinite machines*. Englewood Cliffs, NJ: Prentice-Hall.

Mishking, M., & Forgays, D. G. (1952). Word recognition as a function of retinal locus. *Journal of Experimental Psychology, 43*, 43–48.

Morais, J., Cary, L., Alegria, J., & Bertelson, P. (1979). Does awareness of speech as a sequence of phones arise spontaneously? *Cognition, 7*, 323–331.

Morais, J. (1993). Phonemic awareness, language and literacy. In R. M. Joshi & C. K. Leong (Eds.), *Reading disabilities: Diagnosis and component processes* (pp. 175–184). Dordrecht: Kluwer Academic Publishers.

Newell, A., & Simon, H. (1976). Computer science as empirical inquiry: Symbols and search. *Communications of the Association for Computing Machinery, 19*, 111–126.

Nieuwenhuys, R., Voogd, J., & van Huijzen, C. (1988). *The human central nervous system: A synopsis and atlas* (3rd revised ed.). Berlin: Springer-Verlag.

Nowak, M. A., Komarova, N. L., & Niyogi, P. (2002). Computational and evolutionary aspects of language. *Nature, 417*, 611–617.

Øksendal, B. (2000). *Stochastic differential equations: An introduction with applications* (5th ed.). Berlin: Springer-Verlag.

Olson, D. R. (1996). Towards a psychology of literacy: On the relations between speech and writing. *Cognition, 60*, 83–104.

Ostrosky-Solis, A., Efron, R., & Yund, E. W. (1991). Visual detectability gradients: Effect of illiteracy. *Brain and Cognition, 17*, 42–51.

Ostrosky-Solís, F., Arellano García, M., & Pérez, P. (2004). Can learning to read and write change the brain organization? An electrophysiological study. *International Journal of Psychology, 39*, 27–35.

Ott, E. (1993). *Chaos in dynamical systems*. Cambridge, UK: Cambridge University Press.

Partee, B. H., ter Meulen, A., & Wall, R. E. (1990). *Mathematical methods in linguistics*. Dordrecht: Kluwer Academic Publishers.

Petersson, K. M. (2005a). *Learning and memory in the human brain*. Stockholm: Karolinska University Press.

Petersson, K. M. (2005b). On the relevance of the neurobiological analogue of the finite-state architecture. *Neurocomputing, 65–66*, 825–832.

Petersson, K. M. (2008, in press). On cognition, structured sequence processing, and adaptive dynamical systems. *Proceedings of the American Institute of Physics*, 1060.

Petersson, K. M., Elfgren, C., & Ingvar, M. (1997). A dynamic role of the medial temporal lobe during retrieval of declarative memory in man. *NeuroImage, 6*, 1–11.

Petersson, K. M., Elfgren, C., & Ingvar, M. (1999). Dynamic changes in the functional anatomy of the human brain during recall of abstract designs related to practice. *Neuropsychologia, 37*, 567–587.

Petersson, K. M., Forkstam, C., & Ingvar, M. (2004). Artificial syntactic violations activate Broca's region. *Cognitive Science, 28*, 383–407.

Petersson, K. M., Gisselgård, J., Gretzer, M., & Ingvar, M. (2006). Interaction between a verbal working memory network and the medial temporal lobe. *NeuroImage, 33*, 1207–1217.

Petersson, K. M., Nichols, T. E., Poline, J.-B., & Holmes, A. P. (1999a). Statistical limitations in functional neuroimaging I: Non-inferential methods and statistical models. *Philosophical Transactions of the Royal Society, Series B, 354*, 1239–1260.

Petersson, K. M., Nichols, T. E., Poline, J.-B., & Holmes, A. P. (1999b). Statistical limitations in functional neuroimaging II: Signal detection and statistical inference. *Philosophical Transactions of the Royal Society, Series B, 354*, 1261–1282.

Petersson, K. M., & Reis, A. (2006). Characteristics of illiterate and literate cognitive processing: Implications for brain-behavior co-constructivism. In P. B. Baltes, F. Rösler, & P. A. Reuter-Lorenz (Eds.), *Lifespan development and the brain: The perspective of biocultural co-constructivism* (pp. 279–305). New York: Cambridge University Press.

Petersson, K. M., Reis, A., Askelöf, S., Castro-Caldas, A., & Ingvar, M. (1998). Differences in inter-hemispheric interactions between literate and illiterate subjects during verbal repetition. *NeuroImage, 7*, S217.

Petersson, K. M., Reis, A., Askelöf, S., Castro-Caldas, A., & Ingvar, M. (2000). Language processing modulated by literacy: A network-analysis of verbal repetition in literate and illiterate subjects. *Journal of Cognitive Neuroscience, 12*, 364–382.

Petersson, K. M., Reis, A., & Ingvar, M. (2001). Cognitive processing in literate and illiterate subjects: A review of some recent behavioral and functional data. *Scandinavian Journal of Psychology*, 42, 251–167.

Petersson, K. M., Silva, C., Castro-Caldas, A., Ingvar, M., & Reis, A. (2007). Literacy: A cultural influence on the hemispheric balance in the inferior parietal cortex. *European Journal of Neuroscience*, 26, 791–799.

Quartz, S. R., & Sejnowski, T. J. (1997). The neural basis of cognitive development: A constructivist manifesto. *Behavioral and Brain Sciences*, 20, 537–596.

Reis, A., & Castro-Caldas, A. (1997). Illiteracy: A bias for cognitive development. *Journal of the International Neuropsychological Society*, 3, 444–450.

Reis, A., Faísca, L., Ingvar, M., & Petersson, K. M. (2006). Color makes a difference: Two-dimensional object-naming skills in literate and illiterate subjects. *Brain and Cognition*, 60, 49–54.

Reis, A., Faísca, L., Mendonça, A., Ingvar, M., & Petersson, K. M. (2007). Semantic interference on a phonological task in illiterate subjects. *Scandinavian Journal of Psychology*, 48, 69–74.

Reis, A., Guerreiro, M., & Castro-Caldas, A. (1994). Influence of educational level of non-brain-damaged subjects on visual naming capacities. *Journal of Clinical and Experimental Neuropsychology*, 16 (6), 939–942.

Reis, A., Guerreiro, M., Garcia, C., & Castro-Caldas, A. (1995). How does an illiterate subject process the lexical component of arithmetics? *Journal of the International Neuropsychological Society*, 1, 206.

Reis, A., Guerreiro, M., & Petersson, K. M. (2001). Educational level on a neuropsychological battery. *Journal of the International Neuropsychological Society*, 7 (4), 422–423.

Reis, A., Guerreiro, M., & Petersson, K. M. (2003). A socio-demographic and neuropsychological characterization of an illiterate population. *Applied Neuropsychology*, 10, 191–204.

Reis, A., & Petersson, K. M. (2003). Educational level, socioeconomic status and aphasia research: A comment on Connor et al. (2001): Effect of socioeconomic status on aphasia severity and recovery. *Brain and Language*, 87, 1795–1810.

Reis, A., Petersson, K. M., Castro-Caldas, A., & Ingvar, M. (2001). Formal schooling influences two- but not three-dimensional naming skills. *Brain and Cognition*, 47, 394–411.

Reis, A., Silva, C., Faísca, L., Bramao, I., Mendonça, A., Miranda, P. C., et al. (2007). The impact of reading and writing skills on brain structure: A voxel-based morphometry study. *The International Neuropsychological Society, Federation of Spanish Societies of Neuropsychology, Spanish Neuropsychological Society, Spanish Psychiatry Society Joint Mid-Year Meeting*. Bilbao, Spain.

Sag, I. A., Wasow, T., & Bender, E. M. (2003). *Syntactic theory: A formal introduction* (2nd ed.). Stanford, CA: Center for the Study of Language and Information.

Savage, J. E. (1998). *Models of computation: Exploring the power of computing*. Reading, MA: Addison-Wesley.

Shepherd, G. M. (1997). *The synaptic organization of the brain* (4th ed.). New York: Oxford University Press.

Shieber, S. M. (1986). *An introduction to unification-based approaches to grammar* (Vol. 4). Stanford, CA: CSLI, Stanford University.

Silva, C., Faisca, L., Mendonça, S., Ingvar, M., Petersson, K. M., & Reis, A. (2002). Awareness of words as phonological entities in an illiterate population. *Journal of the International Neuropsychological Society*, 8, 483.

Silva, C. G., Petersson, K. M., Faísca, L., Ingvar, M., & Reis, A. (2004). The effects of formal education on the quantitative and qualitative aspects of verbal semantic fluency. *Journal of Clinical and Experimental. Neuropsychology*, 26, 266–277.

Smith, E. E., & Jonides, J. (1998). Neuroimaging analyses of human working memory. *Proceedings of the National Academy of Sciences, USA*, 95 (20), 12061–12068.

Smith, E. E., & Jonides, J. (1999). Storage and executive processes in the frontal lobes. *Science*, 283 (5408), 1657–1661.

Tanenbaum, A. S. (1990). *Structured computer organization* (3rd ed.). Englewood Cliffs, NJ: Prentice-Hall.

Thompson, P. M., Giedd, J. N., Woods, R. P., MacDonald, D., Evans, A. C., & Toga, A. W. (2000). Growth patterns in the developing brain detected by using continuum mechanical tensor maps. *Nature*, 404, 190–193.

UNESCO (2003). *Literacy, a global perspective*. Paris: UNESCO. (http://unesdoc.unesco.org/images/0013/001318/131817e0.pdf)

Vosse, T., & Kempen, G. (2000). Syntactic structure assembly in human parsing: A computational model based on competitive inhibition and a lexicalist grammar. *Cognition, 75*, 105–143.

Vygotsky, L. S. (1962). *Thought and language*. Cambridge, MA: MIT Press.

Wechsler, D. (1997). *Wechsler Memory Scale (WMS-III) Manual*. San Antonio, TX: The Psychological Corporation.

Wells, A. (2005). *Rethinking cognitive computation: Turing and the science of the mind*. Basingstoke, UK: Palgrave Macmillan.

Wernicke, C. (1874). *Der Aphasiche Symptomen Komplex*. Breslau: Cohn and Weigart.

Zaidel, E., & Iacoboni, M. (Eds.) (2003). *The parallel brain: The cognitive neuroscience of the corpus callosum*. Cambridge, MA: MIT Press.

Ziegler, J. C., & Goswami, U. (2005). Reading acquisition, developmental dyslexia, and skilled reading across languages: A psycholinguistic grain size theory. *Psychological Bulletin, 131*, 3–29.

Part III

LITERACY AND LITERATURES

CHAPTER 10

Ways of Reading

Elizabeth Long

Introduction

The narrative that follows describes two different aspects of the social nature of reading. I wrote the first section while I was at work on a manuscript that became *Book Clubs: Women and the Uses of Reading in Everyday Life*. It arose from my frustration with the "ideology of the solitary reader" – the assumption that reading can be best understood as a wholly individual and very private activity. To unseat that cultural frame, I used autobiographical reflection to describe the ways my own early reading experiences were both shaped and cradled by a complex web of social relationships and cultural beliefs: what is now often referred to as a "culture of reading." Almost as a by-product, this also brought into focus the ways that reading, when it is a deeply experienced cultural practice, contributes to the formation of individual identity.

Some years later, I brought that piece of writing to a group composed of faculty women who read and commented on each other's ongoing projects. At that point, I was still preoccupied with a question that troubled me throughout the *Book Clubs* research: how to make the case that middle-class women's reading and discussion of books was significant or even interesting, given the usual academic tendency to regard women's leisure-time cultural activities as trivial in comparison with larger scale and more public phenomena. Discussing my writing led the group into a collaborative reflection on the nuances of social difference as other people thought and talked about their own "reading stories."

Here, having set the narrative in context, I invite you in, leaving further thoughts for some concluding remarks.

The Personal is Social: Reflections on Reading and Solitude

"Reading my first book" is a significant marker in my remembered childhood. I sat curled up in a big wing-backed chair in our living room and laboriously, excitedly, read all the way through *Pinocchio*. It may have been the little Walt Disney–inspired Golden Book: I remember pictures of Pinocchio's nose and the whale. But, mostly I remember the hard work of making the print on the page into words and the words into the story. There were some rough spots, but there was magic too, powerful magic that transmuted the mundane physical object into a gateway for an imaginary world of feelings and pictures in my head. Those two realities, in fact, would often remain apart in my childhood, so that I would have to plough through marks on the page that stubbornly remained separate blocks of pedestrian syllables and words, opaque and sometimes silly, until suddenly they became not figures in and of themselves but rather the ground upon which the imagination could dance and take wing.

This "first" memory depends on solitude: I had to be alone with the book to truly make its reading mine, to tear it from the context of books my parents read to me. It was only after I finished that I leapt up and ran into the kitchen to tell my mother that I had really read a whole book all by myself. But, when I unpack that originating memory, the solitude dissolves into a complicated network of social relationships.

Reading and the Family

Books and magazines were "everywhere" in the house. They had official locations: bookshelves in the study, in my bedroom and later my brother's, on the beams that ran along the end walls of the house in my parents' room. They lingered in piles on almost every flat surface: on enclosed radiators, on the kitchen table, on counters, on the back of the toilet in the upstairs bathroom. They seemed to breed where they lingered, rising higher in sloppy bunches that would finally so irritate my mother that she would declare war on them and whisk them away to their proper places – where they would be forced into rows of double or even triple thickness if they were paperbacks. Some books were for display: serious hardcover and art books that stayed downstairs. Others – my brother's dinosaur books and war books; my fairy tales, histories, and horse books; my parents' mysteries and science fiction – stayed upstairs out of public view.

From before I can remember, my parents read to my brother and me in the evening. (It must have started even before he was born because for many years I kept *my* copy of *Pat the Bunny*, cherishing it even when the mirror had grown dim, the cloth for "peek-a-boo" had come unstuck, and "Daddy's scratchy face" was smooth.) It was one of the great pleasures of the day – an interval of before-bedtime warmth, coziness, and utter attention from a parent. My mother read to us most often; I particularly remember her readings of the Dr. Seuss books and Winnie the Pooh. We preferred her to my father because she had a repertoire of voices for different characters and would reread any passage we especially enjoyed as often as we wished. Her willingness to "bring the book alive" introduced us to the imaginative and oral levels of textual renditions, and her ease at repetition surely moved us into the transition between orality and literacy with comparative ease, since the way I remember learning to read involved memorizing passages and reciting them with my eyes on the text. My father, on the other hand, grew bored and often skipped whole sentences and paragraphs. We policed him indignantly after we learned how to read. Our policing may have helped us to learn as well, for we had to be constantly on the alert to make sure that what we remembered as the story was not simplified and shortened in his reading.

As I think back over what seems to me on one level like a normal and natural introduction to reading within the family circle, its construction by class and gender seems, on another level, stunningly clear. The wing-backed chair and the privacy of the living room in my "first" memory embody a level of comfort, stability, and spaciousness that is at least middle-class. "Mother-in-the kitchen" during the day is both a middle-class luxury and an exemplification of the feminine mystique that kept even educated middle-class women in a circumscribed suburban routine. (Memory: I dreamt vividly as a young child and once discovered a book on dreams that seemed to accord them the same importance I felt they must have. It was Freud's book, and my mother explained that she had read it for graduate school. When I came across it, it was no longer part of a working library but rather stood among a group of old unsorted books on a remote shelf upstairs.)

"Books everywhere" in the house is itself a complex representation of high income, property, and educational levels. Layers of books indicate disposable income far beyond most people's reach; layers of books from past schooling (and prior generations) testify not only to formal schooling but also to the less formal familiarity with high culture that is so important in establishing and passing on "cultural capital." The role of books in displaying both that capital and loyalty to a stratified literary world was expressed by where books were located in our house and houses like it. Serious, weighty, and beautiful tomes were for public spaces. We banished "light reading" and children's books to the "backstage" areas of the house.

The number of rooms in such houses not only ensures privacy for solitary reading and musing but also the possibility of constructing an identity by assembling a personal, private library. Separate rooms, stability such that we were able to live in the same place for many years, books to guide and express our developing interests and remain as physical and symbolic memorials of our personal histories – these comprise the material foundations for a coherent identity, a self that has the possibility of overcoming the sources of fragmentation so often discussed in accounts of contemporary life.

Books ensured a sense of generational continuity. When I read *The Princess and the Goblins*, it was a copy my grandmother had given to my mother, and it came with stories of my mother's childhood in distant Los Angeles: how she was chased by mockingbirds, smoked cornhusks and got sick, watched movies being filmed on her street (boring), and saw "Zorro" every Saturday at the matinee. My desire to read the Oz books took me to the neighbors' attic, where Florence Burger unpacked boxes of books that had her grandmother's name (Dixon) on inscriptions that marked Florence's own birthdays and Christmases. So my childhood was secured by the thought that the adults in my world had had families and childhoods much like my own. After all, those same mothers took us every Saturday to watch Roy Rogers and Hopalong Cassidy at our local movie theater. This was a disturbing idea on one level, as I watched these responsible and competent women shop, cook, ferry us around and give us orders; organize volunteer activities from the Children's Matinee series and the Girl Scouts; to Democratic Party functions and volunteers for the hospital – and thought of my own tree-climbing, jump-roping, Cowboy and Indian days. How could I become transformed from one to the other? Did I have to? Did I *want* to? But it was also deeply reassuring, for it implied an orderly, continuous, and knowable universe.

Books and magazines also bridged the gap between the private and the wider world. If books were everywhere in the house, then domesticity was equally connected by thousands of tiny and unremarkable filaments to broader horizons of time, place, and knowledge. *Arizona Highways* showed my brother and me romantic pictures of the American West before we had traveled farther than what I used to call "the blue hills" at the end of Cayuga Lake. *Scientific American* introduced me to the intimidating world of science through photographs, diagrams, and impenetrable articles – some of which I would push through even though I understood almost nothing. I remember more fondly a children's book about the atom with diagrams (now hopelessly out of date) of atoms and molecules that convinced me it must be possible, given all the space between particles, for people to walk through walls. I would stand quietly pressing myself against my bedroom wall thinking of those tiny spacious solar systems, trying to vibrate the particles of my flesh in time with those of the solid-seeming wall. Somewhat later, I read a popular science book that advanced as a possible theory what we know now as plate tectonics. Like many ideas from childhood books, this one lodged in my head to blossom later on into a connection that made new knowledge both easier to master and less threatening.

There was a gendered split to the bookish wider worlds my brother and I entered, but it was one we both crossed quite often. I loved fairy tales and myths, and began to read about ancient Greece, the Middle Ages, and other cultures. He took my books on a different tangent and soon knew everything he could about medieval castles and sieges. His passions included dinosaurs and war. I discovered the breathtaking sense of historical time through looking at the time lines and illustrated reconstructions of earlier eras in his dinosaur books, just as I filtered through his World War II books and found an abiding interest in Jewish life and history. So our worlds interpenetrated yet, to a certain degree, remained separate – a separation that continues to mark the reading habits of most men and women as recorded in national surveys and whose causes scholars debate. Biological determinism or socialization? From personal experience, it is impossible to adjudicate.

Once children learn to read, books can, almost by themselves, expand their worlds and make formal education easier. Autobiographical accounts of writers from the working class often focus on the discovery of the neighborhood library or the ways that books provided both the imaginary experience of and the means for movement out of a restricted sphere. In middle-class families, or poorer families that value literacy, parents become the mediators and guides for this movement, which provides for their children an almost taken-for-granted sense of ease and efficacy in the world beyond the home. I remember our parents explaining the references for cartoons and humor books by instructing us about the past and present political scene. In *50 Years of New Yorker Cartoons*, two captions made no sense to me. In one, a group of drunken partygoers yells: "Let's all go hiss Roosevelt." In the second, workers in a coal mine comment about a somewhat bulky woman standing in the light at the head of the shaft, "That must be Eleanor Roosevelt." These cartoons provided the first occasions for my liberal parents to explain their sense of what the New Deal meant and the sources of elite resistance to its programs and to the First Lady's zeal for social reform. Similarly, they connected Wiley Cat in the Pogo cartoons to the Senator McCarthy who gave them nightmares and had forced the father of a schoolmate, Bobby Fischer, to resign from Cornell.

Parental mediation gave us not only conceptual connections but also a sense of resources. Every time the dictionary was pulled out at the dinner table to define a word, we learned how easy it was to access authoritative knowledge. Parental reading also melded knowledge of the outer world with strictures about inner values that, once again, connected books to a sense of coherence and "character" that bridged private and public. The same parents who earnestly unpacked the meaning of Roosevelt's policies so that children could understand them also explained at length the moral implications of Horton the Elephant's "He meant what he said and he said what he meant; an elephant's faithful one hundred percent" for what our behavior should be. In so doing, they were using books to mould identities based on moral integrity and to craft us as selves that would take themselves very seriously.[1]

The earnest mediation of the world of books by parents and, later, teachers and librarians also gave me a strong (although unremarked-on) sense of entitlement. At home, questions about books were important. They engaged creative efforts to help us make sense of what we read. At the children's library, Mrs. Aagard would ask us which of the books we had taken out we enjoyed and why. This was the beginning of a delicious interval of pleasure that made the library stacks like a storehouse of wonders to which she held the key, a feeling that still echoes in my pleasure when a friend or colleague recommends a favorite author or book. Listening to our replies with encouraging attention, Mrs. Aagard would go to the shelves and find us other books and authors we might like as much and, knowing our appetite for reading, she would bend the rules and send us home with huge piles of books due in two weeks. As readers, we merited serious adult attention and nurturance; as children who read, we found that for us authority's rules were flexible. Reading became not only a badge of accomplishment but also a channel through which we acquired a more general sense that we deserved special attention and respect from those around us.

Reading and Peers: School and Competition

Behind the proud sweet memory of my first moment of solitary reading also rests the reality of competition between peers. It, too, gives the innocent value of reading a slightly different cast. I pushed myself to read in part because I badly wanted to go to school with two of my friends who were slightly older than me: if I could read, perhaps I could prove my competence and be accepted early to kindergarten. The roots of competition, in fact, probably go further back than that, because my brother was born when I was three. He absorbed much of my mother's attention, and I turned to my father, whom I could attract by being smarter and quicker than the small creature who could do so little but inexplicably drew everyone's admiration away from me. So, learning to read was a response to tremendous envy. It was part of a strategy for overcoming a deep sense that I was somehow inadequate, a strategy that involved me (reversing Chodorow's traditional women=being/men=doing dichotomy) in continual but never satisfactory attempts to gain loving attention from the adults around me by proving how talented and accomplished I was. The sense of having been displaced by my brother also gave my desire to go to school a quality of desperation: if I could only go to school, I could get out of a home that no longer gave me the security of the unconditionally beloved only child. Reading, then, was not just a gateway but also a getaway, and in a double sense: *in* books imaginatively, and *through* books physically, a means of leaving home. Not everyone, surely, will have such impacted intensities of sibling rivalry as one root of their desire to read, but learning to read often gives the pleasure of mastery, emblematic of the sublimated joys of growing up that help all children wean themselves from the more dependent pleasures of babyhood.

More direct than my competition with a baby brother was rivalry with Henry Bethe, a friend from another academic family whose parents were excelling vicariously by making sure he had early acceptance to school. Henry's mother lent me the "Dick and Jane" books that he was learning, and I pored over them with, I recall, my father's help. At a time when schools were debating the phonetic method, I used a more primitive one: my father would read a page while I stared at his finger moving from word to word. I would memorize the words, take the book away and try to duplicate the narrative, and then return for corrections. At this distance, there seems something driven and compulsive about those endless repetitions, that fierce focus. Certainly, the nostalgia of the little girl curled up alone with her book in the armchair dissolves into a more acid mixture of Oedipal issues, adult status games, and rivalry among siblings and friends. My reading, then, was neither wholly innocent nor entirely private but rather implicated, like all cultural practices in a web of social relationships, mingling competition, power, envy, and desire.

Reading at school brought my first experience of reading in groups. This institutionalized both competition and ranking at the hands of cultural authorities: teachers and "the system." Those of us who had learned to read at home not only had the jump on everyone who had not but also gained special labels and privileges. We were "gifted," and teachers searched to find us challenging tasks while the other students learned the alphabet. The gap in background presented a problem for the social control of the classroom. But because our parents were "gifted" themselves – as well as predictably articulate and powerful players in the politics of schooling – and because our teachers also valued literacy and academic success, those of us who came as readers to school could be smug about our boredom during "easy" lessons and were rewarded rather than punished for knowing too much. Since I attended a predominantly middle-class elementary school, its standards meshed well with those of the community and there was no independent peer culture to contravene scholastic authority.[2] School, peer group, and parents all worked harmoniously to enforce the value of academic excellence and the stigma of failure. By high school, mathematics had become the measure of ability, separating us by gender as well as class, race, and individual talent, but reading was the main sorting mechanism in elementary school.

In the first and second grade, our classrooms were divided into small reading groups. It was immediately apparent to all of us that these were ability groups despite the innocuous names the teachers used to mask the hierarchy: Squirrels, Chipmunks, and Raccoons, or Bluejays, Robins, and Orioles. In such groups, with the specter of falling, the promise of rising, and the possibility of withdrawal into indifference, we practiced reading aloud and the rudiments of textual interpretation: What does this sentence mean? What did Spot do? How did Dick and Jane feel? From very early on, then, reading was not simply a social activity but was suffused with the emotional engagement of competition and its implications for identity and self-esteem.

Here, I am writing from the vantage point of one who was good at school. But most readers, and especially readers who choose to spend their leisure time reading and discussing books in groups with other people, have been good pupils. With some exceptions, only the model schoolchildren of their culture choose to replicate that experience on their own; for the most part, only those who have participated in schooling long and successfully enough to go to college maintain habits of reading for pleasure. So I am writing here from the view of someone who has been very much "inside" that which I am trying to describe.

The social context of reading at school not only worked to constitute a hierarchically organized literary universe that valued certain books and certain responses to them but also helped to constitute our subjectivity along hierarchical lines. Perhaps the most obvious example of this is the way that competition narrowed the focus of attention to make the unsuccessful less visible for those of us who did well at the tasks we were set. However expansive and empowering it was to learn to be good at reading, the excitement of performing well almost automatically led to an unnoticed arrogance of exclusion. The ranked groupings contributed to this: if you were in the top group, its dynamics bounded your horizons. And within groups, the anxieties of competition directed attention to what you had to read next, to how to get your hand up fast to answer the next question. Failure was always embarrassing and sometimes devastating and that made it even harder to identify with others' failures: your own progress was enough to worry about, why spend time and attention on those who couldn't make it? So those of us who did well tended to focus on the other contenders for pride of place. It was too painful and distracting to think about everybody else.

In fact, in my school there were very few children who did not come from middle- or upper-middle-class homes. The school drew university families and other professional or wealthy families who lived in the prestigious neighborhood of Cayuga Heights. At the end of sixth grade, our teacher explained to us that we would be going off to junior high and would meet people who would resent us, who thought of Cayuga Heights as "Snob Hill." I think that she went on to palliate this brute fact with reassurances that we were, of course, not snobs, and that if we were just "nice," just "ourselves," this would not be a problem. But my response was one of shock and uneasy guilt. Shock because I had never thought how I (we) would look from the outside. My horizons had been limited not only at school but in all the other contexts of my daily routines to an essentially middle-class white universe – that was "my world." Guilt because on some level I knew I was privileged (the sidewalks of our town bore testimony to race and class differences) and had perpetuated that privilege at the expense of others in my own striving for first place – without even knowing it.

One day, perhaps during that very same year, for our sixth-grade teacher served as umpire for softball games, my teacher pulled me aside after class and talked to me about a remark I had made to one of the few students who was *not* middle class, and who also wasn't good at school. "Do you remember calling Gary Guidi stupid at recess today when he made a bad play?" I had forgotten. "Well, you must never do such a thing again. I know you didn't intend to be unkind, but school is hard for him, and that remark really hurt him. You're fortunate, things come easy for you, but you must always remember that is not the case for everyone, and that things you may say even without thinking can seem very cruel to other people." I protested that I hadn't meant it, that it was just the kind of thing everybody said in the heat of the moment, that I was sorry, that I had no idea it would bother him – but she stood firm, the voice of conscience for a society at once egalitarian and humanistic in principle and deeply stratified in practice.

Aside from impressing me with the guilty knowledge that my every action might unknowingly become the cause for hurting someone "less fortunate" than I (the acquisition of liberal guilt and responsibility – cf. Coles's *The Privileged Ones*), this incident made it very clear that the academic success that was a source of empowerment for me was based on damaging someone else's self-esteem. But what to do about this dilemma? As I recall, it did not initiate dialogue between Gary and me, since he had confessed his wounded pride to the teacher in confidence. Moreover, she did not discuss the issue in terms of social structure, so it was framed in the language of politeness and personal sensitivity, my privilege and its basis taken as a given. Its net result was to throw me back into concerns about myself: the occasion for crafting a more finely tuned subjectivity (middle-class but with a conscience) rather than exploring either someone else's subjectivity or the possibilities for changing the status quo.

Such incidents are emblematic of the ways that liberal ideology both acknowledges inequality and refocuses its challenge into concern about how to manage inequality's unfortunate *effects* with delicacy and tact. This concern both personalizes structural issues, by centering attention on the individuals involved, and – at least in this conversation between middle-class novice and elder – makes central the issue of crafting a more mannerly and responsible yet always privileged and "managerial" middle-class self. Gary was marginalized, except as the vulnerable victim who must be treated with consideration.

This may seem far from "reading," but we are socialized into reading not simply as solitary individuals but also as children learning their places in a stratified society in which reading serves to demonstrate ability and ensure success at school, with all its consequences for later-life chances. Reading, then, cannot be understood as a "pure" good because it is also, in the Bourdieuian sense, a badge of social distinction and exclusivity. Under the conditions in which it is taught, and within a meritocracy in which it functions as an early and important ranking mechanism, the activity of reading is inevitably colored by issues of prestige, status, and cultural power.

"Dear Readers . . ."

Some years after beginning the research that gave rise to my own reading story, I brought a draft of the preceding narrative to a small all-women's faculty writing group at Rice. The meeting place was both handsome and charmingly urban. Kathryn had a second-story apartment in a rambling old house, with a deck down one side that opened into lush Houston trees; her rooms were airy, well proportioned, and had some appealing contemporary design touches in fixtures and trim. Her furniture was a similar mix: funky graduate-student pieces, ethnic textiles, and witty postmodern accessories.

At the beginning of the meeting, people praised both the substance and style of the draft. Never willing to accept compliments at face value, I pushed for more criticism, while opening up somewhat about what I had been trying to accomplish in the writing. I particularly remember making an emotional statement about studying the middle classes – so often the "standpointless standpoint," the "unmarked category," the dominant social group who defines all others as "other" – to understand the nature of their own sociocultural construction and the dynamics by which they enact and maintain their position as the unremarked-on "standard" or norm. I confessed that although I thought this critique from within had certain strengths, it suffered from lack of confrontation with perspectives from groups and people outside the WASP upper-middle classes, those "others" in relation to whom the center defines itself.

In my memory, it was after this statement that the meeting took a dramatically different turn, as if it – in combination with the work they had read – enabled group members to move to a level of discourse that was at once more personally revealing and more sharply critical and political. People began to speak from their own experience to show the ways my account remained class-bound despite my earnest desire to "see through" my social position. They focused on three main substantive areas: spaces, places, and possessions; Gary's voice; and social class.

Despite my conviction that I had shown the specificities of class and gender by describing books and reading in my family's house, people wanted a more detailed and pointed discussion of the construction of class (and gender) identity through the spaces that contained those books and the "things" that surrounded them. Sharon pointed out that the very differentiation of spaces in houses such as my family's entails compartmentalization, categorization, and the potential not only for solitude but also secretiveness, all of which may characterize middle-class selves.[3] Her own family's social mobility had led to a gradual elaboration of spatial complexity in their houses, and she had observed that their eating and "living" took on a formally distinct quality as they bought houses that separated the living room from the dining room. In like fashion, entryways and porches added a layer of distance between the inner rooms and outside world, and separate rooms for the children allowed privacy and custom-designed "identity packages."

The group pushed me to discuss what besides books was on my brother's bookshelves and my own. And indeed, my brother's books sat in sloppy piles along with model trucks and airplanes, dinosaur figures, rocks, and toy soldiers. His bedroom, too, was much smaller than mine. It had been carved out of part of my parents' room to make way for a television and guest room; as a boy, he was supposed to spend time outside and not care about his "inner" space. Within my large bedroom, which I was continually urged to tidy up, my books kept company with stuffed animals, tiny china figurines of horses, and assorted other pretty small breakable things: bits of coral, "Oriental" umbrellas saved from drinks, a fishbowl with a faded "grow-a-crystal." I used my books to play librarian: cutting cards and envelopes for them out of construction paper, laboring over a classification and "due date" system, and trying to enforce it with my friends. The books we read, then, had life and differential influence on us not just because of their contents, or because of our own individual and gendered "natures," but also because of the physically sedimented contexts of meaning that contained them and helped to construct us as individuals, boy or girl.

Sharon and Gudrun brought up several examples to show how radically different the meaning of an object – like a book – can be depending on the world of other meaningful objects it inhabits.[4] Gudrun's mother, for example, had very ambivalent reactions to books because of how they fit (or failed to) her own social trajectory, even the organization of her workday. As she moved up in the world of postwar Germany, she acquired some "high literature" through a book club, mostly ordering books because of the fame of their authors: for example, Tolstoy or Hemingway. Usually, she found the material so dense, however, that she either gave them away to male friends or saved them for Gudrun, then a young child. They sat in the elaborate family sideboard not as badges of status – that place was reserved for the porcelain dessert settings that were prominently displayed – but rather tucked away on a shelf in a corner behind wooden cabinet doors, awaiting a time that they might actually be used. She explained to Gudrun that she worked all day and wanted something to fall asleep with. For that, she turned to light reading, which Gudrun – familially designated heir to high culture – also learned to love.

Later, when Gudrun herself was a professor's wife, her housekeeper mentioned that her son, who helped her with spring cleaning one year, had said what a terrible nuisance all those books were to clean, adding, "and do they even read them?" This made it startlingly clear to Gudrun how different her beloved books could look from another perspective.

Sharon said that reading my piece made her angry about my kind of childhood, the same kind of anger she felt when as a child visiting rich kids' houses, she saw grand pianos or capacious bookshelves. She thought that these were things people simply should not have in their homes: they belonged in *public* places – at school or in the library. Partly it was envy but partly she felt that it was unfair and they were somehow cheating. Later, she recognized the source of some of these views in her mother. When Sharon, showing off her own adulthood and sophistication, as children in their twenties often do, took her mother to an exhibition of Faberge eggs, her mother's response was, "I just keep thinking of all the poor people who had to pay for this." Books-in-the-house, then, represented for Sharon the ways that not only money but privatization can cheat those who have less, an issue that has continued to resonate for her both personally and intellectually as she herself has acquired the substance and style of cultured prosperity. Sharon's own reading, in fact, began with programs at her local library; without such public support, she might never have begun the trajectory that led her to the professoriate.

Sharon pointed out, as well, that she saw the marks of social class in what one can take for granted that "everyone" knows, a sense of shared cultural reality that she saw in my discussion of the books of my childhood, not simply in my childhood. She had read *The Little Engine That Could*, for instance, but not the A.A. Milne books about Pooh or *Pat the Bunny*, so my attempt to write evocatively called up very little for her. Such blankness, too, can bespeak social and cultural exclusion.

As she spoke, I remembered the climax of a miserable time I spent adjusting to a school year in France. I was rooming with two girls, one mousy, one very popular. The popular one hated me, both because she hated all Americans and because I had established myself as an awkward and defenseless wimp. She also despised her mousy compatriot but made alliance with her to torture me. They finally drove me out of the room with a hysterical cough one night when they collaborated on a conversation about the books they most loved as children, a conversation I recall as dripping with sadistic, nationalistic glee, their "books we had in common" a conscious weapon.[5]

Sharon mentioned, too, the kind of self-masking that is one hallmark of differences in social class. She said that an older cousin had completed, in her lifetime, the same trajectory of social mobility that it had taken Sharon and her mother two generations to cover. In her discussions with her cousin, it emerged that they both tended not to talk with their present-day middle-class friends about the social distance between their own parents' backgrounds and the present realities of their and their friends' lives. Sharon's own choice to speak this personally in our group, in fact, was "not something usual." As she put it, tapping into people's reading histories seemed to be generating a critique of simple notions of social class.

Gudrun characterized the movement as one of both leveling and differentiating: in everyday life, where we all shared not just a workplace but also many other similarities ranging from political orientation to modes of dress, reading had been part of what brought us together as a group and leveled our differences. But within the discussion, it had brought them out again. There was a reverberative quality about talking together about a text that was enabling us to "come out" in unexpected ways to each other, ways that not only allowed us a different perspective on each other but also allowed us to question certain unexamined assumptions about the social world.

This discussion was a powerful demonstration of the complexities of finding a voice within a world where knowledge and its articulation are related to social stratification – for, in a sense, what we were all grappling for was a way to talk about the lived subtleties of gender and social class. In a related critical point, Gudrun, Angela, and Sharon said that my narrative had deprived Gary Guidi of a voice and thus silenced and marginalized him except as an almost abstract marker of a monolithic, victimized working class – an absence whose outlines were filled in by the teacher's and my own assumptions. Angela pointed out that for less-privileged children, school is often a time filler and not a steppingstone. My account was blind to this because it was permeated by the assumption that everyone was competing in the same way I was, whereas in the poor, mainly Mexican American community where she grew up, "doing well" was often seen as going to the "other side." Sharon seconded her remarks, saying that this account clarified why she had not recognized the stories her friends of upper-middle-class origin told of academic competition in high school. In her school, you were weird if you raised your hand too often and very weird if you were seen as a "brain." Girls competed instead to be head cheerleader or "sexiest girl," "most popular," or "most likely to succeed." Here, Kathryn added an account of her Sicilian grandmother, who heartily disapproved of her reading habit because she felt it would hinder Kathryn's chances at a good marriage. Every time she passed Kathryn with her nose in a book, she would shake her head and say disapprovingly, "*Sempre legge! Sempre legge!*"

From Angela's vantage point, too, my teacher's response to Gary was an example of the kind of middle-class pity for the poor that allows those in power both to write off working-class students and simultaneously reaffirm their own compassionate humanitarianism. As she put it, "Tener lastima, lastima," which she translated as both "Pity hurts" and "To pity is to hurt." She linked this deeply personal moment in my past, as well, to larger issues: educational policy has traditionally responded to minority and poor students' low scholastic achievement by treating it as a self-esteem issue; in treating kids' self-esteem, the policies fail to address more substantive *educational* deficits that could, if dealt with, ensure them social mobility.

In response to their urging that I say more about Gary's isolation at that school, about *his* life, I realized I know very little about him. I cannot even remember a word he spoke. Of course, most of the words of those years have vanished; I remember my friends but not our conversations and, although I remember talking a lot at the family supper table, I have no idea what I said.

But Gary stands out from the silence of remembered childhood in two ways, both having to do with the intersection of gender and class. First, some of the boys *did* have memorable voices. They were bold, articulate, and defied authority with its blessing because they were so smart. They made up wicked nicknames for the rest of us and even some of our parents. In fifth grade, they hounded Mrs. Beck out of her new job as kindergarten teacher by their continual verbal harassment. When she walked out the door at the end of each school day, a tiny woman in spike heels, they would scramble among pieces of gravel in the schoolyard and call out, "Speck Beck, speck Beck, where's she gone? Speck Beck!"[6] She walked this gauntlet with her face set in a mask of indifference but her plump ankles trembled with every step.

Gary was not part of this dominant group of boys. In fact, I don't think he was a member of any group at elementary school, where social life was intensely communal as well as hierarchical. When I remember him, he was sitting alone at the back of the class, sometimes drawing intricately beautiful pictures or talking to the teacher – again, alone. So he was isolated from the dense networks of what Connell calls "hegemonic masculinity": those boys who had the kind of authoritative voices that crossed the gap between the often separate worlds of boys and girls to frame at least certain terms of our existence.

Second, Gary became the object of intense scrutiny and discussion among the girls. He arrived at our school in third grade, perhaps older than the rest of us, and certainly much more physically impressive than any of the other boys. He had, in my memory, dark curly hair, a classical profile, broad shoulders, a tan, and muscles. We all thought he was a creature of such exotic beauty that most of us could only whisper about him and worship him from afar. He was a mythic masculine presence: tall, dark, handsome – and silent, in part because we made him into an object of desire who was then too intimidating to talk to.

This same abashed silence fell on me every time I had a crush on one of the boys, but Gary was different because we collectively defined him as a sex object. I think that definition may have isolated him as well, for I cannot remember any of the girls going after him, either that year or the following three we all spent at Cayuga Heights Elementary. I do have a vague memory of a spin-the-bottle party at what I think was his family's house – across the field from ours, on Hanshaw Road – but that has the same flavor of communal giggling and whispering *about* Gary that I remember in general coming from the girls. So Gary was mysterious and unvoiced in my memory in part because of the separation of boys and girls, yet his social class made him more mysterious than the other boys, who lived in the same kinds of houses – if not the same kinds of rooms – as all of the girls, and whose fathers and mothers all knew each other in the dense networks of the upper-middle classes in a small university town. We girls may have dealt with his difference by endowing him with the distance of intense desire: safely objectifying him, as it were.

As soon as I started thinking about Gary, his isolation, and the intersections of class and gender that deprived him of a voice in my account, I also remembered Mr. Padar, the janitor, and our excursions into his basement world of furnace, vents, and pipes. Mr. Padar was a short, bald, middle-aged man who had come from Hungary and still spoke with a marked accent. He was one of the few working-class people around the school. I remember being instructed carefully (but by whom?) always to treat him very politely, in much the same way I had received instruction about "being nice" to Gary. He himself told a group of us about his son's acceptance to medical school with great pride and a faint edge of contempt for us, who had it so easy.

In fifth or sixth grade, a group of us started exploring the basement of the school and discovered a crawl space under the classrooms.[7] Pretty soon, we spent every minute we could – recess, lunch hour, after school – clambering up into that tight dark space and contorting our bodies to travel every inch of it. It had the fascination of the illicit, the excitement of danger, the scandal of dark closeness with other bodies, and the titillation of bringing us under the unknowing feet of our teachers.

Mr. Padar knew what we were doing, but we buttered him up so he would turn a blind eye to us. The boys talked to him with manly deference and the girls flirted with him. He liked small, blonde, cute girls best, though, and being tall and not cute, I always felt awkward around him and caught the dismissiveness he reserved for the kids he didn't like. From this distance, his authority over the dark infrastructure of our enlightened existence, the collusion and highly gendered manipulations we were engaged in with each other, and the forbidden quality of our knowledge – of the school, of each other – all seem to express something metaphorical about the abstractions of class and gender as we learned and lived them through.

The relationships of reading, especially as they intersect with schooling, seem to give a particularly intimate access to broader issues of social identity, perhaps because they are central to the years when children are enacting and reflecting on "who" they are in ever-expanding contexts. Certainly, my story of reading unlocked a very personal discussion of social class in this small group of academic women – a discussion that made me aware of the complexities of social differentiation even among people I thought were much like me.

Angela pointed out that people's knowledge of class and race is severely bounded by their own social location: she became part of her town's Mexican American elite by graduating from high school and although the racial stratification of the town was extremely clear, class stratification among the Mexican American community was relatively narrow: people were lower-middle class or poor. There certainly was ample discrimination at the San Angelo school she attended, and she felt its impact since even though the separation between Anglos and Mexican Americans meant that her networks were mostly Chicano kids – she could see that whites had access to certain privileges. Yet, only when she moved into predominantly white institutions – at college and then at Stanford, where she could for the first time see the resources and opportunities that many people took for granted – did she perceive most concretely and compellingly the wider range of "class" and, indeed, the general complexity of social inequality and stratification in American society. Conversely, she felt that something I had accepted as universal knowledge – a Freudian vision of sibling rivalry – might be part of a very limited class ethos injected into family life through childrearing books and popular psychology.

Sharon highlighted not only the bounded but also the relative nature of class. Even when her family was living what she would now characterize as a working-class life, they considered themselves middle-class because they sent clothes to other relatives and had never lived in cardboard shanties during the Depression.

Kathryn and Anne's stories of social mobility added the complexity of immigration. (Immigration was my word. Neither Kathryn nor Anne characterized their family's experiences as "immigration stories" or their parents or grandparents as "immigrants." This is one example of the way I tended to apply traditional stereotypes even to the narratives of these close colleagues and friends when confronted by real social differences. As the group worked through giving me feedback on the draft of this Coda, my stereotyping became very clear. I had collapsed parts of Gudrun's story and made her mother into a cleaning lady herself – in the "bleak years after World War II." I had also represented Kathryn's and Anne's families as poorer and more "foreign" than they were.)

Kathryn's grandmother (*Sempre legge!*) represented her family's rural Sicilian roots, but her own parents moved definitively into the middle class in her sixth-grade year: a move into a two-story house on a street of other rather suburban-feeling two-story houses. Her parents, especially her mother, felt that affluence entailed assuming certain social responsibilities. So, in part through another woman in the neighborhood, Kathryn's mother became involved with a Social Action League program that organized the "adoption" of an inner-city child. Among other things, this meant having the girl to their house for dinner once a week, an event Kathryn found, in retrospect, disturbing because of the kind of "attitude of charity" it inculcated, and the kind of ideas about social change it entailed.

In her account, for example, the charitable and reformist impulse translated not into effective social action but rather into rendering the lives of the poor as some kind of strange and exotic spectacle. When their mother drove Kathryn and her siblings into the inner city to pick up the girl at her family's place, they would often witness family chaos, even very frightening fights, which made poverty seem terrifying. Kathryn's response was to withdraw into distant fascination. The "adopted" girl also had lice at least once and had to wear a wig to cover her shaved head. She was terrified that her wig would fall off, and the middle-class children in Kathryn's neighborhood whispered about her in the smug and malicious way that kids treat someone different. After this awkward, uncomfortable relationship came to an end, Kathryn's teenaged sister once ran into the girl, who was then a young teenager herself and pregnant. As Kathryn recounted this almost clichéd conclusion to her story, her voice died away to group silence: there seemed no easy commentary on this sad, ironic enactment of the impulse toward social uplift.

Anne's parents were from Eastern Europe, specifically Hungary. Although I used the word, she had never thought of them as "immigrants," in part because the word conjured up images of steerage, while her father had been a practicing architect in Bratislava, so that although both her mother and her father arrived in this country with little money, they were educated, very solidly middle class, and not really part of a community that defined itself as "an immigrant community." Their arrival in this country also had more to do with the situation of Jews in the Third Reich than the typical "immigrant" story, for her father had a harrowing escape from the Nazis in 1939 on the last boat from Italy. Her mother arrived to marry him in 1946 after a separation of seven years, during which she had undergone an equally harrowing wartime experience in Eastern Europe. So, although the family was poor when they came to America, education was always central to their own and their daughter's self-definition. Anne said that in kindergarten, she and her friend Scott used to discuss where they would go to college – much to the amusement of their teacher. By high school, Anne was sent to a private Episcopalian girls' school, where she often felt awkward – although not necessarily because of her family's income, the most popular girls at school were not always wealthy – and rather amazed at the mansions and estates that were homes for some of her schoolmates.

In some ways, Anne's story brought into high relief the differences behind our obvious similarities as academic women, for while her father had fled the Nazis, Gudrun's mother had herself *been* a Nazi during the war. All of these life histories pushed at the simplicity of my narrative and made it clear how inadequate a bipartite and static model was for encapsulating the experiences and emotions that clustered around social class among even such an apparently homogeneous gathering as this writing/reading group.

I heard these narratives and criticisms with mixed emotions, which I think are not atypical for situations where genuine critical and self-reflexive learning is taking place, and where power – in this case, my power to frame a certain representation of the world – is at issue as part of that learning process. On one level, I felt irritated and defensive. I think of this as the response of the upper-middle-class reformer/teacher wanting to reassert her vision and control over a process that threatens genuinely to empower those "others" she wishes (always from above) to help. At another level, I was exhilarated and knew that whatever anxiety it entailed, surrendering tight control of the situation to something more open and multivocal was encouraging a creative kind of dialogue. In fact, I have rarely heard people combine personal life histories with political/intellectual analysis in this fashion outside of the women's movement and, despite my fears, it seemed as if useful collective self-reflection was taking place.

I was reminded here of some conversations I had early in my Houston years with Doug, a welder in the Pasadena oil refineries. I interviewed him as part of an exploratory study of blue-collar oil workers, although having met him at a bike shop, he never seemed simply a "worker." At first, he expressed great pride in his work: welders are well paid and highly respected for their skill and stamina. He was, in a sense, at the top of the refinery hierarchy, and he quickly established that he took home a much bigger salary than I did. Yet, after we had talked two or three times, another story came out. He bitterly resented the engineers, whose book knowledge put them above him in terms of money, prestige, and authority. He was also painfully aware of the limitations of his craft: he may have known more than engineers from experience, but they had a grasp of the whole process that eluded him. Educated people also had an easier life and worked in careers that peaked much higher and later than his. In his early thirties, he was at the top of his powers and already the heat and the danger were getting to him. When I talked to Doug, I thought, within a traditional epistemological framework of surface and depth, that he had finally unveiled his "true" feelings to me (and perhaps to himself) through a process that could be framed in Marxist or Freudian terms as working through either false consciousness or psychological defenses to achieve recognition of what was fundamentally real. And, indeed, it may not be irrelevant that Doug also used our conversations to articulate his desire to become a pilot, which he later did.

However, several years later, as I listened and responded to the women in this small group of readers, the problem of levels seemed less simple. Partially responsible for complexity were the ethnic, religious, and even international overtones of the discussion as well as the shared, although quite different, experiences of social mobility. These women usually did not discuss the details of their class backgrounds in middle-class settings both because they could "pass" as middle class and because by now they *were* middle class. So, like all of us, they lived their lives and enacted their identity on several different levels, and which of these might come into play at any given moment became a contextual, relational, even political question.

In *The Making of the English Working Class*, E. P. Thompson discusses social class as a set of relations. His analysis remains at the level of large-scale social change. Yet, the relational nature of social class (as well as gender and race) can also be posited at the level face-to-face interactions. How you take up and perform your own social identities shifts from one situation to the next. It is equally true, however, that what narratives of identity can be spoken will encourage or silence certain versions of one's own history and orientation – versions that can then be mobilized in later trajectories of personal and social action. I have discussed this reading group because it embodies some of the creative work of narrating self and world that occurs in reading groups more generally, and it shows how reading and talk about reading can encourage reflection about some of the issues that may seem, at first glance, far from reading but are intimately connected to the social relations of reading in our time.

Concluding Remarks

Reading and the narratives that engage and flow from reading are extraordinary cultural practices. They appear in this account mainly as an opening out – onto new horizons of knowledge and experience, into other people's lives and perspectives on the world, and toward life trajectories that bring great rewards. Their shadow is the closed door of exclusion, at least from certain conversations and careers that cannot happen easily without reading.

Writing about reading through this double-looped narrative can, I hope, show the myriad filaments that connect the personal moment of reading to its environing social context, and thus help us open out questions that are more abstract and theoretical. My reading group pounced on questions about the experiential component of social class and its acquisition, making it clear that books, reading itself, and the institutionalization of reading in schools look very different depending on where you stand in the social order. Yet, they also used their readings of my writing to explore the nuances of social difference and to bring their lived experience into a conversation that could complicate frameworks and assumptions that excluded their own self-representations and silenced certain aspects of their lives.

Conclusions are often the place where the expansiveness of exposition is brought under control and stamped with the finality of closure. I am reluctant to do this here. If either the content or the method of this chapter can be helpful in thinking through the nature of reading, it will be because it draws other readers into a similarly creative conversation themselves.

Notes

1 The term comes from Dorinne Kondo's book, *Crafting Selves: Power, Gender, and Discourses of Identity in a Japanese Workplace* (Chicago: University of Chicago Press, 1990).

2 See Arlette Ingram Willis, *Reading comprehension research and testing in the U.S.: Undercurrents of race, class, and power in the struggle for meaning* (New York, NY: Lawrence Erlbaum & Associates, 2008).

3 See Philippe Ariès, *Centuries of childhood* (London: Pimlico, 1996), and Robert Coles, *Privileged ones: The well-off and the rich in America* (Boston: Little, Brown and Co, 1978).

4 See Pierre Bourdieu and Jean-Claude Passeron, *Reproduction in education, society and culture (2nd edition)* (Newbury Park, CA: Sage, 1990); and Mihaly Csikszentmihalyi and Eugene Rochberg-Halton. *The Meaning of Things: Domestic Symbols and the Self* (Cambridge [Eng.]: Cambridge University Press, 1981).

5 When I decided not to care what they thought, I did many things to become happier, one of which was to read every Thomas Hardy book in the school library; his eloquence about despair and exclusion helped end my own paralysis.

6 Their yearlong campaign fascinated me, mostly because they got away with it. From parental gossip, I gather that Mrs. Beck, who had come to our private school from a progressive private school in New York City, made herself cordially disliked among the other teachers by constant negative comparisons of our school with that one. So, the adult authorities gave the boys only token admonishments – allowing the playground mockery but curtailing excursions into Mrs. Beck's room to bang on lockers, for example – since the boys were, in a sense, acting out the adult consensus.

7 Did this begin with the boys? I really can't remember; it seems to me that it followed on the heels of us being forbidden to bring food and eat during the educational movies that were always shown in the gym, which was a basement room.

CHAPTER 11

Conventions of Reading

Heather Murray

The term *convention* is commonly used by critics to refer to the expected features of a literary form or genre.[1] For example, it is conventional for the epic to attempt grand rather than trivial topics and for pastoral poetry to allude to classical mythology. However, as is the case with any convention, a formal or genre convention is an inherently social one: literary conventions are the textual guidelines for communicative writing and knowledgeable reading. They may alter over time or fall from fashion or even be forgotten altogether, shifting as their literary and social contexts change. Although an author may choose to defy genre conventions – to write, as some iconoclastic authors have done, a novel with multiple endings or no conclusion at all – such experimentation depends for its impact on the reader's recognition that the conventions indeed have been flouted. But, must the reader necessarily be knowledgeable of formal and generic precedents? The annals of literary criticism offer a long-running debate as to how far these conventions constrain (or should constrain) readerly activity. Some would argue that the author's intentions for the text (i.e., how he or she wishes it to be understood) are signaled by these generic choices and that a competent reader must comprehend them (Preminger, 1974, p. 153). It is also possible to approach the question of generic knowledge without assuming that the author's intention (even if it can be discerned) should circumscribe the reading result. As Radway (1984) showed in her groundbreaking study of readers of popular romances, genre expertise considerably enhances the reading experience: deep satisfactions are felt by savvy readers who feel in control of the unfolding of the text. But, what about readers who lack specialized genre knowledge? One could encounter with pleasure a haiku or a ghazal without prior exposure to the form, and a detective novel may be even more satisfying for the novice who remains in the dark until the surprising end. However, those readers would require at least an acquaintance with poetry or the novel more generally: without this, misinterpretation or even incomprehension would ensue. Seeing the lines "Go, for the room is cold/and the light is dim" on the blackboard, some students might head for the door, whereas others would take out their poetry notebooks. A reader unable to identify the satiric surround of Swift's essay, "A Modest Proposal," risks radical misunderstanding: Swift is not actually recommending cannibalism as a cure for overpopulation. It should be emphasized, however, that although we often refer to conventions as "literary," they are inherent to all discursive forms. Recipes, for example, are now highly regularized and successful cooking results from following their serial arrangement. The same is true of weather reports, technical manuals, and treatises in analytic philosophy: comprehension depends on the understanding of rules and forms. There is no dividing line between "literacy" and the knowledge of textual conventions.

Similarly, there is a continuum between literacy and the broader conventions that govern readership. To this stage, the term *convention* has been used to refer to identifiable textual features that locate a given work within a genre and the history of that genre. (A poet who uses the "elegiac stanza" to express personal loss has done more than select a pattern of rhyme and meter: she or he has placed that poem in a chain extending back to the eighteenth century and Thomas Gray's famous churchyard meditation.) However, we may also speak more broadly of conventions that guide the use of the book or other print matter. These user conventions point to the who, what, why, when, where, and how of reading. Who, in a given culture, has access to books? What kinds of materials are considered suitable to different demographic groups? Why read in the first place: will certain skills, attributes, even qualities of character be the result? When should one learn to read, at what level should instruction cease, and is reading a lifelong pursuit? Where are the locations and situations of reading: public, familial, or private? How should one read for understanding and for enjoyment, for profit, for self-cultivation, and for social good? Conventions governing book use could involve, for example, the knowledge of how to access books (whether through libraries, bookstores, or vicariously as an auditor); techniques of note taking, "journaling," or collection of quotations; and even more fundamental skills such as the ability to deploy tables of contents and indexes and to understand the relationship of graphic materials to print. These conventions, too, may alter over time: Jackson's (2001) history of marginalia shows how this once-valuable mode of textual commentary is now the mark of antibook vandalism. Knowledge of book-use conventions is not separate from literacy, nor is literacy anterior to it. Understanding of the "book" may well precede any skills in alphabetic decoding: even a young child knows that a book must have a binding and a cover, as she staples pieces of paper together. The toddler nonreader can recognize a book by its cover, carefully turn the pages, and volubly and insistently create the situations where reading aloud will occur. (Similarly, some literary conventions may also precede decoding. The distinctions among a poem, a story, and a song are early ones, as is the plaint that a hurried bedtime narrative is not "really" a story.) Insofar as print-use conventions help to determine who reads which materials, with what intensity and proficiency, and whether reading is incorporated into daily life and into cognitive and emotional patterning, the threads of "literacy" and "use" are not easily teased apart. These are interpenetrative skills, although the disciplinary boundaries of current scholarship mean they are often considered separately (through a neuropsychological approach to literacy acquisition, a literary–theoretical consideration of textual conventions, and a sociological analysis of book use). The point could be stated more strongly and formulaically: *convention* is the place where comprehension and custom meet.

Convention has an additional although etymologically related sense: a coming together of people. In recent years, the understanding of "reading" has been radically reconfigured. No longer viewed as private, individual, and interiorized, reading is now seen as a social activity located in overlapping circles of virtual and actual readership collectivities. This intellectual development has been spurred by assertions, in the fields of linguistics and literary theory, that meaning is context-dependent (rather than absolute, transcendent, or foundational) and that it is located within what reader-response theorist, Stanley Fish (1980), famously termed "interpretive communities." (Such communities are meaning-making rather than solely recipient, as Fish again indicated in his assertion of their "authority." They are also – as Stock (1983) showed in his groundbreaking study of medieval religious sects – brought continually into being through the changing interests and interpretive practices of readers, rather than being defined a priori.) Scholarly work on collective reading also has been encouraged by the appearance of new readership formations: the North American repopularization of the book club, for example, and the exponential rise of Web-based readership and "fanfic" communities. However, associations of readers are not a new phenomenon. From the classroom to the chapel to the Chautauqua tent, the scene of reading has always been a crowded one.[2]

This chapter attempts to align these polyvalent senses of readerly "convention" to the topic of literacy by showing the interdependency of literacy and conventional understanding and the interpersonality of literacy acquisition. It undertakes this through three studies of readers who were literate (i.e., able to decode alphabetically and form meaningful holisms) but deficient in respect to textual and material codes and customs (i.e., genre conventions and book-use conventions) and who attempted to gain this knowledge by coming together as readers in groups (i.e., associative conventions) for mutual instruction. The focus here is the mid-nineteenth century, in the area of central Canada then known as Canada West (now Ontario) – a time and place of varied demographic terrain, a transitional "class" structure, and an educational system undergoing rapid evolutions both institutionally and ideologically.[3] For comparative purposes, I have chosen groups of adult learners engaged in various forms of mutual instruction of a literary nature. These adult learners had a way to describe the transition they wished to effect, and it is helpful to know the terms of their own understanding. Alphabetically literate (or on their way to becoming so), they wanted to precipitate a self-transformation from "lettered" to "literary." Less restrictive than in our current day, the term *literature* in the nineteenth century denoted a range of genres and discursive practices. The adjective *literary* was similarly broad, synonymous with *cultural* or *cultured*, and was often used approvingly to indicate worth or distinction. A literary person was familiar with different textual forms; prepared for public discourse; and ready with quotations, allusions, and historical knowledge – a person for whom reading had become incorporated into character formation and social presentation. Here, three case studies present readers attempting to make the transition from lettered to literary: in a branch of the Mechanics' Institute; in an African Canadian association connected to a newspaper; and in a network of teacher-readers related by a print affiliation. (These three cases all also involve governmental or other regulatory efforts to hinder, restrict, or channel educational efforts.) The conclusion turns to the situation of similarly aspirant readers in North America today. The aim is to present literacy in both its restricted (alphabetic) and expanded (cultural) senses; in its network of sociopolitical, economic, gendered, and "racialized" circumstances; and with reference to the conditions of schooling and of print access of the day – that is, to work on the interface of historical "literacy" and "literary" studies.[4]

Mid–nineteenth-century literacy rates were high in Canada and especially in Canada West, according to data drawn from or correlated to the 1861 census (i.e., the most approximate to the period under discussion). Historian of literacy, Harvey Graff, arrived at a figure of 92.8 percent for Canada West based on the census returns (Graff, 1973, p. 45), whereas Mays and Manzl (1974), surveying deeds, wills, and school records in Ontario's Peel County, recommended just a slight revision downward. Only Scotland,

Denmark, Sweden, and (the polled population of) the United States had comparable national rates at the time. However, there were significant demographic and regional deviations even in the one province. Among the settler groups were Scots who had benefited from a strong system of universal education; the Irish, both "indigent" and educated; and the Black Fugitives, for whom illiteracy rates were as high as 50 percent in some regions. There was further variability within these groups: Irish literacy rates fluctuated according to Protestant or Roman Catholic religious affiliation; and some African Canadians from the northern states had a Quaker education even to the college level. This is to list only some of the English-speaking populations to be encountered at mid-century and in mid-country. There were immigrants from many linguistic groupings, and First Nations people had highly variant chances of alphabetic or syllabic literacy depending on willed or enforced assimilation and the availability of translated materials. Settlers of longer standing had received a differential education, both in duration and quality, in the patchwork of schools, academies, seminaries, home schools, tutoring, and apprenticeships prior to the regularization of the public school system commencing in the late 1840s under superintendent, The Reverend Egerton Ryerson. (There was an overall raising effect, however, whatever the system's flaws: Graff [1979] observed that length of settlement was a positive factor determining literacy rates.) Literacy rates dropped sharply in the northern districts and in two of the counties with hardscrabble land and poorer settlers but were, on the whole, higher in the country (particularly for women) than in the city, perhaps because of the greater educational opportunities offered in rural areas. However, rudimentary literacy did not necessarily lead to competent comprehension, as educational commentators of the day had begun to note. Scholars instructed in the 1840s were usually taught to read by the "letters to words" approach, in which students progressively "sounded out" or "syllabled" words (Curtis, 1988, pp. 283–284; Houston & Prentice, 1988, p. 246), and because sounding was performed aloud, there was limited time per pupil in the crowded classroom.[5] Reading and writing instruction were separated and comprehension was rarely tested. Only at mid-century were new methods of "whole-word" instruction introduced, supported by sequential textbooks (particularly, the *Irish Readers*) distributed through the new agency of the Educational Depository.

To borrow a term from Gilmore's (1989) study of reading in early New England, to how great an extent had literacy become a "necessity of life"? Using both demographic indicators and other evidence (e.g., pictorial street signs) for the city of Hamilton, Canada West, Graff (1979) argued that it was possible to function economically and socially with no or only rudimentary literacy. As the title of his controversial study shows, Graff (1979) sought to overturn "the literacy myth," arguing that literacy acquisition (then as now) strengthened rather than softened class distinctions: education, he showed, could not override the determinants of race, national origin, and religion. More recently, however, statistician Livio di Matteo (1997) located a strong connection between literacy and wealth by correlating probates from 1892 with 1891 census data (although, admittedly, illiteracy would have been more socially anomalous twenty years after the imposition of compulsory schooling).[6] To focus on occupational grouping or economic status is to tell only part of the story, however (see Heath, 2001, pp. 463–465); any historian of Upper Canadian education is familiar with a public discourse praising intellectual cultivation or "improvement" as an end in itself. Readers were motivated by the entertainment, education, and moral guidance that books could provide and by the belief that reading could inculcate self-discipline and self-worth. Although this train of thought ran throughout the century, becoming ever more idealist in its inflections, the discourse of improvement was especially strong at mid-century, as Prentice showed in her study of mid-century school reformers (Prentice, 1977, pp. 45–65). This point stands clear of the debates: adult education was a social necessity, and because the public school system served only the young, new forms of association were required to achieve it.

There is a further variable in the literacy picture and that is the question of access to print materials. Development of literacy and literary skills and the provision of books and journals were interwoven issues for those early associations of readers. Although literacy levels, economic status, and gender all governed access to print materials, geographic location (i.e., town, country, or "bush") probably was the most determinant factor. A well-educated half-pay officer and his family could be starving for print in the backwoods while a young clerk or apprentice in town enjoyed a special cheap membership to the mercantile reading room. However, global or even specific information about book access or ownership does not provide sure indication of reading practices or tastes. The educated backwoods settler, deprived of books and periodicals and perhaps even newspapers, may have developed different habits of "intensive" repeat readings of limited materials: indeed, authors John Dunbar Moodie and Susanna Moodie (1847), themselves backwoods denizens, would extol the merits of such reflective "country" reading practices. The curious clerk or apprentice might chafe at the mercantile library's choice of materials or rebel against a restriction to practical and improving reading, seeking the broader flights of philosophy or poetry. It is to the local Mechanics' Institute that his steps would have turned.

The first institute in Upper Canada, and the third in British North America, was formed at York (now Toronto) in December 1830, only seven years after the birth of the movement in London. (Indeed, one man was present at the origins of both: the English watchmaker Joseph Bates, now emigrated, enlisted the bookseller James Lesslie to the cause.) Although part of a larger movement, the Mechanics' Institutes, along with similar organizations such as debating clubs, played a special role in Upper Canada, functioning as schools in the arts of deliberative democracy (to use the term of historian Jeffrey McNairn [2000]). Furthermore, they helped to develop a sphere of public opinion that extended political discourse beyond the narrow channels of government as then defined (see McNairn, 2000). The Tory ruling clique known as the "Family Compact," alert to the new organization's populist potential, attempted to thwart it by developing a rival and more elite society. The York Mechanics' Institute outflanked this maneuver and stood firmly for reform throughout the turbulent decade. Although it suffered (as did other societies) from the suspicion of voluntary associations that followed the Upper Canada rebellion of 1837–1838, it had begun to recuperate after a decade or more. Incorporated in 1847 and now named the Toronto Mechanics' Institute (TMI), it had a rapidly growing membership of more than 550 members in 1855, having added 100 the previous year (Toronto Mechanics' Institute [TMI], 1855). The cornerstone was laid for an extensive Italianate building, complete with music hall, library, and meeting and reading rooms. The growth was general; by 1853, there were twenty-five institutes in the province and sixty at the end of the decade. The proliferation of this strong network of reform-minded mutual-instruction societies caused both civic congratulation and governmental unease; in 1858, the government placed the institutes under a newly formed Board of Arts and Manufactures, a body responsible for the development of industry in the province. Whereas some institutes were initially drawn by the promise of government funding and shared library resources and lecturers, they were soon suspicious of attempts to impose "efficiencies" and to steer them into practical and vocational pursuits. Many institutes took the path of passive resistance, "neglecting" to send correspondence, or delegates, or membership tithes. (By 1861, fewer than a fifth of the institutes were affiliated.) Because the Board was housed in the Mechanics' Institute building that the government had temporarily leased, and because the TMI may have had more to gain from cooperation, its techniques were cannily different.[7] It would fulfill the letter of the Board's instructions while maintaining its own cultural spirit.

The members of the TMI had always been strong in their literary interests. Before the creation of the Board, for example, "biography" alone outnumbered the library holdings devoted to science, manufacturing, and commerce; by the early 1860s, their impressive collection of six thousand volumes included "all the Standard Works in History, Biography, Poetry and the Drama, Novels and Tales, Voyages and Travels, Science and Art, Periodical Literature, &c." (TMI, 1862). The order of the list is telling. The managing board of the TMI, a group that included some Toronto worthies, expressed reservations when fiction neared a third of the total holdings, assuring the public that works of a "doubtful or improper tendency" had been excluded (TMI, 1865) and wishing for more reading of works of a "higher order." However, the collection reflected the interests of the members, who recorded their suggestions for purchase in a notebook left in the library for that purpose, and voted with their reading tickets as well. The challenge for the TMI was to meet governmental demands while also maintaining its cultural orientation, and this its size and resources allowed it to do. It continued to maintain its own course in library acquisitions. (In 1865 – the first year providing genre-specific circulation statistics – fiction accounted for fully 70 percent of the borrowing.) Although it provided both practical and cultural lectures and courses, over the ensuing decades, its emphasis would fall on the latter. In their precious leisure time, the men – and associated women – of the TMI increasingly sought to improve their literary understanding, to acquire the rudiments of a liberal education, and to turn to books for pleasure.

Throughout the 1850s, the TMI focussed its efforts on public lectures. Building a civic cultural infrastructure was an imperative in this new city, and the TMI then lacked the space for multiple smaller classes and meetings. (Although only men could be members, women were invited to the public events, and female relatives could attend the "teaching lectures." The Institutes were pioneering in this respect.) When the mutual-instruction format eroded as membership swelled, the TMI pressed sympathetic experts into service: clergymen, professors, teachers, and local literati. There were numerous lectures on mental culture but surprisingly few told the members what and how to read: presumably, the audiences resisted more calls for the efficient or "profitable" use of their time. (By contrast, of the six written lectures the Board had commissioned to be read aloud to Institute members, there was only one literary offering, and it was admonitory: "Books – the kind to read; and the way to read them" (Board of Arts and Manufactures, General Committee, 1858).) The few directive lectures were at odds with other Institute practices. The Presbyterian clergyman, The Reverend Dr. Robert Burns, might warn of the moral perils of novel reading (Burns, 1851) but, in the same year, the library catalogued 729 volumes under "Novels-Tales," with sensation fiction well represented (TMI, 1858). On the whole, the cultural lectures were predominantly "literary" in nature and with a special focus on the history of English literature and language. It is possible to discern some specific principles underlying the topics of these talks and the classes later developed from the lectures series.

Toronto audiences were offered a variety of literary evenings throughout the 1850s. The obliging Reverend Burns gave four lectures on Augustan and eighteenth-century literature and another on modern writers; there were further talks on ancient and modern drama, on the anti-slavery poet Cowper, on Spenser's "Faery Queen" [sic], and on "The Poetry of Insanity" (presumably, on the "peasant poet" John Clare). On another occasion, "English Literature and Language" were surveyed. The Chartist song lyricist Charles Mackay, in Toronto at the TMI's invitation in the spring of 1858, gave two lectures on "Poetry and Song." Other eclectic topics would have been classed as "literary" in their day: on antiquity, travel, natural philosophy, and the new principles of species taxonomy, for example; and these were often on speculative themes (e.g., "Science and Revelation" and "The Plurality of Worlds"). Such topics had steadily grown in popularity: whereas the lecture series of 1849–1850 contained only those of a practical or utilitarian nature, liberal education offerings formed half or more of the lectures at mid-decade.[8] However, the literary agenda also took a more specialized turn, when T. J. Robertson of the Toronto Normal School commenced a series of teaching lectures on "The Science and Philosophy of the English Language" in 1850. Reverend Burns followed with "The Dawn of English Literature" and "Early English Literature," the next year surveying Indian languages and legends (plausibly, either of the First Nations or the Asian subcontinent). The eminent ethnohistorian, Daniel Wilson, of the provincial university, presented paired lectures on Anglo-Saxon language and literature. In the 1850s, there was a general interest in philological findings and a sense of their pedagogic utility (as discussed later with reference to teacher education journals), but some sociopolitical considerations were converging in the Institute's choices. For Reverend Burns, the English language developed through "gradual formation" and "through the infusion of new elements" over time (Burns, 1851, p. 187); Professor Wilson was an evolutionist in linguistics as well as in biology. The idea that languages – and their literary manifestations – develop and are enriched through cultural interpenetration would hold an obvious appeal for colonial settlers, but it could also support movements for educational democratization. If language is not a "given," a pure stream flowing from an origin – rather, if language is a malleable product of human interactions – then conscious attempts may be undertaken to make language rational in its principles and more useable by extension. (The ideal of "rational" or clear language use is also flagged by the lectures on eighteenth-century and Augustan style.) Interpreting the literary programme of the 1850s in this way requires recourse to slightly earlier and later events. In the late 1840s, the TMI had featured two different visiting lecturers on the topic of *phonography* (i.e., a synonym for phonetic shorthand or spelling reform) and had attempted to start a class on the topic in 1848; there was another phonological lecture in 1852. (A number of earlier English radicals had proposed schemes for language reform, maintaining that the complexity of "English" – its Latinate constructions, its mismatch of orthography to spoken sounds – was an impediment to universal literacy). In the late 1850s, whether impelled by the demands of its members or by the need to "downsize" given its own financial crises and a depression affecting all the trades – and perhaps in reaction to the Board's new assumption of authority – the TMI initiated classes under the teacher, rhetorician, and language reformer, Richard Lewis.[9]

Lewis was a strong supporter of the Institute movement, who would go on to publish widely used guides to oratory and to reading as well as anthologies of recitation selections, becoming best known for *The Dominion Elocutionist*, which presented "a system of elocution formed on the philosophy of the human voice and the logical structure of language." He offered a first class in English grammar and composition in 1859, which continued for five months in the fall and winter of 1860–1861 for "lessons in English Grammar, the Analysis of Sentences, on Composition and Rhetoric, and on Logic, Elocution and Public Speaking" (TMI, 1860). The keen students vowed to convene during the summer to be better prepared for the next year. The TMI soon added new courses (there were eight by 1862, of which five were devoted to languages, fine art drawing, and music) but Lewis's were so popular that a separate instructor for English was added in 1864. By 1865 and possibly sooner, in addition to French and drawing, the Institute offered separate classes in English and in Elocution, hosted a Ladies Elocution Class and a Ladies Writing Class, and initiated a course in Phonography for which forty-three students registered (TMI, 1866). The library catalogues of the 1850s show that the Institute supported these new directions by increasing its holdings of rhetorical treatises, collections of speeches and elegant extracts, and handbooks of language usage.

Scanty specific evidence remains for the English or phonography classes, but the TMI records in the aggregate hint at the ways TMI members augmented their understanding of textual and book-use conventions and gained a "literary" understanding. The TMI imparted to all of its members the rules of order and the procedures for profitable debate, through insistence on correct practices in all meetings – including those of its committees. It provided, in other words, training in the "deliberative" branch of rhetoric. Institute audiences were exposed to models of sustained disquisition and eloquence as exemplified by visiting speakers on a wide variety of topics. Members learned the conventions of print usage (i.e., book choice, access, and borrowing procedures) through access to and management of a library collection with an unusually broad generic range in both its monograph and periodical holdings. Only a minority elected to take the courses and, according to the annual reports, classes were sometimes smaller than the dedication of the instructor deserved. However, members (and, by the 1860s, women nonmembers) who were so inclined could learn the elements of rhetorical theory and practice, and separate courses on eloquence provided extra training in the spoken arts. Grammar and logic were taught together, in keeping with the TMI's rationalist attitude toward language usage and literary production. Populist in its cultural inclinations, the TMI saw language and literature as a human achievement: something that was and would continue to be *produced* – like other "arts and manufactures." In understanding the specifically political dimensions of the cultural realm, it had much in common with the next association to be considered here.

The Provincial Union Association (PUA), founded in 1854, is known today as an abolitionist society and as a political clearinghouse for the Black Fugitive settlers rather than as a literary–cultural organization. Similarly, one of its central figures, Mary Ann Shadd (later Cary), has been examined as a pioneering woman newspaper editor and publisher, as a teacher, and as a voice in Upper Canadian settlement politics but only in passing as a rhetorician and littérateur. However, the cultural orientation of the PUA is attested in its founding announcement: it was established for the promotion of "literature, general intelligence, active benevolence, the principle of universal freedom, and a British union not based on complexional considerations" (*Provincial Freeman*, 1854–1857, 19 August 1854). The ordering of the mandate is not accidental. Shadd had worked with an earlier organization designed to promote the rhetorical arts and provided literary selections and "literary intelligence" in her newspaper, *The Provincial Freeman*. The mission of the PUA, and Shadd's cultural promotions, can be examined in tandem to gain a sense of the literary work of the Black Fugitives at mid-century.

It might be assumed that cultural associations would not have been a priority for the Black Fugitives: a traumatically displaced and dispersed exile community, whose members faced continuing hardship and racial discrimination after they crossed the border, would need to place mutual assistance and abolitionist mobilization at the forefront of their efforts. Indeed, like their counterpart associations among the freed Black communities of the northern states, the literary societies rarely had study as their sole goal, rather combining it with various forms of community and political work. However, the literary mandate was quickly sensed and met. The mixed-sex Wilberforce Educating Lyceum (Cannonsburg, founded 1850), and a young men's debating club with which Shadd was associated (Windsor [then Sandwich], 1853), preceded the PUA, and at least six organizations were contemporary to it or founded closely after (Murray, 2002, pp. 70–73). In addition, Shadd's sister-in-law, Amelia Freeman Shadd, founder of a Chatham women's group, proposed in 1857 an ambitious program to be followed by reading circles (*Provincial Freeman*, 1854–1857, 15 and 22 August 1857), although it is not known whether these were implemented. It is important to note that the African Canadian community preceded the rest of the settler community by several decades in the formation of both women's and mixed-sex associations.

Some literary societies provided literacy instruction and writing materials to illiterate members, and some also augmented the teaching provided to the younger generation educated in Canada West. As previously mentioned, schools of the period were uneven. However, the picture was even more variant for African Canadian school children, who were sometimes denied admission to rural schools either explicitly or through the gerrymandering of district boundaries, segregated into separate desks and differentially taught if admitted, or educated in the often inferior schools established for the "Coloured population" and licensed by the 1850 School Act (McLaren, 2004). Several cultural associations refer to the needs of the "rising generation" in their founding statements, by which they may mean to include young men and women among their members, or provide support for the schools, or both. However, the principal purpose was to provide a distinctively liberal or "literary" education for adult autodidacts, whose education may have been restricted to practical skills. In 1850, the Willberforce Lyceum Educating Society declared itself "for the promotion of the rising generation in education, scientific attainments, and other such progression in the English language, as will entitle us to mix more freely in the great crowd of her Majesty's subjects that is befitting a people who love Belle letters [sic], and other such polite literature" (Wilberforce Lyceum Educating Society [Ont.], 1850, p. 1). Historian Kristen McLaren detailed the assimilationist goals of this initially separated association (2004); one may further note the role literary study was to play in the process of cultural mixing. The plan is for a mastery of a range of genres and discourses (e.g., science, polite literature) and attainment of advanced rhetorical skills (i.e., "progression" in the English language), necessary for participation in civic affairs and for free movement in the "crowd" of colonial subjects. The syntactic awkwardness of this sentence is itself in eloquent testimony of the author's aspirations to a more formal diction, and it leaves the later analyst with a puzzle. The uncertain referent for "that" makes it unclear whether the love of belles-lettres characterizes the existing colonial public sphere or the Black Fugitives who aim to belong to it. Either reading is satisfactory.[10] McHenry and Heath (2001) have cautioned against seeing African American culture as primarily "oral" in its nature or in its roots; furthermore, McHenry (2002) has shown that rhetorical training in the African American literary societies was broadly based and not overfocussed on oratorical skills. Similarly, the focus of Shadd and of her society was "fine" literature, although widely defined.

The PUA held its founding meeting in the Sayer Street Chapel, Toronto, in August 1854 (*Provincial Freeman*, 1854–1857, 19 August 1854), after the *Freeman* had been in operation for six months. As Shadd's biographer, Jane Rhodes (1998), determined, the death of rival newspaper publisher Henry Bibb provided an opportune moment to realign Black settler politics. Shadd also wished to create a counterbalance to the powerful Anti-Slavery Society of Canada (Rhodes, 1998, p. 94). Among the founders of the PUA were Reverend William P. Newman, an influential Baptist minister; Wilson Abbott, prominent among Toronto's small African Canadian community; and Thomas Cary (later to become Shadd's husband). Reverend Samuel Ringgold Ward, then touring for the Anti-Slavery Society of Canada, was elected president *in absentia*. Some founders had strong literary credentials: Ward, for example, was frequently considered second only to the great Frederick Douglass in his oratorical skills. Shadd had benefited from a Quaker education and possessed a clear, dynamic, balanced prose style. Although occasionally criticized for haste in delivery, she was a powerful platform speaker in an era when women rarely assumed the dais (Rhodes, 1998, p. 79).[11] Ward and Shadd had attempted to impart their rhetorical skills to the young men of Windsor through the formation of a debating society the year before, a scheme aborted when a member was slain after an altercation. Foes saw this as evidence of the intemperate speech stirred by debating clubs, a fear that the careful wording of the PUA statements seems designed to allay.

The PUA and the newspaper were immediately knit tightly together. A principal purpose of the PUA was to lend the *Freeman* moral and financial support and to generate subscriptions. In turn, the paper served as the organ of the PUA and repeatedly published its constitution. Following the successful "branch" model of associations such as the Mechanics' Institutes, smaller local affiliate circles were established in centres such as Brantford, London, and Niagara. Shadd was especially mandated to develop such auxiliaries as she traveled around the province.[12] Whereas men were to convene on a fortnightly basis and women were to meet weekly (in part because they were engaged in fundraising through the manufacture of articles for sale), there was to be a monthly meeting involving both sexes especially "for the purpose of promoting the literary objects specified by reciting of original pieces, reading, debates &c," according to the constitution (*Provincial Freeman*, 1854–1857, 19 August 1854). Members would also be solicited to address the assembly at the semiannual meetings; it is not entirely clear whether this involved statements and speeches pertaining to the business of the association or other types of addresses suited to a social evening or conversazione (either or both are possible). Learning parliamentary procedure, rules of order, and the conventions of debate was a precondition of public participation, as has been seen in the mandate of the Mechanics' Institutes, but literary societies commonly held open meetings to showcase the talents of their members. More direct evidence of literary activities is lacking, however, because the PUA did not publish its minutes; although a corresponding secretary apparently sent the minutes to sister newspapers in the United States, such records have yet to be uncovered.

It is necessary, then, to work inferentially from the pages of the *Freeman*, taking its poetry and fiction selections, items of "literary intelligence," and editorializations on culture and self-education as compatible with the PUA's mission. Some items were authored by Shadd, her affiliates, and correspondents, whereas many were extracted from books or reprinted from journals and newspapers of the day. Reprinting was a common practice, sometimes encouraged by exchanges among editors, but tolerated (and legally sanctioned) even when operating outside this informal system of permissions. Scholars of print culture have learned to value these reprints as evidencing networks of print exchange and ideational circulation (rather than dismissing them as "fill" or, in the case of Canadian literary historians, passing over them in the hunt for early expressions of an authentically national culture). Indeed, the literary programme of the *Freeman* is in most respects a united one; it is noteworthy, too, for making a special place for women as writers and readers. Printing arguments for female education and excerpting women authors, Shadd set a personal, pioneering example. Having "broken the editorial ice" for women of her race and class, she exhorted them to "go to Editing, as many of you as are willing" (*Freeman*, 30 June 1855).

The *Freeman* declared itself devoted to "Anti-Slavery, Temperance and General Literature." Although "General Literature" denoted a wide variety of writings, from its commencement, the paper also presented "literature" more narrowly defined. There were four poems in the first issue; three poems and a travel sketch in the next; and the third issue began the serialization of a two-part story lifted from Charles Dickens's publication, *Household Words*. The fourth issue had three poems, a travel essay, and the conclusion of the story "Mighty Hunters"; the fifth had a character sketch by Dickens, a poem by Longfellow, and Bulwer-Lytton's comic essay prescribing "Books as

Medicine." Also in that issue was an excerpt from G. S. Phillips's essay on "The Value of Books," advocating "*communion* with books" as a way of gaining poise and self-possession in times that are "too busy; too exclusively *outward* in their tendency," whirled by commerce and political strife (*Provincial Freeman*, 22 April 1854). Another essay titled "Scholars," penned probably by Shadd, notes the virtues of self-education: without a teacher, the autodidact is forced into personal application; lacking many books, the student escapes the peril of self-absorbed miscellaneous reading and will become a better and more generous scholar. Despite the pressure put on its pages by the events of the day and the need to provide local and international news as well as advertising, the *Freeman* regularly offered literary selections; the front page was soon categorized according to "Poetry," "Literature," and "Miscellaneous" sections. That these choices and methods of organization reflected Shadd's principles is shown by the striking alteration when she ceded the editorial reins in June 1855 and handed the "literary department" to Reverend Newman. The "Literature" column immediately disappeared, replaced by household hints, comic anecdotes, and amusing "local colour" sketches; the poetry that remained was primarily on abolitionist themes, interspersed with comic or melodramatic ditties. The paper also discontinued its serialization of a translated French novel, *The Maroons*. After eighteen months, when Newman's resignation was announced (19 January 1856), the literary pendulum swung back with a philosophic and formally experimental poem by Browning, and the "Literature" heading reappeared later in the month. These directions were continued under the new editor, H. Ford Douglass, a former slave who had become an accomplished autodidact.

It is possible to locate a literary "canon" of the *Freeman* for the four years of extant issues.[13] The paper published some 184 poems that (with the exception of the more vernacular material under Newman's tenure) would have been recognized by its audience as "literary" although many of the authors are unknown to readers today. As expected, many poems deal with themes of slavery, abolitionism, and the evils of drink; or, by allegorical extension, with freedom, struggle, and the necessity of moral choice. Antislavery poets such as Cowper and Whittier make repeat appearances, although writing sometimes on other topics. Many poems detail beautiful scenes or marvel at natural processes, often using these themes devotionally as evidence of God's handiwork. There are also ballads, narratives, meditations on mortality, some love poetry, and comic or satirical verses. Readers would have encountered not only Longfellow, Browning, Cowper, and Whittier but also William Cullen Bryant, Burns, Oliver Wendell Holmes, Thomas Hood, Keats, and James Russell Lowell, as well as the ever-popular "Mrs. [Lydia] Sigourney" and the bohemian traveller, Bayard Taylor (whose poetry and prose was often reprinted). Some poets were chosen for their social-reform sympathies: the radical Eliza Cook and the Chartist writer Gerald Massey, for example (the latter appearing frequently), and Charles Mackay, visitor to the TMI. Also represented were African American writers such as Frances Ellen Watkins (later Harper), whose lecture trip to Canada West was given special notice in the paper. Myriad anonymous poems were drawn from divergent sources. The *Freeman* also featured literary prose in a variety of genres: travel essays were especially popular, but there were also character sketches, philosophical essays, short stories, fiction serializations, and humorous pieces. The prolific Fanny Fern was a favourite, here as everywhere, while Dickens unknowingly contributed three pieces (and his *Household Words* was mined for nine further items). The *Freeman* drew from a variety of sources: weighty reviews (e.g., the *Athenaeum*), more popular compendia (e.g., Chamber's *Edinburgh Journal* and *Graham's Magazine*), abolitionist papers (e.g., *National Era*, *The Liberator*), and a host of other mainstream, religious, and temperance papers.

The poetry and prose of the *Freeman* was contemporary, topical, and chosen in part for its readability. Noteworthy figures of the day – a George Eliot, for example, or a Carlyle – are missing from its pages, as are the romantic poets (with the exception of one poem by Keats), although Byron and Shelley were often cited in other radical and social-reform newspapers. (They were probably considered unsuited to a temperance publication.) There is no mention of Shakespeare, whose works had not yet become central to autodidactic study, as would be the case later in the century. Literary selections appear to have been based on principles elaborated and exemplified by Shadd elsewhere. She urged her correspondents not to reach for effect, not to "go very 'far' for terms" (22 April 1854) – indeed, her own writing illustrates the balanced plain style favoured by Quaker educationists. Expecting literary understanding to be useful, Shadd sought selections that shed light on the political and moral struggles of the day, and she used contemplative essays and travel narratives to expand the horizons of her readers. Poetry selections were usually short (given the *Freeman*'s four-page constraint), often structured in quatrains, usually cross-rhymed, and characteristically in tetrameter or common measure. If the selections appear lacking in formal sophistication or expressive subtlety to a twenty-first-century eye, it is well to keep in mind Tompkins's (1985) instructions for understanding the sentimental literature of mid–nineteenth-century North America: sentiment was considered a powerful spur to action, and reformers were wary of political programmes that could not change hearts as well as legislation. As to stereotypes, Tompkins reminds us, these were effective, economical shorthands for communicating to an audience versed in their iconography, often drawn from Biblical or other religious sources. Although an African Canadian audience might be well grounded in religious references, they lacked the arsenal of allusions needed to attack most nineteenth-century writing. Thus, the *Freeman* provided multiple items designed to increase its readers' citational range. In its second issue, the *Freeman* began a feature called "Diamond Dust," consisting of sententia and aphorisms; a "Gleanings" column of quips, quotations, and anecdotes soon followed. (These were later replaced by collected "Witticisms.") The "Literature" section might feature items about books and authors – an article on John Bunyan, for example (2 September 1854) or Leigh Hunt and Carlyle (14 October 1854), or even on Yoruba proverbs (21 October 1854) – but smaller items of "literary intelligence" were also scattered throughout the paper. The "Miscellaneous" column contained short items pertaining to science, art, music, and sometimes literature; snippets of biography and history; even comments on current events. More than a source of eclectic information, the "intelligence" and miscellanea gave readers the keys to unlock classical, historical, political, and other textual allusions.

That the *Freeman* readership was increasingly literate is shown both by its correspondence and its advertisements. Shadd relied on correspondents and letter writers – in different corners of the province and beyond – to send news of organizations, events and political affairs in their districts. She addressed them in notices "To Correspondents," stressing the needs of the paper and the requirements to be followed by contributors, whether it was to present original material only or to "write more legibly, friends" for the benefit of the typesetters (17 March 1855). After several years, the paper also began to attract original verse. Twelve poems written "For the Provincial Freeman" appeared in its pages by amateurs in Dresden and Chatham, as well as an original comic sketch. (One poem apostrophized the conductors of the *Freeman*: "Toil on, toil on, ye noble few!" [19 August 1854].) Beginning in mid-1854, the Toronto Circulating Library placed a standing notice in the paper, advising readers of the availability of "over 2000 volumes of standard works in History, Biography, Belles Lettres and Novels" (17 June 1854). A long-running advertisement for Catharine Parr Traill's

The Female Emigrants' Guide is an interesting early example of "niche" marketing to the Black Fugitive community. By the end of the year, other publishers would begin to address this audience. "Good Books by Mail" were advertised by Fowler and Wells in New York: a list of forty-eight titles in self-help, natural health, and phrenology. Soon there were prospectuses for four journals: *Life Illustrated*, the *Saturday Evening Post*, the *Canada Farmer*, and the *Universal Phonographer* (the latter aimed at autodidacts who wished to master phonographic stenography). Whereas these advertisements attest to the efforts of the *Freeman*'s agents to develop revenue sources, they also show that the *Freeman* had helped to generate a literate and reform-minded community of readers and to apprise the wider world of that fact.

As the community of the *Freeman* indicates, readers may be convened through print affiliation as well as through literal meeting. This was a function of educational journals especially at mid-century, before the establishment of associations such as the Ontario Educational Association or more specialized bodies such as the Modern Language Association of Ontario. However, throughout the century, educational journals contained myriad articles intended to both improve the pedagogic skills of language instructors and increase the reading proficiency of the teachers themselves.[14] Such items reflect – and, in some cases, anticipate – the broader shifts in taste and morality of the decades in which they appear and also change along with their target audience, as teachers acquired Normal School or even university training.[15] However, teachers of the 1850s were often in need of instruction themselves. Although district and common schools were rapidly implemented throughout Ontario in the waves of educational acts passed in the late 1840s and early 1850s, the credentials of teachers necessarily lagged behind. Few could have attended the provincial Normal School, established in 1847 (and lacking premises of its own until 1851); nor, as Houston and Prentice (1988, pp. 169–170) observed, would a committee necessarily hire a Normal School graduate if a local applicant were available. A novice might be only slightly older – even, perhaps, younger – than some of the pupils and only marginally advanced in learning.[16] Teachers even of minimal qualification would have been alert to the complaints about transient, temporary, and unskilled teachers that filled the columns of the press of the day and distantly cognizant of the new methods inculcated through the Normal School and its associated Model School.[17] However, it is not easy to haul oneself up by one's intellectual bootstraps, as evidenced in the diaries of Alexander Bickerton Edmison, who at age eighteen was a rural schoolmaster in the late 1850s. His dogged attempts to read Shakespeare and Herodotus, to teach himself Latin and logic, and to trisect a triangle yielded little gain. His only intellectual circle was the debating club of the local Band of Hope, and he was grateful for what he could learn even there: participation in one evening's debate (on whether Napoleon or Wellington was the greater leader) made Edmison "a better teacher, a better talker, a better speaker, and a man of more knowledge" in his estimation (entry 20 October 1857). Edmison's goals are typical of those who wished to become "literary": he is exceptional only in his tenacity. However, the self-elevating intellectual could find more systematic assistance in the pages of the *Journal of Education for Upper Canada* (*JE*), published by the provincial education department commencing in 1848. Distributed free, by 1855 it had a monthly circulation of five thousand in Canada West and beyond (Houston & Prentice, 1988, p. 135). Among its addressees were those occupying the liminal position of the teacher-autodidact.

Given the transitional nature of schooling in the period, the *JE* necessarily assumed that education would occur both inside and outside the classroom. In editorial items and with extracts from sympathetic journals and newspapers, Egerton Ryerson and his affiliates reminded readers of the virtues of self-education. "Great Men Self Educated," one item was titled: both Benjamin

Franklin and the great painter Benjamin West were self-instructed, and the better for it. "Each had a good teacher because he taught himself. Both had a better teacher daily, because both were advancing daily in knowledge and in the art of acquiring it" (February 1853, p. 19). Nor should the autodidact despair when time for study was limited. The greatest thinkers combined literary with practical pursuits, as the reader was reminded with the examples of Cicero, Ben Jonson, and even Shakespeare himself (September 1848, pp. 272–273). The *JE* provided exhortations but also access to information: there was a monthly gathering of "Literary and Scientific Intelligence" as well as similar collations of manual, practical, and agricultural information; more specialized materials could be provided when the curricular occasion arose. As methods of reading instruction altered to a "word" approach, with vocabulary selections introduced to students with comments on their meaning and derivation, instructors required some understanding of the history of the language and etymological principles. Among others, teachers were offered items on "Eastern Etymologies" (April 1850, p. 62), "The Sanskrit Element in the English Language" (April 1855, pp. 55–56), and the history of "The English as a Composite Language" (December 1855, p. 186). A detailed two-part "Papers in Practical Education" series in 1858 focussed on "Studies in English Etymology" and "Oriental [i.e., Indo-Germanic] Studies" (February 1858, pp. 20–22). Teachers could do much in this area through self-study: lacking a classical education, the schoolmaster could still reflect during reading on the "power and virtue" of the words employed (September 1855, pp. 135–136). Those uncertain of their ability to pronounce foreign words, or even the more difficult words in English, were directed to recommended pronunciation guides (July 1858, p. 107). Although the imperative for this knowledge seems to have been tied to the new reading pedagogy, the *JE* audience was witnessing some early moments in the development of a "national" approach to languages and letters, in which story and poetry were viewed as part of the distinctive (and evolving) expression of a people or a "race." This would be become a predominant method of literary analysis in the century's later half and be propounded in Canada with especial vigour.[18] While the new science of philology was wending its way into the pages of the *JE*, there is little of what we would now call "literary criticism," although such analysis would come to occupy an important place in journals and conferences for teachers by the 1880s. At mid-century, however, readers were warned against the scepticism that could result from overly minute analysis, and the elastic category of belles-lettres blurred genre distinctions and made genre-distinctive approaches unnecessary. However, teachers were given ample guidance in the conventions of book selection and book use.

In its opening years, the *JE* counterbalanced its exhortations to "improvement" with equally serious cautions. "Throughout the country, at this moment, thousands are consulting how to obtain and use books," wrote the Irish educator Thomas Osborne Davis. "It is possible that these sanguine young men, who are wildly pressing for knowledge, may grow weary or be misled – to their own and our country's injury" (May 1848, pp. 136–141). The *JE* republished the piece in an early issue, framing it as equally applicable to the Upper Canadian situation. Whereas Davis was concerned about the wasted effort of undirected or random study, other pieces sounded the alarm against "light" reading. The journal reprinted the Reverend Dr. A. Lillie's ineffectual lecture to the TMI on the "pernicious" effects of novel reading (February 1856, pp. 22–23). In a further reprinted lecture, Reverend S. S. Nelles of Victoria College asked the audience of the Cobourg Mechanics' Institute to distinguish between fiction (which could include, after all, *Pilgrim's Progress*) and "the novel" (June 1858, pp. 83–84). A fulmination against "Fictitious Reading" warned that exciting (i.e., sensational) fiction could be delusional and intoxicating in its effects and as addictive as tobacco, liquor, or even opiates (June 1850, p. 86). Positive literary models were provided both indirectly and directly in the pages of the *JE*. The columns of literary intelligence remarked the preparation or publication of worthy books and noted the activities of eminent authors such as Carlyle. Poetry published in the journal was sometimes by students but often by well-known, even popular, writers: Milton, Coleridge, Wordsworth, Longfellow, Felicia Hemans, and Mrs. Sigourney, for example. The majority of the poems were safe in subject matter and moral in tone. (There are an uncanny number about dead children, perhaps in support of the new mandate for teacherly tending of souls; several poems about dead teachers should be referred to the prevailing sentimentality of the day.) However, the education department's monumental effort to direct the reading of teachers, students, and – indeed – entire communities came with the establishment of the provincial textbook depository.[19] Reprinting an essay from a Pennsylvanian educational journal on the need to "Crowd Out the Vicious Literature," the *JE* remarked in a smug asterisked footnote that "This evil has been effectually guarded against in the Upper Canada School Libraries in the selection, by a competent and independent body, of books suitable for these libraries" (December 1859, p. 184).

The catalogue of the nearly thousand works initially approved for provincial school libraries consumed almost three full issues of the *JE* in 1853.[20] (Of special interest is the section headed "Teachers' Library," which included not only works on education, pedagogy, and school management but also sources on English grammar, history of the English language, synonyms, punctuation, and Richard Whateley's *Easy Lessons in Reasoning*. However, the teacher-autodidact now also would have access to a range of literary, scientific, and practical works.) The education department appears to have experienced some anxiety about this massive release of reading material. After the catalogue was concluded, a single issue of the *JE* (September 1853) reprinted two excerpts from previous issues stressing that reading should be profitable rather than "time-passing" – neither too specialized nor general and knitted to practical pursuits – as well as a new essay on "The Use of Knowledge" and a lengthy address on "The Connexion Between Science, Literature, and Religion." An item on Cicero's love of books was balanced by a reminder of the puritan Hannah More's jeremiad against fantasy that, in her formulation, "relaxes the mind, which wants fortifying; stirs the imagination, which wants quieting; irritates the passions, which wants [sic] calming." More specific guidance was provided by the same issue's featured article, a lengthy extract from the 1843 *Handbook for Readers and Students* by the Episcopalian bishop and educator, Alonzo Potter. Although considerably elaborated upon in the essay, Potter's twelve-point program could be encapsulated aphoristically, as follows:

1. Always have some useful and pleasant book ready to take up "odd ends" of time.
2. Be not alarmed because *so many* books are recommended.
3. Do not attempt to read *much* or *fast*.
4. Do not become so far enslaved by any system or course of study as to think it may not be altered. . . .
5. Beware, on the other hand, of frequent *changes* in your plan of study. . . .
6. Read always the *best* and most recent book on the subject on which you wish to investigate.
7. Study *subjects* rather than books [i.e., read comparatively].
8. Seek opportunities to *write* and *converse* on subjects about which you read.
9. Accustom yourself to refer whatever you read to the general head [i.e., principles] to which it belongs. . . .
10. Endeavour to find opportunities to *use* your knowledge and to apply it in practice.
11. Strive, by frequent reviews, to keep your knowledge *always at command*.
12. Dare to be ignorant of many things [i.e., to be selective].

Reading, Potter advised, should be simplified in terms of time expended, systematic in choice of materials and approach, and synthesized through comparative analysis and practical application. The *JE* editorialized that these principles should be taken on board as the "manner by which these [i.e., depository] books may be selected and used to the best advantage by readers generally" (September 1853, p. 138).

The excerpt from Potter was headed "Cautions and Counsels," a title equally applicable to the publication as a whole. The *Journal of Education* was a machine for the distribution of the directions of Egerton Ryerson and his associates. In a manner worthy of a Gilbert and Sullivan operetta, the journal (of which he was editor) published his writings, reprinted his public addresses, and publicized the policies and directives developed under his control. Although clearly the journal was intended to address – *interpellate* might be a better term – the teacher-autodidact among its many audiences, and whereas such teachers were evidently in need of support, we have no way of knowing how successful the journal was in effecting their transition from "literate" to "literary" or even if its readers agreed with the journal's programmatics for reading and self-study. (Ask any teacher today his or her opinion of ministerial communications.) That no letters to the editor were printed by the journal means we have little evidence linking this material to the aspirations and needs of the province's Alexander Edmisons. We do have, however, a concerted attempt to convey the conventions of book use and to knit isolated autodidacts into (what we would now call) a virtual community.

In our own day, the most striking similar endeavour is Oprah's Book Club™ (OBC), a sprawling system of televised book promotion and discussion, Web-based provision of supporting materials, and book and book-accessory marketing. Although praised for perpetuating a time-honoured rhetoric of reading inducement, OBC has attracted criticism for a perceived undemocratic or "top-down" structure (seen as contradictory to its ethos of "sharing")[21] for its commercialization or "commodification" of literature and for its "massification" of the reading public. As well, there were more specific critiques of the selection and presentation of books in the first phase (1996–2002) of the club's existence. Especially in the early years, the chosen books were contemporary, "popular," approachable in language level, and with a more discernable appeal to a female, ethnically plural audience demographic. Whereas some commentators deplored the middlebrow nature of early selections, a more trenchant criticism queried the personal or "bibliotherapeutic" orientation of the first phase, in which discussion centred on personal, emotive, or other experiential forms of response and on the books' themes of growth and empowerment. Coming from both the critical left and right, these observations were licensed to a degree by the different and, in some respects, incompatible meanings of the term *book club* today: on the one hand, denoting a literary discussion group, nonhierarchical in organization and even intimate; on the other hand, referring to a book selection and marketing agency, as in the "Book-of-the-Month Club" and similar organizations. (OBC falls between these definitions. Given the almost-exclusive role of Winfrey and her organization in the selection and framing of materials, it might be more accurately described as a twenty-first-century incarnation of a parlour school.[22]) One could refocus these criticisms by showing that OBC in its first incarnation was designed primarily to teach the conventions of book use: methods of personal (or guided) choice; access to reviews and contextualizing information; functions of reading for pleasure and personal transformation; basics of discussion; and protocols for using the "book" as a token of social interchange. The "critical" approach was largely biographical, with the author, like the reader, shown (e.g., through interviews) as standing in a relationship of lived experience to the text under discussion. It is interesting, however – to refer back to the theoretical contretemps over reader fidelity to author intentionality sketched in the introduction to this chapter – that "Oprah" readers were not expected to have a reduplicative understanding of the text. Divergent, approximate, or "personal" understandings received validation.

Little commentary has focused on the "new" or "all-new" OBC, reconvened in June 2003 after a hiatus of slightly more than a year and initially envisaged as "Travelling with the Classics." The "new" club has presented seventeen selections as of fall 2008, commencing with modern literary classics, but then concentrating on contemporary United States fiction, although one memoir and (most recently) a "new age" spiritual work have also been included. Of this number, three are novels by William Faulkner, which were studied as a trio in the summer of 2005, using the Web resources alone for this particular "Book Club" segment.[23] Although the initial intent was to present three to five books annually, the massive infrastructure of interviews, documentaries, travel footage, professorial video lectures, chapter summaries, study questions, reference materials, and discussion boards underpinning the launch of each selection may have made this unworkable. (A parallel system of book reviews and "picks" now recommends lighter reading and occasional selections.) The Web site was also redesigned to allow (in the press release's terms) an "interactive membership feature": readers may participate in discussion boards that are sometimes calibrated for different demographics (e.g., there are adults, teen, and family forums for Eli Wiesel's *Night*); or may post questions directly to experts (as with the "Q&A with the Professor" feature of the Faulkner unit); or use the Web site to start open or restricted on-line reading groups (although this feature is rarely used). Other interactive elements include quizzes and a "journaling" feature. Underpinning these more evident shifts – to challenging "classic" book selections and to greater interactivity – is a subtle but perhaps more fundamental alteration: from conventions of use to textual conventions, as they have been defined throughout this chapter.[24] Study questions increasingly elicit textual inference and interpretation, often through prompts to show what a setting "says," or a character's behaviour "tells," or what it can be assumed the author "means."[25] Generic and formal categorizations are highlighted with, for example, an elaborate lesson on "magic realism" predating study of Gabriel Garcia Márquez's *One Hundred Years of Solitude*. Readers who need to understand "stream of consciousness" for Faulkner's novels can click on a definition or follow a hands-on exercise in stream-of-consciousness writing. An ingenious sidebar titled "Shift Happens" gives readers "quick tips" to "navigate the shifts in time, and keep the story straight": they are alerted to changes from "normal" typefaces to *italics*, reminded that flashbacks and voiceovers are familiar techniques from television dramas, and that fans of the film *Pulp Fiction* will have a precedent for the play with time and perspective of *The Sound and the Fury*. These materials are user-friendly, display considerably pedagogic creativity, and have the imprimatur of noted scholarly experts who give lectures, post their "notes," and answer student queries.

Scholarship on the "Oprah's Book Club" phenomenon has focused on the first phase to date – in part because the reconvened club is more recent and has covered relatively few selections, in part because the "first phase" enjoyed a higher public profile both within the contours of the televised show and by publicly raising authors and books to stardom. Insofar as it seems more familiarly "academic," the "new" club's presuppositions may seem less worthy of comment to cultural analysts. However, there are questions to be raised both about the "Oprahfication of literacy" (Hall, 2003) and about the "Oprahfication of the literary." Although praising Winfrey as a "sponsor of literacy" (taking a term from Deborah Brandt, 1998), Hall has queried whether OBC's first-phase correlation of reading to "uplift" (and the setting of book discussion in "her" living or dining room) perpetuates a restrictive – indeed, nineteenth-century – correlation of female literacy to spirituality and domesticity. Furthermore, Hall notes of this contemporary propagator of "The Literacy Myth," Winfrey does not acknowledge the severe systemic barriers to literacy faced by African Americans (among others, it should be added), nor that the consequences of literacy acquisition may be negative (Hall, 2003, pp. 661–663).[26] (To continue Hall's list: how does the focus on reading as personal "uplift" prevent recognition of the more tenuous link between literacy and socioeconomic "uplift"?) Similar questions may be registered about the "Oprahfication" of textual conventional understanding. Has the emphasis on "classics" left behind a section of the would-be reading public whose transition from literate to literary was at a more tentative stage? Does the learning of conventions empower Oprah readers or further consolidate the interpretational authority of "Oprah" and the academic authorities who assist her? Does this knowledge open up new paths to readerly satisfaction or constrain interpretation? What are the consequences of severing reading from writing practice and the development of speaking skills, in the Web-based pedagogic context? Finally, does Oprah's Book Club represent an erosion of the mutual instruction format or the impetus to new – actual and virtual – forms of reading convention?

Notes

1 Like several other common terms (i.e., *voice* or *tone*), *convention* is rarely defined in terminology handbooks (the *Princeton Encyclopedia* entry is an exception). So, the understanding of *convention* is itself conventional.

2 Long's work is important in exposing the cultural investment in the "solitary reader" and in arguing for reading and interpretation as forms of "collective action."

3 Earlier, known as Upper Canada. The boundaries of Upper Canada, Canada West, and Ontario are not identical but all circumscribe the places mentioned in this text. The term *class* must be used conditionally for a society that was in many respects pre-industrial (despite the date) and in extreme social flux.

4 Although the theoretical frame for this chapter comes from the field of literary history, it is similar in aim to what Street termed "the new literacy studies" (Street, 2001, p. 431).

5 The "sounded" unit was not necessarily a syllable, however, despite the term: letters were voiced sequentially and cumulatively.

6 Although real estate and assets were relatively unaffected, literates held approximately 35 percent more total wealth than illiterates (Di Matteo, 1997, p. 915).

7 TMI reports, catalogues and broadsides referred to here are all from Toronto Mechanics' Institute fonds, F 2104 (MU 2020) Archives of Ontario; Toronto Mechanics' Institute fonds, L1, Baldwin Room, Toronto Reference Library; Board of Arts and Manufactures for Upper Canada fonds, F 1189 (MU 279), AO.

8 The TMI also resisted confining its art instruction to drafting or other practical modes. On its role in the promotion of the fine arts in Toronto at the same time, see Ramsay (1999).

9 The TMI took possession of its new building just as the government withdrew financial support from the institutes in 1859.

10 Although McHenry and Heath (2001) also treat the relationship between "The Literate and the Literary," they focus on the societies as bases for authorship rather than as educating societies.

11 As further evidence of Shadd's literary inclinations, she was invited to be one of eight corresponding editors for a proposed (although never published) journal titled the *Afric-American Literary Repository* (Rhodes, 1998, p. 120).

12 Rhodes reads "auxiliaries" as meaning women's auxiliaries and sees Shadd as assuming a gender-limited recruiting task. Although Shadd did also belong to the PUA's women's committee, it seems more plausible that "auxiliaries" refers to these affiliated circles.

13 With a few hiatuses, the paper published until September 1857. It apparently continued as a semimonthly in 1858 (no issues extant) and into 1859 (two issues extant). This survey stops with 1857 because it marks the end of Shadd's active involvement with the paper.

14 A survey of educational journals produced in Canada West shows twenty-nine such essays

in the 1850s; thirty-one in the 1860s; twenty in the 1870s; forty-four in the 1880s (twenty-five of which appeared in the *Educational Weekly* in 1886 alone); and ten in the 1890s, not counting smaller items of "literary intelligence." I am grateful to Dr. Daniela Janes for surveying these journals, in her capacity of research assistant on another project.

15 On changing literary tastes throughout the century, see Gerson (1989).

16 Male students in rural areas often attended school only in the agriculturally slow winter months and might still be attending as young adults, a practice especially prevalent in the 1850s and 1860s (Houston & Prentice, 1988, p. 216). Well into the century, teachers served stints in backwoods schools to save money for college or even Normal School.

17 This transitional period, during which a provincial teaching force was developed, is thoroughly delineated in Houston & Prentice (1988, pp. 157–186).

18 Daniel (later Sir Daniel) Wilson, a Scottish antiquarian and proto-archaeologist, became the first professor of English and History at University College, Toronto.

19 Books could be borrowed by family members when not needed by teachers or scholars. The school deposits became de facto public libraries for their communities.

20 There are 944 entries in the first catalogue but, in actuality, there are many more books because series and multivolume works are catalogued as one entry.

21 In fact, Oprah readers make very little use of the possibilities for on-line discussion that are offered and do not appear to form into subgroups or circles. This is in stark contrast to the many reading, reviewing, and fan sites on the Internet. However, McHenry (2002) argues that it is the main impetus to the formation of freestanding book clubs among African American women.

22 Indeed, currently on-line lectures, study guides, and other assistive materials are grouped under the heading "Oprah's Classroom."

23 The other selections (not mentioned in this chapter) are Pearl Buck, *The Good Earth*; Jeffrey Eugenides, *Middlesex*; Ken Follett, *The Pillars of the Earth*; Cormac McCarthy, *The Road*; Carson McCullers, *The Heart is a Lonely Hunter*; Gabriel García Márquez, *Love in the Time of Cholera*; Alan Paton, *Cry, The Beloved Country*; Sidney Poitier, *The Measure of a Man* (described as a "spiritual autobiography"); John Steinbeck, *East of Eden*; Eckhart Tolle, *A New Earth*; and Leo Tolstoy, *Anna Karenina*. The selection of Tolle's *A New Earth*, the study of which occupied the first nine months of 2008, signals a continuance of the preoccupations of the "first" Oprah's Book Club, although the succeeding selection in fall 2008, David Wroblewski, *The Story of Edgar Sawtelle*, marks a return to contemporary fiction.

24 The shift to more expressly "literary" materials is not as dramatic as it might appear. Toni Morrison, for example, was one of the first "Oprah" authors; Anne-Marie MacDonald, Rohinton Mistry, and Jonathan Franzen were chosen at the end of the first phase. Similarly, second-phase readers are still given guidance in elements of book use such as finding, starting, and convening a book club. Many questions continue to focus on feelings and personal response.

25 The present tense is maintained here because all materials are archived and there are continuing discussion groups for the ten retained selections. All following examples are from the Oprah Book Club Archive at *www.oprah.com* accessed 30 August 2006, http:boards.oprah.com/webX?14@173.ofEgc5 MbVII.o@efb8820.

26 Hall's (2003) example is the long-imprisoned Wilbert Rideau, whose outspoken writings may have delayed his release. Hall also notes in passing the use of books in coercive rehabilitative schemes.

References

Board of Arts and Manufactures, General Committee. *Minutes 1857–1868*. Holograph minute book. F 1189, AO.

Brandt, D. (1998). Sponsors of literacy. CCC: *College Composition and Communication*, 49, 165–185.

Burns, Reverend Dr. Robert. (1851). Extract from The dawn of English literature. *Journal of Education of Upper Canada*, 186–187.

Curtis, B. (1988). *Building the educational state: Canada West, 1836–1871*. Lewes, UK, and Philadelphia: The Falmer Press; London, Ontario: The Althouse Press.

Cushman, E., Kintgen. E. R., Kroll, B. M., & Rose. M. (2001). (Eds.) *Literacy: A critical sourcebook*. Boston: Bedford/St. Martin's Press.

Di Matteo, L. (1997). The determinants of wealth and asset holding in nineteenth-century Canada: Evidence from data. *The Journal of Economic History*, 57 (4), 907–934.

Edmison, A. B. (December 1856 – November 1858). Diary. MS 37, Archives of Ontario.

Fish, S. (1980). *Is there a text in this class: The authority of interpretive communities*. Cambridge, MA: Harvard University Press.

Gerson, C. (1989). *A purer taste: The writing and reading of fiction in English in nineteenth-century Canada*. Toronto: University of Toronto Press.

Gilmore, W. J. (1989). *Reading becomes a necessity of life: Material and cultural life in rural New England*, 1780–1835. Knoxville: University of Tennessee Press.

Graff, H. J. (1973). Literacy and social structure in Elgin County, Canada West, 1861. *Histoire Sociale/Social History*, 6 (11), 25–48.

Graff, H. J. (1979). *The literacy myth: Literacy and social structure in the nineteenth-century city*. New York: Academic Press.

Hall, R. M. (2003). The "Oprahfication" of literacy: Reading "Oprah's Book Club." *College English*, 65 (6), 646–667.

Heath, S. B. (2001). Protean shapes in literary events: Ever-shifting oral and literate traditions. In Ellen Cushman et al. (Eds.), *Literacy: A Critical Sourcebook* (pp. 443–466). Boston and New York: Bedford/St. Martin's Press.

Houston, S., & Prentice, A. (1988). *Schooling and scholars in nineteenth-century Ontario*. Toronto: University of Toronto Press.

Jackson, H. (2001). *Marginalia: Readers writing in books*. New Haven, CT: Yale University Press.

Long, E. (1992). Textual interpretation as collective action. In J. Boyarin (Ed.), *The ethnography of reading* (pp. 180–211). Berkeley and Los Angeles: University of California Press.

Mays, H. J., & Manzl, H. F. (1974). Literacy and social structure in 19th-century Ontario: An exercise in historical methodology. *Histoire Sociale/Social History*, 8 (14), 331–345.

McHenry, E. (2002). *Forgotten readers: Recovering the lost history of African American literary societies*. Durham and London: Duke University Press.

McHenry, E., & Heath, S. B. (2001). The literate and the literary: African-Americans as writers and readers: 1830-1940. In E. Cushman, E. R. Kintgen, B.M. Kroll, & M. Rose (Eds.), *Literacy: A critical sourcebook* (pp. 261–274). Boston, MA: Bedford/St. Martin's Pess.

McLaren, K. (2004). "We had no desire to be set apart": Forced segregation of black students in Canada West public schools and myths of British egalitarianism. *Histoire Sociale/Social History*, 37 (73), 27–50.

McNairn, J. (2000). *The capacity to judge: Public opinion and deliberative democracy in Upper Canada*, 1791–1854. Toronto: University of Toronto Press.

Moodie, J. D., & Moodie, S. (1847). To the public. *Victoria Magazine*, 1 (1), 1–2.

Murray, H. (2002). *Come, bright improvement! The literary societies of nineteenth-century Ontario*. Toronto: University of Toronto Press.

Preminger, A. (Ed.) (1974). Convention. In *Princeton Encyclopedia of Poetry and Poetics* (Enlarged ed.) (pp. 152–153). Princeton, NJ: Princeton University Press.

Prentice, A. (1977). *The school promoters: Education and social class in mid-nineteenth-century Upper Canada*. Toronto: McClelland and Stewart.

Provincial Freeman, *The*. (1854–1857). Windsor, Canada West.

Radway, J. (1984). *Reading the romance: Women, patriarchy and popular literature*. Chapel Hill: University of North Carolina Press.

Ramsay, E. L. (1999). Art and industrial society: The role of the Toronto Mechanics' Institute in the promotion of art, 1831–1883. *Labour/Le Travail*, 43, 71–103.

Rhodes, J. (1998). *Mary Ann Shadd Cary*: The Black Press *and protest in the nineteenth century*. Bloomington and Indianapolis: Indiana University Press.

Stock, B. (1983). *The implications of literacy: Written language and models of interpretation in the Eleventh and Twelfth Century*. Princeton NJ: Princeton University Press.

Street, B. (2001). The new literacy studies. In E. Cushman, E. R. Kintgen, B.M. Kroll, & M. Rose (Eds.), *Literacy: A critical sourcebook* (pp. 430–442). Boston, MA: Bedford/St. Martin's Press.

Tompkins, J. P. (1985). *Sensational designs: The cultural work of American fiction, 1790–1860*. London and New York: Oxford University Press.

Toronto Mechanics' Institute [TMI]. (1855). *Report of the General Committee of the Toronto Mechanics' Institute for the year ending May 7th, 1855*. Toronto: Thompson & Co.

TMI. (1858). *Catalogue of books in the library*. Toronto: Rowsell & Ellis, printers.

TMI. (1860). *Report of the General Committee of the Toronto Mechanics' Institute for the year ending May 7th, 1860*. Toronto: Thomas Cuttell.

TMI. (1862). *The Toronto Mechanics' Institute: To the citizens of Toronto*. Broadside. n.p., F 2101, AO.

TMI. (1865). *Report of the General Committee of the Toronto Mechanics' Institute for the year ending May 8th, 1865*. Toronto: Thomas Cuttell.

TMI. (1866). Winter evening classes. Broadside. n.p. F. 2101, AO.

Wilberforce Lyceum Educating Society [Ont.]. (1850). *Constitution and by laws of the Wilberforce Lyceum Educating Society for moral and mental improvement, Cannonsburg township of Colchester, province of Canada, British North America*. CIHM/ICMH Microfiche series, no. 38073. [Amherstburg, Ont.?: s.n.].

CHAPTER 12

Literacy, Reading, and Concepts of the Self

Carolyn Steedman

Making her way from office to library, from library to café, she thought that her exterior self was instructing her interior self, much like someone closing his eyes and mimicking sleep in order to persuade sleep to come.

Ann Tyler, Ladder of Years, 1995, p. 138

In *Ladder of Years,* Delia Grinstead has walked out of her comfortable, maddening, Baltimore doctor's-wife life and made a new life and a new self in Bay Borough (which has no bay, is not by the sea, and is just the place she was set down from her ride). She reads a lot in this little town, as she did as mother and wife: Mills and Boon (gothics) for the main part, preferring the ones with Heathcliffian heroes and heroines who know (and know how to wear) a good negligée when they find one. For the main part, she reads in bed, in the little white boarding-house room that is the setting for her making of a new self. Tyler expects us to understand every nuance of this characterisation, and an entire history of the relationship among the written (and printed) word, reading, and the formation of new, differentiated, self-conscious, interiorised selves. Which – all of us being competent readers of Western modernity – we do understand, very well indeed. We may never have heard, for example, about the considerable erotics of reading and writing established for seventeenth- and eighteenth-century women by modern feminist and literary historians, but we know about it nevertheless; we take for granted that there is and has been a connection between literacy practices and the construction of self in ordinary, everyday lives.[1] We may know all of this so well that we fail to notice how Tyler questions the connection between subjectivity and reading; has Delia ponder a self that is made elsewhere, outside the texts that inscribe her; and suggests that if she does have an interiorised, differentiated, self-fashioned, reflexive self, it may not only come from the gothics and the nights of reading them but also from what she does, the places she goes, the (new) life she lives.

One probably would not learn to question the relationship between reading and self-construction in this way from the history of literacy and literacy practices in the West. Indeed, history-writing itself may have brought the connection between literacy and interiority into being: any historian of the Early Modern and Modern periods in Europe and the Americas works with the heavy freight of a historiography that charts the rise of individualism and individuality in the West. An insistent 'background' stresses the role of literacy in the making of modern social, economic and political persons. From two ends of the twentieth century, two examples: in Weber's *The Protestant Ethic and the Spirit of Capitalism* (1904–1905), spiritual journals, confessional tales, Bunyan's first-person narratives and a whole range of literary texts of the seventeenth and eighteenth centuries are used to chart a relationship between Protestant selfhood and early capitalist development.[2] Then, in a major publishing enterprise of the 1980s, *The History of Private Life*, the volume dealing with the seventeenth and eighteenth centuries elaborates and *illustrates* the thesis in charming and compelling detail so that readers can *see* the things and feelings that proliferate around reading and writing (novels, pens, writing manuals, chairs for reading and *peignoirs* to wear whilst sitting in them, libraries, closets; privacy, intimacy, romantic love...) as the modern subject makes himself or herself. Such techniques of feeling, connected to the practices of reading and writing, were celebrated in Brewer's *Pleasures of the Imagination*, in which the private writing of men and women of the better sort in the English eighteenth century is shown to underpin a deeply pleasurable consciousness of an individual mind, inner thoughts and personal identity.[3] Many of these questions are now pursued in what has become a subdiscipline: the 'history of the book'.[4]

Work on autobiography in the 1980s and 1990s strengthened the assumption of connection between self-writing and self-construction. Feminist literary theorists and critics scrutinised the European autobiographical canon and found it entirely made up of masculine self-writing. The problem was named as the *writing* of normative (and Western) masculinity, reinforcing the connection between written language and the aetiology of the self.[5] A female subject, also self-fashioning, individuated, possessed of an interiority and made in relationship to the written word, was determinedly put in place.[6] At the same time, a vast and proliferating body of postcolonial criticism directed attention away from the Subject of Europe, towards the subaltern and marginalised subjects of the contact zones.[7] The autobiographical canon has been vastly extended and the autobiographical *theory* derived from it is now more likely to be fashioned out of women's writing than that of men.[8]

Charges of elitism against autobiographical scholarship shifted attention away from the chronicles of the privileged to the annals of the labouring poor. There are many more writings of women and of plebeian men *and* women from the past in print and in circulation than there were twenty years ago. Vincent's 2000 account of reading and writing in modern Europe is structured by extraordinarily moving memoires of eighteenth- and nineteenth-century working men (they are exclusively men) coming to literacy.[9] However, working-class writing of whatever sort is seen as the historian's territory – as not belonging to 'literature' or to the literary scholar. When Fox was working on twentieth-century worker-writers, she kept encountering people who assumed that if this were her topic, she *must be* a historian, working on texts that belong to some realm of 'fact' or 'reality' rather than to 'fiction' or 'literature'.[10] Moreover, working-class writing has not been used to construct autobiographical theory, as has women's writing.

Social historians have investigated the literacy experiences of humble seventeenth-century readers and the meaning of reading and writing in eighteenth- and nineteenth-century working lives. This perspective has much to do with the post-Thompsonian mission of the discipline, which is not only to rescue the marginalised and poor from the condescension of history-writing itself but also to propose that a writer with the most minimal skills – telling the story of his (very rarely her) coming with astonishment and intelligence to the world of the book – might have had as rich, as sophisticated a sense of an interior self as any member of a social elite.[11] But, then, working people's first experiences with texts and pens are more open to the historian's scrutiny than those of the privileged. Evidence may be rare but, because plebeian literacy learning was often undertaken in adulthood or was a childhood experience so unusual and striking that it was the first memory written by an adult autobiographer, the first steps of the poorer sort have left traces in a way that the taken-for-granted education of privileged children has not.[12]

In the 1990s, questions about self-fashioning in the past came to be posed via the idea of narrative rather than the idea of literacy. In *Modernity and Self-Identity*, the sociologist, Anthony Giddens, describes a three-hundred-year development in the West, by which personhood and self-identity have come to be understood as 'the self... reflexively understood by the person in terms of his or her biography'. 'Autobiography', he says, is not so much a form of writing or a literary genre but rather a mode of cognition. He described a general 'autobiographical thinking'; in this 'broad sense of an interpretive self-history produced by the individual concerned, [autobiography] whether written down or not... is actually the core of self-identity in modern life'.[13] Historians were grateful for the concept of narrative (even though we may not have acquired it directly from Giddens). There is an extreme difficulty in finding evidence of the effects of reading and writing on hearts, minds and societies in the past, but you certainly can find narrative. The court records, the life stories taken down by charitable organisations, magistrates' clerks, poor law and prison officials, or schematically recorded on preprinted forms for recruits to the army and navy – these are the bread and butter of social history research; they crowd the stacks of county record offices and the National Archives.

In the English eighteenth-century, the largest category of 'self-narration' or 'autobiographical activity' was not written down by the subject concerned and was not voluntarily constructed. Rather, it was demanded of the poorer sort by the administrative state.[14] Under seventeenth-century legislation, magistrates were required to inquire into the origins of those who applied for poor relief. Determining place of settlement – that is, the parish responsible for applicants – involved telling a life story and having it recorded. In answer to a series of legally prescribed questions (What is your name? What was your father?), countless men and women told where they were born, when they were put to work, where they had worked, and, crucially, for how long they had worked in any one place, for working consistently in one parish and receiving wages for a calendar year carried one of the most important entitlements to welfare rights. A century of this kind of self-narration (transcribed by a justice's clerk from the answers to the magistrates' questions) preceded Eleanore Perkins's examination in the parish of Bedworth, Warwickshire, in the summer of 1780.[15] She told the justices that she was about forty years old, had been born in the parish of Withybrooke, and

> *... that when she arrived at a proper age she went to service... [was] hired in several places: that about fourteen years ago she hired herself for a year to Mrs Chambers of ye Parish of St Trinity in the City of Coventry wch term she served & received her full wages: that without any fresh hiring she continued with ysaid Mrs Chambers in said Parish two years longer & received ye same Wages as for ye first year: that leaving Mrs Chambers she went to Oakham in the County of Rutland & lived a servant with John Turner of said Parish Innkeeper...* [16]

Eleanore Perkins did not sign this document; she made her mark. Social histories of literacy and education, of economic development, and of capitalism itself have been built on the little cross that she and others like her inscribed.[17] Signing has been taken as an indicator of the ability to both process and produce writing (particularly by men signing marriage registers); literacy rates for the seventeenth and eighteenth centuries have been calculated in this way. We have assumed it was not very likely that someone like Eleanore Perkins had been taught to write but that probably she could read. If an eighteenth-century girl of the poorer sort received any kind of schooling, it usually stopped short of writing because teaching it was intimately tied to the teaching of Latin, the province of boys. Instruction in writing usually started when a child was about eight years old and could read well enough to cope with the Bible and other simple literature of the faith; eight was also the time when many children of the labouring poor were set to work and schooling stopped. Perhaps we are more aware now of how people in the past understood writing (i.e., what kind of skill and activity it was; what it was *for*), its value carefully calculated by eighteenth-century parents. Some of them decided, perhaps, that the inscription of a name was the only skill with a pen necessary for launching a child into modern commercial society; perhaps a bridegroom signing a marriage register, or a farmer a bill of sale, means nothing much at all.[18]

But Eleanore Perkins did not need to write, nor write her name to (be forced to) survey her life from a fixed standpoint, tell it in chronological sequence, give an account of what it was that brought her to this place, this circumstance now, telling the familiar tale for the justice's clerk to transcribe.[19] Apart from not being written down by the person who lived the life, her brief narrative fulfills the criteria for autobiographical narration; and yet, it was an enforced narrative. As an involuntary narration, was it capable of providing the move from outside to within – the development of an interiorised self? If the historically discernable processes of identity formation can be separated from the question of reading and writing, then how are we to understand the role of literacy and its acquisition in individual lives and the making of individuated selves? We should notice that despite all the historical work surveyed herein, it is possible to write histories of the self without any reference to the practices of reading and writing. Seigal's monumental *Idea of the Self* (2005) tells its story by means of those who have *thought* about self-consciousness and self-identity in Europe – from Locke to Derrida, to scholars who did indeed write about 'the self' and 'le moi' – but not about the literacy practices that underpin most social histories of the individuated self.[20] In such history of ideas (or intellectual history), 'writing' and 'reading' are metaphors for a self; they are ways of describing, philosophising, and thinking about a subjectivity in the past and have very little to do with the social and psychological consequences of reading a prayer on a psalter or picking up a pen.[21] At the very least, we have to entertain the notion that interiorised selves may have been constructed in social worlds that contained texts but which were not congruent with texts. Indeed, the traffic may have run the other way: consciousness of who and what you are (i.e., how made and how fashioned as an individual) may have shaped both acquisition of the written word and all the uses made of it in a lifetime. The remainder of this chapter explores this proposition in relation to one late eighteenth-century life.

The Reverend John Murgatroyd (1719–1806) of Slaithwaite near Huddersfield is of interest because of his relationship with his household servant (Phoebe Beatson, born c.1766), whose life he changed in dramatic and unexpected ways.[22] These lives and this relationship were lived out in the time and place of 'the making of the English working class', the industrialising West Riding of Yorkshire between about 1780 and 1820.[23] Therefore, it has been possible to challenge a received history of state and class formation in England by considering how these historical actors (i.e., a Church of England clergyman, an unwed mother in her late thirties, a wool comber who resolutely refused to marry the mother of his bastard child) were able to buck so many of the trends that their historians have seen them – and people like them – enacting. And the God they all believed in also bucked trends, seemingly allowing them all to think, feel and act in ways contrary to His reputation for underpinning strict social morality and obeisance to the laws of church and state.[24]

About half of the dairies Murgatroyd kept between 1781 and 1806 survive (one for roughly every other year), as does one of his commonplace books and a long essay (folded and handstitched) on the 'Qualifications of a Minister of Christ'. There is also 'A Book of Records' (nine hundred pages long, consisting of bound loose sheets and separate paper-covered notebooks dating back to the 1730s); 'A Cornucopia; or collection of weighty transcripts transcrib'd out of the scarcest, most necessary, & best chosen books &c' (what its compiler said it was and nearly as long as the first); and 'Authors Useful to be Read at School' (smaller and indeed useful, put together in the 1790s but with only two pages actually devoted to its title).[25] All account books are missing from his archive; they might well obviate much of Murgatroyd's silence on his economic, commercial and political context. However, as it is, what we are left with is the writing of a man who considered a diary to be for the purposes of recording the diurnal (e.g., the state of play with the builders on the new house built for his retirement, company at dinner and the contents of the kitchen garden, his maidservant's work for a local spinning master, a new recipe for cooking tainted meat) and his relationship with his God.

Murgatroyd's origins had been as humble as those of the young woman servant who lived in his household for so long: his father had been a Halifax blacksmith.[26] He thought his own rise and progress through the world a sign of God's good grace. He often contemplated his life's story and may have seen his career resonate with that of his maidservant, wondering at the strange conjunction of their courses, in each coming to Slaithwaite to start their life's labour at exactly the same age of not quite nineteen: 'Nota bene itemus Phebe Beatson came to be my servant on 29th May 1785 – 17 years since', he wrote in May 1802. 'I began my 65th year as She began her 18th year'.[27] In his early teens, he had been sent to grammar school to study 'the Greek Testament, Homer, Juvenal and Persius', said his first referee in trying to get him a position with a local clergyman. He was 'a sedate, thinking and promising boy . . . with tolerable judgement . . . '.[28] This was a way into the Church, without benefit of powerful patrons and conventional education; and whilst this attempt failed, the next year, Murgatroyd was appointed schoolmaster at Slaithwaite, a different kind of first rung on the Anglican career ladder. This was a momentous event in his life, to be remembered every year he lived it. In 1786, he noted that 'This afternoon I resign'd Slaithwaite School . . . I have been Master from May 29th 1738 – near 48 years' . . . 'This afternoon / 56 years ago / I came . . . to Slaithwaite to teach School – a noble Undertaking for a person, not quite 19 . . . '.[29] The first day of a new life remained quite clear across the years, always written as a vignette of an ever-present moment of potential. In May 1802, eighty-three years old, after a heavy day of tramping across the valley as the peripatetic minister he became in retirement, he reminded himself, 'Nota bene – May ye 30th 1738 is ye 1st Day of teaching at Slaithwaite ~ . . . [the chapel warden] took down for ye School a Large Elbow Chair & chair'd me by ye window . . . I waited there for Scholars, who came in plenty I look'd on 'em very lovingly & began very chearfully to teach 'em – my willingness was great willingness . . . '. Moreover, 'it was beg.ing to get money, instead of Paying – it was helping my Parents – repaying 'em for Education'.[30] Long before twentieth-century educational and social history provided the category, John Murgatroyd was a Scholarship Boy.[31]

This career did not follow the sociological norms of eighteenth-century Anglicanism, but it was a life well ordered, well financed, and well lived. At his death, John Murgatroyd had nearly £1,000 to leave behind.[32] And Phoebe Beatson did very well, too, out of a life she had shared for such a long time. To do nicely in the end, to reap the rewards of having lived well, was a fitting end to many of the plots, divine and secular, by which this young woman and this old man might interpret their own and each other's life. Murgatroyd bequeathed to his 'faithful Servant Phebe Beatson, Three Hundred pounds... One Hundred & Fifty Pounds of the said Sum for her own use, the other Hundred & Fifty for her child Elizabeths use...', a good deal of furniture, kitchen equipment, and bedding. The house and his books and papers were left to one of his nieces. The globe in the parlour was for the little illegitimate girl, by this time nearly four years old.[33]

He had made notes on the topic of 'Rising in Life' in 1789, emphasising that 'a private independt Station, even when call'd Obscurity, is far more eligible yn. ye most conspicuous Condition of Honour, Emolumnt. & Office, recd as Wages, Vice or Prostitution'.[34] To the modern eye, these reflections seem to miss the point of Murgatroyd's social journey in the way that his nineteenth-century historians also appear to wilfully miscast it. James Horsfall, FRS, eminent scientist and former pupil of Slaithwaite Free School (d.1785), was made much of when they wrote of Murgatroyd's excellencies as a teacher. Horsfall was son of the Slaithwaite blacksmith, and this was one of the points of telling the story of his spectacular social and intellectual rise, but nobody drew the connection between the smithy fathers of teacher and pupil.[35]

The conclusion of the literature surveyed at the beginning of this chapter is that by the late eighteenth century, a life – the idea of a life – was infinitely and inextricably bound up with *having a life story*. To tell, to write, to live a life was an act made by the word; or, to put it another way, the life-narrative, verbal or written, was the dominant (by now, possibly the only) way of imagining or figuring one. A life was not now, as it may possibly once have been, a given thing, a moment in the Deity's mind, the fragment of an eternal stasis but rather, a plot, a sequence: something with a beginning, a story, and an end. Given that we have some understanding of how John Murgatroyd (and Phoebe Beatson, and all their neighbours) may have imagined and understood their own life and represented it to others, what we are most in need of are the interpretive devices for unlocking the ideational and self-reflexive practices of West Yorkshire, 1780–1810, expressed for the main part – for this is the source we have – in John Murgatroyd's writing. There are sixty years' worth of his contemplations, his effusions, the daily recording that he had 'Awaked with God' (always immediately followed by a weather report, such as 'hrd Frost still & fine cold Day')[36]; there is the immense historical detail of a day's doing lost in the effacatory 'my ordinary concerns', the way in which each Sunday he noted that his household had been 'all graciously preserved'. On the face of it, Murgatroyd looks like the majority of Anglican clergy for whom 'the Bible and John Locke had explained the essentials'; whose 'ingrained rationalist assumptions about human nature and social harmony' contributed to the generosity and sympathy with which he viewed what was, for him, an essentially benevolent world.[37] Beliefs like these, in God's rule of order and harmony in a social world that mirrored the divine, have been shown at work in the writings of many clergyman contemporaries of Murgatroyd.[38] However, unlike Parson Woodforde or the Reverend Coles, Murgatroyd wrote – copiously and regularly – about his God and about Anglican theology. Moreover, he found Anglican Protestantism a continual source of intellectual and philosophical interest, a body of ideas and propositions that provided him with food for thought until the very end of his days. He always remained an eager and willing pupil, forever the young man of humble origins and impressive education seeking an increasingly unusual entry to a career in the Church. He was never a beneficed priest; he wasn't quite a gent, in an increasingly gentlemanly Church. His ardour, in understanding and appropriating the theology and social thought of an institution that had denied him a full place within it, was perhaps an expression of being outside a system and a demonstration of his fitness to occupy a position actually denied him. Had he gained a living and actually embodied the tenets he debated with himself and his friends and neighbours for more than sixty years, he may well have devoted more space to his dinner than his God, as did more famous clergymen writers; he may then have written less.

His practice of writing was learned from very old models. He had probably been introduced to it in his own youth and later used it when teaching in the Slaithwaite Free School. 'Commonplacing' had been devised for schoolboys' study of pagan texts. You ruled lines and columns on the pages of a blank notebook, and under different headings you noted the grammatical structures of the Latin tongue and collected your *sententia*, proverbs, maxims and striking passages from the histories, poetry and orations that were more advanced teaching material.[39] It was a method of reading and note-taking designed to enhance memory; it allowed comparisons between different forms of language and served as a storehouse of sentences and formularies for those advanced pupils who went on to compose their own Latin texts. The title of Murgatroyd's 'Ask, Read, Retain, Teach' notebook indicates its pedagogic origins. However, commonplacing was extravagant in its use of the blank page: its columns and headers (means to cross referencing) used up a lot of expensive paper. By way of contrast, Murgatroyd's notebooks are the muddle of a writer trying to save space and money. He did what most users of a notebook do: he transliterated, or copied verbatim, passages from works that had particularly struck him. Sometimes he worked up what he had read into something that had the emphatic form of an essay, with a relatively sustained argument that reached a conclusion. His working out of extended discourses (that may have ended up as sermons) in his 'Ask' notebook often had this form.[40] As many notebook-keepers find themselves doing, he used books that were entitled for one purpose for a quite different one, writing recipes between reflections on chastity and good neighbourliness. His headings are mostly no guide to what followed. A title suggested a topic that he did indeed start to discourse upon but that then (in the space of a few minutes or some days) became a listed compilation from his reading. The passage headed 'Ministers' is typical (possibly written in 1790, if page order is anything to go by, or perhaps in 1788, if the reference to Slaithwaite chapel is current):

> *It's good to keep up Friendship with Families, in whch Relig. Prevails. Let Us nevr. look disdainfully on those below Us, as we know not, how soon we may need 'em. – By ye wise disposal of Providence, one Country has need of anothr, & is benefited by anothr for mutual Correspondence & dependence, to ye Glory of God, our common Parent – strengthen Friendship wth ye honest & fair, lest new Friends prove not so firm & kind as old ones – Great persons sho'd consider their Servants must rest as well as they -. . . Wn a village becomes more numerous ye place of meet.g needs Enlargement. . . .* [41]

Devised for the purposes of secular education, the note-taking method of reading (and listening, to sermons and other forms of public discourse) had been appropriated for religious purposes during the long sixteenth century. 'For Protestant Christians, the school notebook proved a useful aid to worship', notes Masuch, and he gives many examples of its being used for remembering sermons, contemplating the scriptures, and pondering the providential or merely strange experiences recorded.[42] It is clear that the practice of reading over these entries, at the end of a day or a week, was also deeply imbued in writers, so much so that some surviving notebooks have been thumbed over to the point of disintegration. More written reflection might follow on these perusals, a further stage in the devotional technology that commonplacing provided. Often, these collections of odd notes and observations were smoothed into coherent texts by editors, either by family members shortly after the writer's death or much later by academic compilers and commentators. They gave us – either in the seventeenth or the twenty-first century – the form and shape of something with which we are much more familiar: the published diary. These 'diaries' have often been read on the assumption that they are autobiographical in the modern sense, that there is an individual life expressed in the text – self-reflexive and authoring itself.[43] But once you go back to the original writing, says Masuch, you will find something very much like Murgatroyd's 'Ask' notebook: a heterogeneous and, to the modern eye, disorganised collection of notes, observations, prayers, poetry, and instructions for making carrot throat gargle.

When Murgatroyd made notes on what he had read, he used forms of abbreviation and contraction that he did not employ when he was actually composing in writing. (More obviously, he often recorded the title of the work he was noting.) This way of proceeding was typical of the 'Cornucopia', put together in the 1740s. Here, when he writes out of his own resources – or creatively – he uses the extended or full form of most key words (he nearly always contracted prepositions, articles and conjunctions, as his diary writing shows). The much later 'Ask' notebook does contain some unreferenced transcription from published texts; but even when he goes back to the 'Cornucopia' or his 'Book of Records' (compiled fifty years before, and catalogued as part of the library that sat on his parlour shelves), he used extended writing and incorporated the much earlier notes on John Locke, the West Riding *philosophe* Thomas Nettleton (to be discussed herein), *Gil Blas* and *Tom Jones* into his own thinking-in-writing. Extended word form is, then, a fairly reliable marker of originality of composition in his case. There is here the extreme good fortune of possessing so very much of a lifetime's writing as to give a material shape to postmodernist assertions about the realm of intertextuality: that there is nothing ever thought anew, that every written word is the echo and remaking of some other word.[44] This kind of intertextuality operated between the notebooks as well, for Murgatroyd often copied out from earlier volumes into new, a necessary labour that saves on memory and searching for anyone who uses the commonplace method.

Murgatroyd's commonplace books were also a device for Christian devotion, kept a century or so after the practice was developed among the Protestant 'saints' of seventeenth-century England. His diary (and this was a diary in the strictest meaning of the term, for there were daily entries) was also a devotional device, although it seems a much more conventionally autobiographical production to the modern eye. It notes the writer's daily doings with God, as well as describing tea drunk and dinner taken and conversation with fascinating ladies from Manchester who lent him newspapers and journals. It chronicled the building of his new house in very great detail of stone-cutting and timber-sawing until, in despair at the slowness of the builders ('Wt Josh Pogson & his Men are doing, I do not know'), he banished them from the diurnal into another notebook all of their own.[45] The diary is no seamless narrative account of spiritual growth, as we once used to think that earlier, Puritan self-writing might have been; there can be no end-stop to the fully fashioned autonomous self because, after all, this is a diary – but, more profoundly, because Murgatroyd understood that self-effacement rather than self-reflection before his God was what was required.[46]

Even so, to suggest a kind of self-effacement in the diary and the early notebooks is probably to go about things in the wrong way. Murgatroyd did not have, was not conscious of, the kind of self that historians and philosophers might ascribe to him two hundred years on. He did not write nor read to find a self affirmed. For example, he acquired and made extensive notes on Le Sage's *Gil Blas* in the early 1750s.[47] It is truly surprising to the modern historical eye to see what he did with this very long narrative, in which the amiable young hero – from a humble background – moves through social space and varieties of community in a fictionalised Spain (which is actually France but censored as setting under the Ancien Regime) never knowing himself, yet being made plain to the reader through the ways in which he is tricked, duped, liked and made friends with by a remarkably wide range of people. The modern reader expects the identification of a young man from humble circumstances with a literary similar; two centuries of novel-reading have taught us that that is what novels are *for*. However, there is not one moment of textual identification in Murgatroyd's note-taking. Rather, he commonplaces *Gil Blas*, pleased when he can record a maxim from Cicero via its pages ('"Cicero says, Ne'er be so much defeated as to forget you are a Man"'); he lists useful observations, such as '"In these Days all Virtue appears Hypocrisy to young people",' and '"Virtue its:'s too diffict. to be acquir'd, so we're satifd. wth possessing ye appearance of virtue".' As with his reading of *Tom Jones* (1747), the passages he commonplaced were preponderantly to do with love, passion, and ways of women (loose women, in the notes from Le Sage). In the 1740s and 1750s, he was lonely and longing for love. But, as novels, *Gil Blas* and *Tom Jones* were to be treated as any other text: as a source of information about God's creation, not a point of identification for an individuated self.

It was held that the first duty of a Protestant church was to instruct the laity, and Murgatroyd fulfilled this duty through school-teaching and sermonising. Education – of children in parochial schools rehearsing the Catechism or gathered elsewhere to learn their responses, or of adults in a Sunday congregation attending to a sermon – this was what, in its own estimation, marked the Church of England off from the Roman Catholic Church's expectation of unquestioning, superstitious faith in the laity.[48] Slaithwaite Free School was a parochial charity school, first endowed in 1721. Most endowed schools were elementary, common parish schools, established for instruction in reading and writing. Slaithwaite Free School was set up like this; however, in practice under Murgatroyd's regime, the curriculum was much more like that of the grammar school that he himself had attended.[49] It was meant to cater to ten children, boys and girls, 'the poorest objects and chosen out of the townships of Sleigthwaite and Lingards'. The master was to catechise the children once a week in school and make sure that they attended divine service. Boys, when they 'could read competently well', were to be taught to write a fair, legible hand, and be grounded in an arithmetic 'sufficient to qualify them for common apprentices'. Girls were only to be taught to read well and to be catechised, 'except the master has a wife, who can teach them to knit and sew'. The master should be a member of the Church of England, 'of a sober life and conversation, and one who frequents the Holy Communion'. He was required to have 'a good genius for teaching youth to read', possess a fair writing hand, and to understand basic arithmetic.[50]

John Murgatroyd was greatly overqualified for the position and does not appear to have followed the outlines of this elementary curriculum during his mastership of the school. The advertisement for his replacement placed in the *Leeds Mercury* in 1786 mentioned the ability to teach Latin, Greek, other languages, and writing, arithmetic, and bookkeeping, as qualifications.[51] 'Some educated clergymen found it difficult to identify wholeheartedly with the practices and curriculum of a school which taught reading and writing accounts, when their own learning had comprised Latin and Greek'; but this was not a constraint felt by Murgatroyd, nor does he appear to have resented teaching his socially undistinguished scholars.[52] He taught the classics to generations of them during his term of office.[53] His inventory of 'School Books', dated October 1792, counted fifty-seven volumes, of which thirty were works of Latin or Greek, in the original and in translation, including grammars, dictionaries and commentaries.[54] Some of these were very old works that would have been familiar to a seventeenth-century – or, indeed, a sixteenth-century – schoolmaster (some of them were in editions so old that he must have inherited them from friends and relatives in order to undertake his own instruction in the 1720s). He had a 1695 edition of Lily's *Grammar*, originally designated for use in schools during Elizabeth's reign, and an even older *Methodi Practiae*, from 1660.[55] He possessed Hoole's *Accidence* (one of the books he called 'useful') from 1697, a work which suggests a very old teaching method as well, in which the grammatical principles of Latin were learned 'without book', in the question and answer form of the catechism:

> Qust: How many Parts of Speech be there?
> Answ: Eight . . .
> Q: What is the Indicative Mood Present tense of Edo?
> A: Sing. Edo. I eat'.[56]

After learning these rules, the student was meant to proceed to simple texts – epigrams, fables, dialogues – studying them by reading aloud, describing their grammatical structure, and, possibly, by translating them. Again, Murgatroyd owned schoolbooks that would have suggested this traditional teaching method, although he also possessed up-to-date editions of the *Colloquies* of Erasmus and Cordery and Lucian's *History*.[57] The glossaries of rhetorical terms and grammars in his schoolbook library were probably his own teaching aids, as were his several dictionaries. He had half a dozen of these, including Farnaby's *Index Rhetoricus* and Smith's *Rhetorick*.[58]

When he first came to teach in the 1730s, there was a new genre of Latin primers available; he made careful note of their editors in making his inventories. Gentlemen and clerical scholars like John Clarke fulminated much about the arid and impenetrable method of older works. Clarke was particularly scathing about the teaching method implied by someone like Hoole: boys sitting around to hear two or three lines of Cordery construed by the master, maybe twice, if they were lucky. This was meant to keep them occupied for a couple of hours, copying out the lines and parsing them; but, needing more help, 'they must sit doing of nothing, or be continually pacing it up and down the School to the Master'.[59] He thought this a 'tedious, lingering Way of Proceeding' particularly hard on boys not destined for the university. 'The five or six years spent [in school] . . . is Time absolutely thrown away, for almost double the Time is necessary for the Attainment of but a moderate Skill in [Latin]'.[60] Translation was the answer, the absolutely modern method, using text set in parallel if possible.[61] He promoted literal translation for beginners. In his parallel text *Colloquies of Erasmus*, he altered the word order of the English translation rather than of the Latin, for it was, after all, Latin that they were learning: 'All concerned with the Instruction of young Boys in the Latin Tongue cannot but be sensible of how much their Progress is retarded by the Difficulty arising from the perplexed intricate Order of the Words in that Language. This is a continual Rub in their Way . . . '.[62] Others, exercised by the word-order question, went about things differently. In his edition of Phaedrus' *Fables*, John Stirling offered no translation at all. Rather, 'for the greater ease and assistance of Boys, below every Fable, the Words are taken out of their respective Places as they stand in the Text, and ranged in a proper Order, as they are to be construed into our Language'.[63] For the little sons of wool combers, sitting out their five years of Latin, this text could not have produced the startling and arresting effect of the play with English word order in Clarke's *Erasmus*.

Some thought that the translation method had been taken too far. Murgatroyd approved of Bailey's *English and Latin Lessons for School-Boys* (or, at least, listed it twice in his inventories). Bailey thought that the 'great *Heap of Words* with which our common Word Books do so frightfully swell' ought to be discarded, as he had so industriously laboured to do. He meant by this, the efforts of other translators to make Latin more acceptable to English children by inventing words to describe the things of the modern world they inhabited. But 'why should a Person that is to be prepared for the Reading of Corderius, Phaedrus &c be led through a series of *modern Barbarisms*, and loaded with a Multitude of Words which the Romans never heard of?'[64]

Most of Murgatroyd's modern Latin books promised to be as diverting as possible in their instruction or, as Greenwood put it, to be as 'Natural and Entertaining [as] the Subject is capable of', in his preparation of children for a reading of Corderius, the Latin Testament, Phaedrus, Aesop, Cato and Ovid.[65] Incidental entertainment that came with this teaching territory had been available for a very long time as long as you had not restricted your pedagogy to the all-Latin, all-grammar strictness of Hoole. Colloquies proceeded by an amiable mixture of the zany and the utterly familiar, in which in some timeless realm, mothers are too busy in the morning to prepare your lunch box, fathers hand out pocket money when the fair comes around, where fish do swim and birds do fly. Long, shaggy-dog stories proceed by question and answer; they are about a social world, only ever-so-slightly odd, full of people living lives in particular ways. Long, entirely familiar exchanges between teachers and pupils fill their pages – a kind of joke that proceeds by dissolving the boundary between the now of the Slaithwaite schoolroom and the then of the text.[66] Bailey's grammar of 1744 is weirdly arresting because of that great eternal, timeless universe, in which the sun always rises and sets, and dogs and cats behave as they do, but also because of the odd conjunction of visual images in many of his examples of cases, tenses, and moods. Moreover, if you were in a school that allowed you to have *English and Latin Exercises* in your hands (rather than the master reserving it as his method book), then you would not have to be very accomplished in the Latin tongue to discover what going with a whorish woman might do for – and to – you.[67] For two hundred years, at least, a broadly humanist conception of education had encouraged the reading of Ovid's *Metamorphoses*, for example, because of the moral lessons that could be extracted from it, for its retelling of the Greek myths, and for the general knowledge about the natural world that it contained. Murgatroyd had two editions in his schoolbook collection. Like preceding generations of schoolmasters, he would have had to find a way of incorporating the pragmatic approach of the pagans to social and sexual behaviour into the framework of a Christian education.[68]

The material Murgatroyd used for teaching English was far less amusing. Contemporary linguistic theory held that all modern languages, English included, were variants of a universal grammar common to all.[69] Because Latin syntax was understood to be a better representative of universal structures than was English, school readers presented their mother tongue to pupils within the same categorical and analytic framework as Latin.[70] Murgatroyd possessed a copy of Ann Fisher's *Exercises of Bad English* (or perhaps it was the Leeds publication, *Exercises, Instructive and Entertaining, in False English*). Significantly, it was not kept in his schoolbook collection; perhaps he found it as wasteful of school time as Peter Fogg, who described children legging it up and down the schoolroom to have one painful correction after another to a sentence like 'Thi gospil maiks every man my naibour' approved by the master.[71] Fisher divided her text by the topics of Orthography, Prosody, Etymology, and Syntax; it is a very thorough – and mighty dull – exposition of the grammar and structure of the English language. When tense agreement was the fault being corrected, some small West Riding dialect-speakers may have come to doubt their own speech, but that is the closest the text comes to language spoken by an actual human being. This is not the case with the homilies and maxims and moral stories of the *Colloquies* of Erasmus, nor even of Culman's *Senteniae Pueriles*, in which many of the scenes to be imagined out of the text involve people and animals saying and doing things as they did in 1780s Yorkshire – or in the universal Anywhere.[72]

As for the basic instruction in reading and writing that Slaithwaite Free School was set up to provide, we should not expect to find traces of instructional material in Murgatroyd's library. Very early learners may have copied letters and syllables onto slates; before this, they may have learned the names of the letters 'without book' or, indeed, without anything at all except the resources of the Catechism and their master's verbal example.[73] Or, perhaps – which is more likely – the scholars were past this initial stage. The only register surviving from half a century of Murgatroyd's teaching included several groups of brothers and sisters. In these family groups, the oldest children must be assumed to have been taught to read at home.[74]

A curriculum founded on the teaching of Latin was what local parents wanted. West Riding education had long been tailored to commerce: 'the next thing after Learning to be Remark'd in [Halifax], is their manner and way of Trade, into which their Youth, when taken from School are chiefly Educated', it was noted in 1761; 'And this their way of Education hath a principal relation to the Woollen Manufacture, consisting in Making, Buying, & Selling Cloth'.[75] However, even educational programmes for the making of modern commercial man emphasised the importance of Latin. Martin Clare's *Youth's Introduction to Trade and Business* (Murgatroyd acquired this sometime between 1792 and 1799) laid out an entire educational programme for an embryonic man of business, starting with reading and grammar, French, writing, arithmetic, commercial law (enough to understand what a promissory note was and how to interpret a bill of exchange), bookkeeping, drawing, geography, navigation and experimental philosophy. However, he must also learn Latin: it would make him a better master of his own tongue, and the frequent use of English translations would transmit a 'Propriety of Stile . . . [that] elegance and good sense requisite for all, that hope to be considerable in the world'.[76] George Fisher's *Young Man's Companion*, which Murgatroyd also possessed, promised to 'qualify any person for business, without the aid of a Master'. It described a curriculum much like the one Clare recommended, with the exception of Latin.[77] You could not learn Latin without a master; as far as parents were concerned, the possession of Latin may have been what defined a schoolmaster.

Things went on in Slaithwaite Free School in a way so unlike the way the original deed of endowment proposed that we may even entertain the notion that girls were taught Latin. In 1764, the Slaithwaite curate reported to his Bishop that '20 children, boys and girls, are taught reading, writing, arithmetic and Latin'.[78] He made no distinction by gender in its acquisition and, indeed, in a one-room school, where your brother and his friends spend the day getting the *Colloquies* of Cordery and Erasmus by heart, it would have been difficult to avoid the Latin tongue, even if you were (as the Deeds of Trust required but as probably did not happen) restricted to the syllables on your slate and your Testament.

In sermonising, Murgatroyd's teaching was practical, telling best how to push through a troublesome world. His last commonplace book contains notes on slander and defamation ('ye only method for never increasing ye Charge of Calumny, is never of speak to any one's disadvantage'), on how to forget affronts, how to behave fairly in any kind of group endeavour ('ye more they are, ye better is ye Body evry Member hath Use for ye good of ye whole ~ mak.g it by Lot prevents quarrel.g in yr Disposal ~ None can be charg'd with partiality – none can say They had a wrong done'), how friends should behave towards each other, how to avoid the 'fix'd Melancholy' that could develop from grief, and on sexual relations.[79] He told about death and judgment and the irreducible plot line of the Christian narrative; he copied out practical advice about preparation for confirmation and Holy Communion from the printed guides he possessed, and he probably delivered it on a Sunday under the heading of a Biblical text. His Victorian historian accused him of a kind of plagiarism in sermonising. 'I do not think he was very eminent', Canon Hulbert concluded, 'but labourious and conscientious, and took great pains in the preparation of his sermons . . . [his] doctrine . . . not very distinct; the subjects being chiefly practical or rational'.[80] But if you spend, for example, thirty pages, as Murgatroyd did in 1747, extracting from the second volume of Beveridge's sermons, subjecting them to critical analysis, noting the rhetorical moves made, and turning back to the Biblical texts on which each is based, then you can scarcely help using your databank during the coming years.[81]

There is little in the notebooks that cannot be traced back to the books in

Murgatroyd's personal library; 'Ask, Read, Retain, Teach' proclaims its function. That anyone might be interested in the distinction between his own and someone else's thoughts would have struck him as odd. He was a conduit for an accumulated wisdom and body of advice collected by the reformed church during the past two centuries. This was his teaching: the basis of a common conversation between him and his neighbours and the West Riding clergymen he dined with of a Sunday. At a distance of two hundred years, it is only possible to say that he was struck by many arguments and ideas and that in writing them down, he did not disapprove of them. Here, for once, John Murgatroyd does not buck a trend; he *is* a trend or, rather, the amalgam of Anglican theology, working with newish accounts of the historical past and models of the human subject learned from contemporary philosophy and physiology.

Following the course of Murgatroyd's reading through his notebooks, a God of a West Riding Enlightenment is revealed. He first emerged during Murgatroyd's early years in Slaithwaite, when he read Nettleton's *Some Thoughts Concerning Virtue and Happiness*. Through a lifetime's note-taking, Nettleton's (1683–1742) cheerful and rational account of God's Creation reverberates more than any other text.[82] Murgatroyd probably used the second or third edition of Nettleton's work, which expanded the original *Thoughts . . . in a Letter to a Clergyman* of 1729 into something three times as long, with the status of a 'treatise'.[83] The first little book had been written by Nettleton as a token of thanks for a friendship with which an anonymous clergyman had honoured the author for 'many years', and also because the addressee was 'not afraid of any *Freedom* or *Debate*' and would listen to 'anything that can be advanced, provided it is not contrary to Religion and Good Manners'.[84] This kind of epistolary exchange of enlightenment was familiar to Murgatroyd; perhaps it was common across the West Riding for many clergymen and their friends.[85]

Nettleton's *Letter* and the vastly expanded *Treatise* told how to be happy in the light of what recent developments in the philosophy of the human subject told of God's Creatures, as physiological and psychological entities. There could be 'none but who would desire to pass through the world as easily as they can, and to give themselves as little pain as possible: And how we may learn to do this, and also obtain the greatest and most lasting pleasure, is the subject of [my] inquiry'.[86] 'The eighteenth century engaged in obsessional talk about happiness'.[87] The method Nettleton proposed for attaining it was 'attended with some trouble'; it required 'some degree of self-denial'. It was not for everyone but rather of particular use to the reader who understood that the 'chief business in life was to promote his own happiness, and that of others'. Doing this would have discernable effects on civil society – in particular, putting an end to abuses of power and corruption. To be virtuous was the only way to be happy and free. Employing the physiology and psychology of perception, Nettleton explained how modes of grief and joy were excited by external phenomena operating on the senses, or 'powers of affection'. The 'wise author of our beings', having 'endowed us with a power of self and motion, and designated them for action and employment', had also 'subjected us to many unavoidable *pains*, and *uneasiness*; and such is our make and constitution, that whenever we feel any uneasy sensation, we are determined to get quit of it, as soon as possible'.[88] It was 'highly requisite that, in order to be happy . . . we employ that natural talent of thinking, which GOD almighty has given us . . . '.[89] Nettleton also advocated laughter and the pleasures of looking – at the infinite variety of the natural world, at the sky – as great promoters of happiness.[90] However, the God he described was no mere reflection of his Creatures – not their invention but, rather, radically other: 'the *sovereign ruler* of the world' is not like us, influenced by 'weak passions'; neither did this god 'act in partial and capricious manner, but governs by general, steady and inviolable Laws . . . he is not favourable to some of his creatures, and cruel to the rest'. The thinking, feeling, acting and reacting creature made by a wise and just God had been given the faculty to know Him; his existence was to be known within each individual. Nettleton urged his readers to have good and appropriate conceptions of a good and appropriate God making '*free and impartial use* of those natural powers he has given them'.[91]

In Nettleton's account – Murgatroyd had noted this carefully – God had established the same organisation of body and mind in all men and women. Their actions – 'motions' in Nettleton's terminology – were determined by an uneasiness arising from the apprehension of a present evil, representation of an absent good, or an approaching evil. These were the mainsprings of human action; in Nettleton's nice example, it was just the same for the day labourer as it was for Alexander the Great.[92] Of course, much depended on given 'genius and capacity' and even more on what 'rank and station will admit of'; but there was some space here for Murgatroyd to be able to understand his pregnant, unmarried domestic servant as a creature something like himself and to act to make her happier than not.[93]

However, John Murgatroyd did not look at the sky in the way that Thomas Nettleton recommended; or, at least, there is no record in his journals and other notebooks of his gazing at cloud formation in awe and aesthetic wonder. He must have taken note of it to write his daily weather reports, but the sense of wonder at the 'Immensity of Nature' that it promoted in some gentleman scholars, their imagining of that 'Infinite Variety of Creatures, which in all probability swarm through these immeasurable Regions of Matter', was not his.[94] For Joseph Addison, for example, night sky-gazing had been the quickest route to his 'Omniscient God': the enormity of the sky, the smallness of Joseph Addison, was the register of His regard for 'every thing that has Being, especially such of his Creatures who fear they are not regarded by him . . . It is impossible he should overlook any of his Creatures . . . '. Addison knew all of this, as a small figure on a hill, looking at the stars; however, this was not Murgatroyd's way of seeing. His imagination and the deep structure of his responses to God's creation were made by the word and by the book; by the echoing voices of the seventeenth-century saints and churchmen (and their eighteenth-century editors) whose works lined his parlour; by the words of scholars from ancient Rome and seventeenth-century England. If he *saw* the natural or supernatural world with that minute vision and impulse to detail beauty that Daston has called the capacity for attention in the European Enlightenment, then he did not record *looking* or *paying attention* to the natural world in all of the millions of words he wrote.[95] He did not botanise or search for the leaf forms and the habits of insects that might express the divine and the aesthetic, as well as the moral, purposes of Creation. This was not the register of his thought or of his ethics. He could many times have seen the gentleman botanist Mr Bolton of Stannary, mushroom-gathering in the woods and spinneys around Halifax. Indeed, on the occasions when Murgatroyd walked home to visit family in Halifax, he *must* have seen James Bolton in the distance, peering at rotten logs in Bracken-Bed-Wood, or spied him finding 'the Red Agaric' in 'the little wood near Shibden Hall . . . October 29th, 1786', or 'the Noble Agaric at Millsbridge near Huddersfield . . . '.[96] Bolton collected his fungi for the most beautiful expression of what Daston has called a minute attention to the detail of a whole: the hand-coloured plates of his *History of Fungusses growing about Halifax* are quite stunning in their loveliness and a fine West Riding example of a European-wide detailing of the natural world. Indeed, so beautiful are these plates, so minute the description of the circumstances in which 'the Red Agaric', 'the Flat Agaric', the 'Noble Agaric' were acquired, that one suspects Bolton felt something of the guilt of many Christian naturalists of the period, who knew they were paying more attention to the structure and the form of the mushroom, or the beehive, or the aphid – their great importance and loveliness – than they were to the mushroom's Creator.[97] However, John Murgatroyd encountered Nature only as 'a very plashy winterly day'. His God was a god of words – was the Word – transmitted through the writings of the previous century's churchmen and the rational, abstract version of that God, inscribed by the West Riding *philosophe*, Thomas Nettleton.

Writing those words on a daily basis for more than sixty years did not make the uniqueness that was John Murgatroyd: that existed already, a thing made by God and reshaped by His creature throughout a very long life. It is difficult for historians to *believe* this God (not *not to believe in* Him; that is a much easier matter) but rather more difficult to read Murgatroyd's account as a true account of what he knew – as someone meaning what he said – rather than as one deluded, his God masking some other kind of cognitive process. However, the words of others, and God's word, made the self that Murgatroyd wrote. It was *already there* as far as he was concerned – a presence, a fashioned thing – whenever he picked up a pen.

Notes

1 For an erotics of reading and writing in the past, see Carolyn Steedman, *A Woman Writing a Letter*, Rebecca Earle (Ed.), *Epistolary Selves: Letters and Letter-Writers, 1600–1945*, Ashgate, Aldershot, and Brookfield VT, 1999, pp. 111–133, and Notes. I am grateful to David Olson for pointing out that the most overt literary reference embodied in Delia Grinstead is Flaubertian; that she is one in a long line of Emma Bovaries who, through reading, know that *this* is not the life,that real life is elsewhere. Gustave Flaubert, *Madame Bovary. Moeurs de province* (1857).

2 Max Weber, *The Protestant Ethic and the Spirit of Capitalism* (1904–1905), trans. 1930, Harper Collins, London, 1991.

3 Roger Chartier (Ed.), *A History of Private Life, Volume III: Passions of the Renaissance*, Belknap Press of Harvard University Press, Cambridge, MA, 1989. John Brewer, *The Pleasures of the Imagination: English Culture in the Eighteenth Century*, Harper Collins, London, 1997. See also Andrew Taylor, *Into his Secret Chamber: Reading and Privacy in Late Medieval England*, James Raven et al. (Eds.), *The Practice and Representation of Reading in England*, Cambridge University Press, Cambridge, 1996, pp. 41–61; Cecile M. Jagodzinski, *Privacy and Print: Reading and Writing in Seventeenth-Century England*, University Press of Virginia, Charlottesville, VA, 1999. There is an enormous literature on the topic. Reading it, you will come to know that the Western self originates in the reading practices of classical antiquity and that the alphabetic system of writing is deeply implicated in the economic, individuated self who is the hero (or, at least, the central character) of most historical accounts produced from the early eighteenth century onwards. Any list of references is bound to be cursory and incomplete. Readers are invited to consult the Royal Historical Society Website (*www.rhs.ac.uk/bibl/*) with the search term 'literacy' to see the changing shape of historians' interest in reading and writing as subjects of inquiry and 'literacy' as a tool of analysis.

4 Cyndia Susan Clegg, 'History of the Book: An Undisciplined Discipline?' *Renaissance Quarterly*, 54 (2001), pp. 221–245.

5 Sidonie Smith, *Subjectivity, Identity and the Body: Women's Autobiographical Practices in the Twentieth Century*, Indiana University Press, Bloomington, 1993, p. 3.

6 James Daybell, 'Interpreting Letters and Reading Script: Evidence for Female Education and Literacy in Tudor England', *History of Education*, 34, 6 (2005), 695–716; Margaret W. Ferguson, *Dido's Daughters: Literacy, Gender and Empire in Early Modern England and France*, Chicago University Press, Chicago and London, 2003; Patricia Ann Meyer Spacks, *Privacy: Concealing the Eighteenth-century Self*, Chicago University Press, Chicago and London, 2003; Corinne S. Abate, *Privacy, Domesticity, and Women in Early Modern England*, Ashgate, Aldershot, 2003; Rebecca Krug, *Reading Families: Women's Literate Practice in Late Medieval England*, Cornell University Press, Ithaca, NY, 2002; Adam Fox, *Oral and Literate Culture in England, 1500–1700*, Oxford University Press, Oxford, 2000, pp. 173–212; Richard Gameson, 'The Gospels of Margaret of Scotland and the Literacy of an Eleventh-Century Queen', in Jane H. M. Taylor and Lesley Smith (Eds.), *Women and the Book: Assessing the Visual Evidence*, British Library, London, 1996, pp. 149–171; Naomi Tadmor, '"In the even my wife read to me": Women, Reading and Household Life in

the Eighteenth-Century', Raven et al., *Practice and Representation of Reading*, pp. 162–174; Donna Landry, *The Muses of Resistance: Labouring Class Women's Poetry in Britain, 1739–1796*, Cambridge University Press, Cambridge, 1990; Margaret P. Hannay, *Silent But for the Word: Tudor Women as Patrons, Translators, and Writers of Religious Works*, Kent State University Press, Ohio, 1989; Elspeth Graham et al., *Her Own Life: Autobiographical Writings by Seventeenth-Century Englishwomen*, Routledge, London, 1989; Miriam J. Benkowitz, 'Some Observations on Women's Concept of the Self in the Eighteenth Century', in Paul Fritz (Ed.), *Women in the Eighteenth Century and Other Essays*, Hakkert, Toronto, 1976. Again, this is a cursory bibliography of a large topic, confined to the British Isles.

7 Sidonie Smith and Julia Watson, *De/Colonizing the Subject: The Politics of Gender in Women's Autobiography*, University of Minnesota Press, Minneapolis, 1992.

8 Sidonie Smith and Julia Watson (Eds.), *Women, Autobiography, Theory: A Reader*, University of Wisconsin Press, Madison, 1998.

9 David Vincent, *The Rise of Mass Literacy: Reading and Writing in Modern Europe*, Polity, Cambridge, 2000.

10 Pamela Fox, *Class Fictions: Shame and Resistance in the British Working-Class Novel, 1890–1945*, Duke University Press, Durham, NC, 1994, p. 45.

11 For the 'enormous condescension of posterity' in regard to working-class people, see E. P. Thompson, *The Making of the English Working Class* (1963), Penguin, Harmondsworth, 1968. For the post-Thompsonian project, William H. Sewell Jr, 'How Classes are Made: Critical Reflections on E. P. Thompson's Theory of Working-Class Formation', in Harvey J. Kaye and Keith McClelland (Eds.), *E. P. Thompson: Critical Perspectives*, Polity, Cambridge, 1990, pp. 50–77.

12 Margaret Spufford, *Small Books and Pleasant Histories: Popular Fiction and Its Readership in Seventeenth-Century England*, Cambridge University Press, Cambridge, 1981; David Vincent, *Bread, Knowledge and Freedom: A Study of Nineteenth-Century Working-Class Autobiography*, Methuen, London, 1981; Vincent, *Rise of Mass Literacy*, pp. 89–123.

13 Anthony Giddens, *Modernity and Self Identity: Self and Society in the Late Modern Age*, Polity, Cambridge, 1991, pp. 52–54. The making of the self in narrative has also been charted by Franco Moretti, *The Way of the World: The Bildungsroman in European Culture*, Verso, London, 1987; Robert Elbaz, *The Changing Nature of the Self*, Croom Helm, London, 1988; Michael Mascuch, *Origins of the Individual Self: Autobiography and Self-Identity in England, 1591–1791*, Cambridge University Press, Cambridge, 1997. For the Italian philosopher Adriana Caverero, self is impossible without its narration by another. See *Relating Narratives: Storytelling and Selfhood* (1997), Routledge, London, 2000.

14 The major source for Keith Snell's monumental and elegiac account of working-class experience and its expression in rural England between 1660 and 1900 is extant settlement examinations, the many thousands of them that have ended up in county record offices. *Annals of the Labouring Poor: Social Change and Agrarian England, 1660–1900*, Cambridge University Press, Cambridge, 1985.

15 In the later eighteenth century, printed forms for the insertion of relevant details became widely used. This kind of testimony became much more consistently recorded and – for the historian – much less revelatory.

16 Warwickshire Country Record Office, DR 225/327/88-132 (1780–1798). Parish of Bedworth, Examination of Eleanore Perkins, 10 August 1780.

17 Vincent, *Rise of Mass Literacy*, pp. 63–88.

18 Vincent, *Rise of Mass Literacy*, pp. 8–26. See also the important account in David Levine, 'Illiteracy and Family Life During the Industrial Revolution', *Journal of Social History*, 14 (1) (1980), pp. 3–24.

19 I have argued elsewhere that this kind of life story told by the poorer sort laid down the basic structures of the modern literary character. This is a large claim indeed, and, as yet, we know very little about the way in which an understanding of what a character was (what an informal theory of 'character' looked like) moved into the emergent novel, and out again, into the wider society, to be taken and used in innumerable acts of self-fashioning and self-perception. But, the proposition was that one of its points of origin was this kind of enforced narration, particularly in its explanatory aspect: Eleanore Perkins told a story in which her childhood, and what had happened to her since, explained her, now, standing before

the bench in the justicing room of the local magistrate. See Carolyn Steedman, 'Enforced Narratives: Stories of Another Self', in Tess Cosslett et al., *Feminism and Autobiography: Texts, Theories, Methods* (pp. 25–39), Routledge, London and New York, 2000.

20 Jerrold Seigal, *The Idea of the Self: Thought and Experience in Western Europe Since the Seventeenth Century*, Cambridge University Press, Cambridge, 2005.

21 See Roy Porter (Ed.), *Rewriting the Self: Histories from the Renaissance to the Presence*, Routledge, London, 1997. E. J. Hundert's contribution to this collection shows how powerful is the theatrical metaphor in this history of the self – the idea of showing, displaying, self-dramatising, performing a self. 'The European Enlightenment and the History of the Self', idem., pp. 72–83.

22 Carolyn Steedman, *Master and Servant: Love and Labour in the English Industrial Age*, Cambridge University Press, Cambridge, 2007.

23 Thompson, *Making of the English Working Class*.

24 There are disagreements among historians about eighteenth-century Anglicanism, but William Gibson's argument that 'the level of commitment to the Church was . . . much greater than historians allow, and the eighteenth century is perhaps the last period in which popular faith can be taken for granted' has been persuasive. William Gibson, *Church, State and Society*, 1760–1850, Macmillan, London, 1994, p. 10.

25 West Yorkshire Archive Service, Kirklees District, Huddersfield, KC 242/1-7, Reverend John Murgatroyd, Diaries, KC242/1 (1781–2, 1786, 1788, 1789, 1790, 1791), KC242/2 (1794); KC242/3 (1796); KC242/4 (1797); KC242/5 (1800); KC242/6 (1802); KC242/7 (1804). KC242/8, Reverend John Murgatroyd, Notebook, 'The Qualifications of a Minister of Christ', nd. KC249/9, Reverend John Murgatroyd, Notebook, 'Ask, Read, Retain, Teach', Notebook containing miscellaneous observations, University of York, York, 082.2 MUR. John Murgatroyd, 'Authors Useful to be Read at School', Notebook, 1745–1802, unpaginated; Special Collections, Raymond Burton Library, Slaithwaite Parish Collection; 082.2 MUR, John Murgatroyd, 'A Book of Records', Special Collections, Raymond Burton Library, Slaithwaite Parish Collection; 082.2 MUR, John Murgatroyd, 'A Cornucopia: or Collection of weighty Extracts transcribed out of the scarcest, most necessary & best chosen Books &c according to this proper Maxim, that every Man shou'd take down in Writing what He learns for fear of forgetting any useful Circumstance. By John Murgatroyd, Master of Slaithwaite School. Anno Domini 1742', quarto Notebook, nd., unpaginated, Special Collections, Raymond Burton Library, Slaithwaite Parish Collection.

26 Henry James Morehouse, *Extracts from the Diary of the Rev. Robert Meeke . . . Also a Continuation of the History of Slaithwaite Free School and an Account of the Educational Establishments in Slaithwaite-cum-Lingards, by the Rev. Charles Augustus Hulbert*, Bohn, London and *Daily Chronicle* Steam Press, Huddersfield, 1874, pp. 105–116. Morehouse took a lot from Charles Augustus Hulbert, *Annals of the Church in Slaithwaite (near Huddersfield) West Riding of Yorkshire from 1793–1864, in Five Lectures*, Longman, London, 1864.

27 Murgatroyd Diary, KC 242/7 (29 May 1802).

28 Hulbert, *Annals*, pp. 52–53.

29 Murgatroyd Diaries, KC 242/1 (23 January 1786); KC 242/2 (29 May 1794); KC 242/2 (29 May 1794); KC 242/7 (29 May 1804).

30 Murgatroyd Diary, KC 242/6 (30 May 1802).

31 Carolyn Steedman, 'Writing the Self: The End of the Scholarship Girl,' in Jim McGuigan (Ed.), *Cultural Methodologies*, Sage, London, 1997, pp. 106–125. Richard Hoggart, *The Uses of Literacy*, Penguin, Harmondsworth, 1958, pp. 241–263.

32 He may be representative, in a minor way, of the growing wealth of eighteenth-century clergy. John Walsh and Stephen Taylor, 'The Church and Anglicanism in the "long" eighteenth century', in John Walsh, Colin Haydon, and Stephen Taylor (Eds.), *The Church of England, c. 1689–1883: From Toleration to Tractarianism*, Cambridge University Press, Cambridge, 1993, pp. 1–64; p. 7. For the general poverty of northern clergy, see E. J. Evans, 'The Anglican Clergy of Northern England', in Clyve Jones (Ed.), *Britain in the First Age of Party, 1680–1750: Essays Presented to Geoffrey Holmes*, Hambledon, London and Rounceverte, 1987, pp. 221–240. For want of cultural as well as monetary capital among Lancashire clergy in this period, see Michael Snape, 'The Church in a Lancashire Parish: Whalley, 1689–1800', in Geoffrey S. Chamberlain and Jeremy Gregory (Eds.), *The*

National Church in Local Perspective: The Church of England and the Regions, 1660–1800, Boydell Woodbridge (2003), pp. 243–263.

33 Will of the Reverend John Murgatroyd of Lingards, p.[arish] Almondbury, 1806, Borthwicke Institute of Historical Research, University of York.

34 Murgatroyd Notebook, 'Ask, Read, Retain, Teach', KC 242/9, p. 89; 'Rising in Life/1789'.

35 Morehouse, *Extracts*, pp. 111–115. Henry James Morehouse, *Village Gleanings, or Notes and Jottings from the Manuscripts of the Rev. John Murgatroyd, Master of the Free School of Slaithwaite.... Including some Account of his distinguished Scholar, James Horsfall, Born at Slaithwaite, the Son of the Village Blacksmith*, Parkin, Huddersfield, 1886. In Trevor Harvey Levere and G. L. Turner (Eds.), *Discussing Chemistry and Steam: The Minutes of a Coffee House Philosophical Society, 1780–1787*, Oxford University Press, Oxford, 2002, pp. 23–24, 32.

36 Murgatroyd Diary, KC242/1 (1 March 1782).

37 See Judith Jago, *Aspects of the Georgian Church: Visitation of the Diocese of York, 1761–1776*, Associated University Press, London, 1997, pp. 14–17 for an excellent summary of the recent historiography of the Church of England and Anglicanism. Also Alan Smith, *The Established Church and Popular Religion, 1750–1850*, Longman, London, 1971, pp. 8–13, for a preliminary survey of the Anglican belief system. See R. A. Soloway, *Prelates and People: Ecclesiastical Social Thought in England, 1783–1852*, Routledge and Kegan Paul, London, 1969, pp. 19, 5, 22–23, for a more extended survey of Church of England theology and social thought.

38 James Woodforde, *The Diary of a Country Parson: The Reverend James Woodforde 1758–1781*, John Beresford (Ed.), Oxford University Press, Oxford, 1924. Jack Ayres (Ed.), *Paupers and Pig Killers: The Diary of William Holland, A Somerset Parson, 1799–1818* (1984), Sutton, Stroud, 1997. Francis Griffin Stokes (Ed.), *The Blecheley Diary of the Reverend William Cole, MA , FSA, 1765–67*, Constable, London, 1931.

39 Masuch, *Individualist Self*, p. 82. Gugliemo Cavallo and Roger Chartier, *A History of Reading in the West*, trans. Lydia G. Cochrane, Polity, Cambridge, 1999, pp. 25–30. Peter Mack, *Elizabethan Rhetoric: Theory and Practice*, Cambridge University Press, Cambridge, 2002, pp. 31–32, 44–45. M. L. Clarke, *Classical Education in Britain, 1500–1900*, Cambridge University Press, Cambridge, 1959, pp. 38–45.

40 They did not follow the rhetorical structure inherited from the seventeenth century, of proem, and case to be argued, laid out in a legal fashion. James Downey, *The Eighteenth Century Pulpit: A Study in the Sermons of Butler, Berkeley, Secker, Sterne, Whitefield and Wesley*, Clarendon Press, Oxford, 1969, pp. 15–16. Murgatroyd's were not sermons with an ultimate destination in publication. They were directed at the ungrand audiences of the industrial West Riding and not designed to be read by any one but their author. Robert Hoole, *Pulpits, Politics and Public Order in England, 1760–1832*, Cambridge, Cambridge University Press, 1989, p. 85.

41 Murgatroyd Notebook, 'Ask, Read, Retain, Teach', KC 242/9, p. 79. Slaithwaite church was rebuilt and enlarged in 1788, on a new site just up from the River Colne.

42 Masuch, *Individualist Self*, pp. 82–86.

43 Masuch, *Individualist Self*, pp. 84–86.

44 Mary Orr, *Intertextuality: Debates and Contexts*, Polity, Cambridge, 2003.

45 Murgatroyd Diary, KC242/1 (5, 29 May 1786), 'Abt ye Masons &c respecting our intended House, in another Book'.

46 Masuch, *Individualist Self*, p. 84.

47 Alain René Le Sage, *The History and Adventures of Gil Blas of Santillane*, has a complex publishing history. Books I–VI were published in 1715, VII–IX in 1724, and X–XII in 1735. I have used the facsimile reprint of the English translation of 1716 (Garland, New York, 1972). Murgatroyd's notes show him reading beyond the sixth book; maybe he read the lot.

48 Walsh and Taylor, 'Church and Anglicanism', p. 14. Jeremy Gregory, *Restoration, Reformation and Reform, 1660–1828: Archbishops of Canterbury and their Diocese*, Clarendon Press, Oxford, 2000, pp. 235–254.

49 Four thousand endowed schools are estimated for later eighteenth-century England, about seven hundred of them grammar schools ('instituted for instruction which includes classics, which school sends students to universities and/or is staffed by graduates, but which may have gone under any of the common descriptive terms for such a school, i.e., "free school", free grammar school, grammar school, public school'). During the course of the century, these types

of schools were added to by 'charity schools' (endowed elementary schools supported by public subscription). Richard S. Tompson, *Classics or Charity? The Dilemma of the 18th-Century Grammar School*, Manchester University Press, Manchester, 1971, pp. 1–3, 16, Note 2.

50 I have been unable to trace any of the records of Slaithwaite Free School. This account is from D. F. E. Sykes, who transcribed the original deeds of trust and Meeke's will in 1896. D. F. E. Sykes, *The History of the Colne Valley*, F. Walker, Slaithwaite (1896), pp. 138–142, 391–393. See also his *Huddersfield and its Vicinity*, Advertiser Press, Huddersfield, 1898, pp. 415–416.

51 Murgatroyd, 'Authors Useful to be Read at School'. The 'Book of Records' contains the draft advertisement.

52 Jago, *Aspects*, p. 127.

53 Cressida Annesley and Philippa Hoskin (Eds.), *Archbishop Drummond's Visitation Returns 1764 III: Yorkshire S-Y*, Borthwick Texts and Calendars 23, University of York, York, 1998, 'Slaithwaite'.

54 Murgatroyd, 'Book of Records'.

55 For Lily's *Grammar*, see Thompson, *Classics or Charity?*, p. 19. William Lily, *The Royal Grammar Reformed... for the better Understanding of the English and the more speedy Attainment of the Latin Tongue*, A. & J. Churchill, London, 1695. Christopher Wase, *Methodi Practae Specimen: An Essay of Practical Grammar, or an Inquiry after a more easie help to the construing... of authors and the making and speaking of Latin*, privately printed, London, 1660.

56 Charles Hoole, *The Common Accidence Explained by Short Questions and Answers: According to the very Words of the Book*, A. Armstrong, London, 1697, pp. 3, 57.

57 John Clarke, *Erasmi Colloquia Selecta: or, the Select Colloquies of Erasmus*, 22nd ed., J. F. C. Rivington, London, 1789; *Corderii Colloquior mu Centuria Selecta, or, a Century of Cordery's Colloquies*, 15th ed., W. Smith, London, 1773; *A Compendius History of Rome by L. Florus with an English Translation*, 6th ed., Hawes, Clarke & Collins, London, 1763. For the traditional teaching method, see the Preface to any of Clarke's text books; also Mack, *Elizabethan Rhetoric*, pp. 11–47. See Ian Michael, *The Teaching of English from the Sixteenth Century to 1870*, Cambridge University Press, Cambridge, 1987, pp. 317–320 for the relationship between teaching Latin and teaching English.

58 Thomas Farnaby, *Index Rhetoricus et Oratorius: Scholis, & institutioni Aeatis accomodatus*, G. Conyers & J. Clarke, London, 1728. John Smith, *The Mystery of Rhetorick Unveiled*, George Eversden, London, 1693.

59 Clarke, *Coredrii Colloquior*, Preface.

60 Clarke, *Lucius Florus*, Preface.

61 It was not new at all, as a method. From the early seventeenth century, textbook writers had been concerned with innovation in the layout and general presentation of Latin texts. See Mack, *Elizabethan Rhetoric*, pp. 11–47.

62 Clarke, *Erasi Colloquia*, Preface.

63 John Stirling, *Phaedri Fabulae: or, Phaedrus's Fables with... Improvements... in a Method entirely new*, 9th ed., J. Rivington, London, 1771, Preface. Murgatroyd had this, though not necessarily this edition.

64 Nathan Bailey, *English and Latin Exercises for School-Boys: Comprising the Rules of Syntaxis, with Explanations, and other necessary Observations on each Rule*, 11th ed., R. Ware, London, 1744, Preface.

65 James Greenwood, *The London Vocabulary: English and Latin put into a new Method, proper to acquaint the Learner with Things, as well as Pure Latin Words. Adorned with Twenty-six Pictures*, 11th ed., C. Hitch, London, 1749, Preface.

66 Clarke, *Erasmi Colloquia*; *Cordery's Colloquies*.

67 Bailey, *English and Latin Exercises*, p. 107.

68 Mack, *Elizabethan Rhetoric*, pp. 8, 17. Murgatroyd also possessed Ovid's *Art of Love* but did not list it as a book useful for teaching.

69 Hans Aarsleff, *The Study of Language in England, 1780–1860*, University of Minnesota Press, Minneapolis, 1983, pp. 3–43. James Beattie, *The Theory of Language: In Two Parts. Of the Origin and General Nature of Speech...*, Strahan, Cadell & Creech, Edinburgh, 1788.

70 Michaels, *Teaching of English*, pp. 318–330.

71 Ann Fisher, *A New Grammar, with Exercises of Bad English: or, an easy Guide to Speaking and writing the English Language Properly*, 4th ed., I. Thompson, Newcastle-upon-Tyne, 1754. For Fisher, see Michaels, *Teaching of English*, pp. 325–326. Peter Walkden Fogg, *Elementa anglicana; or, the Principles of English*

Grammar Displayed and Exemplified..., J. Clarke, Stockport, 1796. Cited by Michaels, p. 328.

72 Murgatroyd put Leonhard Culmann's *Sentenіae Pueriles* (1639) on his recommendatory 'Authors Useful to be Read at School' list, but does not seem to have possessed a copy.

73 See Michaels, *Teaching of English*, pp. 14–125 for an account of early literacy learning, from the sixteenth century onwards, including the syllabic method.

74 Murgatroyd, 'Authors Useful to be Read at School'. Only two of these children were noted as being 'free' scholars. As Judith Jago remarks, fee-paying children (who appear to have been the majority in Slaithwaite) would be unlikely to be mentioned on Visitation returns, especially in an establishment set up for free education. Jago, *Aspects of the Georgian Church*, p. 131. The last name on the register – 'Smith, Mary – to pay 2 lessons' – suggests a very great flexibility of provision.

75 John Bentley, *Halifax and Its Gibbet-law: Placed in a True Light. Together with a Description of the Town, the Nature of the Soil, the Temper and Disposition of the People*, P. Darby for the Author, Halifax, 1761, pp. 9–11.

76 Martin Clare, *Youth's Introduction to Trade and Business*, 18th ed., G. Keith, London (1769). Clare's emphasis on keeping records and the usefulness of abbreviation in note-taking may have prompted Murgatroyd's interest in shorthand. Perhaps parents asked for it to be included in the curriculum. He devoted twenty pages of the 'Authors Useful' notebook to either practising shorthand or making lesson plans for teaching it, probably the latter. He had no shorthand primer in his library; the length of these notes suggests he was working from a borrowed book.

77 George Fisher (Accomptant), *The Instructor, or Young Man's Best Companion... to which is added The Family's Best Companion... and a Complete Treatise of Farriery*, 13th edn, S. Birt, London, 1755.

78 Annesley and Hoskin, *Archbishop Drummond's Visitation*, 'Slaithwaite'.

79 Murgatroyd 'Ask, Read, Retain, Teach', KC 242/9, p. 17, '1788. Calumny'; p. 90, 'Order and Dealing Justice'; p. 93, 'Duties that shou'd subsist between Friend & Friend'; p. 111, '1788 Grief'.

80 Hulbert, *Annals*, pp. 25–44, 56.

81 Murgatroyd, 'Book of Records', 'January 14 1747: Extracts from Beveridge's Sermons, Vol. 2'. William Beveridge, *The Works of the Right Reverend Father in God, Dr. William Beveridge,... Containining [sic] all his sermons, as well those published by himself, as those since his death*, 2nd ed., 2 vols., William Innys, London, 1729. Some time later, he devoted eighteen pages of densely written foolscap pages to Robert Warren, *Practical Discourses on Various Subjects: Proper for all Families, In two volumes*, Edmund Parker, London, 1723.

82 Murgatroyd, 'A Cornucopia', pp. 625–630, for the notes on Nettleton.

83 Thomas Nettleton, *Some Thoughts Concerning Virtue and Happiness, in a Letter to a Clergyman*, Jeremiah Batley, London, 1729. *A Treatise on Virtue and Happiness*, 2nd ed., Batley and J. Wood, London, 1736.

84 Nettleton, *Some Thoughts*, pp. I, vi.

85 In 1749, he copied out into his 'Book of Records' a letter received from Daniel Eagland (son of the churchwarden who had introduced him to the Slaithwaite schoolroom twenty years before), 'About Human Reason'. 'Bro' Jno', Eagland wrote, 'These Thoughts occur'd to me upon ye July 1, I write 'em to you wth ye utmost Freedom, not in a dictatorial Way, you're entirely at Liberty ei'r to approve or reject...'. This kind of exchange went on until the end of Murgatroyd's life. On New Year's Eve 1802 ('Some Rain and Darkish'), he sat companionably with Rev. Falcon, who 'din'd, drank Tea, sup'd and spent Eveng with me – I read 2 sermons, & we were very instructive & agreeable to one another – his Mothr & Family are tolerably in Health – He would have Moonlight – & I hope, got well Home.' Murgatroyd Diary, KC 242/6 (31 December 1802). Local author Alexander Disney explained his going over to the West Riding Methodists in 1793 in 'three letters to a friend' and gave as a major motivating factor the increased opportunities for 'human happiness' among them. His Friend and addressee was a gloomy kind of man who believed life to be one long series of calamities and a vale of tears; 'Real and experimental Religion' might cheer him up. *Reasons for Methodism, briefly Stated, in three Letters to a Friend*, J. Nicholson, Halifax, 1793, pp. 9, 64–73. For the place of epistolarity in the history of literacy, privacy and interiority,

see Vincent, *Rise of Mass Literacy*, pp. 121–123 and passim; and David Vincent, 'The Progress of Literacy', *Victorian Studies*, 45:3 (2003), pp. 405–431.

86 Nettleton, *Treatise*, p. 11.

87 S. A. Grave, 'Some Eighteenth-Century Attempts to Use the Notion of Happiness', *Studies in the Eighteenth Century. Papers presented at the David Nichol Memorial Seminar*, R. F. Brissenden (Ed.), Australian National University Press, Canberra, 1968, pp. 155–169. Nettleton, *Treatise*, p. ii. For Nettleton's discussion of the social realm, see pp. 132–173. For the dangers of benevolence run riot, p. 265. The *Treatise* was enormously popular, running through fourteen editions before the century's end. Nettleton's arguments bear some resemblance to Francis Hutcheson's and his philosophy of universal benevolence. See T. A Roberts, *The Concept of Benevolence: Aspects of Eighteenth-Century Moral Philosophy*, Macmillan, London (1973); Thomas Mautner (Ed.), *Francis Hutcheson: On Human Nature. Reflections on our Common Systems of Morality. On the Social Nature of Man*, Cambridge University Press, Cambridge, 1993.

88 Nettleton, *Treatise*, p. 26.

89 Nettleton, *Treatise*, p. 118.

90 Nettleton, *Treatise*, pp. 179, 190–191.

91 Nettleton, *Thoughts*, p. 296.

92 Nettleton, *Treatise*, p. 11.

93 Nettleton, *Treatise*, p. 39.

94 Joseph Addison, 'No. 565, Friday July 9, 1714', *The Spectator*, Donald F. Bond (Ed.), Clarendon Press, Oxford, 1965, vol. 4, pp. 529–533.

95 Lorraine Daston, 'Attention and the Values of Nature in the Enlightenment', in Lorraine Daston and Fernando Vidal (eds.), *The Moral Authority of Nature*, University of Chicago Press, Chicago and London, 2004, pp. 100–126.

96 James Bolton, *A History of Fungusses, growing about Halifax* . . . , 4 vols., J. Brook, Huddersfield, 1788–1791, vol. 1, p. 36; vol. 2, pp. 46, 73.

97 Daston, 'Attention', p. 108.

CHAPTER 13

Reading as a Woman, Being Read as a Woman

Lisbeth Larsson

Reading is a two-way affair: to read and to be read. It is an inevitable part of modern life. We read to understand the world, life, ourselves, and we read to define others. Reading is to do things with words, as Austen said. It is also to be formed by words, created by the other's words.

Reading fiction has been and still is an important part of women's lives. In his seminal study *The Rise of the Novel*, Watt showed how the European book market at the end of the eighteenth century developed in intense communication with female readers.[1] In the new bourgeois society, women were cut off from the public sphere and restricted to the private. Their sole task was now to take care of home, children and husband, and in this historically new situation, woman became the reader par excellence. For some reason – less easy to understand – she still is.

The subject matter of the simultaneously appearing new novels was generally about women and their feelings, family and private life. More specifically, they tended to describe a young woman's path from one family to another, following the precarious steps from daughter to wife, from father- to husband-dependency, managing the problems that might disturb this process and the difficulties arising from the outside but even more from within herself.

Several feminist scholars recently have underlined the importance of private reading in the process of becoming a woman in modern society.[2] Making gender has been a decisive part of female reading practices, particularly so at the end of the eighteenth century and the first half of the nineteenth, when the novel was closely connected to another popular and widely reading genre: the manual of manners. This period of social transformation fostered a wide demand for conduct literature and manuals.[3] Most of them treated private matters, gave advice on how to behave in the new society, how and when to make a visit, how to address people and write letters to them. They taught how to dress on different occasions, how to dance and even how to propose (!). However, as Mews, among others, showed, most of them were directed to young unmarried women and young wives[4]: to the former with advice on how to get married, to the latter with advice on how to stay married and make their husband happy. "The art of being a good wife" was a typical title. These manuals were full of good advice but most, interestingly enough, were delivered in the form of short stories or parts of novels. In addition to what Geertz termed the 'thin' stories of advice, there were also 'thick' ones – fictions from which women could acquire more specific knowledge of the risks and possibilities of being a woman.

Thus, reading manuals was, to some extent, like reading novels and, in some cases, it remains difficult to make a clear distinction. So, with Richardson's famous novel *Pamela,* written and first sold as a manual of letter-writing, other writers could mock the manuals but still integrate them into their novels. In *Pride and Prejudice,* Jane Austen makes the pompous Mr. Collin read aloud one of the best known manuals from the eighteenth century: James Fordyce's *Sermon to Young Women* from 1765. In fact, topics and themes of Austen's novels kept close to the manuals.

Despite this promiscuity – or perhaps because of it – reading was a hot topic in the manuals themselves as well as in the novels. Women's reading habits were further discussed in countless newspaper articles and essays. 'I just hate this reading of novels', says the male protagonist of the Swedish romantic Palmblad's essay on the novel at the beginning of the nineteenth century.[5] With his companions, he has set his mind to rescuing the young heroine from the library, where she for days has sought refuge, uncontrollably immersing herself in any foreign or Swedish romance novel on which she can lay her hands. He continues:

> *I cannot but consider such reading detrimental to young women. The tender emotions, the as yet unnamed yearnings budding in their bosom, should not be allowed to ripen prematurely or tempted to seek an external object. Their imagination is as yet too pure, too innocent to dwell among notions appropriate to a more advanced age.*[6]

Although all seem to agree on the importance of women's reading, in particular, the manuals and other conduct literature, there is also general consent about the danger of reading too much and of reading the wrong books. The manuals, many of which are themselves partly novels, are full of almost obsessive laments about women's addiction to novels – what we would now call a "cultural panic."

Reading novels made the married woman forget her duties – kitchen, children and husband – but the effects were considered even worse in younger female readers. They would acquire false notions about married life and, if eventually married, be unable to take care of home and children, and they would neglect their duty to make a husband happy. Reading novels made a woman passive and oversensitive, inclined to weep rather than to act. It kept her, in short, away from the realities of life and fostered a romantic, useless, often even dangerous kind of woman.

Although traditionally disregarded by literary history, this was a serious problem for female writers entering the literary scene in this period, in which female writers were both frequent and important and, like George Eliot in England or George Sand in France, made a deep impact on the development of the novel. The four most purchased, read and translated Swedish writers of the nineteenth century were all women: Fredrika Bremer, Sophie von Knorring, Emily Flygare-Carlén and Marie Sophie Schwartz. I do not expect many readers of today, in Sweden or abroad, to know or to have read any of these authors. However, in their time, they were not only popular but also, at least the first three mentioned, highly respected both at home and abroad. The fourth, Marie Sophie Schwartz, who had started her career writing manuals for young women, later wrote in 1858 the love story of the century, *Mannen af börd och qvinnan af folket* (*The Nobleman and the Woman of the People*).

Common opinion of women's reading was a tricky question for these writers. Because the problem was too controversial to be avoided, the novels abound in meta-discussions of reading habits and the virtues of different kinds of books. It is instructive to see them, on the one hand, defending their chosen genre and, on the other, in the name of political correctness, attacking it. Fredrika Bremer, the first of the four, most explicitly defended in her novels the reading of novels. She pushed the question discreetly but insistently. Her first novel, *Familjen H**** (*The H*** Family*) published in 1832, has a long central scene, where the matter is discussed.[7] With a couple of relatives, friends and persons of the household (e.g., a housekeeper or teacher), the family is gathered in the sitting room. When the conversation turns to reading, all agree that novels are a danger, particularly to young women. An elderly uncle, about sixty and still a bachelor, says, 'If I ever will consider marrying, it would be on the premises that my wife will never read anything but the Bible and the cookbook', and the brother-in-law of the main character, Julia, adds, 'reading is to the soul what opium is to the body', as having already read Marx, he just confused religion with novels. Still worse, because Julia is a novel addict, her fiancée promptly agrees with this statement. At the conclusion of the novel, he has accordingly lost her. She is by then a married woman and seemingly very much in love, but not with the man to whom she was at first engaged. The reader now perceives that the man Julia actually has married is Professor L, the only one to side with her in defending the novel in the earlier discussion. Throughout the novel, he has been treated with the utmost discretion, mentioned as tutor to the boys of the family but described as a rather plain figure. Usually silent in company, in the reading discussion he had suddenly come forward to deliver a fervid speech in favour of novels and their readers. At that crucial moment, this insignificant man, to whom Fredrika Bremer was going to give her heroine's heart, had described the novel as an incomparable tool for the education of soul and heart and particularly recommended it for younger persons.

Defence of novel reading, however, became ever more complicated. Later female novelists, such as von Knorring and Flygare-Carlén, tended to differentiate between commendable and condemnable novels, thus enabling themselves to continue writing novels while remaining politically correct. Still, differences can be noted. In the novels of von Knorring, heroines like Otilia in *Förhoppningar* (*Expectations*) prove their good heart, character and maturity by preferring romantic and idealistic novels and condemning realistic and materialistic ones.[8] Otilia actually manages to save her beloved cousin Hugo by making him read an idealistic and romantic French novel, Lamartine's *Jocelyn*. Conversely, the heroines of the younger Flygare-Carlén (herself baptized Emilie after the heroine of a love novel by Lamartine) are often enchanted by romantic and idealistic novels but, as in *Romanhjeltinnan*, ultimately are redeemed into a more realistic view on life.[9]

In this novel, literally *The Novel Heroine*, the heroine Blenda, as her name intimates, has been blinded by reading novels. Virtually, she has been breast-fed on them. Her mother is an extensive and excessive reader of romantic and idealistic novels, and the daughter inherited her obsession. Her prognosis is, in other words, none too good when she embarks on a steamer from the provincial town of Vänersborg for the capital, Stockholm, to live with her aunt. On board, she gets involved with two men, one of them charming and seductive, the other plain but rather nice. With the latter, she engages in interesting conversation but, of course, she falls in love with the charmer and the outcome looks quite bad. On parting in Stockholm, however, the nice man gives her a parcel that in the end will save her. It contains a whole bunch of realistic novels, and when she reads them after joining her aunt, Blenda acquires a very different view of life – and of men. She comes to her senses, recovers from her romanticism, and when the charming young man comes to see her, she sends him away. When the donor of the realistic novels likewise turns up, she has recognized her feelings for him as genuine love and decides to marry him.

Most novel heroines addicted to novel reading were not that fortunate. The best known of them, Madame Bovary in Gustave Flaubert's novel of that name, actually died from it. Flaubert's novel was published in 1857 and is often acclaimed as the first modern novel. Before *Madame Bovary*, Flaubert had written pompous works such as *The Temptation of Saint Anthony*, but listening to his reading of it aloud for eight days on end, his exasperated friends advised him to write instead a novel on the most boring topic he could imagine. He then wrote his classical novel about a woman with deplorable reading habits, a woman reading herself to death.

It is with a shiver of disgust and indignation that Flaubert comments on his heroine's choice of reading: "They were all about love, lovers, loving", he writes, "martyred maidens swooning in secluded lodges, postilions slain every other mile, horses ridden to death on every page, dark forests, aching hearts, promising, sobbing kissing and tears."[10] He also disapproves of her obsessive way of reading. "Even at table, she had her books with her, and she would be turning the pages, when Charles was eating and talking to her".[11] She does not care about her husband or her daughter, she just keeps reading, lost in the world of books. And when Emma Bovary finally is suffering one of the most painful and disgusting deaths described in literature, there can be no doubt that she is as much a victim of the romances she has imbibed as of the arsenic she has just swallowed.

At the end of the century, the Swedish Nobel prize winner, Selma Lagerlöf, with a magnificent gesture, threw the love novel to the wolves – a gesture which, however, has been difficult to interpret. It happens in her first and most famous novel, *Gösta Berlings saga* (*The Gösta Berling Saga*).[12] The hero, Gösta Berling, is on his way to the Christmas ball, his horse Don Juan harnessed to his sleigh. He makes a stop at the Berga manor, where he has friends, but finds it in bad shape. It is late afternoon, but the lady of the manor is still in bed reading novels. There is hardly anything to eat and the hostess goes to find some horseradish to ameliorate the last piece of bad meat. Their hopes for a marriage between their son and the beautiful and wealthy Anna Stjärnhök are all but gone. She is going to marry a wealthy older man to ensure that she will not be taken for her money, and she is going to declare her decision at the ball. Gösta promises his friends to bring her back. When he is about to leave for the ball and for his mission, his hostess comes running. She wants to give him her dearest possession: Madame de Staehl's *Corinne*, the love novel of the century in four tiny volumes bound in red leather. These will subsequently save not only Gösta Berling's life but also Anna's, the desired marriage, and the Berga manor.

At the ball, Gösta, as befits a romance, falls in love with Anna. He carries her to his sleigh and drives away with her. Running at full speed, Don Juan carries the lovers through the cold night across a frozen lake. Nearing the manor, where the former fiancée is waiting, a pack of wolves emerges from the forest to pursue them, drawing so close that the loving couple fear for their lives. In despair, Gösta throws the four volumes of *Corinne*, one by one, into their jaws. The wolves fall back and Gösta can return Anna to her fiancée. The novel-loving woman gets to keep her manor but, one could conclude, at the price of her favourite novel.[13]

By the turn of the century, the panic about women's novel reading had abated but the discussion of their reading habits continued. In between the wars, when the output of weeklies was expanding rapidly in Sweden, fierce campaigns were launched against women's extensive reading of this "colored slough", which was seen as a dangerous threat particularly to female office workers. After World War II, Swedish media again panicked, first over children's appetites for comicbooks and then over their excessive TV-watching and -exposure to the violence on the screen.

In the 1980s, a new "women's-reading panic" spread that focused on the new type of romantic novels written by Jackie Collins and others. "A new emetic in an enticing package", as one Swedish critic labeled Judith Krantz's bestseller, *Princess Daisy*. "Dirty tricks, obscene gestures, blows below the belt" another critic described Collins's *Hollywood Wives*. The well-known left-wing writer, Jan Myrdal, labeled this type of novel *tantsnusk* ('spinster filth'). A common U.S. synonym was 'shopping-and-fucking' or, in the words of Jane McLoughlin, "a kind of consumer's guide to the best beds in town".[14] Confronted with a new wave of romance, many people now talk of a 'chick lit' with a contempt that may well inaugurate a new disgust debate.

What, then, is the difference between a good and healthy kind of book and a bad, pernicious or even fatal one? It is obviously not just a question of content. Flaubert's *Madame Bovary*, as well as the novels of its heroine, was not very different in subject matter: love, adultery and tears. But his novel about the female reader, Emma Bovary, is classified as a good book, whereas the ones she is reading are deemed bad and destructive.

In the 1960s, the French sociologist, Robert Escarpit, tried to evaluate the differences between novels without passing qualifying judgment.[15] With his seminal study *La Sociologie de la Littérature*, he created a model that became useful in Swedish cultural politics. There is, he wrote, not one book market; rather, there are two circuits of books, one 'popular' and one 'educated'. These books are produced and purchased in different places at different prices and have different readers. In the popular circuit, according to Escarpit, the novels are mass-produced, their authors anonymous and trademarks more important. They are cheap, sold at drugstores or in supermarkets, and are very soon to be maculated and forgotten. In the educated circuit, on the other hand, novels have a long life, they are discussed (not debated as the popular ones), reviewed in newspapers and magazines, read and re-read, researched and remembered. In this circuit, the author is important and production scarce but elaborate. The books are expensive and sold in bookstores or borrowed from public libraries.

However, suppressed in the Escarpit model are two fundamental differences between the two circuits. They look quite similar and comparable, as if equal, but are just the opposite. This is, of course, an illusion: cultural as well as economic accessibility is anything but equal. With this in mind, a cultural–political reform was introduced in Sweden in the 1970s.

A problem of the national book market after World War II had been the rapid growth of popular American paperbacks and the shrinking demand for Swedish novels in the educated circuit. In the 1970s, the popular circuit prospered while the educated circuit steadily declined.[16] Among Social Democrats, with their long tradition of popular education and their ambition to make people read 'good' literature (that is, books from the educated circuit), the Escarpit model now generated a political strategy of economic transference from one circuit to the other. Underlying this desire to push readers in the 'right' direction was another factor suppressed in Escparpit's model. Using a term from Bourdieu, the *cultural capital* invested in the respective circuits is inversely distributed, in that the popular one requires none of it, the educated one a lot. Making books from the educated circuit as available and as inexpensive as the popular books, according to the Social Democrats' conviction, would encourage people to read them rather than the other kind, thereby if not eradicating them, at least decreasing that circuit. This proved to be an optimistic illusion but resulted in three decades' worth of books belonging to the educated circuit very affordable in Sweden. Throughout this period, the government put significant amounts of money into the educated circuit but to no avail. What happened was that the difference between the circuits, as described by Escarpit, all but disappeared; the 'educated' books are now as short-lived as the 'popular' ones. They are sold (at least in the paperback edition) in the same places as the popular books, which have invaded the bookstores. In the first wave came the 'shopping-and-fucking' novels of the 1980s; in the next, the crime fiction of the 1990s; and currently, there are piles of 'chick-lit' books on display and on the shelves of Swedish bookstores. Governmental subsidies notwithstanding, one could conclude that it is the 'educated circuit' that is disappearing. As the latest governmental report on the matter must admit, there are no longer two circuits, the 'popular' having all but swallowed the 'educated' one.[17]

This leads us to two other factors suppressed in Escarpit's model – namely, gender and quality. Mass culture is, as Huyssen underlines in *After the Great Divide*, female-gendered and consumers in the popular circuit, as previously discussed, by tradition and interest are female.[18] As Escarpit noted in *La Sociologie de la Littérature*, the popular circuit built and prospered on female reading habits at the end of the eighteenth century (although this did not prevent him from depicting both circuits as not gendered).

Returning to *Madame Bovary*, we all know it belongs squarely in the educated circuit, whereas the unhappy heroine is reading books exclusively from the popular one. Looking at literary history generally, it is easy to see that popular books and females go together. Novels by women tend to be popular and, if not immediately then in the course of history, labelled as popular literature. The same applies to the novels that women prefer to read.

Following Huyssen, Escarpit's educated circuit was a male circuit focussing on the male writer; the popular circuit was a female circuit focussing on the female reader. This, of course, does not mean that there were no female writers in the educated circuit; there are many. But, as many feminist scholars have shown, they tend to be forgotten or, just as common but much less discussed, defined as popular – if not by contemporary critics, then by literary historians, as was the case of many Swedish female writers of the nineteenth century. Highly rated and often 'queens' of the book market, they are rarely mentioned in our literary manuals. Exceptions such as Fredrika Bremer and Selma Lagerlöf often made comments suggesting that their proper place was in the popular rather than the educational circuit.

The popular circuit, of course, also has many male readers, even if they seldom have been scrutinised or treated with the same contempt as the female readers. When in the 1970s mass culture and its consumption was reevaluated in the context of cultural and reception studies, male consumers and their interests were actually included. Later, when the didactic limitations of *Ideologiekritik* became obvious, German students of popular fiction experimented with new ways of reading and interpretation, more congenial with its past and present readers. Scholars such as Nusser, Spinner and Waldmann claimed that reading popular fiction could strengthen readers' identities.[19] Reading was regarded as a kind of play-acting, a way of distancing oneself from the world in order to master it. The Norwegian writer, Kjartan Fløgstad, drawing on Bakhtin, saw a rebellious potential in popular literature.[20] Like the medieval carnival, he claimed, it acts *within* the established order but directs its zest *against* it. Constructive elements were discovered in crime fiction as well as in Westerns, science fiction, and pornography. Engaging in this literature, it was claimed, the reader distances himself from the disabling reality surrounding him and for a moment is permitted to recognize his actual strength, his possibilities and competence. This new tolerance, however, had its limits. Whereas detective stories could be studied for their description of feats of intelligence, Westerns for their accounts of mental strength, pornography for its depiction of sexual prowess, and science fiction for its mastery of techniques, romance and love stories – the fictions of close relationships and intimacy that women prefer to read – seemed to have no redeeming features. On the contrary, Nusser and Waldmann express an aversion to this kind of literature and see the reading of it as solely destructive. But, is it the content of such books that repels them or the style and the type of reading it invokes?

Returning to *Madame Bovary*, it strikes me that the very style of the novel prevents its reader from reading the way its heroine, Emma, does. Flaubert's ideal as a writer, 'impassivity', was a style of impersonal objectivity, and he consistently undermined the possibility of reading the novel on the romantic premises of the heroine. For example, in the classic scene of seduction – in which Rodolphe, the landed proprietor who has his eye on the doctor's beautiful young wife, meets her at a cattle fair, and takes her upstairs in an empty storehouse – his seductive whispering is constantly interrupted by the bargaining on cows and pigs in the marketplace below. By such means, Flaubert forces the reader to view the situation from the outside and from a distance. Readers cannot simply identify with Emma and experience her feelings, they have to see her from the outside and realise that she is being seduced and cheated. Other scenes, which almost got Flaubert jailed for indecency, are constructed in the same way, and the climactic sexual intercourse is suggested to the reader only by the description of the lovers' carriage swinging through the streets of Rouen.

The basic difference between an 'educated' book and a popular one is the resistances built into the text of the former, making the reader pause from time to time to ponder its meanings. A popular book is a page-turner and is written in a way to eliminate such hindrances, triggering the reader not to stop but rather continue reading. In a literary, educated book, readers have to surmount many obstacles: knots and riddles forcing them to interrupt the reading and reflect on the meaning of the text. In his Balzac analysis *S/Z*, Barthes contends that the difference between a good book and a bad one is the distance between riddles and their solutions, and there may well be some truth to this. It ignores, however, other complications of the matter.[21]

In reader-response studies or any literary criticism considering readers, there are invariably two kinds of readers – I do not now consider readers of high or low culture but rather two styles or ways of reading. One is the reader who strives to keep himself above or outside the text, as if taking a step back while reading to keep an analytical distance. The other kind of reader seeks to get as close to the text as possible and while reading to eliminate any distance between herself and the text. I am saying 'him' and 'her' because in empirical reader studies, the former is generally a man and the latter a woman; the first way of reading – without exception – is now rated as the better of the two.

An example from the American scholar, Norman Holland, elucidates the difference between these two ways of reading.[22] In his book, *Five Readers Reading* from the mid-1970s, he studies some of his students – one girl, four boys – reading a short story, the well-known 'A Rose for Miss Emily' by William Faulkner. Although for his part, Holland seems to ignore gender differences, differences of reading stand out and are easily linked to gender. What Holland sets out to prove is that everybody reads according to his or her psychological character, experience and individual problems. He calls this "identity theme", and his thesis is that we all read in order to bolster our personal identity. Therefore, before discussing their reading of the story, he interviews his students about their life to find out their identity theme.

The students exhibit very different backgrounds and experiences, but what is interesting is that, basically, they turn out to have quite similar identity themes. All are afraid of being abandoned and are doing their best to manage and overcome this fear. All seem to suffer from some kind of fear of separation. Because they seem to have this identity theme in common, and accepting Holland's thesis, one would expect them to read – except for minor personal variations – in a similar way. But they don't. They turn out to read in two very distinct ways. The male students are systematically keeping a distance from the story, whereas the female student, Sandra, seeks to get as close to it as possible.

This difference actually already appears in the interviews. Sandra is a willing object. She does her best to comply with Holland, understand his premises and questions, and give candid answers. Conversely, the male students seek to evade Holland's often personal questions. They say, 'Can you define that?', 'Would you develop your question?', or 'What exactly do you mean?' They elude his recurring and persistent, 'How do you feel?'questions by answering them in strict intellectual terms. Although he persistently asks them to tell him what they feel about the story, they invariably keep their interpretation of it on an abstract level. One of them compares it to a classic Greek tragedy. When Miss Emily's house is opened up after her death, the corpse of a black man is found in her bed, half rotten, half mummified. It is identified as that of a servant working for her years ago. At the time, there had been some gossiping about the two, but in the end, the black man had disappeared – to work somewhere else, as neighbours then believed; now they believe he had been murdered. The student evades Holland's questions about his feelings by comparing the gossip around Miss Emily with a Greek chorus, singing of the inevitable fall of the tragic hero. Another male student interprets the story as describing a conflict between epochs and cultures. In the male readings of the story, the characters are often described not as humans but rather as representatives of values, ideas or principles. They frequently compare the text with other texts, ranging them in hierarchies. "In effect", Holland comments about one male student, "Shep brought in McLuhan to be put down by Faulkner, Sam Fathers, and even the Snoopses, to put down the Griersons, Burroughs to put down Faulkner, and so on – he was acting as a fight promoter, particularly when he changed from intellectual and literary preferences to more tender topics."[23] Faulkner is rated above Burroughs but not as high as Joyce and so on. One and all, they establish hierarchies and differences of value and power. Who in the story has more power than the other, who is right, who is wrong, who is better, who is inferior? To the male students, differences are more important than similarities.

Sandra, conversely, consistently strives to play down differences, both in her relationship to the story and between its characters. She enlarges and reduces, just like her male counterparts, but in a different direction: she strives to bring things and people together. In her discussion of the text, she is concentrating on the story, not constructing patterns or structures but staying with the people in it and the emotional points, as she sees them. 'See' and 'touch' are her favourite words. 'I can see it', she says of the scene in which Miss Emily buys arsenic at the drugstore. 'It is as if I stood behind the cash register myself'.[24] However, when Holland asks her to pass judgment on Miss Emily and tell him whether she thinks her action – presumably to have murdered the man when he wanted to leave her – is right or wrong, she obstinately desists from answering. She does not want to be drawn away from the story or from the heroine to whom she has become attached.

In Swedish reader-response studies of literature-reading in schools, a field in which Norman Holland is an important name, it is also discernable how girls consistently refuse to keep a distance to the texts they read. In descriptions of classroom behaviour, they initially become the teacher's favourites because they love to read.[25] They both read and discuss the texts with an enthusiasm far greater than the boys'. But, ultimately, they invariably disappoint the teacher for the very same reason: they do not want to keep the distance to the text and its characters which teachers deem necessary, nor discuss structures, politics or generally abstract questions.

For more than two hundred years, women have been the mainstay of the book trade, the most reliable clients of public libraries and subscribers of book clubs. And, for more than two hundred years, women's reading habits have been under constant attack. Women's choices of books and their lack of critical distance to what they read make them deficient readers: the common verdict, from the end of the eighteenth century to our own time. However, against these professional litanies about popular literature and their destructive influence on women's sense of identity are the positive accounts of the female readers themselves. In women's diaries and autobiographies from the last two centuries, there is continuous denial of this opinion. But this defense has only lately been (half-) seriously considered in the field of reader research. Not even Radway, in her otherwise pioneering work *Reading the Romance* (1984), dares trust female romance readers' unanimous appraisal of the empowering effects of their kind of reading.[26] After quoting them at length and very loyally letting them express their enjoyment and the healing effect of their reading, she suddenly turns around to criticise their reading in terms borrowed from the long tradition of disapproval. In her opinion, they may well feel stimulated and strengthened – in reality, they are rather debilitated and less capable of dealing with their life.[27] In the second edition of *Reading the Romance*, Radway somewhat modifies her standpoint in an introduction, conceding female readers a higher degree of credibility.[28]

In Radway's study, readers unanimously claim that their identity is strengthened by their reading, as do the female readers in the Swedish study *Inte en dag utan en bok* (*Not a Day Without a Book*) 1988.[29] In its interviews, women consistently testify to a need for intense romance reading as well as to its positive effects in their lives. One describes reading as "a warming up" of her feelings, another feels that she 'becomes whole and alive' by reading.[30]

To read is to confirm and reconstitute one's identity – this is the opinion of Holland and a range of other students of reader response as well as female readers of mass-produced literature. In Radway's study, they describe this reading "a declaration of independence" and how it has variously reaffirmed their sense of self and given them new strength. These women, most of whom also claim to be 'caring beings', make their reading a free space that screens them from their immediate surroundings but simultaneously gives them new impetus to face reality. The moment cherished by female readers of romantic tales is not, as one would expect, the kiss or the happy ending but rather the moment when the male protagonist, at long last, turns around and looks into the heroine's eyes, recognizes her and her values, and tells her that he needs her. To them, such romantic narratives chronicle the 'female triumph, a utopian vision of the virtues of female caring.[31]

In a culture that has for two centuries increasingly celebrated autonomy, self-sufficiency, expansion, efficiency, and rationality, women thus persevere in reading about love, closeness, intimacy, and concern. In a culture enhancing the search for boundless freedom and our need to break away, women prefer to read about the art of making human bonds as strong and intimate as possible.

It may be, of course, that as many observers have assured and still do that this denotes a general regression in reading, that women particularly are looking for some kind of consolation in a world in which it is too difficult to deal with reality. Or, as many others say, that women are quite simply getting cheated: their cherished values may be universally celebrated on the surface but in actual practice, reading is just a way to keep women down and make them continue doing work that society needs but for which it is unwilling to pay.

Still, this reading might also be understood as a reading against the grain, as a way of reaffirming one's identity or what Holland calls one's life-style.[32] By such a reading, a woman makes contact with her theme of identity and her strength and is helped in her attempt to maintain an approach to life and other human beings which is contrary to prevailing cultural values. The vision offered by romantic fiction is of a different society, a utopia in which closeness and intimacy are not equated with weakness and a poor sense of identity but rather with true individuality and self-confidence. In their reading, women do not keep a distance to the text, the way the ideal reader does in studies of reader response. Letting themselves be absorbed by what they read, they maintain their subjectivity and establish a distance to a society that consistently diminishes them.

Notes

1 Watt (1957).
2 Nancy Armstrong and Leonard Tennenhouse (1987); Jones (1996); Hull (1982).
3 J. Hunter (1990), p. 252.
4 Mews (1969), p. 11.
5 Palmblad (1812).
6 Ibid.
7 Bremer (1832/1844).
8 Knorring (1843).
9 Flygare-Carlén (1849).
10 Flaubert (1856/1992) p. 28.
11 Ibid., p. 45.
12 Lagerlöf (1890/1982).
13 Larsson (1993).
14 Larsson (1994), p. 281.
15 Escarpit (1958/1964).
16 SOU (1972) and SOU (1972).
17 SOU (1997).
18 Huyssen (1987).
19 Nusser (1973) and (1975) p. 27 and Spinner (1976) p. 31.
20 Fløgstad (1981).
21 Barthes (1976).
22 Holland (1975).
23 Ibid., p. 158.
24 Ibid., p. 188.
25 Linnér (1984), Malmgren (1986).
26 Radway (1984).
27 Ibid., p. 94.
28 Ibid., p. 81.
29 Gunnar Hansson (1988).
30 Hansson, pp. 103, 108.
31 Janice Radway (1991), introduction.
32 This argument is further developed in Larsson (1989).

References

Armstrong, N., & Tennenhouse, L. (Eds.) (1987). *The ideology of conduct: Essays on literature and the history of sexuality*. New York/London: Routledge.

Barthes, R. (1976). *S/Z*, Points Essais 70. Paris: Seuil.

Bremer, F. (1832/1844). *Domestic life; or, the H-family*. London: T. Allman.

Escarpit, R. (1958/1964). *Sociologie de la littérature*. Paris: Presses universitaires de France.

Flaubert, G. (1856/1992). *Madame Bovary: Provincial Lives*. London/New York: Penguin.

Fløgstad, K. (1981). *Loven vest for Pecos og ander essays om populærkunst og kulturindustri*. Oslo: Gyldendahl Norsk Forlag.

Flygare-Carlén, E. (1849). *Romanhjeltinnan*, Stockholm: Östlund & Berling.

Hansson, G. (1988). *Inte en dag utan en bok. Om läsning av populärfiktion*. Linköping Studies in Art and Science 30. Linköping: Tema Kommunikation.

Holland, N. (1975). *5 readers reading*. New Haven, CT: Yale University Press.

Hull, S. W. (1982). *Chaste, silent and obedient: English books for women 1475–1640*. San Marino, CA: Huntington Library

Hunter, J. P. (1990). *Before novels: The cultural contexts of eighteenth century English fiction*. New York/London: W. W. Norton & Co.

Huyssen, A. (1987). *After the great divide: Modernism, mass culture, postmodernism*. Bloomington: Indiana University Press.

Jones, V. (1996). The Seductions of Conduct: Pleasure and Conduct Literature. In Roy Porter & Marie Mulvey Roberts (Eds.), *Pleasure in the eighteenth century*. Basingstoke, Hants: Macmillian.

Knorring, S. M. von (1843). *Förhoppingar*. Jönköping: JE Lundström & Kompani.

Lagerlöf, S. (1890/1982). *The story of Gösta Berling*. Karlstad: Press.

Larsson, L. (1989). *En annan historia. Om kvinnors läsning och svensk veckopress*. Stehag: Symposion.

Larsson, L. (1993). Den farliga romanen. In Elisabeth Møller Jensen (Ed.), *Fadershuset. Nordisk kvinnolitteraturhistoria II*. Höganäs: Wiken.

Larsson, L. (1994). Lace and the limits of reading. *Cultural Studies*, 8 (2), 278–292.

Linnér, B. (1984). *Litteratur och undervisnig. Om litteraturundervisningens institutionella villkor*. Lund: Liber förlag.

Malmgren, L.-G. (1986). *Den konstiga konsten. En genomgång av några aktuella teorier om litteraturreception*. Lund: Studentlitteratur.

Mews, H. (1969). *Frail vessels: Woman's role in women's novels from Fanny Burney to Georg Eliot*. London: Athlone Press.

Nusser, P. (1973). *Roman für die Unterschicht. Groschenhefte und ihre Leser*. Stuttgart: Metzler

Nusser, P. (1975). Kriminalroman zur Überwindung von Litteraturbarrieren, *Der Deutschunterricht: Beiträge zur seiner Praxis und wissenschaftlichen Grundlegung*, 1, 27.

Palmblad, V. F. (1812). Öfver romanen. *Phosphorous*, 1.

Radway, J. (1984). *Reading the romance: Women, patriarchy, and popular literature*. Chapel Hill: University of North Carolina Press.

Radway, J. (1991). *Reading the romance: Women, patriarchy, and popular literature; with a new introduction by the author*. Chapel Hill: University of North Carolina Press.

Statens Offentliga Utredningar (1972). *En bok om böcker. Litteraturutredningens branschstudier*. Stockholm, Investigations of the Swedish Government, no. 80 and SOU. *Läs – och bokvanor i fem svenska samhällen. Litteraturutredningens läsvanesrudier*. Stockholm, Investigations of the Swedish Government, no. 20.

Statens Offentliga Utredningar (1997). Boken i tiden. Stockholm, Investigations of the Swedish Government, no. 141.

Spinner, K. H. (1976). "Das vergällte Leservergnügen. Zur Didaktik det Unterhaltungsliteratur" in Jörg Hienger (Ed.), *Unterhaltungsliteratur. Zu ihre Theorie und Verteidigung*. Göttingen: Vanderhoeck & Ruprecht.

Waldmann, W. (1981). Triviallitteratur. Ihr dilemma und Wege aus ihn im Problemfeld kommunikations- und produktionsorientierter Unterricht. *Wirkendes Wort. Deutsche Sprache in Forschung und Lehre*, 2, 31.

Watt, I. (1957). *The rise of the novel: Studies in Defoe, Richardson and Fielding*. London: Chatto & Windus.

CHAPTER 14

Literacy and the History of Science

Reflections Based on Chinese and Other Sources

Karine Chemla[1]

REHSEIS, CNRS
Université Paris Diderot
Paris 7

Introduction: Literate Competencies Required for Dealing With Scientific Texts

As far as I can tell, with the exception of some isolated attempts, the issue of literacy has not been a major concern in the history of science thus far.[2] The recent development of research fields such as the history of scientific education could have offered an opportunity to foster the study of literacy but, to my knowledge, this direction of inquiry has not yet been taken up in this context. What kind of research program about literacy would it be meaningful to pursue in the history of science? Of the many directions of research that spring to mind, this chapter attempts to elaborate one in particular: how actors engage with written documents. This question appears specifically necessary and its relevance can be easily demonstrated for the field of the history of science. One may hope that the example from the history of science will prove to be inspiring for the study of literacy more generally.

My starting point is provided by a very simple remark. The scholarly writings produced by the actors constitute a major set of sources for historians of science: these documents require skills to be read and interpreted. The skills in which I am interested here are not the abilities to read a script or to compute. Nor are they the professional skills of the historian, which allow dating a document or identifying the hand that wrote it. They are rather the specific skills required to approach types of scholarly texts; I illustrate them herein with the example of texts for "algorithms." In fact, as will be shown, not only do these skills exist but they also vary, depending on where and when the texts examined were produced. My whole argument in this chapter bears on these skills. It is through them that I approach literacy in the broad sense with which I apply the term here and to which I return later.

My main point is that the skills needed by the historian cannot but reflect specific competencies that the actors acquired to write, make sense of, and use documents. In this sense, these competencies belong to a set of literate skills required to carry out scientific work in a given context. The fact that historians feel aware in some respect of *how* they are illiterate, when they tackle a new set of documents, is the best indicator for the existence of the specific skills that the actors possessed. In my view, without describing the skills and attempting to acquire them, historians of science cannot adequately deal with their sources.

This dimension of literacy is important for the history of science in at least two main respects. First, in relation to the questions they chose to pursue, the environment in which they operated, and the results they expected, actors shaped specific kinds of text and stabilized the skills necessary to work with them.[3] The elaboration of these literate competencies is therefore a dimension of scientific activity that historians of science can aim to account for, one that offers a useful analytical tool for describing scientific practices. Let me stress here that in the way in which I suggest that we approach these competencies, my intention is to concentrate on the literate skills that are social phenomena and to leave aside those that relate to the individual elaboration of personal inscriptions in the course of isolated research. Second, analyzing literacy from this perspective provides historians of science with tools for interpretation that are badly needed if we are to avoid anachronisms in our way of reading.

In what follows, I first provide examples highlighting skills required to engage with specific texts and illustrating a variety of forms these skills could take. I then suggest that in our approach to literacy, we should not limit ourselves to considering the engagement with texts, but rather we should extend our concern more generally to other kinds of "written forms." As a result of these two sections, we should have a fairly broad perspective on the nature of these literate competencies. Moreover, we should have convinced ourselves that literate practices are not uniform and depend on the scholarly or professional cultures in which they take shape. Hence, the tasks confronting the historian are to devise ways of restoring and studying these practices. Last, I evoke some difficulties awaiting us and outline two methods that can be used to describe literate competencies specific to a given milieu, the shape they took, and the institutions through which they could be transmitted. In conclusion, I suggest that the issue is best approached through considering the "scholarly" or "professional cultures," in a sense to define – that is, the cultures within which these practices made sense.

The key examples on which I rely in this chapter are selected from mathematical writings composed in ancient China, although I develop several contrasts with and parallels to other mathematical documents. The reason for this choice is that these were the books that inspired in me the developments that follow. However, there may be something deeper behind these circumstantial reasons; perhaps the nature of mathematics makes it a discipline particularly well suited to studies that aim to capture phenomena related to literacy. In any event, two points must be made clear. First, my intention in examining these writings is by no means to enter into the details of the mathematics behind them. This is not necessary for my purpose, which is to identify literate skills required for engaging with these written documents. Second, even though I take them as my main examples, I intend to focus beyond them, on phenomena that I take to be general.

Let me sketch the main features of the source material from which I draw. Most of the earliest mathematical sources that came down to us from ancient China are composed of problems followed by procedures for solving them. This is the case of the two books on which I mainly rely: *The Nine Chapters on Mathematical Procedures* 九章算術 (*Jiuzhang suanshu*, hereafter, *The Nine Chapters*), which probably reached its present form in the first century CE,[4] and *Mathematical Classic by Zhang Qiujian* 張邱建算經 (*Zhang Qiujian suanjing*). Qian Baocong 錢寶琮 dates the composition of the latter to the second half of the fifth century, whereas he attributes the "details of the procedures 草 *cao*" in it to Liu Xiaosun 劉孝孫, who composed them in the sixth century.[5] These books provide excellent source material to highlight some of the skills required in reading and using a text of a procedure – in modern mathematical terminology, an *algorithm* – and constitute the main example through which I analyze engagement with technical texts.

Reading a Text: The Example of Algorithms

The first text for an algorithm on which I focus deals with a case of multiplication and constitutes the opening section of *Mathematical Classic by Zhang Qiujian*. Let me translate the text of the procedure with its problem to place it in the context in which it occurs in our corpus: [6]

(1.1) 以九乘二十一、五分之三。問得幾何。
答曰: 一百九十四、五分之二。
草曰: 置二十一, 以分母五乘之, 内子三,
得一百八。然以九 乘之, 得九百七十二。
却以分母五而一, 得合所問。

One multiplies 21 and 3/5 by 9. One asks how much it yields.

Answer: 194 and 2/5.

Detail of the procedure (*cao*):

(a) One puts 21, one multiplies it by the denominator 5, and incorporates [the result] with the numerator 3, hence yielding 108.
(b) Then, multiplying this by 9 yields 972.
(c) If, in return, one divides by the denominator, 5, what is yielded conforms to what was asked.

Here, the text of the procedure is quite straightforward. Placed after the statement of a problem and the answer, it starts with the operation: "One puts . . . ," which is quite common in all Chinese mathematical sources. The operation refers to a material surface on which computations are carried out and to the fact that the values to which computations are applied – in our example, to start with, 21 – are represented with counting rods and "put" in appropriate positions on the surface. These representations of numbers are then transformed on the surface during the process of computation, according to the text of the procedure, until the result is achieved.

Let us examine the competencies that using this text presupposes in the reader. The first one is quite obvious: the text prescribes several operations, including multiplication and division. To execute them, the reader must use other procedures that are not provided at this point in the text or, in fact, anywhere in the book. This feature reflects more general and fundamental facts. The text of an algorithm involves terms for higher-level operations, which encapsulate other lower-level procedures. In fact, the way in which these operations are constituted and introduced depends on the scholarly context in which the text was written. The competencies that a given text required from a reader or a user, at least partly, can be approached through the list of higher-level operations that were expected to be understood. Whether these pieces of knowledge were acquired previously or explained orally when first using the text does not make much difference in my view. In both cases, the knowledge remained indispensable to engage with the text as recorded in the book. These remarks lead us to a first conclusion, essential for our purpose: to a given process of computation, there can correspond different texts, and the skills required to use them vary according to their formulation. Yet, it is interesting that a given text usually presents a certain kind of uniformity in the level of detail chosen for writing down the algorithm. In the case under consideration, knowing how to execute the operations involves knowing how to lay them out on the material surface used for computing. We return to this dimension in a subsequent section.

Three additional remarks are useful to highlight other competencies needed to use the text of a procedure. First, the text of the procedure explicitly mentions values to which the computations are to be applied in the framework of the particular problem set out, and it occasionally also indicates the general terms corresponding to them: *numerator, denominator*. However, as one may expect, the text is to be interpreted as referring not only to this particular case but also to all similar cases, in a tradition of expression of a general procedure that dates back at least as early as *The Nine Chapters*.[7] In a grammatical sense, we may say that here the problem and the procedure following it play the part of a paradigm. The way in which a reader determined the degree of generality of a procedure on the basis of the text represents another key skill needed to use the text. There is no reason to assume that the methods put into play to this end were the same in all scholarly environments, and they need to be restored as part of the literate practices involved in making sense of such a text. Note that the skill under consideration does not relate to the interpretation of terms but rather to the use of the text as text. Such skills I specifically aim to bring to light in this chapter.

Second, one may be tempted to imagine that the text of a procedure is purely prescriptive. However, step (c) shows that this view is too schematic and, in any event, does not hold for the text we are reading. The term *in return* indicates the reason why the division should be carried out. By relying on the commentaries composed on the earliest extant Chinese sources, we know how to interpret it: the term points to the fact that the division echoes the multiplication by 5 in step (a) and cancels its effect. Justifying steps to be taken in the very formulation of an algorithm and reading those reasons are other skills required to engage with such texts in the environment in which *Mathematical Classic by Zhang Qiujian* was composed. Again, such phenomena are quite general and also relate to ways of dealing with texts. However, the way in which each of these operations is carried out depends on the literate practices at play in a given scholarly milieu.

Last, in our example, the computations listed in the text straightforwardly correspond to the sequence of actions to be taken on the surface for computing. We may be spontaneously tempted to believe that this holds in general for the relation between the text of an algorithm and the corresponding flow of computations: one reads each operation in turn from the text and carries out the prescribed computation on the instrument before going back to the text. However, this simple circulation is quite far from accounting for the actual variety of links between text and computation that ancient sources evidence.[8] Here, too, the actual diversity in the kinds of texts attested to and how in each case readers in a given milieu establish the link between the given text and the intended computations reveal the heterogeneity of the literate practices required to deal with algorithms and their texts.

To address the previous remarks more deeply, let us turn to another text of an algorithm, one given in *The Nine Chapters* to divide between all kinds of quantities having integers and fractions. Placed after the statement of two problems, the text of the algorithm, which executes the operation designated as "directly sharing," reads as follows:

(1.17)

今有七人, 分八錢三分錢之一。問人得幾何。
荅曰: 人得一錢二十一分錢之四。

Suppose one has 7 persons sharing 8 units of cash and 1/3 of a unit of cash. One asks how much a person gets.

Answer: A person gets 1 unit of cash and 4/21 of a unit of cash.

(1.18)

又有三人三分人之一, 分六錢三分錢之一、
四分錢之三。問人得幾何。
荅曰: 人得二錢八分錢之一。

Suppose again one has 3 persons and 1/3 of a person sharing 6 units of cash, 1/3 and 3/4 of a unit of cash. One asks how much a person gets.

Answer: A person gets 2 units of cash and 1/8 of a unit of cash.

經分
術曰: 以人數爲法, 錢數爲實, 實如法而一。
有分者通之; 重有分者同而通之。

Directly Sharing

Procedure:

(a) One takes the quantity of persons as divisor, the quantity of cash as dividend, and one divides the dividend by the divisor.
(b) If there is one type of part, one *makes* them *communicate*.
(c) If there are several types of parts, one *equalizes* them and hence *makes* them *communicate*.

I translated the text of this algorithm in such a way as to give a flavor of the Chinese original. Probably even more clearly than the previous example and, in any case, in a different way, interpreting and using the text require competencies. Again, we do not discuss the mathematical meaning but rather precisely the kind of competencies presupposed. I italicized the higher-level operations put into play in the text: in contrast to "multiplying" and "dividing," "making communicate" and "equalizing" do not correspond in a natural way to elementary operations we use. This remark, added to the one that each of our examples involves higher-level operations differing from each other, highlights how the literate skill of knowing basic operations varies from context to context. We may go a step further here. The task confronting the historian is not the same in the two cases. In the first example (1.1), even though we may not know how multiplications and divisions were executed in ancient China, we can make sense of the algorithm by supplying our own subprocedures for the operations. This is one way in which texts for algorithms can circulate between different contexts, although the skills required to use them differ. In the second example (1.17 and 1.18), by contrast, the task of interpreting the text is different in nature because we essentially need to restore another way of conceptualizing the process of computation that is expressed by means of different higher-order operations.

But, there is more. The way in which the two sets of higher-level operations are designated differs. The terms *multiplying* and *dividing* refer to the arithmetical operations to be employed by means of a common name for the operation. By contrast, "making communicate" and "equalizing" designate the operations to be carried out in terms of the reasons they should be employed or, in other words, by the intention motivating their use in a given context. As a consequence, in some sense, we meet with a phenomenon analogous to the addition of the nuance "in return" in the text discussed previously. Here, too, the formulation of the text points to a justification for the algorithm. It is probably through a specific training that the reader interpreted the explanations delivered in such a way. In this case, the ancient commentaries on this piece of text make explicit how some concrete readers engaged with the text, and we can rely on their testimony to describe the characteristics of the formulation of the procedure. This property of the text has another consequence for its use, which yet again points to a competency it demands: the practitioners had to translate the intentions into actual actions to be taken and, for this, depending on the situation dealt with, they could fulfill the intentions by means of different sequences of operations.

At first sight, formulating the text of a procedure to indicate a justification may seem odd to us. Yet, the Chinese writings examined are not the only ones evidencing an interest for texts of algorithms that combine prescribing and accounting for the correctness of the procedure. In his study of Paleo-Babylonian Period clay tablets of the beginning of the second millennium BCE, Jens Høyrup suggested that a specific terminology had been elaborated in ancient Mesopotamia to allow formulating algorithms in such a way that, in the same expression, one could prescribe an arithmetic computation and refer to a geometric operation explaining its meaning.[9] Again, we can interpret the perfecting of this terminology as the shaping – by a given milieu – of kinds of text specifically designed to work in a certain way with algorithms. Moreover, engaging with such kinds of texts required acquiring a specific kind of literacy; we come back to this issue in a subsequent discussion. What is important for us here is that Chinese and Mesopotamian texts of algorithms differed in the technique they used to refer to the correctness of the procedures. This remark underlines the fact that the kinds of text designed by scholars of different milieus for writing down the same type of mathematical object – here, a procedure – are specific to those milieus and need to be described as such.

If we go back to early mathematical writings from ancient China, the use of "making communicate" and "equalizing" is not the only example to be found of a speech act of that kind – that is, the indirect prescription of operations by means of a reason to use them. More important, even if we limit ourselves to the ancient Chinese writings, there is already an interesting variety in the way these speech acts are produced. In some cases, the intention designated by the operation relates to a concrete effect to be achieved, quite specific to the situation (e.g., "breaking up units into smaller units"). Yet, this is not the case with "making communicate" and "equalizing." The difference is interesting because it reveals another literate skill involved in the writing of the text and thus required for its reading. The terms *making communicate* and *equalizing* capture the intentions to be realized by means of the operations not in any concrete form but rather in a formal way. This is correlated with the fact that these terms recur in different mathematical contexts, in which the intentions designated are formally the same – one "makes" entities "communicate," for instance – but in which they correspond neither to the same concrete effects nor to the same computations. In other words, the recurring use of these terms to prescribe operations stresses that something formally common happens in algorithms that look different. Quite abstract and philosophically loaded terms are chosen to bring this fact to light here. Seen from the point of view of mathematics, something general in the way of operating is thereby underlined.

From the perspective of the literate skill that the text requires and that this feature discloses, we see that only reading the set of algorithms as a whole and interpreting the intertextuality achieved by the reuse of terms can allow capturing this meaning in the text. This is one of several other examples in our corpus, where we can see how constructing intertextuality by means of correlations between different texts of procedures calls for a specific kind of reading.[10] Only such a specialized reading can uncover this layer of the meaning of the text. But, there is more. Because such a reading relies on the very texts of algorithms, in order to compare them and interpret correlations between them, the texts are revealed as a basis for further scholarly operations. These texts were designed in such a way as to be tools for work. These remarks highlight another way in which the skills engaged in producing the text of an algorithm and, hence, using it may vary.

The issue of generality comes up again, if we compare the way in which the two texts of procedure quoted are written. In contrast to the former procedure, formulated with respect to a paradigm, the latter procedure is expressed in more abstract terms and requires a wholly different kind of processing to be turned into actual computations. The following analysis reveals the artificiality of the text and the literate skills needed for using it. Among the competencies that readers needed to deal with such texts, they must have learned how to interpret the pronoun "them" to determine to precisely which entities the operations should be applied. At the same time, more important here, the text of the latter procedure is composed in such a way as to integrate in a unique text the treatment of all possible cases of division. Following is an outline of its structure.

Step (a) prescribes the operation to be used for the simplest case of division. Steps (b) and (c) both start with a condition and cover two disjoint sets of cases. For the cases corresponding to step (b), "making communicate," adequately applied, transforms them into the case solved by step (a). The solution of such cases is therefore yielded by the succession of "making communicate" and simple division. As for step (c), the cases it covers first require "equalizing" before following the same routine as described in step (b). The solution of the cases step (c) covers is hence provided by the following succession of operations: equalizing, making communicate, and a simple division. We thus see that step (a) not only solves the simplest case but also the most fundamental one – the one to which any other case is reduced. Moreover, behind a seemingly linear structure of the text, we discover a tree-like pattern, the cases being arranged in the text of the procedure according to an order of increasingly long sequences of computations, one embedded in the next one. Note that the use of higher-order operations is essential to make this embedding possible. As a result, the relationship between the text and the variety of actual computations deriving from it is far more complex than was the case in our first example. In correlation with this feature, the degree of generality of the text in our second example is far greater.

The features outlined capture a unique modality of integration of the treatment of all cases within a single text. To summarize, when readers use the text to deal with a special case, they must determine where in the procedure the case falls. On this basis, they can derive from the text the actual computations to be carried out. This operation requires following a specific itinerary within the text itself: either (a), or (b) then (a), or else (c) then (a), because (c) is formulated in such a way as including (b). The itinerary is by no means "natural" and, in any event, it differs from the route that present-day similar texts for algorithms require users to follow to generate an adequate procedure for any given case. This contrast discloses that two different groups of practitioners designed two different kinds of textual solutions for integrating various sequences of computations into a unique text. What is extremely important for us here is that the mathematical writings compiled in ancient China abound with texts of procedures with the same structure as the one just sketched. This confirms that our second example exemplifies a stable and specific kind of technical text, designed by a community of practitioners of mathematics in ancient China to write down algorithms integrating procedures for different cases. Moreover, it shows that norms existed governing the production of such texts. Composing texts of that type or engaging with them required a specific competency to have been acquired.

To recapitulate, the evidence provided herein using the example of algorithms illustrates and supports my claim that in the various milieus engaged in scholarly activities, actors collectively shaped specific kinds of texts and stabilized the skills necessary to work with them relative to the aims they pursued. By sketching contrasts between the types of texts for procedures found in Chinese sources with those in Mesopotamian sources on the one hand, and in present-day publications on the other hand, we can highlight the artificial and technical nature of the texts in the three cases. The literate competencies needed to compose and use such texts in each context embody the dimension of literacy that I concentrate on in this chapter. The key point is that the approach to literacy, to which I point by means of these examples, presupposes in an essential way a widening of the notion of "reading": reading the texts for procedures involved determining a specific itinerary to follow within the text, deploying methods to establish how general the text was, capturing various types of meaning conveyed by terms and by structures of texts, and translating these various elements into actions to be taken. Moreover, literacy in this broad sense appeared as a nonuniform phenomenon, in the sense that we could bring to light – through our analysis of the texts – literate practices proper to each context and indissociable from specific kinds of texts. In all these respects, literacy appears as a potentially fundamental topic of inquiry in the history of science. Furthermore, from this perspective, we can derive a concrete analysis of why a historian must avoid using anachronistic literate practices to interpret texts of the past. One may surmise that the disparaging appreciation that some historians expressed about texts of algorithms from antiquity, which they claimed were obscure or ambiguous, probably stemmed from their failure to interpret the sources in light of contemporary operations required for reading these specific types of texts.[11]

How to describe systematically this dimension of literacy? To what contexts and to which institutions can the shaping of these skills and their transmission be ascribed? These are some of the questions that await further research. Rather than pursuing them, however, in what follows, I suggest a further widening of our approach to literacy, based on the evidence provided by scientific activities.

Reading Other Types of Inscriptions

So far, this discussion has dwelled mainly on texts – in fact, texts of algorithms – and we have emphasized that they were not merely the recording of results but also a support for operations of all kinds that practitioners were carrying out when engaging with them. Another dimension appeared in these texts that we have not focused much attention on yet: the texts are indissociably linked to other objects. For instance, in the case developed here, they are linked to the material surface on which computations were executed in ancient China from at least the third century BCE until the fourteenth century CE. We now briefly consider aspects of the practice of computing on the surface because it will help introduce the second widening of the notions of "reading" and literate competencies that I have in mind.

As has already been described, numbers were represented with counting rods on the material surface and placed in specific positions depending on the computation executed. Using the instrument required knowledge of the rules for arranging the terms of the operations and handling them through a process of computation leading to the result. Let us illustrate these skills linked to "numeracy" with the example of a multiplication.[12] For the sake of simplicity, the digits made with counting rods are replaced by Arabic figures. Moreover, because I cannot represent on paper the dynamic of the computation on the surface, in which the material representations of values with rods succeeded each other, I use instead a sequence of tables. The reader must try to read the sequence as forming a kind of movie, in which the contents in the same positions evolve. Because I am interested *only* in the way of engaging with this dynamic inscription on the surface, I omit all mathematical explanations and suggest that the reader concentrate on operations for "writing" on the surface and reading from it.

Suppose that we have to multiply 23 by 57. The algorithm reproduced in China in several texts without change until the thirteenth century prescribes setting 23 in the lower row and 57 in the upper row, as follows:

upper	5	7
lower	2	3

Were the decimal positions indicated on the surface by the very inscription of the numbers, or were there specific signs marking them? Although we do not know, for several reasons, I find the former hypothesis more plausible. In any case, the presence of numbers to be multiplied on the computing surface implies that its space be divided in columns having decimal values. The algorithm then prescribes that these columns be used to move 23 toward the left, by as many columns as 57 has digits beyond the digit for units, which yields:

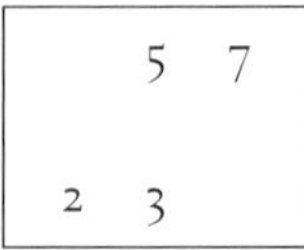

We see that not only is the layout of the numbers fairly strict but also the moves required by the algorithm rely in an essential way on the material features of the values already placed on the surface. Similarly, all the following operations depend on the configuration of numbers on the surface at the moment when they are carried out. After the first move leftward, the transformations continue. The procedure prescribes multiplying 5 by 2, then 3, and adding each of the partial results in the middle row, above the digit multiplied. In the particular example examined, we hence obtain successively:

		5	7
1			
	2	3	

and then:

		5	7
1	1	5	
	2	3	

The multiplication between digits relies on a table, learned by heart, for which we have archeological evidence from early imperial China.[13] After this first subprocedure, the digit 5 is deleted from the surface, and one moves backwards, by one column, the number to be multiplied, 23:

			7
1	1	5	
		2	3

From this point on, the same subprocedure as above is used: one multiples 7 by 2, then 3, and adds the partial results to the middle row, in each case, again, above the digit multiplied. This yields:

			7
1	2	9	
		2	3

and then:

			7
1	3	1	1
		2	3

The same routine is similarly repeated until the digits of the number in the upper row have all vanished. The result is then to be read in the middle row. This point has been reached already in our example, where the final state of the instrument shows:

1	3	1	1
		2	3

Therefore, the result is 1,311. Inscribing the computation on the surface involves placing numbers in positions, moving their representations, and transforming them according to precise rules. Despite the fact that the inscription is temporary, it obeys strict norms that reflect skills acquired by the practitioner. Clearly, such norms ensure that the computation develops correctly and that it can be checked. These are essential functions that more generally standardized texts and inscriptions fulfill in scholarly activities, and achieving such functions is one main reason to stabilize specific literate practices with these texts and inscriptions. However, in our case, the norms serve other functions that are much more important for this argument. In fact, the norms provided the computation with a standard dynamic inscription, which – one can show – was read as such and taken as the support for mathematical operations. This example thus illustrates a peculiar literate competency that was required to engage with the dynamic inscriptions developed on the surface for computing. Let us sketch this literate practice.

To capture the main features of this inscription, we need to go back to the process and observe the events occurring in each row throughout the computation. We note that the digits of the number placed in the upper row at the beginning of the process are progressively deleted, while at the same time, the number in the middle row is fashioned. In contrast, the value of the number below does not change. It is only shifted throughout the computation, first toward the left and then progressively toward the right, by one column at each step. Last, the number in the middle row grows gradually via a process that consists of multiplying one digit above by one digit below and adding the product to the middle row. These remarks would be of no interest were it not that the algorithm for division that accompanied this multiplication procedure for centuries presented – row by row – a behavior either identical to or exactly opposed to what was just described. To capture this phenomenon, we need now to follow the process of division as this algorithm shapes it. We observe it in the inverse example of the division of 1,311 by 23, concentrating on the standardized dynamic inscription that the transformations prescribed to carry out our division drawn on the surface.

The dividend is placed in the middle row, the divisor under it, in the lower row, as follows:

```

1 3 1 1
    2 3
```

The first step consists of moving forward the divisor, as far to the left as possible, with the condition that it still remains under the dividend:

```

1 3 1 1
2 3
```

Note that as before, the positioning of the numbers on the surface determines how the moves should be carried out. Also note that the first event occurring in the lower row is exactly the same as in the process of computation observed previously. This is the first of a series of remarks that will lead us to notice that the dynamic inscriptions of the two operations are tightly correlated to each other. As a result of the first move, 23 comes under 13, which it cannot divide. Hence, the divisor is moved backwards by one column:

```

1 3 1 1
  2 3
```

Here, dividing 131 by 23 produces the digit 5, which is placed in the upper row, above the units digit of the divisor:

```
    5
1 3 1 1
  2 3
```

One then multiplies 5 by 2, then 3, and takes each of the partial results out of the middle row, right above the digit multiplied. Hence, we obtain successively:

```
    5
  3 1 1
  2 3
```

and then:

```
    5
  1 6 1
  2 3
```

When this first step is completed, one moves the divisor backwards by one column:

```
    5
  1 6 1
    2 3
```

There, one repeats the routine: the next digit of the quotient, 7, is added in the upper row:

```
    5 7
  1 6 1
    2 3
```

One multiplies 7 by 2, then 3, and eliminates each of the partial results from the middle row as before, which yields:

```
5 7
2 1
2 3
```

The final operation yields:

5	7
2	3

The middle row being empty, the operation has come to an end and the result of the division is to be read in the upper row: 57.

If we compare this process, as it is dynamically written down in temporary inscriptions, to the process for multiplication, we observe that the upper row starts empty and the digits of the result are progressively added to it, while at the same time, the number in the middle row progressively vanishes. In contrast, the value of the number placed below does not change. It is only shifted throughout the computation, first toward the left and then progressively toward the right, by one column at each step. Last, the number in the middle row vanishes gradually via a process that consists of multiplying one digit above by one digit below and subtracting the product from the middle row. In other words, the relationship of opposition that multiplication and division have, as operations, is displayed through a minutely detailed fashioning of the processes that carry out the operations on the surface. Note that in this respect, the rows and the events occurring in them play a key part.

Several conclusions can be derived from these remarks. Such a precise relationship between the two processes cannot be due to chance. This makes it all the more certain that early Chinese mathematical sources attest to other kinds of relationships between other processes of computation that are "written" in the same dynamic way on the surface.[14] Moreover, the relationship between other similarly matched algorithms has been reworked in a similar way by "rewriting" the inscriptions over several centuries. These facts confirm that we do face here a specific type of "text," which was elaborated within a given scholarly community to inquire into processes of computation in a certain way. Furthermore, the "meanings" thereby expressed related to analyzing the relationship between operations. Even though such inscriptions were only transient "written" forms and would not be recorded for many centuries on the pages of books, we must consider them in our reflection on literacy relative to the history of science because something essential was durably given to be "read" in this way. Composing such inscriptions for a given process of computation, "reading" them dynamically, and working with them required competencies that the practitioners had to acquire. Such competencies belonged to the set of literate practices needed to engage with the "written" forms used in a given scholarly context. They exceed the scope of what is generally designated as "numeracy." At the same time, the form of dynamic writing thereby elaborated on the surface was a scholarly support for further work on the relationships among processes of computation. The mathematical explorations done with these inscriptions do not seem to have been conducted in another way. Far from being ancillary to higher-level mathematical work, the computations as carried out on the surface offered a support essential for part of the mathematical effort.

Taking such inscriptions into account among the written forms to be considered within the framework of our reflection on literacy demands that we widen our conception of the "written" and of "reading." This widening, in turn, invites us to define more broadly the notion of literate competencies. The benefit derived from these moves appears substantial because it leads us to include in our corpus different material ways of creating texts and engaging with them. As a consequence, this opens a space in which we can deal in the same terms as before with milieus that only developed types of texts that were materially different from classical forms of writings. We can think here, for instance, of the *quipus*, the assemblages of colored, knotted cotton cords that were the only written techniques the Incas used for operating with numbers and accounts.[15] We can deal along the same lines with the oral "inscriptions" and texts with which scholarly activities developed in Vedic India.[16] At the same time, the widening allows us to reintroduce – along with classical types of texts – all the ephemera and other material types of inscription with which the classical texts were in conversation.

My claim here is that taking apart the set of written forms, in the large sense I gave to the expression, to deal with them separately – although they were once used together – prevents us from fully attending to the literate practices required for engaging with the books. To explain this point further, we return to the example of the surface for computing used in ancient China and its relation to the texts for algorithms recorded in books. The continuity between practices on the surface for computing and the content of the books is manifested in two ways.

First, in *The Nine Chapters* as well as in *Mathematical Classic by Zhang Qiujian*, the texts for algorithms for carrying out root extraction use the terms *dividend* and *divisor* in a peculiar way that has disconcerted modern historians.[17] All their occurrences can be interpreted if and only if one understands that they refer to rows on the surface for computing and designates them as dynamic entities, much along the same lines as we saw before. In other words, terms such as *dividend* or *divisor* refer to two things: (1) the row itself where the computations are occurring, and (2) the set of events that are described in the text and that are occurring within the row. This means that the use of the terms is essentially dependent on the way in which the computation is dynamically inscribed on the surface, in exactly the same way as we saw before. Such an entity – that is, the row and the set of events occurring in it – is precisely the basis on which the opposition between multiplication and division could be displayed. In conclusion, the use of terms in the books is tightly connected with the practice of dynamically writing processes of computation on the surface. In fact, because terms designate rows as dynamic entities, a reshaping of the process on the surface leads to a redistribution of names in the text. This is how the seventh-century commentator accounted for differences in the use of terms between *The Nine Chapters* and *Mathematical Classic by Zhang Qiujian*.[18] This piece of evidence reveals that a reader makes sense in this way of how the terms are used. Reading the terms used in the text of an algorithm from this additional angle thus appears to be another competency required by the practitioners, a competency that cannot be acquired independently of considering the instrument for computing.

One could make a similar argument with respect to mathematical texts recorded on clay tablets in Mesopotamia during the Paleo-Babylonian Period, even though the nexus between the texts for algorithms and the computing instruments is of a completely different type.[19] Among the tools scribes used for their computations, we know there existed a number of tables learnt by heart during their training period in specialized schools. It is only by reference to these tables – that is, textual objects that had somehow become immaterial for professional scribes – that one can understand the various systems of numbers used in, for instance, mathematical texts and the literate practices used with them. Here, too, texts for algorithms are in conversation with computing instruments, without which the competencies required for reading the former could not be fully achieved.[20] Restoring the web of texts and inscriptions as it once existed and was used is an essential prerequisite for inquiring into the literate skills acquired by scribes. This point is elaborated on in a following discussion.

The second kind of continuity between the surface for computing and the Chinese mathematical writings is of an entirely different nature. Until approximately the tenth century CE, the notation and arrays of numbers on the surface remained strictly with the surface without any illustration being included in the pages of writings. We do not know when what appears to have been a strict separation between books and surface ended. The first extant example of an illustration of numbers represented with counting rods in a piece of writing is found in a manuscript dating from probably shortly before 1000.[21] Thereafter, the extant mathematical writings, mostly from the thirteenth century, abound with illustrations of arrays of numbers on the surface or notations derived from the surface. To interpret them, it was necessary to have acquired the competency of using the instrument. The literate practices linked to using the notations and arrays of numbers on the surface became the basis for competencies to engage with similar marks in the books. In this case, it is even possible to go one step further. In China, probably in the fifteenth century, there seems to have been a change in the instrument used for computing, the surface and the rods eventually being pushed out by the abacus. In correlation with the deep transformations in the way computations were carried out, the meaning in the books from the thirteenth century that depended on the surface for computing was progressively lost in China: practitioners no longer had the literate skills needed to make sense of the writings. The written forms did not impart, in and of themselves, the competencies required to use them. The actors had become illiterate in some sense, much in the same way in which historians can be illiterate when approaching sources that require specific skills they do not possess. Only in Japan, in the seventeenth century, could practitioners of mathematics who knew how to use counting rods to compute make sense of these books and develop the mathematical results they contained. This episode indicates how the literate practices with the surface were so essential to engaging with the books that when the former disappeared, the competencies required for the latter decayed. The example provides a second perspective from which to grasp how artificial it would be to separate too strongly the competencies attached to the computing surface from the skills required for engaging with the books.

I developed the argument that there existed literate competencies that were necessary to engage with "written forms" elaborated on material objects, as well as an adherence of the texts for algorithms to these other "writings," through the example of the computing instrument used in ancient China. In fact, in my view, the argument holds with full generality. For example, one could argue in the same way with respect to the visual tools used to work on geometric questions. I now evoke them to illustrate some basic problems that historians confront with these "written forms" and suggest general methods for approaching literate skills in an historical way.

Restoring Literate Skills and the Cultures Linked to Them

Figure 14.1 shows a 1213 edition of one of the specific "figures" used in relation to the "Pythagorean theorem" and related properties in China, from at least the third century onward.

The fact that among other things, the figure bears a squared grid and that its captions mention singular values and colors allows us to perceive right away that it was not drawn, read, and used using the same operations we learned in school to handle geometric figures. The particular features of the figure point to specific manipulations for which it offered a support. How were such figures supposed to be used?

Before we even start inquiring into the literate skills required to use a given written form in the broad sense I suggested here, we need to ascertain that the text or the inscription under consideration resembles in a reasonable way the ones actually used by actors. Figure 14.1 comes from a 1213 edition: What relation does what it shows have to the figure used in the third century? This leads us to the problem of the methods designed to restore the written forms under consideration. Philology has so far mainly focused on the critical edition of texts in the classical sense of the term. More often than not, however, even though the geometric figures were part of these writings, the critical editions did not deal with them in a way that respected the evidence provided by written testimony. If we take the example of the figure just mentioned, I reproduced in Figure 14.1 the earliest evidence we have about it. Figure 14.2 shows how Qian Baocong,

Figure 14.1. 1213 edition, by Bao Huanzhi, of *The Gnomon of the Zhou* (1st c. CE), with commentary by Zhao Shuang (3rd c. CE).

In translating the text on this diagram from top to bottom, right to left, the two characters at the top, *xian tu*, indicate that this is the "figure of the hypotenuse." Now proceeding from right to left, we read:

> *The square (shi) of the hypotenuse, 25, is vermillion and yellow.// The square of the hypotenuse//The base is 3.//Central yellow area (shi).//(in horizontal characters) The height is 4.//Vermillion area (shi)//(slantwise) The hypotenuse is 5.//The vermillion areas are 6. The yellow area is 1.//*

in his 1963 critical edition, partly proposed to restore the original figure. We see right away that many features were modified. The overall shape of the figure was transformed, which is correlated to the fact that the number of figures was increased – Qian Baocong gave four diagrams for the "figure of the hypotenuse." Yet, I believe that the 1213 edition is much closer to the original material inscription than that which is shown in Figure 14.2.

In fact, the problem is quite general, seriously affecting, for instance, the figures contained in Euclid's *Elements* as they are reproduced in the most commonly used critical edition published by Heiberg. The evidence contained in all the manuscripts is quite different from the figures redrawn by Heiberg according to nineteenth-century standards.[22] Modernizing the inscriptions somehow betrays the hidden assumption that the literate skills needed to engage with geometric figures were at all times and everywhere the same.

Once we have made sure that the texts and inscriptions examined bear some resemblance to those used by the actors, we come to the question of how the historian can restore literate skills required to produce or use the texts: what kind of evidence can we rely on for restoring practices of engagement with written forms of the past? I would like to conclude this chapter by pointing to two types of sources that appear promising for the task of studying competent reading.

First, evidence left by past readers and users relating to how they made use of texts and artifacts certainly constitutes an essential testimony for fulfilling this task, and we must devise ways of identifying sources that allow access to it. In this respect, the

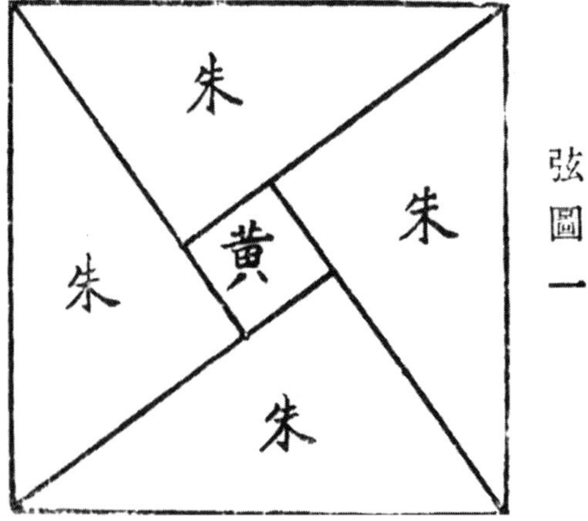

Figure 14.2. One of the figures offered instead of Figure 14.1 in the modern edition by Qian Baocong (1963).[23]

In translating the text on this diagram from top to bottom, right to left, the title on the right indicates "first figure of the hypotenuse." Now, proceeding from right to left, we read:

> *"Vermillion// Vermillion //Yellow// Vermillion // Vermillion."*

commentaries on our texts composed by scholars of the past form a systematic set of sources and prove to be quite precious. The Chinese mathematical writings mentioned previously were all the object of commentaries. In previous discussion, I mentioned several times how we could rely on the evidence they provide, for instance, to make sense of how some terms were used in the text of algorithms. Furthermore, the commentaries bear witness to exegetes' way of reading problems or algorithms, using figures or computations. In each case, this documentation can offer a guide to achieving the competencies that texts and artifacts assumed from the reader. In the same way, the testimonies found in marginalia can be systematically exploited for what they reveal of the readers' engagement with the various components of a writing.

Second, the evidence from schools – and especially professional schools where the producers of our sources studied – should be of paramount importance for us. We do not have such evidence for every historical case and context. However, the available archive allows us to capture how some literate competencies were taught and thereby to grasp them. The example, mentioned previously, of the articulation between mathematical texts and tables for computing in Mesopotamia is quite inspiring in this respect. We do have archives bearing witness to how mathematical knowledge was taught in Mesopotamian scribes' schools. Proust's study of the mathematical tablets produced in such a school, in Nippur, shows, for instance, precisely how school tablets cast light on acquiring the competency to compute by means of articulating various number systems, which more advanced mathematical texts betray. Proust first establishes how and when the scribes learned the set of tables that formed part of the instruments with which they computed. She can then interpret a set of exercises, and the very peculiar layout with which they were solved on the surface of a clay tablet, as the moment when – as well as the means by which – the articulation between various number systems was taught. The correlation between the layout of the exercises and the structure of some tables plays a crucial role in the argument. These school exercises bring to light the link between the tables and the mathematical texts that more advanced writings no longer show.[24] This case illustrates, in my view, quite tellingly what such an approach could yield if school texts were systematically studied from this angle. Not only does it provide evidence for some of the literate skills used in the production and reading of mathematical texts, but it also highlights how the school system taught a specific way of circulating between the different types of written forms with which scholarly activities were carried out.

Restoring piece by piece all the kinds of texts and inscriptions used by different scholarly milieus and the skills that their use required, and bringing to light the network of relationships they once bore to each other in scientific practice – such is the tantalizing task awaiting us to develop fully an inquiry into literacy that would, in my view, be meaningful for the history of science. Beyond presenting an inherent interest, I believe that the study of the various configurations of writings and practices shaped to use them could provide us with a concrete and practicable approach to what is otherwise too loosely designated by the terms of scholarly or professional cultures.

Notes

1 This article was written while I was at the Max Planck Institut für Wissenschaftsgeschichte, Berlin. It is my pleasure to thank this institution for the excellent working conditions it gave me for doing research. The ideas presented here were partially inspired by the program "History of science, history of text," which we developed at REHSEIS (CNRS – University Paris Diderot) beginning in 1996, and especially by the seminar held within this context with Jacques Virbel beginning in 2002. I am grateful to Jacques Virbel and all the participants for the stimulating atmosphere that allowed me to develop these views. My most sincere thanks go to Kelaine Vargas, who played a key part in the

English formulation of this chapter. Needless to say, all remaining mistakes are mine.

2 Among these attempts, let me mention David R. Olson, *The World on Paper: The Conceptual and Cognitive Implications of Writing and Reading* (Cambridge/New York: 1994), Reviel Netz, *The Shaping of Deduction in Greek Mathematics: A Study in Cognitive History* (West Nyack, NY: 1999).

3 The question raised relative to texts was the focus of a collective effort published in Karine Chemla (Ed.), *History of Science, History of Text*, vol. 238, Boston Studies in the Philosophy of Science (Dordrecht, 2004). In an excellent case study related to the kinds of texts that were shaped in the nineteenth century within the various cultures of organic chemistry, Ursula Klein introduced a concept that captures perfectly the dimension I have here in mind: that of "paper tool," although she uses it to designate a larger set of resources. Compare Ursula Klein, *Experiments, Models, Paper Tools: Cultures of Organic Chemistry in the Nineteenth Century*, Timothy Lenoir and Hans Ulrich Gumbrecht (Series Eds.), *Writing science* (Stanford, CA, 2003): 3.

4 For *The Nine Chapters* and the commentaries on it herein, I refer the reader to the critical edition and the French translation in Karine Chemla and Guo Shuchun, *Les neuf chapitres. Le Classique mathématique de la Chine ancienne et ses commentaires* (Paris, 2004). I give arguments for dating the book to the first century CE in my introduction to chapter 6 (pp. 475–478). For both books, I refer to a problem by a pair of numbers: the first refers to the chapter that contains the problem, the second indicates its rank in the sequence of problems.

5 See the discussion of the attribution and the critical edition of the book, respectively, in Qian Baocong, *Suanjing shishu (Qian Baocong jiaodian) (Critical Punctuated Edition of The Ten Classics of Mathematics)*, 2 vols. (Beijing, 1963): 326–327, 329–405. I also refer to another recent critical edition: Guo Shuchun 郭書春 and Liu Dun 劉鈍, *Suanjing shishu. Guo Shuchun, Liu Dun dianjiao*, 2 vols. (Shenyang, 1998).

6 In what follows, to refer to the text of the algorithm in a convenient way, I distinguish steps in the text by introducing letters "(a), (b) . . ." The reader must keep in mind that these do not belong to the original text and are merely a tool for analysis.

7 Arguments for this reading are developed in Karine Chemla, Generality Above Abstraction: The General Expressed in Terms of the Paradigmatic in Mathematics in Ancient China, *Science in Context* 16 (2003). In the case of this passage from *Mathematical Classic by Zhang Qiujian*, this interpretation is confirmed by the evidence given by a seventh-century commentary written under Li Chunfeng's supervision. We return to this remark later.

8 This topic is taken up and developed in much greater detail in Karine Chemla, Describing Texts for Algorithms: How They Prescribe Operations and Integrate Cases. Reflections Based on Ancient Chinese Mathematical Sources, in Karine Chemla and Jacques Virbel (Eds.), *Introduction to Textology Via Scientific Writings* (in preparation).

9 See Jens Høyrup, Algebra and Naive Geometry: An Investigation of Some Basic Aspects of Old Babylonian Mathematical Thought, *Altorientalische Forschungen* 17 (1990).

10 For the sake of brevity, I remain here extremely allusive. Concrete uses of intertextuality in ancient Chinese mathematical sources are described in Karine Chemla, What Is at Stake in Mathematical Proofs From Third-Century China? *Science in Context* 10 (1997); Karine Chemla, Qu'apporte la prise en compte du parallélisme dans l'étude de textes mathématiques chinois? in François Jullien (Ed.), *Parallélisme et appariement des choses. Extrême-Orient, Extrême-Occident. 11* (Saint-Denis, 1989).

11 Examples of the kind abound; compare, for instance, Wang Ling and Joseph Needham, Horner's Method in Chinese Mathematics: Its Origin in the Root-Extraction Procedures of the Han Dynasty, *T'oung-pao*, 43 (1955): 352–353.

12 Texts for these algorithms for multiplying and dividing can be found in the *Mathematical Classic by Sunzi* (*Sunzi suanjing* 孫子算經), dated roughly around 400 CE; see Qian Baocong, *Suanjing shishu (Qian Baocong jiaodian) (Critical Punctuated Edition of The Ten Classics of Mathematics)*: vol. 2, 282–283.

13 Compare Li Yan and Du Shiran, *Chinese Mathematics: A Concise History*, John N. Crossley and Anthony W. C. Lun (trans.), (Oxford [England], 1987): 13–14.

14 Several examples are described in Karine Chemla, Similarities Between Chinese and Arabic Mathematical Writings. I.: Root

Extraction, *Arabic Sciences and Philosophy: A Historical Journal*, 4 (1994).

15 See a brief account and a bibliography in Marcia Ascher, *Ethnomathematics: A Multicultural View of Mathematical Ideas* (Pacific Grove, CA, 1991): 16–29.

16 Despite the fact that these texts were oral, I keep using the word *inscription* to stress the fact that their arrangement was quite rigid and designed to allow an oral use. The formulation of the sentences sometimes depended on where the sentence was placed in the structure. Moreover, the arrangement of the text was the basis on which the "readers'" operations could rely, when they were orally using the text. Compare Pierre-Sylvain Filliozat, Ancient Sanskrit Mathematics: An Oral Tradition and a Written Literature, in Karine Chemla (Ed.), *History of Science, History of Text*, Boston Studies in the Philosophy of Science (Dordrecht, 2004), 140–143. Continuities between writing and speech are approached from another angle in David R. Olson, What Writing Is, *Pragmatics and Cognition*, 9 (2001).

17 Wang Ling and Needham, Horner's Method in Chinese Mathematics: Its Origin in the Root-Extraction Procedures of the Han Dynasty, pp. 350–364.

18 Karine Chemla, Cas d'adéquation entre noms et réalités mathématiques. Deux exemples tirés de textes chinois anciens, in Karine Chemla and François Martin (Eds.), *Le juste nom*, Extrême-Orient-Extrême-Occident (Saint-Denis, 1993).

19 In what follows, for reasons to be explained later, I mainly rely on the clay tablets produced in Nippur before the year 1730 BCE, as studied in Christine Proust, *Tablettes mathématiques de Nippur: Reconstitution du cursus scolaire. Edition des tablettes conservées à Istanbul. Translittération des textes lexicaux et littéraires par Antoine Cavigneaux. Préface de Christian Houzel, Varia Anatolica* (Istanbul, 2007). See pp. 39–40 for the dating.

20 The nature of the "conversation" is beautifully illustrated by Figure 20 in ibid., p. 251.

21 A photo of this Dunhuang manuscript (Stein 930, British Museum) can be found in Li Yan and Du Shiran, *Chinese Mathematics: A Concise History*, p. 15.

22 This problem is discussed in Ken Saito, A Preliminary Study in the Critical Assessment of Diagrams in Greek Mathematical Works, *Sciamus* 7 (2006). For all of Book I of Euclid's *Elements*, the author compares the figures contained in the most important manuscripts with those included by Heiberg in his critical edition. The comparison shows vividly that most of the hints left in the manuscripts of how geometric figures were used were erased from the edition.

23 The 1213 edition has two figures after Figure 14.1. Qian Baocong restores five figures instead; I show the first of them. See Qian Baocong, *Suanjing shishu (Qian Baocong jiaodian) (Critical Punctuated Edition of The Ten Classics of Mathematics)*, p. 15. This "restoring" is adopted by Guo Shuchun 郭書春 and Liu Dun 劉鈍, *Suanjing shishu*: 2. My suggestion for restoring the figure is discussed in my introduction to chapter 9, in Chemla and Guo Shuchun, *Les neuf chapitres*, pp. 673–684, 696–697.

24 Proust, *Tablettes mathématiques de Nippur*, pp. 190–197.

References

Ascher, M. (1991). *Ethnomathematics: A multicultural view of mathematical ideas*. Pacific Grove, CA: Brooks/Cole.

Chemla, K. (1989). Qu'apporte la prise en compte du parallélisme dans l'étude de textes mathématiques chinois? In F. Jullien (Ed.), *Parallélisme et appariement des choses* (pp. 53–80). Extrême-Orient, Extrême-Occident, 11 (F. Jullien, General ed.). Saint-Denis: Presses Universitaires de Vincennes.

Chemla, K. (1993). Cas d'adéquation entre noms et réalités mathématiques. Deux exemples tirés de textes chinois anciens. In K. Chemla & F. Martin (Eds.), *Le juste nom* (pp. 102–138). Extrême-Orient, Extrême-Occident, 15 (F. Martin & K. Chemla, General eds.). Saint-Denis: Presses Universitaires de Vincennes.

Chemla, K. (1994). Similarities between Chinese and Arabic mathematical writings. I. Root extraction. *Arabic Sciences and Philosophy: A Historical Journal*, 4 (2), 207–266.

Chemla, K. (1997). What is at stake in mathematical proofs from third-century China? *Science in Context*, 10 (2), 227–251.

Chemla, K. (2003). Generality above abstraction: The general expressed in terms of the paradigmatic in mathematics in ancient China. *Science in Context*, 16 (3), 413–458.

Chemla, K. (Ed.) (2004). *History of science, history of text*. Boston Studies in the Philosophy of Science, 238 (R. S. Cohen, J. Renn, & K. Gavroglu, General eds.). Dordrecht: Springer.

Chemla, K. (in preparation). Describing texts for algorithms: How they prescribe operations and integrate cases: Reflections based on ancient Chinese mathematical sources. In K. Chemla & J.Virbel (Eds.), *Introduction to textology via scientific writings*.

Chemla, K., & Guo Shuchun. (2004). *Les neuf chapitres. Le Classique mathématique de la Chine ancienne et ses commentaires*, Paris: Dunod.

Filliozat, P.-S. (2004). Ancient Sanskrit mathematics: An oral tradition and a written literature. In K. Chemla (Ed.), *History of science, history of text* (pp. 137–157). Boston Studies in the Philosophy of Science, 238 (R. S. Cohen, J. Renn, & K. Gavroglu, General eds.). Dordrecht: Springer.

Guo Shuchun 郭書春 & Liu Dun 劉鈍 (1998). *Suanjing shishu. Guo Shuchun, Liu Dun dianjiao. 2 vols*. Shenyang: Liaoning jiaoyu chubanshe. Reprinted in Taibei, Jiuzhang chubanzhe (2001).

Høyrup, J. (1990). Algebra and naive geometry: An investigation of some basic aspects of Old Babylonian mathematical thought. *Altorientalische Forschungen*, 17, 27–69, 262–324.

Klein, U. (2003). *Experiments, models, paper tools: Cultures of organic chemistry in the nineteenth century*. Writing Science Series (T. Lenoir & H. U. Gumbrecht, General Eds.). Stanford, CA: Stanford University Press.

Li, Yan, & Du, Shiran (1987). *Chinese mathematics: A concise history*. Translated by J. N. Crossley & A. W. C. Lun. Oxford: Clarendon Press.

Netz, R. (1999). *The shaping of deduction in Greek mathematics: A study in cognitive history*. West Nyack, NY: Cambridge University Press.

Olson, D. R. (1994). *The world on paper: The conceptual and cognitive implications of writing and reading*. Cambridge/New York: Cambridge University Press.

Olson, D. R. (2001). What writing is. *Pragmatics and Cognition*, 9 (2), 239–258.

Proust, C. (2007). *Tablettes mathématiques de Nippur: Reconstitution du cursus scolaire. Edition des tablettes conservées à Istanbul. Translittération des textes lexicaux et littéraires par Antoine Cavigneaux. Préface de Christian Houzel. Varia Anatolica*. Istanbul: IFEA, De Boccard.

Qian Baocong. (1963). *Suanjing shishu (Qian Baocong jiaodian) (Critical punctuated edition of The Ten Classics of Mathematics), 2 vols*. Beijing: Zhonghua shuju.

Saito, K. (2006). A preliminary study in the critical assessment of diagrams in Greek mathematical works. *Sciamus*, 7, 81–144.

Wang, Ling, & Needham, J. (1955). Horner's method in Chinese mathematics: Its origin in the root-extraction procedures of the Han Dynasty. *T'oung-pao*, 43, 345–401.

CHAPTER 15

Scientific Literacy

Stephen P. Norris and Linda M. Phillips

Scientific literacy is a programmatic concept. By this, we mean that its primary use is not to pick out some condition or state of affairs but rather to point in a valued direction or to name a desired goal. Scientific literacy is a good that educators, scientists, and politicians want for citizens and society. Just because it is programmatic in this way, scientific literacy is contested, with different individuals and groups urging their view of the good for adoption by others. We engage in similar urging in this chapter because we believe that prominent conceptions of scientific literacy miss an important element – namely, its connection to what we call the *fundamental* sense of scientific literacy; that is, reading and writing when the content is science (Norris & Phillips, 2003). Instead, these other conceptions are wedded solely to the *derived* sense of scientific literacy – that is, to knowledge of the substantive content of science and to knowledge about science.

In contrast to the specialist education leading to science and science-related degrees and diplomas, generalist science education has two broad aims: (1) to attract the next generation of individuals into scientific careers, and (2) to foster a public understanding of science. It is widely assumed that the science education appropriate for the next generation of scientists is defined by the substantive content of the subject, and that scientific literacy picks out the goals of public understanding for those who will be nonscientists. However, there is a difficulty in dividing generalist science education in this way because we are unable to discern which students fall into which group. Perhaps more by default than by design, therefore, the substantive content of science has become the overwhelming focus of generalist science education. We believe this emphasis to be an unnecessary mistake because there are additional viable alternatives to a focus on content. One of these alternatives is a focus on the nature of science. Another alternative, and the one we address in this chapter, is based on a conception of scientific literacy that emphasizes its fundamental sense. Such an emphasis, we contend, could serve well both future scientists and nonscientist citizens.

The chapter is organized as follows. First, we describe and examine a number of conceptions of scientific literacy and show how all of them fail to include the fundamental sense as explicitly as we urge. Second, we look closely at some typical examples of the language of science as revealed in published journal articles. Third, we draw several general conclusions about the connections among reading and writing and science, arguing that the relationship is constitutive; that is, that science is in part defined by reading and writing. Fourth, we offer an alternative to the conceptions of reading and writing that tend to be found in science education that accords more closely with how language and reading and writing are actually found in science. Finally, we draw some educational implications from our analysis.

Conceptions of Scientific Literacy

In the science education field, scientific literacy is conceptualized variously in one or more of the following ways: (a) knowledge of the substantive content of science and the ability to distinguish science from nonscience (Council of Ministers of Education, Canada (CMEC), 1997; Mayer, 1997; National Research Council (NRC), 1996; Shortland, 1988); (b) understanding science and its applications (DeBoer, 2000; Eisenhart, Finkel, & Marion, 1996; Hurd, 1998; Shen, 1975; Shortland, 1988); (c) knowledge of what counts as science (DeBoer, 2000; Hurd, 1998; Kyle, 1995a, 1995b; Lee, 1997); (d) independence in learning science (Sutman, 1996); (e) ability to think scientifically (DeBoer, 2000); (f) ability to use scientific knowledge in problem solving (American Association for the Advancement of Science (AAAS), 1989, 1993; NRC, 1996); (g) knowledge needed for intelligent participation in science-based social issues (CMEC, 1997; Millar & Osborne, 1998; NRC, 1996); (h) understanding the nature of science, including its relationships with culture (DeBoer, 2000; Hanrahan, 1999; Norman, 1998); (i) appreciation of and comfort with science, including its wonder and curiosity (CMEC, 1997; Millar & Osborne, 1998; Shamos, 1995; Shen, 1975); (j) knowledge of the risks and benefits of science (Shamos, 1995); and (k) ability to think critically about science and to deal with scientific expertise (Korpan, Bisanz, Bisanz, & Henderson, 1997; Shamos, 1995).

Among these portrayals of scientific literacy, several of which reach beyond the singular attention to scientific content, we found only a very few that make any reference at all to features of scientific literacy that would fall under the fundamental sense. For example, Millar and Osborne (1998) claim the "science curriculum should provide sufficient scientific knowledge and understanding to enable students to read simple newspaper articles about science . . . " (p. 9). A similar view was expressed by the National Research Council (1996, p. 22) in claiming, "Scientific literacy entails being able to read with understanding articles about science in the popular press . . . " Shortland (1988) saw the connection between reading and writing and learning science, but his idea of them as basic skills is not the same as our idea that they are fundamental: ". . . literacy has to do not merely with the ability to read and write but with a certain measure of learning which may reasonably be expected to flow from the application of these basic skills . . . " (pp. 313–314). In conceiving of literacy as providing independence in learning science, Sutman (1996) proposed a definition of functional scientific literacy that he saw fitting with the broader goals of language literacy. However, he did not make clear how his conception is related to literacy broadly conceived, except to imply that scientific literacy ought to mean more than memorization of the vocabulary of science.

There have been some studies focussed on the reading and evaluation of scientific news briefs. The conception of scientific literacy that underlies the work of Korpan, Bisanz, Bisanz, and Henderson (1997), for example, includes an understanding of how students read science-related materials for information and critically evaluate the conclusions contained in them. Although he did not explicitly use the notion of scientific literacy, Anderson (1999) contrasted science educators' long-standing attention to "hands-on experience as the essential core of scientific practice" with the comparative neglect of reading and writing in science. Anderson claimed that "reading and writing are the mechanisms through which scientists accomplish [their] task. Scientists create, share, and negotiate the meanings of inscriptions – notes, reports, tables, graphs, drawings, diagrams" (1999, p. 973).

In our judgment, none of the previously mentioned works sufficiently illuminates the fundamental sense of scientific literacy. Anderson's claim is a good example to help frame our point. He says that "reading and writing are the mechanisms through which scientists accomplish [the task of science]". He is, of course, correct – reading and writing do have a functional relationship with respect to science. But reading and writing stand to science not in the same way that glass windows stand to houses. There are houses without glass windows and even houses without structures that serve any of the functions served by glass windows. However, reading and writing are not removable from science in a corresponding manner. Reading and writing are not only functional to science, as tools for storage and transmission, but also constitutive parts of science. Constituents are essential elements of the whole, such that if you remove a constituent, the whole goes with it.

In addition to Anderson's position, consider the positions in the *Beyond 2000* document and in DeBoer's (2000, p. 592) survey of views of scientific literacy. We wholeheartedly endorse the call for a science curriculum that "enables students to read simple newspaper articles about science" (Millar & Osborne, 1998, p. 9) and that promotes an understanding of reports and discussions of science that appear in the popular media. However, these goals acknowledge only an instrumental link between reading and science, and they overlook the intrinsic connection between the two. Reading and writing are inextricably linked to the very nature and fabric of science, just as surely as observation, measurement, and experiment. We have a great deal more to say on this point in the third section, 'Reading as Intrinsic to Science'.

The Language of Science

Although students in schools, colleges, and universities might understandably miss this point about scientists' work, scientists read and write text a great deal of the time (Tenopir & King, 2004). They ponder phrasing that will capture what they mean. They construct what they mean while they write. They search for expressions that will carry the level of exactness they intend. They choose words carefully to distinguish the degrees of certainty they wish to express. They select genres to describe their methods and to provide justifications for them. They puzzle over what other scientists have written, question their own and other scientists' interpretations of text, and they sometimes challenge and at other times endorse what is written. They make choices about what to read and make further choices about how closely and critically to read. These activities of constructing, interpreting, selecting, and critiquing texts are as much a part of what scientists do as are collecting, interpreting, and challenging data. These activities with text are as constitutive of science as are observation, measurement, and calculation.

Suppe (1998) examined more than a thousand data-based papers in science. He concluded that the papers perform the following speech acts:

- present the data arising from an observation or series of observations
- make a case for the relevance of the observations in addressing some scientific problem
- provide detail on the methods used to collect and analyze the data
- provide and justify an interpretation of the data
- identify, acknowledge, and possibly impeach specific doubts that can underpin alternative interpretations of the data

These speech acts create the argumentative structure of the papers. Suppe concluded that the argumentative structure of such papers is not captured by any of the major philosophical theories of scientific reasoning – not by hypothetico-deductivism, not by Popper's falsificationism, not by Bayesian induction, and not by inference to the best explanation. Rather, the central structure of such papers is arguing (in writing) for a favoured interpretation of the results and against the alternatives. Thus, scientists engage a variety of speech acts when they write and read scientific text, including presenting data, making relevance cases, describing methods, justifying interpretations, and impeaching interpretations. These speech acts are artefacts of literacy that are marshaled into an overall argumentative structure that defines the nature of the text.

We conducted our own examination of data-based research reports by some colleagues in physics (Norris & Phillips, 2008). One paper reported a study of *hysteresis*. In hysteresis, a system undergoes a change of state in response to changes in its environment that is not reversible via the backwards route when the environmental changes are run backwards. For example, glass thermometers – once heated and having undergone expansion – do not return to their original size when they are cooled to the original temperature by reversing the path to expansion. If we magnetize a piece of iron by placing it in the magnetic field, decreasing the intensity of the magnetic field does not lead to the piece of iron demagnetizing by simply reversing the route of its magnetization. The states of some physical systems are thus dependent not only on their current states and states of their environments but also on their histories. So it is, apparently, with the adsorption and desorption of helium in silica aerogels, a type of porous media studied in condensed matter physics (Beamish & Herman, 2003).

Beamish's and Herman's paper of just two pages exhibits much of the argumentative structure identified by Suppe (1998). In addition, there is a wide range of speech acts present in the paper. Beamish and Herman:

1. *Motivated* their study: "Silica aerogels . . . provide a unique opportunity to study the effects of disorder on phase transitions" (p. 340).
2. *Reported* relevant past results: "Also, recent experiments . . . showed features characteristic of capillary condensation rather than true two-phase coexistence . . ." (p. 340).
3. *Reported* limitations of past research: ". . . although long thermal time constants made it difficult to determine the equilibrium behavior" (p. 340).
4. *Described* what was done: ". . . a thin (0.6 mm) disc was cut. . . . Copper electrodes (9 mm diameter) were evaporated. . . . This was sealed into a copper cell. . . . Temperatures were measured and controlled. . . . A room temperature gas handling system and flow controller allowed us to admit or remove helium at controlled rates . . . " (p. 340).
5. *Argued* for the suitability of techniques: "This effect [thermal lags when gas was admitted or removed] appears as a rate dependent hysteresis, so it was essential to check directly for equilibrium" (p. 341).
6. *Explained* observations: This behavior [The equilibrium isotherm . . . had a small but reproducible hysteresis loop and did not exhibit the sharp vertical step characteristic of two phase coexistence] is characteristic of surface tension driven capillary condensation in a porous medium with a narrow range of pore sizes" (p. 341).
7. *Conjectured* what might be happening: "At low temperatures we observed hysteresis between filling and emptying, as expected for capillary condensation; this hysteresis disappeared above 5.155 K. The vanishing of the hysteresis may correspond to the critical temperature of the confined fluid" (p. 341).
8. *Challenged* interpretations: "However, this identification [with the critical temperature] is not clear, since all our

isotherms have finite slopes [while theory would suggest an infinite slope at this point]" (p. 341).

The second paper reported a study of the transition from crystalline to amorphous solids in certain nanocrystals under the influence of radiation (Meldrum, Boatner, & Ewing, 2002). In comparison to crystalline solids, amorphous solids (a common example is glass) do not have their molecules arranged in an orderly geometric pattern. They have no definite melting or freezing points (i.e., when heated, they turn soft before becoming liquid; unlike ice, for instance, which jumps from solid to liquid without passing through an intermediary phase); usually have high viscosities (i.e., glass runs very slowly); and fracture along irregular patterns rather than regular cleavage lines. The overall pattern is the argumentative one identified by Suppe (1998), as well as many isolated arguments on particular points that we exemplify:

1. As part of the motivation of the study, whose aim was to provide evidence for the amorphization of nanocrystalline zirconia by ion irradiation, the authors provided a full-paragraph case for the proposition that zirconia is one of the most radiation resistant ceramics known. The point of the argument was to signal that the results of this study were not to be expected, that previous conclusions must be modified, and that therefore this study was significant.
2. In addition to describing what was done to collect data, two justifications were provided for the methods chosen, which were deemed particularly appropriate in that they avoided certain pitfalls that would have led to misleading results.
3. Imbedded in the description of the results, a case was made that the crystals of zirconia that reached the amorphous state were sufficiently small to allow the formation of tetragonal zirconia. However, in the case under study, there was incomplete information for calculating the critical size for such formation. By comparing two related cases in which the relevant calculations could be made, the authors argued that the size of their crystals was smaller than either of these two cases and that therefore they should be adequately small to support the observations made.
4. These authors spent considerable effort arguing against alternative interpretations of the observations they made. They carefully spelled out how various steps of their method made other possible mechanisms implausible.

Scientific language is *textured* in that not all of its statements have the same reported or implied truth status (Norris & Phillips, 1994b). We see this texture in the papers examined. There are statements offered as truths – for example, descriptions of what has been found in the past, of what was done in the current study, and of what was observed. There are statements offered as probable or as having uncertain truth status – for example, conjectured explanations. There are statements offered as false – for example, explanations that the authors aim to impeach. Scientific language is *structured* (meaning that not all of its statements have the same epistemic status and role) by use of a meta-language that includes such terms as *cause, effect, observe, hypothesis, data, results, explanation,* and *prediction*. There also is the structure of argumentation both in the form of justifications for actions taken and of reasons for conclusions drawn. This meta-language and these argumentative forms are found in the papers examined. Each of the meta-language terms and each of the argumentative forms imply a relationship. Taken together, these relationships hold the pieces together.

Myers (1991), who has done an enormous amount of research into the nature of scientific text, made an interesting point that relates to our ideas of texture and structure. Nonspecialists faced with scientific texts often interpret their difficulty in understanding as one of not knowing the vocabulary. However, argued Myers, the problem will not go away by using a dictionary, no matter how good or specialized, because much of the difficulty interpreting scientific text lies in grasping the connections of one statement to another. These questions of scientific vocabulary and its role in understanding scientific text are raised later, where we associate the concern with teaching vocabulary with a simple and particularly narrow view of reading science.

In summary, this section has shown that the language of science at the macro-level is argumentative, in the sense that it is structured so as to support conclusions on the basis of reasons and evidence. At the micro-level, scientific language is usefully characterized as performing a variety of speech acts, which, when taken in combination, create the argumentative structure seen at the larger scale. Scientific language is understood at the macro-level by one who grasps the connections that are made and implied among its micro-level parts.

Reading as Intrinsic to Science

School science education and schooling more generally are dominated by a much simpler view of text and reading than described in the previous section. According to this simple view, reading is equivalent to identifying words and locating information. As a consequence of this view, knowing what a text *means* comes down to knowing what the text *says* (Olson, 1994) – that is, of decoding the words. According to this simple view, texts that cannot be grasped immediately on knowing what they say are problematic because they introduce an obstacle between the reader and the world or theory they depict. Good texts are transparent because once the words are decoded, they can be penetrated immediately to get their meaning.

As must be clear from the previous section, text is related to scientific thought and ideas in a more complex and circuitous way than implied by the simple view of reading. First, text is not speech written down but rather is built on a theory of speech (Olson, 1994). Writing, including scientific writing, is a form of idealization that leaves out much that is included in spoken communication (e.g., intonation, repetition, stammers, incomplete and interrupted thoughts, facial expressions, and gesture), and it is a form of construction that adds in much that is not included in speech (e.g., sentence structure, punctuation, paragraphing, breaks between words, and long chains of expressions connected by tight logical links). Reading involves coping with both the expressed and unexpressed in the written word (Olson, 1994, p. 265). Readers lack the inferential cues provided to listeners by tone, gesture, facial expression, repetition, and stammer. By way of compensation, they have at their disposal the characteristics of text not found in speech. In summary, speech and text are not the same and do not impose the same interpretive demands. This latter point is crucial to science teaching. Readers must learn to cope with science text, must learn to use the resources of text to determine what they mean – or might mean. To accomplish these goals and to be scientifically literate, readers require interpretive strategies, which can be isolated and taught.

Second, the same text can express different thoughts, and the same thought can be expressed through different texts. This means that there is no direct connection between what a text says and what it means. What a text means always must be inferred from what it says plus other extratextual information. There is no alternative when reading but to bring to the text thoughts from outside of it. Readers must learn that neither they nor the text is supreme: each is a required source of information in the interpretive process; their relative weightings change from situation to situation depending on, among other factors, familiarity with what is being read (Phillips & Norris, 1999).

Third, and as a corollary to the second point, although a scientific theory is independent of any given text (because the same theory can be expressed in many different ways), a scientific theory cannot exist outside of text altogether. Any scientific theory requires for its creation and its expression the use of text. Any attempt to provide a scientific theory without appeal to text runs quickly into insurmountable shortcomings of expressive power, memory, and attention. To express even such a simple theory as that of an ideal gas requires appeal to mathematical equations, graphs, and diagrams, all of which are tools of literacy. There is no possible expression of the theory, except for some isolated aspect of it (and even such expressions are parasitic on text), outside of text of some sort. For instance, it is not simply a matter of convenience that the pressure-volume-temperature surface is used centrally in expressions of the theory of ideal gases. We just do not have another way to express the complex of thoughts that this surface represents, portrayed in text as either a three-dimensional graph or a three-variable mathematical function. If somebody were to invent another mode of expression, it too would be within the realm of literacy and would impose the same interpretive demands.

The only contender for the literate tradition is the oral one, and oracy provides neither the tools needed nor the forms of expression required to describe scientific theories. In saying this, we do not intend to denigrate oracy. Just as text provides expressive power not available in speech, speech marshals expressive power not found in text, and speech plays a crucial and irreplaceable role in the development, critique, and refinement of thoughts that go into theories. Also, we acknowledge that oral cultures have gained much knowledge of the world and that this knowledge can play and has played a role in the development of some areas of science. Nevertheless, scientific knowledge has an essential dependence on texts, and the route to scientific knowledgeability is through gaining access to those texts. Although individuals can portray and learn much science within oracy, such access to scientific knowledge is parasitic on access gained through text. This is so because without literacy, the knowledge would not have existed, been preserved, and inherited in the first place. Hence, scientific literacy must be premised on an essential role of text in science.

Fourth, although a scientific theory is independent of any given text, an expression of a theory through text capitalizes on features of textual fixity that allow the *same* text to be transported across time and space – traded, revisited, queried, and reinterpreted. "[W]riting fixes language, controls it in such a way that words do not scatter, do not vanish or substitute for one another. *The same words, time and again* (Ferreiro, 2000, p. 60). Although the text is fixed, the interpretations of it are not. The interpretations are made against the backdrop of the relative fixity of physical presentation and literal meaning. As Olson said, "Consciousness of the fact or possibility that utterances can be taken literally – according to the very words – is at the heart of literate thinking" (1996, p. 149). Although literal meaning is only relatively stable, it affords a level of stability unprecedented in oracy. As argued by Tishman and Perkins (1997): "Written language, stabilized on paper, invites kinds of reflection not so natural to oral exchanges. The written statement is more easily examined, checked, contradicted, doubted, challenged, or affirmed" (p. 371). We would go further than "invitation" and argue that written language is what makes these activities possible in any depth. Readers must understand both the significance of the fixity of text and also that fixed texts invite and allow interpretation and reinterpretation.

Fifth, although the fixities of text make interpretation and reinterpretation possible, they also make some interpretations if not impossible, then highly implausible. That is, the fixities impose constraints on interpretations that readers are obliged to consider. Without the constraints provided by the text, no interpretation would be possible because without constraints, the text could mean anything at all. So, the very fixities of text that make interpretation possible are the same features that ensure that not everything goes, by providing constraints on what can be meant. Therefore, the reader must take note of the very words, the very data, and other textual elements and bears the burden of delivering interpretations under the constraints of those fixities. There is always room to manoeuver, but the degrees of freedom are restricted. Students must learn that the very words and other textual elements matter as constraints on allowable interpretation, and they must learn how to discern the boundaries of those constraints.

Sixth, Halliday and Martin (1993) expanded the notion of the fixity of text to the fixity of what is taken for granted:

> *Until information can be organized and packaged in [written language]... knowledge cannot accumulate, since there is no way one discourse can start where other ones left off. When I can say*
>
> *the random fluctuations in the spin components of one of the two particles*
>
> *I am packaging the knowledge that has developed over a long series of preceding arguments and presenting it as 'to be taken for granted – now we can proceed to the next step'. If I cannot do this... I will never get very far. (pp. 118–119)*

Therefore, science is a result of cumulative discourse that trades on the fixities of text and on what is taken for granted by that text. This is not to imply that scientific knowledge accumulates linearly as in building a monument brick by brick. Yet, students need to learn that scientific discourse always attaches to and is dependent on discourse that has gone before, even if it rejects the former, and it serves as an attachment for discourse that is to come, even if it is rejected by that subsequent discourse.

The implication for the relationship between scientific text and thought is that science would not be possible without text. Science in part is constituted by texts and by our means of dealing with them. Without the expressive power and relative fixity of text, and without the comprehension, interpretive, analytical, and critical capacities we have developed for dealing with texts, then science as we know it could never have come into being. The only alternative to literacy – oracy and the oral tradition – simply does not have at its disposal the tools for developing and sustaining science; however, as we have said, it plays an irreplaceable role in the development, critique, and refinement of scientific thought. Without text, the social practices that make science possible could not be engaged: (a) the recording and presentation and re-presentation of data; (b) the encoding and preservation of accepted science for other scientists; (c) the peer-reviewing of ideas by scientists anywhere in the world; (d) the critical reexamination of ideas once published; (e) the future connecting of ideas that were developed previously; (f) the communication of scientific ideas among those who have never met, even among those who did not live contemporaneously; (g) the encoding of variant positions; and (h) the focusing of concerted attention on a fixed set of ideas for the purpose of interpretation, prediction, explanation, or test. The practices centrally involve texts through their creation in writing and their interpretation, analysis, and critique through reading. The reading and writing practices illustrated in the examples of the second section define partly what it is to engage in scientific inquiry. Thus, reading and writing properly are seen as intrinsic parts of science.

Reading and Writing for Science

"Traditionally science teachers have had little concern for text... [R]eading is not seen as an important part of science education" (Wellington & Osborne, 2001, pp. 41–42). Indeed, criticism of attention given to science text and science reading has "focused the science education community's effort on eliminating text from science instruction" because of a "perception that science reading [is] a passive, text-driven, meaning-taking process" (Yore, Craig, & Maguire, 1998, p. 28). Science educators might be forgiven for these oversights because for those who know how to read well and for those whose primary area of work is not the study of reading, reading can seem a simple process and text can seem transparent. Indeed, there can seem to be little more to reading than knowing the words and locating information in the text. This is a view of reading that has been known for a long time to be flawed because concatenating the meanings of words does not yield the meaning of a proposition, and concatenating the meanings of propositions does not yield the meaning of extended text (Anderson, 1985; Goodman, 1985; Smith, 1978).

We find a reliance on such a simple, word-recognition-and-information-location view of reading throughout the science education field. For example, Miller (1998) considers whether "scientific literacy might be defined as the ability to read and write about science and technology" (pp. 203–204), but he concludes that this definition is too broad because it includes everything that might be read, from simple labels to complex scientific reports. He proposes instead a concept of civic scientific literacy with two dimensions: a vocabulary dimension, referring to "a vocabulary of basic scientific constructs sufficient to read competing views in a newspaper or magazine" (1998, p. 205); and a process of inquiry dimension, referring to "understanding and competence to comprehend and follow arguments about science and technology policy matters in the media" (1998, pp. 205–206). Miller's concept of civic scientific literacy is related to the view we are seeking but has several limitations. First, the vocabulary dimension risks equating successful reading with knowing the meanings of the individual terms. This is the simple view of reading just described. Reading is not the linear process implied by such a model. Second, the vocabulary dimension appears to assume that only scientific constructs need to be known to understand scientific text. However, many literate constructs are not specifically scientific but, nevertheless, are needed to understand scientific text. Third, although the process of inquiry dimension could be interpreted to include the general reading competence necessary to interpret the argumentative structure of text, it really refers, according to Miller's conception, to expository knowledge of the nature of science: the ability of individuals "to describe, in their own words, what it means to study something scientifically" (1998, p. 213) or ability to identify better scientific approaches to solving problems. Although such knowledge and ability are important, they do not yield "competence to comprehend and follow arguments" in text, as the process of inquiry dimension is described by Miller. Such interpretive tasks include but also transcend scientific knowledge and knowledge about science.

What might reading be, if it is not simply decoding words or locating information in text? Fundamentally, reading is inferring meaning from text (Norris & Phillips, 1994a). Inferring meaning from text involves the integration of text information and the reader's knowledge. Through this integration, something new, over and above the text and the reader's knowledge, is created – an interpretation of the text (Phillips, 2002). It is crucial to understanding this view to recognize that interpretations go beyond what is in the text, what was the author's intent, and what was in the reader's mind before reading it. Also crucial is the stance that not all interpretations of a text are equally good but also that usually there can be more than one good interpretation. The possibility of more than one good interpretation exists for all text types, notwithstanding the fact that the leeway for proposing multiple interpretations varies from type to type and from reader to reader. For example, a wave function may be meant to be read in one and only one way; in any field, there are interpretations sanctioned by the experts that novices are not in a position to challenge. However, no text – not even (or, maybe, *especially* not even) a wave function – can be written so as to avoid the need for interpretation by its readers or so as to guarantee that they all will reach the same interpretation; and no reader's interpretation, no matter how expert the reader, is immune to criticism. Thus, the essential nature of reading – that is, inferring meaning from text – is the same no matter what is being read, even though there may be variations in reading purposes and strategies across text types and reading contexts.

Our basic position is that reading is best understood as a constructive process. However, we are at pains to avoid the relativism associated with some versions of constructivism. Relativism is created or avoided in the way readers position themselves with respect to the text. One possible positioning is for readers to adopt a dominant stance toward the text by allowing their background beliefs to overwhelm the text information, thereby forcing interpretations that cannot consistently and completely account for the text. In such a situation, what the text is taken to mean is entirely relative to what the readers believe. On the other hand, readers may adopt a deferential stance, by either accepting whatever the text says or allowing the text to overwhelm their background beliefs by reaching interpretations that would be contradicted by those beliefs if they had been mustered for the interpretive task. In this type of situation, what the text is taken to mean is entirely relative to what it says. Stances of both these types are relativistic because neither is constrained by general standards of completeness and consistency. It is most justifiable for readers to adopt a critical stance by engaging in interactive negotiation between the text and their background beliefs in an attempt to reach an interpretation that, as consistently and completely as possible, takes into account the text information and their background beliefs (Phillips & Norris, 1999).

It is in the fashioning of interpretations that our position is constructivist and in the fashioning under constraints that our position is not relativistic. The previous conception of reading implies a relationship among authors, their texts, and the readers of those texts. Readers are pictured making an array of judgments about text that go beyond surface meaning, including judgments about what is meant or intended in contrast to what is said, what is presupposed in what is said and meant, what is implied by what is said and meant, and what is the value of what is said and meant (Applebee, Langer, & Mullis, 1987; Bereiter & Scardamalia, 1987; deCastell, Luke, & MacLennan, 1986; Torrance & Olson, 1987). The key to reading according to this expansive model is the mastery of literate thought, which brings the thinking involved in interpretation to a conscious level. "Literate thought is the conscious representation and deliberate manipulation of [the thinking involved in reading]. Assumptions are universally made; literate thought is the recognition of an assumption *as an assumption*. Inferences are universally made; literate thought is the recognition of an inference *as an inference*, of a conclusion *as a conclusion*" (Olson, 1994, p. 280).

According to the simple view, reading is knowing all the words and locating information in the text. By contrast, we maintain that reading is not a simple concatenation of word meanings, is not characterized by a linear progression or accumulation of meaning as the text is traversed from beginning to end, and is not just the mere location of information. Rather, reading depends on background knowledge of the reader – that is, on meanings from outside the text; it is dependent on relevance decisions all the way down to the level of the individual word (Norris & Phillips, 1994a); and it requires the active construction of new meanings, contextualization, and the inferring of authorial intentions (Craig & Yore, 1996; Yore, Craig, & Maguire, 1998).

Understanding reading requires a view from the inside, from the perspective of someone who is approaching a text and who does not yet understand it. From that perspective, reading has a number of features (Norris & Phillips, 1987). First, reading is *iterative*. By this, we mean that reading proceeds through a number of stages, each aimed at providing a more refined interpretation. A stage consists of steps, not necessarily followed in order: lack of understanding is recognized; alternative interpretations are created; judgment is suspended until sufficient evidence is available for choosing among the alternatives; available information is used as evidence; new information is sought as further evidence; judgments are made of the quality of interpretations, given the evidence; interpretations are modified and discarded based on these judgments; and, possibly, alternative interpretations are proposed, sending the process back to the third step.

Second, reading is *interactive*. Interaction takes place among information in and about the text, the reader's background knowledge, and interpretations of the text that the reader has created. When reading, people use the information that is available – including their background knowledge – in creative and imaginative ways. They make progress by judging whether what they know fits the current situation, by conjecturing what interpretation would or might fit the situation, and by suspending judgment on the conjectured interpretation until sufficient evidence is available for refuting or accepting it. The reader actively imagines and negotiates between what is imagined and available textual information and background knowledge.

Finally, to carry out such negotiation, reading is *principled*. The principles help determine how conjectured interpretations are to be weighed and balanced with respect to the available information. Completeness and consistency are the two main criteria for judging interpretations. Neither criterion by itself is sufficient; they must be used in tandem. To deal with situations in which there are competing interpretations, the criteria must also be used comparatively. Readers must ask which interpretation is more complete, and more consistent, because often neither interpretation will be fully complete and fully consistent.

Literacy on this view goes beyond skills, no matter how sophisticated those skills are. Literacy incorporates a set of realizations and fundamental understandings about text. One of the most central realizations begins with the recognition that text is a creative product and progresses toward an implication of this mode of production – namely, that text can be subjected to critical evaluation and to judgment concerning what it means (Clay, 1972; Illich, 1987; Olson, 1986, 1996; Wells, 1987). Heath (1986) argued that the belief that text is an artefact is needed in order to have the attitude that text is something that can be evaluated and analyzed. The idea is that unless a person has the attitude and basic understanding that text can be evaluated and analyzed, then the person is unlikely to do the analysis and evaluation when it is needed. A decade later, the same point was made by Kuhn (1997, p. 144) when she argued that "Understanding assertions as belief states carries the implication that they could be false". For most of us, realizations such as these are as common and as assumed as the air we breathe. However, it is not that way for individuals learning to read (Adams, 1991; Astington & Olson, 1990; Gee, 2000; Phillips, 2002). Reading, then, means comprehending, interpreting, analyzing, and critiquing texts. That is what the fundamental sense of scientific literacy encompasses.

If reading is as expansive as we describe, then reading involves many of the same mental activities that are central to science (Gaskins et al., 1994). Moreover, when the reading is of science text, it encompasses a very large part of what is considered doing science. It is not all of science because it does not include the manipulative activities and working with the natural world that are so emblematic of science. However, the relationship between reading and science is so intimate that great care is needed to maintain a distinction between scientific literacy in its fundamental and derived senses (Norris & Phillips, 2003). The need for care is increased by the fact that comprehending, interpreting, analyzing, and critiquing science text requires knowledge of the substantive content of science. This is why attempts to use scientific literacy in the fundamental sense can transmute without notice into uses in the derived sense (Kintgen, 1988; Labbo & Reinking, 1999) and why the fundamental sense is so easy to overlook. Also, if reading is as expansive as we describe, science educators need to be concerned by the possibility that many students will bring to their science classrooms the simple view of reading. If science teachers continue to show little concern for text, see reading as merely a tool to get to science, or see reading as unimportant, then they are likely to reinforce the attraction that this simple view has.

Educational Implications

The school science education goal of fostering scientific literacy must be defined so as to be a suitable ambition both for those students who may someday become scientists or work in science-related careers, as well as for those who will not study science beyond high school. The current overwhelming focus on the substantive content of science cannot suffice, even though that content may distinguish science more so than its method, which was often thought to be its distinguishing feature. Those who do not go on in science quickly forget the minutiae of its content and are thus left with nothing of lasting value for as many as thirteen years of science instruction.

We have argued that there is a way to construe scientific literacy so that it defines a goal of more enduring value for both groups: the future scientists and the others. That construal calls attention to the fundamental role of reading and writing in science, a role that is as basic and constitutive of science as observation, measurement, and data analysis. This aspect of scientific literacy is as important to future scientists as it is to nonscientist citizens, so it helps finesse the fact that during the school years we have, at best, only hunches about students' future career choices by offering a sensible curriculum no matter what their choice.

We also know that the goal of promoting the fundamental sense of scientific literacy is separable empirically from the goal of promoting scientific literacy in its derived sense. We have designed instruments to test the fundamental sense of scientific literacy and given them to students just completing high school with a science focus and to undergraduate university students who had taken several science courses since high school (Norris & Phillips, 1994b; Norris, Phillips, & Korpan, 2003; Phillips & Norris, 1999). The students, by virtue of their high school graduation with a science focus and their success in university science courses, already tested high on the derived sense of scientific literacy. Our instruments, therefore, did not test this aspect of scientific literacy but rather the ability to interpret a variety of pragmatic meanings carried in rather commonplace media reports of science of the type found in newspapers and news magazines. Both groups displayed the same types of errors in their interpretations: systematically overestimating the degree of expressed certainty in the reports, confusing statements providing evidence for conclusions with the conclusions themselves, and misinterpreting descriptions of phenomena with explanations of those phenomena. Furthermore, the students overestimated their own interpretive ability by pronouncing the reading difficulty of the reports to be about right and tended to take a deferential rather than critical stance toward the reports. From such evidence, it is clear that additional teaching directed toward scientific literacy in its derived sense is not likely to achieve the good for citizens and society that we all desire. If citizens are unable to interpret accurately popular reports of science and, furthermore, are disposed to defer to them, then teaching them more of the substantive content of science will not help. Rather, more concerted attention to generalizable literacy skills and attitudes is a better bet.

Construing scientific literacy as we suggest would entail rather dramatic changes to school science and reading education. Instead of the current heavy focus on teaching reading in the context of narrative text, reading of the expository and argumentative genres more typical of science would become more frequent. Also, whereas the prevalent view presumes that learning to read ends sometime in early elementary school – to be replaced by reading to learn – teaching and learning to read scientific texts could conceivably continue into high school and beyond. There is an alternative – the lifelong learning view of reading – that makes better sense of people's reading practices. All of these implications are contingent, of course, on eradicating the educationally destructive view that reading is so simple that it can be mastered by the time a person is nine or ten years old and, once mastered, can be applied without difficulty to any text at all.

Acknowledgments

We acknowledge permission from the publishers to use the following previously published work:

Wiley Periodicals, Inc., for Norris, S. P., and Phillips, L. M. (2003). How literacy in its fundamental sense is central to scientific literacy. *Science Education*, 87, 224–240.

Sense Publishers, B.V., for Norris, S. P. & Phillips, L. M. (2008). Reading as inquiry. In R. A. Duschl & R. E. Grandy (Eds.). *Teaching scientific inquiry: Recommendations for research and implementation* (pp. 233–262). Rotterdam, The Netherlands: Sense.

References

Adams, M. J. (1991). *Beginning to read: Thinking and learning about print*. Cambridge, MA: MIT Press.

American Association for the Advancement of Science (1989). *Science for all Americans: A project 2061 report on literacy goals in science, mathematics, and technology*. Washington, DC: AAAS.

American Association for the Advancement of Science (1993). *Benchmarks for science literacy*. New York: Oxford University Press.

Anderson, C. W. (1999). Inscriptions and science learning. *Journal of Research in Science Teaching*, 36, 973–974.

Anderson, R. C. (1985). Role of the reader's schema in comprehension, learning and memory. In H. Singer & R. B. Ruddell (Eds.), *Theoretical models and processes of reading* (pp. 372–384). Newark, DE: International Reading Association.

Applebee, A., Langer, J., & Mullis, E. (1987). *The nation's report card: Learning to be literate in America*. Princeton, NJ: Educational Testing Service.

Astington, J. W., & Olson, D. R. (1990). Metacognitive and meta-linguistic language: Learning to talk about thought. *Applied Psychology: An International Review*, 39(1), 77–87.

Beamish, J., & Herman, T. (2003). Adsorption and desorption of helium in aerogels. *Physica B*, 329–333, 340–341.

Bereiter, C., & Scardamalia, M. (1987). An attainable version of high literacy: Approaches to teaching higher-order skills in reading and writing. *Curriculum Inquiry*, 17(1), 9–30.

Clay, M. (1972). *The early detection of reading difficulties: A diagnostic survey*. London: Heinemann.

Council of Ministers of Education, Canada (1997). *Common framework of science learning outcomes K to 12*. Toronto.

Craig, M. T., & Yore, L. D. (1996). Middle school students' awareness of strategies for resolving reading comprehension difficulties in science reading. *Journal of Research in Development in Education*, 29, 226–238.

DeBoer, G. E. (2000). Scientific literacy: Another look at its historical and contemporary meanings and its relationship to science education reform. *Journal of Research in Science Teaching*, 37, 582–601.

de Castell, S., Luke, A., & MacLennan, D. (1986). On defining literacy. In S. de Castell, A. Luke, & K. Egan, (Eds.), *Literacy, society, and schooling* (pp. 3–14). Cambridge: Cambridge University Press.

Eisenhart, M., Finkel, E., & Marion, S. F. (1996). Creating the conditions for scientific literacy: A re-examination. *American Educational Research Journal*, 33, 261–295.

Ferreiro, E. (2000). Reading and writing in a changing world. *Publishing Research Quarterly, Fall*, 53–61.

Gaskins, I. W., Guthrie, J. T., Satlow, E., Ostertag, J., Six, L., Byrne, J., et al. (1994). Integrating instruction of science, reading, and writing: Goals, teacher development, and assessment. *Journal of Research in Science Teaching*, 31, 1039–1056.

Gee, J. P. (2000). Discourse and sociocultural studies in reading. In M. L. Kamil, P. Mosenthal, P. D. Pearson, & R. Barr (Eds.), *Handbook of reading research. vol.* 3 (pp. 195–207). Mahwah, NJ: Erlbaum.

Goodman, K. S. (1985). Reading: A psycholinguistic guessing game. In H. Singer & R. B. Ruddell (Eds.), *Theoretical models and processes of reading* (pp. 259–272). Newark, DE: International Reading Association.

Halliday, M. A. K., & Martin, J. R. (1993). *Writing science: Literacy and discursive power*. Pittsburgh, PA: University of Pittsburgh Press.

Hanrahan, M. (1999). Rethinking science literacy: Enhancing communication and participation in school science through affirmational dialogue journal writing. *Journal of Research in Science Teaching*, 36, 699–717.

Heath, S. B. (1986). The functions and uses of literacy. In S. de Castell, A. Luke, & K. Egan,

(Eds.), *Literacy, society, and schooling* (pp. 15–26). Cambridge: Cambridge University Press.

Hurd, P. D. (1998). Scientific literacy: New minds for a changing world. *Science Education, 82*, 407–416.

Illich, I. (1987). A plea for research on lay literacy. *Interchange*, 18 (1 & 2), 9–22.

Kintgen, E. R. (1988). Literacy literacy. *Visible Language*, 1, 149–168.

Korpan, C. A., Bisanz, G. L., Bisanz, J., & Henderson, J. M. (1997). Assessing literacy in science: Evaluation of scientific news briefs. *Science Education*, 81, 515–532.

Kuhn, D. (1997). Constraints or guideposts? Developmental psychology and science education. *Review of Educational Research*, 67, 141–150.

Kyle, W. C., Jr. (1995a). Scientific literacy: How many lost generations can we afford? *Journal of Research in Science Teaching*, 32, 895–896.

Kyle, W. C., Jr. (1995b). Scientific literacy: Where do we go from here? *Journal of Research in Science Teaching*, 32, 1007–1009.

Labbo, L. D., & Reinking, D. (1999). Negotiating the multiple realities of technology in literacy research and instruction. *Reading Research Quarterly*, 34, 478–492.

Lee, O. (1997). Scientific literacy for all: What is it, and how can we achieve it? *Journal of Research in Science Teaching*, 34, 219–222.

Mayer, V. J. (1997). Global science literacy: An earth system view. *Journal of Research in Science Teaching*, 34, 101–105.

Meldrum, A., Boatner, L. A., & Ewing, R. C. (2002). Nanocrystalline zirconia can be amorphized by ion radiation. *Physical Review Letters*, 88, 025503-1-025503-4.

Millar, R., & Osborne, J. (Eds.) (1998). *Beyond 2000: Science education for the future* (the report of a seminar series funded by the Nuffield Foundation). London: King's College London.

Miller, J. D. (1998). The measurement of civic scientific literacy. *Public Understanding of Science*, 7, 203–223.

Myers, G. (1991). Lexical cohesion and specialized knowledge in science and popular science texts. *Discourse Processes*, 14, 1–26.

National Research Council (1996). *National science education standards*. Washington, DC: National Academy of Sciences.

Norman, O. (1998). Marginalized discourses and scientific literacy. *Journal of Research in Science Teaching*, 35, 365–374.

Norris, S. P., & Phillips, L. M. (1987). Explanations of reading comprehension: Schema theory and critical thinking theory. *Teachers College Record*, 89, 281–306.

Norris, S. P., & Phillips, L. M. (1994a). The relevance of a reader's knowledge within a perspectival view of reading. *Journal of Reading Behavior*, 26, 391–412.

Norris, S. P., & Phillips, L. M. (1994b). Interpreting pragmatic meaning when reading popular reports of science. *Journal of Research in Science Teaching*, 31, 947–967.

Norris, S. P., & Phillips, L. M. (2003). How literacy in its fundamental sense is central to scientific literacy. *Science Education*, 87, 224–240.

Norris, S. P., & Phillips, L. M. (2008). Reading as inquiry. In R. A. Duschl & R. E. Grandy (Eds.).*Teaching scientific inquiry: Recommendations for research and implementation* (pp. 233–262). Rotterdam, The Netherlands: Sense.

Norris, S. P., Phillips, L. M., & Korpan, C. A. (2003). University students' interpretation of media reports of science and its relationship to background knowledge, interest, and reading difficulty. *Public Understanding of Science*, 12, 123–145.

Olson, D. R. (1986). Learning to mean what you say: Toward a psychology of literacy. In de Castell, S., Luke, A., & Egan, K. (Eds.), *Literacy, society, and schooling* (pp. 145–158). Cambridge: Cambridge University Press.

Olson, D. R. (1994). *The world on paper*. Cambridge: Cambridge University Press.

Olson, D. R. (1996). Literate mentalities: Literacy, consciousness of language, and modes of thought. In D. R. Olson & N. Torrance (Eds.), *Modes of thought* (pp. 141–151). Cambridge: Cambridge University Press.

Phillips, L. (2002). Making new and making do: Epistemological, normative and pragmatic bases of literacy. In D. R. Olson, D. Kamawar, & J. Brockmeier. (Eds.), *Literacy and conceptions of language and mind* (pp. 283–300). Cambridge: Cambridge University Press.

Phillips, L. M., & Norris, S. P. (1999). Interpreting popular reports of science: What happens when the reader's world meets the world on paper? *International Journal of Science Education*, 21, 317–327.

Shamos, M. H. (1995). *The myth of scientific literacy*. New Brunswick, NJ: Rutgers University Press.

Shen, B. S. P. (1975). Science literacy. *American Scientist*, 63, 265–268.

Shortland, M. (1988). Advocating science: Literacy and public understanding. *Impact of Science on Society*, 38, 305–316.

Smith, F. (1978). *Understanding reading.* New York: Holt, Rinehart & Winston.

Suppe, F. (1998). The structure of a scientific paper. *Philosophy of Science*, 65, 381–405.

Sutman, F. X. (1996). Scientific literacy: A functional definition. *Journal of Research in Science Teaching*, 33, 459–460.

Tenopir, C., & King, D.W. (2004). *Communication patterns of engineers*. Hoboken, NY: Wiley.

Tishman, S., & Perkins, D. (1997). The language of thinking. *Phi Delta Kappan*, 78, 368–374.

Torrance, N., & Olson, D. R. (1987). Development of the meta-language and the acquisition of literacy: A progress report. *Interchange*, 18(1 & 2), 136–146.

Wellington, J., & Osborne, J. (2001). *Language and literacy in science education. Buckingham*, UK: Open University Press.

Wells, G. (1987). Apprenticeship in literacy. *Interchange*, 18(1 & 2), 109–123.

Yore, L. D., Craig, M. T., & Maguire, T. O. (1998). Index of science reading awareness: An interactive-constructive model, text verification, and grades 4–8 results. *Journal of Research in Science Teaching*, 35, 27–51.

CHAPTER 16

Digital Literacy

Teresa M. Dobson and John Willinsky

What is literally *digital* about literacy today is how much of what is read and written has been conveyed electronically as binary strings of ones and zeros before appearing as letters, words, numbers, symbols, and images on the screens and pages of our literate lives. This digital aspect of literacy, invisible to the naked eye, is the very currency that drives the global information economy. Yet, what we see of this literacy is remarkably continuous with the literacy of print culture, right down to the very serifs that grace many of the fonts of digital literacy. So begins the paradox that whereas digital literacy constitutes an entirely new medium for reading and writing, it is but a further extension of what writing first made of language.[1] On the one hand, long-standing scholars of this new medium, such as Leu, favour treating digital literacy as itself a "great transformation," holding that such technologies do nothing less than "rapidly and continuously redefine the nature of literacy."[2] On the other hand, we tend to look to the continuities and extensions achieved through the introduction of digital literacy into a print culture, while seeking to understand how these developments encourage what is most admirable about the nature of literacy.[3]

To begin with an important historical continuity between print and digital forms of literacy that is often overlooked, much is made of the democratic qualities of digital literacy because it affords greater access to knowledge as well as the ability to speak out and make one's views widely available. Yet, such was the nineteenth-century democratic rallying cry for mobilizing wider participation in print literacy through the public library and public school movements of the day. Certainly, digital literacy carries with it the potential for a far wider, more global access to knowledge, as we discuss herein. Additionally, Lanham has been proved all the more right in the decade and a half since he wrote that the "radical democraticization of art and information offered to us by the computer" would be "rigorously opposed by the concepts of fixed property created by print" (1992, p. 242). Within this new realm of digital literacy, however, we are seeing that the emergence of *nonproprietary* and *nonmarket* forces within the networked information economy – to borrow Benkler's terms (2006) – face considerable opposition from among corporate commercial concerns, in an extension of struggles over intellectual property that were no less a part of print culture.

What follows, then, is a roughly chronological discussion of how digital technologies in recent decades have extended contemporary notions of literacy. For the purpose of this chapter, we divide the emergence of digital literacy into three stages: the public uptake of the computer in the 1980s; the rise of hypermedia and the Internet in the 1990s; and the more recent emergence of a networked information economy. We turn more than once to democratic and educational themes because they drive what is most interesting and innovative about digital literacy, whether these themes are realized directly through e-government initiatives to create greater transparency and opportunities for interaction or more generally through increased access and participation in the literate, informed, and knowledgeable quality of our lives through the open-access movement and self-publishing technologies such as blogs and wikis (Kolbitsch & Maurer, 2006). We recognize in what follows, as well, that the new medium does indeed massage the message in aesthetic as well as political ways.

Word Processing

The first hint that computers would give rise to a form of *digital literacy* came with the widespread use of the personal computer for word processing during the 1980s. The term *word processing* may have first found its way into print in 1970, according to the *Oxford English Dictionary*, when it was used in the journal *Administrative Management*, suggesting how word processing was originally a secretarial device for the efficient management of other people's texts. However, it was another decade before those who wrote for a living were drawn to how word processing eased the revision and editing process (Zinsser, 1983). Or, as Fallows stated it, "each maimed and misconceived passage can be made to vanish instantly, by the word or paragraph, leaving a pristine green field on which to make the next attempt" (1982, p. 84). Given as writers are to reflection, it was not long after word processing had caught on that Heim composed a "philosophical study of word processing," in which he considered how "word processing reclaims something of the direct flow of oral discourse" even as it cannot overcome the loss of immediacy that distinguishes written work (1987, p. 209).

Not long afterwards, word processing found its way into the schools, first in business education classes (where it replaced the typewriter, much to the relief of everyone involved) and then to students learning how to write across the subject areas (Smith, 1994). As Cochran-Smith (1991) notes in her review of the literature on word processing in education, which goes back to 1982, this form of digital literacy became a natural ally of the process-writing model, with its emphasis on student creativity, consultation, revisions, and sharing, and its emulation of how professional writers write (Daiute, 1985; Edelsky, 1984). The research at the time certainly demonstrated the integral role that word processing played in classrooms using the writing process (Calkins, 1983; Graves, 1983; Michaels & Bruce, 1989). On the other hand, large-scale surveys in the United States made it clear that teachers were as likely, based on their educational beliefs, to use computers for drill and practice exercises as they were to use them for open-ended work such as word processing (Wiske et al., 1988). For those who did have their students write with computers, the research showed that the ability of students to readily see and comment on each others' work led to improvements in the quality of writing (Bruce, Michaels, & Watson-Gegeo, 1985). Consistent with that finding was research establishing how word processing also proved itself more conducive to collaborative work among students as early as the first grade (Heap, 1989; Levin & Boruta, 1983), as well as collaboration among students and teachers in the primary grades (Cochran-Smith, Paris, & Khan, 1991). Still, it is worth noting Haas's (1989) finding that word processing led to less conceptual planning in the act of writing among both college students and experienced writers.

In those early days, there were those who sought to temper the enthusiasm for what word processing could do for literacy. In his widely cited piece on the "Computer Delusion" in The *Atlantic Monthly*, Oppenheimer (1997) quotes one teacher's concern with students' use of word processors: "They don't link ideas," the teacher says. "They just write one thing, and then they write another one, and they don't seem to see or develop the relationships between them." Some years earlier, Sudol, a teacher of composition at the university level, had noted how professional writers celebrated the trimming and truing of work afforded by word processing, whereas for students, word processing was about the "capacity to generate and accumulate" rather than cut (1990, p. 920). In support of this idea, Bangert-Drowns (1993) found that the thirty-two experimental studies conducted during the 1980s comparing students from elementary to college level revealed that word processing does lead to greater length of composition with slight gains in the quality of writing, especially among weak writers, although there was no indication that it led to a more positive attitude toward writing. The studies that Bangert-Drowns analyzed did not produce clear results on whether word processing reduces the number of mistakes made by school-age writers or on the value of increased revision. Similarly, Cochran-Smith's review of the literature brought to the fore how the numerous instances in which more extensive but "shallow," or micro-structural, revising that resulted from word processing did not appear to improve the overall *quality* of the work (1991, pp. 124, 141).

So, without knowing for sure what word processing has done to our writing, it has become the standard way we write. It does not appear to be "a transitional tool," as Bolter suggested, marking "the transition between conventional writing for print and fully electronic writing" (1992, p. 19). The "electronic writing" – by which Bolter is referring to writing intended to be read on computers involving various forms of hypertext (with more on this in a subsequent discussion) – has certainly become a daily part of what is read and written. Yet, it is still all word processing – whether in preparing documents, sending email, or creating a blog – with its expanded ability to type, copy, and paste texts and its ease of revising, formatting, and distributing. That is, in and of itself, word processing's facilitation of writing may perhaps have led to more letters to public officials, better prepared reports in schools, and more elaborate annual family missives during the 1980s; however, what it afforded was greatly amplified by Internet applications, especially with the rapid, global uptake of email in the 1990s and the enormous growth of blogs in the 2000s. In this way, word processing contributes to an increase in the amount of written communication and the global reach of this writing.

Hypermedia

Although the uptake of hypermedia by the public dates to the 1980s with the marketing of programs for personal computers such as Hypercard™, the conceptualization of networked text environments occurred much earlier. Bush's visionary article in The *Atlantic Monthly* is generally proclaimed the first iteration of the hypertext concept (Bush, 1945). Contemplating where scientists might turn their energies in the postwar period and foreshadowing the birth of the *information literacy* movement, which we discuss shortly, Bush suggested that the growing mass of the human record and our inability to effectively navigate and distribute that record is one of the most pressing concerns of humanity. To combat this problem, he proposed the development of a personal reading machine designed to facilitate information storage and access and to enable the user to demonstrate connections between discrete documents through associative linking.[4] Fifteen years later, Englebart resurrected Bush's ideas in proposing a framework for augmenting or "bootstrapping" intellectual development through a method of computer-based information storage that relied on associative linking of "concept packets" (Engelbart, 1962, p. 60). The paper constituted one of the first descriptions of hypermedia in the context of modern computing.[5] Ultimately, however, it was self-styled philosopher, Theodore Nelson, who coined the term *hypertext* in the early 1960s in the context of exploring a somewhat different question: How might writers use computer technology to compare related texts or different versions of the same text (Nelson, 1965)?[6]

For many years, hypermedia remained an obscure concept: even when prototypes emerged, they were available only on high-end workstations such as the Sun and Apollo (Wiggins & Shiffer, 1990). This scenario changed in the mid-1980s with the publication of the first electronic encyclopedia by Grolier (Marchionini, 1989). Shortly thereafter, in 1987, Apple released a software product called Hypercard™, which allowed users, typically working on stand-alone machines, to create "cards" (nodes containing text and graphics) and to link those cards to others by clicking buttons displayed on the screen. It was possible to link the cards sequentially, but it was also possible to link them associatively, creating a network of text and image. Bolter (2001) argued that this affordance – text as network – facilitates a particular form of writing: "Electronic writing . . . is not the writing of a place, but rather a writing with places as spatially realized topics" (p. 36).

One of the earliest examples of the use of hypermedia in an educational setting was Intermedia™, an extensive hypertext system developed at Brown University in the mid to late 1980s with a view to facilitating the teaching of literature courses (Kahn, Launhardt, Lenk, & Peters, 1990). The network allowed students to access primary and secondary literary materials and permitted them to contribute comments, texts, and links to these materials (Landow, 1997). In reflecting on his experience of teaching with Intermedia, Landow proposed that hypermedia revolutionizes education by freeing students from teacher-centered classrooms, promoting critical thinking, empowering students, easing the development and dissemination of instructional materials, facilitating interdisciplinary work and collaboration, breaking down arbitrary and elitist textual barriers by making all text worthy and immediately accessible, and introducing students to new forms of academic writing (Landow 1997, p. 219ff.). He also claimed that hypermedia blurs the boundaries between reader and writer and is in this sense a form of what Barthes (1974) refers to as "writerly text."

Whether we concede Landow's arguments for hypermedia, we must concede that hypermedia extends in significant ways our notions of textuality and literacy. Writing, for example, has long been deemed a way of making the effervescent word tangible (Ong, 1982). Along these lines, Gelb (1952), a pioneer in the study of writing systems, advocated that writing developed out of "the need for finding a way to convey thoughts and feeling in a form not limited by time or space" and that writing might be defined as "markings on objects or any solid material" (p. 3). The advent of word processing did not particularly challenge this notion because the technology was widely viewed as a means of facilitating the process of preparing documents for printing on paper. Hypermedia, however, gets at the heart of Gelb's definition, for the essence of highly networked documents with multiple pathways lies as much in their linking structures as it does in their content. Such documents are not necessarily amenable to print – or to replication on any solid surface, for that matter. With hypermedia, the McLuhan thesis is undeniable.[7] Clearly, text displayed on screen falls outside of Gelb's definition of marks on solid material. As Hayles (2003) observed, electronic text exists as a "distributed phenomenon," particularly in a network environment, but even when it resides on a stand-alone machine:

> *There are data files, programs that call and process the files, hardware functionalities that interpret or compile the programs, and so on. It takes all of these together to produce the electronic text. Omit any one of them, and the text literally cannot be produced. For this reason it would be more accurate to call an electronic text a process rather than an object. (p. 273)*

Thus, in the wake of the advent of hypermedia, and particularly with the public uptake of the Internet in the early 1990s, orthographers such as Gaur (1992) called for a reassessment of definitions such as Gelb's, suggesting that the digital era is in some respects reminiscent of the preliterate era, for the storage, preservation, and dissemination of knowledge "depends no longer on the actual process of writing. Computers store information in an electronic memory by means of positive and negative impulses – the way information was once (during the age of oral tradition) stored in the human brain" (p. 7).

What, then, are the implications of digital technologies for human engagement with the written word? Considering the luminous character of computer display, there is some question as to whether screen reading might itself pose a literacy challenge. Eyestrain has been linked to reading on computer (Anshel, 1997),[8] and the exceedingly long line lengths that are common in some online environments can be a challenge for readers (Dyson & Haselgrove, 2001). Beyond these considerations, researchers have pondered the affordances of multimedia for learning. For example, Reinking, McKenna, Labbo, and Kieffer (1998) proclaim, *inter alia*, that hypermedia is distinguished from its print predecessors because it is interactive, nonlinear, multimedia, and fluid rather than fixed (p. 1). This sort of understanding of the distinctive features of electronic textuality has become popular but, as some critics have observed (Aarseth, 1997, p. 46ff.), we should be cautious about applying such notions uncritically. The physical properties of earlier technologies for writing such as the codex, for example, do not in and of themselves presume linearity and lack of interactivity. Indeed, it may be argued that books more successfully enable "random access" than their computer-based counterparts, for readers may commence print texts at any point and establish links therein indefinitely. Also, print allows a range of opportunities for interactivity in the form of the addition of intertext or paratext, not least of which is the footnote that acts as a stepping-off point into source texts. Archivists have also argued convincingly against the notion of text "fluidity" – preferring to think in terms of version control – in keeping with long-established practices of working with variant texts in the humanities (Burk, Kerr, & Pope, 2002).

To return to the question of how readers engage hypermedia spaces, Salmerón, Cañas, Kintsch, and Fajardo (2005) reported contradictory findings in studies published since 1999, which they reviewed, with similar results from studies published from 1990 to 1999, which were reviewed by two research teams (Dillon & Gabbard, 1998; Unz & Hesse, 1999). It is difficult to synthesize this body of literature because of the range of variables: in the case of the text, there are questions of linking structures (e.g., hierarchical or networked), the presence or absence of advanced organizers (e.g., maps or overviews), the presence or absence of cues as to link direction, the extent of multimedia integration, and so on; in the case of participants, we must consider expertise with the medium, content-area expertise, learning styles and preferences, and so on. As well, tasks assigned participants in various studies range widely, from simple recall to complex analytical tasks such as essay writing.

With respect to comprehension comparison across hypermedia and paper, Dillon and Gabbard (1998) reported that the majority of experimental findings of controlled, quantitative studies demonstrate no significant difference. Exceptions worth noting are studies by Lehto, Zhu, and Carpenter (1995) and Marchionini and Crane (1994), which reported an advantage for hypermedia in terms of the number of references cited in the context of both search and essay tasks, findings that likely reflect the speed and power of electronic searching. Psotka, Kerst, and Westerman (1993) also reported an advantage for hypermedia in a study requiring participants to compare visual objects. The hypermedia tool appeared to facilitate the activity because it enabled a number of modes of visual comparison not supported in the print context. Dillon and Gabbard (1998) concluded that hypermedia appears to be best suited to tasks involving "substantial amounts of large document manipulation, searching through large texts for specific details, and comparison of visual details among objects" (p. 331).

A second consideration relative to literacy and hypermedia concerns the effects of networked (or multidirectional) text environments on readers' abilities to navigate information. In the first wave of literature about how hypertext may modify and extend literacy practices, proponents of the medium invoked the associationist argument, suggesting that hypermedia was destined to improve comprehension and motivation because it mimics the associative processes of the mind (Delany & Gilbert, 1991). Such claims echo the theories put forth by Bush (1945) and Engelbart (1962) in conceptualizing the medium. Dillon (1996), however, pointed out that these notions are seriously flawed: first, there is no definitive evidence supporting the hypothesis that facilitating associative thinking might improve comprehension; second, even if we were to concede this premise, it does not follow that a given hypertext mimics or facilitates associative thinking for anyone save the author of that hypertext. As Dobrin (1994, p. 310) explained, "The author's conception of the connection's relevance is not the reader's, and the reader gets lost."

Along these lines, early empirical studies with hypertext demonstrated that user disorientation may increase in highly associative networks, particularly for novices in the content area. Mohageg (1992), for example, found that highly networked nonhierarchical environments challenged readers and produced a negative effect on task performance. Hierarchical linking, on the other hand, proved most helpful in enabling readers to complete their tasks, while combined networked-hierarchical linking systems fell somewhere in the middle. Mohageg thus advocates against the use of network linking in isolation from hierarchical linking, a position that is supported by several other researchers (Dee-Lucas & Larkin, 1992; Rouet & Levonen, 1996; Simpson & McKnight, 1990).

In addition, provision for macrostructures such as maps or "fisheye" overviews has been recommended (Foss, 1989; Gray & Sasha, 1989; Kim & Hirtle, 1995; Landow, 1991; Nilsson & Mayer, 2002; Potelle & Rouet, 2003; Rouet & Levonen, 1996). Such advance organizers or literacy supports are advocated because they enable readers to discern, variously, the organization of content, the extent of the text, and their own location in the text. However, as Salmerón et al. (2005) observed on the basis of their extensive review of recent studies, research does not converge respecting whether hierarchical structures and overviews are beneficial for all readers. They pointed to findings with readers of print texts demonstrating that while readers with low knowledge of the content area benefit from reading texts with a high coherence order, those with high knowledge may learn significantly more from a text with low coherence order (McNamara & Kintsch, 1996; McNamara, Kintsch, Songer, & Kintsch, 1996). The work of Spiro and his team with hypermedia readers supports this claim. They showed that domain experts may find immediate utility in relational linking because they are better able to follow connections in a semantic sense, and that the thematic "crisscrossing" afforded by hypermedia documents may encourage readers to apply their knowledge in a more flexible manner (Jacobson & Spiro, 1995; Spiro, Coulson, Feltovich, & Anderson, 1994).

To get at the question of which literacy processes are facilitated or challenged in hypermedia, Salmerón et al. (2005)

suggested that it is worth framing the literature on hypertext literacy from the point of view of the construction-integration model of text comprehension (Kintsch, 1988, 1998; Van Dijk & Kintsch, 1983). This model distinguishes between "two of the mental representations that a reader forms from the text: (a) the textbase, a hierarchical propositional representation of the information within the text, and (b) the situation model, a representation of what the text is about that integrates the information with the readers' prior knowledge" (Salmerón et al. 2005, p. 172). Their experimental work with readers demonstrated that knowledge of the textbase is affected by how many nodes are read in a hypermedia environment but that the situation model is affected by the order in which those nodes are read. This finding supports studies suggesting that domain experts fare better in highly networked environments because they are able to fill in gaps in the situation model with their prior knowledge. Whereas research on the implications of hypermedia for literacy and learning is inconclusive, recent studies such as this point to the need for a more complex analysis that considers the affordances of various network structures for readers with a variety of learning needs and styles.

Literary Hypermedia

Notably, most studies of hypermedia – all of those alluded to herein and all studies in the literature reviews discussed – examine the way in which readers engage expository or informational texts. Although such texts comprise much of what is available in hypermedia environments, it is arguable that some of the most innovative text experiments in online publishing – ones that truly push the boundaries of established conventions of writing and that work to explore the particular affordances of digital media – have occurred in creative contexts in which the literary and design communities converge with a view to generating alternate, innovative, multimedia forms.

One such form is electronic literature, which is defined as a class of "works with important literary aspects that take advantage of the capabilities and contexts provided by the stand-alone or networked computer" (ELO, 2006, n.p.). E-literature includes genres such as hypertext fiction, reactive poetry, blog novels, and collaborative creative writing projects.[9] Older forms, such as hypertext fiction (Jackson, 1995; Joyce, 1987), are said to derive from text-based adventure games (Bolter, 2001), whereas emerging genres such as reactive poetry merge literary arts and multimedia design (Ankerson & Sapnar, 2001). Often presented through Flash, works in this latter class employ animated image and text accompanied by sound in an effort to produce visually dynamic pieces.

Ryan (2005) observed that when it comes to digital texts generated for the purpose of arts and entertainment, particularly those with a narrative component, digital textuality exists in a sort of "split condition." On the one hand are avant-garde forms, such as hypertext fiction and its increasingly multimedia successors; on the other hand are narrative game worlds such as "first-person shooters" (i.e., combat games in which players are provided with a first-person view of the action) and Massively Multiplayer Online Role-Playing Games (MMORPGs), which make use of the network capabilities of computer technology to enable multiple players to interact in a virtual world. The first category – the avant-garde – challenges conventional literary structures and often places a high processing demand on readers, resulting in limited appeal for the genre beyond circles of intellectual elite with an interest in the deconstruction of conventional aesthetic forms. The second category holds wide appeal for popular-culture audiences, and literacy scholars such as Gee have contemplated their implications for literacy and learning (Gee, 2003). Ryan (2005) claimed that there is little between the extremes, that digital texts have yet to reach audiences in the "middle of the spectrum," which she defined as the "educated public" who read for pleasure but who nevertheless pursue challenging literary fiction and nonfiction (Ryan, 2005). Ryan seemed to overlook the possibility of readers who fit into more than one category; nevertheless, her point is well taken: e-literature does not yet have a mainstream audience.

Douglas (2000) observed that there is a dearth of studies examining how the process of literary reading may be modified or extended in the digital realm. Possibly this is because early examples of electronic literature (e.g., hypertext fiction) met with poor reception by many critics, who suggested that the indeterminate, fragmented, open-ended nature of those texts work against our sense of narrative logic and the aesthetics of literary reading, and that examples of the genre lack the quality of their print counterparts (Birkerts, 1994; Platt, 1994). Hayles (2003), however, cautions against judging e-literature, which is still in the incunabular phase, against the standard set by print genres developed over half a millennium. A more appropriate course of action would be to develop models of reading and aesthetic response that account for the diversity of contemporary literature, both print and digital. As Dobson (2006) observed, many of the theories of reading that guide the thinking of literacy educators with respect to how people engage literary texts are based on studies of readers working with normal prose or conventional narratives (Chatman, 1978; Kintsch, 1988; Rabinowitz, 1987). To develop appropriate models for describing the process of reading complex print or digital narratives, it is necessary to examine how people engage these texts and to revise our perspectives of narrative structure, literary reading processes, and methods of teaching literature. This is work that remains to be done.

Computer-Mediated Communication

Roughly concurrent with the public uptake of hypermedia and the Internet was the rise of computer-mediated communication. Baron (1998) identified five different forms of computer-mediated communication: (1) one-to-one dialogue with an identified interlocutor (e.g., electronic mail); (2) one-to-many dialogue with identified interlocutors (e.g., listservs or bulletin boards); (3) postings to the Internet ("finished" pieces made available for public consumption); (4) joint composition (texts written in collaborative spaces); and (5) anonymous dialogue (real-time chat discussion, often within a fictional context in which interlocutors communicate under assumed identities). Notably, Baron's categories do not consider more recent developments, such as Instant Messaging (IM) and text-based communication with handheld digital devices (e.g., "texting"). Nor do they consider how social software applications such as wikis and weblogs have modified the nature of communicative acts such as "posting," which is certainly less formal and more dialogic in a weblog setting than it is in an HTML setting. Nevertheless, these categories serve as a useful starting point in considering the implications for literacy of a broad and growing array of communication technologies.

It is widely acknowledged that computer-mediated communication began with the introduction of electronic mail on ARPANET, the first wide-area computer network, in 1971.[10] Human communication was not the intended use of the network, which was designed for resource-sharing among researchers. Nevertheless, the application was received enthusiastically by the ARPANET community. Licklider and Vezza (1978) reported that by the mid-1970s, the ARPANET was becoming a "human-communication medium" with important advantages over the postal service and the telephone: "one could write tersely and type imperfectly, even to an older person in a superior position and even to a person one did not know very well" (Licklider & Vezza, 1978, p. 1331). Licklider and Vezza attributed this informality to the speed of the network, which encouraged individuals to treat the medium like the telephone. Their assessment was confirmed by early research, which demonstrated that speed, convenience, and asynchronicity were the most appealing features of the medium (Schaefermeyer & Sewell, 1988).[11] Foreshadowing the emergence of a form of shorthand that has come to be known, variously, as "emailese," "chat," and "texting," Licklider and Vezza also remarked on increased informality when two users linked their consoles and "typed back and forth to each other in alphanumeric conversation" (p. 1331).

The uptake of electronic mail by the public in the early 1990s generated pronouncements in the popular media that we are witnessing the biggest explosion of writing since the age of Johnson (Tierney, 1993). However, critics were quick to point out that this writing resurgence was not likely to result in the revitalization of the letter as an art form associated with Johnson's age (Solomon, 1998). On the contrary, the emerging orthography associated with electronic mail and its cousins, IM and Short Message Service (SMS), is marked by lack of punctuation and capitalization, the omission of vowels, the frequent use of alphanumeric abbreviations (e.g., "cul8r" instead of "see you later"), and the addition of paralinguistic footnotes in order to convey tone.[12] To explain this phenomenon, linguists such as Baron (1998) observed that most forms of computer-mediated communication are "speech by other means," marked by a social impulse for speed characteristic of face-to-face communication – a feature that is also noted in the psychology literature (Gackenback, 1998). As such, these communicative modes employ a cross-modality model, which differs from the dichotomous relationship between speech and writing that is widely assumed (e.g., speech is deemed informal, interpersonal, ephemeral, dialogic, and so on, whereas writing is deemed formal, personal, durable, monologic, and so on). Baron (1998, 2005a, 2005b) reminded us that this sort of cross-modality model is not unusual: throughout history, we can find many examples of texts written for oral performance and of oral texts that have been put to the written record. We can also find many examples of primarily oral societies that produced sophisticated written works. It is not inconceivable, therefore, that increasing reliance on digital modes of communication and the linguistic shifts that such reliance promotes might eventually result in "print culture sans print" or even "print sans print culture" (Baron, 2005a, pp. 28, 29).

It is not surprising that any contemplation of the implications of computer-mediated communication practices for literacy inevitably leads to a consideration of whether extensive writing in such environments might erode print-based literacy. As Carrington (2005) observed in speaking of IM, discussions in the popular media exhibit a discursive chain linking "texting to youth to declining standards to poor academic achievement to social breakdown" (p. 163). However, research does not necessarily support this position. In a review of the literature on computer-mediated communication, Cassell and Tversky (2005) observed that there are conflicting results and a number of significant lacunae. For example, networked computer-based communication is known to facilitate global dialogue, yet research is sparse with respect to how language functions in cross-cultural online communities. Among the studies to which they allude, Palfreyman and Khalil (2003) discussed the modification of particular alphabets for the purpose of IM, and Herring (1996) observed a difference in the way men and women communicate, suggesting that the minority gender on a given listserv will conform to the style of the majority. Expanding on this work, Panyametheekul and Herring (2003) suggested that a similar process occurs in cross-cultural forums. This latter study is "often cited as evidence for the 're-construction' of physical categories such as gender in the apparently disembodied space of the Internet" (Cassell & Tversky (2005, n.p.). Finally, Cassell and Tversky note that although debates continue in the popular media regarding the implications of extensive Internet use for the social and psychological well-being of children, studies to date on the matter are inconclusive or contradictory.

Ultimately, Luke and Luke (2001) observed that competence with new technologies – particularly adolescents' competence with new technologies – is often inappropriately reconstrued as incompetence with print-based literacies. They argue against what they see as the representation of a crisis in print literacy as a means to "delay and sublimate the emergence of new educational paradigms around multiliteracies, around new blended forms of textual and symbolic practice and affiliated modes of identity and social relations" (p. 96). To be sure, language and language use have always been fluid and variable, changing over time and in different sociocultural contexts. As Hayles (2003) noted, the advent of electronic textuality reminds us of this, inviting us to reconsider our presuppositions about reading and writing – which are infused with assumptions specific to print – to "re-formulate fundamental ideas about texts and, in the process, to see print as well as electronic texts with fresh eyes" (p. 263).

Digital Divide

As the computer became part of a global business and educational culture during the 1980s and early 1990s, discrepancies in who had access to this technology became strikingly apparent. What became widely known as the *digital divide* has been described by Norris "as shorthand for any and every disparity within the online community," including differences in access between developed and developing nations, the rich and poor – as well as men and women within those nations – and even a democratic divide between "those who do, and do not, use the panoply of digital resources to engage, mobilize and participate in public life" (2001, p. 4). This last point has a special poignancy because digital literacy is so closely connected to the traditional association of literacy and democratic rights, as well as to more specific notions of e-government.

With regard to the gendered dimensions of this divide, Cooper's (2006) overview of research published from Australia, Canada, Egypt, Great Britain, Italy, Romania, Spain, and the United States during the last twenty years demonstrates that females have been disadvantaged relative to men in both learning about computers and in computer-assisted learning. If the occasional study found no gender difference (Solvberg, 2002), Cooper still concludes that "the weight of the evidence strongly suggests a digital divide that has persisted across time and international boundaries" (Cooper, 2006, p. 321). The research demonstrates that males were faster in taking up computers in the first instance (Maurer, 1994) and then the Internet, leading to a shaping of the medium around their interests (Liff & Shepherd, 2004). In addition, reported reasons for the comparative reluctance of women to take up computers and computer applications range from computer anxiety to negative perceptions of self-efficacy (Brosnan, 1998; Colley & Comber, 2003; Colley, Gale, & Harris, 1994; Dundell & Haag, 2002; Farina, Arce, Sobral, & Carames, 1991; Temple & Lips, 1989; Todman & Dick, 1993; Whitley, 1997).

Recent international surveys of the digital divide, such as the UCLA World Internet Project, suggest that a gender gap still persists in many parts of the world, being wider in some countries (e.g., Italy, where 20 percent more men are reported as being online) than in others (e.g., Taiwan, where less than 2 percent more men are reported as being online) (Lebo & Wolpert, 2004). Yet, a survey from the U.S. Census Bureau (2003) claims that the gender gap is now reversed in that country, both in terms of computer and Internet use. Although in 1984 "men's home computer use was 20 percentage points higher than that of women," statistics in 2003 favoured women by 2 percentage points (U.S. Census Bureau, 2003, p. 11). The survey also reports that more women than men use computers and the Internet at work, although this may merely reflect women's prevalence in clerical support jobs.

The gradual closing of the gender gap in many nations has led some researchers to argue that initial concerns about a digital divide along gender lines were premature and that equity initiatives to promote technology use among women and other so-called disenfranchised groups may not be necessary (Compaine, 2001; Fink & Kenny, 2003); however, simple measures of computer and Internet use, which are often cited to support such claims, do not give an accurate sense of the complexity of the situation. A Canadian examination of computer use in school settings, for example, revealed that although "males and females report relatively similar levels of use, males tend to use computers in more diverse ways, such as programming, using graphics and spreadsheet programs, and desktop publishing" (Looker & Thiessen, 2003). Similarly, Bryson, Petrina, Braundy, and de Castell (2003) found that enrolments of males and females in secondary-school courses requiring sophisticated use of computers (i.e., those uses more likely to lead to careers and positions of leadership in computer technology, such as programming) are severely skewed, with males comprising between 79 and 90 percent of the student population in senior-level technology courses. Significantly, these numbers are nearly identical to enrolment patterns observed in such courses in the late 1980s, suggesting that, in certain respects, there has been little movement in the gender gap in the last two decades. Ultimately, we suspect that an analysis of who is in the business of maintaining Web servers, publishing Web materials, designing interfaces, and so on would likely reveal that a significant digital divide in regard to gender remains. As has been the case with the rise of most communication technologies, from print through television, males are the primary adopters and tend to control the content and format of information diffused through various media irrespective of how audiences change through time (Faulkner, 2001; Graff, 1995).

In economic terms, the digital divide has been measured on an international scale in many forms, with, for example, the likelihood of someone in a high-income country being a regular Internet user twenty-two times greater than in a low-income country (Tierney, 1993). Although this divide reflects disparities among nations that have become endemic to the current world economic system, ambitious efforts are underway in developing countries to increase participation in digital literacy through the Internet. In India, the government recently gave $23 million to Mission 2007: Every Village a Knowledge Centre, which will enable, with "training and technical help, local women and men . . . to add value to information and mobilize both dynamic and generic information on a demand-driven principle" (Swaminathan, 2006). Brazil has a PC Connectado campaign underway that is intended to make computers affordable to low-income families in part by using open-source software (Benson, 2005). MIT's Nicholas Negroponte developed a $100 laptop, as part of the One Laptop per Child initiative that is intended to help millions of children acquire basic computing power (Varian, 2006a).

Among universities in the developing world, the online availability of journals has proven something of a boon, enabling them to narrow what had become a growing print divide. The modest growth achieved in research-library collections during the 1970s was almost entirely lost to currency fluctuations, loss of government support for universities, and well-above-inflation increases in subscription prices in the 1980s and into the 1990s. As journals moved online throughout the 1990s, it was possible for a number of organizations to convince publishers to make their online editions available at no or very little cost to developing countries.[13] By the same token, programs such as African Journals Online have been able to take advantage of the Internet and open-source publishing systems to give an increasingly global presence to journals published in developing countries, with similar programs opening up in South East Asia (Cumming, 2005). It is not that the divide between countries has been overcome or even significantly reduced; rather, the recognition of the problem as fundamental to basic rights around literacy is being addressed by a number of initiatives that are taking direct advantage of digital technologies.

Yet, more than basic economic issues are at stake when it comes to literate participation online, as the pervasiveness of English on the Internet can form a further point of exclusion. In a good example of how biases and divides are built into the system on a historic basis, the Internet adopted ASCII (American Standard Code for Information Interchange) as its language standard in 1992, which was a code designed to handle North American English alone. It was only gradually superseded by the Unicode standard, which is capable of handling the full extent of the world's writing systems. By 2001, English prevailed with 230 million Internet users, compared to Chinese, the next most frequently used language online, which was deployed by 60 million users (Paolillo et al., 2005, p. 60). The interest in creating a more multilingual online environment has found eloquent expression in *Wikipedia*, which represents a publicly constructed encyclopedia with entries in more than two hundred languages (discussed further herein).

In the United States, President Bill Clinton spoke in 1996 of the digital divide in the country in his State of the Union message, calling for every library and classroom to be connected to the Internet (Clinton, 1996). Indeed, whereas the distribution of computers in the nation's homes continues to reflect an economic divide that hampers participation in forms of digital literacy, the U.S. schools and libraries have become beacons of equitable public access to the Internet (*Public Libraries and the Internet*, 2005). Libraries, especially, have become important access points for more equitable utilization of e-government, especially in times of crisis (Bertot, Jaeger, Langa, & McClure, 2006).

In considering the scope of the divide, we would do well to heed Warschauer's (2002) caution that current concerns parallel an earlier interest in the "great literacy divide" between oral and literate cultures, which was the object of anthropological research a few decades ago (Goody & Watt, 1963). Warschauer pointed out that those who analyze communities' differential access to computers can treat the differences – in a similar pattern to the way that oral and literate cultures were once distinguished – as a matter of "intellectual differences between simple and complex societies" rather than simply as a concentration of specific material resources. Warschauer pointed to the landmark study by Scribner and Cole of the Vai tribe in Liberia, which made it clear that *literacy*, per se, did not have generalizable cognitive benefits (Scribner & Cole, 1981). Yet, Warschauer (1999) also saw what he termed *electronic literacies* as a "democratic medium," with that democratic element existing in tension with the Internet's top-down economics, as well as its privileging of English-language and masculine cultures. The growing global dimensions of people's participation in digital literacy, with its economic as well as political implications, suggest that efforts to increase opportunities for access remain a worthwhile human-rights goal, much as access to literacy itself has always represented.

New Literacy Studies

Warschauer is hardly alone in drawing attention to how the new uses to which literacy is being put is situated in sociocultural contexts. Graff (1979), for example, argued that it is not appropriate to characterize literacy as a discrete property that individuals possess or lack in varying degrees; rather, literacy should be viewed as a set of complex characteristics and processes that influence and are influenced by social context and personal circumstance. Street (1984) likewise advocated for viewing literacy as a social practice rather than as acquisition and employment of a particular skill set, an approach that came to be known as the New Literacy Studies (Gee, 1991; Street, 1995). In summarizing his own work on the subject, Street (2003, p. 77) observed that the New Literacy Studies recognizes the existence of "multiple literacies" and the social practices with which those literacies become associated. It is a movement that seeks to make problematic what counts as literacy. This paradigm shift in literacy studies through the last half-century is referred to by Gee (1999) as the "social turn" and may be equated with the work of, among others, Barton (1994), Gee (1991, 1996), Graff (1979), Heath (1983), Street (1984), and Willinsky (1990).

Drawing on and expanding this tradition, the New London Group (1996) introduced the term *multiliteracies* with a view to accounting not only for the cultural and linguistic diversity of increasingly globalized societies and the plurality of texts that are exchanged in this context but also for the "burgeoning variety of text forms associated with information and multimedia technologies" (p. 60). Distinguishing multiliteracies from what it terms *mere literacy* (i.e., a focus on letters), the group calls for attendance to broad forms of representation, as well as to the value of these forms of representation in different cultural contexts. It also calls for attendance to the dynamic nature of "language and other modes of meaning," which are "constantly being remade by their users as they work to achieve their various cultural purposes" (Cope & Kalantzis, 2000, p. 5).

Digital technologies are associated with this movement in terms of both their facilitation of global, intercultural exchange, which leads to the convergence of peoples and languages in online communities, and the way in which they allow for the convergence of a range of media, thereby affording multiple modes of representation. Along these lines, Lankshear (1997) proposed that "technological literacies" (what we term *digital literacy*) may be defined as "social practices in which texts (i.e., meaningful stretches of language) are constructed, transmitted, received, modified, shared (and otherwise engaged), with processes employing codes which are digitized electronically" (p. 141). These social practices are undertaken through the means of computers and a range of hand-held devices. Engaging in meaning-making and communication in the digital age, therefore, entails becoming well versed in different semiotic modes – visual, textual, and verbal (Kress & van Leeuwen, 2001).

For Kress (2000), one outcome of this convergence of media is a dominance of the screen. He evokes the image of the twelve-year-old child who "lives in a communicational web structured by a variety of media of communication and of modes of communication" (p. 143). In this scenario, Kress remarked, "the 'screen' may be becoming dominant" and the "visual mode may be coming to have priority over the written, while language-as-speech has new functions in relation to all of these" (2000, p. 143). Bolter (2001, pp. 47ff) likewise identified a "breakout of the visual" in digital culture, viewing this as the continuation of a trend favoring icon over alphabet already evolving in print, television, and cinema – one that has been documented by previous scholars (Gombrich, 1982; Jameson, 1991; Mitchell, 1994). Moreover, Manovich (2001) observed that visual objects in the digital realm have an unusual quality, often having been achieved through "compositing," a process by which the whole is attained through combining a number of disparate elements. Thus, what appears to the user as a single Web "page," or even a single image on a Web page, may in fact consist of many files that are stored as separate units in the file structure and displayed by the browser according to an arrangement specified in the page code. In considering this feature of digital media, Walton (2004) contemplated the significance of the difference between the designer's and user's interface with the Web. Although users generally encounter Web pages as seamless visual artifacts, she observed, "Designers see the Web in its raw, uncomposited state, and work with separate components which they must construct into a whole. They can see the seams of the design and its component pieces: their view reveals the artifact as constructed and composite" (p. 167). Digital literacy, therefore, assumes visual literacy and entails both the ability to comprehend what is represented and the ability to comprehend the internal logics and encoding schemes of that representation (cf. Dobson, 2005).[14]

Digital Archives

One of the great dreams surrounding Western literacy was born in the third century BCE, when Ptolemy II, King of Egypt, came to support the wildly ambitious idea of gathering a copy of all the world's texts in the *Musaion*, or temple, that his father built in Alexandria. Here was the idea of a complete and universal library, which has haunted the committed reader's imagination ever since.[15] This dream has taken on new force with digital literacy, beginning with Hart's typing of the *United States Declaration of Independence* into a networked computer at the University of Illinois in 1971 and then making it available to the entire network, thereby initiating what has since grown into Project Gutenberg, which currently offers readers free online editions of eighteen thousand books that have been entered and checked by volunteers (Hart, 1992). Project Gutenberg was inspired by "dreams of increased world literacy and education," as its Web site describes it, and it was but the first of many expressions of this urge to turn the Internet into a universal library. Google announced its Google Print Library Project in 2004, with the goal of placing online the contents of the libraries at the University of Michigan, Harvard University, Stanford University, Oxford University, and the New York Public Library, for a total of 25 million to 30 million books. For the roughly 15 percent of books in these libraries that are in the public domain, readers would have complete access, whereas for books still subject to copyright restrictions, readers would be able to see only excerpts and a few lines for which terms were searched (Varian, 2006b).[16] Other book-digitization projects, such as the Open Content Alliance and the Million Book Project (which is also distinguished because the majority of books are in languages other than English, with India and China playing leading roles), as well as Project Gutenberg, have taken the more cautious approach of digitizing only material for which copyright is no longer an issue. Today, the sheer quantity and range of texts that are now available online has become a defining aspect of digital literacy.

Against these rising expectations of access to knowledge, a struggle has emerged within the scholarly literature between traditional economic models of relatively expensive access to journals and an *open-access* model that seeks to add this body of work to the universal library developing online and open to all readers. In 1991, Paul Ginsparg, a physicist at the Los Alamos National Laboratory, established what is now known as arXiv.org as a freely accessible database for posting high-energy physics "preprints" that were going to be or had been published in the field's traditional journals. The database grew during the decade from a community of two hundred users to an archive that was receiving forty thousand papers a month in the areas of physics, mathematics, computer science, and quantitative biology (Pinfield, 2001). As a result, as Ginsparg (1996) put it, "the communication of research results occurs on a dramatically accelerated timescale and much of the waste of the hardcopy distribution scheme is eliminated."

Of course, the "hardcopy distribution scheme" that Ginsparg referred to has since been transformed into an online distribution scheme of journals, so that the same published and peer-reviewed paper may be available through a subscription journal in a research library's online collection and through an open-access database like arXiv.org or on the author's Web site. The majority of journal publishers do not permit their authors to post copies of their published work in such archives or on their Web sites, and many journals offer authors a right to purchase open access for their article within the online edition of the journal. Still other journals make their contents open access without charge to authors or readers, either immediately on publication or some time after first making the articles available to subscribers.[17]

The resulting increase in open access to this research has meant that it is read and cited earlier and more often (Eysenbach, 2006; Harnad & Brody, 2004). The new economics of open access to this archived body of research is having a profound impact on scholars in developing countries, as discussed previously. It is also leading to a greater uptake of this work by the public, professionals, and policy makers (Willinsky, 2006). This is especially the case in the area of health and life science research, in which greater access to knowledge is changing the practice of medicine (Diaz et al., 2002; Fox & Rainee, 2000; Murray et al., 2003).

Still, the proportion of the scholarly literature that is open access is still less than 25 percent, by most estimates (Harnad, 2005). The majority of this work is only available through well-endowed research libraries, with no one library providing access to it all. Most faculty members have yet to take advantage of publishers' self-archiving policies to post copies of their published work in their library's open-access archive or on their own Web site. That is, the scholarly wing of the universal library is still a long way from being fully open, but it has demonstrated, at least, that digital literacy holds for readers vast new realms of knowledge and a general right to that knowledge. At the same time that the open-access movement has gained a hold on the scholarly literature, there are similar movements afoot in Benkler's (2006) realm of the nonmarket and nonproprietary approaches to the networked information economy. These include the emergence of open-source biology (Maurer, 2003) and open-data release policies (Rowen, Wong, Lane, & Hood, 2000), as well as the Creative Commons and Wikipedia, discussed in the next section, all of which speak to the development of a knowledge commons that is at once an integral feature of the democratic and educational qualities of digital literacy.

Information Literacy

As digital literacy is leading to significant increases in the quantity and range of information that can be readily accessed, new technologies are adding to the convenience, speed, and accuracy with which readers can work with this wide variety of information sources. Not only is there an ability to locate a single word or phrase in a mountain of digital documents, but also electronic indexes and databases enable readers to readily sort through centuries' worth of publications, finding relevant materials on a given theme. That is, digital literacy can be cast – to a considerable extent – as a form of *information literacy* that demands skilled navigating through, searching for, and making sense of relevant and reliable information. Or, as Lanham noted in *Scientific American*, "the word 'literacy,' meaning the ability to read and write, has gradually extended its grasp in the digital age until it has come to mean the ability to understand information, however presented" (1995, p. 198).

Much as with the concept of word processing, the idea of an *information literacy* was first proposed by those industries that made the sale of information their business in the 1970s (Webber & Johnson, 2000, p. 382). However, it was not long before the idea was to find its larger home within the library community, as a way of making sense of what was required to operate within the new information systems. In 1989, the American Library Association offered a definition of *information literacy* that, although it was technology-free, had an obvious bearing on the growing digitization of information resources: "To be information literate, a person must be able to recognize when information is needed, and have the ability to locate, evaluate, and use effectively the needed information" (American Library Association, 1989). Such abilities are no less pertinent within print culture, but what has changed in the last two decades – particularly with the development of user-friendly Internet search engines in the early 1990s – is the enormous growth in the digital-information resources that are suddenly at far more people's fingertips.[18]

Some within the information science community have suggested that the library community's focus on information literacy represents an effort to consolidate – if not extend – the work that they had been doing for years with programs in library skills and bibliographic studies (Foster, 1993; Miller, 1992). Certainly, information literacy, no less than digital literacy, is an instance of the general proliferation of literacies.[19] It can seem to be based, as Marcum (2002) charged, on too simple of a model for information in which literate people move from data through information to knowledge (see Bruce, 1997), and it is perhaps too much to ask of a literacy that it include, as Marcum also pointed out, a "competency with tools, resources, the research process, emerging technologies, critical thinking and an understanding of the publishing industry and social structures that produce information products" (2002, p. 20).

Yet, the library community has brought to the fore an awareness of *information literacy* that speaks to increasing opportunities and needs now for readers to find their own way across a plethora of information resources and to be able to do so outside of the traditionally supportive bounds of libraries, publishers, and educational institutions. It is a further instance, in that sense, of literacy as a skill not just for decoding text but also for locating texts and establishing the relationships among them. There is something to this approach that parallels the Protestant advocacy of literacy education focused around a reading of the Bible on one's own (Luke, 1989). Lemke provides a similar emphasis on the independence at issue with information literacy when he encourages teachers to pursue a "metamedia literacy" with students that places the emphasis on "access to information, rather than the imposition of learning" (1998, p, 293).[20] This digital form of information literacy would further equip readers in their independent pursuit of a greater understanding, providing them with search and reading strategies for navigating among sources and for dealing with related issues of source reliability, intellectual property, and access rights.[21]

Collaborative Knowledge

A further aspect of the Internet's enormous capacity for the distributed accumulation of knowledge has come with the introduction of software designed to facilitate collaborating on and sharing of information online (Alexander, 2006; Bleicher, 2006; O'Reilly, 2005). Alexander (2006) provided a comprehensive review of Internet-based projects and collaborative services that are associated with what has come to be known as the "Web 2.0" movement.[22] Alexander noted that from the start, many Internet technologies, such as listservs, discussion software, chat spaces, and so forth, have been profoundly social, linking communities and individuals around the world. Extending this trend, a group of Internet-based services and projects that is deemed particularly connective has emerged since the year 2000. These services, collectively termed "social software," include "weblogs, wikis, trackback, podcasting, videoblogs, and enough social networking tools like MySpace and Facebook to give rise to an abbreviation mocking their prevalence: YASN (Yet Another Social Network)" (Alexander, 2006, p. 33).

Alexander observed that much social software is "predicated on microcontent"; in the case of weblogs, for example, the unit of import is the "post" not the "page." This altered rhetoric, he suggested, has "helped shape a different audience, the blogging public, with its emergent social practices of blogrolling, extensive hyperlinking, and discussion threads attached not to pages but to content chunks within them" (2006, p. 33). Similarly, wiki software allows for the creation of collaborative, networked, online writing spaces that are remarkably easy for communities of users to edit on an ongoing basis. The trend in online knowledge-creation appears to be toward "mass amateurisation" (Coates, 2003; Shirky, 2002), a scenario wherein activities once reserved for professional publishers and writers (e.g., journalists, essayists, columnists, critics, and pundits) are taken up by the public *en masse*.

Whereas it is by no means clear what the online literacy economy will look like as it emerges from this formative period in the coming years, it is apparent that there are forces arrayed for increasing public access to and participation in the production of digital texts of every sort, which remains a critical democratic element behind this form of literacy. This increased access is bound to have an effect on how people read and write. One of the strongest – if not strangest – examples of how this digital medium is altering people's relationship to knowledge generally is what can be described as the *Wikipedia* phenomenon.

Wikipedia represents what is perhaps newest about digital literacy. It ranks among the *impossible public goods* that this new age has created, with open-source software, such as Apache and Linux, foremost among those goods, because this software is made freely available with countless people contributing to its development and improvement. In the case of *Wikipedia*, thousands of people all over the world are freely collaborating in creating the world's largest encyclopedia, and doing so with minimal governance, a policy of maintaining a neutral point of view, and a growing multilingual reach (as noted previously). In the process, it is challenging our basic literacy notions of authorship and intellectual property. Historian Roy Rosenzweig pointed out how the "Roosevelt entry, for example, emerged over four years as five hundred authors made about one thousand edits" (2006). Although rules and policies exist for creating entries, as well as rarely invoked policies for locking down articles and banning authors, the project is run, as Rosenzweig notes, "somewhat in the style of 1960s participatory democracy." If the quality of the writing is uneven as a result of so many hands, *Wikipedia*'s accuracy has been pronounced "surprisingly good" by the editors of *Nature* magazine who conducted a study of it and ultimately advised that "researchers should read Wikipedia cautiously and amend it enthusiastically" (Wiki's Wild World, 2005).

In another notable feature for students of digital literacy, *Wikipedia* entries are accompanied by a "discussion" page for contributors and readers to make suggestions and debate issues (whether, for example, Copernicus is rightly considered Polish, German, or Prussian), as well as a "history" page that records all of the changes that have been made to the entry. These meta-pages comprise about a quarter of the site's content and speak to yet another educational aspect of this collaborative digital literacy (Schiff, 2006, p. 41). This sense of public contribution to the representation of knowledge also has been taken up with another Web 2.0 phenomenon known as "folksonomy" (as opposed to taxonomy). Here, people are coming together to share their own classification and indexing of online materials (Alexander, 2006). Whereas traditional metadata classifications are typically hierarchical, structured, and predetermined by content authorities, folksonomic metadata is generated on the fly by users. For example, "social bookmarking" tools such as Furl and del.icio.us allow individuals to create collections of bookmarks, each of which may be "tagged" or categorized with keywords in accordance with the user's interests. When individuals add bookmarks to their lists, the entries are automatically linked to other lists sharing the entry or tag in common, and those collections, in turn, are searched for related sites. Services like del.icio.us thereby allow individuals to learn from and respond to one another's indexing tags, facilitating an inherently social form of information management and exchange.

Social software constitutes a fairly substantial answer to the question of how digital literacy differs from and extends the work of print literacy. It speaks to how people's *literacy* combines the taking in and giving back of words. The contributions that people are making to various collective commons sites extend the connection well beyond what was afforded by print culture, even with its more radically democratic and accessible forms of expression through pamphlets, broadsides, graffiti, mimeographing, and photocopying. This writing back to what had been read and this writing outside of the principal and official media forms have always been a part of literacy's public side. *Wikipedia* in particular provides a constant localization, in languages, places, events, and works, within this otherwise global phenomenon.[23] The very scale of participation in *Wikipedia* – with 100,000 edits a day at the time of the writing of this article – and the resulting quality of work signal a milestone in the long history of the public's literate engagement with knowledge.

Conclusion

We are aware of having painted a fairly Whiggish picture of digital literacy's emergence in the last three decades, tending to treat it as another step forward in the long road of literate development. Digital literacy does appear to be leading to greater literate participation in a wide range of activities, brought on by the ease of writing, greater linking of ideas and texts, and at least the promise of universal access to knowledge. Caught up in the emergence of this medium, we understandably want to highlight and encourage what we find most valuable about this new form. Certainly, serious challenges persist in realizing the benefits of digital literacy across this increasingly global society.

The digital divide may have narrowed during the last two decades as online access has improved through public libraries and Internet cafés, but the opportunity to use this technology remains very much a part of a larger landscape of economic disparities and gender biases. It is not yet clear that the open-access movement and other open-content initiatives – which have begun to increase access to scholarly and other work for scholars and the wider public – will prevail against commercial concerns, including the growing corporate concentration in the publishing of academic journals, which is driving up the cost of access to this knowledge. There are also real issues around too much information, in the form of inundated mailboxes clogged with spam and a World Wide Web that can seem overwhelmingly wide, if never very deep. There are dangers of government and employer surveillance and tracking, which also have long marked literacy's progress across the ages. Terrorist movements, too, continue to advance their cause with the help of digital forms of literacy, among other means.

Against all of that, however, we are still not inclined to temper our enthusiasm for identifying and supporting what is most promising in the emergence of digital literacy. Vigilance is called for, certainly, in recognizing that we are all part of what is giving historical shape to this new medium of expression. We must attend to where exactly and by what means digital literacy can be said to be furthering educational and democratic as well as creative and literary ends. It is by no means given, of course, what such contributions to the public good will look like. For that reason, the nature and value of digital literacy should continue to be the subject of public interest and scholarly inquiry.

Notes

1 See Ong on the line between the spoken and written word, in which "more than any other single invention, writing has transformed human consciousness" (1982, p. 78).

2 Leu identified three sorts of transformations that most researchers working on this topic tend to support in their work: these researchers focus on how the computer has transformed literacy (Labbo & Reinking, 1999); or on how the computer and literacy are transformed in a transactional relation; or on how, in Leu's words (2000), "changing technologies for information and communication and changing envisionments for their use rapidly and continuously redefine the nature of literacy" (Kinzer & Leu, 1997).

3 The historical continuities of a digital literacy go back to the Western invention of moveable type, when within decades of its use, type designers were carefully calculating and artfully configuring the geometry of typeface, which eased reading, while adding to the aesthetic quality of the page (Tufte, 2006, 48).

4 The concept is reminiscent of seventeenth-century inventor Nicolas Grollier de Serviere's sketch of the "reading wheel," a proposed invention for reading wherein multiple texts are set on the steps of a large wheel, presumably allowing readers to consult related documents as necessary without leaving their chair.

5 The roots of hypermedia and the Internet in military culture are significant in contemplating their sociocultural implications.

Bush wrote "As We May Think" while he was Chairman of the National Defense Research Committee under President Roosevelt. Engelbart's report on the augmentation of intellect (Engelbart, 1962) was prepared for the U.S. Air Force Office of Scientific Research during the post-Sputnik period of educational reform legislated by the U.S. National Defense Education Act (1958).

6 As Bardini (1997, n.p.) notes, the enterprise of an individual establishing and displaying connections between well-known texts for the purpose of comparison and "version control" is a substantially different literacy act than following established associative links in a massive body of unknown material. Ultimately, Bardini asserts that there are "two cultures, two world-views, at the origin of hypertext."

7 "The medium is the message" (McLuhan, 1994, p. 7ff.).

8 The problem is primarily with older CRT (cathode ray tube) screens, which have a high degree of flicker; LCD (liquid crystal display) screens, which are backlit and have no flicker, do not pose the same challenge for readers.

9 For examples, see *The Electronic Literature Collection, Volume One* (Hayles, Montfort, Rettberg, & Strickland, 2006).

10 The Advanced Research Projects Agency Network (ARPANET) was developed by the ARPA of the U.S. Department of Defense. It was the first operational "packet switching" network, originally designed for resource-sharing among researchers. The ARPANET is the forerunner of the Internet (Hafner & Lyon, 1996).

11 Synchronous communication is distinguished from asynchronous communication: the former requires both communicators to be present at the time of communication (e.g., telephone conversation or chat rooms); the second allows a written or oral message to be delivered to a mailbox, where it awaits receipt.

12 "Emoticons" (i.e., emotion icons) are a form of iconography employing combinations of keyboard symbols to mimic facial expression and gestures.

13 The World Health Organization worked with publishers in the first instance to provide free access to their medical journals (HINARI, http://www.who.int/hinari/en/); this was followed by arrangements to secure access to agricultural journals (AGORA, http://www.oaresciences.org/en/) and environmental journals (OARE, http://www.oaresciences.org/en/). In addition, the International Network for the Availability of Scientific Publications (INASP, http://www.inasp.org) has negotiated agreements with publishers to provide access to nearly twenty thousand titles across the disciplines to impoverished nations at extremely reduced prices.

14 Wileman (1993) defines visual literacy as "the ability to 'read,' interpret, and understand information presented in pictorial or graphic images" (p. 114). He associates this form of literacy with visual thinking: "the ability to turn information of all types into pictures, graphics, or forms that help communicate the information" (p. 114).

15 The idea of a universal library was introduced earlier in this chapter with Bush's (1945) sketch of the "memex," a machine that would take advantage of new technologies through which "a library of a million volumes could be compressed into one end of a desk," even as "wholly new forms of encyclopedias will appear, ready made with a mesh of associative trails running through them, ready to be dropped into the memex and there amplified." It is also vividly realized in fiction by Borges (1962).

16 At this point, Google is being sued by the Authors Guild of America and the Association of American Publishers in a dispute over *fair use*, a concept that has played such a vital part in the development of print literacy (Ganley, 2006). Fair use is what enables writers to copy, cite, and thus engage another's copyrighted work without having to compensate the cited author. Insofar as writing is so often about what others have written, a well-defined and not overly parsimonious sense of fair use is necessary to a literary economy.

17 On institutional repositories, see Harnad (2005); on the publisher's policies permitting authors to post work published in their journals in open-access institutional repositories or on their Web sites, see SHERPA (http://www.sherpa.ac.uk/). In addition, see Morrison and Waller (2006) and Byrd, Bader, and Mazzaschi (2005) on scholarly journals that make their contents freely available to readers, either immediately or after a period of time.

18 Internet search-engine development is reviewed by Schwartz (1998).

19 Snavely and Cooper (1997, p. 12), for example, identify thirty-five current types of literacy, from agricultural literacy to world literacy. See also the previous discussion of multiliteracies.

20 Lemke (1998, p. 293) opposes metamedia literacy to what he identifies as the "curricular paradigm," which "assumes that someone else will decide what you need to know, and will arrange for you to learn it in a fixed order and on a fixed timetable"; the interactive paradigm, he is advocating, is "how people with power and resources choose to learn" with results that are "usually useful for business or scholarship."

21 See Baldwin (2005, p. 120), for example, on the standards of scientific and technical information literacy, such as "Understands the flow of scientific information and the scientific information life cycle."

22 O'Reilly (2005, n.p.) observed that the concept of "Web 2.0" began with a brainstorming session between O'Reilly and MediaLive International respecting the bursting of the dot.com bubble: "Dale Dougherty, web pioneer and O'Reilly VP, noted that far from having 'crashed,' the web was more important than ever, with exciting new applications and sites popping up with surprising regularity." Many of the sites and services that survived the dot.com collapse come within the rubric of social software.

23 See Kolbitsch and Maurer, who wrote that the "[*Wikipedia*] distorts reality and creates an imbalance in that it emphasizes 'local heroes'" (2006, p. 196).

References

Aarseth, E. (1997). *Cybertext: Perspectives on ergodic literature*. Baltimore, MD: Johns Hopkins University Press.

Alexander, B. (2006). Web 2.0: A new wave of innovation for teaching and learning? *EDUCAUSE Review*, 41 (2), 34–44.

American Library Association (ALA) Presidential Committee on Information Literacy (1989). *Final Report*. Chicago: American Library Association.

Ankerson, I., & Sapnar, M. (2001). *Cruising: Poems that go*, 15. Retrieved May 10, 2006, from http://www.poemsthatgo.com/.

Anshel, J. (1997). Computer vision syndrome: Causes and cures. *Ergonomic News*, 3 (1), 18–19.

Baldwin, V. (2005). Science and technology information literacy: Review of standards developed by an association task force. *Science & Technology Libraries*, Vol. 25 (3), pp. 117–125. http://www.haworthpress.com/Store/E-Text/ViewLibraryEText.asp?s=J122&m=ov=25.

Bangert-Drowns, R. L. (1993). The word-processor as an instructional tool: A meta-analysis of word processing writing instruction. *Review of Education Research*, 63 (1), 69–93.

Bardini, T. (1997). Bridging the gulfs: From hypertext to cyberspace. *Journal of Computer-Mediated Communication*, 3 (2), n.p. Available from http://jcmc.indiana.edu/vol3/issue2/bardini.html.

Baron, N. S. (1998). Letters by phone or speech by other means: The linguistics of email. *Language & Communication*, 18, 133–170.

Baron, N. S. (2005a). The future of written culture. *Ibérica*, 9, 7–31.

Baron, N. S. (2005b). Instant messaging and the future of language. *Communications of the ACM*, 46 (7), 30–31.

Barthes, R. (1974). *S/Z*. R. Millar (Trans.). New York: Hill and Wang.

Barton, D. (1994). *Literacy: An introduction to the ecology of written language*. Oxford: Blackwell.

Benkler, Y. (2006). *The wealth of nations: How social production transforms markets and freedom*. New Haven, CT: Yale University Press.

Benson, T. (2005). Brazil: Free software's biggest and best friend. New York Times, pp. C1, C6, March 29.

Bertot, J. C., Jaeger, P. T., Langa, L. A., & McClure, C. R. (2006). Public access computing and Internet access in public libraries: The role of public libraries in e-government and emergency situations. *First Monday*, 11 (9). http://firstmonday.org/issues/issue11_9/bertot/index.html.

Birkerts, S. (1994). *The Gutenberg elegies: The fate of reading in an electronic age*. New York: Fawcett Columbine.

Bleicher, P. (2006). Web 2.0 revolution: Power to the people. *Applied Clinical Trials*, 15 (8), 34–36.

Bolter, J. D. (1992). Literature in the electronic writing space. In M. C. Tuman (Ed.), *Literacy online: The promise (and peril) of reading and writing with computers* (pp. 19–42). Pittsburgh, PA: University of Pittsburgh Press.

Bolter, J. D. (2001). *Writing space: The computer, hypertext, and the history of writing.* Hillsdale, NJ: Lawrence Erlbaum.

Borges, J. L. (1962). The library of Babel. In *Labyrinths: Selected stories and other writings.* New York: New Directions.

Brosnan, M. J. (1998). The impact of psychology gender, gender-related perceptions, significant others, and the introducer of technology upon computer anxiety in students. *Journal of Educational Computing Research, 18* (1), 63–78.

Bruce, B., Michaels, S., & Watson-Gegeo, K. (1985). How computers can change the writing process. *Language Arts,* 62, 143–149.

Bruce, C. (1997). The relational approach: A new model for information literacy. *The New Review of Information and Library Research,* 3, 1–22.

Bryson, M., Petrina, S., Braundy, M., & de Castell, S. (2003). Conditions for success? Gender in technology-intensive courses in British Columbia secondary schools. *Canadian Journal of Science, Mathematics and Technology Education,* 3 (2), 185–194.

Burk, A., Kerr, J., & Pope, A. (2002). Archiving and text fluidity/version control: The credibility of electronic publishing. *Text Technology, 11* (1), 61–110. Retrieved May 10, 2006, from http://web.mala.bc.ca/hssfc/Final/Credibility.htm.

Bush, V. (1945). As we may think. *The Atlantic Monthly, 176* (1, July), 101–108. Available at http://www.theatlantic.com/unbound/flashbks/computer/bushf.htm.

Byrd, G. D., Bader, S. A., & Mazzaschi, A. J. (2005). The status of open access publishing by academic societies. *Journal of Medical Libraries Association,* 93 (4), 423–424.

Calkins, L. M. (1983). *Lessons from a child: On the teaching and learning of writing.* Exeter, NH: Heinemann.

Carrington, V. (2005). Txting: the end of civilization (again)? *Cambridge Journal of Education,* 35 (2), 161–175.

Cassell, J., & Tversky, D. (2005). The language of online intercultural community formation. *Journal of Computer-Mediated Communication,* 10 (2), n.p. Retrieved December 10, 2006, from http://jcmc.indiana.edu/vol10/issue2/cassell.html.

Chatman, S. (1978). *Story and discourse: Narrative structure in fiction and film.* New York: Cornell University Press.

Clinton, W. (1996). *State of the Union Address.* Washington, DC. Retrieved December 10, 2006, from http://clinton2.nara.gov/WH/New/other/sotu.html.

Coates, T. (2003). The mass amateurisation of (nearly) everything. In J. Engeström, M. Ahtisaari, & A. Nieminen (Eds.), *Exposure: From friction to freedom* (pp. 53–57). Helsinki: Aula.

Cochran-Smith, M. (1991). Word processing and writing in elementary classrooms: A critical review of related literature. *Review of Research,* 61 (1), 107–155.

Cochran-Smith, M., Paris, C. L., & Kahn, J. L. (1991). *Learning to write differently: Beginning writers and word processing.* Norwood, NJ: Ablex.

Colley, A., & Comber, C. (2003). Age and gender differences in computer use and attitudes among secondary school students: What has changed? *Education Research,* 45 (2), 155–165.

Colley, A. N., Gale, M. T., & Harris, T. A. (1994). Effects of gender role identity and experience on computer attitude components. *Journal of Educational Computing Research,* 10 (2), 129–137.

Compaine, B. M. (2001). *The digital divide: Facing a crisis or creating a myth?* Cambridge, MA: MIT Press.

Cooper, J. (2006). The digital divide: The special case of gender. *Journal of Computer Assisted Learning,* 22 (5), 320–334.

Cope, B., & Kalantzis, M. (Eds.) (2000). *Multiliteracies: Literacy learning and the design of social futures.* London: Routledge.

Cumming, S. (2005, June). African Journals OnLine (AJOL). *International Network for the Availability of Scientific Publications Newsletter,* No. 29. Retrieved December 10, 2006, from http://www.inasp.info/newslet/jul05.shtml.

Daiute, C. (1985). *Writing and computers.* Reading, MA: Addison-Wesley.

Dee-Lucas, D., & Larkin, J. H. (1992). *Text representation with traditional text and hypertext.* Pittsburgh, PA: Carnegie Mellon University, Department of Psychology.

Delany, P., & Gilbert, S. (1991). Hypercard stacks for Fielding's Joseph Andrews: Issues of design and content. In P. Delaney & G. Landow (Eds.), *Hypermedia and literary studies* (pp. 287–298). Cambridge, MA: MIT Press.

Diaz, J. A., Griffith, R. A., Ng, J. J., Reinert, S. E., Friedmann, P. D., & Moulton, A. W. (2002). Patients' use of the Internet for medical information. *Journal of General Internal Medicine,* 17 (3), 180–185.

Dillon, A. (1996). Myths, misconceptions, and an alternative perspective on information usage and the electronic medium. In J. F. Rouet, J. J. Levonen, A. Dillon, & R. J. Spiro (Eds.), *Hypertext and cognition* (pp. 25–42). Mahwah, NJ: Lawrence Erlbaum.

Dillon, A., & Gabbard, R. (1998). Hypermedia as an educational technology: A review of the quantitative research literature on learner comprehension, control, and style. *Review of Educational Research*, 68, 322–349.

Dobrin, D. N. (1994). Hype and hypertext. In C. L. Selfe & S. Hilligoss (Eds.), *Literacy and computers: The complications of teaching and learning with technology* (pp. 305–315). New York: Modern Language Association.

Dobson, T. M. (2005). Technologies of text: Reflections on teaching, learning and writing with/in digital environments. *Journal of the Canadian Association for Curriculum Studies*, 3 (1), 123–137.

Dobson, T. M. (2006). For the love of a good narrative: Digitality and textuality. *English teaching: Practice and critique*, 5 (2), 56–68. Retrieved December 10, 2006, from http://education.waikato.ac.nz/research/journal/index.php?id=1.

Douglas, J. Y. (2000). *The end of books – Or books without end? Reading interactive narratives*. Ann Arbor, MI: University of Michigan Press.

Dundell, A., & Haag, Z. (2002). Computer self-efficacy, computer anxiety, attitudes toward the Internet and reported experience with the Internet, by gender, in an East European sample. *Computers in Human Behavior*, 18, 521–535.

Dyson, M. C., & Haselgrove, M. (2001). The influence of reading speed and line length on the effectiveness of reading from screen. *International Journal of Human-Computer Studies*, 54 (4), 585–612.

Edelsky, C. (1984). The content of language arts software: A criticism. *Computers, Reading, and Language Arts*, 1 (4), 8–11.

Electronic Literature Organization (2006). About the ELO. Retrieved January 8, 2007, from http://www.eliterature.org/about.

Englebart, D. (1962). A conceptual framework for the augmentation of man's intellect. In P. W. Hawerton and D. C. Weeks (Eds.), *Vistas in information handling, Volume I: The augmentation of man's intellect by machine*. Washington, DC: Spartan Books. Augmentation of human intellect: A conceptual framework. Available at http://www.bootstrap.org/augment/AUGMENT/133182-0.html.

Eysenbach, G. (2006). Citation advantage of open access articles. *PLoS Biology*, 4 (5): e157.

Fallows, J. (1982). Toys: Living with a computer. *The Atlantic, July*, 84–91.

Farina, F., Arce, R., Sobral, J., & Carames, R. (1991). Predictors of anxiety towards computers. *Computers in Human Behavior*, 7 (4), 263–267.

Faulkner, W. (2001). The technology question in feminism: A view from feminist technology studies. *Women's Studies International Forum*, 24 (1), 79–95.

Fink, C., and Kenny, C. J. (2003) W(h)ither the digital divide? *Info–The Journal of Policy, Regulation and Strategy for Telecommunications*, 5, 15–24.

Foss, C. (1989). Tools for reading and browsing hypertext. *Information Processing and Management*, 25 (4), 407–418.

Foster, S. (1993). Information literacy: Some misgivings. *American Libraries*, 24, 344.

Fox, S., & Rainee, L. (2000). *The online health care revolution: How the Web helps Americans take better care of themselves*. Washington, DC: Pew Internet and American Life Project. Retrieved September 28, 2006, from http://www.pewinternet.org/reports/toc.asp?Report=26.

Gackenback, J. (1998). *Psychology and the Internet: Intrapersonal, interpersonal, and transpersonal implications*. San Diego, CA: Academic Press.

Ganley, P. (2006). Google book search: Fair use, fair dealing and the case for intermediary copying. Working paper, SSRN. Retrieved January 8, 2007, from http://ssrn.com/abstract=875384.

Gaur, A. (1992). *A history of writing*. Revised edition. London: The British Library.

Gee, J. P. (1991). What is literacy? In C. Mitchell and K. Weiler (Eds.), *Rewriting literacy: Culture and the discourse of the other* (pp. 1–11). New York: Bergin and Garvey.

Gee, J. P. (1996). *Social Linguistics and Literacies* (2nd Ed.). London: Falmer Press.

Gee, J. P. (1999). The new literacy studies and the "social turn." Madison: University of Wisconsin–Madison, Department of Curriculum and Instruction. ERIC Document Reproduction Service No. ED442118.

Gee, J. P. (2003). *What video games have to teach us about learning and literacy*. New York: Palgrave Macmillan.

Gelb, I. J. (1952). *A study of writing: The foundations of grammatology*. Chicago: University of Chicago Press.

Ginsparg, P. (1996). Electronic publishing in science. *Scientist's View of Electronic Publishing and Issues Raised*, Conference, UNESCO, Paris. Retrieved January 8, 2007, from http://people.ccmr.cornell.edu/~ginsparg/blurb/pg96unesco.html.

Gombrich, E. H. (1982). *The image and the eye: Further studies in the psychology of pictorial representation*. Ithaca, NY: Cornell University Press.

Goody, J., & Watt, I. (1963). The consequences of literacy. *Comparative Studies in History and Society*, 5 (3), 304–345.

Graff, H. (1979). *The literacy myth: Literacy and social structure in the nineteenth-century city*. New York/London: Academic Press.

Graff, H. (1995). *The labyrinths of literacy*. Pittsburgh, PA: University of Pittsburgh Press.

Graves, D. (1983). *Writing: Children and teachers at work*. Exeter, NH: Heinemann.

Gray, S. H., & Sasha, D. (1989). To link or not to link? Empirical guidance for the design of nonlinear text systems. *Behavior Research Methods, Instruments, & Computers*, 21 (2), 326–333.

Haas, C. (1989). How the writing medium shapes the writing process: Effects of word processing on planning. *Research in the Teaching of English*, 23, 181–207.

Hafner, K., & Lyon, M. (1996). *Where wizards stay up late: The origins of the Internet*. New York: Simon and Schuster.

Harnad, S. (2005). The implementation of the Berlin declaration on open access. *D-Lib Magazine*, *11* (3). Retrieved January 8, 2007, from http://eprints.ecs.soton.ac.uk/10690/.

Harnad, S., & Brody, T. (2004). Comparing the impact of open access (OA) vs. non–OA articles in the same journals. *D-Lib Magazine*, 10 (6), n.p. Retrieved January 8, 2007, from http://www.dlib.org/dlib/june04/harnad/06harnad.html.

Hart, M. S. (1992). *History and philosophy of Project Gutenberg*. Salt Lake City UT: Project Gutenberg Literary Archive Foundation. Retrieved January 8, 2007, from http://www.gutenberg.org/about/history.

Hayles, N. K. (2003). Translating media: Why we should rethink textuality. *The Yale Journal of Criticism*, 16 (2), 263–290.

Hayles, N. K., Montfort, N., Rettberg, S., & Strickland, S. (2006). *The electronic literature collection, volume one*. College Park, MD: Electronic Literature Organization. Available at http://collection.eliterature.org/1/.

Heap, J. (1989). Sociality and cognition in collaborative writing. In D. Bloome (Ed.), *Classrooms and literacy* (pp. 135–151). Norwood, NJ: Ablex.

Heath, S. B. (1983). *Ways with words*. Cambridge: Cambridge University Press.

Heim, M. (1987). *Electric language: A philosophical study of word processing*. New Haven, CT: Yale University Press.

Herring, S. C. (1996). Two variants of an electronic message schema. In S. C. Herring (Ed.), *Computer-mediated communication: Linguistic, social and cross-cultural perspectives* (pp. 81–108). Amsterdam: John Benjamins.

Jackson, S. (1995). *Patchwork girl: A modern monster* [Computer software]. Watertown, MA: Eastgate Systems.

Jacobson, M. J., & Spiro, R. J. (1995). Hypertext learning environments, cognitive flexibility, and the transfer of complex knowledge: An empirical investigation. *Journal of Educational Computing Research*, 12 (4), 301–333.

Jameson, F. (1991). *Postmodernism, or, the cultural logic of late capitalism*. Durham, NC: Duke University Press.

Joyce, M. (1987). *Afternoon, a story* [Computer software]. Cambridge, MA: Eastgate Systems.

Kahn, P., Launhardt, J., Lenk, K., & Peters, R. (1990). Design of hypermedia publications: Issues and solutions. In R. I. Furuta (Ed.), *EP90: Proceedings of the International Conference on Electronic Publishing, Document Manipulation, and Typography* (pp. 107–124). Cambridge, UK: Cambridge University Press. Retrieved January 8, 2007, from http://www.kahnplus.com/download/pdf/ep90.pdf.

Kim, H., & Hirtle, S. C. (1995). Spatial metaphors and disorientation in hypertext browsing. *Behaviour & information technology*, 14 (4), 239–250.

Kintsch, W. (1988). The role of knowledge in discourse comprehension: A construction integration model. *Psychological Review*, 95 (2), 163–182.

Kintsch, W. (1998). *Comprehension: A paradigm for cognition*. New York: Cambridge University Press.

Kinzer, C. K., & Leu, D. J., Jr. (1997). The challenge of change: Exploring literacy and learning in electronic environments. *Language Arts*, 74 (2), 126–136.

Kolbitsch, J., & Maurer, K. (2006). The transformation of the Web: How emerging communities shape the information we consume. *Journal of Universal Computer Science, 12* (2), 187–213.

Kress, G. (2000). A curriculum for the future. *Cambridge Journal of Education*, 30 (1), 133–145.

Kress, G., & van Leeuwen, T. (2001). *Multimodal discourse: The modes and media of contemporary communication.* New York: Oxford University Press.

Labbo, L. D., & Reinking, D. (1999). Theory and research into practice: Negotiating the multiple realities of technology in literacy research and instruction. *Reading Research Quarterly*, 34 (2), 478–492.

Landow, G. P. (1997). *Hypertext 2.0: The convergence of contemporary critical theory and technology* (revised ed.). Baltimore, MD: Johns Hopkins University Press.

Landow, G. P. (1991). The rhetoric of hypermedia: Some rules for authors. In G. P. Landow & P. Delany (Eds.), *Hypermedia and literary studies* (pp. 81–103). Cambridge, MA: MIT Press.

Lanham, R. A. (1992). Digital rhetoric: Theory, practice, and property. In M. C. Tuman (Ed.), *Literacy online: The promise (and peril) of reading and writing with computers* (pp. 221–243). Pittsburgh, PA: University of Pittsburgh Press.

Lanham, R. A. (1995). Digital literacy. *Scientific American, September*, 198–199.

Lankshear, C. (1997). *Changing literacies.* Buckingham & Philadelphia: Open University Press.

Lebo, H., & Wolpert, S. (2004, 14 January). First release of findings from the UCLA World Internet Project shows significant "digital gender gap" in many countries. Los Angeles, CA: UCLA News. Retrieved February 6, 2005, from http://www.digitalcenter.org/.

Lehto, M., Zhu, W., & Carpenter, B. (1995). The relative effectiveness of hypertext and text. *International Journal of Human-Computer Interaction, I*, 293–313.

Lemke, J. (1998). Metamedia literacy: Transforming meanings and media. In D. Reinking et al. (Eds.), *Handbook of Literacy and Technology: Transformations in a Post-Typographic World By Rethinking* (pp. 283–302). Mahwah, NJ: Erlbaum.

Leu, D. J., Jr. (2000). Literacy and technology: Deictic consequences for literacy education in an information age. In M. L. Kamil, P. Mosenthal, P. D. Pearson, & R. Barr (Eds.), *Handbook of reading research, Volume III.* Mahwah, NJ: Erlbaum.

Levin, J., & Boruta, M. (1983). Writing with computers in the classroom: You get EXACTLY the right amount of space. *Theory into Practice*, 22, 291–295.

Licklider, J. C. R., & Vezza, A. (1978). Applications of information networks. *Proceedings of the IEEE*, 66 (11), 1330–1346.

Liff, S., & Shepherd, A. (2004). An evolving gender digital divide? *Oxford Internet Institute Issue Brief No. 2.* Oxford.

Looker, D., & Thiessen, V. (2003). *The digital divide in Canadian schools: Factors affecting student access to and use of information technology.* Ottawa, ON: Statistics Canada. Retrieved January 8, 2007, from http://www.cesc.ca/pceradocs/2002/papers/EDLooker_OEN.pdf.

Luke, A., & Luke, C. (2001). Adolescence lost/childhood regained: On early intervention and the emergence of the techno-subject. *Journal of Early Childhood Literacy, 1*, (1), 91–120.

Luke, C. (1989). *Pedagogy, printing and Protestantism: The discourse on childhood.* Albany, NY: State University of New York Press.

Manovich, L. (2001). *The language of new media.* Cambridge, MA: MIT Press.

Marchionini, G. (1989). Information-seeking strategies of novices using a full-text electronic encyclopedia. *Journal of the American Society for Information Science*, 40 (1), 54–66.

Marchionini, G., & Crane, G. (1994). Evaluating hypermedia and learning: Methods and results from the Perseus Project. *ACM Transactions on Information Systems*, 12, 5–34.

Marcum, R. (2002). Rethinking information literacy. *Library Quarterly*, 72 (1), 1–26.

Maurer, M. M. (1994). Computer anxiety correlates and what they tell us: A literature review. *Computers in Human Behavior*, 10 (3), 369–376.

Maurer, S. M. (2003). New institutions for doing science: From databases to open-source biology. A paper presented to the European Policy for Intellectual Property Conference, University of Maastricht, The Netherlands.

McLuhan, M. (1994). *Understanding media: The extensions of man.* Cambridge, MA: MIT Press.

McNamara, D. S., & Kintsch, W. (1996). Learning from text: Effect of prior knowledge and text coherence. *Discourse Processes*, 22, 247–288.

McNamara, D. S., Kintsch, E., Songer, N., & Kintsch, W. (1996). Are good texts always better? Interaction of text coherence, background knowledge, and levels of understanding in learning from text. *Cognition and Instruction*, 14, 1–42.

Michaels, S., & Bruce, B. (1989). *Classroom contexts and literacy development: How writing systems shape the teaching and learning of composition*. Technical Report No. 476. Urbana-Champaign, IL: Center for the Study of Reading.

Miller, W. (1992). The future of bibliographic instruction and information literacy for the academic librarian. In B. Baker & M. E. Litzinger (Eds.), *The evolving educational mission of the library*. Chicago: American Library Association.

Mitchell, W. J. T. (1994). *Picture theory*. Chicago: University of Chicago Press.

Mohageg, M. F. (1992). The influence of hypertext linking structures on the efficacy of information retrieval. *Human Factors*, 34 (3), 351–367.

Morrison, H., & Waller, A. (2006). Open access for the medical librarian. *Journal of the Canadian Health Libraries Association*, Summer 2006. Retrieved January 8, 2007, from http://eprints.rclis.org/archive/00007201/.

Murray, E., Lo, B., Pollack, L., Donelan, K., Catania, J., White, M., et al. (2003). The impact of health information on the Internet on the physician-patient relationship: Patient perceptions, *Archives of Internal Medicine*, 163, 1727–1734.

Nelson, T. H. (1965). A file structure for the complex, the changing and the indeterminate. *Association for Computing Machinery's 20th National Conference*. New York: Association for Computing Machinery, pp. 84–100.

New London Group (1996). A pedagogy of multiliteracies: Designing social futures. *Harvard Educational Review*, 66 (1), 60–92.

Nilsson, R. M., & Mayer, R. E. (2002). The effects of graphic organizers giving cues to the structure of a hypermedia document on users' navigation strategies and performance. *International Journal of Human–Computer Studies*, 57 (1), 1–26.

Norris, P. (2001). *Digital divide: Civic engagement, information poverty, and the Internet worldwide*. Cambridge: Cambridge University Press.

Ong, W. (1982). *Orality and literacy: The technologizing of the word*. New York: Routledge.

Oppenheimer, T. (1997). The computer delusion. *Atlantic Monthly*, 280 (1), 45–62.

O'Reilly, T. (2005, September 30). What is Web 2.0? *Design Patterns and Business Models for the Next Generation of Software*. O'Reilly Network. Retrieved December 15, 2006, from http://www.oreillynet.com/pub/a/oreilly/tim/news/2005/09/30/what-is-web-20.html.

Palfreyman, D., & Khalil, M. A. (2003). "A funky language for teenzz to use": Representing Gulf Arabic in instant messaging. *Journal of Computer-Mediated Communication*, 9 (1). Retrieved January 9, 2007, from http://jcmc.indiana.edu/vol9/issue1/palfreyman.html.

Panyametheekul, S., & Herring, S. C. (2003). Gender and turn allocation in a Thai chat room. *Journal of Computer Mediated Communication*, 9 (1). Retrieved January 9, 2007, from http://jcmc.indiana.edu/vol9/issue1/panya_herring.html.

Paolillo, J., Pimienta, D., Prado, D., Mikami, Y., & Fantognon, X. (2005). *Measuring linguistic diversity on the Internet*. Montreal, CA: UNESCO Institute for Statistics.

Pinfield, S. (2001). How do physicists use an e-print archive? Implications for institutional e-print services. *D-Lib Magazine*, 7 (12). Retrieved January 9, 2007, from http://www.dlib.org/dlib/december01/pinfield/12pinfield.html.

Platt, C. (1994). Why hypertext doesn't really work. *The New York Review of Science Fiction*, 72 (1), 3–5.

Potelle, H., & Rouet, J. F. (2003). Effects of content representation and readers' prior knowledge on the comprehension of hypertext. *International Journal of Human-Computer Studies*, 58 (3), 327–345.

Psotka, J., Kerst, S., & Westerman, T. (1993). The use of hypertext and sensory-level supports for visual learning of aircraft names and shapes. *Behaviour Research Methods*, 25, 168–172.

Public Libraries and the Internet 2004: Survey Results and Findings (2005). Information Use Management and Policy Institute, College of Information, Florida State University, Tallahassee.

Rabinowitz, P. J. (1987). *Before reading: Narrative conventions and the politics of interpretation*. Ithaca, NY: Cornell University Press.

Reinking, D., McKenna, M., Labbo, L., & Kieffer, R. (Eds.) (1998). *Handbook of literacy and technology: Transformations in a post-typographic world*. Mahwah, NJ: Erlbaum.

Rosenzweig, R. (2006). Can history be open source? Wikipedia and the future of the past. *Journal of American History*, 93 (1), 117–146.

Rouet, J. F., & Levonen, J. J. (1996). Studying and learning with hypertext: Empirical studies and their implications. In J. F. Rouet, J. J. Levonen, A. Dillon, & R. J. Spiro (Eds.), *Hypertext and cognition* (pp. 9–23). Mahwah, NJ: Lawrence Erlbaum.

Rowen, L., Wong, G. K. S., Lane, R. P., & Hood, L. (2000). Publication rights in the era of open data release policies. *Science*, 289 (5486): 1881. Retrieved January 9, 2007, from http://www.sciencemag.org/cgi/content/short/289/5486/1881.

Ryan, M. (2005). Narrative and the split condition of digital textuality. *Dichtung-digital: Journal für digitale ästhetik*, 5 (34), n.p. Retrieved May 10, 2006, from http://www.brown.edu/Research/dichtung-digital/2005/1/Ryan/.

Salmerón, L., Cañas, J. J., Kintsch, W., & Fajardo, I. (2005). Reading strategies and hypertext comprehension. *Discourse Processes*, 40 (3), 171–191.

Schaefermeyer, M., & Sewell, E. H. (1988). Communicating by electronic mail. *American Behavioural Scientist*, 32 (2), 112–123.

Schiff, S. (2006, July 31). Know it all: Wikipedia takes on the experts. New Yorker, 36–43.

Schwartz, C. (1998). Web search engines. *Journal of the American Society for Information Science*, 49 (11), 973–982.

Scribner, S., & Cole, M. (1981). *The psychology of literacy*. Cambridge, MA: Harvard University Press.

Shirky, C. (2002, October 3). Weblogs and the mass amateurization of publishing. Networks, economics, and culture [Internet mailing list]. Retrieved December 15, 2006, from http://www.shirky.com/writings/weblogs_publishing.html.

Simpson, A., & McKnight, C. (1990). Navigation in hypertext: Structural cues and mental maps. In R. McAleese & C. Green (Eds.), *Hypertext: The state of the art* (pp. 74–83). Oxford: Intellect Books Ltd.

Smith, C. (1994). Hypertextual thinking. In C. Selfe & S. Hilligoss (Eds.), *Literacy and computers: The complications of teaching and learning with technology* (pp. 164–281). New York: Modern Language Association of America.

Snavely, L., & Cooper, N. (1997, January). The information literacy debate. *The Journal of Academic Librarianship*, 23 (1), 9–14.

Solomon, S. J. (1998). Corresponding effects: Artless writing in the age of e-mail. *Modern Age*, 40 (3), 319–323.

Solvberg, A. M. (2002). Gender differences in computer-related control beliefs and home computer use. *Scandinavian Journal of Educational Research*, 46, 409–426.

Spiro, R. J., Coulson, R. L., Feltovich, P. J., & Anderson, D. K. (1994). Cognitive flexibility theory: Advanced knowledge acquisition in ill-structured domains. In R. B. Ruddell, M. R. Ruddell, & H. Singer (Eds.), *Theoretical models and processes of reading* (4th ed.). Newark, DE: International Reading Association.

Street, B. (1984). *Literacy in theory and practice*. Cambridge: Cambridge University Press.

Street, B. (1995). *Social literacies: Critical approaches to literacy development, ethnography, and education*. London: Longman.

Street, B. (2003). What's "new" in new literacy studies? Critical approaches to literacy in theory and practice. *Current Issues in Comparative Education*, 5 (2), 77–91.

Sudol, R. A. (1990). Principles of generic word processing for students with independent access to computers. *College Composition and Communication*, 41 (3), 325–331.

Swaminathan, M. S. (2006). *Role of ICT in rural economy proven*. New Delhi: Mission 2007 Secretariat. Retrieved September 6, 2006, from http://www.mission2007.org/mission/.

Temple, L., & Lips, H. M. (1989). Gender differences and similarities in attitudes toward computers. *Computers in Human Behavior*, 5, 215–226.

Tierney, J. (July 5, 1993). In multi-media storm, text survives. *New York Times*. *The Digital Divide Report: ICS Diffusion Index*, 2005 (2006). Geneva: United Nations Conference on Trade and Development (UNCTAD).

Todman, J., & Dick, G. (1993). Primary children and teachers' attitudes to computers. *Computers and Education*, 20, 199–203.

Tufte, E. (2006). *Beautiful evidence*. Cheshire, CT: Graphic Press.

Unz, D. C., & Hesse, F. W. (1999). The use of hypertext for learning. *Journal of Educational Computing Research*, 20, 279–295.

U.S. Census Bureau (2003). Computer and Internet Use in the United States: 2003. U.S. Department of Commerce, Economics and Statistics Administration. Washington, DC: U.S. Census Bureau. Retrieved December 15, 2006, from http://www.census.gov/prod/2005pubs/p23-208.pdf.

U.S. National Defense Education Act of 1958 (1958). Public Law 85-8642, 85th Congress, September 2, 1958. Washington,

DC: Superintendent of Documents, U.S. Government Printing Office.

Van Dijk, T. A., & Kintsch, W. (1983). *Strategies of discourse comprehension*. New York: Academic Press.

Varian, H. R. (2006a). A plug for the unplugged $100 laptop computer for developing nations. *New York Times*, p. C3, February 9.

Varian, H. R. (2006b). *The Google Library Project*. Paper presented at The Google Copyright Controversy: Implications of Digitizing the World's Libraries, AEI-Brookings, Washington, DC. Retrieved December 15, 2006, from http://www.sims.berkeley.edu/~hal/Papers/2006/google-library.pdf.

Walton, M. (2004). Behind the screen: The language of Web design. In I. Snyder & C. Beavis (Eds.), *Doing literacy online: Teaching, learning and playing in an electronic world*. Creskill, NJ: Hampton Press.

Warschauer, M. (1999). *Electronic literacies: Language, culture, and power in online education*. Mahwah, NJ: Erlbaum.

Warschauer, M. (2002). Reconceptualizing the digital divide. *First Monday*, 7 (7), n.p. Retrieved December 15, 2006, from http://firstmonday.org/issues/issue7_7/warschauer/index.html.

Webber, S., & Johnson, B. (2000). Conceptions of information literacy: New perspectives and implications. *Journal of Information Science*, 26 (6), 381–397.

Whitley, B. E., Jr. (1997). Gender differences in computer-related attitudes and behavior: A meta-analysis. *Computers in Human Behavior*, 13, 1–22.

Wiggins, L. L., & Shiffer, M. J. (1990). Planning with hypermedia. *Journal of the American Planning Association*, 56 (2), 226–236.

Wiki's Wild World: Editorial. (2005, December 15). *Nature*, 438, 890 (15 December 2005) | doi:10.1038/438890a.

Wileman, R. E. (1993). *Visual communicating*. Englewood Cliffs, NJ: Educational Technology Publications.

Willinsky, J. (1990). *The new literacy: Redefining reading and writing in the schools*. New York: Routledge.

Willinsky, J. (2006). *The access principle: The case for open access to research and scholarship*. Cambridge, MA: MIT Press.

Wiske, M. S., Zodhiates, P., Wilson, B., Gordon, M., Harvey, W., Krensky, L., et al. (1988, March). *How technology affects teaching*. Cambridge, MA: Harvard Graduate School of Education, Educational Technology Center.

Zinsser, W. K. (1983). *Writing with a word processor*. New York: Harper and Row.

CHAPTER 17

Literacy, Video Games, and Popular Culture

James Paul Gee

School Success

In this chapter, I place the role of popular culture – and video games as one characteristic popular cultural media – squarely in the framework of literacy traditionally conceived. So, let's start with reading. Consider the situation of a child learning to read. What should our goal for this child be? On the face of it, the goal would seem to be that the child should learn to decode print and assign basic or literal meanings to that print. However, the situation is not that simple. We know from the now well-studied phenomenon of the "fourth-grade slump" (i.e., the phenomenon whereby many children, especially poorer children, pass early reading tests but cannot read well enough to learn academic content later on in school) that the goal of early reading instruction has to be more forward-looking than simple decoding and literal comprehension (American Educator, 2003; Chall, Jacobs, & Baldwin, 1990; Snow, Burns, & Griffin, 1998). The goal has to be that children learn to read early on in such a way that this learning creates a successful trajectory throughout the school years and beyond. Such a trajectory is based more than anything else on the child's being able to handle ever increasingly complex language, especially in the content areas (e.g., science and math), as school progresses (Gee, 2004). Children need to get ready for these increasing language demands as early as possible.

Early phonemic awareness and early home-based practice with literacy are the most important correlates with success in first grade, especially success in learning to read in the "decode and literally comprehend" sense (Dickinson & Neuman, 2006). However, the child's early home-based oral vocabulary and early skills with complex oral language are the most important correlates for school success – not just in reading but also in the content areas – past the first grade, essentially for the rest of schooling (Dickinson & Neuman, 2006; Senechal, Ouellette, & Rodney, 2006). This latter claim needs to taken in a certain way: as discussed herein, we are not talking primarily about children's "everyday" vernacular oral language but rather their early exposure to what might be called "school-based" language and practices. Testing a child's oral vocabulary, for instance, is a practice that is not typical of face-to-face, everyday conversational practices.

However, here I must pause, because we are on the brink of what could be a major misunderstanding. Decades of research in linguistics have shown that every normal child's early language and language development are just fine (Chomsky, 1986; Labov, 1979; Pinker, 1994). Every child, under normal conditions, develops a perfectly complex and adequate oral language, the child's "native language" (and, of course, sometimes children develop more than one native language). It never happens, under normal conditions – and "normal" here covers a wide array of variation – that in acquiring English, say, little Janie develops relative clauses but little Johnnie just can't master them.

However, when I say that children's early oral language – vocabulary and skills with complex language – are crucial correlates of success in school, correlates that show up especially after the child has learned to decode in first grade (one hopes) – I am not talking about children's everyday language, the sort of language that is equal for everyone. Rather, I am talking about their early preparation for language that is not "everyday," for language that is "technical" or "specialist" or "academic," language that is used in a range of practices that are not typical of face-to-face, everyday conversational practices (Gee, 2004; Schleppegrell, 2004) and the sorts of thinking and knowledge work that goes with such language (Olson, 1994). I refer to people's "everyday" language – the way they speak when they are not speaking technically or as specialists of some sort – as their "vernacular style." I refer to their language when they are speaking technically or as a specialist as a "specialist style" (people eventually can have a number of different specialist styles, connected to different technical, specialist, or academic concerns).

An Example

Let me give an example of what I am talking about, in terms of both specialist language and of getting ready for later complex specialist language demands early on in life. Crowley talked insightfully about quite young children developing what he called "islands of expertise." Crowley and Jacobs (2002, p. 333) define an *island of expertise* as "any topic in which children happen to become interested and in which they develop relatively deep and rich knowledge." They provide several examples of such islands, including a boy who develops relatively deep content knowledge and a "sophisticated conversational space" (p. 335) about trains and related topics after he is given a *Thomas the Tank Engine* book.

Now consider a mother talking to her four-year-old son, who has an island of expertise around dinosaurs (the following transcript is adapted from Crowley & Jacobs, 2002, pp. 343–344). The mother and child are looking at replica fossil dinosaurs and a replica fossil dinosaur egg. The mother has a little card in front of her that says:

- Replica of a Dinosaur **Egg**
- From the Oviraptor
- Cretaceous Period
- Approximately 65 to 135 million years ago
- The actual fossil, of which this is a replica, was found in the Gobi Desert of Mongolia

In the following transcript, "M" stands for the mother's turns and "C" for the child's:

C: This looks like this is a **egg**.
M: Ok well this . . . That's exactly what it is! How did you know?
C: Because it looks like it.
M: That's what it says, see look ***egg***, ***egg*** . . . . . . Replica of a dinosaur ***egg***. From the oviraptor.
M: Do you have a . . . You have an oviraptor on your game! You know the **egg** game on your computer? That's what it is, an oviraptor.

M: And that's from the Cretaceous Period. And that was a really, really long time ago.

. . .

M: And this is . . . the hind claw. What's a hind claw? (pause) A claw from the back leg from a velociraptor. And you know what . . .

C: Hey! Hey! A velociraptor!! I had that one my [inaudible] dinosaur.

M: I know, I know and that was the little one. And remember they have those, remember in your book, it said something about the claws . . .

C: No, I know, they, they . . .

M: Your dinosaur book, what they use them . . .

C: Have so great claws so they can eat and kill . . .

M: They use their claws to cut open their prey, right.

C: Yeah.

This is a language lesson but not primarily a lesson on vernacular language – although, of course, it thoroughly mixes vernacular and specialist language. It is a lesson on specialist language. It is early preparation for the sorts of academic (school-based) language children see ever more increasingly, in talk and in texts, as they move on in school. It is also replete with "moves" that are successful language-teaching strategies, although the mother is no expert on language development.

Let's look at some of the features that this interaction has as an informal language lesson. First, it contains elements of nonvernacular, specialist language – for example: "**replica** of a dinosaur egg"; "from the **oviraptor**"; "from the **Cretaceous Period**"; "the **hind claw**"; "their **prey**." The specialist elements here are largely vocabulary, although such interactions soon come to involve elements of syntax and discourse associated with specialist ways with words as well.

Second, the mother asks the child the basis of his knowledge: Mother: "How did you know?" Child: "Because it looks like it." Specialist domains are almost always "expert" domains that involve claims to know and evidence for such claims. They are, in Shaffer's (2005) sense, "epistemic games."

Third, the mother publicly displays reading of the technical text, even though the child cannot yet read: "That's what it says, see look ***egg, egg*** . . . . . . Replica of a dinosaur ***egg***. From the oviraptor." This reading also uses print to confirm the child's claim to know, showing one way that this type of print (i.e., descriptive information on the card) can be used in an epistemic game of confirmation.

Fourth, the mother relates the current talk and text to other texts with which the child is familiar: "You have an oviraptor on your game! You know the **egg** game on your computer? That's what it is, an oviraptor"; "And remember they have those, remember in your book, it said something about the claws." This sort of intertextuality creates a network of texts and modalities (e.g., books, games, and computers), situating the child's new knowledge not just in a known background but also in a system the child is building in his head.

Fifth, the mother offers a technical-like definition: "And this is . . . the hind claw. What's a hind claw? (pause) A claw from the back leg from a velociraptor." This demonstrates a common language move in specialist domains – that is, giving relatively formal and explicit definitions (not just examples of use).

Sixth, the mother points to and explicates difficult concepts: "And that's from the Cretaceous Period. And that was a really, really long time ago." This signals to the child that "Cretaceous Period" is a technical term and displays how to explicate such terms in the vernacular (this is a different move than offering a more formal definition).

Seventh, she offers technical vocabulary for a slot the child has left open: Child: "Have so great claws so they can eat and kill. . . . " Mother: "They use their claws to cut open their **prey**, right." This slot-and-filler move co-constructs language with the child, allowing the child to use language "above his head" in ways in line with Vygotsky's concept of a "zone of proximal development" (Vygotsky, 1978).

New digital media – for example, video games; the Internet; DVDs; and software that facilitates production in areas like video, animation, and fan fiction – essentially create the opportunity for more and more young people to form areas of expertise early in life and throughout the school years and beyond. Ironically, as discussed herein, modern businesses are selling our children such centers of expertise built around highly specialized languages and the concomitant knowledge structures.

Specialist Language in Popular Culture

Something very interesting has happened in children's popular culture. It has gotten very complex and it contains a great many practices that involve highly specialist styles of language (Gee, 2004; Johnson, 2005). Young children often engage with these practices socially with each other in informal peer learning groups. Some parents recruit these practices to accelerate their children's specialist language skills (with their concomitant thinking and interactional skills).

To take one example from the many possible, consider the following text, which appears on a *Yu-Gi-Oh* card. *Yu-Gi-Oh* is a card game (with thousands of cards) involving quite complex rules. It is often played face to face with one or more other players – sometimes in formal competitions, more often informally – although it also can be played as a video game.

Armed Ninja
Card-Type: Effect Monster
Attribute: Earth | **Level:** 1
Type: Warrior
ATK: 300 | **DEF:** 300
Description: FLIP: Destroys 1 Magic Card on the field. If this card's target is face-down, flip it face-up. If the card is a Magic Card, it is destroyed. If not, it is returned to its face-down position. The flipped card is not activated.
Rarity: Rare

The "description" is really a rule. It states which moves in the game the card allows. This text has little specialist vocabulary (although it has some; e.g., "activated") unlike the interaction we saw between mother and child, but it contains complex specialist syntax. It contains, for instance, three straight conditional clauses (i.e., the "if" clauses). Note how complex this meaning is: first, if the target is face down, flip it over. Now check to see if it is a magic card. If it is, destroy it. If it isn't, return it to its face-down position. Finally, you are told that even though you flipped over your opponent's card, which in some circumstances would activate its powers, in this case, the card's powers are not activated. This is "logic talk," a matter of multiple, related "either-or," "if-then" propositions.

Note, too, that the card contains classificatory information (e.g., type, attack power, defense power, rarity). All of these linguistic indicators lead the child to place the card in the whole network or system of *Yu-Gi-Oh* cards – and there are more than ten thousand of them – and the rule system of the game itself. This is complex system thinking with a vengeance.

I have watched seven-year-old children play *Yu-Gi-Oh* with great expertise. They must read each card. They endlessly debate the powers of each card by constant contrast and comparison with other cards when they are trading them. They discuss and argue about the rules and, in doing so, use lots of specialist vocabulary, syntactic structures, and discourse features. They can go to Web sites to learn more or to settle their disputes. If and when they do so, following is the sort of information they will see:

***8-CLAWS SCORPION** Even if "8-Claws Scorpion" is equipped with an Equip Spell Card, its ATK is 2400 when it attacks a face-down Defense Position monster.*

The effect of "8-Claws Scorpion" is a Trigger Effect that is applied if the condition is correct on activation ("8-Claws Scorpion" declared an attack against a face-down Defense Position monster.) The target monster does not have to be in face-down Defense Position when the effect of "8-Claws Scorpion" is resolved. So if "Final Attack Orders" is active, or "Ceasefire" flips the monster face-up, "8-Claws Scorpion" still gets its 2400 ATK.

The ATK of "8-Claws Scorpion" becomes 2400 during damage calculation. You cannot chain "Rush Recklessly" or "Blast with Chain" to this effect. If these cards were activated before damage calculation, then the ATK of "8-Claws Scorpion" becomes 2400 during damage calculation so those cards have no effect on its ATK. http://www.upperdeckentertainment.com/yugioh/en/faq_card_rulings.aspx?first=A&last=C

It is not necessary to say much about this text. It is, in every way, a specialist text. In fact, in complexity, it is far above the language many young children see in their schoolbooks until they get to middle school at best and, perhaps, even high school. However, seven-year-old children deal and deal well with this language (although *Yu-Gi-Oh* cards – and, thus, their language – are often banned at school).

Let's consider for a moment what *Yu-Gi-Oh* involves. First and foremost, it involves what I call "lucidly functional language." What do I mean by this? The language on *Yu-Gi-Oh* cards, on Web sites, and in children's discussions and debates is quite complex, as we have seen, but it relates piece by piece to the rules of the game, to the specific moves or actions one takes in the domain. Here, language – complex specialist language – is married closely to specific and connected actions. The relationship between language and meaning (in which meaning here is the rules and the actions connected to them) is clear and lucid. The *Yu-Gi-Oh* company designed such lucid functionality because it allows it to sell ten thousand cards connected to a fully esoteric language and practice. It directly banks on children's love of mastery and expertise. Would that schools did the same. Would that the language of science in the early years of school were taught in this lucidly functional way. It rarely is.

So, we can add "lucidly functional language" to the sorts of informal specialist-language lessons discussed previously as another foundation for specialist-language learning, one currently better represented in popular culture than in school. Note, too, that such lucidly functional language is practiced socially in groups of children as they discuss, debate, and trade with more advanced peers. They learn to relate oral and written language of a specialist sort, a key skill for specialist domains, including academic domains at school. At the same time, many parents (usually, but not always, more privileged parents) have come to know how to use such lucidly functional language practices – like *Yu-Gi-Oh* or *Pokemon* and, as discussed herein, digital technologies like video games – to engage their children in informal specialist-language lessons.

Of course, the sorts of lucidly functional language practices and informal specialist-language lessons that exist around *Yu-Gi-Oh* or *Pokemon* could exist in school – even as early as the first grade – to teach school-valued content. However, it doesn't; the creativity of the capitalist has far out distanced that of the educators.

Video Games and Learning

Following the examples such as *Yu-Gi-Oh*, several people have begun to argue that today's popular culture often organizes learning for problem solving, and for language and literacy, in deep and effective ways (Gee, 2003a, 2005; Johnson, 2005; Shaffer, 2007). To see the case more generally, let's take good video games as an example, games like *Rise of Nations*, *Age of Mythology*, *Deus Ex*, *The Elder Scrolls III: Morrowind*, and *Tony Hawk's Underground*. We discuss just a few of the ways in which good video games recruit good learning.

Such games, first of all, offer players strong identities. Learning a new domain, whether biology or urban planning, requires learning to see and value work and the world in new ways – in the ways that biologists or urban planners do (Collins, 2006; Gee, 1990/1996; Shaffer, 2007). In video games, players learn to view the virtual world through the eyes and values of a distinctive identity (e.g., Solid Snake in *Metal Gear Solid*) or one that they themselves have built from the ground up (e.g., in *The Elder Scrolls III: Morrowind*). It is unfortunate that we have built so few games centered on identities relevant to school and the world of work (however, see Gee, 2005; Shaffer, 2004, 2005, 2007).

Good games are built on a cycle of "hypothesize, probe the world, get a reaction, reflect on the results, re-probe to get better results," a cycle typical of experimental science and of reflective practice (Schön, 1991).

Good games let players be producers, not just consumers. An open-ended game like *The Elder Scrolls III: Morrowind* is a different game for each player. Players co-design the game through their unique actions and decisions. At another level, many games come with software through which players can modify ("mod") them, producing new scenarios or whole new games (e.g., new skate parks in the *Tony Hawk* games).

Good games lower the consequences of failure. When players fail, they can start from their last saved game. Players are encouraged to take risks, explore, and try new things. Good games allow players to customize the game to fit their learning and playing styles. Games often have different difficulty levels, and good games allow problems to be solved in multiple ways. Thanks to all these features, players feel a real sense of agency, ownership, and control. It's *their* game.

However, learning goes yet deeper in good games. In good video games, problems are well ordered so that earlier ones lead to hypotheses that work well for later, more difficult problems.

Good games offer players a set of challenging problems and then let them practice them until they have routinized their mastery. Then, the game throws a new class of problem at the player (this is sometimes called a "boss"), requiring them to rethink their taken-for-granted mastery. In turn, this new mastery is consolidated through repetition (with variation), only to be challenged again. This cycle of consolidation and challenge is the basis of the development of expertise in any domain (Bereiter & Scardamalia, 1993).

Good games stay within – but at the outer edge – of the player's "regime of competence" (diSessa, 2000). That is, they feel "doable" but challenging. This makes them pleasantly frustrating – a flow state for human beings (Csikszentmihalyi, 1990).

Good games encourage players to think about relationships, not isolated events, facts, and skills. In a game like *Rise of Nations*, players need to think how each action they take might impact their future actions and the actions of the other players playing against them as they each move their civilizations through the ages.

Good games recruit smart tools, distributed knowledge, and cross-functional collaborative teams just like modern high-tech workplaces (Scardamalia & Bereiter, 2006). The virtual characters one manipulates in a game are "smart tools." They have skills and knowledge of their own that they lend to the player. For example, the citizens in *Rise of Nations* know how to build cities, but the player needs to know where to build them. In a multiplayer game like *World of WarCraft*, players play on teams in which each player has a different set of skills. Each player must master a specialty – because a Mage plays differently than a Warrior – but also understand enough of each other's specializations to coordinate with them. Thus, the core knowledge needed to play video games is distributed among a set of real people and their smart tools, much as in a modern science laboratory or high-tech workplace.

Good video games operate by a principle of performance before competence. Players can perform before they are competent, supported by the design of the game, the "smart tools" the game offers, and often other, more advanced players (i.e., in the game or in chat rooms).

In my view, the learning features players see in good video games are allwell supported by research in the Learning Sciences (Gee, 2003a, 2004; see also Bransford, Brown, & Cocking, 2000; Sawyer, 2006). All of them could and should be present in school or adult learning – for example, in learning science (diSessa, 2000) – whether or not a game is present.

Situated Meaning and Video Games

Let's turn now not to how learning in general works in games but rather how literacy and language work. Abundant research has shown for years now that in areas like science, many students with good grades and passing test scores cannot actually use their knowledge to solve problems (Gardner, 1991). For example, many students who can list Newton's Laws of Motion for a test cannot correctly say how many forces are acting on a coin when it is tossed into the air and at the top of its trajectory – ironically, this is something that can be deduced from Newton's Laws (Chi, Feltovich, & Glaser, 1981). They cannot apply their knowledge because they do not see how it applies – that is, they do not see the physical world and the language of physics (which includes mathematics) in such a way that it is clear how that language applies to that world.

There are two ways to understand words: I call one way "verbal" and the other way "situated" (Gee, 2004). A situated understanding of a concept or word implies the ability to use the word or understand the concept in ways that are customizable to different specific situations of use (Brown, Collins, & Dugid, 1989; Clark, 1997; Gee, 2004). A general or verbal understanding implies an ability to explicate one's understanding in terms of other words or general principles but not necessarily an ability to apply this knowledge to actual situations. Thus, although verbal or general understandings may facilitate passing certain types of information-focused tests, they do not necessarily facilitate actual problem solving.

Let me quickly acknowledge that, in fact, all human understandings, in reality, are situated. What I am calling verbal understandings aresituated, of course, in terms of other words and, in a larger sense, the total linguistic, cultural, and domain knowledge that a person has. However, they are not necessarily situated in terms of how to apply these words to actual situations of use and vary their applications across different contexts of use. Thus, I continue to contrast verbal understandings to situated understanding, in which the latter implies the ability to do and not just say.

Situated understandings, of course, are the norm in everyday life and in vernacular language. Even the most mundane words take on different meanings in different contexts of use. Indeed, people must be able to build these meanings on the spot in real time as they construe the contexts around them. For instance, people construct different meanings for a word like *coffee* when they hear something like "The coffee spilled, get the mop" versus "The coffee spilled, get a broom" versus "The coffee spilled, stack it again." Indeed, such examples have been a staple of connectionist work on human understanding (Clark, 1993).

Verbal and general understandings are top-down. They start with the general – that is, with a definition-like understanding of a word or a general principle associated with a concept. Less abstract meanings follow as special cases of the definition or principle. Situated understandings generally work in the other direction: understanding starts with a relatively concrete case and gradually rises to higher levels of abstraction through the consideration of additional cases.

The perspective I am developing here, one that stresses knowledge as tied to activity and experiences in the world before knowledge as facts and information – that is, knowledge as situated as opposed to verbal understandings – has many implications for the nature of learning and teaching, as well as for the assessment of learning and teaching (Gee, 2003b). Recently, researchers in several different areas have raised the possibility that what we might call "game-like" learning through digital technologies can facilitate situated understandings in the context of activity and experience grounded in perception (Games-to-Teach, 2003; Gee, 2003a, 2004, 2005; McFarlane, Sparrowhawk, & Heald, 2002; Squire, 2003).

Before I discuss game-like learning in some depth, let me point out a phenomenon of which all gamers are well aware. This phenomenon gets to the heart and soul of what situated meanings are and why they are important: Written texts associated with video games are not very meaningful – certainly not very lucid – unless and until one has played the game. I use the small booklet accompanying the innovative shooter game *Deus Ex* to use as an example of my meaning. Following is a typical piece of language from the booklet:

> *Your internal nano-processors keep a very detailed record of your condition, equipment and recent history. You can access this data at any time during play by hitting F1 to get to the Inventory screen or F2 to get to the Goals/Notes screen. Once you have accessed your information screens, you can move between the screens by clicking on the tabs at the top of the screen. You can map other information screens to hotkeys using Settings, Keyboard/Mouse (http://services.yummy.net/docs/Deusexmanual.pdf, p. 5)*

This makes perfect sense at a literal level, which just goes to show how worthless the literal level is. When you understand this sort of passage only at a literal level, you have only an illusion of understanding, one that quickly disappears as you try to relate the information to the hundreds of other important details in the booklet. Such literal understandings are precisely what children who fuel the fourth-grade slump have. First of all, this passage means nothing real to you if you have no situated idea about what "nano-processors," "condition," "equipment," "history," "F1," "Inventory screen," "F2," "Goals/Notes screen" (and, of course, "Goals" and "Notes"), "information screens," "clicking," "tabs," "map," "hotkeys," and "Settings, Keyboard/Mouse" mean in and for playing games like *Deus Ex*.

Second, although you know literally what each sentence means, they raise a plethora of questions if you have no situated understandings of this game or games like it. For instance: Is the same data (i.e., condition, equipment, and history) on both the Inventory screen and the Goals/Notes screen? If so, why is it on two different screens? If not, which type of information is on which screen and why? The fact that I can move between the screens by clicking on the tabs – but what do these tabs look like; will I recognize them – suggests that some of this information is on one screen and some on the other. But, then, is my "condition" part of my Inventory or my Goals/Notes? It does not seem to be either, but, then, what is my "condition" anyway? If I can map other information screens (and what are these?) to hotkeys using "Setting, Keyboard/Mouse," does this mean there is no other way to access them? How will I access them in the first place to assign them to my own chosen hotkeys? Can I click between them and the Inventory screen and the Goals/Notes screen by pressing on "tabs"? And so on and so forth: 20 pages is beginning to seem like a lot, but remember that there are 199 different headings under which information like this is given at a brisk pace throughout the booklet.

Of course, all these terms and questions can be defined and answered if you closely check and repeatedly cross-check information through the little booklet. You can constantly turn the pages backwards and forwards, but once you have one set of links relating various items and actions in mind, another drops out just as you need it, and you are back to turning pages. Is the booklet poorly written? Not at all. It is written just as well or poorly as, in fact, any of myriad school-based texts in the content areas. Outside the practices in the domain from which it comes, it is just as meaningless, no matter how much one could garner literal meanings from it with which to verbally repeat facts or pass tests.

When you can spell out such information in situation-specific terms in the game by actually playing the game, then its relationships to the other hundreds of pieces of information in the booklet become clear and meaningful. Of course, it is these relationships that really count if you are to understand the game as a system and therefore play it at all well. *Now* you can read the book if you need to in order to fill in missing bits of information, check on your understandings, or solve a particular problem or answer a particular question.

When I first read this booklet before playing *Deus Ex* (at that time, I had played only one other shooter game, a very different one) – yes, I, an overly academic baby-boomer, made the mistake of trying to read the book first, despite my own theories about reading – I was sorely tempted to put the game on a shelf and forget about it. I was simply overwhelmed with details, questions, and confusions. When I started the game, I kept trying to look up information in the booklet, but none of it was understood well enough to be found easily without continually re-searching for the same information. In the end, I had to simply play the game and explore and try everything. Then, at last, the booklet made good sense and it could be used for one's own supplemental and research purposes and goals, not just as preparation for activity long delayed.

I would now make the same claim about any school content domain as I have just made about the video game *Deus Ex*: specialist language in any domain – games or science – has no situated meaning and, thus, no lucid or applicable meaning, unless and until one has "played the game"; in this case, the game of science or, better stated, a specific game connected to a specific science. Such "games"(i.e., "science games") involve seeing the language and representations associated with some part of science in terms of activities one has done, experiences one has had, images one has formed from these, and interactional dialogue one has heard from and had with peers and mentors outside and inside the science activities. School is too often about reading the manual before you get to play the game, if you ever do. This is not harmful for students who have already played the game at home, but it is disastrous for those who have not.

Good video games do not just support situated meanings for the written materials associated with them in manuals and on fan Web sites – which are copious – but also for all language within the game. The meaning of such language is always associated with actions, experiences, images, and dialogue. Furthermore, players get verbal information "just in time," when they can apply it or see it be applied, or "on demand," when they feel the need for it and are ready for it – and, then, in some cases, games will give the player walls of print (e.g., in *Civilization IV*).

So my claim – what I call "game-like learning" – leads to situated and not just verbal meanings. In turn, situated meanings make specialist language lucid, easy, and useful. We saw much the same thing with *Yu-Gi-Oh*. To demonstrate what I mean by "game-like learning," I turn to an example: a situation in which a game-like simulation is built into an overall learning system.

Augmented by Reality: Madison 2020

In their Madison 2020 project, Shaffer and Beckett at the University of Wisconsin developed, implemented, and assessed a game-like simulation of the activities of professional urban planners (Beckett & Shaffer, 2004; Shaffer, 2007; see also Shaffer, Squire, Halverson, & Gee, 2005). I call this a "game" because learners are using a simulation and role-playing new identities; of course, it is not a "game" in a traditional sense.

Shaffer and Beckett's game is not a standalone entity but rather is used as part of a larger learning system. Shaffer and Beckett call their approach to game-like learning "augmented by reality" because a virtual reality – that is, the game simulation – is augmented or supplemented by real-world activities – in this case, further activities of the type in which urban planners engage. Minority high school students in a summer enrichment program engaged with

Shaffer and Beckett's urban-planning simulation game. As they did so, their problem-solving work in the game was guided by real-world tools and practices taken from the domain of professional urban planners.

As in the game *SimCity*, in Shaffer and Beckett's game, students make land-use decisions and consider the complex results of those decisions. However, unlike in *SimCity*, they use real-world data and authentic planning practices to inform those decisions. The game and the learning environment in which it is embedded is based on Shaffer's theory of *pedagogical praxis*, a theory that argues that modeling learning environments on authentic professional practices – in this case, the practices of urban planners – enables young people to develop deeper understandings of important domains of inquiry (Shaffer, 2004, 2007).

Shaffer and Beckett argue that the environmental dependencies in urban areas have the potential to become a fruitful context for innovative learning in ecological education. Whereas ecology is, of course, a broader domain than the study of interdependent urban relationships, cities are examples of complex systems that students can view and with which they are familiar. Thus, concepts in ecology can be made tangible and relevant.

Cities consist of simple components but the interactions among those components are complex. Altering one variable affects all the others, reflecting the interdependent, ecological relationships present in any modern city. For example, consider the relationships among industrial sites, air pollution, and land property values: increasing industrial sites can lead to pollution that, in turn, lowers property values, changing the dynamics of the city's neighborhoods in the process.

Shaffer and Beckett's Madison 2020 project situated student experience at a micro-level by focussing on a single street in their own city (i.e., Madison, Wisconsin):

> *Instead of the fast-paced action required to plan and maintain virtual urban environments such as* SimCity, *this project focused only on an initial planning stage, which involved the development of a land use plan for this one street. And instead of using only a technological simulation [i.e., the game, JPG], the learning environment here was orchestrated by authentic urban planning practices. These professional practices situated the planning tool in a realistic context and provided a framework within which students constructed solutions to the problem. (Beckett & Shaffer, 2004, pp. 11–12)*

The high school students Shaffer and Beckett worked with had volunteered for a ten-hour workshop (conducted over two weekend days) that focussed on city planning and community service. At the beginning of the workshop, the students were given an urban-planning challenge: they were asked to create a detailed redesign plan for State Street, a major pedestrian thoroughfare in Madison that was quite familiar to all the students in the workshop. Professional urban planners must formulate plans that meet the social, economic, and physical needs of their communities. To align with this practice, students received an informational packet addressed to them as city planners. The packet contained a project directive from the mayor, a city budget plan, and letters from concerned citizens providing input about how they wished to see the city redesigned. The directive asked the student city planners to develop a plan that, at the end of the workshop, would be presented to a representative from the planning department.

Students then watched a video about State Street, featuring interviews with people who expressed concerns about the street's redevelopment aligned with the issues in the informational packet (e.g., affordable housing). During the planning phase, students walked to State Street and conducted a site assessment. Following the walk, they worked in teams to develop a land-use plan using a custom-designed interactive geographic information system (GIS) called MadMod. MadMod is a model built using Excel and ArcMap (ESRL 2003) that enables students to assess the ramifications of proposed land-use changes.

MadMod allowed students to see a virtual representation of State Street. It has two components: a decision space and a constraint table. The decision space displays address and zoning information about State Street using official two- or three-letter zoning codes to designate changes in land use for property parcels on the street. As students made decisions about changes they wished to make, they received immediate feedback in the constraint table about the consequences of those changes. The constraint table showed the effects of changes on six planning issues raised in the original information packet and the video: crime, revenue, jobs, waste, car trips, and housing. Following the professional practices of urban planners, students presented their plans to a representative from the city planning office in the final phase of the workshop.

MadMod functions in Shaffer and Beckett's curriculum like a game in much the same way *SimCity* does. In my view, video games are simulations that have "win states" in terms of the goals that players have set for themselves. In this case, the students had certain goals and the game let them see how close or far they were from attaining those goals. At the same time, the game is embedded in a learning system that ensured that those goals and the procedures used to reach them were instantiations of the professional practices and ways of knowing of urban planners.

Through a pre-interview/post-interview design, Shaffer and Beckett showed that students in the workshop were able to provide more extensive and explicit definitions of the term *ecology* after the workshop than before it. The students' explanations of ecological issues in the post-interview were more specific about how ecological issues are interdependent or interconnected than in the pre-interview. Concept maps that the students drew showed an increased awareness of the complexities present in an urban ecosystem. Thus, students apparently developed a richer understanding of urban ecology through their work in the project.

All of the students stated that the workshop changed the way they thought about cities and most said the experience changed the things they paid attention to when walking down a city street in their neighborhood. Shaffer and Beckett were also able to show transfer: students' responses to novel, hypothetical urban-planning problems showed increased awareness of the interconnections among urban ecological issues. All of these effects suggest, as Shaffer and Beckett argued, "that students were able to mobilize understanding developed in the context of the redesign of one local street to think more deeply about novel urban ecological issues" (Beckett & Shaffer, 2004, p. 21).

Conclusions

I have argued that if a child is not to be a victim of the fourth-grade slump, learning to read must involve early preparation for specialist, technical, and academic forms of language – forms that will be seen more and more in speech and, most characteristically, in writing as school progresses. I discussed some of the underpinnings of effective early preparation for such styles of language, including "informal specialist-language lessons," "lucidly functional language" practices, and practices that facilitate "situated meanings." These practices are common in certain homes and in some of the popular cultural practices of children. They are, perhaps, less common in the early years of schooling. More generally, I have argued that a game-like approach to learning – by which I mean not "having fun" but rather thinking inside of and with simulations in a situated and embodied way, an approach well represented even in commercial video games – holds out significant potential as a foundation for learning that leads to problem solving and not just paper and pencil test-passing.

In an important recent paper, Neuman and Celano (2006) show that introducing digital media – for example, science games on computers – into libraries actually widens the literacy and knowledge gaps between rich and poor. Middle-class parents engage in the types of interactional scaffolding that we saw previously with the mother and her three-year-old son talking about dinosaurs; poorer parents do not. The middle-class parents push their children to more complex language, orally and in writing, and to the concomitant knowledge structures that such language supports. Neuman and Celano (2006) argued that modern librarians will have to play just such a role for poorer children. In the end, then, the issue is not about who has access to what in popular culture but rather who has access to powerful popular-culture practices placed in rich scaffolding and mentoring learning systems.

References

American Educator (2003). The fourth-grade plunge: The cause. The cure. Special issue, Spring.

Barsalou, L. W. (1999a). Language comprehension: Archival memory or preparation for situated action. *Discourse Processes*, 28, 61–80.

Beckett, K. L., & Shaffer, D. W. (2004). Augmented by reality: The pedagogical praxis of urban planning as a pathway to ecological thinking. Ms., University of Wisconsin–Madison. See: http://www.academiccolab.org/initiatives/gapps.html.

Bereiter, C., & Scardamalia, M. (1993). *Surpassing ourselves: An inquiry into the nature and implications of expertise*. Chicago: Open Court.

Bransford, J., Brown, A. L., & Cocking, R. R. (2000). *How people learn: Brain, mind, experience, and school: Expanded Edition*. Washington, DC: National Academy Press.

Brown, S. L., Collins, A., & Dugid, P. (1989). Situated cognition and the culture of learning. *Educational Researcher*, 18, 32–42.

Chall, J. S., Jacobs, V., & Baldwin, L. (1990). *The reading crisis: Why poor children fall behind*. Cambridge, MA: Harvard University Press.

Chi, M., Feltovich, P., & Glaser, R. (1981). Categorization and representation of physics problems by experts and novices. *Cognitive Science*, 5.2, 121–152.

Chomsky, N. (1986). *Knowledge of language*. New York: Praeger.

Clark, A. (1989). *Microcognition: Philosophy, cognitive science, and parallel distributed processing*. Cambridge MA: MIT Press.

Clark, A. (1993). *Associative engines: Connectionism, concepts, and representational change*. Cambridge: Cambridge University Press.

Clark, A. (1997). *Being there: Putting brain, body, and world together again*. Cambridge, MA: MIT Press.

Collins, A. (2006). Cognitive apprenticeship. In R. K. Sawyer (Ed.), *The Cambridge handbook of the learning sciences* (pp. 47–60). Cambridge: Cambridge University Press.

Crowley, K., & Jacobs, M. (2002). Islands of expertise and the development of family scientific literacy. In Leinhardt, G., Crowley, K., & Knutson, K. (Eds.), *Learning conversations in museums* (pp. 333–356). Mahwah, NJ: Lawrence Erlbaum.

Csikszentmihalyi, M. (1990). *Flow: The psychology of optimal experience*. New York: Harper Collins.

Dickinson, D. K., & Neuman, S. B. (Eds.) (2006). *Handbook of early literacy research: Volume 2*. New York: Guilford Press.

diSessa, A. A. (2000). *Changing minds: Computers, learning, and literacy*. Cambridge, MA: MIT Press.

Emergent Literacy Project (n.d.). *What is emergent literacy?* [Online]. Available at http://idahocdhd.org/cdhd/emerlit/facts.asp.

Games-to-Teach Team (2003). Design principles of next-generation digital gaming for education. *Educational Technology*, 43 (5), 17–33.

Gardner, H. (1991). *The unschooled mind: How children think and how schools should teach*. New York: Basic Books.

Gee, J. P. (1990/1996). *Sociolinguistics and literacies: Ideology in discourses*. London: Taylor & Francis (Second Edition, 1996).

Gee, J. P. (1992). *The social mind: Language, ideology, and social practice*. New York: Bergin & Garvey.

Gee, J. P. (2003a). *What video games have to teach us about learning and literacy*. New York: Palgrave/Macmillan.

Gee, J. P. (2003b). Opportunity to learn: A language-based perspective on assessment. *Assessment in Education*, 10 (1), 25–44.

Gee, J. P. (2004). *Situated language and learning: A critique of traditional schooling*. London: Routledge.

Gee, J. P. (2005). *Why video games are good for your soul: Pleasure and learning*. Melbourne: Common Ground.

Gee, J. P., Hull, G., & Lankshear, C. (1996). *The new work order: Behind the language of the new capitalism*. Boulder, CO: Westview.

Glenberg, A. M. (1997). What is memory for. *Behavioral and Brain Sciences, 20*, 1–55.

Glenberg, A. M., & Robertson, D. A. (1999). Indexical understanding of instructions. *Discourse Processes, 28*, 1–26.

Gibson, J. J. (1979). *The ecological approach to visual perception*. Boston: Houghton Mifflin.

Johnson, S. (2005). *Everything bad is good for you: How today's popular culture is actually making us smarter*. New York: Riverhead.

Labov, W. (1979). The logic of nonstandard English. In P. Giglioli (Ed.), *Language and social context* (pp. 179–215). Middlesex, UK: Penguin Books.

McFarlane, A., Sparrowhawk, A., & Heald, Y. (2002). *Report on the educational use of games: An exploration by TEEM of the contribution which games can make to the education process*. Cambridge: TEEM, Department for Education and Skills.

Neuman, S. B., & Celano, D. (2006). The knowledge gap: Implications of leveling the playing field for low-income and middle-income children. *Reading Research Quarterly, 41* (2), 176–201.

Olson, D. (1994). *The world on paper: The conceptual and cognitive implications of writing and reading*. Cambridge: Cambridge University Press.

Pinker, S. (1994). *The language instinct: How the mind creates language*. New York: William Marrow.

Sawyer, K. (Ed.) (2006). *The Cambridge handbook of the learning sciences*. Cambridge: Cambridge University Press.

Scardamalia, M., & Bereiter, C. (2006). *Knowledge building: Theory, pedagogy, and technology*. In R. K. Sawyer (Ed.), *The Cambridge handbook of the learning sciences* (pp. 97–115). Cambridge: Cambridge University Press.

Schleppegrell, M. (2004). *Language of schooling: A functional linguistics perspective*. Mahwah, NJ: Lawrence Erlbaum.

Schön, D. A. (1991). *The reflective turn: Case studies in and on educational practice*. New York: Teachers College Press.

Senechal, M., Ouellette, G., & Rodney D. (2006). The misunderstood giant: Predictive role of early vocabulary to future reading. In D. K. Dickinson & S. B. Neuman (Eds.), *Handbook of early literacy research: Volume* 2 (pp. 173–182). New York: Guilford Press.

Shaffer, D. W. (2004). Pedagogical praxis: The professions as models for post-industrial education. *Teachers College Record, 10*, 1401–1421.

Shaffer, D. W. (2005). Epistemic games. *Innovate, 1*, 6, available at http://www.innovateonline.info/index.php?view=article&id=81.

Shaffer, D. W. (2007). *How computer games help children*. New York: Palgrave/Macmillian.

Shaffer, D. W., Squire, K. D., Halverson, R., & Gee, J. P. (2005). Video games and the future of learning. *Phi Delta Kappan*, 87 (2), 105–111.

Snow, C. E., Burns, M. S., & Griffin, P. (Eds.) (1998). *Preventing reading difficulties in young children*. Washington, DC: National Academy Press.

Squire, K. (2003). Video games in education. *International Journal of Intelligent Games & Simulation*, 2 (1). Last retrieved November 1, 2003, at http://www.scit.wlv.ac.uk/~cm1822/ijkurt.pdf.

Squire, K., Barnett, M., Grant, J. M., & Higginbotham, T. (2004). Electromagnetism Supercharged! Learning physics with digital simulation games. In Y. B. Kafai, W. A. Sandoval, N. Enyedy, A. S. Nixon, & F. Herrera (Eds.), *Proceedings of the Sixth International Conference of the Learning Sciences* (pp. 513–520). Mahwah, NJ: Lawrence Erlbaum.

Vygotsky, L. S. (1978). *Mind in society: The development of higher psychological processes*. Cambridge, MA: Harvard University Press.

Part IV

LITERACY AND SOCIETY

CHAPTER 18

Ethnography of Writing and Reading[1]

Brian Street

This chapter locates the ethnographic study of literacy as social practice within the context of the major intellectual currents that have directed literacy debate, outlining the different disciplinary traditions that inform them and detailing the significant changes that they have undergone in recent years. What counts as 'literacy' – or as 'literacies' as some traditions would have it – underpins all of the other considerations addressed by historians, anthropologists, psychologists, and so on – how to measure 'it,' what policies to adopt, what significance, if any, 'it' has for 'human development' and how to teach 'it'. Those intellectual currents also lie beneath the surface of the better known themes and labels under which the literacy debate has been conducted: 'basic literacy' (cf. 'No Child Left Behind' [NCLB] in the United States and the 'National Literacy Strategy' [NLS] in the United Kingdom); 'functional' literacy (Verhoeven, 1994; Verhoeven & Snow, 2001); 'critical' literacy (Muspratt, Luke, & Freebdoy, 1997); 'Freirean' approaches (Freire, 1985; Freire & Macedo, 1987); and, more recently, 'community literacies' (Chitrakar & Maddox, in press); and so forth. This chapter does not focus on those traditions in themselves but rather attempts to elicit and outline the deeper currents of thought that inform them. The aim is neither to arrive at a synthesis of views on the meanings of literacy nor to recommend a particular view, but rather to locate the particular interest in ethnography of literacy within the main strands of debate in the field, in order to put them into perspective and to facilitate the identification of future lines of research.

'Meanings of Literacy' in Different Traditions

The meaning of *literacy* as an object of enquiry and of action – whether for research purposes or in practical programmes – is highly contested and we cannot understand the term and its uses unless we penetrate these contested spaces. I suggest the following four major traditions or areas of enquiry that, despite inevitable overlaps, provide a heuristic by which we can begin to understand different approaches and their consequences: literacy and learning, cognitive approaches to literacy, social practice approaches, and literacy as text.

Whilst attention to reading traditionally has been seen as the main thrust of literacy work, and attention to cognition has driven many academic and policy claims for the 'consequences' of literacy (see other chapters in this volume), recent social and sociocultural approaches and adult-learning theories, as well as the impact of multimodal studies and discourse analysis, have broadened what counts as literacy and challenged claims for its consequences. The authors cited herein represent a variety of responses to these changes: some, like Adams (1993) and Snow (1998), privilege a more decontextualised account of the learning process; others, like Scribner and Cole (1978), attempt to link cognitive processes with social practices; others are moving to locate literacy within broader social and political contexts and to be more sensitive to the variety of backgrounds and language styles that those acquiring literacy bring with them – in and out of schooled contexts – rather than imposing a single standard on all (Street & Street, 1991; Rogers, 1992); and others locate literacy within other semiotic means of communication, such as visual and gestural 'modes', thereby focussing on 'multimodality' or on 'multi-literacies' rather than on just 'literacy', which they see as less central to the communicative needs of a globalising world (Cope & Kalanztis, 2000; Kress & Van Leeuwen, 2001). All of these authors, some more explicitly than others, address contested issues of power and social hierarchy as they affect both definitions and their outcomes for practice. Ethnographers draw on a variety of such theories in addressing literacy as a social practice; before we consider the plethora of such studies in recent years, we need to review the theoretical traditions on which they draw. Conversely, the stance we take with respect to such traditions and the methods we use for researching literacy depend on the theoretical frame underpinning our approach. Studying literacy from an ethnographic perspective, for instance, varies according to which theoretical frame underpins the study. The review of literacy and learning, cognitive approaches to literacy, and literacy as text looks different when surveyed from the perspective of social practice approaches than it might from other perspectives (such as those adopted in other sections of this *Handbook*).

Literacy and Learning

For many, use of the term *literacy* evokes the question of how children learn to read and this, then, is what the concept has been taken to mean. As discussed herein, a similar metonymy is evident in adult-literacy policy, wherein reference to an interest in 'literacy' is taken to be an interest in how to overcome 'illiteracy' by teaching adults how to *read* (even though for many, a major motivation in entering literacy programmes is to learn how to write). Once we have looked more closely at other questions and other traditions of enquiry, it will become evident how this focus on 'literacy as reading' marginalises many other meanings of the term.

The issue of how children learn to read has been highly contested in recent years, and those debates have implications for how adult literacy is conceived. The distinction between a focus on 'phonic' principles on the one hand (Adams, 1993), and on 'reading for meaning' on the other (Goodman, 1996) has led to what is sometimes termed the 'reading wars'. Some researchers have argued for a 'balanced' approach that is less divisive and that recognises the strengths of each perspective (Snow, 1998). In many circles, still, the term *literacy* is interpreted to refer to 'reading' and more particularly to the learning of reading by young children. Adams (1993), for instance, herself a key figure in U.S. National Commission on Literacy, began an overview of the literature on 'literacy' with the following claim:

> *The most fundamental and important issues in the field of reading education are those of how children learn to read and write and how best to help them. (p. 204)*

The piece from which this comes was included in a book titled *Teaching Literacy, Balancing Perspectives* (Beard, 1993), which offers an introduction to some of the key terms in the field of reading – for example, *phonics, whole language, phonemic awareness,* and so on. It also makes claims about what 'scientific' research now tells us about learning to read. There is now a requirement in some countries for 'scientific-based' approaches that can provide sound evidence of which methods and approaches are superior and that can claim to 'soundly refute' some hypotheses in favour of others (Slavin, 2002). Adams's response to these requirements, based on a year of reviewing the literature on the 'reading wars' and looking for alternatives, is that there has been a coming together of different disciplinary strands, that different perspectives are beginning to agree on what counts: the whole-language view of learners engaging in a 'guessing game' (Goodman, 1967) or that the spellings of words are minimally relevant to reading (Smith, 1971) have been rejected in favour of attention to 'phonics.' The key to improvement in literacy, especially amongst the "economically disadvantaged," is "phonic instruction... word recognition, spelling, and vocabulary"(Adams, 1991, p. 42).

If one were only to read such accounts, then the picture would seem clear enough and the task of increasing literacy – not only within the United States, as in this case, but also across the world, for adults as well as children – would be simply a matter of putting those principles into practice. However, once one reads other authors, then other views of what counts as literacy begin to emerge – and these authors speak with as much authority – for instance, about 'what research tells us', as does Adams (1993). Like Adams, Goodman, for instance, a leading international figure in 'whole language' approaches, refers to "what we have learned" and to "scientific knowledge." However, in this case, that requires a different 'knowledge' – namely, of language development, of learning theories, and of teaching and curriculum (Goodman, 1996, p. 117), not just of "spelling-sound relations." For him, learning literacy is a more 'natural' process than described in the phonics approach, and he likens it to the way in which humans learn language. While written language is learned a little later in life, for Goodman (1996, p. 119), it is no less natural than oral language in the personal and social development of individuals.

Whether language and, by analogy, literacy are 'taught' or 'learned naturally' represents extreme poles of what for most educators is a 'continuum'. While Goodman separates *learning* reading and writing from *teaching* reading and writing, he states that he does not do so absolutely (1996, p. 119). What is evident from these accounts, then, is that underpinning approaches to literacy are theories of learning. These too need to be considered in both defining literacy and in developing policies for the spread of literacy, especially with respect to adults.

Learning

Like theories of literacy, theories of learning have themselves been opened up more broadly in academic debate since the 1980s. Social psychologists and anthropologists such as Rogoff, Lave, and Wenger (Lave, 1988; Lave & Wenger, 1991; Rogoff, 2003; Rogoff & Lave, 1984/1999) invoked terms such as *collaborative learning, distributed learning* and *communities of practice* to shift the focus away from the individual mind and towards more social practices. To cite just one example, Rogoff and her colleagues, in their discussions of informal learning, distinguished between the structure of *intent participation* in shared endeavors and *assembly-line preparation* based on transmission of information from experts outside the context of productive activity. For Rogoff, intent participation involves the keen observation of ongoing community events coupled with the anticipation of growing participation in the activity at hand. Whereas intent participation is a collaborative, horizontal structure with varying roles and fluid responsibilities, assembly-line preparation employs a hierarchical structure with fixed roles (Rogoff, et al., 2003).

> *In intent participation, learning is based on participation in ongoing or anticipated activities, with keen observation and listening. Learners observe to figure out processes they expect to engage in. (Rogoff, et al., 2003, p.191)*

In intent participation, experienced people facilitate learners' roles and often participate alongside them; in assembly-line preparation, experienced people are managers, dividing the tasks often without participating. The learners' roles correspond to taking the initiative to learn and contribute versus receiving information. Along with these interrelated facets of the two processes are differences in motivation and purposes, in sources of learning (e.g., observant participation or lessons taken out of the context of productive, purposeful participation), in forms of communication, and in forms of assessment (to aid or test learning).

This account links closely to Rogers's (2003a, 2003b) work in adult education. Drawing on Krashen's (1981) classic distinction with respect to language learning between 'acquisition' and 'learning', Rogers refers to 'task-conscious' learning and 'learning-conscious learning'. For Rogers, these forms of learning are to be distinguished by their methods of evaluation (i.e., task-conscious by the task fulfilment, learning-conscious by measurements of learning). Whilst this may appear at times to differentiate adults from children, Rogers and others argue that both children and adults do both – that, in fact, they form a continuum rather than two categories. Whilst adults do much less of formal learning than children, the difference, he suggests, really lies in the *teaching* of adults (i.e., the formal learning) and in the power relationships, the identities built up through experience, and the experiences adults bring to their formal learning. Much of learning theory in the discipline of psychology has failed to address these features, so that aspects of the more traditional literacy learning of children (including 'assembly-line preparation' and 'test learning') are used for adults. This is evident in many adult literacy programmes: adults are encouraged to join younger age groups, to take tests, to decontextualise learning and ignore their own previous knowledge, and so on.

These debates, like those specifically addressed to literacy learning and to reading, have radical implications for how literacy programmes might be designed and run. Whilst many adult literacy programmes, for instance, have built on the theories of learning that underpin more traditional schooled literacy work (e.g., cited herein from Adams and others), recent accounts suggest that literacy programmes at both levels may do better to focus on the ways of learning evident in everyday life rather than continuing to privilege the formal learning methods of school (Hull & Scultz, 2002). To do so would have major implications for literacy programmes, leading to different emphasis, for instance, with respect to use of curricula and textbooks and/or the use of 'Real Literacy Materials' and to assessment as formative and/or summative (Black & Wiliam, 1998.

Cognitive Approaches to Literacy

Many of these theories of literacy and of learning have rested on deeper assumptions about cognition and, in particular, regarding the 'cognitive consequences' of learning and acquiring literacy. A dominant position, until recently, was to apply the idea of a 'great divide' – originally used to distinguish 'primitive/modern' or 'underdeveloped/developed' – to 'literates' and 'nonliterates', a distinction that implicitly or explicitly still underpins much work in and justification for international literacy programmes. Anthropologists such as Goody (1977) and psychologists such as Olson (1977, 1994) have linked the more precise cognitive argument to broader historical and cultural patterns, regarding the significance of the acquisition of literacy for a society's functioning. These claims often remain part of popular assumptions about literacy and have fed policy debates and media representations of the significance of the 'technology' of literacy. Whilst rejecting an extreme technological determinist position, Goody, for instance, does appear to associate the development of writing with key cognitive advances in human society: the distinction of myth from history; the development of logic and syllogistic forms of reasoning; the ability of writing to help overcome a tendency of oral cultures towards cultural homeostasis; the development of certain mathematical procedures, such as multiplication and division (for early critiques of this position, see Finnegan, 1999; Street, 1984; for further discussion of the debates in mathematics, see Street, Baker, & Tomlin, 2006); and – perhaps the key claim for educational purposes – that "literacy and the accompanying process of classroom education brings a shift towards greater 'abstractedness'" (Goody, 1977, p. 3). Whilst Goody is careful to avoid claiming an "absolute dichotomy between orality and literacy," it is partly on the grounds that his ideas do lend credence to technological determinism that he has been challenged, through the experimental data provided by Scribner and Cole (1977, 1981) and the ethnographic data and arguments by Street (1984) and others (see Finnegan, 1999; Maddox, 2001). Goody himself has criticised many of these counter-arguments as "relativist," a term that might be applied to much contemporary thinking about literacy (and social differences in general) and that has considerable implications for the debates being outlined herein.

During the 1970s, the social psychologists Sylvia Scribner and Michael Cole conducted a major research project amongst the Vai peoples of Liberia to test out the claims of Goody and others about the cognitive consequences of literacy in a 'real life' setting. Their accounts of the outcomes of this research (Scribner & Cole, 1978; 1981) represented a major landmark in our understanding of the issues regarding literacy and cognition considered herein. They quote Farrell as a classic example of claims such as: "the cognitive restructuring caused by reading and writing develop the higher reasoning processes involved in extended abstract thinking" (Farrell, 1977, p. 451, as cited by Scribner & Cole, 1978). Scribner and Cole argue that "our research speaks to several serious limitations in developing this proposition as a ground for educational and social policy decisions" (1978, p. 20). They address the limitations of these claims in both empirical and theoretical terms. For instance, many of the claims derive from abstract hypotheses not based in evidence, or the evidence used is of a very specific form of written text, such as Western scientific 'essay text', as a model for accounts of literacy in general (Olson, 1977; Street, 1984). Many of the assumptions about literacy in general, then, are "tied up with school-based writing" (Scribner & Cole, 1978, p. 24). This, they believe, leads to serious limitations in the accounts of literacy: "The assumption that logicality is in the text and the text is in school can lead to a serious underestimation of the cognitive skills involved in non-school, non-essay writing." (p. 25). The writing crisis, to which many of the reports and commissions cited above (in the *literacy and learning* section) refer, presents itself as purely 'a pedagogical problem' and arises in the first place from these limited assumptions and data.

Scribner and Cole (1978) instead tested out these claims through intensive psychological and anthropological research of actual practice, taking as a case study the Vai peoples of Liberia, who have three scripts – Vai (an invented phonetic script), Arabic, and Roman – each used for different purposes.

> *We examined activities engaged in by those knowing each of the indigenous scripts to determine some of the component skills involved. On the basis of these analyses, we designed tasks with different content but with hypothetically similar skills to determine if prior practice in learning and use of the script enhanced performance (1977, p. 13).*

The tests were divided into three areas: communication skills, memory and language analysis. On the basis of the results, they argued that all we can claim is that "specific practices promote specific skills": the grand claims of the literacy thesis are untenable:

... there is no evidence that writing promotes "general mental abilities." We did not find "superior memory in general" among Qur'anic students nor better language integration skills "in general" among Vai literates.... There is nothing in our findings that would lead us to speak of cognitive consequences of literacy with the notion in mind that such consequences affect intellectual performance in all tasks to which the human mind is put (1978, p. 16).

This outcome suggests that the metaphor of a 'great divide' may not be appropriate "for specifying differences among literates and nonliterates under contemporary conditions. The monolithic model of what writing is and what it leads to ... appears in the light of comparative data to fail to give full justice to the multiplicity of values, uses and consequences which characterize writing as social practice" (Scribner & Cole, 1978, p. 36).

Scribner and Cole, then, were amongst the first to attempt to retheorise what counts as literacy and to look outside of school for empirical data on which to base sound generalisations (Hull & Schultz, 2002). One of the main proponents of the 'strong' thesis regarding the consequences of literacy has been David Olson (1977), who has been and is one of the sources for claims about the 'autonomous' model of iteracy (Street, 1984); indeed, he was cited by Scribner and Cole in their account. However, in a later book, Olson (1994), like them, tried to modify the inferences that can be drawn from his own earlier pronouncements and to set out what is myth and what is reality in our understanding of literacy. He draws an analogy with Christian theologians trying to put faith on a firmer basis by getting rid of unsustainable myths that only weakened the case. As he described the unsustainable myths of literacy, he seemed to be challenging those put forward by Goody, Farrell, and others. In arriving at 'the new understanding of literacy', he described the following six 'beliefs' and the 'doubts' that have been expressed about them as a helpful framework for reviewing the literature on literacy:

- writing as the transcription of speech
- the superiority of writing to speech
- the technological superiority of the alphabetic writing system
- literacy as the organ of social progress
- literacy as an instrument of cultural and scientific development
- literacy as an instrument of cognitive development

Olson then outlined the 'doubts' that modern scholarship has thrown on all of these assumptions. For instance, with respect to literacy and social development, he cited counter-arguments from such anthropologists as Levi-Strauss (1966), who argued that literacy is not only not the royal route to liberation but also is as often a means of enslavement:

It seems to favour rather the exploitation than the enlightenment of mankind.... The use of writing for disinterested ends, and with a view to satisfactions of the mind in the fields either of science or the arts, is a secondary result of its invention – and may even be no more than a way of reinforcing, justifying, or dissimulating its primary function. (Levi-Strauss, 1966, pp. 291–292, as cited in Olson, 1977)

With respect to cultural development, Olson cited the work of cultural historians and anthropologists (Finnegan, 1999) who "have made us aware of the sophistication of 'oral' cultures ... " and from whose work it appears: "No direct causal links have been established between literacy and cultural development."

Like Scribner and Cole, Olson's (1977) conclusion challenged the dominant claims for literacy for adults as well as for children:

[T]he use of literacy skills as a metric against which personal and social competence can be assessed is vastly oversimplified. Functional literacy, the form of competence required for one's daily life, far from being a universalizable commodity turns out on analysis to depend critically on the particular activities of the individual for whom literacy is to be functional. What is functional for an automated-factory worker may not be for a parent who wants to read to a child. The focus on literacy skills

seriously underestimates the significance of both the implicit understandings that children bring to school and the importance of oral discourse in bringing those understandings into consciousness in turning them into objects of knowledge. The vast amounts of time some children spend on remedial reading exercises may be more appropriately spent acquiring scientific and philosophical information. (Olson, 1977, p. 12)

He concluded: "For the first time, many scholars are thinking the unthinkable: is it possible that literacy is over-rated?"

Whatever response we make to this claim, it is apparent that we cannot ignore such findings. As discussed in the next section, for many researchers the rejection of the 'literacy thesis' does not necessarily mean that we should abandon or reduce work in literacy whether of a research or an applied nature; but it does force us to be clearer as to what justifications we use for such work and how we should conduct it. The following sections show how new theoretical perspectives, themselves growing from the debates outlined herein, can provide a way of pursuing productive work in the literacy field without the 'myths,' overstatements and doubtful bases for action of the earlier positions. I deal first with approaches that focus on the textual features of literacy, attempting to move us beyond the over-emphasis on language that has dominated the field of literacy. Finally, I reach the framework on which this chapter is based, social practice approaches, and begin to detail the kinds of ethnographic studies that follow.

Literacy as Text: Multimodality and Multi-Literacies

Linguists, literary theorists and educationalists have tended to look at literacy in terms of the texts that are produced and consumed by literate individuals. Linguists have developed a variety of complex analytic tools for 'unpacking' the meanings of texts, both those that can be extracted by a skilled reader and those that a writer implicitly or explicitly deploys. Educationalists have then applied some of this knowledge to the development of skilled readers and writers. For instance, a movement that began in Australia focused on the analysis of writing into different 'genres' (Cope & Kalantzis, 1993) and became significant in educational contexts more generally (e.g., underpinning aspects of the NLS in the United Kingdom; see Beard, 2000). Theorists and practitioners working from this perspective aim to provide learners with the full range of genres necessary to operate in contemporary society and, indeed, treat this as the crucial dimension of the social justice and 'access' agenda. In doing so, they could be criticised from an ethnography-of-literacies perspective for attempting to genericise 'contemporary society' rather than to particularise it. Similarly building on work by linguists, more radical critics have focussed on stretches of language larger than the sentence, referred to by sociolinguists as 'discourse.' Influenced by broader social theory and by uses of the term *discourse* by Foucault and others, they have developed an approach to what Gee (1990a, 1999) calls "Discourse with a big 'D'." This locates literacy within wider communicative and sociopolitical practices – at times, the term *discourse* looks very like what anthropologists used to mean by *culture* (but see Street, 1993). The work of Gee (1990a, b, 1999) and Fairclough (1995) represents a central plank of this approach.

Kress and others (Kress, Jewitt, Ogborn, & Tsatsarelis, 2000; Kress & van Leeuwen, 2001) developed this position further, arguing that language should be seen as just one of several modes through which communication is conducted: "We suggest that, like language, visual images, gesture and action have been developed through their social usage into articulated or partly articulated resources for representation" (Kress, et al., 2000, p. 12). Individuals make choices from the 'representational resources' available amongst these various modes and a multimodal perspective enables us to identify the traces of these decisions – of the interests of the parties to a text. This approach sees literacy practices as one set amongst many communicative practices at the same time applying the social, ideological and functional interpretations that have been developed with respect to discourse-based studies of communication. It recognises, for instance, that many people, including those defined as 'literate' by standard measures, use other strategies to deal with literacy tasks. For example, in determining bus or train times, or in finding their way to addresses, people do not necessarily 'decode' every word or number but instead 'read off' from a range of signs, including colour, layout, print font, and so on (Cope & Kalanztis, 2000; Street, 1998). Approaches to understanding such 'multimodality' can also be applied to the work of classrooms – science classrooms employ diagrams, objects, notation systems, and so forth in addition to language itself in spoken and written forms, as means whereby pupils learn what counts as 'science' (Kress et al., 2000). Similar analyses can be applied to a range of subject areas in both schooling and adult programmes and less formal educational contexts.

A recent book by Pahl and Rowsell (2006) attempts to bring together the growing field of multimodality and the tradition of New Literacy Studies (discussed herein). Their volume is helpful in guiding us away from extreme versions of these approaches. From the perspective of multimodality, we find uncertainty about what to include and exclude, what goes with what: Do we classify a single mode – say, visual literacy – with its affordances in an entirely separate category from other modes (e.g., writing)? How do we avoid a kind of technical or mode determinism? Can we find ways of describing the overlap and interaction of such modes according to context and 'practice'? (Pahl & Rowsell, 2006; Street, 2000). Likewise, the term *literacy* is sometimes broadened well beyond the NLS conception of social practice to become a metaphor for any kind of skill or competence: at one extreme, we find such concepts as 'palpatory' literacy (i.e., skill in body massage) or 'political' literacy, whereas somewhat closer to the social literacies position, we find reference to 'visual' literacy or computer literacy – both of which do involve some aspects of literacy practices but may not be defined by them.

One way of tracing a path through this semantic and conceptual confusion is to engage in research on the practices described: labelling the object of study forces us to clarify what exactly we include, what we exclude and what the links are between various modes, a principle that is important not only for research but also for policy and practice. And ethnographic-style methods of enquiry may be particularly appropriate to this endeavour, since they involve the reflexivity and the closeness to the ground that enable us to see more precisely what is encompassed by multimodal practices and literacy practices. Future developments, then, both conceptual and applied, may involve some marriage of the last two approaches signalled here – literacy as one component of multimodal communicative practices and literacy as social practice. This is sometimes signalled as a relationship between 'texts and practices,' an approach that may come to inform both research and literacy programmes more in the coming years.

Social Practice Approaches

Whilst the focus on texts reminds us to move beyond the linguistic dimension of literacy and the concerns with cognition and the previously noted 'problems' of acquisition continue, a further recent shift has put all of these approaches into a different perspective that emphasises understanding of literacy practices in their social and cultural contexts. This approach has been particularly associated with an 'ethnographic' perspective, in contrast with the experimental and often individualistic character of cognitive studies, and the textual, etic perspective of linguistic-based studies of text. These social developments have sometimes been referred to as "New Literacy Studies" (Barton, Hamilton, & Ivanic, 1999; Collins, 1995; Gee, 1999; Heath, 1993; Street, 1993). Much of the work in this tradition focusses on the everyday meanings and uses of literacy in specific cultural contexts. In characterising these new approaches to understanding and defining literacy, I referred to a distinction between an 'autonomous' model and an 'ideological' model of literacy (Street, 1984). The autonomous model of literacy works from the assumption that literacy in itself – autonomously – will have effects on other social and cognitive practices, much as in the early 'cognitive consequences' literature cited previously. The model, I have argued, disguises the cultural and ideological assumptions that underpin it and that can then be presented as though they are neutral and universal. Research in the social practice approach challenges this view and suggests that, in practice, dominant approaches based on the autonomous model are simply imposing Western (or urban, e.g., conceptions of literacy on other cultures) (Street, 2001a). The alternative, ideological model of literacy offers a more culturally sensitive view of literacy practices as they vary from one context to another. This model starts from different premises than the autonomous model: it posits instead that literacy is a social practice, not simply a technical and neutral skill; that it is always embedded in socially constructed epistemological principles. The ways in which people address reading and writing are themselves rooted in conceptions of knowledge, identity and being. Literacy, in this sense, is always contested, both its meanings and its practices; hence, particular versions of it are always ideological, they are always rooted in a particular worldview and a desire for that view of literacy to dominate and marginalise others (Gee, 1990b; Gee, Hull & Lankshear, 1996). The argument about social literacies (Street, 1995) suggests that engaging with literacy is always a social act even from the outset. The ways in which teachers or facilitators and their students interact is already a social practice that affects the nature of the literacy being learned and the ideas about literacy held by the participants, especially the new learners and their position in relationships of power. Likewise, the ways in which researchers approach questions of literacy acquisition and learning, of the kind we have seen previously, are also rooted in conceptions of literacy that are ideological. In either case, it is not valid to suggest that literacy can be defined or 'given' neutrally and then its 'social' effects only experienced or 'added on' afterwards.

For these reasons, as well as because of the failure of many traditional literacy programmes (Abadzi, 1996; Street, 1999), academics, researchers and practitioners working in literacy in different parts of the world are coming to the conclusion that the autonomous model of literacy on which much of the research and practice have been based was not an appropriate intellectual tool, either for understanding the diversity of reading and writing around the world or for designing the practical programmes this required that may be better suited to an ideological model (Aikman, 1999; Doronilla 1996; Heath, 1983; Hornberger, 1997, 2002; Kalman 1999; King, 1994; Robinson-Pant 1997; Wagner, 1993). The question this approach raises for researchers and for policy makers then, is not simply that of the 'impact' of literacy – to be measured in terms of a neutral developmental index – but rather of how local people 'take hold' of the new communicative practices being introduced to them, as Kulick and Stroud's (1993) ethnographic description of missionaries bringing literacy to New Guinea villagers made clear. Literacy, in this sense, then, is already part of a power relationship, and how people take hold of it is contingent on social and cultural practices and not just on pedagogic and cognitive factors. This raises questions that need to be addressed in any literacy programme: What is the power relationship between the participants? What are the resources? Where are people going if they take on one literacy rather than another literacy? How do recipients challenge the dominant conceptions of literacy? All of these questions are seen as the focus for those researching literacy within the ideological model.

This approach has implications for both research and practice. Researchers, instead of privileging the particular literacy practices familiar in their own culture, now suspend judgement as to what constitutes literacy among the people they are working with until they are able to understand what it means to the people themselves, and from which social contexts reading and writing derive their meaning. Many people labelled 'illiterate' within the autonomous model of literacy may, from a more culturally sensitive viewpoint, be seen to make significant use of literacy practices for specific purposes and in specific contexts. For instance, studies suggest that even nonliterate individuals find themselves engaged in literacy activities, an indication that the boundary between literate and nonliterate is less obvious than individual measures of literacy suggest (Doronilla, 1996; Chitrakar & Maddox, 2008). Academics, however, have often failed to make explicit the implications of such theory for practical work. In the current conditions of world change, such 'ivory-tower' distancing is no longer legitimate. But likewise, policy makers and practitioners have not always taken on board such 'academic' findings or have adopted one position (most often that identified with the autonomous model) and not taken account of the many others outlined herein. These findings, then, raise important issues for both research and policy in the literacy field.

Key concepts in the field of New Literacy Studies that may enable us to overcome these barriers by applying these new conceptions of literacy to specific contexts and practical programmes include the concepts of *literacy events* and *literacy practices*. Shirley Brice Heath characterised a literacy event as "any occasion in which a piece of writing is integral to the nature of the participants' interactions and their interpretative processes" (Heath, 1982, p. 50). I have employed the phrase *literacy practices* (Street, 1984, p. 1) as a means of focusing on the social practices and conceptions of reading and writing, although later, I elaborated on the term both to take account of events in Heath's sense and to give greater emphasis to the social models of literacy that participants bring to bear upon those events and that give meaning to them (Street, 1998). David Barton, Mary Hamilton and colleagues at Lancaster University, have taken up these concepts and applied them to their own research in ways that have been hugely influential in the United Kingdom as well as internationally (Barton & Hamilton, 1998; Barton, Hamilton, & Ivanic, 1999). The issue of dominant literacies and nondominant – informal or vernacular – literacies is central to their combination of 'situated' and 'ideological' approaches to literacy. There has, however, recently been a critique of this position in turn: Brandt and Clinton (2002) refer to 'the limits of the local' – they and others (cf. Collins & Blot, 2002) question the 'situated' approach to literacy as not giving sufficient recognition to the ways in which literacy usually comes from outside of a particular community's 'local' experience.

Varenne and McDermott (1998) have pursued further the political and ideological questions concerning the marginalisation of particular local literacies. They argue that it is not enough for ethnographers to point out the valuable local literacy practices that schoolchildren come to school experienced in – as Heath (1983) has argued, for instance, with respect to Trackton children. Just getting such literacies accepted does not challenge the framing discourses that marginalise them in the first place. The children of Trackton had lived side by side in the valley with those from Maintown and from Roadville for some hundreds of years, note Varenne and McDermott – so why was it that the literacy practices of the black community had to struggle for acceptance in the first place? If we cannot answer that question, then all we are positing for such children is access to an agenda set elsewhere.

As Gee (1990a) noted, also in an early account of social literacies work, language and literacy are so rich and complex that there is considerable scope always for ruling forces to simply change the local rules: an accent here, a spelling there, a syntactical form again might all be subtly changed in small ways that ensure the maintenance of ruling power. Just 'giving' non-mainstream children access to the language and literacy of the ruling group does not of itself ensure any change in the power structure. As Luke (1996) argued in critiquing the Australian genre approach to literacy pedagogy, there are no intrinsic genres of power; rather, those with the power to name and define can change what counts as a powerful genre including what counts as literacy. The ethnography of literacy, then, has to offer accounts not only of rich cultural forms and situated literacy practices but also broader, more politically charged accounts of the power structures that define and rank such practices, as discussed in the following section.

Such an analysis would hook the account of literacy pedagogy to broader political and ideological questions of the kind raised by Varenne and McDermott (1998) and by Luke (1996) and to broader communicative practices of the kind raised by Kress (2002) and others. These recent accounts, then, challenge Brandt and Clinton's (2002) claim that because for most people literacies come from outside, they are therefore in some ways autonomous of local practices. In my paper (Street, 2005) on how Giddens's (1991) work might help us to understand the complex relationship, I suggest that his account of the salient features of 'Late Modernity,' which at first sight may appear to move in the direction of the autonomous model – "in conditions of modernity, in sum, the media do not mirror realities but in some part form them" – in fact goes on to offer a subtler more dialectical view of the relationship between new and old media – "but this does not mean that we should draw the conclusion that the media have created an autonomous realm of hyper-reality where the sign or image is everything" (Giddens, 1991, p. 27).

I conclude from this that we can take on board Brandt's and others' concern to recognise that literacies are not usually locally invented (Brandt & Clinton, 2002, p. 343) without succumbing to the unwarranted claims of the autonomous model. Indeed, this point needs to be applied not only to literacy but also to multimodal forms of communication, thereby avoiding the tendency to reduce these as well to the autonomous model – what we might term 'mode determinism.' I suggested in that paper that perhaps Giddens' concept of 'disembedding' could be applied to the *potential* of all forms of communication, literacy, electronic media, and so on to create 'distance' from the immediate, local conditions, whilst maintaining ethnographic sensitivity to the local interpretation and mediation of such forms through local practices (Street, 2004, p. 282b). If literacy, as the New Literacy Studies has been at pains to point out, is always instantiated, its potential realised through local practices in the complex ways described herein, then this must also be true of other multimodal communicative practices. I conclude by considering how this complex agenda is being addressed through a new wave of 'ethnographies' of literacy.

Ethnographies of Literacy

In keeping with current reflexive approaches to social science research, I attempt to illustrate what I mean by ethnographic approaches to literacy by describing my own experience. I went to Iran in the 1970s to undertake anthropological field research (Street, 1984). I had not gone specifically to study literacy but found myself living in a mountain village where there was much literacy activity. I was drawn to the conceptual and rhetorical issues involved in representing this variety and complexity of literacy activity at a time when my encounter with people outside of the village suggested the dominant representation was of 'illiterate,' backward villagers. Looking more closely at village life in the light of these characterisations, it seemed that not only was there actually a lot of literacy activity but that there were quite different practices associated with literacy – those in a traditional 'Quranic school, in the new state schools, and among traders using literacy in their buying and selling of fruit to urban markets. If these complex variations in literacy which were happening in one small locale were characterised by outside agencies – state education, UNESCO, literacy campaigns – as illiterate, might this also be the case in other situations? I kept this image in mind as I observed and investigated literacy in other parts of the world – urban Philadelphia, South Africa, Ghana, Nepal, the United Kingdom, and so forth. In all of these cases I hear dominant voices characterising local people as illiterate (currently the UK media are full of such accounts; cf. Street, 1998), whereas on the ground ethnographic and literacy-sensitive observation indicates a rich variety of practices (Barton & Hamilton, 1998; Doronilla, 1996; Heath, 1983; Heath & Street, 2008; Hornberger, 1997; Kalman, 1999; King, 1994; Robinson-Pant, 1997; Street, 2000, 2001a, 2001b). When literacy campaigns and educationalists claim to bring literacy to the illiterate – 'light into darkness,' as it is frequently characterised (cf. NCLB in the United States and the National Literacy Campaign in the United Kingdom as well as international programmes), I find myself asking first what local literacy practices are in place and how do they relate to the literacy practices being introduced by the campaigners and educators? Research, then, is tasked with making visible the complexity of local, everyday, community literacy practices and challenging dominant stereotypes and myopia. I list below some of the wealth of ethnographies of literacy that have attempted to address these issues and conclude with reference to a summary of some of this work by Mike Baynham (1995, 2004).

In his introduction to a special issue of *Language and Education* on 'Ethnographies of Literacy,' Baynham refers to three generations of work in this field:

> *Classic first generation ethnographic studies of literacy are Scribner and Cole (1978), Heath (1983), Street (1984); second generation studies might include Prinsloo and Breier (1996), Besnier (1995), Kulick and Stroud (1993), Barton and Hamilton (1998). In this theme issue we present three current (third generation?) empirical contributions to the ethnography of literacy paradigm. (Baynham, 2004, p. 285)*

Baynham locates all three generations within three overarching concerns: the orientation to literacy pedagogy; the definition of literacy in a period when multimodality is salient; and the relationship between the local and the global. All of these themes are part of the larger debate about theory and methodology in literacy studies that we have been considering in this chapter. Baynham suggests that most ethnographies of literacy have addressed pedagogical issues implicitly if not explicitly, starting of course, from Heath's (1983) explicit concern to bring to the attention of educators the "invisible" home literacies of their pupils. From the perspective of a critical anthropology, however, this concern itself has to be subjected to question. In a paper written for one of the key edited volumes in the Ethnography of Literacy tradition of the last decade, Barton and Ivanic's *Writing in the Community* (1991), Joanna Street and I asked the following question:

> *Among all the different literacies practiced in the community, the home, and the workplace, how is it that the variety associated with schooling has come to be the defining type, not only to set the standard for other varieties but to marginalize them, to rule them off the agenda of the literacy debate? Non-school literacies have come to be seen as inferior attempts at the real thing, to be compensated for by enhanced schooling. (Street & Street, 1991, 143)*

Baynham's second point, regarding the salience of multimodality in literacy work, was addressed previously. His third point – the relationship between local and global practices – was signalled previously in relation to the critique by Brandt and Clinton (2002) and the response by Street (2003). Baynham addresses this question in relation to the papers represented in the special volume on Ethnographies of Literacy: the dominant, universalising literacies can be seen on closer inspection, as profoundly local (2004). The accounts of literacy practices in Nepal, South Africa and Brazil included in that volume demonstrate how supposed global features are all instantiated at local level. This happens at conceptual levels not always recognised by agencies bringing the new literacies: literacy is not just a matter of attitudes or motivation in acquiring a new skill but also is embedded in epistemology, deep notions of identity and what it is to be human. Ahearn (2004) shows how in Nepal, for instance, "conceptions of agency, gender, fate and development shape and reflect new literacy practices" (p. 305). Prinsloo (2004), in describing children's development of new literacy practices in South Africa, argues against a more traditional "bounded community" approach to reception and instead presents an account of "the site of play" which "is shown to be itself a distinctive domain which allows children to practise, learn, innovate around, reflect on, and synthesize the conceptual resources available to them from multiple sites" (p. 292). Cavalcanti (2003) likewise attempts to step back from researcher stereotypes in describing an indigenous teacher education course which takes place in the multilingual and multiethnic context of the southwest Brazilian Rainforest. She shows how from the local perspective, people had more important things to do now than schooling, things such as political organization, self-determination, self-sustained development and environmental preservation. Writing in this context is a new weapon that can help assert local rights where modernisation is stripping out traditional ways of acting and knowing, but the ways in which it is defined by schooling may be part of the problem rather than the solution. In all of these cases, the acquisition of literacy is located in more comprehensive and deeper conceptual ways than those envisaged by the institutions of education and schooling through which it tends to be transmitted. This, then, is what is meant by seeing the outside or the global as embedded in the local: it is at these levels rather than – as perhaps in some dominant conceptions – at the level of local as insular, narrow, embedded, resistant.

More recently, Maddox (2007) has addressed the local/global question by offering a synthesis of the contested positions outlined previously, using his own ethnographic field research in Bangladesh. He critiques NLS for its reluctance in examining the role of literacy capabilities and practices in progressive forms of social change and the production of agency (p. 257). Like Brandt and Clinton (2002), he wants to recognise the force of outside influences associated with literacy, including the potential for helping people move out of local positions and take account of progressive themes in the wider world. In this context, the desire to keep records of household income and expenditure was not just a technical issue but also one of authority, gender relations and kinship – literacy (and numeracy) could play a catalytic role in such women's breaking free from traditional constraints. He wants, then, to shift away from the binary opposition of the ideological and autonomous positions dominating debates in recent years by developing a more inclusive theory that links the local and the global, structure and agency, while resolving some of the theoretical and disciplinary tensions over practice and technology (Maddox, 2007, p. 266). Those conducting ethnographies of literacy within the ideological model have seen their task as addressing these questions and not just describing variety in literacy practices at a local level.

The task of literacy studies in the next phase, then, is to provide rich and complex accounts of literacy practices in the context of such local/global dimensions. It is this agenda that ethnographies of literacy seek to meet. Once we have sufficient such accounts, we might then, as Baynham argues, return full circle to the ethnography of communication's interest in literacy pedagogy and apply it equally to multimodal pedagogy from a perspective that – as Maddox calls for – combines local and global. Hull and Schultz (2002) have argued that for the last decade, the most fruitful accounts of literacy for educational purposes have come from ethnographies of out-of-school literacies. Likewise, we can anticipate that ethnographic accounts of out-of-school communicative practices will inform our understanding of both multimodal pedagogy and local/global relations. Ethnographic studies located in these complex theoretical frameworks will, then, put into broader perspective the earlier studies listed at the outset of this chapter, regarding literacy and learning and the cognitive issues associated with literacy acquisition. Perhaps at that point, we will be ready to follow Olson's (1994) call for a recombination of these different traditions that have, as we have seen, moved apart in such dramatic ways. Marrying ethnographic perspectives from a social practice and ideological approach with observational studies from a cognitive approach may then offer a fruitful way forward for literacy studies.

Note

1 Parts of this chapter were adapted from a paper commissioned as preparatory work for the UNESCO 2005 Global Monitoring Report; these parts are reproduced herein by kind permission of the UNESCO GMR Team, Paris.

References

Abadzi, H. (2003). *Improving adult literacy outcomes*. Washington, DC: World Bank.

Adams, M. (1993). Beginning to read: An overview. In R. Beard (Ed.), *Teaching literacy balancing perspectives* (pp. 204–215). London: Hodder & Stoughton.

Ahearn, L. (2004). Literacy, power, and agency: Love letters and development in Nepal, *Language and Education*, 18(4), 305–312.

Aikman, S. (1999). *Intercultural education and literacy: An ethnographic study of indigenous knowledge and learning in the Peruvian Amazon*. Amsterdam: John Benjamins.

Barton, D. (1999). Literacy practices. In D. Barton, M. Hamilton, & R. Ivanic (Eds.), *Situated literacies: Reading and writing in context* (pp. 7–15). London: Routledge.

Barton, D., & Hamilton, M. (1998). *Local literacies: Reading and writing in one community*. London: Routledge.

Barton, D., Hamilton, M., & Ivanic, R. (Eds.) (1999). *Situated literacies: Reading and writing in context*. London: Routledge.

Barton, D., & Ivanic, R. (1991). *Writing in the community*. Written Communication Annual, Volume 6. Newbury Park: Sage.

Baynham, M. (1995). *Literacy practices*. London: Longman.

Baynham, M. (2004). Ethnographies of literacy: An introduction. *Special Issue of Language and Education*, 18 (4), 285–290.

Beard, R. (1993). *Teaching literacy, balancing perspectives*. London: Hodder & Stoughton.

Beard, R. (2000). Research and the National Literacy Strategy. *Oxford Review of Education*, 26 (3–4), 421–436.

Besnier, N. (1995). *Literacy, emotion and authority: Reading and writing on a Polynesian atoll*. Cambridge [Eng.]: Cambridge University Press.

Black, P., & Wiliam, D. (1998). *Inside the black box: Raising standards through classroom assessment*. London: King's College London School of Education.

Brandt, D., & Clinton, K. (2002). Limits of the local: Expanding perspectives on literacy as a social practice. *Journal of Literacy Research*, 34 (3), 337–356.

Breier, M., & Sait, L. (1996). Literacy and communication in a cape factory. In M. Prinsloo & M. Breier (Eds.), *The social uses of literacy* (pp. 65–84). Amsterdam: John Benjamins.

Cavalcanti, M. C. (2003). It's not writing by itself that is going to solve our problems: Questioning a mainstream ethnocentric myth as part of a search for self-sustained development. In M. Baynham (Ed.), *Special Issue of Language and Education on Ethnographies of Literacy, Volume* 18, No. 4.

Chitrakar, R., & Maddox, B. (2008). The 'Community Literacy Project' in Nepal. In B. V. Street and N. H. Hornberger (Eds.), *Encyclopedia of language and education, 2nd Edition, Volume 2: Literacy*. New York, NY: Springer Science+Business Media LLC.

Collins, J. (1995). Literacy and literacies. *Annual Review of Anthropology*, 24, 75–93.

Collins, J., & Blot, R. (2002). *Literacy and literacies: Texts, Power and Identity*. Cambridge [Eng.]: Cambridge University Press.

Cook-Gumperz, J. (Ed.) (1986). *The social construction of literacy*. Cambridge: Cambridge University Press.

Cope, B., & Kalantzis, M. (1993). Introduction: How a genre approach to literacy can transform the way writing is taught. In B. Cope

& M. Kalantzis (Eds.), *The powers of literacy: A genre approach to teaching writing* (pp. 1–21). Brighton: Falmer Press.

Cope, B., & Kalanztis, M. (2000). *Multi-literacies: Literacy learning and the design of social futures*. London: Routledge.

Department For International Development (DFID) (1994). *Using literacy: New approaches to post-literacy materials*. London: DFID Research Report 10.

Department for International Development (DFID) (1999). *Redefining post-literacy in a changing context*. London: DFID Research Report 29.

Doronilla, M. L. (1996). *Landscapes of literacy: An ethnographic study of funcitonal literacy in marginal Philippine communities*. Hamburg: UIE.

Fairclough, N. (1995). Discourse and text: Linguistics: An intertextual analysis within discourse analysis. In N. Fairclough (Author), *Critical discourse analysis: The critical study of language* (pp. 187–213). Language in social life series. London: Longman.

Farrell, T. J. (1977, January). Literacy, the basics, and all that jazz. *College English*, 443–459.

Finnegan, R. (1999). Sociology/anthropology: Theoretical issues in literacy. In D. Wagner, L. Venezky, & B. Street (Eds.), *Literacy: An international handbook of literacy*. Boulder, CO: Westview Press.

Fordham, P., Holland, D., & Millican, J. (1995). 'Ordinary' materials. In P. Fordham, D. Holland, & J. Millican (Authors), *Adult literacy: A handbook for development workers* (pp. 138–148). Oxford: Oxfam/VSO.

Frank, F., & Hamilton, M. (1993). "Not just a number": The role of basic skills programmes in the changing workplace. Report on *Leverhulme Funded Research Project*, Case Study No. 3, Baxi Heating (pp. 67–89).

Freire, P. (1985). *The politics of education: Culture, power and liberation*. South Hadley, MA: Bergin & Garvey.

Freire, P., & Macedo, D. (1987). Literacy and critical pedagogy. In P. Freire & D. Macedo (Authors), *Literacy: Reading the word and the world* (pp. 141–159). South Hadley, MA: Bergin & Garvey.

Gee, J. P. (1990a). *Social linguistics and literacies: Ideology in discourse*. London/Philadelphia: Falmer Press.

Gee, J. P. (1990b). Orality and literacy: From the savage mind to ways with words. In J. P. Gee (Author), *Social linguistics and literacy: Ideology in discourses*. London: Falmer Press.

Gee, J. P. (1999). *An introduction to discourse analysis: Theory and method*. London: Routledge.

Gee, J. P., Hull, G., & Lankshear, C. (1996). *Introduction. The new work order: Behind the language of the new capitalism* (pp. 1–23). London: Allen & Unwin.

Giddens, A. (1991). *Modernity and self-identity: Self and society in the Late Modern Age*. Stanford, CA: Stanford University Press.

Goodman, K. (1967). Reading: A psycholinguistic guessing game. *Journal of the Reading Specialist*, 6, 126–135.

Goodman, K. (1996). Learning and teaching reading and writing. In K. Goodman (Author), *On reading* (pp. 117–125). Portsmouth, NH: Heinemann.

Goody, J. (1977). Evolution and communication. In J. Goody (Author), *The domestication of the savage mind* (pp. 1–18). Cambridge: Cambridge University Press.

Gowen, S. (1992). *The politics of workplace literacy*. New York: Teachers College Press.

Heath, S. B. (1982), What no bed-time story means: Narrative skills at home and school, *Language in Society*, *11*, pp. 49–78.

Heath, S. B. (1983). *Ways with words: language, life, and work in communities and classrooms*. Cambridge [Cambridgeshire]: Cambridge University Press.

Heath, S. B. (1993). The madness(es) of reading and writing ethnography. *Anthropology & Education Quarterly*, 24 (3), 256–268.

Heath, S. B., & Street, B. (2008). Ethnography. In S. B. Heath, B. V. Street with M. Mills (Authors), *On ethnography: Approaches to language and literacy research*. Commissioned by the National Conference on Research in Language and Literacy. New York: Teachers College Columbia.

Holland, C. (1998). *Literacy and the new work order*. Leicester: National Institute of Adult Continuing Education.

Hornberger, N. H. (1997). Indigenous literacies in the Americas. Introduction in N. H. Hornberger (Ed.), *Indigenous literacies in the Americas: Language planning from the bottom up* (pp. 3–16). Berlin: Mouton de Gruyter.

Hornberger, N. H. (Ed.) (2002). *The continua of biliteracy: A framework for educational policy, research and practice in multiple settings*. Bristol: Multilingual Matters.

Hull, G. (1997). *Changing work, changing workers: Critical perspectives on language, literacy and skills*. New York: State University of New York Press.

Hull, G. (2000). Critical literacy at work. *Journal of Adolescent and Adult Literacy*, 43 (1), 648–652.

Hull, G. (2001). Constructing working selves: Silicon Valley assemblers meet the new work order. *Anthropology of Work Review*, 22 (1), 17–22.

Hull, G., & Schultz, K. (2002). *School's out: Bridging out-of-school literacies with classroom practice*. New York: Teachers College Press.

Jewitt, C. (2006). *Technology, literacy and learning: Aa multimodal approach*. London: Routledge.

Kalman, J. (1999). *Writing on the plaza: Mediated literacy practices among scribes and clients in Mexico City*. Cresskill, NJ: Hampton Press.

Kell, C. (2001). Literacy, literacies and ABET in South Africa: On the knife edge, new cutting edge or thin end of the wedge. In J. Crowther, M. Hamilton, & L. Tett (Eds.), *Powerful literacies* (pp. 94–107). London: National Institute for Adult Continuing Education.

King, L. (1994). *Roots of identity: Language and literacy in Mexico*. Stanford, CA: Stanford University Press.

Krashen, S. D. (1981). *Second language acquisition and second language learning*. Oxford: Pergamon Press.

Kress, G. (2002). *Literacy in the new media age*. London: Routledge.

Kress, G., Jewitt, C., Ogborn, J., & Tsatsarelis, C. (2000). *Multimodal teaching and learning*. Londono Continuum.

Kress, G., & Van Leeuwen, T. (2001). *Multimodal discourse*. London: Arnold.

Kulick, D., & Stroud, C. (1993). Conception and uses of literqcy in a Papua New Guinean Village. In B. Street (Ed.), *Cross-cultural approaches to literacy*. Cambridge [England]: Cambridge University Press.

Lave, J. (1988). *Cognition in practice*. Cambridge: Cambridge University Press.

Lave, J., & Wenger, E. (1991). *Situated learning: Legitimate peripheral participation*. Cambridge: Cambridge University Press.

Levi-Strauss, C. (1966). *The savage mind*. Chicago: University of Chicago Press.

Luke, A. (1996). Genres of power? Literacy education and the production of capital. In R. Hasan & G. Williams (Eds.), *Literacy in society* (pp. 308–335). New York: Longman.

Maddox, B. (2007). What can ethnographic studies tell us about the consequences of literacy? *Comparative Education*, 43(2), 253–271.

Martin-Jones, M., & Jones, K. (Eds.) (2000). *Multilingual literacies: Reading and writing different worlds*. Amsterdam: John Benjamins.

Muspratt, S., Luke, A., & Freebdoy, P. (Eds.) (1997). *Constructing critical literacies*. Cresskill, NJ: Hampton Press.

Olson, D. R. (1977). From utterance to text. *Harvard Educational Review*, 47, 257–281.

Olson, D. R. (1994). *The world on paper*. Cambridge: Cambridge University Press.

Pahl, K., & Rowsell, J. (Eds.) (2006). *Travel notes from the new literacy studies: Case studies in practice*. Clevedon: Multilingual Matters Ltd.

Petersen, C. (2004). Report on Uppingham Seminar: *Measuring literacy: Meeting in collision*. Uppingham Seminar, November 2003. Available at http://www.uppinghamseminars.org/report2003.htm.

Prinsloo, M. (2004). Literacy is Child's Play: Making Sense in Khwezi Park, *Language and Education*, 18 (4), 291–304.

Prinsloo, M., & Breier, M. (1996). Introduction. in M. Prinsloo & M. Breier. (Eds.), *The social uses of literacy* (pp. 11–31). Amsterdam: John Benjamins.

Rainbird, H. (Ed.) (2000). *Training in the workplace: Critical perspectives on learning at work*. London: Macmillan Press.

Robinson-Pant, A. (1997). *Why eat green cucumbers at the time of dying?: The link between women's literacy and development*. Hamburg: UNESCO.

Robinson-Pant, A. (Ed.) (2004). *Women, literacy and development: Alternative perspectives*. London: Routledge.

Rogers, A. (1992). Sharing in development: Adults learning for development (pp 226–238). London: Cassell.

Rogers, A. (2003a). *Teaching adults*. Third edition. Buckingham: Open University Press.

Rogers, A. (2003b). *What is the difference? A new critique of adult learning and teaching*. Leicester: National Institute for Adult Continuing Education.

Rogers, A. (Ed.) (2005). *Urban literacy: Communication, identity and learning in urban contexts*. Hamburg: UIE.

Rogoff, B. (2003). *The cultural nature of human development*. New York: Oxford University Press.

Rogoff, B., & Lave, J. (Eds.) (1984/1999). *Everyday cognition: Development in social context*. Cambridge, MA: Harvard University Press.

Rogoff, B., Paradise, R., Mej a Arauz, R., Correa-Chavez , M., & Angelillo, C. (2003). First-hand learning by intent participation. *Annual Review of Psychology*, 54, 175–203.

Scribner, S. (1984). Studying working intelligence. In B. Rogoff & J. Lave (Eds.), *Everyday cognition: Development in social context*. Cambridge, MA: Harvard University Press.

Scribner, S., & Cole, M. (1978). Unpackaging literacy. *Social Science Information*, 17 (1), 19–40.

Scribner, S., & Cole, M. (1981). *The psychology of literacy*. Cambridge, MA: Harvard University Press.

Slavin, R. (2002). Evidence-based education policies: Transforming educational practice and research. *Educational Researcher*, 31 (7), 15–21.

Smith, F. (1971). *Understanding reading: A psycholoinguistic analysis of reading and learning to read*. New York: Holt, Rinehart & Winston.

Snow, C. (1998). Introduction. In C. Snow, M. Burns, & P. Griffin (Eds.), *Preventing reading difficulties in young children* (pp. 15–31). Washington, DC: National Academy Press.

Street, B. (1984). *Literacy in theory and practice*. Cambridge: Cambridge University Press.

Street, B. (1993). Culture is a verb: Anthropological aspects of language and cultural process. In D. Graddol, L. Thompson, & M. Byram (Eds.), *Language and Culture* (pp. 23–43). Clevedon: BAAL and Multilingual Matters.

Street, B. (1995). *Social literacies*. London: Longman.

Street, B. (1998). New literacies in theory and practice: What are the implications for language in education? *Linguistics and Education*, 10 (1), 1–24.

Street, B. (2000). Literacy 'events' and literacy practices: Theory and practice in the new literacy studies. In K. Jones & M. Martin-Jones (Eds.), *Multilingual literacies: Comparative perspectives on research and practice*. Amsterdam: John Benjamins.

Street, B. (Ed.) (2001a). *Literacy and development: Ethnographic perspectives*. London: Routledge.

Street, B. (2001b). Literacy and development: Challenges to the dominant paradigm. In A. Mukherjee & D. Vasanta (Eds.), *Rethinking literacy: Dominant and alternative discourses*. London: Sage Publications.

Street, B. (2003, May 12). What's 'new' in New Literacy Studies? Critical approaches to literacy in theory and practice. *Current Issues in Comparative Education*, 5 (2), 77–91. ISSN: 1523–1615 http://www.tc.columbia.edu/cice/.

Street, B. (2004). The limits of the local: 'Autonomous' or 'disembedding'? *International Journal of Learning*, 10, 2825–2830.

Street, B. (Ed.) (2005). *Literacies across educational contexts: Mediating teaching and learning*. Philadelphia: Caslon Press.

Street, B., Baker, D., & Tomlin, A. (2006). *Navigating Numeracies: Home/School Numeracy*. Series on Leverhulme numeracy research programme. Kluwer: Dordrecht.

Street, B., & Street, J. (1991). The schooling of literacy. In D. Barton & R. Ivanic (eds.), *Writing in the community* (pp. 143–166). Newbury Park, CA: Sage Publications.

UNESCO (2003). Literacies: New meanings of literacy. Position Paper. Paris: UNESCO/Ed/BA.LIT. Available at (http://unesdoc.unesco.org/images/0013/001362/136246e.pdf).

UNESCO (2005). Global Monitoring Report. Available at http://portal.unesco.org/education/en/ev.php-.

Varenne, H., & McDermott, R. (1998). *Successful failure: The school America builds*. Boulder, CO: Westview Press.

Verhoeven, L. (1994). Modelling and promoting functional literacy: Introduction. In L. Verhoeven (Ed.), *Functional literacy* (pp. 3–34). Amsterdam: John Benjamins.

Verhoeven, L., & Snow, C. (Eds.) (2001). *Literacy and motivation: Reading engagement in individuals and groups*. Mahwah, NJ: Lawrence Erlbaum Associates.

Wagner, D. (1993). *Literacy, culture and development: Becoming literate in Morocco*. Cambridge: Cambridge University Press.

CHAPTER 19

The Origins of Western Literacy

Literacy in Ancient Greece and Rome

Rosalind Thomas

Literacy in the ancient Greco-Roman world has a special place in the study of literacy and its role in society. Our very alphabet was inherited from the Romans, who themselves adopted the alphabet from the Greeks, and they started to use the alphabet in the eighth century BCE. Thus, there is a line of inheritance which prompts a particular fascination with the way both Greeks and Romans used their new alphabets, the origins of Western literacy. The alphabet is more economical and easier to learn than the various other writing systems available, from syllabaries to the single character per word. If this is so, then surely we should be able to see a facility and set of uses of writing in the ancient Greco-Roman world that is powerfully akin to ours. The Greeks actually invented the alphabet as we know it by adapting certain signs to denote vowels, thus adding the vowels to the string of consonants they learned from the Phoenicians. It has been claimed that they thereby created a writing system which could do what previous writing systems could not, enabling the most perfect match of sound and writing and a massive democratisation of literacy. There is something in this: for alphabetic literacy can be learned relatively quickly, but this ease and the extent of the difference can be exaggerated (educational systems can accommodate this greater difficulty if the will is there, even in a complex written system such as Chinese). The alphabet was indeed used in certain ways which we have inherited and which are familiar (e.g., for literature, documents, and laws) but not by all or in all periods, and there are large variations in the uses of literacy which prompt one to look as much at the social and cultural habits of the ancient (or modern) world for explanations of change as at the ease of the alphabet alone. One of the arguments here is that it is misleading and historically naive to assume that ancient attitudes to literacy are essentially 'ours' and to filter out the radically different, or the social or political factors which meant that literacy was manipulated in directions we might think far from obvious. Nor should we neglect the contexts, attitudes and changing uses of writing over the many centuries of Graeco-Roman civilisation.

The Greeks did, indeed, borrow the alphabet from the Phoenicians, a Near Eastern people dwelling on the Levantine coast and in the cities of Tyre and Sidon among others. Speaking a Semitic language, the Phoenicians did not strictly have vowels in their writing system: their opening letter *aleph*, written rather like our capital *A* on its side (ᗉ), became the Greek vowel *alpha* (*A a*), which became our vowel *a*. Yet, strictly they too had discovered the alphabetic principle, which was to denote a single sound by a single letter, thus making possible the combination of a relatively small number of signs. There are good reasons to think that this true alphabetic principle went back to the early Canaanites, who may even have derived it from some elements of the Egyptian writing system (hieroglyphics are mainly syllabic but there are alphabetic elements).[1] Credit for the revolutionary discovery of the alphabetic principle, therefore, has to be rather diffused, and the Phoenicians deserve as much as the Greeks themselves.

It is in another closely related respect that the Greeks have a particular niche in the history of literacy. Classical Greek literature and philosophy have had a formative influence in the Western world, and the educational structures of its modern study imply an intensely bookish, literate culture (more on this later). Yet, when the Greek world began to adopt the alphabet in the eighth century BCE, they had been several centuries without writing, for the Mycenaean Linear B system, a syllabic system, seems to have died out completely, leaving the Dark Ages of Greece without writing. We have, then, a society or set of societies in that fragmented period, which presented the neat picture of a new form of writing being adopted into a completely illiterate one – and the same could be said of the Etruscans adopting the alphabet from the Greeks. It is partly this that prompted the study of the Greeks as a case study for the effects of literacy, 'the consequences of literacy' in the immensely stimulating and influential formulation of Goody and Watt in 1962–1963: they argued that the alphabet itself (rather than writing alone because writing systems were millennia old in the eighth century BCE) was able to promote and encourage mass literacy in the Greek world and bring about the development of historiography, rational thought, and philosophy.[2]

This is not the place to present a critique of this theory which has been much discussed,[3] but it is worth stressing here that such an approach brought together several factors and elements which would have been better distinguished. The *potential* of writing, for instance, and the tasks that writing makes either possible or easier (in theory), need to be distinguished from the uses to which writing is actually put in any particular society. The theoretical opportunities or the potential uses for writing are not necessarily sought out, and it is interesting to ask why. Sparta, for instance, prided herself on not needing written law and this militaristic, highly successful city led Greece for generations without much use of writing. The public decrees and laws written up so conspicuously by democratic Athens are almost wholly absent. (We may contrast, on the other hand, the way canonised written texts are virtually absent in ancient paganism, yet written scriptures became central to early Christians and the development of the Christian church in the first centuries AD.) The development of rational argument and philosophical thought has as much to do with the dynamics of Greek society with its intensely agonistic character – open, public competition – and the willingness of one thinker to take on and better the ideas of a previous thinker, as Lloyd showed, as with the presence of written texts.[4] Socrates, arguably the most famous of all Greek philosophers, wrote nothing down at all, while his pupil and admirer Plato presented his philosophical theories in the form of open verbal dialogues, mimicking real open-air discussions, between Socrates and various speakers with a marked absence of the sense of closure and finality of many written texts. Indeed, Plato criticised writing as a path to education and wisdom, and he argued that true learning and wisdom could only be attained through live dialogue:

one cannot question a piece of writing – it can only say the same thing repeatedly, as he puts it in the *Phaedrus* (275d); writing is useful for storing up things against the forgetfulness of old age, but dialectic is necessary for true wisdom (276e–277a). Criticism and refinement of theories were made considerably easier, of course, from one generation to another by the fact that most philosophers after Socrates were writers who published their ideas, yet such written texts equally had the potential to become 'sacred', revered texts, as it were, as so many written texts do, and we therefore need to give much weight to the spirit of criticism and competition in the development of analytical and critical thought. In the Greek world of the fifth and fourth centuries BCE, written texts did not lead to fossilisation.

The presence of writing, or of 'literacy' in general (whatever that means, for it is a complex concept and is discussed later), evidently has to be approached in a more qualified way, one that considers various forms of literacy, different milieus and practices of literacy. Attitudes towards writing also determine or affect the way that it is used, as did the preceding non-written habits. The Greeks – and, for different reasons, the Romans – do not present a test case for the impact of writing or the effects of literacy taken in general and generalisable terms, but they do offer extremely interesting and important studies of the complexities of 'literacy' in various social, political and cultural settings, and particularly its interaction with non-literate or non-written methods of doing business, communicating, and recording. The nature of ancient Greek and Roman societies encourages us to examine the social and political contexts of writing and, in particular, to ask what is particularly Greek or Roman about Greek or Roman literacy. What we may explore is the tension between the general potential of writing, what writing makes possible, and how writing is used and adapted in a given cultural milieu.

The trend in current research on literacy seems to have turned away from the image of literacy as a 'technology', as a relatively straightforward skill and a force which acts on people, or on society, in a relatively predictable way.[5] Recent work stresses the presence of multiple literacies – that is, different forms of literacy as envisaged, manipulated, adapted – in quite different cultural contexts (we may see this in the contrast between a roughly 'Western model' of literacy and indigenous literacies to be found in colonised countries subject to colonial power and colonial models of education). The ancient world (which henceforth I use as shorthand for the Greek and Roman ancient world) certainly reinforces this; indeed, it perhaps has contributed to strengthening this model. It also serves to emphasise the importance of looking also at what is *not* written, the areas where literacy or written texts are not used, as well as where they are. One cannot achieve a rounded picture of the role of literacy, the place of writing, unless, of course, the total situation is grasped. However, it equally tends to be easier to trace what is written down than what was not, since by definition, the merely spoken word simply disappears into thin air. For any historical period, it is a truism that historians must rely heavily on what survives in writing, whether from the medieval period, the Renaissance or the nineteenth century. Material evidence aside, one learns about oral traditions, songs, festivals, performance, and memories, only if they are written down or described in some way: thus, the oral practices of the illiterate or the literate (i.e., songs, oaths, tales, memories) tend to remain without voice in the historical record. The particular nature of the ancient evidence also encourages an especial stress by the researcher on public monumental writing, – written texts engraved on metal or stone and erected in public spaces in the open air by private individuals or the state in the open air. These are arguably the single most characteristic use of literacy in the ancient world.

Rather than present a general overview for a period covering a thousand years or more, in the remainder of this chapter I concentrate on certain periods, types of literacy, and areas of interesting debate. As will become clear, there is often a fascinating balance or tension between the possibilities offered (in theory) by writing and the apparent manifestations or uses made of it in the Greek or Roman world. We look at (1) the early uses of literacy in Greece; (2) literacy and democracy, literacy and the state, public writing; (3) literacy and literacies in Greece and Rome, how many people were 'literate'?; and (4) literacy and social advancement.

Early Literacy in Greece (Eighth–Sixth Century)

How was writing used when the first Greeks adopted the alphabet in the eighth and seventh centuries BCE and what difference did it make? Our evidence comes in the form of tiny scraps of writing scratched on sherds of broken pottery, either written originally on a whole pot or written on broken pieces – the Greek equivalent of scrap paper. From about the middle of the seventh century BCE, the first inscriptions appear on stone. The earliest examples of so-called graffiti (i.e, informal writing), appearing around the middle of the eighth century BCE or shortly before, are tiny marks on pottery which often state ownership with the proper name prominent. One early example has the scratched message, 'this cup belongs to Tataie'. This is no grandiose public writing, nor is any really extensive piece of writing attested. It is tempting to think that when writing first arrived, it was overwhelmingly used for labelling and marking objects and names, dedications with names, and personal objects. The two most interesting pieces of eighth-century writing – the 'Dipylon vase' of Athens and 'Nestor's cup' – both record a sort of competition or joke about a dinner party: Nestor's cup promises that 'whoever drinks from this cup' will be seized by the desire of Aphrodite.[6] It is in verse, which suggests that it is preserving a song or poem sung at a dinner party, and it makes joking reference to Nestor's cup which was mentioned in the Homeric epic. The Dipylon Oinochoe, in less accomplished writing, seems to promise a reward for the best dancing and then the writing deteriorates into unintelligibility. It begins,

> *He who of all the dancers now performs most daintily . . .*

It has been suggested that the first writing, in fact, was used to write down and record the Homeric epics for all time.[7] Although this romantic idea has its obvious attractions, it is not really borne out by the evidence we have, nor the general considerations of the nature of the Homeric oral epic, and the circumstances and date by which it spread over the Greek world. It seems inconceivable that a type of writing learned from the Phoenicians, who were powerful and adventurous traders and travellers, would be adapted initially to record for the first time an epic which had been orally composed and transmitted for generations rather than for the more prosaic and functional purposes known to the Phoenicians. On present evidence and from more general theoretical factors, it still seems most likely that the new alphabet – now with its fully functioning vowels – spread rapidly around the Greek settlements of the Mediterranean for relatively simple and mundane purposes: writing down names, contents of vases, short messages, marking dedications in the sanctuaries with the name of the dedicator and perhaps the deity in question, and slight pieces of verse to inscribe on vases. The world of poetry and song and the symposium seems to lie in the background, especially when we look at the Nestor Cup and the Dipylon Oinochoe, but it is a world of oral performance – the written word remains on the edge, serving the performance.[8]

Yet, we can trace a gradual extension of writing into other areas of the Greek world during the next two centuries. Dedications (i.e., gifts to the deity) with short pieces of writing generally giving the names of dedicator and deity become more frequent in the sanctuaries, and the prominence of the name of the dedicator suggests that an important purpose was to preserve the memory of the dedicator and his generosity. 'Graffiti' on pots and sherds abound, and some fragments of the alphabet (not usually getting far into the alphabet) have been found: vast numbers consist of personal names, perhaps the first and the main piece of writing some writers could achieve.[9] (It is interesting that when we come to the Roman shrines several centuries later, some sanctuaries might be covered in such dedicatory messages in a virtual forest of names, in which the name is "the fixed written record of one's engagement in ritual".[10]) Funerary monuments also started to record the names of the deceased, and this too was obviously an attempt to record the name and preserve the memory, both for the community when memories of the dead began to fade and for strangers who passed by. Some inscriptions affect to address the passing stranger directly, using the fact that most ancients read aloud, not silently, to make a wry reference to the passerby giving voice, as it were, to the tombstone or to the deceased. One example from Eretria declares in elegiac couplets[11]:

> *Hail, passer-by; I lie low in death: come and read who of men is buried here: a sojourner from Aegina, Mnesitheus his name; my mother Timarete set up this memorial, an imperishable stone on the top of the mound which shall say unceasingly forever to passers-by: Timarete set it up for her dear son dead.*

The Homeric poems themselves were eventually committed to paper, and it is generally thought that once this happened, the poems would start to be enshrined in the written text itself – rather than existing only through the changing performances of the oral poet – and that the creative oral performances would shrivel and die, leaving in their place only performances of the rhapsodists who simply sung the received text. It is unclear when the poems were committed to writing – perhaps in the late eighth century BCE, perhaps in the seventh.[12]

What is more clear is that the lyric poets, poets like Archilochos and Alcaeus and Sappho of Lesbos (mid-seventh century onwards), not only sang their compositions but also knew enough of the Homeric poems to be able to refer to them; and the texts of the lyric poets answer each other as well. This implies that along with the performances, usually accompanied by the lyre, there were at least occasionally written texts which could get passed around. To say this, however, is not to imply that the performances were not the main medium of publication, for they were, and performance was the main context in which the Greeks experienced their poetry. These might be performances during rituals or festivals for a deity, or a big public festival in honour of the main city deity, or private dinner parties. The highly educated elite down to the fifth century BCE were still expected to be able to recite well-known poetry and, indeed, compose their own in the symposium. It remains likely that the texts created by poets such as Sappho were primarily *aides-mémoire*, for they were sung to music and lyre – certainly not texts meant for the silent reading with which modern audiences experience poetry. It should be added that a great deal of this literature was meant primarily for performance at religious festivals, occasions of cult and ritual – therefore, by definition, for public audiences at specific occasions even if it could continue to be sung outside such occasions. This is especially true of the literature of the archaic period and still true of tragedy in the fifth century BCE and beyond. Much lyric poetry seems designed for audiences of similar-minded men and women, and much recent research has been devoted to uncovering those lost occasions or ritual events. The genre of a piece reflected the occasion for which it was meant – for example, marriage, athletic victory celebration, funerals – and when tragedy began, it was performed specifically for the festival of the god Dionysus, rather than the other way round, poetry being determined by genre as an abstract literary phenomenon.[13] As Wallace succinctly stated, one of the changes taking place in the high classical period (i.e., the fifth century BCE) was that performance of literature was becoming separated from any cultic or ritual occasion.[14] In those circumstances, then, the written texts are presumably pale reflections of only one part (i.e., the words, not the music) of the way they were first experienced.

By the time of the Persian Wars (490–479 BCE), however, writing was being exploited for devising written curses, and they continue to occur with spectacular frequency in Sicily (e.g., Selinous): an uttered curse would be just as much a curse, but the written form was perhaps thought even more effective than the oral utterance alone, and the letters of the name of the accursed were sometimes jumbled up in a further act of symbolic malevolence. Short messages and letters are attested around 500 BCE on the edges of the Greek world, Southern France and the Black Sea, for urgent messages between traders or between traders and their subordinates. In at least one case, the so-called Berezan letter, written and sent in the distant northern shore of the Black Sea, we read an urgent cry for help from someone whose property, person and slaves had been seized. The letter begins, "O Protagoras, your father [Achillodorus] sends you this command. He is being wronged by Matasys, for Matasys is enslaving him and has deprived him of his cargo". Some elements of the letter are unclear; however, the gist concerns not only a seizure of the person and goods of Achillodorus, the writer of the lead letter, but also a serious conflict among Achillodorus, Matasys, and Anaxagoras, a third party whose true relationship to Achillodorus remains extremely uncertain; slavery legal and illegal; and an urgent appeal to the son to get his mother and brother away to the city.[15]

Without a postal service, you had to trust to a messenger for communication over distance, and when the messenger could not be entirely relied on, or the message was very long, then you would use a written letter – as the orator Antiphon said in the late fifth century (an admittedly persuasive definition but one which must have sounded plausible; *Herodes* VI 53). Here, we are beginning to see the written word being resorted to for accurate recording not simply of names, dedicators, and the deceased, but also for information which needed to cover long distances. This must have begun earlier than the first examples of such letters which have been found by modern archaeologists: these letters are only preserved because they happen to be on lead; any letters written on wooden sheets or papyrus will have perished.

Similarly, we can see by the fifth century BCE that the Greek city-state had begun to use writing to preserve and enshrine its decisions, mainly in the form of law and sacred calendars (this begs the question of how many people could read them; see subsequent discussion). We turn now to public writing.

Literacy and Democracy, Literacy and the State: Public Writing on Stone in Greece and Rome

The earliest written laws in Greece are attested from the very late seventh century with a series of lawgivers who wrote down their laws and also with isolated examples of laws engraved on stone. This is not the place to discuss the controversy about such lawgivers who often gained almost mythical status. What is interesting for our purposes is that the earliest laws on stone that we still possess are a peculiar and controversial group. They do not tend to record items of customary law, for instance, customs which would be generally in use; the ones committed to stone often have a political import. A law regulating and controlling the actions of the chief official has been found in the tiny town of Dreros on Crete, for example; another law in Chios in the early sixth century sets down the roles of the 'people's council', an enactment covering radical elements of the political structure which can only recently have been established. In Chios, this was an early democratic move; in Dreros the regulation of the highest official may have been a move towards controlling the political and economic elite, the aristocracy, and a partial development towards state-formation. Even with the homicide law of the very early lawgiver, Drakon of Athens, which covers the punishment of unintentional homicide, even a slight alteration to procedure could have profound consequences. These laws were sorting out issues which were *not* widely agreed upon – the controversial or politically charged enactments – and they form a crucial part of the development of the independent city-states of Greece. This hints that writing was now being used by communities to record and enforce some of their most important changes,[16] but the Greek evidence suggests a process more complex and also more faltering than an easy equation of written law and justice (or democracy) would expect. Written law was but one element among many that contributed to the formation of the self-government of the Greek city-state.

To some extent, the early lawgivers in Greece who did much to stabilise or even create a civil society must have formalised or confirmed rules already in place about misdemeanors, crimes and inheritance, but these more political enactments also suggest that often what went up on stone in the public square was a *new* law, a law which might be initiating reforms which were controversial or disliked by some of the most powerful in the city. Clauses mentioning oaths, officials who swear to keep the law, and even the invocation of a deity to act as 'guarantor', all suggest that these stone laws were engraved and erected to enforce and to impress. Sometimes a clause enforces obedience to what is simply called 'the writing' – that is, the law – which suggests that writing is not very common (otherwise 'the writing' would be too vague an expression) and also that it was important that the law was written out. For example, a late-sixth-century law from the important cult-centre of Olympia about improper behaviour in temples adds the severe warning that "If anyone pronounces judgement against the writing, his judgement shall be void", in which the writing obviously refers to the law itself.[17] (It is interesting that this text also lets slip the fact that those who created it were afraid that the written law may not be regarded as authoritative!)

Writing on stone would fix in a permanent manner and could challenge anyone who attempted to overturn what was agreed. The written law also enshrined the decision of the polis in visible form, even if many citizens could not read it: it thus had a powerful symbolic role. However, given the traditional character of the archaic city-states, some early laws may have represented in reality the elite trying to control each other. Moreover, writing alone could not enforce a law, and this was implicit in the archaic laws' addition of swearers, oaths, and religious sanctions; in addition, men and procedures would need to be ready to act when a law was contravened. Nevertheless, written law in archaic Greece did become connected to the collective will of the city-state – or its leaders, posing as the voice of the collective. Even if such written laws did not succeed overnight in stabilising laws and rules, the possibility that written law was necessary (although not sufficient by itself) to avoid arbitrary judgements was grandly declared by authors in the fifth century BCE. In Euripides' *Suppliants*, Theseus declares, "When the laws are written down, then both the weak and the rich have equal justice" (430–434) – a sentiment at the heart of the theory of the Athenian democracy. Similarly, Gorgias declared that "written laws are the guardians of justice" (Diels-Kranz, 82, frag. 11a, 30).

The cities' laws were frequently erected on stone in public. This use of the stone inscription for public enactments, enactments of state, and no longer just for funerary inscriptions became the standard and most characteristic use of writing in the public sphere for the entire Greco-Roman world. The Greek city-states used large stone inscriptions for treaties between cities, often erected in a Pan-Hellenic sanctuary like Olympia, and other forms of public agreements, honours, and alliances. Athens used stone inscriptions most extensively for setting out those decrees of the city which for one reason or another were deemed deserving of an inscription. There is an increase of inscriptions with the advent of the radical democracy in the 460s BCE and some add clauses which become more common later implying a wish for public visibility. Therefore, it does seem that for Athenians, public stone-writing was associated with democracy and it was a democratic attribute: the inscriptions recording in public what the democratic assembly had decided.[18] At least, that was the symbolic meaning in Athens itself. Yet, how widespread this ideal was is doubtful, for some other democracies in Greece did not adopt stone inscriptions for their decrees with the same extravagance. Indeed to judge from the large and extravagant inscriptions in Athens listing payments or monies connected with the gods, there seems also to be a conscious connection between records on stone and the business of the city's deities. The tribute from the allies of the Athenian Empire, for instance, is not inscribed on stone, but the one-sixtieth which was a tithe to the goddess Athena *was* inscribed beautifully at length with care and expense.

The habit became enshrined. Thousands of inscriptions still survive from the ancient world – one estimate is that more than half a million are now published by modern scholars.[19] The Roman port of Ostia alone produced more than three thousand inscriptions[20] – and they survive better than any other texts from the ancient world other than the papyri preserved so well in the dry sands of Egypt. Many interesting questions still remain about the roles, status and nature of the great public inscriptions of the ancient cities, which by any calculation could not be read by the vast mass of the population. At the very least, possible answers must vary with period, place and context; beyond that, they impinge on many of the major debates concerning ancient politics and society. We obviously cannot take inscriptions for granted as a 'natural' or neutral uses of writing: they are an extraordinary and culturally bound use of literacy, although we are not unfamiliar with public stone inscriptions in modern cities. The significance of the ancient ones goes far beyond the simple desire to publish, to make known the content of a decree, or law, or honour. For those who wished to read them, they were there for confirmation, but they also proclaimed in monumental form the significance of whatever it was they recorded. Their erection symbolised the importance of the document (since not all decrees were inscribed on stone) – perhaps the completion of an obligation to the gods[21] – and they gave public importance and weight to those documents regarded as important enough for inscription. Thus, treaties and alliances of importance were regularly inscribed on stone in public, giving historians a mercifully accurate glimpse of the exact text and an identifiable, verifiable text for contemporaries if there was ever a dispute. The cities of the Hellenistic Period and of the Roman Empire also erected many inscriptions honouring prominent individuals, especially benefactors who thus had their virtues (and financial payments) extolled in public places – a phenomenon reflecting the increased importance of the benefactor in maintaining the city and its politics. Somewhat like lists of benefactors in modern museums, these publicised and proclaimed the names of the city's great men – and one imagines that even those who could not actually read them would be impressed by their presence, size and appearance and might well know what they commemorated.

Some eccentric individuals used inscriptions to propagate their favourite philosophical doctrines. Diogenes of Oinoanda, a local Epicurean philosopher from this relatively minor city in southwest Turkey, inscribed his literary works on the walls of a stoa, creating an inscription about 80 metres long (second century AD) – in a town which went in for spectacularly large inscriptions. The North Indian king Asoka in the third century BCE used this medium to publicise Buddhist teachings and explain his conversion in two Greek inscriptions at Kandahar with parallel Aramaic text. The implication was that this was an effective and powerful way to publicise the doctrines, building on the idea that important documents should go up on public; even if not everyone could read them, it gave them a powerful status in the community and ensured the text a long life. When the Roman emperor wrote an important letter to a city detailing a privilege or a decision in a dispute with a neighbour, for instance, the city often erected a stone copy for all to see. In the early years of the Roman Empire, the city of Aphrodisias in southwest Turkey inscribed on the theatre wall a large selection of what they considered their most important documents, including a large collection of documents illustrating their 'special relationship' with Rome.[22]

In Rome, laws, senatorial decrees and grants to individuals were displayed on bronze on the Capitol. They were destroyed by a massive fire towards the end of Nero's reign (i.e., before A.D. 68) and they were mourned by the Roman writer Suetonius in terms that recognise both their symbolic and practical value, their role in embodying as well as recording the decisions and values of the Roman state: "'This was the most beautiful and most ancient record of empire (*instrumentum imperii*), comprising senatorial decrees, decisions made by the Roman people concerning alliance, treaty, and privilege granted to individuals, dating back almost to the foundation of Rome" (Suetonius, *Vespasian* 8.5). Bronze copies of senatorial decrees (*Senatus consulta*) were also sometimes erected in cities of the Roman Empire; several have now been found in Spain. It has been observed that many ancient cities (certainly from the Hellenistic Period, Athens from the fifth century BCE) would present to a contemporary observer a virtual forest of inscriptions – inscriptions public and private jostling for attention amidst the public buildings and public spaces. Public writing on stone may indeed have been the most familiar and common form of writing for many inhabitants. I stress this because it is here that we see the most spectacular gulf between our world of literacy and theirs.

The Greek situation can perhaps best illustrate the range of problems and questions in interpretation: scholars differ in the weight and significance they attach to these public inscriptions which, although our main texts now, were duplicated and shadowed by archive copies which no longer survive.[23] In Athens, for which our evidence is richest, some public documents were kept by the relevant officials, and there was a central archive which kept copies of the Assembly decrees and laws from the late fifth century BCE. It is possible, I believe, to discern a growing complexity and sophistication in Athenian attitudes to documents, to their archives, and to how they used them in the fifth and fourth centuries and beyond. This makes sense in wider historical terms, for documents and a particular attitude to them do not spring up fully formed.[24] The inscriptions record only a selection of these decisions (and it is interesting to wonder why these and not others), but there were other documents we have lost. The nature of the other documents and the degree of archival sophistication must be deduced largely from the inscriptions: some scholars then believe that everything lay in the archives, kept in an orderly fashion, easy to access, and the inscriptions are mere copies, sometimes not complete.[25] However, in that case, we may wonder why so much expense was incurred inscribing certain decrees and laws on stone. In any case, it is certainly true that politicians refer in their speeches to the texts on the inscriptions as the definitive, important text, and to the inscriptions as a sign of an existing and valid treaty. What we probably must accept is that attitudes to documents in the fifth and still in the fourth centuries BCE were evolving, so that the inscriptions were effectively the crucial versions even though there were copies in the archives, and that a 'document mentality' took some time to develop (later, the archive version *was* regarded as the authoritative copy). It is certainly difficult for historians to have it both ways: assuming a modern sophistication in archive-keeping and retrieval of documents and yet a very unmodern attitude to public writing in the public stone inscription.

Rather, we seem to have a situation in which in the Athenian radical democracy of the fourth century BCE, some politicians were able to exploit the decrees in the archives for their arguments. However, at the same time, the inscriptions are widely referred to as the authoritative documents, and the destruction of the inscription of an alliance can be seen as tantamount to the destruction of the alliance: for example, Demosthenes talks about a treaty between Athens and Thebes in terms which assume that the treaty is in force while the stone is still up and vice versa (16.27). Many inscriptions threaten anyone who defaces them. In another treaty, the inscribing in public is expressly seen as making the oaths and alliance valid.[26] Thus, the inscriptions do seem to have a powerful status as embodying the decision, as well as recording it: it is the public statement, set in stone in a public place. To call this a 'symbolic' function is perhaps rather vague, but it should at least be clear that to say inscriptions have symbolic functions is not incompatible with the possibility that at least some people did or were able to refer to them as documents. It gets around the difficulty that many Athenians would probably have been unable to read them word for word – in any case, they could see them, recognise the inscription, and will have heard the text read aloud in the Assembly and know its importance. If we were to say that only the archive documents get official recognition, as some have, the stone documents on inscriptions would be in an even more anomalous position.

The use of archives to deposit documents on wood or papyrus then became increasingly popular and familiar in the Greek world during the fourth century BCE and later into the Hellenistic Period (post–323 BCE). We should also recognise that the inscriptions continue to have an extraordinarily important role, partly for imparting information to literates and illiterates (who learn from others), partly for public display of the action taken by the Assembly or city, and partly for symbolic purposes of various kinds.

The configurations and combinations were somewhat different under the Roman Empire, where archives kept senatorial decrees but where also copies of particularly crucial documents were erected on bronze or stone all over the Empire. For instance, Augustus' *Res Gestae*, a highly tendentious account of his achievements, were erected around the Roman Empire in public. Records were kept of senatorial decrees, laws and the emperor's letters, and copies could be retrieved if needed, as we learn from Pliny when he writes to the emperor Trajan asking about certain edicts and letters of previous emperors (Pliny, *Letters* 10.65 & 66). The practice of widespread posting of Roman statutes throughout the Empire seems to have died out in the Julio-Claudian period (first century AD), but cities across the Empire and in Italy continued to put up inscriptions of locally important documents as well as documents issued from the centre which had especial bearing on their own communities – letters from the emperor in response to a request or petition (e.g., the famous 'archive' on the theatre wall at Aphrodisias mentioned previously).[27] This rich inscriptional presence should be seen in connection with the widespread evidence for the administrative use of writing in business and running estates across the Roman Empire (see subsequent discussion). However, two further points are worth making: even here, there are interesting hints that the function of such writing is not simply to inform, and other social functions overlap. Witnesses to a document, for instance, are added in order of social status and are there to signal not simply witnessing but also support.[28] And, lest we find the image of extensive written administration in Rome familiarly reassuring, the literary accounts of the emperors have a distinct tendency to associate certain literature practices with the arbitrary actions of the tyrant.[29] It is perhaps not any actual machinery of bureaucracy which is regarded with a suspicion familiar to modern audiences from Kafka on (or Levi-Strauss, *Tristes Tropiques*) but rather the smaller scale letter-writing and pen-pushing that could be sinister in the hands of an all-powerful emperor. It is striking that the way in which writing is used by the Roman state seems to be an extension of its use by private individuals – rather than a wholly separate system, let alone one akin to the modern bureaucracy.[30] A nightmarish story of the emperor Domitian impaling house flies with his stylus is recounted by the historian Cassius Dio (66.9.4), which reflects in an exaggeratedly inverted form the sheer fact that the 'good' emperor attended to imperial business in person.

There are important and interesting theoretical points to make here: we create difficulties if we simply assume modern habits in the use of literacy, imposing them automatically on the ancient world (or, for that matter, any other society); writing has manifestations in that world which need to be understood in their own terms. If ancient authors talk of inscriptions in terms which suggest they have a powerful symbolic force, historians need to accept that, asking further what that force is and why. Historians also need to ask about attitudes which were acted out, or implied, but not necessarily consciously described by the actors themselves, as any anthropologist knows. It is likewise highly dubious to assume that uses of writing attested in one century can be read back to an earlier one (or a later one), since the social, cultural and political significance of writing (and its opposite) is related in some way to the surrounding political and social developments of the society at large. There were also large divisions in cultural and educational achievement, political power, and economic wealth throughout the ancient Greco-Roman world. The fact that it was often the slaves – the lowest of the low – who performed the clerical or secretarial tasks (as is most obvious in the Roman Imperial period) went hand in hand with a low valuation of those tasks. Pliny describes an ideal summer day in his country villa, working and writing: most of the physical activities involved are performed by slaves – slaves reading aloud, slaves writing to dictation (Pliny, *Letters* 9.36); although oddly, Pliny also reads speeches aloud very energetically 'to help digestion'. It looks increasingly likely that in the thriving commercial centres of the Roman Empire, there was an everyday use of writing and reading for commercial use, lists, accounts, letter-writing and even games.[31]

As a final point about the hidden social and cultural factors behind the use of inscriptional or stone writing in the Roman world, it is worth mentioning the puzzling problem of private epitaphs. It has been pointed out recently that the surviving epitaphs of Rome may be angled towards a particular social and economic class. The majority of epitaphs on stone in Rome seem to belong to freedmen (i.e., ex-slaves) and to sons of freedmen, and there may be an interesting sociocultural explanation for this fact. Does this mean that the great majority of Rome's population was, in fact, non-Italian and non-Roman, illustrating Juvenal's satirical criticisms of Rome as filled with foreigners? So it has often been assumed, but another possibility is that it is precisely the freedmen, those of lower status and the stigma of slave birth, who were fonder of using stone epitaphs at death than others,[32] resorting to the status symbol of an engraved inscription. Thus, even stone epitaphs dotted around Rome did not exactly reflect the social composition of Rome's population but rather represented a social statement deriving from a particular group: the upwardly mobile lower classes prosperous enough to erect epitaphs and elaborate monuments as a status symbol.

Literacy and Literacies: How Many Were Literate?

I have left till now the question of how many were literate and it should be clear why. Writing has so many facets, manifestations and uses that it seems more profitable to examine how writing was regarded and actually used rather than to try and define the rate of literacy on a single definition of literacy. The definition of 'literacy' is crucial, the answers about its extent quite dependent on whether it is defined as being able to read a literary text in Greek or Latin, or read an inscription, or a simple message or a name – just as today, one might distinguish the ability to fill in a form from the ability to read and appreciate a long book. Harris's extensive study of the evidence was concerned to stress low literacy rates overall, despite the sophisticated achievements of an elite: he showed that it is difficult to argue for more than for very low levels of literacy[33] at any point in the ancient world.[34] However, there are important variations at various times and places. Athens, he thought, showed an exceptionally high level of literacy, with more than 15 percent of the adult males considered 'semi-literate'. Some cities in the Hellenistic Period (c. 323–31 BCE), for example, placed a high premium on schooling even for girls, and even Harris suggested as many as 30 to 40 percent of the adult males has basic literacy in certain Hellenistic cities.[35] In Egypt, the papyrus remains show that a large proportion of the population had direct contact with written documents and had to be able to add signatures at some point (see subsequent discussion). However, this immediately calls into question the utility of working with any single definition of literacy and brings into the picture the wider cultural, economic or social surroundings. Greco-Roman Egypt was dominated by documents and scribes; this document obsession surely was closely aligned with the perceived usefulness of being able to read or write, even though much writing was done by professional scribes. (Therefore, illiterate people could manage by using a scribe but were thus at the scribe's mercy if they could not check the written document to which they put their mark).

Increasingly, then, it seems better to discuss 'literacies' rather than literacy and to separate subgenres of literacy or different literate practices. For instance, 'list literacy', defined as the literacy required to be able to read simple lists, seems relatively common for the ancient world. and since most written texts did not separate the words – writing in continuous lines of letters – the list, with a separate word on each line, would be far easier to read. Commercial literacy (i.e., familiarity with accounts, lists, and contracts) is also a distinguishable subtype, perhaps with its own rules, conventions and habits which may have much in common with list literacy. Cribbiore recently stressed the importance of 'signature literacy' in Egypt, where signatures were often needed.[36] Banking involved habits of writing that were unfamiliar enough for an Athenian orator in the fourth century to explain the manner of keeping records to his large popular audience ([Demosthenes] 49, *Against Timotheus*, c. 362 BCE[37]) – and one would be justified in discussing banking literacy as a subtype. Officials had particular habits of using writing, and the techniques of literary composition would be quite different again.[38]

Nevertheless, it is worth making some remarks which dovetail with this about certain salient features of the distribution of reading and writing skills in the ancient world. Reading and writing in the ancient Greek or Roman worlds never seem to be confined to a scribal class, although we may wonder about the over-powerful scribes who occasionally appear in inscriptions in the archaic period in Greece, and about Crete in general, which produced an early document giving extraordinary privileges to the scribe Spensithios and his entire family.[39] If the diffusion of writing or reading skills is linked to the availability of material to read, we would suspect that the Athenian democracy encouraged such skills quite far down the social or political scale, at least to a very basic level (e.g., name literacy, list literacy). Slaves are often given tasks involving literate skills; thus, 'literacy' itself is not necessarily a mark of the elite alone. The personnel in Athens' public archive in the classical period were public slaves; Pliny notoriously listened to books being read out to him by a slave (discussed previously). There were always skilled writers available for those who could not or did not want to read or write.

As for traders and merchants, more information is emerging as new documents come to light in the Greek world and even more so for the Roman Empire. The sophisticated networks of trade across the Mediterranean during the Roman Empire would be easier to track if merchants could take records, even if they were simple lists. In the earlier classical period (c. 500 BCE), some recently discovered lead letters (e.g., the Berezan letter) show merchants communicating with each other in what often look like crisis letters: these are not contracts but neither are they simply casual letters giving news as a way of keeping in touch. Emergency communications over long distances and written records for transactions between people of different languages and origins were both useful for the trader – but we cannot know from these chance finds, all rather dramatic, how common they actually were. In the Roman Empire, the extensive use of lists, letters, and written records in business and the managing of estates is far clearer and well attested. Indeed, treatises on agriculture and the managing of estates by Cato and Varro recommend the use of written instructions and accounts as advisable in a manner unthinkable or, at the very least, highly unlikely for classical Greece.[40]

In Egypt, however, there was an extensive bureaucratic apparatus, both Greek and Roman, dating to the period of Alexander's conquest and probably earlier. With the tentacles of this bureaucracy and its tax system extending into the smallest village, the accompanying basic skills of literacy were correspondingly useful; people were required to sign their names, receive receipts, and so forth to an extent which seems to be absent elsewhere. It is not surprising that a large number of Egypt's inhabitants could at least sign their name; such was the extent of written documents that Egypt had a special term, 'slow writers', to distinguish between those who could perhaps only sign their name (i.e., Cribbiore's 'signature literacy') and those who could write anything they needed or wished (and 'illiterates' might include those who were literate in Egyptian but not in Greek). Yet, analysis of particular collections of village documents (e.g., those of Tebtynis) shows that the majority of transactions involved men and women who could not sign their name; as Hanson pointed out, the illiterates were not excluded because they relied on a network of literate relatives or friends whom they could trust to write for them or to accompany them on occasions when signatures were needed.[41]

Similarly for the Roman army, an empire-wide machine which required organisation, pay, feeding and clothing on a vast scale, there were extensive lists and recordkeeping, some of which have been discovered. As for the army stationed on what must have seemed the 'back of beyond' at Hadrian's Wall, the recently discovered Vindolanda tablets reveal private letters, letters of recommendation, mundane lists and official administrative records.[42]

We may also consider the connotations of writing in less administrative contexts, the possibility that certain social practices might be dominated by less permanent scraps of writing than the formal inscriptions, and then ask how this presented the world symbolically to both literates and illiterates. We can tell from shrines all over the Roman world in the first century BCE to the third century AD (and, to a lesser extent, in the Greek cities of the fifth and fourth centuries BCE), that popular piety went along with a mass of tiny messages to the deity on stone in formal inscriptions on objects of dedication. In some examples in Italy, fascinatingly discussed by Beard, in the first two centuries AD there are small informal scraps of paper carrying prayers and requests.[43] So, even for people unable to read or write, their shrines and temples were associated in a more vague, more symbolic manner with the written word – writing here conveying an important message to the deity rather than a public enactment of the political system.

Conclusions: Literacy and Social Advancement

One wonders inevitably whether – or to what extent – literacy was seen as an important element in social advancement, or a first step up the ladder. Despite the development of a radical democracy, classical Athens never developed a democratic theory of education which emphasised the need for every male citizen to read and write. So many activities relied mainly on oral presentation, especially in Greece, that illiterates were not excluded to the extent they are today. Much depended on current cultural habits and, just as the mobile phone now facilitates communication across wide distances in Africa without necessarily requiring literacy, much more could be achieved without the written word in the ancient world than we might imagine. Yet, our impression from the ancient sources is that like any other skill, literacy was useful; officials or secretaries would have a greater facility with reading and writing official documents, and when documents became a part of state apparatus, those unable to read would become increasingly disadvantaged. Any Athenians ambitious in political life by the mid-fourth century BCE democracy would not only need to read but also to find their way around the laws and be confident in proposing and drafting decrees.

For social or political advancement, basic literacy was not the issue. For the highly educated elite of either the Greek states, the Hellenistic kingdoms or the Roman Empire, the mere ability to read simple messages was hardly adequate. The accepted form of elite literacy encompassed a host of other skills, such as the ability to extemporise in public speaking or (for the Greek aristocrat) the ability to compose poetry, as well as to read what literature was available and listen intelligently to what was heard on formal or private occasions. We may guess that the elite kept at least one step ahead in the educational attainments that maintained their cultural and political superiority. When Athens developed her radical direct democracy in the fifth century BCE, the ability to speak persuasively to mass audiences of thousands of citizens became even more important; those who could afford to learned the skills of persuasion from the professional teachers who emerged in that period. In the Roman Empire, any self-respecting member of the Roman senatorial class had to be familiar with Greek as well as Roman literature and to be conversant with the great classics of Greek poetry and prose – and young men were sent off to Athens accordingly. The educated elite of the Greek cities of Greece and the Near East now under Roman rule, however, also felt they had to be familiar with the classics of Greek literature as a badge of cultured civilisation. This took a rather surprising twist in that it seems to have been thought necessary to be able not only to read but also to speak this form of Greek, which was now a highly literary form belonging to the literature of five hundred years ago and no longer spoken in ordinary Greek life.[44] So, again, literate skills of a high and specialised order, of course, had to be complemented by a similar ability in speaking and declaiming and public oratory. The spoken word in a highly specialised form remained fundamental.

Notes

1 For an accessible discussion, which stresses the Egyptian origins, John Man, *Alpha Beta. How our alphabet shaped the Western world* (London: Headline, 2000).

2 J. Goody, & I. Watt, The consequences of literacy. In Goody (Ed.), *Literacy in traditional societies* (Cambridge [England]: Cambridge University Press, 1968), pp. 27–68 (article originally published 1962–1963).

3 See, for instance, Brian Street, *Literacy in theory and practice* (Cambridge [Cambridgeshire]: Cambridge University Press, 1984); for its specific application to the ancient world, R. Thomas, *Literacy and orality in Ancient Greece* (Cambridge [England]: Cambridge University Press, 1992), ch. 1–2; and Lloyd in the next footnote. Note, however, the more nuanced later books by Goody: *The domestication of the savage mind* (Cambridge [England]: Cambridge University Press, 1977); *The logic of writing and the organization of society* (Cambridge [Cambridgeshire]: Cambridge University Press, 1986); *The interface between the written and the oral* (Cambridge [Cambridgeshire]: Cambridge University Press, 1987).

4 G. E. R. Lloyd, *Magic, reason and experience: Studies in the origin and development of Greek science* (Cambridge [England]: Cambridge University Press, 1979), and *The revolutions of wisdom* (Berkeley: University of California Press, 1987). Note especially the full study of evidence for literacy by W. V. Harris, *Ancient literacy* (Cambridge, MA: Harvard University Press, 1989); J. H. Humphrey (Ed.), *Literacy in the Roman world*. Journal of Roman Archaeology, Supplementary Series No. 3. (Ann Arbor, MI: Dept. of Classical Studies, University of Michigan, 1991) for a sophisticated and nuanced series of discussions

of very different areas of the ancient world, with Harris's book as a starting point.

5 See, for instance, D. R. Olson & N. Torrance (Eds.), *The making of literate societies* (Malden, MA: Blackwell Publishers, 2001), with a wide range of case studies, and the bibliography there; and chapters in this *Handbook.*

6 See Coldstream, *Geometric Greece* (New York: St. Martin's Press, 1977), ch. 11 for a lucid introduction; and Thomas, *Literacy and orality in Ancient Greece* (1992), ch. 4, and references there.

7 Barry Powell, Why was the Greek alphabet invented? The epigraphic evidence. *Classical Antiquity,* 8 (1989), 321–350; *Homer and the origins of the Greek alphabet* (Cambridge [England]: Cambridge University Press, 1991).

8 See L. H. Jeffery, *The local scripts of Archaic Greece,* 2nd revised edition with supplement by Alan Johnston (Oxford: Clarendon, 1990), ch. 1 for a survey of written texts; R. Thomas, *Literacy and orality in Ancient Greece* (1992), ch. 4.

9 The main evidence is collected in Jeffery, *Local scripts of Archaic Greece* (see previous footnote).

10 See Mary Beard, Writing and religion: Ancient literacy and the function of the written word in Roman religion. In J. H. Humphrey (Ed.), *Literacy in the Roman world* (1991), esp. pp. 46–48.

11 Paul Friedländer, *Epigrammata: Greek inscriptions in verse from the beginnings to the Persian Wars.* (1948; reprinted Chicago: Ares, 1987), no. 140; I used his translation; possibly sixth century BCE or later.

12 There is a vast literature on Homer as oral poetry: a good place to start is Albert Lord, *Singer of tales* (Cambridge, MA: Harvard University Press, 1960); G. S. Kirk, *The songs of Homer* (Cambridge [Eng]: Cambridge University Press, 1962), esp. ch. 4 and 13 (the archaeology, however, is now outdated). See also R. Janko, The Homeric poems as oral dictated texts, CQ 48 (1998), 93–109.

13 See J. Herington, *Poetry into drama: Early tragedy and the Greek poetic tradition.* Sather classical lectures, Volume 49. (Berkeley/Los Angeles: University of California Press, 1985); B. Gentili, *Poetry and its public in Ancient Greece from Homer to the fifth century* (Baltimore: Johns Hopkins University Press, 1988; orig. Italian ed. 1985) on genre/occasion.

14 Robert W. Wallace, Speech, song and text, public and private: Evolutions in communications media and fora in fourth century Athens. In W. Eder (Ed.), *Die Athenische Demokratie im 4. Jahrhundert v. Chr.* (Stuttgart: Franz Steiner, 1995), 1999–1217.

15 See main discussion in B. Bravo, Une lettre sur plomb de Berezan: Colonisation et modes de contact dans le Pont, *Dialogues d'Histoire Ancienne,* 1 (1974), 111–187; J. Chadwick, The Berezan lead letter. *Proceedings of the Cambridge Philological Society,* 199 (1973), 35–37.

16 For this argument and further details, see R. Thomas (*Literacy and orality in Ancient Greece,* 1992), ch. 2, in M. Gagarin & D. Cohen (Eds.), *Cambridge companion to Greek law* (Cambridge: Cambridge University Press, 2005); see also M. Gagarin, *Early Greek law* (Berkeley, CA: University of California Press, 1986).

17 *Inschriften von Olympia,* No. 7.

18 See especially C. Hedrick, Democracy and the Athenian epigraphical habit. *Hesperia, 68* (1999), 387–439, for a comprehensive survey of the evidence of such an idea in the inscriptions themselves.

19 See, e.g., Fergus Millar, Epigraphy. In Michael Crawford (Ed.), *Sources for Ancient history* (Cambridge [Cambridgeshire]: Cambridge University Press, 1983), at p. 80 and generally; see also the excellent entries in S. Hornblower & A. Spawforth (Eds.), *The Oxford classical dictionary,* 3rd edition (Oxford: Oxford University Press, 1996), under Epigraphy, Greek (by H. Pleket), and Epigraphy, Latin (J. Reynolds), for survey; for survey of the value of inscriptions for historians, see J. Bodel (Ed.), Epigraphic evidence: Ancient history from inscriptions (London: Routledge, 2001).

20 G. Woolf, Literacy, in A. K. Bowman, P. Garnsey, & D. Rathbone (Eds.), *Cambridge Ancient History,* Volume XI: The High Empire, AD 70-192 (second edition). (Cambridge: Cambridge University Press, 2000), pp. 886–887.

21 I am thinking here particularly of the large and expensive inventories of temple dedications or of the long temple accounts, painstakingly inscribed on stone in classical Athens.

22 See J. Reynolds, *Aphrodisias and Rome.* Journal of Roman Studies Monographs, 1. (London: Society for the Promotion of Roman Studies, 1982); C. Roueché & N. de Chaisemartin, *Performers and partisans*

at Aphrodisias. Journal of Roman Studies Monographs, 6. (London: Society for the Promotion of Roman Studies, 1993).

23 There was a different relationship between inscriptions and archives in the Hellenistic and Roman periods as archives became more extensive and more important.

24 See R. Thomas, *Oral tradition and written record in classical Athens* Cambridge studies in oral and literate culture, 18. (Cambridge: Cambridge University Press, 1989), ch. 1; *Literacy and orality in Ancient Greece* (1992).

25 P. Rhodes has balanced discussion in two articles: Public documents in the Greek states. Archives and inscriptions, Parts I and II, in *Greece and Rome*, 48 (2001), pp. 33–44 and 136–153; J. P. Sickinger, *Public records and archives in classical Athens* (Chapel Hill, NC : University of North Carolina Press, 1999) argues for maximum sophistication at an early period (see review by R. Thomas, *Journal of Hellenic Studies*, 123 (2003), 230–231).

26 See Thomas, *Literacy and orality in Ancient Greece* (1992), p. 85, for full references.

27 See the wide-ranging survey and analysis by G. Woolf, ch. 30, in *Cambridge Ancient History*, Volume XI (2000).

28 Woolf, ch. 30, in *Cambridge Ancient History* XI (cited in a previous note), p. 885.

29 See A. V. Zadorojnyi, "Stabbed with large pens": Trajectories of literacy in Plutarch's *Lives*. In L. de Blois et al., *The statesman in Plutarch's works, Proc. of 6th International conference of the International Plutarch Society*, May 2002 (Leiden: Brill, 2005), pp.113–137; and his forthcoming piece, Lord of the flies: Literacy and tyranny in imperial biography' (forthcoming). Note also A. K. Bowman & G. Woolf, *Literacy and power in the ancient world* (Cambridge: Cambridge University Press, 1994).

30 Woolf, *Cambridge Ancient History* XI (2000), p. 891 ff., esp. 895–897.

31 See Woolf, op. cit. (2000), and N. Purcell, Literate games: Roman society and the game of alea, *Past and Present*, 147 (1995), 3–37.

32 See most recently H. Mouritsen, Freedmen and decurions: Epitaphs and social history in imperial Italy. *Journal of Roman Studies [JRS]*, 95 (2005), 38–63; also G. Woolf, Monumental writing and the expansion of Roman society in the early empire. *JRS*, 86 (1996), 22–39; R. Macmullen, The epigraphic habit in the Roman Empire, *American Journal of Philology*, 103 (1982), 233–246, showing that stone epitaphs increase with the number of Roman citizens; E. Meyer, Explaining the epigraphic habit in the Roman Empire: The evidence of epitaphs. *JRS*, 80 (1990), 74–96.

33 *Literacy* here meaning the ability to read or write anything easily; but see Harris, *Ancient literacy* (1989), pp. 3–5 for various definitions.

34 W. V. Harris, *Ancient literacy* (1989).

35 See Harris, *Ancient literacy* (1989), Conclusion, pp. 328–329.

36 R. Cribbiore, *Gymnastics of the mind: Greek education in Hellenistic and Roman Egypt* (Princeton, NJ: Princeton University Press, 2001).

37 For example, ch. 5: "Let no one wonder that I know accurately, for bankers are accustomed to write out memoranda of the money they lend, and for what, and the payments a borrower makes, in order that his receipts and his payments should be known for the accounts."

38 This argument is developed, with examples, in a forthcoming paper: R. Thomas, Writing, reading, public and private 'literacies': Functional literacy and democratic literacy in Greece. In *Ancient literacies: The culture of reading in Greece and Rome* (2009), W. A. Johnson and H. N. Parker (Eds.) (New York: Oxford University Press).

39 For this difficult inscription, see R. Thomas, *Literacy and orality in ancient Greece (1992)*, pp. 69–71, and references therein.

40 See Woolf, in *Cambridge Ancient History* XI (2000), esp. pp. 883 ff.

41 See the fascinating discussion by Ann Ellis Hanson: Ancient illiteracy, in J. H. Humphrey (Ed.), *Literacy in the Roman world* (1991); also Keith Hopkins: Conquest by book, in the same volume, with much on Egypt. R. Cribbiore, *Gymnastics of the mind: Greek education in Hellenistic and Roman Egypt* (2001) is also excellent.

42 Woolf, *Cambridge Ancient History XI* (2000), pp. 892–895 for brief survey; A. Bowman, The Roman imperial army: Letters and literacy on the northern frontier, in *Literacy and power in the ancient world*, A. K. Bowman & G. Woolf (Eds.) (1991).

43 Mary Beard, Writing and religion: Ancient literacy and the function of the written word in Roman religion. In J. H. Humphrey (Ed.), *Literacy in the Roman world* (1991), pp. 35–58.

44 See S. Swain, *Hellenism and empire: Language, classicism and power in the Greek world*, AD 50–250 (Oxford, 1996), on the cultivation of classical Attic Greek.

CHAPTER 20

Literacy from Late Antiquity to the Early Middle Ages, c. 300–800 AD

Nicholas Everett

A period which encompasses the fall of the Roman empire and an epoch commonly known as the "Dark Ages" might well be thought of as an inauspicious era in the history of literacy. Yet by the end of the eighth century Arabs called the inhabitants of Europe a "people of the book." No one had ever said this of the Romans, who snuffed out literary languages of conquered peoples, but as their empire waned and fell we witness the emergence of Gothic, Coptic, Syriac, Armenian, Old Irish, Old English, Old High German and Arabic, onto the page. Women became not only respectable subjects of literature but also authors who wrote biography, poetry and prose works. The technological shift from scroll to book, and from papyrus to parchment, profoundly changed how people read, wrote, preserved and decorated the written word. The cultivation of text in churches and monasteries, which combined in one institution the previous separated entities of school, scriptorium and library, fostered an inventiveness in fashioning scripts, layout of text and systems of reference that were the foundation for how we use books today – including our standard minuscule script which you are reading now. The "Dark Ages" lighten up even more when we consider that we have more surviving evidence from the early Middle Ages than we do for the Roman empire, and that this is a fraction of what once existed.

In the following survey, the emphasis, as the title suggests, is upon the exciting developments in literacy in the late antique world (usually defined c. 284–600 AD), and which of these evolved in early medieval Europe. Two themes predominate, each reflecting losses and gains for literacy in this period. Firstly, the collapse of the late Roman empire was disastrous for secular traditions of literacy such as the aristocratic cultivation of classical literature, the uses of literacy in large-scale government, and the system of grammatical education that underpinned these traditions – all of which seem to increase in scale and importance in the fourth and early fifth centuries, thus compounding their loss thereafter. Nonetheless, late antique achievements in law left an enduring legacy of legal literacy that fundamentally shaped the post-Roman world.

Secondly, the impact of Christianity, as it became the religion of the Roman state and the dominant religion of the Mediterranean and early medieval Europe, dramatically affected attitudes toward literacy and its uses, which can be seen in approaches to language, the format of texts, and the subject matter of literate discourse. We address these twin themes in that order, though they obviously overlap, and shall conclude by considering the emergence of new literate languages in this period, all of which reflect the increased importance of religion in the development of literacy.[1]

Literacy in the Late Roman Empire

A sobering assessment of literacy in the Roman world by Max Harris concluded that even in the imperial heydays of the Julio-Claudian or Antonine rulers, no more than 10 to 15 percent of the adult male population was "literate" in any meaningful sense of being able to read and write basic things (what has been termed "craftman's literacy"). When we include women, who were mostly illiterate, the percentage of population is halved.[2] We can easily quibble with these imprecise figures, but in any case, reductionist, numerical considerations of literacy do little to help us understand the role of literacy in society or the values attached to it. Looking toward end of our period, 32.7 percent of witnesses in eighth-century Italian charters wrote their subscriptions in their own hand. However, this is hardly a sound method for determining the general extent of literacy, reading ability, or the importance of documents in everyday life, evocatively attested in (presumed illiterate) slaves holding up their charters of manumission in court to prove their freedom.[3]

Nevertheless, highlighting the elitism of ancient Roman literacy is well taken: Romans never encouraged the extension of literacy to lower orders of society, never imagined large-scale systems of schooling or learning, never required a literate workforce (slaves could meet whatever demand there was), and did not have the technological means for any mass diffusion of texts. These last three points apply equally to the period under discussion here, as they could to pre-modern Europe on the whole.[4] Christianity, however, did encourage literacy, in a manner that shifted the sociological anchors of literacy (see below). In this respect, it is also worth highlighting that a pervasive approach to understanding literacy in the Roman world is the economic-determinist model in which literacy rates are seen as dependent upon the economic and political well-being of the empire. Certainly the high Roman empire was awash with casual, ephemeral uses of writing that reflect a sophisticated society with a rich material culture: labels on merchandise and army supplies shipped from one end of the empire to another; receipts for custom duties on a few amphora of wine; and copious amounts of graffiti scratched on the walls of Pompeii, recording gossip, political intrigue and visits to brothels.[5] Evidence such as Pompeian graffiti, however, raises issues of culture rather than simply economics. Historical studies of literacy have shown that rural, religious settings can produce the highest rates of literacy. The idea that literacy was valued any less in the economically less buoyant world of Late Antiquity is difficult to square with what we know about the role of literacy in late Roman government, the type of education it promoted, and the attitudes toward the written word that Christianity brought with it as it became a state-sponsored religion that eventually became dominant across the Mediterranean and European landscape.

Literary wordiness (even nerdiness) characterises the sources of the late empire, from the high-blown rhetoric of imperial legislation, through the popular genre of panegyric, to pagan and Christian authors alike, such as the orator Libanius of Antioch (c. 314–394), whose surviving corpus of writings amounts to nearly 1,800 items (letters, orations, rhetorical exercises, commentaries on rhetoric), or Augustine of Hippo (354–430), whose oeuvre runs to more than five million words.[6] Behind the achievements of such individuals lay a culture in which rhetoric was revered as a sign of power, privilege and worthiness to rule others. By the fourth century, the ancient Greek ideal of *paideia* (education, in the rounded sense of including lifestyle, diet and behaviour) had been reduced to an exclusively rhetorical education concentrating on the first three "liberal arts," the *trivium* of grammar, rhetoric, and dialectic, and effectively abandoning the *quadrivium* of geometry, arithmetic, music and astronomy. Education involved the line-by-line exposition of a set canon of texts (variable but mainly Virgil, Cicero, Sallust and Terrence in the Latin West; Homer, Euripides, Menander and Demosthenes in the Greek East), under the cane of the grammarian (for ages 11/12–15/16), then *rhetor* (ages 15/16–20) – a process which created a common identity for a ruling class of individuals from varied geographic backgrounds among the landowning classes of the empire.[7] The emphasis on rhetoric certainly encouraged verbose and intellectually vapid writing (late antique authors can be painful to read), but it also garnered contemporary justification from a continued association with legal studies, considered to be the crowning achievement of rhetorical training, and with Greco-Roman philosophical traditions, which prized competitive disputation, and which increasingly focussed on texts as it faced new competition from a religion of the book.[8] Indeed, Roman legal science reached its zenith in Late Antiquity, and as I suggest below, the field of law provided the most enduring legacy of secular literacy for the early Middle Ages. The intellectual combination of forensic persuasion and the nitpicking textual analysis of a grammatical education found a new and explosive outlet in Christianity, for the need to establish correct versions of scripture, and to control its interpretation, channelled rhetoric and philology into a vast amount of commentary and debate in writing about writing.[9] As discussed below, the switch in the format of writing from roll to codex played a suspicious role in these achievements.

While this expensive, grammatical education helped to cement the aristocratic identity of the elite landowning families of the late empire, underwriting it was a genuine need for literate personnel to staff the state bureaucracy. The reforms of the emperors Diocletian (284–305) and Constantine (306–337) not only expanded the size of the army (to c. 600,000 soldiers) but also the imperial bureaucracy (to perhaps two or three times larger than that of the early empire) to control tightly the distribution of resources across the Roman empire by imperial courts in the East (Constantinople from 330) and West (Milan, then Ravenna from 402). The system was also one of short tenures (e.g., one to three years in top jobs like proconsul or praetorian prefect), for which there were long waiting lists, thus maximising the number of people interested in gaining a position within the bureaucracy. Of course, those at the lower levels hardly needed to quote Virgil or Homer in their daily dispatches, and literary education certainly did not automatically confer aristocratic status: Libanius scoffed that imperial notaries were upstarts doing the work for slaves, but his complaints reveal how education and service enabled upward mobility (a few notaries even became emperors).[10] The greatest need for governmental literacy, however, was the need to facilitate the Roman fiscal system, the disintegration of which, in the course of the territorial losses to barbarian rulers during the fifth century, was arguably the biggest blow of all to the survival of secular uses of writing into the early Middle Ages. For paperwork (or papyrus-work) facilitated the chain of command: praetorian prefects calculated the required levels of taxation needed and communicated these to the provincial governors, who then announced them with formal proclamation (often by posting public notices) to cities, whose councillors were responsible for their collection. If these councillors were not armed with official documents naming the amounts required, local landowners, who also kept records, could, and did, refuse to pay.[11] We see this system, and the literate traditions it required, continuing into the sixth and seventh century in Egypt.[12] But in the West, the territorial losses of the fifth century caused its breakdown, although the Visigoths in Spain, the Merovingians in Gaul, and the Ostrogoths in Italy all inherited the land tax and with it some of the Roman infrastructure of offices and personnel that required literate skills for administration. In these new localised, territorial units, barbarian armies were sustained by landowning, and their more rudimentary organisation no longer required a bureaucratic chain of civilian administration to secure its supplies and subsistence. Military leaders still required literate personnel for diplomatic correspondence (even Attila the Hun had secretaries), and barbarian governments continued to rely on literate means for the administration of justice. However, the militarisation of the aristocracy that took place in this period, among Romans and barbarians, meant that literary education was no longer a marker of elite identity, and no longer offered any secure rewards: military capability and service became the key to wealth and status, both East and West.[13] Many aristocrats who became churchmen continued to argue for the worth of grammatical education for elucidating the meaning of scriptures, but by the end of the sixth century, as more ascetic religious sensibilities became dominant, a snowballing Christian polemic against rhetoric wiped out traditions of classical literature in a now radically desecularised world.[14]

The collapse of the Roman empire in the West did not, however, mean the end of record-keeping for fiscal purposes: rents, tolls and fees were still collected, of course, but not on the scale managed by the late Roman state, across vast distances in a centralised system. A group of documents from a remote part of seventh-century Visigothic Spain written in many different hands on slate – a local, cheap alternative to wax tablets – shows the use of writing for estate micro-management: lists of names next to due rents of grain, sheep, even a "notice of cheeses" recording who owed one cheese round, were preserved along with instructions to stewards, the records of court cases before judges (and directly echoing the Visigothic law code), writing exercises, curses and invocations to saints, and so on.[15] We expect to find such evidence for the Roman period, but not for the early Middle Ages, not in remote rural areas, and not on slate: its presence, however, is testimony to the continuity of functional literacy required to manage estates. For documents and accounts were part of the standard, proprietorial culture of landowning, as was a knowledge of local property law and an acquaintance with documentary forms of legal proof, to which we now turn.

Roman legal science reached its greatest heights in Late Antiquity, witnessed in the enormous efforts behind the systematic compilations of Roman law, first under Diocletian (*Codex Gregorianus* 291, *Codex Hermogenianus*, 293–295, both now lost), then under Theodosius II (*Codex Theodosianus*, 438) and finally, Justinian's *Corpus Iuris Civilis* (529–534, comprising the *Codex Justinianus*, the *Digest*, and the *Institutes*). The prime motivator behind this outpouring of legal erudition was the change of the structure of the state itself: the legislative functions of the senate, and of civilian offices like that of praetorian prefect, were largely transferred to imperial courts along with the fiscal mechanisms of state, so that emperors, and their imperial proclamations, were considered the source of Roman law.[16] Barbarian law codes drew heavily from the Theodosian Code, and more often from the same sources of provincial law behind it; and here we find the greatest legacy of Roman law for literacy, namely, the promotion of writing as the highest form of proof in property law. The imperial legislation in these law codes often reflects a dialogue between the ideals of classical, Roman law and the diverse legal practices introduced into the empire after the extension of Roman citizenship to all of its inhabitants in 212 under Caracalla. This process has been labelled by legal historians (with some distaste) as the "vulgarisation" of Roman law, but "popularisation" is a better term, particularly for understanding the role of writing. For what we witness is the increased importance of documents at the expense of classical formalities and ceremonial rituals wherein oral declarations were of supreme importance. This is particularly true of sales, but we also see it in such traditional practices as wills. For example, Constantine declared (in 320/6) that:

> ... *in the execution of last wills, the requirement of formal speech is hereby removed, and those who desire to dispose of their own property can write their wills upon any kind of material whatsoever, and are freely permitted to use any words which they may desire .... and it makes no difference whatever what grammatical forms of the verbs indicate in his will, or what way of speaking pours out.*[17]

The same sense of pressure-from-below for the increasing use of documents is suggested by Emperor Leo's somewhat extravagant decree (in 472) that documents recording any transaction (e.g., sales, loans, and private agreements) performed "secretly" – that is, among friends – were to be considered as "publicly written" and have the full force of public documents in court, whether or not they had been subscribed or witnessed. Despite Justinian's attempts to turn back the clock and reintroduce classical concepts and formalities, writing had become overwhelmingly the source of validity and authority for most transactions.[18]

The point emphasised here is that late Roman law increasingly tended to, and encouraged, private documentation, in terms of both production and preservation, and this legacy continued to be developed in the early Middle Ages. It has often been suggested that this "privatised" world of early medieval documentation emerged from the collapse of late Roman "public" institutions such as the urban notariate or the city archives (*gesta municipalia*). However, this (anachronistically) overestimates the scope and extent of such institutions: use of *gesta municipalia* seems to have been introduced in the fifth century mainly to record the transactions of the fairly wealthy, for state fiscal purposes. One could have employed a *notarius* or *tabellio*, but in late Roman law only the document and its concordance with the law mattered, not the writer (that was a later medieval development).[19] The abundant Egyptian evidence underlines the point: the impressive collections of archives found in Oxyrhynchus and Aphrodito, where the late Roman state still functioned into the seventh century, are from private individuals who held public office but maintained their own records. This was a fundamental aspect of the Roman legal heritage adopted by the post-Roman kingdoms in the West, and its importance for explaining the continued use of literate, legal traditions for property law should not be overlooked. The importance of documents in, for example, Visigothic law, the Merovingian formularies, and Lombard law, derived from the same desire to validate and prove claims to property, and we are only now beginning to understand just how fundamental documentation was in the post-Roman period, and how much has been lost in the Latin West.[20] The switch from papyrus to parchment for documents toward the end of the seventh century in Gaul, Italy and Spain thereafter permitted greater survival rates, although documents concerning the laity usually only survive from their preservation in ecclesiastical archives when the church later acquired the property they concern. In some cases, churches acted as local centres for the production and preservation of lay documents, precisely because they were the only institutional entity that could guarantee continuity across generations. Given that many churches and monasteries were family-owned and -operated, or "proprietary" churches, ecclesiastical–lay conceptual divisions need to be reconsidered.[21]

Before turning to the subject of Christianity's effect on literacy, we should note three aspects of its relevance to law. Firstly, the late antique church borrowed, refined and developed late Roman techniques of legal disputation and documentation for its own purposes, most notably for church councils, where texts, creeds and written statements were painstakingly examined to refute heresy, establish orthodoxy, discipline clergy and promulgate canon law.[22] Secondly, Constantine's grant of authority to bishops to judge private lawsuits, particularly criminal cases, established the need for churches to acquire a knowledge of current secular law, a tradition which we see continuing into the barbarian kingdoms, while a parallel tradition often associated canon law with "Roman" law.[23] Thirdly, when Justinian legislated (in the 530s) that all Roman courtrooms were to display a copy of the Gospels, and that litigants and legal officials alike were to swear an oath of their Christian faith while touching the Gospels before proceedings began, he radically Christianised the operation of Roman law.[24] However, this was also a recognition of common practice which we see continuing into the early Middle Ages, and one which had a double-entendre for legal literacy – on the one hand, oaths upon Gospels enriched the association of authority and truth with writing, yet on the other hand, oaths could be used to bypass or supersede the probative value of writing as evidence. The tension between oral testimony on oaths and the force of documents is one of the major characteristics of post-Roman legislation and legal procedure in the West.[25]

Christianity and Literacy: Belief and Practice

Christianity dramatically affected literacy because of its intensely personal message that one's very salvation depended upon a knowledge of scriptures. All Christians, not simply an aristocratic elite, were encouraged to learn the Bible.[26] Yet there was a paradox embedded within this injunction to know scripture, for Christ also chose uneducated, illiterate men as his disciples, and Christian tradition encouraged the apophatic ideal of the apostles as pure of heart and unsullied by false creeds enshrined in written doctrine or philosophic rationalism. Illiteracy was no bar to holiness: the proto-monk Anthony of Egypt (251–356), for example, was supposedly illiterate, and other illiterate holy heroes were celebrated in Christian literature. However, their beliefs were defined by, and their spirituality was measured against, a canon of texts that they, and all Christians, were meant to know, through others if needed, most commonly the clergy, or friends. One bishop in sixth-century Gaul recommended hiring someone to read the Bible at home if everyone there was illiterate.[27]

The ideals of churchmen aside, that Christianity encouraged the extension of literacy to a broader sector of the population than previously is evident in its attitude toward written language, and its effects on the page. The ideal of *sermo humilis*, simple (humble) speech – the language in which Christ spoke the truth to his uneducated disciples, the language of scripture – opened up the possibilities of acquiring literate skills to the considerable range of people automatically excluded from the grammarian's classroom, notably women, but also the poorer classes, as the Psalter replaced Virgil or Homer as the elementary school text.[28] The emphasis on simple speech developed into reflexive Christian polemic against rhetoric that effectively cut at the roots of late antique education. We witness this struggle first-hand in the well-documented careers of educated Christians like Jerome, whose love of Latin literature caused nightmares in which God accused him of being "not a Christian, but a Ciceronian"; and Augustine, a former hotshot professor of rhetoric, whose disillusionment with his own trade and grammatical education resulted in the first developed theory of reading in the West.[29] By the end of the sixth century, literate discourse was restricted to an exclusively scriptural framework. A seventh-century school text, imitating the dialogue format common in introductory grammars, begins with the teacher asking the student about the individual letters of the alphabet, "from which all branches of scripture spring" (thus playing on the word *scriptura* as "writing"), proceeds to discussing the individual books of the Bible, then finishes by addressing apparent contradictions in scripture as a means of introducing the principles of allegorical reading.[30] Literacy here has become synonymous with knowledge of the Bible.

Whereas ancient practice of writing adhered to a continuous stream of words with little or no punctuation and no word-spacing (*scriptio continua*), early Christians introduced helpful aids to break up the text into intelligible units, such as word-spacing (groups of words), breathing marks, *diaeresis* (a double dot to separate initial vowels from the preceding word), punctuation for sense-units (phrases, clauses, sentences) and paragraph or section divisions, including pushing the first letter of a new section into the left margin (*ekthesis*). Jerome set out a popular method for punctuating the Bible by phrases (*cola et commata*) for those who had not "learned to read in the schools of secular learning."[31] A simple rule of thumb for these developments is that the further we move away from the ancient Mediterranean in time and space, the more punctuation, word-separation and similar reading aids can be found – a pattern that mirrors the spread of Christianity as much as familiarity with the spoken forms of Latin. By the seventh and eighth centuries, Anglo-Saxon and Celtic scribes, for whom Latin was an entirely foreign, visually perceived "dead" language, invented even more ways to break up the text on the page. These included (individual) word-spacing and increased punctuation, and many techniques that one finds in a newspaper today – enlarged initial letters or capitals, titles and subtitles using different types of script from the main text, paragraphing, segmenting typography and so on – an ensemble of reading aids which one scholar has dubbed a "grammar of legibility".[32]

The term "legibility" invites us to consider how changes in script in this period relate to literacy, for the development of minuscule scripts nearly everywhere in the eighth century can easily be viewed in anachronistic terms. The switch to parchment for books (from the third century onwards) encouraged the use of more rounded letter forms, rather than angular, multiple-stroke letters better suited for the rough surface of papyrus. Dubbed "uncial" script by modern palaeographers, this script became the book-hand of the early Middle Ages, which by the seventh and eighth centuries began to morph (often via "half-uncial" and more cursive scripts) into the more economic minuscule script that was the forerunner of Caroline minuscule, the basis of our script today. The inherited nomenclature of palaeography to describe the varieties of script in ethnic terms (Visigothic, Merovingian, Irish, Anglo-Saxon, etc.) can encourage viewing them as a microcosm of the collapse of the empire, as though calligraphic unity of the ancient world was shattered along with Rome's armies.[33] But ancient scripts were just as diverse, and diversity is best understood as a sign of vitality: local elaborations of uncial scripts in parts of Western Europe should best be seen as a maturation of literate traditions in those areas, as scribes and scriptoria developed their own styles to suit their needs. Moreover, Christian written culture was trans-territorial. The Italian monastery of Bobbio, founded c. 613 by the charismatic Irish missionary Columbanus (543–615), is a case in point: there we find scripts betraying Irish, Anglo-Saxon, Merovingian and Italian characteristics, reflecting the polyethnic, multicultural membership of its monks.[34] The diversity of scripts required, and encouraged, familiarity with different kinds of letter forms and scribal traditions, and this should be seen as a cultivation of literacy, not a sign of its decline. Psychological studies of literacy have shown that regularity of script (both letter-forms and layout), and the familiarity of the script to the reader, are crucial factors in facilitating the visual perception of the written word, rather than any particular letter-forms or layout of script. In other words, there is nothing intrinsic about minuscule forms that facilitate or promote literacy, witness the development of Gothic script (and its varieties) soon after minuscule's medieval heyday of the ninth and tenth centuries. The common move towards minuscule script throughout the eighth century must, in part, reflect a loss of expertise in reading and writing cursive scripts, which – with their calligraphic flourishes, suprascript letters, high number of abbreviations and contractions of words, lack of word-separation and minimal punctuation – reflect a higher degree of familiarity with the written word.[35]

Christians took up the codex almost exclusively as their medium for writing by the second century, while secular and pagan works continued to use rolls until the end of the fourth century. The reasons for this are much debated, but clearly the codex offered advantages: it held greater capacity, and was therefore cheaper; it facilitated non-linear access to the text for reference and selective reading purposes; it could be pulled apart and reconstituted with texts added or omitted.[36] By the fourth century, Christians began to exploit the potentials of the new format in a manner that suggests new approaches to reading. Eusebius of Caesarea's canon tables, for instance, were a purely scholarly device intended for the studious Christian to find similar passages among the four Gospels, which he had divided into numbered sections using red ink. The innovation was inspired by his earlier efforts to systematise the chronology of the events in the Old Testament with Greco-Roman history in his *Chronicle*, for which he used a tabular format recording different events from diverse sources and set side-by-side in columns that enabled quick reference and comparison. He was probably inspired by his hero, Origen (185–254), the early Christian scholar whose *Hexapla* used parallel columns to set out the different versions (Hebrew and Greek) of the Old Testament to determine the correct reading.[37] Other devices were soon invented to facilitate reference. Jerome, who borrowed Eusebius' ideas of different coloured inks in his own Latin version of the *Chronicle*, is one of the first to mention numbered chapter headings, and he insults a previous commentator's work as merely an *index capitulorum* – that is, a table of contents. His prolific contemporary, Augustine, never used such devices for his own works, but a century later at Naples, the monk Eugippius (fl. 500–533) carefully divided the great doctor's main works into chapters, provided chapter headings and tables of contents, and in the process also compiled an immensely popular collection of excerpts from Augustine's oeuvre, creating the first "essential Augustine."[38]

Cassiodorus (c. 485–585), whose career and corpus of works traces the demise of the secular, civilian traditions of literature in Italy across the sixth century, applied Eugippius' techniques to the works produced at his own monastery in Vivarium. He went even further in exploiting the visual component of reading that was fostered by the cloistered, meditative environment of the monastery, where silent reading was encouraged.[39] In the preface to his *Institutions*,[40] a bibliographic guide to his library at Vivarium, Cassiodorus lamented his and Pope Agapetus' failure to establish a school of Christian studies in Rome because of the Gothic wars, and showed his monks another way:

> ... *I have prepared for you, with God's aid, these introductory books in place of a teacher* (ad vicem magistri).... *[For] you make a serious teacher angry if you question him often, but however often you want to return to these books you will not be rebuked with any severity... So... [now] you have teachers of a former age always available and prepared to teach you not so much as by their speech as through your eyes.*

The *Institutions* itself included thirty-seven diagrams, setting out divisions of scripture, rhetorical tropes, Aristotle's categories, geometrical figures, the nine different types of syllogism, mathematical schema, and so on. This was nothing short of a revolution in the form of the book, now designed to be read silently, in private study, with visual aids to guide the reader on difficult subjects, without having to ask an angry teacher. Cassiodorus also set out a reference system of marginal notes in red ink to be placed in patristic works in order to mark the particular Biblical book being discussed (OCT for Octateuch, REG for kings, PROP for prophets, etc.). By the early eighth century, the venerable Bede (672–735) had invented source-marks, using a system wherein the first two letters of the author

(AV = Augustine, GR = Gregory, etc.) were separated and placed in the margin to signify the beginning and end of a quotation, effectively the forerunner of our quotation marks.[41] Another eloquent witness to the development of *mise-en-page* potential beyond the fringes of the Roman world is a manuscript (now fragmentary) from Ireland dating from the end of our period which uses three columns, the middle containing the text of Ezechiel, the two side-columns containing commentary on Ezechiel in much smaller, expert Irish minuscule, thus anticipating by centuries the format of later medieval scholastic manuscripts.[42]

The cultivation of literacy evident in these innovations to textual traditions is all the more remarkable when we consider the substantial cost of producing books in this period. A humble manuscript of approximately 90 folios (i.e., 180 pages, c. 182 × 130mm each) may require at least six animal skins (sheep or goat were the most popular). More ambitious or deluxe books required much more slaughter: the famous *Codex Amiatinus*, written in Northumbria in the early eighth century and the earliest surviving manuscript to include the entire contents of the Old and New Testaments, required the skins of 515 calves to make up its 1,030 folios.[43] The biggest early medieval libraries, such as that of Eusebius at Caesarea, or Isidore of Seville, are reckoned to have contained 400 to 500 books, figures comparable to the ninth-century catalogues of Carolingian monasteries (approximately 300 to 600 books)[44] that enjoyed much greater landed wealth. By the ninth century, the church north of the Alps owned around a third of arable land available, and there were more than 650 monasteries, some housing more than 600 monks. These economic factors help explain the explosion in the production and preservation of manuscripts in the Carolingian Renaissance: some 7,000 manuscripts survive from the ninth century alone, compared to 2,000 or so manuscripts and fragments that survive from our period.[45] Of course, these figures pale beside those estimated for the "big" libraries of antiquity, such as that of Alexandria (80,000 books[?]), or Trajan's Ulpian library in Rome (5,000 books), or even the largest libraries of later medieval Europe such as Clairvaux or the papal library at Avignon (2,000 books). However, in terms of numbers of libraries and their geographical spread, from remote corners of Mesopotamia to the even more remote Northern Irish coast, we are witnessing a world in which books became relatively commonplace in areas with little or no previous experience of them.

Women

One profound shift in the social location of literacy encouraged by Christianity was the inclusion of women as authors or subjects of literature as they rejected their traditional and highly restrictive social roles of reproduction and domestic life in both Roman and barbarian society. One of our earliest martyr texts was written by a young mother, Perpetua (d. 203), who has left us a moving, disturbing account of her own suffering and the visions which sustained her before being torn apart by wild animals in the amphitheatre at Carthage.[46] Pious women could now rival men as models of behaviour and belief to be emulated, and hence became subjects of biography. One example is Macrina (d. 389), whose own *Life* was composed by her brother, Gregory of Nyssa (c. 335–394), who also composed a treatise in dialogue form *(On the Soul and Resurrection*), directly modelled on Plato's *Phaedro*, and purporting to be a conversation with Macrina while she was dying. The *Life of Melania the Younger* (written c. 450) recalls how, after her daily readings of scripture (she tried to read the entire Old and New Testaments three or four times a year), Melania then turned to read sermons and hagiography, before copying out the texts she assiduously collected. Melania's grandmother of the same name was included by the monastic historian Palladius (d. 430) among his chapters on "the virile women to whom God granted struggles equal to those of men." The feisty independence of these literate, ascetic women is also witnessed in the pilgrim Egeria, who wrote a long letter in simple yet colourful Latin to her "sisters" describing her visit to the Holy Land (c. 381–384), giving details about church services in Jerusalem.[47] Among the first Christian poems in Latin is the *Cento* of Proba (c. 320–370), which consisted entirely of phrases taken from the poetry of Virgil to narrate Biblical stories and scenes and which served in the West as a school text for centuries to come. A classy copy of the *Cento* was commissioned by Theodosius II, whose wife, the empress Eudocia, also wrote poetical paraphrases in Greek hexameters of the Octoteuch, the martyrdoms of Cyprian and Justina, a panegyric on her husband's defeat of the Persians and, in imitation of Proba, a Homeric *cento* on the life of Christ.[48]

The tradition of women writers continued into the early Middle Ages. Radegund, a sixth-century Frankish queen who become a nun, composed verse and wrote epistles to neighbouring clergy, demonstrating her knowledge of patristic literature. The poet Venantius Fortunatus, who simply adored her, dedicated poems to her and composed her biography, which was continued by her disciple, Baudonivia, a nun from Radegund's convent at Poitiers.[49] The sixth-century *Life of Febronia* was originally composed in Syriac by Febronia's companion nun, Thomaïs, and another work in Greek, the *Life of Matrona of Perge*, may also have been written by a woman. Around 630, the nun Sergia wrote an account of the translation of relics of her convent's founder, the fourth-century holy woman Olympias.[50] Looking to the West, our surviving letter collections from Merovingian Gaul and Lombard Italy include letters sent to women of high status. A little later, the correspondence of the Anglo-Saxon Boniface (672–754) records no less than fourteen women who wrote to, or received letters from, this "apostle of the Germans," many of which refer to the sending and receiving of books, and some include examples of verse by women that attest to the considerable standard of education available in Anglo-Saxon England for both sexes. It is likely that women wrote some of the key narrative sources for Frankish history, and toward the end of our period the duchess of Lombard Benevento, Adelperga commissioned Paul the Deacon to compose not only a brief history of the Romans but also a history of her own people.[51] Such evidence dwarfs that from the ancient world for women's literacy.

Old Languages, New Scripts

Everywhere we look in this period, conversion to Christianity encouraged the redaction of vernacular languages into writing, with the extraordinary exception of Continental Europe. The depth of Romanisation in those areas that are today known as "Romance-speaking" countries (i.e., Italy, France, Spain, and Portugal) is evidenced in the astonishing retention of Latin as the language of law, religion and government, long after the Roman empire had disappeared. Thanks to the work of historical linguists, we now have a much better picture of how Latin could be pronounced in a variety of different ways (a good parallel is modern English as a *lingua franca*, despite its diversity of accent and idiom from, say, Scotland to Texas) and how a situation of diglossia permitted Latin's comprehensibility at a range of different levels, so that the gulfs between the daily, spoken proto-Romance languages and the written traditions of Latin were easily bridged. However, there is still debate as to how much internal, structural metamorphoses of vulgar Latin had weakened its coherence in eighth-century Francia, and how much the Carolingian reforms, which advocated a return to the classical conventions of spelling and one-letter-per-sound for pronunciation, were responsible for cutting off Latin from the Romance-speaking populace to become a literary language restricted to the clergy.[52]

East of the Rhine, Latin retained its prestige as the language of power, be it secular or religious, and it is only toward the end of our period that the first attempts to write Old High German were made, initially as glosses to religious and legal texts, then as translations of prayers, blessings, the Lord's Prayer, baptismal services, and so on. By the ninth century such ambitions were extended to paraphrase parts of the Gospels.[53] Germanic-speakers had used runes for religious and commemorative purposes as early as the fourth century, but it took the presence of Anglo-Saxon missionaries on the Continent to convert Germanic phonemes to the Roman alphabet, for they had generations of experience. Following fast upon the arrival of missionaries sent by Pope Gregory I, converted Anglo-Saxon kings began to draw up law codes on the late Roman model but in their own Germanic dialect, and soon after Old English was being used to translate Latin religious texts. Bede translated the Creed and the Lord's Prayer into Old English, and at the time of his death he was working on translations of the Gospel of St. John and Isidore of Seville's *De natura rerum*. Yet Bede also comments that in his day there were five languages in Britain – Latin, British, [Old] English, Irish and Pictish – and that there were still students around from Bishop Theodore of Tarsus' school at Canterbury who were "as proficient in Latin and Greek as their native tongue." The linguistic diversity of Britain, and the interplay of several different literate languages, facilitated a tremendous degree of experimentation, whether in use of runic inscriptions alongside Latin and scenes of the Bible on the Ruthwell Cross, the use of Old English for boundary clauses in Latin charters, or the redaction of pre-Christian tales like *Beowulf* by clerics sneaking in Old Testament motifs.[54]

In Ireland, Christianity seems to have stirred up an already existing native literacy evidenced in the use of ogam script, which was designed from the Roman alphabet to be cut into stone and used for funerary purposes or territorial markers in "primitive Irish" language (or "proto-Q Celtic") during the fifth century. In the sixth century, ogam inscriptions switched to Old Irish, at the same time the latter also began to be redacted in the Roman alphabet to record poems, mythological tales, and most remarkably, a native tradition of law in the form of legal treatises by a powerful, well-organised and highly trained caste of scholar-poets *(filid)*. Yet the use of documents and charters, which in England and Wales were introduced by the Romans and were subsequently and enthusiastically developed by the church and secular rulers, is not attested until the eleventh century, for Irish property law was reluctant to recognise written evidence as a claim to title. The recalcitrance of this secular, native tradition of literacy is all the more remarkable when we consider the extent to which Christians in Ireland embraced Latin as a sacred language for religious worship and the astounding levels of Latinity achieved only a century after the preaching of Palladius (fl. 431–460s) and Patrick (450s).[55]

For the first two and a half centuries AD, Egyptians were forced to rely on Greek (and to a lesser extent, Latin) as their literary language, as limited use of demotic script to write their own native language faded out almost entirely with the cults and temples that were extinguished under Roman rule. The renewal of native literacy came with the need to translate the Bible, and by the middle of the third century Coptic was created by adding six letters from demotic to a modified Greek alphabet, and borrowing a third of its vocabulary from Greek. A "cultural event of major proportions,"[56] the new means of expression was enthusiastically taken up by clergy and the emerging monastic communities throughout Egypt. It found its apogee in the charismatic Shenoute (348–466), abbot of the White Monastery, whose mastery of Greek rhetoric was channelled into the vernacular and whose works set the literary standard for Coptic. Greek was still required for administration by bilingual functionaries and government personnel up to and beyond the Arab conquest of Egypt. The lawyer and aspiring poet, Dioscorus of Aphrodito (d. 585), could write legal contracts in Coptic then flip the papyrus over and practice encomiastic poetry in Greek on the reverse side. Among his archive is a Greek-Coptic glossary.[57] The fairly recent discovery of 332 Coptic school texts shows that up into the seventh century, phrases from the works of Menander and lists of characters from the *Iliad* were still used to facilitate the linguistic exchange between Greek and Coptic vocabulary.[58]

The Jews and Christians of Edessa had begun to use their particular dialect of Aramaic, now known as Syriac, to translate the Old Testament or *Peshitta* (meaning "common" or "simple," the equivalent to the Latin "Vulgate") as early as the second century, and translations of the four Gospels in a harmonised version (*Diatesseron*) appeared soon after. The new literary language found is first real exponent in the "Aramean philosopher" Bardaisan (154–222), a gnostic Christian of speculative mind who mixed current trends of Greek philosophy with knowledge of Babylonian astrology and science, and who began a distinctive Syriac tradition of using verse as a medium for theology in the stanzaic hymns known as *madrasha*. The prolific Ephrem the Syrian (306–373) used these techniques to create a corpus of liturgical and theological works more in line with orthodox Christian thought.[59] By the fifth century, Syriac, which Jerome called "barbarous gibberish," had become the literary language of Aramaic-speaking Christians within the Roman and Persian empires. The suppression of the Christian school at Edessa by the Emperor Zeno in 489 pushed its scholars and students into the Persian empire to establish their school at Nisibis, where it soon became famous, and where translations of Aristotle and Galen into Syriac complemented scriptural exegesis and the composition of hymns to create a literary culture that facilitated the spread of Nestorian Christianity as far east as China.[60]

Coptic and Syriac could both draw upon cultures in which literacy stretched back millennia, but the examples of Armenian and Gothic demonstrate how Christianity facilitated the creation of literary languages within a few years. The independent kingdom of Armenia was nominally Christian prior to Constantine's conversion, but its conquest and division between the Roman and Persian empires in 387 seems to have spurred the creation of a common literary language by the monk Mesrop Mashtots (c. 360–440). His knowledge of Greek, Syriac and Persian allowed him to chart a new alphabet of thirty-six letters for the new language, although only after several false starts and much collaboration with clerics from Edessa and nearby Samasota, where a Hellenic scribe helped to devise the new letter-forms. The new Bible that resulted was endorsed so enthusiastically by the Armenian king that, according to Mesrop's biographer: "... suddenly, in an instant, Moses, the law–giver, along with the order of the prophets, energetic Paul with the entire phalanx of the apostles, along with Christ's world-sustaining Gospel, became Armenian-speaking."[61]

Whereas the creation of Armenian literate language helped cement the connection between Christianity and independent Armenian identity, the example of Gothic presents a different and somewhat tragic picture. In what appears to have been the first imperially sanctioned missionary enterprise, the priest Ulfilas (fl. 340–360s) devised an alphabet based mostly on Greek characters but with borrowings from Latin and runes to translate the Bible for the Goths living in Moesia (modern north Bulgaria). The vocabulary and syntax of the Gothic Bible was modelled directly on a transliteration of Greek, hence it is difficult to determine its relationship to spoken Gothic, for which we have no other testimony, except for a few pieces of Biblical commentary (known as *skeireins*) and some formulaic subscriptions by Gothic clergy on papyrus documents from mid-sixth-century Ravenna. In fact, most of our evidence for Gothic, including the sumptuous Gothic Bible (known as the *Codex Argenteus)* written in gold and silver on purple-died vellum parchment, and bilingual Latin-Gothic Bibles, dates from fifth- and sixth-century Italy. Hence, Arian clergy in Italy actively promoted the use of Gothic, perhaps to distinguish and defend themselves from Catholic and Roman sectors of the population, on the eve of the Ostrogoths' utter disappearance from history with the emperor Justinian's reconquest of Italy.

With them went Gothic also: the Visigoths in Spain, who mastered Latin learning and law, showed no interest in their ancestral tongue.[62]

But Christianity was hardly alone in this respect: we conclude with two non-Christian examples that further demonstrate how late antique religious culture promoted literacy. The increasing religious intolerance of the Roman state aimed at Jews in particular, and in 425 the suppression of the patriarchate of Jerusalem by Theodosius II caused work on the Talmud of the Land of Israel (or Jerusalem Talmud) to cease. Under the more tolerant Persian empire, the traditions were continued in the Talmud of Babylon, completed in 499 with more than half the text in the local dialect of Babylonian Jews.[63]

But it is the case of Arabic that best highlights the connection among late antique religious culture, literacy and shifts in the political landscape as the empires of Rome and Persia crumbled. Arabic, an already literate Semitic language based on the Aramaic alphabet (via Nabataean script) and used for poetry and inscriptions, was transformed by Mohammad's teaching as the very word of God in the surahs that were gathered into the Qur'an, a word whose root, *qr'*, means to "read out" or "cry aloud" (as with Syriac *qeryana*, "scriptural/liturgical reading"), underlining the oral nature of its reading.[64] Yet the Qur'an was permeated with references to writing that point to the successive promotion of literacy as a fundamental aspect of Islamic culture and society. Mohammad's first revelation was an order to "Recite/read (iqra')," from a God who "taught by the pen" what humans do not know (Q. 96:1–5). His second revelation (entitled "The Pen"), began with an oath to "swear by the pen" (Q. 68). God writes down in a register everything that humans do (Q. 36:12, 54:52–53) or even think (Q. 4:81, as do angels, Q. 10:21, 43:80). However, writing was not only advocated for religious concerns. One surah invites comparison with the practical, common-sense injunctions of late Roman law concerning documents mentioned above:

> ... *When you contract a debt for a fixed period, write it down. Let a scribe (writer) write it down in justice between you. Let not the scribe refuse to write as Allâh has taught him, so let him write. And get two witnesses.... You should not become weary to write it (your contract), whether it be small or big, for its fixed term, that is more just with Allâh, more solid as evidence, and more convenient to prevent doubts among yourselves.*[65]

The cultivation of reading and writing suggested by the Qur'an was quickly followed in practice. Elementary schools (the *kuttab* or *maktab*) were established in the Umayyad period (661–750), where children of six to seven years old learned the rudiments of literacy by studying verses from the Qur'an, a small number of hadiths and some basic principles of Islamic law (*fiqh*). Higher instruction in legal and religious doctrine at the local mosque "college" are attested from the eighth century.[66] Like written Latin in the West, the Qur'an provided the model for elevated, "classical Arabic" that also served, by the beginning of the eighth century, as a *lingua franca* for administration and trade, whereas spoken varieties differed considerably from region to region. The emphasis upon the language of the Qur'an as directly revealed by God to Mohammad, combined with Islam's prohibition of figurative art, resulted in the elevation of calligraphy as the highest of art forms, and a good command of calligraphy was deemed necessary for a position in the bureaucracy of the Abassid court in Baghdad (from 750 onwards).[67] Although this forms an interesting contrast to the emphasis on grammatical education in the late Roman empire, another, more contemporary comparison can be drawn between the language policies of the two monotheistic empires that emerged at the end of our period. While Charlemagne (768–814) promoted the reform of Latin as a means to facilitate religious uniformity and social regeneration across his vast domains, scholars in the early Abassid caliphate, such as Khalíl ibn Ahmad Al Fara-hídi (c. 718–791) and his student Sibawayh (760–793) likewise focussed upon standardising Arabic script, grammar and lexicography to facilitate its accessibility to a far broader audience of non-Arabic native speakers across far wider horizons.[68]

Conclusion

We should not be surprised that our picture of literacy's development from Late Antiquity to the early Middle Ages has changed considerably in the last thirty years. The linguistic turn in philosophy has forced us to ask new questions about the relationship among language, culture and power, and there has been an explosion of historical studies on Late Antiquity and the early Middle Ages that have helped illuminate the role of literacy in this period. Moreover, new evidence keeps turning up. When we consider that only 20 percent of the fifty thousand papyrus fragments from Oxyrhynchus alone have been published to date (a mere sixty-eight volumes so far), it is clear that our picture will change even more.

It is doubtful that literacy declined in the late empire of the fourth century, when it is more likely that literacy increased, in terms of numbers of people who were literate and in terms of literacy's importance in late antique culture, largely due to its extended use in government, the premium placed on grammatical education by elites, and conversion to a religion of the book. Because of this, the breakdown of the imperial system was all the more disastrous for secular uses of literacy in large-scale government, for aristocratic, civilian traditions of classical literature, and for the system of grammatical education that provided the acquisition of literate skills. Christianity went some way toward countering the decline by forcing shifts in the social location of literacy, removing its aristocratic associations and aiming at a wider audience for participation in literate culture, albeit one mainly restricted to religious concerns and a Biblical framework for intellectual discourse. In this context, the institutional, technological and cultural changes meant new purposes and new formats for literacy. If literacy became largely concentrated in the hands of monks and churchmen in early medieval Europe, we need to recognise that churches (rather than the Church) and monasteries were closely linked to secular power, were often proprietary extensions of family interests, and served many different social functions: courts, hospitals, orphanages, schools and, of course, religious services, based on the reading of sacred texts. While we may well look to ideological, cultural, economic and institutional changes to explain the development of literacy, it is also true that good technology has its own way of finding more users. Governments, churches, landowners, trades people, and merchants increasingly relied on literacy because it facilitated communication, aided the storage and retrieval of information, broadened intellectual horizons, and helped to fashion collective identities that eased social cohesion. That Carolingian rulers of the ninth century capitalised on the achievements of earlier developments in literacy is not surprising. But neither should we be surprised at the extent to which literacy was used, valued and further developed from Late Antiquity into the early Middle Ages.

Notes

1 References cleave to publications in English where possible. Surveys very different to that offered here are Briggs (2000), Parkes (1991b), Green (1990), Smith (2005), 13–50. See also the papers in McKitterick (Ed.) (1990). On literacy in the high Middle Ages, two essential studies that have shaped the field in general are Stock (1983) and Clanchy (1993). Mostert (1999) provides a useful bibliographic guide to medieval literacy and related issues. Above: quantity of evidence, Wickham (2005), 829. Romans and languages: Adams (2003), 111–295, 759–760.

2 Harris (1989), 264, 268, 272, 328, 330. Critical responses to Harris's views are collected in Humphrey (1991).

3 Everett (2003), 9, 177–180. The percentage of autograph subscriptions in Italy rise over the next century: Wickham (1981), 125. On the problems of using such evidence, Bäuml (1980), 240–241.

4 Graff (1979), idem (Ed.) (1981); Houston (2002).

5 Ward-Perkins (2005), 151–168. Harris (1989), 285–322, clearly struggles to fit Late Antique evidence into his narrative of decline. On continuity of Roman public display for administrative and legal matters, Matthews (1998). Medieval graffiti (mostly devotional): see Carletti and Otranto (1980); Everett (2003), 265–274.

6 On Libanius, see Cribiore (2007). The literature on Augustine is (appropriately) vast, but essential for the themes under discussion here is Stock (1996). Complementary is G. Clark (2007).

7 Kaster (1988); Irvine (1994); Cribiore (2001). An overview is Browning (2000). For social context of rhetoric, Brown (1992); Cameron (1991).

8 Lim (1995), 31–65; philosophy, Edwards (2006). On the connection between legal studies and our narrative sources, Greatrex (2001).

9 Erhman (1993); Clark (1992); Burton–Christie, D. (1993); McDonald and Sanders (2002). It is worth noting that a good number of medical works (especially in Latin) date from the fourth to sixth centuries: Langslow (2003), 41–63; Nutton (2004), 292–309; Everett (2009).

10 Kelly (1998), idem (2004); Heather (1994b); Jones (1986), 563–606; Barnish, Lee, and Whitby (2000); Harries (1988). On notaries and secretaries, see Teitler (1985).

11 Jones (1986), 462–469; Wickham (2005), 62–80. Of course, tax collectors themselves could be "illiterate," despite their compilation of archives documenting their activities, as witnessed in the early fourth-century archives of Isidoros and Sakoan: Youtie (1971, 1975).

12 Wipszycka (1980); Bagnall (1980); Sarris (2006), 29–49, 81–95.

13 Attila, Heather (1994a); idem (2000); Whitby (2000a); idem (2000b); Innes (2006). For literacy in the Roman army, Bowman (1994); Adams (2003), 617–622. Literacy in early medieval Byzantium, Mullett (1990).

14 Markus (1990), 16–18, 224–227; Everett (2003), 23–45.

15 Ed. in Velázquez Soriano (1988), and idem (2000). Similar estate recordkeeping by a Visigothic noble is noted in a local hagiographic work: Smith (2005), 42–43.

16 Overview, Liebs (2000). The legal scholarship and archival resources behind these collections are revealed by Matthews (2000); Honoré (1978), idem (1994), idem (1998); Harries (1999); Greatrex (2001).

17 *Codex Justinianus* 6.23.15, Ed. Krueger; trans. from Meyer (2004), 270–271.

18 In general, Levy (1951); Zimmermann (1996), 68–94. Leo 472, Codex Justianianus 8.17 (18), 11 Ed. Krueger.

19 Everett (2000), 73–81. The only few surviving examples of *gesta municipalia* are from Italy (c. 450–600): Tjäder (1954–1982).

20 Formularies: Brown (2002). Loss: Kosto (2005). For lost letters, Garrison (1999).

21 Wood, S. (2006), 9–235.

22 Lim (1995); Hanson (1988), 824–875. Teitler (1985); Humfress (2002). On the papacy, Noble (1990).

23 Harries (1999), 191–210; Guterman (1990).

24 Humfress (2005).

25 Davies and Fouracre (Eds.) (1986).

26 Lane Fox (1994); Gamble (1995), 1–41.

27 Anthony: Wipszycka (1980), providing other examples. Bishop Caesarius of Arles, Klingshirn (1994), 183–186.

28 Riché (1976), 447–468. *Sermo humilis*: Auerbach (1965); in the East, Lim (1995) 149–181. On the copying of scripture as a tool for education, see Rapp (1991), and esp. idem (2007) 205–208; also Cribiore (1999) for Coptic.

29 Stock (1996). On Jerome and Augustine, Kaster (1988), 80–90.

30 Everett (2006). Compare a fourth-century school text: Dionisotti (1982).

31 Hurtado (2006). Jerome, Pref. Ezechiel, Isaiah: cf. Cassiodorus, *Inst.* I.9. On early Christian scribal practice, Haines-Eitzen (2000).

32 Parkes (1991a, idem, 1991b). Word separation, Saenger (1997).

33 Origin of *uncia*", Meyvaert (1983). National scripts, Bischoff (1990), 72–112. Minuscule, Ganz (1987). Contemporary Greek manuscripts follow similar trajectories as Latin: Wilson (1973); Cavallo and Maehler (1987).

34 Everett (2003), 279–283.

35 Bischoff (1990),107. Everett (2003), 306–310, 315–316.

36 Hurtado (2006), Gamble (1995), 42–81, updating the fundamental study of Roberts and Skeat (1983).

37 Grafton and Williams (2006). Eusebius' concern for precision and veracious authority spilled over into other innovations, such as the use of maps and diagrams in his *Onomasticon* of Hebrew place-names, or the radical

step of incorporating documents into his historical works. On Canon tables, Nordenfalk (1938); Netzer (1994).

38 O'Donnell (1998), 35. On chapter headings: Petitemengin (1997).

39 The classic study of monastic learning is Leclercq (1961). See also Rousseau (1985), idem (1994); Burton-Christie (1993); and for Byzantine Egypt, Kotsifou (2007).

40 Cassiodorus, *Institutions*, trans. Halporn and Vessey (2004).

41 *Inst.* I.26. See Gorman (2000); Troncarelli (1998); Gorman (2002). Cf. the use of source marks by Simplicius (fl.530s), commentator on Aristotle's works: Wildberg (1993).

42 Zürich, Staatsarchiv W3.19.XII, fols. 24, 25: Lowe (1956) CLA VII.1008. See M. Camillo Ferrari (2001). I have deliberately omitted discussion of illuminated manuscripts and innovations in the interplay between text and image: see Williams (1999), Henderson (1987), Netzer (1994), Nordenfalk (1988).

43 Bruce-Mitford (1967); Gameson (1992). Costs of books: McKitterick (1989), 136: Ganz (1995), 793. Booksellers are rarely attested after the second century, although there was one in sixth-century Ravenna: Tjäder (1972); Bertelli (1998).

44 Carolingian monasteries: Reichenau (415 items), Lorsch (590), Murbach (355), St. Gall (264); Bobbio (tenth century, 600). From Ganz (1995); McKitterick (1989), 165–210. Figures for libraries of Caesarea (400), Isidore (420–480 items), the Ulpian library and Clairvaux/Avignon from Lapidge (2006) 3–33, 58–60, who compares them with Anglo-Saxon libraries: Bede (250 books), Aldhelm (120), Winchester (100), and Alcuin's York (just over 100). A (rightly) skeptic view of the Alexandrian library is Bagnall (2002). Note that the Visigothic King Chindasuinth (642–653) had his own personal library, as did one of his counts: Collins (1990), p. 115. On Augustine's library, Scheele (1978). On Roman aristocratic to Christian libraries, Vessey (2001).

45 Bischoff (1990) suggested a figure of 50,000 manuscripts produced in the ninth century: McKitterick (1989), 163. The figure matches estimates extrapolated from population theories: Cisne (2005). Any attempt to apply this "one seventh survives" rule to the earlier period must consider the substantial number of lost papyrus manuscripts from before c. 600.

46 Musurillo (1972), 107–131; Dronke (1984); Salisbury (1997). On women and hagiography, Coon (1997).

47 Palladius & Meyer (1965); Egeria, Wilkinson (1990). Surveys: Dronke (1984); Ashbrook Harvey (2004).

48 Proba: Clark and Hatch (1981); Eudocia, Holum (1982).

49 Trans. McNamara and Halborg (1992).

50 Ashbrook Harvey (2004), 384, 387.

51 McKitterick (1991/1994), 24–25, 33–34, idem (1992); Wood (1990), 70–71; Nelson (1990b), idem (1991). Everett (2003), 181–182. For Egypt, Bagnall and Cribiore (2006).

52 Herman (2000); Wright (1982), (1991), (2002); emphasising structural change and weakness, Banniard (1992).

53 Green, (1998); Knight Bostock (1976).

54 Kelly (1990); Godden and Lapidge (1991); Lerer (1991); Wormald, (1977), idem (1999); O'Brien, O'Keeffe, and Orchard (2005); Orchard (2003).

55 McManus (1991); Harvey (1987); Stevenson (1990); Charles-Edwards (1998); Sharpe (1986); Davies (1982).

56 Bagnall (1993), 239. For the early Biblical texts, Crum (1909).

57 Emmel (2004); Krawiec (2004); Schroder (2007); MacCoull (1988), idem (1993).

58 Hasitzka (1990); Cribiore (1999).

59 Syriac also served as a vehicle for Manichaean and pagan literature, although only fragments of it survive: Brock (1992), VII, 233.

60 Vööbus (1962) and (1965); Brock (1994), (2004a), (2004b); Jerome Ep. 7.2, in Kelly (1975), 49.

61 Koruin, *Life of Mashtots*, c. 8, 11. Trans. Norehad (1964). Further, Mahé (1987); Garsoian (1999). On Armenian scripts, Stone, Kouymjian, Lehmann (2002). The earliest text in the Georgian language, "Martyrdom of the Holy Queen Shushanik," dates from this period (fifth century), as do the earliest examples of its distinctive *asomtavruli* script, but both may date to an earlier period: see Gamqrelize (1994).

62 Heather and Matthews (1991); Streitberg (1965); Wright (1966); Hunter (1969). *Skeireins*: Holmes Bennet (1960). Gothic in Italy: Amory (1995), 102–108, 237–263. *Codex Argenteus*: Tjäder (1972).

63 Kalmin (2006), implications for literacy, idem (2003), 149–196. Studies of Jewish literacy

are vitiated by dearth of evidence from our period, but see Reif (1990).

64 On Mohammad and literacy: Goldfeld (1980); Lecker (1997); Günther (2002). On orality and writing in the Qur'an, Madigan (2001). On early Arabic script, Gruendler (1993).

65 Q. 2:82. Trans. Muhammad Taqi-ud-Din Al Hilali and Muhammad Muhsin Khan.

66 Makdisi (1981), idem (1991). Versteegh, C. H. M. (1993).

67 Versteegh, K. (1997). Calligraphy, Déroche (1992). For documents and documentary scripts, Khan (1992), idem (1993).

68 Shirbini & Carter (1981); Owens (1988). Charlemagne and Carolingian literacy, McKitterick (1989); Nelson (1990a).

References

Adams, J. (2003). *Bilingualism and the Latin language*. Cambridge: Cambridge University Press.

Amory, P. (1995). *People and identity in Ostrogothic Italy*, 489–554. Cambridge: Cambridge University Press.

Ashbrook Harvey, S. (2004). Women and words: Texts by and about women. In F. Young, L. Ayres, & A. Louth (Eds.), *The Cambridge history of early Christian literature* (pp. 382–390). Cambridge: Cambridge University Press.

Auerbach, E. (1965). *Literary language and its public in Late Antiquity and in the Middle Ages* (Ralph Manhiem, Trans.). New York: Pantheon Books.

Bagnall, R. (1980). 'Papyrus documents in Egypt from Constantine to Justinian'. In R. Pintaudi (Ed.), *Miscellenea papyrologica* (pp. 12–23). Florence: Edizioni Gonnelli.

Bagnall, R. (1993). *Egypt in Late Antiquity*. Princeton, NJ: Princeton University Press.

Bagnall, R. (2002). Alexandria: Library of dreams. *Proceedings of the American Philosophical Society*, 146, 348–362.

Bagnall, R., and Cribiore R. (2006). *Women's letters from ancient Egypt*, 300 BC–AD 800. Ann Arbor: University of Michigan Press.

Banniard, M. (1992). *Viva voce: Communication écrite et communication orale du IVe au IXe siécle en occident latin*. Collection des études augustiniennes, 25. Paris: Institut des études augustiniennes.

Barnish, S., Lee, A. D., & Whitby, M (2000). Government and Administration. In A. Cameron, B. Ward-Perkins, & M. Whitby (Eds.), *The Cambridge ancient history, vol. XIV. Late Antiquity and its successors AD 425–600* (pp. 164–206). Cambridge: Cambridge University Press.

Bäuml, F. (1980). Varieties and consequences of medieval literacy and illiteracy. *Speculum* 55, 237–265.

Bertelli, C. (1998). The production and distribution of books in Late Antiquity. In R. Hodges & W. Bowden (Eds.), *The sixth century: Production, distribution, demand* (pp. 41–60). Leiden/Boston/Cologne: Brill.

Bischoff, B. (1990). *Latin Palaeography: Antiquity and the Middle Ages* (D. Ó Cróinín & D. Ganz, Trans.). Cambridge: Cambridge University Press.

Bowman, A. K. (1994). *Life and letters on the Roman frontier: Vindolanda and its people*. London: Routledge.

Bowman, A. K., & Woolf, G. (Eds.) (1994). *Literacy and power in the ancient world*. Cambridge: Cambridge University Press.

Briggs, C. (2000). Literacy, reading and writing in the medieval West. *Journal of Medieval Studies*, 26, 397–420.

Brock, S. P. (1992). *Studies in Syriac Christianity*. Aldershot: Variorum.

Brock, S. P. (1994). Greek and Syriac in Late Antique Syria. In A. K. Bowman & G. Woolf (Eds.), *Literacy and power in the ancient world* (pp. 149–160). Cambridge: Cambridge University Press.

Brock, S. P. (2004a). The earliest Syriac literate. In F. Young, L. Ayres, & A. Louth (Eds.), *The Cambridge history of early Christian literature* (pp. 161–171). Cambridge: Cambridge University Press.

Brock, S. P. (2004b). Ephrem the Syrian. In F. Young, L. Ayres, & A. Louth (Eds.), *The Cambridge history of early Christian literature* (pp. 362–732). Cambridge: Cambridge University Press.

Brown, P. R. L. (1992). *Power and persuasion in Late Antiquity: Towards a Christian empire*. Madison: University of Wisconsin Press.

Brown, W. (2002). When documents are destroyed or lost: Lay people and archives in the early Middle Ages. *Early Medieval Europe*, 11, 337–366.

Browning, R. (2000). Education in the Roman Empire. In A. Cameron, B. Ward-Perkins, & M. Whitby (Eds.), *The Cambridge ancient history, vol.* XIV. *Late Antiquity and its successors, AD 425–600* (pp. 855–883). Cambridge: Cambridge University Press.

Bruce-Mitford, R. L. S. (1967). *The art of the Codex Amiatinus*. Jarrow lecture, 1967. Jarrow: Parish of Jarrow.

Burton-Christie, D. (1993). *The word in the desert: Scripture and the quest for holiness in early Christian monasticism*. New York: Oxford University Press.

Cameron, A. (1991). *Christianity and the rhetoric of empire: The development of Christian discourse*. Berkeley: University of California Press.

Cameron, A., Ward-Perkins, B., & Whitby, M. (Eds.) (2000). *The Cambridge ancient history, vol. XIV. Late Antiquity and its successors AD 425–600*. Cambridge: Cambridge University Press.

Camillo Ferrari, M. (2001). Die älteste kommentierte Bibelhandschrift und ihr Kontext: Das irische Ezechiel-Fragment Zürich Staatsarchiv W3.19XII. In R. Bergmann, E. Glaser, & C. Moulin-Frankhänel (Eds.), *Mittelalterliche Volksprachige Glossen* (pp. 47–76) (Heidelberg).

Carletti, C., & Otranto, G. (1980). *Il Santuario di S. Michele sul Gargano dal VI al IX secolo: Contributo alla storia della Langobardia meridionale: atti del Convegno tenuto a Monte Sant'Angelo il 9–10 dicembre* 1978. Vetera Christianorum, 2. Bari: Edipuglia.

Cavallo, G., & Maehler, H. (1987). *Greek bookhands of the Early Byzantine Period, A.D. 400–800*. London: University of London, Institute of Classical Studies.

Charles-Edwards, T. M. (1998). The context and uses of literacy in early Christian Ireland. In H. Pryce (Ed.), *Literacy in medieval Celtic societies* (pp. 62–82). Cambridge: Cambridge University Press.

Cisne, J. L. (2005). How science survived: Medieval manuscripts' "demography" and classic text's extinction. *Science*, 307 (25 February 2005), 1305–1307.

Clanchy, M. T. (1993). *From memory to written record: England 1066–1307*. 2nd edition. Oxford: Blackwell.

Clark, E. A. (1984). *Life of Melania the Younger*. Translated introduction and commentary. New York: Edwin Mellen Press.

Clark, E. A. (1992). *The Origenist controversy: The cultural construction of an early Christian debate*. Princeton, NJ: Princeton University Press.

Clark, E. A. (1999). *Reading renunciation: Asceticism and scripture in early Christianity*. Princeton, NJ: Princeton University Press.

Clark, E. A., & Hatch, D. F. (1981). *The Golden Bough, the Oaken Cross: The Virgilian Cento of Faltonia Betitia Proba*. Chico, CA: Scholars Press.

Clark, G. (2007). City of books: Augustine and the world as text. In W. Klingshirn & L. Safran (Eds.), *The early Christian book* (pp. 117–140). Washington, DC: Catholic University of America Press.

Codex Iustinianus (1884). P. Krueger (Ed.). Berolini: Weidmannos.

Codex Theodosianus (1990, 1905). T. Mommsen & P. Krueger (Eds.). 2 vols. Hildesheim: Weidmann.

Collins, R. (1990). Literacy and the laity in early mediaeval Spain. In R. McKitterick (Ed.), *The uses of literacy in early medieval Europe* (pp. 109–133). Cambridge: Cambridge University Press.

Coon, L. (1997). *Sacred fictions: Holy women and hagiography in Late Antiquity*. Philadelphia: University of Pennsylvania Press.

Cribiore, R. (1999). Greek and Coptic education in Late Antique Egypt. In S. Emmel, M. Krause, et al. (Eds.), Ägypten und Nubien in spätantiker und christlicher Zeit: Akten des 6. Internationalen Koptologenkongresses II: 279–286.

Cribiore, R. (2001). *Gymnastics of the mind: Greek education in Hellenistic and Roman Egypt*. Princeton, NJ: Princeton University Press.

Cribiore, R. (2007). *The School of Libanius in Late Antique Antioch*. Princeton, NJ: Princeton University Press.

Crum, W. E. (1909). *Catalogue of the Coptic manuscripts in the collection of the John Rylands Library, Manchester*. Manchester, UK: University Press.

Davies, W. (1982). The Latin charter tradition. In D. Whitelock, R. McKitterick, & D. Dumville (Eds.), *Ireland in early medieval Europe* (pp. 274–280). Cambridge: Cambridge University Press.

Davies, W., & Fouracre, P. (Eds.) (1986). *The settlement of disputes in early medieval Europe*. Cambridge: Cambridge University Press.

Déroche, F. (1992). *The Abbasid tradition: Qur'ans of the 8th to the 10th centuries AD*. Oxford: Oxford University Press.

Dionisotti, A. C. (1982). From Ausonius' schooldays? A schoolbook and its relatives. *Journal of Roman Studies*, 72, 83–125.

Dronke, P. (1984). *Women writers of the Middle Ages: A critical study of texts from Perpetua* to *Marguerite Porete*. Cambridge: Cambridge University Press.

Edwards, M. J. (2006). *Culture and philosophy in the age of Plotinus*. London: Duckworth.

Ehrman, B. D. (1993). *The Orthodox corruption of scripture: The effect of early Christological controversies on the text of the New Testament*. New York/Oxford: Oxford University Press.

Emmel, S. (2004). *Shenoute's literary corpus*, 2 vols., Corpus scriptorum Christianorum Orientalium v. 599–600. Subsidia 111–112. Louvain: Peeters.

Everett, N. (2000). Scribes and charters in Lombard Italy. *Studi Medievali, 41*, 39–83.

Everett, N. (2003). *Literacy in Lombard Italy*. New York/Cambridge: Cambridge University Press.

Everett, N. (2006). The *Interrogationes de littera et de singulis causis*: An early medieval school text. *Journal of Medieval Latin, 16*, 1–78.

Everett, N. (2009). *The Alphabet of Galen. Pharmacology from Antiquity to the Early Middle Ages*. Totonto: University of Toronto Press.

Fink, R. O. (1971). *Roman military records on papyrus*. Cleveland, OH: published for the American Philological Association by the Press of Case Western Reserve University.

Gamble, H. (1995). *Books and readers in the early church: A history of early Christian texts*. New Haven, CT/London: Yale University Press.

Gameson, R. (1992). The cost of the *Codex Amiatinus*. *Notes and Queries, 237*, 2–9.

Gamqrelize, T. V. (1994). *Alphabetic writing and the Old Georgian script: A typology and provenience of alphabetic writing systems*. Delmar, NY: Caravan Books.

Ganz, D. (1987). The preconditions for Caroline minuscule. *Viator, 18*, 23–43.

Ganz, D. (1995). Book production in the Carolingian Empire and the spread of Caroline minuscule. In R. D. McKitterick (Ed.), *The new Cambridge medieval history II c.700–c.900* (pp. 786–808). Cambridge: Cambridge University Press.

Garrison, M. (1999). "Send more socks": On mentality and the preservation context of medieval letters. In M. Mostert (Ed.), *New approaches to medieval communication* (pp. 69–99). Turnhout, Belgium: Brepols.

Garsoian, N. G. (1999). *Church and culture in early medieval Armenia*. Aldershot: Ashgate.

Godden, M., & Lapidge, M. (Eds.) (1991). *The Cambridge companion to Old English literature*. Cambridge: Cambridge University Press.

Goldfeld, I. (1980). The illiterate prophet (nabr ummij): An inquiry into the development of dogma in Islamic tradition. *Der Islam, 57*, 58–67.

Gorman, M. (2000). The diagrams in the oldest manuscripts of Cassiodorus' *Institutiones*. *Revue Bénédictine, 110*, 27–41.

Gorman, M. (2002). Source marks and chapter divisions in Bede's commentary on Luke. *Revue Bénédictine, 112*, 246–290.

Graff, H. J. (1979). *The literacy myth: Literacy and social structure in a nineteenth-century city*. New York: Academic Press.

Graff, H. J. (Ed.) (1981). *Literacy and social development in the West: A reader*. New Haven, CT: Yale University Press.

Grafton, A., & Williams, M. (2006). *Christianity and the transformation of the book*. Cambridge, MA: Belknap Press of Harvard University Press.

Greatrex, G. B. (2001). Lawyers and historians in Late Antiquity. In R. Mathisen (Ed.), *Law, society and authority in Late Antiquity* (pp. 148–161). Oxford: Oxford University Press.

Green, D. H. D. (1990). Orality and reading: The state of eesearch in medieval studies. *Speculum, 65*, 267–280.

Green, D. H. D. (1998). *Language and history in the early Germanic world*. Cambridge: Cambridge University Press.

Gruendler, B. (1993). *The development of the Arabic scripts: From Nabataean era to the first Islamic century according to dated texts*. Atlanta, GA: Scholars Press.

Günther, S. (2002). Muhammad, the illiterate prophet: An Islamic creed in the Qur'an and in Qur'anic exegesis. *Journal of Qur'anic Studies, 4.1*, 1–12.

Guterman, S. (1990). *The principle of the personality of the law in the Germanic kingdoms of Western Europe from the fifth to the eleventh century*. New York: P. Lang.

Haines-Eitzen, K. (2000). *Guardians of letters: Literacy, power and the transmitters of early Christian literature*. Oxford: Oxford University Press.

Halporn, J. W., & Vessey, M. (2004). *Cassiodorus: Institutions of divine and secular learning* and *On the soul*. Translated texts for historians, v. 42. Liverpool: Liverpool University Press.

Hanson, R. P. C. (1988). *The search for the Christian doctrine of God*. Grand Rapids, MI: Zondervan.

Harries, J. (1988). The Roman imperial quaestor from Constantine to Theodosius II. *Journal of Roman Studies*, 78, 148–172.

Harries, J. (1994). *Sidonius Apollinaris and the fall of Rome, AD 407–485*. Oxford: Clarendon Press.

Harries, J. (1999). *Law and empire in Late Antiquity*. Cambridge: Cambridge University Press.

Harris, W. (1989). *Ancient literacy*. Cambridge, MA: Harvard University Press.

Harvey, A. (1987). Early literacy in Ireland: The evidence from ogam. *Cambridge Mediaeval Celtic Studies*, 14 (Winter), 1–14.

Hasitzka, M. R. M. (1990). *Neue Texte und Dokumentation zam Koptischen Unterricht*. Vienna: In Kommission bei B. Hollinek.

Heather, P. (1994a). Literacy and power in the migration period. In A. K. Bowman & G. Wolf (Eds.), *Literacy and power in the ancient world* (pp. 177–197). Cambridge: Cambridge University Press.

Heather, P. (1994b). New men for new Constantines: Creating an imperial elite in the Eastern Mediterranean. In P. Magdalino (Ed.), *The rhythm of imperial renewal in the East from Constantine the Great to Michael Palaiologos* (pp. 11–33). Leiden: Brill.

Heather, P. (2000). State, lordship and community in the West (c. A.D. 400–600). In A. Cameron, B., Ward-Perkins, & M. Whitby (Eds.), *The Cambridge ancient history, vol. XIV. Late Antiquity and its successors AD 425–600* (pp. 437–468). Cambridge: Cambridge University Press.

Heather, P., & Matthews, J. (1991). *The Goths in the fourth century*. Liverpool: Liverpool University Press.

Henderson, G. (1987). *From Durrow to Kells: The insular Gospel books* 650–800. London: Thames and Hudson.

Herman, J. (2000). *Vulgar Latin* (R. Wight, Trans.). University Park, PA: Pennsylvania State University Press.

Hodges, R., & Bowden, W. (1998). *The sixth century: Production, distribution, and demand*. The transformation of the Roman world, v. 3. Leiden/ Boston/Cologne: Brill.

Holum, K. G. (1982). *Theodosian empresses: Women and imperial dominion in Late Antiquity*. Berkeley: University of California Press.

Holmes Bennet, W. (1960). *The Gothic commentary on the Gospel of St John*. New York: Modern Language Association.

Honoré, T. (1978). *Tribonian*. London: Duckworth.

Honoré, T. (1994). *Emperors and lawyers*, 2nd ed. Oxford: Oxford University Press.

Honoré, T. (1998). *Law in the crisis of empire 379–425 A.D.: The Theodosian empire and its quaestors*. Oxford: Oxford University Press.

Houston, R. A. (2002). *Literacy in early modern Europe: Culture and education* 1500–1800, 2nd ed. Harlow: Longman.

Humfress, C. (2002). A new legal cosmos: Late Roman lawyers and the early medieval church. In P. Linehan & J. Nelson (Eds.), *The medieval world* (pp. 557–575). London: Routledge.

Humfress, C. (2005). Law and legal practice in the Age of Justinian. In M. Maas (Ed.), *The Cambridge companion to the Age of Justinian* (pp. 161–184). Cambridge: Cambridge University Press.

Humfress, C. (2007). Judging by the book: Christian codices and Late Antique legal culture. In W. E. Klingshirn & L. Safran (Eds.), *The early Christian book*. CUA studies in early Christianity (pp. 141–158). Washington, DC: Catholic University of America Press.

Humphrey, J. H. (Ed.) (1991). Literacy in the Roman world. *Journal of Roman Archaeology*, Supp. No. 3.

Hunter, M. J. (1969). *The Gothic Bible*. In G. W. H. Lampe (Ed.), *The Cambridge history of the Bible. Volume 2: The West from the fathers to the Reformation*. Cambridge: Cambridge University Press.

Hurtado, L. (2006). *The earliest Christian artifacts: Manuscripts and Christian origins*. Grand Rapids, MI: Eerdmans.

Innes, M. (2006). Land, freedom and the making of the medieval West. *Transactions of the Royal Historical Society*, 16, 39–74.

Irvine, M. (1994). *The making of a textual culture: 'Grammatica' and literary theory*, 350–1100. Cambridge: Cambridge University Press.

Jones, A. H. M. (1986). *The later Roman Empire, 284–602: A social, economic and administrative survey*, 2 vols. Baltimore, MD: Johns Hopkins University.

Kalmin, R. L. (2003). *Jewish culture and society under the Christian Roman Empire* (Leuven).

Kalmin, R. L. (2006). *Jewish Babylonia between Persia and Roman Palestine*. New York: Oxford University Press.

Kaster, R. A. (1988). *Guardians of the language: The grammarian and society in Late Antiquity*. Berkeley: University of California Press.

Kelly, C. M. (1994). Later Roman Bureaucracy: Going through the files. In A. K. Bowman and G. Wolf (Eds.), *Literacy and power in the ancient world* (pp. 161–176). Cambridge: Cambridge University Press.

Kelly, C. M. (1998). Emperors, government and bureaucracy. In A. Cameron & P. Garnsey (Eds.), *The Cambridge Ancient History XIII* (pp. 138–188). Cambridge: Cambridge University Press.

Kelly, C. M. (2004). *Ruling the Later Roman Empire*. Cambridge, MA: Belknap Press of Harvard University Press.

Kelly, J. N. D. (1975). *Jerome: His life, writings and controversies*. New York: Harper & Row.

Kelly, S. (1990). Anglo-Saxon lay society and the written word. In R. McKitterick (Ed.), *The uses of literacy in early medieval Europe* (pp. 36–62). Cambridge: Cambridge University Press.

Khan, G. (1992). *Arabic papyri: Selected material from the Khalili collection*. Oxford: Oxford University Press.

Khan, G. (1993). *Bills, letters and deeds: Arabic papyri of the 7th to 11th centuries*. London: Oxford University Press.

Klingshirn, W. E. (1994). *Caesarius of Arles: The making of a Christian community in Late Antique Gaul*. Cambridge: Cambridge University Press.

Klingshirn, W. E., & Safran, L. (Eds.) (2007). *The early Christian book*. CUA studies in early Christianity. Washington, DC: Catholic University of America Press.

Knight Bostock, J. A. (1976). *Handbook of Old High German literature* (2nd edition). Oxford: Clarendon Press.

Kosto, A. (2005). Laymen, clerics and documentary practices in the early Middle Ages: The example of Catalonia. *Speculum*, 80, 44–74.

Kotsifou, C. (2007). Books and book production in the monastic communities of Byzantine Egypt. In W. E. Klingshirn & L. Safran (Eds.), *The early Christian book*. CUA studies in early Christianity (pp. 48–68). Washington, DC: Catholic University of America Press.

Krawiec, R. (2004). *Shenoute and the women of the White Monastery*. Oxford: Oxford University Press.

Langslow, D. R. (2000). *Medical Latin in the Roman Empire*. Oxford: Oxford University Press.

Lapidge, M. (2006). *The Anglo-Saxon library*. Oxford: Oxford University Press.

Lane Fox, R. (1994). Literacy and power in early Christianity. In A. K. Bowman & G. Wolf (Eds.), *Literacy and power in the ancient world* (pp. 128–148). Cambridge: Cambridge University Press.

Lecker, M. (1997). Zayd b. Thabit, "a Jew with two sidelocks": Judaism and literacy in pre-Islamic Medina (Yatrib). *Journal of Near Eastern Studies*, 56, 259–273.

Leclercq, J. (1961). *The love of learning and the desire for God: A study of monastic culture* (rev. ed.). New York: Fordham University Press.

Lerer, S. (1991). *Literacy and power in Anglo-Saxon literature: Regents studies in medieval culture*. Lincoln: University of Nebraska Press.

Levy, E. (1951). *West Roman vulgar law: The law of property*. Philadelphia: American Philosophical Society.

Liebs, D. (2000). Roman law. In A. Cameron, B. Ward-Perkins, & M. Whitby (Eds.), *The Cambridge ancient history, Vol. XIV* (pp. 238–259). Cambridge: Cambridge University Press.

Lim, R. (1995). *Public disputation, power and social order in Late Antiquity*. Berkeley: University of California Press.

Lowe, E. A. (1956). *Codices Latini Antiquiores*, vol. VII. Oxford: Clarendon Press.

MacCoull, L. S. B. (1988). *Dioscorus of Aphrodito*. Berkeley: University of California Press.

MacCoull, L. S. B. (1993). *Coptic perspectives on Late Antiquity*. Aldershot, UK: Ashgate Publishing.

Madigan, D. A. (2001). *The Qur'an's self-image: Writing and authority in Islam's scripture*. Princeton, NJ: Princeton University Press.

Mahé, J-P. (1987). Quadrivium et cursus d'études au viie siècle en Arménie. *Travaux et Mémoires*, 10, 159–206.

Makdisi, G. (1981). *The rise of colleges: Institutions of learning in Islam and the West*. Edinburgh: Edinburgh University Press.

Makdisi, G. (1991). *Religion, law, and learning in classical Islam*. Aldershot, UK: Ashgate/Variorum.

Markus, R. (1990). *The end of ancient Christianity*. Cambridge: Cambridge University Press.

Matthews, J. F. (1998). Eternity in perishable materials: Law making and literate communication in the Roman Empire. In T. W. Hillard. et al. (Eds.), *Ancient history in a modern university* (pp. 253–265). Grand Rapids, MI: Eerdmans.

Matthews, J. F. (2000). *Laying down the law: A study of the Theodosian Code*. New Haven, CT: Yale University Press.

McDonald, L. M., & Sanders, J. A. (Eds.) (2002). *The canon debate*. Peabody, MA: Hendricksen Publishers.

McKitterick, R. (1989). *The Carolingians and the written word*. Cambridge: Cambridge University Press.

McKitterick, R. (Ed.) (1990). *The uses of literacy in early medieval Europe*. Cambridge: Cambridge University Press.

McKitterick, R. (1991/1994). Frauen und Schriftlichkeit im Frühmittlealter. In H. W. Goetz (Ed.), *Weibliche Lebensgestaltung im frühen Mittelalter* (pp. 65–118). Cologne/Vienna: Weimer-Wiem. English translation in *Books, scribes and learning in the Frankish kingdoms 6th–9th centuries* (ch. XIII). Aldershot, UK: Variorum.

McKitterick, R. (1992). Nuns' scriptoria in England and Francia in the early Middle Ages. *Francia*, 19 (1), 1–35.

McManus, D. (1991). *A guide to ogam*. Maynooth: Maynooth Monographs.

McNamara, J., & Halborg, J. E. (Eds.) (1992). *Sainted women of the Dark Ages* (E. G. Whatley, Trans.). Durham, NC: Duke University Press.

Meyer, E. (2004). *Legitimacy and law in the Roman world. Tabule in Roman belief and practice*. Cambridge: Cambridge University Press.

Meyvaert, P. (1983). 'Uncial letters': Jerome's meaning of the term. *Journal of Theological Studies*, 34, 185–188.

Mostert, M. (Ed.) (1999). *New approaches to medieval communication*. Turnhout, Belgium: Brepols.

Mullett, M. (1990). Writing in early mediaeval Byzantium. In R. McKitterick (Ed.), *The uses of literacy in early medieval Europe* (pp. 156–185). Cambridge: Cambridge University Press.

Musurillo, H. (1972). *The acts of the Christian martyrs*. Oxford: Clarendon.

Nelson, J. (1990a). Literacy in Carolingian government. In R. McKitterick (Ed.), *The uses of literacy in early medieval Europe* (pp. 258–296). Cambridge: Cambridge University Press.

Nelson, J. (1990b). Women and the word in the earlier Middle Ages. In W. Sheils & D. Wood (Eds.), *Women in the church* (pp. 53–87). Oxford/Cambridge: Basil Blackwell.

Nelson, J. (1991). Gender and genre in women historians of the early Middle Ages. In *L'Historiographie médiévale en Europe* (pp. 149–163). Paris: CNRS.

Netzer, N. (1994). *Cultural interplay in the eighth century: The Trier Gospels and the making of a scriptorium at Echternach*. Cambridge: Cambridge University Press.

Noble, T. F. X. (1990). Literacy and the papal government in Late Antiquity and the early Middle Ages. In R. McKitterick (Ed.), *The uses of literacy in early medieval Europe* (pp. 82–108). Cambridge: Cambridge University Press.

Nordenfalk, C. (1938). *Die spätantike Kanontafeln*. Göteburg: Oscar Isacsons.

Nordenfalk, C. (1988). *Early medieval book illumination*. Reprint Geneva: Skira.

Norehad, B. (1964). *Koriun: The life of Mashtots*. New York: Armenian General Benevolent Union of America.

Nutton, V. (2004). *Ancient medicine*. London: Routledge.

O'Brien O'Keeffe, K., & Orchard, A. (Eds.) (2005). *Latin learning and English lore: Studies in Anglo-Saxon literature for Michael Lapidge*, 2 vols. Toronto: University of Toronto Press.

O'Donnell, J. J. (1998). *Avatars of the word: From papyrus to cyberspace*. Cambridge, MA: Harvard University Press.

Orchard, A. (2003). *A critical companion to* Beowulf. Woodbridge/Rochester, NY: D. S. Brewer.

Owens, J. (1988). *The foundations of grammar: An introduction to medieval Arabic grammatical theory*. Amsterdam: J. Benjamins & Co.

Palladius, & Meyer, R. T. (1965). *Palladius: The Lausiac history*. Westminster, MD: Newman Press.

Parkes, M. B. (1991a). *Scribes, scripts and readers: Studies in communication, presentation and dissemination of medieval texts*. London: Hambledon Press.

Parkes, M. B. (1991b). Reading, copying and interpreting text in the early Middle Ages. In G. Cavallo & R. Charier (Eds.), *A history of reading in the West* (L. Cochrane, Trans). Amherst: University of Massachusetts Press.

Parkes, M. B. (1992). *Pause and effect: An introduction to the history of punctuation in the West*. Aldershot, UK: Scholar Press.

Petitemengin, P. (1997). Capitula païens et chrétiens. In Colloque international, de Chantilly & J-C. Fredouille (Eds.), *Titres et articulations du texte dans les oeuvres antiques: Actes du Colloque International de Chantilly 13–15 Décembre 1994* (pp. 491–507). Paris: Institut d'études Augustiniennes.

Pryce, H. (ed.) (1998). *Literacy in medieval celtic societies*. Cambridge: Cambridge University Press.

Rapp, C. (1991). Christians and their manuscripts in the Greek East in the fourth century. In G. Cavallo. et al. (Eds.), *Scritture, libri e testi nelle aree provinciali di Bizanzio* (pp. 127–148). Spoleto: Centro Italiano di Studi sull' alto medioevo.

Rapp, C. (2007). Holy texts, holy men, and holy scribes: Aspects of scriptural holiness in Late Antiquity. In W. E. Klingshirn & L. Safran (Eds.), *The early Christian book*. CUA studies in early Christianity (pp. 194–223). Washington, DC: Catholic University of America Press.

Reif, S. C. (1990). Aspects of mediaeval Jewish literacy. In R. McKitterick (Ed.), *The uses of literacy in early medieval Europe* (pp. 134–155). Cambridge: Cambridge University Press.

Riché, P. (1976). *Education and culture in the barbarian West: Sixth through eighth centuries* (J. Contreni, Trans.). Columbia: University of California Press.

Riché, P. (1979). *Écoles et enseignement dans le haut moyen-age*. Paris: Aubier Montaigne.

Roberts, C. H., & Skeat, T. C. (1983). *The birth of the codex*. London: Published for the British Academy by the Oxford University Press.

Rouse, R., & McNelis, C. (2001). North African literary activity: A Cyprian fragment, the stichometric lists, and a Donatist compedium. *Revue d'Histoire des Texts*, 30, 189–238.

Rousseau, P. (1985). *Pachomius: The making of a community in fourth-century Egypt*. Berkeley: University of California Press.

Rousseau, P. (1994). *Basil of Caesarea*. Berkeley: University of California Press.

Saenger, P. (1997). *Space between words: The origins of silent reading*. Stanford, CA: Stanford University Press.

Salisbury, J. (1997). *Perpetua's passion*. New York: Routledge.

Sarris, P. (2006). *Economy and society in the age of Justinian*. Cambridge, UK: Cambridge University Press.

Scheele, J. (1978). Buch und Bibliothek bei Augustinus. *Bibliothek und Wissenschaft*, 12, 14–114.

Schroeder, C. T. (2007). *Monastic bodies: Discipline and salvation in Shenoute of Atripe*. Philadelphia: University of Pennsylvania Press.

Sharpe, R. (1986). Dispute settlement in medieval Ireland: A preliminary inquiry. In W. Davies & P. Fouracre (Eds.), *The settlement of disputes in early medieval Europe* (pp. 169–190). Cambridge: Cambridge University Press.

Shirbini, M. I. A., & Carter, M. G. (1981). Arab linguistics: An introductory classical text with translation and notes. *Amsterdam Studies in the Theory and History of Linguistic Science*, vol. 24. Amsterdam: J. Benjamins.

Smith, J. M. H. (2005). *Europe after Rome: A new cultural history* 500–1000. New York/Oxford: Oxford Press.

Stevenson, J. (1990). Literacy in Ireland: The evidence of the Patrick dossier in the book of Armagh. In R. McKitterick (Ed.), *The uses of literacy in early medieval Europe* (pp. 11–35). Cambridge: Cambridge University Press.

Stock, B. (1983). *The implications of literacy: Written language and models of interpretation in the eleventh and twelfth centuries*. Princeton, NJ: Princeton University Press.

Stock, B. (1996). *Augustine the reader: Meditation, self-knowledge, and the ethics of interpretation*. Cambridge, MA: Harvard University Press.

Stone, M. E., Kouymjian, D., & Lehmann, H. (2002). *Album of Armenian paleography*. Aarhus, Denmark: Aarhus University Press.

Streitberg, W. (1965). *Die gotische Bibel*. 4th ed. Heidelberg: Universitätsverlag.

Teitler, H. C. (1985). *Notarii and exceptores: An enquiry into the role and significance of the shorthand writers in the imperial and ecclesiastical bureaucracy of the Roman Empire (from the early principate to c. 450 AD)*. Amsterdam: J.C. Gieben Publisher.

Tjäder, J.-O. (1954–1982). *Die nichtliterarischen lateinischen Papyri Italiens aus der Zeit 445–700*. 3 vols. Lund: C.W.K. Gleerup.

Tjäder, J.-O. (1972). Der Codex Argentius in Uppsala und der Buchmeister Viliaric in Ravenna. *Studia Gotica* (pp.144–164). Stockholm: Almqvist & Wiksell.

Troncarelli, F. (1998). *Vivarium: I libri, il destino*. Turnhout, Belgium: Brepols.

Velazquez Soriano, I. (Ed.) (1988). *Las pizarras visigodas*. Murcia: Universidad de Murcia.

Velazquez Soriano, I. (Ed.) (2000). *Documentos de época visigoda escritos en pizarra (siglos VI–VIII)*. 2vols. Turnhout, Belgium: Brepols.

Versteegh, C. H. M. (1993). *Arabic grammar and Qur'anic exegesis in early Islam*. Leiden: E. J. Brill.

Versteegh, K. (1997). *The Arabic language*. Edinburgh: Edinburgh University Press.

Vessey, M. (2001), The *Epistula Rustici ad Eucherium*: From the library of imperial classics to the library of the fathers. In R. Mathisen & D. Shanzer (Eds.), *Society and culture in Late*

Antique Gaul: Revisiting the sources. Aldershot, UK: Ashgate (reprinted in Vessey, 2005).

Vessey, M. (2005). *Latin Christian writers in Late Antiquity and their texts*. Aldershot, UK: Ashgate.

Vööbus, A. (1962). *Statutes of the school at Nisbis*. Stockholm: ETSE.

Vööbus, A. (1965). *History of the school at Nisibis*. Corpus Scriptorum Christianorum Orientalium, Subsidia 26. Louvain: *Secrétariat du* CSCO.

Ward-Perkins, B. (2005). *The fall of Rome and the end of civilisation*. Oxford: Oxford University Press.

Whitby, M. (2000a). The army, c. 420–602. In A. Cameron, B. Ward-Perkins, & M. Whitby (Eds.), *The Cambridge ancient history, vol. XIV. Late Antiquity and its successors* AD 425–600 (pp. 288–314). Cambridge: Cambridge University Press.

Whitby, M. (2000b). Armies and society in the later Roman world. In A. Cameron, B. Ward-Perkins, & M. Whitby (Eds.), *The Cambridge ancient history, vol. XIV. Late Antiquity and its successors* AD 425–600 (pp. 469–495). Cambridge: Cambridge University Press.

Wickham, C. (1981). *Early medieval Italy: Central power and local society, 400—1000*. London: Macmillan.

Wickham, C. (2005). *Framing the early Middle Ages. Europe and the Mediterranean 400–800*. Oxford/New York: Oxford University Press.

Wildberg, C. (1993). Simplicius and das Zitat. Zur Überlieferung des Anführungszeichens. In D. Harlfinger & F. Berger (Eds.), *Symbolae Berolinenses: für Dieter Harlfinger*. Amsterdam: A. M. Hakkert.

Wilkinson, J. (1999). *Egeria's travels: Newly translated*. Warminster: Aris & Phillips.

Williams, J. (Ed.) (1999). *Imaging the early medieval Bible*. University Park: Pennsylvania State University Press.

Wilson, N. (1973). *Mediaeval Greek bookhands*. Cambridge, MA: Mediaeval Academy of America.

Wipszycka, E. (1980). Le degré d'alphabetisation en Égypt byzantine. *Revue des Études Augustiniennes*, 30, 279–296.

Wood, I. (1990). Administration, law and culture in Merovingian Gaul. In R. McKitterick (Ed.), *The uses of literacy in early medieval Europe* (pp. 63–81). Cambridge: Cambridge University Press.

Wood, S. (2006). *The proprietary church in the medieval West*. Oxford/New York: Oxford University Press.

Wormald, P. (1977). The uses of literacy in Anglo-Saxon England and its neighbors. *Transactions of the Royal Historical Society, 5th Series* 27, 95–114.

Wormald, P. (1999). *The making of English law: King Alfred to the twelfth century. I. Legislation and its limits*. Oxford: University of Oxford.

Wright, J. (1966/reprinted 1981). *Grammar of the Gothic language*, 2nd ed. Oxford: Clarendon Press.

Wright, R. (1982). *Late Latin and early romance in Spain and Carolingian France*. Liverpool: F. Cairns.

Wright, R. (Ed.) (1991). *Latin and the romance languages in the early Middle Ages*. London: Routledge.

Wright, R. (2002). *A sociophilological study of Late Latin*. Turnhout, Belgium: Brepols.

Young, F., Ayres L., & Louth, A. (Eds.) (2004). *The Cambridge history of early Christian literature*. Cambridge: Cambridge University Press.

Youtie, H. C. (1971). Agrammatos: An aspect of Greek society in Egypt. *Harvard Studies in Classical Philology*, 75, 161–176. (Reprinted in idem, 1973, *Scriptiunculae II*, pp. 611–628. Amsterdam: Hakkert.)

Youtie, H. C. (1975). Hypographaeus: The social impact of illiteracy in Greco-Roman Egypt. *Zeitschrift für Papyrologie*, 17, 201–221. (Reprinted in idem, 1981, *Scriptiunculae Posteriores* II, 179–199. Bonn: Rudolf Habelt.)

Zimmermann, R. (1996). *The law of obligations: Roman foundations of the civilian tradition*. Oxford: Clarendon Press.

CHAPTER 21

Chinese Literacy[1]

Feng Wang, Yaching Tsai, and William S.-Y. Wang

Abstract

This chapter has two central themes. The first addresses literacy among the Han Chinese. Although writing was invented in China several millennia ago, in the form of hanzi,[2] literacy did not become widespread until recent times. We trace the development of literacy historically and discuss its impact on the culture. The other theme addresses the invention of writing among the non-Hans in China. Although hanzi is the only writing system that is widely used, the other inventions are also of great sociolinguistic interest.

Introduction

Discussions on Chinese literacy are often limited to the reading and writing of hanzi. Although hanzi is the most frequently used form in China, it is not the only writing system used there. Among non-Han ethnic groups, several writing systems, including Written Tibetan, Tangut script, Tomba script, Yi script, and Bai script, play important roles in their culture much as hanzi does in the Han culture.

Literacy plays a fundamental role in cultural development. Questions like the following may be pursued: What is read and written? Who is taught to read and write? Who does the teaching? How is the teaching of reading and writing undertaken? How do people view literacy? What is the difference between a literate and an illiterate person? These questions are all closely related to culture.

In the following sections, the answers to these questions about Chinese literacy are discussed. The first section introduces the history of literacy in the Han culture, focussing on the development of hanzi and its transmission. In the second section, the uniqueness of hanzi is analyzed in terms of historical value, cognition and its influence on other writing systems. The third section observes the role of literacy in the Chinese society. With time, literacy interacts with other cultural elements and has great impact on culture. In the fourth section, the literacy of non-Han groups in China is outlined. The different inventions evolve under the shadow of hanzi. Their development and the history of Han literacy together constitute the wonderful diversity of writing systems in China.

History of Literacy Among Han Chinese

With the expansion of Han culture, hanzi is transmitted to wide areas as a salient characteristic of Han culture. In the long history of China, Han people were not always the victor when fighting with other ethnic groups. For instance, in the Yuan dynasty (1271–1368), China was under the control of the Mongolians. In the Qing dynasty (1644–1911), Manchu people had the dominant power for about three hundred years. These non-Han groups had the right to set their writing systems as the national standard and to suppress the hanzi system. However, they always failed in this direction; Hanzi and the Han culture have always survived.

It might be inappropriate to regard hanzi simply as the written form of the Chinese language. It became a token of Han culture from a very early time. The archaeological excavations at Banpo (半坡) near Xi'an uncovered some abstract symbols etched in pottery. Those symbols are assumed to be the antecedents of the oracle-bone inscriptions (Ho, 1976), although the issue is still controversial.

Nature of Hanzi

Hanzi can be defined as a morphosyllabic writing system (Qiu, 1988; Wang, 1973). In the hanzi system, a character generally represents a syllable and corresponds to a morpheme – for example, 日 (ri 'sun'), 月 (yue 'moon') and 山 (shan 'mountain'). In some cases, more than one character is used to represent a morpheme – for example, 犹豫 (youyu 'hesitate'), 参差 (cenci 'uneven') and 徜徉 (changyang 'wander'). In these examples, each character still corresponds to a single syllable.

Generally, a hanzi can be divided into parts. The principles of hanzi formation were summarized in *Shuowen Jiezi* (121 CE) by Xu Shen 许慎 (c. 58–147). The 9,353 hanzis have been classified into six categories (Liushu 六书): (1) simple ideograms (Zhishi 指事), (2) pictographs (Xiangxing 象形), (3) phonograms (Xingsheng 形声), (4) complex ideograms (Huiyi 会意), (5) derivatives (Zhuanzhu 转注), and (6) phonetic loans (Jiajie 假借).[3] This framework had been followed by Chinese philologists for almost two thousand years, until philologists in the Qing dynasty proposed different ideas. Now, the generally accepted framework is called Sanshu 三书 (i.e., three principles): (1) meaning-representation (Biaoyi 表意) – for example, 三 (san 'three'), 水(shui 'water'), 本 (ben 'root'), 矢 (shi 'arrow'), and 夹 (jia 'nip'); (2) phonetic loan (Jiajie 假借) – for example, 其 (qi 'demonstrative pronoun'), 亦 (yi 'also'), and 彼 (bi 'that, those'); and (3) phonograms (Xingsheng 形声) – for example, 峡 (xia 'gorge'), 胡 (hu 'wattle of animal'), 霖 (lin 'long-continued rain'), 岱 (dai 'Mt. Tai'), 旗 (qi 'flag'), 载 (zai 'carry'), 圆 (yuan 'round'), and 闻 (wen 'hear') (Qiu, 1988, pp. 97–109). The phonogram is always the most numerous category.

Development of the Types of Hanzi

How to differentiate drawing-like writing from real writing is controversial among orthographers. The exact date of hanzi is difficult to determine. Therefore, the question of how the hanzi writing system came into being is more meaningful. In the unearthed materials of ancient hanzi, the earliest can be dated back to the late Shang dynasty, around 1400–1100 BCE. They are well known as oracle-bone characters. In the literature, it is also said that written volumes were made by the ancestors of the Shang dynasty.[4] In the Shang dynasty, brush pens were the major tool of writing. In the oracle character, the character meaning 'writing tool' is [illegible], which is the picture of writing with a brush pen. However, most writings in brush pen could not be preserved due to the perishable material used for them.

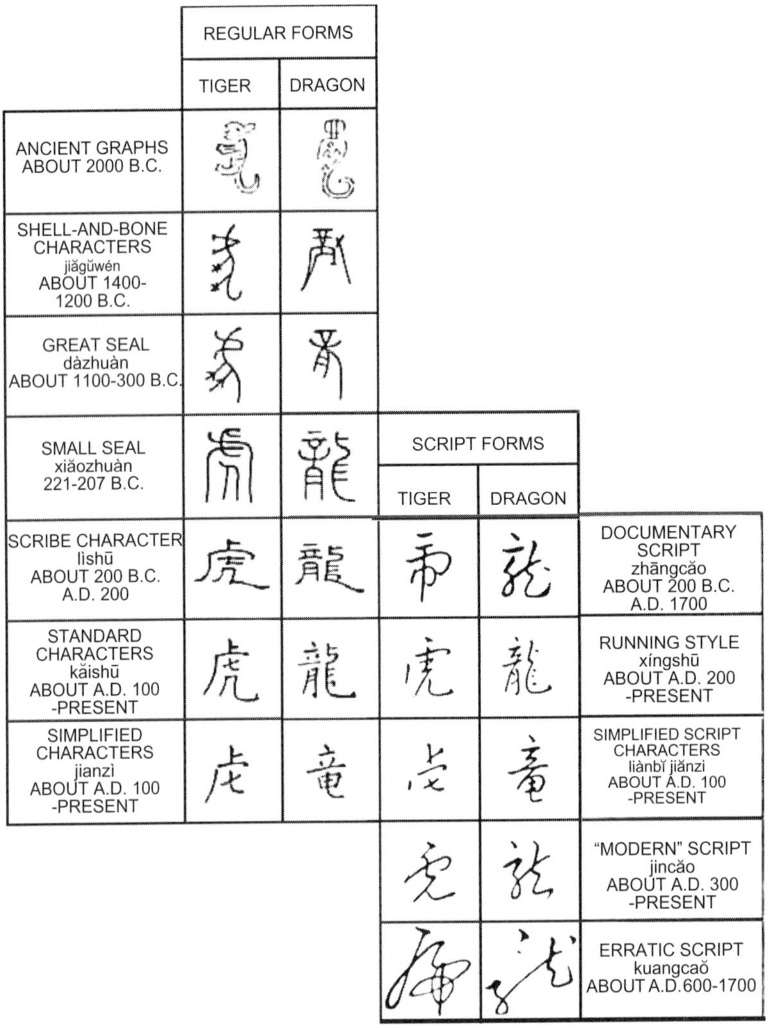

	REGULAR FORMS		SCRIPT FORMS		
	TIGER	DRAGON	TIGER	DRAGON	
ANCIENT GRAPHS ABOUT 2000 B.C.					
SHELL-AND-BONE CHARACTERS jiǎgǔwén ABOUT 1400-1200 B.C.					
GREAT SEAL dàzhuàn ABOUT 1100-300 B.C.					
SMALL SEAL xiǎozhuàn 221-207 B.C.					
SCRIBE CHARACTER lìshū ABOUT 200 B.C. A.D. 200					DOCUMENTARY SCRIPT zhāngcǎo ABOUT 200 B.C. A.D. 1700
STANDARD CHARACTERS kǎishū ABOUT A.D. 100 -PRESENT					RUNNING STYLE xíngshū ABOUT A.D. 200 -PRESENT
SIMPLIFIED CHARACTERS jianzì ABOUT A.D. 100 -PRESENT					SIMPLIFIED SCRIPT CHARACTERS liànbǐ jiǎnzi ABOUT A.D. 100 -PRESENT
					"MODERN" SCRIPT jincǎo ABOUT A.D. 300 -PRESENT
					ERRATIC SCRIPT kuangcaǒ ABOUT A.D.600-1700

Historical Development of pictographic characters for the two most powerful animals in Chinese mythology, the tiger and the dragon, are shown in their various stages. The earliest known pictographic forms of the animals are at the top. The illustration is from *Introduction to Chinese Cursive Script.* by F. Y. Wang of Seton Hall University

Figure 21.1. The evolution of hanzi types (from Wang, 1973).

According to the differences in shape, hanzi can be classified into oracle-bone inscriptions (Jiaguwen 甲骨文), bronze inscriptions (Jinwen 金文), small seal (Xiaozhuan 小篆), clerical script (Lishu 隶书), regular script (Kaishu 楷书[5]), cursive style (Caoshu 草书), and running script (Xingshu 行书) (shown in Figure 21.1).

Oracle-bone inscriptions were used extensively in the late Shang dynasty; however, they were recognized only a hundred years ago. Most oracle-bone characters are inscribed on turtleshells or bones of animals. Some are written by brush pen in ink or vermilion. They were buried in the historic site, Yinxu 殷墟, in the northwest of Anyang City of He'nan province, which was the capital of Shang from ca. 1300 BCE to 1100 BCE. So far, almost 100,000 pieces of shells and bones with characters have been unearthed. Most of them are the record of divinations about activities of the ruling class. The rulers in the Shang dynasty were in awe of the power of the heavens. They used turtle shell or the shoulders blade bone of an ox to auger the idea of the heavens for all kinds of questions (e.g., Is it going to rain tomorrow? Shall we go hunting? Are we going to win the war against our enemy?). After a divination, the specialists usually recorded the reason, the predication and the final result by sculpting characters on shells or bones.

In the Shang dynasty, there was another type of writing of hanzi: inscriptions on bronze. The earliest inscriptions on bronze marked the family name of the person who made the bronzeware and the title of the ancestor that the bronzeware commemorates. Inscriptions on each bronzeware piece mostly consist of several characters; the longest one from the Shang dynasty contains forty-eight characters.

The forms in inscriptions on bronze were the orthography at that time and were used on formal occasions. In comparison, oracle-bone characters were the convenient variant in ordinary life, called 'vulgar type' (Suti 俗体). The strokes in oracle-bone characters are different from inscriptions on bronzeware. Because shells and bones are difficult to inscribe and divination was done frequently, the strokes had to be simplified to improve efficiency of recording. Therefore, inscriptions on bronzeware kept the earlier shapes of hanzi.

From Shang to Western Zhou (1066–771 BCE), the shapes of oracle-bone characters and inscriptions on bronzeware witnessed no major changes. However, during the Warrior States Period (403–221 BCE), the social structure began to change and the landlord class became the new elite. On the one hand, in the new society, the writing system started to be diffused to more people, not just limited to the elite any longer. On the other hand, the writing system was widely used in more domains, without being restricted to the record of divinations. For these reasons, the writing system of hanzi changed abruptly. It developed along two lines: the Qin type and the six-state type. The Qin type of hanzi follows the tradition of Western Zhou because the Qin people lived at the site of Western Zhou. Moreover, the Qin state was located in an enclosed area and its economy developed slowly. The other six states were more advanced.

Because of frequent and wide use, the vulgar type became dominant. It appeared on bronzeware, stamps, coins, pottery, bamboo slips, silk, stone, and so forth. Although among the unearthed ancient written materials, the earliest bamboo slips and silk used for writing were from the Warrior States Period, it does not suggest that they were used for writing so late. Bamboo slips and silk were difficult to preserve. The earlier characters written on them before the Warrior States Period were easily damaged. Based on other indirect evidence, it is estimated that bamboo slips were likely to be used at the beginning of Shang; silk used as a writing material came later. Nevertheless, because of their convenience, both were the major writing materials before paper was invented.

In the Qin state, the characters were modified to be more symmetrical; the shape of the characters became less pictorial. The earlier type of character in Qin, the stone-drum script (Shigu wen 石鼓文), was simplified into the later type, the small seal script (Xiaozhuan 小篆). Compare the following two characters ('horse' and 'complete') written in both types:

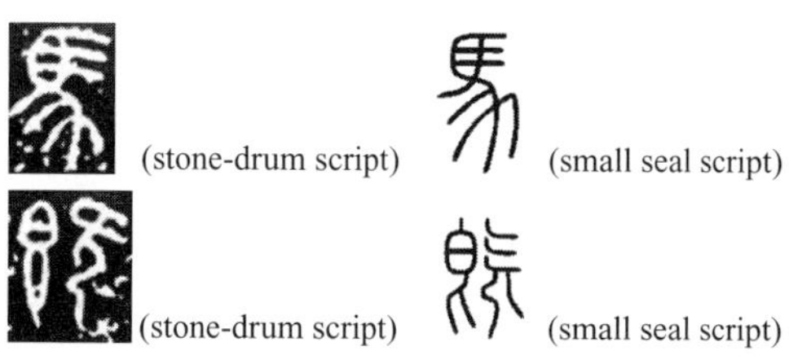

Figure 21.2. Stone-drum script and small seal script of 'horse' and 'complete'.

After the Qin state conquered the other six states in 221 BCE, the emperor, Qinshihuang, realized that different variants of hanzi in different states hindered the development of China as a unified nation. He decided that the writing system, as an important tool of communication, should be unified in the entire territory of China. Therefore, Qinshihuang promulgated a law to establish small seal script as the standard writing of China and other variants of hanzi were abolished. This was a famous event in Chinese history, called 'Writing in the unified characters' (Shutongwen 书同文).

In the Qin state, small seal script was used as the orthodox type on formal occasions. For informal occasions, a type of vulgar script (Suti 俗体) was widely used, which was the early clerical script. During the several hundred years from Qin to Han, clerical script gradually replaced small seal script. Through modification or omission of some small-seal strokes, clerical-script strokes became simpler and smoother. This change greatly improved the speed of writing.

In this transition period, *Shuowen Jiezi* by Xu Shen played an important role. Xu Shen tried to define the original meaning of each character and the standard orthography. Many vulgar scripts and phonetic loans were abandoned.

During the Han-Wei-Jin Period, clerical script was the most popular type. In the Southern and Northern Dynasties Period, a new type of hanzi – the regular script (Kaishu 楷书) – became the major form, which persists today. Although two other types of hanzi emerged, the running script (Xingshu 行书) and the cursive style (Caoshu 草书), they did not replace the regular script, possibly because they were too cursive and not easily recognizable. In comparing the examples of these three types of hanzi in Figure 21.1, the reason why the regular script was immediately accepted as the standard of hanzi after its creation may be apparent.

Simplification is the major direction in the evolution of hanzi types. The government of the People's Republic of China (PRC) tried to establish the standard Hanzi system and to further simplify it. Throughout its history, some hanzi has been written in different forms – for instance, 杯, 盃, 桮. In 1955, the government published 810 sets of such variants and legalized one from each set, which resulted in 1,053 characters being discarded.[6] In 1956, the Chinese Characters Simplification Project (Hanzi jianhua fang'an 汉字简化方案) was established to simplify hanzi. In this project, 515 simplified hanzis and 54 components of character were regulated, resulting in a major stroke reduction, which facilitates writing – for example, 麗 'beautiful' → 丽, 華 'luxurious' → 华, 繫 'tie' → 系. However, it also has some drawbacks, such as ruination of the structure (買 'buy' → 买), increase of similar forms (設 'set' → 设 versus 没 'without'), elimination of the one-to-one match between morpheme and character (幾 'a few, several' → 儿 versus 儿 'teapoy'). Such drawbacks became more obvious in the second proposal of hanzi simplification in 1977.[7] This proposal was abandoned in 1986 because of rejection by society.

Before the twentieth century, a written paragraph was oriented top to bottom and right to left. Perhaps partly motivated by the greater convenience of incorporating such items as English or Arabic numerals, the format from left to right has prevailed in the last few decades.

How to Read Hanzi

The language on which the hanzi system was based varied with the change in capitals of different dynasties. However, the central government of China was always located in the north.[8] Therefore, Northern Chinese played a crucial role in the development of the standard literary language.

For a long time, the standard reading language was called 'Elegant Speech' (Yayan 雅言), which appeared at least in the pre-Qin Period.[9] Yayan is the language of Xia 夏, which was spoken near the Yellow River area. In contrast, languages in Yue[10] and Chu[11] were treated as barbarian languages[12] that should not be used to read hanzi, at least on formal occasions. The standard spoken language was clearly explicated in Yang Xiong's 扬雄 (53–18 BCE) great book, *Fangyan* 方言.[13] The so-called Fanyu 凡语 or Tongyu 通语 was the standard.

Starting with the Sui-Tang dynasties, poem-composition became important in literary life. Because the rhyming of a poem was essential, the standard reading system of hanzi had to be defined. For this purpose, a great rhyme book, *Qieyun* 切韵, was compiled by several leading scholars.[14] In its preface, it was said that the principle of compiling the book was to consider Nanbeishifei 南北是非 (i.e., the right and the wrong of south and north) and Gujintongsai 古今通塞 (i.e., the prevailing and the obsolete of past and present) (Ting, 1998). In other words, *Qieyun* provided a composite system based on more than one single dialect.[15] *Qieyun* soon became the dominant rhyme book. The central government of the Sui dynasty selected it as the standard for Civil Service Examinations (Keju 科举). In the Tang dynasty, it was edited as *Tangyun* 唐韵, with some minor modifications, and used as the standard for rhyming.

In the Song dynasty, Chen Pengnian 陈彭年 (961–1017) and Qiu Yong 邱雍 promulgated a most important revision of *Qieyun*. The new version was entitled *Dasong Chongxiu Guangyun* 大宋重修广韵, abbreviated as *Guangyun*. The phonological system of *Qieyun* was maintained. In other words, the standard reading of hanzi remained almost unchanged during several hundred years, whereas the spoken language evolved and changed over many centuries. This caused a discrepancy between the literary hanzi reading and the spoken language. For the Keju exams, Ding Du 丁度 (990–1053) edited a new rhyme book entitled *Libuyunlüe* 礼部韵略, which considered the colloquial language. Therefore, it simplified 206 rhymes of *Guangyun* into 108 rhymes. This modification minimized the discrepancy between the reading of hanzi and pronunciation in the spoken language. However, *Libuyunlüe* as the standard of hanzi reading lasted only a little more than two hundred years during the Song-Yuan Period.[16] In those two hundred years, the spoken language changed gradually; at the beginning of the Ming dynasty, the pronunciation in the spoken language was already very different from the ancient regulations specified in *Libuyunlüe* 礼部韵略. This status called for a new standard; therefore, *Hongwuzhengyun* 洪武正韵 was promulgated. Its principle was to follow the Elegant Speech of Central China,[17] and the pronunciations that were more intelligible among people of various dialectal backgrounds would be selected as the standard. The common language used by people from different areas was coined as Guanhua (Koine) in the Ming dynasty,[18] which translated in Portuguese to Falla Madarin at the end of the Ming dynasty. The new standard met the need of that time.

In the Qing dynasty,[19] Zhang Yushu 张玉书 was ordered by the emperor Kangxi 康熙 (1654–1722) to edit the rhyme book *Peiwenshiyun* 佩文诗韵, which follows the structure of Ping Shuiyun 平水韵. This standard went back to the Song-Yuan dynasties. Therefore, the distance between hanzi reading and spoken language was even greater than that in the Song-Yuan Period. The literate people had to learn the phonological information of hanzi from rhyme books. For instance, although the entering tone merged into the other tones in Northern Chinese around the eleventh century, the literate people persisted in pronouncing the entering tone in an invented contour for almost five hundred years[20] because the entering tone was regarded as the crucial part of Elegant Speech. This continued until the May Fourth Movement that occurred in Beijing. The movement succeeded in promoting both the sound of Pekingese as the new standard of national language and writing and reading in vernacular. When the PRC was founded in 1949, Putonghua 普通话 (i.e., common language) was legitimized as the national language. Putonghua uses the Beijing sound as the standard, whose foundation is Northern Mandarin and whose grammar standard follows the classic vernacular literature.

There appeared several methods to notate the pronunciation of hanzi. Before Eastern Han (25–220), homophone or near homophone was used to notate a certain character. Sometimes the pronunciation of a character was provided by a near homophone, along with supplementary information on how some of its phonological features were to be modified – for example, 駤读似质，缓气言之，在舌头乃得[21] ("駤" can be pronounced as "质", but the sound should be read slowly). This method failed to notate characters accurately. Possibly stimulated by Sanskrit, another method, Fanqie 反切,[22]

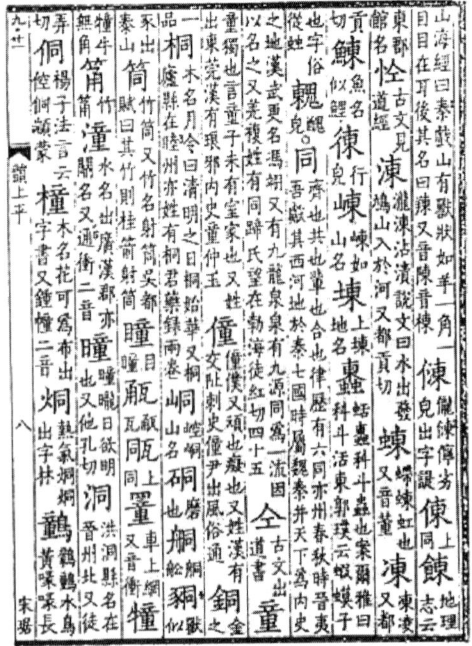

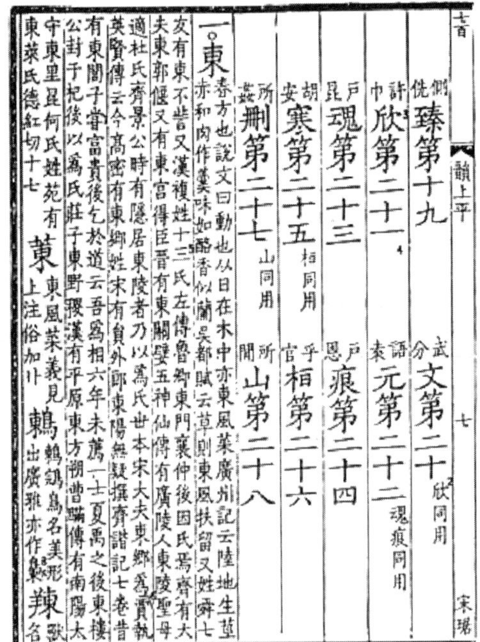

Figure 21.3. A sample from the rhyme book *Guangyun*.

was used to spell a character by means of two other characters, the former sharing the same initial with the notated and the latter sharing the same final; for example: 同[tong2], 徒[tu2]红[hong2]切, 都[du1], 当[dang1]孤[ku1]切.

Rhyme books such as *Qieyun* organized hanzi according to their phonological information. They are classified according to Diao 调 (tone), Yun 韵 (rhyme), and Niu 纽 (homophone set). Under each entry, a gloss was given. Under the first entry of each homophone set, the Fanqie was given. The number following the Fanqie indicated how many characters there are in this set. Figure 21.3 shows an example.

According to tone categories, rhyme books were first divided into four parts because there are four tones in Middle Chinese: Pingsheng 平声 (even tone), Shangsheng 上声 (rising tone), Qusheng 去声 (departing tone), and Rusheng 入声 (entering tone). Each tone part was then subdivided into rhyme groups. All characters of the same rhyme group could rhyme with each other. Each rhyme group was named after the first entry. Each rhyme group was further divided into homophone sets that were separated by a circle. In Figure 21.3, the seventeen entries starting from Dong 東 (counted from right to left) comprise a homophone set, whose end is indicated by the circle above the character Tong 同. If a character had more than one pronunciation, it was notated by another Fanqie spelling or another character. The character You 又 ('also, additionally') was used to mark the additional reading.

In the Song dynasty, a rhyme table tradition was created to represent the phonological information of hanzi. The earliest one was *Yunjing* 韵镜 (mirror of rhymes),[23] which consisted of forty-three charts, called Zhuan 转 (turn) in the Chinese term. Each chart tabulated hanzi in style shown in Figure 21.4.

The twenty-three columns of hanzi were divided into six groups according to the place of articulation[24] of their initials, such as labial, dental, laryngeal, and so on. Within the six groups these initials were subdivided according to their manner of articulation. The sixteen rows were separated into four groups to represent the four tone categories of Middle Chinese. Within the four groups, finals were classified into four categories,

Table 21.1. The Initials in Hanyu Pinyin Fang'an

b[p]	p[pʰ]	m[m]	f[f]	d[t]	t[tʰ]	n[n]	l[l]
ㄅ玻	ㄆ坡	ㄇ摸	ㄈ佛	ㄉ得	ㄊ特	ㄋ讷	ㄌ勒
g[k]	k[kʰ]	h[x]		j[tɕ]	q[tɕʰ]	x[ɕ]	
ㄍ哥	ㄎ科	ㄏ喝		ㄐ基	ㄑ欺	ㄒ希	
zh[tʂ]	ch[tʂʰʰ]	sh[ʂ]	r[ʐ]	z[ts]	c[tsʰ]	s[s]	
ㄓ知	ㄔ蚩	ㄕ诗	ㄖ日	ㄗ资	ㄘ雌	ㄙ思	

called Deng 等 (divisions or grades), and numbered as division 1, division 2, division 3, and division 4. The phonetic value of these Deng and Zhuan was very controversial (Baxter, 1992, 41–43). The organization of the charts was similar to the inventories of syllables in modern linguistics.

Phonetic categories of initials or finals were regarded as crucial in hanzi recognition, whereas the phonetic value of a certain character was ignored for thousands of years. It was not until the beginning of the twentieth century that Pinyin was introduced to notate hanzi. In 1918, Zhuyin zimu 注音字母 (i.e., symbols of phonetic notation) was issued to spell hanzi. These symbols were created by simplifying archaic characters and they consisted of three parts: initial, medial, and rhyme. However, the international trend at that time was to use the Latin alphabet.[25] After a long debate about whether to adopt Zhuyin zimu or the Latin alphabet for the national language of China, the proposal for Romanization was accepted by most people. On the basis of different proposals, the central government of the PRC issued Hanyu pinyin fang'an 汉语拼音方案 (i.e., Chinese Romanization Project). Table 21.1 shows initials with different transcription systems [the symbol under the Latin alphabet is the Zhuyin zimu followed by a hanzi

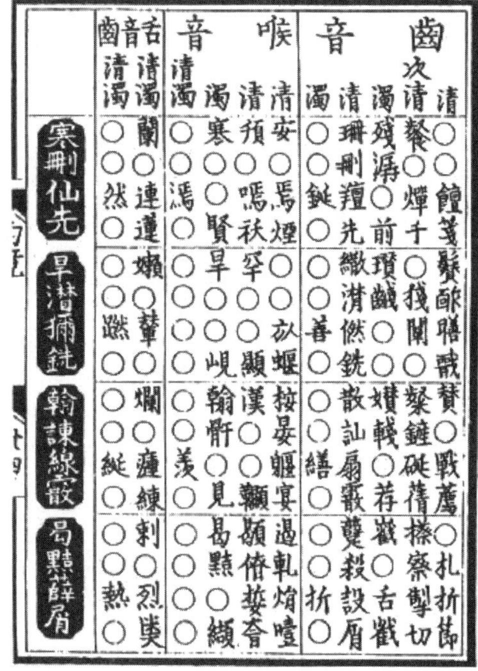

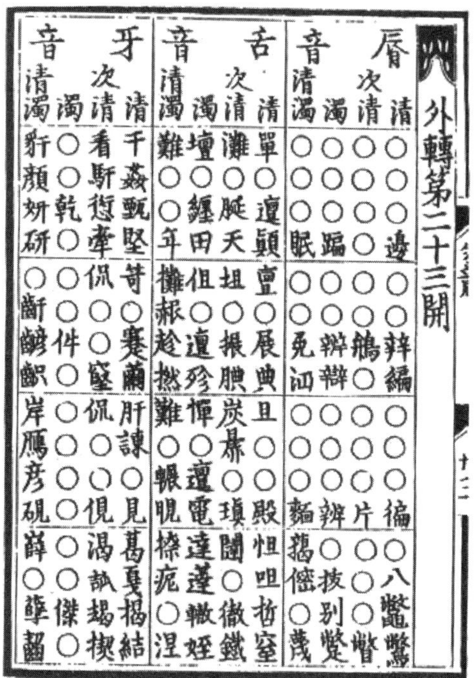

Figure 21.4. A sample from the rhyme table *Yunjing*.

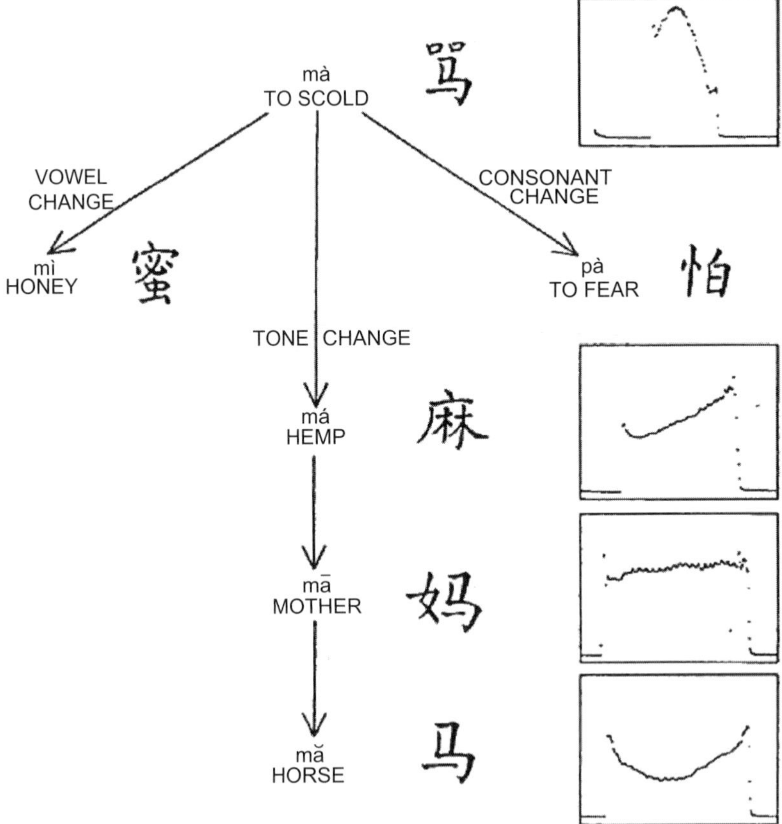

Figure 21.5. The four tones of the Beijing dialect of Chinese (adapted from Wang, 1973).

example; IPA (International Phonetic Alphabet, devised by the International Phonetic Association as a standardized representation of the sounds of spoken language) is added].

Tones are indicated by diacritical marks over the vowels, as shown in Figure 21.5. The computer-generated traces on the right-side show the fundamental frequency of one of the authors as he uttered these words (Wang, 1973).

Thereafter, the pronunciation of hanzi was finally accurately represented by the Pinyin system. More than 3.5 millennia elapsed since hanzi was invented.

School

DEVELOPMENT OF THE SCHOOL SYSTEM

The school for literacy in China is called Xiaoxue 小学 (primary school) or Mengxue 蒙学 (illuminating school). Such an institution was initiated before the Han dynasty. With development throughout Han-Wei-Jin Period, this system became more sophisticated. Textbooks, teaching skills and teachers also cooperated better. These aspects are discussed in this section.

The earliest school, called Xu 序[26] or Xiao 校,[27] presumably appeared in the Xia dynasty (2200–1700 BCE), but it is not clear what was taught there. In the Shang dynasty (1700–1100 BCE), the school for literacy definitely appeared.[28] In the Western Zhou, two types of schools – Guoxue 国学 (national school) and Xiangxue 乡学 (local school) – were established. Guoxue was the national institute for children of nobles and was classified into two grades: Xiaoxue 小学 (junior school) and Daxue 大学 (senior school). Xiangxue was the local school for children of slaveholders or ordinary people. Teachers were appointed by government officials. In these schools, six subjects were taught, the so-called Liuyi 六艺 (six arts): ritual (li 礼), music (yue 乐), archery (she 射), riding (yu 御), writing (shu 书) and arithmetic (shu 数). This order suggests that writing was regarded as more important than reading. The operation of the early school system was clearly portrayed in *Liji-Xueji*:

> *There are three kinds of teaching institutes in ancient time. They are Shu at home, Xiang of town, and Xue of the nation. The Xue recruits students annually. Students thus recruited will be examined every other year. These students will be tested one year later, to see if they are able to parse classics and distinguish directions of their developments; three years later, to see if they respect their career and collaborate well with others; five years later, to see if they have studied extensively and got along with their teachers; seven years later, to see if they know how to argue and how to select friends. Students who pass these tests will be regarded to have 'a minor success.' In the ninth year, students will be tested to see if they can integrate all kinds of knowledge and if they have a determined mind and consistent behavior. All the qualified students are then said to have 'a major success.'*[29]

In the Spring and Autumn Period (770–476 BCE), public schools funded by the government declined whereas private schools gradually gained popularity. The most famous private school was propagandized by Confucius, who accepted students from different social strata. He diffused schooling and educated more students of different backgrounds, enabling them to become literate. Literacy was no longer monopolized by the government. Private schools were flourishing during the Warrior States Period.

When the Qin state united with the other six states in 221 BCE, private schools were banned by the dynasty to enhance the government image in the spiritual domain. The old school system according to the strict principle of learning from government officials was resumed.

In the Han dynasty, both public school (Guanxue 官学) and private school (Sixue 私学) developed prosperously. The full system composed of national schools and local schools was established. The special school for primary literacy, called Shuguan 书馆 (book house), was initiated. In *Hanshu-Yiwenzhi*, it was said:

> *In ancient times, children were sent to the primary school when they reached the age of eight. In the early Zhou dynasty, the official Baoshi was responsible for teaching students the six principles of hanzi-making, which are pictograph, indicative, meaning-compound, onomatopoeic, derivative, and phonetic borrowing. In the beginning of the Han dynasty, Xiao He drafted the regulations and proclaimed that students who wrote more than 9,000 hanzis on the test would be selected as the official Shi. These candidates would thus be tested on writing in the six types of hanzi. The best ones will be appointed as Shangshu, Yushi, Shishu or Lingshi. If the hanzis in the reports to the Emperor by officials or ordinary people are not written in the orthodox type, the authors would be denounced.*[30]

In the Wei-Jin Period (220–420), frequent wars caused disorder in society. Under the tumultuous circumstances, the school system eventually broke down. After that, Sui-Tang (581–960) reached a socioeconomic pinnacle in ancient China. The strong central government advanced the development of Guanxue (public school). The emperors highly regarded schools and issued guidelines to set up all levels of schools in the entire country. In 618, Xiaoxue 小学 was administered by Mishusheng 秘书省 (secretary department), specifically for teaching the children of royal families and meritorious officials, whereas Mengxue 蒙学 (illuminating school) of private schools served the ordinary families. Notably, schools in the Tang dynasty recruited foreign students from contiguous countries, such as Sinla, Gaoli, and Japan.

In the Song dynasty (960–1279), the system of Guanxue 官学 became more sophisticated. Many kinds of institutes were created; for instance, Zongxue 宗学 (royal school), Jiashu 家塾 (home school), and Dongxue 冬学 (winter school). A new type of school, Shuyuan 书院 (book compound), appeared which combined the functions of the classroom, library and cult of Confucius.

The Yuan dynasty (1206–1368) was ruled by the Mongols. Although the number of Mongolian schools increased, the schools of Han literacy still comprised the majority. Textbooks and school systems were copied, but there were stricter requirements of the Han students than the Mongols and non-Han people from Central Asia (called Semu 色目, 'colored eyes'). In 1270, the Shexue 社学 (commune school) was promoted by the central government, which required that every fifty households, comprising one She 社 (commune), set up one school in which children received their schooling in their spare time. In 1288, the number of commune schools had grown to approximately 24,440. One feature that characterized education in the Yuan dynasty is that different ethnic groups learned from each other at school.

The school system in the Ming dynasty (1368–1644) was similar to that in Tang and Song. Guozijian 国子监 recruited students not only from China but also from Korea, Ryukyus, Japan, and other countries, all of whom were called Yisheng 夷生 (foreign student). All their living expenses were provided for by the central government. The requirements of their study program were much stricter than before. The Shexue initiated in Yuan was promoted extensively. However, it was gradually abandoned after the middle Ming dynasty. Although Shuyuan had been prohibited several times by the central government, it continued to develop because of the support of the common people.

The Qing dynasty (1644–1911) before 1840 followed the school system of the Ming dynasty. However, Shuyuan was controlled by the government and became a variant of the public school. After 1840 (i.e., the Opium War), with the intrusion of Western imperialism, the Western style of school became the new model.

At school, Wenyan 文言, the literary speech formed in the Qin-Han Period, was transmitted across different dynasties. Its divergence from the spoken language grew larger and larger, which caused more difficulties in becoming literate. Many people could not afford the expense of educating their children. As soon as the Wenyan system became mainstream, systems close to the spoken language were suppressed.

TEXTBOOKS

Textbooks in the Primary Stage In the traditional literacy education, the most important part is to learn hanzi. At the beginning of primary school, it usually takes about one year to teach students to recognize approximately two thousand characters. The training for writing is arranged in a later stage. It is believed that students will be able to read texts after having learned to recognize the basic hanzis. Therefore, textbooks for Chinese literacy education can be classified into two categories: hanzi-recognition and hanzi-writing.

Let us first look at textbooks for hanzi-recognition in Chinese history. According to the documentation in *Hanshu-Yiwenzhi* 汉书·艺文志, several types of textbooks for hanzi-learning appeared during the Zhou, Qin and Han dynasties, such as *Shizhoupian* 史籀篇, *Cangjiepian* 仓颉篇, *Fanjiangpian* 凡将篇, and *Jijiupian* 急就篇. Among them, the most popular one was *Jijiupian* 急就篇, which was edited by Shi You 史游 of Western Han circa 40 BCE. It contains the 2,144 hanzis[31] that were frequently used in that period. For ease of learning, they were organized in rhymed lines of three, four or seven characters, as shown in the following example:

宋延年, song yan nian
郑子方, zheng zi fang
卫益寿, wei yi shou
史步昌。shi bu chang
边境无事, bian jing wu shi
中国安宁。zhong guo an ning
百姓承德, bai xing cheng de
阴阳和平。yin yang he ping
乘风县钟华洞乐, cheng feng xian zhong hua dong le
豹首落莫兔双鹤。bao shou luo mo tu shuang he

The characters were rarely repeated in the textbooks. The characters are well organized semantically; every line expresses a certain meaning. The lines are grouped into three parts: surnames and names (姓氏名字), things (服器百物), and reasoning (文学法理).

Jijiupian 急就篇 was divided into thirty-four chapters, each chapter serving as a lesson. This textbook was dominant in literacy training until the Tang dynasty.

In the Southern and Northern Dynasties Period, a new textbook, *Qianziwen* 千字文, was compiled by Zhou Xingsi 周兴嗣. After its appearance, it became popular throughout most of China. It was so popular that one could make a living by transcribing it for illiterate people.[32] On many occasions, the character order in *Qianziwen* was used as an index. *Qianziwen* was the primary textbook of hanzi not only among Han people but also among other ethnic groups of China, as well as Japan. Until the Tang dynasty, it had been in circulation for about thousand years, a miracle in the history of literacy.

Qianziwen contains 250 four-character lines; for example:

天地玄黄, tian di xuan huang
宇宙洪荒。yu zhou hong huang
日月盈昃, ri yue ying ze
辰宿列张。chen xiu lie zhang

In those thousand characters, almost none is repeated. Starting from natural phenomena, *Qianziwen* introduced common knowledge of that time, including historical events in Chinese history, agriculture, and so forth. It was a great achievement to express such wide-ranging content with only a thousand characters. It kept the tradition of using rhymed lines for easy reciting. Both the characters and syntactic structures in *Qianziwen* were frequently used at that time. All of these characteristics resulted in *Qianziwen* being the best textbook for beginners.

In the Song dynasty, *Sanzijing* 三字经 appeared, which was a complement of *Qianziwen* in several aspects. The entire book was written in three-character rhymed lines; for example:

人之初, ren zhi chu
性本善。xing ben shan
性相近, xing xiang jin
习相远。xi xiang yuan

Men at birth,
Are naturally good.
Their nature is much the same,
Their habits are widely different.

Compared with *Qianziwen*, the vocabulary used in *Sanzijing* was similar to colloquial language. More noticeably, *Sanzijing* also served as a good grammar book. Although it did not explain syntactic constructions, it helped children become familiar with all types of structures. It is not known whether the author did this deliberately, but the textbook did play an essential role in learning syntax.[33]

In the Song dynasty, another new textbook, *Baijiaxing* 百家姓[34], appeared, which consisted of 472 Chinese surnames composed in four-character lines. Different from *Qianziwen* and *Sanzijing*, the lines in *Baijiaxing* do not bear any meaningful content; for example:

赵钱孙李, zhao qian sun li
周吴郑王. zhou wu zheng wang

It is interesting that the three textbooks complemented each other and constituted an entire set of textbooks for hanzi-recognition. Lü Kun 吕坤 of the Ming dynasty explained the complementary relationship of the three textbooks in terms of language use, as follows:

> *At the very beginning of Shexue, children under 8 years of age are taught to read* Sanzijing *in order to broaden their horizons.* Baijiaxing *is taught to them for the daily use. As for* Qianziwen, *it is mainly used to explain reasoning and tradition.*[35]

The following reasons may explain why the three textbooks prevailed for so many years: (1) rhymed lines were convenient for reciting; (2) there are not too many characters; of the total 2,612, some characters are repeated, so only about 1,000 characters needed to be learned; (3) high-frequency words were selected; and (4) the content expressed common things and principles in everyday life.

Many textbooks were edited for hanzi-recognition on the basis of these three books in the history of Chinese, such as *Kaimengyaoxun* 开蒙要训, *Xuqianwen* 续千文, *Sanzijian* 三字鉴, and *Yuzhi Baijiaxing* 御制百家姓. However, they were often abandoned after temporary use.

During the Ming-Qing Period, another style of textbook, called *Zazi* 杂字 (mixed characters), became popular among people of the lower class; for example:

– From *Shandong zhuangnong riyong zazi* 山东庄农日用杂字
In the human life and the nature,
The most important thing is agriculture.
To record the daily account,
You should learn *Zazi* first.[36]

– *From Shanxi zazi bidu* 山西杂字必读
Living in the world,
The most important things are farming and reading.
While doing business,
Is to earn money.[37]

Compared with *Sanzijing* and *Qianziwen*, such textbooks were more practical because they were edited for particular readers, such as farmers and merchants. These textbooks from different areas all presented their local characteristics. Generally, such textbooks did not contain many words and could be taught in a short period (i.e., two or three months). Therefore, they were good for people who only needed literacy to manage simple aspects of ordinary life, such as account-keeping and letter-writing.

As for training for hanzi-writing, other texts were edited. In the Tang dynasty, a typical textbook for writing looked like the following:

上大人，丘乙己，　化三千，七十士，女小生，
牛羊千，口舌Δ[38]，不受大，不于申，子乙到，
之夫者也。[39]

In the Song dynasty, they were modified as follows:

上大人，　丘乙己。化三千，　七十士。尔小生，
八九子。佳作仁，可知礼也。

It is easy to see that these characters consisted of only a few strokes; they were selected deliberately for beginners.

The separate tasks of training hanzi-recognition and hanzi-writing ended after the PRC; now the two types of training are combined and called Yuwen 语文. The textbooks are available in several levels: every level consists of several identical sections but they are arranged from the simpler to the more complex.

The Hanyu pinyin fang'an (i.e., Chinese Romanization Project) brought a new dimension of literacy to China. In an earlier stage of learning hanzi, the pinyin system is taught. After having been trained for about seven weeks, children know how to use pinyin to spell syllables. They then learn to recognize hanzi and to write or read texts in pinyin at the same time. This new approach undermines the conviction that a certain number of hanzis must be learned before proceeding to any other aspects of literacy.[40] During the first two or three years of primary school, the hanzis in textbooks are usually notated by pinyin. Later, at the higher level of primary school, pinyin notation is restricted to only the new characters.

Textbooks in the Advanced Stage After training in hanzi-recognition and hanzi-writing, children acquire about two thousand characters. The next step is to teach them to read texts. At first, some simple storybooks are used; they no longer rhyme, and often fall into two categories: classic stories or stories about renowned historical figures. Generally, every story is composed of about hundred characters. In these texts, difficult characters have phonetic and semantic footnotes.

In the Ming dynasty, some pictorial storybooks appeared – for example, *Yangzhengtujie* 养正图解 by Jiao Hong 焦竑, *Mengyangtushuo* 蒙养图说 by Tao Zanting 陶赞廷, and *Yangmengtushuo* 养蒙图说 by Tu Shixiang

涂时相. Generally, a story was illustrated with a picture and concise sentences.

Reciting poems is another new practice in the advanced stage of learning. Confucius believed that poem-reciting stimulated students' interests in studying and therefore should be the first stage of teaching. From the Tang dynasty on, it was specified in the teaching curricula to recite simple and famous poems. Many poem anthologies were edited for children, including popular examples such as *Yongshishi* 咏史诗, *Qianjiashi* 千家诗, and *Shentongshi* 神童诗. To illustrate the function of poem-reciting in literacy education, the scholar Lü Kun 吕坤, of the Ming dynasty, commented:

> *When children are tired of studying, they can read a poem aloud. Good poems with easy wording from different times are compiled in a book for children to read. These poems are racy, sensible and touching. The teacher explains these poems to the children and asks them to appreciate and comprehend the connotations.*[41]

Good poems show the beauty of language, and arouse children's study interests. Composing couplets was the third practice in the advanced stage of literacy education. A basic textbook was *Duilei* 对类, from which the following is quoted:

> *Ask children to memorize the characters in* Duilei, *so that they will be acquainted with the grammatical categories of hanzis. Children are required to learn by heart the basic characters of different categories such as Tian 'heaven,' Chang 'long,' Yong 'forever' and Ri 'sun.' Before the class is dismissed, children are asked to complete a couplet with the teacher. This is enough to let them understand the functional distinctions of hanzi*[42] *(Cheng Duanli,* Dushu Fennian Richeng, *Volume 1).*

A couplet consists of two lines: the first is called Shanglian 上联 (upper line) and the second is called Xialian 下联 (lower line). The characters in these two lines should match in their grammatical category. Moreover, couplet-composing requires knowledge of phonology, syntax and logic. In Chinese syntax, characters are classified into the following categories:

- content words: heaven, earth, tree, wood, bird, beast
- semi-content words: literature, power, air, force
- function words (living): blow, fly, soar, sink, run, flow
- function words (dead): high, long, clear, new, hard, soft
- semi-function: up, down, in, out, middle, between
- helping words[43]

Children are asked to do simple couplets first and more complex ones later. They begin with the one-to-one match, such as 雨 (yu 'rain') – 风 (feng 'wind') and 虎 (hu 'tiger') – 龙 (long 'dragon'). Through such simple training, the concepts of word class may be established in a child's mind; he or she then can try the two-to-two match. In these processes, many kinds of syntactical constructions using the previous categories are involved. For example:

虎跃-龙腾 (tigers jump – dragons fly)
云淡-风轻 (clouds soft – wind light)
凿井-耕田 (dig wells – irrigate fields)
行云-流水 (flying clouds – flowing water)
大陆-长空 (vast land – long sky)
父子-兄弟 (father and son – older brother and younger brother)
虎背-熊腰 (tiger's back – bear's waist)
弹唱-跳舞 (sing – dance)
敏捷-迟钝 (swift and sharp – slow and blunt)

As the number of characters increases, more function words are used and more complex syntactic structures may appear. In other words, this type of exercise trains children to compose sentences and understand syntactic rules. Such training leads to the final step of text-composing. Textbooks for couplet composition include *Qidui* 奇对 and *Shenglüfameng* 声律发蒙.

In modern China, the training of poem- or couplet-composition is replaced by phrase-making (Zuci 组词) and sentence-making (Zaoju 造句).

Textbooks for Reading and Composition. In ancient China, after students acquired about two thousand frequently used hanzis, they then learned to read and write essays. Many dynasties selected qualified people from the national exam (Keju) to serve in the government, and the assessment was based mainly on how good their essays were. To master the skills of composition, students were instructed to read and recite the classics from different dynasties; they learned the wording from those models. Many anthologies of the classical prose appeared, especially after the Song dynasty, because the requirements of composition in the Keju exams became stricter than before. In general, two types of anthologies were available. The first was the classics of the past, which may be appended with notation and editors' comments. Some famous examples are *Wenzhang Zhengzong* 文章正宗 by Zhen Dexiu 真德秀, *Guwen Guanjian* 古文关键 by Lü Zuqian 吕祖谦, and *Guwen Guanzhi* 古文观止 by Wu Chucai 吴楚才 and Wu Tiaohou 吴调侯. The second type of anthology was a collection of essays written according to the requirements of Keju, which appeared during the Ming-Qing Period and directly served the needs of the examinees.[44]

TEACHING SKILLS

To teach hanzi, reading aloud and reciting texts are regarded as the most basic methods. Students begin by reading after the teacher. Much time is allowed for the students to read and recite themselves. Two old Chinese sayings exemplify this spirit: (1) "If you read a text for a thousand times, it will be understood naturally" (Dushu qianbian, qiyi zixian 读书千遍，其义自现)[45] (i.e., repetition is helpful for comprehension); and (2) "If you can recite three hundred poems of the Tang dynasty, you will learn how to compose a poem yourself" (Shudu tangshi sanbaishou 熟读唐诗三百首, buhui zuoshi ye huiyin 不会作诗也会吟). Ancient people believed that in the process of literacy education, extensive reading provides structure and materials for composition. The poet Du Fu 杜甫 wrote in a poem: "Read more than ten thousand books, and one will be able to write freely" (Dushu po wanjuan 读书破万卷, xiabi ru youshen 下笔如有神).

A guideline for composition is 'to jot down whatever you have in mind first and to revise the wording afterwards' (Xianfang houshou 先放后收). For a long time, teachers in ancient China insisted on this principle to encourage their students. According to this principle, it is easier for students to get started this way because no rules would limit their brainstorming. After some free exercises, a few requirements of composition are taught. Another guideline is to compose many articles and to revise the same article many times.

The major tool of writing in ancient China was the brush pen. At the very beginning of teaching students to write, teachers help them by holding their hands, the so-called wrist-holding (Bawanr 把腕). Children are first asked to write hanzi in large type. Then they do a handwriting exercise according to the following ordered steps: 'to trace over red characters' (Miaohong 描红), 'to copy the trace of characters via a white paper'(Fangying 仿影), and 'to imitate a model of good handwriting' (Lintie 临帖). After a series of training exercises, children then start to handwrite in smaller type. The order of strokes generally need to follow a certain sequence – that is, from top to bottom, left to right, and periphery to center. Nowadays, pencils, pens, and ballpoint pens have replaced brush pens as the writing instrument. However, these principles for handwriting are still observed. Some special checkers, such as the character 米 or 田, are devised to help learn how to write.

Literate Stratum

The content of oracle-bone characters strongly suggested their function and scope. As mentioned previously, most of them are the record of divination for the emperors. The augurs and the recorders were the literate people in the Shang dynasty.

In the Western Zhou Period, the noble class dominated such important issues as politics, economy, culture, and so on. Literacy as an important resource was thus monopolized by the nobility. Children of the nobles received literacy education in Guoxue (national school), whereas the children of ordinary slaveholders were educated in Xiangxue (local school). Other children rarely had any opportunity for schooling.

Between the Spring and Autumn Period and the Warrior States Period, slavery was abolished. Private schools became popular, and ordinary people could go to school.[46] Confucius tried to diffuse literacy to all people.[47] However, in the Qin dynasty, the central government prohibited private schools, a policy which reduced the literacy rate.

In the Han dynasty, a system for scholar selection was developed. The local government would recommend a certain number of virtuous people according to the total population,[48] and they would be trained in Taixue 太学, funded by the central government. The number of people selected in this way was limited, only about 1/200,000 per year. In the Wei-Jin Period, this system was continued. The reputation of a family guaranteed the opportunity for education.

In the Sui-Tang Period, the unified central government initiated the Civil Service Examinations (Keju 科举) to assemble scholars. Both national and private schools were allowed to recruit children from ordinary families. Such a system was continued by the later dynasties until the end of Qing; therefore, Sui-Tang can be regarded as a turning point for literacy in China. From that time on, the ordinary people could have the opportunity to be educated. In the Song-Yuan Period, the Shexue 社学 were promoted extensively for the children of peasants.

The importance of the Civil Service Examinations was to enhance social mobility of imperial China. Through this system, many literate people from ordinary families were promoted to the administrative level. Table 21.2 shows the impact of Keju on ordinary families.

In the lower classes of society, the Baihua 白话 (i.e., colloquial speech) was used.

Table 21.2. The Impact of Keju Exam on Ordinary Families in the Ming Dynasty. Quoted From Ho 2005:28

Year	*Total of Jinshi* 进士[49]	*From Ordinary Family*	
		Number	*Percentage (%)*
1411	84	70	83
1436	100	76	67
1499	300	165	55
1508	349	196	56
1541	298	177	59
1547	300	181	60
1598	292	186	64
1604	308	188	61
1622	412	245	59
1649	143	114	80
1651	57	35	61
Total	2,643	1,633	61.78

Note: Adapted from Table 5.2 in Elman, 2000.

Compared with articles written in Wenyan, the number of Baihua articles is very small. Because Baihua was based on the contemporary spoken languages, it had variants of different periods; however, there exist few variants of the Wenyan system.

Women generally were denied access to education in ancient China, which continues to be a worldwide problem. It has been reported that there are more than 500 million illiterate women in Third World countries (Chlebowska, 1990); the exact number may be much larger than this estimation. In the Western Zhou Period, females were suppressed. Once children started to learn to speak, gender difference would be emphasized again and again. Only male children had the chance to learn to read and write, female children were forced to learn housework only. The idea that it is a virtue of women to be illiterate (女子无才便是德) originated around the Western Zhou Period. This tragic fate of women lasted several millennia. In the beginning of the twentieth century, the idea that women and men should have equal opportunities was transmitted extensively. Chinese women were first allowed to study at a female school. Later, they won the right to receive education in the same school with men. Before 1949, more than 90 percent of the women in China were illiterate. The PRC government promoted the 'Illiteracy Elimination' (Saomang 扫盲) movements in 1952, 1956, and 1958. Many types of schools to teach reading and writing were established. By 1958, about 16 million illiterate women became literate.

In recent years, a writing system that was only used by females was found in the Jiangyong 江永 county, the Dao 道 county, and the Jianghua 江华 county of the Hunan Province, the so-called Female Writing (Nüshu 女书), a system that is modified from hanzi.[50] It was used by women to complain about their tragic fate, to write their own biography, and to record folk songs (Yuanteng & Huang, 2005). This situation is similar to the kana in Japanese, which was used only by women in the beginning. However, Nüshu did not spread widely and is endangered now, whereas kana is widely used by Japanese people.

Wenjiao

The hanzi system was created circa 3000 BCE. From that time on, the transmission of literacy has been very important. In China, the thoughts that guide literacy education were generally covered by the term *Wenjiao* 文教 (i.e., culture and education). The systematic organization of Wenjiao was developed in Western Zhou after the preparation in Xia and Shang. The basic idea was "to respect four techniques, to establish four arts, and to train literate people with poems, classics, rituals, and music according to previous emperors" (乐正崇四术, 立四教, 顺先王诗、书、礼、乐以造士. From *Liji* 礼记·Wangzhi 王制).

The Qin emperors placed all aspects of Wenjiao under the control of the central government. They decreed that all varieties of hanzi be unified to small seal scripts. In local organizations, a position called Sanlao 三老 (three old) was established for moral education. Private schools were forbidden; students could only learn from the officials. The most radical strategy was to burn the books of Ru 儒 (Confucianism) and to kill those who promoted the art of Ru.

In the Han dynasty, the Ru school was legitimated as the only truth in Wenjiao. The central government established Taixue to train literate people. It also tried to obtain more books and made great efforts to refine them. In this process, studies of the writing, pronunciation and meaning of hanzi became very popular. The famous dictionary, *Shuowen Jiezi*, was compiled in this background.

During the turbulent Wei-Jin Period, Taoist metaphysics was canonized by the literate people. In the Sui-Tang Period, the Ru school resumed its central position in Wenjiao policy. However, it was not the only dominant one; Buddhism and Tao were regarded as important as well. The central government built temples to Confucius and regularly held memorial ceremonies for Confucius. At the same time, the translation of Buddhist classics was supported greatly. Imperial examinations, called Keju 科举, were started and provided many more opportunities for literate people to enter the administrative level.

In the Song dynasty, Wenjiao was regarded as essential to the government. The Ru school prevailed in China. In the beginning of the Song dynasty, imperial examinations were at a high premium; the quota was increased annually. Those who passed the exam were appointed as important governors. The better they scored, the higher position they would be awarded. The emperor Song Zhenzong (986–1022) composed the following poem to promote literacy and it became widely circulated:

> To be wealthy you need not purchase fertile fields,
> Thousands of tons of corn are to be found in the books.
> To build a house you need not set up high beams,
> Golden mansions are to be found in the books.
> To find a wife you need not worry about not having good matchmakers,

Maidens as beautiful as jade are to be
found in the books.
To travel you need not worry about not
having servants and attendants,
Large entourages of horses and carriages
are to be found in the books.
When a man wishes to fulfill the ambition
of his life,
He only needs to diligently study the six
classics by the window.[51]
(Translation from Yu & Suen, 2005, p. 18)

Such policy stimulates the great passion of people to become literate. To amend the degenerate nature of the exam-oriented education at school, there were three reforms on school systems in Northern Song, promulgated by Fan Zhongyan 范仲淹 (989–1052) and Wang Anshi 王安石 (1021–1086). The main purpose of those reforms was to train people to serve society and to avoid the drawbacks of teaching only for tests.

Almost at the same time of Song, Northern China was governed by the non-Han, Liao and Jin. Although they often defeated the Song dynasty in war, they accepted the same policy in literacy as adopted by the Han people in the Song dynasty. Both leaders followed the tradition of respecting Confucius and esteeming the Ru scholars. The governors promoted the Ru classics to their people. Meanwhile, for Liao or Jin students to learn their own writing system, Khitan or Jurchen, they were required to master hanzi. The major content of learning was almost all from classical texts of the Han school.

In the Yuan dynasty, the Mongolian emperors accepted the Ru school of Han culture. The policy was to sinicize the language and other cultural system. The emperors realized that it was important to use literate people to help their administration. Confucius was highly regarded by the government. The neo-Confucianism promoted by Cheng and Zhu (Chengzhu lixue 程朱理学), which developed in the Song dynasty, was adopted as the dominant school of thought. The Keju exam of governors used Sishu 四书 (*The Four Books*) and Wujing 五经 (*The Five Classics*) annotated by the Chengzhu school for guidelines. Although the Phags-pa script was created for the Mongolian language and became the national script, the hanzi system was widely promulgated at the same time.

A rigid organization of composition was created in the Northern Song dynasty, known as Bagu 八股 (i.e., eight-part essay),[52] which was helpful for the beginner to learn to compose an essay. However, in the imperative exams, candidates had to follow the rigid order of the eight parts to compose an essay limited to six hundred characters for a specific topic, which was generally taken from the Ru classics. The Han emperors of the Ming dynasty restored the tradition of setting Ru as the foundation of Wenjiao. The thoughts expressed in the composition had to support their regime. The Bagu essay as the standard writing lasted almost six hundred years, until the Keju exam was abandoned in 1906.[53]

The Manchu emperors of the Qing dynasty tried to take advantage of the literate Han people. They promoted the trend to respect Confucius and the related classics. Neo-Confucianism (Lixue) was esteemed by the government and book compilation was supported. However, if certain writings were regarded as against the Manchu government, their authors would be imprisoned and many were sentenced to death. Therefore, most scholars preferred to deal only with pure academic topics, such as the phonology and semantics of ancient hanzi.

To summarize the traditional literacy education since the Sui-Tang Period, two major tasks, hanzi-recognition and essay-composition, were included for the final purpose of scoring high in the imperial exams.

In 1949, the central government of the PRC accepted the suggestion of Ye Shengtao 叶圣陶 that the courses in Chinese language be unified as the subject Yuwen 语文 (i.e., spoken language and writing).[54] This change aimed to strike a balance between the spoken and the written language. Moreover, the nature of literacy as a tool was emphasized, whose purpose was to help people learn necessary life skills.

The Magic Hanzi

Hanzi as the Centre of Literacy

Because of the nature of hanzi, the basic unit of reading and writing is the single character, and they must be learned one by one. Moreover, about two thousand characters are necessary for text-reading and composition. Morphology in the Chinese language is simple; there are no inflections.[55] The Chinese language is recognized as a typical isolating language. Several millennia before the appearance of *Mashi Wentong* 马氏文通 in 1898, there was no textbook for Chinese morphosyntax. For this reason, in the traditional education of Chinese literacy, the focus was on reading and writing hanzi.

Before the PRC, hanzi-recognition was the most important part of literacy. Many people sent their children to school so they could learn basic Chinese characters. In the traditional perception, illiterate people are those who cannot read Chinese characters. The national guideline of the PRC on the Yuwen (i.e., language and writing) education in the primary school prescribes that approximately two thousand frequent Chinese characters should be taught in the first three years of school. In 1988, *Xiandai Hanyu Changyongzi Biao* 现代汉语常用字表 was published by the Language and Writing Committee and National Education Committee. It consists of 3,500 frequent hanzis, which are classified into two groups: 2,500 more frequent characters and 1,000 less frequent characters. The former covers 97.7 percent of characters in general reading materials; the latter covers 1.51 percent. The percentage of phonograms among the 3,500 hanzis is 85 percent. Such statistical studies on hanzi provide a good basis for hanzi-teaching.

Recently, some Chinese linguists proposed that hanzi is the hub of Chinese where phonology, semantics, syntax and vocabulary converge (Chen, 1999; Wang, 1994; Xu, 1991, 1992, 1994a, 1994b, 1997). Here, hanzi is defined as a basic linguistic unit with a one-character/one-syllable/one-meaning relationship. Chao (1975) pointed out that hanzi in the Chinese language is equal to word in the English language. Although it is still in debate whether hanzi or word should be employed as the basic syntactic unit, it is realized that hanzi may be convenient for Chinese syntax (Chen, 1999, pp. 323–395). Significant evidence is 'hanzilization' (Zihua 字化), a phenomenon that suggests that the pattern of one character/one syllable/one meaning is a strong constraint in Chinese, which causes some characters that do not fit this pattern to adapt into the regular characters. For instance, originally neither 蝴 hu nor 蝶 die (hudie 'butterfly') was considered a morpheme. Therefore, 蝴蝶 shows the two-character/two-syllable/one-meaning pattern, violating the canonical pattern of a hanzi. However, in modern Chinese, constructions like 凤蝶 fengdie 'swallowtail butterfly,' 黑蝶 heidie 'black butterfly,' and 黄蝶 huangdie 'sulfur butterfly' are acceptable. In these constructions, the character 蝶 die seems to have acquired the meaning 'butterfly,' which means it is now a regular hanzi (Chen, 1999, p. 371).

Hanzi and Cognition

It is important to know what role hanzi plays in the acquisition of literacy. The answer may guide us to better understand what would be beneficial in learning to read and write.

In learning to read, hanzi as a logographic system requires different cognitive abilities than those in the process of learning an alphabetic writing system such as English. The correspondence between the written script and the spoken language is considered crucial in learning to read (Tzeng & Singer, 1981). "The relation between script and speech underlying all types of writing systems plays an important role in reading behavior. A reader of a particular script must assimilate the orthographic characteristics of that system. That is to say, if the configuration of a logograph is important in deciphering it, then the reader has to pay special attention to the position of every element it contains. As a consequence, we should expect the processing of logographs to involve more visual memory than the processing of alphabetic script" (Tzeng & Wang, 1983, reprinted in Wang, 1991, p. 288). Therefore, visual memory is prominent in reading hanzi. It has been demonstrated that the strategy to recognize many hanzi characters before learning to write them meets the cognitive requirements.

The memory performance of native Chinese speakers differs from that of native English speakers. Various experiments show that "visual presentation was superior for Chinese readers regardless of whether they were asked to recall the items orally or in writing. This finding suggests that processing logographs involves more visual memory than does processing alphabetic scripts. In fact, it further suggests that the influence of the sensory characteristics of the visual information may not be restricted to the very early stages of processing, and that reading different kinds of script uses different mechanisms of memory that are specific to the individual script" (Tzeng & Wang, 1983, reprinted in Wang, 1991, pp. 289–290). However, recognizing a single logograph is only a step toward comprehending a written sentence. Experiments in sentence-comprehension suggest that "in reading different scripts, the initial perceptual pathways may be different, but later processing may converge on similar linguistics techniques." Findings at different laboratories (Hung & Tzeng, 1981; Seidenberg & Tanenhaus, 1979) have demonstrated that "as soon as our eyes focus on a written symbol, the visual information, combined with the contextual information, is automatically transformed into an abstract 'word' code that carries phonological, orthographic, and semantic information (Wang, 1991, p. 291)."

There is a long-standing misunderstanding about hanzi that reading the logographs does not require phonological information. However, experiments (Polich et al., 1983; Treiman, Baron, & Luk, 1981; Tzeng et al., 1977) tell us that "in every type of writing system, a reader always has access to the phonological information (Wang, 1991, p. 291)." It may be more difficult for a hanzi reader to learn to convert logographs to sound because the phonological information is not specified in the scripts or is specified only indirectly. For this reason, reciting aloud in the early acquisition of hanzi is very effective. From various experiences of learning hanzi, ancient people in China already knew this important skill.

The latest research on hanzi recognition, in both normal and dyslexic children in China using methods of neuron-imaging, reveals some distinctive aspects of Chinese literacy. It shows that hanzi recognition is "critically mediated by the posterior portion of the left middle frontal gyrus, a region just anterior to the motor cortex" (Tan et al., 2005, p. 8784; see also Siok et al., 2004). Research further shows that "the ability to read Chinese is strongly related to a child's writing skills, and that the relationship between phonological awareness and Chinese reading is much weaker than that in reports regarding alphabetic languages" (Tan et al., 2005, p. 8781). A wealth of important psycholinguistic information is contained in the handbook published by Cambridge University Press and edited by Li et al. (2006).

An alphabetic script like Pinyin has been shown to be a helpful tool for Chinese children to learn to read (Hanley, Tzeng, & Huang, 1999). After learning an alphabetic script, the phonological awareness can be improved immediately. The phonological ability will be used when they are attempting to learn new words, no longer in the rote method. Various experiments (Chen & Yuen, 1991; Ko & Lee, 1997; Tzeng et al., 1995) suggested that sensitivity to the phonetic component of compound characters and the ability to read Chinese characters are positively correlated with children's ability in mastering Pinyin (or Zhuyin zimu[56]). Therefore, it may indicate that the phonological information is of the same importance as the visual process is in learning Chinese characters. In fact, ancient Chinese people made use of methods in the spirit of Pinyin to teach children to learn hanzi at a very early stage. Rhymed sentences in the textbooks of primary school and Fanqie in notations improved the phonological sensitivity of students learning hanzi, although indirectly.

In Chinese word recognition, experiments in Hung et al. (1999) suggested that morpheme-construction plays the mediated role. This finding may show why the coupling training is effective in learning Chinese literacy. A recent handbook on psycholinguistic studies in this area addresses these issues in greater depth (Li et al., 2006).

The Spread of Hanzi

With the expansion of the Chinese empire, Chinese culture spread to the surrounding areas. As an important carrier of the Chinese culture, the hanzi system greatly impacted other nations (Lu, 2002). At the beginning of the importation of hanzi, the whole hanzi system was adopted directly. From Han to Tang, the spread of Han culture reached its peak. For instance, the Vietnamese used hanzi as the only writing system from the middle Western Han Period to the thirteenth century. Hanzi was imported into the Korean peninsula as early as the Warrior States Period. In 958, the Keju system was adopted by the central government of Korea. The classics of Ru became the basis of the Keju exam, which lasted until 1486, when the Hangul was decreed as the standard writing system.

Because the hanzi system was not suitable for their native spoken language, hanzi naturally inspired these other peoples to create a similar writing system for their own language – for example, Vietnamese Chu-nom 字喃 (Vietnam's demotic script),[57] Japanese Kana, Khitan large script, Tangut character, Zhuang script, and Bai script. All these variants constitute a cultural circle of hanzi.

In these attempts to use or imitate hanzi, there were several common ways of adoption. First, Chinese characters were borrowed to represent sound or meaning. In Chu-nom of Vietnamese, examples of the former include 没[mot^{6}] 'one,' 碎[tai^{1}] 'I'; examples of the latter are 你[mai2] 'you,'

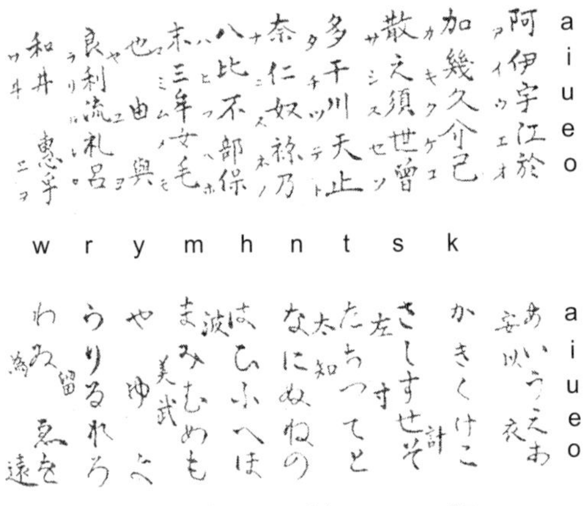

Figure 21.6. Katakana and hiragana of Japanese (adapted from R. A. Miller, 1976, *The Japanese Language*).

才[tai^{4}] 'talent.' In Bai scripts, examples of the former are 波[po^{55}] 'grandfather, male,' 梨[li^{55}] 'also'; examples of the latter 老[ku^{33}] 'old,' 陆[fv^{44}] 'six' (Xu & Zhao, 1984, p. 129). This is like Kanji in Japanese, which uses the meanings of hanzi but is read in Japanese. Second, components of hanzi are used to represent sound or meaning. A typical example of the former is Kana. Two kinds of Kana were originally derived from hanzi: the katakana shown on the top of Figure 21.6 is abbreviated from the regular script of hanzi, whereas the hiragana shown on the bottom is modified from the cursive script of hanzi.

Third, the structures of hanzi served as models in creating new characters for the native languages. As we discussed previously, the six principles of hanzi-formation defined in *shuowen Jiezi* have long been followed as the orthographic principles in Chinese-like scripts. The phonogram (Xingsheng 形声) method is often employed – for instance, in Chu-nom of Vietnamese, 草古[co^{5}] 'grass,' 𢆥 [nam] 'year' (Wang, 1958), and in Bai scripts, 亻昂[ŋa^{55}] 'we,' 亻能; [nɯ^{55}] 'your' (Xu & Zhao, 1984, p. 130).

The Functions of Literacy and its Impacts on Chinese Culture

From very early on in China, literacy was associated with politics. At the beginning of their studies, students were asked to recite three poems in Xiaoya 小雅 of *Shijing* 诗经 (The Book of Odes): Luming 鹿鸣, Simu 四牡, and Huanghuangzhehua 皇皇者华, which eulogize the harmonic relationship between the emperor and officials. This connection is clearly claimed in *Xueji*[58]: "learning the first three poems of Xiaoya is the beginning of being an official (《宵雅》[59] 肄三, 官其始也)." The slogan that "a good scholar should serve in the government (学而优则仕)" has been very popular since it was first stated in *Lunyu* 论语 (Confucian Analects) by Confucius. The Keju exam beginning in the seventh century strengthened the link between literacy and officialdom. This system lasted about 1,300 years. For a long period, the purpose of literacy was limited to only one goal: being an official. A popular poem by Wang Zhu 王洙 in the late Northern Song dynasty exemplified the idea:

> The emperor regards outstanding scholars highly,
> So I teach you how to compose articles.
> All other pursuits are of low value,
> Only studying is of high class.[60]

Ho (1962) demonstrated that a large percentage of ordinary people succeeded in their promotions via the ladder of Keju at least during the thousand years after the Song dynasty, and the percentage was significantly larger than that of any other societies before the Industrial Revolution. Therefore, literacy education was mainly driven by the purpose of establishing a career. The side effects for Chinese culture are salient; China now is known as a nation with all types of exams.

Literacy provided the most important ladder for success. As the transmitter of literacy, teachers became important. Meanwhile, the rulers needed teachers to be the model in supporting the government and to transmit the thoughts they approved. In the Confucian way of thinking, things to be most respected should be "Heaven, Earth, Lord, Parents, and Teacher (天地君亲师)." In such a tradition, what the teachers stated must be followed by the students.[61] Any free thinking of students was suppressed by this system. However, this tradition to respect teachers was destroyed during the Cultural Revolution.

In literacy transmission, the Wenyan system plays the most important role. The Wenyan system was formed during Qin-Han Period (Zhang, 1997) and was based on the common language of that time. After that, this system was followed without major changes, although the spoken language changed significantly. Therefore, the cumulated inheritance from many generations is reflected in the Wenyan system. On the one hand, as the only visible representation of past experience, books written in Wenyan taught people a lot and brought great advantages in life. This caused many ancient Chinese people to believe in everything that was written in books and to respect thoughts of the past. On the other hand, only literate people had the opportunity to achieve the higher level of society. The ability to master the Wenyan system became a symbol of the nobility, which could be used to show their difference from ordinary people. "Free from vulgarity" (Tuosu 脱俗) is an honorable comment for literate people. To win this praise, a convenient way is to employ more ancient phrases and classics.[62] "Literary quotation" (Yongdian 用典) was an important criterion to evaluate an article. In the Tang dynasty, some leading scholars initiated the Old Literature Movement (Guwen yundong 古文运动),[63] which lasted until the Ming dynasty. In this movement, classical writings of the Qin-Han Period were regarded as the model. The Wenyan-oriented thoughts impacted studies of Chinese languages (Ho, 1993). For about two thousand years, Wenyan has been the most important topic and the studies of dialects have been suppressed.

A notable phenomenon is that the hanzi system and the Han culture were transmitted continuously even when the empire was under the control of other ethnic groups. Generally, such continuity is attributed to the refined content and the great value and vitality of the Han culture. However, it may also be due to the stability of hanzi. Because many valuable aspects, such as institutional regulations, historical documents, and classics were all written in hanzi, and the communication among most of the people in China depended heavily on hanzi, Chinese characters became a necessary condition for keeping the empire consolidated.

Hanzi can be read across time and space because the logographs of hanzi are not associated with a particular phonological system. The association between the written form of hanzi and its meaning is relatively stable. In alphabetical writing systems like English, the written alphabetic forms can be related to their meanings via the contemporary pronunciation. Sound changes more frequently than logograph does. Therefore, it becomes a necessary precondition to learn the phonology of the old English when modern people want to read the ancient text. Such an obstacle is minor in the hanzi system. A modern literate Chinese person can read texts written a thousand years ago and understand most of them. For this reason, it is relatively easy for Chinese people to access the written heritage of several millennia ago.

It is well known that in China, varieties of the Chinese language are distributed in vast areas and they are diversified along time. Many varieties are not mutually intelligible. However, people of different dialectal backgrounds can use their own pronunciation to read the same hanzi because the hanzi system is commonly shared. It is not surprising that two people who speak different Chinese dialects can still communicate by writing hanzi. Moreover, official bulletins and all types of documents written in hanzi can be transmitted easily to people in different regions.

Literacy in Non-Han Languages

In China, Tibetan languages are mainly spoken in Tibet, Gansu, Qinghai, Sichuan and Yunnan Provinces. The Written Tibetan system was created around the seventh century. There were three major revisions to this system, with the second at the beginning of the ninth century being the most important. Written Tibetan currently in use maintains the system after the second modification. In this system, scripts of thirty consonants and four vowels are included. The symbols and their IPA transcriptions are shown in Figure 21.7.

ཀ	ཁ	ག	ང	ཅ	ཆ	ཇ	ཉ	ཏ	ཐ	ད	ན
k	kh	g	ŋ	tɕ	tɕh	dʑ	ȵ	t	th	d	n
པ	ཕ	བ	མ	ཙ	ཚ	ཛ	ཝ	ཞ	ཟ	འ	ཡ
p	ph	b	m	ts	tsh	dz	w	ʑ	z	ɦ	j
ར	ལ	ཤ	ས	ཧ	ཨ			ི	ུ	ེ	ོ
r	l	ɕ	s	h	ʔ / a			i	u	e	o

Figure 21.7. Tibetan alphabets for initials and vowels (adapted from Jiang, 2002, p. 2).

The default vowel is /a/. The structure of a most complex graph is shown in Figure 21.8. In the graph, the position of '1' is indispensable.

In the invention of Written Tibetan, the principle of one-symbol/one-sound must have been followed. Most of the thirty consonants are borrowed directly from Indic scripts; the rest are either modified from Indic scripts or innovations.

Written Tibetan faithfully reflects the phonological system of Middle Tibetan. However, not a long time after its creation, the different varieties of Tibetan in vast areas became barely mutually intelligible due to different sound changes. In this sense, Written Tibetan lost its phonetic transparency. People speaking in different Tibetan dialects have to use different rules to interpret words in Written Tibetan. This is similar to what happened when Han people from different dialectal areas read hanzi.

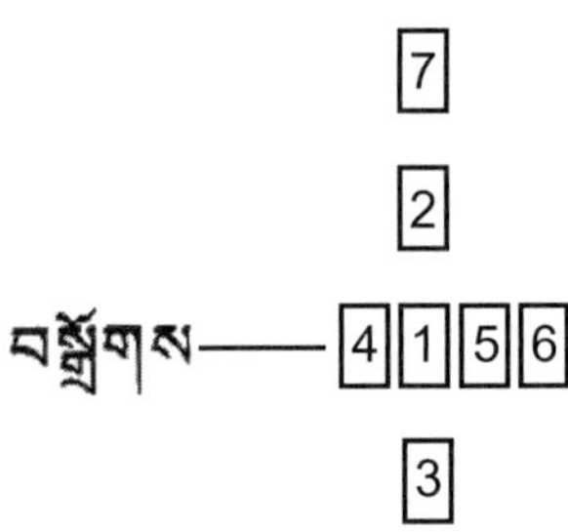

Figure 21.8. The most complex structure of Tibetan graph (adapted from Hu, 1999, p. 10).

Written Tibetan was mainly created for religious use. Many Buddhist classics from India or Han were translated into Written Tibetan with the support of the Tufan government. Most masters of Written Tibetan are lamas of the Tibetan temples. The official files of Tufan governments are also written in this system. Other than for these purposes, Written Tibetan was rarely used before.

In the PRC, the government wants to enhance the popularity of Written Tibetan. Several universities have established departments of Written Tibetan. In Tibetan prefectures, the colleges for Written Tibetan are strengthened. Written Tibetan courses are available in primary and middle schools. Publications in Written Tibetan have increased tremendously. All people are entitled to learn Written Tibetan, unlike in ancient times when this right was monopolized by the religious authorities and Tibetan nobles.

Written Xixia is also called Tangut script. It is generally believed that the creation of Tangut script was led by Li Yuanhao 李元昊 (1004–1048), and Yelirenrong 野利仁荣 (?–1042) was the main contributor.[64] After that, both Tangut script and hanzi were used in all types of documents including diplomatic files, important inscriptions, translated sutra, and bulletins. Dictionaries of Tangut scripts were compiled similar to the form of Chinese rhyme books such as *Guangyun* – for example, *Tongyin* 同音, *Wenhai* 文海, and *Wenhai baoyun* 文海宝韵. Although Tangut script was national writing, hanzi was still held in high esteem and greatly emphasized in school systems. Fanxue 蕃学 was established. Chinese textbooks, such as *Siyanzazi* 四言杂字, *Xiaojing* 孝经, and *Erya* 尔雅, were translated into Tangut. Children of officials, either Dangxiang or Han, were selected for training in schools. Because of the need for bilingualism, an important Tangut-Chinese bilingual glossary was edited by Gulemaocai 骨勒茂才, called *Fan-Han Heshi Zhangzhongzhu* 番汉合时掌中珠. The Tangut scripts preserve many traces of the Chinese influence (Gong, 1982). Two of the six principles (Liushu 六书), phonograms (Xingsheng 形声) and complex ideograms (Huiyi 会意), are made use of in Tangut scripts, whereas examples for the other four are rarely found. Other means of Chinese vulgar scripts are followed, such as component-reversion of graph and graph-formation on the principle of Fanqie. The more direct traces are the resemblances in the shape of graphs and means of composition of graphs.[65]

The double writings employed in Xixia coincided quite well. Hanzi served the need of communication with Central China, and Tangut scripts enhanced interaction within Xixia people and their consolidation as a group. After the defeat by Mongolians in 1227, the Tangut scripts became officially obsolete. After some years, the Xixia language was lost. It is estimated that the Tangut scripts had been used for at least 430 years[66] (Gong, 1981). Currently, this dead language system can be recovered because those documents were written in bilingual scripts. These rich documents help identify this important language in the Sino-Tibetan family, which plays an important role in understanding the phonology of Old Chinese and the evolution from Proto-Sino-Tibetan (Gong, 2002).

In Southwestern China, several writing systems were created by the minorities. The Bai script was created in Nanzhao around the tenth century and was popular among lower-class people. Because the Nanzhao kingdom decreed hanzi as the official writing, the Bai script did not have much opportunity to develop fully. It was mainly used to translate sutra[67] or inscriptions. The structure of Bai script simulates the hanzi system by borrowing Chinese characters or creating new characters in the principles of hanzi-formation. When the Ming dynasty took over the area of the Bai people, the fate of the Bai script worsened. Many books in Bai script were burned. The Bai script was used only by a small group under the great pressure of the dominant hanzi. There is another interesting writing system, the Tomba script of the Naxi people,[68] which is primitive pictograph. The pictographs are similar to drawings and clearly belong to the early

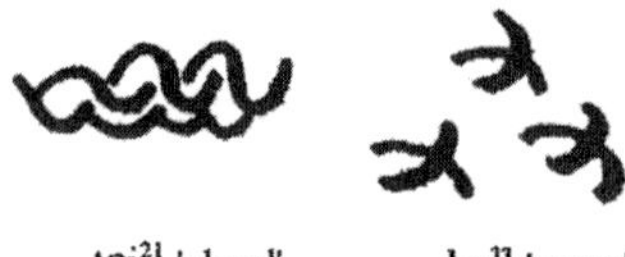

tɕi^{21} 'cloud' be^{33} 'snow'

Figure 21.9. 'Cloud' and 'snow' in Tomba script (He, 2001).

stage in the development of scripts, even more primitive than oracle-bone scripts.[69] For an example, see Figure 21.9.

The Tomba system seems to have originated independently, without obvious traces of influence from Chinese in its creation. For this reason, more comprehensive studies on Tomba scripts will shed light on the evolution of writing. In the western group of Naxi, a syllabic script is used, called Geba, which was created later than the Tomba script (Fang, 1995, p. 42). Due to the drawbacks of the Geba system, such as variant forms, lack of tone markers, and too many homophones, the Tomba script is the main form of Naxi writings. Most Naxi writings are religious. The local religion of Naxi was called Tomba, which is why the scripts they used are called Tomba scripts. Only priests could master this writing and some ordinary people used it to write letters or bills. The large number of religious documents, about twenty thousand manuscripts, contain rich information about folk custom, songs, poems and other kinds of knowledge related to this ethnic group. It is notable that a Tomba symbol can represent a syllable, a sentence, or even several sentences. Some writings are categorized as cartoon type, which can be read by only a few priests.

In Southern China, minorities such as Zhuang, Miao, and Yao invented their writing system using a similar principle as the Bai script. The Zhuang writing[70] may be the one that spread most extensively. All the writing systems of the minorities in China were popular only among the lower-class people because the high classes regarded hanzi as the token of literacy. These writing systems were used mainly to record folk songs, poems, stories, prescriptions, and so on. They are helpful for the preservation of folk culture and all types of cherished experiences.

Since 1949, the central government of the PRC alternated between accommodationism and integrationism when dealing with the relationship between minorities and Han. Eventually, a new framework – duoyuanyiti 多元一体 (i.e., diversity in the unity of the Chinese nation) – proposed by Fei Xiaotong 费孝通 (Fei, 1989) became dominant. In this spirit, the writing reform among minorities was implemented as a crucial step of literacy reform. The experience from almost fifty years of writing reform suggests that the selection of models for the development of a writing system must consider the unique actualities of each minority language and their tradition and religious factors. Throughout the years, the vernacular writing systems of minorities like Miao, Hani, Va, and so forth have undergone conflicts with the Latinized systems promoted by the government. Local minority people would select a system according to their own convenience. Examples include the use of the Sinoform script in Yi communities; Arabic script in the Uygurs and Kazaks; and writing systems created by Christian missionaries in the Yunnan Province for minorities like Lisu, Lahu, Miao and Jingpo (Wang, 2005; Zhou, 2003).

Meanwhile, bilingualism is promoted in minority areas. The Han system and the minority systems are allowed to coexist. However, even with the promotion of the minority writing system, the Han system is still being learned by more people in those areas than before.

Final Remarks

In the ten thousand years or so of human civilization, many peoples have independently devised methods of representing speech graphically (i.e., writing), from the earliest precursors in Western Asia circa seven thousand years ago to recent inventions in the Americas. Until recently, however, access to writing was universally restricted to a privileged few, primarily on political or religious grounds. As the world is shrinking to a global village in recent decades, these diverse methods mostly receded into oblivion, even as literacy is becoming an increasingly common skill.

Of the several methods that remain, two major traditions are thriving in the world today, each with billions of users – the Greco-Phoenician tradition, which is alphabetic, and the Chinese tradition, which is morphosyllabic. In this chapter, we reviewed the historical context in which literacy developed in China and briefly surveyed other non-hanzi writing systems developed in China by various ethnic peoples. Much research awaits for us to delve more deeply into these issues, as well as to expand the scope of the research to neighboring regions. The hanzi, indeed, is the basic ingredient at the root of a large cultural sphere, which includes most of East Asia and part of Southeast Asia.

The fact that hanzi is not alphabetic does not mean that it is not phonetic. By far, the majority of hanzis are phonetic in the sense that they can be grouped into phonetic sets in which all the members of a set share a common phonetic component that is syllable-sized. For example, following is a phonetic set which shares the phonetic component 羊 (yang): 洋, 养, 样, 氧, 痒, 漾, 佯, 恙, 徉, and so forth. Because of this property, sound changes affect Chinese writing and alphabetic writing quite differently. Thus, whereas many different sound changes have separated the major dialects of Chinese from each other over the past two millennia, the phonetic relationships among members of a phonetic set remain largely intact.

The Romance languages are written differently because French, Italian and Portuguese all underwent different sound changes. An extreme case is the French *eau* in contrast with the Italian *acqua*. The Chinese dialects, however, although separated by a comparable time period as the Romance languages, nonetheless have largely retained the original forms for all the hanzis.

Another important property of the hanzis discussed in this chapter is that they group into semantic sets as well. For example, following is a semantic set which shares the semantic component 水 'water': 洋, 海, 江, 河, 湖, and so forth. When readers comes across the character 洋, they are not only reminded of its pronunciation of (yang) but also of its watery association, for its meaning of *ocean*. Thus, the hanzi simultaneously facilitates dual access, albeit imperfectly, to both sound and meaning, which is the fundamental function of a writing system.

Indeed, this uniformity of script and the homogeneity of the culture it promotes are the major reasons for calling Mandarin, Cantonese, and Taiwanese different dialects rather than different languages, even though their spoken forms are no less similar than the Romance languages (Wang, 1997). It remains a challenging question for future cultural historians to investigate the degree of influence writing has had for Chinese unity after the Han dynasty, on the one hand, and for political European fractionation after the Roman Empire on the other.

Notes

1 Research on this chapter is supported in part by a grant from the Hong Kong SAR RGC # 1127/04H to the Chinese University of Hong Kong and a grant from National Social Science Foundation of PRC #07CYY025 to Peking University. We thank Dr. Zhao Tong for providing us some Chinese literature.

2 Han derives from the name of a major dynasty around 200 BCE to 200 CE. Zi refers to a basic unit of writing. Hanzi is also popularly called Chinese character. The Japanese refer to hanzi as 'kanji.'

3 "According to Zhouli, children who reach the age of eight may attend primary school, where the teacher, Baoshi, will teach the Six principles of hanzi-composition to students. The first is called Zhishi (indicative). The meaning of Zhishi characters can be inferred after we see their shape or structure; for example, 上 (shang 'up') and 下 (xia 'down'). The second is called Xiangxing (pictograph). The Xiangxing characters picture the images of objects; for example, 日 (ri 'sun') and 月 (yue 'moon'). The third is Xingsheng (phonograph). The Xingsheng characters consist of phonetic parts and semantic

parts; for example, 江 (jiang 'Yangtzi River') and 河 (he 'Yellow River'). The fourth is Huiyi (complex ideogram). The meaning of Huiyi characters is compounded from its components; for example, 武 (wu 'military') and 信 (xin 'letter'). The fifth is Zhuanzhu (derivative). The Zhuanzhu characters share the same semantic category and may explain each other. The sixth is Jiajie (phonetic loan). The Jiajie character uses the homophone to represent its meaning. For example, 令 (ling 'head of a county') and 长 (zhang 'head of a county'). 周礼八岁入小学，保氏教国子，先以六书。一曰指事。指事者，视而可识，察而见意，上下是也。二曰象形。象形者，画成其物，随体诘诎，日月是也。三曰形声。形声者，以事为名，取譬相成，江河是也。四曰会意。会意者，比类合谊，以见指撝，武信是也。五曰转注。转注者，建类一首，同意相受，考老是也。六曰假借。假借者，本无其字，依声托事，令长是也。" (《说文解字·叙》)

4 In *Shangshu* 尚书·Duoshi 多士, it states 'only the ancestors of the Yin people possessed writing volumes' (Wei yin xianren 惟殷先人, youce youdian 有册有典). The Shang dynasty moved its capital to Yin around 1300 BCE. After that, the dynasty is also called 'Yin Shang.'

5 It is also translated as 'standard script.'

6 cf. Diyipi yitizi zhenglibiao 第一批异体字整理表 [Regular table of the first group of hanzi variants] is issued by the Ministry of Culture of China and Committee for Language Reform of China.

7 cf. Di'erci hanzi jianhua fang'an (cao'an) 第二次汉字简化方案 (草案) [The second project of hanzi simplification (draft)] is drafted by Committee for Language Reform of China and approved by the State Department of China.

8 Western Zhou set the capital in Haojing (镐京), Qin in Xianyang (咸阳), Western Han in Chang'an (长安), Eastern Han in Luoyang (洛阳), Western Jin in Luoyang (洛阳), Sui-Tang in Chang'an (长安), Northern Song in Kaifeng (开封), Yuan, Ming and Qing in Beijing (北京).

9 *Lunyu* (论语): Confucius' frequent themes of discourse were the Odes, the History, and the maintenance of the Rules of Propriety. On all these, he frequently discoursed. (Zi suo yayan 子所雅言, shi 诗、shu 书、zhili 执礼, jie yayan ye 皆雅言也)。In the notation by Zheng Xuan (郑玄): It is necessary to pronounce the sounds right before reading classics by previous emperors. Then they can be understood completely (Du xianwang dianfa 读先王典法, bi zheng yan qi yin 必正言其音, ran hou yi quan 然后义全).

10 Today's Jiangsu and Zhejiang Province.

11 Today's Hubei and Hunan Province.

12 Mencius (372–289 BCE) called a scholar Xu Xing "a southern barbarian speaking strangely (南蛮鴃舌之人)", because Xu spoke the Chu language.

13 The whole title is *Youxuanshizhe juedaiyu shi bieguo fangyan* 輶轩使者绝代语释别国方言.

14 They are Lu Fayan 陆法言, Liu Zhen 刘臻, Yan Zhitui 严之推, Wei Yuan 魏渊, Lu Sidao 卢思道, Li Ruo 李若, Xiao Gai 萧该, Xin Deyuan 辛德源, and Xue Daoheng 薛道衡. Except for Xiao Gai, all are from Northern China.

15 It is still controversial which contemporary dialects form the basis (cf. Tang, 2002).

16 In the *Gujin yunhui juyao* 古今韵会举要·Zixu 自序 by Xiong Zhong 熊忠 of the Yuan dynasty, it was said: "Since the beginning of Keju, all the selected compositions must follow the *Libuyunlüe*, which is the same as a law and no rhyme words should be out of its scope." (迨李唐声律设科，韵略下之礼部，进士词章非是不在选，而有司去取决焉。一部礼韵遂如金科玉条，不敢一字轻易出入). The *Pingshui Xingkan Yunlüe* 平水新刊韵略 with 106 rhymes by Wang Wenyu 王文郁 and the *Renzi Xinkan Libuyunlüe* 壬子新刊礼部韵略 with 107 rhymes by Liu Yuan 刘渊 are modified from *Libuyunlüe* 礼部韵略. They are called Pingshuiyun 平水韵, which are popular in the actual poem composition.

17 In the preface of *Hongwuzhengyun*, it is made clear that the Yayin of Central China is the standard (Yi yi zhongyuan yayin wei ding 一以中原雅音为定). In the notes for use (Fanli 凡例), it is further explained that 'what is the correct sound? It should be intelligible to people of different areas.' (He zhe wei zhengsheng 何者为正声? wufang zhi ren jie neng tongjiezhe wei zhengyin ye 五方之人皆能通解者为正音也).

18 In *Limadou Zhongguo Zhaji* 利玛窦中国札记, it was found that spoken languages in different provinces of China are quite different; that is, they used their own dialects. However, "there is a particular spoken language used in the whole empire," which is called Guanhua (Koine). The Guanhua is very popular among the educated people, and it is employed as the communication tool between people from different areas. It is said that this term first appeared in the literature of Korea (*Lichao Shilu* 李朝实录· Chengzong sishiyi nian jiu yue 成宗四十一年九月) (1483).

19 In the sixth year of Yongzheng emperor (雍正六年), an imperial edict was issued: "The vernaculars of different places could be different. However, the pronunciation of hanzi

should be the same all around the empire. (Wufang xiangyu butong, er ziyin ze sihai ruyi 五方乡语不同，而字音则四海如一).”

20 In *Hengqie wusheng tu* 横切五声图 by Chong Fengwei 崇凤威 of the Qing dynasty, it is depicted that Northern Chinese has no entering tone. The entering tone of ancient Chinese changed into the Yinpin (Upper Even tone), such as 伐扎拉捉, or into the Yangping (Lower Even tone), such as 国格竹菊, or into the Shangsheng (Rising tone), such as 雪北铁笔. Only those who often compose poems will use the entering tone, but its sound is similar to the Qusheng (departing tone). (北圄无入声，其音或呼为阴平，如伐扎拉捉之类是也；或呼为阳平，如国格竹菊之类是也；或呼为上声，如雪北铁笔之类是也。唯素喻诗词者必调此声，然其音仍近于去声也). Prof. Lin Tao of Peking University recalled that the entering tone was taught to be pronounced in a short contour when he attended primary school in Beijing in 1920s.

21 Quoted from the notes (Yanshijiaxunjijie 颜氏家训集解) on *Huainanzi* 淮南子· Xiuwupian 修务篇.

22 Karlgren (1954, p. 213) translated this term as “turning and cutting.”

23 The author is unknown. It is published by Zhang Linzhi 张麟之. He wrote two prefaces to it in 1161 and 1203.

24 Note that the definition of these terms may be not accurate at all.

25 Although in the Ming dynasty, Matteo Ricci used the Roman alphabet to notate hanzi for the first time, this method did not become popular until the May Fourth Movement. Thomas F. Wade (1818–1895) created the so-called Wade system to spell Pekingese in the Latin alphabet. Although twenty Latin letters and other diacritics are used in this famous system, many different sounds are not distinguished.

26 Cf. *Liji* 礼记·Mingtangwei 明堂位.

27 It is called Xiao in the Western Han dynasty (Xia yue xiao 夏曰校) (*Mengzi* 孟子·Tengwen’gong shang 滕文公上).

28 The Yin (殷) people set the right school and the left school [殷人养国老于右学，养庶老于左学 (*Liji* 礼记·Wangzhi 王制)].

29 《礼记·学记》：古之教者，家有塾，党有庠，术有序，国有学。比年入学，中年考校。一年视离经辨志，三年视敬业乐群，五年视博习亲师，七年视论学取友，谓之小成。九年知类通达，强立而不反，谓之大成。

30 《汉书·艺文志》：古者八岁入小学，故周官保氏掌养国子，教之六书，谓象形、象事、象意、象声、转注、假借，造字之本也。汉兴，萧何草律，亦著其法，曰，太史试学童，能讽书九千字以上，乃得为史。又以六体试之，课最者以为尚书御史史书令史。吏民上书，字或不正，辄举劾。

31 According to *Hanzhi Kaozheng* 汉志考证 by Wang Yingling, the last 128 hanzis were added later by someone in Eastern Han.

32 There is a story in the *Tangzhiyan* 唐摭言 by Wang Dingbao 王定保. Gu Meng came to Guangzhou to escape from the disorderly Zhejiang. He was a stranger there and had no money for accommodation. He had to write down the *Qianziwen* to teach illiterate people. Then he could make some money for a living. (顾蒙……淮浙荒乱，避地至广州，人不能知，困于旅食，以至书《千字文》授于聋俗，以换斗筲之资.)

33 For example (here the hanzis are translated literally for better understanding the syntactic structure):

性本善. xing ben shan [nature originally good]
蚕吐丝. can tu si [silkworm spins]
昔孟母，择邻处. xi meng mu, ze lin chu. [previously Mencius’ mother, chose neighborhood]
苟不教，性乃迁. gou bu jiao, xing nai qian. [if not being taught, nature therefore changes]
窦燕山，有义方. dou yan shan, you yi fang. [Dou Yanshan, had right methods]
教五子，名俱扬. jiao wu zi, ming ju yang [taught five sons, reputations all spread]

34 The self-notation of Jiannan Shichao 剑南诗钞 by Lu You 陆游 reports that in October, the peasants send their children to school, which is called Winter School (Dongxue 冬学). Books such as Zazi and Baijiaxing are called Village Books. (农家十月，乃遣子弟入学，谓之冬学．所谓“杂字”《百家姓》之类，谓之村书.)

35 初入社学，八岁以下者，先读《三字经》，以习见闻；《百家姓》，以便日用；《千字文》，亦有义理。

36 人生天地间, ren sheng tian di jian
庄农最为先. zhuang nong zui wei xian
要记日用账, yao ji ri yong zhang
先把杂字观. xian ba za zi guan

37 人生世间, ren sheng shi jian
耕读当先. geng du dang xian
生意买卖, sheng yi mai mai
图赚利钱. tu zhuan li qian

38 The character is missing.

39 In Dunhuang literature, S4106.

40 This idea was proposed by Li Nan 李楠 in 1982. His experiment was promoted all over China by the Education Committee and The National Language Committee of China.

41 每日遇童子倦怠之时，歌诗一首。择古今极浅极切，极痛快，极感发，极关系者，集为一书，令之歌咏，与之讲话，责之体认。(from *Shexueyaolüe* 社学要略)

42 更令记《对类》单字，使知虚实死活字，更记类首"天、长、永、日"字，但临放学时，面属一对即行，使略知轻重虚实足矣。(程端礼《读书分年日程》卷一)

43 1. 实字：天，地，树，木，鸟，兽……
半实：文，威，气，力……
2. 虚字 (活)：吹，腾，升，沈，奔，流……
3. 虚字 (死)：高，长，清，新，坚，柔……
半虚：上，下，里，外，中，间……
4. 助字：者，乎，然，则，乃，于……

44 Such a collection is often called Weimo 闱墨.

45 From *San'guozhi* 三国志. The original text is "Dushu baibian er yi zixian 读书百遍而义自见."

46 It was documented in *Hanfeizi* 韩非子·Waichushuo zuoshang 外储说左上: in Zhongmou, half of the people gave up farming for literacy. [而中牟之民弃田圃而随文学者邑之半]

47 "In education there is no distinction between classes (有教无类)."

48 In *Tongdian* 通典·Xuanju 选举: One "good" person out of a local county with 200,000 people may be recommended to the central government per year, two out of 400,000 people, three out of 600,000, four out of 800,000, five out of 1,000,000, six out of 1,200,000. With a population of no more than 200,000, one candidate could be recommended every two years; with no more than 100,000, one candidate every three years. [自今郡国率二十万口岁举孝廉一人，四十万二人，六十万三人，八十万四人，百万五人，百二十万六人。不满二十万，二岁一人；不满十万，三岁一人。]

49 A successful candidate in the Civil Service Examinations.

50 The exact time of its creation is not yet known.

51 富家不用买良田，书中自有千钟粟。
安房不用架高梁，书中自有黄金屋。
娶妻莫恨无良媒，书中有女颜如玉。
出门莫愁无随人，书中车马多如簇。
男儿欲遂平生志，六经勤向窗前读。

52 The eight parts are named Poti 破题, Chengti 承题, Qijiang 起讲, Tigu 提股, Qigu 起股, Zhonggu 中股, Hougu 后股, and Shugu 束股.

53 The Guangxu 光绪 emperor issued the order to abandon Keju in 1906.

54 "What is Yuwen? Yu is the spoken language, while wen is the written language. The two are put together, called Yuwen. (什么叫语文？……语就是口头语言，文就是书面语言. 把口头语言和书面语言连在一起说，就叫语文.)" From Ye Shengtao 叶圣陶 [1980, p. 138].

55 The pair of 丧 (*s-mang) and 亡 (*mang) is argued to be a kind of causative morphology bearing by s-prefix. However, they are represented by two single Chinese characters.

56 This kind of alphabetic script is mainly used in Taiwan, which is equivalent to Pinyin in Mainland China.

57 Vietnamese created new characters for native Vietnamese words in ways like the *liushu* in hanzi-creation (Nguyen, 1990). Wang (1958) pointed out that only three principles – jiajie, huiyi and xingsheng – are employed in Chu-nom.

58 It is estimated that this book was edited in the period from 403 to 221 BCE.

59 It is another name of Xiaoya 小雅.

60 天子重英豪，文章教尔曹。
万般皆下品，唯有读书高。

61 师之所传，弟之所授，一字毋敢出入，背师说即不用 [What the teacher teaches and what the students learn should be the same. The idea against the teacher should not be accepted] (Pi Xirui 皮锡瑞, *Jingxue Lishi* 经学历史).

62 不学诗，无以言 [Not learning *Shijing*, nothing to say] (*Lunyu* 论语·Jishi 季氏).

63 Han Yu 韩愈 (768–824) is the founder.

64 cf. *Songshi* 宋史·Xiaguo zhuan 夏国传.

65 Gong (1982) analyzed the relationship between Chinese characters and Tangut scripts and listed abundant examples to demonstrate the influence from Chinese to Tangut.

66 The earliest Tangut writing is an official letter in 1072, and the latest scripts were sculpted in stone pillar in 1502.

67 *Huangshinü Duijing* 黄氏女对经 is one of the most famous (cf. Xu, 1988).

68 Their language is classified as Tibeto-Burman.

69 However, it is unknown yet when it was created.

70 The inscription Liuhe jiangu dazhai song 六合坚固大宅颂 sculpted in Shanglin 上林 in 682 is thought to be the landmark of Zhuang writing.

References

Baxter, W. H. (1992). *A handbook of Old Chinese phonology*. Berlin: Mouton De Gruyter.

Chao, Y. R. (1975). Rhythm and structure in Chinese word conceptions. Kaogu renleixuekan *考古人类学刊*. V.37–38, 1–15. Also in Y. R. Chao (1976), *Aspects of Chinese sociolinguistics: Essays* (pp. 275–292). Language, science and national development. Stanford, CA: Stanford University Press.

Chen, B. 陈保亚. (1999). 20 Shiji zhongguo yuyanxue fangfalun 20 *世纪中国语言学方法论* [Methodologies of Chinese linguistics in the 20th century]. Ji'nan 济南: Shandong jiaoyu chubanshe 山东教育出版社.

Chen, M. J., & Yuen, J. C-K. (1991). Effects of Pinyin and script type on verbal processing: Comparisons of China, Taiwan and Hong Kong experience. *International Journal of Behavioral Development*, 14, 429–484.

Chlebowska, K. (1990). *Literacy for rural women in the Third World.* Paris: UNESCO.

Daniel, P. T., & Bright, W. (Eds.) (1995). *The world's writing systems.* New York: Oxford University Press.

Elman, B. A. (2000). *A cultural history of civil examinations in Late Imperial China.* Berkeley: The California University Press.

Fan, K. 樊克政. (2000). Xuexiao shihua *学校史话* [*The history of school*]. Beijing 北京: Zhongguo dabaike quanshu chubanshe 中国大百科全书出版社.

Fang, G. 方国瑜. (1995). Naxi xiangxing wenzipu *纳西象形文字谱* [*A dictionary of Naxi pictographs*]. Kunming 昆明: Yunnan renmin chubanshe 云南人民出版社.

Fei, X. 费孝通 et al. (1989). Zhonghuaminzu duoyuanyiti geju *中华民族多元一体格局* [*Diversity in the unity of the Chinese nation*]. Beijing 北京: Zhongyang minzu xueyuan chubanshe 中央民族学院出版社.

Geng, Z. 耿振生. (1992). Mingqing dengyunxue tonglun *明清等韵学通论* [*Introduction on Dengyunxue of Ming-Qing period*]. Beijing 北京: Yuwen chubanshe 语文出版社.

Gong, H. 龚煌城. (1981). Xixia wenzi de jiegou 西夏文字的结构 [The structure of Tangut characters]. *Bulletin of the Institute of History and Philology*, 52 (1), 79–100.

Gong, H. 龚煌城. (1982). Chinese elements in the Tangut script. *Bulletin of the Institute of History and Philology*, 53 (1), 167–187.

Gong, H. 龚煌城. (2002). Xixia yuwen yanjiu lunwenji *西夏语文研究论文集* [*Studies on the Xixia language and literature*]. Taipei: Institute of Linguistics (Preparatory), Academia Sinica.

Hanley, J. R., Tzeng, O., & Huang, H-S. (1999). Learning to read Chinese. In M. Harris & G. Hatano (Eds.), *Learning to read and write: A cross-linguistic perspective* (pp. 173–195). Cambridge: Cambridge University Press.

He, L. 和力民. (2001). Naxi xiangxing wenzi zitie *纳西象形文字字帖* [*A copybook of Naxi pictographs*]. Kunming 昆明: Yunnan chubabshe 云南出版社.

Ho, D. 何大安 (1993). Cong zhongguo xueshu chuantong lun hanyufangyan yanjiu de guoqu, xianzai yu weilai 从中国学术传统论汉语方言研究的过去、现在与未来 [The past, present and future of studies on Chinese dialects from the perspective of Chinese academic tradition]. *Bulletin of the Institute of History and Philology, Academia Sinica*, 63 (4), 713–731.

Ho, P. (1962). *The ladder of success in Imperial China*, 1368–1911. Columbia: Columbia University Press.

Ho, P. (1976). *The cradle of the East.* Chicago: University of Chicago Press.

Ho, P. 何炳棣 (2005). Dushi yueshi liushinian *读史阅世六十年* [*Sixty years of reading the history and understanding the world*]. Guilin 桂林: Guangxi shifandaxue chubanshe 广西师范大学出版社.

Hu, T. 胡坦 et al. (1999). Lasa kouyu duben *拉萨口语读本* [Spoken language of Lhasa]. Beijing 北京: Minzu chubanshe 民族出版社.

Hung, D. L., & Tzeng, O. J. L. (1981). Orthographic variation and visual information processing. *Psychological Bulletin*, 90, 377–414.

Hung, D. L., Tzeng, O. J. L., & Ho, C. (1999). Word superiority effect in the visual processing of Chinese. In O. J. L. Tzeng (Ed.), The biological basis of language. *Journal of Chinese Linguistics Monograph*, 13, 61–95.

Jiang, D. 江荻. (2002). Zangyu yuyinshi yanjiu *藏语语音史研究* [A study of historic phonetics of Tibetan]. Beijing 北京: Minzu chubanshe 民族出版社.

Karlgren, B. (1954). Compendium of phonetics in Ancient and Archaic Chinese. *Bulletin of the Museum of Far Eastern Antiquities*, 26, 211–367.

Ko, H., & Lee, J. R. (1997). Chinese children's phonological awareness ability and later reading ability: A longitudinal study. *Journal of the National Chung-Cheng University*, 7, 49–66.

Li, P., Tan, L., Bates, E., & Tzeng, O. J. L. (Eds.) (2006). *The Handbook of East Asian Psycholinguistics*. Vol. I: Chinese. Cambridge, UK: Cambridge University Press.

Lin, C. 林崇德. (2002). Fazhan xinlixue *发展心理学* [*Human development*]. Hangzhou 杭州: Zhejiang jiaoyu chubanshe 浙江教育出版社.

Lu, X. 陆锡兴. (2002). Hanzi chuanboshi *汉字传播史* [*A history of hanzi transmission*]. Beijing 北京: Yuwen chubanshe 语文出版社.

Nguyen, D-H. (1990). Graphemic borrowing from Chinese: The case of Chu Nom-Vietnam's Demotic Script. *Bulletin of the Institute of History and Philology, Academia Sinica*, 61, 383–432.

Polich, J. M., McCarthy, G., Wang, W. S-Y., & Donchin, E. (1983). When words collide. *Biological Psychology*, 16, 155–180.

Qiu, X. 裘锡圭. (1988). Wenzixue gaiyao *文字学概要* [*A conspectus of Chinese characters*]. Beijing 北京: The Commercial Press 商务印书馆.

Qu, A. 瞿霭堂. (1996). Zangzu de yuyan he wenzi **藏族的语言和文字** [*The Tibetan language and character*]. Beijing 北京: Zhongguo zangxue chubanshe 中国藏学出版社.

Seidenberg, M. S., & Tanenhaus, M. K. (1979). Orthographic effects on rhyme monitoring. *Journal of Experimental Psychology: Human Learning and Memory*, 5, 546–554.

Siok, W. T., Perfetti, C. A., Jin, Z., & Tan, L. (2004). Biological abnormality of impaired reading is constrained by culture. *Nature*, 431, 71–76.

Tan, L. H., Spinks, J. A., Eden, G. F., Perfetti, C. A., & Siok, W. T. (2005). Reading depends on writing, in Chinese. *Proceedings of National Academy of Science*, 102, 8781–8785.

Tang, Z. 唐作藩. (2002). Yinyunxue jiaocheng *音韵学教程* [A course on Chinese historical phonology]. Beijing 北京: Peking University Press 北京大学出版社. 3rd Edition.

Ting, P. (1998). Some thoughts on reconstructing the phonetic system of ancient Chinese. In B. K. T'sou (Ed.), *Studia linguistica serica: Proceedings of the 3rd international conference on Chinese linguistics* (pp. 27–37). Hong Kong: City University of Hong Kong.

Treiman, R. A., Baron, J., & Luk, K. (1981). Speech recoding in silent reading: A comparison of Chinese and English. *Journal of Chinese Linguistics*, 9, 116–125.

Tsien, T.-H. (1962). *Written on bamboo and silk: The beginnings of Chinese books and inscriptions*. Chicago: University of Chicago Press.

Tzeng, O. J. L., & Singer, H. (Eds.) (1981). *The perception of print: Reading research in experimental psychology*. Erlbaum. Hillsdale, NJ.

Tzeng, O. J. L., & Wang, W. S-Y. (1983). The first two R's. *American Scientist*, 71, 238–243.

Tzeng, O. J. L., Hung, D. L., Cotton, B., & Wang, W. S-Y. (1977). Speech recoding in reading Chinese characters. *Journal of Experimental Psychology*, 3, 621–630.

Tzeng, O. J. L., Zhong, H. L., Hung, D. L., & Lee, W. L. (1995). Learning to be a conspirator: A tale of becoming a good Chinese reader. In B. de Gelder & J. Morais (Eds.), *Speech and reading: A comparative approach* (pp. 227–245). Hove, UK: Erlbaum.

Wang, B. 王炳照, & Guo, Q. 郭齐家 (2000). Zhongguo jiaoyushi yanjiu (Song-Yuan fenjuan) *中国教育史研究(宋元分卷)* [*The history of Chinese education in the Song-Yuan period*]. Shanghai 上海: Huadong shifandaxue chubanshe 华东师范大学出版社.

Wang, F. (2005). Review on multilingualism in China. *Journal of Chinese Linguistics*, 33 (2), 366–368.

Wang, H.王洪君. (1994). Cong zi he zizu kan ci he duanyu 从字和字组看词和短语 [A study of word and phrase from the perspective of zi and combination of zis]. Zhongguo yuwen *中国语文*. 2, 102–112.

Wang, L. 王力. (1958). Hanyueyu yanjiu 汉越语研究 [A study of Sino-Vietnamese]. Hanyushi lunwenji *汉语史论文集*. Beijing 北京: Kexue chubanshe 科学出版社.

Wang, W. S-Y. (1973). The Chinese language. *Scientific American*, 228, 50–60.

Wang, W. S-Y. (1981). Language structure and optimal orthography. In O. J. L. Tzeng & H. Singer (Eds.), *Perception of print: Reading research in experimental psychology* (pp. 223–236). Hillsdale, NJ: Erlbaum.

Wang, W. S-Y. (1991). *Explorations in language*. Taipei: Pyramid Press.

Wang, W. S-Y. (1997). Languages or dialects? *The CUHK Journal of Humanities*, 1, 54–62.

Xu, L. 徐琳. (1988). Baizu *huangshinü duijing* yanjiu 白族黄氏女对经研究 [A study of the Bai story "The Huang family woman and the vajracchedīkā"]. *CAAAL Monograph Series* 12.

Xu, L. 徐琳, & Zhao, Y. 赵衍荪 (1984). Baiyu jianzhi *白语简志* [*The brief introduction to the Bai language*]. Beijing 北京: Minzu chubanshe 民族出版社.

Xu, T. 徐通锵. (1991). Yuyi jufa chuyi 语义句法刍议 [On semantic syntax]. Yuyan jiaoxue yu yanjiu *语言教学与研究*, 3, 38–62.

Xu, T. 徐通锵. (1992). Zai jiehe de daolu shang mosuo qianjin 在"结合"的道路上摸索前进 [Explore in the road of integration]. *Newsletter (Hong Kong)*, No. 13.

Xu, T. 徐通锵. (1994a). Zi he hanyu de jufa yanjiu"字"和汉语的句法研究 [Zi and syntactic studies of Chinese]. Shijie hanyu jiaoxue *世界汉语教学*, 2, 1–9.

Xu, T. 徐通锵. (1994b). Zi he hanyu yanjiu de fangfalun "字"和汉语研究的方法论 [Zi and methodologies of Chinese studies]. Shijie hanyu jiaoxue *世界汉语教学*, 3, 1–14.

Xu, T. 徐通锵. (1997). Yuyan lun *语言论* [Language]. Heilongjiang 黑龙江:: Dongbei shifan daxue chubanshe 东北师范大学出版社.

Ye, S. 叶圣陶. (1980). Yeshengtao yuwen jiaoyu lunji *叶圣陶语文教育论集* [*Ye Shengtao's studies on Chinese education*]. Beijing 北京: Jiaoyu kexue chubanshe 教育科学出版社.

Yu, L., & Suen, H. K. (2005). Historical and contemporary exam-driven education fever in China. *Korean Educational Development Institute (KEDI) Journal of Educational Policy, 2* (1), 17–33.

Yuanteng, Z. 远藤织枝, & Huang, X. 黄雪贞. (2005). Nüshu de lishi yu xianzhuang *女书的历史与现状* [*The past and present of the female writing*]. Beijing 北京: Zhongguo shehui kexue chubanshe 中国社会科学出版社.

Zhang, Z. 张志公. (1962). Chuantong yuwen jiaoyu chutan *传统语文教育初探* [*A preliminary study of traditional Chinese education*]. Shanghai 上海: Shanghai jiaoyu chubanshe 上海教育出版社.

Zhang, Z. 张中行. (1997). Wenyan he baihua *文言和白话* [*Literary language and spoken language*]. Ha'erbin 哈尔滨: Heilongjiang renmin chubanshe 黑龙江人民出版社.

Zhou, M. (2003). *Multilingualism in China: The politics of writing reforms for minority languages 1949–2002*. Berlin: Mouton de Gruyter.

CHAPTER 22

The Elephant in the Room

Language and Literacy in the Arab World

Niloofar Haeri

Perhaps it is fitting to begin a chapter on literacy in the Arab world by stating at the outset that we know little about the subject. With one major exception (Wagner, 1993), we have almost no ethnographic knowledge of what goes on in classrooms at any stage of the twelve-year formal schooling. This is all the more regrettable because literacy rates in the Arab world continue to be low according to the statistics offered in the Arab Human Development Reports of 2002 and 2003 (henceforth, AHDR). Yet, one has little empirical bases to take advantage of. Insofar as children are concerned, there are many basic questions that remain unstudied. What do children learn in elementary school? How do they view their learning material and what kinds of relationships do they develop with the language of instruction? What are the experiences of middle- and secondary-school children? What kinds of relationships with the written word do the educational systems in the Arab world cultivate? Due to the lack of empirical studies, one often has to rely on a kind of backward reasoning – inferring what must be taking place – from statistics on literacy and/or from scattered anecdotal studies written up in academic and nonacademic venues. What about the meanings of literacy? It is well known – as was the case among Christians in the Middle Ages – that for Muslims, literacy has been historically connected to the ability to read the Qur'an. But how have ideas about literacy transformed in the course of the twentiethth century when mass education had its beginnings? Who is considered literate now?

Given the paucity of ethnographic studies, this chapter aims to contribute in this respect by offering a number of ethnographic details based on two periods of my own fieldwork in Cairo in 1987–1988 and 1995–1996. I should mention that literacy was not the primary concern of either period of research but I did make relevant observations. There are perhaps no generalizations that can be made with regard to literacy in the Arab world without being qualified with respect to inequality. Most of the discussion in this chapter has to do with urban lower-middle-class children who have no choice but to attend the public school system. Even when families have minimal money to spare, let alone are comfortably upper class, they make every effort to send their children to private schools, because, in most countries, the public educational systems are in dire states (AHDR, 2002, 2003). In Egypt, until a decade or two ago, private schools were mostly although not exclusively Catholic missionary schools whose main languages of instruction were various European languages. In the past few decades, Islamic private schools have also been opened whose curricula are different and they teach in Arabic, while significantly emphasizing the teaching of English in particular.

Although the ethnographic details offered here are based on research in Egypt, some of the clues, questions and insights they lead to are relevant to the rest of the Arab world. In the first part of this chapter, I begin with a brief background section and go on to pose a number of questions on various aspects of education in Egypt. In the second part, I take advantage of the series of AHDRs that discuss many important matters, including education and literacy. I hope the ideas addressed in this chapter can lead to a dialogue with the authors on as crucial a matter as literacy. All the reports have a constructively critical approach and therefore have received deserved attention and praise in the media. The major concept that is utilized in the 2002 and 2003 reports is "human development," which is defined as a "process of enlarging choices. Every day human beings make a series of choices – some economic, some social, some political, some cultural. . . . Human development is both a process and an outcome. It is concerned with the process through which choices are enlarged" (AHDR, 2002, p. 15). The report notes that human development is a multidimensional concept with a number of central constituents – two of which are human freedom and knowledge acquisition: "human development is inextricably linked with human freedom . . . human development is freedom. However, this freedom, the ability to achieve things that people value, cannot be used if opportunities to exercise this freedom do not exist" (AHDR, 2002, p. 18). In the 2003 report, the Arab world is compared to seven world regions (i.e., North America, Oceania, Europe, Latin America and the Caribbean, South and East Asia, and Sub-Saharan Africa) and is found to have had "the lowest freedom score in the late 1990s" (p. 27).

Some Background Context

In the Arab world, the official language is Classical Arabic, which is the language of the Qur'an and the medium of public education, bureaucracy and print. The nonprint media are dominated by Egyptian Arabic – the majority of radio and television programs are in that language as well as theatre and films. Print media, on the other hand, allow very little Egyptian Arabic. Until the 1800s, there had been little debate about what the language of instruction must be – probably because all institutions of learning belonged to various religious establishments, the most famous of which is the al-Azhar, founded in the tenth century. In the nineteenth century, for the first time, it was the state that founded a variety of professional and vocational schools. At the same time, toward the end of that century, newspapers began to appear. To my knowledge, the historiography of this period with regard to language choice has not been undertaken. One can imagine that there were debates because shortly after the publication of newspapers began, concerns with language matters were among the most frequent topics written about (Haeri, 2003). In any case, the choice was made to 'simplify' [*tabsiit*] and 'modernize' [*tahdith*] Classical Arabic rather than use Egyptian Arabic – the mother tongue of a majority of Egyptians. One can also imagine that the colonization of Egypt in 1882 by the British made Egyptians far keener on preserving Classical Arabic than choosing the 'weaker' unwritten language that had no textual monuments worthy of pride and no relation to their identity as Muslims. The language of the Qur'an is quite different from the various Arabic vernaculars that are spoken as mother tongues across the Arab world. It differs on fundamental grounds so that without studying it formally, one cannot read or write it. In addition, it was perceived as lacking vocabulary for modern technology and the sciences. Simplification has meant avoiding archaic and complex grammatical constructions, using (where possible) constructions that are closer to the vernaculars and also an updated vocabulary. More than a century and a half have passed since the early efforts at simplification and modernization began.[1]

By 'reforming' the language, it was strongly hoped that literacy would spread more easily and, hence, Arab societies would move faster toward modernity and progress. Language reform was seen as essential to social progress. Examining literacy rates at the moment, it is clear that this hope has not been fulfilled. It is possible, given detailed studies, that in certain historical periods various countries were more successful in raising literacy than is the case now, but we lack such research. My central argument in this chapter is that the main reason for exceedingly low literacy in most of the Arab world is that the language of education in the public educational systems is Classical Arabic and various modernized versions of it. That is, I argue that underprivileged, lower-class Arab children are asked to surmount obstacles that no other children in the world are asked to do – namely, learn their subjects while lacking proficiency in the language in which those subjects are written. This is true for Muslim and non-Muslim Arabs such as Copt pupils in Egypt, with the difference that the latter are further marginalized through repeated mentions of the relationship between the language of instruction and Islam in *government* textbooks. Simultaneously, it is also the case that public educational institutions fail at almost all levels from the quality of textbooks, to crowded classrooms, to badly trained teachers, and so on. Hence, even given a language of instruction that is no one's mother tongue, with better textbooks and improved schools, the literacy rates would be higher. As I argue at the end of this chapter, what impedes this move is not entirely due to small budgets for education and other similar factors. A complex web of ideologies with respect to language, nationalism, religion, secularism and the status of Arabic as a former language of empire has made it difficult to make fundamental changes in the public educational systems.

It is by now a truism that standard languages that are the media of education generally belong to the ruling classes (Bourdieu, 1977, 1982). In the case of the Arab world, the upper classes are not, in fact, the ones who speak and use or know the official standard language better than other classes. They are generally far more fluent in foreign languages such as English and French, which they learn while attending private schools as children. In addition to careers in literature or journalism, knowledge of the official language is necessary for the vast bureaucracies in the Arab world. It may not be too unreasonable to say that public schools seem geared to creating armies of low-level civil servants. In the upper echelons of the civil service, those who acquire posts in diplomacy, for example, hire others in the lower rungs expressly because they have better language skills and can write the letters that their bosses would have more difficulty drafting. Hence, those with power occupying the highest paid jobs are fluent in foreign languages. It therefore goes without saying that in this case, the knowledge that brings most power with it is not of the official language of the country but rather of the colonial languages that 'left' but came back with even more power through capitalism and globalization.

Who Is the Pupil Imagined to Be?

Following regular conversations with middle- and secondary-school students during the course of several months in 1995–1996, I examined a number of their textbooks with various questions in mind. My interest lay in trying to understand what kinds of individuals the pupils are imagined to be through an analysis of the form and content of their textbooks. Do the form and content of textbooks show attempts at *persuading* the pupils to learn to read and write? Are they imagined to be intelligent, spirited beings in need of updated material? What kinds of knowledge are considered worth passing on to them? What kinds of future citizens are they hoped to become? Are these children, a majority of whom are economically underprivileged, considered as individuals with potentially important roles to play in the future of their society?

The students that I met had many complaints and a frequent one had to do with their Arabic language classes. Let us remind ourselves of the importance of this subject. In Arabic language classes, students are taught Classical Arabic, the official language of Egypt and of all Arab states, but not the mother tongue of Egyptians or other Arabs. As the official language, public education textbooks are in that language. To learn any subject, whether literature or chemistry, students need to master the official language well – a language that is significantly different from their mother tongues (Maamouri, 1999; Wagner, 1993). Therefore, it is crucial to see how well the Arabic language is taught.

When I looked at the textbook for Arabic for the first year of middle school (Ministry of Education, Egypt, 1989–1990), I understood the complaints of the students I interviewed. To begin with, the textbook is printed on cheap-quality newsprint paper. Other than on its cover, it uses no colors, paintings, photographs and so on, except for a few poor-quality black-and-white drawings. So, it is quite an uninviting book to hold, to look at and then to read. The material in it is dry and outdated. The language used is so stilted and old-fashioned that one truly wonders for whom the textbook writers thought they were writing.

It is surprising that the contemporary or modernized versions of Classical Arabic are barely represented in the lessons. Why is this? Is this a change from other eras? What, then, has been the point of so much (contested) effort expended on linguistic modernization? The textbook begins with an introduction addressed to teachers in which the link between Classical Arabic and Islam is the first thing that is mentioned: "Thanks be to God who honored the Arabic Language with the Nobel Qur'an, and prayers and peace upon its Messenger Muhammad, speaker of the clear Arabic language. . . . " The introduction goes on to describe the contents: "And this book . . . took care to offer to the student these rules [of grammar] through pleasurable stories and human values and . . . useful contemporary scientific discoveries . . . , alongside contemporary culture, and the guarding of the essence of Arab culture [*al-zaatiyya al-thaqaafa al-'arabiyya*], and [of] Islamic values [*al-qiyam al-islamiyya*] that the sons and daughters of the Arab nation are proud of (Ministry of Education, Egypt, 1989–1990, p. x)." The introduction also states that the book does not offer anything new in the "science of grammar." This is a rather curious statement although it is a truthful one. Why not offer a new way of teaching the language? Countless Arab educators have been urging precisely that for decades.

As for the lessons, the first one offers four verses from the Qur'an from the Sura of Luqman (verses 14–17) and begins with "Said Almighty God" followed by verses which appear in large quotation marks and are fully vowelled, as is the case with any edition of the Qur'an in Arabic. That is, Arabic script does not have symbols for short vowels and, because grammatical cases in Classical Arabic are represented by three short vowels, these must be added in the form of diacritics. Hence, a vowelled text means that the short vowels are orthographically present and indicate the case of the word they appear on, for example, whether a noun is in the nominative, accusative or genitive. Because the Qur'an is always printed with orthographically marked vowels, the pages of such textbooks look similar to the Qur'an. The content of the first lesson is about how one should treat one's parents. This lesson is then followed by comprehension and grammatical-analysis exercises. The second lesson is on the pursuit of knowledge from the sayings of the Prophet

Muhammad. Other lessons are on the unity of Arabs, love for Egypt, the contribution of Arabs to mathematics, more verses from the Qur'an, several old morality tales and so on. Most lessons are either directly about religious themes or are verses from the Qur'an. The language of lessons, their vocabulary as well as the particular gramatical constructions they are meant to illustrate, are stunningly archaic, heavy and humorless. It is no wonder that the majority of students feel alienated from such classes and tell countless jokes about the language and teachers of grammar (Haeri, 1996). In this as well as other textbooks, the relationship between the language and Islam is continuously underlined – yet another reason for not assuming that the public school system is "secular" as opposed to those that are within the mosque-university systems, such as the al-Azhar system in Egypt (see also Starrett, 1998).

I would argue that the physical properties, format, language and contents of this book (almost all textbooks looked the same) demonstrate that the pupils are not imagined to be beings in need of any persuasion. It is as though the authors implicitly acknowledge that the readers of their textbook are going to be for the most part poor children with little means for an alternative education. It is unclear on what bases the authors thought they would encourage and motivate the students to pay enthusiastic attention to the lessons. This conclusion is substantiated by the comments of the students who were interviewed. To begin, they as well as older adults who were interviewed about their school experience stated that they found Arabic language classes extremely boring and unbearable – some even said that they *hated* these classes. Students also complained that their grades in other subjects depended in part on whether their answers in exam questions were considered "Classical Arabic enough" by the teacher. Many students said indignantly that their grades are lowered in their exams even when they answer the questions correctly but make a few mistakes with regard to Classical Arabic grammar. Others lamented their lack of mastery of the case system, stating that they had not used it correctly, mistaking accusative for genitive or vice versa. No Arabic vernacular has a case system. They also complained that the language of the textbooks of Classical Arabic was just too difficult. A young man in his early twenties commented that he twice failed the final national exams in secondary school (required for a high school diploma) only because of the exams on Classical Arabic. Dilworth Parkinson, who spent several years researching Egyptians' language abilities and what they consider to be Classical Arabic, has administered detailed written tests to a large sample of subjects. In addition to finding that many educated people are "uncomfortable with the form," he also came to the conclusion that "Some even express resentment toward the form for its difficulty and the effect of the results of their Arabic school tests on their future career choices" (Parkinson, 1991, p. 40).

A Relationship With the Language of Literacy

Perhaps among the concepts in the field of literacy that are in need of further development are the types of relationships that learners come to develop with their language(s) of instruction. This question is important for understanding the impact of affective bonds on the quality of different groups' development of literacy and for why skills such as reading and writing get maintained or not after pupils drop out or finish their schooling. Let us examine this relationship in more detail.

It was mentioned previously that instead of choosing a vernacular as the language to be standardized and taught at schools, the decision was made to 'simplify' Classical Arabic. The problem is that what seems objectively and linguistically 'simple' is not perceived as such by pupils. If ever it is crucial to examine literacy as *social practice*, it is in the case of potentially competing languages of instruction. Familiarity with the language of the Qur'an is part and parcel of a whole series of rituals and celebrations with which children grow up. Muslims must pray in Classical Arabic and read the Qur'an in that language in order for these activities to count as fulfilling their religious obligations. They hear the Qur'an recited live or on radio and television since infancy. The language comes to be associated with countless childhood memories and a deep affective bond is developed. Much encouragement comes in the form of parents teaching their children to recite verses by heart or parts of the five daily prayers and having them perform in front of family and friends. The language does not seem difficult to them.

By contrast, when children go to school, they face *simultaneously* old versions of Classical Arabic and examples of the 'simplified' language. The ratio of the modernized version of Classical Arabic has not been studied and, at least on the surface, seems to vary by subject matter and grade level. In any case, the simplified version they are supposed to learn to read and write in seems to have an odd relationship both to the language of religion and to their mother tongue. Whose language is that? Not theirs and not God's. It is the language of some lessons in their textbooks, books and newspapers. Even children's magazines that run serial comic strips like Mickey (copyright is held by Walt Disney) are in this 'simplified' version of Classical Arabic. They do not see this language as 'simpler' but rather more difficult and more intimidating. While faced with the language of the Qur'an, they are told what various verses mean and are asked to memorize short sections, the language of instruction demands of them active production. Through repeated hearings, performances and their own memorization, they come to perceive of the language of the Holy Book as aesthetically unsurpassed. The sounds of this language soothe and move them. Hence, the language of religion is not put on a scale from simple to difficult – it simply does not enter such comparisons.

A striking comment made both by high school students and older adults, men and women, was that they grew to dislike reading in general, especially "longer pieces" like books. This was true even for the librarians that I interviewed. With few exceptions, people educated in public schools stated that they find the language of books too difficult and it takes them too long to read just a few pages. For fiction and nonfiction reading material, they commented that they found the language "heavy" and "scary" and that they simply did not enjoy the activity. These comments were confirmed in answers to other questions, such as Do you have a favorite author; a favorite book? Do you know X (i.e., name of famous author)? Do you read magazines and newspapers?.

Other than an occasional letter to a friend or a family member, the activity of writing in general was often not a part of the daily routine of most lower-middle-class people that I interviewed. This is because the types of jobs they engaged in, for the most part, did not require them to write, with the exception of those who were teachers. But the same people who found reading difficult commented that they found writing even more so and quite intimidating. The "day-to-day written output" (Street, 1993, p. 2) of people in such occupations and social classes is exceedingly small. There is no reason to believe that these results are due merely to the inevitably small sample of one researcher talking to various people in the course of a few years. All available statistics on literacy and book-reading point to the generality of the conclusion that the public educational systems in most countries in the Arab world produce graduates or dropouts who do not like to read or write beyond a minimum that is required of them. Olson finds writing a "powerful tool of cognition, a tool central to cultural development in the West and perhaps elsewhere as well" (1999, p. 132). In the case of Arab children being taught reading and writing in Classical Arabic, we do not have enough studies to be able to analyze what happens to their cognitive development. Once out of school, writing is used very little unless one's employment requires it and even in that case, it is generally formulaic writing. There is almost no teaching of writing autobiographical works or writing that is intended mainly as self-expression. But the relationship between writing and cognition remains to be investigated.

There has been a long-standing debate among educationalists and others in the Arab world about whether some of the features of the Arabic script pose special problems for mastering reading. Wagner (1993) found some evidence in Morocco to support this view. However, the Arabic script is used in Iran with some modifications and, if anything, the script is even less suited to Persian, which is an Indo-European language and for which the script was not developed. Nevertheless, there is little evidence to suggest that Persian-speaking children have particular difficulties with the script and, in fact, literacy rates are comparatively far higher in Iran. Were it not for the truth of the famous saying that Arab readers have to first understand what they are reading before they actually read it (in reference to figuring out, e.g., what noun is in the nominative in the *absence* of a diacritical mark indicating it), the script does not pose any more special problems for Arab children than other scripts like that of English.

In an article about the poor state of publishing in the Arab world and the "death" of the Arab reader that appeared in *The Chronicle of Higher Education* (Del Castillo, 2001), the head of the publisher's syndicate is among several others who gave his views on the subject:

> *. . . the quantity of books published in the Arab world is small, especially relative to the region's population. . . . There are 275 million Arab speakers in 22 countries, but for Middle Eastern publishers, print runs of 5,000 are considered huge. . . . A best-seller in Egypt is a book that reaches just 10,000 copies sold, a tenth of what a best-seller in the United States might do. Only a few books make it into the stratosphere of 50,000 or more copies. (p. 55)*

The article goes on to present publishers' opinions regarding the question of lack of readership in the Arab world:

> *[the head of the syndicate] . . . says that some of the distaste for books is created by educational institutions, starting at an early age. "Textbooks in most of the Arab countries are a means of torture for students. They are very badly written, very badly illustrated, poorly printed, too long, and tedious," he says. Often, he says, the books are written by employees of the country's education ministries, which are viewed by the public as corrupt. "All of this has the effect of making students hate reading," he says. (p. 56)*

Communities of Practice, Communities of Participation

Given the distinct experiences of many people with the language of religion on the one hand, and the language of education, print media, bureaucracy and most other written material on the other, we should consider one other line of inquiry with respect to low literacy rates in the Arab world. The language of religion is practiced through daily rituals and reinforces the identity of the believer as a member of a moral community. At home, at the mosque, and at work, people pray together – creating and re-creating the bonds of a larger community. They participate alone and with others in performing rituals that have come to have significant meanings in their lives. It is difficult to locate activities and rituals that after decades of mass education have similar features – allowing speakers to become a member of a community of practice and promoting their participation in larger political or cultural activities. These are often accomplished by either performing religious rituals or using *Egyptian* Arabic for various creative purposes. Barton and Hamilton (2000, p. 7) use the concept of "literacy practices" to conceptualize the "link between the activities of reading and writing and the social structures in which they are embedded. . . . Our interest is in social practices in which literacy has a role." As I suggested previously, for those who have attended public schools and must work hard to make ends meet, reading and writing barely figure in any routine activities unless their job requires them. If, however, we include religious rituals among literacy practices, then many people engage in them to various degrees in their daily life.

Newspaper-reading and singing the national anthem come to mind as potential candidates of routine activities one does with the official language. I was unable to find data on the first and I would speculate that the number of people who enjoy reading the newspaper daily is probably not very small but still significantly smaller than those who do the daily prayers. Moreover, I found people who kept a part of a newspaper and read it slowly over the course of weeks. These were generally low-income adults with little money who sought reading material appropriate to their age. For adults whose reading level is about fourth grade, there are few alternatives to newspapers and popular magazines. The former are far less expensive and easily found on the street or in various homes and offices for free. Singing the national anthem probably comes close (at least for a while) to a significant ritual and probably does help in creating a bond among the citizens, the language and the nation. But obviously, it simply is not enough for the creation of persuasive bonds between speakers and the official language – considering the latter is in competition with the language of religion and the language of everyday life.

It seems that the majority of people do not attain a level of literacy that allows for participation in various creative or civic communities when these require proficiency in the official language. This is the case even when people actually do develop enough competence in the language because there is tremendous self-consciousness with regard to the use of the official language. Even grammar teachers, copyeditors, and university-educated people speak routinely of their fear of making mistakes (Haeri, 1996, 2003). The point is that vernacular Arabic is used in most communities of practice and, as a mother tongue, it allows for participation in various dialogues. There is also, as was just stated, the language of religion that is used in many rituals. The place of the official language is unclear – it seems that for most people, it has not turned into a language whose practice allows for social participation.

Literacy and the Production of Knowledge

A variety of statistics are available on literacy in the Arab world and there are significant differences between them, at times as much as 20 percent.[2] As with other statistical compilations of literacy rates, literacy is either not defined at all or is vaguely defined as "adults fifteen years or older who can read and write." Of course, as everyone knows, it all depends on *what* they can read and write. In what follows, I critique the AHDRs of 2002 and 2003, which contain extended discussions of education and literacy. As was mentioned previously, these Reports, written by a team of Arab scholars, put on the table, as it were, a whole host of important problems in the Arab world. The discussions cover topics such as freedom and democracy, knowledge production and acquisition, education and literacy, women's empowerment, youth, economic growth, poverty, governance, political and human rights, public health, technology and Arab cooperation. On most of these issues, the Reports do not shrink from criticism and are forthright although they were written under a variety of difficult constraints.[3] The authors felt they were under pressure not to be critical. Yet, they decided, as they say, to not turn a blind eye to the shortcomings of the region.

In the 2002 report, under the heading "Bridled Minds, Shackled Potential," we read: "About 65 million adult Arabs are illiterate, two thirds of them women. Illiteracy rates are much higher than in much poorer countries" (AHDR, 2002, p. 3). The 2003 report is subtitled "Building the Knowledge Society" and its main focus is on the "knowledge deficit." The goal is defined as helping to build an "Arab knowledge society." In one foreword, the author states that the report "seeks to promote a debate on key questions of knowledge, to help diagnose some of the major challenges facing the Arab states in this area."

The report repeatedly cites different kinds of data that show that low literacy rates play a major role in many different arenas – most notably in "knowledge acquisition" and "knowledge production," but also in low demand for newspapers, the extremely low number of books published, very low readership of books published and so on.

The authors search within diverse kinds of data to find the reasons but, on the whole, they remain somewhat perplexed. For example, as one important explanation they state that family structure in the Arab world is authoritative so the child becomes accustomed to suppressing her or his inquisitive and exploratory tendencies (2003, p. 51). I would argue that, on the one hand, this is not a fair characterization of all Arab families – the structure of the "Arab family" varies greatly across countries, classes, urban versus rural areas, different educational backgrounds, different historical periods, and so on. On the other hand, the countries with which data on literacy are compared, such as Iran and Singapore, could also be argued to have rather authoritarian family structures and yet both countries fare far better in terms of literacy. However, one crucial factor that those countries have in common to the exclusion of Arab countries is that their children are taught either in their own mother tongue or in another vernacular such as a colonial language.

The first AHDR report says nothing on the point. The 2003 report states that "Language is the reservoir of knowledge in general, and a people's mother tongue is the main medium for their *creativity* and *knowledge production* [italics added]" (p. 174). If that is indeed the case, then why aren't Arab children taught in their own mother tongue? And why are both reports silent on this question? In the 2002 report, the question of language is left wholly untouched. It is stated with urgency that:

> *There are many signs of decreasing internal efficiency of education in the Arab world, including high failure and repetition rates, leading to longer periods spent at different stages of education. However, the real problem lies in the quality of education. Despite the scarcity of available studies, complaints concerning the poor quality of education abound. The few available studies identify the key negative features of the real output of education in Arab countries as low level of knowledge attainment and poor and deteriorating analytical and innovative capacity.* (p. 54)

The authors do not consider the fact that knowledge is communicated through a variety of vehicles, and chief among them is language. If pupils do not have enough mastery over the vehicle of knowledge, they will perform poorly. If in their thinking processes, they have to worry primarily and continually about the grammar of Classical Arabic (whether the noun is in the nominative or accusative or whether the vocabulary they have chosen will pass as Classical Arabic), then indeed their "analytical capacity" can deteriorate. Yet, in their discussion, the role of language is only mentioned relative to information technology and the "digital divide." Otherwise, the relationship among education, literacy and language is left silent.

In the 2003 Report, an entire section is devoted to language. It begins with a certain acknowledgment of the language situation: "Classical Arabic is not the language of cordial, spontaneous expression, emotions, feelings and everyday communication. It is not a vehicle for discovering one's inner self or outer surroundings" (p. 7). If Classical Arabic is neither the language of everyday communication nor a vehicle for inner or outer discovery, then what is it doing as the medium of education? Is not education meant to "lead outward" to propel learners toward discovery of themselves and the world? Notwithstanding this explicit statement of the problem, the Report does not entertain the alternative and goes on to make recommendations about reforming the situation. Perhaps to justify why it does not call for changing the status quo, the Report states that

> *In the Arab historical experience, Arabic is also connected with two basic matters that are closely associated with both the existence and the future of Arabs. The first is with 'identity'; the second is the question of the 'sacred.' The Arabic language is the distinctive feature that distinguishes the Arab identity. It is the language of the holy Qur'an. And it was the rallying point for the intellectual, spiritual, literary and social activities incarnated in an entire human civilization, namely the Arab Islamic civilization. (p. 133)*

I interpret the Report to be saying that although we must acknowledge the problem of language, we cannot call for a radical break with the past because of these very reasons.

As for the suggestions the Report makes, most are as old as the modernization project itself and some are rather difficult to comprehend. In the first category are recommendations for the "gradual simplification and rationalization of grammar," increase in translation into Arabic, the use of modern linguistics for better grammatical analysis of the language, the Arabization of all higher education and so on. In the second category, there is a call for "strengthening the relation between the Arabic language and thought... a concerted institutional effort by specialists in psycho-linguistics in order to reveal the relations between the characteristics of Arabic, its morphological, grammatical, lexical and rhetorical resources, and the functions of the brain" (p. 124). This line of suggestion gets only more alarming as the Report proceeds.[4] A second suggestion is offered to prevent "a sense of defeat before the sweeping hurricane of data and information society": "A bold response requires devising a new software toolkit to process texts and to make access to knowledge more efficient, whether in Arabic or other languages... tools for indexing, extraction and abridgement...." (p. 124).

It seems evident that underprivileged Arab children do not *in the first instance* need a "software toolkit" but rather a language that facilitates their development rather than shackles their thinking. This series of recommendations have not worked for decades and there is no reason to believe they will work now. One wonders what is "bold" about repeating what has not worked. The Reports are rightly concerned with knowledge production and, here again, among many other factors, the affective bonds with the language through which knowledge is to be produced are crucial. Without self-confidence in the vehicle of knowledge production, it is difficult to imagine how one would proceed.[5]

We are fortunate to have access to the detailed and longitudinal ethnography of literacy in Morocco – a study that remains unsurpassed in its depth and breadth insofar as the Arab world is concerned. In this study, Wagner (1993) argued against the position of UNESCO that literacy in the mother tongue is best for children: "... the generalization that first language literacy is axiomatically best requires serious reconsideration in light of specific contexts of language use and literacy acquisition; in the case of our data in Morocco, this presupposition can be rejected" (Wagner, 1993, p. 183). In comparing literacy acquisition in Arabic- versus Berber-speaking children, Wagner's team found that "... the difference between language groups [Arabic-speaking versus Berber-speaking] diminished with time and was no longer statistically significant during the later years of primary school. Thus, as hypothesized, there appears to be some advantage to speaking dialectal Arabic as a mother tongue when first beginning to read, but any advantage diminishes substantially over subsequent years of schooling" (p. 176). It was observed that "... the Berber-speaking children of the rural sample, monolingual when they entered primary school, made consistent progress toward Arabic-Berber bilingualism during the 5-year course of this study *as a function of their increased contact with Arabic-speaking peers in the classroom and in the bilingual town environment* (p. 180; emphasis added).

I argue that these findings do not support the assessment that the advantages of mother-tongue literacy can be rejected in the case of Morocco. Wagner (1993) stated that although there are many differences between Moroccan and Classical Arabic, one can still say that they are receiving their education in their mother tongue: "Moroccan Arabic speakers can be thought of as learning literacy in their mother tongue in the same sense that non-standard dialectal English speakers (e.g., African-Americans in the United States; Scottish-English speakers in Great Britain) are learning mother tongue literacy when they learn to read English" (pp. 172–173). In certain respects, the situation of nonstandard speakers is radically different from that of Arabic speakers. Wagner cited the reason for the catching up of Berber with Arab children as a matter of *contact* between the two groups. Why should contact make such a big difference? Whereas Berber children can make friends with children who speak Moroccan Arabic and who can serve as live models for learning the language, Arabic-speaking children will never have friends who speak Classical Arabic (the language of instruction) as their mother tongue or even as a matter of routine. In this sense, they will not have bilingual friends nor will they have the advantage of having peers who speak a language that they need to learn to read, write and comprehend. It is for this reason that the situation of minority children or those who are confronted with learning a former colonial language is fundamentally different. Hence, one could modify the UNESCO position and say that a language that is some group's mother tongue is desirable as a medium of literacy, although even here one needs to investigate the affective bonds between the language and the learners.

Arab children are not confronted, as are other children, with a standardized language of instruction whose most intimidating features could be that it is the language of the upper classes and that of exams. The language that they have to learn, they are told, is the language of God and of the holy Qur'an. In addition to clerics, children also may come across television or radio programs in which intellectuals switch between Classical Arabic and their vernacular. These experiences are very different from, say, Telegu-speaking Indian children learning English or Haitian children learning French. Hence, Wagner's findings do not support the claim that the superiority of mother-tongue instruction can be rejected. There are no native speakers of Classical Arabic just as there are no native speakers of Latin, however 'modernized' a version one would like to consider. Arab children cannot observe or listen to those who speak their language of instruction as their mother tongue because they do not exist. They are confronted with a language that has basically one style – formal and bookish; one cannot speak in a casual style in Classical Arabic not because the language itself lacks the resources but rather because speakers do not and have not used it for casual purposes for centuries.

Crucially, in Wagner's study, the sample population was under fifteen years old (1993, pp. 72–75). As in Egypt, the serious study of Classical Arabic grammar and the corresponding requirement of better knowledge and utilization of it begin in middle school. Up until that point, the pedagogic emphasis is on teaching vocabulary rather than grammar. At higher levels – beginning in sixth grade, the active use of the official language is far more of a requirement. In fact, I argue that the relative success in reading and writing that Wagner found was due to the absence of insistence on grammar during the primary years of schooling. I believe if students in grades higher than the fifth had been considered, the problems with the language of instruction would have become far more easily observable. Based on a background paper for the 2004 AHDR, which was carried out in Morocco, Algeria, and Tunisia, the authors of this report conclude that the material and the exercises in the textbooks are so "standardized" and "rigid" that they become a "vehicle" for the language itself, "dissociated from [the texts's] subject" (2004, p. 149).

Conclusion

I have argued that a major reason for low literacy rates in the Arab world is that lower-class Arab children attending public schools are not taught in their mother tongue but rather in Classical Arabic and various 'modernized' and 'simplified' versions of it simultaneously. Given other contributing factors, such as the poor quality of teaching material, absence of well-trained teachers, crowded classes and so on, the impact of not teaching children in their vernacular is even greater. Children's television programs modeled on *Sesame Street* (*"Iftah ya Simsim"*) and *Electric Company* (*"Al Manaahil"*), in which formal vocabulary was used in entertaining and colorful productions with a certain spirit, seem to have met with success in teaching children the alphabet and some reading (Palmer, 1993). But again, these programs emphasized vocabulary-building far more than grammar.

Many questions, including what happens to the cognitive development of underprivileged Arab children as a result of their experience in public educational systems, remain unanswerable due to the lack of studies. Various bibliographic searches, including one in dissertations, turned up no substantial studies of any aspect of literacy in the Arab world. In a recent conference entitled "The Arab Child's Language Under Globalization," the communiqué offers a clue as to why the concern of many people in the Arab world as expressed in the number of conferences on the themes of children and education still does not translate into some fundamental changes. The 'Arabic Language' is endowed with animacy and humanity. This is also the case with the AHDRs. The language is routinely said to be 'in need of protection,' 'in peril' and danger; it is 'in crisis' and needs 'help.' Television commercials using any language other than Classical Arabic must be banned and parents must not prefer to speak to their children "in the dialect of their country of origin rather than in Classical Arabic" (Gulfnews.com, Kuna.net).[6] Yet, it is, in fact, poor Arab children who are in need of protection and whose future is 'in peril.' Why is saving the language more important than saving the children? As the 2004 AHDR implies, many efforts seem to be intended to service the language itself, divorced from the why and how and the intended audience's needs. It would not be unreasonable to suggest that insofar as education is concerned, there is a class apartheid in place in most of the Arab world. Those with means bypass the perils of the public educational systems and send their children to private schools, where they almost always master a former colonial language and go on to seek their place in the global economy. And the majority, who cannot afford this road to the future, go around in circles created by those who will not change the situation because the children of the poor are not threatening their grip on power.

Notes

1 Some scholars prefer to use the term *Modern Standard Arabic* to refer to the modernized versions of Classical Arabic. In linguistic fact, it is the case that the Classical Arabic of 100 years ago is different from that of today. However, in Arabic, all kinds of Classical Arabic are referred to by the same term *al-lugha al-'arabiyya al-fusha* ('the Eloquent Arabic Language'), or fusha (pronounced fuss-ha) for short. It is only among a minority of intellectuals that terms such as the *third language* or *modern fusha* are used.

2 The CIA, the World Bank, the United Nations Development Program and UNESCO all seem to have their own statistics.

3 In one of the forewords to the second report, the dilemma of open self-criticism carried out in the hostile political context of world politics today is very well described.

4 It seems that part of the strangeness of the whole section on language is that it is probably the result of translation from Arabic into English. The clue to this comes from wanting psycholinguists to reveal the functions of the brain or asserting that Classical Arabic is not the language of "cordial" communication. Classical Arabic provides many means of cordiality and, in fact, it is difficult not to be cordial in, say, greeting interactions

in that language. I surmise that something important has been lost in translation here.

5 In an article that appeared posthumously in the English language al-Ahram weekly published in Egypt (February 2004), Edward Sa'id discusses his experience with learning Classical Arabic. He made a conscious effort when he was already an adult to learn the language because his education had been in English. He asks Anis Frayha, a very prominent linguist at the American University in Beirut, to teach him. Some time after this experience, Sa'id was asked to give a lecture in Arabic. A relative of his went up to him after the lecture and told him that he was very disappointed because Sa'id had failed to be eloquent: "'But you understood what I said,' I asked him plaintively. 'Oh yes, of course,' he replied dismissively, 'no problem: but you weren't rhetorical or eloquent enough.' And that complaint still dogs me when I speak since I am unable to transform myself into a classical faseeh, or eloquent orator." Many years after that experience, Sa'id writes in this article, "I'm still trying to sort out the problem. . . . *still loitering on the fringes of language rather than standing confidently at its center*" (emphasis added). If a world-class erudite scholar like Sa'id keeps 'loitering on the fringes,' unable to muster enough confidence in his linguistic abilities, what can we expect from pupils from the lower classes?

6 Available at http://archive.gulfnews.com/articles/07/02/23/10106278.html; and http://www.kuna.net.kw/home/print/aspx?Language=en&DSNO=953984.

References

Arab Human Development Report (AHDR) (2002). Creating opportunities for future generations. *United Nations Development Program*. Available at http://www.nakbaonline.org/download/UNDP/EnglishVersion/Ar-Human-Dev-2002.pdf.

Arab Human Development Report (AHDR) (2003). Building a knowledge society. *United Nations Development Program*. Available at http://www.miftah.org/Doc/Reports/Englishcomplete2003.pdf.

Arab Human Development Report (AHDR) (2004). Towards freedom in the Arab World. *United Nations Development Program*. Available at http://www.un-ngls.org/Arab_Human_Development_Report_2004_eng.pdf.

Barton, D., & Hamilton, M. (Eds.) (2000). *Situated literacies: Reading and writing in context*. London/New York: Routledge.

Bourdieu, P. (1977). The economics of linguistic exchanges. *Social Science Information*, *16*, 645–668.

Bourdieu, P. (1982). *Ce que parler veut dire: L'économie des échanges linguistique*. Paris: Fayard.

Del Castillo, D. (2001, August 10). The Arabic Publishing Scene Is a Desert, Critics Say. *Chronicle of Higher Education*, *47* (48), A55–A57.

Haeri, N. (1996). *The sociolinguistic market of Cairo: Gender, class and education*. London: Kegan Paul International.

Haeri, N. (2003). *Sacred language, ordinary people: Dilemmas of culture and politics in Egypt*. New York: Palgrave Macmillan.

Maamouri, M. (1999). Literacy in the Arab region. In D. A. Wagner, R. L. Venezky, & B. V. Street (Eds.), *Literacy: An international handbook* (pp. 400–404). Boulder, CO: Westview Press.

Ministry of Education, Egypt. (1989–1990). Qawqaa'id al-lugha al-'arabiyya lil-saff al-awwal al-a'daadi ('The Grammar of the Arabic Language for the First Class of Middle School).

Olson, D. R. (1999). Literacy and language development. In D. A. Wagner, R. L. Venezky, & B. V. Street (Eds.), *Literacy: An international handbook* (pp. 132–136). Boulder, CO: Westview Press.

Palmer, E. (1993). *Toward a literate world: Television in literacy education – lessons from the Arab region*. Boulder/San Francisco/Oxford: Westview Press.

Starrett, G. (1998). *Putting Islam to work: Education, politics, and religious transformation in Egypt*. Berkeley/Los Angeles/London: California University Press.

Street, B. V. (Ed.) (1993). *Cross-cultural approaches to literacy*. Cambridge: Cambridge University Press.

Wagner, D. A. (1993). *Literacy, culture, and development: Becoming literate in Morocco*. Cambridge: Cambridge University Press.

CHAPTER 23

Literacy, Modernization, the Intellectual Community, and Civil Society in the Western World

Frits van Holthoon

Concepts and Thesis

Thesis

The thesis of this chapter is that mass literacy in the course of modernization has produced a civil society that came to be governed by civilizational rather than cultural norms. The intellectual community that has been partly responsible for the creation of these civilizational norms can also be regarded as the victim of this development because it has lost its hegemony as a literate community. The argument presented allows for a descriptive integration rather than a causal explanation. Hence, I begin with a discussion of some concepts that are fundamental in this description.

Modernization

Modernization in this chapter is defined as the rationalization of norms, modes of production and situations. The notion of rationalization is derived from Max Weber, who regarded the transition from magical procedures to scientific methods, empirically derived and formally applied, as the key to the rise of capitalism. *Modernization* as a descriptive term deals with industrialization, economic growth, democratization, the rise of civil society and mass literacy.[1]

The emphasis is on *mass* literacy, for modernization at a certain stage in the process exacts a total mobilization of the population and literacy becomes the precondition for effecting this mobilization. Literacy is a dynamic concept. First, it means the ability to read and write, but this ability becomes the gate to learning new skills, which are demanded in a constantly changing labour market. *Literacy* herein is used in the wider sense as the ability to function in modern society.

Modernization is used as a descriptive term to indicate the tremendous changes that the Western world underwent in the course of its history, but I want to make one more or less theoretical claim. Modernization – as it became manifest in the last two hundred years – is a process of unintended consequences. Individuals create changes but then become confronted with consequences they have not foreseen. Modernization is a blind process (which is, after all, the definition of a process) to which people react and adapt.

Culture and Civilization

Alfred Weber, Max Weber's brother, made the distinction between culture and civilization. Civilization is the repository of knowledge, skills and norms, which make societies function. Culture represents the religious, aesthetic and artistic aspirations of members of a society that find their way into collective representations. Alfred Weber and many others regarded culture as a sympathetic term and civilization as a cold and businesslike term, but this preference is somewhat misleading.[2] As a term, *culture* can mean two different things: (1) the cultivation of the mind through art and thought, and (2) the bonding quality of manners and rules, which preserve the identity of a group or nation. Transactions within civilization often are anonymous and do not presuppose friendship or friendly relationships, but trust is essential for their successful operation. Civilizational norms inspire the trust and spirit of cooperation, which are necessary for transactions in a market economy. Such important values as justice, liberty and democracy are to be associated with these norms. Culture, conversely, can nurture the xenophobic intolerance of a group or nation versus strangers to that particular culture.

The point of introducing this distinction in this chapter is that one aspect of modernization is the shift from cultural to civilizational norms in the history of the Western world.

Civil Society

John Locke used the term *civil society* to distinguish it from political authority. The point of the distinction was that in most fields of human activity, individuals could take care of themselves and learn how to cooperate with others. Political authority is there to protect the civil society from foreign enemies and transgressions of laws within the society. The term has recently acquired new credence because terrorist attacks have made it clear that the peaceful cooperation within society can be easily disrupted. These attacks create a feeling of helplessness among the members of civil societies because they feel defenseless and cannot see the point of the attacks. Modernization leaves us no alternative but to cooperate, nationally as well as internationally. The terrorists can only destroy but can offer no ideology that can function as a realistic alternative.

Locke still had the notion that the traditional (i.e., cultural) norms remained functional for the type of civil society he had in mind. Only at the end of the nineteenth century did some people become conscious of the fact that the norms of civil society should be reformulated in civilizational terms and that the traditional norms were becoming irrelevant or even dysfunctional.

The Intellectual Community

Literacy can mean two things: (1) it is the ability to read and to write, and (2) it is the knowledge a person can acquire using this ability. The ability to read and write has had momentous consequences. Goody writes that the invention of writing and subsequently of printing increased "the technologies of our intellect". He wrote:

> *It is not because we are intellectually better endowed in abilities that we not only live but can operate within the kind of highly developed societies in which we find ourselves, nor yet because we are at the mercy of purely economic forces, on one hand, or highly specific cultural ones, on the other. It is partly the modes of communication that we or our societies have adopted that increase our capacities (as individuals, as agents) to understand and manipulate our world.*[3]

A consequence of this view is that during the greater part of Western history, there was a tremendous gap between the few that achieved a high degree of sophistication by using their literate abilities and the illiterate many. Olson defended the thesis that textual hermeneutics went through several phases.[4] His interesting thesis must be accepted in a skeptical mood. The history of legal hermeneutics demonstrates (as discussed herein) that lawyers have shown a surprising continuity in the way they have interpreted and do interpret legal texts.[5]

The term *community* refers to Tönnies's distinction between *Gemeinschaft* and *Gesellschaft*.[6] A community refers to a group with face-to-face relationships and a strong sense of identity among members of this group. A *society* is characterized by anonymous relationships between individuals. They may feel a sense of belonging to their society, but their regard for their nation (as societies commonly are) is much influenced by the success of that society to manage those relationships.

The intellectual is a person who creates and adapts norms, skills and knowledge and, as such, is indicative of the scholar as well as the priest and artist. Coleridge's term, the *clerisy*, fits their function perfectly. In this light, the term *intellectual community* seems to be a *contradictio in terminis* because intellectuals have universalistic aspirations and they have networks that span groups and nations. Their high degree of literacy guarantees these widespread relationships. However, the intellectuals across borders recognize their equals on the basis of these literary qualifications. They share, in other words, a common culture, which is why I use this term.

Hegemony

Gramsci used the term *hegemony* to define the peculiar power that intellectuals have in the public debate.[7] They have an important say in the selection of issues that are debated, but they cannot dictate them. They may exert political power, but their influence in this respect does not constitute the essence of their hegemony, which is cognitive monopoly. They create the fields of cognition within which norms and issues are created. Traditionally, this made them the guardians of literate culture. The question remains whether they still can be the guardians of civilizational norms.

The Western World

The discovery of a script has been a precondition for all the elaborate political structures in the world. I focus this discussion on the classical world, Europe, and America.

The Rise of Mass Literacy

This chapter is divided into two parts. The first deals with the patterns of literacy as they evolved through history and with certain institutional factors connected with literacy, such as education. Therefore, the first part is about how and why people learned to read and to write. The second part is about those who comprise the literate community, who write in order to communicate.

Patterns of Literacy

The invention of script is closely related to the emergence of "hydraulic" empires. River deltas such as the Nile, the Euphrates and the Indus created the need for bureaucratic controls, and bureaucracy cannot exist or at least develop without the invention of a script.[8] So, a small band of specialists – scribes and craftsmen – acquired a type of literacy, which Harris termed "scribal and craftsman's literacy".[9]

Ancient Greece constitutes a special chapter in the history of literacy because those who acquired the knowledge of that wonderful invention, the Greek alphabet, used it first for literary and philosophical purposes. The bards used script as a mnemonic guide to an audience that knew the stories by oral tradition. These audiences became sophisticated enough to appreciate Euripides' verses, although they (probably) could not read his text. Later, in Classical Athens, the script also came to be used for commercial and political purposes. Yet, the number of literate persons remained small and the ideal of universal education formulated in the Hellenic Period was never reached.

The literate community of Classical Greece was relatively free from political pressure. This changed in the late Roman Republic and the Roman Empire, when the political elite became literate and associated their political ambition with the ideal of a liberal education. Cicero was a typical example of being a politician and a philosopher. Rome donated two important legacies to the Western world: it transmitted Greek philosophy and provided the common language in which to study it. Latin became the principle vehicle of communication during the Middle Ages and remained in use among scholars until the nineteenth century. In fact, if the humanists of the Renaissance had not turned Latin into a highly intricate language with significant 'snob value', Latin instead of English could have remained the lingua franca of the Western world.

The Medieval Western Church made a strenuous effort to Christianize Europe, as the punitive expeditions against the Albigenses demonstrate. These expeditions destroyed the literate Occitan culture of the Count of Toulouse and his court, but stamping out heresy among the shepherds and peasants of Montaillou was a more difficult job.[10] The Church made no effort to educate the peasants of Europe. Its Latin mass symbolizes a powerful but distant authority that many peasants and artisans regarded as their enemy. The miller described by Carlo Ginzberg compared the world to a cheese and the priests as the worms that ate their way into it.[11]

The Church took care of education and so the difference between *clerics* and *clerks* was not very great because clerks were clerics. With urbanization and the ensuing commercial expansion within and outside of Europe, the clerks became secular persons. From the seventeenth century, we have the first quantitative data, which allow us to make a rough sketch of the different patterns of literacy in European countries. The Dutch Republic and Scotland had much higher literacy rates than Catholic countries such as France and Italy. Dutch illiteracy rates decreased from 25 percent for males and 40 percent for females in 1815 to 10 percent in 1900 for both sexes.[12] The performance of Scotland was even better. Colonial America was a major success in terms of literacy. Lockridge tells us that "only" 60 percent of the men signed their wills in 1660; a century later, this increased to 85 percent.[13] The author attaches great importance to the Puritan factor in creating this success. Indeed, authorities in all three countries took great care to establish village schools. However, before we give too much attention to the Calvinist/Puritan factor in the rise of literacy, we must note that the most spectacular success of the rise of literacy was in Prussia; it appears that state intervention was a decisive factor. The Prussian kings were not interested in religion but in the efficiency of their armies.

In Catholic countries such as France and Italy, rates of illiteracy remained spectacularly high, far into the nineteenth century. In Italy, male illiteracy stood at 80 percent in 1875 and only decreased to 20 percent in 1914. These average data obscure the difference between Northern and Southern Italy. In Piedmont, the illiteracy was 42 percent in 1871, decreasing to 11 percent in 1911; in Calabria, the percentages were 87 and 70 percent, respectively.[14]

Imagine what it means that more than 50 percent of the French was illiterate at the time of the French Revolution of 1789 and afterwards. Siéyès's appeal to the French nation echoed in a void. It took the determination of Napoleon to set up a new system on the ruins of the *Ancien Régime,* which survives to this very day. It took the educational system about a century to turn (in E. Weber's phrase) "peasants into Frenchmen".[15] The State and the Church fought a century-long battle for the control of education, and the State eventually won. Next to the school, the army was an important engine of turning peasants into Frenchmen and, undoubtedly, military service helped to boost literacy rates.

In the seventeenth and eighteenth centuries, England teemed with experimenters. Defoe was a striking example. Unsuccessful as a businessman, he was a great propagandist for new ventures. His tour of the British Isles is a splendid account of trades, class and opportunities in 1726.[16] The feverish spirit of invention that manifested itself during the First Industrial Revolution embodied a large element of the self-taught. Robert Stephenson, the builder of the first steam locomotives, started his working career as an illiterate. He is one of the heroes in Smiles's *Self Help*.[17] English politicians and educators believed in the so-called voluntary effort. Civil society, not the State, should take the initiative in establishing schools and universities. It worked but not well enough.

Around 1850, the system of schooling was in a deplorable state. Oxford and Cambridge primarily turned out Anglican clergymen. The curriculum of the best public schools was out of date. Many regions of England had no schools or very poor examples. The much discussed Lancaster–Bell system, in which the older pupils taught the younger ones, is indicative of the effort to have mass education 'on the cheap'. The number of literate persons stagnated compared with a century earlier. When the political decision was made to eliminate the voluntary effort in 1870, elementary and secondary schools were established on a regular basis, and Oxford and Cambridge became regular research universities, open to all denominations, England quickly took its place in the vanguard of educational reform.

A graph in Vincent's book shows a gradual convergence to mass literacy in 1914 in Europe and the United States. This also meant a convergence of literacy rates for males and females. The quantitative data showed that female illiteracy was higher in all countries than for males. In 1914, the gap was closed.[18]

The Creation of National Systems of Education

The national educational system, which provides students with an educational career in primary, secondary and tertiary education, is a product of the nineteenth century. Before and for a long time during that century, there were schools for the poor and the rich. Vocational training was provided by masters and merchants. Latin schools prepared children for universities; sometimes they were taught at home. After having been tutored at home, David Hume became a student in Edinburgh when he was eleven years old. The national educational systems of the nineteenth century linked these schools – sometimes in phases, sometimes at one stroke.

The data gathered on the ability to read and/or to write – often indicating no more than that a person could sign his or her name – provide a minimal definition of literacy, but what was taught at different stages of a student's educational career must be the subsequent question. Data on illiteracy indicate the inaccessibility of the number of persons to certain information. During the rise of mass literacy, the question of what knowledge was taught became increasingly important. National systems were designed to control teachers and students. Even educational reformers did not think that working-class children should be taught more than arithmetic, reading and writing skills. Destutt de Tracy remarked that "in every civilized society there are necessarily two classes, one which works with its hands . . . the other with its minds . . . the first is the working class, the second is that of the intellectuals".[19] His opinion represents the philosophy of many nineteenth-century educational reformers; however, notwithstanding their views, the national systems became instruments of social mobility.

Napoleon and his ministers were the first to regard French education as a system and called it the Imperial University. It included all types of schooling. As a measure of social control, Napoleon was particularly interested in the so-called *lycées* and, to train teachers for these schools, he created the *école normale et supérieure*. Together with other schools such as the *école polytechnique*, it became the 'breeding ground' for high-level bureaucrats. Reality did not correspond to the paper plan for an Imperial University; two factors impeded its success as a system. Napoleon had left the care for the village schools and schools for girls to the Church, but that concession did not appease the clergy. The Jesuits in particular put up a stubborn fight for the right to run their own *lycées*. The conflict eventually led to the *Loi Ferry*, which introduced the secularization of all types of schools; a process, which came to a successful conclusion in the interbellum. The other impediment, mentioned previously, was that the system was not meant to function for the advancement of the working class but rather to protect the privileged position of the bourgeoisie. The reason that the Jesuit schools could maintain their independence so long was that they provided the best classical education in France – and that type of education, as discussed herein, marked the privileged position of the bourgeoisie.

Wilhelm von Humboldt almost singlehandedly created the Prussian school system in less than a year. After 1850, it became the example for the rest of Germany and Europe. It had well-ordered exams and it incorporated science and technology in the educational system. It was the first system that translated a high level of literacy as the result of advanced schooling. The rest of Europe and America followed suit, although most national systems (including the German system) became a cause for social mobility only after World War II. The American republic was an exception. Education was naturally regarded as a means for mobility. First the (elementary) common school, than the (secondary) high school and eventually the colleges fulfilled the promise of an education for the majority of adults.

In an important study, Ringer addressed the "openness" and "closeness" of the merging systems. Openness facilitates ascending the educational ladder, closeness impedes it.[20] At the college level, the American system is more open to students from a nonacademic background than comparable European institutions. However, at the graduate level, the difference disappears. Today, children with an academic background still have an advantage; in the past, classical studies consolidated this advantage.

It is amazing that classical studies dominated the scene of secondary schools and universities during the nineteenth century because they had become totally irrelevant for practical purposes. Matthew Arnold – a poet but also an inspector of schools – explained why the irrelevance was a virtue. Classical studies and the embedding in a foreign culture created the detachment necessary for leaders of men. That was the reason why classical studies were so popular in bourgeois circles. Knowledge from the Classics, however, shielded them from the democratization of knowledge and boosted their class-consciousness because 'the vulgar' could not easily attain it. By the logic of their class-consciousness, they became the elite of society. Needless to say, the classical studies lost their hold on the system, but it was an uphill battle for scientific engineering to earn academic recognition without at least a stint of training in the Classics. Still, in 1879, German engineers complained that engineers without a classical education were admitted to their ranks. In the end, the defeat of classical studies was complete and the study of technology and science prevailed. Even within the haven of classical studies – the English public school or the German and Dutch gymnasium – reading Greek or Latin authors is not what it used to be. In Eton around 1850, students were obliged to write poems in Greek; nowadays, students do have to understand classical texts but are not required to translate them.

Pestalozzi, Froebel, and Herbart propagated child-centered education. Theirs was the Romantics' contribution to pedagogy. Froebel wrote in his *Education of Man*:

> *Educational theory consists in the principles derived from such insight [insight in the practice of life acquired by the science of recognizing the eternal order of things], which enable intelligent beings to become aware of their calling and achieve the purpose for which they are created. The art of education lies in the free application of this knowledge and insight to the development and training of men so that they are enabled to achieve their purpose as rational beings.*[21]

This quotation evokes many questions: What is the eternal order of things and what is the calling of men? Froebel expressed the ambition of many pedagogues in that he hoped to influence the cognitive development of children and adapt that to useful knowledge. Useful to whom: the child or society? Froebel thought the usefulness would coincide, but whether one can draw this conclusion remains an open question. Many middle-class parents enthusiastically welcomed the practical suggestions of the pedagogues. Yet, these failed in their ambition to reach the working class.

The United States and Canada, however, are a special case. Froebel's *kindergarten* became an American household word. The period after World War I became the high tide of educational reform with John Dewey as the central figure. Thousands of immigrants had to be integrated into American society. Dewey's pragmatic approach was ideal for teachers and students: learn to formulate clear ideas and test them in practice. Civic training became an important educational goal and, in this way, child-centered pedagogy became an instrument for socialization. As such, it was spectacularly effective in creating an American culture for all.

Perhaps we do injustice to Dewey when we emphasize the aspect of socialization. He had a high-minded and sympathetic view of people living and working together, but the problem with him and other educational reformers was that their notions of ideal living look insignificant and ineffective next to the tremendous pressure on the individual to adapt to the acquisition of state-mandated practical knowledge. They never managed to ask the question: Knowledge for what? Modernization hollowed the ideal of traditional literate culture and reformers were not able to replace it with something else. Ringer ended his book as follows:

> *The old classical humanism had its faults [it was socially and intellectually narrow].... Yet it had the virtue of endurance; it survived as an incongruent element in a rapidly changing environment. Few of us would be willing to revive it, even if we could. But what shall we put in its place?*[22]

Literacy and Modernization

A discussion on modernization could well start with Max Weber's thesis of the effect of Protestantism on the rise of capitalism. For Weber, the Calvinist who believed in predestination was the ideal type of Protestant. The question is whether this is true. As Protestants, the great merchants and entrepreneurs of the Dutch Golden Age in the seventeenth century did not believe in predestination; one may wonder whether the Calvinists who called themselves the 'bookkeepers of God' had the right mentality of a capitalist. Accountancy does not necessarily give a person the suitable frame of mind to engage in capitalist ventures. For this, the adventurous spirit and the will and power of a robber baron are needed.

Yet, in his essays on Protestantism and the spirit of capitalism, Weber drew attention to two important aspects of the rise of capitalism (read: modernization): its unintended effects and the fact that it made man a prisoner of the process. The Calvinist wanted to serve God and did not want to create a Godless capitalist world, and Western man, in creating it, shut himself in an Iron Cage (as Talcott Parsons translated Weber's "House of Steel").[23] Modernization as it happened and happens on our globe is a blind force to which we can react but which we cannot control.

So literacy (defined as the ability to read and to write) is a product of modernization but in a messy and indirect fashion. The tendency to mobilize a population as part of a market economy finds its expression in a rise of mass literacy. Ad van der Woude and Jan de Vries' wonderful study of the Dutch economy between 1500 and 1815 as an early example of a "modern economy" clearly makes this connection; the high level of literacy in the Dutch Republic makes this a reasonable assumption.[24] However, if we look at educational reformers and politicians, a rise in literacy is not a straightforward result of their intentions and policies. They may have promoted mass literacy but not to enhance economic growth. Only very recently has the link between useful knowledge and economic growth become evident. We now invest, as we call it, in 'human capital' by our educational policies. However, this insight only came to us *after* modernization had effected the total mobilization of the population for demands of the modern economy; that is, when mass literacy had become a fact.

If we interpret literacy in the wider sense as meaning the knowledge and the skills to interpret culture and civilization, literacy and modernization often are contrary forces. Lockridge asked himself[25]:

> *Would it be too much to infer that among the forces behind the rise in literacy in the modern era there is often a similar and equally effective desire to use literacy to reaffirm traditional values in a time of social transition?*

Indeed, education by its very logic has the primary function of preserving existing knowledge rather than creating it. As we have seen, classical studies have been used to build a bulwark against modernization and its threat to existing social and intellectual traditions. Yet, the demand for useful knowledge and the formal skills to use it is has been so great that, in the end, modernization dictated the terms of what to learn. These terms, however, are often contradictory. All modern societies have been plagued by a persistent stream of educational reforms. In part, these reforms result from the illusions of the reformers that they can shape the curriculum for their purposes, but one of the aspects of modernization is that it constantly creates the demand for new skills and makes obsolete existing skills. Because skills have come to depend on formal schooling, it has caused the need for a permanent education of the working force. Permanent is not just a slogan for intellectuals who have done nothing but educate themselves, but it has become an often distasteful reality for adults who no longer can feel satisfied that they have finished their schooling.

The Literate Community, Hegemony, and Civil Society

Hegemony and Civil Society

In her study of the invention of printing, Eisenstein demonstrated that the invention did not immediately create revolutionary changes. In late medieval times, monasteries had become centres for the multiple manual reproductions of manuscripts; when the early presses took over this production, religious tracts and stories of chivalry were published. Only gradually did the enormous potential of printing as a vehicle of communication come to be understood and used. The same can be said about the introduction of written texts. The original impact must have been small, and it took centuries before it seemed inconceivable to live in a world without script, in which an illiterate person could hardly communicate or function.

A script can have the following three functions:

- the *mnemonic function*, which is to preserve oral tradition and commemorate the conquests of kings
- the *storage function*, which is to store knowledge and laws for future use
- the *formalizing function*, which attempts to organize knowledge into systems of law, science and culture

The early river-delta empires could not have come into existence without the invention of script, which is necessary for administering the state. In the more advanced Roman Empire, the organization of its bureaucracy and army would be inconceivable without the use of written texts. Yet, even in Roman times, only a small number of people could read and write and the literate community was an island in a sea of illiteracy. If we define *hegemony* as the mastery of formalized knowledge and norms, the impact of this type of knowledge and formal rules was relatively insignificant on populations of peasants and shepherds, which had only incidental contact (never very positive) with the imperial rulers and their courts. Hence, the literate community had not much use for its hegemony over the common people.

Something similar can be said of the term *civil society*. The imperial court and, in Roman times, the towns and the owners of the villas in the countryside might be considered a civil society, but their polite behaviour was by no means an example for others outside these groups. The hold of their cognitive command on the oral traditions in the Empire was indirect or nonexistent. When Locke introduced the concept of civil society as a counterpart to political authority, commercial development had made the claim that every member of society should adopt a certain type of civilized behaviour – a feasible although not an accomplished desideratum.

The Literate Community and the Legacy of Antiquity

The Greek case of literacy was a special one. The Greeks invented – or rather refurbished – an alphabet which was flexible and which could be transmitted easily. At first, it was a script of merchants and poets who were relatively independent from the *polis*, where they had the status of citizens. This gave the Greek literate community a unique character, which was enhanced by the fact that they had a national audience. The internecine wars between the Greek towns did not extend to trade or literature. The Greek historian, Thucydides, wrote his history of the Peloponnesian Wars as a lesson to all Greeks, not just the Athenians.

Homer's *Iliad* and *Odyssey* were written as mnemonic guides for the bards, and even in Classical Athens, the audience watching Euripides' *Medea* knew the story by heart and complained about the liberties of the poet. In trade, however, literacy spread and "while documents gained authority, they remained subject to a lot of oral control: when an Athenian witness's evidence was read, he had to be present".[26]

After the rule of Alexander the Great during the Hellenistic Period, universal literacy was launched as the goal of Greek civilization, but it remained an impossible dream simply because the infrastructure was lacking. The period, however, is important for another reason. Greek culture – its philosophy, its art and its religion – was transmitted to the Roman Republic. Scribal and craftsman's literacy was converted into the culture of the Roman cultural elite, which became a powerful literate community; however, as previously discussed, its influence remained restricted. Indeed, the elite were not keen on educating the Roman proletariat. Gibbon wrote:

> *The spirit of inquiry, prompted by emulation, and supported by freedom, had divided the public teachers of philosophy into a variety of contending sects; but the ingenious youth, who, from every part, resorted to Athens, and the other seats of learning in the Roman empire, were alike instructed in every school to reject and despise the religion of the multitude.*[27]

The gulf between the elite and the multitude was and remained deep. Yet, as an elite group, it acted as a community and it professed its culture through the expanse of the Roman Empire. In both Britannia and Rome, the 'radical chic' of the day knew Greek and translated the Greek philosophy into Latin. Latin was the lingua franca of the elite and its greatest legacy to the Middle Ages, where it remained the universal vehicle of communication for those who could read and write.

Clerks and Clerics

The spiritual power of the Roman Church, after being supported by the worldly power of Charlemagne, was a tremendous force in medieval Europe. It Christianized the barbarians of Europe and suppressed heretical movements, although the frequency of these movements demonstrates that the common people often regarded the Church as a pack of thieves. The sixteenth-century miller from Friuli could read (although Ginzburg does not tell us whether Menochio could write – by no means a foregone conclusion[28]), but many heretics could not.

The greatest achievement of the Church was that it welded the classical heritage to its version of Christian dogma. Stated in its simplest terms, medieval philosophy cum theology was an amalgam of the Nicaean Creed and the scholastic version of Aristotelianism. Berman pointed out that Pope Gregory VII (1073–1085) started a legal revolution by using the *Ius Civile* and the *Ius Gentium* for a new interpretation of natural law.[29] That powerful paradigm introduced the notion of the rule of law in all European countries and was the major contribution of medieval Christianity to Western civilization.

Originally, all clerks were clerics and even with the growth of the chancelleries of worldly rulers and the administration of towns, this remained the case. All literate people at least had gotten a clerical education at charter schools and universities because it was the only education available. Medieval clerks and clerics exploited the literate culture that was cognitively secure. It explained the relationship between God and man and had clear prescriptive value for the ruler and his subjects. The clerks and clerics were bound by a common code of conduct and achievement. They spoke and wrote in Latin and they often knew each other by correspondence or visitation. They were a tightly knit literate community in an illiterate world.

The Renaissance and the Scientific Revolution

We might have thought that the Renaissance and the scientific revolution would have destroyed this medieval conception of knowledge rooted in sacred or canonical texts. This, however, was not the case, at least not in the beginning. On the contrary, it ensured the literate community hegemony in an expanding world of literacy over a long period. Many humanists and scientific scholars in the period between 1400 and 1800, who were harsh critics of Aristotle, scholasticism and Christian dogma, nevertheless believed that they were adapting the literate tradition rather than destroying it. The authority of Aristotle remained great, if only because Catholic and Protestant theologians supported it. In the field of science, generations of scientists from Albertus Magnus to Descartes grappled with the fundamental problem of motion. Butterfield wrote:

> *Of all the intellectual hurdles which the human mind has confronted and overcome in the last fifteen hundred years, the one which seems to me to have been the most amazing in character and the most stupendous in the scope of its consequences is the one relating to the problem of motion . . . [which] received a definitive form of settlement . . . in the full revised statement of what every schoolboy learns to call the law of inertia.*[30]

Aristotle lanced the commonsense notion that a body moves because there is a force that pushes or pulls it. The abstraction, painfully reached, that a body moves with uniform motion in a vacuum opened the way to Newton's formulation of gravitational force. Obviously, the scientific revolution put an end to Aristotle's scientific teaching; however, what was even more important is that the authority of sacred and canonical texts was subverted. The new knowledge was the product of experimental science and mathematical reasoning, and the printing press was ready to spread that new knowledge.

In moral philosophy, the impact of new ways of thinking was less evident. The Renaissance humanists who wanted to restore the purity of Greek and Latin texts (the very definition of a humanist is a scholar who knows Greek) represented a retrograde force. The attraction of representing classical philosophy in a straightforward secular version was so great that many sixteenth- and seventeenth-century scholars neglected to consider the colossal upheaval of the Reformation. For the majority that did take the upheaval seriously, the problem was how to design a new version under the altered circumstances. Francis Bacon was the great propagandist of experimental science, but Butterfield wrote about him:

> *He has been attacked because there is so much in his writing that savours of the old Aristotle; but that was necessary since his system ranged over all the realms of thought and philosophy. He has been mocked because so many of his beliefs about nature were still medieval – but that was also true of the various scientists of the time.*[31]

The *philosophes* of the Enlightenment finally engineered the liberation from Aristotle. They not only invented a secular moral science, which left no room for theology, but also the style, which was required to reach the public during the Enlightenment. Needless to say, this public consisted of the bourgeoisie and the nobility, but by the time the *philosophes* started their propaganda, the literate and sophisticated public had become quite large.

The greatest monument of this new approach to knowledge undoubtedly was the *Encyclopédie Universelle* of Diderot and d'Alembert. The latter sketched its purpose in his *Discours Préliminaire* as follows:

> *Thus memory, reason (strictly speaking), and imagination are the three different manners in which our soul operates on the objects of its thoughts. . . . These three faculties form at the outset the three general divisions of our system of human knowledge: History, which is related to memory; Philosophy, which is the fruit of reason; and the Fine Arts, which are born of imagination.*[32]

All human efforts in the arts and the sciences were marshaled for the progress of mankind, and the propaganda of the encyclopedists also had a practical side. The text was accompanied by eleven folio volumes of engravings, which gave a unique panorama of eighteenth-century arts and crafts. The literate community put itself firmly in charge and set itself to the task of educating not only the present public but also the generations to come.

Traditional Jurisprudence, Literacy and Civil Society[33]

The history of law and the development of judicial systems illustrate the interchange between the literate community and civil society in the course of the history of the Western world. Legal hermeneutics demonstrate the intense preoccupation of lawyers with texts and their interpretation. We know Vico for his effort to derive truth from ordinary language and common expressions, but jurisprudence was to him "the knowledge of things divine and human" and it became an essential stage in his quest for *philologia perennis*.[34] Scholars seem to have become less conscious of the central position of jurisprudence among the encyclopedia of intellectual efforts. At least until the nineteenth century, intellectuals regarded this centrality as a matter of fact. Conversely, whereas mass literacy diminished the gap between the intellectual community and civil society, magistrates of the law remain aloof and intimidating figures, a fact emphasized by their special garb, esoteric language and heavy legal tomes.

Berman writes that the West has a distinct legal tradition in which legal institutions are singled out in the fabric of society and in which legal officers always have had a special role,[35] principally to protect and execute the rule of law. The papal court in the eleventh and twelfth centuries played a crucial role in defining this rule of law in the Middle Ages. Gratianus constructed the system of Canon Law in his *A Concordance of Discordant Canons* and introduced the supremacy of natural law. This concept proved to be so successful that it became the leading paradigm for all legal systems, spiritual as well as secular.[36]

We have inherited the concept of natural law from the Greeks. Greek philosophers such as Aristotle gave it its moral connotation. It was also, of course, the legacy of the jurists of the Roman Republic and Empire. The idea of a codex was at least as old as Hammurabi, but it was the Romans who started to use law texts systematically. The codex of the emperor Justinianus (527–565) became the model for future legislation in the West as Roman law.

Hume wrote:

> *There was perhaps no event, which tended farther to the improvement of the age, than one, which has not been much remarked, the accidental finding of a copy of Justinian's Pandects, about the year 1130, in the town of Amalfi in Italy.*[37]

Technically, we should make a distinction among *ius civile* (the laws of the city of Rome), *ius gentium* (an interpretation of foreign laws according to Roman convenience) and *ius naturale*, which acted as a stopgap in cases where prescribed laws did not offer precedents. It was the interpretative tool the Romans needed in their expanding Empire to negotiate between different legal systems.

In its medieval conception, natural law, the law of nations and Roman law were indistinguishable for practical purposes. Roman law was used as a model to fashion regional laws and give them a universal orientation. The medieval conception of law was that the existing laws had always been in force as the expression of God's will. This interpretation left little latitude for the creation of new laws, so they crept in surreptitiously under the aegis of established rulings. With the rise of national kingdoms in Europe and particularly since the wars of religion in the sixteenth century, the king as sovereign became, in Jean Bodin's formulation, *legibus solutus*.[38] He had the power to create new laws and act as the supreme arbiter in these murderous conflicts. In fact, the history of English Common Law shows that the medieval kings since William the Conqueror used statutory powers in their courts.

Typically, scholars make a sharp distinction between English Common Law and Continental law systems, and the differences are manifest. However, in both cases, Roman law (in its medieval interpretation) served as a model for further development. At the beginning of the nineteenth century, we can distinguish three developments in legal theory. Common Law had become a conservative system frozen by custom and precedent and was by-passed by the concept of equity practiced in chancery.[39] In France, lawyers such as Poncelet and Dupin stressed the continuity between the jurisprudence of the royal courts and that connected with Napoleon's codes.[40] They developed a conservative attitude towards jurisprudence – relying heavily on the Romanist tradition – in a time when it was no longer necessary to combat feudal particularism because the French Revolution had eradicated it. The great luminary of the German Historical School, Friedrich Karl von Savigny, proclaimed that lawgivers should regard the *Volksgeist* as their leading principle. Logically, this meant that the people were the makers of laws, but they needed to be guided by professional jurists. For them, Roman law (i.e., *ius commune*, according to his usage) remained the stern taskmaster that had to fashion the *Volksgeist*. It was based on precedents and examples from the past, which often stood in the way of the new realities of industrial life. In fact, von Savigny developed a conservative program to block the codification of German national law according to the needs of modernization.[41] So, all three theories harboured a conservative message and all three were overtaken by legislation formulated under the pressure of modernization. The development of European legal systems shows a remarkable convergence leading eventually to a system of European law.

This is not to say that judges, legal officers and jurists in general were only a restraining force blocking innovations at all costs. From jurists also came an impetus for fashioning civil society. Mandrou points out that judicial authorities such as the parliament of Paris made discrete but persistent efforts to dampen accusations of witchcraft, an issue in the judicial system of the seventeenth century.[42] The courts of the *Ancien Régime* in Europe are not noted for their humanity. However, Cesare Beccaria's booklet pleading for a fair system of judging and against the death penalty received immediate and wide acclaim in all of Europe. During the nineteenth century, the death penalty successively was abolished (or put on reserve) in most countries of the West. Britain, its dominions and the United States were notable exceptions, although capital punishment was restricted to certain violent felonies. The movement for humanizing criminal law came from within the literate intellectual community.

Why does capital punishment still exist in the majority of American states? The question is wrongly phrased or, at least, conceals complicated developments. The summary is that until the 1976 Supreme Court decision in *Gregg vs. Georgia*, developments in the West pointed towards the abolition of capital punishment. In Europe (including Britain), capital punishment had been abolished or put on hold (as in France). In the United States, many states still had capital punishment on the books but there was a virtual moratorium on executions. The decision in *Gregg vs. Georgia* reopened the door for further executions. The decision was an expression of a neoconservative revolution, which led to the presidency of Ronald Reagan. The 1950s, according to Garland, were favourable to "penal-welfare", but the 1970s acted as a watershed in which crime "came to function as a rhetorical legitimization for social and economic policies that effectively punished the poor".[43] Capital punishment has never reduced the crime rate and it only became an excuse to avoid welfare for the poor.

However, the explanation of the popularity of capital punishment in recent decades is more complicated than this quotation suggests. Zimring detected a strong ambivalence in American public opinion. On the one hand, there is the vigilante attitude (existing particularly in the South) that was formerly expressed in lynching as a form of judicial self-help and that now makes for the popularity of capital punishment. On the other hand, there is the due-process attitude (particularly in the Northeast) that is concerned about the fairness of the judicial process and the danger of executing innocents.[44] This conflict of values is fundamental and blocks any rational discussion. It is not, according to Zimring, that Americans lack a sense of legality:

> *It is what we have, not what we lack, in American political culture that has produced the singular death penalty policies of the current era.*

I wonder whether this conclusion is entirely correct. Since 1976, the divide between Europe and the United States on the issue of capital punishment has turned into a chasm. European opinion leaders regard capital punishment as a violation of human rights and American practices as barbaric and primitive. The abolition (or euthanasia) of capital punishment in Europe has been a smooth process and was carefully managed by the intellectual elite. The American intellectual elite have never had the clout to force the issue. What is missing is their hegemonic hold over American public opinion. At least, in the case of atrocious crimes and when they are committed, public opinion in most countries of the West is in favour of capital punishment, but the intellectual community in Europe has been able to restrain public opinion. It is revealing for the weakness of the American elite that Zimrich expects that attitudes in Europe will shame Americans into abolishing capital punishment, an end result that Zimrich expects anyway.[45]

The American example highlights a problem with which lawmakers and magistrates have to grapple in modern times. Because people have become literate and, indeed, have become members of civil society through their activities and aspirations, their opinions can no longer be taken for granted. It is not only democracy that puts pressure on legal officers, it is also the character of civil society, which it has been assuming under the influence of modernization and which has a growing influence, albeit indirectly, on law and judicial decisions. For the transactions of mass society, utilitarian considerations have become more important than certain legal traditions. Since Beccaria and Bentham[46] introduced the concept of *utility*, that concept seems to have become the only standard for judging the qualities of laws and the transgressions of those laws. The functional argument takes precedent over custom.

Several distinguished legal theorists, such as Hart, Dworkin, and Rawls,[47] have been concerned about the implications of utilitarian ethics – and with good reason. For example, consider the slogan of "the greatest happiness for the greatest number". Who or what decides what happiness is? Individuals or their government? An even greater difficulty creates the the question: To what extent are the interests of the minority sacrificed to the wishes of the majority? Neumann defined the totalitarian state as a state that, *ad hoc*, can change established rules.[48] Using this method, the Nazis totally subverted the rule of law in Germany. The term *totalitarian state* is, in fact, a *contradictio in terminis*. *State* suggests order but Nazi practices created chaos. Short-term improvisation, even under more honourable conditions, will effectively destroy the legal tradition, which – according to Berman – is a major legacy of the Middle Ages to the modern Western world. It seems to be the case that we cannot do without a sovereign standard; call it the supremacy of natural law. Natural law went into decline because natural rights were turned into human rights and because claims on the basis of human rights became so excessive that they could not be met. Now, natural law comes to the fore again. The trial of Nazi leaders at Nuremberg was clearly inspired by the concept of natural law, and the worldwide agitation for human rights betrays its influence. Utility reflects the myriad transactions of literate people in modern society. However, we need a supreme standard to protect universal human values, which are difficult to define or to justify but which are nevertheless necessary as final considerations when things tend to go seriously wrong.

The Democratization of Knowledge and the Loss of Hegemony

Culture is a problematic concept. For our purposes, I make the distinction between *representative* and *private culture*. In representative culture, the common values and aspirations of a political entity find symbolic expression. Private culture satisfies the artistic and existential needs of individuals. The notion that communities favour cultural expressions is true: culture always needs a group or audience that will acknowledge the cultural expressions. However, Tönnies' concept of *Gemeinschaft* versus *Gesellschaft* will not help much in supporting *representative culture*, for groups have used these expressions to militate against societal arrangements and, therefore, their cultures have acquired a sectarian character that did not add to the mainstream representative culture.

Nineteenth-century representative culture reveals the strains and stresses in the effort of finding a common purpose for societies under the conditions of modernization. Architecture becomes eclectic and imitative. Railway stations take the shape of Gothic cathedrals, and attempts at reaching the people, such as Wagner's *Gesamtkunst*, fail to express the general will. Wagner's attempt is revealing for the failure of representative culture. He appeals powerfully to the needs of individuals but not to the common values of the public as such. Art, literature and music no longer have a general message but rather cater to individual consumers.

Some novelists, such as Charles Dickens, reached a working-class public, but private culture was the domain of the nineteenth-century bourgeoisie; for them, it was primarily an instrument for escaping from the unsympathetic world of business. A nineteenth-century bourgeois male lived in two worlds: the male world of business and the female world of culture. Yet, the bourgeoisie maintained its claim on representative culture and saw it as the way of disciplining and civilizing the masses. The well-established classes realized that *civil society*, which had been their property, had to be enlarged to include all because the masses were needed as workers, consumers, soldiers and voters. In that effort, it was largely unsuccessful except, unfortunately, in one instance: nationalism became the great hoax with disastrous consequences for all involved.

The civilizational offensive reveals a paradox because although representative culture did not do the trick, the inculcation of civilizational norms did. The message got across that all members of society must learn to cooperate and accept responsibility at their level of work. The efforts of housewives, doctors and administrators to teach hygiene and how to manage household budgets was impressive, but schoolmasters and schoolmistresses made the greatest impact. Of course, they taught patriotic lore as a form of representative culture, but the useful knowledge and skills they also taught were far more important because they effected a democratization of knowledge, which – in the long run – enabled their students to become independent human beings under the conditions of modernization. The paradox is that the nineteenth-century bourgeoisie was successful in enlarging the scope of civil society but at the cost of their higher aspirations or, in other words, representative culture.

The working classes were not passive recipients of this civilizational offensive. There was a hunger for knowledge, and schoolmasters rising from the working classes often were the successful upstarts in the world of the bourgeoisie. What these workers were after, however, was useful knowledge, meaning the knowledge derived from applied science and technology as well as the conceptual framework, which the social sciences developed for private and public bureaucracies. We may not be charmed by the jargon of the social sciences, but we have to realize that the rationalization of Western life makes it necessary, at least a moderate dose of it.

Let us return to the subject of the literate community: the democratization of knowledge meant the loss of its hegemony, for that hegemony was based on the 'imponderabilia' of a classical education. Literate erudition made way for expert knowledge. If those experts had a certain authority in society, it is on the basis of their scientific expertise, not their classical education and its derivatives.

The case of the United States is different. No literate American community ever had a comparable hegemonic hold on the public. Benjamin Franklin's remark that it is more useful and productive to read the Classics in translation than in the original is an indication of a different attitude to a classical education, and the emerging society of immigrants in the nineteenth century was ever mistrustful of intellectuals. So, it is only in the guise of the expert that an intellectual can gain authority in American society. Yet, the end result both in Europe and the United States has been the same: for better or for worse, the intellectual and aesthetic standard – which goes beyond the utility of its application – has disappeared.

Perhaps the best example to illustrate the loss of hegemony is the way people write their sentences and spells their words. Sixteenth- and seventeenth-century texts demonstrated a great freedom in the way writers spelled words. In the eighteenth century, grammarians all over Europe and in America (e.g., Samuel Johnson and Noah Webster) made a concerted effort to standardize spelling, which then became the chief preoccupation of schoolmasters in the Western world. As to the construction of sentences, the Latin grammar had been the main influence in determining the do's and don'ts of writing. This discipline has virtually disappeared, notwithstanding the heroic efforts of those who compile dictionaries. Written language has become a repository for free association and mixed metaphor.

Knowledge for What?

Does this development deserve the mournful commentary of the literate community? The *turbo*-texts of youngsters are a form of cultural creativity, which has always been associated with language and writing. Although university students have difficulty in shedding their associationist images in writing, they can be compelled to use writing as a form of clear thinking. There is no reason to declare the decay and fall of civilization on this ground. Nor is the jargon introduced by scientists into our languages a reason for concern. In his *Rationalism in Politics*, Oakeshott confronted his opponent, the "rationalist", with "practical knowledge" that is superior to technical knowledge and indispensable, if the latter can be applied with profit. Practical knowledge "exists only in use, is not reflective and (unlike technique) cannot be formulated in rules".[49]

> *[It] can neither be taught nor learned, but only imparted and acquired. It exists only in practice, and the only way to acquire it is by apprenticeship to a master – not because the master can teach it (he cannot), but because it can be acquired only by continuous contact with one who is practicing it.*[50]

The contempt for "technical knowledge" is a sign of obscurantism. Our modern world cannot exist without technical knowledge, even in politics, and we have to learn it the hard way. Yet, this verdict of a great teacher contains a kernel of truth. Knowledge for the sake of knowing it, *savoir pour savoir*, creates detachment, and detachment is a step to wisdom. Cicero wrote:

> *The genuine philosopher, who aims at truth and not ostentation, while refusing on the other hand to deny all value to the things which even those high sounding teachers themselves admit to be in accordance with nature will on the other hand realize that virtue is so potent, Moral Worth invested so to speak with such prestige, that all those other goods, though not worthless, are so small as to appear worthless.*[51]

The literate community can no longer prescribe how we read and write, let alone what we read and write, but it can set an example of clear-headed and responsible literacy. In this respect, nothing has changed since people discovered the script and since the time Cicero used it.

Notes

1 See F. L. van Holthoon, *State and civil society, theories, illusions, realities, a survey of political theories in the 19th century world* (Maastricht, The Netherlands, 2003: Shaker), 5.

2 A. Weber, *Prinzipien der Geschichts- und Kultursoziologie* (Munich, 1951: R. Piper), 44ff.

3 J. Goody, *The power of the written tradition* (Washington, DC, 2000: Smithsonian Institution Press), 150.

4 D. Olson, *The world on paper: The conceptual and cognitive implications of writing and reading* (Cambridge, 1994: Cambridge University Press). The phases are (1) readers interpret texts loosely; they read on and between the lines; they are mnemonic tools; (2) then they come to be read with a great deal of strictness; (3) under the influence of the Reformation, texts and their literal wording become sacred; and () texts come to express the personal intentions of the writer.

5 See D. R. Kelley, Hermes, Clio, Themis: Historical Interpretation and Legal Hermeneutics, *History, law and the human sciences* (London, 1984: Variorum Reprint), XV, 644–668.

6 F. Tönnies, *Community and society* (East Lansing, 1957: Michigan State University Press), C. Loomis (ed. and transl.), 202.

7 A. Gramsci, *Selections from prison notebooks* (London, 1978: Lawrence & Wishart), *passim*.

8 K.Wittfogel, *Oriental despotism* (New Haven, CT, 1978: Yale University Press).

9 W. V. Harris, *Ancient literacy* (Cambridge, MA, 1989: Harvard University Press), 24.

10 E. B. Le Roy Ladurie, *Montaillou, Village Occitan de 1294 à 1324* (Paris, 1985: Gallimard).

11 C. Ginzberg, *The cheese and the worms: The cosmos of a sixteenth-century miller* (London, 1980: Routledge & Kegan Paul), J. Tedeschi and A. Tedeschi, translators.

12 D. Vincent, *The rise of mass literacy* (Cambridge, 2000: Polity), 9–10.

13 K. Lockridge, *Literacy in colonial New England: An enquiry into the social context of literacy in the early modern West* (New York, 1974: Norton), 19.

14 C. M. Cipolla, *Literacy and development in the West* (Harmondsworth, 1969: Penguin), 19, Table 3.

15 E. Weber, *Peasant into Frenchmen: The modernization of rural France, 1870–1914* (Stanford, CA, 1976: Stanford University Press).

16 D. Defoe, *A tour through the whole island of Great Britain* (Harmondsworth, 1986: Penguin).
17 S. Smiles, *Self-help with illustrations of conduct and perseverance* (London, 1905: Murray).
18 D. Vincent, *The rise of mass literacy*, 9–10.
19 In his *Observations sur le Système Actuel d'Instruction Publique* (Paris, 1801), cited by J. Bowen, *A history of the modern world*, vol. 3, *The modern West, modern Europe and the New World* (London, 1981: Methuen), 251.
20 F. K. Ringer, *Education and society in modern Europe* (Bloomington, 1979: Indiana University Press), 169, 254–255.
21 J. Bowen, *A history of Western education*, 339.
22 F. K. Ringer, *Education and society in modern Europe* (Bloomington, 1979: Indiana University Press), 270.
23 M. Weber, "Die Berufsethik des Asketischen Protestantismus", *Die Protestantische Ethik* (Gütersloh, 1981: Mohn), 188. See F. L. van Holthoon, *State and civil society, theories, illusions, realities, a survey of political theories in the 19th century Western world* (Maastricht, 2003: Shaker), 5.
24 J. de Vries & A. van de Woude, *The first modern economy, success, failure, and perseverance of the Dutch economy*, 1500–1815 (Cambridge, 1997: Cambridge University Press), 170–171.
25 K. A. Lockridge, *Literacy in colonial New England: An enquiry into the social context of literacy in the early modern West* (New York, 1974: Norton), 101.
26 W. V. Harris, *Ancient literacy*, 72.
27 E. Gibbon, *The history of the decline and fall of the Roman Empire*, H. Milman (ed.) (London, s.a.: Ward, Lock and Co.), vol. 1, 21–22.
28 C. Ginzberg, *The cheese and the worms: The cosmos of a sixteenth-century miller* (London, 1980: Routledge and Kegan Paul).
29 H. J. Berman, *Law and revolution: The formation of the Western legal tradition* (Cambridge, MA, 1983: Harvard University Press).
30 H. Butterfield, *The origins of modern science* (London, 1957: Bell), 3.
31 H. Butterfield, *The origins of modern science*, 103.
32 *D' Alembert: Preliminary discourse to the encyclopedia of Diderot* (Chicago, 1995: University of Chicago Press), 50–51, cited by J. G. A. Pocock, *Barbarism and religion*, vol. 1, *The enlightenment of Edward Gibbon*, 1737–1764 (Cambridge, 1999: Cambridge University Press), 178.
33 I am grateful to Bernard Stolte for his remarks on this section.
34 D. R. Kelley, *History, law and the human sciences*, IX, 30; and XII, 27; Vico borrowed this quotation from Ulpianus (*Digests*, 1, 1, 10, 2).
35 H. J. Berman, *Law and revolution: The formation of the Western legal tradition* (Cambridge, MA, 1983: Harvard University Press), 7.
36 The Canonists created an intricate system of marriage laws. By increasing the number of interdicts within the extended family, they accentuated the focus on the nuclear family. See J. Goody, *The development of the family and marriage in Europe* (Cambridge, 1985: Cambridge University Press), 115.
37 D. Hume, *The history of England* (Indianapolis, IN, 1985: Liberty Classics), vol. 2, p. 520, *Variorum* edition (Charlottesville, VA: 2000), F. L. van Holthoon (Ed.), rec. 6124.
38 J. Bodin, *Les six livres de la republique*. (A Lyon, 1589: De l'Imprimerie de Iean de Tovrnes). For English language edition, see J. Bodin, *Six books of the commonwealth*. (Oxford, 1967: Basil Blackwell).
39 T. Pluckett, *A concise history of the common law* (London, 1940: Butterworth), 612.
40 D. R. Kelley, *Historians and the law in post-revolutionary France* (Princeton, NJ, 1984: Princeton University Press), 56.
41 D. R. Kelley, *Historians and the law*, 77.
42 R. Mandrou, *Magistrats et Sorciers en France au XVIIe Siècle, Une Analyse de Psychologie Historique* (Paris, 1968: Plon), 491–492.
43 D. Garland, *The culture of control, crime and the social order in contemporary society* (Chicago, 2001: University of Chicago Press), 102.
44 F. E. Zimring, *The contradictions of American capital punishment*, (Oxford, 2003: Oxford University Press), 119.
45 F. E. Zimrich, *The contradictions of American capital punishment*, 205.
46 J. Bentham, *An Introduction to the Principles of Morals and Legislation*, (London 1970: Athlone Press), eds J. H. Burns & H. L. A. Hart; C. Beccaria, *Dei delitti et delle pene* (Milan 1964: Giuffrè). Beccaria and Bentham were the first authors who introduced utility as an instrument of legal reform. Utility as a concept became widely used during the eighteenth century. In England it is associated with the names of Priestley, Hutcheson, Hume and Adam Smith.

47 See J. M. Kelly, *A short history of Western legal history* (Oxford, 1992: Clarendon Press), 403ff.

48 F. Neumann, *Behemoth, the structure and practice of national socialism* (New York, 1963).

49 Ibid., 12.

50 Ibid., 15.

51 Cicero, *De Finibus Bonorum et Malorum* (Cambridge, MA, 1971: Loeb Library), H. Rackham (ed. and transl.), 475.

Part V

LITERACY AND EDUCATION

CHAPTER 24

The Teaching of Literacy Skills in Western Europe

An Historical Perspective

A.-M. Chartier

The Evolving Meaning of Literacy

According to the Church Examination Register of the rural Swedish parish of Leksand, Kerstin Ersdotter, born in 1617, was one of the few women of her times who received the reading mark L (*Litteratus*) and was able to answer the *Questiones* of the catechism. She had been taught at home during her childhood and, as an adult, she helped parents instruct their own children until a school was founded in 1672 in Leksand. "She has been a widow for fifty years and has led her life as one would expect of a Christian," said the text read at her funeral in 1706.[1]

Henry Facy, an English schoolboy who died in 1667 at the age of fourteen, was a good pupil as well. As his schoolmaster testified, "Henry did learn what was taught him very well, as well as could be expected from a boy of his age, about thirteen or fourteen years old," and "he was able to write a good hand after a copy and could read in the Bible." He had been learning to write for five or six months at the time of his death and had only recently achieved full literacy. Kerstin and Henry learnt relatively easily even though they did not belong to the upper class; under the same circumstances, "some people were still emerging into literacy in their late teens, while many of their contemporaries made no progress at all."[2]

However, it was not uncommon for young adults to learn informally to read from other adults. Born in 1695, Valentin Jamerey-Duval was a fifteen-year-old shepherd in the Lorraine countryside near Épinal when fellow shepherds taught him spelling using a collection of *Aesop's Fables*. This proved to be the beginning of an intellectual adventure, as he finally became a librarian at the court of the Duke of Lorraine and wrote his *Memories* around 1730.[3] Angela Veronese was born the daughter of a gardener in Treviso in 1779. At the age of six, she behaved so badly that she was expelled from school; several adults then failed to teach her to read. At the age of eleven, she overcame her disgust of the alphabet and learnt it from the local postman's son, whom she told fairy tales in exchange. She first deciphered poetry books (Metastasio, Ariosto – which her father promptly confiscated – and Petrarch) and soon became an avid reader.

At the age of fourteen, she secretly taught herself writing by drawing letters on blank sheets of paper which she applied on printed poems. She then wrote her first sonnets, later became a renowned poet and writer under the pen name of Aglaia Anassillide, and finally wrote her own memories.[4]

Uses of written culture which were common until the nineteenth century differ from contemporary literacy practices, so that the current distinction between *literate* and *illiterate* persons cannot describe them in a meaningful way. International tests implemented since the latter decades of the twentieth century illustrate the current concept of *literacy*, defined as the ability to process the information provided by various sorts of texts that are in common use in social life. Furthermore, reading and writing skills are measured in reference to school practices that are being universalised as enrolment ratios increase worldwide.[5]

The life histories of Kerstin Ersdotter, Henry Facy, Valentin Jamerey-Duval and Angela Veronese cannot be understood in the same perspective. Henry did acquire literacy through schooling, but the testimony left by his schoolmaster shows that his pupils progressed at a pace that would have led them all to score low on tests such as the Programme for International Student Assessment (PISA). Indeed, his pupils would learn to read only the Bible. The only profane texts that were introduced (towards the end of the curriculum) were title deeds, lease agreements, contracts, wills – that is, legal documents through which the functioning of civil society was linked to written culture. Those texts were used as templates for pupils who were learning to write. Before he died, Henry "made a will which was challenged in the ecclesiastic courts for three years and his teacher was called to testify Henry's literacy"; "exceptionally for a minor," Henry's literacy thus left a mark that historians could study.[6] The ability to read and write legal documents – which more or less resembles what international organisations like the United Nations Educational, Scientific and Cultural Organization (UNESCO) or the Organisation for Economic Co-operation and Development (OECD) today define as functional or basic literacy – was then considered a vocational skill, useful for future merchants or artisans. The ability to read religious texts was the only skill that was considered necessary for all to acquire.

For Kerstin, Valentin and Angela, learning to read or write, having access to written culture, and schooling were distinct realities. Kerstin learnt to write in a society in which schools did not yet exist and in which written culture was limited to religious culture. On the contrary, Valentin would read the tales of "Jean of Paris, Pierre from Provence and marvellous Mélusine" from chapbooks sold by peddlers. Angela was still illiterate when she left school, where she had learnt knitting and saying prayers in Latin and had been taught the Christian dogma in Italian. But she also knew folk and fairy tales that blended oral tradition with literary written culture. She thus had some knowledge of Shakespeare plays, which an English servant narrated to the chaplain of the villa where her father worked, so that her mind was full of stories about "poisoned kings, queens, somnambulists, witches and compassionate murderers." Angela would not have made a clear-cut distinction between educated, literate persons and uneducated, illiterate ones. It is not through reading that, as a young illiterate woman, she discovered literature. On the contrary, the culture she had acquired orally was for a long time a deterrent to her becoming literate: as she already knew by rote so many tales, novels and poetries, she had little incentive to engage in learning an alphabet which she later wrote that she loathed so much. She finally learnt to write by herself, reproducing printed characters rather than handwriting, with the aim of writing poetry rather than keeping accounts or drafting legal documents. According to current criteria, Angela would be a 'functionally illiterate' person who would have jumped from oral literature to written literary creation.

Writing about the teaching of literacy skills in Europe from the sixteenth century until the beginning of the twentieth century thus requires considering the evolution of the social aims of teaching and of the circumstances under which learning took place during that period.

The Evolving Methodology of Research in the History of Literacy

The curriculum used in elite institutions is well known through college regulations, written curricula, textbooks, examination topics, and memories of former pupils or teachers. The acquisition of basic skills made by the majority of the population did not leave such marks. How then could historians reconstruct a history of literacy?

Literacy and Schooling: Research Conducted between 1880 and 1960

The first historical studies published on literacy all focussed on Western European countries. As historians kept debating about the diffusion and impact of popular literacy in their own country, distinct 'histories of literacy' were successively written. A first set of historical narratives was elaborated on in the latter half of the nineteenth century as compulsory schooling laws were passed in many countries.[7] According to those retrospective narratives, which celebrated the 'progress'of 'civilization,' formal teaching of literacy skills actually began at the time of Gutenberg. The invention of the printing press allowed a democratisation of written culture because Latin was losing ground to national languages, especially those used in Protestant countries to translate the Bible. A second period began when innovators belonging to the Church (e.g., La Salle) and philanthropists (e.g., Bell and Lancaster) developed new curricula and new pedagogical processes suited to teaching large classes. Learning was divided into distinct tasks that could be ranked according to their degree of complexity, and pupils were distributed in grades. A third period began when literacy was universalised through mass editorial production. Between 1830 and 1880, children would still recite lists of syllables, but prayers and the Bible were replaced with didactic texts emphasising moral and patriotic principles, specifically written for children and reflecting the modernity of the day.

Those narratives analysed the past through the criteria of the late nineteenth century. They considered that genuine literacy appeared only when religion receded and the time devoted to scientific and moral instruction increased. In Protestant countries, schools would pursue the teaching of 'objective knowledge' without rejecting religious traditions that were linked to national identity. On the contrary, in France, there was a conflict between the supporters of 'religion-free' schooling and Catholics who accused the French Revolution of having led to a decline of education levels, owing to the destruction of the earlier Christian schools network. The methodology of quantitative surveys on popular literacy was first developed around 1880 to settle this very argument, based on the evidence provided by signatures in marriage registers.[8] Survey results showed that the French Revolution had led to neither a collapse nor a dramatic increase in literacy levels. The gap between Northern and Southern France remained and would remain until a compulsory schooling law was passed under Jules Ferry in 1882. French national tradition still envisages Ferry as the 'founder of the Republican school' and the man responsible for making France fully literate, including its most isolated rural areas.[9]

Literacy and Popular Culture: Research Conducted since the Late 1960s

From the end of the nineteenth century until the end of the 1960s, governments hoped that compulsory schooling would lead to the eradication of illiteracy.[10] During the 1950s, when UNESCO implemented large-scale literacy campaigns in underdeveloped countries, the Western model seemed the only option: mass schooling, teacher training, state control over the curricula and textbook publishing. It was thought that economic development and democracy would necessarily result from an increase in literacy levels achieved through mass schooling.

The intellectual context has significantly altered since the late 1960s. First, the spread of new media, such as television and the telephone, has been challenging the supremacy of written communication.[11] Its impact on culture has been debated, as some fear that it is leading to cultural impoverishment while others emphasise that it could lead to a democratisation of elite culture. Second, in the context of decolonisation, ethnologists have questioned what the West used to consider as its superiority and, as a consequence, the superiority of written culture on supposedly archaic oral cultures, the disappearance of which 'the progress of civilisation' had been meant to imply.[12] Third, the duration of schooling has dramatically increased and Western school systems have failed to reduce inequality in achievement. In the United States, the United Kingdom and France,[13] teachers, theories of learning and primers have been questioned.[14] The inability of former pupils to understand texts that are common in everyday life, officially termed 'functional adult illiteracy,' has become a major social issue in the United States and, since the 1980s, in Europe as well. How can the inefficiency of the school system be explained? Has pupil achievement actually decreased? Or have literacy levels required by the school system and more generally by society increased? Current understandings of reading, writing and arithmetic may well encompass different basic skills than the '3Rs' as defined at the beginning of the twentieth century.

In this context, historians have been studying the written culture of past centuries and have investigated the impact of *The Coming of the Book*[15] or *The Printing Revolution*[16] on popular literacy practices. Drawing on the methodology pioneered in the French survey conducted in the 1880s, historians have used documents in which signatures were used (e.g., testimonies, wills, contracts, baptism or marriage registers) to evaluate rural and urban literacy levels. Debates about which inferences can be drawn from individuals' ability to sign their name have led to a conclusion that "the level of signatures runs below but closely parallels reading skills."[17] The ability to sign spread dramatically between 1500 and 1800, more quickly in Northern than in Southern Europe and in urban rather than rural areas. Craftsmen were able to sign earlier than peasants and men earlier than women. Pioneering countries were Great Britain, the Netherlands, Lutheran States of Germany and Scandinavian countries. According to a first synthesis published in 1969, by 1850, adult literacy levels reached 10 percent in Russia, 25 percent in Italy and Spain, 60 percent in France, 70 percent in England, 80 percent in Scotland and 90 percent in Sweden.[18]

The publication of those data has allowed international comparisons in literacy levels and led to three conclusions. First, mass popular instruction was initiated during the Reformation, well before the secularisation of the school system took place in the nineteenth century. In several countries, reading skills had been widespread for generations when formal schooling was made compulsory. Second, churches promoted reading among populations that had little opportunity of using it in their everyday life. Thus, at the end of the eighteenth century, in predominantly rural Sweden, almost all girls could read. In that case, universal literacy was not an answer to the economic or social needs that underlie the current demand for functional literacy.[19] The supply of religious instruction preceded any demand for it, even though Protestant pastors, who availed of Bibles translated into local languages, were more successful than Catholic priests, who relied on Latin prayers. Third, the emphasis was on reading religious texts: The reading of texts of other types (which may well rely on distinct cognitive processes) was relatively neglected as was writing. This may bias comparisons between historical and contemporary estimates of literacy rates.

Teaching to Read from the Reformation to the Age of the Enlightenment

Learning to Read as Part of Catechism: Reading and Oral Memory

Learning to read was not an aim in itself. It bore sense only in that it was useful to ensure the population's elementary religious knowledge, and the tools for reading were none other than prayers and catechism books. Those books reflected the basic pattern of medieval Christian instruction as it was preserved in all religious traditions: Lutheran, Anglican, and Calvinist, as well as Catholic and probably Slavonic Orthodox. It was considered that a book had been read properly only if it had become a part of the reader's mind, whether through personal reading or public lectures.

Since the nineteenth century, a distinction has been made between memory and literacy: "Because oral cultures must obviously depend on memory and hence value memory highly, such valorisation has come to be seen as a hallmark of orality, as opposed to literacy. This has led to a further assumption that literacy and memory are per se incompatible."[20] Education thinkers continue to argue against the "mechanical reciting" that a literal knowledge of texts would produce as being inconsistent with an "intelligent reading" that would allow understanding.

However, an opposite certainty prevailed from the sixteenth until the eighteenth century. Reading did not consist in treating information but rather in learning and memorising. Learning by rote was not a pedagogical tool to be used only by children or the uneducated. It was practised in the training of clerics at all stages of the curriculum, and many "arts of memory" were elaborated to facilitate the accumulation and use of knowledge. Nevertheless, two distinct modes of reading religious texts coexisted and competed with each other: the fundamentalist and the textualist modes. "Fundamentalism denies legitimacy to interpretation. Instead of interpreting, a reader is engaged at most only in rephrasing the meaning of the written document, a meaning which is really transparent, simple and complete. . . . In the process of textualising, the original work acquires commentary and gloss."[21]

Many dissident churches defined themselves through their refusal of textualist interpretations of the Bible imposed by their hierarchy, and they emphasised direct, literal reading instead.[22] They followed closely young Luther's principle that there should be no intermediation between the text of the Scriptures and the faithful, whatever their social condition, sex and age ("a miserable farmer's daughter or even a nine-year-old child"[23]). In rural Sweden, the New Readers community resisted the introduction by the State Church of Sweden of new ecclesiastical books in the 1810s (i.e., catechism, manual and hymnal). "As the new books contained some moderate religious rationalism, the New Readers refused to accept them, and continued to use the old ones."[24] According to the New Readers, it was necessary to come back to the first Luther, and to follow him literally, because "Luther's reformation was the true restoration of the evangelical order."

In school practice, both modes of reading were used. A text was introduced with comments and explanations in a first stage; it could then be read again and recited, focussing on "rephrasing the meaning of the written document." In the *Small Catechism* (1529), Luther explained how the Head of the Family should teach in a simple way to his household the Ten Commandments, the Creed and the Lord's Prayer, giving before each sentence a short explanation. For instance, for the Lord's Prayer:

"Give us this day our daily bread.

- What does this mean?
- Answer: God gives daily bread, even without our prayer, to all wicked men; but we pray in this petition that He would lead us to know it, and to receive our daily bread with thanksgiving.
- What is meant by daily bread?

- Answer: Everything that belongs to the support and wants of the body, such as meat, drink, clothing, shoes, house, homestead, field, cattle, money, goods, a pious spouse, pious children, pious servants, pious and faithful magistrates, good government, good weather, peace, health, discipline, honour, good friends, faithful neighbours, and the like."

Prayer could then take place. The example of the Lord's Prayer is significant: it is through this prayer which everybody knew by rote that all children would learn to spell letters and to separate words into syllables, whether in Latin or in their mother tongue.[25] Children would thus practice their reading skills using a text that had already been read and explained to them several times.

Arts of Memory for Schoolchildren: Reciting, Singing, Verse, Questions and Answers

Pedagogies based on repetition could be efficient only if texts did not vary across time and space. All communities referred to the same texts: the Bible, hymns, prayers, and catechism. During the English Reformation, new catechisms and primers flourished between 1530 and 1560, as "the first instinct of both Protestants and orthodox Catholics trying to respond to Protestant challenges was to adapt (them) to suit the new situation."[26] "The one that Cranmer issued in Henry VIII's name in 1545 was sufficiently different at a number of points from the earlier primers to be deemed a protestant work on balance."[27] Prayers translated from Latin soon took on a definitive form (e.g., the *Book of Common Prayer* in England) that preserved archaic language (e.g., the use of 'thou' for 'you') and became part of collective memory: any rephrasing would be resisted, as exemplified by the New Readers.

Liturgy also included hymns and canticles, the text of which was memorised with the help of the melody. Religious music performed during the sixteenth, seventeenth and eighteenth centuries did not include only the cantatas, passions, oratorios and motets of classical music. For instance, in 1720, in the Swedish parish of Rättvik (800 families, 3,400 inhabitants), "the hymn book from 1695 comprised of close to a thousand pages of songs" and "92 percent of the households had at least one Hymn Book, 28 percent had two, and those households with three and more totalled 34 percent."[28] Thousands of prayers, invocations and psalms were sung to melodies to which the faithful were accustomed.

In the (Catholic) Christian Schools founded by La Salle, the daily catechism lecture would begin with a canticle, of which La Salle himself composed more than a hundred about sacraments, virtues or sins, often using then-fashionable melodies.[29] Indeed, as much as the Protestant Reformation, the Catholic Reformation sought to capture popular piety and religious fervour in canticles written in vulgar language.

What could not be sung could still be written in verse: the alphabet, grammar rules,[30] maxims, psalms, the Ten Commandments, Holy History.[31] In 1644, Claude Lancelot wrote a Latin grammar for beginners, stating rules in French – an innovation – but in verse. Jean-Jacques Rousseau had a bitter experience of that book, which he made responsible for his dislike of Latin, thus expressing a new sensitivity: what had been designed to help the pupil a century before his time had then become a barrier to learning. According to Rousseau, those absurd verses made the meaning of the text impossible to grasp.

Mnemotechnic versification was applied to the alphabet and first readings. In some primers, such as the *New England Primer*, each letter would be illustrated with a Biblical picture and commented on by a distich:

A: In Adam's Fall / We sinned all;
B: Heaven to find / The Bible Mind;
C: Christ crucify'd / For sinners dy'd' (etc).[32]

A syllabary printed in Mexico in 1811 ended on the following somewhat threatening advice:

Si cultivas / Tu talento / Cuando joven / Vendrá tiempo / Que te alegres / En estremo

Mas si tratas / Com desprecio / Los estudios / Serás necio / E infelice / Quando viejo.[33]

[If you cultivate / Your talent / When you are young / A time will come / When you rejoice / In your last days /

But if you treat / Study with contempt / You will be stupid / And unhappy / In your old days.]

The Ten Commandments were expressed in verse in all European languages. Verse was also in use in the Mediterranean tradition of books titled *Catos*, after Cato the Elder, whose work epitomised the concise statement of moral truths using Latin rhetoric.[34] *Catos* published during the Renaissance, especially in Spain,[35] comprised maxims written as distiches or quatrains. After the Council of Trent, *Catos* were used to Christianise the populace: They summarised everything a Christian ought to know, from the alphabet to prayers, the truths of faith, and advice on life given by a father to his son:

Guárdate de la mujer y amor desordenado

Porque no vivas triste y por ella menguado.[36]

[Keep clear of women and their disordered love
Lest you lead a sad and submissive life.]

Catechisms relied on questions and answers, which allowed public readings or recitations by one or two persons. They were very similar across persuasions and epitomised memory-based pedagogy because they comprised all truths that were worth knowing. 'Large catechisms' intended for pastors or professors exposed theological doctrine. 'Small catechisms' were always written in national, regional languages or local dialects, even in Catholic areas, because they were designed to help beginners memorise essential truths. Luther's is the most famous catechism but, after the Council of Trent, the Catholic catechism was also abridged into small catechisms which all bishops would distribute widely. La Salle wrote two versions of his *Duties of a Christian* (270 printings): the first version consisted of a treaty designed for schoolmasters, with a companion volume following the same structure and presenting the same materials on 110 pages of questions and answers; the second consisted of two abridged texts, the *Grand Abrégé* (50 pages) and the *Petit Abrégé* (15 pages) for beginners. Young readers would first study the *Petit Abrégé* and then the *Grand Abrégé*, in which the same material was found together with new questions and answers.

A defining feature of this pedagogy is that the first articles of faith to be introduced were not those that pupils could understand most easily but rather those deemed to be the most important: by the time of their 'solemn communion' (a ceremony specific to French Catholicism that takes place between First Communion and Confirmation), children would have heard, read, learnt and recited them several times. This pedagogy based on progression through repetition, or 'concentric teaching,' had a long-lasting influence on French primary schools. Until 1923, the grammar, history, geography and science curricula of the first grade were rehearsed in the second and then third grades, with additions and new developments. In Christian Schools, only basic skills devoid of intrinsic intellectual content such as reading (i.e., being able to read letters, to combine them into syllables and to spell words), writing and arithmetic were taught using a pedagogy based on linear progression. They were mere tools that had to be first acquired systematically and then practised regularly. In stark contrast, religion comprised truths which all children had to remember textually (i.e., reading and reciting religious texts) as well as practically (i.e., believing in the texts that had been read and learnt) to ensure their salvation.

Exams of Literacy and Participation in Sacraments

Religious authorities required each faithful person to be able to read so that he could confess his faith, participate in divine service and say his prayers with the help of the immutable text of a book: eternal life depended on this. The Holy Communion and the Lord's Supper (among Protestants) and Communion (among Catholics) should thus be understood as exams that the faithful had to pass to belong to the community and receive sacraments, in addition to being graduation ceremonies for most schoolchildren.

In Sweden and Finland, the Church Law of 1686 made it compulsory for pastors to conduct a formal annual examination of all adolescents who were preparing for confirmation. "The parents were the teachers of their children, till they reached the age of fourteen or thereabouts, when they attended the pastor or his assistant, to be prepared for confirmation and being admitted to the Lord's Supper. And as no person can be confirmed till he can read and repeat his catechism, or until confirmed, can give his oath in court of justice, or get married, a great disgrace is attached not to being able to read; indeed, one who cannot read is nobody in the eye of the law."[37] Examination registers, in which pastors would evaluate both 'book reading' and 'knowledge of catechism,' thus provide precise, annual information on literacy levels reached by rural populations of Sweden and Finland: "The words of the Lord's Prayer, the Articles of Faith, the Ten Commandments (*Partes simpliciter*) and the Confession of Sins (*Confessio*) served as a general measure of knowledge for which reading proficiency apparently was not absolutely essential. Here, there was a long verbal tradition. But to be able to know Luther's explanation of the Catechism's five major texts (the *Small Catechism*) was something new. Those who were book-learned were, of course, a step ahead."[38] There was a continuum of literacy skills, from oral memory to an ability to read, approaching that of the literary tradition but excluding writing. By the mid-eighteenth century, only 5 to 10 percent of girls and 44 percent of boys could write. More emphasis was given to writing in Germany, where churches established schools for both girls and boys. For instance, according to the Church Examination Register of Oldenburg in 1750, almost all children could read (about 99 percent), and 44 percent of girls and 75 percent of boys could write.[39]

Protestant confirmation took place at the age of fourteen or fifteen, so that the school curriculum developed during the nineteenth century, based on the earlier tradition of religious education, extended beyond elementary education and included adolescents. In Catholic countries, religious education would end with communion, at the age of eleven or twelve. For a long time, formal teaching and compulsory schooling did not extend beyond this age,[40] which is one of the main sources of the education gap between Northern and Southern Europe.

A crucial question emerges: If belonging to a community and being recognised as a Christian required having received religious education and passing an examination, what was the fate of those who failed? Were they excluded from the community? Children who attended elite institutions passed the examinations at the expected age, but it was not so simple for other children. Church authorities were faced with a dilemma: maintaining high educational requirements would result in the rejection of children of lower social background, but lowering the requirements would defeat the very purpose of compulsory education.

The question was most acute in Catholic countries where communion took place at an early age, instruction time was short and children's maturity was very low for taking an examination on the mysteries of faith. For instance, children had to answer questions on the communion sacrament which they were about to receive and to explain what *transubstantiation* meant – this question was at the core of the theological debates of the

Reformation. In many regions, the clergy would require only oral knowledge (prayers, the Ten Commandments, confession of sins, answers to the questions of the *Petit Abrégé*) and the goodwill of the child. This was the case in Spain, Portugal and Southern Italy, where the religious meaning of collective practice seemed to be understood more easily by people and controlled by priests than the meaning of religious texts.[41] However, in France, priests who had been influenced by Jansenism (i.e., a doctrine which, to some extent, was similar to Protestantism) insisted on an actual understanding of the mysteries of the Eucharist – and sometimes realised that nothing had been understood.[42] Priests had children repeat a school year, causing discontent among parents whose children could not really participate in adult society or enter apprenticeship because they had not been admitted to communion even though they were thirteen, fourteen, or even fifteen years old.[43] This led to a rejection of religion: in France, areas under Jansenistic influence became strongly anticlerical and the Catholic Church lost much of its influence earlier in those regions than in the rest of France, from the Revolution onwards.

Literacy and the School Curriculum

American Primers between 1750 *and* 1850

Three widely distributed American primers reflect the extent to which schooled literacy was transformed between 1750 and 1850. The *New England Primer*, first published in London in 1683 and reprinted in Boston as soon as the eighteenth century, constituted "the standard textbook of reading instruction throughout the colonial period."[44] Religious tradition still pervades this book that relies on a rhymed and illustrated alphabet (e.g., "In Adam's fall / We sinned all"), lists of syllables and words sorted by length, and texts to be read or recited by rote (i.e., prayers, hymns, a summary of Holy History, and catechism).

By 1790, the Stars and Stripes had replaced the Union Jack and Noah Webster published *The American Spelling Book*, commonly referred to as the *Blue Back Speller*, a bestseller (24 million copies sold). Alphabets, lists of syllables and words sorted by length still appeared in that book (74 of 158 pages), but religious content had almost disappeared and had been replaced by texts written for children which refer to a religious moral that does not depend on a specific confession.

Published in 1836, McGuffey's primer, reprinted until 1907, is much closer to today's primers: pages that introduce the alphabet are no longer followed with lists of syllables or words. Each lesson is printed on a single page, comprising a picture (Lesson 1: an ox) and, below, two columns, in which the same short sentences are printed twice: in the left-hand column as distinct syllables, without capital letters and no punctuation, and in the right-hand column in usual types. Sentences do no deliver any message, whether Christian, moral, or educational. The aim of a lesson is not to teach anything else but how to encode and decode written language.

> Lesson 1: "is it an ox /it is an ox/it is my ox" (left-hand column)
> Lesson 64: "Can a pup run? Yes, a pup can run. All the pups can run. But a pup can not run as fast as a dog." (right-hand column)

Thus, teaching materials designed for beginners changed dramatically within fifty years. The *Blue Back Speller* retained the structure of earlier primers but substituted profane material for the earlier religious material. With McGuffey, the instructive content itself disappeared. His main innovation was to simultaneously teach to read syllables, words and phrases, using one-syllable words, which are common in English. The book progresses, combining linguistic didactic and psychological criteria: it uses only regular words and includes a small number of words which are often repeated and belong to the vocabulary of nursery-age children.

The other innovation was the constitution of a curriculum through a series of more advanced textbooks. *The American Spelling Book* is followed by *The Little Reader's Assistant*, a grammar book, and *An American Selection in Reading and Speaking*. McGuffey kept updating the book series that made his publisher extremely wealthy[45] because school attendance had become more regular and the duration of schooling had increased. Parents would no longer withdraw their children from school as soon as they could read.

How was the material that replaced religion defined? Elite grammar schools relied on the teaching of Latin, but this tradition was irrelevant for popular education. Until the nineteenth century, the traditional 3R's had combined the reading of religious texts and, for those who like Henry Facy could learn beyond that level, writing and arithmetic. The latter skills were conceived of as vocational skills linked to the activities of merchants and artisans (i.e., accounting, contracts, commercial correspondence).[46] Understanding the new purposes of elementary education that emerged at the beginning of the nineteenth century thus requires understanding the contemporary evolution of written culture.

Schooled Literacy in an Age of Novels and Newspapers

A profane culture had become pervasive in eighteenth-century publishing. This phenomenon increased during the nineteenth century, as technical progress in printing and the availability of cellulose paper reduced the price of books and newspapers. Reading that had been taught as an activity aimed at salvation or the acquisition of knowledge now belonged also to the realm of leisure, relaxation, pleasure and even passion.

The 'taste for reading' that used to be a privilege of the elite extended to urban populations. At the beginning of the French Revolution, a survey was conducted on the theme: "Do country people have a taste for reading?" "How could they have one?" answered some respondents who considered the question meaningless. Others underlined that "they only read when they are on benches, that is until their first communion." But others remarked: "Since the Revolution, they have taken up a certain taste for writings that are relative to it." "Everywhere the people are beginning to read"; there were "enough men avid for instruction to make the taste universal sooner or later."[47]

In addition to traditional reading, which was collective, solemn, slow, repetitive and restricted to religious texts, a new way of reading emerged, which extended to profane texts and was individual, fast, pleasurable, and a favoured novelty.[48] This new way of reading did not imply the disappearance of earlier ones because many more persons had been taught at elementary school and could read the Bible or their Psalter. However, reading for pleasure was in contradiction with the "intensive reading" which educators used to teach. The emergence of "extensive reading" is correlated with the growing production of gazettes and novels.[49]

The novel was then an expanding genre that made emotional reading possible. Rationalists of the Age of The Enlightenment and Church authorities were astonished to observe the progress of such "narcotic" reading, as Fichte wrote,[50] in all European countries. In England, in France, in Germany, men and women of all ages and conditions cried while reading Richardson's *Pamela, or Virtue Rewarded* (1740), Rousseau's *Julie, or the New Heloise* (1761) and Goethe's *The Sufferings of Young Werther* (1774). Kant himself complained that reading novels led to distraction, among other dysfunctions of the mind.

Newspapers constituted another new medium. Gazettes fed on events: princely weddings and political treaties, miracles and natural tragedies, victories and defeats. The French Revolution and Napoleonic Wars fascinated all Europeans and reading newspapers became, as Hegel wrote, "modern man's morning prayer."[51] This provocative reference to religion, pertaining to absent-minded reading of often insignificant pieces of news, is revealing. The value of religious books – which stated universal truths and sought to dictate behaviour – lay on their demands on the reader. Gazettes, which reported about events or opinions, and novels, which narrated specific histories, were not the least demanding.

Anybody – whether man, woman or child, servant, soldier or artisan – could thus become an apt reader without becoming a professional user of written matter. In workshops and in taverns, workers were seen reading aloud newspapers for their coworkers.[52] Novels published as feuilletons in newspapers made famous authors such as Honoré de Balzac and Eugène Sue[53] in France, Thackeray and Trollope in England. Novels were much easier to understand than prayers and led simple minds to become confused between fiction and reality; the more intense the emotions, the more intense the feeling was that the books told the truth. This understanding through emotions stood in contradiction with reading habits that used to be taught earlier. Texts no longer had to be learnt by rote nor explained by masters. They could be rephrased, summarised, retold, commented and distorted, as if they had belonged to oral tradition.

Among the numerous books published, male[54] and female[55] readers had to find those that would suit their tastes. Whereas religious literacy used to be a controlled, collective practice, dominated by the upper class, novels and newspapers now allowed an individual practice of reading, in which books were chosen in one's own social network or through recommendations published in the press. This change first occurred in social contexts in which reading as leisure already existed, but it soon exerted an influence on schools. The way educators conceived of reading – of its patterns, aims and impacts – was transformed, and this led to a concern about the responsibility of state authorities in promoting education. Indeed, it was widely felt that the new literacy practices were as threatening as they were promising.

In the same way that religious authorities had invented catechisms to establish and control religious orthodoxy, political authorities now envisaged schooled literacy as a protection against literacy practices over which they had no control. Schools were expected to defeat ignorance, promote "useful knowledge" and fight transgressive writings, which could belong to either the private sphere (i.e., immoral novels) or political life (i.e., revolutionary newspapers).[56] Flaubert's characters are typical of these pitiful 'new readers' who fell prey to their naïve enthusiasm for sentimental novels (i.e., *Madame Bovary*, 1858) or encyclopaedic knowledge (i.e., *Bouvard et Pécuchet*, 1881). For Wilkie Collins, the three million readers of the lower class who for a penny bought illustrated magazines full of scandals constituted "The Unknown Public" that deserved to be taught "the difference between a good book and a bad one."[57]

The Distinction between Primers and First Readers

Educational answers to this taste for reading concerned adult as well as child education. Religious or philanthropic associations (e.g., the Society for the Diffusion of Useful Knowledge or the Franklin Society) organised the lending of 'good books' and published specific series to compete with commercial products. The same concern with education was found in British and American networks of public libraries[58] and later in firm libraries or workers' libraries constituted by trade unions in Germany.[59]

Schools followed the way that these institutions had paved. At the beginning of the nineteenth century, primers participated in the encyclopaedic vulgarisation of knowledge:[60] travel and scientific discovery narratives, descriptions of plants and animals, advice on hygiene, biographies of great men, edifying anecdotes. Primers were thus composite books which included both literacy lessons and instructive reading, as in the *Blue Back Speller*. Among the French equivalents of American primers, the *Abécédaire et Premier Livre de Lecture*, published by Hachette in 1832, was massively bought by the Ministry (one million copies) to be distributed to poor pupils.[61] The first lessons were devoted to syllables and words, but the seventy-five following lessons dealt with various topics such as stars, the Earth, volcanoes, plants, animals, and parts of the body (one page each). There were also lessons on numbers and measurement units. As in Webster's book, maxims drawn from the Bible were printed on the last pages as well as elements of public law.

However, these textbooks, which sought to vulgarise "any useful or instructive knowledge," proved to be difficult to use in class. Pupils were still unable to read their textbook as if it had been written as an encyclopaedia for youth. It seemed absurd to teach them those texts as if they had constituted a new catechism, yet this was what happened: Each morning, class would start with pupils "learning lessons aloud. Pupils would cover their ears with both hands so as not to hear each other, and thus shout even more loudly. Teachers were used to such noise, and devoted that time to preparing impressive amounts of quill pens, an unpleasant task which most teachers nowadays would be reluctant to perform."[62] Then, "each child successively recites five or six lessons by rote: French, history, geography, arithmetic, etc. Those who had a better memory or were more studious knew the whole book, while others endlessly repeated the first pages." Every pupil thus progressed through the book at his own pace without any collective lesson or explanation. This individual mode allowed apt pupils to help the schoolmaster: as monitors, they made beginners repeat syllables printed on large charts. However, thirty years later, this method would be unanimously condemned: "Methods that relied only upon memorisation were loathsome."[63]

Indeed, a revolution occurred in schools between the 1850s and the 1880s: beginners were made to learn reading and writing simultaneously, as soon as they entered school. This pedagogical change was made possible through the spread of slates, cheap paper and metal penpoints (quill pens had been so fragile and difficult to handle that pupils would hardly use them before reaching the age of nine or ten). Why would such an innovation radically alter the learning of reading?

In catechism-based learning, by spelling prayers that had been learnt by rote (F-A, FA; T-H-E-R, THER; FA-THER), pupils would learn to separate a text into its components, naming letters and pronouncing syllables. Such elementary deciphering would be consolidated as pupils read more, until it could be applied to unknown texts belonging to the same corpus. When the universe of texts that could be read started expanding endlessly, schoolmasters – who now aimed to teach 'extensive reading' – wanted their pupils to be able to 'read everything.' Early and systematic learning of all correspondences between oral and written forms became a necessary precondition for reading words. In English and in French, the disjunction between pronunciation and spelling made this learning an endless and tedious task. "Reading is the plague of childhood," Rousseau said, denouncing formal exercises that would suppress children's taste for reading. Indeed, those exercises led children to believe that reading did not consist in discovering a message but rather in practicing meaningless combinations of letters.

The early and simultaneous teaching of reading and writing transformed schooling. During a visit to Prussia in 1843, Horace Mann[64] reported that the teacher "wrote the word *Haus* in German script and printed it also in German letters. . . . He ran over the forms of the letters, the children following the movements of the pointer with their fingers in the air. Then the children copied the word on their slates. Drill in the sounds of the letters followed: the names of the letters were not given, merely their sounds."[65] The regularity of German spelling facilitated the development of a phonic method based on writing whole words, without naming their component letters.

Similar methods were developed in France, England and the United States at the same time, but it took a generation or two for both cursive and printed characters to appear in the primers. Each reading lesson was then followed with a writing exercise: "While, in the reading lesson, the quick pronunciation of vowels and consonants does not allow the pupil to perfectly distinguish letters that compose words, in the writing lesson . . . , he has to notice them all."[66] Pupils who studied with McGuffey's primer would write 'P, U, P,' but directly read 'PUP.' The practice of writing facilitated the memorisation of syllables and one-syllable words, and some pedagogues soon believed that the same would apply to long or irregular words. This led to the first whole-word reading methods, which were developed in the United States before the 1900s and the twentieth-century controversies.

The Creation of a Primary School Curriculum and of Academic Disciplines

The simultaneous teaching of reading and writing thus facilitated the organisation of the primary-school curriculum around new types of knowledge. The mastery of the 3R's was no longer an aim of schooling but rather a means of all further learning. Between 1850 and 1900, all primers became books meant to cover an entire school year and to be read by all pupils at the same pace. They were structured in progressively difficult lessons and included regular reviews to ensure that reading and writing skills were definitively acquired and became automatic. At more advanced levels, graded readers progressively introduced longer texts that would further improve reading skills while providing access to knowledge. Hence, authorities would ask schoolmasters to explain words, check what pupils had understood, require clear articulation and, above all, provide an example of "sound reading." All pupils, whether apt or weak readers, would thus understand the contents of the lesson by listening to the schoolmaster or to other pupils reading aloud what each of them would read at the same time.

Sound reading was defined as being able to show 'that one understands what one is reading.' Fluent, expressive reading had been given as an example to children of literate families as soon as the beginning of the nineteenth century. In 1829, Leavitt wrote in *Easy Lessons in Reading*: "Try to understand every word as you go along," and "try to read as if you were telling a story to your mother, or talking with some of your playmates. Reading is talking from a book."[67] However, the schooled pronunciation of working-class children was a far cry from such natural elocution. To help children go through the three steps of reading each syllable, then reading fluently and finally reading expressively, pedagogues would practice a triple-paced pedagogy. Apt readers would be taken as an example for their classmates and would then read books from the school library; average readers would further practice reading aloud; weak readers would learn to follow the text being read and join collective reading. Visiting American schools in Cincinnati during the 1890s, Dr. J. M. Rice thus observed that "the lesson was conducted as follows: One child was called upon to read a paragraph, then another pupil was told to read the same paragraph over again, and lastly, this paragraph was read by the class in concert. The same course was pursued in all the paragraphs read. Taken all in all, this reading sounded like a piece of music consisting of a solo, an echo and a chorus. How interesting the story must have been to the children!"[68]

Silent, individual reading long remained an exception. However, during the 1930s in the United States and the 1950s in Europe, it became an urgent social need, and the usual practice of reading aloud finally appeared as a condemnable archaism.[69]

During the 1900s, the material to be read in class was structured into distinct disciplines (e.g., morals, geography, history, science, hygiene) – a structure that would persist until the 1960s. This structure differed across countries, but everywhere a national history and geography introduced each pupil to the genesis of the country, with its dynasties or its Founding Fathers, its wars and heroes, its territory and its (well- or ill-defined) frontiers. Ideological or cultural orientations of history books may have varied with political regimes, but the definition and functions of the discipline remained untouched.

At different dates according to the countries, the name of the national language started referring to an academic discipline (e.g., German in the nineteenth century, English and French at the beginning of the twentieth century). Although society seemed to be threatened by conflicting interests and ideologies,[70] all citizens of a nation were to have a common literature and history, regardless of their religious beliefs, social class or political opinions. National literature was envisaged as a new corpus of sacred texts, with poetry anthologies to be learnt and recited like prayers. In France, after 1882, religion was no longer part of 'knowledge' taught to schoolchildren, but it remained so in Germany. In all countries, morals, the 'science of duties,' was part and parcel of knowledge. The set of academic disciplines that constituted the curriculum soon appeared to define legitimate knowledge and suffered little contestation from pupils or parents – the arbitrariness of that definition was not perceived. National knowledge also became the benchmark against which all 'foreign' schools were evaluated. Earlier literacy practices became 'illiteracy' and the school of yore now appeared as a school of ignorance in which 'almost nothing' had been taught – that is, almost nothing of what would now be considered worth teaching.

Conclusion

Between the invention of printing and World War I, the same idea kept emerging in radically different social contexts: education is an imperative social need. During the Reformation, it appeared imperative to teach truths that would lead to salvation. In this era of intense religious conflicts, everyone had to confess his or her faith, to participate in divine service and to learn prayers with the help of the immutable text of a book. In the Age of The Enlightenment, as profane texts supplanted sacred ones, it became imperative to teach the people to be emancipated through printed knowledge. Everyone must be able to read to learn beyond their own experience, to compare their opinions with 'public opinion,' to enjoy fiction. In the course of the nineteenth century, political and economic changes resulted in the fragmentation of society, and it became imperative to impart to children a sense of belonging to the same nation. National languages, histories, geographies and literatures were now central to identity-building.

The teaching of literacy always aimed to ensure common destinies – whether religious, political or social – through access to the written culture of the times. This entailed conflict because the supply of education preceded demand for it and was imposed on society. Reading and writing were always used in economic life or for practical purposes, but the legitimacy of public instruction never derived from such uses. The innovation that occurred at the end of the twentieth century thus was not to define literacy as a set of basic skills that would be necessary at work or on the market of cultural consumption. It was to consider that the sense and value of compulsory education derive chiefly from the economic and practical uses of literacy.

Notes

1 Johansson, Egil, Women and the tradition of reading around 1700: Examples from Sweden and Germany. In *Women and literacy yesterday, today and tomorrow*, Symposium for Study of Education in Developing Countries, Stockholm, June 1989, Stockholm: Svenska Unescorådets Skriftserie, Nr 1/1992, pp. 77–94.

2 Cressy, David, *Literacy and the social order: Reading and writing in Tudor & Stuart England*, Cambridge: Cambridge University Press, 1980, p. 29.

3 Valentin Jamerey-Duval, *Mémoires: Enfance et éducation d'un paysan au XVIIIe siècle*, introduction and notes by J-M. Goulemot, Paris: Le Sycomore, 1981. Also see Jean Hébrard, Comment Valentin Jamerey-Duval apprit-il à lire? L'autodidaxie exemplaire, in Roger Chartier (Ed.), *Pratiques de la lecture*, Marseille: Rivages, 1985, pp. 23–60.

4 Angela Veronese, *Notizie della sua vita scritte de lei medesima*, Firenze, Le Monnier, 1973 [1826]. Also see Marina Roggero, L'alphabétisation en Italie: Une conquête

féminine?, *Annales ≪ Pratiques d'écriture ≫*, 4–5, July–October 2001, pp. 903–925.

5 Education for all. Global Monitoring Report, *Literacy for Life*, UNESCO, 2006.

6 Cressy, ibid. p. 29.

7 In Prussia in 1736, Saxony in 1764, Bavaria in 1802, Sweden in 1842, Norway in 1848, Austria in 1869, the German States around 1870, Scotland in 1872, Switzerland in 1874, Italy in 1877, Portugal in 1878, England in 1880, France in 1882. In the *Dictionnaire Pédagogique* edited by Ferdinand Buisson in 1887, literacy rates are given for each country, based on contemporary official sources.

8 To evaluate 'the number of illiterates prior to the French Revolution and during the first years of our century,' the Ministry of Public Instruction had 16,000 primary schoolteachers working under education officer Maggiolo count the number of signatures on marriage registers. Results of this survey were reprinted during the 1970s by Furet and Ozouf, *Lire et écrire: L'alphabétisation des Français, de Calvin à Jules Ferry*, Paris: Ed. de Minuit, 1977.

9 Ballet-Baz, Illettrés, in Ferdinand Buisson, *Dictionnaire pédagogique*, 1887.

10 Institutions that aim to create schools where they do not yet exist still share the same belief. The Education for All Global Monitoring Report published by UNESCO, for instance, wrote in 2006: "Literacy for all is at the heart of basic education for all and creating literate environments and societies is essential for achieving the goals of eradicating poverty, reducing child mortality, curbing population growth, achieving gender equality and ensuring sustainable development, peace and democracy."

11 McLuhan, *The Gutenberg galaxy: The making of typographic man*, University of Toronto Press, 1962.

12 Lévi-Strauss, *Tristes tropiques*, Paris: Plon, 1955; R. Hoggart, *The uses of literacy*, Harmondsworth, 1958; Jack Goody (Ed.), *Literacy in traditional societies*, Cambridge, 1968, pp. 311–325; Clifford Geertz, *The interpretation of cultures*, New York: Basic Books, 1973; Jack Goody, *The domestication of the savage mind*, Cambridge: Cambridge University Press, 1977.

13 In those three countries, statistical studies (Coleman Report, USA, 1966; Lady Plowden Report, UK, 1967; INED surveys, France, published in 1970) led to a criticism of investment levels in 'human capital' as being too low and to a consideration of low achievement levels as a failure of the school system and not only as the result of pupils' lack of individual ability.

14 Rudolf Flech, *Why Johnny can't read, and what you can do about it*, New York, Harper and Brothers, 1955. This book initiated an endless debate about the relative efficiency of alternative 'reading methods' (phonic versus visual) that extended from the US to the UK, and later to France as well. See Jane Chall, *The great debate*, McGraw Hill, Inc., 1967, for an exposition of the American debate.

15 Febvre, L., and Martin, H.-J., *L'Apparition du livre*, Paris: A. Michel, 1958; English translation: *The coming of the book*, London: Verso, 1976.

16 Eisenstein, Elizabeth, *The printing revolution in early modern Europe*, Cambridge, UK, and New York: Cambridge University Press, 1983.

17 Burke, Peter, *Popular culture in early modern Europe*, p. 251. Research on the 'ability to sign' conducted about England (Schofield), New England (Lockridge), France (Furet), Sweden (Johansson), Portugal (Magalhães) and other European regions led to endless debates among researchers.

18 Cipolla, C. M., *Literacy and development in the West*, Harmondsworth, 1969.

19 Gilmore, William, *Reading becomes a necessity of life*, Knoxville, 1988.

20 Carruthers, Mary, *The book of memory: A study of memory in medieval culture*, Cambridge University Press: Cambridge, UK, 1990, p. 10.

21 Ibid., pp. 11–12.

22 Leszek Kolakowski, *Chrétiens sans Église*, Paris: Gallimard, 1969.

23 Martin Luther, *M.L.O.*, IX, ed. Labor et Fides, Genève, p. 111. Jean-François Gilmont, Réformes protestantes et lecture, in Gugliemo Cavallo and Roger Chartier (Eds.), *Histoire de la lecture dans le monde occidental*, Paris: Seuil, 1997, pp. 249–278.

24 Daniel Lindmark, *Reading, Writing and Schooling*, Umea, 2004, pp. 218 and 221–222.

25 Monnagan, Jennifer E., *Learning to read and write in colonial America*, University of Massachusetts Press: Amherst and Boston, 2005, Part 1: The Ordinary Road.

26 Green, Ian, *The Christian ABC: Catechisms and catechising in England, c. 1530–1740*, Oxford: Oxford University Press, 1996; *Print and Protestantism in early modern*

England, Oxford: Oxford University Press, 2000.

27 Thomas Cranmer (1489–1556), the Archbishop of Canterbury during the reigns of Henry VIII and Edward VI, is credited with writing and compiling the first two *Books of Common Prayer*, which were the basis of Anglican liturgy for centuries and influenced the English language (along with King James' Version of the Bible, or *Authorized Version*, published in 1611). Cranmer, burnt in 1556 for heresy, was one of the first Anglican martyrs.

28 Johansson, Egil, Women and the tradition of reading around 1700: Examples from Sweden and Germany, in *Women and Literacy Yesterday, Today and Tomorrow*, op. cit.

29 Jean-Baptiste de La Salle (1651–1719) founded the *Institute of the Brothers of the Christian Schools*, a religious order that provided free Catholic education to children living in cities. Reading, writing and arithmetic were taught in French.

30 Villedieu's *Doctrinale*, written around 1200 in verse, was the most commonly used of medieval grammars because it was easier to learn by rote than Donatus' (written around 350) and its examples were drawn from classical Latin and Christian authors. It remained in use throughout the Renaissance (i.e., more than 260 printings between 1570 and 1620). Bernard Colombat, Les manuels de grammaire latine des origines à la Révolution: Constantes et mutations, *Histoire de l'Éducation, Les Humanités Classiques*, May 1997, 74, pp. 89–114.

31 Ian Green quotes the official prose psalter and Sternold and Hopkins' metrical psalms which were in use from the 1550s in England. *Print and Protestantism in early modern England*, Oxford: Oxford University Press, 2000, p. 246.

32 *The New-England Primer*, improved for the more easy attaining of the true reading of English, to which is added the Assembly of Divines and Mr. Cotton's Catechism, Boston, 1777.

33 Valdés, Alejandro, *Cartilla o silabario para uso de las escuelas*, México, 1811 [BCEHM, Condumex]. Quoted in Castañeda, Carmen, Libros para la enseñaza de la lectura en la Nueva España, siglo XVIII y XIX: Cartillas, silabarios, catones y catecismos, in Castañeda, C., Galván, L. E., Martínez-Moctezuma, L. (Eds.), *Lecturas y lectores en la historia de México*, México: CIESAS, 2004, pp. 35–66.

34 Viınao, Antonio, Notas para una tipologïa de las cartillas para aprender a leer (c. 1496–1825), *El Libro y la educacíon*, International Standing Conference for the History of Education, ISCHE XXII, Universidad de Alcalá, Alcalá de Henares, 2000.

35 For instance, Dioniso Caton, *Libri Minoris et primum Catonis disticha Moralia, com Antonij Nebriissensis annotattionibus. Apud Inclytam Apuli*, s.i., 1545.

36 *El Sabio Catón, Avisos y ejemplos del Sabio Catón Censorino Romano*, reprint in Puebla de los Angeles, México, 1815, quoted by C. Castenada, op. cit., p. 47.

37 Johansson, Egil, The history of literacy in Sweden. In Harvey J. Graff (Ed.), *Literacy and social development in the West: A reader*, Cambridge University Press, 1981, pp. 151–182.

38 Johansson, Egil, Women and the tradition of reading around 1700: Examples from Sweden and Germany, in *Women and literacy yesterday, today and tomorrow*, op. cit., p. 84.

39 Ibid.

40 Caspard, Pierre, Les trois âges de la première communion en Suisse, in *Lorsque l'enfant grandit*, Paris: Presses de l'Université de Paris-Sorbonne, 2002, pp. 173–181.

41 In 1559, the Spanish Inquisition forbade approximately seven hundred books translated from Latin into Castilian, most of which were used for individual devotion or home prayer. Such devotion was considered dangerous for ignorant souls (*idiotes*) and appropriate only for Latinists (*lettrados*). Indeed, in Spain, Portugal and Southern Italy, the Church favoured collective religious practice over the individual reading of religious texts because the former seemed to be better understood by the populace and could be controlled by the clergy. Reading and writing in vernacular languages thus remained vocational skills that had chiefly economic and social uses and were not universally needed. In Portugal, it was deemed sufficient for one person in each family to be able to read, sign and write.

Justino Magalhães, *Ler e ascrever no mundo rural do antigo regime. Um contributo para a historia da alfabetização em Portugal*, Universidade do Minho, Braga 1994. Rita Marquilhas, *A Faculdade das Letras: Leitura e Escrita em Portugal no Século XVII*. Lisboa, Imprensa Nacional-Casa da Moeda, 2000.

42 Bouchard, Gérard, *Le village immobile, Sennely-en-Sologne au XVIIIe siècle*, Paris: Plon, 1971.

43 Delumeau, J. (Ed.), *La première communion, Quatre siècles d'histoire*, Paris: Desclée de Brouwer, 1987.

44 Benton Smith, Nila, *American reading instruction*, International Reading Association, 1965 [1934], p. 19.

45 Between 1836 and 1920, 132 million copies of the McGuffey readers (one book for each level) were bought. Mathews, Mitford, *Teaching to read, historically considered*, Chicago and London: University of Chicago Press, 1966, p. 102.

46 Hébrard, Jean, La scolarisation des savoirs élémentaires,. *Histoire de l'Éducation*, 38, May 1988, 7–58.

47 Chartier, Roger, Figures of the other. Peasant reading in the Age of the Enlightenment, in *Cultural History*, Ithaca, NY: Cornell University Press, 1988, pp. 151–170.

48 Hall, David D., *Cultures of print: Essays in the history of the book*, Amherst: University of Massachusetts Press, 1996.

49 Engelsing, *Der Bürger als Leser*, Stuttgart, 1974. Engelsing considers that the distinction between 'intensive' and 'extensive' reading was the basis of a reading revolution in the eighteenth century.

50 Quoted by Reinhard Wittmann, "Une révolution de la lecture à la fin du XVIIIe siècle?" in Gugliemo Cavallo and Roger Chartier (Eds.), op cit, pp. 331–364.

51 Quoted by Reinhard Wittmann, ibidem.

52 Lyons, Martin, Les nouveaux lecteurs au XIXe siècle, in Cavallo and Chartier (Eds.), *L'histoire de la lecture dans le monde occidental*, Seuil, 1996, p. 427 (Reprint: Seuil Poche, 2001).

53 Lyon-Caen, Judith, *La lecture et la Vie, Les usages du roman au temps de Balzac*, Paris: Tallandier, 2006.

54 Lyons, Martin, *Le Triomphe du Livre: Une histoire sociologique de la lecture dans la France du XIXe siècle*, Paris, 1987; Vincent, David, *Literacy, popular culture, England 1750–1914*, Cambridge: Cambridge University Press, 1989.

55 Flint, Kate, *The woman reader, 1837–1914*, Oxford: Oxford University Press, 1993.

56 Chartier, Anne-Marie, and Hébrard, Jean, *Discours sur la lecture, 1880–2000*, Paris: Fayard, 2000.

57 Quoted by Lyons, Martin, Les nouveaux lecteurs, op. cit., p. 395.

58 Hassenforder, Jean, *Développement comparé des bibliothèques publiques en France, en Grande-Bretagne et aux Etats-Unis (1830–1914)*, Paris, 1967.

59 Schön, Erich, *Der Verlust der Sinnlichkeit oder die Verwandlungen des Lesers. Mentalitätswandel um 1800*, Stuttgart, Klette-Cotta, 1987.

60 Bensaude-Vincent, Bernadette, and Ramussen, Anne (Eds.), *La Science populaire dans la presse et l'édition, XIXe –XXe siècles*, Paris: CNRS éditions, 1997.

61 Chartier, Anne-Marie, L'école et la lecture obligatoire, *Paris: Retz, 2007, chapitre* 5, "Des abécédaires aux méthodes de lecture: la genèse du manuel moderne" pp. 99–130.

62 Vauclin, Noël, *Les mémoires d'un instituteur français*, Paris: Alcide Picard, 1895, p. 25.

63 Ibid., p. 25.

64 As First Secretary of the Massachusetts State Board of Education, Horace Mann inspected and favorably appraised the Prussian school system.

65 Mathews, Mitford, *Teaching to read, historically considered*, Chicago and London: University of Chicago Press, 1966, p. 49.

66 A. Adrien, government-school teacher, *Enseignement gradué et simultané de la lecture et de l'écriture: Méthode nouvelle où les leçons de lecture et celles d'écriture sont mises en corrélation*, Paris: Hachette, 1853.

67 Quoted by Benton Smith, Nila, *American reading instruction*, International Reading Association, 1965 [1934], p. 40.

68 Rice, J. M., *The public-school system of the United States* (New York, 1893). Quoted in Mathews, Mitford, op. cit., p. 110–111.

69 Chartier, Anne-Marie, L'école et la lecture obligatoire, Paris : Retz, 2007, chapitre 6 "La crise de la lecture à voix haute", pp. 131–158.

70 In *Culture and anarchy* (1869), Matthew Arnold (1822–1888) expressed his worry about social fragmentation to which social segregation in the English school system contributed. 'British' literature could unite nations (Scotland, Wales, Ireland), social classes and religious groups (non-Anglican Protestants or Catholics). The first literature chairs were created in Oxford in 1893 and in Cambridge in 1904. The risk of social fragmentation was a central concern to Durkheim (1858–1917) as well as to Dewey (1859–1952).

CHAPTER 25

The Configuration of Literacy as a Domain of Knowledge

Liliana Tolchinsky

As children grow up, they interact with a variety of people and other living creatures as well as a diverse range of physical objects. They also grow up surrounded by a particular type of visual marks intentionally created to transmit different messages. These marks appear on a particular types of artifacts that include pamphlets, road signs, labels, calendars, and books. They belong to different notational systems used, for example, in mathematics, logic, chemistry, and writing and perform a diversity of functions from the mundane to the sacred. In a sense, becoming literate means learning how to interpret and create these marks. This chapter focuses on one specific kind of visual marks, those of writing. I describe how children make sense of these marks in the process of becoming literate. I examine this process from a developmental perspective, exploring how literacy is constituted as a domain of knowledge. In contrast to other perspectives that consider literacy as an issue within teaching – pondering over *what* children are or *should* be taught at school – a developmental approach to literacy assumes that the steps by which children become literate cannot be equated with the way in which they happen to be formally instructed.

Throughout the history of writing, there has been "a constant concern for the structured transmission of the system from generation to generation and the method of instruction was passed along with the practical knowledge of the script" (Cooper, 1996, p. 37). Even among the earliest ancestors of our writing system, it is possible to find "writing manuals." These constituted lists of words (lexical lists) used for teaching how to write. It is no exaggeration to say that school was born hand in hand with writing (Halliday, 1987). However, noting that literacy is an institutionally supported cultural practice *and* believing that what children know about written language is what they are institutionally taught are two different things. Children access the meaning of written language by interacting with the artifacts that carry written messages and, in particular, by participating with other people in using these artifacts. The process of interpretation is crucial for triggering changes in the conceptualization of writing; here,

I refer not only to the interpretation performed by those readers that children may witness (e.g., an adult reading a storybook to a child) but also children's own attempts at interpreting any material and at reading back what they have written.

In what follows, I first explain what is meant by a domain of knowledge in this context and in what sense literacy constitutes such a domain. Second, I show that the configuration of literacy as a domain of knowledge begins in a domain-specific manner and then proceeds from being a universal to an orthographically specific phenomenon and from being concerned with formal aspects to being concerned with functional aspects. However, it should not be seen as an additive process. Finally, I discuss the psychological and educational implications of adopting a developmental approach to literacy.

Literacy as a Domain of Knowledge

From the point of view of the developing child, a domain is a set of representations sustaining a specific area of knowledge (Karmiloff-Smith, 1992, p. 6). Thus, to the extent that knowledge about notations is a special kind of knowledge – although not one that should be confused with a child's knowledge about their different domains of reference – the beliefs and conceptualizations that subjects construct about notations constitute a domain of knowledge. Here, I am distinguishing what subjects may know about music, number, physics, language, and so on from what they know about the notational systems created for externally representing these different domains. The representations that subjects construct about writing can be thought of as a subdomain of notational knowledge.

Subjects that behave in a domain-specific manner attribute certain *properties* to one domain but not to the other (e.g., self-propelled movement is attributed to living things but not to notational objects), and they are aware that certain *activities* can be performed in one domain but not in the other (e.g., it is appropriate to feed a duck but not a book).

During the initial stages of the configuration of a domain, subjects hold implicit knowledge about the domain. This implicit knowledge is evidenced in the way they react, sort, and denominate entities. However, they are unable to justify verbally their reactions or sorting behavior. Later, this knowledge becomes more explicit and subjects are able to justify verbally the differences, properties, and activities in each domain. Some subjects may be able to develop formal models or even theories about them, such as a formal model of writing (Sproat, 2000).

Studies conducted in developmental literacy (Ferreiro, 1988; Scheuer, de la Cruz, Pozo, & Neira, 2006) aim at tapping this implicit knowledge about literacy. One of the strongest views in both psycholinguistic research and public discussions of literacy is the conceptualization of learning literacy as a set of skills (Barton, 1994, p. 162). Cognitive psychology has shown that there are a number of specific processes (e.g., visual analysis of letters, categorical perception of letters, parallel processing of each letter in a word, and grapheme to phoneme conversion) that interact in attaining the goal of reading to discover the meaning of written words (Morais, 1991). This skills view of learning maintains that the components of the reading process can be divided into parts that can be taught and tested and that this is the way children become literate (Barton, 1994).What, then, is the difference between considering literacy as the configuration of a domain of knowledge and considering literacy as the learning of a set of reading and writing skills?

My point is that there is much more to becoming literate than learning a set of skills. Both the possibility of acquiring such skills and the consequences of having actually acquired those skills take on a much wider range of meanings and implications. Indeed, one aspect of literacy involves competence with a particular writing system, but there are other aspects to literacy – in particular, the discursive competences that are appropriate for participating in the literate community of which the learner forms a part. Many of the features that characterize later language development are related to literacy – not just in the narrow sense of learning to read and write but also in the sense of participating in the communicative activities of a literate community (Ravid & Tolchinsky, 2002). The way children deploy, recruit, organize, select, and modify specific linguistic structures in different communicative circumstances develop well into late childhood. Vocabulary becomes more specialized and the semantic specificity of the lexicon changes dramatically with age (Tolchinsky, 2004b); children learn to distinguish linguistic registers to make appropriate distinctions between, for example, colloquial and more formal usage, while the capacity to reflect on language increases, heightening children's sensibility to figurative expression. This discursive competence is not only a result of the type of communicative interaction promoted by literacy but also a result of the very nature of writing as a particular mode of production. Writing frees language-processing from the time pressures that are characteristic of oral language; in so doing, it facilitates control over language production (Reilly, Wulfeck, & Tolchinsky, 2006) and enables the consideration of sounds and words in isolation (Tolchinsky & Teberosky, 1998). As discussed in the next section, the discursive dimension of literacy and the properties of the written mode mediate the acquisition of the basic skills throughout the process of the acquisition of reading and writing.

The Configuration of a Domain of Knowledge

Obviously, children do not move from a state of complete ignorance about literacy to a state of full command. Rather, there are a number of steps during which their conceptualization of and their beliefs concerning the writing system to which they are exposed and its related discourse competence evolve. Having focused on this developmental process elsewhere (Tolchinsky, 2003, 2004b, 2005), in this chapter I instead highlight the distinctive features of the configuration of literacy as a domain of knowledge. Almost from birth, children – in certain environments – *process* patterns of notational information and participate in a web of social literate interactions. It is through these interactions that children build literacy as a domain of knowledge. However, I am not suggesting a processing of different sensory-input through specialized modules without this processing being affected by any central processor. Neither am I suggesting a priori domain-specific specializations for different kinds of information patterns corresponding to real word categories such as social agents, living things, and faces. My proposal differs from the modular conceptualization of domains suggested by Fodor (1982). I believe literacy is a domain of expertise that does not result from evolutionary processes but rather from an organism's learning experiences (Keil, 2006) – in this case, learning experiences involving a special type of cultural artifacts and from seeing them put to use.

A Domain-Specific Onset

According to Indian chronicles, South American indigenous peoples called the Spanish conquerors "Those barbed men that move sheets while talking." Seeing the conquerors reading long scrolls of parchment, they were able only to grasp the behavioral signs but not the kind of activity they were performing. Such a description would never be obtained from a literate community. Behavioral signs are interpreted at a very early age by a child growing in a literate community as representing a special kind of activity. The youngest participants in our studies were thirty months old, but there are no reports elsewhere of any lack of understanding in even younger participants (Brennemann, Massey, Machado, & Gelman, 1996; Karmiloff-Smith, 1992). Even illiterate individuals living in literate communities are able to infer the kind of activity being performed from behavioral signs

(Ferreiro, 1983). Anybody gazing at a sheet of paper and talking is assumed to be reading, even when what is being said cannot be heard or when what is written on the paper cannot be seen.

However, children raised in isolated communities with no experience of book-reading practices develop a representation of writing before developing a meaning for reading. For three-year-olds born and raised in these communities, writing means the production of marks on paper, but reading has no clearly defined meaning and is confused with writing (Ferreiro, 1986). Thus, children who had just jotted down some marks on a sheet of paper and were asked to read them back responded that they had already done so. Other children claimed that pencils are needed for reading. Such manifestations are not terminological issues; rather, they indicate that the concept of writing is understood earlier than reading because it leaves traces. Writing changes the object visibly whereas reading does not. Access to notational objects and to people using them seems to be a condition for children developing an idea of the kind of activity that certain objects afford.

Children not only recognize reading and writing as special activities, but they also react differently to writing instruments. At eighteen months or even earlier, a child given a tool and a surface will produce graphic marks. The child does so not for the mere sake of the activity or as a simple exercise but rather for the traces themselves (Gibson & Levin, 1975). In so doing, children recognize the main feature of writing – leaving permanent traces.

Children also react differently to the prosody of reading. Between the ages of eight and eighteen months, children engaged in the reading of picture books progress from attempting to eat the page to being able to participate fully in verbal dialogue while looking at the books (Bus, van IJzendorm, & Pellegrini, 1995; Snow & Ninio, 1986). As for the notational dimension, the acquisition of writing does not emerge from the acquisition of drawing. Levin and Bus (2003) analyzed the drawing and writing of children aged twenty-eight to fifty-three months using tasks in which the children, in addition to writing their name, were asked to draw and write the same eight referents. From their results, the authors concluded that children up to the age of three draw and write indistinguishable, nonrepresentational graphic products. However, the authors only analyzed the products of drawing and writing; when observing the process of production, a different picture emerges.

Even when their products are indistinguishable, three- to four-year-olds' motor plans can be clearly identified as being for either drawing or writing. By examining procedural competence through the analysis of children's videotaped action sequences, Brennemann et al. (1996) showed that children's action plans differ for writing and drawing. When drawing, children make wide continuous circular movements, whereas when writing, they lift their pencils off the page and interrupt their movements much more frequently. Although the graphic product does not look like writing to an external observer, as long as children are acting, they will act differently when writing and drawing.

Children not only differentiate between drawing and writing but also between writing and numbers. A study carried out with Spanish children whose ages ranged from three years and eight months to six and a half years showed that they are sensitive to the constraints inherent to each system (Tolchinsky Landsmann & Karmiloff-Smith, 1993). We used two sets of cards: one set for the *writing-domain* task and the other for the *numbers-domain* task. For each set of cards, we asked children *which cards were not good for writing* or *not good for counting*. The cards varied according to the following features: iconicity, linearity, identical elements, length of the string, conventionality of elements, and pronounceability of the string. The same features were used in designing the cards for both the numbers and the writing domains. Thus, some cards bore figurative drawings, others abstract schematic drawings, and others conventional letters or numerals. Some cards bore strings of the same letter (or the same numeral) repeated many times, others included different letters (or different numerals) without any of them being repeated, and others bore certain letters (or numbers) that were repeated whereas others were different. Some cards contained a single letter (or a single numeral), whereas others contained between two and eight units. Finally, some cards showed pronounceable words, whereas others consisted solely of consonants and were thus unpronounceable.

The sorting task showed that more than 95 percent of the children at all ages clearly separated the cards belonging to writing or numbers from those belonging to drawing. The subjects overwhelmingly concluded that cards containing drawings were good for neither writing nor expressing numbers. Mixtures of elements from different domains ($*M*#&©) were also rejected by 85 percent of the children because they were considered bad examples of the two domains. However, the most revealing finding was that the children drew a clear distinction between writing and number notation. Of the subjects at all ages, 80 percent identified strings containing repeated identical letters as not being good for writing, although they did not do so for number notation when presented with strings of identical numerals. Thus, the children clearly imposed a constraint on writing that stipulates that strings must include a variety of different elements, while realizing that for number notation such a constraint does not hold. Moreover, they chose a card containing linked numerals imitating cursive writing as a bad example of number notation, but they accepted cursive writing for written notation. In the context of this task, four-year-olds were quite clear regarding the formal distinctions between writing and numbers.

How then is the knowledge that serves to distinguish between systems internally represented? If it is implicit knowledge, embedded in the sorting procedure, then it should be automatic, difficult to access and to change. If, on the other hand, children have some internal access to this knowledge, they should be able to manipulate it and adapt it to different situations.

To determine whether children do have internal access to their knowledge, we applied the "transgression technique" – initially devised for a drawing study (Karmiloff-Smith, 1990) – to the domain of writing and numbers. The children who participated in our study (Tolchinsky Landsmann, & Karmiloff-Smith, 1992) were successful in the sorting task, but we wished to determine whether the differentiating constraints could be accessed or whether they were implicitly represented. Children between the ages of three and a half and six and a half years were first asked to write on a piece of paper their own name, other names, words, letters, and any numbers they knew. Irrespective of whether the children were able to write in a conventional way, they succeeded in writing letters, numbers, and what they considered to be words. To test whether the knowledge they demonstrated was implicitly embedded in writing and number procedures or whether it could be accessed and manipulated, the investigator pointed to one of the child's productions – for example, a letter – and said: *Here you have put a letter, now put a letter that doesn't exist.* The same process was repeated with the children's productions of words and letters.

Some four-year-olds produced exemplars of nonexistent numbers, letters, and words that were barely distinguishable from those they produced for ones that actually exist. From this behavior, we were able to deduce that they could not yet purposefully manipulate the procedures they used for sorting and for writing "normally." These children displayed no capacity to produce nonexistent exemplars; nonetheless, they clearly distinguished between notational domains in their productions. For written notation they used, for example, a form that looked like writing, although it was not conventional writing, whereas for the number domain, they used ill- or well-formed numerals; but their knowledge proved inaccessible to internal scrutiny. However, a

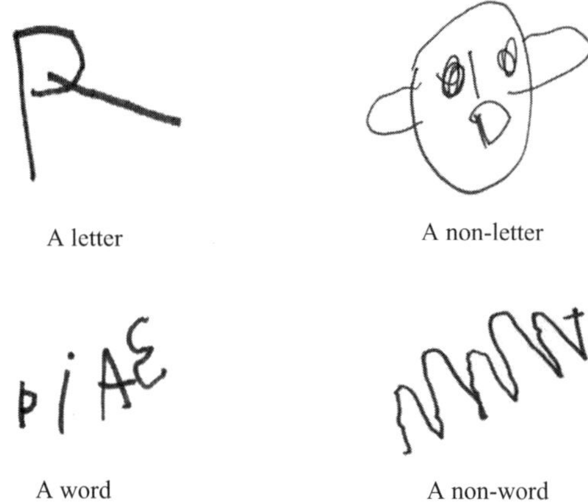

Figure 25.1. Examples of transgression.

small number of four-year-olds and the majority of the five- and six-year-olds were capable of transgressing certain constraints on writing and number notation.

An example from a five-year-old who, like many others, produced a drawing for a non-letter (as well as a non-number and a non-word) is shown at the top of Figure 25.1. The children that did this transgressed the relative closure of each domain. In the bottom part of the same figure is an example from another five-year-old who produced a string of different letters for a real word, following her self-imposed constraint of intra-string variety together with a string of linked repeated identical letters for a non-word, violating the same constraint. Finally, there were children who focused on the function of notations as referential-communicative tools. Thus, for non-words, they announced that they would write "words that cannot be said." On occasions, by this, they meant words that were unpronounceable but, on others, they meant words that cannot be said "in public" and so wrote *pipi* and *caca*.

In short, our aim in undertaking this study was to determine how knowledge about numerals and writing is internally represented. Working with three age groups, we assumed that there might be different levels at which this knowledge is represented. We reasoned that if the knowledge was completely implicit, embedded in sorting procedures that are triggered by particular material, or embedded in writing procedures, children would be unable to create an example of an element that was *not* a letter or *not* a number, or a string that was *not* a word, and so forth. This assumption was based on the belief that in order to do this, children must know about elements and strings at a level that allows some analysis of their features and meaning. That is, only at a certain level of internal explicitness of knowledge could children violate the constraints they had shown themselves able to impose on each system. We found that few children as young as four but the majority of five- and six-year-olds had explicit representations of the constraints that they imposed on different notational systems. They were able to purposefully violate these constraints to produce nonexistent exemplars.

This initial differentiation between systems is, indeed, a favorable beginning because it guides children in the mass of notational input and in the attribution of meaning to the notational elements – sounds to letters and numerosity to numerals. Nevertheless, more mature applications of the systems require the use of letters and numerals for multiple functions. The use of the same notational forms with multiple meanings is a rule in mass media, advertisement, and computers. It seems, then, that rather than learning to differentiate between the systems, what children learn as they become literate in our communities is to blur these distinctions.

From Formal Constraints of Writing to its Referential-Communicative Functions

The configuration of literacy as a domain of knowledge begins by being domain-specific. Children single out reading and writing as specific activities, the instruments of writing as having the specific purpose of leaving traces, and the marks of writing as obeying different constraints to those of drawings and numbers. But, what about the representational meaning of these marks? Are children aware of *the kind* of linguistic information that the written symbols represent? Are they aware of how the particular writing system to which they are exposed represents this linguistic information?

> *Making marks which can serve mnemonic and communicative purposes is as old as human culture itself. What such marks may be taken as representing by those who make and those who read those marks is the critical question.* (Olson, 1994, p. 65)

Even when children are aware that someone is saying something while standing in front of a written text, an induction problem is still present – namely, what aspect of the saying is represented? How are the links established between the saying and the written text?

In the following discussion, I show that in developmental terms, formal aspects take over from referential-communicative functions; that is, children impose formal constraints before grasping the referential-communicative meaning of writing. But, the formal constraints that they impose facilitate their attribution of meaning. *Formal* here refers to features of form: linear arrangement, similarity or distinctiveness of elements, the number of elements, the shape and spacing between elements. *Referential-communicative* is the meaning attributed to these forms. One possibility is that sensitivity to formal differences develops as a result of understanding the different functions of notational elements. An alternative possibility is that an awareness of formal differences *precedes* children's understanding of the meaning and function of notations.

The way to examine children's developing grasp of the representational meaning of written symbols is to ask three- to five-year-olds to write words, sentences, and stories and to see which links they establish between the marks they make and the utterances they are attempting to represent. Conversely, we are also interested in seeing the links they establish when asked to read words, sentences, and texts in different contexts. Sometimes the words they are asked to read appear as captions under certain images; on other occasions, the adult says isolated words or sentences and the children must say where these words are written; or the interviewer might say a spoken sentence for a written one that is in front of the child and ask the child to look for parts of the spoken sentence in the written one. Most of these tasks exceed a child's expected level of expertise. They are used with the assumption that in solving these tasks, children will put into practice the implicit knowledge they have constructed about the representational meaning of writing. Details of these procedures are provided elsewhere (Tolchinsky, 2003); here, I restrict my discussion to the most important findings regarding our initial questions.

In the studies that have been carried out in a diverse range of languages and orthographies, the youngest children are found to produce similar "scrawls" regardless of the word or sentence they have been asked to write (Ferreiro, 1988; Harste, Woodward, & Burke, 1984; Luria, 1929/1978; Tolchinsky, 2003). Neither the child nor the adult can distinguish what has been written, be it a short word or a sentence. From an examination of what the child produces, it is impossible to recognize which "scrawl" represents the word, which the noun phrase (NP), and which the sentence. There are no letters, no correspondence to the acoustic length of the utterances, no marks to distinguish between the meanings of the sentences. The marks may appear organized around a horizontal axis, relatively separated from each other with more or less regular spacing between them and usually written in the same direction, whether from right to left or left to right. Some children – instead of wavy lines with more or less regular spacing between them – may produce conventional letters or sometimes one single letter. Figure 25.2 shows the written output of three Spanish-speaking children: one using the typical long, linearly arranged, discontinuous graphic patterns; a second producing a single sign; and a third using conventional letters in any order to write a word: *pelota* (ball), an NP: *una flor roja* (a red flower), and a sentence: *La niña está bailando* (The girl is dancing).

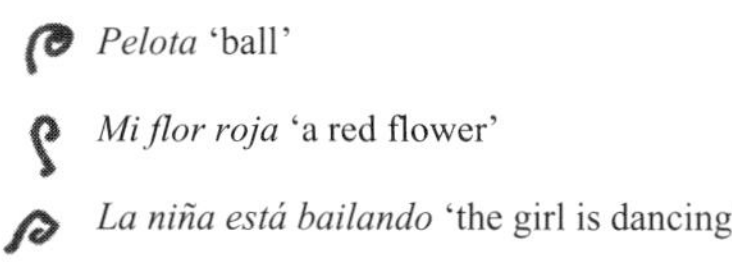

Pelota 'ball'
Mi flor roja 'a red flower'
La niña está bailando 'the girl is dancing'

Pelota 'ball'
Mi flor roja 'a red flower'
La niña está bailando 'the girl is dancing'

Figure 25.2. Examples of different kinds of undifferentiated writing.

The point is not what kind of graphic marks they are making – because this depends on the social information at their disposal – but rather to note that they are unable to adapt either the amount or the type of graphic marks to the different utterances that they are asked to write.

Therefore, when separated from the "writer" and the writing task, the traces "do not mean." One crucial characteristic of written outputs is that they can be interpreted outside the context of production, even when separated from the person who has produced them. In the first stages of literacy, this characteristic has yet to be attained because the product has not yet been detached from the process of production and from the producer. The dependency of written outputs on the context and the producer is also evident in children's reading behavior. Similar as the written outputs may look, when children are asked to read back what they have written, they usually repeat the different utterances they have been asked to write. For the first writing pattern, they said *pelota* (ball), for the second *flor roja*'(red flower),[1] and so on. Thus, they were saying different things when referring to similar written outputs. We discuss this apparently trivial reading behavior later in this chapter, but here it serves to illustrate that at this stage, the meaning of writing is circumstantial; it depends on the child's intention and it changes with the adult's instructions or with the context in which the writing is presented.

Further illustration comes from a study conducted with three- to four-year-olds in which the children were shown pictures bearing a caption (e.g., a picture of a boat with the caption BOAT). Either as a result of their own guesswork or following a suggestion from an adult, they agreed that BOAT was written under the drawing of a boat. However, when the written caption was "accidentally" moved to another picture, the reading of the word also changed (Bialystok, 1992; Ferreiro, 1984, 1988). So, the same written word could come to mean "pipe" under the drawing of a pipe. Apparently, they did not see the written word BOAT as being a representation of "boat" independent of the changes in contexts, referents, or conditions of productions.

After a period of undifferentiated writing, the graphic patterns children produce are substituted for short strings, usually containing between three and five of either the same or different letters. Children gradually become more selective as to what forms or combinations of forms are accepted as "writable" or "readable." Their written output becomes formally constrained in terms of the number and variety of marks they think they should include. The constraints of number and variety are applied when writing almost every utterance children are asked to write, and they are applied as sorting criteria when children are asked to separate what is "good for reading" from what is "not good for reading."

In conjunction with this – and in contrast with what happened during the phase of *undifferentiated* writing – at a given point, children began to introduce graphic differences when writing different utterances. Many years ago, Luria (1929/1978) noted, for example, that some "scrawls" took on a longer or more rounded appearance. This occurred when the sentences referred to objects that differed in size and shape. For example, when writing that "The monkey has a long tail," children were found to use longer lines than when writing "It's cold in winter." It seemed that children were trying to represent the content of the sentence rather than their sounds. Similar findings were reported by Ferreiro (1985) more than fifty years after Luria. She also found that children suggested, for example, that "bear" should be written with more letters than "duck" because a bear is bigger than a duck. Similarly, Chan & Nunes (1998) found that even five-year-olds, when producing accurate Chinese symbols, would retain a figurative correspondence between what they wrote and the object of reference. Likewise, Hebrew-speaking four- to six-year-olds were found to use figurative elements when attempting to write pairs of words that had contrasting references – for example, "elephant" (in Hebrew *pil*) and "ant" (in Hebrew *nemala)* (Levin & Korat, 1993).

Luria and Vygotsky both argued that from the moment children resort to referential devices, the natural development of writing becomes one of cultural development because children grasp the fundamental relationship that something *stands for something else* (Luria, 1929/1978; Scinto, 1986, p. 73). That is, a symbolic relation has been established, although not one that is connected with the sound patterns of words. In my view, this is the point at which children start to look at writing as a communicative tool; for that reason, they start to look for ways of introducing elements into their writing to show (to themselves or to others) what they have heard, what words they are attempting to represent. They look for ways of correlating variation in spoken utterances, albeit in their content, with variations in written displays because the features of the written output have now acquired an additional importance in communicating particular meanings. In other words, children begin to understand that in order to mean, they must put some cue in writing that the meaning does not just depend on the reader's intention or the context. Writing is beginning to become a potential source of information in itself; that is, by looking at it, one can discover what was said.

Even when children produce similar "scrawls" for different utterances, there is no doubt that they perceive the differences between the utterances they are asked to write; it is not a perceptual problem. The point is that these young children do not find (or do not search for) any way of recording the perceived differences. The search for graphic means to record the differences implies that children realize that what they do when making their marks (during the encoding process) will help afterwards when decoding the marks. Only when children attempt to demonstrate via the graphic medium the differences they perceive do we have a manifestation of children linking writing and reading. Before this, when they write, they merely write, and when they read (or participate in reading activities) they do no more than read. The two activities are juxtaposed but they are not integrated.

The production of differences using referentialization might not be a necessary step in development because it emerged mostly when children were presented with pairs of words or series of sentences that contrasted in selected features. What does seem necessary, however, is the introduction of certain graphic changes in the written output that co-vary with differences in the words the child is attempting to write. Children's concerns are not only formal but also referential-communicative.

The next turning point occurs when children are able to attune the graphic modifications in their written outputs and interpret the graphic differences they perceive in print to differences in the linguistic features of words. Before this, when children are engaged in exploring the formal features of writing, their behavior shows that they are aware that writing is somehow related to language. They are also aware that utterances can be segmented. We have seen how three- to four-year-olds, when required to read what they have written, will repeat verbatim the words they were asked to write. They can do it in one breath, without pausing between syllables or any part of the word, or cutting the words so as to start and end the reading together with the written string. These behaviors are not systematic; they are produced as a sort of justification of what the children have read, but they are crucially scaffolding the conceptualization of the links between what is written and what is said.

When children repeat verbatim what they were asked to write for what they have just written, the occasion is created for a mapping of a verbal utterance onto a written display. At this point, it is important to consider the characteristics of the graphic pattern to which children attempt to match the verbal utterance. If the reduction in number and variety of letters has already been established, then the features of the written string will help to go beyond the global mapping of an utterance and a written pattern; they will pave the way to the possibility of providing a pronunciation for each of the graphic elements they are attempting to interpret. Then, parts of the utterance can be mapped onto parts of the written display and, vice versa, parts of the written display can be mapped onto parts of the utterance. The emergence of the phonetic principle (Olson, 1994), by which written signs and the sound aspect of words are linked, has been triggered and marks a turning point in the development of literacy. It constitutes the discovery of a stable frame of reference. Let me elaborate on this.

In the previous discussion, I commented on children adding referential elements to their writing to hint at the meaning of the words they are representing. However, the idea that writing represents referential differences can be applied only in certain circumstances; that is, when there is some type of contrast between the words children are attempting to write. Children were found to use this strategy when they had to write words that contrasted in size (e.g., ant and elephant), color (e.g., tomato and cucumber), or in any other feature. It is in this sense that the idea of referential correspondence functions as an *ad hoc* model, a model suitable for solving particular situations. The emergence of this model shows a child's capacity to accommodate particular situations and to take advantage of the features of writing, but it is limited and it is not based on the working principle of the writing system that children are acquiring. When children turn to the phonetic principle to guide their writing, they turn to a general model – a model suitable for every writing task – because every word and sentence has a phonic aspect. The "phonetization" of writing implies a shift from co-variation of graphic changes with some spoken words to the discovery of the general principle on which our writing system is based. Children have discovered that the number and variety of graphic elements (i.e., letters) is related to the phonological aspect of words. Written symbols have stopped being distinctive, formally constrained graphic patterns to become referential-communicative tools.

I have tried to show the extent to which formal constraints precede a child's attribution of meaning and also the role of formal constraint in paving the way to the possibility of attributing an articulate meaning to the written symbols. The data from the transgression study (Tolchinsky Landsmann & Karmiloff-Smith, 1992) provide additional evidence of this. We found that there was a developmental order in the type of transgressions children were able to produce. At four years of age, they were barely capable of any transgression; however, with age, they moved to formal transgressions in each domain and finally to referential-communicative transgressions. That is, the children first differentiated between systems by the formal constraints internal to each of them and then by their referential-communicative constraints. These findings confirm – by adopting a different approach – that formal differentiation is a point of departure and that it constrains children's further experience with notations. Only once these features have become relatively explicit for the subject can they manipulate them to create nonexisting exemplars and, more than likely, adapt these features to their representational needs.

The constraints children applied to their writing are neither a direct application of social learning nor can they be said to have emerged from the functional use of writing. Children apply these constraints before they know how to or, indeed, are willing to produce a written message. If literate adults were asked why they think that there are so few one-letter words, they would probably answer that it is because there are very few spoken words of one sound. We know that many of the formal constraints (although by no means all of them) result from the use of the system. However, for children in the process of becoming literate, it is the formal features that they initially see. The first things they observe in writing are the differing lengths of strings, spaces between words, and the graphic variations in size and shape. These features are informative sources that guide children in their sorting of written materials.

From Universal to Orthography-Specific Development

The two characteristics of the configuration of literacy as a domain of knowledge – that it begins as being domain-specific and then proceeds from formal to referential-communicative functions – are common across languages and writing systems. It might also be argued that similar stages exist despite orthographic differences. A child's grasp of the nature of writing and the formal features that distinguish written artifacts from other kinds of artifact precedes their grasp of the properties of the specific orthography to which they are exposed. Another cross-orthography phenomenon concerns the initial production of undifferentiated writing and the further imposition of formal constraints.

Some of the earliest written output, appearing in Luria's (1929/1978) research with Russian children during the 1920s, does not differ substantially from that produced by German-speaking children and described by Hildreth (1936) in the 1940s, or from that reported by Tolchinsky Landsmann and Levin (1985) in the 1980s when working with Hebrew-speaking children, or from that described by Chan (1998) with Chinese children. In a sense, it might be considered an imitation of the graphics in the environment, which – like any imitation – is never a copy (Zelazo, 2000). What children imitate from their environment functions as a sort of raw material with which they work out the constraints on interpretability. These constraints were found to reappear

Figure 25.3. Examples of the same word in two writing systems.

in Hebrew and Spanish, two languages that use different writing systems (Tolchinsky & Teberosky, 1998). The resorting to figurative elements when exploring the referential-communicative function of writing was also found in different languages and writing systems, discussed previously herein.

Another phenomenon that was also found to be general across the two writing systems was the phonetization of writing. It was at this juncture, however, that the two developmental paths – which, up to this point, had been very similar – became differentiated. Thus, Hebrew-speaking children use consonants for writing the same words for which Spanish-speaking children use vowels, despite the fact that both groups of children had been exposed to the same word and the fact that they had analyzed the same word into syllables. This divergence is illustrated in Figure 25.3.

The same word *Coca Cola*™ – a word that appears with great frequency in both Tel Aviv and Barcelona, the two cities where the children who participated in the study live – was analyzed by the two children into syllables. However, for each syllable, the Hebrew-speaking boy used consonants whereas the Spanish-speaking girl used vowels. At this point, the phonological structure of each language and the way the orthography relates to it emerge as the main factors; therefore, literacy becomes language-specific development. Although Spanish-speaking children prefer vowels, Hebrew-speaking children prefer consonants, which also English-speaking children tend to prefer. It is clear why that because in Spanish there are only five vowels to remember that they are obligatory constituents of syllables. In addition, Spanish spelling is completely transparent as far as vowels are concerned: there is a one-to-one mapping between vowels and letters, and the names of the vowels coincide with their sounds. In English, in contrast, there are at least fourteen vowels and their reading is instable and context-dependent; there is no term-to-term correspondence and the names of the vowels do not coincide with their sounds. It would seem indisputable that it is the combined effect of these factors that determines the massive presence of vowels in Spanish and its scarcity in English speakers at similar levels of knowledge about writing. Several authors, as well as many parents and teachers, have noted that English-speaking preschoolers and first-graders "miss" vowels out (writing, e.g., VKT for vacation). Kamii, Long, Manning, and Manning (1993) suggested that in English there must be a sort of consonantal stage rather than a syllabic using of vowels.

Children approach reading and writing through their universal features – as an activity that produces language, as a formal pattern displaying certain formal features – with time and with literate experience, they are increasingly sensitive to the specific properties of the writing systems to which they are exposed, particularly the way writing represents language.

The Configuration of Literacy Is Not an Additive Process

A common assumption about the development of literacy is that it begins with the recognition of elements – letters, then progressing to the identification of words, then to the interpretation of sentences, and finally reaching the level of extended discourse. In the previous sections, however, we have seen that before looking for letter-to-sound correspondences, children establish a set of distinctive, formal principles that set writing apart from other notational systems and separate what is readable and writeable from what is not. These principles attain the key notion of notation and embrace the whole domain of writing. Knowledge of these principles denotes a basic understanding of the structural properties of written language independently of specific instantiations.

A notation is a limited set of elements, each having a distinctive form, a name, and a given position in the set: "They are structured systems of which the members may be defined by their internal relationships to one another, *independently* of any function each may acquire when integrated into (used for) some specific set of communicational practices" (Harris, 1995, p. 169). Consequently, a young child may be able to recite the alphabet yet not know how to read, and be familiar with the names of the digits without knowing how to use them for calculation. The fact that notation has a limited number of clearly distinct elements facilitates learning and further establishes the generalization of the notation.

When children establish the conditions of legibility and when they use the same limited number of elements for producing different messages, they are working out the main feature of a notation. These constraints will guide their exploration and production of every type of written material. Children are working on general aspects of notations even before they work out the particular meaning of individual letters. This is not to say that they are ignoring individual elements or that knowledge of individual elements is unimportant; it simply means that it is not a prerequisite. Attention to notational constraints was found in children with very different knowledge of letters (Ferreiro, 1988) and it is also apparent when children from poor literate environments recount their own experiences of learning to write (Scheuer et al., 2006).

A further point refuting an additive conceptualization of literacy learning relates to the fact that discursive constraints – the features of extended discourse – are present from the very beginning of literacy. A brief clarification is required here to understand this point. Discourse does not exist in a void but rather within the specific constraints of genre and modality. There is no such thing as *neutral* use of language: people constantly attune their speech to specific intentions, purposes, and interlocutors. We speak narrative, description, poetry or whatever discourse genre the circumstances demand (Tolchinsky, 2004b). The point is that prior to gaining a full command of the phonographic conventions of the written system – that is, the conventions that link elements to sound units – the graphic layout of children's texts imitates the features of different genres and the linguistic expression they use denotes an awareness of genre and modality differences.

For example, Hebrew-speaking five-year-olds were asked to write a fairy tale, *Ami ve'tami* (Hansel and Gretel), and to describe what the chocolate house in the tale looks like. Their knowledge of the phonographic conventions of written Hebrew was very poor; most of them could draw Hebrew letters but they did not always know their phonic value. Nevertheless, their written output for narratives and descriptions differed markedly. The narrative was written in long lines of one letter after the other with hardly any internal spacing between them, except for the name of the protagonists, which sometimes appeared with blanks on both sides. The description, however, looked much like a list of isolated words (Sandbank, 2001). A similar graphic differentiation was found when comparing the way preschoolers wrote shopping lists with the way they wrote news stories, advertisements and poetry (Pontecorvo & Zucchermaglio, 1988; Tolchinsky Landsmann, 1993). Studies of young children's use of genre (Hudson & Shapiro, 1991; Pontecorvo & Morani, 1996; Sandbank, 2001) found that they employ different forms distinctly to reflect different communicative purposes. The problem of casting information into a given genre is solved at a very early age (Berman & Nir, 2004).

Moreover, throughout the conceptualization of writing, children are concerned with the semantic level of the utterances they are requested to write, particularly with the written representation of absence, negation, impossibility, and falsity (Olson, 1996; Tolchinsky Landsmann, 1989). By way of illustration, Italian-speaking children were asked to write down null quantity (e.g., *one pear, two pears, three pears* and then *zero pears*); impossible situations (e.g., *children and cats fly*); falsity (e.g., *the birds are not flying*, when presented with a picture in which some birds are flying) and negative phrases (e.g., *there are no pears*, when shown a drawing of a tree bearing many apples) (Pontecorvo & Rossi, 2001). Sentences with these characteristics create a sort of conflict between their semantic meaning and the features of writing. If *nothing* equates to zero and if there are no objects in a void set, there are no good reasons for using any letters – tangible marks – to express an absence; if identity and ownership are "proven" by written documents, how can we possibly write down falsity (Ferreiro, 1981)? In effect, 38 percent of the children whose writing was not yet regulated by phonographic correspondences refused to write any of these particular sentences. However, with the phonetization of writing, they increasingly agreed to write sentences of negation and absence, but the written representation of impossibility and falsity was still a problem for some children, even those who already wrote alphabetically.

Findings like these clearly show that children are sensitive to both to the semantic meaning of what they are attempting to represent and the properties of written representation. There is no question of four- to six-year-olds being unable to understand or produce these kinds of expression in the spoken modality (Bombi & Marotti, 1998). However, writing is not understood by the child as merely putting words on paper but rather as a representational issue; hence, the struggle between meaning and the formal properties of writing. Further, and in support of the nonadditive nature of literacy learning, is the awareness that children show of the full embracing properties rather than of particular elements.

The research discussed up to this juncture suggests that writing actually develops simultaneously at many levels. Children do not move unidirectionally from smaller to larger units. Rather, what children come to know about texts and about the representational meaning of writing permeates the whole process of learning and, as discussed in the next section, constrains their grasp of letter-sound correspondences which in turn guides and constrains their way of writing texts.

The Process of Interpretation Gears the Development of Literacy

The developmental changes that occur in the process of becoming literate are strongly dependent on the learning activities that children engage in with the notational artifacts. What children do with books, calendars, road signs, and newspapers and, specifically, what they do when faced with a written text, not only provides them with information but also gears their development.

I commented previously that the tasks set for children in psycholinguistic studies typically exceed their expected level of expertise. In none of the countries in which the studies described herein were carried out were three- to five-year-olds expected to know how to read decontextualized sentences or to write stories. Indeed, many children refused to try to read or write, convinced that they did not know how to do so. In this setting, the studies depend on the interviewer's ability (and insistence) to convince the children to try despite their lack of knowledge. In a school, it is up to the teacher to create a situation that triggers children's attempts to write and to interpret. Teachers and interviewers need to change children's attitude to their own knowledge so that they dare to explore the graphic features of texts, the shape of the letters and the relationships between what is said and what is written. In each case, it is notable how the children's understanding of written texts guides their interpretation but also how their own interpretative behavior brings about a shift in their understanding of written texts. I illustrate this general feature by focusing on one particular moment in literacy development: the transition to phonetically sensitive writing. Recall that at this particular point in development, children's writing is usually formally constrained. A common strategy they display for interpreting what they have written is to make use of the words the investigator asked them to write or – in contextualized or real-life situations – if a text appears under a picture, they may use what they see in the picture to interpret the text.

No matter which source of information children use for interpreting what is written, the fact that they produce a verbal utterance when faced by a limited number of graphic elements enables a link to be established between parts of the verbal utterance and the graphic elements. A child's first attempt at mapping letters onto parts-of-utterance appears when he reads back what he has just finished writing. Initially, such attempts are nonsystematic. The child follows the written marks while segmenting the words into parts (e.g., saying *choco#late*), syllables, or a mixture of both. The need to accommodate the reading to the written elements leads to different ways of breaking up words. Sometimes a child elongates the sound of a part, sometimes she cuts it short. It is at this point when the social information plays a crucial role and when general across-writing systems development turns into language- and orthography-specific development. If children can identify one or more letters by their sound-value, they will use them – albeit in a nonsystematic way – when they recognize the presence of that sound in a word. If the name of the letter coincides with the analysis children are performing, they will use that particular letter (Ehri, 1984). It is at this juncture in their development that we found Hebrew-speaking children resorting to consonantal writing and Spanish-speaking children resorting to vowel writing (Tolchinsky & Teberosky, 1998). At any rate, it is the interpretation process that brings about the increasing articulation of the links between what is written and what is pronounced.

A similar process of interaction between graphic features and their interpretation is found at the level of extended discourse. The formal constraints on legibility that we previously discussed at length typically appear when children are asked to write single words. By contrast, when children attempt to write texts – stories, lists or poems – other constraints enter the picture: the constraints of genre. As previously discussed, prior to mastering the phonographic conventions of the writing system to which they are exposed, children are able to distinguish between different text types. Thus, shopping lists look different than news stories, advertisements or poetry (Pontecorvo & Rossi, 2001) and narratives look different than descriptions (Sandbank, 2001). One plausible explanation for this finding is that it is a case of iconicity resulting from the effect of previous experience with text layouts of different kinds (Pontecorvo & Rossi, 2001). This would be an explanation in terms of visual information. An alternative explanation, however, is that children's knowledge of the kind of linguistic elements that are included in each kind of text guides their graphic layout. For genres in which isolated words (mainly nouns) are used, they put together strings of letters, usually each on a different line. For fuller utterances, they are reluctant to create internal blanks among strings of letters and therefore produce longer unsegmented strings of letters. Indeed, while writing their narratives, five-year-olds produce full utterances for parts of the tale. For the description, however, they named the different elements in the house (e.g., *chocolates, candies, cookies*). Children's off-line interpretation of the text, however, produced interesting changes. When reading back the lists they had produced, they might sometimes add a conjunction (e.g., *chocolates, candies* and *cookies*) that led them to link strings of letters (Sandbank, 2001). Likewise, when pronouncing the names of the characters on reading back the narrative, the children sometimes produced a separation between strings of letters. Here, they would seem to be working on word separation in order to accommodate the graphics to the interpretation. At the level of the written elements and phonological segmentation and at the level of extended discourse, we found a similar role of interpretation in both shaping and enhancing written representation.

Psycholinguistic and Educational Implications

The configuration of literacy as a domain of knowledge is interesting in itself because it shows how active children are in their learning of a cultural artifact such as written language. They are not merely absorbing piecemeal information from the printed material present in their environment or from adults' explicit instruction. Rather, there is a constant interaction between children's own ideas, the specific properties of the written modality, the notational features of writing, and the discursive characteristics of written language. One of the main aims of the developmental approach to literacy is to describe this process – to show how children build their knowledge about the practices of reading and writing, the notion of texts and discourse, the regularities of writing systems and written strings, and the rules of particular writing systems. In other words, the approach has demonstrated that it is a domain that can be approached developmentally in a sense similar to physical or mathematical knowledge. As useful and as interesting as this might be, there are a number of additional benefits to this approach. In effect, children's behavior in the face of a written text that they have produced, or that has been produced by another person, is a source of information not only for the child but also for the researcher. Whereas for a child, it is a motor for development, for the researcher, it is a window on a child's understanding of the meaning of written texts, as well as on the linguistic notions that mediate the learning processes at a time when the learner does not have the ability to verbalize his or her conceptualizations or even to be aware of them. Consider, for example, the drawing of distinctions between syntactic word categories. It is obvious that five- or six-year-olds are not able to explain verbally the difference between verbs and nouns; yet, through their way of writing (i.e., their way of laying out texts graphically), a researcher is able to infer that the child sees them as being different. The same is true of phonological segmentation. When observing preschoolers' attempts at writing words they do not know, it is possible to witness segmentation of words into sound components that they are unable to manipulate explicitly. Segmenting into subsyllabic segments *for-writing-it* is possible even for children who failed typical metalinguistic tasks (Tolchinsky & Teberosky, 1998). In general, the writing activity is a privileged context for assessing levels of knowledge, which are in between implicit automatic procedures and verbally stayed explanations. These intermediate levels roughly correspond to what Culioli (1990) termed "epilinguistic" activity or what Karmiloff-Smith (1992) described as a level of knowledge that is implicit for the subject but that can be accessed to fulfill certain tasks. The transgression task produced further evidence of these different levels of knowledge at which the constraints of writing systems are grasped.

A further benefit to be derived from considering literacy as a developing domain of knowledge is evident in the increase in the number of activities devoted to literacy in preschool education. Currently, a large number of schools all over the world take a child's out-of-school knowledge as the starting point for instructional processes. At a very early age, a child's knowledge about writing is taken into account and expanded upon. Spontaneous writing and multiple types of texts are integrated in daily school activities. Whatever the project that is being undertaken, kindergartens, preschools and first grades include reading and writing activities without any limitation on the letters or the text to be used. The criterion for inclusion is the interest of the theme or project and the need to write, not the particular difficulty of a sound combination.

No less important is the awareness that early literacy is related to literate growth beyond the early years of schooling. Seventeen years ago, Adams (1991) expressed this point most succinctly in her review of the factors involved in successful literacy learning: "across the literature I reviewed, children's first-grade reading achievement depends most of all on how much they know about reading before they get to school" (p. xx). Ten years later, the same reasoning still holds as "the differences in children's skills and knowledge usually seen in later grades appears to be present as children begin school and persist after 1 and 2 years of school" (Denton, West, & Walston, 2003, p. xx). The resources children possess when they start kindergarten, such as their early literacy skills and the richness of their home literacy environment, are related to their reading proficiency in the later grades across kindergarten and first grade (Denton, West, & Walston, 2003).

The process of becoming literate builds on a precocious sensibility to the features of the written modality and to the presence and characteristics of different modes of discourse. *Interpretation* of written strings is crucial for children to establish links between written elements and sound segments, and it will eventually lead to their establishing the alphabetic principle. In every one of these processes, the availability of written input and participation in literate experiences are crucial: if there is no *what* to look at, to explore and to interpret, if there is no *with whom* to participate, there is no chance for increasing sensibility and interpretation.

Note

1 Children usually delete undefined determinants when reading back or when attempting to interpret written words. That is the reason why, when asking children to write a word, we can delete the determinant.

References

Adams, M. J. (1991). *Beginning to read: Thinking and learning about print*. Cambridge, MA: MIT Press.

Barton, D. (1994). *Literacy: An introduction to the ecology of written language*. Oxford: Basil Blackwell.

Berman, R. A., & Nir, B. (2004). Linguistic indicators of inter-genre differentiation in later language development. *Journal of Child Language*, 31, 339–380.

Bialystok, E. (1992). Symbolic representation of letters and numbers. *Cognitive Development*, 7, 301–316.

Bombi, A. S., & Marotti, A. (1998). Bugie, errori e scherzi [Lies, Mistakes, and Jokes]. *Psicologia Generale*, 1, 122–134.

Brennemann, K., Massey, C., Machado, S., & Gelman, R. (1996). Notating knowledge about words and objects: Pre-schoolers' plans differ for "Writing" and "Drawing." *Cognitive Development*, 11, 397–419.

Bus, A. G., van IJzendorm , M. H., & Pellegrini, A. D. (1995). Joint book reading makes for success in learning to read. A meta-analysis on intergenerational analysis of literacy. *Review of Educational Research*, 65, 1–21.

Chan, L., & Nunes, T. (1998). Children's understanding of the formal and functional characteristics of written Chinese. *Applied Psycholinguistics*, 19, 115–131.

Cooper, J. (1996). Summerian and Akkadian. In P. T. Daniels & W. Bright (Eds.), *The world's writing systems* (pp. 37–40). New York: Oxford University Press.

Culioli, A. (1990). *Pour une linguistique de l'énonciation. Tome 1*. Paris: Ophrys.

Denton, K., West, J., & Walston, J. (2003). *Reading – Young children's achievement and classroom experiences: Findings from the condition of education, 2003* (Report No. NCES-2003-070). Washington, DC: National Center for Education Statistics, U.S. Department of Education.

Ehri, L. C. (1984). How orthography alters spoken language competencies in children learning to read and spell. In J. Downing & R. Valtin (Eds.), *Language awareness and leaning to read* (pp. 119–147). New York: Springer-Verlag.

Ferreiro, E. (1981). La posibilidad de la escritura de la negación y la falsedad. *Cuadernos de Investigación Educativa*, 4, Departamento de Investigaciones Educativas, Mexico D.F.

Ferreiro, E. (1983). Los adultos no alfabetizados y sus conceptualizaciones del sistema de escritura [Illiterate adults and their conceptualization of the system of writing]. *Cuadernos de Investigaciòn Educativa*, 10, Departamento de Investigaciones Educativas, Mexico D.F.

Ferreiro, E. (1984). The underlying logic of literacy development. In H. Goelman, A. Oberg, & F. Smith (Eds.), *Awakening to literacy* (pp. 154–173). Porthmouth, NH: Heinemann Educational Books.

Ferreiro, E. (1985). Literacy development: A psychogenetic perspective. In D. R. Olson, N. Torrance, & A. Hildyard (Eds.), *Literacy, language and learning* (pp. 217–228). Cambridge: Cambridge University Press.

Ferreiro, E. (1986). The interplay between information and assimilation in beginning literacy. In W. Teale & E. Sulzby (Eds.), *Emergent literacy: Writing and reading* (pp. 15–49). Norwood, NJ: Ablex.

Ferreiro, E. (1988). L'écriture avant la lettre. In H. Sinclair (Ed.), *La production de notations chez le jeune enfant: Langage, nombre, rythmes et melodies* [The production of notations in young children: Language, number, rhythms, and melodies] (pp. 17–70). Paris: Press Universitaire de France.

Fodor, J. (1982). *The modularity of mind*. Cambridge, MA: MIT Press.

Gibson, E., & Levin, H. (1975). *The psychology of reading*. Cambridge, MA: MIT Press.

Halliday, M. K. S. (1987). Language and the natural order. In N. Fabb, D. Attridge, A. Durant, & C. MacCabe (Eds.), *The linguistics of writing* (pp. 147–164). Manchester: Manchester University.

Harris, R. (1995). *Signs of writing*. London: Routledge & Kegan Paul.

Harste, J. C., Woodward, V. A., & Burke, C. L. (1984). *Language stories and literacy lessons*. Portsmouth, NH: Heinemann Educational Books.

Hildreth, G. (1936). Developmental sequences in name writing. *Child Development*, 7, 291–303.

Hudson, J. A., & Shapiro, L. R. (1991). From knowing to telling: Children's scripts, stories, and personal narratives. In A. McCabe & C. Peterson (Eds.), *Developing narrative structure* (pp. 89–136). Hillsdale, NJ: Lawrence Erlbaum.

Kamii, C., Long, R., Manning, G., & Manning, M. (1993). Les conceptualisations du système alphabétique chez les jeunes enfants anglophones [The conceptualization of the alphabetic system in small English-speaking children]. *Etudes de Lingüistique Appliquée*, 91, 34–47.

Karmiloff-Smith, A. (1990). Constraints on representational change: Evidence from children's drawing. *Cognition*, 34, 57–83.

Karmiloff-Smith, A. (1992). *Beyond modularity: A developmental perspective on cognitive science*. Cambridge, MA: MIT Press/Bradford Books.

Keil, F. C. (2006). Cognitive science and cognitive development. In W. Damon & R. Lerner (Series Eds.), D. Kuhn & R. S. Siegler (Vol. Eds.), *Handbook of child psychology: Vol. 2: Cognition, perception, and language* (6th ed.) (pp. 609–635). New York: Wiley.

Levin, I., & Bus, A. (2003). How is emergent writing based on drawing? Analyses of children's products and their sorting by children and mothers. *Developmental Psychology*, 39, 891–905.

Levin, I., & Korat, O. (1993). Sensitivity to phonological, morphological and semantic cues in early reading and writing in Hebrew. *Merrill-Palmer Quarterly*, 392, 233–251.

Luria, A. R. (1929/1978). The development of writing in the child. In M. Cole (Ed.), *The selected writings of A. R. Luria*. New York: M.E. Sharpe, Inc. (Original work published 1929.)

Morais, J. (1991). *L'art de lire* [The art of reading]. Paris: Odile Jacob.

Olson, D. R. (1994). *The world on paper: The conceptual and cognitive implications of writing and reading*. Cambridge: Cambridge University Press.

Olson, D. R. (1996). Literate mentalities: Literacy consciousness of language, and modes of thought. In D. R. Olson (Ed.), *Modes of thought* (pp. 141–151). Cambridge, UK: Cambridge University Press.

Pontecorvo, C., & Morani, R. M. (1996). Looking for stylistic features in children's composing stories: Products and processes. In C. Pontecorvo, M. Orsolini, & L. Resnick (Eds.), *Early text construction in children* (pp. 229–258). Hillsdale, NJ: Lawrence Erlbaum.

Pontecorvo, C., & Rossi, F. (2001). Absence, negation, impossibility and falsity in children's first writings. In L. Tolchinsky (Ed.), *Developmental aspects in learning to write* (pp. 13–33). Amsterdam: Kluwer.

Pontecorvo, C., & Zucchermaglio, C. (1988). Modes of differentiation in children's writing construction. *European Journal of Psychology of Education*, 3 (4), 371–384.

Ravid, D., & Tolchinsky, L. (2002). Developing linguistic literacy: A comprehensive model. *Journal of Child Language*, 29 419–448.

Reilly, J., Wulfeck, B., & Tolchinsky, L. (2006). Neuroplasticity and development: Spoken and written narratives in children with early focal lesions and children with specific language impairment. Paper presented at the *VI SIG Writing Conference*, Antwerp, September 2006.

Sandbank, A. (2001). On the interplay of genre and writing conventions in early text writing. In L. Tolchinsky (Ed.), *Developmental aspects in learning to write* (pp. 55–77). Dordrecht: Kluwer Academic Publishers.

Scheuer, N., de la Cruz, M., Pozo, J. I., & Neira, S. (2006). Children's autobiographies as learners of writing. *British Journal of Educational Psychology*, 76 (4), 709–725.

Scinto, L. (1986). *Written language and psychological development*. London: Academic Press.

Snow, C. E., & Ninio, A. (1986). The contracts of literacy: What children learn from learning to read books. In W. Teale & E. Sulzby (Eds.), *Emergent literacy: Writing and reading* (pp. 116–138). Norwood, NJ: Ablex.

Sproat, R. (2000). *A computational theory of writing systems: ACL studies in natural language processing*. Cambridge: Cambridge University Press.

Tolchinsky, L. (2003). *The cradle of culture and what children know about writing and numbers before being taught*. Mahwah, NJ: Lawrence Erlbaum.

Tolchinsky, L. (2004a). Childhood conceptions on literacy. In T. Nunes & P. Bryant (Eds.), *The handbook of children's literacy* (pp. 11–30). Dordrecht: Kluwer Academic Publishers.

Tolchinsky, L. (2004b). The nature and scope of later language development. In R. Berman (Ed.), *Language development across childhood and adolescence. TiLAR Vol.* 3 (pp. 238–248). Amsterdam: John Benjamins.

Tolchinsky, L. (2005). The emergence of writing. In C. A. MacArthur, S. Graham, & J. Fitzgerald (Eds.), *Handbook of writing research* (pp. 83–96). New York: Guilford Press.

Tolchinsky, L., & Teberosky, A. (1998). The development of word segmentation and writing in two scripts. *Cognitive Development*, 13, 1–21.

Tolchinsky Landsmann, L. (1989). Form and meaning in the development of written representation. *European Journal of Educational Psychology*, 3, 385–398.

Tolchinsky Landsmann, L. (1993). *El aprendizaje del lenguaje escrito*. Barcelona: Anthropos.

Tolchinsky Landsmann, L., & Karmiloff-Smith, A. (1992). Children's understanding of notations as domains of knowledge versus referential-communicative tools. *Cognitive Development*, 7, 287–300.

Tolchinsky Landsmann, L., & Karmiloff-Smith, A. (1993). Las restricciones del conocimiento notacional. *Infancia y Aprendizaje*, 62–63, 19–51.

Tolchinsky Landsmann, L., & Levin, I. (1985). Writing in preschoolers: An age-related analysis. *Applied Psycholinguistics*, 6, 319–339.

Zelazo, P. (2000). Minds in the (re)making: Imitation and the dialectic of representation. In J. W. Astington (Ed.), *Minds in the making* (pp. 143–164). Oxford: Blackwell Publishers.

CHAPTER 26

Literacy and Metalinguistic Development

Bruce D. Homer

Of the many cognitive skills that have been linked to literacy, none has been as closely associated with learning to read and write as metalinguistic development. The process of becoming a competent member of a linguistic community begins early in life. By the age of two, most children produce simple two-word sentences and understand more complex utterances. However, this early linguistic competence demonstrates an understanding of language that is largely implicit. More explicit awareness of language typically does not develop until children are older – usually sometime between the ages of six and eight, depending on the specific tasks being used. With the acquisition of metalinguistic skill, children gain the ability to reflect on the formal properties of language.

Various explanations have been given for metalinguistic development. Traditionally, theories have focused their causal explanations on either individual, cognitive factors (Hakes, 1980; Piaget, 1929; Sinclair, 1978) or language acquisition (Bialystok, 1993; Karmiloff-Smith, 1992; Smith & Tager-Flusberg, 1982). Researchers with this perspective typically consider metalinguistic development, particularly in phonological awareness, to be an essential precursor to literacy acquisition (Adams, 1990; Bradley & Bryant, 1985). In contrast, other researchers have focused on the ways that literacy supports the development of metalinguistic knowledge, arguing, for example, that literacy brings aspects of language into consciousness (Homer, 2002; Morais, 1991; Olson, 1994; Vygotsky, 1934/1986). These apparently contradictory claims – that metalinguistic knowledge is essential for literacy acquisition and that metalinguistic knowledge is a product of literacy acquisition – are resolved, in part by considering the multifaceted and mutually influencing nature of metalinguistic development and literacy.

This chapter reviews theory and research on the relationship between literacy and metalinguistic development. An overview of metalinguistic development is provided, with particular emphasis on two domains that are closely related to literacy: phonemic awareness and word awareness. Evidence is given of the influence of metalinguistic abilities on literacy as well as literacy's influence on metalinguistic development. It is argued that although some basic level of linguistic awareness is present from early on in life, it is literacy that allows children to develop more explicit and conscious awareness of the properties of language.

The Nature of Metalinguistic Development

The most common explanations for metalinguistic development suggest that it is either a part of more general cognitive developments (Hakes, 1980; Piaget, 1929; Sinclair, 1978) or an aspect of language acquisition (Bialystok, 1993; Karmiloff-Smith, 1992; Smith & Tager-Flusberg, 1982). Theories linking metalinguistic development to general cognitive developments are typically grounded in Piagetian theory. Piaget addressed the issue of "awareness" in two of his later books, *The Grasp of Consciousness* and *Success and Understanding* (Piaget, 1977; 1978). Piaget and his colleagues investigated the delay between children's ability to perform an action (i.e., *know-how*) and their ability to correctly describe how they performed that action (*know-that*). For example, children were asked to hit a target with a wooden ball using a sling. Although most children could do this by five years of age, younger children could not explain how they did it (i.e., they had know-how, but lacked know-that); only the older children were able to state correctly that they had released the ball when it was at a tangent to the target (i.e., know-that). Based on these and similar findings, Piaget argued that know-how and know-that constitute autonomous yet reciprocally influencing forms of knowledge. Although the basis for "knowing-that" is procedural knowledge (i.e., know-how), children are not able to access this information directly; there is no "direct illumination" of the knowledge implicit in their procedural schemas. Instead, implicit knowledge must be assimilated by coordinating actions and forming new concepts, a process that is "as laborious as if it corresponded to nothing already known by the child... [and] presents the same risks of omissions and distortions as if the subject were required to explain to himself an external system of physical connections" (Piaget, 1977, p. 339).

According to Piaget (1977), the process of children becoming aware proceeds from "the periphery to the centre," by which he meant that children's knowledge does not originate in either the "subject" (i.e., the child) or in the "object" (i.e., the world) but, instead, from the interaction of the two. Children's knowledge passes through several levels in this process. Initially, children are aware of only the goals and results of their actions. This is the level of know-how, or "action without conceptualization," in which children have isolated assimilation schemes that are linked to specific objects. Gradually, children come to understand the internal mechanisms of their actions (e.g., the means employed, the reasons for modifying the actions) by making empirical abstraction of "observable features," which are "anything that can be recorded through a simple factual (or empirical) observation" – for example, the covariance of two events (Piaget, 1977, p. 345). The next step is marked by the beginning of conceptualization as children make "inferential coordinations" of properties that are not directly observable but must be deduced. This occurs through a process of reflexive abstraction, in which children are unconscious of the inferences they are making. Ultimately, children are able to engage in reflected abstraction, in which inferences are made consciously and intentionally, often as the result of them carrying out two or more actions in order to discern common factors. Concepts are added at this level, which Piaget hypothesized to be contemporaneous with formal operations. Also emerging at this last stage is the ability to engage in "second-power operations" that allow abstractions to be made from previous abstractions. Although concepts are derived from actions, there is also a retroactive effect of the concepts on action – for example, through planning or devising new actions.

Although Piaget did not directly address how children become aware of the properties of language, several researchers have applied his theory to explain children's metalinguistic development. For example, Sinclair (1978) argued that by characterizing language (i.e., speaking) as an action, Piaget's general theory of the development of awareness could be applied to explain children's acquisition of metalinguistic skill. Children's ability to speak indicates know-how, whereas metalinguistic ability requires know-that. Sinclair argued that as with other forms of awareness, cognizance of language progresses from the periphery to the center. For language, this means that children are first aware of the goals and success or failure of their speech-acts and then start to become aware of both the meaning and the form of language as they compare their utterances to their intended meaning and to linguistic regularities (both morphosyntactic and phonetic).

Hakes (1980) also applied Piaget's model of cognitive development to children's development of metalinguistic abilities. According to Hakes, language developments, including metalinguistic developments, are continuous with other, more general cognitive developments. He suggested that the same set of underlying cognitive skills underlie both the transition from preoperational to concrete-operational thought and children's development of metalinguistic ability. More specifically, Hakes claimed that in addition to task-specific knowledge (e.g., knowing the meaning of words and sentences used in a task), the development of metalinguistic ability involves an increase in the ability to engage in deliberate, controlled activities and, in particular, an increase in the ability to "decenter" (i.e., to mentally "stand back" and simultaneously consider multiple aspects of a situation). These are the skills that Piaget described as being part of "reflected abstraction," which is acquired with the advent of concrete operations. Hakes supported his claim with data showing that children's performance on metalinguistic tasks correlate with their performance on conservation tasks.

Smith and Tager-Flusberg (1982) criticized Hakes (1980) and others who argued that the cognitive abilities required to engage in metalinguistic activities are different from those used in language acquisition and develop only in middle childhood. Smith and Tager-Flusberg (1982) called this view (i.e., that language acquisition and metalinguistic ability are two distinct cognitive abilities) the "autonomy hypothesis." They disagreed with the autonomy hypothesis, arguing instead for the "interaction hypothesis, which is that basic language processes, such as comprehension and production, and metalinguistic abilities develop together, each influencing the other (Smith & Tager-Flusberg, 1982). In support of their hypothesis, Smith and Tager-Flusberg pointed out that detecting and correcting errors in speech, which begins in early childhood, requires a certain level of metalinguistic ability. This observation does not necessarily disprove the "autonomy hypothesis" because any intentional action (including speech) requires the actor to be aware of at least the goals and the success or failure of the action, an awareness that Piaget (1977) dubbed "minimal consciousness." However, Smith and Tager-Flusberg seem to be suggesting that children have more than "minimal consciousness" of language from a very young age. The data they provide indicate that children as young as five years of age are able to perform correctly modified metalinguistic tasks. Furthermore, children's success on these tasks is correlated with performance on tests of language skills. These findings are not inexplicable by the "autonomy" theories, but they do suggest that the development of metalinguistic ability is a gradual and continuous process rather than stage-like.

Bialystok (1986a, 1993, 1999) also argued that metalinguistic development is continuous with language learning and use. Bialystok proposed that two distinct processes are involved in metalinguistic problem solving: analysis (i.e., representation of language) and control (i.e., selective attention). *Analysis* is defined as "the ability to represent increasingly explicit and abstract structures"

(Bialystok, 1999, p. 636) and *control* is "the ability to selectively attend to specific aspects of a representation" (Bialystok, 1999, p. 636). According to the "analysis and control" framework, developments in children's linguistic abilities (including metalinguistic problem solving) are due to incremental developments of analysis and control. Bialystok suggested that these two components are related. For example, increased analysis means that children's representations of language are more explicit and abstract, allowing them to engage in activities that require higher levels of control.

Bialystok examined metalinguistic development primarily as part of her larger body of work on bilingualism. She showed, for example, that bilingual children are better than their monolingual counterparts on tasks that require selective attention (e.g., control), with no significant difference between monolinguals and bilinguals on tasks requiring analysis (Bialystok, 1988; Bialystok & Herman, 1999; for a review, see Bialystok, 2005). According to the analysis and control framework, analysis increases via qualitative changes in how language is represented by children. Bialystok proposed that there are at least three levels of language representation: conceptual representation, formal representation, and symbolic representation. With conceptual representations, children "encode the world of meaning" (Bialystok, 1993, p. 223) but do not represent the structure of language. Children's understanding of language at this level is procedurally based. At the next level, formal representation, children begin to represent the "explicit codings of language structure . . . including the units of language: word, sound, sentence" (Bialystok, 1993, p. 223). Finally, with the development of symbolic representations, children are able to represent explicitly the ways in which the components of speech relate to one another; language is understood as a symbolic system. Bialystok and Herman (1992) suggested that Karmiloff-Smith's (1992) *Representational Redescription* model of cognitive development may explain the means by which children's representation of language passes through qualitatively distinct levels.

Karmiloff-Smith's theory of representational redescription was initially derived from her work on children's language acquisition and metalinguistic knowledge (Karmiloff-Smith, 1979). According to Karmiloff-Smith's (1992) model, developmental change is a three-phase process, during which children's knowledge passes through four levels of representation. This process occurs repeatedly within a domain (e.g., language) at the "micro-domain" level (e.g., pronoun use). Initially, children learn how to respond to a certain stimulus (or type of stimulus) and, in so doing, they acquire an encapsulated procedure that does not interact with prior representations. For example, children may have a procedure for using the word *played* instead of *play* and another for using *went* instead of *go*. In both cases, the procedure marks past tense; however, at this phase, children are not aware of this functional correspondence between the procedures – they have linguistic knowledge but not metalinguistic knowledge. The end of the first phase is marked by consistently successful performance, which Karmiloff-Smith (1992) labeled "behavioral mastery." During the next two phases, change is not brought about by external stimuli but, instead, it occurs spontaneously through "system internal dynamics." Procedural representations, which were formed in the first phase, are recoded into more abstract formats, a process called *representational redescription*. Through representational redescription, knowledge that was implicitly contained in the procedural representations becomes explicit (Phase 2) and conscious (Phase 3) as it is recoded into more abstract representational formats.

During the second phase (when the knowledge is explicit but unconscious), internal representations dominate over external, incoming data. This can lead to new behavioral errors where performance was previously successful. For example, children may overgeneralize the rule for forming past tense and say 'goed' even though they previously were able to use 'went' correctly. It is at this phase that children first begin to demonstrate metalinguistic knowledge. Finally, in the third phase, internal representations and external data are reconciled. Children no longer make the errors typical of Phase 2; they have explicit and conscious knowledge and will succeed on standard metalinguistic tasks. This process is repeated independently in all linguistic microdomains.

Although there are some important differences in the theories of metalinguistic development described previously, there are also several key commonalities. First, all of the theories suggest that children acquire cognitive flexibility and a more abstract and explicit understanding of language as their linguistic representations proceed through different levels. Second, all of the theories posit that metalinguistic development requires an increase in children's attentional control; children must be able to "distance" themselves from the use and meaning of language to attend to the form of language. Third, there is a common assumption that children are able to abstract from speech the units of language that are used by the (literate) adults in their communities. Finally, the theories all suggest that metalinguistic abilities are acquired through normal cognitive developments and/or language acquisition. In contrast, other theorists have argued that the literacy is responsible for the development of at least some aspects of metalinguistic ability. This reverses the more commonly held belief about the causal relationship between literacy and metalinguistic development, which is briefly presented in the next section.

Metalinguistic Development as a Predictor of Literacy

Most of the research on the relationship between metalinguistic development and literacy examined how metalinguistic skills underlie children's learning to read and write (for reviews, see Adams, 1990; Ehri, 2005; Stanovich, 1992; Whitehurst & Lonigan, 1998). Researchers have examined how a number of metalinguistic skills, including *phonological awareness* (Bradley & Bryant, 1985; Torgesen, Morgan, & Davis, 1992), *knowledge of grammatical rules* (Blackmore & Pratt, 1997; Bowey, 2005; Muter, Hulme, Snowling, & Stevenson, 2004), and *vocabulary knowledge* (Carlisle & Fleming, 2003; Nation & Snowling, 1999; Rego & Bryant, 1993) contribute to the acquisition of reading.

One of the strongest predictors of subsequent reading ability is phonological awareness, or the explicit understanding of the sound structures of spoken language (Brady & Shankweiler, 1991; Goswami & Bryant, 1990; Wagner & Torgesen, 1987.) Many studies have found that children's abilities to segment spoken language into smaller sound units are related to reading. For example, Bradley and Bryant (1983) presented four- and five-year-olds with a list of three or four words and asked the children to identify the words that had a different initial sound (i.e., onset) when all but one of the words shared a common onset. The authors found that success on this task predicted reading and spelling ability (as indicated by standardized reading measures) three years later. Bradley and Bryant also found that children who were trained in detecting onset, rhyme, and ending sounds of words over a two-year period scored significantly better on tests of reading and spelling than matched children who did not receive this training. Many subsequent studies found that the ability to detect onset and rhyme is predictive of later reading abilities (Bryant, MacLean, & Bradley, 1990; Goswami, 1999 – however, see MacMillan, 2002, for a critical review of this literature). It was argued that the ability to detect onset and rhyme enables the development of phonemic awareness, which is essential for children to map out letter–sound correspondences (Goswami, 1999; chapter 8, this volume).

The predictiveness of phonological awareness for reading ability was found in a number of longitudinal, correlational studies (Bradley & Bryant, 1983; Bryant et al., 1990; Juel, Griffith, & Gough, 1986; Lundberg, Olofsson, & Wall, 1980; Muter et al., 2004). For example, Muter at al. (2004) conducted a two-year longitudinal study with ninety four-year-olds (mean age = 4;9). During initial testing, the authors assessed a number of linguistic and metalinguistic skills, including rhyme awareness, phoneme sensitivity, letter knowledge, vocabulary knowledge, and grammar. At the end of two years, the authors gave the same tests of linguistic and metalinguistic skills as well as tests that assessed two aspects of reading: word recognition and comprehension. The results indicated that children's word-reading ability was predicted only by phoneme sensitivity and letter knowledge, whereas reading comprehension was predicted only by grammatical knowledge and vocabulary.

There have also been a number of experimental intervention studies that found phonological training to improve children's reading acquisition (Bradley & Bryant, 1983; Torgesen et al., 1992; for a review, see Bus & Van Ijzendoorn, 1999). For example, Torgesen et al. (1992) examined the effects of two different phonological training programs. One program taught children how to make phoneme segmentations (e.g., "Say 'lake' without the /l/"). The second program taught children to combine isolated phonemes (e.g., "What word is this, /d/, /o/, /g/?") The authors found that compared to controls, children demonstrated significantly improved performance on the specific phonological task in which they were trained. Only children trained in both tasks demonstrated significant improvements in reading. Torgensen et al. concluded that training in both tasks allowed children to decontextualize their phonological knowledge that then allowed it to be utilized in the novel situation of learning to read.

The studies reviewed herein and similar studies provide clear evidence that metalinguistic development influences literacy acquisition. However, there is also compelling evidence of the influence of literacy on developing metalinguistic ability. The following section presents theories of why literacy affects metalinguistic development and summarizes some of the empirical evidence of this relationship.

Literacy as a Predictor of Metalinguistic Development

Vygotsky (1934/1986) was one of the first to argue that writing restructures how we think about language. He focused on the differences between writing and speech, pointing out that they are fundamentally different activities: speech is "spontaneous, involuntary, and nonconscious," whereas writing is "abstract, voluntary, and conscious." According to Vygotsky, these differences are responsible for the cognitive effects of literacy, the foremost of which is bringing "awareness to speech." For Vygotsky, writing provided a means by which language can be thought about in an abstract way. Piagetian (e.g., Piaget, Sinclair, and Hakes) and neo-Piagetian (e.g., Bialystok and Karmiloff-Smith) explanations of metalinguistic development also argue that children's difficulty with metalinguistic tasks stems from an inability to think abstractly about language. Where the theories differ is in what is proposed to be responsible for children being able to engage in this mode of abstract thought: the advent of reflected abstraction emerging with concrete operations (e.g., Piaget), the recoding of representations of language into more abstract formats that allows conscious reflection (e.g., Bialystok, Karmiloff-Smith), or the abstractness of writing, an external representational system (e.g., Vygotsky).

All of these theories suggest that once children are able to engage in "abstract thought" about language, they then have access to linguistic categories such as "words" and "phonemes." These units of language are assumed either to be known implicitly by children before they become metalinguistically aware or else to be observable by children once they have reached a sufficient level of competency with speech and can cognitively distance themselves from language. In other words, the theories assume that the linguistic categories used by literate adults in a culture are "real" and directly observable. Harris (1980, 1997) criticized linguists for using writing as a model of speech, a practice he calls "scriptism." According to Harris, writing presents an idealized form of language that does not concur with actual speech. Furthermore, he claimed that linguistic categories such as phonemes and words are "second-order constructs, belonging not to nature but to culture" (Harris, 1997, p. 270). This suggests that literacy may not only be providing "cognitive distance" (or "control," to use Bialystok's terminology) but may also be providing a model of the categories that are used to reflect on language.

In his *model* theory of literacy, Olson (1994) claimed that writing provides a model for understanding the structure of language; we become aware of the particular aspects of speech that are represented or codified by our culture's script. Olson argued that writing is responsible for bringing aspects of language into consciousness by providing the set of categories that is used to reflect on and analyze speech. Which aspects of language are brought into consciousness are dependent on the nature of the writing system – different writing systems bring different aspects of speech into consciousness. For example, the advent of writing systems that represented verbal form rather than meaning allowed for the differentiation between what is said and what is meant; what is said are the words written on the paper whereas what is meant is how those words are to be taken. With the development of each script, language is thought of in terms of the units of writing that are used in that script. With syllabic scripts like Vai, for example, the syllable becomes an object of thought; with alphabetic scripts like Greek or English, phoneme-like sound units (corresponding to letters) become available for conscious reflection. Although Olson focused primarily on cultural and historical implications of the model theory, he did suggest that children undergo a similar process. He claimed that for children, "learning to read is learning to hear speech in a new way" (Olson, 1994, p. 85).

There is considerable empirical evidence for the influence of literacy on metalinguistic development. Although a number of studies found that phonological awareness is predictive of subsequent reading ability, other studies found the opposite relationship, with literacy being predictive of phonological awareness. Morais, Cary, Alegria, and Bertelson (1979), for example, administered phoneme deletion and phoneme addition tasks to two similar groups of Portuguese adults who had limited education. Half of the participants had never learned to read and half had learned to read later in life (i.e., after the age of fifteen). The participants who had never learned to read had great difficulty with the phoneme deletion and addition tasks, whereas the participants who were able to read had no difficulty with those tasks. Morais et al. concluded that explicit awareness of phonemes is not spontaneous but instead requires some specific training that is provided by learning to read an alphabetic system.

Further evidence for the importance of literacy for phonemic awareness comes from Read, Zhang, Nie, and Ding (1986) who asked Chinese adults to add and delete consonants in spoken Chinese words. (An English example of this task would be to say "fish" without the "/f/".) Some of the participants had previously learned the alphabetic script, Pinyin, whereas others had only ever been taught to read and write in traditional Chinese characters. Read et al. found that only the participants with prior exposure to the alphabetic script were able to segment words into phonemes. This effect was found even if exposure to the script had occurred many years previous and the subjects could no longer read or write in Pinyin.

In a longitudinal study with Chinese-speaking children, Huang and Hanley (1997) had similar findings. During their first year of school, the children in Huang and Hanley's study were initially taught an alphabetic script and then taught Chinese characters. Phonemic-awareness tasks were given to the children several times throughout the school year: once at the beginning of the year; once ten weeks later, after having been taught the alphabetic script; and a final time at the end of the year, after having been taught to read and write Chinese characters. Huang and Hanley found that there was a significant increase in phonological awareness after the children had learned the alphabetic script, but there was no significant change after the children learned Chinese characters. These findings led the authors to conclude that at least to some extent, phonemic awareness depends on learning an alphabetic script.

Vernon adopted an emergent literacy approach to more closely examine the relationship between literacy acquisition and phonemic awareness. In her work with Spanish-speaking children, Vernon (1993; Vernon & Ferreiro, 1999) found that only children who had begun to relate letters to subsyllabic units (i.e., phonemes) were able to pass either a phoneme-deletion task (Vernon, 1993) or a word-segmentation task (Vernon & Ferreiro, 1999). Based on these findings, Vernon concluded that children's understanding of writing determines the way in which they analyze spoken language.

Additional evidence for the effects of literacy on metalinguistic development comes from research on children's understanding of the concept of word. A number of studies have found that children's understanding of the concept of word increases significantly around the age of six, when they begin school and formal literacy instruction. For example, in one of the first empirical investigations of children's concept of word, Downing and Oliver (1974) presented four- to eight-year-old children with a series of auditory stimuli. The stimuli included words and distracters (including nonverbal sounds, phonemes, syllables, phrases, and sentences). After each presentation, the children were asked if the sound that they had just heard was a word. All of the children overextended the use of word; however, the youngest group (4;5 to 5;5) did so significantly more than the oldest children (6;6 to 8;0). Similarly, Bialystok (1986b) investigated children's concept of word using a variety of Piagetian-style tasks. For example, children were read a sentence and then asked to move a marker for each word in the sentence. In another task, children had to judge which of two spoken words was bigger: "train" or "caterpillar." In both tasks, there was a significant improvement from Junior Kindergarten to Grade 1, the age that children begin their formal literacy instruction.

The importance of literacy for developing a concept of word was questioned by Karmiloff-Smith et al. (1996). The authors developed a word-identification task that was designed to tap into children's "on-line" language-processing capabilities. Children were read a passage of text by an experimenter who would occasionally stop and ask the child to "repeat the last word I said." (Prior to the testing, children were given a brief training session to segment speech into words.) With this technique, many children as young as four demonstrated some understanding of words. Karmiloff-Smith et al. concluded that the four-year-olds had an explicit but unconscious concept of word that was developed independently of literacy. The authors further suggested that "metalinguistic awareness could turn out to be a part of language acquisition itself rather than the mere product of literacy" (Karmiloff-Smith et al., 1996, p. 215).

Homer and Olson (1999) used Karmiloff-Smith et al.'s (1996) "on-line" technique to assess children's metalinguistic concept of word, but the authors also assessed children's emergent literacy knowledge. Children (four to six years of age) were given a version of the Karmiloff-Smith et al. task to assess their understanding of "word" in speech. In this task, children were read a story and the experimenter stopped occasionally to ask the child to say "the last word." The children were also given two tasks to assess their understanding of "word" as a unit of text. In one of the tasks, children were shown and read a piece of text and then asked to circle one of the words. For example, children were shown a piece of text that said "The bird flew" and were asked to circle where it said "bird." In the second text-based task, children were shown and read a piece of text (e.g., "Three little pigs"). The first word of the text was then covered and the children were asked, "what does this say now" (e.g., "XXX little pigs"). Similar to Karmiloff-Smith et al., Homer and Olson found that even some four-year-olds were able to segment spoken language into words. However, the results of Homer and Olson suggested that those children who were successfully able to "repeat the last word" in the speech-based task succeeded in the text-based tasks, with no child doing well on the speech task but poorly on the text-based task. The authors interpreted their findings as supporting the claim that children's metalinguistic understanding of word develops as children attempt to relate written language to speech.

Similar results were found for languages other than English. Kurvers and Uri (2006), for example, used Karmiloff-Smith et al.'s (1996) method to examine four- and five-year-old Dutch- and Norwegian-speaking children's conception of word. They found that, contrary to Karmiloff-Smith et al. (1996), the children in their sample performed poorly on the awareness of word task. However, Kurvers and Uri (2006) reported on the results of an informal follow-up study with comparable children who had had approximately seven months of literacy training. The authors found that those children had dramatically improved performance, leading the authors to suggest that literacy is responsible for introducing new representations of language to children.

Similar effects were found by Homer, Xu, Lee, and Olson (2007), who examined Mandarin-speaking children's awareness of the linguistic concepts of word (/ci/) and character (/zi/). In the Chinese writing system, words are not explicitly marked; instead, characters (which correspond to English syllables and morphemes) are the main unit of text. The authors compared two groups of five- and six-year-old Chinese children ($N = 82$). Half of the children had begun school (and formal literacy instruction) at age five (early literacy group) and half had begun at age six (late literacy group). Homer et al. found that although age alone accounted for variance in children's metalinguistic understanding of word, both age and literacy education accounted for variance in the children's understanding of character. The authors interpreted the results as additional evidence of writing providing a model for reflecting on spoken language.

The studies reviewed herein are part of a growing body of work that provides insight into the ways in which literacy mediates children's development of metalinguistic ability. The effects of literacy are due in part to writing providing an idealized model of language that is then use to reflect on and analyze spoken language. When these findings are considered in conjunction with the studies from the previous section on the effects of metalinguistic development on literacy, a picture begins to emerge of the reciprocal nature of the relationship between the acquisition of literacy and metalinguistic development.

Reciprocal Nature of Literacy Acquisition and Metalinguistic Development

Considered together, the two bodies of work reviewed previously provide compelling evidence of the reciprocal nature of the relationhip between metalinguistic development and literacy acquisition: Although some awareness of the structure of language is required to learn to read and write, acquiring literacy also transforms children's representation of language. These two claims can be reconciled by considering three issues that have contributed to confusion about the nature of the relationhip between literacy and metalinguistic understanding. First, metalinguistic understanding encompasses a constellation of skills rather than a single skill (Birdsong, 1989; Homer & Olson, 1999). Earlier writing would often discuss metalinguistic ability as if it were a singular phenomenon with results obtained from testing a single component of children's metalinguistic skill being generalized to all aspects of metalinguistic ability. Second, some confusion was the result of differences in how researchers were conceptualizing and measuring literacy. Most of the studies that examined how metalinguistic developments influence literacy used word reading (often of decontextualized word lists) as their measure of literacy. This type of task requires fairly advanced literacy skills. In contrast, studies that examined how literacy affects metalinguistic ability tended to use literacy measures that assess more basic literacy skill. They adopted a view of literacy as an emergent process with different components that begins well before formal school-based instruction (Ferreiro & Teberosky, 1982; Whitehurst & Lonigan, 1998). Third, the nature of children's understanding of the components of language changes over time – becoming more abstracted and explicit – in part because of the contributions made by literacy. Different assessment tasks of metalinguistic knowledge have had different requirements for the degree to which the knowledge must be explicit. For example, there have been dramatic differences in what has been taken as evidence for children's awareness of grammatical rules. Tasks have ranged from the very implicit to the very explicit. Examples of metalinguistic tasks to assess knowledge of grammar include spontaneous repair of speech (Karmiloff-Smith, 1979, 1986); judging which of two sentences "sounds better" (de Villiers & de Villiers, 1972; Gleitman, Gleitman, & Shipley, 1972), being able to conjugate a word on request (Vygotsky, 1934/1986), and the very explicit task of being asked to state verbally the grammatical rule in question (Karmiloff-Smith, 1979, 1986). It is not surprising that children's performance varies according to the degree to which the task requires explicit knowledge.

In the past, there has been significant theoretical debate about the directionality of the relationship between metalinguistic ability and literacy, with some researchers arguing that metalinguistic ability must be in place before children learn to read and write (Bradley & Bryant, 1983; McBride-Chang & Kail, 2002; Stanovich, Cunningham, & Cramer, 1984; Yopp, 1988) and other researchers focusing more on how literacy – in the sense of exposure to printed models of oral utterances – affects children's metalinguistic development (Homer & Olson, 1999; Kurvers & Uri, 2006; Morais et al., 1987; Read et al., 1986). Most contemporary researchers, however, acknowledge that literacy and metalinguistic ability interact. The challenge for researchers is to track developmental changes in the nature of children's metalinguistic and literacy knowledge in different domains of metalinguistics.

It seems likely that any child who can speak has some sort of basic metalinguistic understanding, similar to what Piaget (1977) referred to as "minimal consciousness," in that they are aware of only the objectives and outcomes of their linguistic behaviors. For phonological awareness, for example, this means that children are able to determine if the utterance they just made corresponds to what they had intended to say and, if not, make spontaneous repairs. With development and experience – including experiences with written language – metalinguistic ability changes from being implicit and minimally conscious to being explicit and conscious. For example, with increased linguistic experiences, children become able to compare immediate linguistic stimuli (e.g., identifying which of three words "sounds the same") and engage in new forms of language play (e.g., rhyming). In literate cultures, exposure to letters and knowledge of letter names and sounds facilitates this development (Blaiklock, 2004; Foy & Mann, 2006). With exposure to oral language only, children may be able to form implicit representations of some metalinguistic units, such as morphemes and syllables. However, for this implicit knowledge to become explicit seems to require some additional experience – specifically those experiences that are associated with the acquisition of literacy.

One implication of this reciprocal model is that literacy should change how individuals process phonological information. A number of studies – some of which are reviewed herein – have found behavioral evidence that changes in phonological processing are associated with literacy (e.g., being able to manipulate words at the phonemic level is associated with learning an alphabetic script). There is also evidence that literacy causes functional-organizational changes in how the brain processes oral language (Castro-Caldas, Petersson, Reis, Stone-Elander, & Ingvar 1998; for a review, see Petersson, Ingvar, & Reis, Chapter 9, this volume). For example, Castro-Caldas et al. (1998) compared brain activation during language processing of two groups of Spanish-speaking adults who were similar in most respects except that one group had never learned to read (due to social issues). Castro-Caldas et al. used positron emission tomography (PET) and statistical parameter mapping to compare brain activations as their two groups of participants engaged in word and pseudoword repetition tasks. Their behavioral data corresponded to previous studies in that the literate adults performed significantly better than the illiterate adults on the pseudoword repetition task. There was also evidence of significant physiological differences in how the two groups processed phonological information: when repeating the pseudowords, only the literate participants engaged components of the phonological processing system. The authors claimed that that was due to the literate participants making phoneme-grapheme connections in order to facilitate their perception and subsequent production of the pseudowords. Castro-Caldas et al. conclude that having a writing system permanently alters the functional organization of the human brain.

A second implication of this interacting model of literacy and metalinguistic development is that the effects of literacy start early in life, well before children are functionally literate. Ravid and Tolchinsky (2002), in their theory of *linguistic literacy*, argued that linguistic and literacy developments are closely interwoven in literate societies. They suggest that literacy and literate activities play a crucial role in the development of metalinguistic ability throughout development – even before children are able to read and write – and continue throughout advanced levels of education as they learn to manage more complex literate and literary forms (see Berman & Ravid, Chapter 6, this volume). Linguistic literacy, which includes control over linguistic variation and the acquisition of an awareness of language, is theorized to become possible as children become increasingly familiar with written language. The authors pointed out that although children can display some metalinguistic ability in natural contexts (e.g., through repair of speech), more explicit and controlled linguistic awareness develops only later, in conjunction with literacy acquisition. Ravid and Tolchinsky concluded that the relative importance of different factors, including literacy and general cognitive developments, for language development (including metalinguistic ability) varies at different developmental stages. However, by virtue of living in a literate society, literacy is a factor for children's language knowledge at all stages; therefore, literacy should be included as a factor in studies of language acquisition and development.

In conclusion, the question of how literacy and metalinguistic skill interact has implications not only for our understanding of metalinguistic development and children's acquisition of literacy but also for our more general understanding of the nature of children's cognitive development. The investigation of how literacy affects children's conception of language serves as a specific instance of a more general question pertinent to developmental psychology – namely, how do external representations or symbols operate to affect changes in mental-knowledge structures (Homer & Hayward, 2008; Nelson, 1996; Olson, 1994). It seems clear that learning to read and write plays a critical role in transitioning children from thinking about things to thinking about the linguistic representations of those things. In other words, literacy enables language to become an object of thought that can be analyzed, dissected, and manipulated.

References

Adams, M. J. (1990). *Beginning to read: Thinking and learning about print*. Cambridge, MA: MIT Press.

Bialystok, E. (1986a). Factors in the growth of linguistic awareness. *Child Development*, 57, 498–510.

Bialystok, E. (1986b). Children's concept of word. *Journal of Psycholinguistic Research*, 15 (1), 13–32.

Bialystok, E. (1988). Levels of bilingualism and levels of linguistic awareness. *Developmental Psychology*, 24, 560–567.

Bialystok, E. (1993). Metalinguistic awareness: The development of children's representations of language. In C. Pratt & A. F. Garton (Eds.), *Systems of representation in children: Development and use* (pp. 211–233). New York: John Wiley & Sons Ltd.

Bialystok, E. (1999). Cognitive complexity and attentional control in the bilingual mind. *Cognitive Development*, 70, 636–644.

Bialystok, E. (2005). Consequences of bilingualism for cognitive development. In J. F. Kroll & A. M. B. De Groot (Eds.), *Handbook of bilingualism: Psycholinguistic approaches* (pp. 417–432). New York: Oxford University Press.

Bialystok, E., & Herman, J. (1999). Does bilingualism matter for early literacy? *Bilingualism: Language and Cognition*, 2 (1), 35–44.

Birdsong, D. (1989). *Metalinguistic performance and interlanguage competence*. New York: Springer.

Blackmore, A. M., & Pratt, C. (1997). Grammatical awareness and reading in Grade 1 children. *Merrill-Palmer Quarterly*, 43 (4), 567–590.

Blaiklock, K. E. (2004). The importance of letter knowledge in the relationship between phonological awareness and reading. *Journal of Research in Reading*, 27 (1), 36–57.

Bowey, J. A. (2005). Grammatical sensitivity: Its origins and potential contribution to early word-reading skill. *Journal of Experimental Child Psychology*, 90 (4), 318–343.

Bradley, L., & Bryant, P. E. (1983). Categorizing sounds and learning to read: A causal connection. *Nature*, 301 (5899), 419–421.

Bradley, L., & Bryant, P. E. (1985). *Rhyme and reason in reading and spelling*. Ann Arbor: University of Michigan Press.

Brady, S., & Shankweiler, D. (Eds.) (1991). *Phonological processes in literacy*. Hillsdale, NJ: Lawrence Erlbaum Associates.

Bryant, P. E., MacLean, M., & Bradley, L. L. (1990). Rhyme, language, and children's reading. *Applied Psycholinguistics*, 11 (3), 237–252.

Bryant, P. E., MacLean, M., Bradley, L. L., & Crossland, J. (1990). Rhyme and alliteration, phoneme detection, and learning to read. *Developmental psychology*, 26 (3), 429–438.

Bus, A. G., & Van Ijzendoorn, M. H. (1999). Phonological awareness and early reading: A meta-analysis of experimental training studies. *Journal of Educational Psychology*, 91, 403–414.

Carlisle, J. F., & Fleming, J. (2003). Lexical processing of morphologically complex words in the elementary years. *Scientific Studies of Reading*, 7 (3), 239–253.

Castro-Caldas, A., Petersson, K. M., Reis, A., Stone-Elander, S., & Ingvar, M. (1998). The illiterate brain: Learning to read and write during childhood influences the functional organization of the adult brain. *Brain*, 121 (6), 1053–1063.

de Villiers, P. A., & de Villiers, J. G. (1972). Early judgments of semantic and syntactic acceptability by children. *Journal of Psycholinguistic Research*, 1 (4), 299–310.

Downing, J., & Oliver, P. (1974). The child's concept of a word. *Reading Research Quarterly*, 9, 568–582.

Ehri, L. C. (2005). Learning to read words: Theory, findings, and issues. *Scientific Studies of Reading*, 9, 167–188.

Ferreiro, E., & Teberosky, A. (1982). *Literacy before schooling* (S. Veintiuno, Trans.). Exeter, NH: Heinemann.

Foy, J. G., & Mann, V. (2006). Changes in letter sound knowledge are associated with development of phonological awareness in pre-school children. *Journal of Research in Reading*, 29 (2), 143–161.

Gleitman, L. R., Gleitman, H., & Shipley, E. F. (1972). The emergence of the child as grammarian. *Cognition*, 1 (2–3), 137–164.

Goswami, U. (1999). Causal connections in beginning reading: The importance of rhyme. *Journal of Research in Reading*, 22, 217–240.

Goswami, U., & Bryant, P. (1990). *Phonological skills and learning to read*. Hillsdale, NJ: Lawrence Erlbaum Associates.

Hakes, D. H. (1980). *The development of metalinguistic abilities in children*. New York: Springer-Verlag.

Harris, R. (1980). *The language-makers*. London: Duckworth.

Harris, R. (1997). From an integrational point of view. In G. Wolf & N. Love. (Eds.), *Linguistics inside out: Roy Harris and his critics* (Vol. 148, pp. 229–310). Philadelphia: John Benjamins Publishing Co.

Homer, B. D. (2002). Literacy and metalinguistic thought: Development through knowledge construction and cultural mediation. In J. Brockmeier, M. Wang, & D. R. Olson. (Eds.), *Literacy, narrative & culture* (pp. 266–287). London: Routledge/Curzon.

Homer, B. D., & Hayward, E. (2008). Cognitive and representational development in children. In K. B. Cartwright (Ed.), *Literacy processes: Cognitive flexibility in learning and teaching* (pp. 19–41). New York: Guilford Publishing.

Homer, B. D., & Olson, D. R. (1999). The role of literacy in children's concept of word. *Written language and literacy*, 2, 113–140.

Homer, B. D., Xu, F., Lee, K., & Olson, D. R. (2007). *The role of literacy in young English- and Chinese-speaking children's acquisition of metalinguistic awareness*. [Manuscript under review.]

Huang, H. S., & Hanley, J. R. (1997). A longitudinal study of phonological awareness, visual skills, and Chinese reading acquisition among first-graders in Taiwan. *International Journal of Behavioral Development*, 20 (2), 249–268.

Juel, C., Griffith, P. L., & Gough, P. B. (1986). Acquisition of literacy: A longitudinal study of children in first and second grade. *Journal of Educational Psychology*, 78 (4), 243–255.

Karmiloff-Smith, A. (1979). Micro- and macro-developmental changes in language acquisition and other representational systems. *Cognitive Science*, 3, 91–118.

Karmiloff-Smith, A. (1986). From meta-processes to conscious access: Evidence from children's metalinguistic and repair data. *Cognition*, 23 (2), 95–147.

Karmiloff-Smith, A. (1992). *Beyond modularity: A developmental perspective on cognitive science*. Cambridge, MA: MIT Press.

Karmiloff-Smith, A., Grant, J., Sims, K., Jones, M.-C., & Cuckle, P. (1996). Rethinking metalinguistic awareness: Representing and accessing knowledge about what counts as a word. *Cognition*, 58, 197–219.

Kurvers, J., & Uri, H. (2006). Meta-lexical awareness: Development, methodology or written language? A cross-linguistic comparison. *Journal of Psycholinguistic Research*, 35 (4), 353–367.

Lonigan, C. J., Burgess, S. R., & Anthony, J. L. (2000). Development of emergent literacy and early reading skills in preschool children: Evidence from a latent-variable longitudinal study. *Developmental Psychology*, 36 (5), 596–613.

Lundberg, I., Olofsson, Å, & Wall, S. (1980). Reading and spelling skills in the first school years predicted from phonemic awareness skills in kindergarten. *Scandinavian Journal of Psychology*, 21 (3), 159–173.

MacMillan, B. M. (2002). Rhyme and reading: A critical review of the research methodology. *Journal of Research in Reading*, 25 (1), 4–42.

McBride-Chang, C., & Kail, R. V. (2002). Cross-cultural similarities in the predictors of reading acquisition. *Child Development*, 73 (5), 1392–1407.

Morais, J. (1991). Constraints on the development of phonemic awareness. In S. A. Brady & D. P. Shankweiler. (Eds.), *Phonological processes in literacy: A tribute to Isabelle Y. Liberman* (pp. 5–27). Hillsdale, NJ: Erlbaum.

Morais, J., Cary, L., Alegria, J., & Bertelson, P. (1979). Does awareness of speech as a sequence of phones arise spontaneously? *Cognition*, 7 (4), 323–331.

Morais, J., Castro, S. L., Scliar-Cabral, L., Kolinsky, R., & Content, A. (1987). The effects of literacy on the recognition of dichotic words. *Quarterly Journal of Experimental Psychology*, 39*A*, 451–465.

Morais, J., & Kolinsky, R. (1994). Perception and awareness in phonological processing: The case of the phoneme. *Cognition*, 50, 287–297.

Muter, V., Hulme, C., Snowling, M. J., & Stevenson, J. (2004). Phonemes, rimes, vocabulary, and grammatical skills as foundations of early reading development: Evidence from a longitudinal study. *Developmental Psychology*, 40 (5), 665–681.

Nation, K., & Snowling, M. J. (1999). Developmental differences in sensitivity to semantic relations among good and poor comprehenders: Evidence from semantic priming. *Cognition*, 70, 1–13.

Nation, K., & Snowling, M. J. (2004). Beyond phonological skills: Broader language skills contribute to the development of reading. *Journal of Research in Reading*, 27 (4), 342–356.

Nelson, K. (1996). *Language in cognitive development: The emergence of the mediated mind*. New York: Cambridge University Press.

Olson, D. R. (1994). *The world on paper*. New York: Cambridge University Press.

Piaget, J. (1929). *The child's conception of the world* (J. Tomlinson & A. Tomlinson, Trans.). London: Routledge & Kegan Paul Ltd.

Piaget, J. (1977). *The grasp of consciousness: Action and concept in the young child*. Cambridge, MA: Harvard University Press.

Piaget, J. (1978). *Success and understanding*. London: Routledge & Kegan Paul Ltd.

Ravid, D., & Tolchinsky, L. (2002). Developing linguistic literacy: A comprehensive model. *Journal of Child Language*, *29*, 417–447.

Read, C. A., Zhang, Y., Nie, H., & Ding, B. (1986). The ability to manipulate speech sounds depends on knowing alphabetic reading. *Cognition*, *24*, 31–44.

Rego, L. L., & Bryant, P. E. (1993). The connection between phonological, syntactic and semantic skills and children's reading and spelling. *European Journal of Psychology of Education. Special Issue: Prediction of Reading and Spelling Evidence from European Longitudinal Research*, 8 (3), 235–246.

Sinclair, H. (1978). Conceptualization and awareness in Piaget's theory and its relevance to the child's conception of language. In A. Sinclair, R. J. Jarvella, & W. J. M. Levelt. (Eds.), *The child's conception of language* (pp. 191–200). New York: Springer-Verlag.

Smith, C. L., & Tager-Flusberg, H. (1982). Metalinguistic awareness and language development. *Journal of Experimental Child Psychology*, *34*, 449–468.

Stanovich, K. E. (1992). Speculations on the causes and consequences of individual differences in early reading acquisition. In P. B. Gough, L. C. Ehri, & R. Treiman. (Eds.), *Reading acquisition* (pp. 307–342). Hillsdale, NJ: Erlbaum.

Stanovich, K. E., Cunningham, A. E., & Cramer, B. (1984). Assessing phonological awareness in kindergarten children: Issues of task comparability. *Journal of Experimental Child Psychology*, *38*, 175–190.

Torgesen, J. K., Morgan, S., & Davis, C. (1992). Effects of two types of phonological awareness training on word learning in kindergarten children. *Journal of Educational Psychology*, *84*, 364–370.

Vernon, S. (1993). Initial sound/letter correspondences in children's early written productions. *Journal of Research in Childhood Education*, 8 (1), 12–22.

Vernon, S. A., & Ferreiro, E. (1999). Writing development: A neglected variable in the consideration of phonological awareness. *Harvard Educational Review*, 69 (4), 395–415.

Vygotsky, L. S. (1934/1986). *Thought and language* (A. Kazulin, Trans.). Cambridge, MA: MIT Press. (Original work published in 1934.)

Wagner, R., & Torgesen, J. (1987). The nature of phonological processing and its causal role in the acquisition of reading skills. *Psychological Bulletin*, *101*, 192–212.

Whitehurst, G. J., & Lonigan, C. J. (1998). Child development and emergent literacy. *Child Development*, 69, 848–872.

Yopp, H. K. (1988). The validity and reliability of phonemic awareness tests. *Reading Research Quarterly*, 23, 159–177.

CHAPTER 27

Cultural and Developmental Predispositions to Literacy

Alison F. Garton and Chris Pratt

Most cultural explanations of children's development have their origins in cognitive theories of learning, such as those of Piaget and Vygotsky. Vygotsky's theory, in particular, laid the basis for the subsequent sociocultural explanations of children's learning. This chapter charts these theoretical foundations and how they are linked, via children's cognitive development and learning, through various pathways to the development of literacy. Sociocultural theories are outlined, leading to the identification of cultural practices in learning, which are then applied to the development of literacy. Home-literacy practices serve as an example of how literacy is encouraged and fostered. The chapter concludes with some brief observations about how valuing literacy in the home benefits children on starting school and during the early years of formal education.

Cognitive and Cultural Explanations of Learning

Vygotsky's theory is important to our understanding of children's cognitive, language and literacy development both directly through its own contributions to our understanding of children's learning and indirectly through its influence on subsequent theoretical and explanatory frameworks. A fundamental tenet in Vygotsky's theory is the "zone of proximal development" (ZPD), which is a theoretical construct specifying the area in which learning takes place and where children's potential learning transforms into actual learning through interaction with another, more competent partner. This is in contrast with Piaget's model that can be characterised as an individualistic, equilibration model which is aligned more closely with biology and philosophy than mainstream psychology. In the two theories, the means and processes by which learning occur are not the same, and the form of the social environment considered important for learning and development varies in subtle yet important ways. These positions have influenced later theorising about the role cognitive development and learning has in the acquisition of literacy.

Vygotsky's observations and experiments emphasise the nature of the social process for learning in a teaching/learning co-constructive environment. By definition, this requires a teacher – usually an adult or more capable peer – and a learner. These areas of difference between the theories are important when considering the role of the cultural and social world in supporting, promoting, facilitating and benefiting children's cognitive, language and literacy development.

Research and theorising in children's learning and development are often premised on the view that adults are the experts who support, scaffold or otherwise assist children's learning. Rogoff coined the phrase "guided participation" (1990) to characterise the social embodiment of knowledge, specifically instructional communication between the adult expert and the child learner. In line with Vygotskian theory, instruction refers to both teaching and learning; therefore guided participation recognises social participation and the contribution the novice or the child makes to the process of learning. Attention shifts to consider the roles of both participants in learning, and only when the roles are mutual can opportunities for learning be created. These opportunities for learning require that partners can adjust their roles and responsibilities to meet the levels of understanding of the other person and contribute to changing that understanding. There are large social and cultural differences in the extent to which either participant is involved in shared learning because norms and institutions vary.

School is an example where there are formalised cultural (often called 'institutionalised') roles for both the expert and the novice. The role of the expert – in this case, the teacher – is to select suitable activities that provide relevant learning opportunities. It is also possible for the novice – in this case, the child – to select activities. These activities are perhaps not necessarily nor intentionally those that provide maximum learning opportunities but may be intrinsically interesting to the child. Because they are selected by the child, they may be activities that have been mastered or learned to a certain extent and are not new. In such circumstances, teachers can raise their expectations regarding the child's performance to ensure that learning takes place. The child makes choices about how to use the opportunity to learn. In general terms, this may entail working out roles and responsibilities between partners, learning to use and monitor cues from the expert and working out with whom it is best to work.

Rogoff (1990) cited the example of language learning as one in which the adult takes a leadership role but in which the capacity to manage their own learning by establishing eye contact or smiling are examples of infants taking a leading role, and, she conjectures, may be the origin of intersubjectivity. In both cases, we are reminded that intersubjectivity – its establishment and how it changes over the course of the interaction, as partners work together and children learn – is fundamental to a theoretical explanation of cognitive development or learning that considers both partners and their sociocultural environment.

A study conducted by Garton, Harvey, and Pratt (cited in Garton, 2004) gave particular attention to the language used in problem-solving interactions between individual four-year-old children and their parents. The interactions involved sorting toy furniture into a number of model rooms. This study highlighted how intersubjectivity is established and maintained and how parental scaffolding is managed through different language forms and functions, and how these assist children's learning. In teaching, parents deliberately focus the child's attention on the problem and demonstrate directly and clearly the strategy required to achieve the outcome. Scaffolding, on the other hand, is more indirect, with parents providing a framework, not direct instruction, for strategy selection and task management. The language used during parent–child interactions was coded into seven categories, including planning, description, meta (self) talk, off task and checking. The latter was included to capture the elements of scaffolding, whereby a collaborative partner monitored the performance of the child and encouraged and/or reinforced appropriate problem-solving skills. Coded commands such as "put the table there" were also included as a more direct measure of parental involvement. Finally, procedural language, in which parents and children demonstrated their knowledge of the 'how to' of the task (e.g., saying 'this goes here' when managing furniture placement), was coded to capture ongoing involvement in the collaborative task.

In general, the results demonstrated that four-year-old children showed an improved individual problem-solving capacity or learning after participating in collaboration with one of their parents. The results demonstrated that there were specific differences in the types of language used by parents and children within the collaborative process. Parents primarily used their language for checking and commanding their child during the collaboration so were both teaching and scaffolding the children in the sorting task, but there was also a significant association between the planning language used by parents and improved problem-solving outcomes by the children.

Much of the descriptive language used by children was elicited by parents' use of checking statements, such as "are you sure that goes there?" to which the child replies "yes, it's a bed" (as the model bed is placed in the room designated as the bedroom), and "what else goes in the bedroom?" to encourage item selection. In general terms, parental questioning and agreement were used to encourage children to think about the problem-solving task in a concrete and purposeful way (as demonstrated by the child's use of procedural and descriptive language). The use of feedback is known to lead to successful and improved collaboration outcomes (Tudge, Winterhoff, & Hogan, 1996). The significant association between planning language used by parents and children's improved problem solving clearly supported a scaffolding explanation for children's learning. Permitting the adults to select their means of supporting learning shows a preference for indirect teaching through language, although undoubtedly any form of experienced support will assist learning. Planning language highlights what parents want the child to do and compliance means that success at the task occurs. This was then generalised to the related post-test task. The relationship of planning language to subsequent child performance also pointed to the role of children paying attention to or being aware of the role of the adult in assisting them during problem solving.

In conclusion, it was argued that the parents' strategic approach to the collaborative task allowed them to support the child to generate more effective problem-solving skills leading to cognitive change. The results lend support to the notion that adults scaffold children's learning through their use of specific language functions that aid and support the child. It also demonstrates that experts use direct and indirect language in the ZPD rather than nonverbal strategies to "teach" their children to learn. Cognitive change and learning are thus supported by sociocultural conventions – in this case, the use of different forms of language.

A recent study by Fidalgo and Pereira (2005) compared how mothers with two different levels of education adjusted their speech to three- to five-year-old children's cognitive and language skills while they engaged in a variety of problem-solving tasks. This study also adopted a scaffolding analogy to show how mothers' behaviour is contingent on children's ages and current skill levels. The authors related the different uses of language explicitly to cultural values and practices. They also highlighted the need to differentiate the scaffolding discourse of the mothers that is due to their educational levels and how they interpret the various problem-solving tasks used in the research study from that due to their child's cognitive and language development level. The study included two didactic problem-solving tasks (a jigsaw puzzle and two versions of a seriation task) and a domestic task (setting a table for three people).

In brief, analysis of the mothers' speech revealed that all mothers adjusted their speech to the child's level of development and that there were few differences between the various tasks. More highly educated mothers, however, were more demanding and challenging, irrespective of the skill level of the child, and used more abbreviated directives such as "where does this one go?" and "now it's a green one" in which there are few if any aspects of the situation provided explicitly. These mothers also used a greater number of referential expressions to direct their children's attention to aspects of the task. Fidalgo and Pereira interpreted the patterns of language found in terms of the functions of abbreviation and referential expressions to mediate the learning process from the interpsychological level (i.e., between the mother and her child) to the intrapsychological level as seen in the child's successful performance on the task or learning (even though this was not reported). The different levels of mediation are claimed to reflect the mothers' interpretation of the cognitive and linguistic skills of their children at a particular age, as well as limitations imposed by the social interactions encouraged in the research. Again, this research demonstrated the critical role of the social and cultural environment in supporting children's learning.

Cognitive Tools for Literacy

Many cognitive approaches to literacy and education have also been derived from both Piaget's theory and Vygotsky's theory. Piaget's stage theory provides a solid framework to describe children's learning in areas such as mathematics, science, language and physical development. Children move from intuitive preoperational thinking, through the mental manipulation of objects and events, to more complex problem solving. The final, formal operational stage is characterised by abstract thinking. This stage is usually not reached until the teenage years and its accomplishment is often recognised to be linked to formal schooling.

In terms of literacy development, Piaget's theory has been influential in the widespread adoption of a constructive and active approach to teaching. It can be seen in the 'whole language' approach in which reading and writing in particular are regarded as developing from the language the child uses to communicate and the goal-directed activities and social practices in which the child engages. These are largely untutored activities that allow literacy to 'emerge.' Children engage in activities using pictures, letters and other playful symbolic experiences, and they communicate with others through talking or by early attempts at letter-writing. In this 'emergent literacy' view, children approach text and signs in whatever form as sources of meaning and they try to derive meaning from these. There is a natural progression in the development of literacy; exposure to and familiarity with conventional print, particularly in books, increasingly leads to conventional forms of writing. Teaching requires the provision of appropriate experiences to assist children in learning to decode meaning and to transfer that to their own writing. Developing children and their ability to deal with increasingly complex material is at the centre of this view of literacy, although it does support an interactionist view of children and how they learn. Teachers are there to provide the necessary experiences to enable the natural development process.

In contrast, Vygotsky's theory suggested that teachers are necessary not just to accommodate a model of psychological development but also to initiate and sustain the transformation of knowledge and learning. So, instead of schools providing cognitive tools necessary for literacy, it can be argued that cultural tools support changes in behaviour. Vygotsky (1978), for example, argued that writing cannot be acquired naturally as in a whole-language approach, but that language is a system of signs and symbols, the acquisition of which culturally transforms children to take their place in the society in which they are developing. Literacy itself brings new cultural tools to children: They not only learn the mechanics of writing, they also are introduced to new ways of thinking and understanding. With the development of literacy comes the development of dispositions or ways of thinking which affect how children engage with their world and interpret their experiences. Spoken language itself serves as a cultural tool that mediates human activities. This reciprocally mediates higher psychological processes such as writing and includes the mind and cultural behaviour. In turn, this higher or second-order system of representation, formed during the cultural development of the child, requires formal teaching or instruction. Reading and writing are among those "... definite areas of school instruction" (Vygotsky, 1962, p. 97).

Cultural Practices, Literacy and Cognitive Development

Literacy can be related to cognitive development through examination of children's performance on cognitive tasks designed to measure aspects of thinking. Success on cognitive tasks often requires the use of cultural tools like literacy and numeracy, themselves the product of formal schooling. Literacy influences the ways in which we think – seen, for example, in a reduction in the use of memory for recording oral narratives with the development of writing and written records. Cultures that rely on oral transmission of knowledge thus privilege memory as an essential tool for maintaining records of those stories, skills and experiences. Indigenous Australians, for example, do better on tasks that rely on spatial memory than verbal memory. In one study, Kearins (1986) used a nonverbal version of 'Kim's Game,' which involved rearranging objects in a grid. On all tasks, Aboriginal adolescents and children performed significantly better than white Australians, even controlling for familiarity with the materials. Kearins noted that the Aboriginal children sat very still and concentrated on the task, taking their time to relocate objects. White children, by contrast, fidgeted and responded hastily. She inferred that the Aboriginal children were using a visual strategy to solve the problem whereas the white children, as evidenced by their 'muttering,' were using a verbal strategy. These superior visuospatial memory skills of Aboriginal children were regarded as part of a set of wider cognitive skills that are maintained by the culture.

Scribner and Cole (1981) were among the first to claim that literacy influenced children's cognitive abilities. They examined the relationship between literacy and cognitive skills, looking particularly at the Vai people from Liberia, whose use of literacy encompassed various written forms. These include Vai script, which was used for personal and most of their professional needs. It is used for informal writing and does not involve writing essay-style or expository text. Some of the Vai people are also literate in Arabic, mainly through study of the Qur'an (i.e., the Koran), the religious text of the Muslims. Study of the Qur'an requires recitation and memorising the text. Finally, a few Vai people are literate in English because they have attended English-speaking schools. Scribner and Cole predicted that because of differences in the forms of literacy, those people who only use Vai script would not have the cognitive and intellectual outcomes of the other language users. They found, however, few differences in cognitive skills between those who only used Vai written scripts and the others who had been exposed to different forms of literacy.

However, like the Australian Aborigines, the Vai people demonstrated superior skills in certain circumstances. For example, in a communication task that required describing an absent board game, literate Vai people were better than the nonliterate people and Arabic literates at giving and organising information. Scribner and Cole (1981) attributed this superiority in communication skills to the Vai scriptwriters' fluent use of writing – hence, with the text conveying the message and little support coming from the context. In general, results of their work with the Vai people demonstrated that literacy is related to cognitive skills but only when specific aspects of the literacy activities were considered. Different types of literacy, both in terms of its forms and functions, are linked to an individual's use of the cultural tools that comprise that literacy.

Cultural tools vary from simple writing implements to typewriters to modern software packages in computers. As societies become more technologically advanced, increased expectations about skill and competence with the various cultural tools mean that literacy itself must increase. In the twenty-first century, there is a strong expectation for adults to be able both to read and to operate efficiently a means of communication that relies on the written word – namely, the Internet. Spinillo and Pratt (2005) noted that street children in Brazil, with little or no formal schooling, showed high levels of awareness of newspaper articles as a type of text genre. Exposure to this literacy environment gives children familiarity and competence with newspapers as a particular form of literacy. Newspapers themselves can be regarded as a cultural tool.

Sociocultural Theory

Contemporary sociocultural theory can be applied generally to children's cognitive and language development (Bearison & Dorval, 2002; Gauvain, 2001b; Hatano & Wertsch, 2001; Rogoff, 1998; Shweder et al., 1998). Sociocultural theory places the individual in the centre of sociocultural activities and regards interaction with others and with 'cultural tools' as essential to the development of cognition (Hatano & Wertsch, 2001). Cultural tools are artefacts created at particular times in particular cultures that support cognitive and linguistic activity. Westernised tools include such things as clocks, street signs, dressmaking patterns, architectural plans and recipes, as well as alphabets (Gauvain, 2001a). Children observe adults using these cultural tools to obtain goals, or to learn, and they gradually form part of the child's competence. Cultural tools also include such things as reading and writing systems and various forms of representational activity, as determined and shaped by the culture, usually via social means.

The unit of analysis in sociocultural theory is not the individual but the interaction itself. Cultural or sociocultural approaches and theories consider the broader context in which humans live and develop, and link these to the development of mind or cognition. According to Rogoff (1998), both "... development and learning entail individuals' *transformation of participation* (her italics) in sociocultural activity" (p. 687). In this way, the roles adopted by individuals in any activity are not separate from the activity itself. So, an advantage of the sociocultural approach is that it moves away from the isolated individual and from a universal description of mind and its development. Gauvain (2001b) promoted the notion of cognition as a socially mediated process insofar as the social context indirectly influences learning. What resides in the mind and what is learned cannot be distinguished from the social and cultural processes that support such learning.

There are five characteristics of development and learning viewed from a sociocultural perspective (Rogoff, 1998). First, there is an interdependence of individual, interpersonal and community processes. Second, learning can be regarded as the changing participation in activities that leads to individual change. Such participation is active and creative, and – in a strong version of this view – children can transform their understanding and role depending on the activity and become people who can adopt various roles in society and in the cultural context, changing their understanding and their interpersonal relationships. Participation in sociocultural activities can be flexible, dynamic and creative. Third, in a sociocultural view, the development of knowledge comes from participation in shared activity, so knowledge is not static but rather arises as a consequence of cognitive transformation resulting from interaction. Fourth, Rogoff comments that the distinction between competence and performance is not relevant to sociocultural theory as the focus shifts from what children can do, think or act in certain situations (e.g., experimental or natural) to what they are capable of thinking or doing. Developmental change, or transition, focussing on the acquisition of individual competence, gives way to a focus on the roles of children in particular sociocultural activities. Change is qualitative and varies according to cultural values, interpersonal needs and specific circumstances. Finally, participation in different activities does not reflect generalisation or transfer (which implies knowledge is stored); instead, the sociocultural approach recognises regularities in the structure of human activities.

Sociocultural Practices

Rogoff (1998) pointed to the roles that belong to the institutional and cultural traditions that frame the collaboration relationship between children and their teachers. Rogoff termed this perspective the 'sociocultural view,' suggesting that children's learning takes place in a broader social context than is usually considered. Learning through or by participating in sociocultural activities requires us to consider individuals as learning not only in the company of peers, parents and teachers but also through participation in family, community and cultural activities and how these various forms of activities are interlinked. One way of establishing sociocultural practices is by studying cultures other than the prevailing or Westernised dominant culture. For other researchers, culture is defined and represented by educated societies.

A sociocultural view is not only consistent with Vygotskian theory, it also gives rise to studies that consider the interaction itself, how relationships are formed and maintained between participants, how individuals contribute differentially to solving a common problem or participate in jointly working on an activity, and how these aspects of the interaction "... are constituted by and themselves constitute cultural practices and institutions" (Rogoff, 1998, p. 722). This reminds us that language, cognition and literacy should not be regarded as separate from all other aspects of development. Literacy development derives from social processes and transforms as a consequence of participation in relevant cultural activities. Areas for investigation include the dynamics of groups in the learning of literacy and the role of observation as a form of participation.

The sociocultural view also owes some of its origins to Bourdieu's (1977) view that literacy is a form of 'cultural capital,' or competencies or skills. According to Bourdieu, educational success involves a range of cultural behaviours of which literacy is one. Privileged children learn these from their teachers whereas unprivileged children do not. Privileged children fit into school with apparent ease and can meet educational expectations. This ease is seen as an ability that is a product of the social environment – in this case, the parents. Privileged children are equipped by their parents with favourable dispositions to school, as well as the intellectual capacity to succeed, to ensure that they take their parents' place in the wider social system. To be specific, in the case of literacy, there are different forms of literacy available and different ways of 'doing' literacy, some of which are regarded as more legitimate than others. Children become familiar with certain literacy practices at home but, when they get to preschool or school, these are not regarded as legitimate or valid (Barratt-Pugh, 2000). In the formal setting of school, the literacy practices that children bring (e.g., watching television) may be in conflict with those valued by the school and, as such, they hold little cultural capital. Such children would thus be regarded as unprivileged because the literacy practices of home are not recognised or built on. Children are unprivileged because of cultural, ethnic, socioeconomic and community differences in the value placed on literacy activities regarded as important in the formal teaching of reading and writing.

More recently, Rogoff and colleagues discussed 'intent participation' (Correa-Chávez, Rogoff, & Mejìa Arauz, 2005; Mejìa-Arauz et al., 2005; Rogoff, 2003; Rogoff, Paradise, Mejìa Arauz, Correa-Chávez, & Angelillo, 2003) and 'intent community participation' (Rogoff, 2006), which refers to learning via active observation of and participation in shared cultural activities. It is seen in parent–child interaction (specifically, e.g., shared book-reading) as well as in communities that segregate children from some but not all adult activities although engaging them actively and jointly in others. Current industrialised societies tend to segregate children completely from adult activities in that children are educated separately from but by adults who transmit knowledge and skills to children. Features of intent participation include differential roles taken by both more and less experienced participants in activities; the use of observation rather than instruction for learning activities; the use of communication between participants; and how learning is assessed. As can be seen, these are features of collaborative classrooms and effective language and literacy learning in the home. Children learn by active involvement in and listening to more experienced others, including their parents. This is not simply passive observation as psychologists traditionally described it but rather observation as a precursor to participation. Knowing when to enter, when to take part, and how to participate are all gleaned from observation: in other words, intent participation.

Rogoff et al. (2003) draw comparisons between intent participation and what they term 'assembly-line instruction' which include differential roles of the teachers and of the learners in the two models and differences in motivation. In intent participation, motivation is inherent in the activity; the setting and achieving of a goal are intrinsically rewarding. School learning, however, requires artificial motivators such as rewards and praise. Teachers consequently must learn behaviour-management techniques to keep children focussed on their learning. Because learning is based on observation and engagement, in intent participation, children actively take part and share the opportunities, activities and experiences.

In intent participation, language is learned because it serves a purpose. It is learned in joint activity and joint action (cf. Bruner, 1983). According to Rogoff, language learning is embedded in a familiar context and language is used to request something that is needed or to seek answers that are not already known. Assembly-line instruction often requires children to reply to questions to which the teacher, for example, already knows the answer (cf. Garton & Pratt, 1998). What *is* the purpose of classroom question-and-answer routines? To guess what is in the mind of the teacher, not to obtain new information. Finally, in intent participation, assessment is built in to the process of learning. It is intrinsic to and integrated with the setting and achievement of goals, in the context of being a willing participant in the activity and sharing it with another, more knowledgeable and skillful person. School instruction requires that assessment be undertaken to measure compliance with participation in that instruction.

An example of intent participation is described by Mejía-Arauz et al. (2005), who studied children's observation of an adult's demonstration of paper folding (i.e., origami) or of an older child's attempt at demonstrating the same task. The researchers were careful to point out that it is the cultural practices, not the populations themselves, that were the object of the study. Children were not to request any further information as they watched the demonstration. Mexican-heritage children in the United States were compared with U.S.-European–heritage children. Mexican children had mothers with only a basic education and those communities have a tradition of observation among the indigenous communities. Migration to central California has meant that these cultural practices have been retained as they reflect the original culture. In contrast, U.S.-European–heritage children would have been exposed to Western cultural practices such as questioning and praise, which is more akin to instruction in formal schooling. To see which cultural group they more closely resembled, a midway sample also included Mexican-heritage children of mothers who had completed high school. The aim was not to isolate schooling as a variable but rather to regard maternal education and family ethnicity as features of community lives.

Six- to ten-year-old children in triads viewed a scripted origami demonstration and each child made two figures – a pig and a jumping frog – during the demonstration. The prediction for the study was that Mexican-heritage children whose mothers had limited schooling would more often observe without asking for further information than their U.S.–European-heritage counterparts whose mothers had high levels of education. U.S.–European children did indeed make more requests during the demonstration, although both groups of children intently studied the folding activity (both from the scripted adult and the spontaneous peers who participated). Mexican-heritage children, however, more often followed both the adult and the peers by observation alone, without making any requests for more information, when compared with their European peers, whose mothers had higher levels of education. This finding was taken as evidence for the priority accorded to observation in the Mexican community compared with other cultures in which verbal instruction is paramount. This was further supported by U.S.–European-heritage children whose mothers had high levels of schooling making more requests for additional information during the demonstrations. The pattern for Mexican children whose mothers had high levels of schooling resembled more closely the U.S.–European-heritage children, adding weight to the argument that children's learning occurs in an instructional context once mothers have reached high levels of formal education. It had been shown previously that Mexican children typically do not ask questions because questioning and challenging authority are regarded as impolite (Goody, 1978). Such a social convention also prevents children from asking questions in the classroom, an impediment to teaching and learning.

The sociocultural approach draws attention to the distinction between culture and social class relative to the values held about education, instruction and literacy. Tudge et al. (2006) defined culture as a social group that has "... a shared set of values, beliefs, practices, access to resources, social institutions, a sense of identity, and that passes on the values, beliefs, etc., to the next generation" (p. 1447). Different cultural groups can be formed of different ethnic groups as well as different societies. Culture is regarded as multidimensional. Culture is contrasted with social class, defined loosely as upper, middle and lower class based on socioeconomic indicators. Tudge et al. argued, however, that there could be another view – namely, that different classes may be regarded as different cultures because their members hold different views and values about child development and educational instruction, stemming from different life experiences. Most of the work on literacy development has been conducted on middle class and upper-to-middle class educated families who value literacy and reading highly. This may underestimate the value placed on literacy (not simply reading) in cultures in which oral language and storytelling are valued. In other words, these cultures may value literacy more than we originally thought

Cultural Practices and Literacy

Some research that adopts a sociocultural approach to literacy has looked at how families' interpretation of literacy informs and influences their practices with respect to their children as they develop. Serpell, Sonnenschein, Baker, and Ganapathy (2002) summarised some of these various approaches and discussed 'cultural models' as implicit theories about child development held by parents, such as how to "... cultivate the child's appropriation of various valued, cultural practices" (p. 391). These practices include reading and writing, as well as literacy more broadly construed. This is linked with Rogoff's (1993) theoretical framework which here is called 'participatory appropriation,' similar to 'intent participation.' The cultural practice of literacy is generally regarded as an activity that is an instrument of cognitive development

(Olson, 1994); it is a recurrent activity, it is associated with particular technological advances (or artefacts) and it is highly functional. Sociocultural theory assumes that the family is the major context through which social activities and cultural meanings are interpreted and transmitted. According to Serpell et al., the family "... generates a filter between the larger cultural formations and the developing child" (p. 391). Learning is noticed and charted at the individual child level, but this is simply a manifestation of more general systemic change and development. In addition, theories such as those of Bronfenbrenner (1979) placed the developing child at the centre of interdependent social systems, representing increasing levels of broader society. The family is one of the immediate social systems and acts as an intermediary between the child and the broader social systems.

According to Serpell et al. (2002), even if the school is the primary agent of literacy teaching, the family can influence children's literacy development by offering a range of opportunities for children to participate in literacy activities, such as joint storybook reading (Bus, van IJzendoorn, & Pellegrini, 1995), visits to the library and other social routines like shopping, and language games such as recitation of nursery rhymes (Garton & Pratt, 2004). Other researchers have placed more emphasis on informal opportunities for language such as casual conversations and arguments; however, sometimes these too (e.g., dinnertime discussions) could be regarded as structured as well as social activities. Literacy can be regarded as both a set of skills to be acquired or developed and as a source of entertainment (Serpell et al., 2002). This distinction, however, blurs the fact that children can be having fun while engaging in and learning from literacy activities. Nonetheless, it is claimed that parental emphasis on fun and play predicts faster rates of literacy development than does a purely skills orientation. Other major factors often considered when looking at family processes are issues such as the socioeconomic class, race or language group to which the parents belong, which influence not only literacy development but also the socialisation processes and beliefs held by parents.

Serpell et al.'s (2002) study examined a number of characteristics of family life relative to literacy, such as the frequency of the child's engagement in reading and writing activities with an older person; the parents' orientation to literacy socialisation (entertainment- or skill-based); and family routines such as reading books at bedtime, doing homework, and dinnertime conversations. These characteristics were then examined relative to children's literacy competencies using a standard measure of reading ability. Sixty-six children participated in the reported longitudinal study. Children were aged about seven and a half years at the time of the final inventory (measuring the frequency of engagement in literacy activities), and they were evenly distributed across socioeconomic and racial groups. In general, the data supported a view that found reading skills at Grade 3 were predicted by parental endorsement of literacy entertainment, parental endorsement of literacy as a skill and parental investment in doing homework. General social variables such as family income and ethnicity did not account for significant amounts of variance. Other relationships amongst the variables were also of interest; for example, the extent to which parents reported that the family spent time in regular reading out loud was correlated with the frequency with which that activity occurred. Serpell et al. (2002) concluded that, in general, the recurrent activities during a child's literacy development are organised and driven by the parents' implicit views on child development, socialisation and literacy practices.

Home Literacy Practices

In a description of his extensive longitudinal study of language development in children, Bruner (1983) examined the growth of reference through what he termed 'book reading' but which is better characterised as early shared book experiences. This activity is what Bruner termed a 'format' with a routinised structure, requiring the mother and child to sit down together and 'read.' The early books were picture books and much of the shared book experiences consisted of the mother pointing at things (objects, actions) on the pages and naming or commenting on them. As discussed by Bruner and then later by Garton and Pratt (1998), by the time 'book reading' appeared as a format, the children were able to take turns and knew many of the conventions of conversations. Over time, this early form of book reading through sharing books showed clearly how mothers used the format to scaffold and enable her child to achieve more with language. So, for example, when one of the mothers in Bruner's study initially pointed to a picture and asked her son what it was, she would accept any noise that signalled he was looking and listening. Over time, she became more demanding in the answer she found acceptable, providing feedback on the acceptability of the answer given to her and commenting on both the picture and the language used. The criteria of acceptability were constantly moved and the 'bar raised.' Over time too, the mother's role became more instructional and pedagogical, and the shared book experiences led into shared book reading. The child's contribution to book reading also increased. This involved the child taking on the questioning role and turning the pages when ready, as well as rudimentary approximations to reading.

In later book-reading routines, the mother took the opportunity to turn it into a language and reading learning lesson. The principles she used were to support, scaffold and encourage her child to strive for greater and more accurate language use. She provided the context and the constraints within which the child could demonstrate his current language attainment and reading. She was also encouraging further achievement, supporting her child's attempts to use language and to approximate more closely what would be considered reading. Finally, the mother became more particular in what she found acceptable language and reading behaviour on the part of her child.

In the case of literacy, Garton and Pratt (2004) described how parents facilitate entry into literacy for children from a young age, pointing out that the social context in which literacy takes places is extremely important for both facilitating and restraining the rate and direction of reading development. Some parents read stories and look at picture books with their children from an early age, and this activity can assist the 'what' as well as the 'how' of reading development. It is argued that there are two phases – early book reading and reading comprehension – when children start to learn to read these storybooks (Garton & Pratt, 1998). These are sometimes combined in the term *emergent literacy*, which refers to the acquisition of the skills, knowledge and attitudes toward learning to read. With the present focus on only early shared book experiences, as noted previously, we can discuss how the regular framework and routine provide the child with a context in which language – its words and their meanings – can be learned and how the experience fosters a child learning to *use* language.

Researchers have argued that parents have a fundamental role to play in the development of reading (Bus, 1994; Garton & Pratt, 1998, 2004). Studies have examined the active role played by children in book reading, drawing on Bruner's (1983) seminal early work. The scaffolding analogy best describes the role played by the parent in guiding the child through being sensitive and aware of his or her abilities, interests and knowledge. It also has been claimed that there is a direct link among early shared book experiences, shared book reading and later reading and literacy skills at school. In addition, a link between early shared book experiences and later vocabulary acquisition was found (deLoache & deMendoza, 1987).

Sénéchal and colleagues published a number of studies examining the relationship between preschool children's exposure to and knowledge of storybooks in the family home from an early age and later language and reading skills. The work reported by Sénéchal and LeFevre (2002) was a longitudinal study examining the relationships between home literacy experiences, children's receptive language and emergent literacy skills, and reading achievement. It was conducted during a five-year period with children from middle- and upper-middle-class homes being educated in English-language schools. Informal home-literacy activities were those that involved parents reading storybooks to children for enjoyment and pleasure, whereas formal home-literacy activities – which may also involve parents and children sharing storybooks – were those in which parents specifically taught their children to read and write. Sénéchal and LeFevre noted that most previous work on parents reading to children has focussed on informal activities. Formal teaching of reading is less often studied and is tied up with parental expectations of and beliefs about their roles relative to literacy and numeracy (as well as other cultural and educational responsibilities).

Sénéchal, LeFevre, Hudson, and Lawson (1996) examined the influence of early book reading on subsequent vocabulary development. The researchers made some assumptions that were supported through their study. They noticed that shared book reading has many characteristics that can assist in the development of a vocabulary, including encountering words that may not be used in everyday spoken language and may even be more sophisticated than that encountered when adults speak to children. Second, book reading means that the child has the (more or less) undivided attention of the adult and the focus is on language, which can only be beneficial to the development of the child's language skills. However, Sénéchal et al. claimed that previous research studies of the relationship between shared book reading and subsequent language development were poorly designed and had low reliability, relying as they typically do on correlational evidence from parental reports of reading frequency. To overcome these problems, Sénéchal et al. devised checklist measures of exposure to storybooks through parental knowledge of storybooks, as well as including some self-report measures. The hypothesis was that book exposure would enhance vocabulary acquisition, once parental education level and parental exposure to adult books were controlled. Correlational data were again the main source of evidence to support the conclusion that storybook exposure made a unique and significant contribution to children's subsequent vocabulary development.

In a second part of this study, Sénéchal et al. (1996) measured children's knowledge of storybooks directly and how this predicted later vocabulary development. The knowledge was obtained through showing children illustrations from storybooks and asking them to identify characters, the book title and so on. Correlational analyses were again conducted and showed a strong relationship between children's knowledge of books and their vocabulary, controlling for other factors including verbal ability, recall ability and age. It was therefore concluded that both children's and parents' knowledge of storybooks are good predictors of preschool children's vocabulary development. However, this work was conducted in an environment in which language skills were regarded as important, and English was the predominant language used at home and school. It is reasonable to assume that language and reading would be important skills to be nurtured and developed, given these environments and circumstances.

Sénéchal and LeFevre (2002) again used the checklist method of children's exposure to books by asking parents which book titles, from a list of sixty, they recognised and which children's authors, from a list of sixty, they recognised. As discussed previously, storybook exposure is regarded as a reliable predictor of later vocabulary development. The longitudinal study had three aims: (1) to examine the importance of informal storybook reading versus more formal reading teaching by parents to children's language and literacy; (2) to evaluate the relationship between early literacy experiences and later reading acquisition; and (3) to assess the relationship between these early literacy experiences and reading fluency. Children were followed from their early school years (when they were aged four or five years) through to the end of Grade 3.

The main outcome from this research was a clear link from home-literacy experiences through reading acquisition in Grade 1 to reading fluency in Grade 3. A model was developed to explore these relationships. Storybook reading was related to children's language development, whereas parental reports of teaching reading were related to children's early literacy skills. Language and literacy were linked, in turn, through the children's developing phonological awareness to reading acquisition and reading fluency. Early literacy also was related to reading acquisition, which moderated its influence on later reading fluency. It is interesting that children's exposure to storybooks (as reported by parents) was not linked to their emergent literacy skills, such as early decoding and phonological awareness, but did have direct relationships with reading acquisition in Grade 1 and reading fluency in Grade 3. Sénéchal and LeFevre (2002) suggested that this is perhaps because these informal literacy experiences are insufficient to facilitate the development of specific literacy skills such as early decoding, knowledge of the alphabet or phonological awareness. They also hinted that the indirect checklist measure may not tap into children's interest in books. The overall conclusion was that parental teaching was directly related to early literacy and later reading achievements, whereas shared storybook reading was only indirectly related to literacy achievements through language and phonological abilities. Both teaching and shared storybook reading were indirectly related to phonological awareness. Early literacy skills themselves were good predictors of later reading, a finding that was reported previously and in other research.

Another way that families can support literacy development is through conversations, often at mealtimes. Rogoff (2003) reported research that examined and analysed mealtime conversations amongst middle-class families. Such conversations often took the form of the parents asking children about their day at school. Parents guided their children through these reports, requesting additional and new information, background information and a summing up or evaluation of the day's events. Other devices used by parents included ensuring that each child completed his or her turn before another child was asked to furnish a report. Parents' own reports were likewise conventionally structured and children were expected to wait until they were finished and not interrupt. This research (Martini, 1995) found that such discourse structures recorded at mealtimes led to success at school, where the same structures were used in the classroom. Exposure to language structures, as well as to books and literacy practices, gave children advantages on reading tests and in constructing narratives.

Valuing literacy and encouraging literacy (i.e., reading and writing) has benefits for both further literacy development and learning at school in general. Parents who encourage thinking, talking, reading and writing with their children will privilege the children on starting school, but we must be careful not to suggest that one set of home-literacy practices is better than another (Rivalland, 2000). Many of these practices are based in cultural beliefs about parental roles in providing either formal or informal instruction in literacy to their children. These practices, particularly in terms of examination by researchers, are dominated by parents who hold beliefs about the importance of literacy as written language, often seen as reading. Different kinds of literacy practices must be made available to all children to enable their successful learning at school. In addition, it should be recognised that school literacy practices may be very different than home literacy practices, and early experiences should not be either overvalued or devalued on children's entry to school. Rivalland (2000) drew attention to children in remote Aboriginal communities in Australia who were familiar with the contents of an advertising catalogue of a major toy manufacturer and who could also participate in oral storytelling and reading activities. There are many ways in which children can learn about literacy, including through watching television, playing board games and puzzles, and reading advertising material. There are also myriad opportunities for social interaction, for talking and taking photographs, as well as attending church, going to the local health centre and engaging in a hobby. Each of these activities, and more, contributes to literacy development. They need to translate that into (or bridge the gap between) school learning and literacy. Various home literacy practices make this transition easy; for other children, the types of activities they have been exposed to or engaged in at home are not as helpful for early learning at school. They have to learn the links between their home literacy practices and those expected at school.

Differences in family environments that can affect literacy include the health of the children; the geographical location in which they are growing up (i.e., country versus city); and socioeconomic status or parental income and household circumstances, such as living conditions, stability of accommodation and number of people in the household. Under these different circumstances, children come to school with different dispositions to and knowledge about reading and writing. They also have varying degrees of knowledge of and cultural views about schools and schooling. All of these must be considered when children start school. Children's home experiences in general and their home literacy experiences in particular are not always recognised by educators and teachers. These predispositions, however, affect early school literacy learning. Some children have made connections between, for example, early shared book experiences and reading; others have not had the experiences or made the connections. Some children can benefit from being taught; others will not do so immediately. They have to be socialised into school and the nature of learning at school.

Furthermore, children's backgrounds vary greatly. They may be bilingual, from disadvantaged homes, of minority ethnic or indigenous descent, from single-parent homes, from a remote community or farm, or from intact families. These are background factors which may increase or decrease the likelihood that a child will have been introduced to reading and writing and socialised into understanding the value of school. If literacy is generally valued by communities, cultures and societies (and all pointers suggest that it is), then research must inform practice about how children can best learn to read and write. Early school practices build on what children already know and this relies on teachers understanding what different children know. Teachers are often criticised for not considering differences between children's past and existing experiences and literacy skills. Differences in home life and experiences influence literacy learning. School practices include shared book reading (as is seen in many homes); language activities such as rhymes, songs and poems; and explicit teaching of the alphabet, phonemic awareness and early writing. School literacy learning also relies heavily on speaking, such as the question-and-answer routines discussed previously that are dependent on children knowing that they must listen to and understand the teacher. However, many of the early school literacy experiences are embedded in 'fun' activities, not too different from many of those experienced at home and – for the fortunate ones – in preschool.

Finally, some children's experience with spoken and written language can be limited and their literacy experiences varied. Spinillo and Pratt (2005) examined differential experiences with texts between Brazilian middle-class children who lived at home and attended school and street children with no education. They found that children who were living on the streets experienced as important a literacy environment as children who lived at home and attended school. Middle-class children produced and understood texts such as letters and stories, whereas street children, although illiterate, had greater familiarity with newspaper articles perhaps by having newspapers read to them or by viewing television news stories. These differences were noted in the children's production of the different texts and their metatextual awareness or their capacity to reflect on the structure and organisation of texts. Spinillo and Pratt concluded that children's generic literacy knowledge is mediated by the social practices, such as being read to by adults, around the text types that are experienced by children from different social backgrounds and is not just a product of participating in the educational system which street children will never do.

Conclusion

Parents and children in the work conducted by researchers examining early literacy, such as that discussed herein, have been predominantly educated, middle- to upper-class families, whose expectations about literacy would be high. These parents place a high value on language development, reading and writing as cultural tools that ultimately lead to educational success. Research examining families where literacy is highly valued can provide us with useful information about how children's early experiences with books and language can furnish them with a platform from which they can tackle formal schooling. This work needs to be extended to families and cultures in which early literacy is not as highly prized but is regarded as something that is taught in school. Even informal language activities can promote skills that assist in reading, and their value needs to be encouraged and supported in cultural groups other than those who often participate in research (see, e.g., a recent study by Raikes et al., 2006). Any literacy environment, however, must be supplemented with teaching the alphabet and phonological awareness, either at home or in school, because these are fundamental building blocks for literacy.

Cultural and social practices, particularly those of parents with regard to their children's literacy development, must also be seen relative to the children's own developing cognitive and linguistic abilities and how they also contribute to literacy (both reading and writing). Language, thought and literacy are inter-related systems of representation of knowledge. As representations, they can be argued to be culturally determined formal systems. How they are acquired, learned and integrated are questions that must be examined in sociocultural contexts. If education and literacy are the key to economic success in a nation, as the Organisation for Economic Co-operation and Development would have us believe, then it is important to continue to conduct research into how children learn to read and write, especially research that considers the impact of different sociocultural contexts on learning. In comparison with less-developed countries and with the industrialised times in the past, to be able to function in the twenty-first-century 'knowledge economies,' high levels of literacy are essential to adapt to and profit from technological advances. Without such a high value being placed on literacy and education, less educated, less technologically developed and more traditional cultures are disadvantaged. Educating parents to provide environments that support early literacy seems a key to social and economic success.

Exposure to books and other forms of print in the home-literacy environment provides a clear benefit to children in their later language and reading skills. The link of early book reading with later reading abilities has been shown to benefit spoken language as well as reading. A recent Australian review of the teaching of reading (Department of Education, Science and Training [DEST], 2005) recommended the following:

> *The Committee recommends that programs, guides and workshops be provided for parents and carers to support their children's literacy development. These should acknowledge and build on the language and literacy that children learn in their homes and communities.*

This recommendation is an endorsement of the research that claims that parents and the home environment can influence children's reading and literacy development, engagement and achievement. As well as providing early opportunities through book reading, parents are further encouraged to take an active role in '. . . discussing, monitoring and supporting their children's learning. . . .' (DEST, 2005, p. 40). Highly effective schools are characterised by such high levels of parental engagement irrespective of all other characteristics such as socioeconomic status and ethnic background. This is an affirmation of good literacy practices, identified through research.

References

Barratt-Pugh, C. (2000). The socio-cultural context of literacy learning. In C. Barratt-Pugh & M. Rohl (Eds.), *Literacy learning in the early years* (pp.1–26). Buckingham: Open University Press.

Bearison, D., & Dorval, B. (2002). *Collaborative cognition: Children negotiating ways of knowing.* Westport, CT: Ablex Publishing.

Bourdieu, P. (1977). *Outline of a theory of practice.* Cambridge: Cambridge University Press.

Bronfenbrenner, U. (1979). *The ecology of human development.* Cambridge, MA: Harvard University Press.

Bruner, J. S. (1983). *Child's talk: Learning to use language.* Oxford: Oxford University Press.

Bus, A. (1994). The role of social context in emergent literacy. In E. Assink (Ed.), *Literacy acquisition and social context* (pp. 9–24). London: Harvester Wheatsheaf.

Bus, A., van IJzendoorn, M. H., & Pellegrini, A. D. (1995). Joint book reading makes for success in learning to read: A meta-analysis on intergenerational transmission of literacy. *Review of Educational Research*, 65, 1–21.

Correa-Chávez, M., Rogoff, B., & Mejìa Arauz, R. (2005). Cultural patterns in attending to two events at once. *Child Development*, 76, 664–678.

deLoache, J., & deMendoza, O. (1987). Joint picturebook interactions of mothers and their 1-year-old children. *British Journal of Developmental Psychology*, 5, 111–123.

Department of Education, Science and Training (DEST) (2005). *Teaching reading.* Canberra: Australian Government.

Fidalgo, Z., & Pereira, F. (2005). Socio-cultural differences and the adjustment of mothers' speech to their children's cognitive and language comprehension skills. *Learning and Instruction*, 1, 1–21.

Garton, A. F. (2004). *Exploring cognitive development: The child as problem solver.* Oxford: Blackwell Publishing.

Garton, A. F., & Pratt, C. (1998). *Learning to be literate: The development of spoken and written language* (2nd Ed.). Oxford: Blackwell Publishing.

Garton, A. F., & Pratt, C. (2004). Reading stories. In P. E. Bryant & T. Nunes (Eds.), *Handbook of literacy* (pp. 323–350). Dordrecht: Kluwer.

Gauvain, M. (2001a). Cultural tools, social interaction and the development of thinking. *Human Development*, 44, 126–143.

Gauvain, M. (2001b). *The social context of cognitive development.* New York: Guildford Press.

Goody, E. (Ed.) (1978). *Questions and politeness: Strategies in social interaction.* Cambridge: Cambridge University Press.

Hatano, G., & Wertsch, J. V. (2001). Sociocultural approaches to cognitive development: The constituents of culture in the mind. *Human Development*, 44, 77–83.

Kearins, J. (1986). Visual spatial memory in Aboriginal and white Australian children. *Australian Journal of Psychology*, 38, 203–214.

Martini, M. (1995). Features of home environments associated with children's school success. *Early Child Development and Care*, 111, 49–68.

Mejìa-Arauz, R., Rogoff, B., & Paradise, R. (2005). Cultural variation in children's observation during a demonstration. *International Journal of Behavioural Development*, 29, 282–292.

Olson, D. R. (1994). *The world on paper.* Cambridge: Cambridge University Press.

Piaget, J. (1932). *The moral judgment of the child.* London: Routledge and Kegan Paul.

Raikes, H., Pan, B. A., Luze, G., Tamis-LeMonda, C. S., Brooks-Gunn, J., Constantine, J., et al. (2006). Mother-child bookreading in low-income families: Correlates and outcomes during the first three years of life. *Child Development*, 77, 924–953.

Rivalland, J. (2000). Linking literacy learning across different contexts. In C. Barratt-Pugh & M. Rohl (Eds.), *Literacy learning in the early years* (pp. 27–56). Buckingham: Open University Press.

Rogoff, B. (1990). *Apprenticeship in thinking: Cognitive development in social context.* New York: Oxford University Press.

Rogoff, B. (1998). Cognition as a collaborative process. In D. Kuhn & R. S. Siegler (Volume Eds.), W. Damon (Ed. in Chief), *Handbook of child psychology: Volume Two: Cognition, perception and language (5th ed.)* (pp. 679–744). New York: John Wiley and Sons.

Rogoff, B. (2003). *The cultural nature of human development*. New York: Oxford University Press.

Rogoff, B. (2006). Learning through observation and collaboration in sociocultural activities. Keynote address at the 19th ISSBD meeting, Melbourne.

Rogoff, B., Paradise, R., Mejìa Arauz, R., Correa-Chávez, M., & Angelillo, C. (2003). Firsthand learning through intent participation. *Annual Review of Psychology*, 54, 175–203.

Scribner, S., & Cole, M. (1981). *The psychology of literacy*. Cambridge, MA: Harvard University Press.

Sénéchal, M., & LeFevre, J. (2002). Parental involvement in the development of children's reading skill: A five-year longitudinal study. *Child Development*, 73, 445–460.

Sénéchal, M., LeFevre, J., Hudson, E., & Lawson, E. P. (1996). Knowledge of storybooks as a predictor of young children's vocabulary. *Journal of Educational Psychology*, 88, 520–536.

Serpell, R., Sonnenschein, S., Baker, L., & Ganapathy, H. (2002). Intimate culture of families in the early socialisation of literacy. *Journal of Family Psychology*, 16, 391–405.

Shweder, R. A., Goodnow, J. J., Hatano, G., Levine, R. A., Markus, H., & Miller, P. (1998). The cultural psychology of development: One mind, many modalities. In R. M. Lerner (Ed.) and W. Damon (Ed. in Chief), *Handbook of child psychology: Volume One: Theoretical models of human development (5th ed.)* (pp. 865–937). New York: John Wiley & Sons.

Spinillo, A. G., & Pratt, C. (2005). Socio-cultural differences in children's genre knowledge. In T. Kostouli (Ed.), *Writing in context(s): Textual practices and learning processes in sociocultural settings* (pp. 27–28). New York: Springer.

Tudge, J. R. H., Doucet, F., Odero, D., Sperb, T. M., Piccinini, C. A., & Lopes, R. S. (2006). A window into different cultural worlds: Young children's everyday activities in the United Sates, Brazil and Kenya. *Child Development*, 77, 1446–1469.

Tudge, J. R. H., Winterhoff, P. A., & Hogan, D. M. (1996). The cognitive consequences of collaborative problem solving with and without feedback. *Child Development*, 67, 2892–2909.

Vygotsky, L. (1962). *Thought and language*. Cambridge, MA: MIT Press.

Vygotsky, L. (1978). *Mind in society*. Cambridge, MA: Harvard University Press.

CHAPTER 28

Literacy and International Development

Education and Literacy as Basic Human Rights[1]

Joseph P. Farrell

Through a series of international conventions and declarations in the course of the twentieth century, a basic primary education, generally thought of as at least five to six years of traditional formal schooling, has come to be understood as one of the Universal Rights of the Child and, thus, as a basic human right. This 'movement' started, in a formal international sense, in 1924, when the League of Nations adopted the Geneva Resolution of the Rights of the Child. After many years of interim efforts, interrupted by World War II, this Resolution was followed, sixty-five years later, by the International Convention on the Rights of the Child, adopted in 1989 by the United Nations General Assembly, and thereafter ratified by 192 nations. As UNICEF's report on *The State of the World's Children 2006* noted:

> *As the most widely endorsed human rights treaty in history, the Convention . . . lays out in specific terms the legal duties of governments to children. Children's survival, development and protection are now no longer matters of charitable concern but of moral and legal obligation. Governments are held to account for their care of children by an international body, the Committee on the Rights of the Child, to which they have agreed to report regularly. (UNICEF, 2006, p. 1)*

In both of these international agreements, basic (primary) education was noted as one of those fundamental human rights.

This emphasis on education as a basic human right was reinforced at the 1990 World Conference on Education for All in Jomtien, Thailand. The Conference was attended by ministers of education (or their senior representatives) from almost every nation in the world; representatives of such international agencies as UNESCO, UNICEF, The World Bank, and the United Nations Development Program; most bilateral donor agencies; and many international non-governmental organizations (NGOs). These delegates unanimously declared that access to a full primary education (and its equivalent for unschooled adults) was a basic human right. A target date for universal access to free primary education was set at 2000, and elaborate international monitoring and reporting mechanisms were set in place. During the ensuing decade, it became clear that in many nations this target date was not attainable. At a follow-up meeting in 2000 in Dakar, Senegal, the goal was reaffirmed but the target date was set back to 2015. These international identifications of free primary education for all (EFA) were reconfirmed at the United Nations Millennium Summit in 2000, which resulted in a list of eight Millennium Development Goals (MDGs) which were reaffirmed at the United Nations General Assembly's Special Session on Children held in May 2002. The second of these eight MDGs was to "achieve universal primary education," meaning "ensure that all boys and girls complete a full course of primary education" (UNICEF, 2006, p. 2).

Many justifications have been advanced, from many different theoretical and ideological perspectives, for this call for universal access to primary education as a basic human right, ranging from matters of individual personal development and fulfillment to collective economic, social or political development. Underlying all of these justifications is a claim – sometimes implicit but usually explicit in the full texts of the declarations and conventions and the supporting documents – that whatever else may be accomplished in terms of curricular learning objectives by a 'full course of primary education,' it will develop graduates who are *literate* and *numerate*, at least to the level expected at the end of formal primary schooling. Thus, the international establishment of a full course of primary education (or its adult equivalent) as a basic and universal human right is also a call for literacy (and numeracy, but I do not have space here to explore the debates about whether or under what circumstances numeracy is different from or part of literacy; see Chrisomalis, Chapter 4, this volume) as a basic and universal human right.

This connection between *schooling* and *literacy* has long been well understood and assumed. It has been established for many years that the majority of people in our world who are literate (to whatever level) have become so through exposure to traditional formal schooling. In the other direction, because 'real' estimates of literacy rates for various nations and population groups are extremely difficult and expensive to establish through tests of one type or another, a large share of the international statistical series which list cross-national comparisons of literacy rates – for entire populations or subgroups thereof – are derived from estimates of the proportion of the relevant population who have completed a full course of primary education. This conflation of literacy with formal primary education is based on an assumption (or assertion), which is widely held by such international agencies as UNESCO and UNICEF, that it ordinarily requires at least five or six years of reasonable quality primary education for young people to attain a minimal level of literacy, sufficient to sustain them as well-functioning adult members of their society if they proceed no further in formal schooling, or to succeed in further levels of schooling if such are available to them.

Unfortunately, this long and long-standing chain of international declarations and the assumptions undergirding them have proven to be unattainable for hundreds of millions of young people and not empirically sustainable. In the next section, I briefly outline the problem involved herein. In the subsequent section, I analyze and compare some promising possibilities based on an ongoing international analysis of more than two hundred cases, mostly from developing nations, where implementation of a radically alternative form of primary schooling has dramatically increased the enrolment, retention in school, and, most important, levels of learning, especially among highly marginalized young people in very poor places in our world.

The Problem

There are several aspects of 'the problem' to consider here. The first is that even after the major national and international efforts over the span of several decades, there remain millions of young people who have no access whatsoever to school, and millions more who begin to attend primary school and drop out after one or two years, and thus have effectively no chance of acquiring even a basic level of literacy. Consider, for example, the three nations of the Indian Subcontinent, whose combined population is about that of China's. Their net primary enrolment ratios (i.e., percentage of age-eligible children enrolled in school) are India, 77 percent; Bangladesh, 79 percent; and Pakistan, 56 percent. The enrolment ratios are generally even lower in much of sub-Saharan Africa and parts of the Middle East. Moreover, during the decade of the 1980s, primary enrolment ratios actually declined in forty-five developing nations, leading many observers to refer to that period as a "disastrous decade for education" from which many nations have not yet recovered (Farrell, 2007a, p. 157). A recent UNESCO document noted the not-surprising causes for lack of access to primary education. "Where are the missing children? Most live in remote rural areas or in urban slums. Most are girls. Most belong to population groups outside the mainstream of society: they pass their days in overcrowded refugee camps, displaced by man-made or natural disasters, or wander with their herds. Others are marginalized by language, life-style or culture" (UNICEF, 2001, p. 34). After the Jomtien Education for All Conference, some progress was made. In the decade following that 1990 conference, the absolute number of children with no access to school declined slightly, from 123 million to 111 million, and many very populous nations, such as China, Indonesia and Brazil, achieved near-universal enrolment. The follow-up conference in Dakar referred to these as "tangible but modest gains" (Farrell, 2007a, p. 158). It remains the case, however, that well over 100 million children have never enrolled in school, as well as hundreds of millions more youth and adults, and no international agency seems to have a serious idea about how to change that fact.

The second part of the problem is that among those who do manage to enrol in primary education, many do not finish the full course. Among middle-income developing nations, the noncompletion rates range around 20 percent. Among very poor nations, they range up to 50 percent – in some cases even higher (Farrell, 2007a). Thus, the total numbers of children, youth and adults in the world who have never entered formal school, or left too early to achieve even a minimal level of basic literacy, is well over the hundreds of millions estimate noted previously.

A third part of the problem is that even among those young people who do manage one way or another to enrol and stay the full course, many do not become 'literate.' Hartwell noted in 2005 that in many low-income nations, more than one third of primary-school graduates have very limited reading skills (Hartwell, 2005, p. 3). He also noted that in Ghana, where English is the language of instruction, the results of a Criterion Referenced Test administered annually to a 10 percent sample of last-year primary students show that only 8.7 percent achieve the minimal competence level in English (Hartwell, 2005, p. 12). In 2006, Abadzi reported the following levels of minimum mastery of literacy among last-year primary students based on international or national tests: Malawi, 7 percent; Mauritius, 52 percent; Namibia, 19 percent; Tanzania, 18 percent; Colombia, 27 percent; Morocco, 59 percent; Burkina Faso, 21 percent; Cameroon, 33 percent; Cote d'Ivoire, 38 percent; Papua New Guinea, 21 percent; Madagascar, 20 percent; Senegal, 25 percent; Togo, 40 percent; Uruguay, 66 percent; and Yemen, 10 percent (Abadzi, 2006, p. 6). Even in Latin America, generally considered a region with relatively high educational development within the developing world (i.e., primary enrolment ratios generally range above 90 percent), Schiefelbein reported that among the 63 percent of each cohort of entering students who actually complete the primary cycle, "no more than half of those who completed their primary education understand a short text published on the front page of a ['popular'] newspaper (Schiefelbein, 2006, p. 1).

Thus, in the developing world, there are more than 100 million children who never enter primary school. Of those who do enter, hundreds of millions do not complete the full cycle. Of those who do complete the full cycle, hundreds of millions do not attain even a minimal level of literacy. Thus, the internationally acclaimed goal of education and literacy as a basic human right is far from being attained. What is the problem here? Most of the diagnoses and attendant policy and practice prescriptions are essentially 'technicist' in nature. Many claim, for example, that the problem is primarily one of resources and investment, that there are not enough schools or they are not in the appropriate locations, that there are not enough teachers and/or teachers are not well prepared, or that there is a lack of basic learning materials. The attendant solution is more money, better spent. Where exactly this extra money is to come from, given that many of the nations with the most serious learning problems are desperately poor, is not clear, except by borrowing externally, which will only land them once again in the debt trap in which they have already been engulfed. However, I submit that even if the problem of resource scarcity and/or misallocation were somehow to be magically solved, this would not address a far more fundamental problem.

As educators and scholars of education, we are observers of and parties to a most peculiar pattern. In the past century or more, we have come to learn much about how human beings, young and old, actually learn best. Yet, almost none of this new knowledge has penetrated the standard practices of formal schools, which generally carry on the rituals and traditions of the conceptions of how learning occurs and what is most worth knowing. These rituals and traditions were developed more than a century ago, first in Western Europe and then spread around the world through a combination of colonial imposition and cultural borrowing. Although I have been making this point for many years, I am certainly neither the first to observe it nor the latest (see Farrell, 1989, 2007a, and other authors cited therein; Hayhoe & Mundy, 2008). In 1995, two major books were published which chronicled and tried to understand a century of failed attempts at educational reform in the United States (Ravitsch & Vinovskis, 1995; Tyack & Cuban, 1995; for an essay review of both, see Farrell, 2000). The stories told there of dysfunctional formal schooling and of failed reform initiatives were noted in another review article that I published in 1997, which indicated that the patterns found in the United States are generalizable to most of the world:

> *One general lesson is that planning educational change is a far more difficult and risk-prone venture than had been imagined in the 1950s and 1960s. There are many more examples of failure, or of minimal success, than of relatively complete success. Much more is known about what does not work, or does not usually work, than about what does work. . . . Moreover, when planned educational reform attempts have been successful, the process has usually taken a long time, frequently far longer than originally anticipated. In recent decades there have been a few examples where an unusual combination of favorable conditions and politically skilled planners has permitted a great deal of educational change in a relatively brief period, but these have been rare and idiosyncratic. (Farrell, 1997, p. 298)*

During the latter years of the twentieth century and the early years of the current millennium, several other major state-of-the-art papers came to roughly the same conclusion (see, e.g., Caillods, 1989; Davies, 1996; Fagerlind & Sjosted, 1990; Polyzoi, Fullan, & Anchan, 2003). A review of educational reform efforts in Africa, published in 2002, notes that the experience has

> *. . . demonstrated that there are serious difficulties inherent in implementing the comprehensive, multifaceted educational policy reforms being proposed by the international community. . . . Even if the time, funds, and other resources had been adequate [which they never were] however, it is unlikely the reforms would have been implemented as planned. (Moulton, Mundy, Welmond, & Williams, 2002, pp. 2, 210)*

- one hundred to several hundred children/youth assembled (often compulsorily for at least a period) in a building called a school
- from approximately the age of 6 or 7 up to somewhere between 11 to 16
- for 3 to 6 hours per day, where
- they are divided into groups of 20 to 60
- to work with a single adult, a 'certified' teacher, in a single room
- for (especially at the 'upper grades') discrete periods of 40 to 60 minutes, each devoted to a separate 'subject'
- to be 'studied and learned' by a group of young people of roughly the same age
- with supporting learning materials (e.g., books, chalkboards, notebooks, workbooks and worksheets, increasingly computers, and in 'technical' areas, such things as laboratories, workbenches, and so forth), all of which is organized by
- a standard curriculum set by an authority level much beyond the individual school, normally the central or provincial/state government, which all are expected to 'cover' in an 'age-graded' fashion
- adults, assumed to be more knowledgeable, 'teach' and students 'receive' instruction from them
- in a broader system in which the students are expected to 'repeat back' to the adults what they have been taught if they are to progress any higher
- teachers and/or (a) central exam system(s) evaluate students' ability to repeat back to them what the students have been taught and provide formal recognized certificates for 'passing' particular 'grades' or 'levels'
- most or all of the financial support comes from national or regional governments, or other kinds of authority levels (e.g., religion-related schools) well above the local community level

Figure 28.1. The traditional forms of formal schooling.

A 1997 review of educational reform efforts in Latin America observed: "...there is a high degree of failure of reform plans. We don't know what factors favor the implementation of reform plans, nor what conditions or institutional capacity are needed for the reform plans to affect wide sectors of society" (Alvarez & Ruiz-Casares, 1997, p. 7). In short, these many reviews of the experience – whether focussing on one or a few wealthy nations or regional groupings of developing nations – all come to roughly the same conclusion. Proposals for educational change or reform are seldom enacted. If enacted (i.e., via legislation, regulation or experimental program), they are seldom implemented well and widely. If implemented, they tend after a few years to fade away as the 'system' slowly moves back to its normal state. If implemented well and widely and sustainably, there is little evidence of long-term and wide-scale impact on the primary mission of the schooling enterprise – that is, enabling and enhancing the learning and capacity to learn of the young people who are in its charge.

What we have come to understand about human learning has almost nothing to do with how schooling generally continues to be conducted. What I have come to call the "forms of formal schooling" (Farrell, 2002, p. 247), which were set in the mid to late nineteenth century, reflected the misconceptions about human learning of the intellectual and political-economic elites of that very different time and place. However, now that we have them and have set them firmly in place, we do not seem to know how to change them, at least on any large scale. Figure 28.1 outlines those forms of formal schooling:

When looked at as a set, this list of characteristics well illustrates the degree to which they are taken for granted. A striking feature of almost all of the reform proposals, whether for a system as a whole or school-by-school (as in the 'school improvement' movement), is that they rarely (if ever) question the basic model, the *forms* of formal schooling. Typically, they aim to alter one or a few bits of it, while taking the rest for granted, unquestioned.

Table 28.1. What Cognitive Science Says versus What Schools Do

What Cognitive Science Says	*What Schools Do*
What people learn depends on what they already know	What they learn depends on what the school mandates
People learn because they are intrinsically interested or because they love learning	They pursue knowledge because they need the credit
Learning is inspired by the search for meaning and growth and understanding	What they learn depends on what books, chapters and pages they are responsible for
The growth of the mind is spontaneous and continuous	It is a matter of obligation and duty

(Adapted from Olson, 2003, p. ix)

The continued and near-universal existence of these forms of formal schooling and their seeming intractability to efforts at change have been a source of great frustration to many scholars of learning who have consistently seen their hard-won findings knocking fruitlessly on the schoolhouse door, to well-intentioned reformers who see their efforts regularly fail, and to many individual citizens seeking a better and more productive form of organized learning for their children.

Among the first group, Olson published the following 'cry of desperation' in a recent work:

> *For some time I have been struck by the fact that whereas the psychological understanding of children's learning and development has made great strides . . . the impact on schooling as an institutional practice has been modest if not negligible. With most of my colleagues I had assumed that if only we knew more about how the mind works, how the brain develops, how interests form, how people differ, and, most centrally, how people learn, educational practice would take a great leap forward. But while this knowledge has grown, schools have remained remarkably unaffected. (Olson, 2003, p. ix)*

He then outlines a series of key distinctions between what cognitive science now knows and what schools do. These distinctions are summarized in Table 28.1.

A leading spokesman for the well-intentioned reformers foreshadowed Olson's comments in 2001. In a special issue of *Harpers Magazine* entitled "New Hope for American Education," Sizer noted the following (his comments refer to the United States, but the point is near-universal):

> *You are assuming that Americans make educational policy rationally. But I think history will show that the system follows a kind of* mindless *thread. In the sixties, Charles Silverman wandered around and visited all of these schools and listened to all these state superintendents and concluded that the whole thing was mindless, that we do what we do because we've always done it. The basic structure and ideas behind the high school [for example] haven't changed in a fundamental way since Charles Eliot and the Committee of Ten designed it in the 1890s. We know more about human learning. We understand that the culture and the economy have changed. But we are so stuck in what has become the conventional way of schooling that we don't think twice about it. So we still think that the mainline subjects that Charles Eliot and his colleagues established in 1893 are the core of the school. We still assume that one can test children's mastery of those subjects in a way which is rigorous and useful. We still persist in thinking that school is a school is a school. It runs for 180 days. You take English, math, social studies science, in forty-seven-minute periods, taught by teachers who have more than a hundred students, sometimes two hundred. The students march forward on the basis of their birthdays, in things called*

"grades" – like eggs – and we tell ourselves that we can ascertain whether these kids have profound intellectual competence. The system is mindless. (Sizer, 2001, p. 56)

These observations well sum up the dilemma we face around the world. What we now know about how humans learn has little or nothing to do with how we try to enable young people to learn in places called 'school,' and we seem generally unable to change those places in any fundamental way. Even with enormous efforts in some nations, what we mostly get is small changes, dearly bought, with small effects (if any) in terms of the actual learning of young people, especially those who arrive at the school door most disadvantaged.

Many explanations have been advanced for this situation but, whatever the explanation, the phenomenon remains: whatever we learn about learning, schooling systems of the traditional sort seem generally unable to produce significant change. This is the core of the problem, what I have elsewhere called 'the bad news' (Farrell, 2007a).

The Quiet Revolution in Schooling: The Good News

Although schooling as we generally know it appears relatively impervious to sustained and spreading change, except in very special circumstances (e.g., some parts of post-communist Central Europe) (Kochan, 2005; Polyzoi et al., 2003), the good news is that there is a quiet revolution in schooling developing in a large number of nations. Typically, these new programs develop initially on the margins of the standard system, among groups where traditional schooling has been unable to penetrate, or has manifestly failed. In some cases that have been in place for a few decades, there are signs of diffusion of the new patterns into the mainstream schools. This section draws on some of the results of a long-term international research study of such programs, drawing on work by scholars and graduate students, international agency officials, and local program developers, of which I am, in a loose sense, a co-coordinator. Thus far, we are working with a database of well over two hundred cases, some new and still rather small (i.e., perhaps fifty to a hundred schools), which are essentially still at a pilot project stage, and others, which have survived and thrived for several decades and have grown to systems of tens of thousands of schools. Following is a representative list of some of these many programs, taken from our large and growing dataset.

Escuela Nueva (New School) in Colombia. This is the oldest and perhaps internationally best known of these programs. It started on a very small scale in the late 1970s and was carefully grown and nurtured with constant experimentation and learning from experience until it had spread to about eight thousand schools in the mid-1980s. It was then declared by the government as the 'standard model' for rural schooling and has now spread to most rural schools there, with varying degrees of faithful implementation in close to thirty thousand schools, and is currently spreading slowly into urban schools as well. It has been adapted for adoption in at least ten other Latin American nations, and core features of the model have been used to build new educational programs in many parts of Africa, the Middle East and Asia. It is also noteworthy that this model, in one region of Colombia, has spread upward to the post-primary level of formal schooling. This allows us to consider how this successful primary-level alternative model may adapt as youngsters move to more senior levels of schooling (Arboleda, 1994; Colbert & Arboleda, 1990; McEwan, 1998; Pitt, 2002, 2004; Psacharopolous, Rojas, & Velez, 1993; Schiefelbein, 1991; Siabato, 1997).

The Non-formal Primary Education Program of the Bangladesh Rural Advancement Committee (BRAC). This program is another of the 'grandparents' here. It started in the mid-1980s, has grown to involve approximately thirty-five thousand rural schools in that nation, and is slowly moving into urban schools and ethnic-minority regions of the nation, partly through a diffusion

Table 28.2. The Spread of Alternative Schooling Programs from 1992 to 1998

Nueva Escuela Unitaria	**Guatemala**	
Start	1992	18 schools
Growth	1998	1,300 schools; 140,000 students (Kraft, 1998)
Multi-Grade Program	**Guinea**	
Start	1991	18 schools
Growth	1998	1,300 schools; 40,000 students (Bah-Layla, 1998)
Multi-Grade and Community Schools Programs	**Zambia**	
Start	1985	8 schools
Growth	1998	600 schools; 40,000 students (Kelly, 1998)
Concurrent Pedagogy Program	**Mali**	
Start	1988	10 schools
Growth	1998	700 schools; 40,000 students (Republique du Mali, 1998)
MECE Rural and P900 Programs	**Chile**	
Start	1990	1,000 schools
Growth	2000	3,900 schools; 230,000 students (Garcia-Huidobro, 2000)

program with other local NGOs. It is also being adapted/adopted in nations such as Ethiopia, Sudan, Somalia and Afghanistan (Ahmed, 1993; Haiplik, 2004; Sarker, 1994; Scott, 1996; Sweetser, 1999).

The Community Schools Program of UNICEF–Egypt. This program started in the early 1990s, drawing upon the experience of the two programs discussed previously, and adapted to the particular local situation in small hamlets in Upper Egypt, where girls' access to schooling was problematic, and the boys who attended school at all had low levels of learning. It has now grown to a core system of close to three hundred schools with carefully planned diffusion, in conjunction with the Ministry of Education, of its nonformal pedagogy to roughly eight thousand government-managed one-classroom schools and then to the broader system of mainstream schools. Its core pedagogical model is being adapted to many other Islamic nations of the Middle East (Farrell, 2004; Farrell & Connelly, 1998; Hartwell, 1995; Zaalouk, 1995, 2004).

School for Life in Ghana. This program was started on a small scale in 1996 in the northern region of Ghana and by 2004 had grown to 760 schools. It is managed jointly by the Dagbon Traditional Council and the Ghana Education Service, with some support by the Danish International Development Agency (Danida). It aims at youth aged eight to fifteen in rural villages with no or limited access to regular primary education. In a nine-month program, it provides literacy in the mother tongue, numeracy, and general knowledge equivalent to the first three grades of the standard primary schools. Plans are underway for a major spread of its pedagogical model to mainstream schools (DeStefano, Hartwell, & Benbow, 2004; Hartwell, 2005).

Other examples are listed in Table 28.2 and illustrate the geocultural spread of these alternative programs (the numbers of schools and students are approximate).

As mentioned previously, these are just a few of the representative and best-documented examples of such programs – some still relatively small in scale, others large and growing steadily. They are not identical; each is adapted to the local conditions and culture (as it should be) as well as the history of educational thought and practice in the nation and culture in

- child-centred rather than teacher-driven pedagogy
- active rather than passive learning
- multi-graded classrooms with continuous progress learning
- combinations of fully trained teachers, partially trained teachers and community resources – parents and other community members – are heavily involved in the learning of the children and the management of the school
- peer-tutoring: older and/or faster-learning children assist and 'teach' younger and/or slower-learning children
- carefully developed self-guided learning materials which children, alone or in small groups, can work through themselves, at their own pace, with help from other students and the teacher(s) as necessary; the children are responsible for their own learning.
- teacher- and student-developed learning materials
- active student involvement in the governance and management of the school
- use of radio, correspondence lesson materials, in some cases television, in a few cases computers
- ongoing, regular and intensive in-service training and peer-mentoring for teachers
- ongoing monitoring/evaluation/feedback systems allowing the 'system' to learn from its own experience, with regular modification of the methodology
- free flows of children and adults between the schools and the community
- community involvement includes attention to the nutrition and health needs of young children long before they reach school age
- locally adapted changes in the school day or school year
- the focus is much less on 'teaching' and much more on 'learning'

Figure 28.2. The emergent model: Common features of the alternative school programs.

which it operates. However, there are some conclusions which now seem reasonably well established.

In Figure 28.2, what seem to be the most common characteristics of these alternative programs are listed. It is obvious that this is a model or style of 'schooling' that is very different from the forms of formal schooling outlined in Figure 28.1.

In the comparative-analysis section which follows, I explore some of these differences in more detail. It should be mentioned that although all of these alternative programs share most of these characteristics, not all programs share all of them. In comparing Figures 28.1 and 28.2, it should also be noted that they have different kinds of truth-value. I assert that Figure 28.1 is a reasonably accurate representation of most of the schools in most of the world. There are, of course, minor variations on the theme (e.g., in some parts of Asia, students regularly stay with the same teacher throughout their primary schooling) (Hayhoe, 2008), but this represents more or less what happens to most youngsters in school in most places most of the time. Figure 28.2 is closer to a Weberian scheme of the 'ideal type.' It is an intellectual construct to capture what we now understand about these alternative programs; however, there is much more variation and much more we need to know than can be seen in Figure 28.2.

Let us turn to a detailed comparison of the four 'core' cases listed previously: the Escuela Nueva in Colombia (which is actually two cases: Escuela Nueva Primary and Escuela Nueva Secondary); the BRAC Non-formal Primary Education Program in Bangladesh; the UNICEF Community Schools Program in Egypt; and the School for Life Program in Ghana. These cases were chosen for this comparative exercise for several reasons: they are exceptionally well documented and evaluated, including both formal outsider evaluations and insider insights; they are exemplars of different approaches to alternative pedagogy, with a common core of understanding, in different cultural locations; three of the cases have been widely adapted in other cultural locations; and they have all had detailed case studies done for the EQUIP2 program of the Academy for Educational Development, funded by USAID. This includes not only the facts of the case but also history, management and planning systems, curriculum, and costs and cost–benefit analyses conducted by scholars who know the programs intimately and thus could also provide detailed pedagogical day-in-the-life-of-the-school accounts. Consider first the most fundamental questions: How do we understand *success*? What are the measurable and measured outcomes of these programs, particularly in terms of achieving literacy, compared to traditional schooling? Proceed then to core questions of pedagogy: What do the teachers and learners actually *do* in these programs to accomplish what they are achieving?

The Results: What Constitutes Success and How Do We Know?

There would be little point in comparing and analyzing these programs – and the broader set which they represent – unless they can demonstrate that they are producing good learning results, particularly in the core areas of literacy and numeracy, and not just for a few young people who manage to 'survive' and complete the schooling process but rather for most if not all of the young people involved. Thus, the issue involves not only measured academic achievement but also cohort survival and completion rates. This is obviously a complex and difficult issue. All of these programs are targeted at young people who are severely marginalized and who usually are not reached by or quickly fail at traditional schooling: those who are the hardest to reach and hardest to teach, at least in the standard-issue fashion. In all of our cases, the youngsters who pass through these alternative programs do at least as well as and typically much better than those who have gone through the traditional forms of formal schooling. Given the circumstances from which these young people come, this can be considered a major triumph, truly succeeding against the odds. In economic terms, this is a *value added* accomplishment of high degree.

Escuela Nueva has been formally evaluated many times by both national and international agencies. These studies have consistently found that Escuela Nueva students score higher than students in traditional schools (who ordinarily come from much higher socioeconomic groups) in standardized tests of Spanish language and mathematics, and they have markedly lower repetition and dropout rates. About 90 percent of these primary graduates continue on to the secondary level and do well there. They also have higher levels of self-esteem and more developed civic values. In a 1998 UNESCO study of academic achievement in eleven Latin American nations, Colombia was the only location where rural students outperformed urban students in literacy and numeracy achievement. This remarkable result was attributed to Escuela Nueva (Pitt, 2004, pp. 22–23). This 'discrepancy' was widely reported in the Colombian media and has led to considerable political pressure from middle-class parents to expand the program into urban areas, which is now underway with careful experimentation (Vicky Colbert, personal communication, March 2006).

With reference to the BRAC NFPE program, Haiplik (2004, pp. 12–13) observed that students in those schools perform academically, especially in literacy and numeracy, at a much higher level than students in traditional schools, who again are typically from families of much higher socioeconomic status. The completion rate is about 95 percent, markedly higher than in traditional schools, and more than 90 percent of those students go on to secondary schooling and do well there. By 2002, 2.4 million children had graduated from the BRAC schools, two thirds of whom were girls. It is noteworthy that the BRAC schools 'cover' the core elements of the standard five-year primary curriculum in four years. These are quite astonishing accomplishments in one of the poorest nations in the world.

The Egyptian Community Schools Program has also been regularly evaluated by both national and international agencies. Its students also take standard government achievement tests in Grades 3 and 5 (end-primary). Dropout rates are extremely low; of those who enrol, between 95 and 99 percent complete the program. On Grade 5 achievement tests, focussed on literacy in Arabic and numeracy, 95 percent pass compared to 73 percent in traditional government schools. Among its graduates, 92 percent continue on to junior secondary schooling, of which 96 percent successfully complete that cycle. About 70 percent of these successful students are girls. Observational evidence from international and national studies also consistently shows that the young people exhibit high levels of self-esteem and confidence, have enthusiasm for learning, are well mannered and collaborative among themselves and with adults, and act as conduits of knowledge to their families and wider communities regarding such matters as health, sanitation, child-care and the environment (Farrell, 2004, pp. 16–18; Zaalouk, 2004, pp. 104, 109–110, 130).

Regarding School for Life, in 2003 the Ghana Education Service administered tests of mother-tongue literacy, numeracy and general knowledge to students about to complete the program that year. Just over 80 percent achieved the minimal standards of success for Grade 3 students in literacy and numeracy, and more than 50 percent had reached the government-defined 'mastery' level for that grade level. A subsequent tracer study of the program's graduates indicated that approximately two thirds continue on to the Grade 4 level in standard primary schools and do very well there, adapting quickly and successfully to instruction in English, which is the standard language of instruction in Ghana. These results are in marked and vastly superior contrast to results in the standard primary schools in that nation, where about two thirds of those who enter complete Grade 6; of those in Grade 6, only about 10 percent have achieved the minimum level of reading competence in English (Hartwell, 2005; Ash Hartwell, personal communication, September, 2006). These quite remarkable results reinforce what cognitive science and second-language-learning experts have long claimed: children need to become literate first in their home language and can then more easily transfer their basic literacy skills to another language of instruction (Abadzi, 2006).

In summary, in terms of results in all of these cases, as in most of the other cases studied (although the data are firmer in some cases than in others), extremely poor children come to school, stay in school, finish the primary cycle, become literate and numerate and master all of the other general knowledge of the primary curriculum, develop self-confidence and self-esteem, and in large proportions continue on to the next level of formal schooling. All of this is at much superior levels, on average, than their compatriots in standard schools who are usually from more advantaged social backgrounds.

The core question then becomes: How do they do this? There are many ways to address this question. Here, I concentrate on the pedagogy: What actually goes on in these schools?; and, more briefly, on teachers: Who are they and how do they quickly learn, as they generally do, to 'teach' in a radically different pedagogical mode?

Pedagogy

A sense of the actual pedagogy used in these programs can be obtained by reviewing Figure 28.2. All of these programs have moved in one way or another away from the traditional age-graded 'egg crate' pedagogical model. This both encourages and permits continuous progress learning (i.e., children advance individually or in small groups at their own pace, and at different paces in different learning areas; e.g., a child may at any given age and stage be really good at reading but not so skilled at math) and peer-tutoring (i.e., older and/or more advanced children assisting younger and/or less advanced learners). Three of these cases are fully multigraded (i.e., Escuela Nueva Primary, Egyptian Community Schools, and School for Life). The BRAC program is age-graded in a sense because the children in any given school go together through Grade 1, Grade 2, and so on., However, these grades are not set by the calendar but rather by the judgment of the facilitators regarding when students are ready to move to the next stage in a learning area. Thus, a given class may be working at the Grade 3 level in reading, Grade 2 level in math, and Grade 4 level in science at any given time, with the usual accommodations of individual variations that occur in any classroom. However, the class group is composed of children of different ages, and they move through the primary curriculum with the same teacher(s) from start to finish (a pattern which is common in many Asian school systems) (Hayhoe, 2008), which allows many opportunities for a form of continuous-progress learning and peer tutoring. It is thus a locally adapted means of accomplishing the same core pedagogical objectives. Escuela Nueva Secondary is formally age-graded, and classes are divided by subject matter reflecting the subject-content orientation and testing routines of standard secondary schooling. However, they still manage to maintain much multi-grade and multi-age work and peer tutoring as part of the pedagogy. Again, we see a locally adapted way of addressing the same core pedagogical changes.

Within this model, young people typically spend a large proportion of the school-day working individually or in small groups, in learning 'centres' or 'corners,' using learning materials which are specially designed for such self-guided learning. Standard textbooks also are used often but only in conjunction with such specially designed materials. It is not surprising that standard texts, which are designed for age-graded classes, do not work well as a sole learning resource for a multi-grade, multi-age school. When individual learners or small learning groups encounter a problem, they first ask older or more advanced students for assistance. If that does not 'solve' the problem, they ask the teacher/facilitator for help. Thus, the adults in the classroom spend much of their time moving about, checking the progress of various learning groups, solving problems and asking/answering questions, and recording the progress and obstacles of various individuals and learning groups for planning future work (e.g., from my own observation notes: "Jose and his group need special work in two-column multiplication"; "Tasneem is having real difficulty with verbs in the future tense, but she has just written a wonderful story that she should share with the class, maybe as a puppet play with her group"; or "Ali and Ahmed seem to be having real difficulty with the science-corner material on the human body, and are avoiding it. Most of the children love this material. Are they embarrassed by it, or what? Must ask Mr. G. [her supervisor] for suggestions").

This does not mean that the teachers do not teach. Rather, they teach differently. They work mostly with individuals or small groups (although there is almost always some whole-class activity), responding to learning needs as they arise. They also concentrate effort on teaching each new group of children how to read, using a variety of teaching approaches that would be familiar to most early-primary teachers in the world, until the new students have reached a level of decoding and comprehension of written text which permits them to work with self-guided material. They can concentrate their efforts on such essential learning challenges as they arise precisely because they can depend on the fact that most of the young people most of the time are engaged in their own self-guided learning. Such classrooms are busy places, with much movement and activity, and are generally rather noisy; however, that is not the disruptive noise of children acting up or acting out but rather the productive noise of young people working together on their own learning.

The Teachers: Who They Are and How They Learn

Within our overall dataset, there are two different patterns of teacher selection. In most of the programs, the teachers are not formally 'certified' according to the standard system of teacher preparation, whether by a university faculty of education or a 'normal school.' Rather, they are young people, mostly women, who have a modest degree of formal schooling (usually Grade 10 or equivalent), which means that they are ordinarily among the most formally educated members of their community area. They are locally known individuals, selected by a local school committee, and trained in the local area to teach in the locality. They are very much *of* the local community and known to that community. They are often called 'facilitators' rather than teachers to avoid potential problems with national or regional teacher organizations. The Egyptian, Bangladeshi and Ghanaian programs exemplify this pattern. The two Colombian programs represent the other common pattern in which the teachers are university-educated and certified as are all teachers in the nation, and they regularly move from place to place under the standard rules of the administrative systems which govern teacher career mobility.

What is striking, however, is that whichever model of teacher selection used, in all of these cases the adults learn very quickly how to work in a radically alternative form of pedagogy with excellent learning results for their students. Generally, the pre-service teacher-development activities for working in the new mode are brief (a few weeks at most) but intensive. This is followed by several years of intensive in-service teacher-to-teacher mentoring programs and regular supervisory support.

It is important to mention just how different this approach to teacher development and learning is from that typically found in North America and other 'developed' regions. Here, we generally 'front-end load' the process, devoting most of our teacher-development resources and energy to the pre-service period. Once the new teachers are trained and hired and in their new classrooms, they are essentially abandoned to their own devices. Opportunities for collaboration with and learning from other teachers are scarce, and ongoing professional learning experiences are rare, sporadic, and most commonly devised by authority levels far from the individual classrooms. (There are exceptions in the rich world, especially Japan and France, but the general pattern holds.) One recent article maintained that this pattern of "on their own" may account for the fact that in North America, overall about 50 percent of any new cohort of teachers abandons the profession in the first five years (Kardos & Johnson, 2007).

Conclusion

In summary, literacy, as well as numeracy, and the basic primary education assumed to provide them, have become enshrined in international declarations and covenants as basic universal human rights. However, in reality, in much of the developing world, that right is far from being attained and many are claiming that it is, in fact, unattainable – at least in any near term, except with massive infusions of resources which cannot be found. Hundreds of millions of young people have no access at all to primary schooling, or they start but never finish, or they finish but do not attain literacy. To a degree, the problem is a question of lack of resources or resources poorly used, but the argument here is that the problem is much more fundamental: the traditional model of education – which is now well-nigh universal in the world and what is called the *forms of formal schooling* – does not fit with what we now understand about how humans learn, and it inherently serves poorly the learning needs of vast numbers of youngsters, particularly those most marginalized by circumstances of birth. We generally seem to be unable to change it on any large scale.

In the midst of that rather gloomy scenario, the alternative programs considered in the latter part of this chapter offer at least a modest ray of hope. By following a radically alternative form of pedagogy, they are achieving remarkable learning results, even among some of the poorest children in the world. The achieved literacy levels can only be considered spectacular, compared to traditional schools generally – and the learning rates and levels among the adults who work with the children – the teachers/facilitators – are also astonishing. So these are very hopeful indications but, as noted previously, it is also the early days in this long-term international research program. There is still much that we do not understand or on which we have only a rather weak and tentative grip. I conclude with a quick review of some of the major questions still pending.

The *pedagogical* question: How exactly do these students learn as well as they do? The answer is far from clear. We have good descriptions of the day-to-day learning routines in many of these programs, and the learning results, as discussed previously. However, *why* they work as well as they do remains a mystery. All of us involved in this long multinational venture at understanding how they work have our own hunches (it would be far too early to label them elegantly as 'hypotheses'). It is worth noting that none of the pedagogical ideas embedded in these programs are particularly new; they have been around in the literatures of pedagogical theory, curriculum theory, learning theory, and philosophy of education for a long time – in many cases for well over a century. As discussed previously, the problem has been that we have never figured out how to implement these ideas in standard schools, on a large scale. My own hunch is that these radically alternative programs demonstrate, among other things, that Maria Montessori and Robert Baden-Powell were right all along. (He was the founder of the Scouting movement, which now enrols approximately 40 million young people in any given year in most nations of the world. He was an ardent disciple of Montessori, and she was an admirer of his work with older youth [Jeal, 1989]). However, there is much we still need to learn.

The *teacher learning* question: How do these adults learn so quickly and so successfully a radically alternative form of pedagogy? Again, we have good descriptive accounts, and the results in terms of student learning are clear. An early clue is that these teacher-development systems seem to reflect rather well what adult educators have been saying for a long time about what they call *andragogy* (see the classic works of Kidd, 1973, and Knowles, 1984). Yet, again, this is long-standing knowledge, which we have not generally figured out how to implement within the forms of formal schooling. Most teacher-education programs in the world deal with their students not as adult learners, which they are, but rather essentially as students in secondary school. However, *how* and *why* this happens in these alternative programs remain a mystery.

The third major puzzle is the *planning and implementation* question, or perhaps better stated, the *institutionalization* question. This is perhaps the most fundamental question of all because if the developers and managers of these radically alternative programs had not been able to solve this puzzle, the other two questions would have no relevance. From the standard literature on educational change, as noted previously, this is not supposed (in both senses of the term) to happen, at least not usually. In all of these cases, people have managed within or alongside the bureaucratic systems, which have long enshrined the forms of formal schooling, to design and implement some form of the radically alternative model shown in Figure 28.2. *How* have they done this? Here, too, the answer is far from clear. There are three general patterns of system organization and management within our dataset and in the several cases considered in detail herein. Some programs develop and thrive within the standard Ministry of Education framework; Escuela Nueva in Colombia is an example. As discussed previously, this model has now been adopted by the Ministry as the 'standard' for all rural schools in that nation, and it is spreading slowly, under Ministry direction, into urban areas. It is also strongly supported by the Federation of Coffee-Growers (i.e., a sort of production and marketing cooperative organization) and by a major social foundation in Colombia. The BRAC program in Bangladesh represents a different common model. It is entirely outside of the standard Ministry of Education administrative framework, although there are linkages in the sense that BRAC program graduates easily move into standard government schools and do well there. However, it must be noted that BRAC itself is a huge administrative organization (its headquarters in the capital, Dhaka, is the largest and tallest building in the city). Yet, it works with significant agility and flexibility in responding to reports and needs from the thousands of villages in which its programs are located. A third common pattern is seen in the Egyptian and Ghanaian cases, which are mixed models with complex collaboration among international organizations, local civil society groups, and the government.

It is essential to mention that in all of these programs there are complex bureaucracies, including functionaries who routinely carry out all the necessary tasks of any Ministry of Education. There are policymakers, curriculum designers, evaluators, text and learning-materials developers, local coordinators and organizers, supervisors of teachers, and so on. However, they somehow manage to do all those necessary administrative tasks in a way which encourages and promotes, rather than blocks, major educational change. Detailed case studies on how this has actually happened are planned, but much work needs to be done.

So, there are many fundamental questions still at issue, many things we are only beginning to understand. However, one core lesson to be learned, even at this early stage, is that this sort of fundamental educational change, which ultimately leads schools closer to the learning principles established in the cognitive science literature (see Table 28.1), *can* occur, and often on quite large a scale, even in desperately poor parts of our world. There is much that we need to learn from these cases. Therein lies the hope.

Note

1 Portions of this chapter were adapted for this particular readership from previously written work (Farrell, 2007a, 2007b, in press).

References

Abadzi, H. (2006). *Efficient learning for the poor: Insights from the frontier of cognitive neuroscience*. Washington, DC: The World Bank.

Ahmed, M. (1993). *Primary education for all: Learning from the BRAC experience. A case study*. Dhaka: Abel Press.

Alvarez, H. B., & Ruiz-Casares, M. (1997). *Senderos de cambio: Genesis y ejecucion de las reformas educativas en America Latina y el Caribe*. Washington, DC: U.S. Agency for International Development.

Arboleda, J. (1994). Participation and partnership in the Colombian Escuela Nueva. In S. Shaeffer (Ed.), *Partnerships and participation in basic education* (Vol. 2, Case 5). Paris: International Institute for Educational Planning.

Bah-Layla, I. (1998). Les classes multigrades en Guinea: Formation et emploi des formateurs, les centres NAFA ou ecoles de seconde chance. *Le programme de petite subventions aux ecoles. Prepared for the improving learning: Perspectives for primary education in rural Africa seminar sponsored by UNESCO & World Bank*. Lusaka, Zambia.

Caillods, F. (Ed.) (1989). *The prospects for educational planning*. Paris: International Institute for Educational Planning.

Colbert, V., & Arboleda, J. (1990). *Universalization of primary education in Colombia – the New School Program*. Paper presented at the World Conference on Education for All. Jomtien, Thailand.

Davies, L. (1996). The management and mismanagement of school effectiveness. In J. D. Turner (Ed.), *The state and the school: An international perspective* (pp. 91–107). London: Falmer Press.

DeStefano, J., Hartwell, A., & Benbow, J. (2004). *Achieving education for all – The challenge: Quality basic education in underserved areas*. EQUIP2 Policy Brief. Washington, DC: Academy for Education Development EQUIP2.

Fagerlind, I., & Sjosted, B. (1990). *Review and prospects of educational planning and management in Europe*. Paris: UNESCO/International

Congress on Planning and Management of Educational Development.

Farrell, J. P. (1989). International lessons for school effectiveness: The view from the Third World. In M. Holmes, et al. (Eds.), *Policy for effective schools*. New York and Toronto: Teachers College Press and OISE Press.

Farrell, J. P. (1997). A retrospective on educational planning in comparative education. *Comparative Education Review, 41*, 270–313.

Farrell, J. P. (2000). Why is educational reform so difficult? Similar descriptions, different prescriptions, failed explanations, *Curriculum Inquiry*, 30, 83–103.

Farrell, J. P. (2001). Can we really change the forms of formal schooling, and would it make a difference if we could? *Curriculum Inquiry*, 31, 289–308.

Farrell, J. P. (2002). The Aga Khan Foundation experience compared with emerging alternatives to formal schooling. In S. Anderson (Ed.), *Improving schools through teacher development: Case studies of the Aga Khan Foundation Projects in East Africa* (pp. 247–270). *Contexts of Learning*, 11. Lisse, The Netherlands: Swets & Zeitlinger.

Farrell, J. P. (2004). *The Egyptian Community Schools Program: A case study*. Washington, DC: *Academy for Educational Development*.

Farrell, J. P. (2007a). Equality of education: A half century of comparative experience as seen from a new millennium. In R. Arnove & C. A. Torres (Eds.), *Comparative education: The dialectic of the local and the global* (3rd ed.) (pp. 146–175). Lanham, MD: Rowman & Littlefield.

Farrell, J. P. (2007b). Community education in developing countries: The quiet revolution in schooling. In F. M. Connelly, M. F. He, & J. A. Phillion (Eds.), *The Sage handbook of curriculum and instruction* (pp. 369–389). Thousand Oaks, CA: Sage Publications.

Farrell, J. P. (2007c). Education in the years to come: What we can learn from alternative education. In P. D. Hershock, M. Mason, & J. Hawkins (Eds.), *Changing education: Leadership, innovation, and development in a globalizing Asia Pacific* (pp. 199–224). CERC 20. Honolulu and Hong Kong: Springer & Comparative Education Research Center, Hong Kong University.

Farrell, J. P. (2008). Teaching and learning to teach: Successful radical alternatives from the developing world. In R. Hayhoe & K. Mundy (Eds.), *Comparative and international education: Issues for teachers* (pp. 107–131). Toronto and New York: Canadian Scholars Press International and Teachers College Press.

Farrell, J. P., & Connelly, F. M. (1998). *Final retrospective report: Forum workshops on educational reform in Egypt*. Report to UNICEF, Egypt and the Ministry of Education, Egypt.

Garcia-Huidobro, J. E. (2000). Educational policies and equity in Chile. In F. Reimers (Ed.), *Unequal schools, unequal chances: The challenges to equal opportunity in the Americas* (pp. 160–181). Cambridge, MA: Harvard University Press.

Haiplik, B. (2004). *BRAC's Non-formal Education (NFPE) Program*. Washington, DC: Academy for Educational Development.

Hartwell, A. (1995). *Review of Egypt's Community School Project*. Cairo: UNICEF–Egypt.

Hartwell, A. (2005). *EQUIP 2 case study: School for Life, Northern Ghana*. Washington, DC: *Academy for Educational Development*.

Hayhoe, R. (2008). *Philosophy and comparative education: What can we learn from East Asia?* In R. Hayhoe & K. Mundy (Eds.), *Comparative and international education: Issues for teachers* (pp. 23–48). Toronto and New York: Canadian Scholars Press International and Teachers College Press.

Hayhoe, R., & Mundy, K. (Eds.) (2008). *Comparative and international education: Issues for teachers*. Toronto and New York: Canadian Scholars Press International and Teachers College Press.

Jeal, T. (1989). *Baden-Powell*. London: Pimlico.

Kardos, S., & Johnson, S. (2007). On their own and presumed expert: New teachers' experience with their colleagues. *Teachers College Record*, 109 (9), 2083–2106. Available at http://www.tcrecord.org. ID#12812.

Kelly, M. J. (1998, December). Initiatives from Zambia: Multigrade teaching, initial literacy in a local language, community schools, determining learning outcomes for the improvement of quality. *Prepared for the improving learning: Perspectives for primary education in rural Africa seminar sponsored by UNESCO & World Bank*. Lusaka, Zambia.

Kidd, J. R. (1973). *How adults learn*. New York: Cambridge University Press.

Knowles, M. (1989). *The adult learner: A neglected species*. Houston, TX: Gulf Publishing.

Kochan, A. (2005). *The decade of uncertainty: Educational change in Poland, 1992–2002*. Unpublished Ph.D. dissertation. Toronto: University of Toronto.

Kraft, R. J. (1998). *Rural educational reform in the Nueva Escuela Unitaria of Guatemala*. Washington, DC: Academy for Educational Development.

McEwan, P. (1998). The effectiveness of multigrade schools in Colombia. *International Journal of Educational Development*, 18, 435–452.

Moulton, J., Mundy, K., Welmond, M., & Williams, J. (2002). *Education reform in sub-Saharan Africa: Paradigm lost?* London: Greenwood Press.

Mundy, K. (2008). Education for all and the comparative sociology of schooling. In R. Hayhoe & K. Mundy (Eds.), *Comparative and international education: Issues for teachers* (pp. 49–76). Toronto and New York: Canadian Scholars Press International and Teachers College Press.

Olson, D. R. (2003). *Psychological theory and educational reform: How school remakes mind and society*. Cambridge, UK: Cambridge University Press.

Pitt, J. (2002). *Civic education and citizenship in Escuela Nueva schools in Colombia*. Unpublished M. A. thesis. Toronto: University of Toronto.

Pitt, J. (2004). *Case study for Escuela Nueva program*. Washington, DC: Academy for Educational Development.

Polyzoi, E., Fullan, M., & Anchan, J. P. (Eds.) (2003). *Change forces in post-communist Eastern Europe: Education in transition*. London: Routledge/Falmer.

Psacharopolous, G., Rojas, C., & Velez, E. (1993). Achievement evaluation of Colombia's "Escuela Nueva": Is multigrade the answer? *Comparative Education Review*, 37, 263–276.

Ravitsch, D., & Vinovskis, M. (Eds.) (1995). *Learning from the past: What history teaches us about school reform*. Baltimore, MD: Johns Hopkins University Press.

Republique du Mali, Ministere del'Education de Base (1998). Amélioration de l'apprentissage: Les perspectives pour l'enseignment primaire en milieu rural en Afrique. *Prepared for the seminar improving learning: Perspectives for primary education in rural Africa sponsored by UNESCO & World Bank*. Lusaka, Zambia.

Sarkar, S. (1994). The BRAC non-formal primary education centres in Bangladesh. In S. Shaeffer (Ed.), *Partnerships and participation in basic education*. (Volume 2, Case 7). Paris: International Institute for Educational Planning.

Schiefelbein, E. (1991). *In search of the school of the 21st century: Is Colombia's Escuela Nueva the right pathfinder?* Santiago: UNESCO Regional Office for Education in Latin America and the Caribbean.

Schiefelbein, E. (2006). *School performance problems in Latin America: The potential role of the Escuela Nueva system*. Paper prepared for the Second International New Schools Congress, Medellin, Colombia.

Scott, S. (1996). *Education for child garment workers in Bangladesh*. Unpublished M. A. thesis. Toronto: University of Toronto.

Siabato, R. C. (1997). *Educacion basica primaria en zonas rurales: La escuela nueva y su relacion con la evaluacion del plan de universalization de la educacion basica primaria*. Bogotá: Ministerio de la Educacion Nacional.

Sizer, T. (2001). Forum discussion. *Harpers Magazine*, September, 148–160.

Sweetser, A. T. (1999). *Lessons from the BRAC Non-formal Primary Education Program*. Washington, DC: Association for Basic Education and Learning.

Tyack, D., & Cuban, L. (1995). *Tinkering toward Utopia: A century of public school reform*. Cambridge, MA: Harvard University Press.

UNICEF (2001). *The state of the world's children 2001*. New York: UNICEF.

UNICEF (2006). *The state of the world's children 2006*. New York: UNICEF.

Zaalouk, M. (1995). *The children of the Nile: The community schools project in Upper Egypt*. Paris: UNICEF.

Zaalouk, M. (2004). *The pedagogy of empowerment: Community schools as a social movement in Egypt*. Cairo: The American University in Cairo Press.

CHAPTER 29

Adult Literacy Education in Industrialized Nations

Thomas G. Sticht

For decades, most industrialized nations have conducted adult literacy programs for what were often considered 'pockets' of adults with low literacy. However, in the last decade of the twentieth century, a number of these nations were challenged by the results of international adult literacy assessments which indicated that rather than isolated pockets of illiteracy or low literacy, upwards of one to two fifths of their adult populations appeared to have low literacy skills (OECD, 1995).

In light of such findings, a number of industrialized nations have focused additional attention on the policies and programs of adult literacy education. They have engaged in various activities aimed at transforming what have historically been a plethora of independent literacy programs – often consisting of community-based charitable programs staffed largely by volunteer tutors or teachers – into systems of government-funded education programs. These new systems of adult literacy education provide greater numbers of full- and part-time teachers who view themselves as professionals in an emerging field of adult literacy education (or basic skills education when English language and numeracy instruction are included).

This chapter discusses five areas of activity that can be identified in the recent reform movements. Across nations, the five areas to be examined include activities to determine the scale of need for adult literacy education, the extent of participation in adult literacy education, the system of provision, the quality of provision, and the accountability of provision.

Three nations with which the author has had considerable experience for fifteen years are the primary focus of this chapter, including Canada, the United Kingdom (UK), and the United States (US). However, many of the issues and findings presented are also relevant to other industrialized nations, and references to resources which will provide readers with additional sources of information about industrialized nations beyond the three focused on herein are listed.

Determining the Scale of Need

One of the questions policy makers ask when considering support for adult literacy education is how many adults are in need of such education. A major effort for determining the scale of need for adult literacy education took place in the mid-1990s when Canada, the UK and the US joined with what was eventually nineteen other member nations of the Organisation for Economic Co-operation and Development (OECD) to take part in the International Adult Literacy Survey (IALS) (OECD, 1995; Tuijnman, 2000). The IALS developed performance tasks for prose, document and quantitative literacy scales that were used to assess adult literacy skills using door-to-door sampling methods. Adults were assigned to literacy levels from Level 1 (low) to Level 5 (high) depending on their performance on the literacy tasks.

Additionally, the IALS developed a scale for the adults' self-assessment of their literacy ability, including rating categories of poor, moderate, good, excellent and no response.

Performance Scales: On the *document* literacy scale, 23.7 percent of U.S. adults aged sixteen to sixty-five were assigned to Level 1, the lowest level, whereas in Canada 18.2 percent of adults and in the UK 23.3 percent of adults were assigned to Level 1. Similar percentages, with a little variation, held for the assignment of adults to Level 1 on the *prose* and *quantitative* literacy scales. Using the performance scales, then, about one fifth of adults aged sixteen to sixty-five in these three countries were considered 'at risk' for social problems due to poor literacy, which would result in about 32 million adults in the US, 3.3 million in Canada, and 7 million in the UK.

Self-Perceived Literacy Skills: Using the adults' self-assessments of their reading abilities for work and daily life, grouped by the document scale results, fewer than 5 percent of adults in either Canada, the UK, or the US rated their reading as poor. Using a 5 percent estimate for these three nations, some 8 million adults in the US, less than 1 million in Canada, and fewer than 2 million in the UK considered themselves at risk for poor reading. Similar results held for self-assessments of writing and numeracy and with self-assessments grouped by the prose and quantitative scales (OECD, 1995).

As indicated, there was considerable discrepancy between the performance tests and the self-assessments of the IALS in determining the percentages and numbers of adults at risk for poor literacy in these three nations. In an extensive analysis of the IALS and the discrepancies between the standardized test and the self-assessment results, Sticht (2001a) noted that the IALS assigned a skill level to adults based on their having an 80 percent chance of performing a given item correctly. A person assigned to the lowest level of literacy had an 80 percent chance of performing the average item at that level correctly and was therefore assigned to that level. However, it was also the case that a person assigned to Level 1 could perform approximately half of the average Level 2 items, a fourth of the average Level 3 items, and even some of the more difficult Levels 4 and 5 items. So, in fact, adults assigned to the lowest levels of literacy had a greater than zero chance of correctly performing many tasks at higher levels. This may account for some of the discrepancy between the adults' self-perceived literacy abilities and their abilities as designated by the test administrators.

In 2005, a report from a U.S. National Academy of Sciences study group concluded that the response probability of 80 percent used by the IALS was overly stringent (Hauser, Edley, Koenig, & Elliot, 2005). It recommended that the 2003 National Assessment of Adult Literacy (NAAL) being developed in the US use a 67 percent response probability for declaring adults proficient at some given level. The report also indicated that referring to adults with less than Level 3 literacy skills as unable to cope with modern society, as was done in the reports on the IALS, was an "unsupported inference" and not based on any empirical evidence.

In the early 1990s, in an OECD report leading up to the IALS, it was stated that there was a growing interest among educational policy makers and analysts in "the direct measurement of literacy levels in the labor force of industrialized nations" (Benton & Noyelle, 1992, p. 11). However, it is now clear that one cannot 'directly measure' the literacy skills of the adult labor force. Rather, following certain methodologies, one creates a particular representation of the literacy skills of the labor force. Depending on the methodological choices, one can construct a variety of representations of literacy skills. All measurements depend on the making of many decisions that are essentially arbitrary. This renders problematic the task of determining the scale of need for adult literacy education. For instance, in the IALS, the question arises as to which is the more valid estimate of the scale of need for adult literacy in the industrialized nations discussed previously, the 20 to 40 percent of adults determined to be at risk using the standardized tests or the 5 percent using self-assessments of literacy skills?

Participation in Adult Literacy Education

Regardless of the relatively large scale of need for adult literacy education that governments in industrialized nations have declared using the standardized tests of the IALS, the actual number of adults who participate in programs to improve their literacy skills has remained small. Activities relating to improving participation in provision have taken the approach of conducting studies to better determine why adults do or do not participate in adult literacy or basic skills programs and ways to increase outreach to and recruitment of adults into programs.

In Canada, it has been reported based on IALS data that 42 percent of Canadians have serious difficulties with any type of printed material, yet only a small fraction, 5 to 10 percent, of adults eligible for literacy education have ever enrolled in literacy courses (Long, 2000). Some 43 percent of Canadians who were seeking information about literacy and upgrading education across Canada in the study by Long did not enroll because of program or policy-related problems, such as not being called back, long waiting lists, inconvenient course times, wrong content or teaching structure, and unhelpful program contact.

In the UK, the IALS assigned around 23 percent of adults to literacy level 1, some 7 million adults (OECD, 1995), whereas participants in adult literacy programs around that time included fewer than 5 percent of that number. To increase participation in provision, in 2001, the UK set up a Skills for Life initiative (Blunkett, 2001). In a report to the House of Commons in 2005, it was stated that the Skills for Life initiative had an initial goal of getting some 750,000 adults to improve their skills and that by July 2004, this goal had been achieved (House of Commons, 2006). However, instead of consisting strictly of those adults identified by the IALS as the least skilled in literacy Level 1, more than half of those reached were sixteen to eighteen year olds, many of whom were in school and already working on educational qualifications at higher levels of literacy. New targets of reaching a total of 2.25 million adults by 2010 were established by the UK government, and new efforts were to be taken to reach those adults most in need of literacy education.

To determine what might motivate adults with poor basic skills to seek to improve them, the Basic Skills Agency of the UK conducted a study called *Getting Better Basic Skills* (Basic Skills Agency, 2001). The research focused on adults' perceptions of their own skills, why they wanted to improve their skills, their access to learning programs, the content of the programs and what would encourage them to try and improve their skills. It was found that one third of adults thought that their basic skills needed improving; 29 percent of those questioned said they would definitely take up a basic skills course and 42 percent said they would probably do so.

The main reasons for wanting to improve basic skills were both emotional (*to feel better about yourself/ your skills*) and practical (*to be better at everyday tasks which involve basic skills*). The largest percentage of adults (41 percent) preferred teaching to be in their own home, yet most adults preferred to learn with a teacher. Information, communications and technology (ICT) facilities were also important; the factors motivating adults to improve their basic skills included being able to learn on a computer – being able to improve computer skills and basic skills at the same time – getting an educational qualification and being able to attend a course near home.

The Basic Skills Agency concluded that the research clearly indicated that there was an existing interest in improving basic skills among those adults in need in the UK and that only by considering what the learners want would it be possible to make progress towards the targets set out in the Skills for Life strategy for improving adult literacy and numeracy skills.

In the US, the National Adult Literacy Survey (NALS), the predecessor to the IALS, reported in 1993 that 90 million adults (47 percent) scored below literacy Level 3 and were therefore at risk of social exclusion and other social problems because of low literacy. Yet, in 1998, only 4 million adults were enrolled in the Adult Education and Literacy System (AELS) (Sticht, 1998). Despite the NALS report of tens of millions of adults with low literacy, no initiatives with major funding, unlike in the UK, were undertaken to reach out to adults in the US.

In fact, in 1998, a new National Reporting System (NRS) was implemented by the federal government for the four thousand or so programs that were funded in part by the federal government and comprised the AELS of the US. The NRS requires that states report a number of outcomes, including learning gains determined by the use of standardized tests. Following the implementation of the NRS, there was a decline in enrollments in the AELS of more than 1 million students (Sticht, 1998; U.S. Department of Education, 2005). No official explanation for this decline was given by any official government entity. It has been speculated, however, that many community-based programs that had been providing literacy education in the AELS before the NRS was implemented left the system because they lacked the resources to do the testing and other outcome measurements that the NRS required.

Systems of Provision

Unlike public schools or higher education, which are well-developed systems with stable funding and more-or-less uniform classrooms, the provision of basic skills education for adults in industrialized nations tends to be a marginalized activity, often with only year-to-year funding under grants that must be applied for annually. Literacy education for adults in most industrialized nations, including Canada, the UK and the US, takes place in numerous settings ranging from formal schoolhouses or learning centers to storefronts, prison cells, homes for the elderly, church buildings, private homes, workplaces, and so on. Students range in age from sixteen to older than eighty; within a given classroom, there may be many different cultural and language backgrounds; and educational levels can range from zero to college. As well, many adult literacy students have had distressing experiences with schooling and are afraid to take part in educational activities. Furthermore, within a classroom, there may be a range of learning disabilities (Quigley, 1997).

In Canada, the federal government funds a National Literacy Secretariat which offers some central coordination and support for research and development, but adult literacy education is primarily a provincial activity and involves a plethora of providers working under different rules, regulations, and procedures for the conduct of adult literacy programs across Canada (Shohet, 2001). To bring order into adult literacy education across Canada, participants in a National Summit on Literacy and Productivity in October 2000 called for an integrated, pan-Canadian system of adult education and lifelong learning with appropriate structures to support such a system (ABC Canada, 2000).

Five years later, an Advisory Committee on Literacy and Essential Skills submitted a report to the Minister of State for Human Development and reiterated the need for a pan-Canadian strategy for addressing adult literacy. The Committee stated, "...we need to build a Canada-wide system of high-quality adult literacy/basic education services. We have created effective K-12 and post-secondary systems. Canada also needs an adult learning system that has a strong infrastructure and sustained financial support" (Advisory Committee on Literacy and Essential Skills, 2005). As of this writing, such a system has yet to be formed.

In the UK, about 60 percent of basic-skills students receive basic-skills provision in Further Education colleges, and 20 percent receive such training in Local Education Agencies. The remaining 20 percent of programs occur in prisons, training organizations, voluntary organizations, employer-based settings and other contexts (Brooks et al., 2001a, p. 60).

Unlike Canada, in the UK, funding for adult basic skills provision is very much a central government responsibility. In 2000, this central government role was enhanced by the formation of a new Adult Basic Skills Strategy Unit in the Department for Education and Employment (now the Department for Education and Skills [DfES]) (Blunkett, 2001). This unit oversees a new adult literacy provision scheme for the UK that involved the expenditure of some £1.5 billion during the first three years to provide adult basic skills education. The unit works closely with Learning and Skills Council regional offices that have responsibilities for assessing local need and ensuring that opportunities exist for adult basic skills education in local settings.

In the US, as in Canada and the UK, there are numerous organizations that provide adult literacy education. However, in the US, the main body of providers can be grouped into the Adult Education and Literacy System (AELS) which was formed in 1966 when the Adult Education Act (AEA) was enacted (Sticht, 2002). The AEA brought adult educators at the local, state, and federal levels together to work under an agreed-to set of common rules and regulations that began the process of systematizing adult literacy education in the United States. Since then, the AEA has undergone numerous amendments and name changes. It was renamed the National Literacy Act in 1991, and in 1998 it was incorporated into the Workforce Investment Act as Title 2, the Adult Education and Family Literacy Act (AEFLA). This is the legislation under which the AELS operates today.

When the Adult Education Act of 1966 was passed, the federal funds for the AELS provided most of the funds for the states to provide this education. Today, however, the federal funds are just one fourth of the total funding for the AELS and the states make up the major source of funds (U.S. Department of Education, 2003).

In Program Year 2000–2001, 3,500 to 4,000 programs comprised the AELS in the US and offered adult education and literacy provision under the AEFLA of 1998 (U.S. Department of Education, 2003, p. 1). A report to the U.S. Congress (U. S. Department of Education, 2006) indicated that the purpose of the AELS, which is supported in part at the federal level by the AEFLA, is "to provide educational opportunities to adults sixteen and older, not currently enrolled in school, who lack a high school diploma or the basic skills to function effectively in society or who are unable to speak, read, or write the English language" (p. iii). The report went on to say that in "program year (PY) 2003–2004, the program enrolled 2,677,119 learners, of which just under 40% (39.7) were enrolled in Adult Basic Education, 16.5% were enrolled in Adult Secondary Education, and 43.8% were enrolled in English Literacy programs" (p. iii).

Across these three nations, Canada has the least nationally systematized adult literacy education system, with each province controlling its own system of provision. The UK (England and Wales) has the most centrally controlled system, with funding, instruction, and accountability all under the jurisdiction of the federal government. The US has the most formally structured partnership of federal and state provision, with a joint federal/state funding scheme and a national accountability system but with a decentralized instructional system run by each state.

Quality of Provision

Definitions of adult literacy education program quality may include a number of factors, including the extent to which programs overcome barriers to participation in provision; the rate of dropping out of programs, the professionalism and preparation of the teaching staff; and the availability of skills, content, and curriculum standards.

Participation in Provision

As discussed previously, in Canada, the UK and the US, only a small proportion of adults deemed in need of provision actually enroll. Cross (1982) identified three major categories of barriers to participation in adult education in general, which have also been applied in studies of participation in adult literacy education (Sticht, McDonald, & Erickson, 1998). These categories address the concept of the 'quality' of programs in terms of whether the programs actually address the life circumstances of adults with literacy-education needs.

Situational barriers include childcare problems, work schedules, transportation problems, and so on. In Canada, Long (2000) referred to these as "socioeconomic-circumstantial" factors and found that 30 percent of adults in her research reported such factors as deterrents to participation in adult literacy education. In this case, the quality of programs suffers if they lack provision of supports for adult learners to help them overcome these barriers where possible.

Dispositional barriers stem from the psychological, personality, and attitudinal disposition of the students and their beliefs about their abilities to learn. Long (2000) referred to these as "cognitive-emotive" factors and reported that 15 percent of adults in her Canadian study cited such factors as deterrents to enrollment in programs. Here, a program is defined as lacking in quality when it fails to offer counseling, social supports, or other services that help adults overcome these psychological barriers to program participation.

Institutional barriers involve the instruction, policies, practices and requirements of programs. Long (2000) reported that in Canada, 43 percent of those adults in her study reported what she called "program/policy-related" barriers to participation. Better-quality programs are aware of these types of barriers and implement activities to reduce them where possible.

In the UK, the National Foundation for Educational Research (NFER) (Brooks et al., 2001a) reported barriers to participation in adult basic skills provision that were similar to those reported by Cross (1982) and Long (2000). Sticht, McDonald, and Erickson (1998) in the US engaged adult literacy students to interview people they knew whom they thought should be but were not participating in adult literacy provision. Barriers reported by adult student interviewers that make it difficult for adults they interviewed to pursue education were similar to those reported by Long (2000) for Canada and by the NFER (Brooks et al., 2001a) for the UK.

Dropout Rates

Another indicator of program quality that is sometimes cited is the dropout rate – that is, failure of the student to complete a program. Dropout rates are high in all three nations. Long (2000) reported dropout rates of 41 percent for males and 23 percent for females across Canada. NFER (Brooks et al., 2001a) reported dropout rates in the UK of 20 to 50 percent depending on the type of program being attended. Generally, dropouts from briefer (i.e., about twelve-week) intensive courses, eight or so hours per week, were lower than from courses attended for only two to four hours per week.

In the US, dropout rates in excess of 50 percent were found in some studies and, as in the UK, greater persistence was found in intensive programs of shorter duration that are highly focused on specific goals, such as getting a job or helping one's children with school (Sticht, McDonald, & Erickson, 1998). Quigley (1997) noted that dropout rates as high as 18 percent within the first twelve hours may occur in adult literacy programs in the AELS of the US. He discusses the importance of the first three weeks in helping adults overcome barriers to retention in programs. In research on persistence in library literacy programs, Comings, Cuban, Bos, and Taylor (2001) pointed out that many dropouts actually re-engage in programs at a later time. Such intermittent engagement in literacy education complicates the meaning of dropout rates in terms of how much adult literacy education adults may actually participate in over time.

Professionalism of the Teaching Staff

The professionalism and preparation of teaching staff is another indicator used to refer to the quality of provision. Paid teachers in adult literacy education are generally part-time in Canada, the UK and the US, and large numbers of tutors are unpaid volunteers. For 13,201 teachers in the UK, Brooks et al. (2001a, p. 73) reported that more than 90 percent were part-time and that there were an additional 12,046 volunteers, almost equal the number of paid staff. Data from the U.S. Department of Education indicate that in the Adult Education and Literacy System of the US in program year 2003–2004, of 148,039 personnel, 23,954 were employed full-time, 72,988 were part-time, and 51,097 were unpaid volunteers (U.S. Department of Education, 2005). Hoddinott (1998) reported similar findings for Canada, with most teachers being part-time and the widespread use of volunteers.

Based on the studies of teaching in adult literacy education, all three nations have taken steps to improve the profession of adult literacy teaching. In addition to advocating for more funds to support more full-time teachers, all three nations have developed teacher training materials and procedures.

In Canada, *literacy.ca*, the newsletter of the Movement for Canadian Literacy, discussed the professionalization of adult literacy education in its February 2000 issue. It reports on work by the Ontario Literacy Coalition to produce the *Adult Literacy Educators Skills List*. Provision of training for adult educators was also recommended by the *National Literacy Summit on Literacy and Productivity* in October 2000 (ABC Canada, 2000).

In the US, the U.S. Department of Education's Division of Adult Education and Literacy has implemented the Pro-Net Project to develop competencies and performance indicators for adult literacy educators (Sherman et al., 1999) (Table 29.1).

In the UK, major efforts to improve adult literacy education through teacher training have been undertaken as called for by the Department for Education and Skills' Adult Basic Skills Strategy Unit as part of the implementation of a new national core curriculum for adult literacy and numeracy (Blunkett, 2001).

It is interesting that although all three of these nations have engaged in extensive professional development activities to improve the quality of the teaching staffs in their adult literacy programs, as yet no evidence has been provided that indicates that these efforts have actually had beneficial effects for student learning or other outcomes.

Curriculum Standards

Skills, content, and curriculum standards as quality indicators have been the focus of government and literacy agencies in Canada, the US and the UK. For instance, Human Resources and Skills Development Canada (2005) produced a list of essential skills that people are claimed to use to carry out a wide variety of everyday life and occupational tasks (Table 29.2, column A). The different essential skills are arrayed by low to high

Table 29.1. The Pro-Net Project for Professional Development in the United States: Competency Categories for Adult Educators

1. *Maintains Knowledge and Pursues Professional Development.* Competencies for this area include those for obtaining and maintaining the requisite skills and content knowledge to guide the instructional process.
2. *Organizes and Delivers Instruction.* Competencies for this area include the development of instructional plans, sequence and pacing of classroom activities, and linking instruction to learner needs and abilities.
3. *Manages Instructional Resources.* Providing quality instruction requires an emphasis on competencies for managing instructional and planning time as well as learner time-on-task.
4. *Continually Assesses and Monitors Learning.* The competencies in this section focus on collecting and sharing information about learner needs and progress, and using the information to plan appropriate instruction.
5. *Manages Program Responsibilities and Enhances Program Organization.* Competencies in this section focus on collecting, managing, and sharing data and ideas to improve instruction and program quality.
6. *Provides Learner Guidance and Referral.* Relevant competencies in this area include the knowledge of appropriate referral services and the ability to communicate learner needs to other service providers within the program.

Source: Sherman et al., 1999.

complexity levels to indicate progression in skills development.

The Equipped for the Future project in the US (Stein, 2000) developed content standards for what adults should know and be able to do to fulfill their life roles as parents/family members, citizen/community members, or workers (Table 29.2, column B).

In the UK, the Qualification and Curriculum Authority (2000) published national standards for adult literacy and numeracy (Table 29.2, column 3). The standards also present competencies of progression through three entry levels of skill and two more advanced levels of skill. These standards were used to develop a national curriculum, and the Basic Skills Agency of the UK conducted teacher training and certification programs to implement the new standards and basic skills curriculum across England.

As indicated in Table 29.2, the standards presented in these three nations are all presented in terms of abstract 'skills' that are thought to be needed by all adults. However, Hirsch (2006) presented an extensive review of research that demonstrated that approaches to the teaching of literacy that focus on abstract skills while largely ignoring the importance of content knowledge (e.g., specific facts, concepts, principles, rules) are likely to result in students with poor comprehension ability. The so-called content standards put forth in Table 29.2 ignore the specification of specific content (e.g., vocabulary words, conceptual information, and so forth) that must be obtained in large quantities to render adults literate beyond some low level. The general idea behind such lists is that one can develop the *skills* in any number of specific knowledge *contents* and the latter must be determined based on the interests and contexts of the adult learners. Mismatches between the content that is taught in literacy programs and the content on standardized tests can produce underestimates in the measurement of learning gains which are called for in accountability measures.

Accountability of Provision

With the greater interest in adult literacy stimulated by the results of the International Adult Literacy Survey (IALS) of the mid-1990s and the calls for increased funding for adult literacy education came a greater concern by policy makers and funding agencies for accountability. One concern was whether adult literacy provision is effective in increasing adult literacy skills. To evaluate this at the national level, several nations took part in a second administration of an IALS-type assessment of adult literacy skills. Called the International Adult Literacy and Lifeskills (ALL) Survey, the

Table 29.2. Examples of Skills, Content and Curriculum Standards Efforts for Canada, the United States and the United Kingdom

A. ESSENTIAL SKILLS *Canada*	*B. EQUIPPED FOR THE FUTURE STANDARDS* *United States*	*C. NATIONAL STANDARDS FOR ADULT LITERACY AND NUMERACY* *United Kingdom*
Reading Text Use of Documents Writing Numeracy Oral Communication Thinking Skills – Problem Solving – Decision Making – Job Task Planning & Organizing – Significant Use of Memory – Finding Information Working with Others Computer Use Continuous Learning	COMMUNICATION SKILLS Read with understanding Convey ideas in writing Speak so others can understand Listen actively Observe critically DECISION-MAKING SKILLS Solve problems and make decisions Plan Use math to solve problems and communicate INTERPERSONAL SKILLS Cooperate with others Guide others Advocate and influence Resolve conflict and negotiate LIFELONG LEARNING SKILLS Take responsibility for learning Learn through research Reflect and evaluate Use information and communications technology	LITERACY Speaking and listening – Listen and respond – Speak to communicate – Engage in discussion Reading – Read and understand – Read and obtain information Writing – Write to communicate NUMERACY Understanding and using mathematical information – Read numbers and understand – Specify and describe practical problems Calculating and manipulating mathematical information – Generate results which make sense Interpreting results and communicating mathematics information – Present and explain results

Note: All three nations have also produced standards for English language [ESL/ESOL] instruction through government or professional association auspices.

assessment was conducted in 2003 and the results were reported in 2005.

Desjardins, Clermont, Murray, and Werguin (2005) provided a first report of the ALL findings for several of the nations that participated in the survey. Both Canada and the US took part, but this time the UK did not. Instead, it developed its own assessment to determine how well progress in advancing adult literacy was proceeding.

For Canada, the ALL survey produced data showing that the percentage of adults in the lowest level of literacy on the earlier IALS, Level 1, dropped by 2 percent on the *prose* scale of literacy and 2.4 percent on the *document* scale. In the US, the comparable figures showed a drop of 0.8 percent in literacy Level 1 for the *prose* scale and 3.4 percent for the *document* scale. This indicates a reduction in adults within the lowest level of literacy in Canada and the US from the mid-1990s to 2003.

A surprising finding, however, was that in both Canada and the US, at the highest levels of literacy (Levels 4 and 5 combined), there were larger percentages of declines. In Canada, the drop in the higher literacy levels for the *prose* scale was 2.8 percent and for the *document* scale it was 5.2 percent. The corresponding numbers for the US were 9.1

and 5.0 percent. These data indicate that the two nations were losing their higher literacy adults at rates faster than they were improving the literacy of the least literate. Similar findings were obtained for several of the other nations that took part in the ALL survey, but no explanation for this was given in the report on the results.

In the UK, the DfES reported the results of a followup to the IALS called the Skills for Life (SFL) survey. The results of the survey were used by the DfES to infer that following their SFL Strategy activities, there had been a decrease in the numbers of poorly literate adults from 7.0 million identified using the IALS in 1997 to 5.2 million in 2003.

Unfortunately, there were major differences between the IALS and the SFL survey that render comparisons of the results of the two surveys invalid. Important differences include each survey used different test items with different content and formats; the IALS used short-answer responses whereas the SFL used multiple-choice items; the IALS used an 80 percent criterion to assign adults to literacy levels whereas the SFL used a 70 percent criterion; and the matches of the SFL to the IALS levels were subjective judgments with no separate objective validation.

Measuring Learning Gains in Programs

In addition to these types of national test surveys to determine if adult literacy is improving – and indirectly whether adult literacy provision is being effective in reducing the percentages of adults with low levels of literacy – in both the UK and the US, new initiatives for accountability in the form of measuring learning gains made by adults in programs have been formally integrated into new national adult basic skills reform strategies. Brooks, et al. (2001b) conducted studies in the UK measuring pre-program post-program reading skills. They found that although most adults showed gains, about 30 percent did poorer on the post-test than they did on the pre-test. Reasons for the negative gain scores were not explained. Also in the UK, new national literacy and numeracy examinations were developed to evaluate and certify the outcomes of adult learning in basic skills programs (Blunkett, 2001). As of this writing, tests are available for higher ability adult literacy learners, and there have been calls for tests to certify the literacy skills of lower ability learners (House of Commons, 2006).

In the US, a National Reporting System was implemented to capture a wide variety of data on demographics, attendance, and outcomes in programs that are a part of the AELS (Sticht, 1998). One of the goals of the new accountability system was to make possible the measurement of improvements in learning gains. To measure these gains, the National Reporting System requires states to report the numbers of students who progress from one of six levels of performance, from low to high, in Adult Basic Education (ABE), Adult Secondary Education (ASE), and English Literacy/Language. In Program Year 2000–2001 (PY00–01), averaged over the fifty states and US territories, 36 percent of students in ABE/ASE combined made enough educational gain to move from one level to a higher level. In PY01–02, this increased to 37 percent; in PY02–03, to 38 percent; and in PY03–04, it remained constant at 38 percent. Similar data for gains in English Literacy/Language indicated that in PY00–01, 32 percent moved from one level to a higher level; in PY01–02, this increased to 34 percent; in PY02–03, to 36 percent; and in PY03–04, data remained constant at 36 percent.

Clearly, the first four years of data on educational gains collected by the National Reporting System in the US indicate only little or, in the last two years, no improvement in the overall national data. There is, however, considerable variation among the fifty states and territories. For instance, in California, the largest state in terms of the numbers of students served, data show that in PY01–02, 29 percent of students in ABE/ASE made educational gains from one level to a higher level; this stayed the same in PY02–03 but dropped to 28 percent in PY03–04. Thus, the gains in ABE/ASE in California were well below the national gains and there was no improvement in the three years of data. There was, however, a small improvement in English Literacy/Language, rising from 33 percent in PY01–02 to 35 percent in PY03–04. Whether data collected by the National Reporting System actually lead to major improvements in learning gains in the coming years is yet to be determined.

In Canada, the National Summit on Literacy and Productivity (ABC Canada, 2000) recommended that adult literacy education programs be integrated into a pan-Canadian system of adult education and lifelong learning and that structures be created to support such a system. Participants thought this should include an accountability framework that considered evaluation and assessment, best practices, benchmarks, and reporting-back processes. As of this writing, such an accountability system has not been developed.

Discussion

The last decade of the twentieth century witnessed the broadening of attention to adult literacy in industrialized nations. In this chapter, the focus has been on efforts in three industrialized nations to transform adult literacy education from a disparate collection of individual programs into systems of education similar to the preschool, primary, and secondary education systems of these nations.

Although such transformations may lead to the creation of tax-supported educational systems for adults so that full-time teachers and other professionals can be provided to meet the needs of many of those most difficult to reach, it is important that adult literacy education maintain the focus on the adult learner that has been characteristic of its past. It should not succumb to excessive demands for accountability that can drive community-based organizations and their learners out of the system, which seems to have happened in the US. It is also necessary to keep the needs of the most undereducated in mind and not commit the adult literacy education system to simply a degree- or qualification-granting system for secondary-school dropouts who need to complete a credential to find a good job or enter post-secondary education or training. In the UK, this has led to declarations of almost 80 percent of the adult population as lacking in 'basic skills' because they lack certain secondary-school qualifications. This can reduce attention to and provision of services for meeting the needs of those adults with the least-developed skills and knowledge.

This chapter reviewed five categories of activities that have been undertaken in Canada, the UK and the US to bring about the transformation from disparate programs to educational systems. The review revealed difficulties in identifying the scale of need for adult literacy education using psychometric tests, as well as the problems of increasing participation in programs when large percentages of the adult population do not think they have basic-skills problems.

One activity that has been focused on is the expansion of professional development for those working in the field. Most of those who work in adult literacy education have entered into this work with little education and training about the field (Quigley, 1997, p. 9). Indeed, there may be little understanding by those working in it that there is such a field of educational professionalism, and that it has a history, a body of professional wisdom, and sustained efforts that have endured for decades.

Today, there are numerous resources that advance this idea of the professionalism of the field of adult literacy education. The National Center for the Study of Adult Learning and Literacy (NCSALL) in the US published a series of books with chapters that provide succinct histories and contemporary practices of adult literacy activities in several industrialized nations. These include chapters on adult literacy education in Canada (Shohet, 2001), Ireland (Bailey, 2006), New Zealand (Johnson & Benseman, 2005), the United Kingdom (Hamilton & Merrifield, 2000), and the United States (Sticht, 2002). These chapters reveal the international growth and development among industrialized nations of adult literacy education as a field of professional education. Additionally, numerous information sources on the Internet's World Wide Web expand on the ideas presented herein and take the discussion of adult literacy in industrialized nations into areas not covered. Three major online resources are the National Adult Literacy Database (www.nald.ca) in Canada, the Basic Skills Agency (www.basic-skills.co.uk) in the UK, and the National Institute for Literacy (www.nifl.gov) in the US.

With the chapters in volumes from the National Center for the Study of Adult Learning and Literacy cited herein and the vast resources available on the World Wide Web, it is possible to point to the field of adult literacy education as a field with a history in each of these nations and a continuing need for its services among their adult populations. The psychologist Edwin G. Boring of Harvard wrote the first history of the field of experimental psychology (Boring, 1950). In the introduction to the book, he said (paraphrasing) that psychology has a long past but a short history, meaning by this that although ideas about human psychology had been around for centuries, there has been just a brief period in which it has emerged as an academically recognized field of study.

Similarly, adult literacy education has had a long past and now it has at least the beginnings of a brief history documented in the resources and activities outlined herein. Perhaps it will continue with its development, overcome many of the difficulties identified in this chapter, and move from the marginalized field that it has been until now, and become a well-recognized and well-funded system of adult lifelong education in each of the industrialized nations of the world.

References

ABC Canada (2000, October). *National summit on literacy and productivity*. Toronto: ABC Canada Literacy Foundation.

Advisory Committee on Literacy and Essential Skills (2005, November). Towards a fully literate Canada: Achieving national goals through a comprehensive pan-Canadian literacy strategy. Retrieved July 19, 2006, from www.nald.ca/fulltext/towards/cover.htm.

Bailey, I. (2006). Overview of the adult literacy system in Ireland and current issues in its implementation. In: In J. Comings, B. Garner, & C. Smith (Eds.), *The annual review of adult learning and literacy. Vol. 6* (pp. 197–240). Mahwah, NJ: Lawrence Erlbaum Associates, Inc.

Basic Skills Agency (2001). *Getting better basic skills*. London: Basic Skills Agency.

Benton, L., & Noyelle, T. (Eds.) (1992). *Adult illiteracy and economic performance*. Paris: Organisation for Economic Co-operation and Development, Centre for Educational Research and Innovation.

Blunkett, D. (2001). *Skills for Life: The national strategy for improving adult literacy and numeracy skills*. London: DfES Publications.

Boring, E. G. (1950). *A history of experimental psychology*. New York: Appleton-Century-Crofts.

Brooks, G., Giles, K., Harman, J., Kendall, S., Rees, F., & Whittaker, S. (2001a, January). *Assembling the fragments: A review of research on adult basic skills*. Research Report No. 220. London: Her Majesty's Stationery Office.

Brooks, G., Davies, R., Ducke, L., Hutchinson, D., Kendall, S., & Wilkin, A. (2001b, January). *Progress in adult literacy: Do learners learn?* London: Basic Skills Agency.

Comings, J., Cuban, S., Bos, J., & Taylor, C. (2001, September). *"I did it for myself": Studying efforts to increase adult student persistence in library literacy programs*. New York: Manpower Demonstration Research Corporation.

Cross, K. P. (1982). *Adults as learners*. San Francisco: Jossey-Bass.

Desjardins, R., Clermont, Y., Murray, T., & Werguin, P. (2005). *Learning a living: First results of the adult literacy and life skills survey*. Paris: Organisation for Economic Co-operation and Development.

Hamilton, M., & Hillier, Y. (2006). *Changing faces of adult literacy, language, and numeracy: A critical history*. Stoke-on-Trent: Trentham Books.

Hamilton, M., & Merrifield, J. (2000). Adult learning and literacy in the United Kingdom. In J. Comings, B. Garner, & C. Smith. (Eds.),

The annual review of adult learning and literacy. Vol. 1 (pp. 243–303). San Francisco: Jossey-Bass.

Hauser, R., Edley, Jr., C., Koenig, J., & Elliot, S. (Eds.) (2005). *Measuring literacy: Performance levels for adults*. Washington, DC: National Academy of Sciences Press.

Hirsch, E. (2006). *The knowledge deficit: Closing the shocking education gap for American children*. New York: Houghton Mifflin.

Hoddinott, S. (1998). *Something to think about: Please think about this*. Ottawa, ON: Ottawa Board of Education.

House of Commons (2006, January). *Skills for Life: Improving adult literacy and numeracy*. Twenty-first Report of Session 2005–06, HC 792. London: The Stationery Office.

Human Resources and Skills Development Canada (2005). Understanding essential skills. Retrieved August 1, 2006, from http://srv600.hrdc-drhc.gc.ca/esrp/english/general/Understanding_ES_e.shtml.

Johnson, A., & Benseman, J. (2005). Adult literacy in New Zealand. In J. Comings, B. Garner, & C. Smith. (Eds.), *Review of adult learning and literacy. Vol. 5* (pp. 155–185). Mahwah, NJ: Lawrence Erlbaum Associates, Inc.

Long, E. (2000). *Who wants to learn?* Toronto: ABC Canada Literacy Foundation.

OECD (1995). *Literacy, economy and society: Results of the first International Adult Literacy Survey*. Paris: Organisation for Economic Co-operation and Development.

Qualifications and Curriculum Authority (2000). *National standards for adult literacy and numeracy*. London: Department for Education and Skills.

Quigley, B. A. (1997). *Rethinking literacy education*. San Francisco: Jossey-Bass.

Sherman, R., Tibbetts, J., Woodruff, D., & Weidler, D. (1999, February). *Instructor competencies and performance indicators for the improvement of adult education programs*. Washington, DC: U.S. Department of Education, Division of Adult Education and Literacy.

Shohet, L. (2001). Adult learning and literacy in Canada. In J. Comings, B. Garner, & C. Smith. (Eds.), *The annual review of adult learning and literacy. Vol. 2* (pp. 189–241). San Francisco: Jossey-Bass.

Smithers, R. (2006, June 15). *Minister promises to end adult illiteracy by 2020*. The online *Education Guardian*. Retrieved August 3, 2006, from http://education.guardian.co.uk/further/story/0,1797968,00.html.

Stein, S. (2000, January). *Equipped for the future content standards: What adults need to know and be able to do in the 21st century*. Washington, DC: National Institute for Literacy.

Sticht, T. G. (1998, September). *Beyond 2000: Future directions for adult education*. Washington, DC: U.S. Department of Education, Division of Adult Education and Literacy.

Sticht, T. G. (2001). The International Adult Literacy Survey: How well does it represent the literacy abilities of adults? *The Canadian Journal for the Study of Adult Education, 15*, 19–36.

Sticht, T. G. (2002). The rise of the Adult Education and Literacy System in the United States: 1600–2000. In J. Comings, B. Garner, & C. Smith. (Eds.), *The annual review of adult learning and literacy, Vol. 3* (pp. 10–43). San Francisco: Jossey-Bass.

Sticht, T. G., McDonald, B., & Erickson, P. (1998, January). *Passports to paradise: The struggle to teach and to learn on the margins of adult education*. El Cajon, CA: Applied Behavioral and Cognitive Sciences, Inc.

Tuijnman, A. (2000, September). *International Adult Literacy Survey: Benchmarking adult literacy in America: An international comparative study*. Jessup, MD: U.S. Department of Education, Education Publishing Center.

U.S. Department of Education (2003). *Adult education and family literacy act: Program Year 2000–2001. Report to Congress*. Washington, DC: U.S. Department of Education, Office of Vocational and Adult Education, Division of Adult Education and Literacy.

U.S. Department of Education (2005, March). *State-administered adult education program: Program Year 2003–2004 enrollment*. Washington, DC: U.S. Department of Education, Office of Vocational and Adult Education, Division of Adult Education and Literacy.

U.S. Department of Education (2006). *Adult education and family literacy act: Program Year 2003–2004. Report to Congress*. Washington, DC: U.S. Department of Education, Office of Vocational and Adult Education, Division of Adult Education and Literacy.

CHAPTER 30

New Technologies for Adult Literacy and International Development[1]

Daniel A. Wagner

[L]iteracy proficiency . . . has a substantial effect on earnings, a net effect that is independent of the effects of education.

OECD/Statistics Canada, 2000, p. 84

[T]he ICT revolution can provide powerful new tools both for addressing people's basic needs and for enriching the lives of poor people and communities in unprecedented ways.

G8 DOT, 2001, p. 10

Literacy is a human right.

Kofi Annan, 2003

Literacy and International Development

Few areas of social and economic development have received as much attention and as few proportionate resources as adult literacy. Across the world – in both industrialized and developing countries alike – it is widely acknowledged that at most, 5 percent of national education budgets is spent on the roughly 50 percent of the adult population in need of increased literacy skills.

For several centuries, it has been variously claimed that literacy – a key (if not *the* key) product of schooling – would lead to economic growth, social stability, a democratic way of life, and other social 'good things.' Detailed historical reviews have not been so kind to such generalizations (see several chapters in Wagner, Venezky & Street, 1999; also UNESCO, 2005), in that literacy 'campaigns,' in particular, were often more politically inspired than practically implemented (Wagner, 1986). General notions of national economic growth have been said to have a similar set of positive consequences for the poor. However, both universal literacy and universal economic growth have suffered from what has been called at times 'development fatigue' – namely, that governments and international agencies have come to feel that significant toil and funding have led to only limited return on investment.

Thus, as we near the halfway point of the United Nations (UN) Literacy Decade (declared initially in February 2003), one might legitimately ask what progress have we made and how far will the Decade take us? What has changed that leads us to believe that the goals and means for a special Decade will succeed when decades of prior effort have not? Do we have new or better ideas? One way to begin to answer such questions is to see whether the concepts and activities related to literacy work have remained the same or whether we have entered, to some extent, a changed era – where the needs and contexts for literacy, and our capabilities for promoting it, may have changed. In this chapter, it is first suggested that the need for literacy and basic skills has grown importantly, along with the contexts in which such skills need to be deployed. We then turn to some new capabilities for literacy promotion – more specifically, that of new technologies and how they are beginning to change what can be done to promote universal education for the twenty-first century. We draw connections between these new technologies and both the improvement of literacy and economic development.

In summary, this chapter suggests that there are important implications for the use of new technologies for the delivery of literacy education and for a new vision of what it means to be literate in a world fundamentally transformed by technology. The prospect exists that technological developments could offer new tools to help meet the substantive goals of literacy and education improvement, poverty reduction, and more. Finally, it is the contention of this chapter that a UN Decade that does not place technology at its forefront will be relegated to repeat the benevolent and ineffective efforts of the past – efforts that have meant relatively little for poor people in both wealthy and poor countries alike.

Although numerous national campaigns have been undertaken globally in the last half-century (Arnove & Graff, 1988), it comes as no surprise that the fundamental problems and the global statistics on literacy have changed only moderately, whether in industrialized or developing countries. Nonetheless, due in large part to the growth of competitive and knowledge-based economies across the world, most governments and international/bilateral agencies have expressed increasing concern about illiteracy and low literacy. Resource allocations, however, have remained as a disproportionately small fraction of what is contributed to formal schooling. As discussed herein, even substantial progress in primary-school attendance has driven quality downward in many poor countries, thereby giving an erroneous policy impression that literacy problems have been 'solved' by primary-school attendance (Greaney, Khandker, & Alam, 1999).

The 1990 UN World Conference on Education for All (EFA) in Jomtien, Thailand, included adult literacy as one of its six major worldwide goals. Specifically, a number of national educational goals related to youth and adult education were agreed upon, including (1) to reduce the number of adult illiterates to half of the 1990 level by 2000, while reducing the male–female disparity; and (2) to improve learning achievement to an agreed percentage of an appropriate age cohort (which might vary from country to country). As part of the Jomtien EFA goals, a new approach to learning was emphasized, one that focused on measurable learning achievement rather than mere class attendance or participation. These challenges, then, formed the basis for some renewed interest in literacy and adult education in the past two decades.

The UN General Assembly proclaimed the years 2003–2012 to be the UN Literacy Decade (United Nations, 2002a), which was officially launched in February 2003. The founding resolution (i.e., 56/116) reaffirmed the Dakar Framework for Action (UNESCO, 2000) in which the commitment was made to achieve a 50 percent improvement in adult literacy by 2015, especially for women, and equitable access to basic and continuing education for all adults. The International Action Plan for implementing Resolution 56/116 states that "literacy for all is at the heart of basic education for all and that creating literate environments and societies is essential for achieving goals of eradicating poverty, reducing child mortality, curbing population growth, achieving gender equality and ensuring sustainable development, peace, and democracy" (UN, 2002b, p. 3). The Plan calls for a *renewed vision* of literacy that goes beyond the limited view of literacy that has dominated in the past. The Plan elaborates: ". . . it has become necessary for all people to learn new literacies and develop the ability to locate, evaluate and effectively use information in multiple manners" (p. 4).

These proposals and plans came during a period of significant, interconnected economic, social, and technological changes in which literacy and education have become ever more important to personal, social, and national development. Economists acknowledge that a profound shift occurred in the role that knowledge and technology play in driving productivity and global economic growth (Stiglitz, 2000), a phenomenon referred to as the "knowledge economy" (OECD, 1996). From this perspective, knowledge is both the engine and the product of economic growth (OECD, 1999). The production, distribution, and use of new knowledge and information are major contributors to increased innovation, productivity, and creation of new, high-paying jobs. Developments in human, institutional, and technological capabilities are, in turn, major sources of new knowledge and innovation.

A parallel, linked consequence – sometimes referred to as the "information society" (European Commission, 2000) – is the broader social transformation resulting from the convergence of computers and communication technologies and their assimilation throughout society. As information and communication technologies (ICTs) – ranging now from laptops wirelessly connected to the Internet to cell-phones, Web browsers, personal digital assistants, and low-cost video cameras – become more accessible and embedded in society, they are said to offer the potential to make education and health care more widely available, foster cultural creativity and productivity, increase democratic participation and the responsiveness of governmental agencies, and enhance the social integration of individuals and groups with different abilities and of different cultural backgrounds. Of course, these claims remain largely untested to date (Cuban, 2003), but there is nonetheless great public hope for ICT impact, as described in the next section.

Technology and Literacy

The UN Development Program (UNDP, 2001) provided a model that illustrates the relationship among technology, skill development, and economic development. According to this model, a country's ICT investments can directly enhance the capabilities of its citizens. Increased skill capacity, in turn, can support the further development and increase the productive use of the technological infrastructure. The growing sophistication of the skill base and the technological infrastructure can lead to innovation and the creation of new knowledge and new industries. New knowledge and innovation support the growth of the economy that, in turn, provides resources needed to further develop the human, economic, and technological infrastructure and the welfare of society.

Personal participation in this technology-knowledge-economic development cycle begins with literacy. ICT is viewed here primarily as a set of potential delivery and instructional tools that can be used to help people acquire the skills associated with traditional notions of literacy. In this approach, computer-assisted tutorials and other technology-supported resources can make education more accessible and help adults improve their ability to decode and comprehend prose text, thus increasing their literacy, employability, and continued use of literacy skills to become life-long learners. The policy implications of this approach are relatively straightforward: Are the expenses associated with providing the hardware, software and delivery infrastructure for literacy learning less than those required to provide this training by some other means? Or, if not less expensive, are technology-based means more effective than traditional means and sufficiently so to justify the added costs?

The goal of this chapter is to present a set of possible visions on the ways that technology can support the development of youth and adult literacy, as well as nonformal education in a global perspective (with an emphasis on developing countries). We start with a description of the status, trends, and problems related to adult literacy and issues related to the application of technology to address these problems. We then analyze various approaches to using ICT to support adult literacy and basic education. Discussion follows on ways in which ICT developments can be relevant to industrialized and developing countries alike. We build a case for new notions of literacy and how technology influences and supports the basic literacy and information skills so crucial for economic and social development. The chapter concludes with implications and options for the use – or rather, necessity – of expanded roles for new ICTs in literacy development.

Status and Trends

Many countries have been actively striving to achieve Jomtien's major goal of meeting the basic learning needs for all children, youth and adults, as well as the conjoint necessity for an adequate methodology to understand whether such goals are being met. Current national and international capacities remain limited, however, for a variety of historical reasons. In the literacy domain, there is a long tradition of statistics-gathering; however, due to changing definitions of literacy as well as a dearth of human capacity in the educational measurement field, the data on and definitions of literacy have long been open to question and debate.

Concepts and Definitions

All definitions of literacy relate in some way, at their core, to an individual's ability to understand and communicate through written text (printed or digital). Most contemporary definitions portray literacy in *relative* rather than absolute terms – gone are the days when the 'scourge' of illiteracy (and illiterates) needed to be 'eradicated.' Four of the better known definitions of literacy are as follows:

> *A person is literate who can with understanding both read and write a short simple statement on his everyday life. . . . A person is functionally literate who can engage in all those activities in which literacy is required for effective functioning of his group and community. . . . (UNESCO, 1978)*

> *[Literacy is] using printed and written information to function in society to achieve one's goals and to develop one's knowledge and potential. (OECD/Statistics Canada, 1995)*

> *The ability to understand and employ printed information in daily activities, at home, at work and in the community – to achieve one's goals, and to develop one's knowledge and potential. (OECD/Statistics Canada, 2000)*

> *[Literacy has moved] beyond its simple notion as the set of technical skills of reading, writing and calculating. . . to a plural notion encompassing the manifold meanings and dimensions of these undeniably vital competencies. Such a view, responding to recent economic, political and social transformations, including globalization, and the advancement of* information and communication technologies, *recognizes that there are many practices of literacy embedded in different cultural processes, personal circumstances and collective structures. (UNESCO, 2005; emphasis added)*

Traditional definitions of literacy have been used to develop national and international assessments of literacy. International literacy data from UNESCO are widely used for making country-level cross-sectional and longitudinal comparisons. As with other aggregated country-level indicators, these data suffer reliability and validity weaknesses that stem from some chronic methodological flaws. Because the definitions of literacy are continually evolving, measures that remain the same have increasingly narrow and limited use. Constantly changing measures, however, render data invalid for across-time comparisons. However, for lack of suitable alternatives, the UNESCO data are deemed sufficient for aggregate-level analyses, provided that the limitations they present to making inferences are properly acknowledged. More detailed literacy assessments for specific populations need to be undertaken separately.

Contemporary definitions of learning competencies are prompting the development of new approaches to assessment that consider new ICTs (ETS, 2002; OECD/Statistics Canada, 2000; UNESCO, 2004; Wagner, 2005a). These approaches often emphasize the use of technology to search for and select relevant information, interpret and analyze data, and use this information to communicate effectively with others, create new knowledge products, and solve practical problems. Such assessments are currently in the development and pilot-testing phase and are scheduled for wider implementation later in this decade. Their implementation will allow researchers and policy makers to chart the development of these new skills, connect the impact of literacy programs to the requirements of the knowledge economy, and adjust policies and programs accordingly. As part of this effort, a definition of "ICT literacy" has now become important; following is one example:

> *ICT literacy proficiency is the ability to use digital technology, communication tools and networks appropriately to solve information problems in order to function in an information society. This includes the ability to use technology as a tool to research, organize, evaluate and communicate information, and the possession of a fundamental understanding of the ethical/legal issues surrounding the access and use of information. (Educational Testing Service, 2002)*

Trends in Technology Development

There has always been a strong relationship between the development of new technologies, major social transformations, and changing definitions of what it takes to be a literate person. These changes have not always been viewed as positive by contemporaries. In Plato's *Phaedrus*, Socrates bemoaned the introduction of written text because he felt it would reduce the skill of memory and the ability to engage in active discourse – skills that were necessary for an informed citizen of his day. He felt that written text was inferior to oral discourse because of its lack of interactivity – the reader could not engage in dialog with it. Yet, skills in decoding and comprehending written text have become the core of our conception of literacy. The invention of the printing press made the knowledge encoded in text available to a larger number of people and it made mass literacy an important part of everyday life. The press and the knowledge made available with it spawned significant social transformations, such as the rise of Protestantism and the scientific revolution.

Recent years have seen a tremendous growth in technological development, much of it related to the invention of the computer (see Figure 30.1; adapted from UN Development Program (UNDP), 2001).

In the sixty years from the end of World War II to the beginning of the second millennium, computers evolved from bulky, room-sized machines designed to calculate military firing tables to the compact, typewriter-sized devices found in a third of American homes, in half of American workplaces, and in classrooms serving more than 70 percent of American students (Newburger, 2001), and these numbers will have increased to near asymptote in industrialized countries as we approach 2010. In less than thirty years – roughly half the evolutionary time of computers – the Internet grew from a top-secret military computer network (designed to survive a nuclear first strike) into a popular and nearly-ubiquitous information system. Its structural growth has been astounding – from a network of approximately 160,000 Internet host computers in 1989 to 100 million by 1999, to billions today. In less than a decade – about half the time it took the Internet to

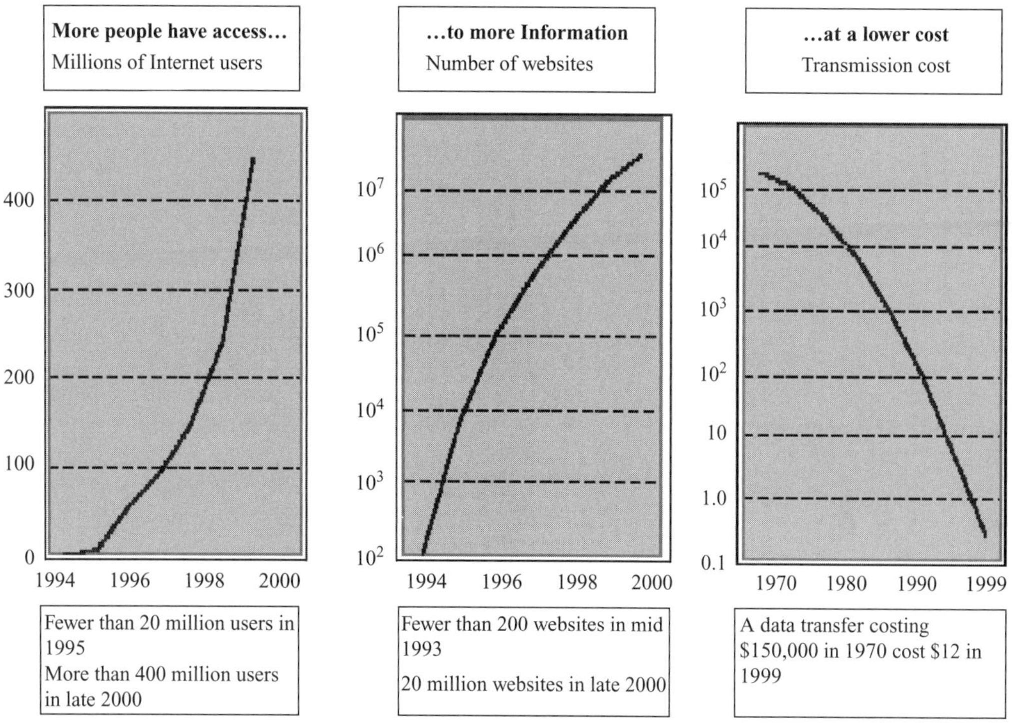

Figure 30.1. Changes in global Internet consumption.

grow – the World Wide Web developed from an information-swapping technology serving a close-knit community of Swiss particle physicists into a cultural tidal wave of nearly uncountable numbers Web sites. It was estimated that there were 550 billion individual documents on the Web as of 2000 (Bergman, 2001), with these numbers growing exponentially every year.

Such dramatic technological developments cannot help but be associated with significant social transformations, such as the economic and societal developments referenced at the beginning of this chapter (European Commission, 2000; OECD, 1996, 1999). However, although these technological and social trends are global, they have not benefited equally all nations and groups of people. The concept of a *digital divide* between the haves and have-nots in the United States and globally is nearly a decade old, and it remains a constant concern, especially in global perspective (OECD, 2001, 2002). Whereas this term originally referred to simple access to personal computers and other 'new' technologies, the accelerating growth of the Internet in the 1990s quickly became the major thrust of what it meant to 'be connected' (i.e., to the Web). Even as late as 2001, there were huge differences among the industrialized countries that form the OECD, such that Scandinavian countries had nearly five times the per-capita connectivity of countries such as Hungary, Greece and France (Figure 30.2). Although dramatic changes occurred in access to hardware and in Internet connectivity in the first few years of this century, major differences still exist between industrialized and developing nations (International Telecommunication Union, 2003). Furthermore, as noted in a major government publication (U.S. Department of Commerce, 2002), the digital divide in the United States may well be shrinking if one considers the primary parameter to be 'getting connected.' Indeed, Figure 30.3 suggests that the poor in the United States are gaining connectivity at least as rapidly as the more affluent.

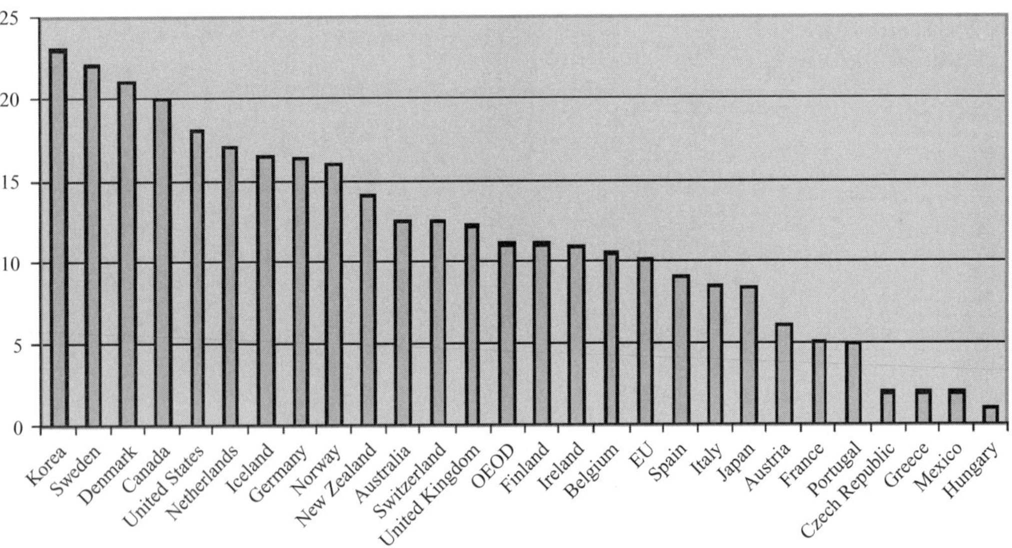

Figure 30.2. Percent Internet subscriber (per 100 inhabitants) in OECD countries, 2000.

However, some critics reviewed the same data and suggested that the key parameter in the first decade of the twenty-first century is not simply connectivity but rather the *bandwidth* possessed. In terms of bandwidth, the poor are still as far behind the rich as when the rich were far ahead in ICT access alone (Warschauer, 2004). This is not a minor issue, of course, because educational multimedia is increasingly taking advantage of still and moving images that require large digital files that cannot be effectively utilized on low-bandwidth, modem-based retrieval. Nowhere is this more obvious than in telecommunications-poor Africa, where Internet access has been crippled by low bandwidth. In summary, in one form or another, the digital divide in hardware and connectivity is likely to remain *divisive* for a long time to come and will clearly affect education and development choices.

There is another more subtle digital divide that is rarely discussed: the *digital language* divide. In the field of literacy, there is probably no other issue that has engendered as much debate and concern as language of instruction (Wagner, 2005b). There are those who strongly assert the need for literacy in the mother tongue and those who say that such programs are far too expensive – that social and economic dynamics are such that international languages are simply more cost-effective. Although not a major focus of this chapter, the issue of language

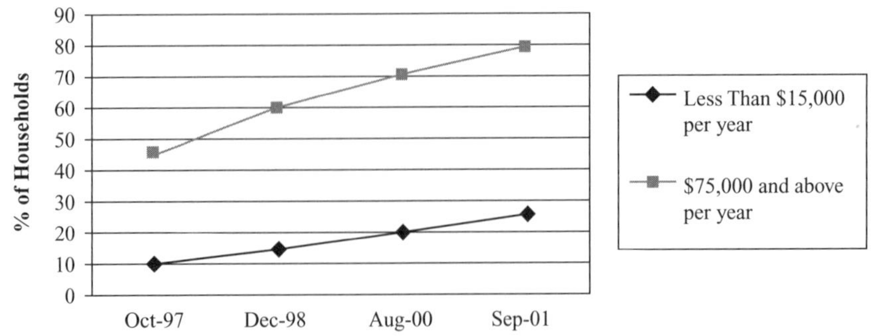

Figure 30.3. Percentage of U.S. households with Internet access by income, 1997–2001.

of instruction (LOI) is one that has special meaning when taken in conjunction with ICTs.

One reason for this is that the Internet itself is *not* language-neutral. Indeed, recent research shows that English is more present (with 60 percent of total volume) on the World Wide Web (Web) than all other languages combined (Langer, 2001). It is interesting that the dominance of English has dropped somewhat from an even greater dominance only a couple of years earlier (i.e., 65 percent in mid-1999). Still, no other language exceeds even 10 percent of the English total (German was in second place, at 6 percent of overall Web presence). Although similar data are not available for software production, a substantial dominance is likely to be found for English, at the expense of other languages: even the major international (e.g., French, Spanish), metropolitan (e.g., Hindi, Swahili) and national/local 'minority' languages (e.g., Telugu in India, with 60 million speakers; or Mayan in Mexico, with several million speakers) receive relatively little digital attention.

Of course, the digital revolution did not create this situation of language dominance, which has gone on for centuries. Simply stated, literacy programs have found it difficult to teach in local LOIs for a set of well-known reasons (Wagner, 2000), including poor and insufficient materials in local LOIs, lack of research-based materials in local LOIs, and teachers who are poorly trained in local LOIs. These problems in local LOI print-based programs have been in existence for a long time – and this is precisely an area in which digital materials can make a difference. It is very possible that the language-based digital divide can be bridged more easily than the language-in-print divide, if only because translation and production costs in digital media are decreasing regularly, whereas the costs of hardcopy printed materials are continually increasing. See one recent example, described further below, in the state of Andhra Pradesh in India, where the local LOI (Telugu) has been integrated into a multimedia platform via CD-ROM to teach basic skills to out-of-school youth as well as to elementary school children (Wagner & Daswani, 2006).

Technology in Support of Literacy and Basic Skills

There are two interconnected approaches by which ICT can be used to develop literacy and adult education. The first is to use technology to support the development of basic literacy skills. With this approach, the computational capabilities of computers can be used to deliver instruction in support of the cognitive skills needed to read and understand text. Basic literacy skill is not only of value in itself but is also essential for using text to learn other important skills. Second, as literacy in society increases, technology also can be used to efficiently support education at a distance when instruction and other resources might not be otherwise available. Furthermore, the capabilities of ICTs are improving dramatically and have significant implications for the support of cognitive skills. These advanced technologies also have significant costs with implications for policy decisions. We explore these possibilities and issues in the following sections.

Basic Literacy Skills

Traditional approaches to literacy focus on the skills of reading and writing text. Text-reading involves processes of decoding and comprehension, and it is a cognitively demanding task for new readers (Just & Carpenter, 1987; Perfetti, 1989; Sabatini, 1999; Snow & Strucker, 2000). The reader must use decoding skills to convert the printed text into the mental equivalent of spoken words while also constructing a mental understanding of what the words mean – that is, comprehend what the text is saying. These two processes interact and they can help or detract from each other. For fluent readers, the process of text-decoding is automatic and most of the reader's cognitive resources are used to understand the meaning of the text. Conversely, an understanding of the text topic helps the reader figure out an unfamiliar word or difficult passage. However, the process is slow for readers with limited decoding skills who spend more of their cognitive resources on the act of decoding. Consequently, there are fewer cognitive resources available for understanding the meaning of the text, and the slowness of the process makes it more difficult for readers to keep their understanding in memory so as to support decoding and continued comprehension. Also, the more unfamiliar or complex the subject matter of the text, the more challenging is the task of comprehension.

Decoding, especially the sounding out of words (in alphabetic scripts), is a major problem for adult illiterates, as shown in the United States (Perfetti & Marron, 1995) and in developing countries (Abadzi, 2003). However, adult literacy learners have an advantage over young readers in that they often bring a strong sense of purpose, a significant amount of world knowledge, and – for those learning to read their mother tongue – a significant spoken vocabulary that they can use to help with decoding. Whereas the specific purposes and background knowledge vary significantly among adults, the more the text deals with topics that are familiar and interesting to adults (rather than topics that are familiar and interesting to children), the more mental resources will be available to focus on building and using decoding skills and the more motivated students will be to continue their engagement in the reading process. As decoding skills and comprehension strategies develop, these literacy skills can become more self-regulated and can be used to understand increasingly challenging texts. They become a significant resource for further learning throughout one's lifetime (Chall, 1987). Thus, these basic literacy skills become the foundation for further text-based instruction and learning.

The main productive component of literacy is writing in terms of text created (although many have argued that reading is mentally productive as well). Whereas those new to writing may struggle with the psychomotor competencies needed to create simple letters and words, the emphasis in most writing assessments is on the cognitive skills needed to generate, draft, revise, and edit ideas in written form (National Assessment Governing Board, 1998). At the most basic level, this involves a command of spelling, grammar, punctuation, and capitalization sufficient enough to communicate to the reader. However, more advanced writers should be able to express analytical, critical, and creative thinking in well-crafted, cohesive written text whether it is for narrative, informative, or persuasive purposes.

In considering the use of new technologies for basic literacy skills, we focus both on how to structure effectively the use of technology to support the development of literacy skills in and out of school and how to provide access to educational opportunities for adult learners.

ICTs in Support of Basic Literacy Skills

Increasingly, the use of new (and old) ICTs has become a topic of great interest to adult literacy educators, both in the United States and abroad (Askov, Johnston, Petty, & Young, 2003; Rosen, 2000; Sabatini, 2001; Stites, 2004; Wagner & Hopey, 1998; Wagner, 2001). Technology can be used in two primary ways to support the acquisition of literacy skills, as traditionally defined. First, the capabilities of technology can be used to support development of the cognitive processes and basic skills involved in literacy. For the purposes of this discussion, the focus is on beginning reading, which has received the most attention in ICT-based instruction. Second, technology can be used effectively to support the development of literacy skills for learning at a distance when instruction and other resources might not be otherwise available.

The first application of ICT draws on the interactive abilities of the computer. The computer has the nearly unique capability – compared with other (older) technologies – to accept 'input' and use this to determine its subsequent presentation of information or 'output.' This input-processing-output capability can be used to develop computer-based tutorials that support the cognitive processes involved in reading, primarily those related to decoding. New developments in hardware and software are increasing the computer's ability to provide such support; and, it should be mentioned, there are new tools based on computer chips called 'talking books' that do not require a computer but offer some of the same enhanced interactive capabilities, as may be seen in the "Kindle" of Amazon.com (Wagner & Kozma, 2005).

One-to-one human tutors were found to have substantial positive and long-lasting effects on the skill development of early youth readers, especially when certified teachers were used as tutors (Wasik & Slavin, 1993); the data are less clear with adult readers in the United States (Wagner & Venezky, 1999). Unfortunately, many developing countries have a significant shortage of trained teachers for classroom instruction, let alone one-to-one tutoring. Computer-based tutorials – sometimes referred to as 'computer-assisted instruction' (CAI) – augmented by multimedia capabilities may be able to provide learners with the skillful interaction that human tutors otherwise can provide. The available data on CAI innovations in early reading instruction to date come primarily from research on American schoolchildren. A typical lesson involves the presentation of instructional information in any or several of a variety of forms, such as text, sound, pictures, and video (Alessi & Trollip, 2000). This multimedia capability is particularly important for new readers because it supplements their limited ability to use text for instruction by providing spoken information and pictorial content. In turn, the student is asked to enter some type of response into the computer, such as selecting the best choice of multiple choices presented. The software then provides feedback on this response, which usually tells the learner if the response is correct and, if not, why it is not and what the right answer should be. With newer and better designed tutorials, feedback will be specifically tailored to the type of error that the learner has made. The analysis of the learner's response will also determine the information that the learner receives next. This type of interactivity is rarely available for individual students in classes with large enrolments and the customization of subsequent instruction is perhaps not feasible at all. These characteristics of tutorial software represent – at least, in principle – a potential benefit or advantage over classroom instruction and account for their appeal.

More powerful computers are needed to present multimedia instruction. Until recently, the software for even the newer multimedia computers has been limited in its ability to accept and analyze a variety of responses. However, these capabilities are changing, and the changes have significant implications for the needs of literacy learners.

ICTs in Support of Distance Learning

Another major application of ICT to support adult education is distance learning, which is often used where there are insufficient numbers of qualified and trained teachers. For this reason, distance learning is playing an increasingly important role in developing countries (UNESCO, 2002). The roots of distance learning go back to correspondence programs, primarily in higher education; the earliest programs in developing countries were in the Philippines (in 1940) and Indonesia (in 1955). With the development and dissemination of radio and television, developing countries used these technologies to address the educational needs of remote populations. Beyond these traditional technologies, ICTs are now playing a role in creating 'virtual classrooms' that support distance learning. E-learning at present is focused mainly within higher education and is growing rapidly in adult education in the United States (Askov et al., 2003). Each technology may allow adult learners to access otherwise unavailable resources and use their growing literacy skills to further their education. Because the primary use of technology in poor countries remains in radio and television where there has been some evaluation research, it is useful to provide a summary before moving on to new ICTs for which less solid research exists.

As broadcast technologies, radio and television have the advantage of leveraging costs (initially for the production and distribution facilities and subsequently for the production of individual programs) to address the needs of a large number of users over distance and, with rebroadcast, over time. For example, the UNESCO/UNICEF Gobi Desert Project in Mongolia used radio to deliver education to fifteen thousand nomadic women in literacy skills, livestock-rearing techniques, family care, income generation and basic business skills (Robinson, 1997). The radio program included visiting teachers and small information centers that served as meeting places for learning groups. *Telesecundaria*, a secondary-level education television series in Mexico, served more than 800,000 students during the 1997–1998 school year (Kelley-Salinas, 2001; Wolf, Castro, Navarro & Garcia, 2002). By 1990, China, India, Indonesia, Iran, the Islamic Republic of Pakistan, the Republic of Korea, Sri Lanka, Thailand and Turkey had all used broadcast media to set up national open universities, with most of these institutions having more than 100,000 students and 400,000 at the China Radio and TV University (Perraton & Creed, 2002).

Historically, educational broadcast programs started off in 'talking-head' format and were designed to distribute information very inexpensively to large numbers of students. However, the lack of interactivity and, in the case of radio, the lack of visuals significantly limited the instructional support that can be provided to students. More recent developments have found ways to work around some of those limitations.

For example, interactive radio instruction (IRI) uses a methodology that requires learners to stop and react to questions and exercises through verbal response to radio characters and engages them in group work and physical and intellectual activities while the radio program is on the air (Bosch, Rhodes, & Kariuki, 2002). Short pauses are provided throughout the lessons, after questions and during exercises, to ensure that students have time to think and respond adequately. Typically used in formal classroom settings, the program also encourages interaction between the teacher and learners as they work together on problems, activities or experiments. Materials and activities in the classroom compensate for the limited ability that radio has to provide information in various forms and to give students feedback on their responses. Probably the best known application of educational television is *Sesame Street*, which airs in 140 countries around the world. Called *Zhima Jie* in China, *Takalani Sesame* in South Africa, and *Alam SimSim* in Egypt, it is preparing children in 140 countries around the world to begin school and literacy. For example, in Egypt, more than 90 percent of children under age eight (i.e., more than 4 million children) in urban areas and 86 percent of children in rural areas watch the show (Ward-Bent, 2002). Significantly, 54 percent of mothers regularly view the series.

Whereas broadcast radio and television have had a long history in distance education, the use of the computer to create virtual classrooms at a distance is quite new and has not yet taken hold in most developing countries. However, despite its recency, the practice has become quite common in industrialized countries. Relying extensively on the Internet and Web, virtual learning can either supplement an existing face-to-face class or entirely replace the face-to-face experience, with learners never meeting their teacher or other students (Harasim et al., 1995; Hiltz, 1995; Palloff & Pratt, 1999, 2000; Zucker & Kozma, 2003). Indeed, some virtual experiences eliminate the teacher's role altogether or reduce it to an available online advisor, relying instead on the student's interaction with extensive online materials. Alternatively, the program may try to reproduce the face-to-face experience online, with teachers and students holding electronic discussions in a virtual space, either synchronously or asynchronously. These meetings may be conducted as online 'text chat' or using more sophisticated and expensive teleconferencing equipment. These environments make significant demands on text-comprehension skills, as well as on motivation and the self-direction of learning (Wagner & Hopey, 1999).

Technology in Support of a Broader Vision of Literacy

Another approach to the use of technology is to consider ICT in the broader context of economic and social development and to examine the way technology is changing what it means to be a literate person. Clearly, the welfare of both the economy and the society more generally depends on the creation, exchange, and use of information – information that is increasingly in digital form. In this regard, a broader vision of literacy seems to be warranted, as acknowledged by the UN Literacy Decade Action Plan (United Nations, 2002b). As networked computers, wireless PDAs, video cameras and other information and communication technologies become integrated into everyday life, additional skills are needed to operate the technology and use it to benefit from and contribute to society. Beyond the traditional skills needed to read and write text, new skills are needed to use technology to search for, organize, and manage information; interpret and analyze data; work with distributed teams; communicate with others; and use information to solve problems and create new knowledge and cultural artifacts.

Furthermore, literacy has come to be viewed by researchers more recently as not just a cognitive process but also a social process by which people in a community use spoken and written language to understand, communicate and accomplish important tasks in their everyday lives at school, home, the workplace and other social settings (Olson & Torrance, 2000; Street, 1999; Wagner, 1995, 2000). This *broader* notion of literacy fits the needs and reality of adult literacy learners and users better than the narrower notion of literacy as the cognitive processes of reading and writing text. It provides a purpose and value for literacy, comprising the skills and activities of a community that generates, shares, and uses knowledge for the betterment of its members.

The previous section focused on ICTs as delivery tools that can support the acquisition and use of basic skills needed to read and write text. This section adds these new 'information skills' to the definition of literacy and emphasizes ICT as a productive technology that can be used to communicate and create new knowledge in a variety of forms within a social context in which information and knowledge are used to solve problems, share cultural practices, and advance the welfare and economic development of a community. Clearly, these may be seen, for the most part, as more 'advanced' literacy skills that build on the more basic skills of reading and writing. Although this broader definition may seem to be largely theoretical and conceptual, it is shown in the following discussion that there are a number of important practical implications.

Information Literacy and the Use of Digital Information

At the intersection of technology and literacy, one must consider what is already part of both mainstream and lay thinking. Notions of 'computer literacy,' 'technological literacy' and 'information literacy' not only borrow terminology from text literacy but also begin to redefine what 'text' is and the tools and skills that literate people need to use and create it (Murray, 2000; Tyner, 1998). However, it must be understood that these terms do not necessarily connote the same thing in the present discussion. An important distinction in this chapter is between the skills that are specifically required to manage technology (e.g., in 'computer literacy,' this would be using a mouse, connecting to the Internet, and so forth) and those skills that are required to manage information (e.g., how to organize, search, and produce digital information). This is what is referred to as 'information literacy.'

Information literacy and text literacy have different implications for the skills needed to use, produce, and share information. Whereas text literacy remains the foundation for information literacy, the latter involves the convergence of text, sound, and video, and it offers the reader/viewer information in multiple media. Information presented in additional and sometimes redundant forms may reduce the skill level that is required to use information; this can be particularly important for adult literacy learners. However, the storage of and instant access to millions of digital documents on the Web and the unique navigational conventions of hypertext require a different set of strategies to find, read, and use these documents. As a consequence, information literacy has come to encompass a broader range of human competencies needed to access and manage information, analyze and interpret this information, critically evaluate its relevance and credibility, and to use information to solve everyday problems, collaboratively create knowledge products, and communicate ideas in a variety of media for purposes valued by a community (21st Century Partnership, 2003; Committee on Information Technology Literacy, 1999; ETS, 2002; ISTE, 1998; OECD/Statistics Canada, 2000).

Literacy, the Internet, and the Creation of Digital Products

As learners acquire and solidify basic literacy skills, these skills can be used to acquire the more advanced information literacy skills needed to be productive and successful in a knowledge economy and information society that is increasingly influenced by technology. To participate and contribute to these changes, learners must not only be able to access and manage the information of others, they also will need to be able to produce their own digital, multimedia content.

The ability to use equipment such as computers, video cameras, and recording equipment will become more important but so will the skills needed to use authoring packages – that is, the set of software tools that can help users create multimedia or hypertext products that will appear on the Web. Hypertexts are electronic documents that contain embedded links to yet other Web pages, texts, images, sounds, definitions, examples, and so on. Common Web-design packages help users create multimedia hypertext Web sites without the need to know a lower-level scripting language such as Hypertext Markup Language (HTML). They make it relatively easy to format text and pictures, embed other media, and create navigational devices. To date, the educational use of these tools has been primarily the domain of vocational or technical education, where students are taught skills that prepare them for jobs (Eisenberg & Johnson, 2002). However, training in their use can be of significant value for adult education programs in developing countries that are trying to build their technological infrastructure and human capacities.

Information Literacy and New Approaches to Learning and Teaching

Information literacy relies on and supports new approaches to curriculum, learning and teaching. An educational goal that values the collaborative creation and use of knowledge conflicts in a fundamental way with approaches to teaching and learning that emphasize only the authoritative role of teachers and textbooks and the rote memorization of facts and procedures. New approaches to learning and teaching emphasize not only the importance of established knowledge in the curriculum but also the primary responsibility of students for their own learning; the importance of group and community in supporting the learning process; and the role of assessment in providing ongoing information that students, teachers, and others can use to monitor progress and measure success (Bransford, Brown, & Cocking, 2000).

In their review, Nunes and Gaibel (2002) provided a useful schema for thinking about the connections between ICT and such new approaches to learning and teaching. Their schema is adapted herein as follows:

- *Learner centered.* Increasingly, ICT environments will be sensitive to specific and diverse learner needs. Information will be customized to the interests of the learner, presented in appropriate modalities, addressing his or her specific educational goals, and building on his or her everyday experiences and cultural and linguistic strengths.
- *Knowledge centered.* Sophisticated tutorial environments will support students in their mastery of knowledge and skills in specific subject domains, including literacy. Rather than merely cover or include a wide range of topics, technology will be used to help students to accomplish important specific learning standards, interconnect and integrate what they learn, develop a deep understanding and use this as a base to learn more.
- *Assessment centered.* Technology will actively assess students' learning throughout the educational process, not just at the end of a course or school year. Software will provide regular feedback to the learner so that the learner, if working alone, can gain sufficient insight as to what may be best learned next.
- *Community centered.* Context is important to the success of learning. Literacy programs will be more successful when skills can be used to accomplish multiple social and economic goals. Learners can gain an awareness of their place in the broader world around them, at the village, regional, national and global levels.

Case studies of innovative schools in twenty-eight countries in North and South America, Europe, Asia, and Africa found important similarities in how teaching and learning is changing and how ICT supports these changes (Kozma, 2003a, 2003b). The studies found that in a large majority of these innovative classrooms, teachers were engaged in advising and guiding their students' work along with more traditional practices such as creating structure and monitoring or assessing student performance. Students used productivity tools, Web resources, email and multimedia software, and they collaborated with each other to search for information, publish or present the results of their projects or research, and design or create various digital products. As a result, teachers claimed that students acquired ICT skills, developed positive attitudes toward learning or school, and acquired new subject-matter knowledge and collaborative skills.

Social Structures and Information Literacy in Developing Countries

Information literacy activities occur with great variation across cultures in both industrialized and developing nations, but it is clear that they are most often associated with formal schooling where such information-based knowledge products have substantial inherent value. However, these processes, purposes and contexts – and the technologies that support them – may seem quite far removed from the lives of youth and adult learners in developing countries. This seeming contrast is likely more apparent than real. Indeed, the use of technology to support adult literacy and learning in developing counties may require especially those types of skills that are described herein, which may be the most efficient route to improving literacy in poor countries. As counterintuitive as it may seem at first glance, it is the present contention that *only by using ICTs will the promotion of adult literacy succeed* in making substantial inroads in the ongoing dismal world statistics. More important, only by using ICTs will we be preparing low-literate adults for a future that will increasingly require the types of flexible skill sets that are needed in a competitive, global economy and a society increasingly influenced by ICT. Even so, the use of ICT to advance literacy in developing countries presents significant challenges that require novel social structures that reach beyond the classroom and into the community.

An example of this approach may be seen in the *Bridges to the Future Initiative* (BFI; www.bridgestothefuture.org), which is designed to provide basic and information-literacy skills for the poorest of the poor, including minorities, indigenous-language speakers, and the unschooled. There are three components to the BFI: (1) development of community learning and technology centers for lifelong learning, basic and ICT skill acquisition, and high-impact information resources in local languages; (2) development of ICT-based tools to improve teacher training; and (3) development of innovative ICT applications for human development and sustainability. Initiated by the International Literacy Institute, the BFI has active programs in India, South Africa, and Ghana. In the Indian state of Andhra Pradesh, the BFI has thirteen dual-purpose community learning and technology centers, mainly located in secondary schools to save on ICT costs. These centers, which are open after regular school hours, have begun to provide Telugu-language resources for helping children and youth get back into school, literacy and life skills instruction for out-of-school youth and adults, and e-government resources that are both online and offline. An additional two hundred primary schools have now been added to the BFI–India project. In collaboration with other partners, the program is providing culturally and linguistically appropriate learning resources for illiterate and low-literate youth and adults. Recent evaluation research has confirmed the significant impact of the BFI program on children and young adults in India (Wagner & Daswani, 2008).

Conclusions

We have now reached the halfway mark of the UN Literacy Decade. Its success will depend on the mobilization of the best talents that can be brought to bear on worldwide literacy problems. The use – indeed, the increased use – of effective and appropriate technologies can play a significant role in creating a more literate world. Conversely, the failure to take appropriate advantage of ICTs to help improve the lives of the poorest and least-schooled populations of the world make it all the more difficult to achieve the goals of the UN Decade.

At the same time, if this argument is correct, it is essential to understand that neither more hardware nor more connectivity *alone* will have much effect on the positive consequences for poor people. At the policy level, most ICT resources still end up where they are least likely to be effective for poor people. At the professional level, human resources (whether in content or in ICT design), as well as teacher training, remain heavily weighted toward the formal K–12 education sector, where the majority of national budgets reside. This needs to change if literacy is to be increased. Furthermore, literacy and technology are becoming *interdependent*. Literacy and technology are 'tools' that have much in common. Neither is an end unto itself, but each can amplify human skills and human development. Literacy education needs to take advantage of the power of technology, especially as national economies require an ever more skilled population of workers.

In this chapter, the main focus was on literacy for the poor and underserved. However, as statistics indicate worldwide, there are substantial differences between what 'being poor' means and represents in different countries, even within the poorest developing countries. As discussed, there are ICT 'digital divide' programs that may widen the divide by investing in the top (i.e., easier to reach) parts of the spectrum of the disadvantaged population. Thus, it is suggested that if the UN Decade is to succeed, it must also try to reach those at the bottom end of the literacy divide and to pay attention to how ICTs can make a special contribution.

Note

1 Prepared at the International Literacy Institute (ILI) and the National Center on Adult Literacy (NCAL) with support from the U.S. Department of Education, Spencer

Foundation, JPMorganChase Foundation, and UNESCO. This chapter is drawn in part from earlier work by Wagner and Kozma (2005), originally prepared for the UN World Summit on Information Societies (Tunis, Tunisia).

References

21st Century Partnership (2003). *Learning for the 21st Century*. Washington, DC: 21st Century Partnership.

Abadzi, H. (2003). *Improving adult literacy outcomes: Lessons from cognitive research for developing countries*. Operations and evaluation department. Washington, DC: World Bank.

Alessi, S. M., & Trollip, S. R. (2000). *Multimedia for learning: Methods and development* (3rd Ed.). Boston: Allyn & Bacon.

Annan, K. (2003, February 13). Remarks by UN Secretary-General Kofi Annan at the New York Public Library, New York.

Arnove, R. F., & Graff, H. J. (Eds.) (1988). *National literacy campaigns*. New York: Plenum.

Askov, Eunice N., Johnston, Jerome, Petty, Leslie I., & Young, Shannon J. (2003). Expanding access to adult literacy with online distance education. Cambridge, MA.: National Center for the Study of Adult Learning and Literacy (NCSALL). (http://www.ncsall.net/fileadmin/resources/research/op_askov.pdf)

Bergman, M. (2001). The deep Web: Surfacing hidden value. *The Journal of Electronic Publishing*, 7 (1). Available at http://www.press.umich.edu/jep/07-01/bergman.html.

Bosch, A., Rhodes, R., & Kariuki, S. (2002). Interactive radio instruction: An update from the field. In W. Haddad (Ed.), *Technologies for education: Potentials, parameters, and prospects* (pp. 134–143). Paris: UNESCO.

Bransford, J., Brown, A., & Cocking, R. (2000). *How people learn: Brain, mind, experience, and school*. Washington, DC: National Academic Press.

Bruce, B., Peyton, J., & Batson, T. (1993). *Network-based classrooms: Promises and realities*. New York: Cambridge University Press.

Chall, J. (1987). Developing literacy in children and adults. In D. A. Wagner (Ed.), *The future of literacy in a changing world* (pp. 65–80). New York: Pergamon Press.

Committee on Information Technology Literacy (1999). *Being fluent with information technology*. Washington, DC: National Academy Press.

Cuban, L. (2003). *Oversold and underused: Computers in the classroom*. Cambridge, MA: Harvard University Press.

Educational Testing Service (ETS) (2002). *Digital transformation: A framework for ICT literacy*. Princeton, NJ: ETS.

Eisenberg, M., & Johnson, D. (2002). Learning and teaching information technology computer skills in context. *ERIC Digest* (Technical Report EDO-IR-2002-04). Syracuse, NY: ERIC Clearinghouse on Information and Technology.

European Commission (2000). *Europe: An information society for all*. Brussels: European Commission.

G8 Digital Opportunities Task Force (G8 DOT) (2001). *Digital opportunities for all: Meeting the challenge*. Siena, Italy: G8 DOT.

Greaney, V., Khandker, S. R., & Alam, M. (1999). *Bangladesh: Assessing basic learning skills*. Washington, DC: World Bank.

Haddad, W. D., & Jurich, S. (2002). ICT for education: Prerequisites and constraints. In W. D. Haddad & A. Draxler (Eds.), (2002). *Technologies for education: Potentials, parameters, and prospects* (pp. 28–40). Washington, DC/Paris: AED/UNESCO.

Harasim, L., Hiltz, S., Teles, L., & Turoff, M. (1995). *Learning networks*. Cambridge, MA: MIT Press.

Hiltz, S. (1995). *The virtual classroom: Learning without limits via computer networks*. Norwood, NJ: Ablex.

International Society for Technology in Education (ISTE) (1998). *National Educational Technology Standards for Students*. Eugene, OR: ISTE.

International Telecommunication Union (ITU) (2003). *World telecommunication report: Access indicators for the information society*. Geneva: ITU.

James, T., Hesselmark, O., Akoh, B., & Mware, L. (2003, in press). *Review of basic ICT skills and training software for educators in Africa*. Report to DFID/Imfundo. Johanessburg: self-published.

Jamison, D. T., & Moock, P. R. (1984). Farmer education and farm efficiency in Nepal: The role of schooling, extension services, and cognitive skills. *World Development*, 12, 67–86.

Just, M. A., & Carpenter, P. A. (1987). *The psychology of reading and language comprehension*. Newton, MA: Allyn Bacon.

Kelley-Salinas, G. (2001). Different education inequalities: ICT as an option to close the gaps. *Learning to bridge the digital divide*. Paris: OECD.

Kozma, R. (2003a). Technology and classroom practices: An international study. *Journal of Research on Computers in Education*, 36 (1), 1–14.

Kozma, R. (2003b). *Technology, innovation, and educational change: A global perspective*. Eugene, OR: International Society for Technology in Education.

Langer, S. (2001). Natural languages on the Word Wide Web. In S. Franc-Comtoises, *Bulag: Revue annuelle*. Presses Universitaire, 89–100.

Murray, D. (2000). Changing technologies, changing literacy communities? *Language Learning and Technology*, 4 (2), 43–58.

National Assessment Governing Board (1998). *Writing framework and specifications for the 1998 National Assessment of Educational Progress*. Washington, DC: National Assessment Governing Board.

Newburger, E. C. (2001). *Home Computers and Internet Use in the United States: August 2000* (P23-207). U.S. Department of Commerce. Washington, DC: Bureau of the Census.

OECD (1996). *The Knowledge-Based Economy*. Paris, OECD.

OECD (1999). *Knowledge Management in the Learning Society*. Paris, OECD.

OECD (2001). *Learning to bridge the digital divide*. Paris: OECD.

OECD (2002). *Measuring the information economy*. Paris: OECD.

OECD/Statistics Canada (1995). *Literacy, economy and society*. Paris: OECD.

OECD/Statistics Canada (1997). *Literacy skills for the knowledge society: Further results from the International Adult Literacy Survey*. Paris: OECD.

OECD/Statistics Canada (2000). *Literacy in the information age*. Paris: OECD.

Olson, D. R. (1995). *The world on paper*. New York: Cambridge University Press.

Olson, D. R., & Torrance, N. (2000). *The making of literate societies*. Oxford: Blackwell.

Nunes, C. A. A., & Gaibel, E. (2002). Development of multimedia materials. W. D. Haddad, & A. Draxler (Eds.), *Technologies for Education: Potentials, Parameters and Prospects*. Washington DC/Paris, AED/UNESCO.

Perraton, H., & Creed, C. (2002). Applying New Technologies and Cost-Effective Delivery Systems in Basic Education. Paris, UNESCO.

Palloff, R., & Pratt, K. (1999). *Building learning communities in cyberspace: Effective strategies for the online classroom*. San Francisco: Jossey-Bass.

Palloff, R., & Pratt, K. (2000). *Lessons from the cyberspace classroom: The realities of online teaching*. San Francisco: Jossey-Bass.

Perfetti, C. (1989). There are generalized abilities and one of them is reading. In L. B. Resnick (Ed.), *Knowing and learning: Essays in honor of Robert Glaser* (pp. 307–334). Hillsdale, NJ: Erlbaum.

Perfetti, C., & Marron, M. (1995). *Learning to read: Literacy acquisition by children and adults*. Philadelphia, PA: National Center on Adult Literacy.

Proenza, F., Bastidas-Buch, R., & Montero, G. (2001). *Telecenters for socioeconomic and rural development in Latin America and the Caribbean: Investment opportunities and design recommendations, with special reference to Central America*. Washington, DC: Inter-American Development Bank.

Robinson, B. (1997). *In the Green Desert: Non-formal distance education project for nomadic women of the Gobi Desert, Mongolia*. UNESCO's Education for All Innovations Series, No. 12.

Rosen, D. (2000). Using electronic technology in adult literacy education. In J. Coming, B. Garner, & C. Smith (Eds.), *The annual review of adult learning and literacy. Vol. 1* (pp. 304–315). San Francisco: Jossey-Bass.

Sabatini, J. (1999). Adult reading acquisition. In D. A. Wagner, R. L. Venezky, & B. L. Street (Eds.), *Literacy: An international handbook*. Boulder, CO: Westview Press.

Sabatini, J. (2001). *Designing multimedia learning systems for adult learners: Basic skills with a workforce emphasis*. Philadelphia, PA: National Center on Adult Literacy.

Snow, C. E., & Strucker, J. (2000). Lessons from *Preventing reading difficulties in young children* for adult learning and literacy. In J. Comings, B. Garner, & C. Smith (Eds.), *Annual review of adult learning and literacy, Vol. 1* (pp. 25–73). San Francisco: Jossey-Bass.

Stiglitz, J. (2000). *Economics of the public sector* (3rd ed.). New York: Norton.

Stites, R. (2004). Implications of new learning technologies for adult literacy and learning. In J. Coming, B. Garner, & C. Smith (Eds.),

Review of adult learning and literacy. Vol. 4 (pp. 109–155). Mahwah, NJ: Erlbaum.

Street, B. V. (1999). The meanings of literacy. In D. A. Wagner, R. L. Venezky, & B. L. Street (Eds.), *Literacy: An international handbook* (pp. 34–40). Boulder, CO: Westview Press.

Tyner, K. (1998). *Literacy in a digital world: Teaching and learning in the age of information.* Mahwah, NJ: Erlbaum.

UNDP (2001). *Human development report 2001: Making new technologies work for human development.* New York: UN.

UNESCO (1978). *Revised recommendation concerning the international standardization of educational statistics.* Paris: UNESCO.

UNESCO (1998). *World education report.* Paris: UNESCO.

UNESCO (2000). *The Dakar framework for action.* Paris: UNESCO.

UNESCO (2002). *Open and Distance Learning: Trends, Policy and Strategy Considerations.* Paris, UNESCO.

UNESCO (2004). *Integrating ICTs into education: Lessons learned.* Bangkok: UNESCO Asia and the Pacific Regional Bureau for Education.

UNESCO (2005). *Literacy for life: Education for All global monitoring report.* Paris: UNESCO.

United Nations (2002a). *Resolution adopted by the General Assembly: 56/116. United Nations Literacy Decade: Education for all.* New York: UN.

United Nations (2002b). *United Nations Literacy Decade: Education for all. International plan of action: Implementation of General Assembly Resolution 56/116.* New York: UN.

U.S. Department of Commerce (2002). *A nation online.* Washington, DC: U.S. Printing Office.

Wagner, D. A. (1986). Review of H. S. Bhola, *Campaigning for literacy,* and V. Miller, *Between struggle and hope: The Nicaraguan literacy campaign. Comparative Education Review,* August, 450–454.

Wagner, D. A. (1995). Literacy and development: Rationales, myths, innovations, and future directions. *International Journal of Educational Development,* 15, 341–362.

Wagner, D. A. (2000). *Literacy and adult education.* Global Thematic Review prepared for the UN World Education Forum (EFA), Dakar, Senegal. Paris: UNESCO.

Wagner, D. A. (2001, August). IT and education for the poorest of the oor: Constraints, possibilities, and principles. *TechKnowlogia: International Journal for the Advancement of Knowledge and Learning.* Washington, DC.

Wagner, D. A. (Ed.) (2005a). *Monitoring and evaluation of ICT in education projects: A handbook for developing countries.* Washington, DC: World Bank/InfoDev.

Wagner, D. A. (2005b). Pro-equity approaches to monitoring and evaluation: Gender, marginalized groups and special needs populations. In D. A. Wagner, B. Day, T. James, R. B. Kozma, J. Miller, & T. Unwin (Eds.), *Monitoring and evaluation of ICT in education projects: A handbook for developing countries* (pp. 93–110). Washington, DC: World Bank/InfoDev.

Wagner, D. A., & Daswani, C. J. (2008). Bridges to the Future Initiative in India: Impact on children and adults. Technical Report, International Literacy Institute, University of Pennsylvania, Philadelphia.

Wagner, D. A., & Hopey, C. (1999). Literacy, electronic networking and the Internet. In D. A. Wagner, R. L. Venezky, & B. L. Street (Eds.), *Literacy: An international handbook* (pp. 475–480). Boulder, CO: Westview Press.

Wagner, D. A., & Kozma, R. (2005). *New technologies for literacy and adult education: A global perspective.* Paris: UNESCO. (In English, French, and Arabic.)

Wagner, D. A., & Venezky, R. L. (1999). Adult literacy: The next generation. *Educational Researcher,* 28 (1), 21–29.

Wagner, D. A., Venezky, R. L., & Street, B. V. (Eds.) (1999). *Literacy: An International Handbook.* Boulder, CO: Westview Press.

Ward-Bent, M. (2002). "Sesame Street" runs along the Nile. In W. Haddad (Ed.), *Technologies for education: Potentials, parameters, and prospects* (pp. 154–157). Paris: UNESCO.

Warschauer, M. (2004). *Technology and social inclusion: Rethinking the digital divide.* Boston: MIT Press.

Wasik, B., & Slavin, R. (1993). Early reading failure with one-to-one tutoring: A review of five programs. *Reading Research Quarterly,* 28 (2), 178–200.

Wolf, L., Castro, C., Navarro, J., & Garcia, N. (2002). Television for secondary education: Experience of Mexico and Brazil. In W. Haddad (Ed.), *Technologies for education: Potentials, parameters, and prospects* (pp. 144–152). Paris: UNESCO.

Zucker, A., & Kozma, R., with Yarnall, L., & Marder, C. (2003). *Teaching Generation V: The Virtual High School and the Future of Virtual Secondary Education.* New York, Teachers College Press.

CHAPTER 31

Literacy, Literacy Policy, and the School

David R. Olson

The focus of education [is] raising the levels of literacies for all students.

Royal Commission on Learning, Ontario, Canada 1994, p. 35

We're recommending a new body, an Office of Learning Assessment and Accountability, consisting of a small number of experts in education and assessment, and reporting directly to the legislature . . . to evaluate and report on the success of Ontario's education policy.

Royal Commission on Learning, Ontario, Canada 1994, p. 53

Universal literacy has been a goal of developed countries for more than a century and has been designated as a basic human right by the United Nations (UN). Yet, most nations declare that literacy levels fail to reach an 'acceptable standard,' and the spread of literacy to developing countries has been slow to negligible. Each generation proposes a solution to these putative problems, proposals ranging from improving the writing system, to improved materials, to improved teaching, and – in our own generation – to increased accountability through mandatory testing, as the epigram to this chapter attests and, in the United States, to the policy initiative called No Child Left Behind (U.S. Department of Education, 2002). Here, too, the results are usually judged as disappointing. The deeper inquiry into the nature of literacy explored in this volume may, on the one hand, better help to approach these acceptable standards. On the other hand, this inquiry may help to develop more realistic policy.

Literacy policy, in many cases, consists of extravagant wish lists combined with the distribution of blame for failure to deliver. Literacy policy addressed in terms of a universal standard and an idealized pedagogy, it may be argued, has doomed the project to failure. A more realistic policy may be formulated by, first, defining literacy in terms of the goals relevant to the personal and social lives of those affected; second, setting the criteria for the achievement of those goals in terms of the responsibilities and entitlements of those agencies involved in advancing literacy; and, third, sketching procedures that may be useful in helping various agents to meet their responsibilities.

The formation of educational policy is the responsibility of governments, not academics. Yet, academics can usefully enter this discourse both by acquainting policy makers with the literature – that is, with the state of the art – and the successes and failures of previous attempts at reform. Previous reviews have shown that policy initiatives in the past are largely addressed to 'remedying abuse' of earlier failed policies rather than addressing the second responsibility of academics – namely, to set out, as far as possible, the dimensions and choices amongst which policy makers are free to choose. Primary amongst those dimensions is whether to define literacy narrowly, following the *Oxford English Dictionary* (OED), as "the ability to read and write" or more broadly, again following the OED, as "an acquaintance with literature." It is to our conception of literacy that the chapters in this volume have made the most important contributions.

Literacy as the Ability to Read and Write

The primary definition of a literate person is one who is able to read and write (OED) – that is, literacy as a basic personal competence. To turn the definition into a policy, one must address two more specific questions: (1) *how well*, which is the question of standards; and (2) *read what*, which is the question of content. Neither of these questions is straightforward and ignoring them has resulted in many of the failures of attempted educational reforms.

Consider first the question of how well. It is a relatively straightforward matter to define competence in terms of years of schooling. Children are said to read at a fourth- or a twelfth-grade level if their performance is equivalent to the average or mean performance of children at that grade level. Traditional 'norm-referenced' tests readily allow such classifications. Yet, it is well known that reading level, in fact, is poorly correlated with actual grade level in that the reading levels of children in a single sixth-grade class typically range six years – some children reading at the third-grade level others at the ninth-grade level. If graduation from one grade to the next were based on reading at one's grade level, half of the children would fail. That is just the logical implication of norm-referenced testing. For this reason, many jurisdictions have attempted to spell out standards for 'criterion-referenced' tests that would detail what one must know to pass, to graduate or to earn a credential. Although enthusiasm for this tack continues to run high, it quickly runs into the more general constraint on all such initiatives, as pointed out by Satz and Ferejohn (1994, p. 72) – namely, that only if one narrows the goals sufficiently can one design an efficient method for their achievement; the more broadly defined the less likely they are to be achieved. To illustrate, the British press recently reported that only 40 percent of middle-school graduates could spell the word *particularly*. There is no doubt that if the goal of literacy were narrowed to bringing that level to 100 percent for that word, a system could be developed to achieve that specific end. However, no one knows how to design a system to get all or most children to spell all or most words competently; yet, that is the educational goal. Policy makers, therefore, have a choice to either (1) define precisely and narrowly goals of dubious value and ensure that all children achieve them, or (2) define goals more broadly and validly with the unwanted consequence that some children will fail to meet them. Policy formation requires some decision and, in what follows, I attempt to indicate criteria that are relevant to judgments of basic and more advanced levels of literacy.

In fact, if we define literacy strictly in terms of the ability to read and write and ignore fixed standards and content, school literacy programs are successful. By the fourth grade, most children can read and write to some basic level. Nevertheless, improvements in achievement levels have more or less 'flat-lined'; in Ontario,

Canada, from where I write, this is clearly so (www.eqao.com). However, worldwide, about 1 billion people are unable to read and write, and even in developed countries about 25 percent "had problems reading texts that required inferences" (Triebel, 2005, p. 798; Sticht, Chapter 29, this volume). Furthermore, although there are many local successes, the overall picture remains as it has been for the last four decades.

What has had an enduring effect – and this occurred in developed societies well over a century ago – was the establishment of mass public schooling. Years-of-schooling is a suitable proxy for assessing the literacy level of groups of individuals and entire societies. Individual children's literacy achievements advance in a stepwise fashion with each year of schooling. Making quality schooling attractive, systematic and available remains the best way of raising the literacy levels of individuals and entire societies. Despite the diverse forms it takes, schooling tends to have uniform effects on basic literacy, so much so that international comparisons of literacy levels are not only meaningful but also tend to indicate that learners everywhere are learning much the same things to much the same levels, dependent primarily on years of schooling. The variability that does remain in large part depends on the 'transparency' of the link between the script and the language being represented. As Daniels (Chapter 2, this volume) shows, writing systems were first invented for languages with a rich inventory of monosyllabic morphemes that could be represented by a single visual sign. Alphabets, in which signs represent only phonemic constituents of syllables, are more difficult, and writing systems that are only indirectly related to the oral vernacular are the most difficult of all (Haeri, Chapter 22, this volume). The remaining variability is attributable to basic demographic factors such as poverty, urbanization, parental educational levels, employment opportunities and religious background (Garton & Pratt, Chapter 27, this volume).

Thus, basic literacy – the mere ability to read and write, to master the relationship between sound and script – is relatively easily mastered by most children as long as the signs of the writing system map on to comprehensible properties of the learner's speech and appropriate learning environments are available (Venezky, 2004). However, that skill in itself has little to do with turning literacy into an instrument of use and power (Wang, Tsai, & Wang, Chapter 21, this volume). Indeed, the very mechanical or algorithmic procedures of reading and writing have made it seem that reading is everywhere the same for all people and in all times and places – a matter of reconstructing an appropriate oral equivalent, silent or aloud. What that assumption overlooks is the fact that reading is a social practice in which readers and writers engage with text for quite different purposes, in quite different ways, and they evolve somewhat unique conventions for expression and interpretation. Some of these ways of dealing with written texts require a high level of expertise and years of involvement to master. These literacy practices are sufficiently different from the more basic processes of learning to read and write that they are more correctly described by the second meaning of literacy – namely, literacy as "an acquaintance with literature."

Literacy as an Acquaintance with Literature

In its most general sense, an acquaintance with literature means the ability to deal with an encyclopedic range of written materials (Langacker, 1991). These abilities, sometimes described as linguistic or academic literacy (Berman & Ravid, Chapter 6, this volume; Snow & Uccelli, Chapter 7, this volume), go beyond those involved in the basic ability to read and write as well as beyond those skills involved in oral discourse. These are reflective skills with language that allow one to express thoughts that are largely or uniquely associated with literacy and a literate tradition. This knowledge involves a grasp of conventions, only some of which are marked in the orthography that have evolved over time in diverse "textual communities" (Stock, 1983; Long, Chapter 10, this volume; Steedman, Chapter 12, this volume; Larsson, Chapter 13, this volume). These distinctive ways of writing and reading are central to such social practices as science, law, economics and government, but they also take shape in such local social practices as reading circles (Murray, Chapter 11, this volume). These textual communities are composed of groups of readers who evolve conventions for the interpretation and use of texts for their own purposes in their distinctive ways. Writers such as Heath (1983), Gee (1990, Chapter 17, this volume) and Street (1995, Chapter 18, this volume; Dobson and Willinsky (Chapter 16, this volume) have explored the variety of ways in which persons and groups engage with text and the ways that these uses of writing are rooted in conceptions of knowledge, authority and identity. The same text may be read for instruction, for meditation or simply for establishing group membership. Historians have appealed to different ways of reading to explain the charge of heresy leveled at a sixteenth-century miller who was subsequently burned at the stake (Ginzburg, 1982), as well for more pervasive religious change (Stock, 1983). Different ways of reading the same texts distinguish all religious groups – whether Catholics, Protestants, Christians, Jews and Muslims or Fundamentalists – from their more liberally minded neighbors (Olson, 1994). There is a world of difference between reading the Bible as scripture and reading it as literature even if both may involve mouthing the same text. This re-emphasis on the diverse uses that readers make of texts is perhaps what Barthes (1977) had in mind when he spoke of the death of the author and the birth of the reader. The reader, it turns out, has more to do with how a text is taken than the quasi-algorithmic processes of reading and comprehension that schools have taken as normative. The community of readers, the textual community, evolve conventions for reading and interpreting documents and texts as well as for writing new texts – conventions that may take years to master.

Those of us schooled in the Western tradition pick up these conventions of reading as part of everyday social practices – so much so that they are often thought of as simply a part of learning how to read and write 'better.' How to consult a book for information, how to formulate a claim or an argument in writing, how to 'correctly' interpret a text, and the like are social practices that we mistakenly take to be *given* by the very nature of reading itself. Rather, the competence required to participate in these social practices is essential to becoming literate in the sense of 'being acquainted with literature.' These conventions are extremely important, they are extremely diverse, and their mastery is essential for participation in any social practice, including those central to the major institutions of a modern society. Knowing how to read the literature is an essential part of any discipline, including mathematics and physics.

Thus, it would be a mistake to think that the conventions for reading that are inculcated through learning to read and write in school are the only conventions at play. Each textual community, the community of readers, and the writers who write for them evolve their own ways of understanding what they read and write. This is what makes reading a social practice rather than strictly an individual skill (Long, Chapter 10, this volume). One comes to know how the others in the group will tend to take a text. When one grants that there are many ways of forming, taking and using texts, it turns out that even within so-called nonliterate societies, many people are engaged with texts in some way or another (Street, Chapter 18, this volume).

Normative Conventions of Reading

What are these conventions of reading – these ways of writing and reading – that modern Western societies have evolved for advancing knowledge and organizing society? For these are the conventions that have come to possess a particularly valued place in modern literate societies. These are the conventions that the school is charged with passing on to students.

It is important that these are conventions that are essentially unique to writing as opposed to speaking and that, consequently, tend to create a gulf between utterance and text. In other words, these are conventions that are more readily established and monitored in written than in spoken form and, for that reason, are particularly tied to literacy, particularly to higher levels of literacy. Some of these are basic and more or less universal (Goswami, Chapter 8, this volume), such as phonological, word and sentence awareness, and some are more abstract and specialized, such as an awareness of the properties distinguishing narrative from argument and conventions involved in various forms of technical writing.

The most basic of these understandings is the ability – indeed, the tendency – to think of one's speech as if it were written (Harris, Chapter 3, this volume). Writing is an ideal medium for taking language 'offline' and for thinking about language as an object. Once offline, oral speech comes to be seen as defective in comparison to its written counterpart. However, there are some benefits. The first is what is usually referred to as *linguistic awareness*, the ability to reflect on the properties of language as opposed to the meanings conveyed. It is the ability to think about words, their decontextualized meanings, their intensional relationships; about synonyms, antonyms, hyponyms; about equivalences of meaning; of paraphrase; and, more generally, about the relationships between what is said and what is meant. There is a vast literature that includes Piaget's simple demonstration that young children have difficulty switching from thinking of a thing to thinking about the name of a thing (Homer, Chapter 26, this volume). Learning to read and write requires that children recognize that the script represents not things but rather language about things (Tolchinsky, Chapter 25, this volume). Pre-reading children believe that to write "two little pigs" requires two written symbols because there are two pigs rather than three written symbols because there are three words. Words as grammatical objects, as objects of thought, are to some extent products of a writing system (Petersson et al., Chapter 9, this volume). In general, literacy brings such aspects of language into awareness. Anthropologists also have reported the difficulty they had in convincing their nonliterate informants that they should use "the same words" on each telling of a song or story so that the anthropologists could make a written record. The informants insisted they *were* using the same words (Finnegan, 1977; Goody, 1987). Yet, it should be acknowledged that much of this attentiveness to language may be advanced orally, through verbal games such as "Simon says . . . " and "I spy . . . " independent of reading – so much so that critics of the literacy hypothesis often assume that writing plays little or no role in such awareness. This is despite the fact that schooling and literacy instruction are primarily responsible for teaching children to pay attention to "the very words."

However, some of these new understandings about language are tied to higher levels of literacy and to advanced levels of reading and writing employed in quite complex social practices – namely, the academic disciplines, themselves importantly tied to a *written* language. The properties of such a language have been described in several ways. Ong (1982) examined forms of writing in the early modern period and detected a shift from a more open narrative form, which he described as "additive rather than subordinative" (1982, p. 37), to a more hierarchical, expository form. van der Toorn (2007, p. 110) described the activities of one "scribal culture," that involved in writing the Hebrew Bible, as reforming an oral tradition to meet the "conventions of the written genre" (p. 111). Whereas oral conventions tended to be 'paratactic' – that is, linked by *and thens* – the written conventions tended to be 'hypotactic,' implying the logical connective *consequently*. Halliday (1987; see also Chafe, 1985) described these evolved written structures in terms of "grammatical metaphor" essentially using words from one syntactic class as members of a different class, thereby constructing the more complex clauses that have become a distinguishing feature of written language. Berman and Ravid (Chapter 6, this volume) showed that it is only more advanced writers who are able to manage the lexical and syntactic resources needed for academic writing: "written language and expository discourse combine to create a favoured habitat for rich and complex use of language." Biber's (Chapter 5, this volume) examination of texts similarly reveals an interaction between modality and genre. Snow and Uccilli (Chapter 7, this volume) suggest that academic literacy involves the grammatical resources (i.e., lexical, syntactic, register and genre) that make modern scientific writing – indeed, modern scientific thought – possible. Although some of these resources were available in antiquity and manifest in such oral forms as oratory (Thomas, Chapter 19, this volume), the skills soon came to be more often confined to the writing, reading, commenting and criticizing of texts and other documents (Everett, Chapter 20, this volume).

These advanced literary forms exist within the social practices we think of as the academic disciplines, and they have a meaning and a use primarily within well-defined "textual communities." Membership in those communities requires that one be able to produce and understand the conventions of writing and the assumptions involved in reading the fundamental texts of the discipline (Chemla, Chapter 14, this volume). Some of these higher level conventions are exclusively tied to writing and reading about a domain rather than comprising part of the disciplinary knowledge itself. As Norris and Phillips (Chapter 15, this volume) show, "scientific literacy" is misleading when applied to the sciences themselves and would be more appropriately restricted to mastering the conventions involved in reading and writing about the sciences. Yet, it is also the case that an important aspect of expertise in a discipline involves the construction and interpretation of the formative texts of that discipline.

Societal Literacy

In addition to the two meanings of literacy examined to this point, there is a third concept of literacy that has more recently come to the fore. Societal literacy, to borrow a concept from Elwert (2001), is the type of literacy that underwrites a modern bureaucratic society. Indeed, to understand the formation of knowledge and the distribution of power in a modern society, it is essential to examine the documentary practices of that society (Smith, 1990). Documentary practices are carried out within a textual community, but a textual community *writ large*. It involves the formulation and implementation of explicit procedures for the ordering of activities in terms of rules, norms, formal procedures or algorithms that are set out in codes, documents and manuals. Examples include the early use of notations for numbers (Chrisomalis, Chapter 4, this volume) and the later Robert's Rules of Order, the first attempt to spell out how to conduct a public meeting. However, they also include constitutions, charters, contract law, rules for production, rules for interpretation of documents, and the like, as well as an understanding of the institutions that give such documents force. Such rules not only depend on explicit procedures but also rely on mechanisms to monitor and enforce such rules. The entire machinery of a bureaucratic state, whether ancient empire or modern democracy, is so ordered as to make explicit, establish and enforce these rules. The conventions implicit in any less formal textual community have become, in a modern state, explicit procedures for regulating action. Power goes hand in hand with such procedure but if the procedure is explicit and rule governed, it may gain, as we say, 'the consent of the governed.' Schools are seen as essential to learning the rules of the bureaucratic systems charged with the management of knowledge and power in a society, and schools have some responsibility for teaching the young to respect and honour those rules and, indeed, to use them for their own purposes. These include the rules and conventions for participation as citizens with rights and responsibilities, including understanding and complying with 'the rule of law,' as well as with the rights and responsibilities as a student or a teacher or other professional (von Holthoon, Chapter 23, this volume). Although some roles, such as father or big brother or headman, may be filled without appeal to literacy, those mentioned herein are spelled out in terms of contracts and other explicit rules documented in writing. Filling those roles, therefore, depends on both a general level of literacy and the special type of literacy that we think of as credentials appropriate to particular roles and responsibilities.

A literate society is held together by a set of contentions for using language and writing in ordering and carrying out actions in such a way that they are easily anticipated by others. 'Others' include not only the member of one's tribe or local textual community but also those of the state as a whole. Only when one grasps these conventions and acts in terms of them do actions become predictable and understandable and congruent with the rule of law – and only then can one usefully speak of a literate society. This need not imply that everyone be a skilled reader but rather that they have access to written documents and their interpretation and an appropriate respect for the conventions involved in their application and use. The absence of these shared conventions is what puts large-scale societies at risk; although schools cannot, on their own, instill allegiance to such conventions, they have some responsibility for developing them. In a modern society, literacy is at the core.

Literacy Policy: Responsibility for the Acquisition of Basic and Higher Levels of Literacy

As discussed at the beginning of this chapter, foremost in the formation of a literacy policy is defining literacy in terms of the criteria to be met in judging that one is or is not literate. These criteria vary dramatically from one social group to another, depending on whether literacy is seen as instrumental to one's own goals. Yet, policy makers are, by and large, committed to a more or less universal standard and a universal pedagogy. Beyond that, a literacy policy would set out who is responsible for meeting the criteria that have been agreed upon. Third, it would set out how each agent is to accomplish meeting their responsibilities. Setting out an account of learning in terms of responsibilities and the entitlements earned by meeting those responsibilities provides a distinctive approach to thinking about literacy policy. Such an analysis would permit one to answer in a court of law: "Who is at fault in case of failure?" and "Who earned their entitlements in case of success?"

Contrary to conventional educational wisdom, it is the learner, not the teacher, who is responsible for his or her own learning. No one can do the learning for the learner; it is the student who must do the learning. The teacher's responsibility is not only to make it possible for the learner to learn but also to hold the learner responsible for his or her learning. It is a crude oversimplification to assume that learning is a direct consequence of teaching – namely, that if there is no learning, there is no teaching. Rather, learning is the learner's responsibility and meeting that responsibility earns some entitlement, whether in the form of satisfaction in having learned, gaining approval from teachers and peers, or advancing to the next grade or level. Indeed, programs that focus on the learner's own agency and responsibility tend to be more successful than those that assign it directly and exclusively to the teacher (Farrell, Chapter 28, this volume). Students' responsibility for their own learning, although the centrepiece of adult learning (Wagner, Chapter 30, this volume), is largely overlooked in most theories of education, yet it is essential to issues of accountability.

The teacher's responsibilities include providing materials, directions, explanations and a suitable environment for learning to occur. Specifically, the teacher's responsibility is to engineer the conditions that allow the learner to meet his or her responsibility for learning. Equally important, the teacher's responsibilities include setting out and monitoring the criteria for successful performance of the learner. Tests and other forms of performance are essential for helping students judge whether the performance meets the required standards and earns the appropriate entitlement. There is considerable ambiguity as to just what these criteria are or should be, and I return to this point in the next section.

Just as the teacher's responsibility is to provide the conditions that make it possible for the learner to meet his or her responsibilities for learning, so also do school authorities have the responsibility for providing the conditions that make it possible for the teacher to meet his or her responsibilities – and so on through the entire educational bureaucracy. In each case, meeting one's responsibilities earns some entitlement, whether as satisfaction, promotion or salary.

Setting and Monitoring Criteria for Judging that One is Literate

Setting goals for the acquisition of literacy contrasts with the view that there is no such thing as 'literacy' but only locally defined 'literacies' – that is, the specific processes involved in using writing for special purposes within a social practice in a particular culture. Indeed, such local literacies are essential for understanding much out-of-school learning where the literacy learned is adapted to a particular function, such as the production and marketing of produce, crafts and technical skills. Even in school contexts, these local literacy practices are critical in that they may either contribute to or interfere with the more generalized schooled literacy. Most advanced societies assume that there is some set of generalizable literacy skills and practices that can be applied in a variety of contexts somewhat independently of the content expressed and that, therefore, may be taught and assessed (Norris & Phillips, Chapter 15, this volume). While the generalizability question remains open, it is possible to use the criteria set out in our definitions of literacy to set realistic policy goals.

The criteria to be met if one is to be judged as achieving 'basic literacy' are importantly different from those involved in achieving higher, academic literacy. Basic literacy involves learning the relationship between written marks and the phonological properties of one's own speech (Goswami, Chapter 2, this volume; Daniels, Chapter 8, this volume). Learning to read is relatively easy if there is a clear relationship between the visible marks and the constituents of one's speech; if not, it may pose a formidable hurdle (Haeri, Chapter 22, this volume). Pedagogical methods for helping students achieve basic literacy have changed historically (Chartier, Chapter 24, this volume) to reflect the importance of understanding in mastering these basic relationships. The ability to read simple texts or, ideally, to read the texts that one has been able to write for oneself, it may be argued, constitutes a suitable criterion for defining basic literacy. Basic literacy is the universal goal of primary schooling.

The criteria to be met, if one is to be judged as achieving an advanced level of literacy, are much disputed as this level is easily conflated with specialized knowledge for particular purposes in particular domains such as reading law books, computer manuals, parts catalogues or telephone bills. A more defensible set of criteria may be derived from the previous discussion of the conventions of reading. Although each domain of knowledge and practice has a somewhat specialized vocabulary and conventions of use, they all share a certain attitude to texts – namely, the ability to reflect on those texts, to paraphrase, summarize, extrapolate from, and recontextualize texts. Furthermore, these criteria include knowledge of how to classify texts – as to type (e.g., report or opinion); register (e.g., formal or informal); genre (e.g., poetry or prose) – and to adopt the appropriate interpretive stance for each. Furthermore, it involves the ability to manage the complex grammatical forms employed in literary and expository texts.

This more advanced level of literacy requires that one master the accompanying metalanguage – that is, the concepts and words for 'talking about text,' the explicit set of concepts for referring to the genres, their properties and their normative interpretations. As Haas and Flower (1988) discovered, many able readers identify words, locate information, and recall content and yet provide a paraphrase when asked to analyze, summarize when asked to criticize, and simply retell when asked to interpret. The abilities to summarize, paraphrase, compare, discuss, and outline are more general than any specific content and, therefore, constitute an important part of advanced literate competence.

Other metalinguistic concepts essential for referring to, discussing, editing, and interpreting various types of documents are also essential aspects of literate competence. These include both obvious concepts such as words, sentences, and paragraphs and more subtle concepts such as main point, topic sentence, assumptions, arguments, implications, conclusions, evidence, and theory – and still more subtle concepts such as literal and metaphorical meaning as well as truth and validity. These metalinguistic concepts are frequently taken for granted rather than made into objects of instruction, an oversight with unfortunate consequences because these concepts tend to be well known by children in highly literate families but not by those from less literate ones (Olson & Astington, 1990). To the extent that content-based forms of knowledge such as literature or science are document-based, they may be viewed as an outgrowth of literacy without being central to literacy skills themselves. That is, it may be argued that it is legitimate to examine a person's literate competence independently of the more specialized knowledge of the disciplines or other specialized literacy practices. The relationship of literate competence to specialized branches of knowledge, nonetheless, is important and is highlighted by programs that examine writing across the curriculum.

The concepts of basic and advanced levels of literacy are embarrassingly close to those at play in much current educational practice. And, like that practice, they are limited in the sense that highlighting the criteria leaves hidden the social communicative practices that these criteria are designed to serve. The danger of enumerating criteria is that, too readily, they become the direct object of instruction rather than remaining, as they should be, specialized devices for advancing communication and understanding in particular domains. It is on this point that major educational battles are fought between the traditionalists and the progressives, both of whom are prone to overstating their cases.

Literacy is deeply implicated in modern bureaucratic societies, and literate competence, both basic and advanced, is essential to participation in such a society (Brockmeier & Olson, Chapter 1, this volume). Although many agencies have some responsibility for making it possible for learners to acquire literacy skills, in modern societies, the school has been charged with the responsibility for developing those competencies. This volume examines just what is involved in being and becoming literate, thereby allowing us to specify more achievable goals for literacy programs and some of the means for achieving them.

References

Barthes, R. (1977). *Image-music-text* (S. Heath, trans.). Glasgow: Fontana Collins.

Berman, R., & Ravid, D. (this volume). *Becoming a literate language user: Oral and written text construction across adolescence*.

Biber, D. (this volume). *Are there linguistic consequences of literacy? Comparing the potentials of language use in speech and writing*.

Brockmeier, J., & Olson, D. R. (this volume). *The literacy episteme (from Innis to Derrida)*.

Chafe, W. (1985). Linguistic differences produced by differences between speech and writing. In D. R. Olson & N. Torrance (Eds.), *Literacy, language and learning*. Cambridge, UK: Cambridge University Press.

Chartier, A.-M. (this volume). *The teaching of literacy skills in Western Europe: An historical perspective (sixteenth to twentieth centuries).*

Chemla, K. (this volume). *Literacy and the history of science.*

Chrisomalis, S. (this volume). *The origins and coevolution of literacy and numeracy.*

Daniels, P. T. (this volume). *Grammatology.*

Dobson, T. M., & Willinsky, J. (this volume). *Digital literacy.*

Elwert, G. (2001). Societal literacy: Writing culture and development. In D. R. Olson & N. G. Torrance (Eds.), *The making of literate societies* (pp. 54–67). Oxford: Blackwell.

Everett, N. (this volume). *Literacy from Late Antiquity to the early Middle Ages, c. 300–800.*

Farrell, J. (this volume). *Literacy and international development: Education and literacy as human rights.*

Finnegan, R. (1977). *Oral poetry: Its nature, significance, and social context.* Cambridge, UK: Cambridge University Press.

Garton, A., & Pratt, C. (this volume). *Cultural and developmental predispositions to literacy.*

Gee, J. (1990). *Social linguistics and literacies: Ideology in discourse.* London: Falmer.

Gee, J. (this volume). *Literacy, video games, and popular culture.*

Ginzburg, C. (1982). *The cheese and the worms: The cosmos of a sixteenth-century miller.* Markham, ON: Penguin Books.

Goody, J. (1987). *The interface between the oral and the written.* Cambridge, UK: Cambridge University Press.

Goswami, U. (this volume). *The basic processes in reading: Insights from neuroscience.*

Haas, C., & Flower, L. (1988). Rhetorical reading strategies and the recovery of meaning. *College Composition and Communication,* 39, 30–47.

Haeri, N. (this volume). *The elephant in the room: Language and literacy in the Arab world.*

Halliday, M. A. K. (1987). Spoken and written modes of meaning. In R. Horowitz & S. J. Samuels (Eds.), *Comprehending oral and written language* (pp. 55–82). San Diego, CA: Academic Press.

Harris, R. (this volume). *Speech and writing.*

Heath, S. (1983). *Ways with words.* Cambridge: Cambridge University Press.

Homer, B. (this volume). *Literacy and metalinguistic development.*

Langacker, R. (1991). *Concept, image, and symbol: The cognitive basis of grammar.* Berlin: Mouton de Gruyter.

Larsson, L. (this volume). *Reading as a woman, being read as a woman.*

Long, E. (this volume). *Ways of reading.*

Murray, H. (this volume). *Conventions of reading.*

Norris, S. P., & Phillips, L. M. (this volume). *Scientific literacy.*

Olson, D. R. (1994). *The world on paper: The conceptual and cognitive implications of writing and reading.* Cambridge: Cambridge University Press.

Olson, D. R., & Astington, J. A. (1990). Talking about text: How literacy contributes to thought. *Journal of Pragmatics,* 14, 705–721.

Ong, W. (1982). *Orality and literacy: The technologizing of the word.* London: Methuen.

Petersson, K. M., Ingvar, M., & Reis, A. (this volume). *Language and literacy from a cognitive neuroscience perspective.*

Royal Commision on Learning (1994). *For the love of learning.* Toronto: Publications Ontario.

Satz, D., & Ferejohn, J. (1994). Rational choice and social theory. *Journal of Philosophy,* 9102, 71–87.

Smith, D. (1990). *The conceptual practices of power: A feminist sociology of knowledge.* Boston: Northeastern University Press.

Snow, C., & Uccelli, P. (this volume). *The challenge of academic language.*

Steedman, C. (this volume). *Literacy, reading, and concepts of the self.*

Sticht, T. (this volume). *Adult literacy education in industrialized nations.*

Stock, B. (1983). *The implications of literacy.* Princeton, NJ: Princeton University Press.

Street, B. V. (this volume). *Ethnography of writing and reading.*

Street, B. V. (1995). *Social literacies: Critical approaches to literacy in development, ethnography and education.* London: Longman.

Stock, B. (1983). *The implications of literacy.* Princeton, NJ: Princeton University Press.

Thomas, R. (this volume). *The origins of Western literacy: Literacy in Ancient Greece and Rome.*

Tolchinsky, L. (this volume). *The configuration of literacy as a domain of knowledge.*

Triebel, A. (2005). Literacy in developed and developing countries. In N. Bascia, A. Cumming, A. Datnow, K. Leithwood, & D. Livingstone (Eds.), *International handbook of educational policy* (pp. 793–812). Dordrecht, The Netherlands: Springer.

U.S. Department of Education (2002). *No Child Left Behind: A desktop reference.* Washington,

DC: U.S. Department of Education, Office of Elementary and Secondary Education.

van der Toorn, K. (2007). *Scribal culture and the making of the Hebrew Bible*. Cambridge, MA: Harvard University Press.

Venezky, R. L. (2004). In search of the perfect orthography. *Written language & literacy*, 7, 139–163.

von Holthoon, F. (this volume). *Literacy, modernization, the intellectual community, and civil society in the Western world.*

Wagner, D. (this volume). *New technologies for adult literacy and international development.*

Wang, F., Tsai, Y., & Wang, W.S.-Y. (this volume). *Chinese literacy.*

Index